What's New in This Edition

Java Unleashed, Second Edition, is an all-new version of the best-selling First Edition. It includes the best chapters from many different Java books published by Sams.net. All these chapters have been modified and updated to reflect the state of Java as the 1.1 specification approaches release.

Three new parts have been added to this edition:

- **Part VIII, "Integrating Java with Other Technologies,"** which provides a close look at how Java can be used with other emerging technologies such as VRML, JavaScript, ActiveX, and VBScript.
- **Part IX, "Applied Java,"** includes examples of Java as you can apply it to several fields such as intranets, game programming, image processing, and databases.
- **Part X, "Emerging Java Technologies,"** looks at the upcoming Java technologies including JIT compilers, remote objects, the standard extension APIs, JavaOS, Java Beans, Java microprocessors, JAR files, and Jeeves.

These additional parts greatly expand the scope of the book and give you new insights into the current and future use of Java. In particular, be sure to check out these powerful new chapters, new to the Second Edition:

- **Chapter 9, "Threads and Multithreading,"** covers the basics of programming with threads including the use of monitors.
- **Chapter 21, "Creating User Interface Components,"** explains some advanced tricks accomplished using the AWT such as password-protected text fields and scrolling-image panels.
- **Chapter 25, "Client/Server Fundamentals,"** presents the basics of client/server architectures and includes an example of programming using live data.
- **Chapter 26, "Java Socket Programming,"** explains the details of programming sockets in Java for advanced networking programs.
- **Chapter 28, "Java Debugging,"** now includes a look at debugging using Café's Visual Debugger.
- **Chapter 29, "Documenting Your Code,"** has been rewritten. It explains the reasons why documentation is important and describes the process of documenting code along with examples of using the javadoc utility.
- **Chapter 30, "Optimizing Java Code,"** provides you with techniques that can be used to speed up your Java programs without the help of a JIT compiler.
- **Chapter 31, "Exploring Database Connectivity with JDBC,"** explains the details of JDBC and shows you how to build database connectivity into your Java programs.
- **Chapter 33, "Integrating Native Code,"** shows how to use the native method interface to speed up your Java programs and to interfac

- **Chapter 34, "Java Under the Hood: Inside t** etails of the virtual machine and shows how you can nder-lying power of the virtual machine.

D1511252

continues

continued

- **Chapter 35, "Java Security,"** provides an in-depth look at the security issues of Java including why security is important, what kinds of threats Java protects against, and the details of how Java security works.

- **Chapter 37, " Integrating Java and JavaScript,"** details the workings behind JavaScript and how it can be used to connect to Java applets and how to control them from an HTML file.

- **Chapter 38, "Integrating Java and ActiveX,"** starts by comparing these two different technologies and then shows how they can be integrated to harness the power of both.

- **Chapter 39, "Using Java with VBScript,"** gives a quick overview of VBScript and shows how VBScript can be used to control Java applets.

- **Chapter 40, "Developing Intranet Applications with Java,"** explains how intranets are being used in the corporate world and how Java is becoming the programming language of choice for creating intranet applications. This chapter includes a framework that allows you to quickly and easily create intranet applications.

- **Chapter 42, "Advanced Image Processing,"** presents the basics of Java's image model and then shows how to program some advanced image filters including an example applet that displays the Mandelbrot fractal set.

- **Chapter 43, "Developing Your Own Database Application,"** explains basic database concepts and shows an example of developing a guest book database applet using relational databases.

- **Chapter 44, "Just-in-Time Compilers,"** shows how just-in-time compilers can speed up your Java applications and takes a close look at some of the more popular JIT compliers that are starting to appear.

- **Chapter 45, "Remote Objects and the Java IDL System,"** teaches you how to invoke methods on objects running on a remote virtual machine with the RMI facility. It also covers the CORBA and IDL compiler libraries used to create a platform for client/server applications.

- **Chapter 47, "The Scoop on JavaOS, Java Microprocessors, and JAR Files,"** explores the newly announced technologies that will shape the Java market.

- **Chapter 48, "Serving the Net with Jeeves,"** looks at the Jeeves initiative and how servlets can add functionality to the server.

A complete set of reference appendixes to enable programmers to quickly get the information they need.

The remaining chapters have been modified and updated with the latest information to provide you with a complete and timely reference to aid you in your Java programming tasks.

Visual J++ 1.0 Publishers Edition

Microsoft© Corp. Visual J++™ Publishers Edition, included on the accompanying CD, allows you to create your own Visual J++™ programs without purchasing the commercial version. The Publishers Edition does differ from the commercial version in some ways: No Database support for SQL and ODBC databases through Data Access Objects (DAO) and Remote Data Objects (RDO); no JET engine for creating programs that work with Access and other DAO databases; no Zoomin and WinDiff tools; no third-party tools and libraries that integrate with Visual J++™; no redistribution of Java virtual machine and Internet Explorer; no code samples; no Microsoft technical support; no free or discounted upgrades to later versions of Visual J++™ Professional Edition.

Microsoft Corp. Visual J++™ Publishers Edition requires the following to operate:

- Personal computer with a 486 or higher processor running MS Windows© 95 or Windows NT© Workstation version 4 or later operation system
- 8M of memory (12M recommended) if running Windows 95; 16M (20M recommended) if running Windows NT Workstation
- Hard-disk space:

   Typical installation: 20M

   Minimum installation: 14M

   CD-ROM installation (tools run from the CD): 50M
- A CD-ROM drive
- VGA or higher resolution monitor (super VGA recommended)
- Microsoft mouse or compatible point device

Java™
Second Edition

Michael Morrison, et al.

sams
net

201 West 103rd Street
Indianapolis, IN 46290

UNLEASHED

Copyright © 1997 by Sams.net Publishing

SECOND EDITION

International Standard Book Number: 1-57521-197-1

Library of Congress Catalog Card Number: 96-70387

2000 99 98 97   4 3 2 1

Interpretation of the printing code: the rightmost double-digit number is the year of the book's printing; the rightmost single-digit, the number of the book's printing. For example, a printing code of 96-1 shows that the first printing of the book occurred in 1997.

Composed in Garamond and MCPdigital by Macmillan Computer Publishing

Printed in the United States of America

Trademarks

President, Sams Publishing   *Richard K. Swadley*

Publishing Manager   *Mark Taber*

Managing Editor   *Cindy Morrow*

Director of Marketing   *John Pierce*

Assistant Marketing Managers   *Kristina Perry, Rachel Wolfe*

Acquisitions Editor
Beverly M. Eppink

Development Editor
Kelly Murdock

Software Development Specialist
Bob Correll

Production Editor
Alice Martina Smith

Technical Editor
Ramesh Chandak

Editorial Coordinator
Katie Wise

Technical Edit Coordinator
Lorraine E. Schaffer

Resource Coordinator
Deborah Frisby

Editorial Assistants
Carol Ackerman
Andi Richter
Rhonda Tinch-Mize

Cover Designer
Tim Amrhein

Book Designer
Gary Adair

Copy Writer
Peter Fuller

Production Team Supervisors
Brad Chinn
Charlotte Clapp

Production
Mona Brown
Jennifer Dierdorff
Polly Lavrick
Mark Matthews
Andrew Stone

Indexer
Tom Dinse

Contents

Part III   The Standard Packages

Part VI Programming Strategies

To my best friend in the whole world, Mahsheed, who now just so happens to be my wife.

—Michael Morrison

Acknowledgments

I would like to thank Beverly Eppink for giving me the opportunity to lead such a fun project and to everyone else at Sams.net who contributed to making this book a reality.

I'd also like to thank all the contributing authors, without whom this book would not have been possible.

I would like to thank my family and friends, especially my mom and dad, who give me unyielding encouragement and support.

Finally, I'd like to thank my Nashville skateboarding cronies, Keith, Josh, Heath, and Squirrel, who are kind enough to keep my legend alive.

—Michael Morrison

About the Authors

Lead Author:

Michael Morrison (mmorrison@thetribe.com, www.thetribe.com) is a freelance writer and gearhead living in Scottsdale, Arizona. Michael is the author of *Teach Yourself Internet Game Programming with Java in 21 Days*, as well as a contributing author to *Teach Yourself Java in 21 Days, Premier Edition*, and *Tricks of the Java Programming Gurus*. When not unleashing Java on unsuspecting friends and family, Michael can be found resurrecting his youth on skateboard ramps. Michael wrote Chapters 4, 6, 7, 8, 11, 12, 14, 19, 30, 38, 44, 46, 47, and Appendix D; he coauthored Chapter 3.

Contributing Authors:

Jerry Ablan (munster@mcs.net) is best described as a computer nut. He has been involved in computers since 1982 and has worked on and owned a variety of microcomputers including several that are no longer manufactured. Jerry has programmed in many languages, including several that are not cool (for example, RPG II), and is a senior software engineer at the Chicago Board Options Exchange. He lives in a Chicago suburb with his wife Kathryn, and when not playing WarCraft II with his friends, working, writing, or otherwise cavorting, Jerry and his brother Dan operate NetGeeks (http://www.netgeeks.com), an Internet consulting firm. He is the author of *Developing Intranet Applications with Java*, coauthor of the *Web Site Administrator's Survival Guide*, and a contributing author to *Special Edition: Using Java*; *Platinum Edition: Using CGI, HTML, and Java*; and *Intranets Unleashed*. Jerry wrote Chapter 40.

Michael Afergan (mikea@ai.mit.edu) began working with Java as early as the spring of 1995 through his research work at the MIT AI Labs. Since then, he has carefully studied its growth, developing practical applets for companies as an independent consultant. Michael is the author of *Java Quick Reference* and has taught Java overseas to both managers and programmers. Although only 18, Michael has been programming for 11 years and has even taught a class on computer science at MIT. Captain of his high school wrestling team, he is currently attending Harvard University. Michael wrote Chapter 27.

Rogers Cadenhead (rcade@airmail.net, http://www.cruel.com/rcade) is a Web developer, computer programmer, and writer who created the multiuser games Czarlords and Super Video Poker. Thousands of readers see his work in the *Fort Worth Star-Telegram* question-and-answer column "Ask Ed Brice." Rogers has developed Java applets for Tele-Communications Inc. and other clients, and is the coauthor of *Teach Yourself SunSoft's Java Workshop in 21 Days*. Rogers wrote Chapters 1, 5, 17, and 18 and contributed to Chapter 2.

David R. Chung (dchung@inav.net, http://soli.inav.net/~dchung) is a senior programmer in the Church Software Division of Parsons Technology in Hiawatha, Iowa. His current projects include Windows and the Internet, and he moonlights teaching C and C++ to engineers for a local community college. In his spare time, David enjoys bicycling, teaching adult Sunday school, rollerblading, skiing, windsurfing, preaching in a nursing home, tennis, 2-player and 6-player volleyball, playing the clarinet, and speaking French. He is the father of six children whose names all begin with *J* and contributed to *Tricks of the Java Programming Gurus*. David wrote Chapters 10, 16, and 21.

Justin Couch (justin@vlc.com.au, http://www.vlc.com.au/~justin) works as software engineer for ADI Ltd. He also runs The Virtual Light Company, a small VRML and Java Web publishing company located in Sydney, Australia. Coauthor of *Laura Lemay's Web Workshop: 3D Graphics and VRML 2*, Justin is an active member of both the VRML standards and Java-VRML mailing lists. Currently, he is involved in research on using VRML to create seamless worlds on the Internet and can be found most days in the CyberGate community Point World, under the name Mithrandir. When not pushing the limits, he relaxes by playing bassoon and clarinet and going gliding. Justin wrote Chapter 36.

Rick Darnell (darnell@montana.com), a contributing author to *FrontPage Unleashed* and *Microsoft Internet Explorer 3 Unleashed*, is a midwest native currently living with his wife and two daughters in Missoula, Montana. He began his career in print at a small weekly newspaper after graduating from Kansas State University with a degree in broadcasting. While spending time as a freelance journalist and writer, Rick has seen the full gamut of personal computers, since starting out with a Radio Shack Model I in the late 1970s. When not in front of his computer, he serves as a volunteer firefighter and member of a regional hazardous materials response team. Rick wrote Chapter 37.

John December (john@december.com, http://www.december.com) is owner of December Communications, the publisher of *Computer-Mediated Communication Magazine*, and several widely used and frequently accessed World Wide Web-based reference publications about the Internet and the Web. An experienced Internet writer, teacher, software developer, and author, he holds an M.S. degree in computer science, an M.F.A. degree in creative writing, and is a Ph.D. candidate in communication and rhetoric at Rensselaer Polytechnic Institute. He is coauthor of *The World Wide Web Unleashed*, *HTML & CGI Unleashed*, and *Presenting Java*, all published by Sams.net Publishing. He wrote Appendix E.

Mike Fletcher (fletch@ain.bls.com) graduated from Georgia Institute of Technology in 1994 and now works for BellSouth Wireless's AIN Services Group as a system administrator. Mike was a contributing author to the first edition of *Java Unleashed*. He once played tuba on stage with Jimmy Buffet, and his interests include reading science fiction and juggling. Mike wrote Chapters 15, 23, 24, 45, and 48.

Michael Girdley (girdleyj@allwilk.com, http://www.lafayette.edu/~girdleyj/) contributed to *Web Programming with Java* and is the chief consultant at Allwilk Consulting (http://www.allwilk.com/), an organization specializing in Web site creation and Java programming. He is currently pursuing a Bachelor of Science degree in computer science at Lafayette College in Easton, Pennsylvania, and will earn his fourth varsity letter in 1996-1997 as a member of the varsity swimming team. Originally from San Antonio, Texas, Michael hopes to find a job or go to graduate school after possibly graduating on time in May 1997. Michael coauthored Chapter 13.

K.C. Hopson (chopson@universe.digex.net, http://www.universe.digex.net/~chopson) is President of Geist Software and Services, Inc., an independent consulting firm in the Baltimore/Washington D.C. metro area. He specializes in distributed computing solutions and has deep experience in GUI programming (especially Windows), relational databases, and client/server products. K.C. received a B.S. degree in applied mathematics from the University of California, Irvine, and an M.S. in computer science from the University of Maryland, Baltimore County, and was a lead architect of the software used in Bell Atlantic's Stargazer interactive television system. Coauthor of *Developing Professional Java Applets,* K.C. thrives in cyberspace and enjoys using it to work anywhere in the world. In his spare time, he enjoys his family, plays music of all kinds, and studies history and literature. K.C. wrote Chapter 22 and coauthored Chapter 42.

Steve Ingram (singram@qnet.com) is a computer consultant in the Washington D.C. metro area specializing in embedded data communications and object-oriented design. Coauthor of *Developing Professional Java Applets* and contributor to *Tricks of the Java Programming Gurus,* Steve holds an electrical engineering degree from Virginia Tech and has been programming for 15 years. He was the architect behind the language of Bell Atlantic's Stargazer interactive television project, where he first encountered Java. When he's not working, Steve likes to sail the Chesapeake Bay with his wife and son. Steve wrote Chapters 26 and 34 and coauthored Chapter 42.

John J. Kottler (73157.335@compuserve.com, jkottler@aol.com, or jay_kottler@msn.com) has been programming for 14 years and has spent the past 6 years developing applications for the Windows platform. He has programmed multimedia applications for more than two years and has spent this past year developing for the Web. His knowledge includes C/C++, Visual Basic, Lotus Notes, PowerBuilder, messaging-enabled applications, multimedia and digital video production, and Web page development. John contributed to *Presenting ActiveX, Web Publishing Unleashed, Netscape 2 Unleashed,* and *Programming Windows 95 Unleashed;* he codeveloped the shareware application Virtual Monitors. A graduate of Rutgers University with a degree in computer science, he enjoys rollerblading, cycling, and playing digital music in his spare time. John wrote Chapter 39.

Laura Lemay (lemay@lne.com, http://www.lne.com/lemay/) is the author of several best-selling books about the Internet and the World Wide Web, including *Teach Yourself Java in 21 Days* and *Teach Yourself Web Publishing with HTML.* After receiving her degree in technical writing from Carnegie-Mellon University in 1989, she wrote documentation at various Silicon Valley software companies before writing her first book in 1994. She also writes a monthly column on HTML and Web page design for *Web Techniques Magazine.* Laura has won Awards of Merit and Excellence from the Society of Technical Communication for her work and has spoken to diverse audiences ranging from programmers to industry pundits to librarians and to junior high school girls. She makes frequent appearances and lectures in the San Francisco Bay Area. She is the original author of Chapter 2 and Appendixes A and C.

Richard Lesh (rich@micros.umsl.edu) is an instructor with the microcomputing program at the University of Missouri, St. Louis. He has developed a variety of applications for the Macintosh, PC, and various UNIX platforms. A number of software products that he has developed are in national distribution, including PLANMaker, a business plan-building product, and a number of screen saver modules published by Now Software in Now Fun! and by Berkeley Systems in After Dark. Richard contributed to Chapter 13.

Tim Macinta (twm@mit.edu) is currently working towards a degree in computer science and electrical engineering at the Massachusetts Institute of Technology. He has been working with Java since the summer of 1995 when he joined Dimension X, one of the leaders in Java development. While at Dimension X, Tim developed the first commercial-quality Java chat applet along with several applets for commercial sites such as the Disney and Monopoly sites. More recently, he has been using Java to write several client/server applications (SMTP, POP, and IRC, to name a few) from the ground up. After graduating from MIT, Tim plans to start a company whose sole purpose will be to grab market share from Microsoft. Tim wrote Chapter 41.

Bryan Morgan is a software engineer with TASC, Inc. in Fort Walton Beach, Florida. He holds a B.S. degree in electrical engineering from Clemson University and is currently using Java to build Web applications as well as to perform Web-based distributed interactive simulations. Bryan and his wife, Becky, are expecting their first child in November 1996. Bryan is the coauthor of *Teach Yourself SQL in 14 Days* and *Teach Yourself ODBC in 21 Days*. Bryan coauthored Chapter 3.

Tim F. Park (tpark@leland.stanford.edu) is a recent graduate of the Stanford Graduate School of Electrical Engineering. Now employed by a major computer company in Silicon Valley, he is currently working on a Java 3D graphics library for the Internet. He contributed to *Tricks of the Java Programming Gurus,* and his interests include distributed computing, computer graphics, and mountain biking. Tim wrote Chapters 28 and 33.

Charles L. Perkins (virtual@rendezvous.com) is the founder of Virtual Rendezvous (http://rendezvous.com/java), a company building a Java-based service that fosters socially focused, computer-mediated, real-time, filtered interactions between people's personas in the virtual environments of the near future. In previous lives, he has evangelized NeXTSTEP, Smalltalk, and UNIX, and has degrees in both physics and computer science. He is the author of Appendix B.

George Reese (borg@imaginary.com) holds a philosophy degree from Bates College in Lewiston, Maine. He currently works as a consultant with York and Associates, Inc. and as a magazine columnist for the *Java Developer's Journal.* George has written some of the most popular mud software on the Internet, including the Nightmare Object Library and the Foundation Object

Library. For Java, he was the creator of the first JDBC implementation, the Imaginary JDBC Implementation for mSQL. He contributed to *Tricks of the Java Programming Gurus,* and his Internet publications include the free textbooks on the LPC programming language, *LPC Basics* and *Intermediate LPC.* George lives in Bloomington, Minnesota, with his two cats, Misty and Gypsy. George wrote Chapters 25, 29, 31, and 43.

Chris Seguin (seguin@uiuc.edu) is an Eagle Scout. He completed a B.S. degree in computational mathematics at the University of Delaware in 1991, and on June 25, 1994, married his long-time sweetheart, Angela DiNunzio. Chris is currently working toward his Ph.D. at the University of Illinois in computer science in the area of artificial intelligence. For the past three years, he has been a teaching assistant for the introductory computer science class for majors. His research interests include using artificial neural networks for signal processing and developing teaching and collaboration tools on the World Wide Web in Java. Chris wrote Chapter 20.

Glenn Vanderburg (glv@vanderburg.org, http://www.vanderburg.org/~glv/) is a software architect with BusinessWorks, Inc., where he is using Java to support multimedia educational systems. Glenn lives in Plano, Texas, with his wife, Deborah. He holds a B.S. degree in computer science from Texas A&M University. Glenn is the lead author of *Tricks of the Java Programming Gurus* and is interested in using Java to build dynamically extensible, upgradable network applications. Glenn wrote Chapter 35.

Eric Williams (williams@sky.net, http://www.sky.net/~williams) is a team leader and software engineer for Sprint's Long Distance Division. Although currently focusing on C++ and Smalltalk development, Eric is active in the Java community, contributing to the comp.lang.java newsgroup and delivering presentations about Java to various user groups. Eric is also responsible for identifying a Java 1.0.1 security flaw related to sockets and DNS. Eric wrote Chapters 9 and 32.

Tell Us What You Think!

As a reader, you are the most important critic and commentator of our books. We value your opinion and want to know what we're doing right, what we could do better, what areas you'd like to see us publish in, and any other words of wisdom you're willing to pass our way. You can help us make strong books that meet your needs and give you the computer guidance you require.

Do you have access to CompuServe or the World Wide Web? Then check out our CompuServe forum by typing **GO SAMS** at any prompt. If you prefer the World Wide Web, check out our site at http://www.mcp.com.

> **NOTE**
>
> If you have a technical question about this book, call the technical support line at (800) 571-5840, ext. 3668.

As the team leader of the group that created this book, I welcome your comments. You can fax, e-mail, or write me directly to let me know what you did or didn't like about this book—as well as what we can do to make our books stronger. Here's the information:

Fax: (317) 581-4669

E-mail: newtech_mgr@sams.mcp.com

Snail mail: Mark Taber
                Comments Department
                Sams.net Publishing
                201 W. 103rd Street
                Indianapolis, IN 46290

Introduction

Just over a year after its inception, Java is still the dominant technology bringing interactive content to the World Wide Web. In a world where just about everyone has his or her own opinion about where the future of the Web is headed, this is no small feat. JavaSoft, the division of Sun Microsystems responsible for Java, has managed to stay ahead of the development curve and steadily improve Java to accommodate the rapidly changing environment known as the Web. Even so, Java is still a new technology and has plenty of room to evolve to meet the demands of Web developers.

The fact that Java is an evolving technology has played a critical role in its wide acceptance by Web developers; many developers who struggle with limitations in the current release of Java feel confident that JavaSoft will quickly remedy the situation in a future release. This confidence depends greatly on JavaSoft's willingness and desire to solicit input from experts in the field when expanding Java to solve new problems and provide new features. Since initially releasing Java, JavaSoft has been steadily improving Java to meet the needs of the demanding Web community. More recently, JavaSoft has been busily working on significant features that will impact almost every aspect of Java development.

As of this writing, JavaSoft is closing in on the release of Java 1.1, which is the next major Java release since Java 1.02. JavaSoft has been relatively open about the enhancements and additions that will appear in Java 1.1, although they have evaded mentioning anything conclusive. A strong effort has been made in this book to highlight areas of Java that may change or be impacted by the imminent release of Java 1.1. Just keep in mind that any Java 1.1 material mentioned here is based on preliminary reports from JavaSoft and is subject to change in the final release of Java 1.1. Nevertheless, this coverage of Java 1.1 should give you a great deal of insight into the future of Java.

Aside from including references to Java 1.1, you may wonder exactly why we think a Second Edition of this book is necessary. The truth is that there is just too much new material that isn't covered anywhere else. More specifically, this edition includes completely new coverage of topics such as custom user interface components, client/server networking, code optimization, database connectivity, persistence, ActiveX integration, VBScript integration, intranet applications, image processing, just-in-time compilers, remote objects, and emerging Java technologies. As if those topics aren't enough to warrant this edition, the First Edition material that managed to make it into this edition has been completely revised to accommodate both the incremental changes in Java 1.02 and the projected changes in Java 1.1.

Our goal in this edition is to explore the Java technology from a variety of angles so that you can see the bigger picture of what Java has to offer as a Web technology. Our contention is that if you understand Java in its entirety, you will be much better suited to make decisions regarding its efficient use in your own Web development projects. Beyond that, we also thought it would be a lot of fun to chart some new territory and see for ourselves what Java could do!

In this book, you learn about the following topics related to the Java technology:

- Getting started with Java
- The Java language
- The standard Java programming packages
- Creating Java applets
- Networking with Java
- Java programming strategies
- Advanced Java programming
- Integrating Java with other technologies
- Applied Java
- Emerging Java technologies

This book is divided into 10 parts that neatly cover each of these topics.

Part I: Getting Started with Java

Every exploration has to start somewhere—you're ready to begin learning about the vast world of Java. You want to know why Java is an object-oriented language and what this really means in a practical sense. You'd also like to know exactly where to begin as far as setting up your own Java development environment.

Part II: The Java Language

The cornerstone of the Java technology is the Java programming language. You understand Java in general terms, but you want to know more about the Java language and what it can do for you. You are curious about Java classes and how they relate to all the object-oriented hype you've heard about Java. You also want to know what in the world *threads* and *exceptions* are, and why so many people seem so worried about them.

Part III: The Standard Java Programming Packages

The real power of Java is spelled out in the standard Java programming packages. You're ready to move past the Java language and see exactly what Java provides in the way of specific programming features such as mathematical functions, I/O, and networking. You're also curious about graphical user interfaces and what kinds are available in the standard Java packages.

Part IV: Creating Java Applets

How popular would Java be without applets? Probably not very, which is why you just have to know how to start developing your own. You don't just want to develop run-of-the-mill applets, however, you want to create applets with graphics, animation, and fancy user interfaces.

Part V: Networking with Java

Can you possibly imagine a programming language for the Web that doesn't provide extensive support for networking? Of course not! You want to know all about networking with Java and exactly what it can do for you. You've heard a lot about client/server networking and want to know how it is supported in Java. You're also interested in writing a multiuser applet in Java.

Part VI: Java Programming Strategies

You realize the importance of smart programming and want to know some Java programming strategies to help improve development efficiency. You understand the inherent nature of programming bugs and want to know how to debug Java code. You want to employ a documentation strategy so that your code can be better maintained. You are also interested in speeding up your code, because performance is a very critical issue in Java programming.

Part VII: Advanced Java Programming

You are ready to press on to some more advanced areas of Java programming. More specifically, you have an interest in connecting Java programs to existing databases. You want to learn about *persistence*, a technique for storing and retrieving the state of Java objects. You are also interested in how Java integrates with native C code, as well as finding out more about the Java virtual machine and Java security.

Part VIII: Integrating Java with Other Technologies

Although Java is a pretty complete technology, there are still instances where you may want to integrate Java with another technology such as ActiveX. You want to know some details surrounding the integration of Java with technologies such as VRML, ActiveX, JavaScript, and VBScript.

Part IX: Applied Java

A software development technology is only as useful as its range of application. Knowing this, you want to see some specific areas of application where Java can be used. More specifically, how can Java be applied to intranets, games, image processing, and custom databases?

Part X: Emerging Java Technologies

Even though Java has come a long way, the story of Java is still very much being written. You're interested in emerging Java technologies because they play a significant role in determining the future of software development for the Web. More specifically, you want to know more about just-in-time compilers, remote objects, the standard extension APIs, JavaOS, Java microprocessors, and JAR files.

We can certainly use Java's past as a means of forecasting its future, but ultimately, we must keep an open mind and be willing to adapt to changes in Java as they unfold. Knowing that, I encourage you to set out on your own exploration of Java using this book as your guide. Have fun!

—*Michael Morrison*

IN THIS PART

PART

I

Getting Started

Introducing Java

by Rogers Cadenhead

IN THIS CHAPTER

CHAPTER 1

> *This represents the end result of nearly 15 years of trying to come up with a better programming language and environment for building simpler and more reliable software.*
>
> —*Sun Microsystems cofounder Bill Joy*

A year ago, Java was just an island and one of the cooler synonyms for *coffee* (along with *joe* and *demitasse*). But anyone who has come within five feet of a Web page, computer magazine, or business newspaper in 1996 has heard of Java, the programming language from Sun Microsystems.

If you haven't been initiated into the Secret Personhood of Java yet, you might be wondering what all the fuss is about. It's just a programming language, for cryin' out loud! It's not some kind of cross-dressing basketball player, Latino dance craze, or teeth whitener.

Figure 1.1 shows a Java program being used to test students on Egyptian history.

FIGURE 1.1.

A Java program to administer student testing (courtesy of David Benjamin and Auburn University).

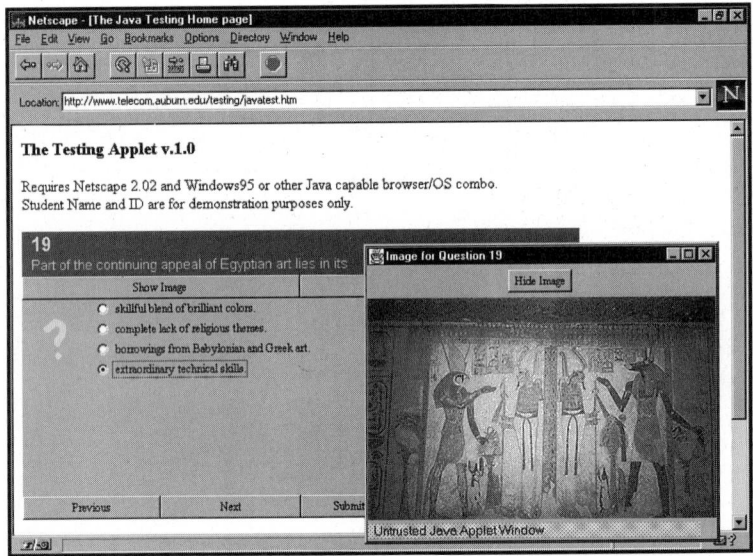

The test software itself isn't remarkable—numerous computer-based education programs are being used in schools today. What *is* noteworthy about the program are the following points:

- It runs on a World Wide Web page, making the test instantly accessible to the entire planet.
- The types of computer and operating system being used by the student don't matter—the student can use a Windows 95 PC clone, an Apple MacOS computer, or any other setup that has a Java interpreter.
- No special installation was required. The program loads itself when needed and unloads when it's done.

Java represents a fundamental shift in the way software can be designed and experienced. This, more than anything else, is why Sun's invention is the computer nerd's Macarena.

> **NOTE**
>
> The Macarena is a Latino dance craze that involves lots of repetitive motion, arm gyration, and an occasional pelvic swivel. If you're unfamiliar with the term, insert your own annoying aerobic trend into the previous paragraph and repeat as desired.

Shortly after Sun introduced Java in late 1995, company cofounder Bill Joy described the language as follows:

> Java is just a small, simple, safe, object-oriented, interpreted or dynamically optimized, byte-coded, architecture-neutral, garbage-collected, multithreaded programming language with a strongly typed exception-handling mechanism for writing distributed, dynamically extensible programs.

At this point, you probably are saying one of two things: "Duh!" or "Huh?"

If you're in the "huh?" camp, this chapter is for you. It discusses what Java is, where Java came from, and where Java is going. The "duh!" camp can benefit from this overview as well—and there's enough advanced material in *Java Unleashed* for even the most grizzled Java veteran.

> **NOTE**
>
> Java's first official beta release was in November 1995, two months after Netscape became the first company to license the language from Sun. You may be questioning whether someone can become a "grizzled veteran" after little more than a year. However, many of us in the computer programming community have rather—shall we say—*unique* approaches to wellness and diet which contribute to premature grizzling.

The first thing to discuss, before getting into what Bill Joy meant in that Mother of All Sentences, is where Java came from.

How Java Was Developed

The story of Java is a tale of two situations—the worst of times followed by the best of times. It's a story about how a promising language didn't amount to a hill of coffee beans in this crazy world—until the crazy world got a little crazier and a new mass medium was born: the World Wide Web.

One for the Toasters

Five years ago, James Gosling was part of Green, an isolated research project at Sun that was studying how to put computers into everyday household items. The researchers wanted to make smart appliances like thoughtful toasters, lucid lamps, and sagacious Salad Shooters—the Jetsons' vision of the future realized. The group also wanted these devices to communicate with each other.

To get a hands-on look at the issue, the Greens built a prototype device called Star7. This gadget was a handheld remote control operated by touching animated objects on the screen. A Star7 user could navigate by fingertip through a universe of rooms and objects. The universe featured Duke—immortalized later as Java's mascot (see Figure 1.2).

Figure 1.2.

Duke, Java's mascot.

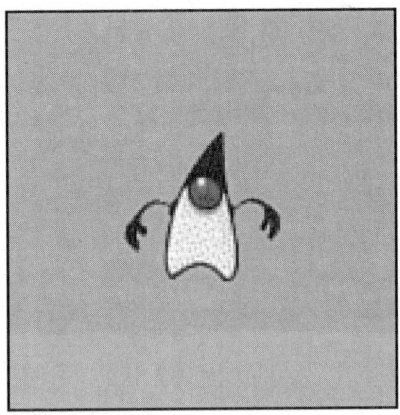

The most remarkable ability of the Star7 device was how it communicated with other Star7 devices. An on-screen object could be passed from one device to another. The prototype was a distributed operating system in which each device was a part of the whole—exactly the kind of thing that would be needed for the freezer to tell the vacuum to tell the humans that the ice machine is on strike until someone cleans it.

The original plan was for the Star7 operating system to be developed in C++. However, as Gosling said in a speech at the JavaOne conference in May 1996, "The tools kept breaking. It was at a fairly early breaking point when I was so disgusted that I went to my office and started typing." He wasn't writing hate mail to Bjarne Stroustrup, the primary developer of C++. Instead, Gosling holed up in his office and wrote a new language that was better for the purposes of the Green project than C++. He called the language Oak in honor of a tree that could be seen from his office window.

From the start, Gosling's language was created so that simple, bug-free, network-capable programs could be written with it. Like C++, Oak was object oriented—a powerful way of developing computer programs that has many advantages over other methods but is difficult to master. Oak was designed to be easier to learn and use than other object-oriented languages.

Oak programs had to be platform independent because consumer appliance manufacturers need the ability to replace a higher-priced CPU with a cheaper one whenever possible to cut costs. Unlike computer owners, an appliance consumer isn't looking for a math coprocessor and 33MHz of added computational speed when buying a lawn edger. The consumer also is less likely to tolerate a bug in the edger's software or hardware, especially if said glitch causes unexpected limb loss.

The Green project had an impressive demonstration device, operating system, and programming language. Sun's higher-ups gave the go-ahead and the project was incorporated as FirstPerson in November 1992. The group focused its efforts on cable set-top boxes and the potentially billion-dollar interactive television (ITV) industry. Don't laugh—this was the early 1990s.

As the FirstPerson team was busy gunning to do Time-Warner's interactive TV trial in Spring 1993, an event took place that would become very important later to the FirstPerson people, long after they struck out in the ITV business. The first visual World Wide Web browser, Mosaic 1.0, was developed by Marc Andreesen, an undergraduate student working at the National Center for Supercomputing Applications.

Caught in the Web

For the next 12 months, the FirstPerson project tried to sell one of the ITV or consumer electronics companies on the use of Oak and the Green operating system. The future of Java can trace its roots back to the project's failure to attract a big client in its chosen field. After Time-Warner chose SGI over FirstPerson, and a deal with 3DO for the FirstPerson OS did not materialize, the project was cut in half and it started scrambling for a new *raison d'être*.

In mid-1994, the folks who stuck with Oak found their reason for being: the World Wide Web. When Oak was created, the Web was a little-known service bouncing around the high-energy physics community. However, Andreesen's graphical Web browser had sparked an international phenomenon, and the Web was rapidly becoming a mass medium. The Oak technology was well-suited for this medium, especially because of its ability to run on multiple platforms. More importantly, it introduced something that wasn't available anywhere else— programs that could be run on user's computers safely from a Web page.

Patrick Naughton and Jonathan Payne finished WebRunner, a Web browser that brought back the star of the Star7, Duke. Sun realized it had something promising on its hands, but soon found that Oak could not be trademarked because of a product already using the name.

NOTE

When Sun needed to rename Oak, no one used Gosling's "look out the office window" method of naming. This is perhaps fortunate. Ask yourself if Java would have been as successful under any of the following names:

- Shrubbery
- OfficeBuildingNextDoor
- LightPole
- WindowWasher
- SecretaryLeavingForLunch
- WeirdSecurityGuard
- FatGuyMowing

After brainstorming sessions in January 1995 to supplant the *Oak* name, *Java* won for the language and *HotJava* replaced *WebRunner* as the browser's name. Java does not stand for Just Another Vague Acronym, or any other acronym or meaningful term. Like rock bands (Deep Blue Something, Smashing Pumpkins) and celebrity offspring (Moon Unit Zappa, Chastity Bono), Java was the name chosen because it sounded the coolest. It won out over DNA, Silk, Ruby, and WRL (WebRunner Language).

The project now had a cool name, a cool new purpose, and a HotJava browser to show it off. On March 23, 1995, it attracted a cool new admirer: that Andreesen kid. In a front-page story, the *San Jose Mercury News* reported that Sun was working on a project to make Web pages "as lively as a CD-ROM." The story included the following quote from Andreesen, who had become a vice president at Netscape (and a Bill Gates starter kit): "What these guys are doing is undeniably, absolutely new," Andreesen told the *Mercury News*. "It's great stuff. There's so much stuff people want to do over the network that they haven't had the software to do. These guys are really pushing the envelope."

The phenomenon was on. Netscape licensed the Java language for use in its browser a few months after the article ran, putting the language in front of millions of Netscape users. The first beta release of Java was made available for download in November 1995. Sun made a developer's kit and the source code for its product freely available to anyone who wanted it—and by that time, thousands of people and companies did.

Toasters are no smarter today than they were in 1991, so in that regard, Sun's research project has been a total failure. However, a new object-oriented, made-for-the-Internet programming language was created instead.

Now that you know about Java's ancestors, it's time to be introduced to the language.

1
INTRODUCING
JAVA

What Java Is

The basics: Java is an object-oriented programming language developed by Sun Microsystems that plays to the strengths of the Internet.

Object-oriented programming (OOP) is an unusual but powerful way to develop software. In OOP, a computer program is considered to be a group of objects that interact with each other. Consider an embezzlement program implemented with Java: A Worker object skims some Money objects from the CompanyFunds object and puts them in its own BankAccount object. If another Worker object uses the DoublecheckFunds object, a Police object will be called.

The feature that is best known about Java is that it can be used to create programs that execute from World Wide Web pages. These programs are called *applets*. A check of the AltaVista search engine at http://www.altavista.digital.com finds more than 4,800 Web pages running applets as of this writing.

Java programs made such a big splash on the Web because they offered interactivity in a medium that was largely one way. The Web distributes almost all information in a passive manner. Someone using a browser asks for a page, looks it over, asks for another, looks it over, and so on. Lather, rinse, repeat.

A Java applet running on a Web page provides a much richer experience—both in terms of information and user interaction. Information can change in response to user input or be updated dynamically as a Web page is viewed. Figure 1.3 shows an example of a Java applet that dynamically updates itself. The applet, offered by *JavaWorld* magazine (at the URL http://www.javaworld.com) in conjunction with Quote.Com, updates a stock portfolio dynamically with quotes updated in real time.

FIGURE 1.3.

A Java applet that updates a stock portfolio in real time (courtesy of JavaWorld *magazine).*

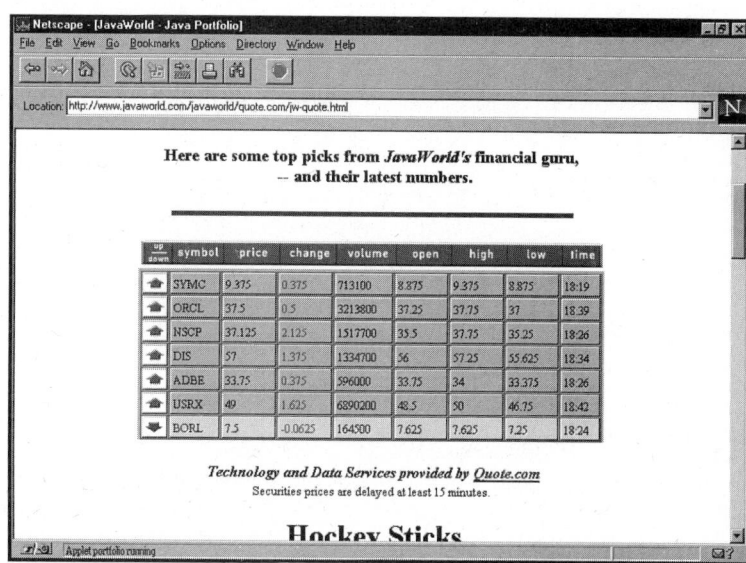

Although Web-based programs are a strength of the language, Java is a general-purpose language that can be used to develop all kinds of programs.

A Java program is created as a text file with the file extension .java. It is compiled into one or more files of bytecodes with the extension .class. *Bytecodes* are sets of instructions similar to the machine code instructions created when a computer program is compiled. The difference is that machine code must run on the computer system it was compiled for, and bytecodes can run on any computer system equipped to handle Java programs.

The next section describes why Java is being used and takes a closer look at Bill Joy's adjective-stuffed description of the language.

Why Java Is Internationally Beloved

Although "internationally beloved" might be pushing it a bit, Java has quickly become a popular choice for computer programming—both on and off the Internet. A lot of the initial interest undoubtedly came from people who wanted to know whether Java lived up to the hype. In a short time, the language has become one of the biggest buzzwords of the Internet, spawning magazines, Web sites, training courses, conferences, and more than 120 books.

Even if Java was as underpublicized as Tonya Harding's singing career, the programming language has some advantages over other languages such as C++ and Visual Basic. These can be found in Bill Joy's description of the language.

As a reminder, Joy sang its praises as follows:

> Java is just a small, simple, safe, object-oriented, interpreted or dynamically optimized, byte-coded, architecture-neutral, garbage-collected, multithreaded programming language with a strongly typed exception-handling mechanism for writing distributed, dynamically extensible programs.

These adjectives can be tackled by dividing them into more manageable groups.

Java Is Small and Simple

When James Gosling retreated to his office to write the language that became Java, it was modeled after C and C++. The object-oriented approach, and most of Java's syntax, is adapted from C++. Programmers who are familiar with that language (or with C) will have a much easier time learning Java because of the common features.

However, Java has been described as "C++ minus" because of elements of C++ that were omitted. Gosling wanted to avoid the problems that the Green project had encountered when using C++ as it developed the Star7 prototype. The most complex parts of C++ were excluded from Java, such as pointers and memory management. These elements are complicated to use, and are thus easier to use incorrectly. Finding a pointer error in a large program is an experience not unlike searching for the one-armed man who framed you for murder. Memory management occurs automatically in Java—programmers do not have to write their own garbage-collection routines to free up memory.

Another design decision to make Java simpler is its elementary data types and objects. The language enforces very strict rules regarding variables—in almost all cases, you have to use variables as the data type they were declared to be, or use explicit casts to manipulate them. This arrangement permits mistakes in variable use to be caught when the program is compiled, rather than letting them creep into a running program where they're harder to find. As a result, programs behave in a more predictable manner.

Experienced programmers may have trouble adjusting to some of the changes and reductions from C++. However, Java's developers were trying to make the language easier to write, debug, and learn.

Java Is Object Oriented

Object-oriented programming (OOP) is a powerful way of organizing and developing software. The short-form description of OOP is that it organizes a program as a set of components called *objects*. These objects exist independently of each other, and they have rules for communicating with other objects and for telling those objects to do things. Think back to how Star7 devices were developed as a group of independent devices with methods for communicating with each other. Object-oriented programming is highly compatible with what the Green project was created to do and, by extension, for Java as well.

Java inherits its object-oriented concepts from C++ and other languages such as Smalltalk. The fact that a programming language is object oriented may not seem like a benefit to some. Object-oriented programming can be an intimidating subject to tackle, even if you have some experience programming with other languages. However, object-oriented programs are more adaptable for use in other projects, easier to understand, and more bugproof.

The language includes a set of class libraries that provide basic variable types, system input and output capabilities, and other functions. It also includes classes to support networking, Internet protocols, and graphical user interface functions.

There's a lot of excitement in the programming community because Java provides a new opportunity to use object-oriented techniques on the jobs. Smalltalk, the language that pioneered object-oriented programming in the 1970s, is well-respected but has never been widely adopted as a software-development choice. As a result, getting the go-ahead to develop a project using Smalltalk can be an uphill struggle. C++ is object oriented, but concerns about its use have already been described. Java is overcoming the hurdle in terms of usage, especially in regard to Internet programming and the development of distributed applications.

Tim Berners-Lee, the inventor of the World Wide Web, told the attendees at the JavaOne conference one big reason he's excited about the language: "We now have an excuse to really use object-oriented programming."

Java Is Safe

Another thing essential to Java's success is that it be safe. The original reason for Java to execute reliably was that people expect their waffle irons not to kill them or to exhibit any other unreliable behavior. This emphasis on security was well-suited for Java's adaptation to the World Wide Web.

A Java program that executes from a Web page is called an *applet*. All other Java programs are called *applications*. When an applet is encountered on a Web page (if the user's browser can handle Java), the browser downloads the applet along with the text and images on the page. The applet then runs on the user's computer. This act should raise a red flag—danger! danger!—because a lot of harmful things can occur when programs are executed: viruses, Trojan horses, the Microsoft Network, and so on.

Java provides security on several different levels. First, the language was designed to make it extremely difficult to execute damaging code. The elimination of pointers is a big step in this regard. Pointers are a powerful feature, as the programmers of C-like languages can attest, but pointers can be used to forge access to parts of a program where access is not allowed, and to access areas in memory that are supposed to be unalterable. By eliminating all pointers except for a limited form of references to objects, Java is a much more secure language.

Another level of security is the bytecode verifier. As described earlier, Java programs are compiled into sets of instructions called bytecodes. Before a Java program is run, a verifier checks each bytecode to make sure that nothing suspicious is going on.

In addition to these measures, Java has several safeguards that apply to applets. To prevent a program from committing random acts of violence against a user's disk drives, an applet cannot open, read, or write files on the user's system. Also, because Java applets can open new windows, these windows have a Java logo and text that identifies their identity. This prevents one of these pop-up windows from pretending to be something such as a user name and password dialog box.

There is no system of security that is completely foolproof, and there were several instances in the first year after Java's release where security bugs were brought to Sun's attention by programmers such as David Hopwood. The following Web site describes some of these incidents and outlines the issues regarding safe Internet programming:

```
http://www.cs.princeton.edu/sip/News.html
```

Because of the multiple levels of security, and the continued efforts to improve these measures, Java is generally regarded as a secure means to execute code over the World Wide Web.

CAUTION

These safeguards are not an absolute guarantee against malicious programming. Several security experts have found ways to circumvent Java applet security during the first year of the language's availability, and the details were sent to JavaSoft and browser developers. There will undoubtedly be new security holes found in the future with Java, as there are with any system. If you are concerned about running Java applets on your computer, you should run only applets that have been approved by a Java directory such as Gamelan or another trusted source. Gamelan, which can be found at the URL `http://www.gamelan.com`, tests applets before offering them. You also should back up any essential data on your computer regularly—which is good practice in any case.

Java Is Platform Independent

Platform independence is another way of saying that Java is architecture neutral. If both terms leave you saying "huh?", they basically mean that Java programs don't care what system they're running on.

Most computer software is developed for a specific operating system. If Sid Software wanted its two-fisted 17th-century shoot-'em-up *Quaker* to run on Windows and Mac systems, it had to develop two versions of the software at a significant effort and expense. *Platform independence* is the ability of the same program to work on different operating systems; Java is completely platform independent.

Java's variable types have the same size across all Java development platforms—so an integer is always the same size, no matter which system a Java program was written and compiled on. Also, as shown by the use of applets on the Web, a Java `.class` file of bytecode instructions can execute on any platform without alteration.

Sun Microsystems has been aggressive in making Java available on different systems. As JavaSoft President Alan Baratz says, "Anything that feels, smells, walks, or talks like it has a processor— we'd like the Java platform to live on it." There are Java interpreters that can run programs for Microsoft Windows 95 and NT, Apple Macintosh 7.5, SPARC Solaris 2.3 or higher, and Intel x86 Solaris; other systems have Java versions under development.

Java's declaration of platform independence is often trumpeted by Java advocates as a major accomplishment because it opens up a much larger audience for programs than has been readily available in the past. Although no major commercial releases of Java-based software have been introduced as of this writing (other than JavaSoft products such as HotJava and the Java WorkShop programming environment), several have been announced.

Java Is That Other Stuff, Too

One adjective that has been left out thus far is that Java is *multithreaded*. Threads represent a way for a computer program to do more than one task at the same time. Many operating systems are multitasking. Windows 95, for example, enables a person to write a book chapter with Word in one window while using Netscape Navigator to download every known picture of E! host Eleanor Mondale in the other. (Speaking hypothetically, of course.)

A multithreaded language extends this schizophrenic behavior to programs so that more than one set of instructions can be executed concurrently. Java provides the tools to write multithreaded programs and to make these programs reliable in execution.

Another thing that should be highlighted is Java's network-centric nature. Sun, the company that trademarked the phrase, "the network is the computer," has created a language that backs it up. Star7 was able to pass an object from one device to another using radio signals, and Java makes it possible to create applications that communicate across the Internet in the same way.

Its networkability may be the area in which Java truly separates itself from other languages that can be used for development. As language creator James Gosling has remarked, "The thing that distinguishes Java is its approach to distributed programming."

Most of Bill Joy's accolades should make more sense to you at this point, although it may take a complete reading of *Java Unleashed* before you're ready to string together technical jargon like his with the proficiency of a *Dilbert* character.

Java Today

Now that you have an idea about what Java is and why you should use it, forsaking all others (or maybe not), you're ready to get started. To understand the status of Java development today, you should learn more about the Java Developer's Kit, the language Application Programming Interface (API), future APIs, and some examples of Java in action.

The Java Developers Kit

The Java Developers Kit (JDK) is a set of command-line tools that can be used to create Java programs. As of this writing, version 1.0.2 is the current release of the JDK, and it can be downloaded from the following Web address:

```
http://java.sun.com/java.sun.com/products/JDK/index.html
```

Sun supports the following platforms: Microsoft Windows 95 and NT, Solaris 2.x for SPARC and x86 systems, and Apple MacOS. The JDK includes the following tools: a compiler, an interpreter to run compiled Java standalone applications, an applet viewer to run Java applets, and other utilities.

There are numerous alternatives to JDK 1.0.2 that offer graphical user interfaces, tools to speed up debugging and program development, and other niceties. Some of these alternatives use the JDK transparently during use, while others replace the JDK's tools.

JavaSoft, the division of Sun Microsystems responsible for Java development, plans to release a new, expanded version of the JDK that may be available as you read this. The successor to JDK 1.0.2 will be version 1.1, and it is expected to include improved security, new windowing design classes, a way to group files into archives, and other enhancements.

The Java API

The Java Application Programming Interface (API) is a set of classes used to develop Java programs. These classes are organized into groups called *packages*. There are packages for the following tasks:

- Numeric variable and string manipulation
- Image creation and manipulation
- File input and output
- Networking
- Windowing and graphical user interface design
- Applet programming
- Error handling

The API includes enough functionality to create sophisticated applets and applications. The Java API must be supported by all operating systems and Web software equipped to execute Java programs, so you can count on the existence of Java API class files when developing programs.

The Java API is at version 1.0.2 at this time; Sun will make no changes in future versions that would require changes to source code. Although enhancements are planned for future releases of the API, there will be no removals or changes to class behavior.

Extended APIs

In addition to the basic API that must be present with all Java implementations, Sun is developing extended APIs that extend the features of the language.

All but one of the following classes are in various stages of development at Sun:

- Commerce API, for secure commercial transactions
- Security API, which adds advanced security features, an improved bytecode verifier, encryption, and other features
- Three Enterprise APIs, to connect programs with enterprise database and legacy applications
- Media API, which adds multimedia classes for graphics, sound, video, 3D, VRML, and telephony
- Java Beans component APIs, to connect Java to reusable software component schemes such as Microsoft ActiveX, Netscape LiveConnect, and OpenDoc
- Servlet API, which creates applet-like Java programs that can run on a Web server
- Management API, to integrate with network management systems, which will be offered as part of the Solstice WorkShop development tool
- Additional Abstract Windowing Toolkit classes, to extend the capabilities of Java's graphical user interface

- An object serialization API, which enables objects to be stored on and loaded from disks
- A Socratic API, which answers the questions that have befuddled mankind for centuries, including the chicken-or-egg dilemma, the doctrine of original sin, the noise caused by trees falling in uninhabited forests, and actress Susan Lucci's lack of success at the Daytime Emmy awards

Java Beans is the most likely of the extended APIs to appear first, although the enhanced security APIs are close to completion. If you guessed that the Socratic API was the false one, move forward two spaces—you're right. However, Microsoft could not take the risk that another company would be first to implement it—the Socratic API will begin development with ActiveX later this year.

JavaOS

In May 1996, JavaSoft announced plans to develop JavaOS, a compact operating system intended to run Java programs. The stated goal is to be the fastest and smallest platform that can handle Java. In addition to being a competitor to operating systems such as Microsoft Windows 95, JavaOS will put the language where it was originally intended to be: in appliances.

The operating system will be embedded on processor chips being developed by Sun. At the JavaOne conference, Mitsubishi demonstrated its own Java chip, which was being used to run a mobile Java terminal called the MonAMI.

The JavaOS and similar efforts are in a much earlier stage of development than other Java-related projects from Sun. However, JavaOS or some other hardware-based Java solutions should be available by early 1997.

Web Sites

One of the advantages of a Web-based phenomenon like Java is that it generates megabytes of information on the World Wide Web. Documentation, news, source code, and other material about Java is offered at thousands of sites. The following should get you started:

- `http://java.sun.com` is the official JavaSoft site. It offers online documentation, news on the latest developments, Java software to download or purchase, and links to other pertinent sites. The Java Developers Kit is available from this site, and a trial version of the Java WorkShop integrated development environment can be downloaded also.
- `http://www.gamelan.com` is the largest directory of Java applets and Java-related Web sites. It also offers links to the winners of the Java Cup applet programming contest, and a chat applet that uses Java to offer America Online-style discussions.
- `http://www.jars.com` is the Java Applet Rating Service, a group that reviews Java applets. If you see an apple logo accompanying a Java program on the Web, it has been reviewed by JARS.

- `http://www.j-g.com/java/` is another directory of Java applets that is smaller than Gamelan's collection. However, a nice collection of Java programs has been assembled here.

- `http://www.mbmdesigns.com/macjava/` is Apple-flavored Java, a site devoted to Macintosh implementations of Java development software and Java programs.

- `http://sunsite.unc.edu/javafaq/javafaq.html` is a list of frequently asked questions about Java programming answered by participants in the Java-related Usenet newsgroups.

- `http://k2.scl.cwru.edu/~gaunt/java/java-faq.html` is another list of questions about Java. Called the "Unofficial Obscure Java FAQ," it was established for some answers to infrequently asked questions about the language.

- `http://www.javaworld.com/` is the home page of *JavaWorld* magazine, which puts a lot of articles, sample source code, and news stories online.

- `http://www.yahoo.com/Computers_and_Internet/Programming_Languages/Java/` is a section of the Yahoo Directory devoted to Java, with more than 300 links to Web sites.

Usenet Newsgroups

Numerous messages are posted on Usenet newsgroups each day by people who are interested in Java. Some are from developers with experience in the language who can comment on advanced aspects of the language. Many are from newcomers who need help in their efforts to learn Java. In any case, Usenet is a great place to get technical assistance. (Some other Usenet messages are from America Online users who have become lost in their search for pictures of Pamela Anderson Lee, but that's another story entirely.)

The following newsgroups currently are available on Usenet, which can be accessed with an Internet account, a subscription to online services such as CompuServe and America Online, and other means:

- `comp.lang.java.advocacy` is a newsgroup for debate and diatribes about Java and other languages that can be compared to it.

- `comp.lang.java.announce` is a moderated newsgroup with announcements related to Java—often used for company press releases, Web site launches, and similar information.

- `comp.lang.java.api` is a newsgroup for discussion of the Java Application Programming Interface, the full class library that comes with Java WorkShop, and other development environments for the language.

- `comp.lang.java.programmer` is a newsgroup for questions, answers, and other talk related to Java programming.

- `comp.lang.java.security` is a newsgroup where the security issues related to Java are discussed, with an emphasis on the security of executing Java applets over the World Wide Web.

- ■ `comp.lang.java.setup` is a newsgroup for the discussion of installation problems regarding Java development tools and similar issues.
- ■ `comp.lang.java.tech` is an advanced newsgroup where technical issues of the Java language are discussed.
- ■ `comp.lang.java.misc` is a newsgroup for everything else related to Java. It generally is the most active of the newsgroups.

Java Tomorrow

During its first year of release, Java has enjoyed the same advantages bestowed on child prodigies. Most of the talk has been about its great potential, and criticism is overshadowed by excited anticipation about what it will do in the future.

As an example of this, consider the words of Marc Andreesen, himself a child prodigy of sorts, after creating Mosaic while he was an undergraduate. Andreesen's endorsement was one of the reasons for Java's astonishing growth. He said the following at the JavaOne conference:

> Java is a huge opportunity for all of us, all the developers in the industry, who are, all of a sudden, able to develop applications in days or weeks, instead of months or years; who have new ways of distributing those applications, making money from those applications without having to fight for retail shelf space.

One of the applications that has been announced is the WordPerfect Office Suite. Corel has stated that Office Suite will be redesigned entirely using Java, making it available for a wide range of platforms. IBM is redesigning its OS/2 Warp operating system to make it optimized for Java programs.

The technology venture capital firm, Kleiner, Perkins, Caufield, and Byers (KPCB), has offered $100 million to support companies doing work with Java.

Year two is going to be a little tougher on the tyke. If Java is to remain the object-oriented language of people's affections, it has to start fulfilling some of its promises.

Growing up isn't always an easy process for those who have achieved outlandish success early in life. Ask any former child star who has traded in a Screen Actors Guild card for a life of crime or a career in talk shows.

By picking up a book of this kind and learning about Java, you're one of the people who is expected to do something remarkable with it. The developers of Java, the nation's press, and those of us who make our living writing Java books by the ton are depending on you. Not to mention the folks at KPCB who gave up $100 million of their allowances to fund Java-related programming.

It's one of the prices you pay for being in the right place at the right time.

CHAPTER 2

Object-Oriented Programming and Java

by Laura Lemay and Rogers Cadenhead

IN THIS CHAPTER

Object-oriented programming (OOP) is one of the biggest programming ideas in recent years—and it's also one of the biggest sources of consternation for programmers unfamiliar with how it works. You may fear that years must be spent learning about OOP and how it makes life easier than other ways to program. The central idea of object-oriented programming is simple: Organize programs in ways that echo how things are put together in the real world.

This chapter provides an overview of object-oriented programming concepts in Java and how they relate to the structure of your programs. The following topics are covered:

- Classes and objects, and how they relate to each other
- The two main parts of a class or object: behavior and attributes
- Class inheritance, and how inheritance affects the way programs are designed
- Packages and interfaces

If you already are familiar with object-oriented programming, much of this material will be a review for you. Even if you skim over the introductory sections, you may want to create the Java examples in this chapter to get more experience using the language.

Thinking in Objects: An Analogy

Consider, if you will, LEGO building bricks. LEGO bricks, for those of you who do not spend much time with children, are small plastic building blocks in various colors and sizes. They have small round studs on one side that fit snugly into round holes on other bricks to create larger shapes. With different LEGO pieces (wheels, engines, hinges, pulleys, and the like), you can make castles, automobiles, giant robots, or just about anything else you can imagine. Each LEGO piece is a small object that fits together with other small objects in specific ways to create other, larger objects.

Consider another example. You can walk into a computer store and, with a little expertise and some help, assemble an entire personal computer system from various components: a motherboard, a CPU chip, a video card, a hard disk, a keyboard, and so on. Ideally, when you finish assembling the various self-contained units, you have a system in which all the units work together to create a larger system. You can use this larger system to solve the problems you bought the computer for in the first place.

Internally, each of those computer components might be extremely complicated and engineered by different companies using different methods of design. But you don't need to know how each component works, what every chip on the board does, or how an *A* gets sent to your computer when you press the A key. Each component you use is a self-contained unit, and as the assembler of the overall system, you are interested only in how the units interact with each other. Will this video card fit into a slot on the motherboard? Will this monitor work with this video card? Will each component speak the right commands to the other components it interacts with, so that each part of the computer is understood by every other part? Once you know about the interactions between the components and can match those interactions, putting together the overall system is easy.

What do these examples have to do with programming? Everything. Object-oriented programming is a lot like building structures from LEGO bricks or assembling a PC. When you use object-oriented programming, your overall program is made up of lots of different self-contained components called objects. Each object has a specific role in the program, and all the objects can talk to each other in defined ways.

Objects and Classes

Object-oriented programming is modeled on the observation that, in the real world, objects are made up of many kinds of smaller objects. However, the capability to combine objects is only one general aspect of object-oriented programming. Object-oriented programming provides several other concepts and features to make the creation and use of objects easier and more flexible. The most important of these features is the class.

A *class* is a template for multiple objects with similar features. Classes embody all the features of a particular set of objects. When you write a program in an object-oriented language, you don't define individual objects. You define classes of objects.

For example, you might have a Tree class that describes the features of all trees (each tree has branches and roots, grows, and creates chlorophyll). The Tree class serves as an abstract model for the concept of a tree. To reach out and grab, or interact with, or cut down a tree, you must have a concrete instance of that tree. Of course, once you have a Tree class, you can create lots of different instances of that tree, and each different tree instance can have different features (it can be short, tall, bushy, drop leaves in autumn, and so on), yet still behave like a tree and be immediately recognizable as one (see Figure 2.1).

An *instance* of a class is an actual object of that class. The class is the general, abstract representation of an object, and an instance is its concrete representation. So what, precisely, is the difference between an instance and an object? Nothing, really. The term *object* is used more generally, but both instances and objects are the concrete representations of a class. In fact, the terms *instance* and *object* often are used interchangeably in OOP terminology. A Tree instance and a Tree object are the same thing.

In an example closer to the kind of thing you may want to do with Java, you can create a class for an on-off switch (an item you intend to use on dialog boxes and other windows). The LightSwitch class defines the following features of an on-off switch:

■ Its label (if any)

■ Its size

■ Its appearance

The class also defines how an on-off switch behaves, as follows:

- Whether it needs a single click or a double click to be activated
- Whether it changes color when clicked
- What it does when it's activated

Once you define the LightSwitch class, you easily can create instances of that switch—in other words, LightSwitch objects. The instances all take on the basic features of a switch as defined by the class, but each instance can have different appearances and behavior based on what you want that particular switch to do. By creating a LightSwitch class, you don't have to keep rewriting the code for each switch you want to use in your program. Also, you can reuse the LightSwitch class to create different kinds of switches as you need them—in this program and in other programs.

FIGURE 2.1.

The Tree *class and* Tree *instances.*

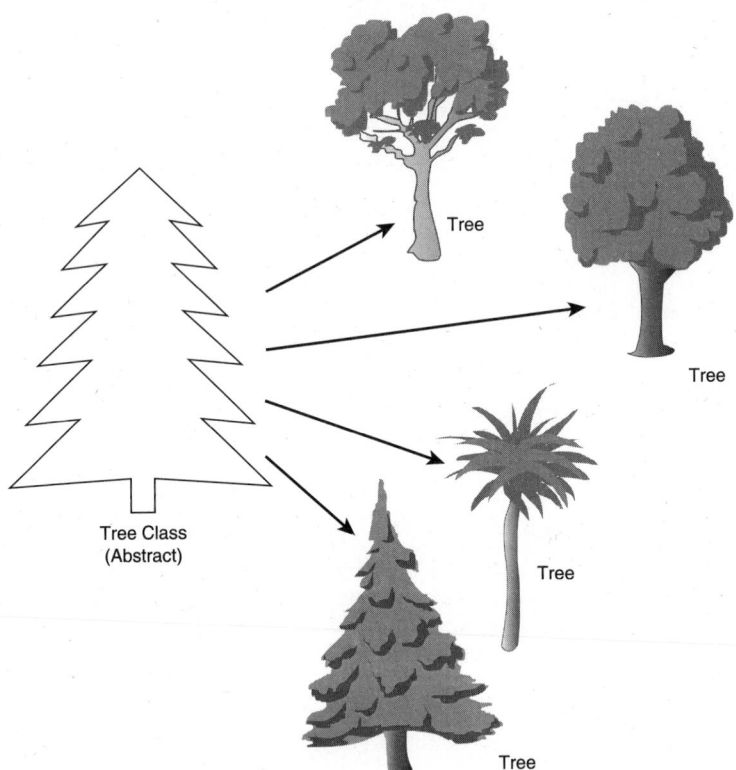

Tree

Tree

Tree Class
(Abstract)

Tree

Tree

> **TIP**
>
> If you're used to programming in C, you can think of a class as a way to create a new composite data type that is analogous to using `struct` and `typedef` statements in C. Classes, however, can provide much more functionality than just a collection of data, as you'll discover in the rest of this chapter.

When you write a Java program, you design and construct a set of classes. When your program runs, instances of those classes are created and discarded as needed. Your task, as a Java programmer, is to create the right set of classes to accomplish what your program needs to accomplish.

Fortunately, you don't have to start from scratch. The Java environment comes with a library of classes that implement a lot of the basic behaviors you need. A *class library* is a set of classes. The Java library has classes to handle basic programming tasks (math functions, arrays, strings, and so on) as well as classes to handle graphics and networking behavior. In many cases, the Java class libraries may be sufficient for your needs; all you have to do in your Java program is to create a single class that uses the standard class libraries. For complicated Java programs, however, you may have to create a whole set of classes with defined interactions between them.

Attributes and Behavior

Generally, every class you write in Java is made up of two components: attributes and behavior. In the following sections, you learn about each component as it applies to a theoretical class called `Jabberwock`. To wrap up this discussion, you'll create the Java code to implement a representation of a jabberwock—a dragon-like monster from the Lewis Carroll poem *Jabberwocky*.

Attributes of an Object

Attributes are the individual things that differentiate one object from another and determine the appearance, state, or other qualities of that object. Consider how a theoretical class called `Jabberwock` could be created. The attributes of a jabberwock might include the following:

- **Color:** red, orange, yellow
- **Sex:** male, female
- **Appetite:** full, hungry

Attributes of an object also can include other information about its state. For example, you can have features for the jabberwock's attitude (enraged or calm) or its current health (alive or dead).

Attributes are defined by variables; in fact, you can consider attributes to be analogous to global variables for the entire object. Because each instance of a class can have different values for its variables, each variable is called an instance variable. *Instance variables* define the attributes of an object. The class defines the type of the attribute, and each instance stores its own value for that attribute.

Each attribute, as the term is used here, has a single corresponding instance variable; changing the value of a variable changes the attribute of that object. Instance variables can be set when an object is created and stay constant throughout the life of the object, or they can change at will as the program runs.

Class variables apply to the class itself and to all of its instances. Instance variable values are stored in the instance; class variable values are stored in the class itself.

How Objects Behave

Behavior is the only way objects can do anything to themselves or have anything done to them. The behavior of a class determines what instances of that class do to change their internal state. Behavior also determines what class instances do when asked to do something by another class or object. For example, the Jabberwock class might have some of the following behaviors:

- Get angry
- Calm down
- Eat a peasant
- Skip dinner
- Recuperate

To define an object's behavior, you create methods. *Methods* are just like functions in other languages, but they are defined inside classes. Methods operate on instances of their class. Unlike C++, Java does not have functions of any kind defined outside of classes.

Although methods operate within their own class, methods do not affect only a single object. Objects communicate with each other using methods. A class or object can call methods in another class or object to communicate changes in the environment or to ask that an object change its state.

For example, consider the swordsman in the poem *Jabberwocky*. When he attacked the jabberwock with his vorpal blade, here's what happened:

> *One, two! One, two! And through and through*
> *The vorpal blade went snicker-snack!*
> *He left it dead, and with its head*
> *He went galumphing back.*

In Java, the swordsman could be created as a Knight object. When the swordsman chops the head off the jabberwock, it definitely causes a change in the jabberwock's internal state. The Knight object would use a method to tell the Jabberwock object, "I chopped your head off. You're dead."

Just as there are instance and class variables, there are also instance and class methods. Instance methods (which are so common they're usually just called methods) apply and operate on an instance of a class. Class methods apply and operate on a class itself.

Creating a Class

Up to now, this chapter has been pretty theoretical. In this section, however, you create a working example of the Jabberwock class so that you can see how instance variables and methods are defined in a class. You also create a Java applet that creates a new instance of the Jabberwock class, displays its instance variables, and modifies one of its instance variables.

> **NOTE**
>
> The syntax of this example is not covered in great detail in this chapter. Don't worry too much if you're not completely sure what's going on. All you need to focus on in this example are the basic parts of the Jabberwock class definition.

The Jabberwock Class

We'll name the applet you are creating JabberwockApplet to distinguish the applet from the Jabberwock class that it uses. With your Java development software, create a source file called JabberwockApplet.java. If you're using the Java Developers Kit, you can create this file with any text editor that can work with plain text files. If a project name is required, call it JabberwockApplet.

You start by creating a basic class definition. Enter the following into your source code editor:

```
class Jabberwock {

}
```

Congratulations! You have designed a class. Of course, it doesn't do much at the moment, but that's a Java class at its simplest.

To make Jabberwock more sophisticated, create three instance variables for this class. Just below the class Jabberwock { line, add the following three lines:

```
String color;
String sex;
boolean hungry;
```

These lines create three instance variables. Two, `color` and `sex`, can contain `String` objects. (`String` is part of that standard class library mentioned earlier.) The third, `hungry`, is a `boolean` that refers to whether the jabberwock is hungry (`true`) or full (`false`).

NOTE

In Java, boolean is a real data type that can have the values `true` or `false`. Booleans are not numbers, as they are in C.

You can add some behavior to the class by adding methods. There are all kinds of things a jabberwock can do (claws that catch, jaws that bite, and so on), but to keep things short, just add one method—a method to feed the monster. Add the following lines below the three instance variables in your class definition:

```
void feedJabberwock(Graphics g, int y) {
    if (hungry == true) {
        g.drawString("Yum -- a peasant!", 25, y);
        hungry = false;
    } else
        g.drawString("No, thanks -- already ate.", 25, y);
}
// more to come
```

TIP

The last line, `// more to come`, is a comment line. *Comments* are used for the benefit of programmers looking at source code to figure out what it's doing. Everything from the initial `//` to the end of the line will be ignored by the compiler. In this case, the comment is being used as a placeholder. You'll replace it soon.

The `feedJabberwock()` method tests to see whether the jabberwock is hungry (in the line `if (hungry == true) {`). If it is hungry, the jabberwock is fed (much to its delight), and the state of `hungry` is changed to `false`. If the jabberwock is not hungry, a message is displayed that the monster already ate. Here's what your program should look like so far:

```
class Jabberwock {
    String color;
    String sex;
    boolean hungry;

    void feedJabberwock(Graphics g, int y) {
        if (hungry == true) {
            g.drawString("Yum -- a peasant!", 25, y);
            hungry = false;
        } else
            g.drawString("No, thanks -- already ate.", 25, y);
```

```
        }

    // more to come
}
```

> **TIP**
>
> The indentation of each part of the class and the insertion of blank lines aren't required for the program to work correctly—the compiler ignores these blanks. Using some form of indentation, however, makes your class definition easier to read. This readability pays dividends when you or another programmer tries later on to figure out what the code is doing. The indentation used here, with instance variables and methods indented from the class definition, is a commonly used style for Java programs. The Java class libraries use a similar indentation. You can choose any indentation style that you like.

Before you compile this class, you should add one more method. The showAtts() method displays the current values of the instance variables in an instance of your Jabberwock class. In the program, delete the comment line // more to come and replace it with the following:

```
void showAtts(Graphics g, int y) {
    g.drawString("This is a " + sex + " " + color
        + " jabberwock.", 25, y);
    if (hungry == true)
        g.drawString("The jabberwock is hungry.", 25, y+20);
    else
        g.drawString("The jabberwock is full.", 25, y+20);
}
```

The showAtts() method displays two lines to the screen: the sex and color of the Jabberwock object, and whether the monster is hungry. Save your source code file after adding the showAtts() method.

At this point, you have a Jabberwock class and methods that can be used to modify or display its instance variables. To do something with the class (for example, to create instances of that class and play with them), you must create the code for a Java applet that uses the Jabberwock class.

Listing 2.1 shows the full source code for JabberwockApplet.java. Return to your text editor and enter lines 1 through 20 above the source code you already have entered. When you're done, save the file.

> **CAUTION**
>
> It is important to note that Java is case sensitive. In this example, if you enter g.drawstring as a method name instead of g.drawString, it will result as a compiler error because drawstring will not be found in the java.awt.Graphics class.

Listing 2.1. JabberwockApplet.java.

```java
1: import java.awt.Graphics;
2:
3: public class JabberwockApplet extends java.applet.Applet {
4:
5:     public void paint(Graphics g) {
6:         Jabberwock j = new Jabberwock();
7:         j.color = "orange";
8:         j.sex = "male";
9:         j.hungry = true;
10:        g.drawString("Calling showAtts ...", 5, 50);
11:        j.showAtts(g, 70);
12:        g.drawString("Feeding the jabberwock ...", 5, 110);
13:        j.feedJabberwock(g, 130);
14:        g.drawString("Calling showAtts ...", 5, 150);
15:        j.showAtts(g, 170);
16:        g.drawString("Feeding the jabberwock ...", 5, 210);
17:        j.feedJabberwock(g, 230);
18:    }
19: }
20:
21: class Jabberwock {
22:     String color;
23:     String sex;
24:     boolean hungry;
25:
26:     void feedJabberwock(Graphics g, int y) {
27:         if (hungry == true) {
28:             g.drawString("Yum — a peasant!", 25, y);
29:             hungry = false;
30:         } else
31:             g.drawString("No, thanks — already ate.", 25, y);
32:     }
33:
34:     void showAtts(Graphics g, int y) {
35:         g.drawString("This is a " + sex + " " + color
36:             + " jabberwock.", 25, y);
37:         if (hungry == true)
38:             g.drawString("The jabberwock is hungry.", 25, y+20);
39:         else
40:             g.drawString("The jabberwock is full.", 25, y+20);
41:     }
42: }
```

Before you can test the applet, you must compile it. If you're using the Java Developers Kit (JDK), the command to compile the file JabberwockApplet.java is the following:

```
javac JabberwockApplet.java
```

javac is the compiler included with the JDK. It takes one or more .java source code files as input and creates class files of compiled Java bytecode, which have the file extension .class. When JabberwockApplet.java is compiled, two .class files are created: JabberwockApplet.class and Jabberwock.class.

If the source code has been entered correctly, it should compile without any errors.

Running the Applet

Although most of the code in the Jabberwock class definition has been described, the contents of the JabberwockApplet class in Listing 2.1 are largely new to you. This section more fully explains the lines that involve the Jabberwock class to give you an idea of how classes are used.

Line 6, Jabberwock j = new Jabberwock(), creates a new instance of the Jabberwock class and stores a reference to it in the variable j. Remember that you usually do not operate directly on classes in your Java programs. Instead, you create objects from those classes and call methods in those objects. Lines 7, 8, and 9 set the instance variables for the Jabberwock object j. The color is set to orange, the sex is set to male, and the hungry boolean instance variable is set to true.

Line 11 calls the showAtts() method, defined in your Jabberwock object, with the parameters (g, 70). (The parameters used here and elsewhere in the program determine where text will be displayed in the applet. Disregard them for now.) The showAtts() method displays the values of the instance variables sex and color for the Jabberwock object j. It also displays the value of the instance variable hungry.

Line 13 calls the feedJabberwock() method in Jabberwock to feed object j. Jabberwock object j is hungry when the applet starts because hungry is initially set to true, so the object eats the food. As you saw in the feedJabberwock() method described previously, the instance variable hungry is set to false after the Jabberwock object eats.

Line 15 calls the showAtts() method again, displaying the values of the instance variables for a second time. A change in state for hungry is shown. Line 17 tries to feed the jabberwock again to see what happens. Because Jabberwock object j is no longer hungry, the object refuses to eat the food.

Now that you have become familiar with what the program is doing, you should be ready to run JabberwockApplet. If you're using the Java Developers Kit or some other tool that does not have the facility to immediately test applets, you must create a simple Web page that can load the applet. Enter the text from Listing 2.2 into a file called JabberwockApplet.html. Using the Java Developers Kit, you can see the output of this applet by using the following command:

```
appletviewer JabberwockApplet.html
```

Listing 2.2. The HTML code of JabberwockApplet.html.

```
1: <html>
2: <body>
3: <applet code=JabberwockApplet.class height=250 width=300>
4: </applet>
5: </body>
6: </html>
```

The output should look like the following:

```
Calling showAtts ...
    This is a male orange jabberwock.
    The jabberwock is hungry.
Feeding the jabberwock ...
    Yum -- a peasant!
Calling showAtts ...
    This is a male orange jabberwock.
    The jabberwock is full.
Feeding the jabberwock ...
    No, thanks -- already ate.
```

With a basic grasp of classes, objects, methods, and variables, you have put them together successfully in a Java program. But this is only part of the story of object-oriented programming. It's time to learn about the features that make this style of programming so powerful.

Understanding Inheritance, Interfaces, and Packages

Inheritance, interfaces, and packages are all mechanisms for organizing classes and class behaviors. The Java class libraries use all these concepts—and so will the best class libraries you write for your own programs.

Inheritance

Inheritance is one of the most crucial concepts in object-oriented programming, and it has a direct effect on how you design and write Java classes. Inheritance is a powerful mechanism that allows a class to inherit functionality from an existing class. To create the new class, you only have to specify how that class is different from an existing class, and inheritance gives you automatic access to the existing class.

With inheritance, all classes—those you write, those from other class libraries that you use, and those from the standard utility classes as well—are arranged in a strict hierarchy such as the one shown in Figure 2.2.

Each class has a *superclass* (the class above it in the hierarchy)—except for the topmost class in the hierarchy. Each class can have one or more *subclasses* (classes below it in the hierarchy). Classes in the hierarchy inherit from classes above them in the hierarchy.

Subclasses inherit all the methods and variables from their superclasses. In practical terms, this means that if the superclass defines behavior your class needs, you don't have to redefine that behavior or copy that code from some other class. Your class automatically receives that behavior from its superclass, the superclass gets behavior from its superclass, and so on, all the way up the hierarchy. Your class becomes a combination of all the features of the classes above it in the hierarchy, as well as its own features.

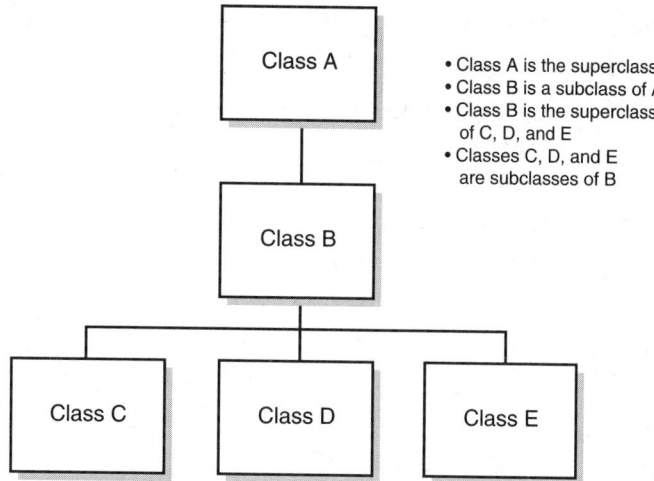

FIGURE 2.2.

A class hierarchy.

- Class A is the superclass of B
- Class B is a subclass of A
- Class B is the superclass of C, D, and E
- Classes C, D, and E are subclasses of B

At the top of the Java class hierarchy is the `Object` class—all classes inherit from this one superclass. `Object` is the most general class in the hierarchy; it defines behavior inherited by all the classes in the Java class hierarchy. Each class further down the hierarchy adds more information and becomes more tailored to a specific purpose. A class hierarchy defines abstract concepts at the top of the hierarchy, and those concepts become more concrete the further you go down the chain of subclasses.

Most of the time when you create a new class in Java, you will want your class to have all the functionality of an existing class with some new additions or modifications of your own creation. For example, you may want a version of a `LightSwitch` class with images for the switch. To receive all the `LightSwitch` functionality, all you have to do is define your class as a subclass of `LightSwitch`. Your class automatically has all the behavior defined in `LightSwitch`, and all the behavior defined in the superclasses of `LightSwitch`. All you have to worry about are the things that make your new class different from `LightSwitch` itself. The mechanism of defining new classes as the differences between them and their superclasses is called *subclassing*.

Subclassing is the creation of a new class that inherits from an existing class in the class hierarchy. Using subclassing, you only have to define the differences between your class and its parent (superclass). The basic behavior is available to your class through inheritance.

What if your class defines entirely new behavior, and it isn't really a subclass of another class? Your class also can inherit directly from `Object`, which still allows it to fit neatly into the Java class hierarchy. In fact, if you create a class definition that doesn't indicate its superclass in the first line, Java assumes that the new class is inheriting directly from `Object`. The `Jabberwock` class you created in the previous section inherited from the `Object` class.

Creating a Class Hierarchy

If you're creating a larger set of classes, it makes sense for your classes not only to inherit from the existing class hierarchy, but also to make up a hierarchy themselves. Creating this hierarchy can take some planning beforehand when you're trying to figure out how to organize your Java code. However, the advantages are significant:

■ When you develop your classes in a hierarchy, you can put functionality that is common to multiple classes into superclasses. This arrangement allows that functionality to be reused repeatedly because each subclass receives that common information from its superclass.

■ Changing or inserting a class further up in the hierarchy automatically changes the behavior of the lower classes. There is no need to change or recompile any of the lower classes because they receive the new information through inheritance and not by copying any code.

Imagine that you have created a Java class to implement all the features of a Jabberwock. It's done, it works, and everything is fine. Your next task is to create a Java class called Dragon.

Dragon and Jabberwock have many similar features—both are large monsters that eat peasants. Both have sharp claws, powerful teeth, and fiery breath. Your first impulse may be to open up your Jabberwock class file and copy a lot of the functionality from it into the new Dragon class.

A far better plan is to factor out the common information for Dragon and Jabberwock into a more general class hierarchy. This can be a lot of work just for the classes Jabberwock and Dragon, but when you add classes for Medusa, Yeti, Sasquatch, and so on, having common behavior in a reusable superclass significantly reduces the overall amount of work you have to do.

To design a class hierarchy that serves this purpose, start at the top with the class Object, the pinnacle of all Java classes. The most general class to which Jabberwock and Dragon both belong might be called Monster. A monster, generally, is defined as a ferocious creature of some kind that terrorizes people. In the Monster class, you define only the behavior that qualifies something as ferocious and terrifying to people, and nothing more.

Below Monster? How about two classes: FlyingMonster and WalkingMonster? FlyingMonster is different from WalkingMonster because it can fly (obviously). The behaviors of flying monsters might include swooping down on prey, carrying people off into the sky, dropping them from great heights, and so on. Walking monsters behave differently. Figure 2.3 shows what you have so far.

Now the hierarchy becomes even more specific. With FlyingMonster, you may have several subclasses: Mammal, Reptile, Amphibian, and so on. As an alternative, you can factor out still more behavior and have intermediate classes for TwoLegged and FourLegged monsters, with different behaviors for each (see Figure 2.4).

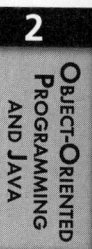

FIGURE 2.3.

The basic Monster *hierarchy.*

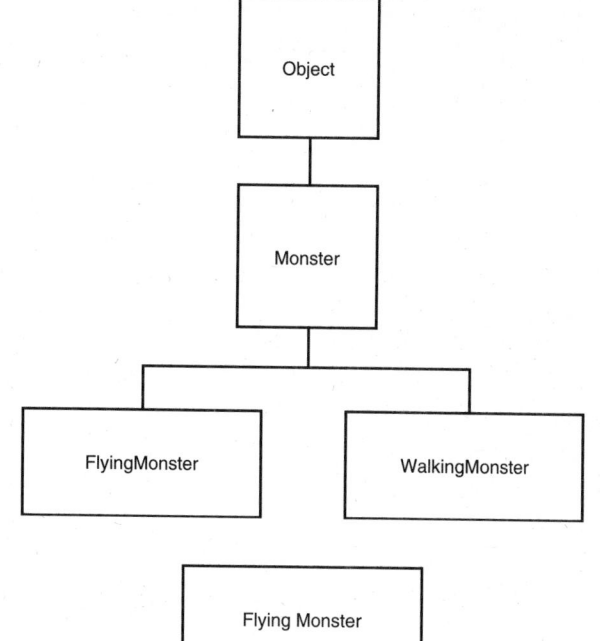

FIGURE 2.4.

Two-legged and four-legged flying monsters.

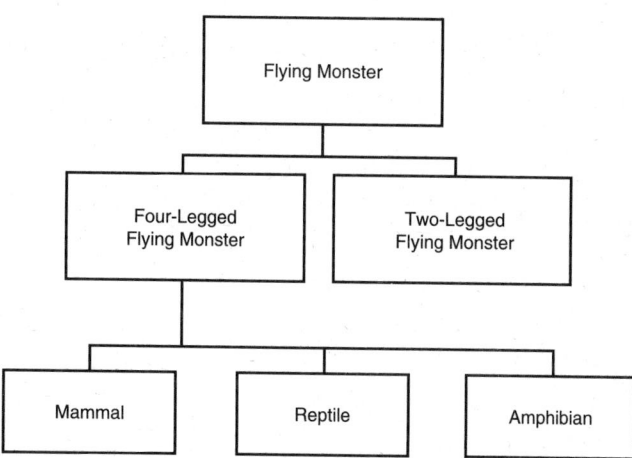

Finally, the hierarchy is done, and you have a place for Jabberwock. It can be a subclass of reptile, four-legged, flying monsters. (Actually, going all the way up the class hierarchy, Jabberwock would be a subclass of reptile, four-legged, flying monster objects, because FlyingMonster is a subclass of Object.)

Where do qualities such as sex, color, or appetite come in? They come in at the place they fit into the class hierarchy most naturally. If you define sex and color as instance variables in Monster, all subclasses will have those variables as well. Remember that you need to define a feature or a behavior only once in the hierarchy, and it is automatically reused by each subclass.

How Inheritance Works

How does inheritance work? How is it that instances of one class automatically receive variables and methods from the classes further up in the hierarchy? For instance variables, when you create a new instance of a class, you get a slot for each variable defined in the current class and a slot for each variable defined in all its superclasses. In this way, all the classes combine to form a template for the current object, and each object fills in the information appropriate to its situation.

Methods operate similarly. New objects have access to all the method names of the object's class and its superclasses, but method definitions are chosen dynamically when a method is called. That is, if you call a method of a particular object, Java first checks the object's class for the definition of that method. If the method is not defined in the object's class, Java looks in the superclass of that class, and so on up the chain until the method definition is found (see Figure 2.5).

FIGURE 2.5.

How methods are located.

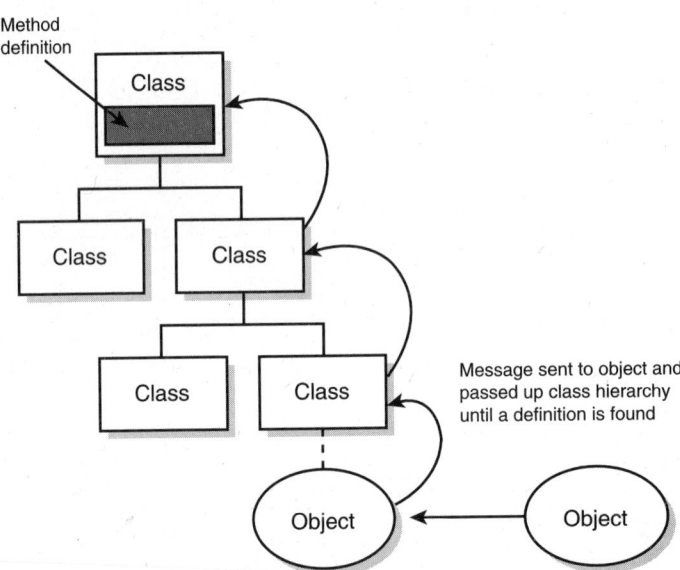

Things get complicated when a subclass defines a method that has the same name, return type, and arguments as a method defined in a superclass. In this case, the method definition that is found first (starting at the bottom of the hierarchy and working upward) is the one that is executed. Because of this, you can intentionally create a new method in a subclass to hide a method in the superclass by defining the new method with the same name, return type, and arguments as the superclass method. This procedure is called *overriding* (see Figure 2.6).

FIGURE 2.6.
Overriding methods.

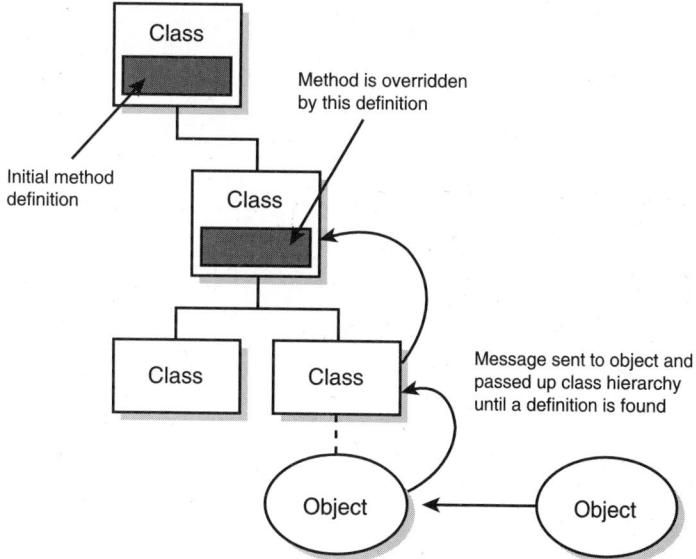

Single and Multiple Inheritance

Java's form of inheritance, as described in the previous sections, is called single inheritance. The rule of *single inheritance* is that each Java class can have only one superclass (although any superclass can have multiple subclasses).

In other object-oriented programming languages, such as C++, classes can have more than one superclass, and they inherit the variables and methods from all those superclasses. This arrangement is called *multiple inheritance*. Multiple inheritance provides enormous power (classes can be created that encompass just about any imaginable behavior), but it also significantly complicates class definitions and the code needed to produce them. Java makes inheritance simpler by allowing only single inheritance.

Interfaces

Because of single inheritance, any Java class has only a single superclass. It inherits variables and methods from all superclasses above it in the hierarchy. This makes subclassing easier to implement and design, but it also can be restricting—especially when you have similar behavior that must be duplicated across different branches of a class hierarchy. Java solves the problem of shared behavior by using interfaces.

An *interface* is a collection of method names, without actual definitions, which indicate that a class has a set of behaviors in addition to the behaviors it receives from its superclasses. Although a single Java class can have only one superclass, that superclass can also implement any number of interfaces. By implementing an interface, a class provides method definitions for the method names defined by the interface. If two very different classes implement the same interface, they both can respond to the same method calls as defined by that interface. However, what each class does in response to those method calls can be completely different.

You don't need to know much about interfaces right now, so don't panic if this information is confusing. You'll learn more as the book progresses.

Using Packages

In Java, *packages* are a way of grouping together related classes and interfaces. Packages enable groups of classes to be available only if they are needed. Packages also eliminate potential conflicts between class names in different groups of classes.

For now, you need to know the following things about packages:

- The class libraries in the JDK are contained in a package called java. The classes in the java package are guaranteed to be available in any Java implementation and are the only classes guaranteed to be available in any implementation. The java package contains other packages for classes that define the language itself, the input and output classes, some basic networking classes, and the windowing toolkit functions. Classes in other packages (for example, those in the sun or netscape packages) might be available only in specific implementations.

- By default, your Java classes have access only to the classes in java.lang (the base language package inside the java package). To use classes from any other package, you have to either refer to them explicitly by package name or import them into your source file.

- To refer to a class within a package, you list all the packages that the class is contained in followed by the class name—separated by periods. For example, consider the Color class. It is contained in the awt package, which in turn is contained in the java package. To refer to the Color class in your program, you use the notation java.awt.Color.

Creating a Subclass

As a final exercise in this chapter, you will create a subclass of another class and override some methods. You also will get a better feel for how packages work.

When you start programming in Java, the most common use of subclassing is when applets are created. You already relied on subclassing when you wrote JabberwockApplet. All applets are subclasses of the class Applet, which is part of the java.applet package. By creating a subclass of Applet, you automatically received behavior from windowing and layout classes that enabled your applet to be drawn in the right place and to interact with system operations such as mouse clicks and key presses.

The `BigPalindrome` Applet

To become familiar with subclassing, we'll create an applet called `BigPalindrome`, a program that displays a line of text that reads the same backwards as forwards (and does so with some panache). Begin developing a new applet with the filename `BigPalindrome.java`.

To start the example, first construct the class definition for the applet. Enter the following class definition:

```
public class BigPalindrome extends java.applet.Applet {
    // placeholder
}
```

This definition creates a class called `BigPalindrome`. Take a look at the phrase `extends java.applet.Applet`—this phrase is what makes `BigPalindrome` a subclass of the `Applet` class. Because the `Applet` class is contained in the `java.applet` package, as opposed to the `java.lang` package, you do not have automatic access to the class. You have to refer to it explicitly by package and class name.

The other new part of this class definition is the `public` keyword. The `public` keyword means that your class is available to the Java system at large once it is loaded. Most of the time, you need to make a class `public` only if you want it to be visible to all other classes in your Java program. However, applets *must* be declared as `public`.

A class definition with nothing in it is pointless—if you don't add anything new, or override the variables or methods of its superclasses, why is the new class needed at all? Let's add some things to make this class different from its superclass.

First, add an instance variable to contain a `Font` object. Replace the `// placeholder` line with the following:

```
Font f = new Font("TimesRoman", Font.BOLD, 30);
```

The `f` instance variable now contains a new instance of the class `Font`, part of the `java.awt` package. This particular font object is a 30-point Times Roman font in boldface style. If a `Font` object is not used and text is displayed, it defaults to 12-point Times Roman. By using a `Font` object, you can change the font of the text displayed in your applet.

By creating an instance variable to hold this `Font` object, you make the object available to all the methods in your class. Now, you will create a method that uses the object.

Overriding a Method

When you write applets, there are several standard methods defined in the `Applet` superclass that you normally will override in the class of your applet. These standard methods include methods to initialize the applet, to start it running, to handle operations such as mouse movements, and to clean up when the mouse stops running.

One of the methods in the `Applet` superclass is the `paint()` method, which displays your applet on-screen. The default definition of `paint()` does nothing at all—it's an empty method. By overriding `paint()`, you tell the applet what should be drawn on-screen. After the `Font` line, enter the following definition for `paint()`:

```
public void paint(Graphics g) {
    g.setFont(f);
    g.setColor(Color.red);
    g.drawString("Go hang a salami, I'm a lasagna hog.", 5, 25);
}
```

Note that this method is declared `public`, just as the applet itself was. Unlike the applet, however, the `paint()` method is `public` because the method it is overriding also is `public`. If the method of a superclass is defined as `public`, the method to override it also has to be `public` or an error will occur when the class is compiled.

Also note that the `paint()` method takes a single argument: an instance of the `Graphics` class. The `Graphics` class provides platform-independent behavior for rendering fonts, colors, and basic drawing operations. You learn more about the `Graphics` class in Chapter 18, "Programming Applets," when you create more extensive applets.

Inside your `paint()` method, you have done the following:

- You told the `Graphics` object that the default drawing font will be the one contained in the instance variable `f`.

- You told the `Graphics` object that the default color is an instance of the `Color` class for the color red.

- You told the `Graphics` object to draw the palindrome, `Go hang a salami, I'm a lasagna hog.`, on the applet window at the x and y positions of 5 and 25. The string will be rendered in the new font and color.

Importing a Package

For an applet this simple, no more code seems necessary. However, something is missing. If you don't know what it is, save the source file and compile it. You will get a bunch of errors like the following:

```
BigPalindrome.java:3: Class Font not found in type declaration.
```

These errors occur because classes such as `Font` and `Graphics` are part of a package. Remember that the only package you automatically have access to is `java.lang`. You referred to the `Applet` class in the first line of the class definition by referring to its full package name (`java.applet.Applet`). Further down in the program, however, you referred to several other classes as if they already were available.

There are two ways to solve this problem. You can refer to all external classes by full package name, or you can import the appropriate class or package at the beginning of your class file.

The solution you choose is mostly a matter of personal choice, but if you refer to a class in another package numerous times, you may want to use the `import` statement to cut down on the typing required.

In the `BigPalindrome` example, import the needed classes: `Graphics`, `Font`, and `Color`. All three are part of the `java.awt` package. Before the first line of the program, insert the following three lines:

```
import java.awt.Graphics;
import java.awt.Font;
import java.awt.Color;
```

TIP

You also can import an entire package of `public` classes by using an asterisk (*) in place of a specific class name. For example, to import all classes in the awt package, you can use the following statement:

```
import java.awt.*;
```

Listing 2.3 shows the full source code of the `BigPalindrome` applet.

Listing 2.3. BigPalindrome.java.

```
 1: import java.awt.Graphics;
 2: import java.awt.Font;
 3: import java.awt.Color;
 4:
 5: public class BigPalindrome extends java.applet.Applet {
 6:
 7:     Font f = new Font("TimesRoman", Font.BOLD, 30);
 8:
 9:     public void paint(Graphics g) {
10:         g.setFont(f);
11:         g.setColor(Color.red);
12:         g.drawString("Go hang a salami, I'm a lasagna hog.", 5, 25);
13:     }
14: }
```

Now that the proper classes have been imported into your program, it should work successfully. Compile the applet, and if you have to create an HTML page to see it, enter the code in Listing 2.4 into a file called `BigPalindrome.html`. Java Developers Kit users can see the output of the applet by using the following command:

```
appletviewer BigPalindrome.html
```

Listing 2.4. The HTML code of `BigPalindrome.html`.

```
1: <html>
2: <body>
3: <applet code=BigPalindrome.class height=150 width=500>
4: </applet>
5: </body>
6: </html>
```

Run the applet and the output should look like Figure 2.7.

FIGURE 2.7.

The output of the
`BigPalindrome` *applet.*

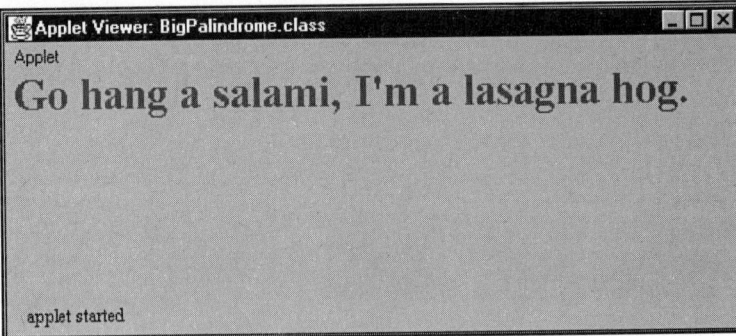

Summary

If this chapter was your first encounter with object-oriented programming, a lot of the information probably seems both theoretical and overwhelming at this point. You do not have to fully understand the information yet because you will be using object-oriented techniques for the rest of this book. The information will become more familiar to you as you gain more experience.

One of the biggest hurdles of object-oriented programming is not necessarily the concepts, it's the names. There is a lot of jargon. To summarize the material in this chapter, here's a glossary of terms and concepts that were covered:

class
A template for an object that contains variables to describe the object, and methods to describe how the object behaves. Classes can inherit variables and methods from other classes.

object
A concrete instance of a class—in other words, a real instance that has been created using a class as its template. Multiple instances of the same class have access to the same methods, but they often have different values for their instance variables.

instance	An object made real through the use of a class.
superclass	A class further up the class hierarchy than another class (its subclass). The subclass inherits variables and methods from all superclasses above it in the hierarchy.
subclass	A class further down the class hierarchy than another class (its superclass). When you create a new class to inherit the behavior of another class, the process is called *subclassing*.
instance method	A method defined in a class that operates on an instance of that class. Instance methods usually are just called *methods*.
class method	A method defined in a class that operates on the class itself and can be called through the class or any of its instances.
instance variable	A variable owned by an individual instance of a class, and whose value is stored in that instance.
class variable	A variable owned by the class and all its instances as a whole, and whose value is stored in the class.
interface	A collection of abstract behavior specifications that can be implemented by individual classes.
package	A collection of related classes and interfaces. Classes from packages other than `java.lang` must be imported explicitly or referred to by their full package names.

Browsing Java

by Bryan Morgan and
Michael Morrison

IN THIS CHAPTER

CHAPTER 3

Java applets wouldn't be very useful without a client Web browser to run them in. Sure, we could all download applets and run them using the JDK (Java Developers Kit) applet viewer tool but that wouldn't be quite the same. Because Java applets are so dependent on quality Java-enabled Web browsers, this entire chapter explores the available Web browsers that currently offer Java support. The three big browsers that support Java as of this writing are Sun's HotJava 1.0, Netscape Navigator 3.0, and Microsoft Internet Explorer 3.0.

The HotJava 1.0 browser is actually still in pre-beta form, but it will be an important browser in the near future because it is being developed by JavaSoft. The other two Web browsers, Netscape Navigator 3.0 and Microsoft Internet Explorer 3.0, are currently battling it out over who dominates the Web client software market. This chapter doesn't bother trying to rate one browser over another because all we're concerned with is Java. Instead, you learn about what each browser has to offer in terms of Java support.

HotJava 1.0

The HotJava browser is a product of JavaSoft, the subsidiary of Sun Microsystems that is responsible for Java. It is the only Web browser that not only supports Java applets but also is actually written in Java. Although the browser market is dominated at the present time by Netscape Navigator and Microsoft Internet Explorer, HotJava stands a chance to rock the boat a little when it ships in final form.

What is now known as the HotJava product was actually introduced as a standalone Web browser back in the spring of 1995. As Java's potential was recognized by the public and its popularity skyrocketed, HotJava came to be much more than a Web browser. The HotJava product now also refers to a set of Java class libraries that simplify the creation of Internet-aware applications. The HotJava browser is provided as a showcase of these class libraries' capabilities. The HotJava class library will be available from JavaSoft as a licensable product in the near future, possibly at the release of Java 1.1.

At this time, HotJava can best be explored by downloading and installing the HotJava Web browser. You can download the HotJava browser from JavaSoft's Web site:

`http://www.javasoft.com.`

In the following sections, you learn about some of the features in HotJava that make it unique among other Web browsers.

HotJava Features

The HotJava Web browser supports many of the most popular browser features. More important to this discussion is its support for the execution of Java applets. HotJava also has the following features that make it somewhat unique among other browsers:

- **Security**—Because HotJava was written using the Java language, it provides a very secure environment for Java applets to run in.
- **External Viewers**—Although the HotJava browser will natively display a number of file formats such as HTML, GIF, and JPEG, its designers realized the need to occasionally view documents of other types. HotJava allows the user to configure viewers based on the file's MIME (Multipurpose Internet Mail Extensions) type.
- **Configurable User Interface**—The HotJava user interface is completely contained within files included with the HotJava installation. These files can be changed or replaced, allowing users to completely modify the appearance of the HotJava browser.

Navigating in HotJava

Figure 3.1 shows the navigation buttons available to the HotJava user.

FIGURE 3.1.

The HotJava navigator buttons.

These buttons, from left to right, perform the following functions:

- Go back a page
- Go forward a page
- Go to home page
- Reload a page
- Stop a page's loading
- Show HTML errors

The last button bears some special mention because this feature is unique to the HotJava Web browser. HotJava features a sophisticated HTML parser that can detect errors in HTML pages. The last button on the HotJava toolbar is used to display any HTML errors found within a page.

Setting Preferences

HotJava provides a means to alter its preferences, which means that you can configure the browser display and applet security, among other things. You access these preferences by selecting Preferences from the Edit menu. The following list briefly explains the submenu items of interest available under the Preferences menu:

■ **Display**—This option loads a form that contains several entry fields (see Figure 3.2). This form allows the user to change default font sizes, set a home page, and control the display of the HotJava welcome screen.

FIGURE 3.2.

Contents of the Preferences/Display form.

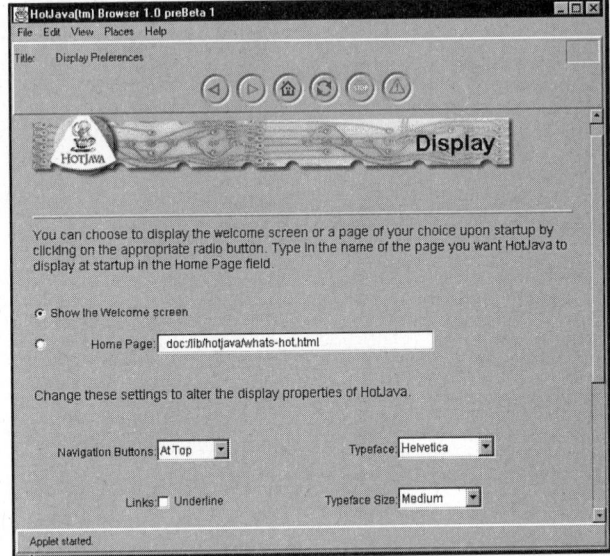

■ **Applet Security**—This is the most interesting of the Edit menu options. HotJava actually allows the user to disable (or weaken) the default security precautions to allow applets complete file access on your local machine, as well as the ability to communicate with other computers across the Internet (in addition to the server from which the applet was sent). Unless you have good reason for not doing so, these security settings should be set to the following:

```
Network Access = Applet Host
```

```
Class Access = Restricted
```

If, for some reason, you want to configure your HotJava browser to allow applets to read and write files on your local drive, you can do so by modifying the Access Control List in the HotJava properties file. This file is located in the ./.hotjava directory. Although the Access Control List is blank by default, it can be modified by adding the acl_read and acl_write properties, using the following syntax:

```
acl_read=[directory_name1 or file_name1]:[directory_nameN or file_nameN]
```

```
acl_write=[directory_name1 or file_name1]:[directory_nameN or file_nameN]
```

> **NOTE**
>
> These security settings are completely browser dependent and do not rely in any way on Java or the Java virtual machine. Developers who complain that Java is too restrictive are generally misinformed (or underinformed). In general, it is the Java *default* implementations that are designed to be restrictive—and for good reason!

Setting View Options

HotJava's View menu contains a set of options that apply specifically to the current page being viewed. The following list briefly explains some of the more important menu items:

- **Monitor**—The Monitor option contains the following submenus: Progress, Memory, and Thread. These submenus load HTML pages that can be used to see the current state of various operations. Remember to press the Shift key when selecting any of these options to load a *separate* HotJava window. Otherwise, these pages *replace* the current HTML page you are viewing.

- **Monitor Progress**—This submenu selection loads a form that shows the progress of the current form load process. Note that a miniature version of the progress bar is located in the right corner of the HotJava browser window. When the progress bar is completely filled, the loading process is finished.

- **Monitor Memory**—This selection loads a form that shows a bar graph illustrating the amount of total free memory and the amount of memory that HotJava is currently using. At the bottom of this page is a button that allows you to clean up memory previously allocated by HotJava.

- **Monitor Thread**—This submenu selection loads a form showing all active threads in HotJava with their respective priorities and thread groups. It includes options that allow the user to raise and lower thread priorities as well as kill active threads (see Figure 3.3).

Content and Protocol Handlers

HotJava is the only Web browser with direct support for dynamic content and protocol handlers. In case you aren't familiar with these concepts, a *protocol handler* is a piece of code that handles the details of transferring different types of information between a server and client across an Internet connection. A *content handler* takes information that has been transmitted or received with a protocol handler and determines how that information is processed.

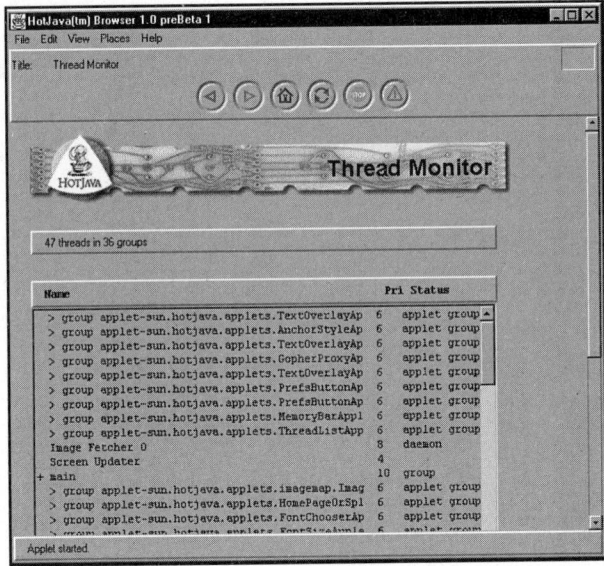

FIGURE 3.3.

The HotJava Thread Monitor page.

A good example of a protocol is HTTP (HyperText Transfer Protocol), which defines the means in which hypertext documents are transferred between a Web server and client browser. Both the server and client in this case have HTTP protocol handlers that determine how the hypertext information is packaged and transferred. Likewise, an example of a content handler is the component of a Web browser that interprets and displays Web pages based on HTML content sent with the HTTP protocol. All Web browsers must support content and protocol handlers at this level.

HotJava offers a whole new level of abstraction by supporting dynamic content and protocol handlers—meaning that you can add support for new protocol and content types to the HotJava browser without getting a new version of the browser. This modularization of protocol and content types allows the structure of the Web to evolve and change without requiring significant reworking of the browser itself; if a new protocol or content type emerges, you just plug in the handler for it and go!

You learn all about writing your own content and protocol handlers in Chapter 24, "Developing Content and Protocol Handlers."

Netscape Navigator 3.0

If you are like the average Web user, chances are extremely good that you use or have used the Netscape Navigator Web browser. Netscape Navigator is by far the most popular Web browser. In fact, Netscape claims to currently control around 80 percent of the Web browser market with Navigator, although this number is no doubt dropping as Microsoft aggressively pursues

Netscape with its Internet Explorer. However, one number Microsoft can't compete with at present is the number of platforms for which Navigator is available. Currently, Navigator is available for a whopping 16 different platforms including Windows 3.1, Windows 95/NT, Apple Macintosh 68K/PowerPC, and Sun Solaris, among others.

Because Navigator—and Internet Explorer, for that matter—has features similar to those discussed earlier in the HotJava Web browser, there's no need to spend a great deal of time discussing each individual feature. Instead, let's turn our attention to its support of Java and related technologies.

Java Support

The most recent version of Netscape Navigator, version 3.0, represents Netscape's most complete support for Java to date. Navigator 3.0 includes full support for both Java applets and JavaScript programs. It even supports the latest version of JavaScript (version 1.1). I guess this doesn't come as too much of a surprise considering that Netscape developed JavaScript! Figure 3.4 shows Netscape Navigator 3.0 in action. You can download Netscape Navigator 3.0 from Netscape's Web site, which is located at `http://www.netscape.com`.

FIGURE 3.4.

Netscape Navigator 3.0.

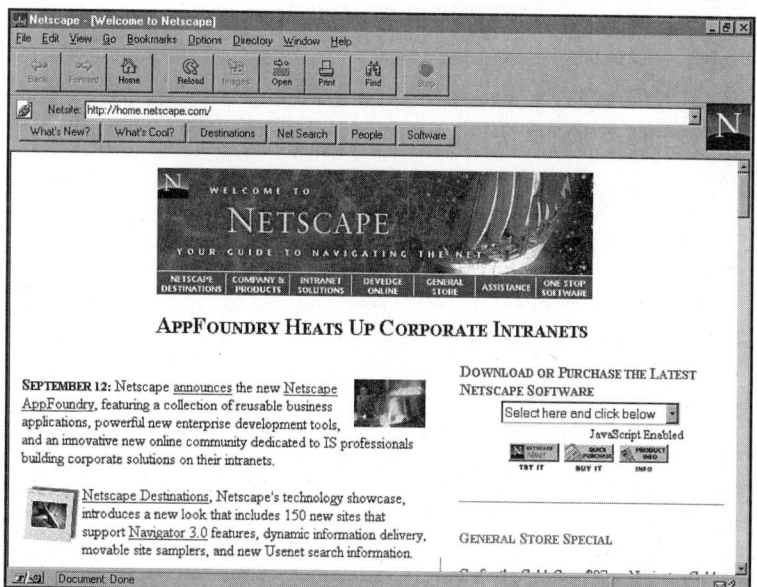

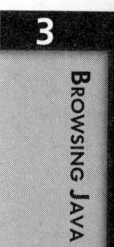

Even though core support for Java and JavaScript is extremely important, one of the more exciting features of Navigator is its inclusion of a just-in-time Java compiler in the Windows 95/NT version. If you aren't familiar with just-in-time compilers, they compile Java executables into native machine code on the fly to allow much faster execution speeds. For the details about just-in-time Java compilers, check out Chapter 44, "Just-in-Time Compilers."

Along with all this Java support behind the scenes, Navigator also has a nice feature not found in many other Web browsers: the Java console (see Figure 3.5).

FIGURE 3.5.

Netscape Navigator's Java console.

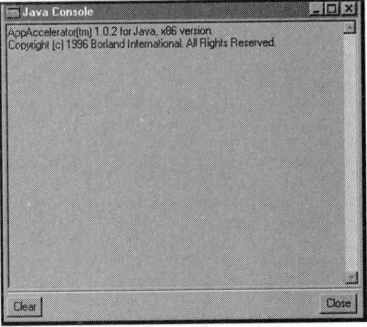

The Java console allows the user to see exactly which Java applets are being loaded and executed without having to examine the HTML source directly. This feature can come in handy when you are trying to debug Java and HTML forms.

You just learned that Navigator supports JavaScript 1.1, which is a scripting language that allows you to embed scripted programs directly into HTML code. JavaScript was initially introduced by Netscape in an earlier version of Navigator as a feature known as LiveScript. Because Java applets generally do not interact with other elements on HTML pages, JavaScript is useful in providing a means to tie these types of elements together. Although much of the syntax is similar to Java, there are some major differences. Most notably, JavaScript does not allow you to define new types of objects. Additionally, inheritance is not allowed and JavaScript code is not compiled. Instead, it is embedded within the <SCRIPT> and </SCRIPT> tags in an HTML form. Nevertheless, JavaScript is still a very viable alternative for people who want to add a little interactivity to their Web pages without becoming Java experts.

Security

The approach Navigator 3.0 takes in handling applet security is what separates its Java support from the HotJava browser. HotJava allows the user to set security options, but Navigator does not. With Navigator, Java applets are not allowed to read or write to the local file system under any circumstances; applets are restricted to communicating only with the computer from which they came. In addition, unlike users of HotJava, users of Navigator can turn off Java applet support altogether. This feature was provided primarily to pacify users who were concerned over security problems with early versions of Java. Figure 3.6 shows Navigator's Java options.

FIGURE 3.6.
Netscape Navigator's Preferences dialog box.

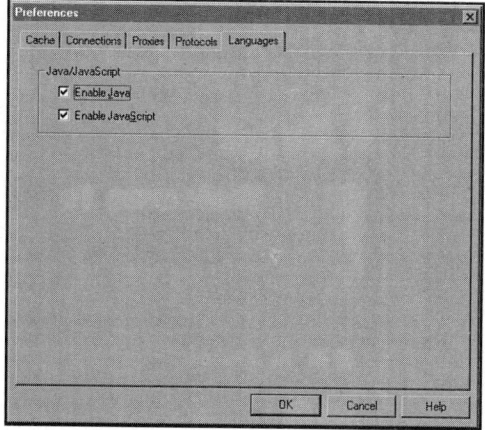

Microsoft Internet Explorer 3.0

Although late to the game, Microsoft's latest version of the Web browser, Internet Explorer 3.0, is actually full of features—not the least of which is its support for Java and other interactive technologies. Even though Netscape beat Microsoft to the punch with Java support in earlier versions of Netscape Navigator, Microsoft has managed to make up ground fast and even to throw in a few related extras. Internet Explorer 3.0 includes full support for Java applets and JavaScript, including a just-in-time Java compiler. However, Internet Explorer doesn't support the latest version of JavaScript (version 1.1). Figure 3.7 shows Internet Explorer 3.0 in action. You can download Internet Explorer 3.0 from Microsoft's Web site, which is located at `http://www.microsoft.com`.

Perhaps more exciting than Internet Explorer's direct Java support is the inclusion of Microsoft's own ActiveX technology. ActiveX is a powerful new technology built on Microsoft's popular OLE component technology. ActiveX allows Web developers to embed prebuilt software components, called *controls*, directly in Web pages, much like Java applets are embedded. Also included in ActiveX is a scripting language called VBScript, which is a scaled-down version of the popular Visual Basic programming language. Both ActiveX controls and VBScript programs can be integrated with Java applets, resulting in an interesting mix of new technologies. For more information about the specifics regarding Java and ActiveX, refer to Chapter 38, "Integrating Java and ActiveX."

FIGURE 3.7.

*Microsoft Internet
Explorer 3.0.*

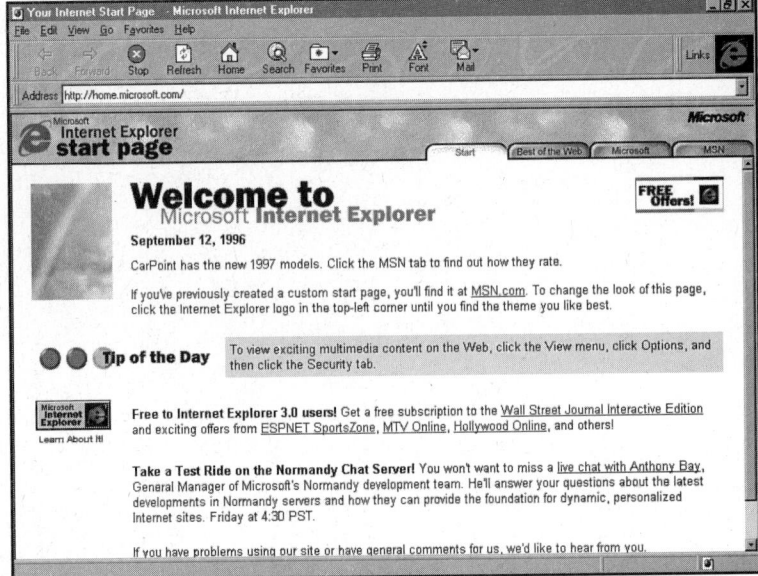

Java Support

Similar to Netscape Navigator, Internet Explorer supports Java, JavaScript, and a just-in-time
Java compiler. Unlike Navigator, Internet Explorer currently supports only version 1.0 of
JavaScript (it does not support the newer version 1.1). Also unlike Navigator, Internet Explorer
allows you to disable the just-in-time Java compiler. This is done through the Advanced tab of
the Options dialog box, shown in Figure 3.8.

FIGURE 3.8.

*Microsoft Internet
Explorer's Advanced
Options dialog box.*

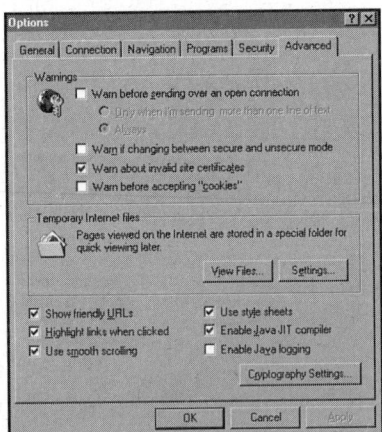

In the Advanced Options dialog box, you may also notice that you can enable or disable Java logging, which is a feature that tracks all Java program activity. In a way, this feature is much like the Java console in Navigator, except that it writes information to a file rather than presenting it in a window.

Security

Internet Explorer, like Navigator, takes a hard line when it comes to Java security. As is true in Navigator, Java applets executing in Internet Explorer are not allowed to read or write to the local file system and are restricted to communicating only with the host computer from which they came. Internet Explorer also provides a means to completely disable Java applets. You set this option using the Security tab in the Options dialog box, shown in Figure 3.9.

FIGURE 3.9.

Microsoft Internet Explorer's Security Options dialog box.

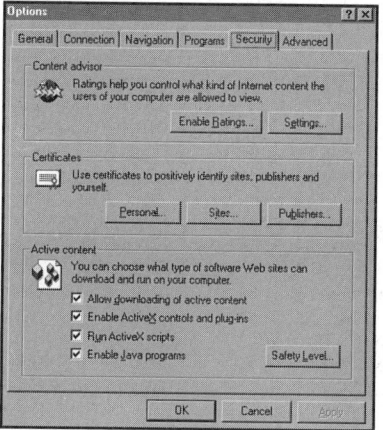

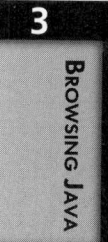

In the Security Options dialog box, you may also notice that Internet Explorer allows you to disable ActiveX controls and plug-ins, as well as ActiveX scripts, which includes both JavaScript and VBScript.

Summary

Because Java applets are only as useful as the Web browsers that support them, this chapter introduced you to the latest Java-enabled browsers. Even though Java is still very young, Web browsers have already come a long way in their internal support for Java. And with the competition heating up over which browser will rule the Web, we can only expect better and faster Java support from all these browsers in subsequent versions.

Each browser you learned about in this chapter took a different approach in how it positioned Java next to its other features. HotJava, which is itself entirely written in Java, is the browser most closely wedded to Java. Netscape Navigator, which was the only commercial browser to adopt Java early on, is probably second to HotJava in its support for Java because it includes the latest release of JavaScript. Internet Explorer, although not as firmly linked to the Java camp, includes a very competitive implementation of Java, JavaScript, and a just-in-time Java compiler. Couple this support with ActiveX and VBScript, and Internet Explorer ultimately provides the most options for Web developers.

Now that you have an idea of what's out there in regard to Java browsers, you're probably eager to find out what's available in terms of Java programming tools. Chapter 4 explores the Java Developers Kit, which is JavaSoft's set of tools for Java development.

The Java
Developers Kit

by Michael Morrison

IN THIS CHAPTER

CHAPTER 4

The Java Developers Kit (JDK) is a comprehensive set of tools, utilities, documentation, and sample code for developing Java programs. Without it, you wouldn't be able to do much with Java. This chapter focuses on the JDK and the tools and information supplied with it. Although some of the tools are discussed in more detail in later chapters, this chapter gives you a broad perspective on using the tools to develop Java programs with the JDK.

In this chapter, you learn which tools are shipped in the JDK and how they are used in a typical Java development environment. With the information presented in this chapter, you will be well on your way to delving further into Java development; the Java Developers Kit is the first step toward learning to program in Java.

Getting the Latest Version

Before you get started learning about the Java Developers Kit, it's important to make sure that you have the latest version. As of this writing, the latest version of the JDK is release 1.02. Version 1.1 is expected in the very near future; you can check Sun's Java Web site at `http://www.javasoft.com/` to see what the latest version is. This Web site provides all the latest news and information regarding Java, including the latest release of the JDK. Keep in mind that Java is a new technology, still in a state of rapid change. Be sure to keep an eye on the Java Web site for the latest information.

 The JDK version 1.0.2 for Windows 95, Windows NT, Macintosh, and Solaris is provided on the CD-ROM that accompanies this book.

The JDK usually comes as a compressed self-extracting archive file. To install the JDK, simply execute the archive file from the directory where you want the JDK installed. The archive will automatically create a `java` directory within the directory you extract it from and build a directory structure to contain the rest of the JDK support files. All the related files are then copied to the correct locations in the JDK directory structure automatically.

Overview

The Java Developers Kit contains a variety of tools and Java development information. Following is a list of the main components of the JDK:

- ■ The runtime interpreter
- ■ The compiler
- ■ The applet viewer
- ■ The debugger
- ■ The class file disassembler
- ■ The header and stub file generator
- ■ The documentation generator

■ Applet demos

■ API source code

The runtime interpreter is the core runtime module for the Java system. The compiler, applet viewer, debugger, class file disassembler, header and stub file generator, and documentation generator are the primary tools used by Java developers. The applet demos are interesting examples of Java applets, which all come with complete source code. And finally, if you are interested in looking under the hood of Java, the complete source code for the Java API (Application Programming Interface) classes is provided.

The Runtime Interpreter

The Java runtime interpreter (`java`) is a stand-alone version of the Java interpreter built into the HotJava browser. The runtime interpreter provides the support to run Java executable programs in compiled, bytecode format. The runtime interpreter acts as a command-line tool for running nongraphical Java programs; graphical programs require the display support of a browser. The syntax for using the runtime interpreter follows:

```
java Options ClassName Arguments
```

The `ClassName` argument specifies the name of the class you want to execute. If the class resides in a package, you must fully qualify the name. For example, if you want to run a class called `Roids` that is located in a package called `ActionGames`, you would execute it in the interpreter like this:

```
java ActionGames.Roids
```

When the Java interpreter executes a class, what it is really doing is executing the `main()` method of the class. The interpreter exits when the `main()` method and any threads created by it are finished executing. The `main()` method accepts a list of arguments that can be used to control the program. The `Arguments` argument to the interpreter specifies the arguments passed into the `main()` method. For example, if you have a Java class called `TextFilter` that performs some kind of filtering on a text file, you would likely pass the name of the file as an argument, like this:

```
java TextFilter SomeFile.txt
```

The `Options` argument specifies options related to how the runtime interpreter executes the Java program. Following is a list of the most important runtime interpreter options:

■ `-debug`

■ `-checksource` (equivalent to `-cs`)

■ `-classpath Path`

■ `-verbose` (equivalent to `-v`)

■ `-verbosegc`

■   -verify

■   -verifyremote

■   -noverify

■   -D*PropertyName=NewValue*

The -debug option starts the interpreter in debugging mode, which enables you to use the Java debugger (jdb) in conjunction with the interpreter. The -checksource option causes the interpreter to compare the modification dates of the source and executable class files. If the source file is more recent, the class is automatically recompiled.

> **NOTE**
>
> The -checksource and -verbose options have shorthand versions: -cs and -v. You can use these shorthand versions as a convenience to save typing.

The Java interpreter uses an environment variable, CLASSPATH, to determine where to look for user-defined classes. The CLASSPATH variable contains a semicolon-delimited list of system paths to user-defined Java classes. Actually, most of the Java tools use the CLASSPATH variable to know where to find user-defined classes. The -classpath option informs the runtime interpreter to override CLASSPATH with the path specified by *Path*.

The -verbose option causes the interpreter to print a message to standard output each time a Java class is loaded. Similarly, the -verbosegc option causes the interpreter to print a message each time a garbage collection is performed. A *garbage collection* is performed by the runtime system to clean up unneeded objects and to free memory.

The -verify option causes the interpreter to run the bytecode verifier on all code loaded into the runtime environment. The verifier's only default function is to verify code loaded into the system using a class loader. This default behavior can also be explicitly specified using the -verifyremote option. The -noverify option turns all code verification off.

The -D option enables you to redefine property values. *PropertyName* specifies the name of the property you want to change, and *NewValue* specifies the new value you want to assign to it.

The Compiler

The Java compiler (javac) is used to compile Java source code files into executable Java bytecode classes. In Java, source code files have the extension .java. The Java compiler takes files with this extension and generates executable class files with the .class extension. The compiler creates one class file for each class defined in a source file. This means that it is possible for a single Java source code file to compile into multiple executable class files. When this happens, it means that the source file contains multiple class definitions.

NOTE

Even though Java source files and classes are typically given the extensions `.java` and `.class`, it is important to note that some operating systems aren't capable of fully representing these extensions because of their length. For example, Windows 3.1 is limited to three character extensions, in which case Java source files and classes use the extensions `.jav` and `.cla`.

NOTE

Even though you are allowed to include multiple classes in a single Java source code file, only one of them can be declared as public. This means that any other classes defined in the file must be private support classes used only by the public class. You learn all about public and private classes in Chapter 6, "Java Language Fundamentals."

The Java compiler is a command-line utility that works in a manner similar to the Java runtime interpreter. The syntax for the Java compiler follows:

```
javac Options Filename
```

The `Filename` argument specifies the name of the source code file you want to compile. The `Options` argument specifies options related to how the compiler creates the executable Java classes. Following is a list of the compiler options:

- `-classpath Path`
- `-d Dir`
- `-g`
- `-nowarn`
- `-verbose`
- `-O`

The `-classpath` option tells the compiler to override the CLASSPATH environment variable with the path specified by `Path`. Use of this option causes the compiler to look for user-defined classes in the path specified by `Path`. The `-d` option determines the root directory where compiled classes are stored. This is important because classes are frequently organized in a hierarchical directory structure. With the `-d` option, the directory structure will be created beneath the directory specified by `Dir`. An example of using the `-d` option follows:

```
javac -d ..\ Flower
```

In this example, the output file `Flower.class` is stored in the parent directory of the current directory. If the file `Flower.java` contained classes that were part of a package hierarchy, the subdirectories and output classes would fan out below the parent directory.

The `-g` compiler option causes the compiler to generate debugging tables for the Java classes. Debugging tables are used by the Java debugger and contain information such as local variables and line numbers. The default action of the compiler is to generate only line numbers.

The `-nowarn` option turns off compiler warnings. Warnings are printed to standard output during compilation to inform you of potential problems with the source code. In general, it isn't a good idea to suppress warnings using the `-nowarn` option because warnings can be useful in pointing out problems in your code. The `-verbose` option has a somewhat opposite effect as `-nowarn`; it prints out extra information about the compilation process. You can use `-verbose` to see exactly what source files are being compiled.

The `-O` option causes the compiler to optimize the compiled code. In this case, *optimization* simply means that static, final, and private methods are compiled inline. When a method is compiled inline, it means that the entire body of the method is included in place of each call to the method. This speeds up execution because it eliminates the method call overhead. Optimized classes are usually larger in size (to accommodate the duplicate code). The `-O` optimization option also suppresses the default creation of line numbers by the compiler. You learn all about optimization in Chapter 30, "Optimizing Java Code."

The Applet Viewer

The applet viewer is a tool that serves as a minimal test bed for final release Java applets. You can use the applet viewer to test your programs instead of using a full-blown Web browser. You invoke the applet viewer from a command line, like this:

```
appletviewer Options URL
```

The *URL* argument specifies a document URL containing an HTML page with an embedded Java applet. The *Options* argument specifies how to run the Java applet. There is only one option supported by the applet viewer: `-debug`. The `-debug` option starts the applet viewer in the Java debugger, which enables you to debug the applet. To see the applet viewer in action, check out Figure 4.1.

Figure 4.1 shows the `MoleculeViewer` demo applet (which comes with the JDK) running in the applet viewer. This program was launched in the applet viewer by changing to the directory containing the `MoleculeViewer` HTML file and executing the following statement at the command prompt:

```
appletviewer example1.html
```

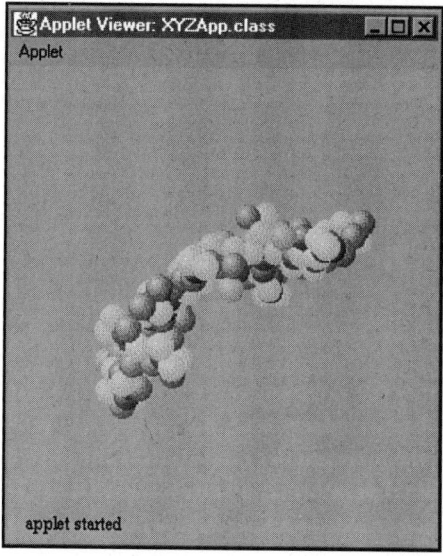

example1.html is the HTML file containing the embedded Java applet. As you can see, there's nothing complicated about running Java applets using the applet viewer. The applet viewer is a useful tool for testing Java applets in a simple environment.

The Debugger

The Java debugger (jdb) is a command-line utility that enables you to debug Java applications. The Java debugger uses the Java Debugger API to provide debugging support within the Java runtime interpreter. The syntax for using the Java debugger follows:

```
jdb Options
```

The Options argument is used to specify different settings within a debugging session. Because the Java debugger is covered in detail in Chapter 28, "Java Debugging," you won't learn any more details about it in this chapter. If you are just dying to know more about Java debugging, feel free to jump ahead to Chapter 28 and get the whole scoop.

The Class File Disassembler

The Java class file disassembler (javap) is used to disassemble executable Java class files. Its default output consists of the public data and methods for a class. The class file disassembler is useful in cases where you don't have the source code for a class, but you'd like to know a little more about how it is implemented. The syntax for the disassembler follows:

```
javap Options ClassNames
```

The `ClassNames` argument specifies the names of one or more classes to be disassembled. The `Options` argument specifies how the classes are to be disassembled. The disassembler supports the following options:

- ■ `-c`
- ■ `-p`
- ■ `-h`
- ■ `-classpath` *Path*
- ■ `-verify`
- ■ `-version`

The `-c` option tells the disassembler to output the actual bytecodes for each method. The `-p` option tells the disassembler to also include private variables and methods in its output. Without this option, the disassembler outputs only the public member variables and methods. The `-h` option specifies that information be created that can be used in C header files—useful when you are attempting to interface C code to a Java class for which you don't have the source code. You'll learn much more about interfacing Java to C code in Chapter 33, "Integrating Native Code."

The `-classpath` option specifies a list of directories in which to look for imported classes. The path given by *Path* overrides the `CLASSPATH` environment variable. The `-verify` option tells the disassembler to run the verifier on the class and output debugging information. Finally, the `-version` option causes the disassembler to print its version number.

The Header and Stub File Generator

The Java header and stub file generator (`javah`) is used to generate C header and source files for implementing Java methods in C. The files generated can be used to access member variables of an object from C code. The header and stub file generator accomplishes this by generating a C structure whose layout matches that of the corresponding Java class. The syntax for using the header and stub file generator follows:

```
javah Options ClassName
```

The `ClassName` argument is the name of the class from which to generate C source files. The `Options` argument specifies how the source files are to be generated. Because you learn how to use the Java header and stub file generator in Chapter 33, "Integrating Native Code," you don't get into it in any more detail in this chapter.

The Documentation Generator

The Java documentation generator (`javadoc`) is a useful tool for generating API documentation directly from Java source code. The documentation generator parses through Java source files and generates HTML pages based on the declarations and comments. The syntax for using the documentation generator follows:

```
javadoc Options FileName
```

The `FileName` argument specifies either a package or a Java source code file. In the case of a package, the documentation generator creates documentation for all the classes contained in the package. The `Options` argument enables you to change the default behavior of `javadoc`.

Because the Java documentation generator is covered in detail in Chapter 29, "Documenting Your Code," you'll have to settle for this brief introduction for now. Or you could jump to Chapter 29 to learn more.

Applet Demos

The JDK comes with a variety of interesting Java demo applets, all of which include complete source code. Following is a list of the demo Java applets that come with the JDK:

- Animator
- ArcTest
- BarChart
- Blink
- BouncingHeads
- CardTest
- DitherTest
- DrawTest
- Fractal
- GraphicsTest
- GraphLayout
- ImageMap
- ImageTest
- JumpingBox
- MoleculeViewer

- NervousText
- ScrollingImages
- SimpleGraph
- SpreadSheet
- TicTacToe
- TumblingDuke
- UnderConstruction
- WireFrame

Rather than go through the tedium of describing each of these applications, I'll leave most of them for you to explore and try out on your own. However, it's worth checking out a few of them here and discussing how they might impact the Web.

The first demo applet is the BarChart applet, shown in Figure 4.2.

FIGURE 4.2.

The BarChart *Java applet.*

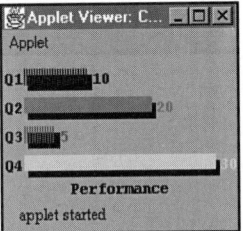

The BarChart applet is a good example of how Java can be used to show statistical information on the Web graphically. The data represented by the bar graph could be linked to a live data source, such as a group of stock quotes. Then you could actually generate a live, to-the-minute, dynamically changing stock portfolio.

The GraphicsTest applet is a good example of how to use Java graphics. Java includes an extensive set of graphics features, including support for drawing primitive shapes as well as more elaborate drawing routines. Figure 4.3 shows what the GraphicsTest applet looks like.

Keeping the focus on graphics, the SimpleGraph applet shows how Java can be used to plot a two-dimensional graph. There are plenty of scientific and educational applications for plotting. Using Java, data presented in a Web page can come to life with graphical plots. SimpleGraph is shown in Figure 4.4.

FIGURE 4.3.

The `GraphicsTest` *Java applet.*

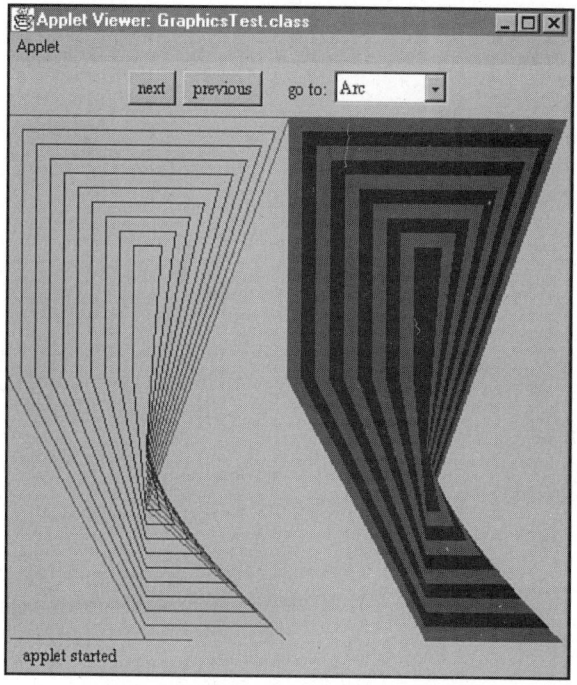

FIGURE 4.4.

The `SimpleGraph` *Java applet.*

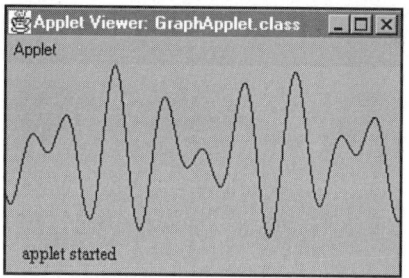

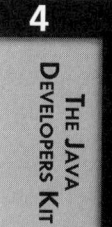

On the business front, there's nothing like a good spreadsheet. The `SpreadSheet` Java applet shows how to implement a simple spreadsheet in Java. I don't think I even need to say how many applications there are for interactive spreadsheets on the Web. Check out the `SpreadSheet` applet in Figure 4.5.

FIGURE 4.5.

The SpreadSheet *Java applet.*

			Example	
1 10	500	10000		
2 30	1000	30000		
3		40000		
4				
A	B	C	D	E

applet started

Once you've gotten a headache playing with the SpreadSheet applet, it's time to blow off a little steam with a game. The TicTacToe applet demonstrates a simple Java version of TicTacToe. This demo opens a new window of opportunity for having fun on the Web. Games will no doubt be an interesting application for Java, so keep your eyes peeled for new and interesting ways to have fun on the Web with Java games. The TicTacToe applet is shown in Figure 4.6.

FIGURE 4.6.

The TicTacToe *Java applet.*

The last applet mentioned in this chapter is the UnderConstruction applet, which is a neat little applet that can be used to jazz up unfinished Web pages. This applet shows an animation of the Java mascot, Duke, with a jackhammer. Because the applet also has sound, it's a true multimedia experience! Although this applet is strictly for fun, it nevertheless provides a cool alternative to the usual "under construction" messages that are often used in unfinished Web pages. The UnderConstruction applet is shown in Figure 4.7.

FIGURE 4.7.

The UnderConstruction *Java applet.*

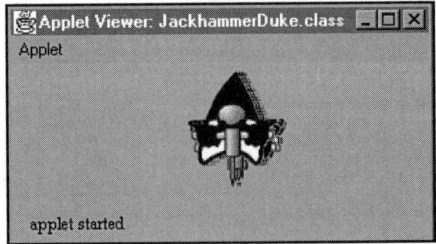

Although running these demo applets is neat, the real thing to keep in mind is that they all come with complete source code. This means that you can rip them apart and figure out how they work, and then use similar techniques in your own Java programs. The most powerful way to learn is by example, and the demo applets that come with the JDK are great examples of robust Java applets.

API Source Code

The final component of the Java Developers Kit is the source code for the Java API. That's right—the JDK comes with the complete source code for all the classes that make up the Java API. Sun isn't concerned with keeping the internals of Java top secret. They followed the lead of the UNIX world and decided to make Java as available and readily understood as possible. Besides, the real value of Java is not the specific code that makes it work, it's the idea behind it.

The API source code is automatically installed to your hard drive when you decompress the JDK, but it remains in compressed form. The assumption is that not everyone is concerned about how the internals of Java are implemented, so why waste the space. However, it is sometimes useful to be able to look under the hood to see how something works. Because Java is no exception, the API source code comes compressed in a file called `src.zip`, located in the `java` directory created on your hard drive during installation of the JDK. All the classes that make up the Java API are included in this file.

Summary

The Java Developers Kit provides a wealth of information, including the tools essential to Java programming. In this chapter, you learned about the different components of the JDK, including tools, applet demos, and the Java API source code. Although you learn more about some of these tools throughout the rest of the book, it's important to understand what role each tool plays in the development of Java programs. A strong knowledge of the information contained in the Java Developers Kit is necessary to becoming a successful Java developer.

However, you shouldn't stop with the Java Developers Kit. Many third-party tools are available or are in the works to supplement the JDK and enable you to put together a more complete Java programming toolkit. The next chapter highlights these tools and describes how they impact Java development now, and what they may mean for the future.

Third-Party Development Tools

by Rogers Cadenhead

IN THIS CHAPTER

CHAPTER 5

When the Java programming language was introduced in 1995, the only development tool available was the Java Developers Kit (JDK) from Sun. This set of command-line tools makes it possible to write, compile, and debug Java programs. However, the JDK is a far cry from the software used to write programs in languages such as Visual Basic and Borland C++. These languages make good use of integrated development environments.

An *integrated development environment* (IDE, pronounced *I'd*) is software that combines several development tools into a single, cohesive package. The assortment usually includes a source code editor, compiler, debugger, and other utilities. These tools work together through the development process; most packages use windows, drag-and-drop, and other graphical elements. The goal is to make software design faster, more efficient, and easier to debug.

Many IDEs make use of *rapid application development* (RAD) methods in their approach. RAD is a broad strategy to use tools such as an interface designer and prototyping to speed up the design process. For most of the Java programming environments that have been released, the RAD tools in evidence are graphical user interface builders. Some of these have a direct connection from the interface design tool to the source code so that you can design a component such as a button and go directly to the event-handling code to make something happen when the button is clicked.

As further evidence of Java's enormous popularity, the number of Java development environments has gone from 1 to more than 40 in a matter of months. Although many of these programs are in early beta release or are unreleased in any form, several have reached the market.

This chapter focuses on some of the environments you are most likely to have heard about and seen available at retail outlets. As you evaluate each to see whether any of them fits your own programming needs, you will become better prepared to choose from among the on-rushing march of IDEs becoming available.

> **NOTE**
>
> A frequently updated list of Java IDEs, with reviews and notes regarding these tools, is presented at the following URL:
>
> ```
> http://www.cybercom.net/~frog/javaide.html
> ```

The following development environments are described in this chapter:

- Symantec Café
- SunSoft Java WorkShop
- SourceCraft NetCraft
- Pro-C WinGEN for Java
- Rogue Wave JFactory

You learn about the features of each environment, the systems they can run on, and some factors to consider when choosing which to use. Other Java development environments such as Microsoft Visual J++ are described briefly, to provide a full picture of the choices available to you.

Selecting an IDE

When you are evaluating an integrated development environment for any language, you should ask yourself some questions about what you need to have on hand when you're ready to develop a program. Although this approach is true for any language and any environment, you should consider some specific issues related to Java's unique programming features (such as portability). Ask yourself the following questions:

- How important is graphical interface design to your programs?
- Do your programs have to be completely portable across platforms?
- What is your comfort zone with IDE tools?
- Do you want to program in other languages at the same time?

GUI Development Tools

The popularity of windowing systems is well established; users have begun to shy away from software that does not make use of these features. Although some of us grizzled veterans have an Amish-like love of the old ways—DOS utilities, the command prompt, batch processing, 1970s dance funk—most users today expect their software to have features such as mouse control, point-and-click, and resizable program windows.

Because these requirements make graphical user interface design an important element of most Java programming, it is important to select an IDE that is strong in this area.

Most Java IDEs are distinguishing themselves from each other by their approach to interface design and the functionality possible from within the interface development tool. Also, software such as Rogue Wave's JFactory is primarily an interface builder rather than an entire IDE.

Most Java interface builders work in largely the same way—like a painting program. You start with a blank form and a palette of user interface components. These components are usually abstract windowing toolkit (AWT) objects, and the interface builder generates AWT code that can be modified by a programmer who is fluent in dealing with the toolkit. Some IDEs, such as SunSoft Java WorkShop, introduce a layer between the AWT and the programmer's source code. The goal of a layer such as this is to make it easier to deal with windowing and interface issues. The IDE handles things behind the scenes so that the programmer can concentrate on larger issues.

For some programmers, especially those who spent a lot of time learning the intricacies of the AWT, this may not be an attractive feature. Others may be more interested in the power offered by these interface builders or may be ready to leave the complexity of the AWT behind.

One of the nicest features of these interface builders is their capability to generate event-handling code at the same time they create a user interface component. Anyone who has used Visual Basic is familiar with this approach: You plunk down a text field where you want it on a dialog box, double-click the text field, and then begin entering the source code to control how it operates.

Portability of Code

One of the features to watch for when choosing an IDE is whether it produces code that is fully compatible with the Java class library. Several of the development environments such as Café and Java WorkShop come with their own versions of the JDK instead of using an existing implementation of the JDK.

This usually does not matter because one of the goals of any Java IDE is to take advantage of the language's ability to be portable across any platform. Many development environments such as SourceCraft NetCraft work entirely within the JDK, and they create software that does not enhance those features with proprietary extensions.

Others environments, such as Microsoft Visual J++, add features that require new classes. J++ (formerly known under the code name Jakarta) has extensions to the Java language that are specific to the Windows operating system. For an applet or application designed with Visual J++ to be fully portable, it must not make use of these extensions. Because this IDE is just now becoming available, it remains to be seen whether the advantage of extended features makes up for the significant disadvantage of platform specificity. This issue is hotly debated within the community of Java developers because many believe that the continued growth of the language depends on its ability to stay cohesive and fully cross platform.

An interesting side issue to the portability question is that most Java development environments are not cross platform themselves—even when the IDE is touted as being a Java program. All the major IDEs that have been introduced to date are offered for specific platforms—primarily because of the use of native code.

IDE Experience

One element of IDE use that sometimes gets lost in the shuffle is the skill level required to use one. If the idea of an IDE is to improve your programming, this can't happen if you can't figure out the IDE! An integrated development environment is a complex type of software. It often makes use of a multiple-document interface where you can have several windows open at once and be faced with a dizzying array of options.

For experienced programmers, this functionality is a great boon. You want to have as much power in your control as possible. A new programmer can easily get lost in the IDEs that are available—especially if the programmer is still learning the language. When you are busy clearing out space in your brain for a new programming language, you shouldn't have to find room for an IDE at the same time.

Several of the IDEs available for Java are more suited for the code warrior—the multilingual veteran who can throw around jargon like *OOP, MUMPS*, and *male-female connector* with the greatest of ease. However, a few of the development environments are more suited for the newcomer because their interface is more approachable and less complex.

The best example of this kind of interface is Java WorkShop from SunSoft—it uses the familiar Web browser interface. People coming to Java from a limited programming background—such as HTML developers looking to upgrade their skills—can find this kind of IDE more suited to their tastes.

There is a trade-off for this ease of use, of course. An environment like Java WorkShop may require more steps to get a task done—either because the functions are not immediately available or because they may not offer some of the functionality of a more complex IDE.

Multiple Language Development

Another factor regarding the use of an IDE for some programmers is its use with other languages. Several of these environments, including MetroWerks CodeWarrior and Borland 5.0 C++ IDE with Java Enhancements, are designed to handle more than one language or are fully equivalent to the company's other development tools.

If the IDE is a complex one (as these are), you learn how to use it and don't have to learn another when you shift gears and program in a non-Java language.

Also, if you write native methods for use in your Java programs, you can use some multilanguage IDEs to write that code. The Borland 5.0 Java environment comes with a C and a C++ compiler, so native methods can be written alongside Java methods in an integrated manner.

The Bottom Line

The goal of an IDE is to make you a better programmer. As Java developer Chuck McManis wrote in his August 1996 *JavaWorld* column, "I rate the IDEs by my ability to get productive work done while using them."

As you go over the details of the software products discussed in the following sections, you get a clearer picture of how each environment can help you. Given the number of IDEs already available for Java, you should be able to match one with your skill level, programming tasks, and personal taste.

If not, as the Amish coder might tell you—there's always the JDK. You can match it with word processors, custom interface builders, and other single-feature design tools to create a personalized IDE.

CAUTION

If you are downloading tryout or beta copies of several IDEs—as I did in the course of preparing this material—be advised that these rival products may not coexist peacefully. Many Java development tools make use of environment variables such as CLASSPATH and JAVAHOME, and they are not happy if another software tool has claimed these variables for its own purposes. As an example, Café and Java WorkShop are the Prince Charles and Lady Diana of software—they should be kept apart for the benefit of everyone involved. If possible, de-install one IDE before installing the next one on your system and make sure that your bootup files are cleaned out as well. If you need more than one IDE active on your system, you can establish multiple configuration files that are executed when a particular environment is used.

Symantec Café

Symantec Café, released in March 1996, is the first development environment that became widely available for Java programming after the JDK. Symantec calls it an *integrated development and debugging environment* (IDDE), but the added *D* doesn't make it different than most IDEs—the others usually include a debugger, too.

Café is based on Symantec's C++ environment, but Café is a standalone product that does not require a C++ platform to run.

Figure 5.1 shows an example of Café at work.

System Requirements

Symantec has released versions of Café for the Microsoft Windows 95, Windows NT 3.5x, and Macintosh systems.

For Microsoft users, an Intel 386 processor and 8M memory are required, but a 486 or better and 16M memory are recommended. A VGA monitor is needed, but Symantec recommends that an SVGA monitor be used if available. The software, and all its sample files and Help files, requires 60M of disk space and a CD-ROM drive.

For Macintosh owners, a Power Macintosh, 68030, or 68040 Macintosh is required, and 16M memory is recommended. The full installation of the software requires 30M of disk space.

FIGURE 5.1.

A screen capture of Symantec Café.

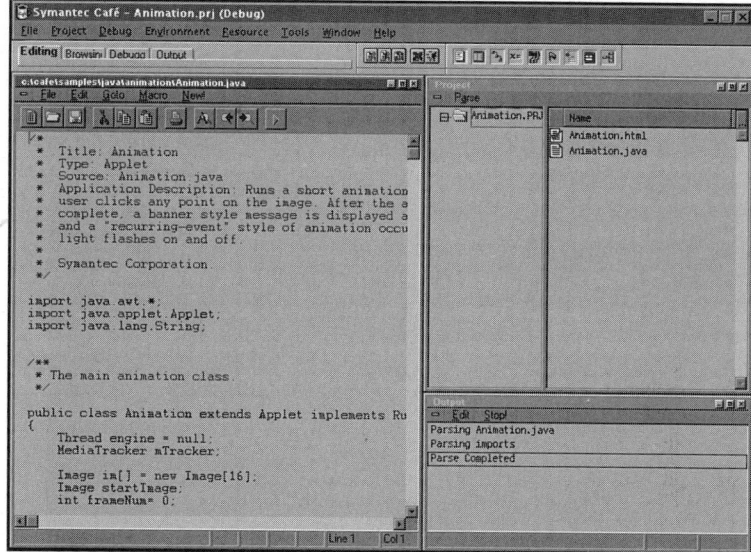

Café incorporates the JDK into its release with a full implementation of the Java class libraries and source code samples. You do not have to have the JDK before installing Café. In fact, it is prudent to de-install the JDK before implementing Café to avoid system conflicts between the two.

Overview

Café is a sophisticated IDE that offers an excellent source editor with color highlighting of syntax, an editor for class and hierarchy modification, a Studio tool for interface design, and numerous example applets.

Because it has been on the market for a long time relative to its competitors, Café has the advantage of being more robust than some other IDEs. Café also has been documented more completely in books such as *Teach Yourself Java in Café in 21 Days*, available now from Sams.net Publishing.

To aid in the design of a class hierarchy, Café has a class editor for navigating through classes and editing class methods, and a hierarchy editor for viewing and modifying Java class relationships. Changes in the source code that affect the class hierarchy can be seen as the program is being written, instead of requiring that it be compiled before changes are reflected in the hierarchy. You can also change the source code from within the class editor—clicking the function or method within a class brings up its source code in a window that can be used to edit the code.

With AppExpress, the process of creating a skeleton Java program speeds up. This and several other *Express Agents*—Café's term for wizards—make it easier to begin projects and new programs.

In the source editor, Java syntax is highlighted, making it easier to spot typos and other errors immediately. The editor can be customized to behave like several popular programmers' editors such as Brief, Emacs, and Epsilon. The editor also uses standard Windows cut, copy, and paste commands.

With Café Studio, designing a graphical user interface for your Java programs can be done in a visual, drag-and-drop manner. Studio enables programmers to develop the dialog boxes and other visual elements visually, and it creates event handlers for these components automatically. There's also a menu editor with an active window in which you can test the menu. These resources are saved in separate .rc files that can be edited later (just as source files are edited); the .rc format is compatible with other design tools that generate .rc files.

One interesting aspect of Café Studio is the ability it gives you to design a form and dictate exactly how it looks. With the JDK and its abstract windowing toolkit, graphical user interface designers have to allow their work to be changed depending on the platform the applet or application was running on. This approach is similar to the way HTML can be modified to fit the large number of platforms used on the World Wide Web. It's an approach well suited to cross-platform design.

With Café Studio, programmers can choose to use one of these variable layout managers or to dictate the position and size of all interface elements.

When you're ready to compile a program, Café provides the option to use Sun's JDK compiler or the Café compiler, which operates more quickly than the current JDK version.

The Café debugger provides several different ways to temporarily halt the execution of code, including a quick-breakpoint feature for a one-time run that stops at a specific line. The debugger also enables a large amount of control over threads in multithreaded programs. During debugging, a watch view can be used to monitor the contents of variables.

The environment of Symantec Café is highly customizable—all toolbars and palettes can be resized and placed where you want them on-screen. Several windows can be open at the same time, making it possible to view the object hierarchy while entering source code and using the form editor, for example.

There are 54 sample Java programs included with Windows versions of Café and more than 90 with the Macintosh version. Many of these are duplicates of the sample applets Sun offers with the JDK or on its Web site at http://java.sun.com.

Pricing and Additional Information

Pricing is subject to change, of course, but the most recent retail price for Café, quoted on the company's Web site, is $299.95 for Windows users. An introductory price of $99.95 is currently being offered to Macintosh owners for 90 days—an offer that is to be followed by a $299.95 price. Café can be purchased from Symantec's Web site in addition to retail and mail-order outlets.

The home page for Symantec Café is at the following URL:

```
http://cafe.symantec.com/
```

The customer service number for the company is (800) 441-7234, and its e-mail address for Java-related comments and questions is `javainfo@symantec.com`.

SunSoft Java WorkShop

SunSoft Java WorkShop, the development tool offered by the language's home team, is scheduled for release in the Fall of 1996 and may already be on the market as you read this.

According to its designers, the IDE is written almost entirely in Java, and its development has been used to help improve the Java language. The mindset at Sun is that committing to such a large-scale undertaking in the company's own language gives them insight into the issues other developers are facing and reveals any kinks in Java that still have to be straightened out.

However, all that talk doesn't benefit the developer looking for a tool to write software. Java WorkShop is evaluated here on the basis of its applicability to this task.

Figure 5.2 shows an example of Java WorkShop in use.

FIGURE 5.2.

Java WorkShop in use.

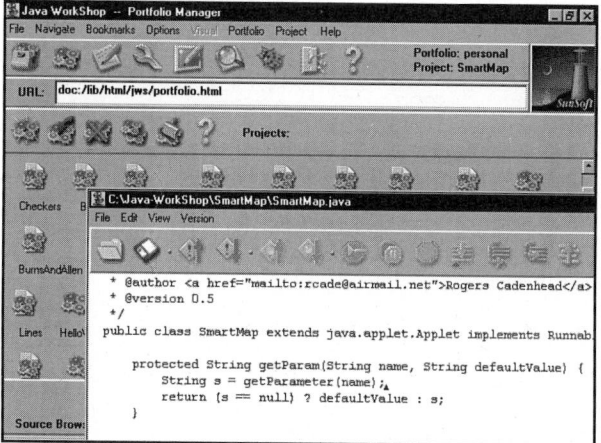

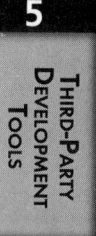

System Requirements

Versions of Java WorkShop are available for the following systems: Microsoft Windows 95, Windows NT 3.5.1, SPARC Solaris (2.4 or later), and Intel x86 Solaris systems.

Microsoft Windows 95 and NT systems must be running a 90-megahertz Pentium or better with 16M of memory and 45M of hard disk space. Solaris systems must have 32M of memory, 45M of disk space, and an OSF/Motif 1.2.3-compliant windowing system. The recommended display resolution to use with Java WorkShop is 800×600 pixels.

Java WorkShop comes with its own modified version of the JDK, so it cannot be used in conjunction with an existing installation of the kit. Like Café, Java WorkShop requires that any existing JDK copies be de-installed before you can install and run WorkShop correctly.

Overview

Java WorkShop, one of the most approachable IDEs for a novice programmer, uses a Web interface to offer the following features: a source editor, class browser, debugger, project management system, and Visual Java (a tool for the visual design of a graphical interface and an easier means to create windowing software). WorkShop is fully detailed in *Teach Yourself SunSoft Java WorkShop in 21 Days*, available now from Sams.net Publishing. (This is a book I can personally recommend—I coauthored it!)

Although still in beta release as of this writing, Java WorkShop has been available long enough to assess the kind of functionality it will offer when it hits the market. The most striking difference between it and other IDEs is its interface. Java WorkShop looks more like a Web browser than a programming development environment. It *is* a Web browser, in fact—users of Sun's HotJava browser will recognize elements from that software in the design of WorkShop. In addition, you can view any Web page while working in Java WorkShop.

Java WorkShop's browser interface is easier to use for programmers who are unfamiliar with IDEs and similar software; the browser interface is frustrating to some of those who are comfortable with these tools.

WorkShop has a source browser for viewing a class hierarchy, public methods, and variables. The browser creates HTML pages in the same format as HTML documentation generated by the JDK's javadoc utility.

The WorkShop source editor is still in an early stage of development and lacks some of the cut-and-paste functionality of other, more established editors. The editor works in conjunction with WorkShop's debugger—compile errors create links directly into the source editor for fixing. The WorkShop debugger provides breakpoints and other methods of debugging.

The Visual Java feature provides a way to graphically design an interface, much as Café Studio does. Visual Java enables programmers to develop dialog boxes and other visual elements and automatically creates event handlers for these components. There's also a menu editor. Resources are saved in separate `.gui` files that can be edited later, just as source files are edited.

In its current release, Java WorkShop requires the use of runtime classes that make Visual Java work, but developers have said that this will not be the case when the software hits the market.

The environment is not customizable in the way Café is, but the Web interface makes it easy to integrate other tools and programs into WorkShop. The program is a collection of Web pages with Java programs embedded in and around them. You can go to a different page from within Java WorkShop as easily as you can enter a URL in a Web browser. This approach makes it possible for a user to create original pages of Java development tools that can be linked to WorkShop pages. This arrangement may be unusual for someone accustomed to development environments written as cohesive, single-executable files that can't be changed (as most are). However, it suits the spirit of Java—independent programs linked together by HTML pages, which can be modified as individual elements without affecting the other parts of the whole.

Pricing and Additional Information

When it is released, SunSoft Java WorkShop is expected to retail for $295. While it still is in beta release, the software can be downloaded freely for evaluation. For more details, and the opportunity to download a beta release, visit the following URL:

`http://www.sun.com/sunsoft/Developer-products/java/index.html`

The customer service number to use for the company is (800) 786-7638 (SUN-SOFT) in the United States, or (512) 434-1511 elsewhere. The company's e-mail address for comments and questions is `sunsoft@selectnet.com`.

SourceCraft NetCraft

SourceCraft, the developer of the ObjectCraft development environment, is making its NetCraft Java IDE available as freeware. For those unfamiliar with the term, *freeware* is software available for no cost as long as you comply with the developer's terms and conditions for use.

This fact makes NetCraft attractive if cost is a criteria, obviously, but the IDE still must be well designed or you will pay in terms of lost time and efficiency.

Figure 5.3 provides a look at the NetCraft environment.

FIGURE 5.3.

NetCraft at work.

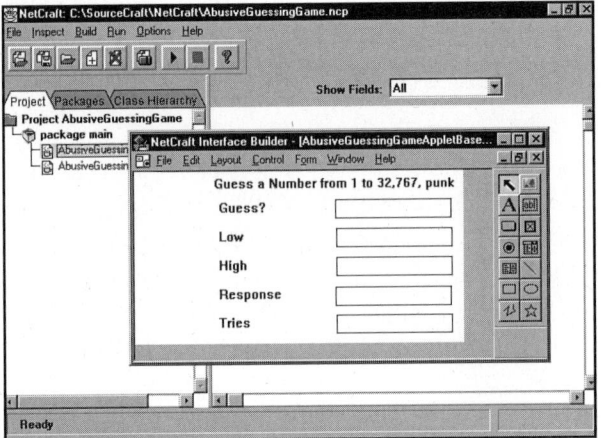

System Requirements

Versions of NetCraft are available for Microsoft Windows 95 and Windows NT 3.5.1 systems running a 486 or better with 8M of memory. NetCraft comes bundled with the current version of the JDK; SourceCraft also makes NetCraft available for download without the JDK if you already have the JDK installed.

Overview

SourceCraft NetCraft is somewhat less ambitious in its approach than other IDEs because it has a smaller set of available features. However, it is a fully featured replacement for the JDK, and it creates Java programs compatible across all Java implementations. NetCraft has an editor, a class inspector, a user interface designer, and a compiler.

NetCraft is an IDE that can be used for any type of Java applet or application. In its approach to the software, SourceCraft focuses on Java's applicability in intranet environments.

The Package Inspector, part of NetCraft's system for organizing projects, includes a way to browse the methods used in a class. NetCraft also has a Class Inspector for looking at the following aspects of a class: its position in the hierarchy, its methods, and its variables. When you are looking at a method with this tool, you can view the source code of the method and how it is used in a program.

NetCraft, like Café and Java WorkShop, includes a way to visually develop a graphical user interface. The NetCraft UI Builder generates Java code that uses the abstract windowing toolkit as its raw material, so the code does not rely on any new classes introduced with the development environment. When you create an interface component, NetCraft generates source code for that component, complete with a TODO comment line where the event-handling code for that component is placed. It's a simpler approach than some of the alternatives and a programmer comfortable with the AWT should be comfortable with it.

The source editor uses Windows cut-and-paste commands and is similar to other small word processors with which you are probably familiar. And the NetCraft UI Builder is not much more difficult to use than a word processor. Although the components in the release available at this writing have the odd habit of moving around a little when clicked, a nice feature of the Builder is its ability to set the specific coordinates (height and width) of a component by entering numbers into text fields. This approach makes it easy to bring wandering components in line with each other.

The environment is simpler to use and master than other IDEs. However, this may be a problem when you are developing sophisticated programs with numerous windows and interactions; some of the tools you need to manage this software are not available in NetCraft. Its strength for use with complex programs depends on where SourceCraft, the maker of other development tools, plans to go with this freeware product.

For basic tasks and applets, NetCraft appears to be a good substitute for JDK users seeking to migrate to a graphical interface. Because it is free, it is a fitting place for novices to start when choosing a Java IDE.

Pricing and Additional Information

For more details, and the opportunity to download NetCraft at no cost, visit the home page for NetCraft at the following URL:

```
http://www.sourcecraft.com:4800/about/netcraft/
```

The customer service number for the company is (617) 221-5665; the company's e-mail address for comments and questions is edc@sourcecraft.com.

Pro-C WinGEN for Java

WinGEN for Java, development software from Pro-C, is an IDE designed with the nonprogrammer in mind. The focus is on automatically generating code so that HTML designers and other programming novices can develop Java applets and applications. The graphical interface of a program can be developed using drag-and-drop features; elements such as animation can be introduced without writing a single line of code. The IDE calls the Java Developers Kit from within WinGEN to compile and run programs.

Figure 5.4 shows a look at the WinGEN environment.

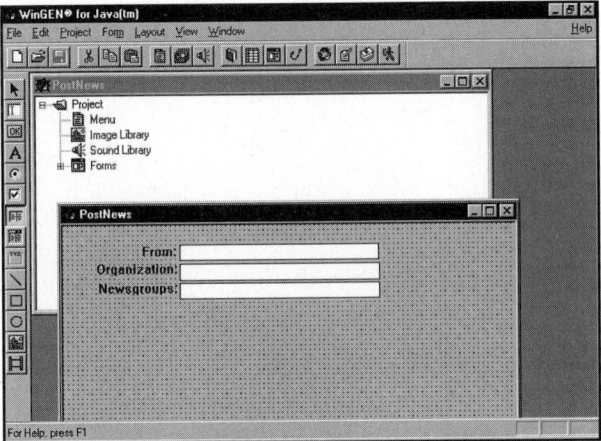

FIGURE 5.4.

*WinGEN for Java
at work.*

System Requirements

Versions of WinGEN are available for Microsoft Windows 95 and Windows NT 3.5.1 systems running a 486 or better with 8M of memory and 10M of hard disk space. Unpacking WinGEN Lite, the evaluation edition of the software, requires a program that can unpack ZIP files into long filenames. (For users of Windows systems, the Windows 95 operating system introduced filenames longer than eight characters and a three-character extension.) If you use a ZIP unpack program that does not support long filenames, files are not named correctly and the setup will fail. WinGEN includes the current version of the JDK, which must be installed *before* WinGEN is installed so that the IDE will function.

Overview

WinGEN augments the existing JDK rather than replacing it, enabling you to run the compiler and interpreter from within WinGEN rather than using the JDK's command-line tools.

As software that strives to put nonprogrammers to work developing Java applets and applications, WinGEN puts its emphasis on its point-and-click approach to the creation of graphical user interfaces. Many simple user events can be created through WinGEN without writing any Java code; graphics and animation features can also be created without programming.

The user interface is designed in a manner that should be familiar to programmers who have used other GUI design tools—especially Visual Basic developers. The version currently available is a bit difficult to use when it comes to aligning components (because of the lack of a snap-to-grid feature). Otherwise, laying out things such as text fields and labels is easier than doing so in some other IDEs.

The IDE takes a resource-centric view of development. Instead of starting from the code and using it to create things such as menus and dialog boxes, you start with the menus and dialog boxes and use them to generate the required code. One feature missing from WinGEN is the ability to see the interface before any code has been generated. The Java program that uses the interface must be compiled and run in order to see how the interface will look.

The commercial version of WinGEN for Java includes some features not commonly available in other IDEs at this time, such as support for specific types of ASCII text databases and tables.

A system called CodeHooks handles advanced programming—for writing Java code to handle special circumstances that WinGEN can't handle. These *hooks*—blocks of code that accomplish specific tasks such as a special event handler—are kept separate from the code WinGEN automatically generates. This separation of code enables programmers to change the GUI and plug CodeHooks back in without reentering any code.

WinGEN is an interesting approach that can be especially useful in the development of simple applets and applications or as a tool for Java novices. Although the lack of a debugger, source browser, and other features might limit its use, the IDE still is in an early phase of development and may yet implement some of these tools.

Pricing and Additional Information

The retail price of WinGEN is listed at $349, but it can be purchased online for $199. For more details, the opportunity to download WinGEN Lite at no cost, or to purchase the full version online, visit the home page for WinGEN at the following URL:

```
http://www.pro-c.com/products/wfj/java.html
```

The phone number at Pro-C for inquiries related to the software is (813) 227-7762; the company's e-mail address for comments and questions regarding WinGEN is support@pro-c.com.

Rogue Wave JFactory

Unlike most of the development tools being introduced for Java, JFactory is being offered as an interface builder rather than an IDE. However, because JFactory enables the placement of event-handling code from within the program and also provides a way to compile and test programs during development, it's close enough to a full IDE to be worthy of consideration. Although JFactory can be used in conjunction with any editor and Java compiler, a default editor is provided and JFactory is initially set up to use the JDK compiler.

Figure 5.5 gives you a look at the JFactory environment.

FIGURE 5.5.

*Rogue Wave JFactory
at work.*

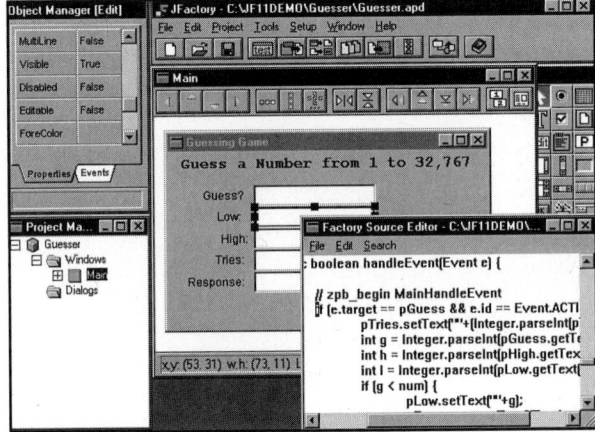

System Requirements

Versions of JFactory are available for the following platforms:

- Microsoft Windows 95 and Windows NT systems running a 486 or better with 16M of memory, 25M of hard disk space, and the Java Developers Kit version 1.0.2.

- SPARC Solaris 2.4 or 2.5 running UNIX with 25M of hard disk space, an applet browser, JDK version 1.0.2, and X11R5. You must have enough memory to run X11R5, the JDK compiler, and an applet browser.

- HP-UX 10.01 systems with 25M of hard disk space, an applet browser, JDK version 1.0.2, and X11R5. The memory requirements are the same as for Solaris systems.

- IBM OS/2 Warp 3.0 systems with 25M of hard disk space, 4M of memory not used by OS/2, a two-button mouse or pointing device, and JDK version 1.0.2, build os2-19960412.

Overview

JFactory is a sophisticated interface builder based on zApp Factory, a multiplatform C++ application framework from Rogue Wave. The software has a large number of features that facilitate rapid application design, and the product benefits from the experience Rogue Wave has accumulated with its other programming tools. The primary offering of JFactory is its visual, drag-and-drop editor for interface creation. This graphical user interface developer is head-and-shoulders above many of the other visual development tools currently available.

The JFactory software is not considered to be a full IDE because it does not provide its own compiler, debugger, or other tools. However, JFactory's visual editor is so easy to use, and so capable, that it may compensate for the loss of some integrated development offerings. This open environment, a trait of Rogue Wave's programming software, enables any compiler or debugger to be used from within JFactory.

At any stage in the development process, you can test the interface you have created. Another useful feature is that custom components can be integrated easily into the toolbar alongside standard components such as text labels, text fields, and radio buttons. One thing JFactory offers that sets it apart from most other IDEs is the ability to import `.rc` and `.dlg` files created with other programming environments.

A lot of the source code associated with interface components is generated automatically by JFactory. Custom code that must be added is protected from modification so that you can change the interface afterward without overwriting your changes to the source code.

JFactory has a robust system for creating the interface: You can use drag-and-drop and mouse movements to place components, and you can also place components with numeric input. The height, width, and (x,y) coordinates of a component can be set from a properties dialog box. This approach makes it much easier to cure the problem of wandering components that are difficult to align correctly.

When a menu, window, or dialog box has been created, you can save it in an object library for reuse with other programs.

If the lack of tools such as a class browser and integrated debugger are not detrimental to your programming tasks, JFactory may be an excellent choice for your needs.

Pricing and Additional Information

JFactory retails for $195; a multiplatform package that includes the Microsoft Windows, UNIX, and OS/2 versions is available for $390. For more details and the opportunity to download a demo version or to purchase JFactory online, visit the home page for JFactory at the following URL:

```
http://www.roguewave.com/products/jfactory/jfactory.html
```

The e-mail address for comments and questions regarding JFactory is support@roguewave.com.

Other Offerings

The following products for Java development cannot be described fully here (because they are not yet available or for some other consideration). However, they're profiled here so that you can get a fuller picture of the IDEs that will be available to you.

Borland C++ 5.0 with Java Enhancements

Borland C++ 5.0 with Java Enhancements is a C++ development environment that has been extended to include Java programming tools. The advantages of this approach are multilanguage development within the same environment for native method use, the ability to program in three languages (C, C++, and Java) without learning three IDEs, and software that has become robust from several years of use by the C and C++ development community.

The home page for Borland's Internet development tools is given here:

```
http://www.borland.com/internet/
```

MetroWerks CodeWarrior

CodeWarrior is one of several IDEs that have been made available in prerelease or beta form for Macintosh Java development. CodeWarrior is a multilanguage development environment with an introductory version called Discover Programming with Java that is intended for novices. CodeWarrior can be used to develop programs in C, C++, ObjectPascal, and Java.

The home page for MetroWerks CodeWarrior 9 is at the following URL:

```
http://www.metrowerks.com/products/announce/cw9.html
```

Java WebIDE

The Java WebIDE development environment is worth looking at to see what's being attempted: A fully Web-based programming tool that doesn't require downloading. You run it off the Web page over the Internet, which is how many software packages will be run as Java development matures (according to the language's adherents). WebIDE is an experiment that does not supplant a more traditional IDE at this time, because it offers only source creation, compilation, and syntax highlighting in its present incarnation. However, as more tools are added, it will become more interesting. WebIDE is one of the only development environments for Java that attempts full cross-platform support. Its home page is at the following URL:

```
http://www.chamisplace.com/prog/javaide/
```

Kalimantan

Before it was christened as Kalimantan, this IDE was one of several Java-related products that staked a claim to the name *Espresso*. The developers have been kind enough to offer links to the other Espressos, so the Kalimantan Web page is a good place to sort out any Espresso confusion you may have. Kalimantan is another cross-platform IDE. It has been tested for use with Solaris 2.4 and up, as well as Windows 95 systems. Kalimantan's current beta release includes only an inspector to look at the values of internal variables and a debugger, but it is bundled with the `teikade` suite of utilities from PFU Limited. This suite includes a class browser that is familiar to those who have used class browsers with the Smalltalk programming language. The home page for Kalimantan is at the following URL:

```
http://www.real-time.com/java/kalimantan/index.html
```

Natural Intelligence Roaster

Roaster was made available to developers in January 1996, making it the first Java IDE for the Macintosh. The current version at this writing is Developer Release 2.1. The Roaster Professional Edition includes a visual interface builder, compilation that can be targeted for Macintosh or Microsoft Windows systems, and an extended class library. The Sams.net book *Teach Yourself Java for the Macintosh in 21 Days* was written for the Roaster environment. Details on Roaster are available from the following URL:

```
http://www.natural.com/pages/products/roaster/index.html
```

Microsoft Visual J++

Microsoft Visual J++ is just becoming available in beta release as of this writing, but the company developing Visual J++ makes the product worth keeping an eye on. Visual J++ is Microsoft's machine-proprietary answer to Java development. It features extensions to the Java class library that are specific to Microsoft's operating system. It integrates Java with the component object model (COM) integration through Microsoft ActiveX and is integrated with the Internet Explorer browser that implemented Java with its 3.0 release.

Details about Visual J++ can be found at the following URL:

```
http://www.microsoft.com/visualj/
```

Microsoft Java Software Development Kit

Microsoft has recently released a Software Development Kit (SDK) for Java programming. The Microsoft Java SDK is not an IDE, but instead is a package that includes Microsoft's implementation of the Java language for 32-bit Windows machines, a special just-in-time (JIT) compiler that makes Java applications execute more quickly, and other platform-specific enhancements.

Like Visual J++, the Java SDK offers improvements for Microsoft Java programming at the cost of platform independence. Some of the SDK's offerings (such as 3D programming through DirectX) offer new features that aren't readily available in other implementations.

Microsoft has an extensive Web site that promotes its approach to Java development and its tools for programming. The current version of the Java SDK is available at the following URL:

```
http://www.microsoft.com/java/sdk
```

Cosmo Code

Cosmo Code is an integrated development environment for Java that runs on Silicon Graphics IRIX operating system versions 5.3 and 6.2. The product includes a compiler, interpreter, debugger, and a class browser. The compiler can create machine-independent code, symmetric multiprocessing on SGI systems, and can create executable native code files. The Cosmo Code home page is available at the following URL:

```
http://www.sgi.com/Products/cosmo/code/index.html
```

Summary

As you have probably discovered by this point, the decision about which IDE to use depends on your programming experience, personal taste, and the tasks you have to accomplish with your software creations.

Because developments occur at such a rapid pace in regard to Java (a trend that will continue for the foreseeable future), it is worthwhile to use the Internet to keep up with changes. As stated earlier, one Web site has been established to offer the latest news on IDEs, links to reviews, and a full listing of announced software. It's available at the following URL:

```
http://www.cybercom.net/~frog/javaide.html#reviews
```

The Java newsgroups such as `comp.lang.java.misc` and `comp.lang.java.programmer` are another way to get a range of user opinions on the IDEs you are considering. Many IDE developers also participate in these forums, including the folks who created Café and Java WorkShop.

Most of the IDEs that have not yet reached the market can be downloaded as beta versions over the World Wide Web. You ought to make use of this availability before you choose a development environment. It's a hassle to install the software and de-install its rivals, but even if the IDE doesn't suit your needs, it gives you a much better idea about what you *do* need in a development environment.

When it comes down to choosing the right one, it's what IDE do.

PART

IN THIS PART

The Java Language

Java Language Fundamentals

by Michael Morrison

IN THIS CHAPTER

CHAPTER 6

Java is an object-oriented language. This means that the language is based on the concept of an *object*. Although a knowledge of object-oriented programming is necessary to put Java to practical use, it isn't required to understand the fundamentals of the Java language. This chapter focuses on the language and leaves the object-oriented details of Java for Chapter 8, "Classes, Packages, and Interfaces."

If you already have some experience with another object-oriented language such as C++ or Smalltalk, much of Java will be familiar territory. In fact, you can almost consider Java a new, revamped C++. Because Java evolved from C++, many of the similarities and differences between Java and C++ will be highlighted throughout the next few chapters. Additionally, Appendix D provides a more thorough look at the differences between Java and C++.

This chapter covers the essentials of the Java language, including a few sample programs to help you hit the ground running.

Hello, World!

The best way to learn a programming language is to jump right in and see how a real program works. In keeping with a traditional introductory programming example, your first program is a Java version of the classic "Hello, World!" program. Listing 6.1 contains the source code for the HelloWorld class, which also is located on the CD-ROM that accompanies this book in the file HelloWorld.java.

Listing 6.1. The HelloWorld class.

```
class HelloWorld {
  public static void main(String args[]) {
    System.out.println("Hello, World!");
  }
}
```

After compiling the program with the Java compiler (javac), you are ready to run it in the Java interpreter. The Java compiler places the executable output in a file called HelloWorld.class. This naming convention might seem strange considering that most programming languages use the .EXE file extension for executables. Not so in Java! Following the object-oriented nature of Java, all Java programs are stored as Java classes that are created and executed as objects in the Java runtime environment. To run the HelloWorld program, type **java HelloWorld** at the command prompt. As you may have guessed, the program responds by displaying Hello, World! on your screen. Congratulations! You just wrote and tested your first Java program!

Obviously, HelloWorld is a very minimal Java program. Even so, there's still a lot happening in those few lines of code. To fully understand what is happening, let's examine the program line by line. First, you must understand that Java relies heavily on classes. In fact, the first statement of HelloWorld reminds you that HelloWorld is a class, not just a program. Furthermore, by looking at the `class` statement in its entirety, you can see that the name of the class is defined as `HelloWorld`. This name is used by the Java compiler as the name of the executable output class. The Java compiler creates an executable class file for each class defined in a Java source file. If there is more than one class defined in a `.java` file, the Java compiler stores each class in a separate `.class` file.

The `HelloWorld` class contains one *method*, or member function. For now, you can think of this function as a normal procedural function that happens to be linked to the class. The details of methods are covered in Chapter 8, "Classes, Packages, and Interfaces." The single method in the `HelloWorld` class is called `main()`, and should be familiar if you have used C or C++. The `main()` method is where execution begins when the class is executed in the Java interpreter. The `main()` method is defined as being `public static` with a `void` return type. `public` means that the method can be called from anywhere inside or outside the class. `static` means that the method is the same for all instances of the class. The `void` return type means that `main()` does not return a value.

The `main()` method is defined as taking a single parameter, `String args[]`. `args` is an array of `String` objects that represents command-line arguments passed to the class at execution. Because `HelloWorld` doesn't use any command-line arguments, you can ignore the `args` parameter. You learn a little more about strings later in this chapter.

The `main()` method is called when the `HelloWorld` class is executed. `main()` consists of a single statement that prints the message `Hello, World!` to the standard output stream, as follows:

```
System.out.println("Hello, World!");
```

This statement may look a little confusing at first because of the nested objects. To help make things clearer, examine the statement from right to left. First, notice that the statement ends in a semicolon, which is standard Java syntax borrowed from C/C++. Moving to the left, you see that the `"Hello, World!"` string is in parentheses, which means it is a parameter to a function call. The method being called is actually the `println` method of the `out` object. The `println` method is similar to the `printf` method in C, except that it automatically appends a newline (`\n`) at the end of the string. The `out` object is a member variable of the `System` object that represents the standard output stream. Finally, the `System` object is a global object in the Java environment that encapsulates system functionality.

That pretty well covers the `HelloWorld` class—your first Java program. If you got lost a little in the explanation of the `HelloWorld` class, don't be too concerned. `HelloWorld` was presented with no previous explanation of the Java language and was only meant to get your feet wet with Java code. The rest of this chapter focuses on a more structured discussion of the fundamentals of the Java language.

Tokens

When you submit a Java program to the Java compiler, the compiler parses the text and extracts individual tokens. A *token* is the smallest element of a program that is meaningful to the compiler. (Actually, this definition is true for all compilers, not just the Java compiler.) These tokens define the structure of the Java language. All the tokens that comprise Java are known as the Java *token set*. Java tokens can be broken into five categories: identifiers, keywords, literals, operators, and separators. The Java compiler also recognizes and subsequently removes comments and whitespaces.

The Java compiler removes all comments and whitespaces while tokenizing the source file. The resulting tokens are then compiled into machine-independent Java bytecode capable of being run from within an interpreted Java environment. The bytecode conforms to the hypothetical Java virtual machine, which abstracts processor differences into a single virtual processor. For more information on the Java virtual machine, check out Chapter 34, "Java Under the Hood: Inside the Virtual Machine." Keep in mind that an interpreted Java environment can be either the Java command-line interpreter or a Java-capable browser.

Identifiers

Identifiers are tokens that represent names. These names can be assigned to variables, methods, and classes to uniquely identify them to the compiler and give them meaningful names for the programmer. `HelloWorld` is an identifier that assigns the name `HelloWorld` to the class residing in the `HelloWorld.java` source file developed earlier.

Although you can be creative in naming identifiers in Java, there are some limitations. All Java identifiers are case sensitive and must begin with a letter, an underscore (_), or a dollar sign ($). Letters include both uppercase and lowercase letters. Subsequent identifier characters can include the numbers 0 to 9. The only other limitation to identifier names is that the Java keywords, which are listed in the next section, cannot be used. Table 6.1 contains a list of valid and invalid identifier names.

Table 6.1. Valid and invalid Java identifiers.

Valid	*Invalid*
`HelloWorld`	`Hello World` (uses a space)
`Hi_Mom`	`Hi Mom!` (uses a space and punctuation mark)
`heyDude3`	`3heyDude` (begins with a numeral)
`tall`	`short` (this is a Java keyword)
`poundage`	`#age` (does not begin with letter)

In addition to the mentioned restrictions of naming Java identifiers, you should follow a few stylistic rules to make Java programming easier and more consistent. It is standard Java practice to name multiple-word identifiers in lowercase except for the beginning letter of words in the middle of the name. For example, the variable toughGuy is in correct Java style; the variables toughguy, ToughGuy, and TOUGHGUY are all in violation of this style rule. The rule isn't etched in stone—it's just a good rule to follow because most other Java code you run into follows this style.

Another more critical naming issue regards the use of underscore and dollar-sign characters at the beginning of identifier names. Using either of these characters at the beginning of identifier names is a little risky because many C libraries use the same naming convention for libraries, which can be imported into your Java code. To eliminate the potential problem of name-clashing in these instances, it's better to stay away from the underscore and dollar-sign characters at the beginning of your identifier names. A good use of the underscore character is to use it to separate words where you normally would use a space (Hi_Mom).

Keywords

Keywords are predefined identifiers reserved by Java for a specific purpose and are used only in a limited, specified manner. Java has a richer set of keywords than C or C++, so if you are learning Java with a C/C++ background, be sure to pay attention to the Java keywords. The following keywords are reserved for Java:

abstract	double	int	super
boolean	else	interface	switch
break	extends	long	synchronized
byte	false	native	this
byvalue	final	new	threadsafe
case	finally	null	throw
catch	float	package	transient
char	for	private	true
class	goto	protected	try
const	if	public	void
continue	implements	return	while
default	import	short	
do	instanceof	static	

Literals

Program elements used in an invariant manner are called *literals* or *constants*. Literals can be numbers, characters, or strings. Numeric literals include integers, floating-point numbers, and booleans. Booleans are considered numeric because of the C influence on Java. In C, the boolean values for true and false are represented by 1 and 0. Character literals always refer to a single Unicode character. Strings, which contain multiple characters, are still considered literals even though they are implemented in Java as objects.

> **NOTE**
>
> If you aren't familiar with the Unicode character set, you should know that it is a 16-bit character set that replaces the ASCII character set. Because it is a 16-bit character set, there are enough entries to represent many symbols and characters from other languages. Unicode is quickly becoming the standard for modern operating systems.

Integer Literals

Integer literals are the primary literals used in Java programming. They come in a few different formats: decimal, hexadecimal, and octal. These formats correspond to the base of the number system used by the literal. Decimal (base 10) literals appear as ordinary numbers with no special notation. Hexadecimal numbers (base 16) appear with a leading 0x or 0X, similar to the way they do in C/C++. Octal (base 8) numbers appear with a leading 0 in front of the digits. For example, an integer literal for the decimal number 12 is represented in Java as 12 in decimal, 0xC in hexadecimal, and 014 in octal.

Integer literals default to being stored in the int type, which is a signed 32-bit value. If you are working with very large numbers, you can force an integer literal to be stored in the long type by appending an l or L to the end of the number, as in 79L. The long type is a signed 64-bit value.

Floating-Point Literals

Floating-point literals represent decimal numbers with fractional parts, such as 3.142. They can be expressed in either standard or scientific notation, meaning that the number 563.84 also can be expressed as 5.6384e2.

Unlike integer literals, floating-point literals default to the double type, which is a 64-bit value. You have the option of using the smaller 32-bit float type if you know the full 64 bits are not required. You do this by appending an f or F to the end of the number, as in 5.6384e2f. If you are a stickler for details, you also can explicitly state that you want a double type as the storage unit for your literal, as in 3.142d. But because the default storage for floating-point numbers is double already, this addition isn't necessary.

Boolean Literals

Boolean literals are certainly welcome if you are coming from the world of C/C++. In C, there is no boolean type, and therefore no boolean literals. The boolean values `true` and `false` are represented by the integer values 1 and 0. Java fixes this problem by providing a `boolean` type with two possible states: `true` and `false`. Not surprisingly, these states are represented in the Java language by the keywords `true` and `false`.

Boolean literals are used in Java programming about as often as integer literals because they are present in almost every type of control structure. Any time you need to represent a condition or state with two possible values, a `boolean` is what you need. You learn a little more about the `boolean` type later in this chapter. For now, just remember the two boolean literal values: `true` and `false`.

Character Literals

Character literals represent a single Unicode character and appear within a pair of single quotation marks. Similar to C/C++, special characters (control characters and characters that cannot be printed) are represented by a backslash (\) followed by the character code. A good example of a special character is \n, which forces the output to a new line when printed. Table 6.2 shows the special characters supported by Java.

Table 6.2. Special characters supported by Java.

Description	Representation
Backslash	\\
Continuation	\
Backspace	\b
Carriage return	\r
Form feed	\f
Horizontal tab	\t
Newline	\n
Single quote	\'
Double quote	\"
Unicode character	\udddd
Octal character	\ddd

An example of a Unicode character literal is \u0048, which is a hexadecimal representation of the character *H*. This same character is represented in octal as \110.

> **NOTE**
>
> To find out more information about the Unicode character set, check out the Unicode home page at this URL:
>
> http://www.unicode.org

String Literals

String literals represent multiple characters and appear within a pair of double quotation marks. Unlike all the other literals discussed in this chapter, string literals are implemented in Java by the String class. This arrangement is very different from the C/C++ representation of strings as an array of characters.

When Java encounters a string literal, it creates an instance of the String class and sets its state to the characters appearing within the double quotes. From a usage perspective, the fact that Java implements strings as objects is relatively unimportant. However, it is worth mentioning at this point because it is a reminder that Java is very object oriented in nature—much more so than C++, which is widely considered the current object-oriented programming standard.

Operators

Operators, also known as *operands*, specify an evaluation or computation to be performed on a data object or objects. These operands can be literals, variables, or function return types. The operators supported by Java follow:

+	-	*	/	%	&	¦
^	~	&&	¦¦	!	<	>
<=	>=	<<	>>	>>>	=	?
++	--	==	+=	-=	*=	/=
%=	&=	¦=	^=	!=	<<=	>>=
>>>=	.	[	]	(	)	

Just seeing these operators probably doesn't help you a lot in determining how to use them. Don't worry—you'll learn a lot more about operators and how they are used in the next chapter, "Expressions, Operators, and Control Structures."

Separators

Separators are used to inform the Java compiler of how things are grouped in the code. For example, items in a list are separated by commas much like lists of items in a sentence. Java separators go far beyond commas, however, as you discover in the next chapter. The separators supported by Java follow:

```
{       }       ;       ,       :
```

Comments and Whitespaces

Earlier in this chapter, you learned that comments and whitespaces are removed by the Java compiler during the tokenization of the source code. You might be wondering, "What qualifies as whitespace and how are comments supported?" First, *whitespace* consists of spaces, tabs, and linefeeds. All occurrences of spaces, tabs, or linefeeds are removed by the Java compiler, as are comments. *Comments* can be defined in three different ways, as shown in Table 6.3.

Table 6.3. Types of comments supported by Java.

Type	Usage
/* comment */	All characters between /* and */ are ignored.
// comment	All characters after the // up to the end of the line are ignored.
/** comment */	Same as /* */, except that the comment can be used with the javadoc tool to create automatic documentation.

The first type of comment (/* comment */) should be familiar if you have programmed in C before. All characters inside the /* and */ comment delimiters are ignored by the compiler. The second type of comment (// comment) should also be familiar if you have used C++. All characters appearing after the // comment delimiter up to the end of the line are ignored by the compiler. These two comment types are borrowed from C and C++. The final comment type (/** comment */) works in the same fashion as the C-style comment type, with the additional benefit that it can be used with the Java documentation generator tool, javadoc, to create automatic documentation from the source code. The javadoc tool is covered in Chapter 29, "Documenting Your Code." Following are a few examples of using the various types of comments:

```
/* This is a C style comment. */
// This is a C++ style comment.
/** This is a javadoc style comment. */
```

Data Types

One of the fundamental concepts of any programming language is data types. *Data types* define the storage methods available for representing information, along with how the information is interpreted. Data types are linked tightly to the storage of variables in memory because the data type of a variable determines how the compiler interprets the contents of the memory. You already have received a little taste of data types in the discussion of literal types.

To create a variable in memory, you must declare it by providing the type of the variable as well as an identifier that uniquely identifies the variable. The syntax of the Java declaration statement for variables follows:

```
Type Identifier [, Identifier];
```

The declaration statement tells the compiler to set aside memory for a variable of type `Type` with the name `Identifier`. The optional bracketed `Identifier` indicates that you can make multiple declarations of the same type by separating them with commas. Finally, as in all Java statements, the declaration statement ends with a semicolon.

Java data types can be divided into two categories: simple and composite. *Simple data types* are core types not derived from any other types. Integer, floating-point, boolean, and character types are all simple types. *Composite types*, on the other hand, are based on simple types and include strings, arrays, and both classes and interfaces in general. You learn about arrays later in this chapter. Classes and interfaces are covered in Chapter 8, "Classes, Packages, and Interfaces."

Integer Data Types

Integer data types are used to represent signed integer numbers. There are four integer types: byte, short, int, and long. Each of these types takes up a different amount of space in memory, as shown in Table 6.4.

Table 6.4. Java integer types.

Type	*Size*
byte	8 bits
short	16 bits
int	32 bits
long	64 bits

To declare variables using the integer types, use the declaration syntax mentioned previously with the desired type. Following are some examples of declaring integer variables:

```
int i;
short rocketFuel;
long angle, magnitude;
byte red, green, blue;
```

Floating-Point Data Types

Floating-point data types are used to represent numbers with fractional parts. There are two floating-point types: `float` and `double`. The `float` type reserves storage for a 32-bit single-precision number and the `double` type reserves storage for a 64-bit double-precision number.

Declaring floating-point variables is very similar to declaring integer variables. Following are some examples of floating-point variable declarations:

```
float temperature;
double windSpeed, barometricPressure;
```

Boolean Data Type

The boolean data type (`boolean`) is used to store values with one of two states: `true` or `false`. You can think of the `boolean` type as a 1-bit integer value (because 1 bit can have only two possible values: 1 or 0). However, instead of using 1 and 0, you use the Java keywords `true` and `false`. `true` and `false` aren't just conveniences in Java; they are actually the only legal boolean values. This means that you can't interchangeably use booleans and integers as you can in C/C++. To declare a boolean value, just use the `boolean` type declaration:

```
boolean gameOver;
```

Character Data Type

The *character data type* is used to store single Unicode characters. Because the Unicode character set is composed of 16-bit values, the `char` data type is stored as a 16-bit unsigned integer. You create variables of type `char` as follows:

```
char firstInitial, lastInitial;
```

Remember that the `char` type is useful only for storing single characters. If you come from a C/C++ background, you may be tempted to fashion a string by creating an array of `char`s. In Java, this isn't necessary because the `String` class takes care of handling strings. This doesn't mean that you should never create arrays of characters, it just means that you shouldn't use a character array when you really want a string. C and C++ do not distinguish between character arrays and strings, but Java does.

Casting Types

Inevitably, there will be times when you have to convert from one data type to another. The process of converting one data type to another is called *casting*. Casting is often necessary when a function returns a type different than the type you need to perform an operation. For example, the `read` member function of the standard input stream (`System.in`) returns an `int`. You must cast the returned `int` type to a `char` type before storing it, as in the following:

```
char c = (char)System.in.read();
```

The cast is performed by placing the desired type in parentheses to the left of the value to be converted. The System.in.read function call returns an int value, which then is cast to a char value because of the (char) cast. The resulting char value is then stored in the char variable c.

> **CAUTION**
>
> The storage size of the types you are attempting to cast is very important. Not all types can be safely cast to other types. To understand this, consider the outcome of casting a long to an int. A long is a 64-bit value and an int is a 32-bit value. When casting a long to an int, the compiler chops off the upper 32 bits of the long value so that it will fit into the 32-bit int. If the upper 32 bits of the long contain any useful information, that information will be lost and the number will change as a result of the cast. Information loss can also occur when you cast between different fundamental types, such as integer and floating-point numbers. For example, casting a double to a long results in the loss of the fractional information, even though both numbers are 64-bit values.

When casting, the destination type should always be equal to or larger in size than the source type. Furthermore, you should pay close attention to casting across fundamental types, such as from floating-point to integer types. Table 6.5 lists the casts that are guaranteed to result in no loss of information.

Table 6.5. Casts that result in no loss of information.

From Type	*To Type*
byte	short, char, int, long, float, double
short	int, long, float, double
char	int, long, float, double
int	long, float, double
long	float, double
float	double

Blocks and Scope

In Java, source code is broken into parts separated by opening and closing curly braces: { and }. Everything between curly braces is considered a *block* and exists more or less independently of everything outside of the braces. Blocks aren't important just from a logical sense—they are required as part of the syntax of the Java language. If you don't use braces, the compiler will have trouble determining where one section of code ends and the next section begins. From a purely aesthetic viewpoint, it would be very difficult for someone else reading your code to understand what was going on without the braces. For that matter, it wouldn't be very easy for you to understand your own code without the braces!

Braces are used to group related statements together. You can think of everything between matching braces as being executed as one statement. In fact, from an outer block, that's exactly what an inner block appears like: a single statement. But what's a block? A *block* is simply a section of code. Blocks are organized in a hierarchical fashion, meaning that code can be divided into individual blocks *nested* under other blocks. One block can contain one or more nested subblocks.

It is standard Java programming style to identify different blocks with indentation. Every time you enter a new block, you should indent your source code by a number of spaces—preferably two. When you leave a block, you should move back, or *deindent*, two spaces. This is a fairly established convention in many programming languages. However, indentation is just a style issue and is not technically part of the language. The compiler produces identical output even if you don't indent anything. Indentation is used for the programmer, not the compiler; it simply makes the code easier to follow and understand. Following is an example of the proper indentation of blocks in Java:

```java
for (int i = 0; i < 5; i++) {
  if (i < 3) {
    System.out.println(i);
  }
}
```

Following is the same code without any block indentations:

```java
for (int i = 0; i < 5; i++) {
if (i < 3) {
System.out.println(i);
}
}
```

The first code listing clearly shows the breakdown of program flow through the use of indentation; it is obvious that the `if` statement is nested within the `for` loop. The second code listing, on the other hand, provides no visual cues about the relationship between the blocks of code. Don't worry if you don't know anything about `if` statements and `for` loops; you'll learn plenty about them in the next chapter, "Expressions, Operators, and Control Structures."

The concept of *scope* is tightly linked to blocks and is very important when working with variables in Java. Scope refers to how sections of a program (blocks) affect the lifetime of variables. Every variable declared in a program has an associated scope, meaning that the variable is used only in that particular part of the program.

Scope is determined by blocks. To better understand blocks, take a look again at the `HelloWorld` class in Listing 6.1, earlier in this chapter. The `HelloWorld` class is composed of two blocks. The outer block of the program is the block defining the `HelloWorld` class:

```
class HelloWorld {
...
}
```

Class blocks are very important in Java. Almost everything of interest is either a class itself or belongs to a class. For example, methods are defined inside the classes they belong to. Both syntactically and logically, everything in Java takes place inside a class. Getting back to `HelloWorld`, the inner block defines the code within the `main()` method, as follows:

```
public static void main (String args[]) {
...
  }
```

The inner block is considered to be nested within the outer block of the program. Any variables defined in the inner block are local to that block and are not visible to the outer block; the scope of the variables is defined as the inner block.

To get an even better idea behind the usage of scope and blocks, take a look at the `HowdyWorld` class in Listing 6.2.

Listing 6.2. The HowdyWorld class.

```
class HowdyWorld {
  public static void main (String args[]) {
    int i;
    printMessage();
  }
  public static void printMessage () {
    int j;
    System.out.println("Howdy, World!");
  }
}
```

The `HowdyWorld` class contains two methods: `main()` and `printMessage()`. `main()` should be familiar to you from the `HelloWorld` class, except that in this case, it declares an integer variable `i` and calls the `printMessage()` method. `printMessage()` is a new method that declares an integer variable `j` and prints the message `Howdy, World!` to the standard output stream, much like the `main()` method did in `HelloWorld`.

You've probably figured out already that `HowdyWorld` results in basically the same output as `HelloWorld` because the call to `printMessage()` results in a single text message being displayed. What you may not see right off is the scope of the integers defined in each method. The integer `i` defined in `main()` has a scope limited to the body of the `main()` method. The body of main() is defined by the curly braces around the method (the method block). Similarly, the integer j has a scope limited to the body of the printMessage() method. The importance of the scope of these two variables is that the variables aren't visible beyond their respective scopes; the HowdyWorld class block knows nothing about the two integers. Furthermore, main() doesn't know anything about j, and printMessage() knows nothing about i.

Scope becomes more important when you start nesting blocks of code within other blocks. The GoodbyeWorld class shown in Listing 6.3 is a good example of variables nested within different scopes.

Listing 6.3. The GoodbyeWorld class.

```
class GoodbyeWorld {
  public static void main (String args[]) {
    int i, j;
    System.out.println("Goodbye, World!");
    for (i = 0; i < 5; i++) {
      int k;
      System.out.println("Bye!");
    }
  }
}
```

The integers i and j have scopes within the main() method body. The integer k, however, has a scope limited to the for loop block. Because k's scope is limited to the for loop block, it cannot be seen outside that block. On the other hand, i and j still can be seen within the for loop block. What this means is that scoping has a top-down hierarchical effect—variables defined in outer scopes can still be seen and used within nested scopes; however, variables defined in nested scopes are limited to those scopes. Incidentally, don't worry if you aren't familiar with for loops—you learn all about them in the next chapter, "Expressions, Operators, and Control Structures."

For more reasons than visibility, it is important to pay attention to the scope of variables when you declare them. Along with determining the visibility of variables, the scope also determines the lifetime of variables. This means that variables are actually destroyed when program execution leaves their scope. Look at the GoodbyeWorld example again: Storage for the integers i and j is allocated when program execution enters the main() method. When the for loop block is entered, storage for the integer k is allocated. When program execution leaves the for loop block, the memory for k is freed and the variable is destroyed. Similarly, when program execution leaves main, all the variables in its scope are freed and destroyed (i and j). The concepts of variable lifetime and scope become even more important when you start dealing with classes. You'll get a good dose of this in Chapter 8, "Classes, Packages, and Interfaces."

Arrays

An *array* is a construct that provides for the storage of a list of items of the same type. Array items can have either a simple or composite data type. Arrays also can be multidimensional. Java arrays are declared with square brackets: [ ]. Following are a few examples of array declarations in Java:

```
int numbers[];
char[] letters;
long grid[][];
```

If you are familiar with arrays in another language, you may be puzzled by the absence of a number between the square brackets specifying the number of items in the array. Java doesn't allow you to specify the size of an empty array when declaring the array. You must always explicitly set the size of the array with the new operator or by assigning a list of items to the array at time of creation. The new operator is covered in the next chapter, "Expressions, Operators, and Control Structures."

NOTE

It may seem like a hassle to have to explicitly set the size of an array with the new operator. The reason for doing this is because Java doesn't have pointers like C or C++ and therefore doesn't allow you to just point anywhere in an array to create new items. Because the Java language handles memory management this way, the bounds-checking problems common with C and C++ have been avoided.

Another strange thing you may notice about Java arrays is the optional placement of the square brackets in the array declaration. You can place the square brackets after either the variable type or the identifier.

Following are a couple examples of arrays that have been declared and set to a specific size by using the new operator and by assigning a list of items in the array declaration:

```
char alphabet[] = new char[26];
int primes = {7, 11, 13};
```

More complex structures for storing lists of items, such as stacks and hash tables, are also supported by Java. Unlike arrays, these structures are implemented in Java as classes. You'll get a crash course in some of these other storage mechanisms in Chapter 13, "The Utilities Package."

Strings

In Java, *strings* are handled by a special class called String. Even literal strings are managed internally by an instantiation of a String class. An *instantiation of a class* is simply an object that has been created based on the class description. This method of handling strings is very different from languages like C and C++, where strings are represented simply as an array of characters. Following are a few strings declared using the Java String class:

```
String message;
String name = "Mr. Blonde";
```

At this point, it's not that important to know the String class inside and out. You'll learn all the gory details of the String class in Chapter 12, "The Language Package."

Summary

In this chapter, you took a look at the core components of the Java language. Hopefully, you now have more insight about why Java has become popular in such a relatively short time. With vast improvements over the weaknesses of the C and C++ languages—arguably the industry's language standards—Java will no doubt become more important in the near future. The language elements covered in this chapter are just the tip of the iceberg when it comes to the benefits of programming in Java.

Now that you are armed with the fundamentals of the Java language, you are no doubt ready to press onward and learn more about the Java language. The next chapter, "Expressions, Operators, and Control Structures," covers exactly what its title suggests. In it, you learn how to work with and manipulate much of the information you learned about in this chapter. In doing so, you will be able to start writing programs that do a little more than display cute messages on the screen.

Expressions, Operators, and Control Structures

by Michael Morrison

IN THIS CHAPTER

CHAPTER 7

In the previous chapter, you learned about the basic components of a Java program. This chapter focuses on how to use these components to do more useful things. Data types are interesting, but without expressions and operators, you can't do much with them. Even expressions and operators alone are somewhat limited in what they can do. Throw in control structures and you have the ability to do some interesting things.

This chapter covers all these issues and pulls together many of the missing pieces of the Java programming puzzle you've begun to assemble. You'll not only expand your knowledge of the Java language a great deal, you'll also learn what it takes to write some more interesting programs.

Expressions and Operators

Once you create variables, you typically want to do something with them. *Operators* enable you to perform an evaluation or computation on a data object or objects. Operators applied to variables and literals form expressions. An *expression* can be thought of as a programmatic equation. More formally, an expression is a sequence of one or more data objects (operands) and zero or more operators that produce a result. An example of an expression follows:

```
x = y / 3;
```

In this expression, x and y are variables, 3 is a literal, and = and / are operators. This expression states that the y variable is divided by 3 using the division operator (/), and the result is stored in x using the assignment operator (=). Notice that the expression was described from right to left. Although this approach of analyzing the expression from right to left is useful in terms of showing the assignment operation, most Java expressions are, in fact, evaluated from left to right. You get a better feel for this in the next section.

Operator Precedence

Even though Java expressions are typically evaluated from left to right, there still are many times when the result of an expression would be indeterminate without other rules. The following expression illustrates the problem:

```
x = 2 * 6 + 16 / 4
```

Strictly using the left-to-right evaluation of the expression, the multiplication operation 2 * 6 is carried out first, which leaves a result of 12. The addition operation 12 + 16 is then performed, which gives a result of 28. The division operation 28 / 4 is then performed, which gives a result of 7. Finally, the assignment operation x = 7 is handled, in which the number 7 is assigned to the variable x.

If you have some experience with operator precedence from another language, you might already be questioning the evaluation of this expression, and for good reason—it's wrong! The problem is that using a simple left-to-right evaluation of expressions can yield inconsistent results, depending on the order of the operators. The solution to this problem lies in *operator precedence*, which determines the order in which operators are evaluated. Every Java operator has an associated precedence. Following is a list of all the Java operators from highest to lowest precedence. In this list of operators, all the operators in a particular row have equal precedence. The precedence level of each row decreases from top to bottom. This means that the [ ] operator has a higher precedence than the * operator, but the same precedence as the ( ) operator.

.	[ ]	( )	
++	- -	!	~
*	/	%	
+	-		
<<	>>	>>>	
<	>	<=	>=
==	!=		
&			
^			
&&			
||			
? :			
=			

7

EXPRESSIONS AND
CONTROL
STRUCTURES

Evaluation of expressions still moves from left to right, but only when dealing with operators that have the same precedence. Otherwise, operators with a higher precedence are evaluated before operators with a lower precedence. Knowing this, take another look at the sample equation:

```
x = 2 * 6 + 16 / 4
```

Before using the left-to-right evaluation of the expression, first look to see whether any of the operators have differing precedence. Indeed they do! The multiplication (*) and division (/) operators both have the highest precedence, followed by the addition operator (+), and then the assignment operator (=). Because the multiplication and division operators share the same precedence, evaluate them from left to right. Doing this, you first perform the multiplication operation 2 * 6 with the result of 12. You then perform the division operation 16 / 4, which results in 4. After performing these two operations, the expression looks like this:

```
x = 12 + 4;
```

Because the addition operator has a higher precedence than the assignment operator, you perform the addition operation 12 + 4 next, resulting in 16. Finally, the assignment operation x = 16 is processed, resulting in the number 16 being assigned to the variable x. As you can see, evaluating the expression using operator precedence yields a completely different result.

Just to get the point across, take a look at another expression that uses parentheses for grouping purposes:

```
x = 2 * (11 - 7);
```

Without the grouping parentheses, you would perform the multiplication operation first and then the subtraction operation. However, referring back to the precedence list, the () operator comes before all other operators. So the subtraction operation 11 - 7 is performed first, yielding 4 and the following expression:

```
x = 2 * 4;
```

The rest of the expression is easily resolved with a multiplication and an assignment to yield a result of 8 in the variable x.

Integer Operators

There are three types of operations that can be performed on integers: unary, binary, and relational. Unary operators act on only single integer numbers, and binary operators act on pairs of integer numbers. Both unary and binary integer operators typically return integer results. Relational operators, on the other hand, act on two integer numbers but return a boolean result rather than an integer.

Unary and binary integer operators typically return an int type. For all operations involving the types byte, short, and int, the result is always an int. The only exception to this rule is when one of the operands is a long, in which case the result of the operation is also of type long.

Unary Integer Operators

Unary integer operators act on a single integer. Table 7.1 lists the unary integer operators.

Table 7.1. The unary integer operators.

Description	Operator
Increment	++
Decrement	- -
Negation	-
Bitwise complement	~

The increment and decrement operators (++ and --) increase and decrease integer variables by 1. Similar to their complements in C and C++, these operators can be used in either prefix or postfix form. A *prefix operator* takes effect before the evaluation of the expression it is in; a *postfix operator* takes effect after the expression has been evaluated. Prefix unary operators are placed immediately before the variable; postfix unary operators are placed immediately following the variable. Following are examples of each type of operator:

```
y = ++x;
z = x--;
```

In the first example, x is *prefix incremented*, which means that it is incremented before being assigned to y. In the second example, x is *postfix decremented*, which means that it is decremented after being assigned to z. In the latter case, z is assigned the value of x before x is decremented. Listing 7.1 contains the IncDec program, which uses both types of operators. Please note that the IncDec program is actually implemented in the Java class IncDec. This is a result of the object-oriented structure of Java, which requires programs to be implemented as classes. When you see a reference to a Java *program*, keep in mind that it is really referring to a Java *class*.

Listing 7.1. The IncDec class.

```
class IncDec {
  public static void main (String args[]) {
    int x = 8, y = 13;
    System.out.println("x = " + x);
    System.out.println("y = " + y);
    System.out.println("++x = " + ++x);
    System.out.println("y++ = " + y++);
    System.out.println("x = " + x);
    System.out.println("y = " + y);
  }
}
```

The IncDec program produces the following results:

```
x = 8
y = 13
++x = 9
y++ = 13
x = 9
y = 14
```

The negation unary integer operator (-) is used to change the sign of an integer value. This operator is as simple as it sounds, as indicated by the following example:

```
x = 8;
y = -x;
```

In this example, x is assigned the literal value 8 and then is negated and assigned to y. The resulting value of y is -8. To see this code in a real Java program, check out the Negation program in Listing 7.2.

Listing 7.2. The Negation class.

```
class Negation {
  public static void main (String args[]) {
    int x = 8;
    System.out.println("x = " + x);
    int y = -x;
    System.out.println("y = " + y);
  }
}
```

The last Java unary integer operator is the *bitwise complement operator* (~), which performs a bitwise negation of an integer value. *Bitwise negation* means that each bit in the number is toggled. In other words, all the binary 0s become 1s and all the binary 1s become 0s. Take a look at an example very similar to the one for the negation operator:

```
x = 8;
y = ~x;
```

In this example x is assigned the literal value 8 again, but it is bitwise complemented before being assigned to y. What does this mean? Well, without getting into the details of how integers are stored in memory, it means that all the bits of the variable x are flipped, yielding a decimal result of -9. This result has to do with the fact that negative numbers are stored in memory using a method known as *two's complement* (see the following note). If you're having trouble believing any of this, try it yourself with the BitwiseComplement program shown in Listing 7.3.

NOTE

Integer numbers are stored in memory as a series of binary bits that can each have a value of 0 or 1. A number is considered negative if the highest-order bit in the number is set to 1. Because a bitwise complement flips all the bits in a number—including the high-order bit—the sign of a number is reversed.

Listing 7.3. The BitwiseComplement class.

```
class BitwiseComplement {
  public static void main (String args[]) {
    int x = 8;
    System.out.println("x = " + x);
    int y = ~x;
    System.out.println("y = " + y);
  }
}
```

Binary Integer Operators

Binary integer operators act on pairs of integers. Table 7.2 lists the binary integer operators.

Table 7.2. The binary integer operators.

Description	Operator
Addition	+
Subtraction	-
Multiplication	*
Division	/
Modulus	%
Bitwise AND	&
Bitwise OR	¦
Bitwise XOR	^
Left-shift	<<
Right-shift	>>
Zero-fill-right-shift	>>>

The addition, subtraction, multiplication, and division operators (+, -, *, and /) all do what you expect them to. An important thing to note is how the division operator works; because you are dealing with integer operands, the division operator returns an integer divisor. In cases where the division results in a remainder, the modulus operator (%) can be used to get the remainder value. Listing 7.4 contains the `Arithmetic` program, which shows how the basic binary integer arithmetic operators work.

Listing 7.4. The `Arithmetic` class.

```
class Arithmetic {
  public static void main (String args[]) {
    int x = 17, y = 5;
    System.out.println("x = " + x);
    System.out.println("y = " + y);
    System.out.println("x + y = " + (x + y));
    System.out.println("x - y = " + (x - y));
    System.out.println("x * y = " + (x * y));
    System.out.println("x / y = " + (x / y));
    System.out.println("x % y = " + (x % y));
  }
}
```

The results of running the `Arithmetic` program follow:

```
x = 17
y = 5
x + y = 22
x - y = 12
x * y = 85
x / y = 3
x % y = 2
```

These results shouldn't surprise you too much. Just notice that the division operation x / y, which boils down to 17 / 5, yields the result 3. Also notice that the modulus operation x % y, which is resolved down to 17 % 5, ends with a result of 2 (the remainder of the integer division).

Mathematically, a division by zero results in an infinite result. Because representing infinite numbers is a big problem for computers, division or modulus operations by zero result in an error. To be more specific, a runtime exception is thrown. You learn a lot more about exceptions in Chapter 10, "Exception Handling."

The bitwise AND, OR, and XOR operators (&, ¦, and ^) all act on the individual bits of an integer. These operators are sometimes useful when an integer is being used as a bit field. An example of this is when an integer is used to represent a group of binary flags. An int is capable of representing up to 32 different flags because it is stored in 32 bits. Listing 7.5 contains the program Bitwise, which shows how to use the binary bitwise integer operators.

NOTE

Java actually includes a class that provides specific support for storing binary flags. The class is called BitSet, and you learn about it in Chapter 13, "The Utilities Package."

Listing 7.5. The Bitwise class.

```java
class Bitwise {
  public static void main (String args[]) {
    int x = 5, y = 6;
    System.out.println("x = " + x);
    System.out.println("y = " + y);
    System.out.println("x & y = " + (x & y));
    System.out.println("x ¦ y = " + (x ¦ y));
    System.out.println("x ^ y = " + (x ^ y));
  }
}
```

The output of running Bitwise follows:

```
x = 5
y = 6
x & y = 4
x ¦ y = 7
x ^ y = 3
```

To understand this output, you must first understand the binary equivalents of each decimal number. In Bitwise, the variables x and y are set to 5 and 6, which correspond to the binary numbers 0101 and 0110. The bitwise AND operation compares each bit of each number to see whether they are the same. It then sets the resulting bit to 1 if both bits being compared are 1; it sets the resulting bit to 0 otherwise. The result of the bitwise AND operation on these two numbers is 0100 in binary, or decimal 4. The same logic is used for both of the other operators, except that the rules for comparing the bits are different. The bitwise OR operator sets the resulting bit to 1 if either of the bits being compared is 1. For these numbers, the result is 0111 binary, or 7 decimal. Finally, the bitwise XOR operator sets resulting bits to 1 if exactly one of the bits being compared is 1, and 0 otherwise. For these numbers, the result is 0011 binary, or 3 decimal.

The left-shift, right-shift, and zero-fill-right-shift operators (<<, >>, and >>>) shift the individual bits of an integer by a specified integer amount. Following are some examples of how these operators are used:

```
x << 3;
y >> 7;
z >>> 2;
```

In the first example, the individual bits of the integer variable x are shifted to the left three places. In the second example, the bits of y are shifted to the right seven places. Finally, the third example shows z being shifted to the right two places, with zeros shifted into the two leftmost places. To see the shift operators in a real program, check out Shift in Listing 7.6.

Listing 7.6. The Shift class.

```
class Shift {
  public static void main (String args[]) {
    int x = 7;
    System.out.println("x = " + x);
    System.out.println("x >> 2 = " + (x >> 2));
    System.out.println("x << 1 = " + (x << 1));
    System.out.println("x >>> 1 = " + (x >>> 1));
  }
}
```

The output of Shift follows:

```
x = 7
x >> 2 = 1
x << 1 = 14
x >>> 1 = 3
```

The number being shifted in this case is the decimal 7, which is represented in binary as 0111. The first right-shift operation shifts the bits two places to the right, resulting in the binary number 0001, or decimal 1. The next operation, a left-shift, shifts the bits one place to the left, resulting in the binary number 1110, or decimal 14. The last operation is a zero-fill-right-shift, which shifts the bits one place to the right, resulting in the binary number 0011, or decimal 3. Pretty simple, eh? And you probably thought it was difficult working with integers at the bit level!

Based on these examples, you may be wondering what the difference is between the right-shift (>>) and zero-fill-right-shift (>>>) operators. The right-shift operator appears to shift zeros into the leftmost bits, just like the zero-fill-right-shift operator, right? Well, when dealing with positive numbers, there is no difference between the two operators—they both shift zeros into the upper bits of a number. The difference arises when you start shifting negative numbers. Remember that negative numbers have the high-order bit set to 1. The right-shift operator preserves the high-order bit and effectively shifts the lower 31 bits to the right. This behavior yields results for negative numbers similar to those for positive numbers. That is, -8 shifted right by one results in -4. The zero-fill-right-shift operator, on the other hand, shifts zeros into *all* the upper bits, including the high-order bit. When this shifting is applied to negative numbers, the high-order bit becomes 0 and the number becomes positive.

Relational Integer Operators

The last group of integer operators is the relational operators, which all operate on integers but return a type boolean. Table 7.3 lists the relational integer operators.

Table 7.3. The relational integer operators.

Description	Operator
Less-than	<
Greater-than	>
Less-than-or-equal-to	<=
Greater-than-or-equal-to	>=
Equal-to	==
Not-equal-to	!=

These operators all perform comparisons between integers. Listing 7.7 contains the Relational program, which demonstrates the use of the relational operators with integers.

Listing 7.7. The Relational class.

```
class Relational {
  public static void main (String args[]) {
    int x = 7, y = 11, z = 11;
    System.out.println("x = " + x);
    System.out.println("y = " + y);
    System.out.println("z = " + z);
    System.out.println("x < y = " + (x < y));
    System.out.println("x > z = " + (x > z));
    System.out.println("y <= z = " + (y <= z));
```

```
    System.out.println("x >= y = " + (x >= y));
    System.out.println("y == z = " + (y == z));
    System.out.println("x != y = " + (x != z));
  }
}
```

The output of running `Relational` follows:

```
x = 7
y = 11
z = 11
x < y = true
x > z = false
y <= z = true
x >= y = false
y == z = true
x != y = true
```

As you can see, the `println()` method is smart enough to print boolean results correctly as true and `false`.

Floating-Point Operators

Similar to integer operators, there are three types of operations that can be performed on floating-point numbers: unary, binary, and relational. Unary operators act only on single floating-point numbers, and binary operators act on pairs of floating-point numbers. Both unary and binary floating-point operators return floating-point results. Relational operators, however, act on two floating-point numbers but return a boolean result.

Unary and binary floating-point operators return a `float` type if both operands are of type `float`. If one or both of the operands is of type `double`, however, the result of the operation is of type `double`.

Unary Floating-Point Operators

The unary floating point operators act on a single floating-point number. Table 7.4 lists the unary floating-point operators.

Table 7.4. The unary floating-point operators.

Description	Operator
Increment	++
Decrement	--

As you can see, the only two unary floating point operators are the increment and decrement operators. These two operators respectively add and subtract 1.0 from their floating-point operand.

Binary Floating-Point Operators

The binary floating-point operators act on a pair of floating-point numbers. Table 7.5 lists the binary floating-point operators.

Table 7.5. The binary floating-point operators.

Description	Operator
Addition	+
Subtraction	-
Multiplication	*
Division	/
Modulus	%

The binary floating-point operators consist of the four traditional binary operations (+, -, *, /), along with the modulus operator (%). You might be wondering how the modulus operator fits in here, considering that its use as an integer operator relied on an integer division. If you recall, the integer modulus operator returned the remainder of an integer division of the two operands. But a floating-point division never results in a remainder, so what does a floating-point modulus do? The floating-point modulus operator returns the floating-point equivalent of an integer division. What this means is that the division is carried out with both floating-point operands, but the resulting divisor is treated as an integer, resulting in a floating-point remainder. Listing 7.8 contains the FloatMath program, which shows how the floating-point modulus operator works along with the other binary floating-point operators.

Listing 7.8. The FloatMath class.

```
class FloatMath {
  public static void main (String args[]) {
    float x = 23.5F, y = 7.3F;
    System.out.println("x = " + x);
    System.out.println("y = " + y);
    System.out.println("x + y = " + (x + y));
    System.out.println("x - y = " + (x - y));
    System.out.println("x * y = " + (x * y));
    System.out.println("x / y = " + (x / y));
    System.out.println("x % y = " + (x % y));
  }
}
```

The output of `FloatMath` follows:

```
x = 23.5
y = 7.3
x + y = 30.8
x - y = 16.2
x * y = 171.55
x / y = 3.21918
x % y = 1.6
```

The first four operations no doubt performed as you expected, taking the two floating-point operands and yielding a floating-point result. The final modulus operation determined that `7.3` divides into `23.5` an integral amount of 3 times, leaving a remaining result of `1.6`.

Relational Floating-Point Operators

The relational floating-point operators compare two floating-point operands, leaving a boolean result. The floating-point relational operators are the same as the integer relational operators listed in Table 7.3, earlier in this chapter, except that they work on floating-point numbers.

Boolean Operators

Boolean operators act on `boolean` types and return a boolean result. The boolean operators are listed in Table 7.6.

Table 7.6. The boolean operators.

Description	Operator
Evaluation AND	&
Evaluation OR	¦
Evaluation XOR	^
Logical AND	&&
Logical OR	¦¦
Negation	!
Equal-to	==
Not-equal-to	!=
Conditional	?:

The evaluation operators (&, ¦, and ^) evaluate both sides of an expression before determining the result. The logical operators (&& and ¦¦) avoid the right-side evaluation of the expression if it is not needed. To better understand the difference between these operators, take a look at the following two expressions:

```
boolean result = isValid & (Count > 10);
boolean result = isValid && (Count > 10);
```

The first expression uses the evaluation AND operator (&) to make an assignment. In this case, both sides of the expression are always evaluated, regardless of the values of the variables involved. In the second example, the logical AND operator (&&) is used. This time, the isValid boolean value is first checked. If it is false, the right side of the expression is ignored and the assignment is made. This operator is more efficient because a false value on the left side of the expression provides enough information to determine the false outcome.

Although the logical operators are more efficient than the evaluation operators, there still may be times when you want to use the evaluation operators to ensure that the entire expression is evaluated. The following code shows how the evaluation AND operator is necessary for the complete evaluation of an expression:

```
while ((++x < 10) && (++y < 15)) {
  System.out.println(x);
  System.out.println(y);
}
```

In this example, the second expression (++y < 15) is evaluated after the last pass through the loop because of the evaluation AND operator. If the logical AND operator had been used, the second expression would not have been evaluated and y would not have been incremented after the last time around.

The three boolean operators—negation, equal-to, and not-equal-to (!, ==, and !=)—perform exactly as you might expect. The negation operator toggles the value of a boolean from false to true or from true to false, depending on the original value. The equal-to operator simply determines whether two boolean values are equal (both true or both false). Similarly, the not-equal-to operator determines whether two boolean operands are unequal.

The conditional boolean operator (?:) is the most unique of the boolean operators and is worth a closer look. This operator also is known as the *ternary operator* because it takes three items: a condition and two expressions. The syntax for the conditional operator follows:

```
Condition ? Expression1 : Expression2
```

The Condition, which itself is a boolean, is first evaluated to determine whether it is true or false. If Condition evaluates to a true result, Expression1 is evaluated. If Condition ends up being false, Expression2 is evaluated. To get a better feel for the conditional operator, check out the Conditional program in Listing 7.9.

Listing 7.9. The Conditional class.

```
class Conditional {
  public static void main (String args[]) {
    int x = 0;
    boolean isEven = false;
    System.out.println("x = " + x);
```

```
    x = isEven ? 4 : 7;
    System.out.println("x = " + x);
  }
}
```

The results of the `Conditional` program follow:

```
x = 0
x = 7
```

The integer variable x is first assigned a value of 0. The boolean variable isEven is assigned a value of false. Using the conditional operator, the value of isEven is checked. Because it is false, the second expression of the conditional is used, which results in the value 7 being assigned to x.

String Operators

Just as integers, floating-point numbers, and booleans can, strings can be manipulated with operators. Actually, there is only one string operator: the concatenation operator (+). The concatenation operator for strings works very similarly to the addition operator for numbers—it adds strings together. The concatenation operator is demonstrated in the `Concatenation` program shown in Listing 7.10.

Listing 7.10. The Concatenation class.

```
class Concatenation {
  public static void main (String args[]) {
    String firstHalf = "What " + "did ";
    String secondHalf = "you " + "say?";
    System.out.println(firstHalf + secondHalf);
  }
}
```

The output of `Concatenation` follows:

```
What did you say?
```

In the `Concatenation` program, literal strings are concatenated to make assignments to the two string variables, `firstHalf` and `secondHalf`, at time of creation. The two string variables are then concatenated within the call to the `println()` method.

Assignment Operators

One final group of operators you haven't seen yet is the assignment operators. Assignment operators actually work with all the fundamental data types. Table 7.7 lists the assignment operators.

Table 7.7. The assignment operators.

Description	Operator
Simple	=
Addition	+=
Subtraction	-=
Multiplication	*=
Division	/=
Modulus	%=
AND	&=
OR	¦=
XOR	^=

With the exception of the simple assignment operator (=), the assignment operators function exactly like their nonassignment counterparts, except that the resulting value is stored in the operand on the left side of the expression. Take a look at the following examples:

```
x += 6;
x *= (y - 3);
```

In the first example, x and 6 are added and the result stored in x. In the second example, 3 is subtracted from y and the result multiplied by x. The final result is then stored in x.

Control Structures

Although performing operations on data is very useful, it's time to move on to the issue of program flow control. The flow of your programs is dictated by two different types of constructs: branches and loops. *Branches* enable you to selectively execute one part of a program instead of another. *Loops*, on the other hand, provide a means to repeat certain parts of a program. Together, branches and loops provide you with a powerful means to control the logic and execution of your code.

Branches

Without branches or loops, Java code executes in a sequential fashion, as shown in Figure 7.1.

In Figure 7.1, each statement is executed sequentially. But what if you don't always want every single statement executed? Then you use a branch. Figure 7.2 shows how a conditional branch gives the flow of your code more options.

FIGURE 7.1.

A program executing sequentially.

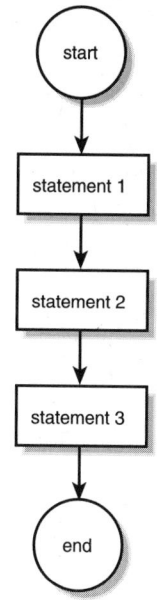

7

EXPRESSIONS AND
CONTROL
STRUCTURES

FIGURE 7.2.

A program executing with a branch.

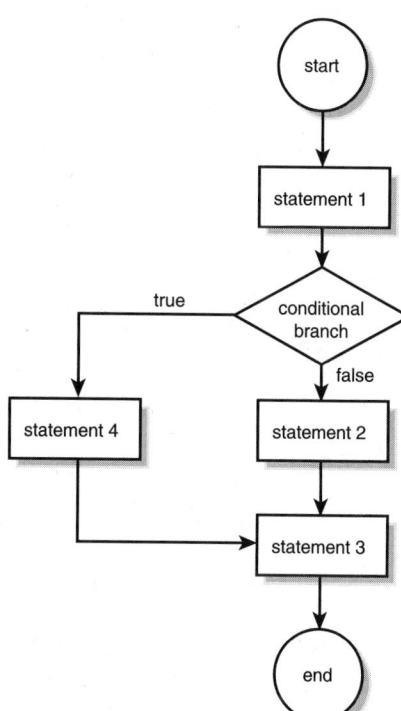

By adding a branch, you give the code two optional routes to take, based on the result of the conditional expression. The concept of branches might seem trivial, but it would be difficult if not impossible to write useful programs without them. Java supports two types of branches: `if-else` branches and `switch` branches.

if-else Branches

The `if-else` branch is the most commonly used branch in Java programming. It is used to select conditionally one of two possible outcomes. The syntax for the `if-else` statement follows:

```
if (Condition)
  Statement1
else
  Statement2
```

If the boolean `Condition` evaluates to `true`, `Statement1` is executed. Likewise, if `Condition` evaluates to `false`, `Statement2` is executed. The following example shows how to use an `if-else` statement:

```
if (isTired)
  timeToEat = true;
else
  timeToEat = false;
```

If the boolean variable `isTired` is `true`, the first statement is executed and `timeToEat` is set to `true`. Otherwise, the second statement is executed and `timeToEat` is set to `false`. You may have noticed that the `if-else` branch works in a manner very similar to the conditional operator (`?:`) described earlier in this chapter. In fact, you can think of the `if-else` branch as an expanded version of the conditional operator. One significant difference between the two is that you can include compound statements in an `if-else` branch, which you cannot do with the conditional operator.

> **NOTE**
>
> *Compound statements* are blocks of code surrounded by curly braces {} that appear as a single, or simple, statement to an outer block of code.

If you have only a single statement that you want to execute conditionally, you can leave off the `else` part of the branch, as shown in the following example:

```
if (isThirsty)
  pourADrink = true;
```

On the other hand, if you need more than two conditional outcomes, you can string together a series of `if-else` branches to get the desired effect. The following example shows multiple `if-else` branches used to switch between different outcomes:

```
if (x == 0)
  y = 5;
else if (x == 2)
  y = 25;
else if (x >= 3)
  y = 125;
```

In this example, three different comparisons are made, each with its own statement executed on a true conditional result. Notice, however, that subsequent if-else branches are in effect nested within the previous branch. This arrangement ensures that at most one statement is executed.

The last important topic to cover in regard to if-else branches is compound statements. As mentioned in the preceding note, a compound statement is a block of code surrounded by curly braces that appears to an outer block as a single statement. Following is an example of a compound statement used with an if branch:

```
if (performCalc) {
  x += y * 5;
  y -= 10;
  z = (x - 3) / y;
}
```

Sometimes, when nesting if-else branches, it is necessary to use curly braces to distinguish which statements go with which branch. The following example illustrates the problem:

```
if (x != 0)
  if (y < 10)
    z = 5;
else
  z = 7;
```

In this example, the style of indentation indicates that the else branch belongs to the first (outer) if. However, because there was no grouping specified, the Java compiler assumes that the else goes with the inner if. To get the desired results, you must modify the code as follows:

```
if (x != 0) {
  if (y < 10)
    z = 5;
}
else
  z = 7;
```

The addition of the curly braces tells the compiler that the inner if is part of a compound statement; more importantly, it completely hides the else branch from the inner if. Based on what you learned from the discussion of blocks and scope in the last chapter, you can see that code within the inner if has no way of accessing code outside its scope, including the else branch.

Listing 7.11 contains the source code for the IfElseName class, which uses a lot of what you've learned so far.

Listing 7.11. The IfElseName class.

```
class IfElseName {
  public static void main (String args[]) {
    char firstInitial = (char)-1;
    System.out.println("Enter your first initial:");
    try {
      firstInitial = (char)System.in.read();
    }
    catch (Exception e) {
      System.out.println("Error: " + e.toString());
    }
    if (firstInitial == -1)
      System.out.println("Now what kind of name is that?");
    else if (firstInitial == 'j')
      System.out.println("Your name must be Jules!");
    else if (firstInitial == 'v')
      System.out.println("Your name must be Vincent!");
    else if (firstInitial == 'z')
      System.out.println("Your name must be Zed!");
    else
      System.out.println("I can't figure out your name!");
  }
```

When typing the letter **v** in response to the input message, IfElseName yields the following results:

```
Your name must be Vincent!
```

The first thing in IfElseName you probably are wondering about is the read() method. The read() method simply reads a character from the standard input stream (System.in), which is typically the keyboard. Notice that a cast is used because read() returns an int type. Once the input character has been successfully retrieved, a succession of if-else branches is used to determine the proper output. If there are no matches, the final else branch is executed, which notifies users that their names could not be determined. Notice that the value of read() is checked to see whether it is equal to –1. The read() method returns –1 if it has reached the end of the input stream.

NOTE

You may have noticed that the call to the read() method in IfElseName is enclosed within a try-catch clause. The try-catch clause is part of Java's support for exception handling and is used in this case to trap errors encountered while reading input from the user. You'll learn more about exceptions and the try-catch clause in Chapter 10, "Exception Handling."

switch Branches

Similar to the if-else branch, the switch branch is specifically designed to conditionally switch among multiple outcomes. The syntax for the switch statement follows:

```
switch (Expression) {
  case Constant1:
    StatementList1
  case Constant2:
    StatementList2

  default:
    DefaultStatementList
}
```

The switch branch evaluates and compares *Expression* to all the case constants and branches the program's execution to the matching case statement list. If no case constants match *Expression*, the program branches to the *DefaultStatementList*, if one has been supplied (the *DefaultStatementList* is optional). You might be wondering what a statement list is. A *statement list* is simply a series, or list, of statements. Unlike the if-else branch, which directs program flow to a simple or compound statement, the switch branch directs the flow to a list of statements.

When the program execution moves into a case statement list, it continues from there in a sequential manner. To better understand this, take a look at Listing 7.12, which contains a switch version of the name program developed earlier with if-else branches.

Listing 7.12. The SwitchName1 class.

```java
class SwitchName1 {
  public static void main (String args[]) {
    char firstInitial = (char)-1;
    System.out.println("Enter your first initial:");
    try {
      firstInitial = (char)System.in.read();
    }
    catch (Exception e) {
      System.out.println("Error: " + e.toString());
    }
    switch(firstInitial) {
      case (char)-1:
        System.out.println("Now what kind of name is that?");
      case 'j':
        System.out.println("Your name must be Jules!");
      case 'v':
        System.out.println("Your name must be Vincent!");
      case 'z':
        System.out.println("Your name must be Zed!");
      default:
        System.out.println("I can't figure out your name!");
    }
  }
}
```

When typing the letter **v** in response to the input message, SwitchName1 produces the following results:

```
Your name must be Vincent!
Your name must be Zed!
I can't figure out your name!
```

Hey, what's going on here? That output definitely does not look right. The problem lies in the way the switch branch controls program flow. The switch branch matched the **v** entered with the correct case statement, as shown in the first string printed. However, the program continued executing all the case statements from that point onward, which is *not* what you wanted. The solution to the problem lies in the break statement. The break statement forces a program to break out of the block of code it is currently executing. Check out the new version of the program in Listing 7.13, which has break statements added where appropriate.

Listing 7.13. The SwitchName2 class.

```java
class SwitchName2 {
  public static void main (String args[]) {
    char firstInitial = (char)-1;
    System.out.println("Enter your first initial:");
    try {
      firstInitial = (char)System.in.read();
    }
    catch (Exception e) {
      System.out.println("Error: " + e.toString());
    }
    switch(firstInitial) {
      case (char)-1:
        System.out.println("Now what kind of name is that?");
        break;
      case 'j':
        System.out.println("Your name must be Jules!");
        break;
      case 'v':
        System.out.println("Your name must be Vincent!");
        break;
      case 'z':
        System.out.println("Your name must be Zed!");
        break;
      default:
        System.out.println("I can't figure out your name!");
    }
  }
}
```

When you run SwitchName2 and enter **v**, you get the following output:

```
Your name must be Vincent!
```

That's a lot better! You can see that placing break statements after each case statement kept the program from falling through to the next case statements. Although you will use break statements in this manner the majority of the time, there may still be some situations where you will want a case statement to fall through to the next one.

Loops

When it comes to program flow, branches really tell only half the story; loops tell the other half. Put simply, *loops* enable you to execute code repeatedly. There are three types of loops in Java: for loops, while loops, and do-while loops.

Just as branches alter the sequential flow of programs, so do loops. Figure 7.3 shows how a loop alters the sequential flow of a Java program.

Figure 7.3.

A program executing with a loop.

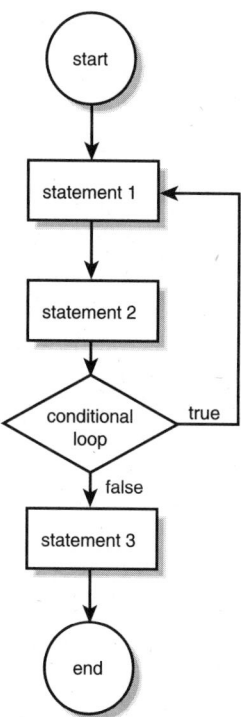

for Loops

The for loop provides a means to repeat a section of code a designated number of times. The for loop is structured so that a section of code is repeated until some limit has been reached. The syntax for the for statement follows:

```
for (InitializationExpression; LoopCondition; StepExpression)
    Statement
```

The for loop repeats the *Statement* the number of times that is determined by the *InitializationExpression*, the *LoopCondition*, and the *StepExpression*. The *InitializationExpression* is used to initialize a loop control variable. The *LoopCondition* compares the loop control variable to some limit value. Finally, the *StepExpression* specifies how the loop control variable should be modified before the next iteration of the loop. The following example shows how a for loop can be used to print the numbers from 1 to 10:

```java
for (int i = 1; i < 11; i++)
  System.out.println(i);
```

First, i is declared as an integer. The fact that i is declared within the body of the for loop might look strange to you at this point. Don't despair—this is completely legal. i is initialized to 1 in the *InitializationExpression* part of the for loop. Next, the conditional expression i < 11 is evaluated to see whether the loop should continue. At this point, i is still equal to 1, so *LoopCondition* evaluates to true and the *Statement* is executed (the value of i is printed to standard output). i is then incremented in the *StepExpression* part of the for loop, and the process repeats with the evaluation of *LoopCondition* again. This continues until *LoopCondition* evaluates to false, which is when x equals 11 (10 iterations later).

Listing 7.14 shows the ForCount program, which shows how to use a for loop to count a user-entered amount of numbers.

Listing 7.14. The ForCount class.

```java
class ForCount {
  public static void main (String args[]) {
    char input = (char)-1;
    int  numToCount;
    System.out.println("Enter a number to count to between 0 and 10:");
    try {
      input = (char)System.in.read();
    }
    catch (Exception e) {
      System.out.println("Error: " + e.toString());
    }
    numToCount = Character.digit(input, 10);
    if ((numToCount > 0) && (numToCount < 10)) {
      for (int i = 1; i <= numToCount; i++)
        System.out.println(i);
    }
    else
      System.out.println("That number was not between 0 and 10!");
  }
}
```

When the ForCount program is run and the number 4 is entered, the following output results:

```
1
2
3
4
```

ForCount first prompts the user to enter a number between 0 and 10. A character is read from the keyboard using the read() method and the result stored in the input character variable. The static digit method of the Character class then is used to convert the character to its base 10 integer representation. This value is stored in the numToCount integer variable. numToCount is then checked to make sure that it is in the range 0 to 10. If so, a for loop is executed that counts from 1 to numToCount, printing each number along the way. If numToCount is outside the valid range, an error message is printed.

Before you move on, there is one small problem with ForCount that you may not have noticed. Run it and try typing in a number greater than 9. What happened to the error message? The problem is that ForCount grabs only the first character it sees from the input. So if you type 10, ForCount just gets the 1 and thinks everything is fine. You don't have to worry about fixing this problem right now because it will be resolved when you learn more about input and output in Chapter 14, "The I/O Package."

while Loops

Like the for loop, the while loop has a loop condition that controls the execution of the loop statement. Unlike the for loop, however, the while loop has no initialization or step expressions. The syntax for the while statement follows:

```
while (LoopCondition)
    Statement
```

If the boolean LoopCondition evaluates to true, the Statement is executed and the process starts over. It is important to understand that the while loop has no step expression as the for loop does. This means that the LoopCondition must somehow be affected by code in the Statement or the loop will infinitely repeat, which is a bad thing. It is bad because an infinite loop causes a program to never exit, which hogs processor time and can ultimately hang the system.

Another important thing to notice about the while loop is that its LoopCondition occurs before the body of the loop Statement. This means that if the LoopCondition initially evaluates to false, the Statement is never executed. Although this may seem trivial, it is in fact the only thing that differentiates the while loop from the do-while loop, which is discussed in the next section.

To better understand how the while loop works, take a look at Listing 7.15, which shows how a counting program works using a while loop.

Listing 7.15. The WhileCount class.

```
class WhileCount {
  public static void main (String args[]) {
    char input = (char)-1;
    int  numToCount;
    System.out.println("Enter a number to count to between 0 and 10:");
    try {
      input = (char)System.in.read();
```

continues

Listing 7.15. continued

```
    }
    catch (Exception e) {
      System.out.println("Error: " + e.toString());
    }
    numToCount = Character.digit(input, 10);
    if ((numToCount > 0) && (numToCount < 10)) {
      int i = 1;
      while (i <= numToCount) {
        System.out.println(i);
        i++;
      }
    }
    else
      System.out.println("That number was not between 0 and 10!");
  }
}
```

Arguably, WhileCount doesn't demonstrate the best usage of a while loop. Loops that involve counting should almost always be implemented with for loops. However, seeing how a while loop can be made to imitate a for loop can give you insight into the structural differences between the two types of loops.

Because while loops don't have any type of initialization expression, you first have to declare and initialize the variable i to 1. Next, the loop condition for the while loop is established as i <= numToCount. Inside the compound while statement, you can see a call to the println() method, which outputs the value of i. Finally, i is incremented and program execution resumes back at the while loop condition.

do-while Loops

The do-while loop is very similar to the while loop, as you can see in the following syntax:

```
do
  Statement
while (LoopCondition);
```

The major difference between the do-while loop and the while loop is that, in a do-while loop, the LoopCondition is evaluated *after* the Statement is executed. This difference is important because there may be times when you want the Statement code to be executed at least once, regardless of the LoopCondition.

The Statement is executed initially, and from then on it is executed as long as the LoopCondition evaluates to true. As with the while loop, you must be careful with the do-while loop to avoid creating an infinite loop. An infinite loop occurs when the LoopCondition remains true indefinitely. The following example shows a very obvious infinite do-while loop:

```
do
  System.out.println("I'm stuck!");
while (true);
```

Because the `LoopCondition` is always `true`, the message `I'm Stuck!` is printed forever, or at least until you press Ctrl+C and break out of the program.

break and continue Statements

You've already seen how the `break` statement works with the `switch` branch. The `break` statement is also useful when dealing with loops. You can use the `break` statement to jump out of a loop and effectively bypass the loop condition. Listing 7.16 shows how the `break` statement can help you out of the infinite loop problem shown earlier.

Listing 7.16. The BreakLoop class.

```
class BreakLoop {
  public static void main (String args[]) {
    int i = 0;
    do {
      System.out.println("I'm stuck!");
      i++;
      if (i > 100)
        break;
    }
    while (true);
  }
}
```

In `BreakLoop`, a seemingly infinite `do-while` loop is created by setting the loop condition to `true`. However, the `break` statement is used to exit the loop when `i` is incremented past `100`.

Another useful statement that works similarly to the `break` statement is the `continue` statement. Unlike `break`, the `continue` statement is useful only when working with loops; it has no real application to the `switch` branch. The `continue` statement works like the `break` statement in that it jumps out of the current iteration of a loop. The difference with `continue` is that program execution is restored to the test condition of the loop. Remember that `break` jumps completely out of a loop. Use `break` when you want to jump out and terminate a loop; use `continue` when you want to jump immediately to the next iteration of the loop. The following example shows the difference between the `break` and `continue` statements:

```
int i = 0;
while (i++ < 100) {
  System.out.println("Looping with i.");
  break;
  System.out.println("Please don't print me!");
}
int j = 0;
while (j++ < 100) {
  System.out.println("Looping with j!");
  continue;
  System.out.println("Please don't print me!");
}
```

In this example, the first loop breaks out because of the break statement after printing the looping message once. Note that the second message is never printed because the break statement occurs before we get to it. Contrast this with the second loop, which prints the looping message 100 times. The reason for this is that the continue statement allows the loop to continue its iterations. In this case, the continue statement serves only to skip over the second message, which still isn't printed.

Summary

This chapter covered a lot of territory. You started off by learning about expressions and then moved right into operators, learning how they work and how they affect each data type. You won't regret the time spent working with operators in this chapter—they are at the core of almost every mathematical or logical Java expression.

From operators, you moved on to control structures, learning about the various types of branches and loops. Branches and loops provide the means to alter the flow of Java programs and are just as important as operators in Java programming.

With the concepts presented in this chapter firmly set in your mind, you are ready to dig a little deeper into Java. Next stop: object-oriented programming with classes, packages, and interfaces!

Classes, Packages, and Interfaces

by Michael Morrison

CHAPTER 8

IN THIS CHAPTER

So far, you've managed to avoid the issue of object-oriented programming and how it relates to Java. This chapter aims to remedy that hole in your education. It begins with a basic discussion of object-oriented programming in general. With this background in place, you can then move into the rest of the chapter, which covers the specific elements of the Java language that provide support for object-oriented programming—namely, classes, packages, and interfaces.

You can think of this chapter as the chapter that finishes helping you to your feet in regard to learning the Java language. Classes are the final core component of the Java language you must learn before becoming a proficient Java programmer. Once you have a solid understanding of classes and how they work in Java, you'll be ready to write some serious Java programs. So, what are you waiting for? Read on!

Object-Oriented Programming Primer

You may have been wondering what the big deal is with objects and object-oriented technology. Is it something you should be concerned with, and if so, why? If you sift through the hype surrounding the whole object-oriented issue, you'll find a very powerful technology that provides a lot of benefits to software design. The problem is that object-oriented concepts can be difficult to grasp. And you can't embrace the benefits of object-oriented design if you don't completely understand what they are. Because of this, a complete understanding of the theory behind object-oriented programming is usually developed over time through practice.

A lot of the confusion among developers in regard to object-oriented technology has led to confusion among computer users in general. How many products have you seen that claim they are object oriented? Considering that object orientation is a software design issue, what can this statement possibly mean to a software consumer? In many ways, "object oriented" has become to the software industry what "new and improved" is to the household cleanser industry. The truth is that the real world is already object oriented, which is no surprise to anyone. The significance of object-oriented technology is that it enables programmers to design software in much the same way they perceive the real world.

Now that you've come to terms with some of the misconceptions surrounding the object-oriented issue, try to put them aside and think of what the term *object-oriented* might mean to software design. This primer lays the groundwork for understanding how object-oriented design makes writing programs faster, easier, and more reliable. And it all begins with the object. Even though this chapter ultimately focuses on Java, this object-oriented primer section really applies to all object-oriented languages.

Objects

Objects are software bundles of data and the procedures that act on that data. The *procedures* are also known as *methods*. The merger of data and methods provides a means of more accurately representing real-world objects in software. Without objects, modeling a real-world problem in software requires a significant logical leap. Objects, on the other hand, enable programmers to solve real-world problems in the software domain much easier and more logically.

As is evident by its name, objects are at the heart of object-oriented technology. To understand how software objects are beneficial, think about the common characteristics of all real-world objects. Lions, cars, and calculators all share two common characteristics: state and behavior. For example, the state of a lion includes its color, weight, and whether the lion is tired or hungry. Lions also have certain behaviors, such as roaring, sleeping, and hunting. The state of a car includes the current speed, the type of transmission, whether it is two-wheel or four-wheel drive, whether the lights are on, and the current gear, among other things. The behaviors for a car include turning, braking, and accelerating.

As with real-world objects, software objects also have these two common characteristics (state and behavior). To relate this back to programming terms, the state of an object is determined by its data; the behavior of an object is defined by its methods. By making this connection between real-world objects and software objects, you begin to see how objects help bridge the gap between the real world and the world of software inside your computer.

Because software objects are modeled after real-world objects, you can more easily represent real-world objects in object-oriented programs. You can use the lion object to represent a real lion in an interactive software zoo. Similarly, car objects would be very useful in a racing game. However, you don't always have to think of software objects as modeling physical real-world objects; software objects can be just as useful for modeling abstract concepts. For example, a thread is an object used in multithreaded software systems that represents a stream of program execution. You'll learn a lot more about threads and how they are used in Java in the next chapter, "Threads and Multithreading."

Figure 8.1 shows a visualization of a software object, including the primary components and how they relate.

FIGURE 8.1.

A software object.

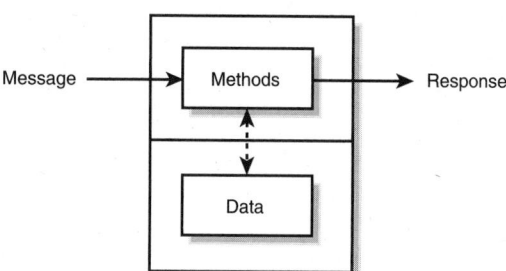

The software object in Figure 8.1 clearly shows the two primary components of an object: data and methods. The figure also shows some type of communication, or access, between the data and the methods. Additionally, it shows how messages are sent through the methods, which result in responses from the object. You learn more about messages and responses later in this chapter.

The data and methods within an object express everything that the object represents (state), along with what it can do (behavior). A software object modeling a real-world car would have variables (data) that indicate the car's current state: It's traveling at 75 mph, it's in 4th gear, and the lights are on. The software car object would also have methods that allow it to brake, accelerate, steer, change gears, and turn the lights on and off. Figure 8.2 shows what a software car object might look like.

FIGURE 8.2.

A software car object.

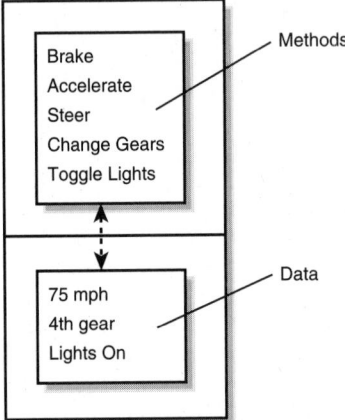

In both Figures 8.1 and 8.2, notice the line separating the methods from the data within the object. This line is a little misleading because methods have full access to the data within an object. The line is there to illustrate the difference between the visibility of the methods and the data to the outside world. In this sense, an object's *visibility* refers to the parts of the object to which another object has access. Because object data defaults to being invisible, or inaccessible, to other objects, all interaction between objects must be handled through methods. This hiding of data within an object is called *encapsulation.*

Encapsulation

Encapsulation is the process of packaging an object's data together with its methods. A powerful benefit of encapsulation is the hiding of implementation details from other objects. This means that the internal portion of an object has more limited visibility than the external portion. This arrangement results in the safeguarding of the internal portion against unwanted external access.

The external portion of an object is often referred to as the object's *interface* because it acts as the object's interface to the rest of the program. Because other objects must communicate with the object only through its interface, the internal portion of the object is protected from outside tampering. And because an outside program has no access to the internal implementation of an object, the internal implementation can change at any time without affecting other parts of the program.

Encapsulation provides two primary benefits to programmers:

■ **Implementation hiding.** This refers to the protection of the internal implementation of an object. An object is composed of a public interface and a private section that can be a combination of internal data and methods. The internal data and methods are the hidden sections of the object. The primary benefit is that these sections can change without affecting other parts of the program.

■ **Modularity.** This means that an object can be maintained independently of other objects. Because the source code for the internal sections of an object is maintained separately from the interface, you are free to make modifications with confidence that your object won't cause problems to other areas. This makes it easier to distribute objects throughout a system.

Messages

An object acting alone is rarely useful; most objects require other objects to do much of anything. For example, the car object is pretty useless by itself with no other interaction. Add a driver object, however, and things get more interesting! Knowing this, it's pretty clear that objects need some type of communication mechanism to interact with each other.

Software objects interact and communicate with each other through *messages*. When the driver object wants the car object to accelerate, it sends the car object a message. If you want to think of messages more literally, think of two people as objects. If one person wants the other person to come closer, he or she sends the other person a message. More accurately, he or she may say to the other person "Come here, please." This is a message in a very literal sense. Software messages are a little different in form, but not in theory—they tell an object what to do.

Many times, the receiving object needs—along with a message—more information so that it knows exactly what to do. When the driver tells the car to accelerate, the car must know by how much. This information is passed along with the message as *message parameters*.

From this discussion, you can see that messages consist of three things:

1. The object to receive the message (car)
2. The name of the action to perform (accelerate)
3. Any parameters the method requires (15 mph)

These three components are sufficient information to fully describe a message for an object. Any interaction with an object is handled by passing a message. This means that objects anywhere in a system can communicate with other objects solely through messages.

So that you don't get confused, understand that "message passing" is another way of saying "method calling." When an object sends another object a message, it is really just calling a method of that object. The message parameters are actually the parameters to a method. In object-oriented programming, messages and methods are synonymous.

Because everything an object can do is expressed through its methods (interface), message passing supports all possible interactions between objects. In fact, interfaces allow objects to send and receive messages to each other even if they reside in different locations on a network. Objects in this scenario are referred to as *distributed objects*. Java is specifically designed to support distributed objects.

> **NOTE**
>
> Actually, complete support for distributed objects is a very complex issue and isn't entirely handled by the standard Java class structure. However, new extensions to Java do provide thorough support for distributed objects.

Classes

Throughout this discussion of object-oriented programming, you've dealt only with the concept of an object that already exists in a system. You may be wondering how objects get into a system in the first place. This question brings you to the most fundamental structure in object-oriented programming: the class. A *class* is a template or prototype that defines a type of object. A class is to an object what a blueprint is to a house. Many houses may be built from a single blueprint; the blueprint outlines the makeup of the houses. Classes work exactly the same way, except that they outline the makeup of objects.

In the real world, there are often many objects of the same kind. Using the house analogy, there are many different houses around the world, but all houses share common characteristics. In object-oriented terms, you would say that your house is a specific instance of the class of objects known as houses. All houses have states and behaviors in common that define them as houses. When builders start building a new neighborhood of houses, they typically build them all from a set of blueprints. It wouldn't be as efficient to create a new blueprint for every single house, especially when there are so many similarities shared between each one. The same thing is true in object-oriented software development; why rewrite tons of code when you can reuse code that solves similar problems?

In object-oriented programming, as in construction, it's also common to have many objects of the same kind that share similar characteristics. And like the blueprints for similar houses, you can create blueprints for objects that share certain characteristics. What it boils down to is that classes are software blueprints for objects.

As an example, the car class discussed earlier would contain several variables representing the state of the car, along with implementations for the methods that enable the driver to control the car. The state variables of the car remain hidden underneath the interface. Each instance, or instantiated object, of the car class gets a fresh set of state variables. This brings you to another important point: When an instance of an object is created from a class, the variables declared by that class are allocated in memory. The variables are then modified through the object's methods. Instances of the same class share method implementations but have their own object data.

Where objects provide the benefits of modularity and information hiding, classes provide the benefit of reusability. Just as the builder reuses the blueprint for a house, the software developer reuses the class for an object. Software programmers can use a class over and over again to create many objects. Each of these objects gets its own data but shares a single method implementation.

Inheritance

What happens if you want an object that is very similar to one you already have, but that has a few extra characteristics? You just inherit a new class based on the class of the similar object. *Inheritance* is the process of creating a new class with the characteristics of an existing class, along with additional characteristics unique to the new class. Inheritance provides a powerful and natural mechanism for organizing and structuring programs.

So far, the discussion of classes has been limited to the data and methods that make up a class. Based on this understanding, all classes are built from scratch by defining all the data and all the associated methods. Inheritance provides a means to create classes based on other classes. When a class is based on another class, it inherits all the properties of that class, including the data and methods for the class. The class doing the inheriting is referred to as the *subclass* (or the *child class*), and the class providing the information to inherit is referred to as the *superclass* (or the *parent class*).

Using the car example, child classes could be inherited from the car class for gas-powered cars and cars powered by electricity. Both new car classes share common "car" characteristics, but they also add a few characteristics of their own. The gas car would add, among other things, a fuel tank and a gas cap; the electric car might add a battery and a plug for recharging. Each subclass inherits state information (in the form of variable declarations) from the superclass. Figure 8.3 shows the car parent class with the gas and electric car child classes.

FIGURE 8.3.
Inherited car objects.

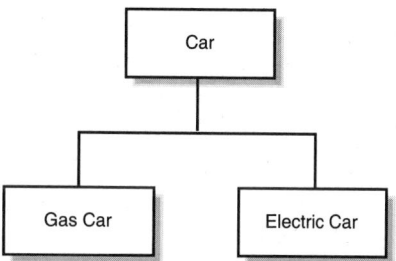

Inheriting the state and behaviors of a superclass alone wouldn't do all that much for a subclass. The real power of inheritance is the ability to inherit properties and methods and add new ones; subclasses can add variables and methods to the ones they inherited from the superclass. Remember that the electric car *added* a battery and a recharging plug. Additionally, subclasses have the ability to override inherited methods and provide different implementations for them. For example, the gas car would probably be able to go much faster than the electric car. The accelerate method for the gas car could reflect this difference.

Class inheritance is designed to allow as much flexibility as possible. A group of interrelated classes is called an *inheritance tree*, or *class hierarchy*. An inheritance tree looks much like a family tree: it shows the relationships between classes. Unlike a family tree, the classes in an inheritance tree get more specific as you move down the tree. You can create inheritance trees as deep as necessary to carry out your design, although it is important to not go so deep that it becomes cumbersome to see the relationship between classes. The car classes in Figure 8.3 are a good example of an inheritance tree.

By understanding the concept of inheritance, you understand how subclasses can allow specialized data and methods in addition to the common ones provided by the superclass. This arrangement enables programmers to reuse the code in the superclass many times, saving extra coding effort and eliminating potential bugs.

One final point to make in regard to inheritance: It is possible and sometimes useful to create superclasses that act purely as templates for more usable subclasses. In this situation, the superclass serves as nothing more than an abstraction for the common class functionality shared by the subclasses. For this reason, these types of superclasses are referred to as *abstract classes*. An abstract class cannot be instantiated, meaning that no objects can be created from an abstract class. The reason an abstract class can't be instantiated is that parts of it have been specifically left unimplemented. More specifically, these parts are made up of methods that have yet to be implemented—abstract methods.

Using the car example once more, the accelerate method really can't be defined until the car's acceleration capabilities are known. Of course, how a car accelerates is determined by the type of engine it has. Because the engine type is unknown in the car superclass, the accelerate method could be defined but left unimplemented, which would make both the accelerate method and the car superclass abstract. Then the gas and electric car child classes would implement the accelerate method to reflect the acceleration capabilities of their respective engines or motors.

The Java Class Hierarchy

No doubt, you're probably about primered out by now and are ready to get on with how classes work in Java. Well, wait no longer! In Java, all classes are subclassed from a superclass called `Object`. Figure 8.4 shows what the Java class hierarchy looks like in regard to the `Object` superclass.

As you can see, all the classes fan out from the `Object` base class. In Java, `Object` serves as the superclass for all derived classes, including the classes that make up the Java API.

FIGURE 8.4.

Classes derived from the
Object *superclass.*

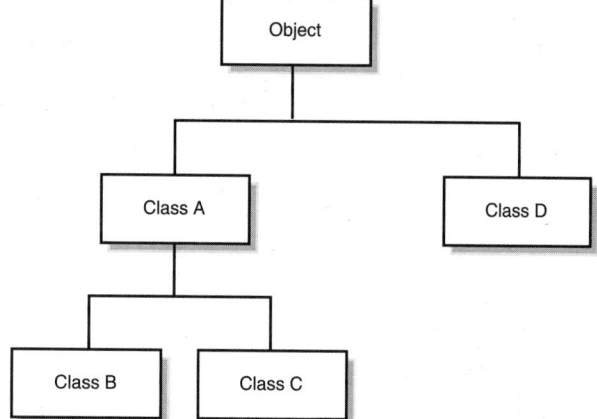

Declaring Classes

The syntax for declaring classes in Java follows:

```
class Identifier {
   ClassBody
}
```

Identifier specifies the name of the new class, which is by default derived from Object. The curly braces surround the body of the class, *ClassBody*. As an example, take a look at the class declaration for an Alien class, which could be used in a space game:

```
class Alien {
   Color  color;
   int    energy;
   int    aggression;
}
```

The state of the Alien object is defined by three data members, which represent the color, energy, and aggression of the alien. It's important to notice that the Alien class is inherently derived from Object. So far, the Alien class isn't all that useful; it needs some methods. The most basic syntax for declaring methods for a class follows:

```
ReturnType Identifier(Parameters) {
   MethodBody
}
```

ReturnType specifies the data type that the method returns, *Identifier* specifies the name of the method, and *Parameters* specifies the parameters to the method, if there are any. As with class bodies, the body of a method, *MethodBody*, is enclosed by curly braces. Remember that in object-oriented design terms, a method is synonymous with a message, with the return type being the object's response to the message. Following is a method declaration for the morph() method, which would be useful in the Alien class because some aliens like to change shape:

```
void morph(int aggression) {
   if (aggression < 10) {
```

```
      // morph into a smaller size
    }
    else if (aggression < 20) {
      // morph into a medium size
    }
    else {
      // morph into a giant size
    }
  }
```

The morph() method is passed an integer as the only parameter, aggression. This value is then used to determine the size to which the alien is morphing. As you can see, the alien morphs to smaller or larger sizes based on its aggression.

If you make the morph() method a member of the Alien class, it is readily apparent that the aggression parameter isn't necessary. This is because aggression is already a member variable of Alien, to which all class methods have access. The Alien class, with the addition of the morph() method, looks like this:

```java
class Alien {
  Color color;
  int    energy;
  int    aggression;

  void morph() {
    if (aggression < 10) {
      // morph into a smaller size
    }
    else if (aggression < 20) {
      // morph into a medium size
    }
    else {
      // morph into a giant size
    }
  }
}
```

Deriving Classes

So far, the discussion of class declaration has been limited to creating new classes inherently derived from Object. Deriving all your classes from Object isn't a very good idea because you would have to redefine the data and methods for each class. The way you derive classes from classes other than Object is by using the extends keyword. The syntax for deriving a class using the extends keyword follows:

```java
class Identifier extends SuperClass {
  ClassBody
}
```

Identifier refers to the name of the newly derived class, *SuperClass* refers to the name of the class you are deriving from, and *ClassBody* is the new class body.

Let's use the Alien class introduced in the preceding section as the basis for a derivation example. What if you had an Enemy class that defined general information useful for all enemies?

You would no doubt want to go back and derive the Alien class from the new Enemy class to take advantage of the standard enemy functionality provided by the Enemy class. Following is the Enemy-derived Alien class using the extends keyword:

```
class Alien extends Enemy {
  Color color;
  int   energy;
  int   aggression;

  void morph() {
    if (aggression < 10) {
      // morph into a smaller size
    }
    else if (aggression < 20) {
      // morph into a medium size
    }
    else {
      // morph into a giant size
    }
  }
}
```

This declaration assumes that the Enemy class declaration is readily available in the same package as Alien. In reality, you will likely derive from classes in a lot of different places. To derive a class from an external superclass, you must first import the superclass using the import statement.

> **NOTE**
>
> You'll get to packages a little later in this chapter. For now, just think of a package as a group of related classes.

If you had to import the Enemy class, you would do so like this:

```
import Enemy;
```

Overriding Methods

There are times when it is useful to *override* methods in derived classes. For example, if the Enemy class had a move() method, you would want the movement to vary based on the type of enemy. Some types of enemies may fly around in specified patterns, while other enemies may crawl in a random fashion. To allow the Alien class to exhibit its own movement, you would override the move() method with a version specific to alien movement. The Enemy class would then look something like this:

```
class Enemy {
...
  void move() {
    // move the enemy
  }
}
```

8

CLASSES,
PACKAGES,
AND INTERFACES

Likewise, the `Alien` class with the overridden `move()` method would look something like this:

```java
class Alien {
  Color color;
  int   energy;
  int   aggression;

  void move() {
    // move the alien
  }

  void morph() {
    if (aggression < 10) {
      // morph into a smaller size
    }
    else if (aggression < 20) {
      // morph into a medium size
    }
    else {
      // morph into a giant size
    }
  }
}
```

When you create an instance of the `Alien` class and call the `move()` method, the new `move()` method in `Alien` is executed rather than the original overridden `move()` method in `Enemy`. Method overriding is a simple yet powerful usage of object-oriented design.

Overloading Methods

Another powerful object-oriented technique is method overloading. *Method overloading* enables you to specify different types of information (parameters) to send to a method. To overload a method, you declare another version with the same name but different parameters.

For example, the `move()` method for the `Alien` class could have two different versions: one for general movement and one for moving to a specific location. The general version is the one you've already defined: it moves the alien based on its current state. The declaration for this version follows:

```java
void move() {
  // move the alien
}
```

To enable the alien to move to a specific location, you overload the `move()` method with a version that takes x and y parameters, which specify the location to move to. The overloaded version of `move()` follows:

```java
void move(int x, int y) {
  // move the alien to position x,y
}
```

Notice that the only difference between the two methods is the parameter lists; the first `move()` method takes no parameters; the second `move()` method takes two integers.

You may be wondering how the compiler knows which method is being called in a program, when they both have the same name. The compiler keeps up with the parameters for each method along with the name. When a call to a method is encountered in a program, the compiler checks the name and the parameters to determine which overloaded method is being called. In this case, calls to the `move()` methods are easily distinguishable by the absence or presence of the `int` parameters.

Access Modifiers

Access to variables and methods in Java classes is accomplished through access modifiers. *Access modifiers* define varying levels of access between class members and the outside world (other objects). Access modifiers are declared immediately before the type of a member variable or the return type of a method. There are four access modifiers: the default access modifier, `public`, `protected`, and `private`.

Access modifiers affect the visibility not only of class members, but also of classes themselves. However, class visibility is tightly linked with packages, which are covered later in this chapter.

The Default Access Modifier

The default access modifier specifies that only classes in the same package can have access to a class's variables and methods. Class members with default access have a visibility limited to other classes within the same package. There is no actual keyword for declaring the default access modifier; it is applied by default in the absence of an access modifier. For example, the `Alien` class members all had default access because no access modifiers were specified. Examples of a default access member variable and method follow:

```
long length;
void getLength() {
  return length;
}
```

Notice that neither the member variable nor the method supplies an access modifier, so each takes on the default access modifier implicitly.

The `public` Access Modifier

The `public` access modifier specifies that class variables and methods are accessible to anyone, both inside and outside the class. This means that `public` class members have global visibility and can be accessed by any other object. Some examples of `public` member variables follow:

```
public int count;
public boolean isActive;
```

The protected Access Modifier

The protected access modifier specifies that class members are accessible only to methods in that class and subclasses of that class. This means that protected class members have visibility limited to subclasses. Examples of a protected variable and a protected method follow:

```
protected char middleInitial;
protected char getMiddleInitial() {
  return middleInitial;
}
```

The private Access Modifier

The private access modifier is the most restrictive; it specifies that class members are accessible only by the class in which they are defined. This means that no other class has access to private class members, even subclasses. Some examples of private member variables follow:

```
private String firstName;
private double howBigIsIt;
```

The static Modifier

There are times when you need a common variable or method for all objects of a particular class. The static modifier specifies that a variable or method is the same for all objects of a particular class.

Typically, new variables are allocated for each instance of a class. When a variable is declared as being static, it is only allocated once, regardless of how many objects are instantiated. The result is that all instantiated objects share the same instance of the static variable. Similarly, a static method is one whose implementation is exactly the same for all objects of a particular class. This means that static methods have access only to static variables.

Following are some examples of a static member variable and a static method:

```
static int refCount;
static int getRefCount() {
  return refCount;
}
```

A beneficial side effect of static members is that they can be accessed without having to create an instance of a class. Remember the System.out.println() method used in the last chapter? Do you recall ever instantiating a System object? Of course not. out is a static member variable of the System class, which means that you can access it without having to actually instantiate a System object.

The final Modifier

Another useful modifier in regard to controlling class member usage is the final modifier. The final modifier specifies that a variable has a constant value or that a method cannot be overridden in a subclass. To think of the final modifier literally, it means that a class member is the final version allowed for the class.

Following are some examples of `final` member variables:

```
final public int numDollars = 25;
final boolean amIBroke = false;
```

If you are coming from the world of C++, `final` variables may sound familiar. In fact, `final` variables in Java are very similar to `const` variables in C++; they must always be initialized at declaration and their value can't change any time afterward.

The synchronized Modifier

The `synchronized` modifier is used to specify that a method is *thread safe*. This means that only one path of execution is allowed into a `synchronized` method at a time. In a multithreaded environment like Java, it is possible to have many different paths of execution running through the same code. The `synchronized` modifier changes this rule by allowing only a single thread access to a method at once, forcing the other threads to wait their turn. If the concept of threads and paths of execution are totally new to you, don't worry; they are covered in detail in the next chapter, "Threads and Multithreading."

The native Modifier

The `native` modifier is used to identify methods that have native implementations. The `native` modifier informs the Java compiler that a method's implementation is in an external C file. It is for this reason that `native` method declarations look different from other Java methods; they have no body. Following is an example of a `native` method declaration:

```
native int calcTotal();
```

Notice that the method declaration simply ends in a semicolon; there are no curly braces containing Java code. This is because `native` methods are implemented in C code, which resides in external C source files. To learn more about `native` methods, check out Chapter 33, "Integrating Native Code."

Abstract Classes and Methods

In the object-oriented primer earlier in this chapter, you learned about abstract classes and methods. To recap, an *abstract class* is a class that is partially implemented and whose purpose is solely as a design convenience. Abstract classes are made up of one or more *abstract methods*, which are methods that are declared but left bodiless (unimplemented).

The `Enemy` class discussed earlier is an ideal candidate to become an abstract class. You would never want to actually create an `Enemy` object because it is too general. However, the `Enemy` class serves a very logical purpose as a superclass for more specific enemy classes, like the `Alien` class. To turn the `Enemy` class into an abstract class, you use the `abstract` keyword, like this:

```
abstract class Enemy {
  abstract void move();
  abstract void move(int x, int y);
}
```

8

CLASSES,
PACKAGES,
AND INTERFACES

Notice the usage of the abstract keyword *before* the class declaration for Enemy. This tells the compiler that the Enemy class is abstract. Also notice that both move() methods are declared as being abstract. Because it isn't clear how to move a generic enemy, the move() methods in Enemy have been left unimplemented (abstract).

There are a few limitations to using abstract of which you should be aware. First, you can't make constructors abstract. (You'll learn about constructors in the next section, which covers object creation.) Second, you can't make static methods abstract. This limitation stems from the fact that static methods are declared for all classes, so there is no way to provide a derived implementation for an abstract static method. Finally, you aren't allowed to make private methods abstract. At first, this limitation may seem a little picky, but think about what it means. When you derive a class from a superclass with abstract methods, you must override and implement all the abstract methods or you won't be able to instantiate your new class, and it will remain abstract itself. Now consider that derived classes can't see private members of their superclass, methods included. This results in you not being able to override and implement private abstract methods from the superclass, which means that you can't implement (non-abstract) classes from it. If you were limited to deriving only new abstract classes, you couldn't accomplish much!

Casting

Although casting between different data types was discussed in Chapter 6, "Java Language Fundamentals," the introduction of classes puts a few new twists on casting. Casting between classes can be divided into three different situations:

- Casting from a subclass to a superclass
- Casting from a superclass to a subclass
- Casting between siblings

In the case of casting from a subclass to a superclass, you can cast either implicitly or explicitly. *Implicit casting* simply means that you do nothing; *explicit casting* means that you have to provide the class type in parentheses, just as you do when casting fundamental data types. Casting from subclass to superclass is completely reliable because subclasses contain information tying them to their superclasses. When casting from a superclass to a subclass, you are required to cast explicitly. This cast isn't completely reliable because the compiler has no way of knowing whether the class being cast to is a subclass of the superclass in question. Finally, the cast from sibling to sibling isn't allowed in Java. If all this casting sounds a little confusing, check out the following example:

```
Double d1 = new Double(5.238);
Number n = d1;
Double d2 = (Double)n;
Long l = d1;  // this won't work!
```

In this example, data type wrapper objects are created and assigned to each other. If you aren't familiar with the data type wrapper classes, don't worry, you'll learn about them in Chapter 12, "The Language Package." For now, all you need to know is that the Double and Long sibling classes are both derived from the Number class. In the example, after the Double object d1 is created, it is assigned to a Number object. This is an example of implicitly casting from a subclass to a superclass, which is completely legal. Another Double object, d2, is then assigned the value of the Number object. This time, an explicit cast is required because you are casting from a superclass to a subclass, which isn't guaranteed to be reliable. Finally, a Long object is assigned the value of a Double object. This is a cast between siblings and is not allowed in Java; it results in a compiler error.

Object Creation

Although most of the design work in object-oriented programming is creating classes, you don't really benefit from that work until you create instances (objects) of those classes. To use a class in a program, you must first create an instance of it.

The Constructor

Before getting into the details of how to create an object, there is an important method you need to know about: the *constructor*. When you create an object, you typically want to initialize its member variables. The constructor is a special method you can implement in all your classes; it allows you to initialize variables and perform any other operation when an object is created from the class. The constructor is always given the same name as the class.

Listing 8.1 contains the complete source code for the Alien class, which contains two constructors.

Listing 8.1. The Alien class.

```
class Alien extends Enemy {
  protected Color color;
  protected int   energy;
  protected int   aggression;

  public Alien() {
    color = Color.green;
    energy = 100;
    aggression = 15;
  }

  public Alien(Color c, int e, int a) {
    color = c;
    energy = e;
    aggression = a;
  }
```

continues

Listing 8.1. continued

```java
public void move() {
  // move the alien
}

public void move(int x, int y) {
  // move the alien to the position x,y
}

public void morph() {
  if (aggression < 10) {
    // morph into a smaller size
  }
  else if (aggression < 20) {
    // morph into a medium size
  }
  else {
    // morph into a giant size
  }
}
}
```

The Alien class uses method overloading to provide two different constructors. The first constructor takes no parameters and initializes the member variables to default values. The second constructor takes the color, energy, and aggression of the alien and initializes the member variables with them. As well as containing the new constructors, this version of Alien uses access modifiers to explicitly assign access levels to each member variable and method. This is a good habit to get into.

 This version of the Alien class is located in the source file Enemy1.java on the CD-ROM that accompanies this book. The CD-ROM also includes the Enemy class. Keep in mind that these classes are just example classes with little functionality. However, they are good examples of Java class design and can be compiled into Java classes.

The new Operator

To create an instance of a class, you declare an object variable and use the new operator. When dealing with objects, a declaration merely states what type of object a variable is to represent. The object isn't actually created until the new operator is used. Following are two examples that use the new operator to create instances of the Alien class:

```java
Alien anAlien = new Alien();
Alien anotherAlien;
anotherAlien = new Alien(Color.red, 56, 24);
```

In the first example, the variable anAlien is declared and the object is created by using the new operator with an assignment directly in the declaration. In the second example, the variable anotherAlien is declared first; the object is created and assigned in a separate statement.

NOTE

If you have some C++ experience, you no doubt recognize the new operator. Even though the new operator in Java works in a somewhat similar fashion as its C++ counterpart, keep in mind that you must *always* use the new operator to create objects in Java. This is in contrast to the C++ version of new, which is used only when you are working with object pointers. Because Java doesn't support pointers, the new operator must always be used to create new objects.

Object Destruction

When an object falls out of scope, it is removed from memory, or deleted. Similar to the constructor that is called when an object is created, Java provides the ability to define a destructor that is called when an object is deleted. Unlike the constructor, which takes on the name of the class, the destructor is called `finalize()`. The `finalize()` method provides a place to perform chores related to the cleanup of an object, and is defined as follows:

```
void finalize() {
  // cleanup
}
```

It is worth noting that the `finalize()` method is not guaranteed to be called by Java as soon as an object falls out of scope. The reason for this is that Java deletes objects as part of its system garbage collection, which occurs at inconsistent intervals. Because an object isn't actually deleted until Java performs a garbage collection, the `finalize()` method for the object isn't called until then either. Knowing this, it's safe to say that you shouldn't rely on the `finalize()` method for anything that is time critical. In general, you will rarely need to place code in the `finalize()` method simply because the Java runtime system does a pretty good job of cleaning up after objects on its own.

Packages

Java provides a powerful means of grouping related classes and interfaces together in a single unit: packages. (You learn about interfaces a little later in this chapter.) Put simply, *packages* are groups of related classes and interfaces. Packages provide a convenient mechanism for managing a large group of classes and interfaces, while avoiding potential naming conflicts. The Java API itself is implemented as a group of packages.

As an example, the `Alien` and `Enemy` classes developed earlier in this chapter would fit nicely into an `Enemy` package—along with any other enemy objects. By placing classes into a package, you also allow them to benefit from the default access modifier, which provides classes in the same package with access to each other's class information.

Declaring Packages

The syntax for the `package` statement follows:

```
package Identifier;
```

This statement must be placed at the beginning of a compilation unit (a single source file), before any class declarations. Every class located in a compilation unit with a `package` statement is considered part of that package. You can still spread classes out among separate compilation units; just be sure to include a `package` statement in each.

Packages can be nested within other packages. When this is done, the Java interpreter expects the directory structure containing the executable classes to match the package hierarchy.

Importing Packages

When it comes time to use classes outside of the package you are working in, you must use the `import` statement. The `import` statement enables you to import classes from other packages into a compilation unit. You can import individual classes or entire packages of classes at the same time if you want. The syntax for the `import` statement follows:

```
import Identifier;
```

Identifier is the name of the class or package of classes you are importing. Going back to the `Alien` class as an example, the `color` member variable is an instance of the `Color` object, which is part of the Java AWT (abstract windowing toolkit) class library. For the compiler to understand this member variable type, you must import the `Color` class. You can do this with either of the following statements:

```
import java.awt.Color;
import java.awt.*;
```

The first statement imports the specific class `Color`, which is located in the `java.awt` package. The second statement imports all the classes in the `java.awt` package. Note that the following statement doesn't work:

```
import java.*;
```

This statement doesn't work because you can't import nested packages with the * specification. This only works when importing all the classes in a particular package, which is still very useful.

There is one other way to import objects from other packages: *explicit package referencing.* By explicitly referencing the package name each time you use an object, you can avoid using an `import` statement. Using this technique, the declaration of the `color` member variable in `Alien` would look like this:

```
java.awt.Color color;
```

Explicitly referencing the package name for an external class is generally not required; it usually serves only to clutter up the class name and can make the code harder to read. The exception to this rule is when two packages have classes with the same name. In this case, you are required to explicitly use the package name with the class names.

Class Visibility

Earlier in this chapter, you learned about access modifiers, which affect the visibility of classes and class members. Because class member visibility is determined relative to classes, you're probably wondering what *visibility* means for a class. Class visibility is determined relative to packages.

For example, a `public` class is visible to classes in other packages. Actually, `public` is the only explicit access modifier allowed for classes. Without the `public` access modifier, classes default to being visible to other classes in a package but not visible to classes outside the package.

Interfaces

The last stop on this object-oriented whirlwind tour of Java is a discussion of interfaces. An *interface* is a prototype for a class and is useful from a logical design perspective. This description of an interface may sound vaguely familiar... Remember abstract classes?

Earlier in this chapter, you learned that an abstract class is a class that has been left partially unimplemented because it uses abstract methods, which are themselves unimplemented. Interfaces are abstract classes that are left completely unimplemented. *Completely unimplemented* in this case means that *no* methods in the class have been implemented. Additionally, interface member data is limited to static final variables, which means that they are constant.

The benefits of using interfaces are much the same as the benefits of using abstract classes. Interfaces provide a means to define the protocols for a class without worrying about the implementation details. This seemingly simple benefit can make large projects much easier to manage; once interfaces have been designed, the class development can take place without worrying about communication among classes.

Another important use of interfaces is the capacity for a class to implement multiple interfaces. This is a twist on the concept of multiple inheritance, which is supported in C++ but not in Java. *Multiple inheritance* enables you to derive a class from multiple parent classes. Although powerful, multiple inheritance is a complex and often tricky feature of C++ that the Java designers decided they could do without. Their workaround was to allow Java classes to implement multiple interfaces.

The major difference between inheriting multiple interfaces and true multiple inheritance is that the interface approach enables you to inherit only method *descriptions*, not *implementations*. If a class implements multiple interfaces, that class must provide all the functionality for the methods defined in the interfaces. Although this approach is certainly more limiting than multiple inheritance, it is still a very useful feature. It is this feature of interfaces that separates them from abstract classes.

Declaring Interfaces

The syntax for creating interfaces follows:

```
interface Identifier {
  InterfaceBody
}
```

Identifier is the name of the interface and *InterfaceBody* refers to the abstract methods and static final variables that make up the interface. Because it is assumed that all the methods in an interface are abstract, it isn't necessary to use the abstract keyword.

Implementing Interfaces

Because an interface is a prototype, or template, for a class, you must implement an interface to arrive at a usable class. Implementing an interface is similar to deriving from a class, except that you are required to implement any methods defined in the interface. To implement an interface, you use the implements keyword. The syntax for implementing a class from an interface follows:

```
class Identifier implements Interface {
  ClassBody
}
```

Identifier refers to the name of the new class, *Interface* is the name of the interface you are implementing, and *ClassBody* is the new class body. Listing 8.2 contains the source code for Enemy2.java, which includes an interface version of Enemy along with an Alien class that implements the interface.

Listing 8.2. The Enemy interface and Alien class.

```
package Enemy;

import java.awt.Color;

interface Enemy {
  abstract public void move();
  abstract public void move(int x, int y);
}

class Alien implements Enemy {
  protected Color color;
  protected int    energy;
  protected int    aggression;

  public Alien() {
    color = Color.green;
```

```
      energy = 100;
      aggression = 15;
   }

   public Alien(Color c, int e, int a) {
      color = c;
      energy = e;
      aggression = a;
   }

   public void move() {
      // move the alien
   }

   public void move(int x, int y) {
      // move the alien to the position x,y
   }

   public void morph() {
      if (aggression < 10) {
         // morph into a smaller size
      }
      else if (aggression < 20) {
         // morph into a medium size
      }
      else {
         // morph into a giant size
      }
   }
}
```

Summary

This chapter covered the basics of object-oriented programming as well as the specific Java constructs that enable you to carry out object-oriented concepts: classes, packages, and interfaces. You learned the benefits of using classes—and how to implement objects from them. The communication mechanism between objects—messages (methods)—was covered. You also learned how inheritance provides a powerful means of reusing code and creating modular designs. You then learned how packages enable you to logically group similar classes together, making large sets of classes easier to manage. Finally, you saw how interfaces provide a template for deriving new classes in a structured manner.

You are now ready to move on to more advanced features of the Java language, such as threads and multithreading. The next chapter covers exactly these topics.

Threads and Multithreading

by Eric Williams

IN THIS CHAPTER

CHAPTER 9

Multithreading

One of the characteristics that makes Java a powerful programming language is its support of multithreaded programming as an integrated part of the language. This is unique because most modern programming languages either do not offer multithreading or provide multithreading as a nonintegrated package. Java, however, offers a single, integrated view of multithreading.

Multithreaded programming is an essential aspect of programming in Java. To master the Java programming language, you should first become familiar with the concepts of multithreaded programming. Then you should learn how multithreaded and concurrent programming are done *in Java.*

This chapter presents a complete introduction and reference to Java threads, including these topics:

- How to write and start your own threads
- A comprehensive reference to the `Thread` and `ThreadGroup` classes
- How to make your classes thread-safe
- An introduction to Java monitors
- How to coordinate the actions of multiple threads

> **NOTE**
>
> Multithreading and concurrent programming are unfamiliar concepts for most new Java programmers. If you are familiar with only single-threaded languages like Visual Basic, Delphi, Pascal, COBOL, and so on, you may be worried that threads are too hard to learn. Although learning to use Java threads is not trivial, the model is simple and easy to understand. Threads are a normal everyday aspect of developing Java applications and applets.

What Is a Thread?

In the early days of computing, computers were *single-tasking*—that is, they ran a single job at a time. The big lumbering machine would start one job, run that job to completion, then start the next job, and so on. When engineers became overly frustrated with these batch-oriented systems, they rewrote the programs that ran the machines and thus was born the modern multitasking operating system.

Multitasking refers to a computer's ability to perform multiple jobs concurrently. For the most part, modern desktop operating systems like Windows 95 or OS/2 have the ability to run two or more programs at the same time. While you are using Netscape to download a big file, you can be playing Solitaire in a different window; both programs are running at the same time.

Multithreading is an extension of the multitasking paradigm. But rather than multiple programs, multithreading involves multiple threads of control within a single program. Not only is the operating system running multiple programs, each program can run multiple threads of control within the program. For example, using a Web browser, you can print one Web page, download another, and fill out a form in a third—all at the same time.

A *thread* is a single sequence of execution within a program. Until now, you have probably used Java to write single-threaded applications, something like this:

```
class MainIsRunInAThread {
    public static void main(String[] args) {
        // main() is run in a single thread
        System.out.println(Thread.currentThread());
        for (int i=0; i<1000; i++) {
            System.out.println("i == " + i);
        }
    }
}
```

This example is simplistic, but it does demonstrate the use of a single Java thread. When a Java application begins, the VM runs the main() method inside a Java thread. (You have already used Java threads and didn't even know it!) Within this single thread, this simple application's main() method counts from 0 to 999, printing out each value as it counts it.

Programming within a single sequence of control can limit your ability to produce usable Java software. (Imagine using an operating system that could execute only one program at a time, or a Web browser that could load only a single page at a time.) When you write a program, you often want to do multiple things at the same time. For example, you may want to retrieve an image over the network at the same time you are requesting an updated stock report, and you also want to run several animations—all concurrently. This kind of situation is where Java threads become useful.

Java threads allow you to write programs that do many things at once. Each thread represents an independently executing sequence of control. One thread can write a file out to disk while a different thread responds to user keystroke events.

Before jumping into the details about Java threads, let's take a peek at what a multithreaded application looks like. Listing 9.1 modifies the preceding single-threaded application to take advantage of threads. Instead of counting from 0 to 999, this application uses five different threads to count from 0 to 999—each thread counts 200 numbers: 0 to 199, 200 to 399, and so on. Don't worry about understanding the details of this example yet; it is presented only to introduce you to threads.

9

THREADS AND
MULTITHREADING

Listing 9.1. A simple multithreaded application.

```
class CountThreadTest extends Thread {
    int from, to;

    public CountThreadTest(int from, int to) {
        this.from = from;
        this.to = to;
    }

    // the run() method is like main() for a thread
    public void run() {
        for (int i=from; i<to; i++) {
            System.out.println("i == " + i);
        }
    }

    public static void main(String[] args) {
        // spawn 5 threads, each of wich counts 200 numbers
        for (int i=0; i<5; i++) {
            CountThreadTest t = new CountThreadTest(i*200, (i+1)*200);

            // starting a thread will launch a separate sequence
            // of control and execute the run() method of the thread
            t.start();
        }
    }
}
```

When this application starts, the VM invokes the `main()` method in its own thread. `main()` then starts five separate threads to perform the counting operations. Figure 9.1 shows the threads in the `CountThreadTest` application.

FIGURE 9.1.

Parallel Java threads.

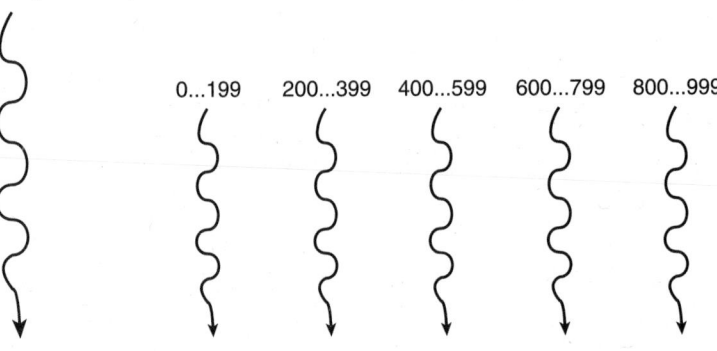

NOTE

Even though threads make it appear that a program is performing multiple tasks *at the same time*, technically speaking, this may not be true. Even today, most computers are equipped with a single processor—such computers can perform at most one task at a time. On single-processor systems, threads give the appearance of performing multiple tasks simultaneously by scheduling each thread to run one at a time, occasionally switching between threads. This subject is discussed in detail in "Thread Scheduling," later in this chapter.

Java Threads

Support for multiple threads of execution is not a Java invention. Threads have been around for a long time and have been implemented in many programming languages. However, programmers have had to struggle with a lack of thread standards. Different platforms have different thread packages, each with a different API. Operating systems do not have uniform support for threads; some support threads in the OS kernel, and some do not. Only recently has a standard emerged for threads—POSIX threads (IEEE standard 1003.1c-1995). However, the POSIX threads standard defines a C programming interface and is not yet widely implemented.

One of the greatest benefits of Java is that it presents the Java programmer with a unified multithreading API—one that is supported by all Java virtual machines. When you use Java threads, you do not have to worry about what threading packages are available on the underlying platform or whether the operating system supports kernel threads. The virtual machine isolates you from the platform-specific threading details. The Java threading API is identical on all Java implementations.

Creating New Threads

The first thing you need to know about threads is how to create and run a thread. This process involves two steps: writing the code that is executed in the thread and writing the code that starts the thread.

As discussed earlier, you are already familiar with how to write single-threaded programs. When you write a main() function, that method is executed in a single thread. The Java virtual machine provides a multithreaded environment, but it starts user applications by calling main() in a single thread.

An application's main() method provides the central logic for the main thread of the application. Writing the code for a thread is similar to writing main(). You must provide a method that implements the main logic of the thread. This method is always named run() and has the following signature:

```
public void run();
```

Notice that the run() method is not a static method, like main(). The main() method is static because an application starts with only one main(). But an application may have many threads, so the main logic for a thread is associated with an object—the Thread object.

You can provide an implementation for the run() method in two ways. Java supports the run() method in subclasses of the Thread class. Java also supports run() through the Runnable interface. Both methods for providing a run() method implementation are described in the following sections.

Subclassing the Thread Class

In this section, we'll discuss how to create a new thread by subclassing java.lang.Thread. The Thread class is the objectification of a Java sequence of control.

Let's start with a plausible situation in which a thread might be useful. Suppose that you are building an application. In one part of this application, a file must be copied from one directory to a different directory. But when you run the application, you find that if the file is large, the application stalls during the time that the file is being copied. Because the application is copying the file, it is unable to respond to user-interface events.

To improve this situation, you decide that the file-copy operation should be performed concurrently, in a separate thread. To move this logic to a thread, you provide a subclass of the Thread class that contains this logic, implemented in the run() method. The FileCopyThread class shown in Listing 9.2 contains this logic.

Listing 9.2. The file-copy logic in FileCopyThread.

```
// subclass from Thread to provide your own kind of Thread
class FileCopyThread extends Thread {
    private File from;
    private File to;
    public FileCopyThread(File from, File to) {
        this.from = from;
        this.to = to;
    }

    // implement the main logic of the thread in the run()
    // method [run() is equivalent to an application's main()]
    public void run() {
        FileInputStream in = null;
        FileOutputStream out = null;
        byte[] buffer = new byte[512];
        int size = 0;
        try { // open the input and output streams
            in = new FileInputStream(from);
            out = new FileOutputStream(to);
```

```
            // copy 512 bytes at a time until EOF
            while ((size = in.read(buffer)) != -1) {
                out.write(buffer, 0, size);
            }
        } catch(IOException ex) {
            ex.printStackTrace();
        } finally {
            // close the input and output streams
            try {
                if (in != null) { in.close(); }
                if (out != null) { out.close(); }
            } catch (IOException ex) {
            }
        }
    }
}
```

Let's analyze the FileCopyThread class. The first thing to note is that FileCopyThread subclasses from Thread. By subclassing from Thread, FileCopyThread inherits all the state and behavior of a Thread—the property of "being a thread."

The FileCopyThread class implements the main logic of the thread in the run() method. (Remember that the run() method is the initial method for a Java thread, just as the main() method is the initial method for a Java application.) Within run(), the input file is copied to the output file in 512-byte chunks. When a FileCopyThread instance is created, the entire run() method is executed in one separate sequence of control (you'll see how this is done soon).

Now that you are familiar with how to write a Thread subclass, you have to learn how to use that class as a separate control sequence within a program. To use a thread, you must *start* the concurrent execution of the thread by calling the Thread object's start() method. The following code demonstrates how to launch a file-copy operation as a separate thread:

```
File from = getCopyFrom();
File to = getCopyTo();

// create an instance of the thread class
Thread t = new FileCopyThread(from, to);

// call start() to activate the thread asynchronously
t.start();
```

Invoking the start() method of a FileCopyThread object begins the concurrent execution of that thread. When the thread starts running, its run() method is called. In this case, the file copy begins its execution concurrently with the original thread. When the file copy is finished, the run() method ends (as does the concurrent execution of the thread). This process is shown in Figure 9.2.

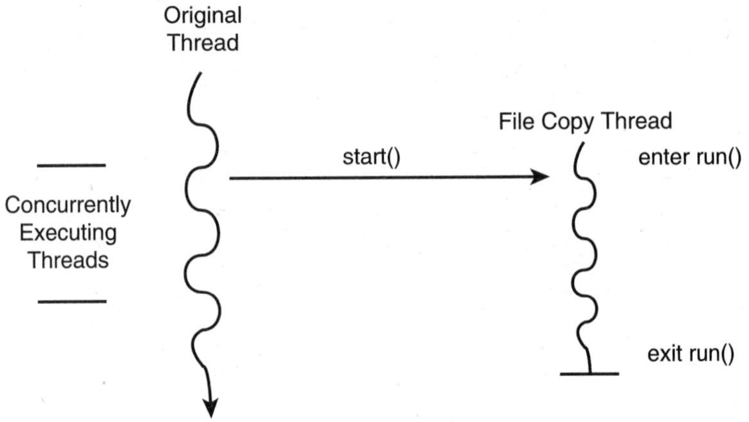

FIGURE 9.2.
Concurrent file copy.

Implementing the Runnable Interface

There are situations in which it is not convenient to create a Thread subclass. For example, you may want to add a run() method to a preexisting class that does not inherit from Thread. The Java Runnable interface makes this possible.

The Java threading API supports the notion of a thread-like entity that is an interface: java.lang.Runnable. Runnable is a simple interface, with only one method:

```
public interface Runnable {
    public void run();
}
```

This interface should look familiar. In the previous section, we covered the Thread class, which also supported the run() method. To subclass Thread, we redefined the Thread run() method. To use the Runnable interface, you must write a run() method and add implements Runnable to the class. Reimplementing the FileCopyThread (of the previous example) as a Runnable interface requires few changes:

```
// implementing Runnable is a different way to use threads
class FileCopyRunnable implements Runnable {
    // the rest of the class remains mostly the same
    ...
}
```

Using a Runnable interface as a separate control sequence requires the cooperation of a Thread object. Although the Runnable object contains the main logic, Thread is the only class that encapsulates the mechanism of launching and controlling a concurrent thread. To support Runnable, a separate Runnable parameter was added to several of the Thread class constructors. A thread that has been initialized with a Runnable object will call that object's run() method when the thread begins executing.

Here is an example of how to start a thread using `FileCopyRunnable`:

```
File from = new File("file.1");
File to = new File("file.2");

// create an instance of the Runnable
Runnable r = new FileCopyRunnable(from, to);

// create an instance of Thread, passing it the Runnable
Thread t = new Thread(r);

// start the thread
t.start();
```

Thread States

Although you have learned a few things about threads, we have not yet discussed one aspect that is critical to your understanding of how threads work in Java—thread states. A Java thread, represented by a `Thread` object, traverses a fixed set of states during its lifetime (see Figure 9.3).

FIGURE 9.3.

Thread states.

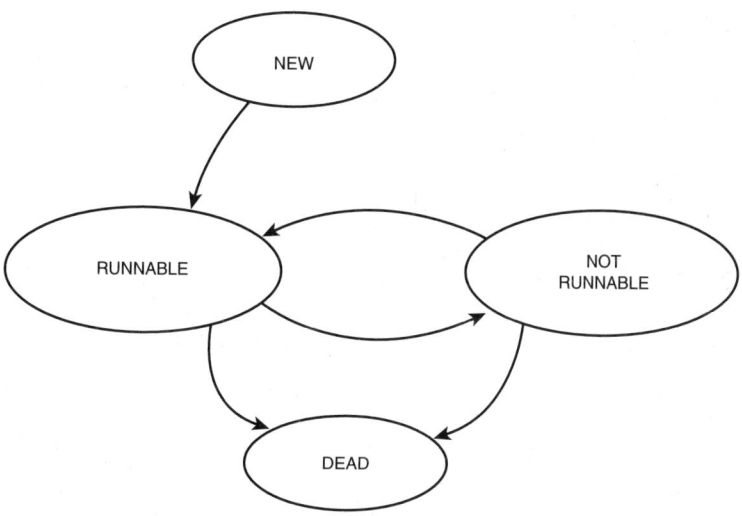

When a `Thread` object is first created, it is NEW. At this point, the thread is not executing. When you invoke the `Thread`'s `start()` method, the thread changes to the RUNNABLE state.

When a Java `Thread` object is RUNNABLE, it is *eligible* for execution. However, a `Thread` that is RUNNABLE is not necessarily *running*. RUNNABLE implies that the thread is alive and that it can be allocated CPU time by the system when the CPU is available—but the CPU may not always be available. On single-processor systems, Java threads must share the single CPU; additionally, the Java virtual machine must also share the CPU with other programs running on the system. How a thread is allocated CPU time is covered in greater depth in "Scheduling and Priority," later in this chapter.

When certain events happen in a RUNNABLE thread, the thread may enter the NOT RUNNABLE state. When a thread is NOT RUNNABLE, it is still alive, but it is not eligible for execution. The thread is not allocated time on the CPU. Some of the events that may cause a thread to become NOT RUNNABLE include these:

- The thread is waiting for an I/O operation to complete
- The thread has been put to sleep for a certain period of time (using the sleep() method)
- The wait() method has been called (as discussed in "Synchronization," later in this chapter)
- The thread has been suspended (using the suspend() method)

A NOT RUNNABLE thread becomes RUNNABLE again when its state changes (I/O has completed, the thread has ended its sleep() period, and so on). During the lifetime of a thread, the thread may frequently move between the RUNNABLE and NOT RUNNABLE states.

When a thread terminates, it is said to be DEAD. Threads can become DEAD in a variety of ways. Usually, a thread dies when its run() method returns. A thread may also die when its stop() or destroy() method is called. A thread that is DEAD is permanently DEAD—there is no way to resurrect a DEAD thread.

> **NOTE**
>
> When a thread dies, all the resources consumed by the thread—including the Thread object itself—are immediately eligible for reclamation by the garbage collector (if, of course, they are not referenced elsewhere). Programmers are responsible for cleaning up system resources (open files, graphics contexts, and so on) *while* a thread is terminating, but no cleanup is required *after* a thread dies.

The Thread API

The following sections present a detailed analysis of the Java Thread API.

Constructors

The Thread class has seven different constructors:

```
public Thread();
public Thread(Runnable target);
```

```
public Thread(Runnable target, String name);
public Thread(String name);
public Thread(ThreadGroup group, Runnable target);
public Thread(ThreadGroup group, Runnable target, String name);
public Thread(ThreadGroup group, String name);
```

These constructors represent most of the combinations of three different parameters: thread *name*, thread *group*, and a Runnable *target* object. To understand the three constructors, you must understand the parameters:

- *name* is the (string) name to be assigned to the thread. If you fail to specify a name, the system generates a unique name of the form Thread-*N*, where *N* is a unique integer.

- *target* is the Runnable instance whose run() method is executed as the main method of the thread.

- *group* is the ThreadGroup to which this thread will be added. (The ThreadGroup class is discussed in detail later in the chapter.)

Constructing a new thread does not begin the execution of that thread. To launch the Thread object, you must invoke its start() method.

CAUTION

Although it is possible to allocate a thread using new Thread(), it is not useful to do so. When constructing a thread directly (without subclassing), the Thread object requires a target Runnable object because the Thread class itself does not contain your application's logic.

Naming

```
public final String getName();
public final void setName(String name);
```

Every Java thread has a name. The name can be set during construction or with the setName() method. If you fail to specify a name during construction, the system generates a unique name of the form Thread-*N*, where *N* is a unique integer; the name can be changed later using setName().

The name of a thread can be retrieved using the getName() method.

Thread names are important because they provide the programmer with a useful way to identify particular threads during debugging. You should name threads in such a way that you (or others) will find the name helpful in identifying the purpose or function of the thread during debugging.

Starting and Stopping

To start and stop threads once you have created them, you need the following methods:

```
public void start();
public final void stop();
public final void stop(Throwable obj);
public void destroy();
```

To begin a new thread, create a new Thread object and call its start() method. An exception will be thrown if start() is called more than once on the same thread.

As discussed in "Thread States," earlier in this chapter, there are two main ways a thread can terminate: The thread may return from its run() method, ending gracefully. Or the thread may be terminated by the stop() or destroy() method.

When invoked on a thread, the stop() method causes that thread to terminate by throwing an exception *to* the thread (a ThreadDeath exception). Calling stop() on a thread has the same behavior as executing "throw new ThreadDeath()" within the thread, except that stop() can also be called from other threads (whereas the throw statement affects only the current thread).

To understand why stop() is implemented this way, consider what it means to stop a running thread. Active threads are part of a running program, and each runnable thread is in the middle of *doing* something. It is likely that each thread is consuming system resources: file descriptors, graphics contexts, monitors (to be discussed later), and so on. If stopping a thread caused all activity on the thread to cease immediately, these resources might not be cleaned up properly. The thread would not have a chance to close its open files or release the monitors it has locked. If a thread were stopped at the wrong moment, it would be unable to free these resources; this leads to potential problems for the virtual machine (running out of open file descriptors, for example).

To provide for clean thread shutdown, the thread to be stopped is given an opportunity to clean up its resources. A ThreadDeath exception is thrown to the thread, which percolates up the thread's stack and through the exception handlers that are currently on the stack (including finally blocks). Monitors are also released by this stack-unwinding process.

Listing 9.3 shows how calling stop() on a running thread generates a ThreadDeath exception.

Listing 9.3. Generating a ThreadDeath exception with stop().

```
class DyingThread extends Thread {
    // main(), this class is an application
    public static void main(String[] args) {
        Thread t = new DyingThread();          // create the thread
        t.start();                             // start the thread

        // wait for a while
        try { Thread.sleep(100); } catch (InterruptedException e) { }
```

```
        t.stop();                                // now stop the thread
    }


    // run(), this class is also a Thread
    public void run() {
        int n = 0;
        PrintStream ps = null;
        try {
            ps = new PrintStream(new FileOutputStream("big.txt"));
            while (true) {                        // forever
                ps.println("n == " + n++);
                try { Thread.sleep(5); } catch (InterruptedException e) { }
            }
        } catch (ThreadDeath td) {               // watch for the stop()
            System.out.println("Cleaning up.");
            ps.close();                          // close the open file

            // it is very important to rethrow the ThreadDeath
            throw td;
        } catch (IOException e) {
        }
    }
}
```

The `DyingThread` class has two parts. The `main()` method spawns a new `DyingThread`, waits for a period of time, and then sends a `stop()` to the thread. The `DyingThread` `run()` method, which is executed in the spawned thread, opens a file and periodically writes output to that file. When the thread receives the `stop()`, it catches the `ThreadDeath` exception and closes the open file. It then rethrows the `ThreadDeath` exception.

When you run the code shown in Listing 9.3, you see the following output:

```
Cleaning up.
```

9

THREADS AND
MULTITHREADING

NOTE

Java provides a convenient mechanism for programmers to write "cleanup" code—code that is executed when errors occur or when a program or thread terminates. (Cleanup involves closing open files, releasing graphics contexts, hiding windows, and so on.) Exception handler `catch` and `finally` blocks are good locations for cleanup code.

Programmers use a variety of styles to write cleanup code. Some programmers place cleanup code in `catch(ThreadDeath td)` exception handlers (as in Listing 9.3). Others prefer to use `catch(Throwable t)` exception handlers. Both of these methods are good, but writing cleanup code in a `finally` block is the best solution for most situations. A `finally` block is executed unconditionally, whether the exception handler exited because of a thrown exception or not. If an exception was thrown, it is automatically rethrown after the `finally` block has completed.

Although the ThreadDeath solution allows the application a high degree of flexibility, there are problems. By catching the ThreadDeath exception, a thread can actually prevent stop() from having the desired effect. The code to do this is trivial:

```
// prevent stop() from working
catch (ThreadDeath td) {
    System.err.println("Just try to stop me. I'm invincible.");
    // oh no, I've failed to rethrow td
}
```

Calling stop() is not sufficient to guarantee that a thread will end. This is a serious problem for Java-enabled Web browsers; there is no guarantee that an applet will terminate when stop() is invoked on a thread belonging to the applet.

The destroy() method is stronger than the stop() method. The destroy() method is designed to terminate the thread without resorting to the ThreadDeath mechanism. The destroy() method stops the thread immediately, without cleanup; any resources held by the thread are not released().

CAUTION

The destroy() method is not implemented in the Java Developers Kit, version 1.0.2. Calling this method results in a NoSuchMethodError exception. Although there has been no comment about when this method will be implemented, it is likely that it will not become available until JavaSoft is able to implement it in a way that cleans up the dying thread's environment (locked monitors, pending I/O, and so on).

Scheduling and Priority

Thread *scheduling* is the mechanism used to determine how RUNNABLE threads are allocated CPU time (that is, when they actually get to execute for a period of time on the computer's CPU). In general, scheduling is a complex subject that uses terms such as *preemptive, round-robin scheduling, priority-based scheduling, time-sliced,* and so on.

A thread-scheduling mechanism is either *preemptive* or *nonpreemptive.* With preemptive scheduling, the thread scheduler preempts (pauses) a running thread to allow different threads to execute. A nonpreemptive scheduler never interrupts a running thread; instead, the nonpreemptive scheduler relies on the running thread to *yield* control of the CPU so that other threads may execute. Under nonpreemptive scheduling, other threads may *starve* (never get CPU time) if the running thread fails to yield.

Among thread schedulers classified as preemptive, there is a further classification. A preemptive scheduler can be either *time-sliced* or *nontime-sliced.* With time-sliced scheduling, the scheduler allocates a period of time that each thread can use the CPU; when that amount of time has elapsed, the scheduler preempts the thread and switches to a different thread. A nontime-sliced scheduler does not use elapsed time to determine when to preempt a thread; it uses other criteria such as priority or I/O status.

Different operating systems and thread packages implement a variety of scheduling policies. But Java is intended to be platform independent. The correctness of a Java program should not depend on what platform the program is running on, so the designers of Java decided to isolate the programmer from most platform dependencies by providing a single guarantee about thread scheduling: *The highest priority* RUNNABLE *thread is always selected for execution above lower priority threads.* (When multiple threads have equally high priorities, only one of those threads is guaranteed to be executing.)

Java threads are guaranteed to be preemptive—but not time sliced. If a higher priority thread (higher than the current thread) becomes RUNNABLE, the scheduler preempts the current thread. However, if an equal or lower priority thread becomes RUNNABLE, there is no guarantee that the new thread will ever be allocated CPU time until it becomes the highest priority RUNNABLE thread.

The current implementation of the Java virtual machine uses different thread packages on different platforms; the behavior of the Java thread scheduler differs slightly for each platform. The Java implementation on Windows 95/NT uses the underlying Win32 thread scheduler (which *is* time-sliced). On Solaris and other UNIX platforms, the 1.0.2 JDK uses a custom package developed by Sun called Green Threads (which is *not* time-sliced). In the future, the Solaris JDK will likely use the Solaris thread package (which is also *not* time-sliced).

Even though Java threads are not guaranteed to be time-sliced, this should not be a problem for the majority of Java applications and applets. Java threads release control of the CPU when they become NOT RUNNABLE. If a thread is waiting for I/O, is sleeping, or is waiting to enter a monitor, the thread scheduler will select a different thread for execution. Generally, only threads that perform intensive numerical analysis (without I/O) will be a problem. A thread would have to be coded like the following example to prevent other threads from running (and such a thread would block other threads only on some platforms—on Windows NT, for example, other threads would still be allowed to run):

```
int i = 0;
while (true) {
    i++;
}
```

There are a variety of techniques you can implement to prevent one thread from consuming too much CPU time:

- Don't write code such as `while (true) { }`. This code has no purpose in the first place. It is acceptable to have infinite loops—as long as what takes place inside the loop involves I/O, `sleep()`, or interthread coordination (using the `wait()` and `notify()` methods, discussed later in this chapter).

■ Occasionally call `Thread.yield()` when performing operations that are CPU intensive. The `yield()` method allows the scheduler to spend time executing other threads.

■ Lower the priority of CPU-intensive threads. Threads with a lower priority run only when the higher priority threads have nothing to do. For example, the Java garbage collector thread is a low priority thread. Garbage collection takes place when there are no higher priority threads that need the CPU; this way, garbage collection does not needlessly stall the system.

By using these techniques, your applications and applets will be well behaved on any Java platform.

Setting Thread Priority

```
public final static int MAX_PRIORITY = 10;
public final static int MIN_PRIORITY = 1;
public final static int NORM_PRIORITY = 5;
public final int getPriority();
public final void setPriority(int newPriority);
```

Every thread has a priority. When a thread is created, it inherits the priority of the thread that created it. The priority can be adjusted subsequently using the `setPriority()` method. The priority of a thread may be obtained using `getPriority()`.

There are three symbolic constants defined in the `Thread` class that represent the range of priority values: `MIN_PRIORITY`, `NORM_PRIORITY`, and `MAX_PRIORITY`. The priority values range from 1 to 10, in increasing priority. An exception is thrown if you attempt to set priority values outside this range.

Waking Up a Thread

```
public void interrupt();
public static boolean interrupted();
public boolean isInterrupted();
```

To send a wake-up message to a thread, call `interrupt()` on its `Thread` object. Calling `interrupt()` causes an `InterruptedException` to be thrown in the thread and sets a flag that can be checked by the running thread using the `isInterrupted()` method. `Thread.interrupt()` is the same thing as `Thread.currentThread().isInterrupted()`.

The `interrupt()` method is useful in waking a thread from a blocking operation such as I/O, `wait()`, or an attempt to enter a `synchronized` method.

> **CAUTION**
>
> The `interrupt()` method is not fully implemented in the 1.0.x JDK. Calling `interrupt()` on a thread sets the `interrupted` flag but does not throw an `InterruptedException` or end a blocking operation in the target thread; threads must check `interrupted()` to determine whether the thread has been interrupted.

Suspending and Resuming Thread Execution

```
public final void suspend();
public final void resume();
```

Sometimes, it is necessary to pause a running thread. You can do so using the `suspend()` method. Calling the `suspend()` method ensures that a thread will not be run. The `resume()` method reverses the `suspend()` operation.

A call to `suspend()` puts the thread in the NOT RUNNABLE state. However, calling `resume()` does not guarantee that the target thread will become RUNNABLE; other events may have caused the thread to be NOT RUNNABLE (or DEAD).

Putting a Thread to Sleep

```
public static void sleep(long millisecond);
public static void sleep(long millisecond, int nanosecond);
```

To pause the current thread for a specified period of time, call one of the varieties of the `sleep()` method. For example, `Thread.sleep(500)` pauses the current thread for half a second, during which time the thread is in the NOT RUNNABLE state. When the specified time expires, the current thread again becomes RUNNABLE.

> **CAUTION**
>
> In the 1.0.2 JDK, the `sleep(int millisecond, int nanosecond)` method uses the nanosecond parameter to round the millisecond parameter to the nearest millisecond. Sleeping is not yet supported in nanosecond granularity.

Making a Thread Yield

```
public static void yield();
```

The `yield()` method is used to give a hint to the thread scheduler that now would be a good time to run other threads. If many threads are RUNNABLE and waiting to execute, the `yield()` method is guaranteed to switch to a different RUNNABLE thread only if the other thread has at least as high a priority as the current thread.

Waiting for a Thread to End

```
public final void join();
public final void join(long millisecond);
public final void join(long millisecond, int nanosecond);
```

Programs sometimes have to wait for a specific thread to terminate; this is referred to as *joining* the thread. To wait for a thread to terminate, invoke one of the join() methods on its Thread object. For example:

```
Thread t = new OperationINeedDoneThread();
t.start();
....           // do some other stuff
t.join();      // wait for the thread to complete
```

The two join() methods with time parameters are used to specify a timeout for the join() operation. If the thread does not terminate within the specified amount of time, join() returns anyway. To determine whether a timeout has happened, or whether the thread has ended, use the Thread method isAlive().

join() with no parameters waits forever for the thread to terminate.

CAUTION

In the 1.0.2 JDK, the join(int *millisecond*, int *nanosecond*) method uses the nano-second parameter to round the millisecond parameter to the nearest millisecond. Joining is not yet supported in nanosecond granularity.

Understanding Daemon Threads

```
public final boolean isDaemon();
public final void setDaemon(boolean on);
```

Some threads are intended to be "background" threads, providing service to other threads. These threads are referred to as *daemon* threads. When only daemon threads remain alive, the Java virtual machine process exits.

The Java virtual machine has at least one daemon thread, known as the garbage collection thread. The garbage collection thread is a low-priority thread, executing only when there is nothing else for the system to do.

The setDaemon() method sets the daemon status of this thread. The isDaemon() method returns true if this thread is a daemon thread; it returns false otherwise.

Miscellaneous Thread Methods

The countStackFrames() method returns the number of active stack frames (method activations) currently on this thread's stack. The thread must be suspended when this method is invoked. Following is this method's signature:

```
public int countStackFrames();
```

The getThreadGroup() method returns the ThreadGroup class to which this thread belongs. A thread is always a member of a single ThreadGroup class. Following is this method's signature:

```
public final ThreadGroup getThreadGroup();
```

The isAlive() method returns true if start() has been called on this thread and if this thread has not yet died. In other words, isAlive() returns true if this thread is RUNNABLE or NOT RUNNABLE and false if this thread is NEW or DEAD. Following is this method's signature:

```
public final boolean isAlive();
```

The currentThread() method returns the Thread object for the current sequence of execution. Following is this method's signature:

```
public static Thread currentThread();
```

The activeCount() method returns the number of threads in the currently executing thread's ThreadGroup class. Following is this method's signature:

```
public static int activeCount();
```

The enumerate() method returns (through the *tarray* parameter) a list of all threads in the current thread's ThreadGroup class. Following is this method's signature:

```
public static int enumerate(Thread tarray[]);
```

The dumpStack() method is used for debugging. It prints a method-by-method list of the stack trace for the current thread to the System.err output stream. Following is this method's signature:

```
public static void dumpStack();
```

The toString() method returns a debugging string that describes this thread. Following is this method's prototype:

```
public String toString();
```

The ThreadGroup API

Each Java thread belongs to exactly one ThreadGroup instance. The ThreadGroup class is used to assist with the organization and management of similar groups of threads. For example, thread groups can be used by Web browsers to group all threads belonging to a single applet. Single commands can be used to manage the entire group of threads belonging to the applet.

ThreadGroup objects form a tree-like structure; groups can contain both threads and other groups. The top thread group is named system; it contains several system-level threads (such as the garbage collector thread). The system group also contains the main ThreadGroup object; the main group contains a main Thread—the thread in which main() is run. Figure 9.4 is a graphical representation of the ThreadGroup tree.

FIGURE 9.4.

The ThreadGroup *tree.*

Java Thread Tree

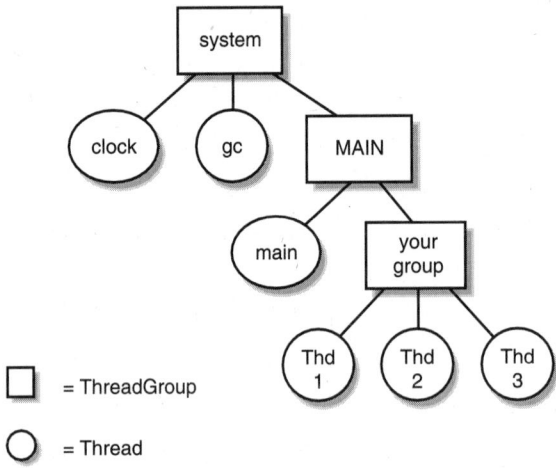

Constructors

The ThreadGroup class has two constructors. Both constructors require that you specify a name for the new thread group. One of the constructors takes a reference to the parent group of the new ThreadGroup; the constructor that does not take the *parent* parameter uses the group of the currently executing thread as the parent of the new group.

```
public ThreadGroup(String name);
public ThreadGroup(ThreadGroup parent, String name);
```

Initially, the new ThreadGroup object contains no threads or other thread groups.

Thread Helper Methods

The ThreadGroup class contains a few methods that operate on the threads within the group. These methods are "helper" in nature; they invoke the same-named Thread method on all threads within the group (recursively, to thread groups within this group).

```
public final void suspend();
public final void resume();
```

```
public final void stop();
public final void destroy();
```

The "helper" methods include suspend(), resume(), stop(), and destroy(). Here is an example of how to stop an entire group of threads with a single method call:

```
ThreadGroup group = new ThreadGroup("client threads");
while (some_condition) {
    Thread t = new Thread(group);
    t.start();
    ...
}
...
if (kill_em_all) {    // stop all of the threads
    group.stop();
}
```

The other thread group "helper" methods can be called in a similar manner.

Priority

ThreadGroup trees can assist in the management of thread priority. After calling setMaxPriority() on a ThreadGroup object, no thread within the group's tree will be able to use setPriority() to set a priority higher than the specified maximum value. (Priorities of threads already in the group are not affected.)

```
public final int getMaxPriority();
public final void setMaxPriority(int pri);
```

The getMaxPriority() method returns the maximum priority value of this ThreadGroup tree.

ThreadGroup Tree Navigation

Each thread group can contain both threads and thread groups. The activeCount()and activeCountGroup()methods return the number of contained threads and groups respectively. Following are the method signatures:

```
public int activeCount();
public int activeGroupCount();
```

The activeCount() method returns the number of threads that are members of this ThreadGroup tree (recursively).

The activeCountGroup() method returns the number of ThreadGroups that are members of this ThreadGroup tree (recursively).

The following enumerate()methods can be used to retrieve the list of threads or groups in this ThreadGroup object:

```
public int enumerate(Thread list[]);
public int enumerate(Thread list[], boolean recurse);
public int enumerate(ThreadGroup list[]);
public int enumerate(ThreadGroup list[], boolean recurse);
```

9

THREADS AND
MULTITHREADING

The *recurse* parameter, if `true`, causes the retrieval of all the threads or groups within this `ThreadGroup` tree (recursively). If *recurse* is `false`, only threads or groups in this immediate `ThreadGroup` object are retrieved. The `enumerate()` methods lacking the *recurse* parameter perform the same as the `enumerate()` method with *recurse* set to `true`.

The `parentOf()` method returns `true` if this thread group is the parent of the specified group; it returns `false` otherwise. Following is this method's syntax:

```
public final boolean parentOf(ThreadGroup g);
```

The `getParent()` method returns the parent of this thread group, or `null` if this `ThreadGroup` is the top-level `ThreadGroup`. Following is this method's syntax:

```
public final ThreadGroup getParent();
```

The `list()` method prints debugging information about this `ThreadGroup`'s tree (threads and groups) to `System.out`. Following is this method's syntax:

```
public void list();
```

Miscellaneous ThreadGroup Methods

The `getName()` method returns the name of this thread group. Following is this method's syntax:

```
public final String getName();
```

Some thread groups, like some threads, can be referred to as *daemons*. When a `ThreadGroup` object is a daemon group (`setDaemon(true)` has been called), the group is destroyed once all its threads and groups have been removed.

```
public final boolean isDaemon();
public final void setDaemon(boolean daemon);
```

The `isDaemon()` method returns `true` if this thread group is a daemon; it returns `false` otherwise.

The `toString()` method returns debugging information about this. Following is this method's syntax:

```
public String toString();
```

When a thread exits because it failed to catch an exception, the `uncaughtException()` method of the thread's group is invoked with the `Thread` object and the exception (`Throwable`) as parameters:

```
public void uncaughtException(Thread t, Throwable e);
```

The default behavior of `uncaughtException()` is to pass the thread and exception to the parent of this thread group. The `system` thread group, if reached, calls the `Throwable` exception's `printStackTrace()` method, dumping the stack trace of the exception to `System.err`.

Security Features

Threads and thread groups are considered a critical system resource that can be protected by Java's security features. The precise implementation of the security policy depends on the environment. When running a Java application, there is no security unless you install a `SecurityManager` using `System.setSecurityManager()`. Applets, however, use the `SecurityManager` installed by the browser environment. When you run an applet under Netscape Navigator 3.0, the applet is allowed to modify only the threads and thread groups created by the current applet; attempts to modify other threads or groups result in a `SecurityException`.

The `Thread` class has security (as implemented by the current `SecurityManager` object) implemented for the following methods:

- `Thread(ThreadGroup group)`
- `Thread(ThreadGroup group, Runnable target, String name)`
- `Thread(ThreadGroup group, String name)`
- `stop()`
- `suspend()` and `resume()`
- `setPriority()`
- `setName()`
- `setDaemon()`

The `ThreadGroup` class has security (as implemented by the current `SecurityManager` object) implemented for the following methods:

- `ThreadGroup(ThreadGroup parent, String name)`
- `setDaemon()`
- `setMaxPriority()`
- `stop()`
- `suspend()` and `resume()`
- `destroy()`

Concurrency

One of the most powerful features of the Java programming language is its ability to run multiple threads of control. Performing multiple tasks at the same time seems natural from the user's perspective—for example, simultaneously downloading a file from the Internet, performing a spreadsheet recalculation, and printing a document. From a programmer's point of view, however, managing concurrency is not as natural as it seems. Concurrency requires the programmer to take special precautions to ensure that Java objects are accessed in a thread-safe manner.

There is nothing *obvious* about threads that makes threaded programs unsafe; nevertheless, threaded programs can be subject to hazardous situations unless you take appropriate measures to make them safe.

The following example demonstrates how a threaded program may be *unsafe*:

```java
public class Counter {
    private int count = 0;
    public int incr() {
        int n = count;
        count = n + 1;
        return n;
    }
}
```

As Java classes go, the Counter class is simple, having only one attribute and one method. As its name implies, the Counter class is used to count things, such as the number of times a button is pressed or the number of times the user visits a particular Web site. The incr() method is the heart of the class, returning and incrementing the current value of the counter. However, the incr() method has a problem; it is a source of unpredictable behavior in a multithreaded environment.

Consider a situation in which a Java program has two runnable threads, both of which are about to execute this line of code (affecting the same Counter object):

```java
int cnt = counter.incr();
```

The programmer cannot predict or control the order in which these two threads are run. The Java thread scheduler has full authority over thread scheduling. There are no guarantees about which thread will receive CPU time, when the threads will execute, or how long each thread will be allowed to execute. Either thread can be interrupted by the scheduler at any time (remember that Java's thread scheduler is preemptive). On a multiprocessor machine, both threads may execute concurrently on separate processors.

Table 9.1 describes one possible sequence of execution of the two threads. In this scenario, the first thread is allowed to run until it completes its call to counter.incr(); then the second thread does the same. There are no surprises in this scenario. The first thread increments the Counter value to 1, and the second thread increments the value to 2.

Table 9.1. Counter scenario I.

Thread 1	Thread 2	Count
`cnt = counter.incr();`	—	0
`n = count;    // 0`	—	0
`count = n + 1; // 1`	—	1
`return n;    // 0`	—	1
—	`cnt = counter.incr();`	1
—	`n = count;    // 1`	1
—	`count = n + 1;  // 2`	2
—	`return n;    // 1`	2

Table 9.2 describes a somewhat different sequence of execution. In this case, the first thread is interrupted by a *context switch* (a switch to a different thread) during execution of the `incr()` method. The first thread remains temporarily suspended, and the second thread is allowed to proceed. The second thread executes its call to the `incr()` method, incrementing the `Counter` value to 1. When the first thread resumes, a problem becomes evident. The `Counter`'s value is not updated to the value 2, as you would expect, but is instead set again to the value 1.

Table 9.2. Counter scenario II.

Thread 1	Thread 2	Count
`cnt = counter.incr();`	—	0
`n = count;    // 0`	—	0
—	`cnt = counter.incr();`	0
—	`n = count;     // 0`	0
—	`count = n + 1;  // 1`	1
—	`return n;     // 0`	1
`count = n + 1; // 1`	—	1
`return n;    // 0`	—	1

By examining Thread 1 in Table 9.2, you can see a problematic sequence of operations. After entering the `incr()` method, the value of the count attribute (0) is stored in a local variable, n. The thread is then suspended for a period of time while a different thread executes. (It is important to note that the count attribute is modified by the second thread during this time.) When Thread 1 resumes, it stores the value n + 1 (1) back in the count attribute. Unfortunately, this is no longer a correct value for the counter because the counter was already incremented to 1 by Thread 2.

The problem outlined by Table 9.2 is called a *race condition*—the outcome of the program was affected by the order in which the program's threads were allocated CPU time. It is usually considered inappropriate to allow race conditions to affect a program's result. Consider a medical device that monitors a patient's blood pressure. If this device were affected by race conditions in its software, it might report an incorrect reading to the physician. The physician would base medical treatment decisions on incorrect information—a bad situation for the patient, doctor, insurance company, and software vendor!

All multithreaded programs, even Java programs, can suffer from race conditions. Fortunately, Java provides the programmer with the necessary tools to manage concurrency—monitors.

Monitors

Many texts on computer science and operating systems deal with the issue of concurrent programming. Concurrency has been the subject of much research over the years, and many concurrency-control solutions have been proposed and implemented. These solutions include the following:

- Critical sections
- Semaphores
- Mutexes
- Database record locking
- Monitors

Java implements a variant of the monitor approach to concurrency.

The concept of a *monitor* was introduced by C.A.R. Hoare in a 1974 paper published in the *Communications of the ACM*. Hoare described a special-purpose object, called a *monitor*, which applies the principle of mutual exclusion to groups of procedures (*mutual exclusion* is a fancy way of saying "one thread at a time"). In Hoare's model, each group of procedures requiring mutual exclusion is placed under the control of a single monitor. At run time, the monitor allows only one thread at a time to execute a procedure controlled by the monitor. If another thread tries to invoke a procedure controlled by the monitor, that thread is suspended until the first thread completes its call.

Java monitors remain true to Hoare's original concept, with a few minor variations (which are not discussed here). Monitors in Java enforce mutually exclusive access to methods; more specifically, Java monitors enforce mutually exclusive access to `synchronized` methods. (The `synchronized` keyword is an optional method modifier. If the `synchronized` keyword appears before the return type and signature of the method, the method is referred to as a "synchronized method.")

Every Java object has an associated monitor. `Synchronized` methods that are invoked on an object use that object's monitor to limit concurrent access to that object. When a `synchronized` method is invoked on an object, the object's monitor is consulted to determine whether any other thread is currently executing a `synchronized` method on the object. If no other thread is executing a `synchronized` method on that object, the current thread is allowed to *enter* the monitor. (Entering a monitor is also referred to as *locking* the monitor, or *acquiring ownership of* the monitor.) If a different thread has already entered the monitor, the current thread must wait until the other thread *leaves* the monitor.

Metaphorically, a Java monitor acts as an object's gatekeeper. When a `synchronized` method is called, the gatekeeper allows the calling thread to pass and then closes the gate. While the thread is still in the `synchronized` method, subsequent `synchronized` method calls to that object from other threads are blocked. Those threads line up outside the gate, waiting for the first thread to leave. When the first thread exits the `synchronized` method, the gatekeeper opens the gate, allowing a single waiting thread to proceed with its `synchronized` method call. The process repeats.

In plain English, a Java monitor enforces a one-at-a-time approach to concurrency. This is also known as *serialization* (not to be confused with "object serialization," which is the Java library for reading and writing objects on a stream).

> **NOTE**
>
> Programmers already familiar with multithreaded programming in a different language often confuse monitors with *critical sections*. Java monitors are not like traditional critical sections. Declaring a method as `synchronized` does not imply that only one thread at a time may execute that method, as would be the case with a critical section. It implies that only one thread may invoke that method (or any synchronized method) on a particular object at any given time. Java monitors are associated with objects, not with blocks of code. Two threads can concurrently execute the same synchronized method, provided that the method is invoked on different objects (that is, `a.method()` and `b.method()`, where `a != b`).

To demonstrate how monitors operate, let's rewrite the `Counter` example from the preceding section to take advantage of monitors, using the `synchronized` keyword:

```
public class Counter2 {
    private int count = 0;
    public synchronized int incr() {
```

```
        int n = count;
        count = n + 1;
        return n;
    }
}
```

Note that the incr() method has not been modified except for the addition of the synchronized keyword.

What would happen if this new Counter2 class were used in the scenario presented in Table 9.2 (the race condition)? The outcome of the same sequence of context switches is listed in Table 9.3.

Table 9.3. Counter scenario II, revised.

Thread 1	Thread 2	Count
cnt = counter.incr();	—	0
(acquires the monitor)	—	0
n = count; // 0	—	0
—	cnt = counter.incr();	0
—	(can't acquire monitor)	0
count = n + 1; // 1	(blocked)	1
return n; // 0	(blocked)	1
(releases the monitor)	(blocked)	1
—	(acquires the monitor)	1
—	n = count; // 1	1
—	count = n + 1; // 2	2
—	return n; // 1	2
—	(releases the monitor)	2

In Table 9.3, the sequence of operations begins the same as the earlier scenario. Thread 1 starts executing the incr() method of the Counter2 object but is interrupted by a context switch. In this example, however, when Thread 2 attempts to execute the incr() method on the same Counter2 object, the thread can't acquire the monitor and is blocked; the monitor is already owned by Thread 1. Thread 2 is suspended until the monitor becomes available. When Thread 1 releases the monitor, Thread 2 becomes able to acquire the monitor and continue running.

The synchronized keyword is Java's solution to the concurrency control problem. As you saw in the Counter example, the potential race condition was eliminated by adding the synchronized modifier to the incr() method. All accesses to the incr() method of a counter was serialized by the addition of the synchronized keyword. Generally speaking, any method that modifies an object's attributes should be synchronized. It is easy to mark all object-modifying methods as synchronized and be done with it.

> **NOTE**
>
> You may be wondering when you will see an actual monitor object. Anecdotal information has been presented about monitors, but you probably want to see some official documentation about what a monitor is and how you access it. Unfortunately, that is not possible. Java monitors have no official standing in the language specification, and their implementation is not directly visible to the programmer. Monitors are not Java objects—they have no attributes or methods. Monitors are a concept beneath Java's implementation of multithreading and concurrency. It is possible to access Java monitors at the native code level in the 1.x release of the Java virtual machine from Sun.

Non-synchronized Methods

Java monitors are used only in conjunction with synchronized methods. Methods that are not declared synchronized do not attempt to acquire ownership of an object's monitor before executing—they ignore monitors entirely. At any given moment, at most one thread can execute a synchronized method on an object, but an arbitrary number of threads may be executing non-synchronized methods. This can lead to some surprising situations if you are not careful in deciding which methods should be synchronized. Consider the Account class in Listing 9.4.

Listing 9.4. The Account class.

```
class Account {
  private int balance;

  public Account(int balance) {
    this.balance = balance;
  }

  public synchronized void transfer(int amount, Account destination) {
    this.withdraw(amount);
    Thread.yield();      // force a context switch
    destination.deposit(amount);
  }

  public synchronized void withdraw(int amount) {
    if (amount > balance) {
      throw new RuntimeException("No overdraft protection!");
    }
    balance -= amount;
  }
```

continues

Listing 9.4. continued

```
public synchronized void deposit(int amount) {
  balance += amount;
}

public int getBalance() {
  return balance;
  }
}
```

The attribute-modifying methods of the Account class are declared synchronized, but the getBalance() method is not synchronized. It appears that this class has no problem with race conditions—but it does!

To understand the race condition to which the Account class is subject, consider how a bank deals with accounts. To a bank, the correctness of its accounts is of the utmost importance— a bank that makes accounting errors or reports incorrect information would not have happy customers. To avoid reporting incorrect information, a bank would likely disable "inquiries" on an account while a transaction involving the account is in progress. This prevents the customer from viewing the result of a partially complete transaction. The Account class getBalance() method is not synchronized, and this can lead to problems.

Consider two Account objects, and two different threads performing actions on these accounts. One thread is performing a balance transfer from one account to the other. The second thread is performing a balance inquiry. This code demonstrates the suggested activity:

```
public class XferTest implements Runnable {
  public static void main(String[] args) {
    XferTest xfer = new XferTest();
    xfer.a = new Account(100);
    xfer.b = new Account(100);
    xfer.amount = 50;

    Thread t = new Thread(xfer);
    t.start();

    Thread.yield();    // force a context switch

    System.out.println("Inquiry: Account a has : $" + xfer.a.getBalance());
    System.out.println("Inquiry: Account b has : $" + xfer.b.getBalance());
  }

  public Account a = null;
  public Account b = null;
  public int amount = 0;

  public void run() {
    System.out.println("Before xfer: a has : $" + a.getBalance());
    System.out.println("Before xfer: b has : $" + b.getBalance());
    a.transfer(amount, b);
```

```
    System.out.println("After xfer: a has : $" + a.getBalance());
    System.out.println("After xfer: b has : $" + b.getBalance());
  }
}
```

In this example, two Account objects are created, each with a $100 balance. A transfer is then initiated to move $50 from one account to the other. The transfer is not an operation that should affect the total balance of the two accounts; that is, the sum of the balance of the two accounts should remain constant at $200. If the balance inquiry is performed at just the right time, however, it is possible that the total amount of funds in these accounts could be incorrectly reported. If this program is run using the 1.0 Java Developers Kit (JDK) for Solaris, the following output is printed:

```
Before xfer: a has : $100
Before xfer: b has : $100
Inquiry: Account a has : $50
Inquiry: Account b has : $100
After xfer: a has : $50
After xfer: b has : $150
```

The Inquiry reports that the first account contains $50 and the second account contains $100. That's not $200! What happened to the other $50? Nothing has "happened" to the money, except that it is in the process of being transferred to the second account when the balance inquiry scans the accounts. Because the getBalance() method is not synchronized, a customer would have no problem executing an inquiry on accounts involved in the balance transfer. The lack of synchronization can leave some customer wondering why the accounts are $50 short.

If the getBalance() method is declared synchronized, the application has a different result. The modified code follows:

```
public synchronized int getBalance() {
  return balance;
}
```

The balance inquiry is blocked until the balance transfer is complete. Here is the modified program's output:

```
Before xfer: a has : $100
Before xfer: b has : $100
Inquiry: Account a has : $50
Inquiry: Account b has : $150
After xfer: a has : $50
After xfer: b has : $150
```

Advanced Monitor Concepts

Monitors sound pretty simple. Add the synchronized modifier to your methods, and that's all there is to it. Well, not quite. Monitors themselves may be simple, but taken together with the rest of the programming environment, there are a few issues you should understand before you use monitors. This section presents a few tips and techniques you should master to become expert in concurrent Java programming.

static synchronized Methods

Methods that are declared `synchronized` attempt to acquire ownership of the target object's monitor. But what about methods that do not have an associated object (`static` methods)?

The language specification is fairly clear, if brief, about `static synchronized` methods. When a `static synchronized` method is called, the monitor acquired is said to be a *per-class* monitor —that is, there is one monitor for each class that regulates access to all `static` methods of that class. Only one `static synchronized` method in a class can be active at a given moment.

The synchronized Statement

It is not possible to use `synchronized` methods on some types of objects. For example, it is not possible to add *any* methods to Java array objects (much less `synchronized` methods). To get around this restriction, Java has a second method of interacting with an object's monitor. The `synchronized` *statement* is defined to have the following syntax:

```
synchronized ( Expression ) Statement
```

Executing a `synchronized` statement has the same effect as calling a `synchronized` method— ownership of an object's monitor is acquired before a block of code can be executed. With the `synchronized` statement, the object whose monitor is up for grabs is the object resulting from *Expression* (which must be an object type, not an elemental type).

One of the most important uses of the `synchronized` statement involves controlling access to array objects. The following example demonstrates how to use the `synchronized` statement to provide thread-safe access to an array:

```
void safe_lshift(byte[] array, int count) {
    synchronized(array) {
        System.arraycopy(array, count, array, 0, array.size - count);
    }
}
```

Before modifying the array in this example, the virtual machine assigns ownership of array's monitor to the currently executing thread. Other threads trying to acquire array's monitor are forced to wait until the array-copy operation is complete. Of course, accesses to the array that are not guarded by a synchronized statement are not blocked; so be careful!

The `synchronized` statement is also useful when modifying an object's public variables directly. Here's an example:

```
void call_method(SomeClass obj) {
    synchronized(obj) {
        obj.variable = 5;
    }
}
```

PUBLIC OR NOT?

There is debate within the Java community about the potential danger of declaring attributes to be `public`. When concurrency is considered, it becomes apparent that `public` attributes can lead to thread-unsafe code. Here's why: `public` attributes can be accessed by any thread without the benefit of protection by a `synchronized` method. When you declare an attribute `public`, you relinquish control over updates to that attribute; any programmer using your code has a license to access (and update) `public` attributes directly.

In general, it is not a good idea to declare (non-`final`) attributes to be `public`. Not only can it introduce thread-safety problems, it can make your code difficult to modify and support in later revisions.

Note, however, that Java programmers frequently define immutable symbolic constants as `public final` class attributes (such as `Event.ACTION_EVENT`). Attributes declared this way do not have thread-safety issues. (Race conditions involve only objects whose values can be modified.)

When Not to Be synchronized

By now, you should be able to write thread-safe code using the `synchronized` keyword. When should you really use the `synchronized` keyword? Are there situations in which you should not use `synchronized`? Are there drawbacks to using `synchronized`?

The most common reason developers don't use `synchronized` is that they write single-threaded, single-purpose code. For example, CPU-bound tasks do not benefit much from multithreading. A compiler does not perform much better if it is threaded. The Java compiler from Sun does not contain many `synchronized` methods. For the most part, it assumes that it is executing in its own thread of control, without having to share its resources with other threads.

Another common reason for avoiding `synchronized` methods is that they do not perform as well as non-`synchronized` methods. In simple tests in the 1.0.1 JDK from Sun, `synchronized` methods have been shown to be three to four times slower than their non-`synchronized` counterparts. Although this doesn't mean your entire application will be three or four times slower, it is a performance issue nonetheless. Some programs demand that every ounce of performance be squeezed out of the runtime system. In this situation, it may be appropriate to avoid the performance overhead associated with `synchronized` methods.

Deadlocks

Sometimes referred to as a *deadly embrace*, a *deadlock* is one of the worst situations that can happen in a multithreaded environment. Java programs are not immune to deadlocks, and programmers must take care to avoid them.

A deadlock is a situation that causes two or more threads to *hang*, that is, they are unable to proceed. In the simplest case, two threads are each trying to acquire a monitor already owned by the other thread. Each thread goes to sleep, waiting for the desired monitor to become available—but the monitors never become available. (The first thread waits for the monitor owned by the second thread, and the second thread waits for the monitor owned by the first thread. Because each thread is waiting for the other, each never releases its monitor to the other thread.)

The sample application in Listing 9.5 should give you an understanding of how a deadlock happens.

Listing 9.5. A deadlock.

```
public class Deadlock implements Runnable {
  public static void main(String[] args) {
      Deadlock d1 = new Deadlock();
      Deadlock d2 = new Deadlock();
      Thread t1 = new Thread(d1);
      Thread t2 = new Thread(d2);

      d1.grabIt = d2;
      d2.grabIt = d1;
      t1.start();
      t2.start();
      try { t1.join(); t2.join(); } catch(InterruptedException e) { }
      System.exit(0);
  }

  Deadlock grabIt;
  public synchronized void run() {
      try { Thread.sleep(2000); } catch(InterruptedException e) { }
      grabIt.sync_method();
  }

  public synchronized void sync_method() {
      try { Thread.sleep(2000); } catch(InterruptedException e) { }
      System.out.println("in sync_method");
  }
}
```

In this class, main() launches two threads, each of which invokes the synchronized run() method on a Deadlock object. When the first thread wakes up, it attempts to call the sync_method() of the other Deadlock object. Obviously, the second Deadlock's monitor is owned by the second thread; so, the first thread begins waiting for the monitor. When the second thread wakes up, it tries to call the sync_method() of the first Deadlock object. Because that Deadlock's monitor is already owned by the first thread, the second thread begins waiting. Because the threads are waiting for each other, neither will ever wake up.

NOTE

If you run the deadlock application shown in Listing 9.5, you will notice that it never exits. That is understandable; after all, that is what a deadlock is. How can you tell what is really going on inside the virtual machine? There is a trick you can use with the Solaris/UNIX JDK to display the status of all threads and monitors: press Ctrl+\ in the terminal window where the Java application is running. This sends the virtual machine a signal to dump the state of the VM. Here is a partial listing of the monitor table dumped several seconds after launching the deadlock application:

```
Deadlock@EE300840/EE334C20 (key=0xee300840):      monitor owner: "Thread-5"
    Waiting to enter:
        "Thread-4"
Deadlock@EE300838/EE334C18 (key=0xee300838):      monitor owner: "Thread-4"
    Waiting to enter:
        "Thread-5"
```

Numerous algorithms are available for preventing and detecting deadlock situations, but those algorithms are beyond the scope of this chapter (many database and operating system texts cover deadlock-detection algorithms in detail). Unfortunately, the Java virtual machine itself does not perform any deadlock detection or notification. There is nothing that prevents the virtual machine from doing so, however, so this behavior may be added to future versions of the virtual machine.

Using `volatile`

It is worth mentioning that the `volatile` keyword is supported as a variable modifier in Java. The language specification states that the `volatile` qualifier instructs the compiler to generate loads and stores on each access to an attribute, rather than caching the value in a register. The intent of the `volatile` keyword is to provide thread-safe access to an attribute, but `volatile` falls short of this goal.

In the 1.0 JDK virtual machine, the `volatile` keyword is ignored. It is unclear whether `volatile` has been abandoned in favor of monitors and `synchronized` methods or whether the keyword was included solely for C and C++ look and feel. Regardless, `volatile` is useless—use `synchronized` methods rather than the `volatile` keyword.

Synchronization

After learning how `synchronized` methods are used to make Java programs thread-safe, you may wonder what the big deal is about monitors. They are just object locks, right? Not true! Monitors are more than locks; monitors can also be used to coordinate multiple threads by using the `wait()` and `notify()` methods available in every Java object.

9

THREADS AND MULTITHREADING

The Need for Thread Coordination

In a Java program, threads are often interdependent—one thread may depend on another thread to complete an operation or to service a request. For example, a spreadsheet program may run an extensive recalculation as a separate thread. If a user-interface (UI) thread attempts to update the spreadsheet's display, the UI thread should coordinate with the recalculation thread, starting the screen update only when the recalculation thread has successfully completed.

There are many other situations in which it is useful to coordinate two or more threads. The following list identifies only two of the possibilities:

- Shared buffers are often used to communicate data between threads. In this scenario, one thread writes to a shared buffer (the writer) and one thread reads from the buffer (the reader). When the reader thread attempts to read from the buffer, it should coordinate with the writer thread, retrieving data from the shared buffer only after the writer thread has put it there. If the buffer is empty, the reader thread should wait for the data. The writer thread notifies the reader thread when it has completed filling the buffer so that the reader can continue.

- Many threads may have to perform an identical action, such as loading an image file across the network. These threads can reduce the overall system load if only one thread performs the work while the other threads wait for the work to be completed. (The waiting threads must wait without consuming CPU time by temporarily transitioning into the NOT RUNNABLE thread state—this is possible, and is discussed later in this chapter.) This is precisely the model used in the java.awt.MediaTracker class.

It is no accident that the previous examples repeatedly use the words *wait* and *notify*. These words express the two concepts central to thread coordination: a thread *waits* for some condition event to occur, and you *notify* a waiting thread that a condition or event has occurred. The words *wait* and *notify* are also used in Java as the names of the methods you call to coordinate threads: wait() and notify(), in class Object.

As noted in "Monitors," earlier in this chapter, every Java object has an associated monitor. That fact turns out to be useful at this point because monitors are also used to implement Java's thread-coordination primitives. Although monitors are not directly visible to the programmer, an API is provided in class Object that enables you to interact with an object's monitor. This API consists of two methods: wait() and notify().

Conditions, wait(), and notify()

Threads are usually coordinated using a concept known as a condition, or a condition variable. A *condition* is a logical statement that must hold true in order for a thread to proceed; if the condition does not hold true, the thread must wait for the condition to become true before continuing. In Java, this pattern is usually expressed as follows:

```
while ( ! the_condition_I_am_waiting_for ) {
    wait();
}
```

First, check to see whether the desired condition is already true. If it is true, there is no need to wait. If the condition is not yet true, call the `wait()` method. When `wait()` ends, recheck the condition to make sure that it is now true.

Invoking `wait()` on an object pauses the current thread and adds the thread to the *condition variable wait queue* of the object's monitor. This queue contains a list of all the threads that are currently blocked inside `wait()` on that object. The thread is not removed from the wait queue until `notify()` is invoked on that object from a different thread. A call to `notify()` wakes a single waiting thread, notifying the thread that a condition of the object has changed.

There are two additional varieties of the `wait()` method. The first version takes a single parameter—a timeout value in milliseconds. The second version has two parameters—a more precise timeout value, specified in milliseconds *and* nanoseconds. These methods are used when you do not want to wait indefinitely for an event. If you want to abandon the wait after a fixed period of time (referred to as *timing out*), you should use either of the following methods:

- `wait(long milliseconds);`
- `wait(long milliseconds, int nanoseconds);`

Unfortunately, these methods do not provide a means to determine how the `wait()` was ended—whether a `notify()` occurred or whether it timed out. This is not a big problem, however, because you can recheck the wait condition and the system time to determine which event has occurred.

> **CAUTION**
>
> In the 1.0.2 JDK, the `wait(int millisecond, int nanosecond)` method uses the nanosecond parameter to round the millisecond parameter to the nearest millisecond. Waiting is not yet supported in nanosecond granularity.

The `wait()` and `notify()` methods must be invoked from within a `synchronized` method or from within a `synchronized` statement. This requirement is discussed in further detail in "Monitor Ownership," later in this chapter.

A Thread Coordination Example

A classic example of thread coordination used in many computer science texts is the *bounded buffer* problem. This problem involves using a fixed-size memory buffer to communicate between two processes or threads. To solve this problem, you must coordinate the reader and writer threads so that the following are true:

■ When the writer thread attempts to write to a full buffer, the writer is suspended until some items are removed from the buffer.

■ When the reader thread removes items from the full buffer, the writer thread is notified of the buffer's changed condition and may continue writing.

■ When the reader thread attempts to read from an empty buffer, the reader is suspended until some items are added to the buffer.

■ When the writer adds items to the empty buffer, the reader thread is notified of the buffer's changed condition and may continue reading.

The following class listings demonstrate a Java implementation of the bounded buffer problem. There are three main classes in this example: the Producer, the Consumer, and the Buffer. Let's start with the Producer:

```java
public class Producer implements Runnable {
  private Buffer buffer;

  public Producer(Buffer b) {
      buffer = b;
  }

  public void run() {
      for (int i=0; i<250; i++) {
          buffer.put((char)('A' + (i%26)));    // write to the buffer
      }
  }
}
```

The Producer class implements the Runnable interface (which should give you a hint that it will be used in a Thread). When the Producer's run() method is invoked, 250 characters are written in rapid succession to a buffer.

The Consumer class is as simple as the Producer:

```java
public class Consumer implements Runnable {
  private Buffer buffer;

  public Consumer(Buffer b) {
      buffer = b;
  }

  public void run() {
      for (int i=0; i<250; i++) {
          System.out.println(buffer.get());    // read from the buffer
      }
  }
}
```

The Consumer is also a Runnable interface. Its run() method greedily reads 250 characters from a buffer.

The Buffer class has been mentioned already, including two of its methods: put(char) and get(). Listing 9.6 shows the Buffer class in its entirety.

Listing 9.6. The Buffer class.

```
public class Buffer {
  private char[] buf;    // buffer storage
  private int last;      // last occupied position

  public Buffer(int sz) {
      buf = new char[sz];
      last = 0;
  }

  public boolean isFull()  { return (last == buf.length); }
  public boolean isEmpty() { return (last == 0);          }

  public synchronized void put(char c) {
      while(isFull()) {                      // wait for room to put stuff
        try { wait(); } catch(InterruptedException e) { }
      }
      buf[last++] = c;
      notify();
  }

  public synchronized char get() {
      while(isEmpty()) {                      // wait for stuff to read
        try { wait(); } catch(InterruptedException e) { }
      }
      char c =  buf[0];
      System.arraycopy(buf, 1, buf, 0, --last);
      notify();
      return c;
  }
}
```

NOTE

When you first begin using wait() and notify(), you may notice a contradiction. The wait() and notify() methods must be called from synchronized methods, so if wait() is called inside a synchronized method, how can a different thread enter a synchronized method in order to call notify()? Doesn't the waiting thread own the object's monitor, preventing other threads from entering the synchronized method?

The answer to this paradox is that wait() temporarily releases ownership of the object's monitor; before wait() can return, however, it must reacquire ownership of the monitor. By releasing the monitor, the wait() method allows other threads to acquire the monitor (which gives them the ability to call notify()).

The Buffer class is just that—a storage buffer. You can use put() to put items into the buffer (in this case, characters), and you can use get() to get items out of the buffer.

Note the use of wait() and notify() in these methods. In the put() method, a wait() is performed while the Buffer is full; no more items can be added to the buffer while it is full. At the end of the get() method, the call to notify() ensures that any thread waiting in the put() method will be activated and allowed to continue adding an item to the buffer. Similarly, a wait() is performed in the get() method if the buffer is empty; no items can be removed from an empty buffer. The put() method calls notify() to ensure that any thread waiting in get() will be wakened.

> **NOTE**
>
> Java provides two classes similar to the Buffer class presented in this example. These classes, java.io.PipedOutputStream and java.io.PipedInputStream, are useful in communicating streams of data between threads. If you unpack the src.zip file shipped with the 1.0 JDK, you can examine these classes to see how they handle interthread coordination.

Advanced Thread Coordination

The wait() and notify() methods simplify the task of coordinating multiple threads in a concurrent Java program. However, to make full use of these methods, you should understand a few additional details. The following sections present more material about thread coordination in Java.

Monitor Ownership

The wait() and notify() methods have one major restriction you must observe: you can call these methods only when the current thread owns the monitor of the object. Most frequently, wait() and notify() are invoked from within a synchronized method, as in the following example:

```
public synchronized void method() {
    ...
    while (!condition) {
      wait();
    }
    ...
}
```

In this case, the synchronized modifier guarantees that the thread invoking the wait() call already owns the monitor when it calls wait().

If you attempt to call `wait()` or `notify()` without first acquiring ownership of the object's monitor (for example, from a non-synchronized method), the virtual machine throws an `IllegalMonitorStateException`. The following example demonstrates what happens when you call `wait()` without first acquiring ownership of the monitor:

```
public class NonOwnerTest {
  public static void main(String[] args) {
       NonOwnerTest not = new NonOwnerTest();
       not.method();
  }

  public void method() {
       try { wait(); } catch(InterruptedException e) { }    // a bad thing to do!
  }
}
```

If you run this Java application, the following text is printed to the terminal:

```
java.lang.IllegalMonitorStateException: current thread not owner
       at java.lang.Object.wait(Object.java)
       at NonOwnerTest.method(NonOwnerTest.java:10)
       at NonOwnerTest.main(NonOwnerTest.java:5)
```

When you invoke the `wait()` method on an object, you must own the object's monitor if you are to avoid this exception.

MONITORS AND THE synchronized STATEMENT

All Java objects can participate in thread synchronization by using the `wait()` and `notify()` methods. However, the "monitor ownership" requirement introduces a quirk for some object types, such as arrays. (Strangely enough, Java array types inherit from the `java.lang.Object` class, where the `wait()` and `notify()` methods are defined.) The `wait()` and `notify()` methods can be called on Java array objects, but monitor ownership must be established using the synchronized statement rather than a synchronized method. The following code demonstrates monitor usage as applied to a Java array:

```
// wait for an event on this array
Object[] array = getArray();
synchronized (array) {
  array.wait();
}

...

// notify waiting threds
Object[] array = getArray();
synchronized (array) {
  array.notify();
}
```

Multiple Waiters

It is possible for multiple threads to be waiting on the same object. This can happen when multiple threads wait for the same event. For example, recall the Buffer class described earlier; the Buffer was operated on by a single Producer and a single Consumer. What would happen if there were multiple Producers? If the Buffer filled, different Producers might attempt to put() items into the buffer; they would all block inside the put() method, waiting for a Consumer to come along and free up space in the Buffer.

When you call notify(), there may be zero, one, or more threads blocked in a wait() on the monitor. If there are no threads waiting, the call to notify() is a *no-op*—it does not affect any other threads. If there is a single thread in wait(), that thread is notified and begins waiting for the monitor to be released by the thread that called notify(). If two or more threads are in a wait(), the virtual machine picks a single waiting thread and notifies that thread. (The method used to "pick" a waiting thread varies from platform to platform—your programs should not rely on the VM to select a specific thread from the pool of waiting threads.)

Using notifyAll()

In some situations, you may want to notify *every* thread currently waiting on an object. The Object API provides a method to do this: notifyAll(). The notify() method wakes only a single waiting thread, but the notifyAll() method wakes every thread currently waiting on the object.

When would you want to use notifyAll()? Consider the java.awt.MediaTracker class. This class is used to track the status of images being loaded over the network. Multiple threads may wait on the same MediaTracker object, waiting for all the images to be loaded. When the MediaTracker detects that all images have been loaded, notifyAll() is called to inform every waiting thread that the images have been loaded. notifyAll() is used because the MediaTracker does not know how many threads are waiting; if notify() were used, some of the waiting threads would not receive notification that the transfer was completed. These threads would continue waiting, probably hanging the entire applet.

Listing 9.6, earlier in this chapter, can also benefit from the use of notifyAll(). In that code, the Buffer class used the notify() method to send a notification to a single thread waiting on an empty or a full buffer. However, there was no guarantee that only a single thread was waiting; multiple threads may have been waiting for the same condition. Listing 9.7 shows a modified version of the Buffer class (named Buffer2) that uses notifyAll().

Listing 9.7. The Buffer2 class, using notifyAll().

```
public class Buffer2 {
  private char[] buf;              // storage
  private int last = 0;            // last occupied position
```

```
    private int writers_waiting = 0;  // # of threads waiting in put()
    private int readers_waiting = 0;  // # of threads waiting in get()

    public Buffer2(int sz) {
        buf = new char[sz];
    }

    public boolean isFull()  { return (last == buf.length); }
    public boolean isEmpty() { return (last == 0);          }

    public synchronized void put(char c) {
        while(isFull()) {
            try     { writers_waiting++;  wait(); }
            catch   (InterruptedException e) { }
            finally { writers_waiting--; }
        }
        buf[last++] = c;
        if (readers_waiting > 0) {
            notifyAll();
        }
    }

    public synchronized char get() {
        while(isEmpty()) {
            try     { readers_waiting++;  wait(); }
            catch   (InterruptedException e) { }
            finally { readers_waiting--; }
        }
        char c =  buf[0];
        System.arraycopy(buf, 1, buf, 0, --last);
        if (writers_waiting > 0) {
            notifyAll();
        }
        return c;
    }
}
```

The get() and put() methods have been made more intelligent. They now check to see whether any notification is necessary and then use notifyAll() to broadcast an event to all waiting threads.

Summary

This chapter was a whirlwind tour of multithreaded programming in Java. Among other things, the chapter covered the following:

■ Creating your own thread classes by subclassing Thread or implementing Runnable

■ Using the ThreadGroup class to manage groups of threads

■ Understanding thread states and thread scheduling

■ Making your classes thread-safe by using the `synchronized` keyword to protect objects from concurrent modification

■ Understanding how monitors affect concurrent programming in Java

■ Coordinating the actions of multiple threads by calling the `wait()` and `notify()` methods

Java threads are not difficult to use. After reading this chapter, you should begin to see how threads can be used to improve your everyday Java programming.

Exception Handling

by David R. Chung

IN THIS CHAPTER

CHAPTER 10

Errors are a normal part of programming. Some of these errors are flaws in a program's basic design or implementation—these are called *bugs*. Other types of errors are not really bugs; rather, they are the result of situations like low memory or invalid filenames.

The way you handle the second type of error determines whether they become bugs. Unfortunately, if your goal is to produce robust applications, you probably find yourself spending more time handling errors than actually writing the core of your application.

Java's exception handling mechanism lets you handle errors without forcing you to spend most of your energy worrying about them.

What Is an Exception?

As the name implies, an *exception* is an exceptional condition. An exception is something that is out of the ordinary. Most often, exceptions are used as a way to report error conditions. Exceptions can be used as a means of indicating other situations as well. This chapter concentrates primarily on exceptions as an error handling mechanism.

Exceptions provide notification of errors and a way to handle them. This new control structure allows you to specify exactly where to handle specific types of errors.

> **NOTE**
>
> Other languages such as C++ and Ada provide exception handling. Java's exception handling is similar to the one used by C++.

Tennyson Understood the Problem

In his poem, *Charge of the Light Brigade*, Alfred, Lord Tennyson describes an actual battle. In this battle, a cavalry brigade is ordered to attack a gun emplacement. It turns out that the valley the troops attack is a trap. There are big guns on three sides and the brave soldiers on horseback with their sabers are massacred. The poem describes an actual battle from the Crimean War.

The battle as Tennyson describes it highlights a classic problem. Someone (probably far from the front) had given the order to attack. The men who led the charge very quickly became aware that an error had been made. Unfortunately, they did not have the authority to do anything about it. In Tennyson's immortal words, "Theirs not to reason why, theirs but to do and die: into the valley of Death rode the 600."

Using exceptions in Java allows you to determine exactly who handles an error. In fact, low-level functions can detect errors while higher-level functions decide what to do about them. Exceptions provide a means of communicating information about errors up through the chain of methods until one of them can handle it.

If Exceptions Are the Answer, What Is the Question?

Most procedural languages like C and Pascal do not use exception handling. In these languages, a variety of techniques are used to determine whether an error has occurred. The most common means of error checking is the function's return value.

Consider the problem of calculating the retail cost of an item and displaying it. For this example, the retail cost is twice the wholesale cost:

```
int retailCost( int wholesale ) {

    if ( wholesale <= 0 ) {
        return 0 ;
    }

    return (wholesale * 2 ) ;
}
```

The `retailCost()` method takes the wholesale price of an item and doubles it. If the wholesale price is negative or zero, the function returns zero to indicate that an error has occurred. This method can be used in an application as follows:

```
int wholesalePrice = 30 ;
int retailPrice    = 0 ;

retailPrice = retailCost( wholesalePrice ) ;

System.out.println( "Wholesale price = " + wholesalePrice ) ;
System.out.println( "Retail price = "    + retailPrice ) ;
```

In this example, the `retailCost()` method calculates the correct retail cost and prints it. The problem is that the code segment never checks whether the `wholesalePrice` variable is negative. Even though the method checks the value of `wholesalePrice` and reports an error—there is nothing that forces the calling method to deal with the error. If this method is called with a negative `wholesalePrice`, the function blindly prints invalid data. Therefore, no matter how diligent you are in ensuring that your methods return error values, the callers of your methods are free to ignore them.

You can prevent bad values from being printed by putting the whole operation in a method. The `showRetail()` method takes the wholesale price, doubles it, and prints it. If the wholesale price is negative or zero, the method does not print anything and returns the `boolean` value `false`:

```
boolean showRetail( int wholesale ) {

    if ( wholesale <= 0 ) {
        return false ;
    }

    int retailPrice ;
```

```
    retailPrice = wholesalePrice * 2 ;

    System.out.println( "Wholesale price = " + wholesale ) ;
    System.out.println( "Retail price = "    + retailPrice ) ;

    return true ;

}
```

Using this new and improved method guarantees that *bad* values are never printed. However, once again, the caller does not have to check to see whether the method returned `true`.

The fact that the caller can choose to ignore return values is not the only problem with using return values to report errors. What happens if your method returns a `boolean` and both `true` and `false` are valid return values? How does this method report an error?

Consider a method to determine whether a student passes a test. The `pass()` method takes the number of correct answers and the number of questions. The method calculates the percentage; if it is greater than 70 percent, the student passes. Consider the `passingGrade()` method:

```
boolean passingGrade( int correct, int total ) {

    boolean returnCode = false ;

    if ( (float)correct / (float)total > 0.70 ) {
        returnCode = true ;
    }

return returnCode ;
}
```

In this example, everything works fine as long as the method arguments are well behaved. What happens if the number correct is greater than the total? Or worse, if the total is zero (because this causes a division by zero in the method)? By relying on return values in this case, there is *no way* to report an error in this function.

Exceptions prevent you from making your return values do double duty. Exceptions allow you to use return values to return only useful information from your methods. Exceptions also *force* the caller to deal with errors—because exceptions cannot be ignored.

Some Terminology

Exception handling can be viewed as a nonlocal control structure. When a method *throws* an exception, its caller must determine whether it can *catch* the exception. If the calling method can catch the exception, it takes over and execution continues in the caller. If the calling method cannot catch the exception, the exception is passed on to its caller. This process continues until either the exception is caught or the top (or bottom, depending on how you look at it) of the call stack is reached and the application terminates because the exception has not been caught.

Java exceptions are class objects subclassed from `java.lang.Throwable`. Because exceptions are class objects, they can contain both data and methods. In fact, the base class `Throwable` implements a method that returns a String describing the error that caused the exception. This is useful for debugging and for giving users a meaningful error message.

Don't Throw Up Your Hands— throw an Exception

The passingGrade() method presented in the preceding section was unable to report an error condition because all its possible return values were valid. Adding exception handling to the method makes it possible to uncouple the reporting of results from the reporting of errors.

The first step is to modify the passingGrade() method definition to include the throws clause. The throws clause lists the types of exceptions that can be thrown by the method. In the following revised code, the method throws only an exception of type Exception:

```
static boolean passingGrade( int correct, int total )
                            throws Exception {

    boolean returnCode = false ;
```

The rest of the method remains largely unchanged. This time, the method checks to see whether its arguments make sense. Because this method determines passing grades, it would be unreasonable to have more correct responses than total responses. Therefore, if there are more correct responses than total responses, the method throws an exception.

The method instantiates an object of type Exception. The Exception constructor takes a String parameter. The String contains a message that can be retrieved when the exception is caught. The throw statement terminates the method and gives its caller the opportunity to catch it:

```
    if( correct > total ) {
        throw new Exception( "Invalid values" ) ;
    }

    if ( (float)correct / (float)total > 0.70 ) {
        returnCode = true ;
    }

    return returnCode ;
}
```

throw, try, and catch Blocks

To respond to an exception, the call to the method that produces it must be placed within a try block. A try block is a block of code beginning with the try keyword followed by a left and a right curly brace. Every try block is associated with one or more catch blocks. Here is a try block:

```
try
    {
    // method calls go here
    }
```

If a method is to catch exceptions thrown by the methods it calls, the calls must be placed within a try block. If an exception is thrown, it is handled in a catch block. Different catch blocks handle different types of exceptions. This is a try block and a catch block set up to handle exceptions of type Exception:

```
try
    {
    // method calls go here
    }
catch( Exception e )
    {
    // handle exceptons here
    }
```

When any method in the try block throws any type of exception, execution of the try block ceases. Program control passes immediately to the associated catch block. If the catch block can handle the given exception type, it takes over. If it cannot handle the exception, the exception is passed to the method's caller. In an application, this process goes on until a catch block catches the exception or the exception reaches the main() method uncaught and causes the application to terminate.

An Exceptional Example

Because *all* Java methods are class members, the passingGrade() method is incorporated in the gradeTest application class. Because main() calls passingGrade(), main() must be able to catch any exceptions passingGrade() might throw. To do this, main() places the call to passingGrade() in a try block. Because the throws clause lists type Exception, the catch block catches the Exception class. Listing 10.1 shows the entire gradeTest application.

Listing 10.1. The gradeTest application.

```
import java.io.* ;
import java.lang.Exception ;

public class gradeTest {

    public static void main( String[] args ) {

        try
            {
            // the second call to passingGrade throws
            // an excption so the third call never
            // gets executed

            System.out.println( passingGrade( 60,  80 ) ) ;
            System.out.println( passingGrade( 75,   0 ) ) ;
            System.out.println( passingGrade( 90, 100 ) ) ;
            }
        catch( Exception e )
            {
            System.out.println( "Caught exception --" +
                            e.getMessage() ) ;
```

```
            }

    }

    static boolean passingGrade( int correct, int total )
                                  throws Exception {

        boolean returnCode = false ;

        if( correct > total ) {
            throw new Exception( "Invalid values" ) ;
        }

        if ( (float)correct / (float)total > 0.70 ) {
            returnCode = true ;
        }

        return returnCode ;
    }

}
```

The second call to `passingGrade()` fails in this case, because the method checks to see whether the number of correct responses is less than the total responses. When `passingGrade()` throws the exception, control passes to the `main()` method. In this example, the `catch` block in `main()` catches the exception and prints `Caught exception -- Invalid values`.

Multiple catch Blocks

In some cases, a method may have to catch different types of exceptions. Java supports multiple `catch` blocks. Each `catch` block must specify a different type of exception:

```
try
    {
    // method calls go here
    }
catch( SomeExceptionClass e )
    {
    // handle SomeExceptionClass exceptions here
    }
catch( SomeOtherExceptionClass e )
    {
    // handle SomeOtherExceptionClass exceptions here
    }
```

When an exception is thrown in the `try` block, it is caught by the first `catch` block of the appropriate type. Only one `catch` block in a given set will be executed. Notice that the `catch` block looks a lot like a method declaration. The exception caught in a `catch` block is a local reference to the actual exception object. You can use this exception object to help determine what caused the exception to be thrown in the first place.

Does Every Method Have to Catch Every Exception?

What happens if a method calls another method that throws an exception but chooses not to catch it? In the example in Listing 10.2, main() calls foo(), which in turn calls bar(). bar() lists Exception in its throws clause; because foo() is not going to catch the exception, it must also have Exception in its throws clause. The application in Listing 10.2 shows a method, foo(), that ignores exceptions thrown by the called method.

Listing 10.2. A method that ignores exceptions thrown by the method it calls.

```java
import java.io.* ;
import java.lang.Exception ;

public class MultiThrow {

    public static void main( String[] args ) {

        try
            {
            foo() ;
            }
        catch( Exception e )
            {
            System.out.println( "Caught exception " +
                            e.getMessage() ) ;
            }

    }

    static void foo() throws Exception {

        bar() ;

    }

    static void bar() throws Exception {

        throw new Exception( "Who cares" ) ;

    }

}
```

In the example in Listing 10.3, main() calls foo() which calls bar(). Because bar() throws an exception and doesn't catch it, foo() has the opportunity to catch it. The foo() method has no catch block, so it cannot catch the exception. In this case, the exception propagates up the call stack to foo()'s caller, main().

Listing 10.3. A method that catches and rethrows an exception.

```java
import java.io.* ;
import java.lang.Exception ;
public class MultiThrow {

    public static void main( String[] args ) {

        try
            {
            foo() ;
            }
        catch( Exception e )
            {
            System.out.println( "Caught exception " +
                                e.getMessage() ) ;
            }

    }

    static void foo() throws Exception {

        try
            {
            bar() ;
            }
        catch( Exception e )
            {
            System.out.println( "Re throw exception -- " +
                                e.getMessage() ) ;
            throw e ;
            }    }

    static void bar() throws Exception {

        throw new Exception( "Who cares" ) ;

    }

}
```

The foo() method calls bar(). The bar() method throws an exception and foo() catches it. In this example, foo() simply *rethrows* the exception, which is ultimately caught in the application's main() method. In a *real* application, foo() could do some processing and then rethrow the exception. This arrangement allows both foo() and main() to handle the exception.

The finally Clause

Java introduces a new concept in exception handling: the finally clause. The finally clause sets apart a block of code that is always executed. Here's an example of a finally clause:

```java
import java.io.* ;
import java.lang.Exception ;
public class MultiThrow {
    public static void main( String[] args ) {
```

```
    try
        {
        alpha() ;
        }
    catch( Exception e }
        {
        System.out.println( "Caught exception " ) ;
        }
    finally()
        {
        System.out.println( "Finally. " ) ;
        }
    }

}
```

In normal execution (that is, when no exceptions are thrown), the `finally` block is executed immediately after the `try` block. When an exception is thrown, the `finally` block is executed before control passes to the caller.

If `alpha()` throws an exception, it is caught in the `catch` block and *then* the `finally` block is executed. If `alpha()` does not throw an exception, the `finally` block is executed after the `try` block. If any code in a `try` block is executed, the `finally` block is executed as well.

The Throwable Class

All exceptions in Java are subclassed from the class `Throwable`. If you want to create your own exception classes, you must subclass `Throwable`. Most Java programs do not have to subclass their own exception classes.

Following is the `public` portion of the class definition of `Throwable`:

```
public class Throwable {

    public Throwable() ;
    public Throwable(String message) ;
    public String getMessage()
    public String toString() ;
    public void printStackTrace() ;
    public void printStackTrace(java.io.PrintStream s) ;
    private native void printStackTrace0(java.io.PrintStream s);
    public native Throwable fillInStackTrace();

}
```

The constructor takes a string that describes the exception. Later, when an exception is thrown, you can call the `getMessage()` method to get the error string that was reported.

Types of Exceptions

The methods of the Java API and the language itself also throw exceptions. These exceptions can be broken into two classes: `Exception` and `Error`.

Both the `Exception` and `Error` classes are derived from `Throwable`. `Exception` and its subclasses are used to indicate conditions that may be recoverable. `Error` and its subclasses indicate conditions that are generally not recoverable and should cause your applet to terminate.

The various packages included in the Java Developers Kit throw different kinds of `Exception` and `Error` exceptions, as described in the following sections.

`java.lang` Exceptions

The `java.lang` package contains much of the core Java language. The exceptions subclassed from `RuntimeException` do not have to be declared in a method's `throws` clause. These exceptions are considered *normal* and nearly any method can throw them. Figure 10.1 and Table 10.1 show the recoverable exceptions from the `java.lang` package. Figure 10.2 and Table 10.2 show the nonrecoverable errors in the `java.lang` package.

Table 10.1. The `java.lang` exceptions.

Exception	Cause
ArithmeticException	Arithmetic error condition (for example, divide by zero).
ArrayIndexOutOfBoundsException	Array index is less than zero or greater than the actual size of the array.
ArrayStoreException	Object type mismatch between the array and the object to be stored in the array.
ClassCastException	Cast of object to inappropriate type.
ClassNotFoundException	Unable to load the requested class.
CloneNotSupportedException	Object does not implement the `cloneable` interface.
Exception	Root class of the exception hierarchy.
IllegalAccessException	Class is not accessible.
IllegalArgumentException	Method receives an illegal argument.
IllegalMonitorStateException	Improper monitor state (thread synchronization).
IllegalThreadStateException	The thread is in an improper state for the requested operation.
IndexOutOfBoundsException	Index is out of bounds.
InstantiationException	Attempt to create an instance of the abstract class.
InterruptedException	Thread interrupted.

10

EXCEPTION HANDLING

continues

Table 10.1. continued

Exception	Cause
NegativeArraySizeException	Array size is less than zero.
NoSuchMethodException	Unable to resolve method.
NullPointerException	Attempt to access a null object member.
NumberFormatException	Unable to convert the string to a number.
RuntimeException	Base class for many java.lang exceptions.
SecurityException	Security settings do not allow the operation.
StringIndexOutOfBoundsException	Index is negative or greater than the size of the string.

Table 10.2. The java.lang errors.

Error	Cause
AbstractMethodError	Attempt to call an abstract method.
ClassCircularityError	This error is no longer used.
ClassFormatError	Invalid binary class format.
Error	Root class of the error hierarchy.
IllegalAccessError	Attempt to access an inaccessible object.
IncompatibleClassChangeError	Improper use of a class.
InstantiationError	Attempt to instantiate an abstract class.
InternalError	Error in the interpreter.
LinkageError	Error in class dependencies.
NoClassDefFoundError	Unable to find the class definition.
NoSuchFieldError	Unable to find the requested field.
NoSuchMethodError	Unable to find the requested method.
OutOfMemoryError	Out of memory.
StackOverflowError	Stack overflow.
ThreadDeath	Indicates that the thread will terminate. May be caught to perform cleanup. (If caught, must be rethrown.)
UnknownError	Unknown virtual machine error.
UnsatisfiedLinkError	Unresolved links in the loaded class.
VerifyError	Unable to verify bytecode.
VirtualMachineError	Root class for virtual machine errors.

FIGURE 10.1.

The java.lang *exception hierarchy.*

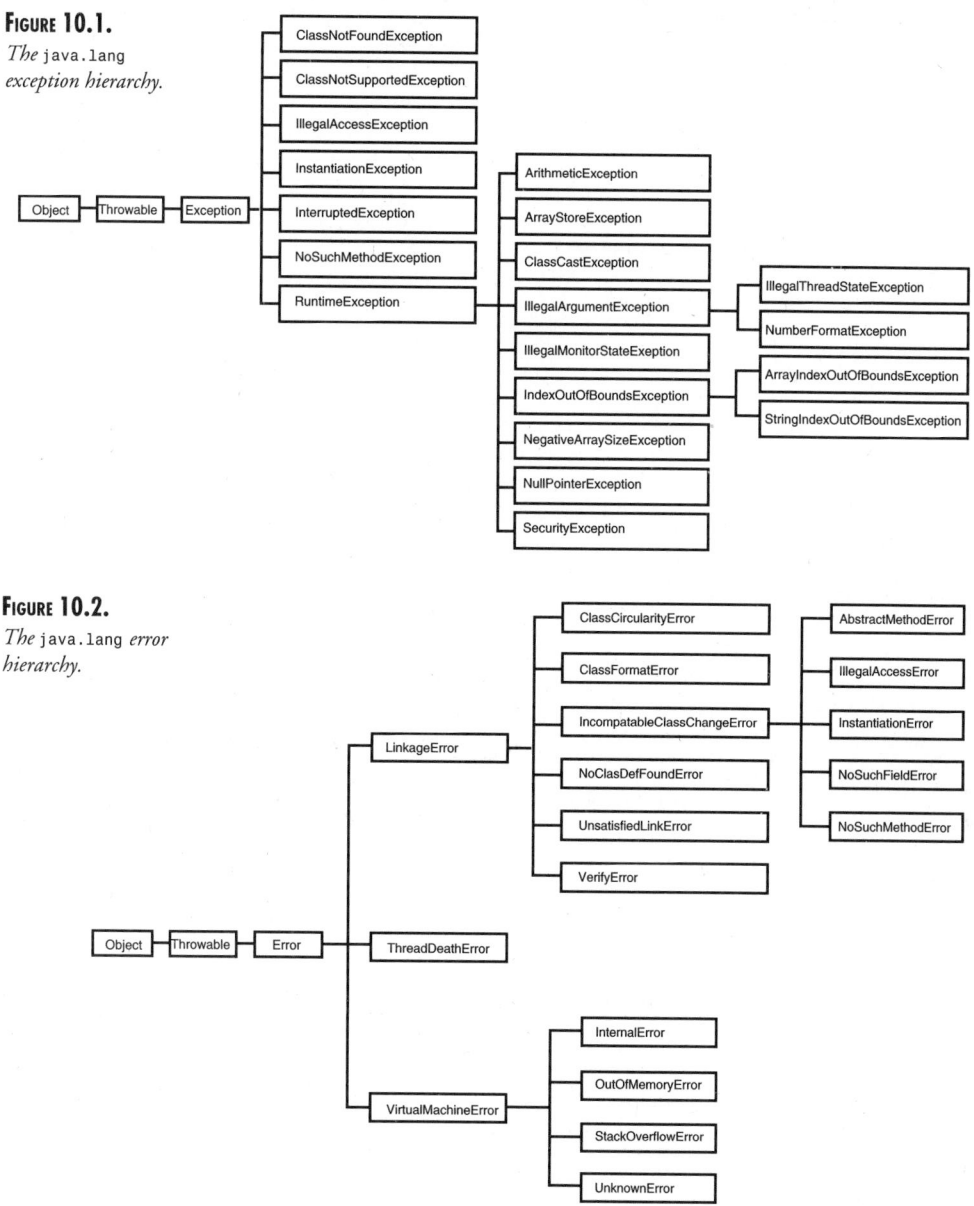

FIGURE 10.2.

The java.lang *error hierarchy.*

java.io Exceptions

The classes in java.io throw a variety of exceptions, as shown in Table 10.3 and Figure 10.3. Any classes that work with I/O are good candidates to throw recoverable exceptions. For example, activities such as opening files or writing to files are likely to fail from time to time. The classes of the java.io package do not throw errors at all.

Table 10.3. The java.io exceptions.

Exception	Cause
IOException	Root class for I/O exceptions.
EOFException	End of file.
FileNotFoundException	Unable to locate the file.
InterruptedIOException	I/O operation was interrupted. Contains a bytesTransferred member that indicates how many bytes were transferred before the operation was interrupted.
UTFDataFormatException	Malformed UTF-8 string.

FIGURE 10.3.

The java.io exception hierarchy.

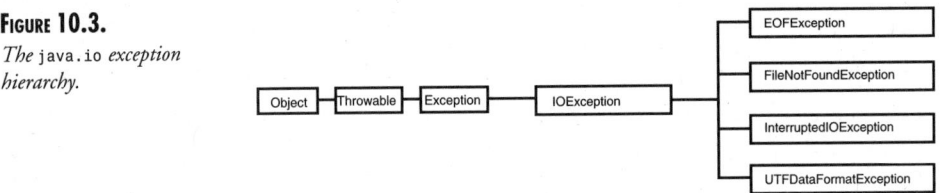

java.net Exceptions

The java.net package handles network communications. Its classes most often throw exceptions to indicate connect failures and the like. Table 10.4 and Figure 10.4 show the recoverable exceptions from the java.net package. The classes of the java.net package do not throw errors at all.

Table 10.4. The java.net exceptions.

Exception	Cause
MalformedURLException	Unable to interpret URL.
ProtocolException	Socket class protocol error.
SocketException	Socket class exception.
UnknownHostException	Unable to resolve the host name.
UnknownServiceException	Connection does not support the service.

FIGURE 10.4.
The java.net *exception hierarchy.*

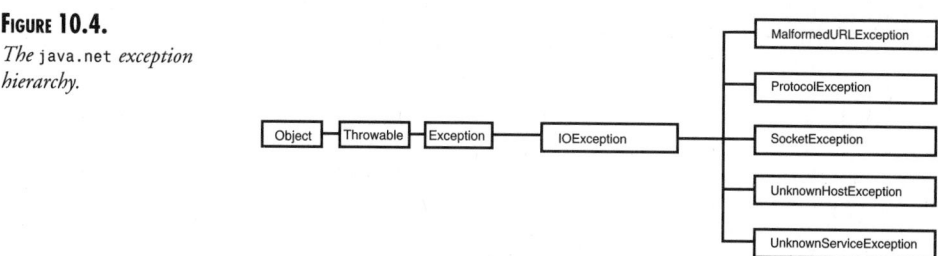

java.awt Exceptions

The AWT classes have members that throw one error and one exception:

- AWTException (exception in AWT)

- AWTError (error in AWT)

java.util Exceptions

The classes of java.util throw the following exceptions:

- EmptyStackException (no objects on stack)

- NoSuchElementException (no more objects in collection)

Built-In Exceptions

In the example in Listing 10.4, you see how the *automatic* exceptions in Java work. This application creates a method and forces it to divide by zero. The method does not have to explicitly throw an exception because the division operator throws an exception when required.

Listing 10.4. An example of a built-in exception.

```
import java.io.* ;
import java.lang.Exception ;

public class DivideBy0 {

    public static void main( String[] args ) {

    int a = 2 ;
    int b = 3 ;
    int c = 5 ;
    int d = 0 ;
    int e = 1 ;
    int f = 3 ;
```

continues

10

Listing 10.4. continued

```
    try
        {
        System.out.println( a+"/"+b+" = "+div( a, b ) ) ;
        System.out.println( c+"/"+d+" = "+div( c, d ) ) ;
        System.out.println( e+"/"+f+" = "+div( e, f ) ) ;
        }
    catch( Exception except )
        {
        System.out.println( "Caught exception " +
                                except.getMessage() ) ;
        }
    }

    static int div( int a, int b ) {

        return (a/b) ;

    }

}
```

The output of this application is shown here:

```
2/3 = 0
Caught exception / by zero
```

The first call to `div()` works fine. The second call fails because of the divide-by-zero error. Even though the application did not specify it, an exception was thrown—and caught. So you can use arithmetic in your code without writing code that explicitly checks bounds.

Summary

The exception handling mechanism in Java allows your methods to report errors in a manner that cannot be ignored. Every exception that is thrown must be caught or the application terminates. Exceptions are actually class objects derived from the `Throwable` class. Therefore, exceptions combine data and methods; an exception object generally contains a string explaining what the error is.

Exception handling helps you combine error processing in one place. It uncouples the reporting of results and the reporting of errors. If you use exception handling, you can create much more powerful and robust code.

PART

III

IN THIS PART

The Standard Packages

Overview of the Standard Packages

by Michael Morrison

IN THIS CHAPTER

CHAPTER 11

Code reuse is one of the most significant benefits of using object-oriented design practices. Creating reusable, inheritable classes can save amazing amounts of time and energy—which in turn greatly boosts productivity. Java itself takes code reuse to heart in its implementation of a wide variety of standard objects available to Java programmers. The standard Java objects are known collectively as the Java *standard packages.*

The Java standard packages contain groups of related classes. Along with classes, the standard Java packages also include interfaces, exception definitions, and error definitions. Java is composed of six standard packages: the language package, the utilities package, the I/O package, the networking package, the windowing package, and the applet package. In this chapter, you learn what each package is and what classes and interfaces comprise each.

The Language Package

The Java language package, also known as `java.lang`, provides classes that make up the core of the Java language. The language package contains classes at the lowest level of the Java standard packages. For example, the `Object` class, from which all classes are derived, is located in the language package.

It's impossible to write a Java program without dealing with at least a few of the elements of the language package. You'll learn much more about the inner workings of the language package in the next chapter. The most important classes contained in the language package follow:

- The `Object` class
- Data type wrapper classes
- The `Math` class
- `String` classes
- `System` and `Runtime` classes
- Thread classes
- `Class` classes
- Exception-handling classes
- The `Process` class

The `Object` Class

The `Object` class is the superclass for all classes in Java. Because all classes are derived from `Object`, the methods defined in `Object` are shared by all classes. This results in a core set of methods that all Java classes are guaranteed to support. `Object` includes methods for making copies of an object, testing objects for equality, and converting the value of an object to a string.

Data Type Wrapper Classes

The fundamental data types (`int`, `char`, `float`, and so on) in Java are not implemented as classes. It is frequently useful, however, to know more information about a fundamental type than just its value. By implementing class wrappers for the fundamental types, additional information can be maintained—you can also define methods that act on the types. The data type wrapper classes serve as class versions of the fundamental data types and are named similarly to the types they wrap. For example, the type wrapper for `int` is the `Integer` class. Following are the Java data type wrapper classes:

- `Boolean`
- `Character`
- `Double`
- `Float`
- `Integer`
- `Long`

Type wrappers are also useful because many of Java's utility classes require classes as parameters, not simple types. It is worth pointing out that type wrappers and simple types are *not* interchangeable. However, you can get a simple type from a wrapper through a simple method call, which you learn about in the next chapter.

The Math Class

The `Math` class serves as a grouping of mathematical functions and constants. It is interesting to note that all the variables and methods in `Math` are `static` and that the `Math` class itself is `final`. This means that you can't derive new classes from `Math`. Additionally, you can't instantiate the `Math` class. It's best to think of the `Math` class as just a conglomeration of methods and constants for performing mathematical computations.

The `Math` class includes the `E` and `PI` constants, methods for determining the absolute value of a number, methods for calculating trigonometric functions, and minimum and maximum methods, among others.

String Classes

For various reasons (mostly security related), Java implements text strings as classes, rather than forcing the programmer to use character arrays. The two Java classes that represent strings are `String` and `StringBuffer`. The `String` class is useful for working with constant strings that can't change in value or length. The `StringBuffer` class is used to work with strings of varying value and length.

The System and Runtime Classes

The System and Runtime classes provide a means for your programs to access system and runtime environment resources. Like the Math class, the System class is final and is entirely composed of static variables and methods. The System class basically provides a system-independent programming interface to system resources. Examples of system resources include the standard input and output streams, System.in and System.out, which typically model the keyboard and monitor.

The Runtime class provides direct access to the runtime environment. An example of a runtime routine is the freeMemory() method, which returns the amount of free system memory available.

Thread Classes

Java is a multithreaded environment and provides various classes for managing and working with threads. Following are the classes and interfaces used in conjunction with multithreaded programs:

- Thread: Used to create a thread of execution in a program.
- ThreadDeath: Used to clean up after a thread has finished execution.
- ThreadGroup: Useful for organizing a group of threads.
- Runnable: Provides an alternative means of creating a thread without subclassing the Thread class.

Threads and multithreading are covered in detail in Chapter 9, "Threads and Multithreading."

Class Classes

Java provides two classes for working with classes: Class and ClassLoader. The Class class provides runtime information for a class, such as the name, type, and parent superclass. Class is useful for querying a class for runtime information, such as the class name. The ClassLoader class provides a means to load classes into the runtime environment. ClassLoader is useful for loading classes from a file or for loading distributed classes across a network connection.

Exception-Handling Classes

Runtime error handling is a very important facility in any programming environment. Java provides the following classes for dealing with runtime errors:

- Throwable: Provides low-level error-handling capabilities such as an execution stack list.
- Exception: Derived from Throwable to provide the base level of functionality for all the exception classes defined in the Java system. Used to handle normal errors.

■ Error: Derived from Throwable (as is the Exception class) but is used to handle abnormal errors that aren't expected to occur. Very few Java programs worry with the Error class; most use the Exception class to handle runtime errors.

Error handling with exceptions is covered in detail in Chapter 10, "Exception Handling."

The Process Class

Java supports system processes with a single class, Process. The Process class represents generic system processes that are created when you use the Runtime class to execute system commands.

The Utilities Package

The Java utilities package, also known as java.util, provides various classes that perform different utility functions. The utilities package includes a class for working with dates, a set of data structure classes, a class for generating random numbers, and a string tokenizer class, among others. You'll learn much more about the classes that make up the utilities package in Chapter 13, "The Utilities Package." The most important classes contained in the utilities package follow:

■ The Date class
■ Data structure classes
■ The Random class
■ The StringTokenizer class
■ The Properties class
■ The Observer classes

The Date Class

The Date class represents a calendar date and time in a system-independent fashion. The Date class provides methods for retrieving the current date and time as well as computing days of the week and month.

Data Structure Classes

The Java data structure classes and interfaces implement popular data structures for storing data. The data structure classes and interfaces are as follows:

■ BitSet: Represents a set of bits, also known as a *bitfield*.
■ Dictionary: An abstract class that provides a lookup mechanism for mapping keys to values.

- ■ `Hashtable`: Derived from `Dictionary` to provide additional support for working with keys and values.
- ■ `Properties`: Derived from `Hashtable` to provide the additional functionality of being readable and writable to and from streams.
- ■ `Vector`: Implements an array that can dynamically grow.
- ■ `Stack`: Derived from `Vector` to implement a classic stack of last-in-first-out (LIFO) objects.
- ■ `Enumeration`: This interface specifies a set of methods for counting (iterating) through a set of values.

The Random Class

Many programs, especially programs that model the real world, require some degree of randomness. Java provides randomness with the `Random` class. The `Random` class implements a random-number generator by providing a stream of pseudo-random numbers. A slot-machine program is a good example of one that would make use of the `Random` class.

The StringTokenizer Class

The `StringTokenizer` class provides a means of converting text strings into individual tokens. By specifying a set of delimiters, you can parse text strings into tokens using the `StringTokenizer` class. String tokenization is useful in a wide variety of programs, from compilers to text-based adventure games.

The Observer Classes

The model-view paradigm is becoming increasingly popular in object-oriented programming. This model divides a program into data and views on the data. Java supports this model with the `Observable` class and the `Observer` interface. The `Observable` class is subclassed to define the observable data in a program. This data is then connected to one or more observer classes. The observer classes are implementations of the `Observer` interface. When an `Observable` object changes state, it notifies all its observers of the change.

The I/O Package

The Java I/O package, also known as `java.io`, provides classes with support for reading and writing data to and from different input and output devices—including files. The I/O package includes classes for inputting streams of data, outputting streams of data, working with files, and tokenizing streams of data. You'll learn a lot more about the classes that make up the I/O package in Chapter 14, "The I/O Package." The most important classes contained in the I/O package follow:

- Input stream classes
- Output stream classes
- File classes
- The StreamTokenizer class

Input Stream Classes

Java uses input streams to handle reading data from an input source. An *input source* can be a file, a string, memory, or anything else that contains data. The input stream classes follow:

- InputStream
- BufferedInputStream
- ByteArrayInputStream
- DataInputStream
- FileInputStream
- FilterInputStream
- LineNumberInputStream
- PipedInputStream
- PushbackInputStream
- SequenceInputStream
- StringBufferInputStream

The InputStream class is an abstract class that serves as the base class for all input streams. The InputStream class defines an interface for reading streamed bytes of data, finding out the number of bytes available for reading, and moving the stream position pointer, among other things. All the other input streams provide support for reading data from different types of input devices.

Output Stream Classes

Output streams are the counterpart to input streams; they handle writing data to an output source. Similar to input sources, *output sources* include files, strings, memory, and anything else that can contain data. The output stream classes defined in java.io follow:

- OutputStream
- BufferedOutputStream

- ByteArrayOutputStream
- DataOutputStream
- FileOutputStream
- FilterOutputStream
- PipedOutputStream
- PrintStream

The OutputStream class is an abstract class that serves as the base class for all output streams. OutputStream defines an interface for writing streamed bytes of data to an output source. All the other output streams provide support for writing data to different output devices. Data written by an output stream is formatted to be read by an input stream.

File Classes

Files are the most widely used method of data storage in computer systems. Java supports files with two different classes: File and RandomAccessFile. The File class provides an abstraction for files that takes into account system-dependent features. The File class keeps up with information about a file including the location where it is stored and how it can be accessed. The File class has no methods for reading and writing data to and from a file; it is useful only for querying and modifying the attributes of a file. In actuality, you can think of the File class data as representing a filename, and the class methods as representing operating system commands that act on filenames.

The RandomAccessFile class provides a variety of methods for reading and writing data to and from a file. RandomAccessFile contains many different methods for reading and writing different types of information, namely the data type wrappers.

The StreamTokenizer Class

The StreamTokenizer class provides the functionality for converting an input stream of data into a stream of tokens. StreamTokenizer provides a set of methods for defining the lexical syntax of tokens. Stream tokenization can be useful in parsing streams of textual data.

The Networking Package

The Java networking package, also known as java.net, contains classes that allow you to perform a wide range of network communications. The networking package includes specific support for URLs, TCP sockets, IP addresses, and UDP sockets. The Java networking classes make it easy and straightforward to implement client/server Internet solutions in Java. You

Overview of the Standard Packages

CHAPTER 11

231

11

OVERVIEW OF THE
STANDARD
PACKAGES

learn much more about the classes that make up the networking package in Chapter 15, "The Networking Package." The classes included in the networking package follow:

- The InetAddress class
- URL classes
- Socket classes
- The ContentHandler class

The InetAddress Class

The InetAddress class models an Internet IP address and provides methods for getting information about the address. For example, InetAddress contains methods for retrieving either the text name or raw IP representation of the host represented by the address. InetAddress also contains static methods that allow you to find out about hosts without actually creating an InetAddress object.

URL Classes

The URL classes are used to represent and interact with Uniform Resource Locators (URLs), which are references to information on the Web. Following are the URL classes included in the networking package:

- URL: Represents a Uniform Resource Locator. URL objects are constant, meaning that their values cannot change once they have been created. In this way, URL objects more closely represent physical URLs, which are also constant.

- URLConnection: An abstract class that defines the overhead necessary to facilitate a connection through an URL. This class must be subclassed to provide functionality for a specific type of URL connection.

- URLStreamHandler: An abstract class that defines the mechanism required to open streams based on URLs.

- URLEncoder: Allows you to convert a string of text information into a format suitable for communication through a URL.

Socket Classes

The socket classes are perhaps the most important classes contained in the networking package. They provide the entire framework for performing network communication through a couple of different approaches. The classes that comprise Java's socket support follow:

- SocketImpl: An abstract class that defines a base level of functionality required by all sockets. This functionality includes both member variables and a substantial collection of methods. Specific socket implementations are derived from SocketImpl.

- `Socket`: Provides client-side streamed socket support. *Streamed sockets* are sockets that communicate in real time over a live connection with a high degree of reliability.

- `ServerSocket`: Used to implement the server side of streamed socket support.

- `DatagramSocket`: Contains everything necessary to perform datagram socket communication. A *datagram socket* is a socket that sends out packets of information with little regard for reliability or timing. Unlike streamed sockets, datagram sockets don't rely on a live connection, meaning that they send and receive data whenever it is convenient. Data being transferred with a datagram socket must be encapsulated by a `DatagramPacket` object.

- `DatagramPacket`: Includes information critical to a packet of information being transferred with a datagram socket.

The `ContentHandler` Class

The `ContentHandler` class serves as a framework for handling different Internet data types. For example, you can write a content handler to process and display a proprietary file format. To do this, you would derive a class from `ContentHandler` and write code to build an object from a stream of data representing the object type.

The Windowing Package

The Java windowing package, also known as `java.awt`, consists of classes that provide a wide range of graphics and user interface features. This package includes classes representing graphical interface elements such as windows, dialog boxes, menus, buttons, checkboxes, scroll bars, and text fields, as well as general graphics elements such as fonts. You learn much more about the classes in the windowing package in Chapter 16, "The Windowing (AWT) Package." The most important classes included in the windowing package follow:

- Graphical classes
- Layout manager classes
- Font classes
- Dimension classes
- The `MediaTracker` class

NOTE

The windowing package is also often referred to as the Abstract Windowing Toolkit (AWT), which is where the name `java.awt` comes from.

Graphical Classes

The graphical classes are all based on serving a particular graphical user input or display need. For this reason, the graphical classes are often indispensable in applet programming. The graphical classes include support for everything from checkboxes and menus to canvases and color representations.

> **NOTE**
>
> Although I mention the graphical classes here only in terms of Java applets, these classes are equally useful in graphical standalone Java applications. Just keep in mind that standalone applications must create their own frame window to house any graphical elements; applets can simply use the applet window that has been allotted on the containing Web page.

One of the most important GUI classes is the `Graphics` class, which serves as an all-purpose graphical output class capable of performing all kinds of different drawing functions. The `Graphics` class is ultimately responsible for all graphical output generated by a Java applet.

The `Component` class is another very fundamental graphical class and serves as the parent for many of the other graphical classes. It is used this way primarily because `Component` provides all the overhead necessary for a basic graphical element.

Layout Manager Classes

The layout manager classes provide a framework for controlling the physical layout of GUI elements. For example, you may want to have a row of buttons arranged in a certain way across the top of an applet window. You would use a layout manager to accomplish this. Following are the layout manager classes implemented in the windowing package:

- `BorderLayout`: Arranges graphical elements, or components, along a window border, with one element in each position (north, south, east, west, and center).

- `CardLayout`: Arranges components on top of each other like a stack of cards; you can flip through the "cards" to display different components.

- `FlowLayout`: Arranges components from left to right across a window until no more will fit, in which case they are wrapped around to another line.

- `GridLayout`: Arranges equally sized components in a grid with a specific number of rows and columns.

- `GridBagLayout`: Similar to the `GridLayout` class except that the components in `GridBagLayout` don't have to be the same size, resulting in much more flexibility.

All the layout classes are derived from the LayoutManager interface, which defines the core functionality required of a graphical layout manager.

Font Classes

The font classes consist of the Font class and the FontMetrics class. The Font class represents graphical font objects with attributes such as name, size, and style. Furthermore, Font objects can also be made **bold** or *italic*. The FontMetrics class provides a means to find information about the size of a font. For example, you can use a FontMetrics object to ascertain the height of a font, or something more specific such as a font's line spacing (leading).

Dimension Classes

The dimension classes provide a convenient way to represent different graphical dimensions in Java. The following dimension classes are defined in the windowing package:

- Dimension: Represents the basic rectangular dimensions of a graphical element. The class includes two public member variables for storing the width and height of a rectangular object.
- Rectangle: Similar to Dimension, except that Rectangle also includes the x and y coordinates of the upper-left corner of a graphical element. In other words, the Rectangle class keeps up with the dimension of a graphical element as well as its position.
- Point: Similar to the Rectangle class, except that Point keeps up only with an xy position.
- Polygon: Represents a polygon, which is basically a series of connected points.

The MediaTracker Class

The MediaTracker class provides a means to track when media resources have finished transmitting across a network connection. Currently, the MediaTracker class supports only the tracking of images, but a future release of Java will no doubt add support for sounds and other media types as they gain popularity. The MediaTracker class serves a very useful purpose for applets because it allows them to know when a particular image is ready to be displayed. For some applets, this knowledge is critical.

The Applet Package

The Java applet package, also known as java.applet, contains only one class: Applet. The Applet class contains all the overhead required of a Java applet—which is quite a lot. The Applet class includes methods for accessing applet parameters, loading images, and playing sounds, along with plenty of general behind-the-scenes applet support. One other interesting component of the applet package is the AudioClip interface, which defines the basic functionality required of a Java audio clip.

Summary

This chapter provided a thumbnail sketch of the contents of the six Java standard packages: the language package, the utilities package, the I/O package, the networking package, the windowing package, and the applet package. Although you didn't learn a lot of gritty details, or how to use any of these classes in a real program, you should now have a general sense of what these packages can do. The Java standard packages provide a rich set of classes for overcoming a wide variety of programming obstacles.

A common problem when using programming environments that have a lot of support libraries is knowing what functionality is provided and what functionality you must write yourself. This chapter has given you an idea of what standard classes you can reuse in your own Java programs, and what classes you will have to implement yourself.

Having seen what each package in the Java standard packages contains, you're probably eager to start learning how to use the classes in each package. The next six chapters focus on the packages that make up the Java standard packages.

The Language Package

by Michael Morrison

IN THIS CHAPTER

The Java language package is the heart of the Java language. In this chapter, you learn more about some of the classes that make up the language package (java.lang). You'll find that many of the classes in the language package are indispensable in writing Java programs.

The language package contains many classes, each with a variety of member variables and methods. You don't learn about every class and every method in this chapter (that would simply be too much material to cover in a single chapter). Rather, you focus on the most important classes in the language package; classes that come in the most useful as you begin developing your own Java classes. Please note that although the multithreading and error-handling classes are part of the language package, they aren't covered in this chapter; Chapter 9, "Threads and Multithreading" and Chapter 10, "Exception Handling," are devoted to these classes.

The Object Class

The Object class is probably the most important of all Java classes, simply because it is the superclass of all Java classes. It is important to have a solid understanding of the Object class because all the classes you develop inherit the variables and methods of Object. The Object class implements the following important methods:

- ▧ `Object clone()`
- ▧ `boolean equals(Object obj)`
- ▧ `int hashCode()`
- ▧ `final Class getClass()`
- ▧ `String toString()`

The clone() Method

```
Object clone()
```

The Object clone() method creates a clone of the object it is called on. clone() creates and allocates memory for the new object being copied to. clone() actually creates a new object and then copies the contents of the calling object to the new object. An example of using the clone() method follows:

```
Circle circle1 = new Circle(1.0, 3.5, 4.2);
Circle circle2 = circle1.clone();
```

In this example, the circle1 object is created, but the circle2 object is only declared. circle2 is not created by using the new operator; it is created when circle1 calls the clone() method to create a clone of itself.

The equals() Method

```
boolean equals(Object obj)
```

The equals() method compares two objects for equality. equals() is applicable only when both objects have been stored in a hash table.

The hashCode() Method

```
int hashCode()
```

The hashCode()method returns the hashcode value for an object. *Hashcodes* are integers that uniquely represent objects in the Java system.

The getClass() Method

```
final Class getClass()
```

The getClass()method returns the runtime class information for an object in the form of a Class object. The Class object keeps up with runtime class information such as the name of a class and the parent superclass.

The toString() Method

```
String toString()
```

The toString() method returns a string representing the value of an object. Because the value of an object varies depending on the class type, it is assumed that each class will override the toString() method to display information specific to that class. The information returned by toString() can be very valuable for determining the internal state of an object when debugging.

Data Type Wrapper Classes

The data type wrapper classes provide object versions of the fundamental Java data types. Type wrapping is important because many Java classes and methods operate on classes rather than fundamental types. Furthermore, by creating object versions of the simple data types, it is possible to add useful member functions for each type. Following are the type wrapper classes supported by Java:

- Boolean
- Character
- Double

- Float
- Integer
- Long

Although each wrapper implements methods specific to each data type, a handful of methods are applicable to all the wrappers. These methods follow:

- `ClassType(`*type*`)`
- `type typeValue()`
- `int hashCode()`
- `String toString()`
- `boolean equals(Object `*obj*`)`
- `static boolean valueOf(String `*s*`)`

> **NOTE**
>
> Actually, the `valueOf()` method isn't implemented in the `Character` class, but it is implemented in all the other wrapper classes.

The `ClassType()` Method

```
ClassType(type)
```

The `ClassType()` method is actually the constructor for each class. The wrapper constructors take as their only parameter the type of data they are wrapping. This enables you to create a type wrapper from a fundamental type. For example, you can use the constructor for the `Character` class like this:

```
Character c1 = new Character('x');
```

The `typeValue()` Method

```
type typeValue()
```

The `typeValue()` method is used to get the fundamental type back from a wrapper. `typeValue()` returns a value of the same type as the fundamental type it wraps. Following is an example of how a fundamental type can be extracted from a wrapper object:

```
char c2 = c1.charValue();
```

> **NOTE**
>
> Remember that fundamental types are not represented in Java by classes or objects. Data type wrapper classes provide a means of representing a fundamental type as an object, which is often useful. Wrapper classes are different from other Java classes in that their only purpose is to allow fundamental types to be represented as objects. You can easily distinguish wrapper classes from primitive types because the first letter of wrapper class names is always capitalized.

The hashCode() Method

```
int hashCode()
```

The hashCode() method returns the hashcode for a type wrapper object. This hashCode() method is simply an overridden version of the hashCode() method contained in the Object class.

The toString() Method

```
String toString()
```

The toString() method is used to get a string representation of the internal state of an object. toString() is typically overridden in each class so that it reflects unique state implementations. Following is an example of how you can output the state of a wrapper variable using toString():

```
System.out.println(c1.toString());
```

The equals() Method

```
boolean equals(Object obj)
```

The equals() method is used to test for equality between two wrapper objects. This is the same equals() method that is implemented in Object and inherited by all other objects in Java.

The valueOf() Method

```
static boolean valueOf(String s)
```

The valueOf() method is implemented in all the type wrappers except Character. valueOf(), which is static, is used to convert a string to a value of a particular wrapper type. valueOf() parses the String parameter s and returns the value of it.

Now that you have an idea of what functionality all the wrapper classes share, it's time to take a look at some of the specifics of each class.

The Boolean Class

The `Boolean` class wraps the `boolean` fundamental data type. `Boolean` implements only one method in addition to the common wrapper methods already mentioned: `getBoolean()`.

The getBoolean() Method

`static boolean getBoolean(String name)`

The `getBoolean()` method returns a type `boolean` that represents the boolean property value of the `String` parameter *name*. The *name* parameter refers to a property name that represents a boolean property value. Because `getBoolean()` is `static`, it is typically meant to be used without actually instantiating a `Boolean` object.

NOTE

Java properties are system variables that define the characteristics of the Java runtime environment. For example, there is a property called `os.name` that specifies the name of the operating system in which the Java runtime is executing. In my case, `os.name` is set to `"Windows 95"`.

Member Variables

The `Boolean` class also includes two `final static` (`constant`) data members: `TRUE` and `FALSE`. `TRUE` and `FALSE` represent the two possible states that the `Boolean` class can represent. It is important to note the difference between `true` and `false` and `Boolean.TRUE` and `Boolean.FALSE`. The first pair applies to `boolean` fundamental types; the second pair applies to `Boolean` classes; they cannot be interchanged.

The Character Class

The `Character` class wraps the `char` fundamental type and provides some useful methods for manipulating characters. The methods implemented by `Character`, beyond the common wrapper methods, follow:

- `static boolean isLowerCase(char ch)`
- `static boolean isUpperCase(char ch)`
- `static boolean isDigit(char ch)`
- `static boolean isSpace(char ch)`
- `static char toLowerCase(char ch)`
- `static char toUpperCase(char ch)`

- static int digit(char *ch*, int *radix*)
- static char forDigit(int *digit*, int *radix*)

All these methods are static, which means that they can be used without instantiating a Character object.

The isLowerCase() and isUpperCase() Methods

```
static boolean isLowerCase(char ch)
static boolean isUpperCase(char ch)
```

The isLowerCase() and isUpperCase() methods return whether or not a character is an upper-case or lowercase character. An example of using the isLowerCase() method follows:

```
Character c = new Character('g');
boolean isLower = Character.isLowerCase(c);
```

In this case, the boolean variable isLower is set to true because 'g' is a lowercase character.

The isDigit() Method

```
static boolean isDigit(char ch)
```

The isDigit()method simply returns whether or not a character is a digit (0 to 9). Following is an example of how to use the isDigit() method:

```
boolean isDigit = Character.isDigit('7');
```

The boolean variable isDigit is set to true here because '7' is in fact a numeric digit.

The isSpace() Method

```
static boolean isSpace(char ch)
```

The isSpace() method returns whether or not a character is whitespace. (*Whitespace* is defined as any combination of the space, tab, newline, carriage return, or linefeed characters.) Following is an example of how to use isSpace():

```
boolean isSpace = Character.isSpace('\t');
```

In this example, the isSpace boolean variable is set to true because the tab ('\t') character is considered whitespace.

The toLowerCase() and toUpperCase() Methods

```
static char toLowerCase(char ch)
static char toUpperCase(char ch)
```

The toLowerCase()and toUpperCase() methods convert a character to a lowercase or upper-case character. If a character is already lowercase and toLowerCase() is called, the character is not changed. Similarly, `toUpperCase()` does nothing to uppercase characters. Following are a few examples of using these methods:

```
char c1 = Character.toUpperCase('g');
char c2 = Character.toLowerCase('M');
```

In the first example, c1 is converted from `'g'` to `'G'` with the call to the `toUpperCase()` method. In the second example, c2 is converted from `'M'` to `'m'` with the call to `toLowerCase()`.

The `digit()` Method

```
static int digit(char ch, int radix)
```

The `digit()` method returns the numeric (integer) value of a character digit in base 10. The *radix* parameter specifies the base of the character digit for conversion. If the character is not a valid digit, `-1` is returned. Following are a few examples of using the `digit()` method:

```
char c1 = '4';
char c2 = 'c';
int four = Character.digit(c1, 10);
int twelve = Character.digit(c2, 16);
```

In the first example, the character `'4'` is converted to the integer number 4 using the `digit()` method. In the second example, the hexadecimal number represented by the character `'c'` is returned as the base 10 integer number 12.

The `forDigit()` Method

```
static char forDigit(int digit, int radix)
```

The `forDigit()` method performs the reverse of the `digit()` method: it returns the character representation of an integer digit. Once again, *radix* specifies the base of the integer number. Following is an example of how to use `forDigit()`:

```
int i = 9;
char c = Character.forDigit(i, 10);
```

In this example, the integer number 9 is converted to the character `'9'` by the `forDigit()` method.

Member Variables

The `Character` class provides two `final static` data members for specifying the radix limits for conversions: `MIN_RADIX` and `MAX_RADIX`. The radix for a number is its base, such as binary, octal, or hexadecimal. These common radixes have values of 2, 8, and 16, respectively. `MIN_RADIX` specifies the minimum radix (base 2) for performing numeric-to-character conversions and vice-versa. Likewise, `MAX_RADIX` specifies the maximum radix (base 36) for conversions.

The Integer and Long Classes

The `Integer` and `Long` classes wrap the fundamental integer types `int` and `long` and provide a variety of methods for working with integer numbers. The methods implemented by `Integer` follow:

- `static int parseInt(String s, int radix)`

- `static int parseInt(String s)`

- `long longValue()`

- `float floatValue()`

- `double doubleValue()`

- `static Integer getInteger(String name)`

- `static Integer getInteger(String name, int val)`

- `static Integer getInteger(String name, Integer val)`

The parseInt() Methods

```
static int parseInt(String s, int radix)
static int parseInt(String s)
```

The `parseInt()` methods parse strings for an integer value and return the value as an `int`. The version of `parseInt()` with the `radix` parameter enables you to specify the base of the integer; the other version of `parseInt()` assumes a base of 10.

The longValue(), floatValue(), and doubleValue() Methods

```
long longValue()
float floatValue()
double doubleValue()
```

The `longValue()`, `floatValue()`, and `doubleValue()` methods return the values of an integer converted to the appropriate type. For example, the following code shows how to convert an integer to a double:

```
Integer i = new Integer(17);
float f = i.floatValue();
```

In this example, the value of the `Integer` variable `i` is converted to a `float` value and stored in the `float` variable `f`. The result is that the `Integer` value `17` is converted to the `float` value `17.0`.

The getInteger() Methods

```
static Integer getInteger(String name)
static Integer getInteger(String name, int val)
static Integer getInteger(String name, Integer val)
```

The getInteger() methods return an integer property value specified by the String property name parameter *name*. Notice that all three of the getInteger() methods are static, which means that you don't have to instantiate an Integer object to use these methods. The differences between these methods is what happens if the integer property isn't found. The first version returns 0 if the property isn't found, the second version returns the int parameter val, and the last version returns the Integer object value val.

Member Variables

The Integer class also includes two final static (constant) data members: MINVALUE and MAXVALUE. MINVALUE and MAXVALUE specify the smallest and largest numbers that can be represented by an Integer object.

The Long class is similar to the Integer class except that it wraps the fundamental type long. Long actually implements similar methods as Int, with the exception that they act on long-type numbers rather than int-type numbers.

Floating-Point Classes

The Float and Double classes wrap the fundamental floating-point types float and double. These two classes provide a group of methods for working with floating-point numbers. The methods implemented by the Float class follow:

- ◼ boolean isNaN()
- ◼ static boolean isNaN(float *v*)
- ◼ boolean isInfinite()
- ◼ static boolean isInfinite(float *v*)
- ◼ int intValue()
- ◼ long longValue()
- ◼ double doubleValue()
- ◼ static int floatToIntBits(float *value*)
- ◼ static float intBitsToFloat(int *bits*)

The isNaN() Methods

```
boolean isNaN()
static boolean isNaN(float v)
```

The isNaN() method returns whether or not the Float value is the special not-a-number (NaN) value. The first version of isNaN() operates on the value of the calling Float object. The second version is static and takes the float to test as its parameter, *v*.

The isInfinite() Methods

```
boolean isInfinite()
static boolean isInfinite(float v)
```

The isInfinite() method returns whether or not the Float value is infinite, which is represented by the special NEGATIVE_INFINITY and POSITIVE_INFINITY final static member variables. Like the isNaN() method, isInfinite() comes in two versions: a class value version and a static version that takes a float as an argument.

The intValue(), longValue(), and doubleValue() Methods

```
int intValue()
long longValue()
double doubleValue()
```

The intValue(), longValue(), and doubleValue() methods return the values of a floating-point number converted to the appropriate type. For example, the following code shows how to convert a Float to a long:

```
Float f = new Float(5.237);
long l = f.longValue();
```

In this example, the value of the Float variable f is converted to a long and stored in the long variable l. This action results in the floating-point value 5.237 being converted to the long value 5.

The floatToIntBits() and intBitsToFloat() Methods

```
static int floatToIntBits(float value)
static float intBitsToFloat(int bits)
```

The last two methods implemented by the Float class are floatToIntBits() and intBitsToFloat(). The floatToIntBits() and intBitsToFloat() methods convert floating-point values to their integer bit representations and back.

Member Variables

The Float class also has a group of final static (constant) data members: MINVALUE, MAXVALUE, NEGATIVE_INFINITY, POSITIVE_INFINITY, and NaN. MINVALUE and MAXVALUE specify the smallest and largest numbers that can be represented by a Float object. NEGATIVE_INFINITY and POSITIVE_INFINITY represent negative and positive infinity, while NaN represents the special not-a-number condition.

The Double class is very similar to the Float class. The only difference is that Double wraps the fundamental type double instead of float. Double implements similar methods as Float, with the exception that the methods act on double rather than float-type numbers.

The Math Class

The Math class contains many invaluable mathematical functions along with a few useful constants. The Math class isn't intended to be instantiated; it is basically just a holding class for mathematical functions. Additionally, the Math class is declared as final—you can't derive from it. The most useful methods implemented by the Math class follow:

- `static double sin(double a)`
- `static double cos(double a)`
- `static double tan(double a)`
- `static double asin(double a)`
- `static double acos(double a)`
- `static double atan(double a)`
- `static double exp(double a)`
- `static double log(double a)`
- `static double sqrt(double a)`
- `static double pow(double a, double b)`
- `static double ceil(double a)`
- `static double floor(double a)`
- `static int round(float a)`
- `static long round(double a)`
- `static double rint(double a)`
- `static double atan2(double a, double b)`
- `static synchronized double random()`
- `static int abs(int a)`
- `static long abs(long a)`
- `static float abs(float a)`
- `static double abs(double a)`
- `static int min(int a, int b)`
- `static long min(long a, long b)`
- `static float min(float a, float b)`
- `static double min(double a, double b)`
- `static int max(int a, int b)`
- `static long max(long a, long b)`

■ `static float max(float a, float b)`

■ `static double max(double a, double b)`

Trigonometric Methods

```
static double sin(double a)
static double cos(double a)
static double tan(double a)
static double asin(double a)
static double acos(double a)
static double atan(double a)
```

The trigonometric methods `sin()`, `cos()`, `tan()`, `asin()`, `acos()`, and `atan()` perform the standard trigonometric functions on `double` values. All the angles used in the trigonometric functions are specified in radians. Following is an example of calculating the sine of an angle:

```
double dSine = Math.sin(Math.PI / 2);
```

Notice in the example that the `PI` constant member of the `Math` class was used in the call to the `sin()` method. You learn about the `PI` constant member variable of `Math` at the end of this section.

The `exp()`, `log()`, `sqrt()`, and `pow()` Methods

```
static double exp(double a)
static double log(double a)
static double sqrt(double a)
static double pow(double a, double b)
```

The `exp()` method returns the exponential number E raised to the power of the `double` parameter a. Similarly, the `log()` method returns the natural logarithm (base E) of the number passed in the parameter a. The `sqrt()` method returns the square root of the parameter number a. The `pow()` method returns the result of raising a number to a power. `pow()` returns a raised to the power of b. Following are some examples of using these `Math` methods:

```
double d1 = 12.3;
double d2 = Math.exp(d1);
double d3 = Math.log(d1);
double d4 = Math.sqrt(d1);
double d5 = Math.pow(d1, 3.0);
```

The `ceil()`, `floor()`, `round()`, and `rint()` Methods

```
static double ceil(double a)
static double floor(double a)
static int round(float a)
static long round(double a)
static double rint(double a)
```

The `ceil()` and `floor()` methods return the "ceiling" and "floor" for the passed parameter a. The *ceiling* is the smallest whole number greater than or equal to a; the *floor* is the largest whole

12

THE LANGUAGE PACKAGE

number less than or equal to *a*. The round() methods round float and double numbers to the nearest integer value, which is returned as type int or long. Both round() methods work by adding 0.5 to the number and then returning the largest integer that is less than or equal to the number. The rint() method returns an integral value, similar to round(), that remains a type double. Following are some examples of using these methods:

```
double d1 = 37.125;
double d2 = Math.ceil(d1);
double d3 = Math.floor(d1);
int i = Math.round((float)d1);
long l = Math.round(d1);
double d4 = Math.rint(d1);
```

Notice in the first example of using round() that the double value d1 must be explicitly cast to a float. This is necessary because this version of round() takes a float and returns an int.

The atan2() Method

```
static double atan2(double a, double b)
```

The atan2() method converts rectangular coordinates to polar coordinates. The double parameters *a* and *b* represent the rectangular x and y coordinates to be converted to polar coordinates, which are returned together as a single double value.

The random() Method

```
static synchronized double random()
```

The random() method generates a pseudo-random number between 0.0 and 1.0. random() is useful for generating random floating-point numbers. To generate random numbers of different types, you should use the Random class, which is located in the utilities package, java.util. The utilities package, including the Random class, is covered in the next chapter.

The abs() Methods

```
static int abs(int a)
static long abs(long a)
static float abs(float a)
static double abs(double a)
```

The abs() methods return the absolute value of numbers of varying types. There are versions of abs() for the following types: int, long, float, and double. Following is an example of using the abs() method to find the absolute value of an integer number:

```
int i = -5, j;
j = Math.abs(i);
```

The `min()` and `max()` Methods

```
static int min(int a, int b)
static long min(long a, long b)
static float min(float a, float b)
static double min(double a, double b)
static int max(int a, int b)
static long max(long a, long b)
static float max(float a, float b)
static double max(double a, double b)
```

The `min()` and `max()` methods return the minimum and maximum numbers given a pair of numbers to compare. Like the `abs()` methods, the `min()` and `max()` methods come in different versions for handling the types `int`, `long`, `float`, and `double`. Following are some examples of using the `min()` and `max()` methods:

```
double d1 = 14.2, d2 = 18.5;
double d3 = Math.min(d1, d2);
double d4 = Math.max(d1, 11.2);
```

Beyond the rich set of methods provided by the `Math` class, there are also a couple of important constant member variables: `E` and `PI`. The `E` member represents the exponential number (`2.7182...`) used in exponential calculations. The `PI` member represents the value of Pi (`3.1415...`).

String Classes

Text strings in Java are represented with classes rather than character arrays (as they are in C and C++). The two classes that model strings in Java are `String` and `StringBuffer`. The reason for having two string classes is that the `String` class represents constant (immutable) strings and the `StringBuffer` class represents variable (mutable) strings.

The `String` Class

The `String` class is used to represent constant strings. The `String` class has less overhead than `StringBuffer`, which means that you should use it if you know that a string is constant. The constructors for the `String` class follow:

- `String()`
- `String(String value)`
- `String(char value[])`
- `String(char value[], int offset, int count)`
- `String(byte ascii[], int hibyte, int offset, int count)`
- `String(byte ascii[], int hibyte)`
- `String(StringBuffer buffer)`

It should be readily apparent from the number of constructors for `String` that there are many ways to create `String` objects. The first constructor simply creates a new string that is empty. All the other constructors create strings that are initialized in different ways from various types of text data. Following are examples of using some of the `String()` constructors to create `String` objects:

```
String s1 = new String();
String s2 = new String("Hello");
char cArray[] = {'H', 'o', 'w', 'd', 'y'};
String s3 = new String(cArray);
String s4 = new String(cArray, 1, 3);
```

In the first example, an empty `String` object (s1) is created. In the second example, a `String` object (s2) is created from a literal `String` value, `"Hello"`. The third example shows a `String` object (s3) being created from an array of characters. The fourth example shows a `String` object (s4) being created from a subarray of characters. The subarray is specified by passing 1 as the *offset* parameter and 3 as the *count* parameter. This means that the subarray of characters is to consist of the first three characters starting at one character into the array. The resulting subarray of characters in this case consists of the characters `'o'`, `'w'`, and `'d'`.

Once you have some `String` objects created, you are ready to work with them using some of the powerful methods implemented in the `String` class. Some of the most useful methods provided by the `String` class follow:

- ◼ `int length()`
- ◼ `char charAt(int index)`
- ◼ `boolean startsWith(String prefix)`
- ◼ `boolean startsWith(String prefix, int toffset)`
- ◼ `boolean endsWith(String suffix)`
- ◼ `int indexOf(int ch)`
- ◼ `int indexOf(int ch, int fromIndex)`
- ◼ `int indexOf(String str)`
- ◼ `int indexOf(String str, int fromIndex)`
- ◼ `int lastIndexOf(int ch)`
- ◼ `int lastIndexOf(int ch, int fromIndex)`
- ◼ `int lastIndexOf(String str)`
- ◼ `int lastIndexOf(String str, int fromIndex)`
- ◼ `String substring(int beginIndex)`
- ◼ `String substring(int beginIndex, int endIndex)`
- ◼ `boolean equals(Object anObject)`
- ◼ `boolean equalsIgnoreCase(String anotherString)`

- int compareTo(String *anotherString*)
- String concat(String *str*)
- String replace(char *oldChar*, char *newChar*)
- String trim()
- String toLowerCase()
- String toUpperCase()
- static String valueOf(Object *obj*)
- static String valueOf(char *data*[])
- static String valueOf(char *data*[], int *offset*, int *count*)
- static String valueOf(boolean *b*)
- static String valueOf(char *c*)
- static String valueOf(int *i*)
- static String valueOf(long *l*)
- static String valueOf(float *f*)
- static String valueOf(double *d*)

The length(), charAt(), startsWith(), and endsWith() Methods

```
int length()
char charAt(int index)
boolean startsWith(String prefix)
boolean startsWith(String prefix, int toffset)
boolean endsWith(String suffix)
```

The length() method simply returns the length of a string, which is the number of Unicode characters in the string. The charAt() method returns the character at a specific index of a string specified by the int parameter *index*. The startsWith() and endsWith() methods determine whether or not a string starts or ends with a prefix or suffix string, as specified by the *prefix* and *suffix* parameters. The second version of startsWith() enables you to specify an offset to begin looking for the string *prefix*. Following are some examples of using these methods:

```
String s1 = new String("This is a test string!");
int len = s1.length();
char c = s1.charAt(8);
boolean b1 = s1.startsWith("This");
boolean b2 = s1.startsWith("test", 10);
boolean b3 = s1.endsWith("string.");
```

In this series of examples, a String object is first created with the value "This is a test string!". The length of the string is calculated using the length() method and stored in the integer variable *len*. The length returned is 22, which specifies how many characters are contained in the string. The character at offset 8 into the string is then obtained using the charAt() method. As is true with C and C++, Java offsets start at 0, not 1. If you count eight characters into the string, you can see that charAt() returns the 'a' character. The next three examples use the startsWith() method to determine whether specific strings are located in the String object. The first startsWith() example looks for the string "This" at the beginning of the String object. This example returns true because the string is in fact located at the beginning of the String object. The second startsWith() example looks for the string "test" beginning at offset 10 into the String object. This call also returns true because the string "test" is located 10 characters into the String object. The last example uses the endsWith() method to check for the occurrence of the string "string." at the end of the String object. This call returns false because the String object actually ends with "string!".

The indexOf() and lastIndexOf() Methods

```
int indexOf(int ch)
int indexOf(int ch, int fromIndex)
int indexOf(String str)
int indexOf(String str, int fromIndex)
int lastIndexOf(int ch)
int lastIndexOf(int ch, int fromIndex)
int lastIndexOf(String str)
int lastIndexOf(String str, int fromIndex)
```

The indexOf() method returns the location of the first occurrence of a character or string within a String object. The first two versions of indexOf() determine the index of a single character within a string; the second two versions determine the index of a string of characters within a string. Each pair of indexOf() methods contains a version for finding a character or string based on the beginning of the String object, as well a version that enables you to specify an offset into the string to begin searching for the first occurrence. If the character or string is not found, indexOf() returns -1.

The lastIndexOf() methods work very much like indexOf(), with the exception that lastIndexOf()searches backwards through the string. Following are some examples of using these methods:

```
String s1 = new String("Saskatchewan");
int i1 = s1.indexOf('t');
int i2 = s1.indexOf("chew");
int i3 = s1.lastIndexOf('a');
```

In this series of examples, a String object is created with the value "Saskatchewan". The indexOf() method is then called on this string with the character value 't'. This call to indexOf() returns 5 because the first occurrence of 't' is 5 characters into the string. The second call to indexOf() specifies the string literal "chew". This call returns 6, since the substring "chew" is located 6 characters into the String object. Finally, the lastIndexOf() method is called with a character parameter of 'a'. The call to lastIndexOf() returns 10, indicating the position of the third 'a' in the string. (Remember that lastIndexOf() searches *backward* through the string to find the first occurrence of a character.)

The substring() Methods

```
String substring(int beginIndex)
String substring(int beginIndex, int endIndex)
```

The substring() methods return a substring of the calling String object. The first version of substring() returns the substring beginning at the index specified by *beginIndex*, through the end of the calling String object. The second version of substring() returns a substring beginning at the index specified by *beginIndex* and ending at the index specified by *endIndex*. Following is an example of using some of the substring() methods:

```
String s1 = new String("sasquatch");
String s2 = s1.substring(3);
String s3 = s1.substring(2, 7);
```

In this example, a String object is created with the value "sasquatch". A substring of this string is then retrieved using the substring() method and passing 3 as the *beginIndex* parameter. This results in the substring "quatch", which begins at the string index of 3 and continues through the rest of the string. The second version of substring() is then used with starting and ending indices of 2 and 7, yielding the substring "squat".

The equals(), equalsIgnoreCase(), and compareTo() Methods

```
boolean equals(Object anObject)
boolean equalsIgnoreCase(String anotherString)
int compareTo(String anotherString)
```

There are two methods for determining equality between String objects: equals() and equalsIgnoreCase(). The equals() method returns a boolean value based on the equality of two strings. isEqualNoCase() performs a similar function except that it compares the strings with case insensitivity. Similarly, the compareTo() method compares two strings and returns an integer value that specifies whether the calling String object is less than, greater than, or equal to the *anotherString* parameter. The integer value returned by compareTo() specifies the numeric difference between the two strings; it is a positive value if the *calling* String object is greater; it is negative if the *passed* String object is greater. If the two strings are equal, the return value is 0.

Wait a minute—if strings are just text, how can you get a numeric difference between two strings, or establish which one is greater than or less than the other? When strings are compared using the compareTo() method, each character is compared to the character at the same position in the other string until they don't match. When two characters are found that don't match, compareTo() converts them to integers and finds the difference. This difference is what is returned by compareTo(). Check out the following example to get a better idea of how this works:

```
String s1 = new String("abcfj");
String s2 = new String("abcdz");
System.out.println(s1.compareTo(s2));
```

Each pair of characters is compared until two are encountered that don't match. In this example, the `'f'` and `'d'` characters are the first two that don't match. Because the `compareTo()` method is called on the s1 String object, the integer value of `'d'` (100) is subtracted from the integer value of `'f'` (102) to determine the difference between the strings. Notice that all characters following the two nonmatching characters are ignored in the comparison.

The concat() Method

```
String concat(String str)
```

The `concat()` method is used to concatenate two String objects. The string specified in the str parameter is concatenated onto the end of the calling String object. Following are a few examples of string concatenation:

```
String s1 = new String("I saw sasquatch ");
String s2 = new String(s1 + "in Saskatchewan.");
String s3 = s1.concat("in Saskatchewan.");
```

In these concatenation examples, a String object is first created with the value "I saw sasquatch". The first concatenation example shows how two strings can be concatenated using the addition operator (+). The second example shows how two strings can be concatenated using the `concat()` method. In both examples, the resulting string is the sentence "I saw sasquatch in Saskatchewan.".

The replace() Method

```
String replace(char oldChar, char newChar)
```

The `replace()` method is used to replace characters in a string. All occurrences of *oldChar* are replaced with *newChar*. Using the strings from the previous concatenation examples, you can replace all the s characters with m characters like this:

```
String s4 = s3.replace('s', 'm');
```

This results in the string "I maw mamquatch in Samkatchewan.". Notice that the uppercase 'S' character wasn't replaced.

The trim(), toLowerCase(), and toUpperCase() Methods

```
String trim()
String toLowerCase()
String toUpperCase()
```

The `trim()` method trims leading and trailing whitespace from a String object. The `toLowerCase()` and `toUpperCase()` methods are used to convert all the characters in a String object to lowercase and uppercase. Following are some examples of these methods using the strings from the previous two examples:

```
String s5 = new String("\t  Yeti\n");
String s6 = s5.trim();
```

```
String s7 = s3.toLowerCase();
String s8 = s4.toUpperCase();
```

In this example, the `trim()` method is used to strip off the leading and trailing whitespace, resulting in the string `"Yeti"`. The call to `toLowerCase()` results in the string `"i saw sasquatch in saskatchewan."`. The only characters modified were the `'I'` and `'S'` characters, which were the only uppercase characters in the string. The call to `toUpperCase()` results in the string `"I MAW MAMQUATCH IN SAMKATCHEWAN."`. All the lowercase characters were converted to uppercase, as you might have guessed!

The `valueOf()` Methods

```
static String valueOf(Object obj)
static String valueOf(char data[])
static String valueOf(char data[], int offset, int count)
static String valueOf(boolean b)
static String valueOf(char c)
static String valueOf(int i)
static String valueOf(long l)
static String valueOf(float f)
static String valueOf(double d)
```

Finally, the `valueOf()` methods all return `String` objects that represent the particular type taken as a parameter. For example, the `valueOf()` method that takes an `int` returns the string `"123"` when passed the integer number `123`.

The `StringBuffer` Class

The `StringBuffer` class is used to represent variable, or nonconstant, strings. The `StringBuffer` class is useful when you know that a string will change in value or in length. The constructors for the `StringBuffer` class follow:

- `StringBuffer()`

- `StringBuffer(int length)`

- `StringBuffer(String str)`

The first constructor simply creates a new string buffer that is empty. The second constructor creates a string buffer that is `length` characters long, initialized with spaces. The third constructor creates a string buffer from a `String` object. This last constructor is useful when you need to modify a constant `String` object. Following are examples of using the `StringBuffer` constructors to create `StringBuffer` objects:

```
String s1 = new String("This is a string!");
String sb1 = new StringBuffer();
String sb2 = new StringBuffer(25);
String sb3 = new StringBuffer(s1);
```

Some of the most useful methods implemented by StringBuffer follow:

- `int length()`
- `int capacity()`
- `synchronized void setLength(int newLength)`
- `synchronized char charAt(int index)`
- `synchronized void setCharAt(int index, char ch)`
- `synchronized StringBuffer append(Object obj)`
- `synchronized StringBuffer append(String str)`
- `synchronized StringBuffer append(char c)`
- `synchronized StringBuffer append(char str[])`
- `synchronized StringBuffer append(char str[], int offset, int len)`
- `StringBuffer append(boolean b)`
- `StringBuffer append(int I)`
- `StringBuffer append(long l)`
- `StringBuffer append(float f)`
- `StringBuffer append(double d)`
- `synchronized StringBuffer insert(int offset, Object obj)`
- `synchronized StringBuffer insert(int offset, String str)`
- `synchronized StringBuffer insert(int offset, char c)`
- `synchronized StringBuffer insert(int offset, char str[])`
- `StringBuffer insert(int offset, boolean b)`
- `StringBuffer insert(int offset, int I)`
- `StringBuffer insert(int offset, long l)`
- `StringBuffer insert(int offset, float f)`
- `StringBuffer insert(int offset, double d)`
- `String toString()`

The `length()`, `capacity()`, and `setLength()` Methods

```
int length()
int capacity()
synchronized void setLength(int newLength)
```

The length() method is used to get the length of, or number of characters in, the string buffer. The capacity() method is similar to length() except that it returns how many characters a string buffer has allocated in memory, which is sometimes greater than the length. Characters are allocated for a string buffer as they are needed. Frequently, more memory is allocated for a string buffer than is actually being used. In these cases, the capacity() method returns the amount of memory allocated for the string buffer. You can explicitly change the length of a string buffer using the setLength() method. An example of using setLength() is to truncate a string by specifying a shorter length. The following example shows the effects of using these methods:

```
StringBuffer s1 = new StringBuffer(14);
System.out.println("capacity = " + s1.capacity());
System.out.println("length = " + s1.length());
s1.append("Bigfoot");
System.out.println(s1);
System.out.println("capacity = " + s1.capacity());
System.out.println("length = " + s1.length());
s1.setLength(3);
System.out.println(s1);
System.out.println("capacity = " + s1.capacity());
System.out.println("length = " + s1.length());
```

The resulting output of this example follows:

```
capacity = 14
length = 0
Bigfoot
capacity = 14
length = 7
Big
capacity = 14
length = 3
```

In this example, the newly created string buffer shows a capacity of 14 (based on the value passed in the constructor) and a length of 0. After appending the string "Bigfoot" to the buffer, the capacity remains the same but the length grows to 7, which is the length of the string. Calling setLength() with a parameter of 3 truncates the length down to 3, but leaves the capacity unaffected at 14.

The charAt() and setCharAt() Methods

```
synchronized char charAt(int index)
synchronized void setCharAt(int index, char ch)
```

The charAt() method returns the character at the location in the string buffer specified by the *index* parameter. You can change characters at specific locations in a string buffer using the setCharAt() method. The setCharAt() method replaces the character at *index* with the *ch* character parameter. The following example shows the use of these two methods:

```
StringBuffer s1 = new StringBuffer("I saw a Yeti in Yellowstone.");
char c1 = s1.charAt(9);
System.out.println(c1);
s1.setCharAt(4, 'r');
System.out.println(s1);
```

In this example, the call to charAt() results in the character 'e', which is located 9 characters into the string. The call to setCharAt() results in the following output, based on the 'w' in "saw" being replaced by 'r':

```
I sar a Yeti in Yellowstone.
```

The append() and insert() Methods

```
synchronized StringBuffer append(Object obj)
synchronized StringBuffer append(String str)
synchronized StringBuffer append(char c)
synchronized StringBuffer append(char str[])
synchronized StringBuffer append(char str[], int offset, int len)
StringBuffer append(boolean b)
StringBuffer append(int I)
StringBuffer append(long l)
StringBuffer append(float f)
StringBuffer append(double d)
synchronized StringBuffer insert(int offset, Object obj)
synchronized StringBuffer insert(int offset, String str)
synchronized StringBuffer insert(int offset, char c)
synchronized StringBuffer insert(int offset, char str[])
StringBuffer insert(int offset, boolean b)
StringBuffer insert(int offset, int I)
StringBuffer insert(int offset, long l)
StringBuffer insert(int offset, float f)
StringBuffer insert(int offset, double d)
```

The StringBuffer class implements a variety of overloaded append() and insert() methods. The append() methods allow you to append various types of data onto the end of a String object. Each append() method returns the String object on which it was called. The insert() methods enable you to insert various data types at a specific offset in a string buffer. insert() works in a manner similar to append(), with the exception of where the data is placed. Following are some examples of using append() and insert():

```
StringBuffer sb1 = new StringBuffer("2 + 2 = ");
StringBuffer sb2 = new StringBuffer("The tires make contact ");
sb1.append(2 + 2);
sb2.append("with the road.");
sb2.insert(10, "are the things on the car that ");
```

In this set of examples, two string buffers are first created using the constructor for StringBuffer that takes a string literal. The first StringBuffer object initially contains the string "2 + 2 = ". The append() method is used to append the result of the integer calculation 2 + 2. In this case, the integer result 4 is converted by the append() method to the string "4" before it is appended to the end of the StringBuffer object. The value of the resulting StringBuffer object is "2 + 2 = 4". The second string buffer object begins life with the value "The tires make contact ". The string "with the road." is then appended onto the end of the string buffer using the append() method. Then the insert() method is used to insert the string "are the things on the car that ". Notice that this string is inserted at index 10 within the StringBuffer object. The string that results after these two methods are called follows:

The tires are the things on the car that make contact with the road.

The toString() Method

String toString()

The last method of interest in the StringBuffer class is the toString() method. toString() returns the String object representation of the calling StringBuffer object. toString() is useful when you have a StringBuffer object but need a String object.

System and Runtime Classes

The System and Runtime classes provide access to the system and runtime environment resources. The System class is defined as final and is composed entirely of static variables and methods, which means that you never actually instantiate an object of it. The Runtime class provides direct access to the runtime environment and is useful for executing system commands and determining things like the amount of available memory.

The System Class

The System class contains the following useful methods:

- static long currentTimeMillis()
- static void arraycopy(Object *src*, int *src_position*, Object *dst*, int *dst_position*, int *length*)
- static Properties getProperties()
- static String getProperty(String *key*)
- static String getProperty(String *key*, String *def*)
- static void setProperties(Properties *props*)
- static void gc()
- static void loadLibrary(String *libname*)

The currentTimeMillis() Method

static long currentTimeMillis()

The currentTimeMillis() method returns the current system time in milliseconds. The time is specified in GMT (Greenwich Mean Time) and reflects the number of milliseconds that have elapsed since midnight on January 1, 1970. This is a standard frame of reference for computer time representation.

The `arraycopy()` Method

```
static void arraycopy(Object src, int src_position, Object dst,
  int dst_position, int length)
```

The arraycopy() method copies data from one array to another. arraycopy() copies *length* elements from the *src* array beginning at position *src_position* to the *dst* array starting at *dst_position*.

The `getProperties()`, `getProperty()`, and `setProperties()` Methods

```
static Properties getProperties()
static String getProperty(String key)
static String getProperty(String key, String def)
static void setProperties(Properties props)
```

The getProperties() method gets the current system properties and returns them using a Properties object. There are also two getProperty() methods in System that allow you to get individual system properties. The first version of getProperty() returns the system property matching the *key* parameter passed into the method. The second version of getProperty() does the same as the first except that it returns the default *def* parameter if the property isn't found. The setProperties() method takes a Properties object and sets the system properties with it.

The `gc()` Method

```
static void gc()
```

The gc() method stands for *garbage collection* and does exactly that. gc() forces the Java runtime system to perform a memory garbage collection. You can call gc() if you think the system is running low on memory, because a garbage collection usually frees up memory.

The `loadLibrary()` Method

```
static void loadLibrary(String libname)
```

The Java system supports executable code in dynamic link libraries. A *dynamic link library* is a library of Java classes that can be accessed at run time. The loadLibrary() method is used to load a dynamic link library. The name of the library to load is specified in the *libname* parameter.

The System class contains three member variables that are very useful for interacting with the system: in, out, and err. The in member is an InputStream object that acts as the standard input stream. The out and err members are PrintStream objects that act as the standard output and error streams.

The Runtime Class

The Runtime class is another very powerful class for accessing Java system-related resources. Following are a few of the more useful methods in the Runtime class:

- ■ static Runtime getRuntime()
- ■ long freeMemory()
- ■ long totalMemory()
- ■ void gc()
- ■ synchronized void loadLibrary(String *libname*)

The getRuntime(), freeMemory(), and totalMemory() Methods

```
static Runtime getRuntime()
long freeMemory()
long totalMemory()
```

The static method getRuntime() returns a Runtime object representing the runtime system environment. The freeMemory() method returns the amount of free system memory in bytes. Because freeMemory() returns only an estimate of the available memory, it is not completely accurate. If you need to know the total amount of memory accessible by the Java system, you can use the totalMemory() method. The totalMemory() method returns the number of bytes of *total* memory; the freeMemory() method returns the number of bytes of *available* memory. Listing 12.1 contains the source code for the Memory program, which displays the available free memory and total memory.

Listing 12.1. The Memory class.

```
class Memory {
  public static void main (String args[]) {
    Runtime runtime = Runtime.getRuntime();
    long freeMem = runtime.freeMemory() / 1024;
    long totalMem = runtime.totalMemory() / 1024;
    System.out.println("Free memory : " + freeMem + "KB");
    System.out.println("Total memory : " + totalMem + "KB");
  }
}
```

An example of the output of running the Memory program follows:

```
Free Memory : 3068KB
Total Memory : 3071KB
```

The Memory class uses the getRuntime(), freeMemory(), and totalMemory() methods of the Runtime class. Note that you can convert the amount of memory returned by each method from bytes to kilobytes by dividing by 1024.

The `gc()` and `loadLibrary()` Methods

```
void gc()
synchronized void loadLibrary(String libname)
```

The other two methods of importance in the `Runtime` class (`gc()` and `loadLibrary()`) work exactly the same as the versions belonging to the `System` class.

Class Classes

Java provides two classes in the language package for dealing with classes: `Class` and `ClassLoader`. The `Class` class allows you access to the runtime information for a class. The `ClassLoader` class provides support for dynamically loading classes at run time.

The Class Class

Some of the more useful methods implemented by the `Class` class follow:

- `static Class forName(String className)`
- `String getName()`
- `Class getSuperclass()`
- `ClassLoader getClassLoader()`
- `boolean isInterface()`
- `String toString()`

The `forName()` Method

```
static Class forName(String className)
```

The `forName()` method is a `static` method used to get the runtime class descriptor object for a class. The `String` parameter `className` specifies the name of the class about which you want information. `forName()` returns a `Class` object containing runtime information for the specified class. Notice that `forName()` is `static` and is the method you typically use to get an instance of the `Class` class for determining class information. Following is an example of how to use the `forName()` method to get information about the `StringBuffer` class:

```
Class info = Class.forName("java.lang.StringBuffer");
```

The `getName()` Method

```
String getName()
```

The `getName()` method retrieves the string name of the class represented by a `Class` object. Following is an example of using the `getName()` method:

```
String s = info.getName();
```

The `getSuperClass()`, `getClassLoader()`, and `isInterface()` Methods

```
Class getSuperclass()
ClassLoader getClassLoader()
boolean isInterface()
```

The `getSuperclass()` method returns a `Class` object containing information about the superclass of an object. The `getClassLoader()` method returns the `ClassLoader` object for a class or `null` if no class loader exists. The `isInterface()` method returns a boolean indicating whether or not a class is an interface.

The `toString()` Method

```
String toString()
```

Finally, the `toString()` method returns the name of a class or interface. `toString()` automatically prepends the string `"class"` or `"interface"` to the name based on whether the `Class` object represents a class or an interface.

The `ClassLoader` Class

The `ClassLoader` class provides the framework that enables you to dynamically load classes into the runtime environment. Following are the methods implemented by `ClassLoader`:

- `abstract Class loadClass(String name, boolean resolve)`
- `final Class defineClass(byte data[], int offset, int length)`
- `final void resolveClass(Class c)`
- `final Class findSystemClass(String name)`

The `loadClass()` and `defineClass()` Methods

```
abstract Class loadClass(String name, boolean resolve)
final Class defineClass(byte data[], int offset, int length)
```

The `loadClass()` method is an `abstract` method that must be defined in a subclass of `ClassLoader`. `loadClass()` resolves a class name passed in the `String` parameter *name* into a `Class` runtime object. `loadClass()` returns the resulting `Class` on success or `null` if not successful. The `defineClass()` method converts an array of `byte` data into a `Class` object. The class is defined by the *data* parameter beginning at *offset* and continuing for *length* bytes.

The `resolveClass()` Method

```
final void resolveClass(Class c)
```

A class defined with `defineClass()` must be resolved before it can be used. You can resolve a class by using the `resolveClass()` method, which takes a `Class` object as its only parameter.

The `findSystemClass()` Method

```
final Class findSystemClass(String name)
```

Finally, the `findSystemClass()` method is used to find and load a system class. A *system class* is a class that uses the built-in (primordial) class loader, defined as `null`.

Summary

In this chapter, you learned a great deal about the classes and interfaces that make up the Java language package. The language package lays out the core classes, interfaces, and errors of the Java class libraries. Although some of the classes implemented in the language package are fairly low level, a solid understanding of these classes is necessary to move on to other areas of the Java class libraries.

This chapter explained how fundamental data types can become objects using the data type wrappers. You then learned about the many mathematical functions contained in the `Math` class. And don't forget about the string classes, which provide a powerful set of routines for working with strings of text. You finished up with a tour of how to access the system and runtime resources of Java, along with the lower-level runtime and dynamic class support.

The following chapter provides the next stop on this guided tour of the Java class libraries: the Java utilities package.

The Utilities Package

by Michael Girdley and Richard Lesh

IN THIS CHAPTER

This chapter describes the classes in the java.util package in the Java class library. These classes implement many of those features or functions usually left for the programmer or someone else to implement. In programming experiences, I regularly find myself saying, "It would be so much easier if there were a built-in object that would do *some common but complicated task.*" The java.util package is a well-designed and effective attempt to satisfy many of these specialized needs.

In many languages, you find yourself implementing a stack or a hash table class and all the corresponding methods. Java has a built-in stack type that enables you to quickly and efficiently include your own stack data structures in your Java programs. This frees you to deal with more important design and implementation issues. These classes are also useful in a variety of other ways and are the fundamental building blocks of the more complicated data structures used in other Java packages and in your own applications.

This chapter covers the following topics:

- Each of the features of the utilities package
- The implementation of each of the different classes in the utilities package

NOTE

Unless otherwise noted, all the interfaces and classes discussed in this chapter extend the java.lang.Object class.

Table 13.1 shows the classes that are part of the utilities package and that are discussed in this chapter.

Table 13.1. Utilities package classes.

Class	Description
BitSet	Implements a collection of binary values
Date	Used for date and time data storage and use
Dictionary	Used to store a collection of key and value pairs
Hashtable	Used to store a hash table
Observable	Used to store observable data
Properties	Used to store and make use of a properties list that can be saved
Random	Used to generate a pseudo-random number
Stack	Used to store and implement a stack
StringTokenizer	Used to tokenize a string
Vector	Used to store a vector data type

> **NOTE**
>
> You may not be familiar with some of these data types. The Dictionary class is used to implement a dictionary in your program. A Hashtable is a storage data type whose speed in searching is much greater than that of other data structures because it stores data items based on a key derived from some given formula. A Stack, of course, functions as if you were stacking data items on the floor, one on top of the other, in a single stack. As a consequence, the only two manipulations you can make to the stack are to remove the top item or to place another item on top. The Vector class implements an interesting data structure that has the capability to begin with a limited capacity and then change in size to accommodate the data items you insert into it. The Vector class can be described as a "growable array."

Linked Lists, Queues, Search Trees, and Other Dynamic Data Structures

One would expect that the Vector class would eliminate the necessity for creating your own data structures. But there may be times when you want to conserve space to the maximum or access your data in a specialized way. In these cases, there is a technique to implement such data structures in Java.

As you know, Java has no pointers. Because dynamically linked lists and queues are implemented using pointers, is it then impossible to create these two data structures in Java? Not quite. Just as with many other tasks in Java, you have to do a little "funky stepping" to get it right because the implementation of lists, queues, and other dynamic data structures is not intuitive.

To define your own dynamic data structures, you will want to make use of the fact that references to *objects* in Java are already dynamic. This is demonstrated and necessitated by the practices Java uses, such as interfaces and abstract implementations.

If you are accustomed to implementing dynamically linked lists or queues in C++, the format you use in Java to create your own version of these structures should seem very familiar to you. For example, the following code creates a Node class for the list that contains a string:

```
class Node {
    String Name;
    Node Prev;
    Node Next;
}
```

Of course, this code creates a *doubly linked list*, which has links backward and forward to other nodes containing strings. You could easily convert this type to link objects in just about any way to exhibit just about any behavior you want: queues, stacks (remember, there is already a `Stack` object in the class library), doubly linked lists, circular lists, binary search trees, and so on.

To implement such a list, you create a `DoubleList` class that contains one such `Node` object and links strung out from there. You can use the keyword `null` to represent an empty object. Here is an example of the `DoubleList` declaration:

```
class DoubleList {
    // Declare the listhead to be of the Node type we created earlier.
    // Also, set it to be an empty object.
    Node ListHead = null;
.
.
.
}
```

You then create methods to act on the list, such as `InsertNode()` or `ClearMyListJerk()`—whatever you want.

You may also want to create a constructor method for the `Node` class that accepts parameters to set the previous and next nodes at construction time; or you may want to create a method such as `SetNext()` or `SetNextToNull()`. Either choice would work just fine.

> **NOTE**
>
> Out of all this you get a surprise bonus: No worry about freeing space allocated to create nodes because the Java garbage collection processes take care of all that for you. Just create objects when you need them and let Java take care of it.

Using the Utilities Package

The utilities package has two interfaces you can use in classes of your own design: `Enumeration` and `Observer`. An interface is a set of methods that must be written for any class that claims to *implement* the interface. This arrangement provides a way to consistently use all classes that implement the interface. Following is a summary of the `Enumeration` and `Observer` interfaces:

`Enumeration`	Interface for classes that can enumerate a vector
`Observer`	Interface for classes that can observe observable objects

The `Enumeration` interface is used for classes that can retrieve data from a list, element by element. For example, there is an `Enumeration` class in the utilities package that implements the `Enumeration` interface for use with the `Vector` class. This frees you from hard-core traversal of the different classes of data structures.

The `Observer` interface is useful in designing classes that can watch for changes that occur in other classes.

> **CAUTION**
>
> Some of the examples in this chapter are not applets—they are applications. Many of these data structures are best exhibited by just plain text input and output. Removing the baggage that would have come along with applets allows the examples to be simplified so that the topic being demonstrated is clearer.
>
> When you apply any code segments from this chapter in your own applets, remember that some of the examples are not true applets; you must deal with the differences inherent between applets and applications.

The Enumeration Interface

The Enumeration interface specifies a set of methods used to enumerate—that is, iterate through—a list. An object that implements this interface can be used to iterate through a list only once because the Enumeration object is consumed through its use.

For example, an Enumeration object can be used to print all the elements of a Vector object, v, as follows:

```
for (Enumeration e=v.elements();e.hasMoreElements();)
    System.out.print(e.nextElement()+" ");
```

The Enumeration interface specifies only two methods: hasMoreElements() and nextElement(). The hasMoreElements() method must return true if there are elements remaining in the enumeration. The nextElement() method must return an object representing the next element within the object that is being enumerated. The details of how the Enumeration interface is implemented and how the data is represented internally are left up to the implementation of the specific class.

The Observer Interface

The Observer interface, if implemented by a class, allows an object of the class to observe other objects of the class Observable. The Observer interface is notified whenever the Observable object that it is watching changes.

The interface specifies only one method, update(Observable, Object). This method is called by the observed object to notify the Observer of changes. A reference to the observed object is passed along with any additional object that the observed object wants to pass to the Observer. The first argument enables the Observer to operate on the observed object; the second argument is used to pass information from the observed to the Observer.

Classes

The utilities package supplies 10 different classes that provide a wide variety of functionality. Although these classes don't generally have much in common, they all provide support for the most common data structures used by programmers. The techniques described in the next sections enable you to create your own specialized classes to supplement those missing from the package.

The classes supplied in the `java.util` package, however limited they are, do provide a great advantage over other languages. The main advantage is that these classes simplify some things and eliminate a lot of the garbage you were stuck with in the past, in terms of freeing memory and doing mundane programming tasks.

However, there are a number of limitations. For example, you have to "dance a little bit" to implement some of the more complicated data structures. And if you want speed, there are much faster languages to choose from. Java provides a combination of power and simplicity while sacrificing speed. However, don't worry that your programs will be slugs. Although Java is not nearly as efficient as C++ and C, it still beats Visual Basic in terms of size and speed.

The BitSet Class

The `BitSet` class implements a data type that represents a collection of bits. The collection grows dynamically as more bits are required. The class is useful for representing a set of `true` and `false` values. Specific bits are identified using nonnegative integers. The first bit is bit 0.

The `BitSet` class is most useful for storing a group of related `true`/`false` values, such as user responses to Yes and No questions. For example, if the applet has a number of radio buttons, you can slap those values into an instance of the `BitSet` class.

The class is also useful in terms of bitmapping your own graphics. You can create bitsets that represent a pixel at a time (of course, it would be much easier to use the `Graphics` class for this purpose instead).

Individual bits in the set are turned on or off with the `set()` and `clear()` methods. Individual bits are queried with the `get()` method. These methods all take the specific bit number as their only argument. The basic boolean operations AND, OR, and XOR can be performed on two bitsets using the `and()`, `or()`, and `xor()` methods. Because these methods modify one of the bitsets, you generally use the `clone()` method to create a duplicate of one bitset, and then use the AND, OR, or XOR operation on the clone with the second bitset. The result of the operation then ends up in the cloned bitset. The `BitSet1` program in Listing 13.1 shows the basic `BitSet` operations.

Listing 13.1. BitSet1.java: a sample BitSet program.

```
import java.io.DataInputStream;
import java.util.BitSet;
```

```
class BitSet1 {
    public static void main(String args[])
        throws java.io.IOException
    {
        DataInputStream dis=new DataInputStream(System.in);
        String bitstring;
        BitSet set1,set2,set3;
        set1=new BitSet();
        set2=new BitSet();

        // Get the first bit sequence and store it
        System.out.println("Bit sequence #1:");
        bitstring=dis.readLine();
        for (short i=0;i<bitstring.length();i++){
            if (bitstring.charAt(i)=='1')
                set1.set(i);
            else
                set1.clear(i);
        }
        // Get the second bit sequence and store it
        System.out.println("Bit sequence #2:");
        bitstring=dis.readLine();
        for (short i=0;i<bitstring.length();i++){
            if (bitstring.charAt(i)=='1')
                set2.set(i);
            else
                set2.clear(i);
        }
        System.out.println("BitSet #1: "+set1);
        System.out.println("BitSet #2: "+set2);

        // Test the AND operation
        set3=(BitSet)set1.clone();
        set3.and(set2);
        System.out.println("set1 AND set2: "+set3);

        // Test the OR operation
        set3=(BitSet)set1.clone();
        set3.or(set2);
        System.out.println("set1 OR set2: "+set3);

        // Test the XOR operation
        set3=(BitSet)set1.clone();
        set3.xor(set2);
        System.out.println("set1 XOR set2: "+set3);
    }
}
```

13

**THE UTILITIES
PACKAGE**

The output from this program looks like this:

```
Bit sequence #1:
1010
Bit sequence #2:
1100
BitSet #1: {0, 2}
BitSet #2: {0, 1}
```

```
set1 AND set2: {0}
set1 OR set2: {0, 1, 2}
set1 XOR set2: {1, 2}
```

Table 13.2 summarizes all the methods available in the BitSet class.

Table 13.2. Methods in the BitSet interface.

Method	Description
Constructors	
BitSet()	Constructs an empty BitSet
BitSet(int)	Constructs an empty BitSet of a given size
Methods	
and(BitSet)	Logically ANDs the object's bitset with another BitSet object
clear(int)	Clears a specific bit
clone()	Creates a clone of the BitSet object
equals(Object)	Compares this object against another BitSet object
get(int)	Returns the value of a specific bit
hashCode()	Returns the hash code
or(BitSet)	Logically ORs the object's bitset with another BitSet object
set(int)	Sets a specific bit
size()	Returns the size of the set
toString()	Converts bit values to a string representation
xor(BitSet)	Logically XORs the object's bitset with another BitSet object

In addition to extending the java.lang.Object class, BitSet implements the java.lang.Cloneable interface. This, of course, allows instances of the object to be cloned to create another instance of the class.

The Date Class

You will regularly run into instances in which you have to access and manipulate dates and times in your applets on the Web. For example, you may want an applet to display the current time or date during its execution. If you are programming a game, you may want to use the system clock to get your elapsed time right.

The Date class is used to represent dates and times in a platform-independent fashion. For example, the current date or a specific date can be printed as shown in Listing 13.2.

Listing 13.2. Date1.java: A sample Date program.

```java
import java.util.Date;

public class Date1{
    public static void main (String args[]){
        Date today=new Date();
        System.out.println("Today is "+today.toLocaleString()+
            " ("+today.toGMTString()+")");

        Date birthday=new Date(89,10,14,8,30,00);
        System.out.println("My birthday is"+
            birthday.toString()+" ("+birthday.toGMTString()+")");

        Date anniversary=new Date("Jun 21, 1986");
        System.out.println("My anniversary is "+
            anniversary+" ("+anniversary.toGMTString()+")");
    }
}
```

The output from this program looks like this:

```
Today is 01/21/97 19:55:17 (22 Jan 1997 01:55:17 GMT)
My birthday is Thu Nov 14 08:30:00  1989 (14 Nov 1989 14:30:00 GMT)
My anniversary is Sat Jun 21 00:00:00  1989 (21 Jun 1986 05:00:00 GMT)
```

The default constructor is used when the current date and time are needed. A specific date and time can be used to initialize a Date object using the constructors that take three, five, and six integers. These constructors allow the date and time to be specified using YMD, YMDHM, or YMDHMS formats. Any parts of the time not specified by the three-integer and five-integer constructors are set to zero.

> **NOTE**
>
> Date and time formats can be conveniently summarized using notations of the form YMD, YMDHMS, HMS, or MDY. These abbreviated formats indicate the order in which the various numeric parts of the date appear. Each letter refers to a specific component of the date or time: year (Y), month (M), day (D), hour (H), minute (M), and second (S). Whether the letter M refers to month or minute depends on the context.

Alternatively, a Date object can be constructed using a single string that represents a date and time using a variety of different syntax. One of the most important is the international standard date syntax of the form, "Sun, 14 Aug 1995 9:00:00 GMT." Continental U.S. time zone abbreviations are understood, but time zone offsets should be considered for general use; for

13

THE UTILITIES
PACKAGE

example, "Sun, 14 Aug 1995 9:00:00 GMT+0600" (six hours west of the Greenwich meridian). The local time zone to the computer executing the code is assumed if none is supplied.

> **NOTE**
>
> The Date class intends to store date and time information in UTC (Coordinated Universal Time). However, the class does not necessarily achieve this goal. UTC is a time standard based on an atomic clock. Time specifications using UTC are considered equal to GMT (Greenwich Mean Time). The implementation of the Date class is limited by the time set by the underlying operating system. Because modern operating systems typically assume that a day is always 86,400 seconds, the extra leap seconds, which are needed about once a year to accurately reflect UTC, are usually not added.

The date can be converted to a text representation using the methods toString(), toGMTString(), and toLocaleString(), which convert the date and time to the standard UNIX, GMT, or local time formats. The toLocaleString() function is very useful because you do not have to determine what your system's date format is. This may not sound like much, but it is just another piece of the very complicated puzzle that Sun has put together to allow your applets and applications to flow seamlessly into the system on which they are running.

When a date is converted to a string by an automatic coercion, the toString() method is used. The resulting string returned by the toString() function follows UNIX time and date standards.

The Date class also has methods for setting and querying the date and time component values once the Date object is constructed. The individual parts of the date (month, date, year) and time (hours, minutes, seconds) are always specified in local time. When referring to the various parts of the date and time, the first letter of each part is typically used in an abbreviation. For example, YMDHMS indicates that all six parts (year, month, date, hour, minute, second) are present. Each of these parts of the date and time have a specific range of acceptable values, as shown in Table 13.3.

Table 13.3. Date component ranges.

Component	Range
Year	Year minus 1900
Month	0 to 11 (January=0)
Date	1 to 31
Day	0 to 6 (Sunday=0)
Hour	0 to 23

Component	Range
Minute	0 to 59
Second	0 to 59

The date and time also can be specified using a single integer UTC value that represents the number of milliseconds that have elapsed since a specific starting date (which may vary from system to system). For UNIX systems, this date is January 1, 1970. The program `Date2` in Listing 13.3 shows how this single value corresponds to the normal YMDHMS representation.

Listing 13.3. Date2.java: A sample Date program.

```java
import java.util.Date;

public class Date2{
    public static void main (String args[]){
        Date beginning=new Date(0);
        Date anniversary=new Date("Jun 21, 1986");
        Date today=new Date();

        System.out.println(beginning+"="+beginning.getTime());
        System.out.println(anniversary+"="+anniversary.getTime());
        System.out.println(today+"="+today.getTime());
    }
}
```

The output from this program looks like this:

```
Wed Dec 31 18:00:00  1969=0
Sat Jun 21 00:00:00  1986=519714000000
Sun Jan 21 19:55:17  1996=822275717000
```

Dates can be compared to each other by using this UTC value or by using the method `after()`, `before()`, or `equals()`.

CAUTION

Don't try to launch space shuttles or coordinate nuclear attacks based on your operating system's local time as reflected by Java. Although the API is intended to reflect UTC (Coordinated Universal Time), it doesn't do so exactly. This inexact behavior is inherited from the time system of the underlying OS. The vast majority of all modern operating systems assume that one day equals 3600 seconds/hour times 24 hours, and as such, they reflect time to the accuracy that UTC does.

continues

continued

Under the UTC, about once a year, there is an extra second, called a "leap second," added to account for the wobble of the earth. Most computer clocks are not accurate enough to reflect this distinction.

Between UTC and standard OS time (UT/GMT), there is this subtle difference; one is based on an atomic clock, and the other is based on astronomical observations—which, for all practical purposes, is an invisibly fine hair to split.

For more information, Sun suggests you visit the U.S. Naval Observatory site, particularly the Directorate of Time at `http://tycho.usno.navy.mil` and its definitions of different systems of time at `http://tycho.usno.navy.mil/systime.html`.

Table 13.4 summarizes all the methods available in the `Date` class.

Table 13.4. Methods available in the `Date` interface.

Method	Description
Constructors	
`Date()`	Constructs a date using today's date and time
`Date(long)`	Constructs a date using a single UTC value
`Date(int, int, int)`	Constructs a date using YMD format
`Date(int, int, int, int, int)`	Constructs a date using YMDHM format
`Date(int, int, int, int, int, int)`	Constructs a date using YMDHMS format
`Date(string)`	Constructs a date from a string
Static Methods	
`UTC(int, int, int, int, int, int)`	Calculates a UTC value from YMDHMS format
`parse(string)`	Returns the single UTC value of a date in text format
Methods	
`after(Date)`	True if the date is later than the specified date
`before(Date)`	True if the date is earlier than the specified date
`equals(Object)`	True if the date and the specified date are equal
`getDate()`	Returns the day of the month
`getDay()`	Returns the day of the week

Method	*Description*
	Methods
getHours()	Returns the hour
getMinutes()	Returns the minute
getMonth()	Returns the month
getSeconds()	Returns the second
getTime()	Returns the time as a single UTC value
getTimezoneOffset()	Returns the time zone offset, in minutes, for this locale
getYear()	Returns the year after 1900
hashCode()	Computes a hash code for the date
setDate(int)	Sets the date
setHours(int)	Sets the hours
setMinutes(int)	Sets the minutes
setMonth(int)	Sets the month
setSeconds(int)	Sets the seconds
setTime(long)	Sets the time using a single UTC value
setYear(int)	Sets the year
toGMTString()	Converts a date to text using Internet GMT conventions
toLocaleString()	Converts a date to text using locale conventions
toString()	Converts a date to text using UNIX ctime() conventions

One of the most helpful methods available in the Date class is the parse() method. This void takes an instance of the String type and then parses that string. The result of that parse() is then placed in the calling instance of the class. If you have a date called ADate, you can set its value to be the date in the SomeString class with this code line:

```
ADate.parse(SomeString);
```

You will also find the before() and after() functions useful. They enable you to send in another instance of the Date class and compare that date to the value in the calling instance.

The sample applet in Listing 13.4 demonstrates the use of the Date class.

Listing 13.4. Using the Date class.

```java
import java.awt.*;
import java.util.*;

public class MichaelSimpleClock extends java.applet.Applet {

    Date TheDate = new Date();
    Button DateButton = new Button(
        "                    Click me!                    ");

    public void init()  {
        add(DateButton);
    }

    public boolean handleEvent(Event e) {
        if (e.target == DateButton) {
            DateButton.setLabel(TheDate.toString());
        }
        return true;
    }

}
```

Figure 13.1 shows the MichaelSimpleClock applet. Note that the clock in the applet is wrong: it is not actually 8:00 A.M. There is no way I would write that early in the morning.

FIGURE 13.1.

The
MichaelSimpleClock
applet.

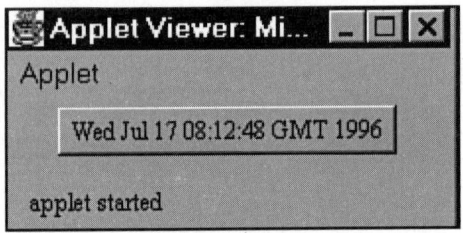

What about a real-time clock that updates as the clock changes? To accomplish this small feat, you must include in the applet a loop that has each iteration reconstructing the internal Date instance. Then, you regularly repaint that value inside the applet's paint() method. You also have to include threading to keep your system from locking up during the applet's execution. Threading is covered in Chapter 9, "Threads and Multithreading," so a real-time clock was not included in this chapter.

The Random Class

For the programming of games and many other program types, it is important to be able to generate random numbers. Java includes the capability to generate random numbers efficiently and effectively.

The Random class implements a pseudo-random number data type that generates a stream of seemingly random numbers. To create a sequence of different pseudo-random values each time the application is run, create the Random object as follows:

```
Random r=new Random();
```

This statement seeds the random generator with the current time. On the other hand, consider the following statement:

```
Random r=new Random(326);    // Pick any value
```

This statement seeds the random generator with the same value each time, resulting in the same sequence of pseudo-random numbers each time the application runs. The generator can be reseeded at any time using the setSeed() method.

TIP

Want to get really random numbers? Well, you can't. But a common practice to simulate actual random numbers in computer programs is to seed the random number generator with some variant of the current time or date. If, for example, you want to seed a random number generator with the sum of the current seconds, minutes, and hours, you could use this code, which should suffice for most tasks:

```
int OurSeed = ADate.getSeconds() + ADate.getHours() + ADate.getMinutes();
Random = new Random(OurSeed);
```

Pseudo-random numbers can be generated using one of these functions: nextInt(), nextLong(), nextFloat(), nextDouble(), or nextGaussian(). The first four functions return *integers*, *longs*, *floats*, and *doubles*. For more information about the Gaussian distribution, refer to the following sidebar. The program Random1 in Listing 13.5 prints out pseudo-random uniformly distributed values using these functions.

Listing 13.5. Random1.java: A sample Random program.

```
import java.lang.Math;
import java.util.Date;
import java.util.Random;

class Random1 {
    public static void main(String args[])
        throws java.io.IOException
    {
        int count=6;
        Random randGen=new Random();

        System.out.println("Uniform Random Integers");
        for (int i=0;i<count;i++)
        System.out.print(randGen.nextInt()+" ");
        System.out.println("\n");
```

13

THE UTILITIES
PACKAGE

continues

Listing 13.5. continued

```
        System.out.println("Uniform Random Floats");
        for (int i=0;i<count;i++)
        System.out.print(randGen.nextFloat()+" ");
        System.out.println("\n");

        System.out.println("Gaussian Random Floats");
        for (int i=0;i<count;i++)
            System.out.print(randGen.nextGaussian()+" ");
        System.out.println("\n");

        System.out.println("Uniform Random Integers [1,6]");
        for (int i=0;i<count;i++)
            System.out.print((Math.abs(randGen.nextInt())%6+1)+" ");
        System.out.println("\n");
        }
}
```

The output from the preceding program looks like this:

```
Uniform Random Integers
1704667569 -1431446235 1024613888 438489989 710330974 -1689521238

Uniform Random Floats
0.689189 0.0579988 0.0933537 0.748228 0.400992 0.222109

Gaussian Random Floats
-0.201843 -0.0111578 1.63927 0.205938 -0.365471 0.626304

Uniform Random Integers [1,6]
4 6 1 6 3 2
```

If you want to generate uniformly distributed random integers within a specific range, the output from nextInt(), nextLong(), or nextDouble() can be scaled to match the required range. However, a simpler approach is to take the remainder of the result of nextInt() divided by the number of different values plus the first value of the range. For example, if the values 10 to 20 are needed, you can use the formula nextInt()%21+10. Unfortunately, although this method is much simpler than scaling the output of nextInt(), it is guaranteed to work only on truly random values. Because the pseudo-random generator may have various undesired correlations, the modulus operator may not provide acceptable results—you might get all odd numbers, for example. In other words, don't plan on simulating the detonation of your new H-bomb in Java because you may find yourself a couple miles too close.

GAUSSIAN AND NORMAL DISTRIBUTIONS

Uniformly distributed random numbers are generated using a modified linear congruential method with a 48-bit seed. Uniformly distributed random numbers within a given range all appear with the same frequency. The Random class can also generate random numbers in a

Gaussian or Normal distribution. The Gaussian frequency distribution curve is also referred to as a *bell curve*. For information on the Gaussian frequency distribution curve, see *The Art of Computer Programming*, Volume 2, by Donald Knuth.

Table 13.5 summarizes the complete interface of the `Random` class.

Table 13.5. The methods available in the Random interface.

Method	Description
	Constructors
`Random()`	Creates a new random number generator
`Random(long)`	Creates a new random number generator using a seed
	Methods
`nextDouble()`	Returns a pseudo-random uniformly distributed double
`nextFloat()`	Returns a pseudo-random uniformly distributed float
`nextGaussian()`	Returns a pseudo-random Gaussian distributed double
`nextInt()`	Returns a pseudo-random uniformly distributed integer
`nextLong()`	Returns a pseudo-random uniformly distributed long
`setSeed(long)`	Sets the seed of the pseudo-random number generator

The applet shown in Listing 13.6 demonstrates a bit of what you can do with the `Random` class.

Listing 13.6. Using the Random class.

```
import java.awt.*;
import java.util.*;

public class TheWanderer extends java.applet.Applet {

        int xpos = 100;
        int ypos = 100;


    // Our current date
    Date D = new Date();
```

continues

13

THE UTILITIES PACKAGE

Listing 13.6. continued

```
        // The movement button
        Button theButton = new Button("Click Me");

        // Our random number generator
        Random R;

        public void init() {
                add(theButton);
                setBackground(Color.white);

        // Our random number generator seeded with the current seconds
        int seed = D.getSeconds();
                R = new Random(seed);
        }

        public boolean handleEvent (Event e) {
                if (e.target == theButton) {
                        // Move our thing.
                        xpos = xpos + (Math.abs(R.nextInt())%10-7);
                        ypos = ypos + (Math.abs(R.nextInt())%10-7);

            // repaint the sucker
                        repaint();
        }
                return super.handleEvent(e);
    }

    public void paint(Graphics g) {
                g.setColor(Color.black);
                g.fillOval(xpos,ypos, 50, 50);
    }
}
```

Figure 13.2 shows TheWanderer applet during its execution.

FIGURE 13.2.

TheWanderer *applet.*

The StringTokenizer Class

This section describes the function of the StringTokenizer class, which also could have been appropriately grouped with other classes in Chapter 14, "The I/O Package," because it is so vital to the input and output functions demonstrated in that chapter. The StringTokenizer class enables you to parse a string into a number of smaller strings called *tokens*. This class works specifically for what is called "delimited text," which means that each individual substring of the string is separated by a delimiter. The delimiter can be anything ranging from a * to YabaDaba. You simply specify what you want the class to look for when tokenizing the string.

This class is included in this chapter because it has uses that prove helpful in everything from a spreadsheet applet to an arcade game applet.

The delimiter set can be specified when the StringTokenizer object is created, or it can be specified on a per-token basis. The default delimiter set is the set of *whitespace* characters. With this delimiter set, the class would find all the separate words in a string and tokenize them. For example, the StringTokenizer1 code in Listing 13.7 prints out each word of the string on a separate line.

Listing 13.7. StringTokenizer1.java: A sample StringTokenizer program.

```
import java.io.DataInputStream;
import java.util.StringTokenizer;

class StringTokenizer1 {
    public static void main(String args[])
        throws java.io.IOException
    {

        DataInputStream dis=new DataInputStream(System.in);

        System.out.println("Enter a sentence: ");
        String s=dis.readLine();
        StringTokenizer st=new StringTokenizer(s);
        while (st.hasMoreTokens())
            System.out.println(st.nextToken());
    }
}
```

Here is the output from this listing:

```
Enter a sentence:
Four score and seven
Four
score
and
seven
```

Pure excitement. The method countTokens() returns the number of tokens remaining in the string using the current delimiter set—that is, the number of times nextToken() can be called before generating an exception. This is an efficient method because it does not actually construct the substrings that nextToken() must generate.

In addition to extending the java.lang.object class, the StringTokenizer class implements the java.util.Enumeration interface.

Table 13.6 summarizes the methods of the StringTokenizer class.

Table 13.6. The methods available in the StringTokenizer interface.

Method	Description
Constructors	
StringTokenizer(string)	Constructs a StringTokenizer given a string using whitespace as delimiters.
StringTokenizer(string, string)	Constructs a StringTokenizer given a string and a delimiter set.
StringTokenizer (string, string, boolean)	Constructs a StringTokenizer given a string and a delimiter set. The final parameter is a boolean value which, if true, says that the delimiters must be returned as tokens. If this parameter is false, the tokens are not returned.
Methods	
countTokens()	Returns the number of tokens remaining in the string.
hasMoreTokens()	Returns true if more tokens exist.
nextToken()	Returns the next token of the string.
nextToken(string)	Returns the next token, given a new delimiter set.
hasMoreTokens()	Returns true if more elements exist in the enumeration.
nextElement()	Returns the next element of the enumeration using the current delimiter set.

The Vector Class

As stated earlier in this chapter, Java doesn't include dynamically linked list, queue, or other data structures of that type. Instead, the designers of Java envisioned the Vector class, which handles the occasions when you need to dynamically store objects. Of course, there are positive and negative consequences of this decision by the designers at Sun. On the positive side, the Vector class contributes to the simplicity of the language. The major negative point is that, at face value, the Vector class severely limits programmers from using more sophisticated programs.

In any case, the Vector class implements a dynamically allocated list of objects. It attempts to optimize storage by increasing the storage capacity of the list when needed by increments larger than just one object. Typically, with this mechanism, there is some excess capacity in the list. When this capacity is exhausted, the list is reallocated to add another block of objects at the end of the list. Setting the capacity of the Vector object to the needed size before inserting a large number of objects reduces the need for incremental reallocation. Because of this mechanism, it is important to remember that the *capacity* (the available elements in the Vector object) and the *size* (the number of elements currently stored in the Vector object) usually are not the same.

Suppose that a Vector with capacityIncrement equal to 3 has been created. As objects are added to the Vector, new space is allocated in chunks of three objects. After five elements have been added, there is still room for one more element without the need for any additional memory allocation.

After the sixth element has been added, there is no more excess capacity. When the seventh element is added, a new allocation is made to add three additional elements, giving a total capacity of nine. After the seventh element is added, there are two remaining unused elements.

The initial storage capacity and the capacity increment can both be specified in the constructor. Even though the capacity is automatically increased as needed, the ensureCapacity() method can be used to increase the capacity to a specific minimum number of elements; the trimToSize() method can be used to reduce the capacity to the minimum number of elements needed to store the current amount. New elements can be added to the Vector using the addElement() and insertElementAt() methods. The elements passed to be stored in the Vector must be derived from type Object. Elements can be changed using the setElementAt() method. Removal of elements is accomplished with the removeElement(), removeElementAt(), and removeAllElements() methods. Elements can be accessed directly using the elementAt(), firstElement(), and lastElement() methods; elements can be located using the indexOf() and lastIndexOf() methods. Information about the size and the capacity of the Vector are returned by the size() and capacity() methods. The setSize() method can be used to directly change the size of the Vector.

For example, the Vector1 code in Listing 13.8 creates a Vector of integers by adding new elements to the end. Then, using a variety of techniques, it prints the Vector.

Listing 13.8. Vector1.java: A sample Vector program.

```
import java.lang.Integer;
import java.util.Enumeration;
import java.util.Vector;
```

continues

Listing 13.8. continued

```
class Vector1 {
    public static void main(String args[]){
        Vector v=new Vector(10,10);
        for (int i=0;i<20;i++)
            v.addElement(new Integer(i));

        System.out.println("Vector in original order using an Enumeration");
        for (Enumeration e=v.elements();e.hasMoreElements();)
            System.out.print(e.nextElement()+" ");
        System.out.println();

        System.out.println("Vector in original order using elementAt");
        for (int i=0;i<v.size();i++)
            System.out.print(v.elementAt(i)+" ");
        System.out.println();

        // Print out the original vector
        System.out.println("\nVector in reverse order using elementAt");
        for (int i=v.size()-1;i>=0;i++)
            System.out.print(v.elementAt(i)+" ");
        System.out.println();

        // Print out the original vector
        System.out.println("\nVector as a String");
        System.out.println(v.toString());
    }
}
```

The output from this program looks like this:

```
Vector in original order using an Enumeration
0 1 2 3 4 5 6 7 8 9 10 11 12 13 14 15 16 17 18 19
Vector in original order using elementAt
0 1 2 3 4 5 6 7 8 9 10 11 12 13 14 15 16 17 18 19

Vector in reverse order using elementAt
19 18 17 16 15 14 13 12 11 10 9 8 7 6 5 4 3 2 1 0

Vector as a String
[0, 1, 2, 3, 4, 5, 6, 7, 8, 9, 10, 11, 12, 13, 14, 15, 16, 17, 18, 19]
```

> **NOTE**
>
> The expression new Integer() was used to create integer objects to store because the fundamental types, such as int, are not objects in Java. This technique is used many times throughout this chapter.

Notice the use of the Enumeration object as one way to access the elements of a Vector. Look at the following lines:

```
for (Enumeration e=v.elements();e.hasMoreElements();)
    System.out.print(e.nextElement()+" ");
```

You can see that an Enumeration object, which represents all the elements in the Vector, is created and returned by the Vector method elements(). With this Enumeration object, the loop can check to see whether there are more elements to process using the Enumeration method hasMoreElements(); the loop can get the next element in the Vector using the Enumeration method nextElement().

The Vector2 program in Listing 13.9 shows some of the vector-accessing techniques. It first generates a vector of random integers; then it allows the user to search for a specific value. The locations of the first and last occurrences of the value are printed by the program using the indexOf() and lastIndexOf() methods.

Listing 13.9. Vector2.java: Another sample Vector program.

```java
import java.io.DataInputStream;
import java.lang.Integer;
import java.lang.Math;
import java.util.Enumeration;
import java.util.Random;
import java.util.Vector;

class Vector2 {
    public static void main(String args[])
        throws java.io.IOException
    {
        int numElements;
        DataInputStream dis=new DataInputStream(System.in);
        Vector v=new Vector(10,10);
        Random randGen=new Random();

        System.out.println("How many random elements? ");
        numElements=Integer.valueOf(dis.readLine()).intValue();
        for (int i=0;i<numElements;i++)
            v.addElement(new Integer(Math.abs(
                randGen.nextInt())%numElements));

        System.out.println(v.toString());

        Integer searchValue;
        System.out.println("Find which value? ");
        searchValue=Integer.valueOf(dis.readLine());
        System.out.println("First occurrence is element "+
            v.indexOf(searchValue));
        System.out.println("Last occurrence is element "+
            v.lastIndexOf(searchValue));
    }
}
```

The output from this program looks like this:

```
How many random elements?
10
[0, 2, 8, 4, 9, 7, 8, 6, 3, 2]
```

```
Find which value?
8
First occurrence is element 2
Last occurrence is element 6
```

In addition to extending the java.lang.Object class, the Vector class implements the java.lang.Cloneable interface. Table 13.7 summarizes the methods of the Vector class.

Table 13.7. The variables and methods available in the Vector interface.

Variable or Method	Description
Variables	
capacityIncrement	Size of the incremental allocations, in elements
elementCount	Number of elements in Vector
elementData	Buffer in which the elements are stored
Constructors	
Vector()	Constructs an empty vector
Vector(int)	Constructs an empty vector with the specified storage capacity
Vector(int, int)	Constructs an empty vector with the specified storage capacity and capacityIncrement
Methods	
addElement(Object)	Adds the specified object at the end of the Vector
capacity()	Returns the capacity of the Vector
clone()	Creates a clone of the Vector
contains(Object)	True if the specified object is in the Vector
copyInto(Object[])	Copies the elements of this vector into an array
elementAt(int)	Returns the element at the specified index
elements()	Returns an Enumeration of the elements
ensureCapacity(int)	Ensures that the Vector has the specified capacity
firstElement()	Returns the first element of the Vector
indexOf(Object)	Returns the index of the first occurrence of the specified object within the Vector

Variable or Method	Description
Methods	
indexOf(Object, int)	Returns the index of the specified object within the Vector, starting the search at the index specified and proceeding toward the end of the Vector
insertElementAt(Object, int)	Inserts an object at the index specified
isEmpty()	True if the Vector is empty
lastElement()	Returns the last element of the Vector
lastIndexOf(Object)	Returns the index of the last occurrence of the specified object within the Vector
lastIndexOf(Object, int)	Returns the index of the specified object within the Vector, starting the search at the index specified and proceeding toward the beginning of the Vector
removeAllElements()	Removes all elements of the Vector
removeElement(Object)	Removes the specified object from the Vector
removeElementAt(int)	Removes the element with the specified index
setElementAt(Object, int)	Stores the object at the specified index in the Vector
setSize(int)	Sets the size of the Vector
size()	Returns the number of elements in the Vector
toString()	Converts the Vector to a string
trimToSize()	Trims the Vector's capacity down to the specified size

13

THE UTILITIES PACKAGE

The Stack Class

The stack data structure is key to many programming efforts, ranging from building compilers to solving mazes. The Stack class in the Java library implements a *Last In, First Out* (LIFO) stack of objects. Even though they are based on (that is, they extend) the Vector class, Stack objects are typically not accessed in a direct fashion. Instead, values are pushed on and popped off the top of the stack. The net effect is that the values most recently pushed are the first to pop.

The Stack1 code in Listing 13.10 pushes strings onto the stack and then retrieves them. The strings end up printed in the reverse order from which they were stored.

Listing 13.10. Stack1.java: A sample Stack program.

```java
import java.io.DataInputStream;
import java.util.Stack;
import java.util.StringTokenizer;

class Stack1 {
    public static void main(String args[])
        throws java.io.IOException
    {
        DataInputStream dis=new DataInputStream(System.in);

        System.out.println("Enter a sentence: ");
        String s=dis.readLine();
        StringTokenizer st=new StringTokenizer(s);
        Stack stack=new Stack();
        while (st.hasMoreTokens())
            stack.push(st.nextToken());
        while (!stack.empty())
            System.out.print((String)stack.pop()+" ");
        System.out.println();
    }
}
```

The output from this program looks like this:

```
Enter a sentence:
The quick brown fox jumps over the lazy dog
dog lazy the over jumps fox brown quick The
```

Even though Stack objects normally are not accessed in a direct fashion, it is possible to search the Stack for a specific value using the search() method. search() accepts an object to find and returns the distance from the top of the Stack where the object was found. It returns -1 if the object is not found.

The peek() method returns the top object on the Stack without actually removing it from the Stack. The peek() method throws an EmptyStackException if the stack has no items.

Table 13.8 summarizes the complete interface of the Stack class.

Table 13.8. The methods available in the Stack interface.

Method	Description
	Constructor
Stack()	Constructs an empty Stack

Method	Description
Methods	
empty()	True if the Stack is empty
peek()	Returns the top object on the Stack without removing the element
pop()	Pops an element off the Stack
push(Object)	Pushes an element onto the Stack
search(Object)	Finds an object on the Stack

The Dictionary Class

The Dictionary class is an abstract class used as a base for the Hashtable class. It implements a data structure that allows a collection of key and value pairs to be stored. Any type of object can be used for the keys or the values. Typically, the keys are used to find a particular corresponding value.

Because the Dictionary class is an abstract class that cannot be used directly, the code examples presented in this section cannot actually be run. They are presented only to explain the purpose and use of the methods declared by this class. The following code would, hypothetically, be used to create a Dictionary with these values:

```
Dictionary products = new Dictionary();
products.put(new Integer(342), "Widget");
products.put(new Integer(124), "Gadget");
products.put(new Integer(754), "FooBar");
```

The put() method is used to insert a key and value pair into the Dictionary. Both arguments must be derived from the class Object. The key is the first argument, and the value is the second argument.

A value can be retrieved using the get() method and a specific key to be found. get() returns the null value if the specified key is not found. Here's an example:

```
String name = products.get(new Integer(124));
if (name != null) {
    System.out.println("Product name for code 124 is " + name);
}
```

Although an individual object can be retrieved with the get() method, it is sometimes necessary to access all the keys or all the values. Two methods, keys() and elements(), return Enumerations that can be used to access the keys and the values.

Table 13.9 summarizes the complete interface of the Dictionary class.

13

THE UTILITIES
PACKAGE

Table 13.9. The methods available in the `Dictionary` interface.

Method	Description
	Constructors
`Dictionary()`	Constructs an empty `Dictionary`
	Methods
`elements()`	Returns an `Enumeration` of the values
`get(Object)`	Returns the object associated with the specified key
`isEmpty()`	True if the `Dictionary` has no elements
`keys()`	Returns an `Enumeration` of the keys
`put(Object, Object)`	Stores the specified key and value pair in the `Dictionary`
`remove(Object)`	Removes an element from the `Dictionary` based on its key
`size()`	Returns the number of elements stored

The Hashtable Class

The `Hashtable` data structure is very useful when searching for and manipulating data. You should use the `Hashtable` class if you will be storing a large amount of data in memory and then searching it. The time needed to complete a search of a hash table is decidedly less than what it takes to search a `Vector`. Of course, for small amounts of data, it doesn't make much difference whether you use a hash table or a linear data structure because the overhead time is much greater than any search time would be. See the following sidebar for more information on search times in the different classes.

Hash table organization is based on *keys*, which are computed based on the data being stored. For example, if you want to insert a number of words into a hash table, you can base your key on the first letter of the word. When you come back later to search for a word, you can then compute the key for the item being sought. By using this key, search time is drastically reduced because the items are stored based on the value of their respective keys.

The `Hashtable` class implements a hash table storage mechanism for storing key and value pairs. Hash tables are designed to quickly locate and retrieve information stored by using a key. Keys and values can be of any object type, but the key object's class must implement the `hashCode()` and `equals()` methods.

SEARCH TIMES

Big "O" notation is used to measure the "worst case scenario" time requirements in terms of searching while using different data structures. Linear searching, such as that used in the Vector class, is O(n); hash table searching is O(log n). This means that for a large number of objects, you can save a lot of search time when you use a Hashtable because the *log* of a number is always less than the number itself. If you will be doing a large amount of searching through data, a hash table is likely to be much more efficient.

The sample Hashtable1 in Listing 13.11 creates a Hashtable object and stores 10 key and value pairs using the put() method. It then uses the get() method to return the value corresponding to a key entered by the user.

Listing 13.11. Hashtable1.java: A sample Hashtable program.

```java
import java.io.DataInputStream;
import java.lang.Integer;
import java.lang.Math;
import java.util.Random;
import java.util.Hashtable;

class Hashtable1 {
    public static void main(String args[])
        throws java.io.IOException
    {
        DataInputStream dis=new DataInputStream(System.in);
        int numElements=10;
        String keys[]={"Red","Green","Blue","Cyan","Magenta",
            "Yellow","Black","Orange","Purple","White"};
        Hashtable ht;
        Random randGen=new Random();

        ht=new Hashtable(numElements*2);
        for (int i=0;i<numElements;i++)
            ht.put(keys[i],new Integer(Math.abs(
                randGen.nextInt())%numElements));

        System.out.println(ht.toString());

        String keyValue;
        System.out.println("Which key to find? ");
        keyValue=dis.readLine();
        Integer value=(Integer)ht.get(keyValue);
        if (value!=null) System.out.println(keyValue+" = "+value);
    }
}
```

13

THE UTILITIES PACKAGE

The output from this program looks like this:

```
{Cyan=4, White=0, Magenta=4, Red=5, Black=3,
Green=8, Purple=3, Orange=4, Yellow=2, _Blue=6}
Which key to find?
Red
Red = 5
```

In addition to the get() method, the contains() and containsKey() methods can be used to search for a particular value or key. Both return true or false depending on whether the search was successful. The contains() method must perform an exhaustive search of the table and is not as efficient as the containsKey() method, which can take advantage of the hash table's storage mechanism to find the key quickly.

Because hash tables must allocate storage for more data than actually is stored, a measurement called the *load factor* indicates the number of used storage spaces as a fraction of the total available storage spaces. The load factor is expressed as a value between 0 and 100 percent. Typically, the load factor should not be higher than about 50 percent for efficient retrieval of data from a hash table. When specifying the load factor in a program, use a fractional value in the range 0.0 to 1.0 to represent load factors in the range 0 to 100 percent.

Hash tables can be constructed in three different ways: By specifying the desired initial capacity and load factor; by specifying only the initial capacity; or by specifying neither the initial capacity nor the load factor. If the load factor is not specified, the Hashtable is rehashed into a larger table when it is full—otherwise, it is rehashed when it exceeds the load factor. The constructors throw an IllegalArgumentException if the initial capacity is less than or equal to zero, or if the load factor is less than or equal to zero.

The clone() method can be used to create a copy (a clone) of the Hashtable. However, it creates a *shallow copy* of the Hashtable, which means that the keys and values themselves are not clones. This local method overrides the inherited clone() method.

CAUTION

The clone() method is a relatively expensive operation to perform in terms of memory usage and execution time. Because the new Hashtable still refers directly to the objects (keys and values) stored in the old table, use caution to avoid making changes that will disrupt the original Hashtable.

The Hashtable class extends the java.util.Dictionary class and implements the java.lang.Cloneable interface. Table 13.10 summarizes the methods of the Hashtable class.

Table 13.10. The methods available in the Hashtable interface.

Method	Description
	Constructors
Hashtable()	Constructs an empty Hashtable
Hashtable(int)	Constructs an empty Hashtable with the specified capacity
Hashtable(int, float)	Constructs an empty Hashtable with the given capacity and load factor
	Methods
clear()	Deletes all elements from the Hashtable
clone()	Creates a clone of the Hashtable
contains(Object)	True if the specified object is an element of the Hashtable
containsKey(Object)	True if the Hashtable contains the specified key
elements()	Returns an Enumeration of the Hashtable's values
get(Object)	Returns the object associated with the specified key
isEmpty()	True if the Hashtable has no elements
keys()	Returns an Enumeration of the keys
put(Object, Object)	Stores the specified key and value pair in the Hashtable
rehash()	Rehashes the contents of the table into a bigger table
remove(Object)	Removes an element from the Hashtable based on its key
size()	Returns the number of elements stored
toString()	Converts the contents to a very long string

The Properties Class

The Properties class is what enables end-users to customize their Java programs. For example, you can easily store values such as foreground colors, background colors, font defaults, and so on and then have those values available to be reloaded. This arrangement is most useful for Java applications, but you can also implement them for applets. If you have an applet that is regularly used by multiple users, you can keep a properties file on your server for each different user; the properties file is accessed each time that user loaded the applet.

The Properties class is a Hashtable, which can be repeatedly stored and restored from a stream. It is used to implement persistent properties. The Properties class also allows for an unlimited level of nesting by searching a default property list if the required property is not found. The fact that this class is an extension of the Hashtable class means that all methods available in the Hashtable class are also available in the Properties class.

The sample Properties1 program in Listing 13.12 creates two properties lists. One is the default property list and the other is the user-defined property list. When the user property list is created, the default Properties object is passed. When the user property list is searched, if the key value is not found, the default Properties list is searched.

Listing 13.12. Properties1.java: A sample Properties program.

```
import java.io.Data7InputStream;
import java.lang.Integer;
import java.util.Properties;

class Properties1 {
    public static void main(String args[])
        throws java.io.IOException
    {
        int numElements=4;
        String defaultNames[]={"Red","Green","Blue","Purple"};
        int defaultValues[]={1,2,3,4};
        String userNames[]={"Red","Yellow","Orange","Blue"};
        int userValues[]={100,200,300,400};
        DataInputStream dis=new DataInputStream(System.in);
        Properties defaultProps=new Properties();
        Properties userProps=new Properties(defaultProps);

        for (int i=0;i<numElements;i++){
            defaultProps.put(defaultNames[i],
                Integer.toString(defaultValues[i]));
            userProps.put(userNames[i],
                Integer.toString(userValues[i]));
        }
        System.out.println("Default Properties");
        defaultProps.list(System.out);
        System.out.println("\nUser Defined Properties");
        userProps.list(System.out);

        String keyValue;
        System.out.println("\nWhich property to find? ");
        keyValue=dis.readLine();
        System.out.println("Property '"+keyValue+"' is '"+
            userProps.getProperty(keyValue)+"'");
    }
}
```

Notice that the getProperties() method is used instead of the inherited get() method. The get() method searches only the current Properties object. The getProperties() method must be used to search the default Properties list. An alternative form of the getProperties() method has a second argument: a Properties list that is to be searched instead of the default specified when the Properties object was created.

The propertyNames() method can be used to return an Enumeration, which can be used to index through all the property names. This Enumeration includes the property names from the default Properties list. Likewise, the list() method, which prints the Properties list to the standard output, lists all the properties of the current Properties object and those in the default Properties object.

Properties objects can be written to and read from a stream using the save() and load() methods. In addition to the output or input stream, the save() method has an additional string argument that is written at the beginning of the stream as a header comment.

Table 13.11 summarizes the methods of the Properties class.

Table 13.11. The variables and methods available in the Properties interface.

Variable or Method	Description
Variable	
defaults	Default Properties list to search
Constructors	
Properties()	Constructs an empty property list
Properties(Properties)	Constructs an empty property list with the specified default
Methods	
getProperty(string)	Returns a property given the key
getProperty(string, string)	Returns a property given the specified key and default
list(PrintStream)	Lists the properties to a stream for debugging
load(InputStream)	Reads the properties from an InputStream
propertyNames()	Returns an Enumeration of all the keys
save(OutputStream, string)	Writes the properties to an OutputStream

The Observable Class

The Observable class acts as a base class for objects you want to have observed by other objects that implement the Observer interface. An Observable object can notify its Observers whenever the Observable object is modified using the notifyObservers() method. This method accomplishes the notification by invoking the update() method of all its Observers, optionally passing a data object that is passed to notifyObservers(). Observable objects can have any number of Observers.

Table 13.12 summarizes the complete interface of the Observable class.

Table 13.12. The methods available in the Observable interface.

Method	Description
	Constructor
Observable()	Constructs an instance of the Observable class
	Methods
addObserver(Observer)	Adds an Observer to the observer list
clearChanged()	Clears an observable change
countObservers()	Returns the number of Observers
deleteObserver(Observer)	Deletes an Observer from the observer list
deleteObservers()	Deletes all Observers from the observer list
hasChanged()	True if an observable change has occurred
notifyObservers()	Notifies all observers when an observable change has occurred
notifyObservers(Object)	Notifies all observers of a specific observable change
setChanged()	Sets a flag to indicate that an observable change has occurred

Summary

This chapter described the classes that make up the Java utilities package. This package provides complete implementations of the basic data structures and some of the most useful data types (other than the fundamental numeric types) needed by programmers. Many of the data types and data structures that you will develop using Java will be based on the classes found in the utilities package. For smaller applets, many of these classes are not necessary. However, as your applets increase in complexity, you will find these classes to be very useful. In any case, this chapter has been a good starting point for understanding the utility of these important Java classes and for understanding how to use them effectively.

The I/O Package

by Michael Morrison

IN THIS CHAPTER

It would be impossible for a program to do anything useful without performing some kind of input or output of data. Most programs require input from the user; in return, they output information to the screen, printer, and often to files. The Java I/O package provides an extensive set of classes that handle input and output to and from many different devices. In this chapter, you learn about the primary classes contained in the I/O package, along with some examples that show off the capabilities of these classes.

The I/O package, also known as `java.io`, contains many classes, each with a variety of member variables and methods. This chapter does not take an exhaustive look at every class and method contained in the I/O package. Instead, you can view this chapter as a tutorial on how to perform basic input and output using the more popular I/O classes. Armed with the information from this chapter, you will be ready to begin using the Java I/O classes in your own programs. And should you choose to explore the more complex I/O classes supported by Java, you will be prepared for the challenge.

Input Stream Classes

The Java input model is based on the concept of an input stream. An *input stream* can be thought of much like a physical (and certainly more literal) stream of water flowing from a water plant into the pipes of a water system. The obvious difference is that an input stream deals with binary computer data rather than physical water. The comparison is relevant, however, because the data going into an input stream flows like the water being pumped into a pipe. Data pumped into an input stream can be directed in many different ways, much like water is directed through the complex system of pipes that make up a water system. The data in an input stream is transmitted a byte at a time, which is roughly analogous to individual drops of water flowing into a pipe.

More practically speaking, Java uses input streams as the means of reading data from an *input source*, such as the keyboard. The basic input stream classes supported by Java follow:

- `InputStream`
- `BufferedInputStream`
- `DataInputStream`
- `FileInputStream`
- `StringBufferInputStream`

The `InputStream` Class

The `InputStream` class is an abstract class that serves as the base class for all other input stream classes. `InputStream` defines a basic interface for reading streamed bytes of information. The methods defined by the `InputStream` class will become very familiar to you because they serve a similar purpose in every `InputStream`-derived class. This design approach enables you to learn the protocol for managing input streams once and then apply it to different devices using an `InputStream`-derived class.

The typical scenario when using an input stream is to create an `InputStream`-derived object and then tell it you want to input information (by calling an appropriate method). If no input information is currently available, the `InputStream` uses a technique known as *blocking* to wait until input data becomes available. An example of when blocking takes place is the case of using an input stream to read information from the keyboard. Until the user types information and presses Return or Enter, there is no input available to the `InputStream` object. The `InputStream` object then waits (blocks) until the user presses Return or Enter, at which time the input data becomes available and the `InputStream` object can process it as input.

The `InputStream` class defines the following methods:

- `abstract int read()`
- `int read(byte b[])`
- `int read(byte b[], int off, int len)`
- `long skip(long n)`
- `int available()`
- `synchronized void mark(int readlimit)`
- `synchronized void reset()`
- `boolean markSupported()`
- `void close()`

`InputStream` defines three different `read` methods for reading input data in various ways. The first `read()` method takes no parameters and simply reads a byte of data from the input stream and returns it as an integer. This version of `read()` returns `-1` if the end of the input stream is reached. Because this version of `read` returns a byte of input as an `int`, you must cast it to a `char` if you are reading characters. The second version of `read()` takes an array of bytes as its only parameter, enabling you to read multiple bytes of data at once. The data that is read is stored in this array. You have to make sure that the byte array passed into `read()` is large enough to hold the information being read or an `IOException` will be thrown. This version of `read()` returns the actual number of bytes read or `-1` if the end of the stream is reached. The last version of `read()` takes a byte array, an integer offset, and an integer length as parameters. This version of `read()` is very similar to the second version except that it enables you to specify where in the byte array you want to place the information that is read. The `off` parameter specifies the offset into the byte array to start placing read data, and the `len` parameter specifies the maximum number of bytes to read.

The `skip()` method is used to skip over bytes of data in the input stream. `skip()` takes a `long` value *n* as its only parameter, which specifies how many bytes of input to skip. It returns the actual number of bytes skipped or `-1` if the end of the input stream is reached.

14

THE I/O PACKAGE

The available() method is used to determine the number of bytes of input data that can be read without blocking. available() takes no parameters and returns the number of available bytes. This method is useful if you want to ensure that there is input data available (and therefore avoid the blocking mechanism).

The mark() method marks the current position in the stream. You can later return to this position using the reset() method. The mark() and reset() methods are useful in situations in which you want to read ahead in the stream but not lose your original position. An example of this situation is verifying a file type, such as an image file. You would probably read the file header first and mark the position at the end of the header. You would then read some of the data to make sure that it follows the format expected for that file type. If the data doesn't look right, you can reset the read pointer and try a different technique.

Notice that the mark() method takes an integer parameter, *readlimit*. *readlimit* specifies how many bytes can be read before the mark becomes invalidated. In effect, *readlimit* determines how far you can read ahead and still be able to reset the marked position. The markSupported() method returns a boolean value representing whether or not an input stream supports the mark/reset functionality.

Finally, the close() method closes an input stream and releases any resources associated with the stream. It is not necessary to explicitly call close() because input streams are automatically closed when the InputStream object is destroyed. Although it is not necessary, calling close() immediately after you are finished using a stream is a good programming practice. The reason for this is that close() causes the stream buffer to be flushed, which helps avoid file corruption.

The System.in Object

The keyboard is the most standard device for retrieving user input. The System class contained in the language package contains a member variable that represents the keyboard, or standard input stream. This member variable is called in and is an instance of the InputStream class. This variable is useful for reading user input from the keyboard. Listing 14.1 contains the ReadKeys1 program, which shows how the System.in object can be used with the first version of the read() method. This program can be found in the file ReadKeys1.java on the CD-ROM that accompanies this book.

> **NOTE**
>
> I mentioned the keyboard as being the standard input stream. This isn't totally true because the standard input stream can receive input from any number of sources. Although the keyboard certainly is the most common method of feeding input to the standard input stream, it is not the only method. An example of the standard input stream being driven by a different input source is the redirection of an input file into a stream.

Listing 14.1. The ReadKeys1 class.

```
class ReadKeys1 {
  public static void main (String args[]) {
    StringBuffer s = new StringBuffer();
    char c;
    try {
      while ((c = (char)System.in.read()) != '\n') {
        s.append(c);
      }
    }
    catch (Exception e) {
      System.out.println("Error: " + e.toString());
    }
    System.out.println(s);
  }
}
```

The `ReadKeys1` class first creates a `StringBuffer` object called s. It then enters a `while` loop that repeatedly calls the `read` method until a newline character is detected (the user presses Return). Notice that the input data returned by `read()` is cast to a `char` type before being stored in the character variable c. Each time a character is read, it is appended to the string buffer using the `append()` method of `StringBuffer`. It is important to see how any errors caused by the `read()` method are handled by the `try/catch` exception-handling blocks. The `catch` block simply prints an error message to the standard output stream based on the error that occurred. Finally, when a newline character is read from the input stream, the `println()` method of the standard output stream is called to output the string to the screen. You learn more about the standard output stream a little later in this chapter.

Listing 14.2 contains `ReadKeys2`, which is similar to `ReadKeys1` except that it uses the second version of the `read()` method. This `read()` method takes an array of bytes as a parameter to store the input that is read. `ReadKeys2` can be found in the file `ReadKeys2.java` on the CD-ROM that accompanies this book.

Listing 14.2. The ReadKeys2 class.

```
class ReadKeys2 {
  public static void main (String args[]) {
    byte buf[] = new byte[80];
    try {
      System.in.read(buf);
    }
    catch (Exception e) {
      System.out.println("Error: " + e.toString());
    }
    String s = new String(buf, 0);
    System.out.println(s);
  }
}
```

In ReadKeys2, an array of bytes is created that is 80 bytes long. A single read() method call is performed that reads everything the user has typed. The input is blocked until the user presses Return, at which time the input becomes available and the read() method fills the byte array with the new data. A String object is then created to hold the constant string previously read. Notice that the constructor used to create the String object takes an array of bytes (buf) as the first parameter and appends the high-byte value specified in the second parameter to each byte, thus forming 16-bit Unicode characters. Because the standard ASCII characters map to Unicode characters with zeros in the high byte, passing 0 as the high byte to the constructor works perfectly. Finally, println() is again used to output the string.

 The ReadKeys3 program in Listing 14.3 shows how to use the last version of the read() method. This version of read() again takes an array of bytes, as well as an offset and length for determining how to store the input data in the byte array. ReadKeys3 can be found in the file ReadKeys3.java on the CD-ROM that accompanies this book.

Listing 14.3. The ReadKeys3 class.

```
class ReadKeys3 {
  public static void main (String args[]) {
    byte buf[] = new byte[10];
    try {
      System.in.read(buf, 0, 10);
    }
    catch (Exception e) {
      System.out.println("Error: " + e.toString());
    }
    String s = new String(buf, 0);
    System.out.println(s);
  }
}
```

ReadKeys3 is very similar to ReadKeys2, with one major difference: The third version of the read() method is used to limit the maximum number of bytes read into the array. The size of the byte array is also shortened to 10 bytes to show how this version of read() handles it when more data is available than the array can hold. Remember that this version of read() can also be used to read data into a specific offset of the array. In this case, the offset is specified as 0 so that the only difference is the maximum number of bytes that can be read (10). This useful technique guarantees that you don't overrun a byte array.

The BufferedInputStream Class

As its name implies, the BufferedInputStream class provides a buffered stream of input. This means that more data is read into the buffered stream than you might have requested, so that subsequent reads come straight out of the buffer rather than from the input device. This arrangement can result in much faster read access because reading from a buffer is really just reading from memory. BufferedInputStream implements all the same methods defined by InputStream.

As a matter of fact, it doesn't implement any new methods of its own. However, the BufferedInputStream class does have two different constructors, which follow:

- BufferedInputStream(InputStream *in*)
- BufferedInputStream(InputStream *in*, int *size*)

Notice that both constructors take an InputStream object as the first parameter. The only difference between the two is the size of the internal buffer. In the first constructor, a default buffer size is used; in the second constructor, you specify the buffer size with the *size* integer parameter. To support buffered input, the BufferedInputStream class also defines a handful of member variables, which follow:

- byte *buf*[]
- int *count*
- int *pos*
- int *markpos*
- int *marklimit*

The *buf* byte array member is the buffer in which input data is actually stored. The *count* member variable keeps up with how many bytes are stored in the buffer. The *pos* member variable keeps up with the current read position in the buffer. The *markpos* member variable specifies the current mark position in the buffer as set using the mark() method. *markpos* is equal to -1 if no mark has been set. Finally, the *marklimit* member variable specifies the maximum number of bytes that can be read before the mark position is no longer valid. *marklimit* is set by the *readlimit* parameter passed into the mark() method. Because all these member variables are specified as protected, you will probably never actually use any of them. However, seeing these variables should give you some insight into how the BufferedInputStream class implements the methods defined by InputStream.

 Listing 14.4 contains the ReadKeys4 program, which uses a BufferedInputStream object instead of System.in to read input from the keyboard. ReadKeys4 can be found in the file ReadKeys4.java on the CD-ROM that accompanies this book.

Listing 14.4. The ReadKeys4 class.

```
import java.io.*;

class ReadKeys4 {
  public static void main (String args[]) {
    BufferedInputStream in = new BufferedInputStream(System.in);
    byte buf[] = new byte[10];
    try {
      in.read(buf, 0, 10);
    }
    catch (Exception e) {
```

14

THE I/O PACKAGE

continues

Listing 14.4. continued

```
    System.out.println("Error: " + e.toString());
    }
    String s = new String(buf, 0);
    System.out.println(s);
  }
}
```

Notice first that the BufferedInputStream class must be imported from the I/O package. Actually, in this case, the * qualifier is used to import all the classes in the I/O package. The BufferedInputStream object is created by passing the System.in InputStream into its constructor. From there on, the program is essentially the same as ReadKeys3, except that the read() method is called on the BufferedInputStream object rather than on System.in.

The DataInputStream Class

The DataInputStream class is useful for reading primitive Java data types from an input stream in a portable fashion. There is only one constructor for DataInputStream, which simply takes an InputStream object as its only parameter. This constructor is defined as follows:

DataInputStream(InputStream *in*)

DataInputStream implements the following useful methods beyond those defined by InputStream:

- final int skipBytes(int *n*)
- final void readFully(byte *b*[])
- final void readFully(byte *b*[], int *off*, int *len*)
- final String readLine()
- final boolean readBoolean()
- final byte readByte()
- final int readUnsignedByte()
- final short readShort()
- final int readUnsignedShort()
- final char readChar()
- final int readInt()
- final long readLong()
- final float readFloat()
- final double readDouble()

The skipBytes() method works in a manner very similar to skip(); the exception is that skipBytes() blocks until all bytes are skipped. The number of bytes to skip is determined by the integer parameter *n*. There are two `readFully()` methods implemented by `DataInputStream`. These methods are similar to the `read()` methods except that they block until *all* data has been read. The normal `read()` methods block only until *some* data is available, not all. The `readFully()` methods are to the `read()` methods what `skipBytes()` is to `skip()`.

The `readLine()` method is used to read a line of text that has been terminated with a newline (\n), carriage return (\r), carriage return/newline (\r\n), or end-of-file (EOF) character sequence. `readLine()` returns the line of text in a `String` object. Listing 14.5 contains the `ReadFloat` program, which uses the `readLine()` method to read a floating-point value from the user.

Listing 14.5. The ReadFloat class.

```
import java.io.*;

class ReadFloat {
  public static void main (String args[]) {
    DataInputStream in = new DataInputStream(System.in);
    String s = new String();
    try {
      s = in.readLine();
      float f = Float.valueOf(s).floatValue();
      System.out.println(f);
    }
    catch (Exception e) {
      System.out.println("Error: " + e.toString());
    }
  }
}
```

In `ReadFloat`, a `DataInputStream` object is first created based on `System.in`. A `String` object is then created to hold the input line of text. The `readLine()` method is called with the resulting line of text being stored in the `String` object `s`. A floating-point number is extracted from the string by first getting a `Float` object from the string using the `valueOf()` static method of the `Float` class. The `floatValue()` method is then called on the `Float` object to get a `float` value, which is then stored in the `float` variable `f`. This value is then output to the screen using `println()`.

The rest of the methods implemented by `DataInputStream` are variations of the `read()` method for different fundamental data types. The type read by each method is easily identifiable by the name of the method.

The `FileInputStream` Class

The `FileInputStream` class is useful for performing simple file input. For more advanced file input operations, you will more than likely want to use the `RandomAccessFile` class, discussed a little later in this chapter. The `FileInputStream` class can be instantiated using one of the in three following constructors:

14

■ `FileInputStream(String name)`

■ `FileInputStream(File file)`

■ `FileInputStream(FileDescriptor fdObj)`

The first constructor takes a `String` object parameter called *name*, which specifies the name of the file to use for input. The second constructor takes a `File` object parameter that specifies the file to use for input. You learn more about the `File` object near the end of this chapter. The third constructor for `FileInputStream` takes a `FileDescriptor` object as its only parameter.

 The `FileInputStream` class functions exactly like the `InputStream` class except that it is geared toward working with files. Listing 14.6 contains the `ReadFile` program, which uses the `FileInputStream` class to read data from a text file. `ReadFile` can be found in the file `ReadFile.java` on the CD-ROM that accompanies this book.

Listing 14.6. The ReadFile class.

```
import java.io.*;

class ReadFile {
  public static void main (String args[]) {
    byte buf[] = new byte[64];
    try {
      FileInputStream in = new FileInputStream("Grocery.txt");
      in.read(buf, 0, 64);
    }
    catch (Exception e) {
      System.out.println("Error: " + e.toString());
    }
    String s = new String(buf, 0);
    System.out.println(s);
  }
}
```

In `ReadFile`, a `FileInputStream` object is first created by passing a string with the name of the file (`"Grocery.txt"`) as the input file. The `read()` method is then called to read from the input file into a byte array. The byte array is then used to create a `String` object, which is in turn used for output. Pretty simple!

The `StringBufferInputStream` Class

Aside from having a very long name, the `StringBufferInputStream` class is a pretty neat class. `StringBufferInputStream` enables you to use a string as a buffered source of input. `StringBufferInputStream` implements all the same methods defined by `InputStream`, and no more. The `StringBufferInputStream` class has a single constructor, which follows:

`StringBufferInputStream(String s)`

The constructor takes a `String` object, from which it constructs the string buffer input stream. Although `StringBufferInputStream` doesn't define any additional methods, it does provide a few of its own member variables, which follow:

- String *buffer*
- int *count*
- int *pos*

The *buffer* string member is the buffer where the string data is actually stored. The *count* member variable specifies the number of characters to use in the buffer. Finally, the *pos* member variable keeps up with the current position in the buffer. As is true with the `BufferedInputStream` class, you will probably never see these member variables, but they are important in understanding how the `StringBufferInputStream` class is implemented.

 Listing 14.7 shows the `ReadString` program, which uses a `StringBufferInputStream` to read data from a string of text data. `ReadString` can be found in the file `ReadString.java` on the CD-ROM that accompanies this book.

Listing 14.7. The ReadString class.

```
import java.io.*;

class ReadString {
  public static void main (String args[]) {
    // Get a string of input from the user
    byte buf1[] = new byte[64];
    try {
      System.in.read(buf1, 0, 64);
    }
    catch (Exception e) {
      System.out.println("Error: " + e.toString());
    }
    String s1 = new String(buf1, 0);

    // Read the string as a string buffer and output it
    StringBufferInputStream in = new StringBufferInputStream(s1);
    byte buf2[] = new byte[64];
    try {
      in.read(buf2, 0, 64);
    }
    catch (Exception e) {
      System.out.println("Error: " + e.toString());
    }
    String s2 = new String(buf2, 0);
    System.out.println(s2);
  }
}
```

The ReadString program enables the user to type text, which is read and stored in a string. This string is then used to create a StringBufferInputStream that is read into another string for output. Obviously, this program goes to a lot of trouble to do very little; it's only meant as a demonstration of how to use the StringBufferInputStream class. It's up to you to find an interesting application to which you can apply this class.

The first half of the ReadString program should look pretty familiar; it's essentially the guts of the ReadKeys3 program, which reads data entered by the keyboard into a string. The second half of the program is where you actually get busy with the StringBufferInputStream object. A StringBufferInputStream object is created using the String object (s1) containing the text entered from the keyboard. The contents of the StringBufferInputStream object are then read into a byte array using the read() method. The byte array is in turn used to construct another String object (s2), which is output to the screen.

Output Stream Classes

In Java, output streams are the logical counterparts to input streams; they handle writing data to output sources. Using the water analogy from the discussion of input streams earlier in this chapter, an *output stream* is equivalent to the water spout on your bathtub. Just as water travels from a water plant through the pipes and out the spout into your bathtub, so must data flow from an input device through the operating system and out an output device. A leaky water spout is an even better way to visualize the transfer of data out of an output stream: Each drop of water falling out of the spout represents a byte of data. Each byte of data flows to the output device just like the drops of water falling one after the other out of the bathtub spout.

Getting back to Java, you use output streams to output data to various output devices, such as the screen. The primary output stream classes used in Java programming follow:

- OutputStream
- PrintStream
- BufferedOutputStream
- DataOutputStream
- FileOutputStream

The Java output streams provide a variety of ways to output data. The OutputStream class defines the core behavior required of an output stream. The PrintStream class is geared toward outputting text data, such as the data sent to the standard output stream. The BufferedOutputStream class is an extension to the OutputStream class that provides support for buffered output. The DataOutputStream class is useful for outputting primitive data types such as int or float. And finally, the FileOutputStream class provides the support necessary to output data to files.

The OutputStream Class

The OutputStream class is the output counterpart to InputStream; it serves as an abstract base class for all the other output stream classes. OutputStream defines the basic protocol for writing streamed data to an output device. As with the methods for InputStream, you will become accustomed to the methods defined by OutputStream because they act very much the same in every OutputStream-derived class. The benefit of this common interface is that you can essentially learn a method once and then apply it to different classes without starting the learning process over again.

You typically create an OutputStream-derived object and call an appropriate method to tell it you want to output information. The OutputStream class uses a technique similar to the one used by InputStream: it will block until data has been written to an output device. While blocking (waiting for the current output to be processed), the OutputStream class does not allow any further data to be output.

The OutputStream class implements the following methods:

- abstract void write(int *b*)
- void write(byte *b*[])
- void write(byte *b*[], int *off*, int *len*)
- void flush()
- void close()

OutputStream defines three different write() methods for writing data in a few different ways. The first write() method writes a single byte to the output stream, as specified by the integer parameter *b*. The second version of write() takes an array of bytes as a parameter and writes it to the output stream. The last version of write() takes a byte array, an integer offset, and a length as parameters. This version of write() is very much like the second version except that it uses the other parameters to determine where in the byte array to begin outputting data, along with how much data to output. The *off* parameter specifies an offset into the byte array from which you want to begin outputting data, and the *len* parameter specifies how many bytes are to be output.

The flush() method is used to flush the output stream. Calling flush() forces the OutputStream object to output any pending data.

Finally, the close() method closes an output stream and releases any resources associated with the stream. As with InputStream objects, it isn't usually necessary to call close() on an OutputStream object because streams are automatically closed when they are destroyed.

The PrintStream Class

The PrintStream class is derived from OutputStream and is designed primarily for printing output data as text. PrintStream has two different constructors:

14

THE I/O PACKAGE

■ `PrintStream(OutputStream out)`

■ `PrintStream(OutputStream out, boolean autoflush)`

Both `PrintStream` constructors take an `OutputStream` object as their first parameter. The only difference between the two methods is how the newline character is handled. In the first constructor, the stream is flushed based on an internal decision by the object. In the second constructor, you can specify that the stream be flushed every time it encounters a newline character. You specify this through the boolean *autoflush* parameter.

The `PrintStream` class also implements a rich set of methods, which follow:

■ `boolean checkError()`

■ `void print(Object obj)`

■ `synchronized void print(String s)`

■ `synchronized void print(char s[])`

■ `void print(char c)`

■ `void print(int i)`

■ `void print(long l)`

■ `void print(float f)`

■ `void print(double d)`

■ `void print(boolean b)`

■ `void println()`

■ `synchronized void println(Object obj)`

■ `synchronized void println(String s)`

■ `synchronized void println(char s[])`

■ `synchronized void println(char c)`

■ `synchronized void println(int I)`

■ `synchronized void println(long l)`

■ `synchronized void println(float f)`

■ `synchronized void println(double d)`

■ `synchronized void println(boolean b)`

The `checkError()` method flushes the stream and returns whether or not an error has occurred. The return value of `checkError()` is based on an error ever having occurred on the stream, meaning that once an error occurs, `checkError()` always returns `true` for that stream.

`PrintStream` provides a variety of `print()` methods to handle all your printing needs. The version of `print()` that takes an `Object` parameter simply outputs the results of calling the `toString()` method on the object. The other `print()` methods each take a different type parameter that specifies which data type is printed.

The `println()` methods implemented by `PrintStream` are very similar to the `print()` methods. The only difference is that the `println()` methods print a newline character following the data that is printed. The `println()` method that takes no parameters simply prints a newline character by itself.

The `System.out` Object

The monitor is the primary output device on modern computer systems. The `System` class has a member variable that represents the standard output stream, which is typically the monitor. The member variable is called out and is an instance of the `PrintStream` class. The out member variable is very useful for outputting text to the screen. But you already know this because you've seen the out member variable in most of the sample programs developed thus far.

The `BufferedOutputStream` Class

The `BufferedOutputStream` class is very similar to the `OutputStream` class except that it provides a *buffered* stream of output. This class enables you to write to a stream without causing a bunch of writes to an output device. The `BufferedOutputStream` class maintains a buffer that is written to when you write to the stream. When the buffer gets full or when it is explicitly flushed, it is written to the output device. This output approach is much more efficient because most of the data transfer takes place in memory. And when it does come time to output the data to a device, it all happens at once.

The `BufferedOutputStream` class implements the same methods defined in `OutputStream`, meaning that there are no additional methods except for constructors. The two constructors for `BufferedOutputStream` follow:

■ `BufferedOutputStream(OutputStream out)`
■ `BufferedOutputStream(OutputStream out, int size)`

Both constructors for `BufferedOutputStream` take an `OutputStream` object as their first parameter. The only difference between the two is the size of the internal buffer used to store the output data. In the first constructor, a default buffer size of 512 bytes is used; in the second constructor, you specify the buffer size with the *size* integer parameter. The buffer itself within the `BufferedOutputStream` class is managed by two member variables, which follow:

■ `byte buf[]`
■ `int count`

The *buf* byte array member variable is the actual data buffer in which output data is stored. The *count* member keeps up with how many bytes are in the buffer. These two member variables are sufficient to represent the state of the output stream buffer.

Listing 14.8 shows the WriteStuff program, which uses a BufferedOutputStream object to output a byte array of text data. WriteStuff can be found in the file WriteStuff.java on the CD-ROM that accompanies this book.

Listing 14.8. The WriteStuff class.

```java
import java.io.*;

class WriteStuff {
  public static void main (String args[]) {
    // Copy the string into a byte array
    String s = new String("Dance, spider!\n");
    byte[] buf = new byte[64];
    s.getBytes(0, s.length(), buf, 0);

    // Output the byte array (buffered)
    BufferedOutputStream out = new BufferedOutputStream(System.out);
    try {
      out.write(buf, 0, 64);
      out.flush();
    }
    catch (Exception e) {
      System.out.println("Error: " + e.toString());
    }
  }
}
```

The WriteStuff program fills a byte array with text data from a string and outputs the byte array to the screen using a buffered output stream. WriteStuff begins by creating a String object containing text, and a byte array. The getBytes() method of String is used to copy the bytes of data in the string to the byte array. The getBytes() method copies the low byte of each character in the string to the byte array. This works because the Unicode representation of ASCII characters has zeros in the high byte. Once the byte array is ready, a BufferedOutputStream object is created by passing System.out into the constructor. The byte array is then written to the output buffer using the write() method. Because the stream is buffered, it is necessary to call the flush() method to actually output the data.

The DataOutputStream Class

The DataOutputStream class is useful for writing primitive Java data types to an output stream in a portable way. DataOutputStream has only one constructor, which simply takes an OutputStream object as its only parameter. This constructor is defined as follows:

DataOutputStream(OutputStream *out*)

The DataOutputStream class implements the following useful methods beyond those inherited from OutputStream:

- `final int size()`
- `final void writeBoolean(boolean v)`
- `final void writeByte(int v)`
- `final void writeShort(int v)`
- `final void writeChar(int v)`
- `final void writeInt(int v)`
- `final void writeLong(long v)`
- `final void writeFloat(float v)`
- `final void writeDouble(double v)`
- `final void writeBytes(String s)`
- `final void writeChars(String s)`

The `size()` method is used to determine how many bytes have been written to the stream thus far. The integer value returned by `size()` specifies the number of bytes written.

The rest of the methods implemented in `DataOutputStream` are all variations on the `write()` method. Each version of `writeType()` takes a different data type that is in turn written as output.

The `FileOutputStream` Class

The `FileOutputStream` class provides a means to perform simple file output. For more advanced file output, you should check out the `RandomAccessFile` class, discussed a little later in this chapter. A `FileOutputStream` object can be created using one of the following constructors:

- `FileOutputStream(String name)`
- `FileOutputStream(File file)`
- `FileOutputStream(FileDescriptor fdObj)`

The first constructor takes a `String` parameter, which specifies the name of the file to use for input. The second constructor takes a `File` object parameter that specifies the input file. You learn about the `File` object later in this chapter. The third constructor takes a `FileDescriptor` object as its only parameter.

The `FileOutputStream` class functions exactly like the `OutputStream` class except that it is specifically designed to work with files. Listing 14.9 contains the `WriteFile` program, which uses the `FileOutputStream` class to write user input to a text file. `WriteFile` can be found in the file `WriteFile.java` on the CD-ROM that accompanies this book.

14

THE I/O PACKAGE

Listing 14.9. The `WriteFile` class.

```java
import java.io.*;

class WriteFile {
  public static void main (String args[]) {
    // Read the user input
    byte buf[] = new byte[64];
    try {
      System.in.read(buf, 0, 64);
    }
    catch (Exception e) {
      System.out.println("Error: " + e.toString());
    }

    // Output the data to a file
    try {
      FileOutputStream out = new FileOutputStream("Output.txt");
      out.write(buf);
    }
    catch (Exception e) {
      System.out.println("Error: " + e.toString());
    }
  }
}
```

In `WriteFile`, user input is read from the standard input stream into a byte array using the `read()` method of `InputStream`. A `FileOutputStream` object is then created with the filename `"Output.txt"`, which is passed in as the only parameter to the constructor. The `write()` method is then used to output the byte array to the stream.

You can see that working with output file streams is just as easy as working with input file streams.

File Classes

If the `FileInputStream` and `FileOutputStream` classes don't quite meet your file-handling expectations, don't despair! Java provides two more classes for working with files that are sure to meet your needs. These two classes are `File` and `RandomAccessFile`. The `File` class models an operating system directory entry, providing you with access to information about a file—including file attributes and the full path where the file is located, among other things. The `RandomAccessFile` class, on the other hand, provides a variety of methods for reading and writing data to and from a file.

The File Class

The `File` class can be instantiated using one of three constructors, which follow:

- `File(String path)`
- `File(String path, String name)`
- `File(File dir, String name)`

The first constructor takes a single `String` parameter that specifies the full pathname of the file. The second constructor takes two `String` parameters: *path* and *name*. The *path* parameter specifies the directory path where the file is located; the *name* parameter specifies the name of the file. The third constructor is similar to the second except that it takes another `File` object as the first parameter instead of a string. The `File` object in this case is used to specify the directory path of the file.

The most important methods implemented by the `File` class follow:

- `String getName()`
- `String getPath()`
- `String getAbsolutePath()`
- `String getParent()`
- `boolean exists()`
- `boolean canWrite()`
- `boolean canRead()`
- `boolean isFile()`
- `boolean isDirectory()`
- `boolean isAbsolute()`
- `long lastModified()`
- `long length()`
- `boolean mkdir()`
- `boolean mkdirs()`
- `boolean renameTo(File dest)`
- `boolean delete()`
- `String[] list()`
- `String[] list(FilenameFilter filter)`

The `getName()` method gets the name of a file and returns it as a string. The `getPath()` method returns the path of a file—which may be relative—as a string. The `getAbsolutePath()` method returns the absolute path of a file. The `getParent()` method returns the parent directory of a file or `null` if a parent directory is not found.

The `exists()` method returns a boolean value that specifies whether or not a file actually exists. The `canWrite()` and `canRead()` methods return boolean values that specify whether a file can be written to or read from. The `isFile()` and `isDirectory()` methods return boolean values that specify whether a file is valid and whether the directory information is valid. The `isAbsolute()` method returns a boolean value that specifies whether a filename is absolute.

14

THE I/O PACKAGE

The `lastModified()` method returns a `long` value that specifies the time at which a file was last modified. The `long` value returned is only useful in determining differences between modification times; it has no meaning as an absolute time and is not suitable for output. The `length()` method returns the length of a file in bytes.

The `mkdir()` method creates a directory based on the current path information. `mkdir()` returns a boolean indicating the success of creating the directory. The `mkdirs()` method is similar to `mkdir()` except that it can be used to create an entire directory structure. The `renameTo()` method renames a file to the name specified by the `File` object passed as the *dest* parameter. The `delete()` method deletes a file. Both `renameTo()` and `delete()` return a boolean value indicating the success or failure of the operation.

Finally, the `list()` methods of the `File` object obtain listings of the directory contents. Both `list()` methods return a list of filenames in a `String` array. The only difference between the two is that the second version takes a `FilenameFilter` object that enables you to filter out certain files from the list.

 Listing 14.10 shows the source code for the `FileInfo` program, which uses a `File` object to determine information about a file in the current directory. The `FileInfo` program is located in the `FileInfo.java` source file on the CD-ROM that accompanies this book.

Listing 14.10. The `FileInfo` class.

```java
import java.io.*;

class FileInfo {
  public static void main (String args[]) {
    System.out.println("Enter file name: ");
    char c;
    StringBuffer buf = new StringBuffer();
    try {
      while ((c = (char)System.in.read()) != '\n')
        buf.append(c);
    }
    catch (Exception e) {
      System.out.println("Error: " + e.toString());
    }
    File file = new File(buf.toString());
    if (file.exists()) {
      System.out.println("File Name  : " + file.getName());
      System.out.println("    Path   : " + file.getPath());
      System.out.println("Abs. Path  : " + file.getAbsolutePath());
      System.out.println("Writable   : " + file.canWrite());
      System.out.println("Readable   : " + file.canRead());
      System.out.println("Length     : " + (file.length() / 1024) + "KB");
    }
    else
      System.out.println("Sorry, file not found.");
  }
}
```

The `FileInfo` program uses the `File` object to get information about a file in the current directory. The user is first prompted to type a filename; the resulting input is stored in a `String` object. The `String` object is then used as the parameter to the `File` object's constructor. A call to the `exists()` method determines whether the file actually exists. If so, information about the file is obtained through the various `File()` methods and the results are output to the screen.

Following are the results of running `FileInfo` and specifying `FileInfo.java` as the file for which you want to get information:

```
File Name  : FileInfo.java
      Path : FileInfo.java
Abs. Path  : C:\Books\JavaUnleashedProRef\Source\Chap14\FileInfo.java
Writable   : true
Readable   : true
Length     : 0KB
```

The RandomAccessFile Class

The `RandomAccessFile` class provides a multitude of methods for reading and writing to files. Although you can certainly use `FileInputStream` and `FileOutputStream` for file I/O, `RandomAccessFile` provides many more features and options. Following are the constructors for RandomAccessFile:

- `RandomAccessFile(String name, String mode)`
- `RandomAccessFile(File file, String mode)`

The first constructor takes a `String` parameter specifying the name of the file to access, along with a `String` parameter specifying the type of mode (read or write). The mode type can be either `"r"` for read mode or `"rw"` for read/write mode. The second constructor takes a `File` object as the first parameter, which specifies the file to access. The second parameter is a mode string, which works exactly the same as it does in the first constructor.

The `RandomAccessFile` class implements a variety of powerful file I/O methods. Following are some of the most useful ones:

- `int skipBytes(int n)`
- `long getFilePointer()`
- `void seek(long pos)`
- `int read()`
- `int read(byte b[])`
- `int read(byte b[], int off, int len)`
- `final boolean readBoolean()`
- `final byte readByte()`
- `final int readUnsignedByte()`
- `final short readShort()`

■ `final int readUnsignedShort()`

■ `final char readChar()`

■ `final int readInt()`

■ `final long readLong()`

■ `final float readFloat()`

■ `final double readDouble()`

■ `final String readLine()`

■ `final void readFully(byte b[])`

■ `final void readFully(byte b[], int off, int len)`

■ `void write(byte b[])`

■ `void write(byte b[], int off, int len)`

■ `final void writeBoolean(boolean v)`

■ `final void writeByte(int v)`

■ `final void writeShort(int v)`

■ `final void writeChar(int v)`

■ `final void writeInt(int v)`

■ `final void writeLong(long v)`

■ `void writeFloat(float v)`

■ `void writeDouble(double v)`

■ `void writeBytes(String s)`

■ `void writeChars(String s)`

■ `long length()`

■ `void close()`

From looking at this method list, you no doubt are thinking that many of these methods look familiar. And they should look familiar—most of the methods implemented by `RandomAccessFile` are also implemented by either `FileInputStream` or `FileOutputStream`. The fact that `RandomAccessFile` combines them into a single class is a convenience in and of itself. But you already know how to use these methods because they work just like they do in `FileInputStream` and `FileOutputStream`. What you are interested in are the new methods implemented by `RandomAccessFile`.

The first new method you may have noticed is the `getFilePointer()` method. `getFilePointer()` returns the current position of the file pointer as a `long` value. The file pointer indicates the location in the file where data will next be read from or written to. In read mode, the file pointer is analogous to the needle on a phonograph or the laser in a CD player. The `seek()` method is the other new method that should catch your attention. `seek()` sets the file pointer to the absolute position specified by the `long` parameter *pos*. Calling `seek()` to move the file pointer is analogous to moving the phonograph needle with your hand. In both cases, the read point of the data or music is being moved. It is a similar situation when you are writing data as well.

 Listing 14.11 shows the source code for FilePrint, a program that uses the RandomAccessFile class to print a file to the screen. The source code for the FilePrint program can be found in the file FilePrint.java on the CD-ROM that accompanies this book.

Listing 14.11. The FilePrint class.

```java
import java.io.*;

class FilePrint {
  public static void main (String args[]) {
    System.out.println("Enter file name: ");
    char c;
    StringBuffer buf = new StringBuffer();
    try {
      while ((c = (char)System.in.read()) != '\n')
        buf.append(c);
      RandomAccessFile file = new RandomAccessFile(buf.toString(), "rw");
      while (file.getFilePointer() < file.length())
        System.out.println(file.readLine());
    }
    catch (Exception e) {
      System.out.println("Error: " + e.toString());
    }
  }
}
```

The FilePrint program begins very much like the FileInfo program in Listing 14.10 in that it prompts the user to type a filename and stores the result in a string. It then uses that string to create a RandomAccessFile object in read/write mode, which is specified by passing "rw" as the second parameter to the constructor. A while loop is then used to repeatedly call the readLine() method until the entire file has been read. The call to readLine() is performed within a call to println() so that each line of the file is output to the screen.

Summary

Whew! This chapter covered a lot of ground! Hopefully, you've managed to make it this far relatively unscathed. On the up side, you've learned almost all there is to know about fundamental Java I/O and the most important classes in the I/O package. That's not to say that there isn't still a wealth of information inside the I/O package that you haven't seen. The point is that the Java class libraries are very extensive, which means that some of the classes are useful only in very special circumstances. The goal of this chapter was to highlight the more main-stream classes and methods within the I/O package.

14

THE I/O PACKAGE

One of the neatest uses of I/O streams is in sending and receiving data across a network. You're in luck because the next chapter takes a look at the Java networking package, `java.net`. You learn all about the built-in networking support provided by the networking package and how it can be used to build network Java programs.

The Networking Package

by Mike Fletcher

IN THIS CHAPTER

CHAPTER 15

This chapter serves as an introduction to the package containing Java's networking facilities. It covers the classes, interfaces, and exceptions that make up the `java.net` package.

Unless otherwise noted, classes, exceptions, and interfaces are members of the `java.net` package. The full package name is given for members of other classes—such as `java.io.IOException`. Method names are shown followed by parentheses (), such as `close()`.

These descriptions are not intended to be a complete reference. For a more detailed description of the components of the `java.net` package and the arguments of their various methods, see Appendix C, "The Java Class Library."

Classes

The classes in the networking package fall into three general categories:

- **Web interface classes.** The `URL` and `URLConnection` classes provide a quick and easy way to access content using Uniform Resource Locators. This content may be located on the local machine or anywhere on the WWW. The `URLEncoder` class provides a way to convert text for use as arguments for CGI scripts.

- **Raw network interface classes.** `Socket`, `ServerSocket`, `DatagramSocket`, and `InetAddress` are the classes that provide access to plain, bare-bones networking facilities. They are the building blocks for implementing new protocols, talking to preexisting servers, and the like. Chapter 26, "Java Socket Programming," covers using these classes in detail.

- **Extension classes.** The `ContentHandler` and `URLStreamHandler` abstract classes are used to extend the capabilities of the `URL` class. Chapter 24, "Developing Content and Protocol Handlers," explains how to write handlers for new protocols and content types.

Keep in mind that some of the `java.net` classes (such as `URLConnection` and `ContentHandler`) are abstract classes and cannot be directly instantiated. Subclasses provide the actual implementations for the different protocols and contents.

Table 15.1 lists all the classes in the package along with brief descriptions of the functionality each provides.

Table 15.1. Classes of the `java.net` package.

Class	Purpose
URL	Represents a Uniform Resource Locator
URLConnection	Retrieves content addressed by URL objects
Socket	Provides a TCP (connected, ordered stream) socket
ServerSocket	Provides a server (listening) TCP socket

Class	Purpose
DatagramSocket	Provides a UDP (connectionless datagram) socket
DatagramPacket	Represents a datagram to be sent using a DatagramSocket object
InetAddress	Represents a host name and its corresponding IP number or numbers
URLEncoder	Encodes text in the x-www-form-urlencoded format
URLStreamHandler	Subclasses implement communications streams for different URL protocols
ContentHandler	Subclasses know how to turn MIME objects into corresponding Java objects
SocketImpl	Subclasses provide access to TCP/IP facilities

The URL Class

The URL class represents a Web Uniform Resource Locator. Along with the URLConnection class, the URL class provides access to resources located on the World Wide Web using the HTTP protocol or on the local machine using file: URLs.

Constructors. The constructors for the URL class allow the creation of absolute and relative URLs. One constructor takes a whole String as a URL; other constructors allow the protocol, host, and file to be specified in separate String objects. The class also provides for relative URLs with a constructor that takes another URL object for the context and a String as the relative part of the URL.

Constructor	Description
URL(String *url*)	Takes the entire URL as a String.
URL(String *protocol*, String *host*, int *port*, String *file*)	Takes each component of the URL as a separate argument.
URL(String *protocol*, String *host*, String *file*)	As above, but uses the default port number for the protocol.
URL(URL *context*, String *file*)	Replaces the file part of the URL with the second argument.

Methods. The methods for the URL class retrieve individual components of the represented URL (such as the protocol and the host name). The class also provides comparison methods for determining whether two URL objects reference the same content.

Probably the most important method is getContent(). This method returns an object representing the content of the URL. Another method, openConnection(), returns a URLConnection object that provides a connection to the remote content. The connection object then can be used to retrieve the content, as it can be with the getContent() method.

The URLConnection Class

The URLConnection class does the actual work of retrieving the content specified by URL objects. This class is an abstract class; as such, it cannot be directly instantiated. Instead, subclasses of the class provide the implementation to handle different protocols. The subclasses know how to use the appropriate subclasses of the URLStreamHandler class to connect and retrieve the content.

Constructor. The only constructor provided for the URLConnection class takes a URL object and returns a URLConnection object for that URL. However, because URLConnection is an abstract class, it cannot be directly instantiated. Instead of using a constructor, you will probably use the URL class openConnection() method. The Java runtime system creates an instance of the proper connection subclass to handle the URL.

Methods. The getContent() method acts just like the URL class method of the same name. The URLConnection class also provides methods to get information such as the content type of the resource or HTTP header information sent with the resource. Examples of these methods are getContentType(), which returns what the HTTP content-type header contained, and the verbosely named guessContentTypeFromStream(), which tries to determine the content type by observing the incoming data stream.

Methods also are provided to obtain a java.io.InputStream object that reads data from the connection. For URLs that provide for output, there is a corresponding getOutputStream() method. The remaining URLConnection methods deal with retrieving or setting class variables.

Variables. Several protected members describe aspects of the connection, such as the URL connected to and whether the connection supports input or output. A variable also notes whether or not the connection uses a cached copy of the object.

The Socket Class

A Socket object is the Java representation of a TCP connection. When a Socket is created, a connection is opened to the specified destination. Stream objects can be obtained to send and receive data to the other end.

Constructors. The constructors for the Socket class take two arguments: the name (or IP address) of the host to connect to, and the port number on that host to connect to. The host name can be given as either a String or as an InetAddress object. In either case, the port number is specified as an integer.

Constructor	Description
`Socket( String host, int port, boolean stream )`	Takes the hostname and port to contact, and whether to use a stream (`true`) or datagram connection.
`Socket( String host, int port )`	As above, but defaults to a stream connection.
`Socket( InetAddress host, port, boolean stream )`	Uses an `InetAddress` object to specify the `int` hostname rather than a `String`.
`Socket( InetAddress host, int port )`	As above, but defaults to a stream connection.

Methods. The two most important methods in the `Socket` class are `getInputStream()` and `getOutputStream()`, which return stream objects that can be used to communicate through the socket. A `close()` method is provided to tell the underlying operating system to terminate the connection. Methods also are provided to retrieve information about the connection such as the local and remote port numbers and an `InetAddress` representing the remote host.

The ServerSocket Class

The `ServerSocket` class represents a listening TCP connection. Once an incoming connection is requested, the `ServerSocket` object returns a `Socket` object representing the connection. In normal use, another thread is spawned to handle the connection. The `ServerSocket` object is then free to listen for the next connection request.

Constructors. Both constructors for this class take as an argument the local port number to listen to for connection requests. One constructor also takes the maximum time to wait for a connection as a second argument.

Constructor	Description
`ServerSocket( int port, int count )`	Takes the port number to listen for connections on and the amount of time to listen.
`ServerSocket( int port )`	As above, but the socket waits until a connection is received.

Methods. The most important method in the `ServerSocket` class is `accept()`. This method blocks the calling thread until a connection is received. A `Socket` object is returned representing this new connection. The `close()` method tells the operating system to stop listening for requests on the socket. Also provided are methods to retrieve the host name the socket is listening on (in `InetAddress` form) and the port number being listened to.

The DatagramSocket Class

The DatagramSocket class represents a connectionless datagram socket. This class works with the DatagramPacket class to provide for communication using UDP (User Datagram Protocol).

Constructors. Because UDP is a connectionless protocol, you do not have to specify a host name when creating a DatagramSocket—only the port number on the local host. A second constructor takes no arguments. When this second constructor is used, the port number is assigned arbitrarily by the operating system.

Constructor	Description
DatagramSocket(int *port*)	Creates a socket on the specified port number.
DatagramSocket()	Creates a socket on an available port.

Methods. The two most important methods for the DatagramSocket class are send() and receive(). Each takes as an argument an appropriately constructed DatagramPacket (described in the following section). In the case of the send() method, the data contained in the packet is sent to the specified host and port. The receive() method blocks execution until a packet is received by the underlying socket, at which time the data is copied into the packet provided.

A close() method is also provided, which asks for the underlying socket to be shut down, as is a getLocalPort() method, which returns the local port number associated with the socket. This last method is particularly useful when you let the system pick the port number for you.

The DatagramPacket Class

DatagramPacket objects represent one packet of data that is sent using UDP (using a DatagramSocket).

Constructors. The DatagramPacket class provides two constructors: one for outgoing packets and one for incoming packets. The incoming version takes as arguments a byte array to hold the received data and an int specifying the size of the array. The outgoing version also takes the remote host name (as an InetAddress object) and the port number on that host to send the packet to.

Constructor	Description
DatagramPacket(byte[] *buffer*, int *length*)	Creates a packet to receive the specified number of bytes into the given buffer.
DatagramPacket(byte[] *buffer*, int *length*, InetAddress *addr*, int *port*)	Creates a packet to send the specified number of bytes from the given buffer to the host and port given.

Methods. Four methods in the DatagramPacket class allow the data, datagram length, and addressing (InetAdress and port number) information for the packet to be extracted. The methods are named, respectively, getData(), getLength(), getAddress(), and getPort().

The InetAddress Class

The InetAddress class represents a host name and its IP numbers. The class itself also provides the functionality to obtain the IP number for a given host name—similar to the C gethostbyname() function on UNIX and UNIX-like platforms.

Constructors. There are no explicit constructors for InetAddress objects. Instead, you use the static class method getByName(), which returns a reference to an InetAddress. Because some hosts may be known by more than one IP address, there also is a getAllByName() method, which returns an array of InetAddress objects.

Methods. In addition to the static methods just listed, the getHostName() method returns a String representation of the host name that the InetAddress represents; the getAddress() method returns an array of the raw bytes of the address. The equals() method compares address objects. The class also supports a toString() method, which prints out the host name and IP address textually.

The URLEncoder Class

The URLEncoder class provides a method to encode arbitrary text in the x-www-form-urlencoded format. The primary use for this format is when you are encoding arguments in URLs for CGI scripts. Nonprinting or punctuation characters are converted to a two-digit hexadecimal number preceded by a percent (%) character. Space characters are converted to plus (+) characters.

Constructors. There is no constructor for the URLEncoder class. All the functionality is provided by means of a static method.

Methods. The URLEncoder class provides one static class method, encode(), which takes a String representing the text to encode and returns the translated text as a String.

The URLStreamHandler Class

The subclasses of the URLStreamHandler class provide the implementation of objects that know how to open communications streams for different URL protocol types. More information on how to write handlers for new protocols can be found in Chapter 24, "Developing Content and Protocol Handlers."

Constructors. The constructor for the URLStreamHandler class cannot be called because URLStreamHandler is an abstract class.

Methods. Each subclass provides its own implementation of the openConnection() method, which opens an input stream to the URL specified as an argument. The method should return an appropriate subclass of the URLConnection class.

The ContentHandler Class

Subclasses of the ContentHandler abstract class are responsible for turning a raw data stream for a MIME type into a Java object of the appropriate type.

Constructors. Because ContentHandler is an abstract class, ContentHandler objects cannot be instantiated. An object implementing the ContentHandlerFactory interface decides what the appropriate subclass is for a given MIME content type.

Methods. The important method for ContentHandler objects is the getContent() method, which does the actual work of turning into a Java object the data read using URLConnection. This method takes as its argument a reference to a URLConnection that provides an InputStream at the beginning of the representation of an object.

The SocketImpl Class

The SocketImpl abstract class provides a mapping from the raw networking classes to the native TCP/IP networking facilities of the host. This means that the Java application does not have to concern itself with the operating system specifics of creating network connections. At runtime, the Java interpreter loads the proper native code for the implementation, which is accessed by means of a SocketImpl object. Each Socket or ServerSocket then uses the SocketImpl object to access the network.

This scheme also allows for flexibility in different network environments. An application does not have to bother with details such as being behind a firewall because the interpreter takes care of loading the proper socket implementation (such as one that knows how to use the SOCKS proxy TCP/IP service).

TIP

SOCKS provides TCP and UDP access through a firewall. A SOCKS daemon runs on the firewall (or the inside machine of a DMZ setup). Clients on the inside network call up the SOCKS daemon and ask it to make a connection to an outside host. The daemon connects to the outside host directly or through another SOCKS daemon. SOCKS is pretty cool because the client application doesn't even know it's there if things are set up properly.

For more information about SOCKS, take a look at this URL:

http://www.socks.nec.com/socks5.html

Unless you are porting Java to a new platform or adding support for something such as connecting through a firewall, you probably will never see or use SocketImpl.

Constructors. The SocketImpl abstract class has one constructor that takes no arguments.

Methods. The methods provided by the SocketImpl class look very familiar to anyone who has done socket programming under a UNIX variant. All the methods are protected and may be used only by subclasses of SocketImpl that provide specific socket implementations.

The create() method creates a socket with the underlying operating system. It takes one boolean argument that specifies whether the created socket should be a stream (TCP) or datagram (UDP) socket. Two calls, connect() and bind(), cause the socket to be associated with a particular address and port.

For server sockets, there is the listen() method, which tells the operating system how many connections may be pending on the socket. The accept() method waits for an incoming connection request. It takes another SocketImpl object as a parameter, which represents the new connection once it has been established.

To allow reading and writing from the socket, the class provides the getInputStream() and getOutputStream() methods, which return a reference to the corresponding stream. Once communication on a socket is finished, the close() method may be used to ask the operating system to close the connection. The remaining methods allow read access to the member variables as well as a toString() method for printing a textual representation of the object.

Variables. Each SocketImpl object has four protected members:

Member	Description
fd	A java.io.FileDescriptor object used to access the underlying operating system network facilities.
address	An InetAddress object representing the host at the remote end of the connection.
port	The remote port number, stored as an int.
localport	The local port number, stored as an int.

Exceptions

Java's exception system allows for flexible error handling. The java.net package defines five new exceptions, which are described in the following sections. All these exceptions provide the same functionality as any java.lang.Exception object. Because each exception is a subclass of java.io.IOException, the exceptions can be handled with code such as that in the following fragment:

```
try {
    // Code that might cause an exception goes here
} catch( java.net.IOException e ) {
    System.err.println( "Error on socket operation:\n" + e );
    return;
}
```

This code could be put inside a for loop—for example, when trying to create a Socket to connect to a heavily loaded host.

The UnknownHost Exception

The UnknownHostException exception is thrown when a host name cannot be resolved into a machine address. The most probable causes for this exception are listed here:

- The host name is misspelled.
- The host does not actually exist.
- There is a problem with the network and the host, or the host that is providing name-to-IP number mapping is unreachable.

> **TIP**
>
> If you are sure that you are using the right host name and are still getting this exception, you may have to fix the name-to-IP number mapping. How to go about this depends on the platform you are using. If you are using DNS, you must contact the administrator for the domain. If you are using Sun's NIS, you must have the system administrator change the entry on the NIS server. Finally, you may have to change the local machine's host file, usually named hosts or HOSTS (/etc/hosts on UNIX variants, \WINDOWS\HOSTS on Windows 95). In any case, using the IP number itself to connect to the host should work.

The UnknownService Exception

The URLConnection class uses the UnknownServiceException exception to signal that a given connection does not support a requested facility such as input or output. If you write your own protocol or content handlers and do not override the default methods for getting input or output stream objects, the inherited method throws this exception. An application to which a user can give an arbitrary URL should watch for this exception. (Users being the malicious creatures they are!)

The Socket Exception

The SocketException exception is thrown when there is a problem using a socket. One possible cause is that the local port you are asking for is already in use (that is, another process already has the socket open). Some operating systems might wait for a period of time after a socket has been closed before allowing it to be reopened.

Another cause is that the user cannot bind to that particular port. On most UNIX systems, ports numbered less than 1024 cannot be used by accounts other than the root or superuser account. This is a security measure because most well-known services reside on ports in this range. Normal users are not able to start their own server in place of the system version. While you are developing a service, you may want to run the server on a higher numbered port. Once the service has been developed and debugged, you can move it to the normal port.

The SocketException exception is also thrown if you try to use the setSocketImplFactory() method of the Socket or ServerSocket class when the SocketImplFactory already has been set. Usually, the Java interpreter sets this to a reasonable value for you, but if you are writing your own socket factory (for example, to provide sockets through a firewall), this exception may be thrown.

The Protocol Exception

The ProtocolException exception is raised by the underlying network support library. It is thrown by a native method of the PlainSocketImpl class when the underlying socket facilities return a protocol error.

The MalformedURL Exception

The URL class throws the MalformedURLException exception if it is given a syntactically invalid URL. One cause can be that the URL specifies a protocol that the URL class does not support. Another cause is that the URL cannot be parsed. A URL for the HTTP or FILE protocols should have the following general form:

```
protocol://hostname[:port]/[/path/_/path]/object
```

In this syntax, the following components are used:

Component	Description
protocol	The protocol to use to connect to the resource (http or file).
hostname[:port]	The host name to contact, optionally followed by a colon (:) and the port number to connect to (for example, kremvax.gov.su:8000). The host name also may be given as an IP address.
[/path/.../path]	The (optional) path to the object, separated by / characters.
object	The name of the actual object itself.

This syntax for a URL depends on the protocol. The complete URL specification can be found in RFC 1738 (see Chapter 23, "Introduction to Network Programming," for details on retrieving RFC documents, or check out the World Wide Web Consortium's site at http://www.w3.org/ for the latest version).

Other Exceptions

In addition to the exceptions in the `java.net` package, several methods throw exceptions from the `java.io` package. The most common of these is `java.io.IOException`—which is thrown when there is a problem reading a Web resource by the `URL` class or if there is a problem creating a `Socket` object.

Interfaces

The `java.net` package defines three interfaces. These interfaces are used primarily behind the scenes by the other networking classes rather than by user classes. Unless you are porting Java to a new platform or are extending it to use a new socket protocol, you probably will have no need to implement these interfaces in a class. They are included here for completeness and for those people who like to take off the cover and poke around in the innards to find out how things work.

The `SocketImplFactory` Interface

The `SocketImplFactory` interface defines a method that returns a `SocketImpl` instance appropriate to the underlying operating system. The socket classes use an object implementing this interface to create the `SocketImpl` objects they need to use the network.

The `URLStreamHandlerFactory` Interface

Classes that implement the `URLStreamHandlerFactory` interface provide a mapping from protocols such as HTTP or FTP into the corresponding `URLStreamHandler` subclasses. The `URL` class uses this factory object to obtain a protocol handler.

The `ContentHandlerFactory` Interface

The `URLStreamHandler` class uses the `ContentHandlerFactory` interface to obtain `ContentHandler` objects for different content types. The interface has one method, `createContentHandler()`, which takes the MIME type for which a handler is desired as a `String`.

Summary

This chapter provided a quick introduction to the networking facilities that the `java.net` package provides. Appendix C, "The Java Class Library," contains more detailed information about the specific arguments and return types for the various methods.

The Windowing (AWT) Package

by David R. Chung

IN THIS CHAPTER

The Java Abstract Windowing Toolkit (AWT) is a general-purpose, multiplatform windowing library. The AWT provides classes that encapsulate many useful graphical user interface (GUI) components (also called *widgets* or *controls*). The AWT also includes classes to manage component layout and utility classes to handle fonts, colors, and other GUI-related items. Because Java is a multiplatform solution, the AWT provides a common interface to the native GUI components on a wide variety of platforms. This abstraction makes the AWT highly portable.

The tradeoff is that the AWT does not fully encapsulate the machine-specific GUI features of *any* specific platform. Even so, the AWT is a fully capable GUI, and you can use it to create powerful user interfaces that run on a wide variety of platforms.

The AWT classes can be divided into three groups:

- Control classes
- Layout classes
- Menu classes

This chapter examines the classes of the AWT and explains how to incorporate them into your applets and applications. Example applets demonstrate the various AWT controls.

Control Classes

The control classes of the AWT provide a platform-independent *wrapper* for the basic GUI widgets. These classes include most of the components necessary to create a modern user interface for your Java applets or applications.

The Component Class

The AWT component classes are all derived from a common base class: the Component class. The Component class is an abstract class. This class defines the elements common to all GUI components. The Component class is derived from the Object class. The Component class also implements the ImageObserver interface.

> **NOTE**
>
> An *abstract class* is a class that contains one or more methods declared to be abstract. (Abstract methods are similar to pure virtual functions in C++.) Abstract classes cannot actually be instantiated. To make use of these classes, you must derive a class from the abstract class and provide an implementation for each abstract method.

The Component class provides a unified interface to all the graphic components of the AWT. Figure 16.1 shows all the AWT widgets derived from the Component class.

FIGURE 16.1.
The Java Component *class hierarchy.*

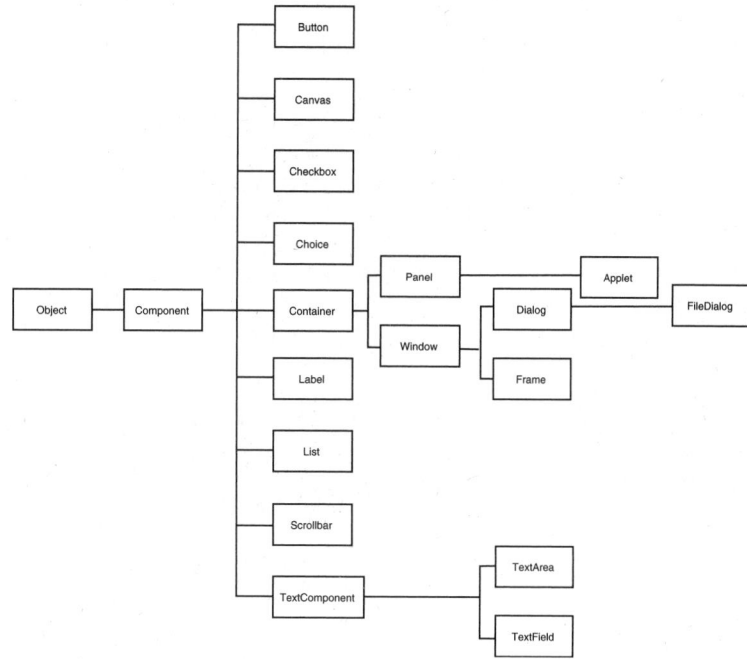

The components in this hierarchy can be divided into the following functional groups:

- Simple widgets (buttons, checkboxes, and so on)
- Text controls
- The Canvas class

Simple Widgets

The Java AWT encapsulates many of the controls common to most GUIs. Specifically, these are the Button, Checkbox, Choice, Label, List, and Scrollbar classes. Figure 16.2 shows an applet that displays the AWT simple widgets.

The following code shows the Simple applet, which contains the simple AWT widgets. The applet's init() method creates an example of each simple widget and adds it to the applet.

```
import java.awt.*;

public class Simple extends java.applet.Applet {

    public void init() {

        Button      button      = new Button( "Quit" ) ;
        Checkbox    checkbox    = new Checkbox( "Test" ) ;
```

FIGURE 16.2.
The simple AWT components.

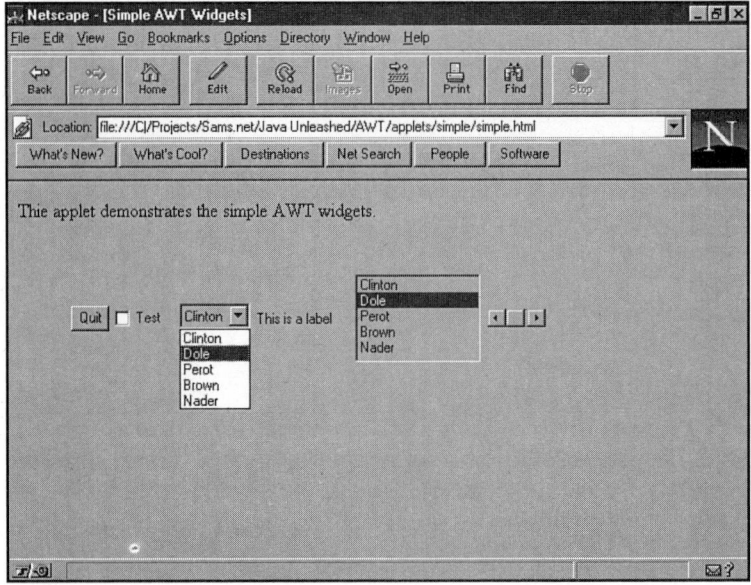

Both the Choice and List objects include addItem() methods. These methods allow you to fill the control with the items you specify. Unlike some GUIs, the AWT Choice and List controls do not sort the items they contain. They are displayed in the order in which you add them.

```
Choice       choice     = new Choice() ;
 // fill the Choice
choice.addItem( "Clinton" ) ;
choice.addItem( "Dole" ) ;
choice.addItem( "Perot" ) ;
choice.addItem( "Browne" ) ;
choice.addItem( "Nader" ) ;

Label        label      = new Label( "This is a label" ) ;

List         list       = new List( 5, false ) ;
// fill the List
list.addItem( "Clinton" ) ;
list.addItem( "Dole" ) ;
list.addItem( "Perot" ) ;
list.addItem( "Browne" ) ;
list.addItem( "Nader" ) ;

Scrollbar    scrollbar  = new Scrollbar( Scrollbar.HORIZONTAL ) ;
```

To display these controls, you must add them to the applet's layout using the add() method:

```
// add the controls to the default layout
add( button ) ;
add( checkbox ) ;
add( choice ) ;
```

```
        add( label ) ;
        add( list ) ;
        add( scrollbar ) ;

    }

}
```

This applet displays the simple widgets. To be truly useful, an applet should do more than just display the controls—the applet must also be interactive. This brings up the topic of *event handling*. The DemoFrame applet presented later in this chapter demonstrates event handling.

Text Controls

The AWT contains a group of controls whose purpose is to allow users to enter and display text. Unlike the simple widgets just discussed, the text controls let users enter freeform text into applications. The TextField and TextArea classes are derived from TextComponent as shown in Figure 16.3.

FIGURE 16.3.
The AWT text component hierarchy.

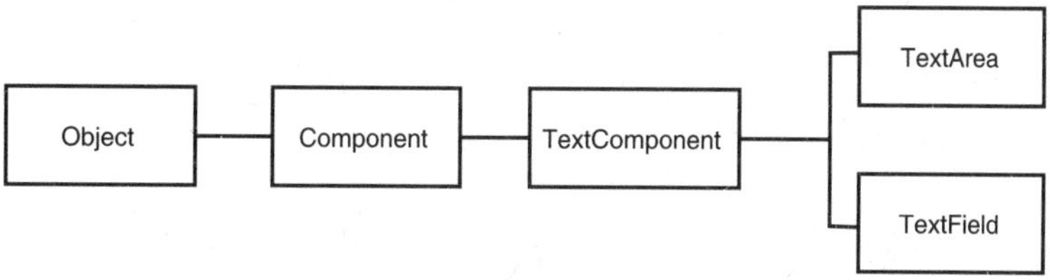

TextComponent is an abstract base class. It provides common methods for displaying text, getting text from the user, and selecting portions of text. The base class also allows the control to be made editable or read-only.

The TextField class encapsulates a nonscrollable text box. TextField controls are commonly used to allow users to enter single values.

TextArea controls are more versatile and allow multiple lines and scrolling. Both TextField and TextArea components can be used to get user input or to display values.

Now let's work through the code for the Text applet that shows the use of the AWT text components:

```
import java.awt.*;

public class Text extends java.applet.Applet {

    public void init() {
```

Both the TextArea and TextField classes (and many other Component-derived classes) have overloaded constructor methods.

NOTE

Overloaded methods are methods with the same name that take different parameters. Constructors are commonly overloaded to provide different types of initialization for a class.

This applet uses the `TextArea` and `TextField` constructors to specify the number of rows and columns displayed in each control. These constructors also specify the text that will be initially displayed in the control.

```
TextArea  textarea  = new TextArea(
    "This text area has 3 rows and 40 columns",
    3, 40 ) ;

TextField textfield = new TextField(
    "This text field has 30 columns",
    30 ) ;

add( textarea ) ;
add( textfield ) ;

    }

}
```

The `Text` applet demonstrates the AWT text components. Figure 16.4 shows the `Text` applet.

FIGURE 16.4.

The AWT text components.

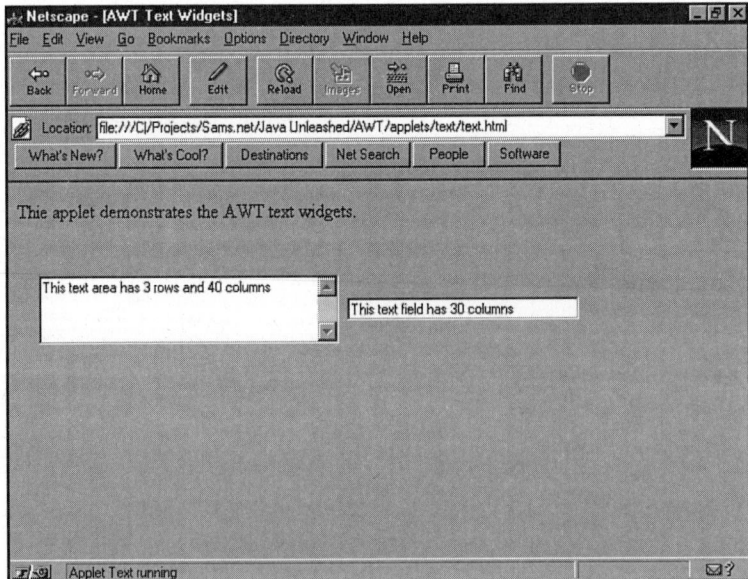

The Canvas Class

The AWT Canvas class is a generic Component class. The Canvas class is most often used to display images. It is also used as the background for user drawing. Chapter 21, "Creating User Interface Components," contains an example that uses the Canvas class to draw an image.

The Container Class

The AWT Container class is a Component class that can contain other Component objects. Although Container is an abstract class, its derived classes are among the most useful in the AWT. Figure 16.5 shows the Container class hierarchy.

FIGURE 16.5.
The Container *class hierarchy.*

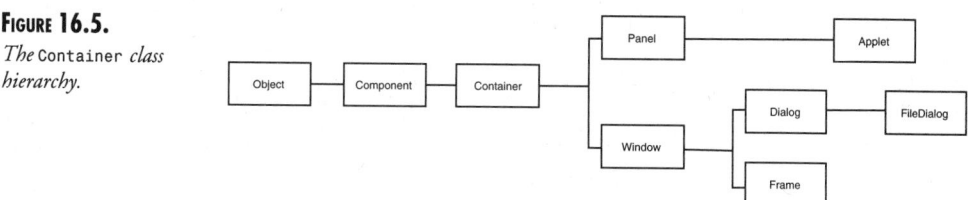

Container classes are the basic framework from which you build the GUI components of your applets. The Container hierarchy can be divided into two categories: the Panel and Window classes.

The Panel Class

The Panel class is a generic Container class. Panel is not an abstract class and can be instantiated or subclassed. *Panels* are Java's multipurpose containers and do not provide any special functionality—except for the capability to embed other GUI objects. Panels give you a convenient method of forming *composite* controls. In Chapter 21, you use the Panel class to combine other controls. Sample applets in that chapter demonstrate many of the GUI components available in the AWT.

The Panel class performs one other important function: It is the superclass of the AWT Applet class. This makes sense because one of the things you do with applets is embed controls in them.

> **NOTE**
>
> The Applet class is not actually part of the java.awt package. Applet is contained in the java.applet package.

The Window Class

Like the Panel class, the Window class is derived from the Container class. Although it is not an abstract class, you rarely create Window objects. However, the Window class is the root class for two *very* useful classes: Frame and Dialog. The Window class and its derived classes allow you to create windows that can float over or even outside the browser window. These Window objects can be resizable and can have their own titles and menus.

Because Frame objects are derived from the Container class, they can contain other controls. The FrameTest applet creates a Frame with embedded Button and Label objects. Figure 16.6 shows the FrameTest applet in operation.

FIGURE 16.6.

The FrameTest *applet (with* Frame *displayed).*

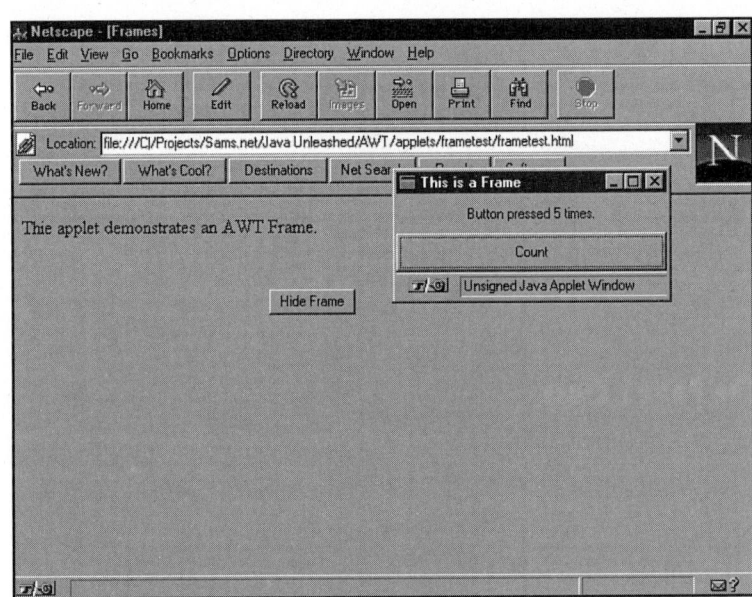

This applet has a Button object that displays or hides a Frame. The button is an AWT Button; the Frame object is the DemoFrame class derived from Frame. The applet doesn't actually create a Frame, rather it creates a DemoFrame object derived from Frame.

```
class DemoFrame extends Frame {

    Label  label ;
    Button button ;

    // variable to store button presses
    int count ;
```

The DemoFrame Class

The DemoFrame constructor takes a String parameter. This string is passed to the *superclass constructor*. Because DemoFrame is derived from Frame, the constructor called is Frame (String txt). It is the Frame constructor that actually makes the string the window title.

> **NOTE**
>
> Calls to a superclass constructor should be made only from a derived class constructor. They must be the first line of code in the derived class constructor.
>
> Other superclass methods can be called from *any* derived class method. The syntax is super.superclassMethod().

The constructor also creates the embedded Label object and sets its text to an empty string. The Label.CENTER parameter indicates that the label text should be centered in the control.

```
DemoFrame( String title ) {

        super( title ) ;

        label = new Label( "", Label.CENTER ) ;
```

The resetCount() and showCount() methods are defined a little later in this section. These methods set the value of count and display it in the embedded Label. Both of these methods are public so that the *owner* of this Frame (in this case, the FrameTest applet) can use them to reset and display the count value:

```
        resetCount() ;
        showCount() ;
```

Next, the constructor creates the Button object. The Button face displays the label *Count.* To display the Label above the Button, you must set the Frame's Layout to GridLayout and add the controls. GridLayout lets you lay out controls in a regular grid—in this case, two rows and one column:

```
        button = new Button( "Count" ) ;

        setLayout( new GridLayout( 2,1 ) ) ;

        add( label ) ;
        add( button ) ;

    }
```

The resetCount() method is a public method. This method is designed to allow access to the count variable. Of course, you can make the count variable public, but then count could be modified by anyone. By using a public access method, you can control who accesses your data members and what they can do with them.

```
public void resetCount(){
    count = 0 ;
}
```

The showCount() method updates the Label text. Every time the Frame's button is pressed, the count variable is incremented and the showCount() method is called to display the results:

```
public void showCount(){
    label.setText( "Button pressed " + count + " times." ) ;
}
```

Event Handling

In Java, most of the programming you do is *event driven.* This means that Java programs spend a lot of time waiting for someone to do something. For example, when a user presses a button, your applet must provide a method that is executed in response to that event. The DemoFrame class uses the action() method to respond to events.

The action() method takes two parameters: an Event and an Object. Both parameters are objects. Event provides information about the type of event and the control that originated it. The Object argument is a generic argument that contains information specific to the type of event that occurs.

> **NOTE**
>
> Object is the superclass to all Java classes; therefore, the Object parameter can be used to pass *any* type of object. To make use of this parameter, you must cast it to some specific type.

The action() method is supposed to respond to the Frame's button. The first thing the method must do is determine the type of event this is. The if statement checks the target member of the Event argument to see whether it is a Button (or a class derived from Button).

The expression in the if statement uses the instanceof operator. This operator is similar to the == and > operators. It compares its right and left operands to see whether they are of the same type. This is an example of runtime type checking. (C++ is just now getting runtime type checking.)

If the Event was generated by a Button, the next if statement checks to see which Button was pressed. Because this is a Button Event, the Object parameter is a String containing the text on the Button face. Because the parameter is of type Object (remember that all Java classes, including String, are derived from Object), you must cast the parameter to a String.

If this Event was generated by the Count button, the action() function increments count. Next, the function calls the showCount() method to display the new value.

Finally, if the action() method has completely handled the Event, it should return true. If further processing is required, the method returns false.

```
public boolean action( Event evt, Object arg ) {

    if ( evt.target instanceof Button ) {

        if ( ((String)arg).equals( "Count" ) ){

            count++ ;
            showCount() ;

            // the event has been handled
            return true ;

        }

    }

    // the event has not been handled
    return false ;
}

}
```

The FrameTest Applet

The `DemoFrame` class is used to create a `Frame` for the applet. The applet creates a button that alternately displays or hides the `Frame`:

```
import java.awt.*;

public class FrameTest extends java.applet.Applet {
    DemoFrame  frameWindow ;
    Button showFrame ;
```

The applet's `init()` method creates the `Button` and the `DemoFrame`. Notice that the button is added to the applet's `Layout` but the `DemoFrame` is not. Because `Frame` objects are *top-level* windows, they cannot be embedded in other containers. Frames actually float outside the applet and browser windows. They can be hidden by other windows or tiled along with other top-level windows.

In this example, the `Frame` object is created and a `String` is passed to the `Frame` constructor. The `String` is used as the `Frame` window title.

When you create a `Frame`, it is initially invisible. When the user presses the button, the applet displays (or hides) the `Frame`. The `Frame` must also be given a size; this is done by calling its `resize()` method:

```
public void init() {
    showFrame = new Button( "Show Frame" ) ;
    add( showFrame ) ;

    frameWindow = new DemoFrame( "This is a Frame" ) ;
    frameWindow.resize( 200, 100 ) ;
}
```

The FrameTest applet handles Button events the same way the DemoFrame class does. A subtle difference is that each time the button is pressed, the text on its face changes. When the Button says *Show Frame*, it resets the count to zero and shows the Frame. The method also changes the text on the button to *Hide Frame*. Likewise, if the Button face says *Hide Frame*, the Frame is hidden.

```
public boolean action( Event evt, Object arg ) {

        if ( evt.target instanceof Button ) {

            if (((String)arg).equals( "Show Frame" )){

                frameWindow.resetCount() ;
                frameWindow.showCount() ;

                frameWindow.show() ;
                showFrame.setLabel( "Hide Frame" ) ;

                // the event has been handled
                return true ;

            }
            else if (((String)arg).equals( "Hide Frame" )){

                frameWindow.hide() ;
                showFrame.setLabel( "Show Frame" ) ;

                // the event has been handled
                return true ;

            }

        }

        // the event has not been handled
        return false ;
    }
}
```

If you run this applet in a browser, you may notice that the Frame window has a status bar with the message Untrusted Applet Window, Warning Applet Window, or Unsigned Java Applet Window. These warnings are displayed by browser implementations of Java whenever a Java applet creates a Frame window. This prevents Frame windows from masquerading as a local application.

Layout Classes

The AWT contains a group of classes designed to handle placement of controls in Container objects. These are the layout classes. All layout classes are derived directly from Object. These classes all implement the LayoutManager interface.

The AWT implements the following layout classes:

- `FlowLayout`
- `BorderLayout`
- `CardLayout`
- `GridLayout`
- `GridBagLayout`

These classes provide a flexible, platform-independent means of arranging `Component` objects in your `Container` objects. It is possible that these five classes provide all the flexibility your applets and applications need. If you have specific needs, you can implement your own layout class by deriving it from `Object` and implementing the `LayoutManager` interface.

The `FlowLayout` Class

The `FlowLayout` class allows you to lay out controls in rows. Controls are placed in rows as long as there is room. After a row has been filled, subsequent controls are placed in the next row. Figure 16.7 shows the `flow` applet.

FIGURE 16.7.

The `flow` *applet.*

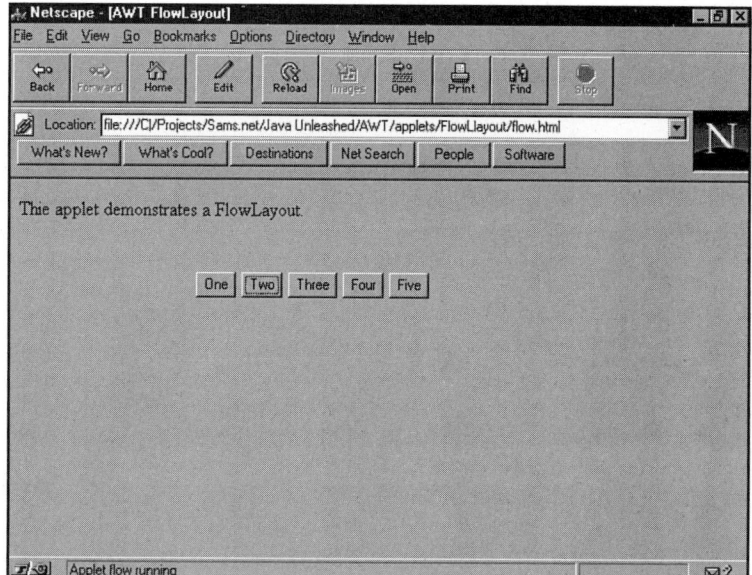

The `flow` applet creates a simple `FlowLayout`:

```
import java.awt.*;

public class flow extends java.applet.Applet {

    public void init() {

        setLayout( new FlowLayout() ) ;

        add( new Button( "One"   ) ) ;
        add( new Button( "Two"   ) ) ;
        add( new Button( "Three" ) ) ;
        add( new Button( "Four"  ) ) ;
        add( new Button( "Five"  ) ) ;

    }
}
```

In this applet, the `FlowLayout` constructor is called with no parameters. There are two other overloaded constructors for the `FlowLayout` class. These allow you to fine tune the `FlowLayout` to meet your particular needs.

The first constructor takes one parameter. By passing `FlowLayout.LEFT`, `FlowLayout.CENTER`, or `FlowLayout.RIGHT`, you specify the alignment for the controls. The default alignment (when you don't specify one) is `FlowLayout.CENTER`. Therefore, to align the buttons on the left in the `flow` applet, you replace the call to `setLayout()` with this call:

```
setLayout( new FlowLayout( FlowLayout.LEFT ) ) ;
```

Layouts also give you control over the amount of space between controls. The `FlowLayout()` method fills the first row and then each subsequent row as necessary. If the layout requires more than one row, you can specify the vertical spacing as well. The constructor that does this takes an alignment parameter followed by two parameters specifying the spacing between controls. To make the `flow` applet place its controls centered with ten pixels of horizontal gap and five pixels of vertical gap, use the following code:

```
setLayout( new FlowLayout( FlowLayout.CENTER, 10, 5 ) ) ;
```

The BorderLayout Class

The AWT `BorderLayout` class places controls so that they fill their `Container` object. The controls are placed according to a geographic position that you specify. Controls can be placed on the north, south, east, and west edges of the `Container`. You can also place a control in the center of the `Container`. The centered control is then expanded to fill the remaining space.

Figure 16.8 shows the `border` applet with five controls.

FIGURE 16.8.

The border *applet.*

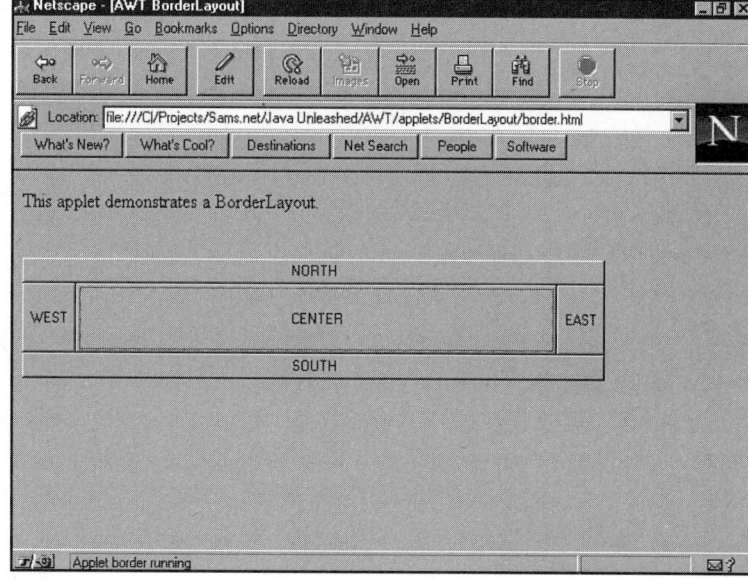

The border applet creates a simple BorderLayout:

```
import java.awt.*;

public class border extends java.applet.Applet {

    public void init() {

        setLayout( new BorderLayout() ) ;

        add( "North",  new Button( "NORTH"  ) ) ;
        add( "South",  new Button( "SOUTH"  ) ) ;
        add( "East",   new Button( "EAST"   ) ) ;
        add( "West",   new Button( "WEST"   ) ) ;
        add( "Center", new Button( "CENTER" ) ) ;

    }

}
```

When you create a BorderLayout, you can specify vertical and horizontal gap values as you can with the setLayout() method (described in the flow applet).

The CardLayout Class

The AWT CardLayout class is unique. Rather than placing multiple controls in a Container object, this layout displays the controls one at a time (much like the familiar deck of cards in the ubiquitous Solitaire game). The controls that are displayed may, in fact, be composite controls. Therefore, you can present entirely different sets of controls to the user in a manner similar to the tabbed dialog boxes that Microsoft Windows uses. Figure 16.9 shows an applet with five buttons laid out in a CardLayout fashion.

FIGURE 16.9.

The card *applet.*

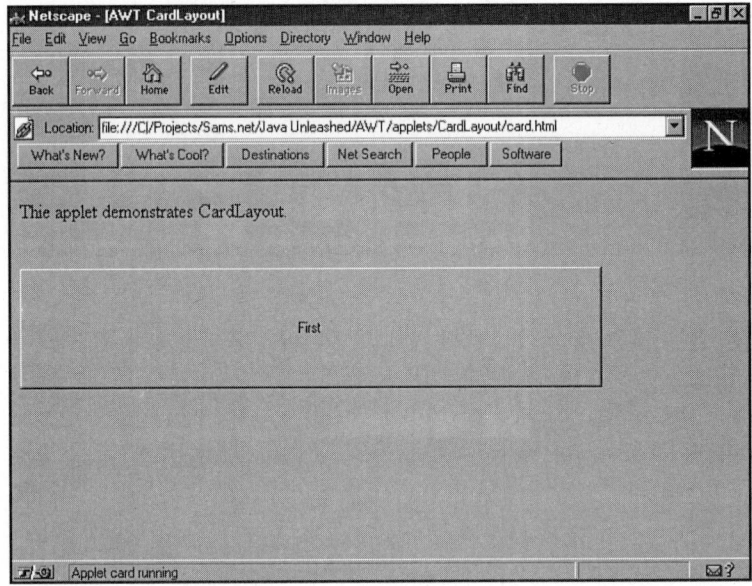

The card applet creates a CardLayout with five buttons:

```
import java.awt.*;

public class card extends java.applet.Applet {

    CardLayout layout ;

    public void init() {

        layout = new CardLayout() ;

        setLayout( layout ) ;

        add( new Button( "First"  ) ) ;
        add( new Button( "Second" ) ) ;
        add( new Button( "Third"  ) ) ;
        add( new Button( "Fourth" ) ) ;
        add( new Button( "Fifth"  ) ) ;
    }

    public boolean action( Event evt, Object arg ) {
```

```
        if ( evt.target instanceof Button ) {
            layout.next(this) ;
            return true ;
            }

        return false ;
    }

}
```

The card applet places five Button objects in a CardLayout. When any button is pressed, the action() method calls the CardLayout's next() method to display the next card in order. This layout also allows you to label the various controls that are added.

The add() method takes an optional String parameter that labels the controls you add. The following call adds a Button labeled my button with the label *Push Me*:

```
add( "my button", new Button( "Push Me" ) ;
```

Once the controls have labels, you can display them without having to show them in order, without calling the layout's next() method. To display my button, simply call the layout's show() method:

```
show( this, "my button" ) ;
```

The show() method displays a specified control; the next() method displays the next control in order. The CardLayout class provides the following functions to navigate the controls in the layout:

- first(Container)
- last(Container)
- next(Container)
- previous(Container)
- show(Container, String)

All these navigational functions take a reference to a Container object as a parameter. The show() method takes a String containing the label given to the control when it was added.

NOTE

What's this? In Java, this is a keyword that represents a reference to a given object. When an applet calls one of the CardLayout's navigational methods, it needs a Container as a parameter. Because these functions are called in the context of a Container member method, this represents the current Container.

The GridLayout Class

As its name suggests, the GridLayout class places controls in the Container in a grid. It is important to note that this is a *regular* grid—all the grid cells are the same size. The applet in Figure 16.10 shows a GridLayout.

FIGURE 16.10.

The grid *applet.*

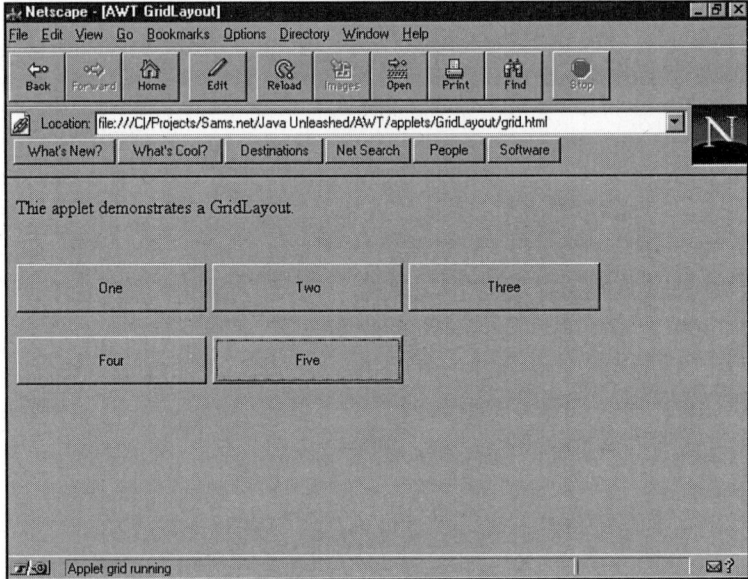

The grid applet defines a grid with two rows and three columns. The add() method adds each control starting with row 1, column 1 followed by row 1, column 2 and so on.

```java
import java.awt.*;

public class grid extends java.applet.Applet {

    public void init() {

        setLayout( new GridLayout( 2, 3 ) ) ;

        add( new Button( "One"   ) ) ;
        add( new Button( "Two"   ) ) ;
        add( new Button( "Three" ) ) ;
        add( new Button( "Four"  ) ) ;
        add( new Button( "Five"  ) ) ;

    }

}
```

You can also create a GridLayout with vertical and horizontal gap values by using the setLayout() method as you do with the FlowLayout and BorderLayout classes.

The GridBagLayout Class

The GridBagLayout class is complex enough to fill an entire chapter by itself. This class was added to the AWT very late in the Java beta. Therefore, many early acceptors of Java didn't use this layout at all. Some early books omit it completely.

Of all the layouts offered by the AWT, GridBagLayout is the most versatile. Despite its funny name, once you learn how to use GridBagLayout, it will become an indispensable part of your Java toolkit.

Like GridLayout, GridBagLayout places controls in a Container in a grid. The difference is that in a GridBagLayout, controls can span any number of grid cells vertically, horizontally, or both. Controls can be placed in any grid cell. Cells can be of differing sizes as well. Figure 16.11 shows the gridbag applet.

FIGURE 16.11.

The gridbag *applet.*

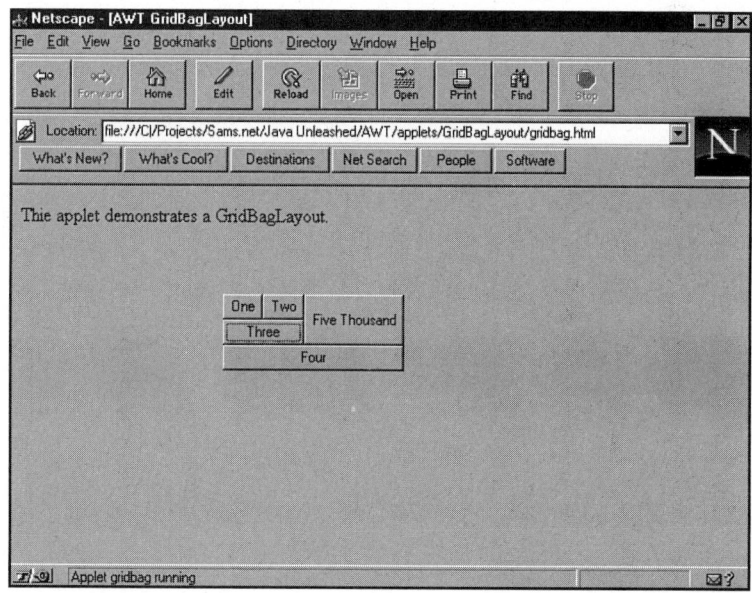

The gridbag applet displays five buttons in a GridBagLayout arrangement:

```
import java.awt.*;

public class gridbag extends java.applet.Applet {

    public void init() {

        Button b1 = new Button( "One"   ) ;
        Button b2 = new Button( "Two"   ) ;
        Button b3 = new Button( "Three" ) ;
        Button b4 = new Button( "Four"  ) ;
        Button b5 = new Button( "Five Thousand"  ) ;
```

```
GridBagLayout gridbag = new GridBagLayout();
setLayout( gridbag ) ;
{
GridBagConstraints c = new GridBagConstraints();

c.fill      = GridBagConstraints.BOTH ;
c.gridx     = 1 ;
c.gridy     = 1 ;
gridbag.setConstraints(b1, c);
add( b1 ) ;
}


{
GridBagConstraints c = new GridBagConstraints();

c.anchor      = GridBagConstraints.WEST ;
c.gridx       = 2 ;
c.gridheight  = 2 ;
gridbag.setConstraints(b2, c);
add( b2 ) ;
}


{
GridBagConstraints c = new GridBagConstraints();

c.fill       = GridBagConstraints.BOTH ;
c.gridx      = 1 ;
c.gridy      = 2 ;
c.gridwidth  = 2 ;
gridbag.setConstraints(b3, c);
add( b3 ) ;
}


{
GridBagConstraints c = new GridBagConstraints();

c.fill       = GridBagConstraints.BOTH ;
c.gridx      = 1 ;
c.gridy      = 3 ;
c.gridwidth  = 3 ;
gridbag.setConstraints(b4, c);
add( b4 ) ;
}


{
GridBagConstraints c = new GridBagConstraints();

c.fill        = GridBagConstraints.VERTICAL ;
c.gridx       = 3 ;
c.gridy       = 1 ;
c.gridheight  = 2 ;
gridbag.setConstraints(b5, c);
add( b5 ) ;
}
}


}
```

The key to using GridBagLayout is the GridBagConstraints class. This class is used to encapsulate information about each control that is added to the layout. Setting the class data members determines how the controls will be placed.

To use a GridBagLayout, you must create a GridBagConstraints object. Then set the data members of the GridBagConstraints object to appropriately lay out the given control. Next, call the GridBagLayout's setConstraints() method to associate a GridBagConstraints object with a control. Finally, add the control.

NOTE

C and C++ programmers may be asking why GridBagConstraints is a class. It appears to have only data members. In fact, if this were C or C++, GridBagConstraints would be a structure. Because Java does not support structures, GridBagConstraints must be implemented as a class.

The following GridBagConstraints public data members determine how your controls are placed:

- The anchor member specifies how a control is displayed if it is smaller than the grid cell in which it is placed. This member can be set to CENTER, NORTH, SOUTH, EAST, WEST, NORTHEAST, SOUTHEAST, NORTHWEST, or SOUTHWEST.

- The fill member lets a control grow to fill its allotted grid cells if the cells are larger than the control's default size. The choices for this member are BOTH, HORIZONTAL, VERTICAL, and NONE.

- The gridheight and gridweight members determine how many grid cells a control takes up.

- The gridx and gridy members specify the row and column (in grid coordinates) at which to place the control.

- The ipadx and ipady members specify the vertical and horizontal gap (or padding) for components.

- The weightx and weighty members specify how *excess* space is assigned to the various components if the container in which they are embedded is resized.

- The Insets member is a class that specifies the *margins* of a Container that has a GridBagLayout.

By using the GridBagLayout and GridBagConstraints classes, you can produce layouts to meet nearly all your needs. If these are not flexible enough for you, there is always the option of creating your own LayoutManager. You create your own LayoutManager by creating a class (subclassed from Object) that implements the LayoutManager interface.

Menu Classes

The AWT provides a hierarchy of classes that allow you to include menus in your applets and applications. Figure 16.12 shows the AWT menu classes.

FIGURE 16.12.

The AWT menu class hierarchy.

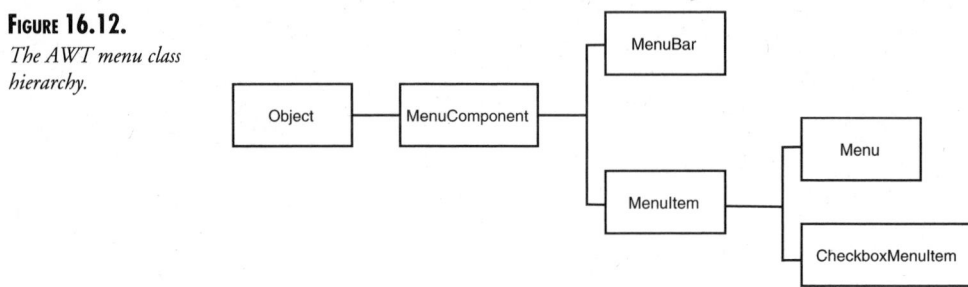

All the menu classes are derived from the `MenuComponent` class. The `MenuBar` and `Menu` classes both implement the `MenuContainer` interface.

The `MenuFrame` applet shows a `Frame` with a menu. Selecting Hide Frame from the menu closes the frame window. Figure 16.13 shows the `MenuFrame` applet.

FIGURE 16.13.

The `MenuFrame` *applet.*

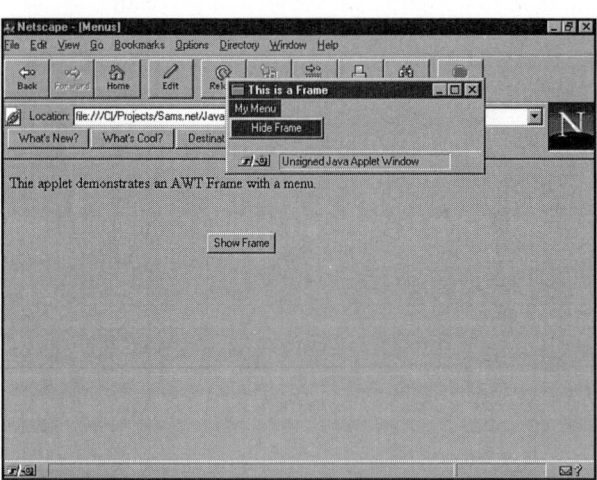

The `MenuFrame` applet creates `MenuItem`, `Menu`, and `MenuBar` objects. The `Frame`'s `action()` method determines whether the Hide Frame menu item has been selected.

```java
import java.awt.*;

public class MenuFrame extends java.applet.Applet {

    DemoFrame   frameWindow ;
    Button      showFrame ;
```

```java
    public void init() {
        showFrame = new Button( "Show Frame" ) ;
        add( showFrame ) ;

        frameWindow = new DemoFrame( "This is a Frame" ) ;
        frameWindow.resize( 200, 100 ) ;
    }

    public boolean action( Event evt, Object arg ) {

        if ( evt.target instanceof Button ) {
            if ( !frameWindow.isShowing() ) {
                frameWindow.show() ;
                return true ;
            }
        }
        return false ;
    }
}

class DemoFrame extends Frame {

    MenuItem    menuItem ;
    Menu        menu ;
    MenuBar     menuBar ;

    Label  label ;

    DemoFrame( String title ) {
        super( title ) ;

        menuItem = new MenuItem( "Hide Frame" ) ;

        menu = new Menu( "My Menu" ) ;
        menu.add( menuItem ) ;

        menuBar = new MenuBar() ;
        menuBar.add( menu ) ;

        setMenuBar( menuBar ) ;
    }

    public boolean action( Event evt, Object arg ) {

        if ( evt.target instanceof MenuItem ) {
            if ( ((String)arg).equals( "Hide Frame" ) ) {
                hide() ;
                return true ;
            }
        }
        return false ;
    }
```

Summary

The Java AWT contains a rich collection of controls. By using these controls, you can create a variety of truly multiplatform GUI applications. The AWT also provides generic container and window classes you can use to create your own custom controls.

The layout classes of the AWT answer the question of how to place controls so that they appear properly on all platforms. You can even create custom layout managers.

Java and the AWT provide a credible solution to developing fully featured GUI applications for a wide variety of target platforms.

Applet Programming

IV

PART

## CHAPTER 17

Introduction to Applet Programming

by Rogers Cadenhead

IN THIS CHAPTER

Although Java is a general-purpose programming language suitable for a large variety of tasks, the task most people use it for is applet programming. An *applet* is a Java program that executes on a World Wide Web page.

When the prerelease versions of the Java Developers Kit were made available in 1995, the demonstration programs that drew international attention to the language were applets. Your first experience with Java might have been one of these demos—spinning heads, the animated Duke character doing cartwheels, a dancing headline, and so on. Those applets are still available on the JavaSoft site at the following URL:

```
http://java.sun.com/java.sun.com/applets/applets.html
```

Today, applets are being used to accomplish far more than demonstrative goals. There are working examples of applets on Web sites throughout the Internet—a check of the AltaVista search engine finds more than 4,200 Web pages that have applets embedded on them.

The current uses of applets include the following:

- Tickertape-style news and sports headline updates
- Animated graphics
- Video games
- Student tests
- Image maps that respond to mouse movement
- Advanced text displays
- Database reports

Figure 17.1 shows a noteworthy example of an applet: the Instant Ballpark program from Instant Sports.

Instant Ballpark takes real-time data from live baseball games and updates its display to reflect what's happening in the game. Players run the bases, the ball goes to the place it was hit, and sound effects are used for strike calls, crowd noise, and other elements. The program, which was unique enough to qualify for a U.S. patent, is reminiscent of the old-time baseball tradition of presenting the play-by-play for road games by moving metal figures on the side of a building. In addition to the live coverage, Instant Ballpark can be used to review the play-by-play action of past games.

The applet shows one of the advantages of a Web program over a Web page. With HTML and some kind of gateway programming language such as Perl, a Web page can offer textual updates to a game in progress. However, Instant Ballpark offers a *visual* presentation of a live game in addition to text, and the applet can respond immediately to user input. Java can be used to provide information to Web users in a more compelling way, which is often the reason site providers are offering applets.

To try this applet, visit the following Web site:

```
http://www.instantsports.com/ballpark.html
```

FIGURE 17.1.

The Instant Ballpark applet (courtesy of Instant Sports).

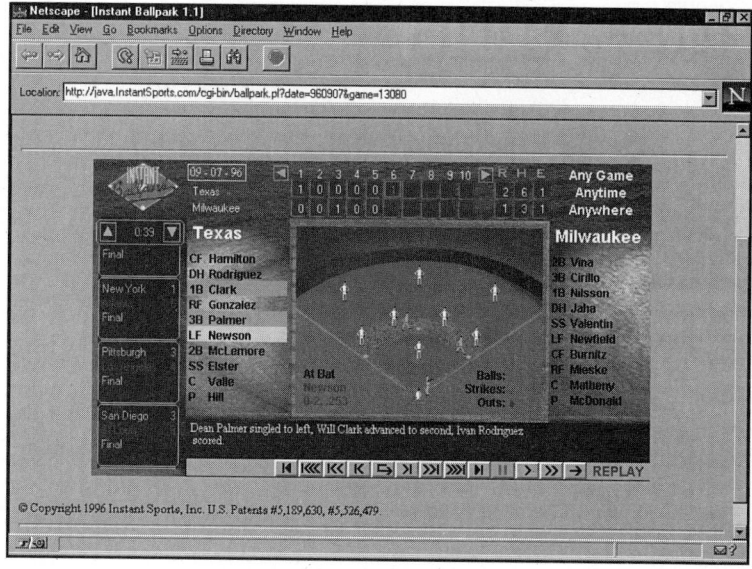

Viewing Applets

As you know, applets are displayed as a part of a Web page. A special HTML tag, `<APPLET>`, is used to attach a Java applet to an HTML page. Running an applet requires the use of a Web browser or other software that serves the function of a browser, such as the applet viewer program that ships with the Java Developers Kit from JavaSoft.

The browser acts as the operating system for applets—you cannot run an applet as a standalone program in the same way you can run an executable file.

At the time of this writing, there are three widely available Web browsers that can run Java applets:

- Netscape Navigator version 2.02 or higher
- Microsoft Internet Explorer 3.0
- JavaSoft HotJava 1.0 pre-beta 1

These programs load applets from a Web page and run them remotely on the Web user's computer. This arrangement raises security issues that must be handled by the Java language itself and by Java-enabled browsers. These browsers are covered in detail in Chapter 3, "Browsing Java."

Providing Security

Java applets are programs that run on a Web user's machine. Anything that can execute code is a potential security risk because of the damaging things that can occur. Viruses can damage a computer's file system and reproduce onto other disks, Trojan horses can masquerade as helpful programs while doing harmful things, and programs can be written to retrieve private information surreptitiously. Even Microsoft Word has been a security risk because of Word Basic—an executable programming language that can be used in conjunction with Word documents.

Security is one of the primary concerns of Java's developers, and they have implemented safeguards at several levels. Some of these safeguards affect the language as a whole: The removal of pointers, the verification of bytecodes, and other language issues have been discussed elsewhere in this book.

Some of Java's functionality is not possible when programming applets because of security concerns. The following safeguards are in place:

■ Applets cannot read or write files on the Web user's disk. If information must be saved to disk during an applet's execution (as in the case of a video game saving the top 10 scores), the storage of information must be done on the disk from which the Web page is served.

■ Applets cannot make a network connection to a computer other than the one from which the Web page is served.

■ Pop-up windows opened by applets are identified clearly as Java windows. A Java cup icon and text such as `Untrusted Applet Window` appear in the window. These elements are added to prevent a window opened by Java from pretending to be something else, such as a Windows dialog box requesting a user's name and password.

■ Applets cannot use dynamic or shared libraries from any other programming language. Java can make use of programs written in languages such as Visual C++ by using a `native` statement from within Java. However, applets cannot make use of this feature because there's no way to adequately verify the security of the non-Java code being executed.

■ Applets cannot run any programs on the Web user's system.

As you can see, Java applets are more limited in functionality than standalone Java applications. The loss is a tradeoff for the security that must be in place for the language to run remotely on users' computers.

The security restrictions discussed here are current as of the 1.0.2 release of the Java Developers Kit. JDK version 1.1 is in development as of this writing, but it is expected to add more security rather than lessening any of the existing safeguards. Refer to Chapter 35, "Java Security," for more information.

A WORD ABOUT APPLICATIONS

This chapter focuses on applets, but it's important to make clear the distinction between the two types of Java programs. *Applets* are programs offered on Web pages that require the use of a Web browser to execute. *Applications* are everything else: general-purpose programs run by executing the Java interpreter with the name of the Java program as an argument. For example, to run the Java program ReadNews.class, enter the following at a command-line prompt:

```
java ReadNews
```

Applications do not have any of the restrictions that are in place for applets.

The Basics of Applet Programming

Now that you understand what applets are, it's time to get out the tools and build one. Before starting the project, however, the following sections introduce some basic elements of applet programming.

The java.applet.Applet Class

Each applet starts out with a class definition such as the following:

```
public class LearnPigLatin extends java.applet.Applet {
    // to do
}
```

In this example, LearnPigLatin is the name of the applet's class. An applet must be declared as a public class. Applets are subclasses of java.applet.Applet, which is a subclass of the java.awt.Panel class. Figure 17.2 shows the full class hierarchy tree of the Applet class.

FIGURE 17.2.

The hierarchy of
java.applet.Applet.

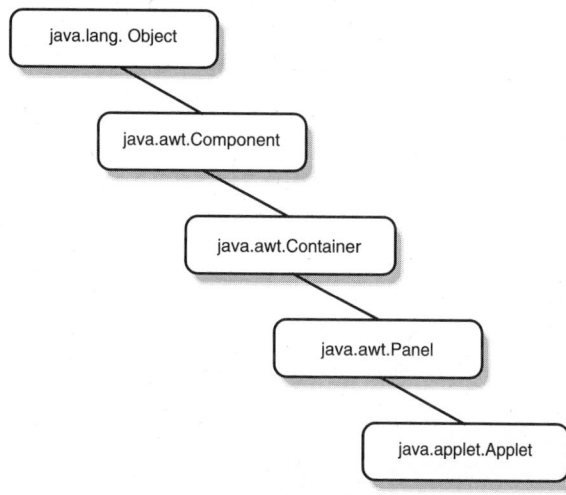

The superclasses of `Applet` give all applets a framework on which you can build user interface elements and mouse events. These superclasses also provide a structure for the applet that must be used when the program is developed.

Applet Methods

The structure of an applet takes the form of five events that can take place as an applet is running. When the events occur, a method is automatically called. The methods also can be called directly within the applet. The methods are the following:

- **Initialization:** The `init()` method is called the first time the applet is loaded.
- **Destruction:** The `destroy()` method is called the final time the applet is exited.
- **Stopping:** The `stop()` method is called each time an applet is stopped. A *stop* happens automatically when a Web page containing the applet is exited and also when the `stop()` method is called directly in a program.
- **Starting:** The `start()` method is called each time an applet is loaded or reloaded. A *start* follows initialization and also takes place each time the applet is restarted. A *start* happens when a Web user comes back to the applet's page after leaving it; you can also call `start()` directly.
- **Painting:** The `paint()`method is called any time the applet window must be re-painted. This occurs automatically at certain times, such as when the applet window is covered up by another window and then uncovered. It also can be called by using a `repaint()` call when a program needs a screen update to take place.

The last of the methods, `paint()`, must take a parameter—an instance of the `Graphics` class—as in the following method definition:

```
public void paint(Graphics g) {
    g.drawString("One moment, please", 5, 50);
}
```

A `Graphics` object is used to indicate where something should be drawn. The `Graphics` object used as the parameter to `paint()` is created automatically, and it represents the applet window. The `g.drawString()` line uses this `Graphics` object to indicate where a string should be drawn. Every time the `repaint()` method is called and the applet window must be updated, the string `One moment, please` is drawn at the x, y position (in this example, `5, 50`).

The `Graphics` object does not have to be declared. However, the `.Graphics` class must be imported at the beginning of an applet's source code. Here's what that import statement should look like:

```
import java.awt.Graphics;
```

Each of these applet methods—`init()`, `destroy()`, `start()`, `stop()`, and `paint()`—is inherited by an applet. You do not have to write your own methods for any of these.

However, each of the applet methods is empty by default. If something is supposed to happen in an applet, some or all of these methods must be overridden.

The <APPLET> Tag

For a Java applet to be run when a Web page is loaded, information about that applet must be put on the page. This requires the use of two special HTML tags: <APPLET> and <PARAM>. This HTML code is included on a Web page along with all other HTML code. In this respect, putting a Java applet on your home page is no different than putting a picture there.

Java applets can be viewed by Web browsers and any other software that is equipped to load applets, such as the applet viewer utility that comes with the Java Developers Kit.

Following is an example of an applet tag:

```
<APPLET CODE="NowShowing.class" CODEBASE="progdir" WIDTH=376 HEIGHT=104>
<PARAM NAME="speed" value="100">
<PARAM NAME="blink" value="5">
<PARAM NAME="text" value="FREE THE BOUND PERIODICALS!">
<PARAM NAME="fontsize" value="21">
<PARAM NAME="pattern" value="random">
<H5>This applet requires the use of a Java-enabled browser!</H5>
</APPLET>
```

When included on a Web page, this HTML code causes the following to take place on a Java-enabled browser:

1. An applet called NowShowing.class is loaded from a directory called progdir. The CODE attribute specifies the applet to load, and the optional CODEBASE attribute refers to a directory where the applet can be found.

2. The applet is set to a width of 376 pixels and a height of 104 pixels using the WIDTH and HEIGHT attributes.

3. A parameter named speed is sent to the applet with a value of 100. Four other parameters are sent to the applet: blink, text, fontsize, and pattern. Parameters are optional; you can include as many as you want. The NAME attribute indicates the name a parameter should be given, and the VALUE attribute indicates the value to associate with the parameter.

4. The line <H5>This applet requires a Java-enabled browser!</H5> is ignored.

The HTML code causes the following to take place on a browser that is *not* equipped to run Java programs:

1. The line <H5>This applet requires a Java-enabled browser!</H5> is shown.

2. Everything else is disregarded.

Browsers that do not handle Java programs disregard everything within the <APPLET>, </APPLET>, and <PARAM> tags. As shown in the preceding HTML code of an applet tag, an alternative can be provided for browsers that do not handle Java.

The CODE attribute must be used in conjunction with the <APPLET> tag because it specifies the name of the applet's class file. This is the file that will be run after it has been loaded onto the Web user's computer.

If the CODEBASE attribute is used, it indicates the path from the Web page's directory to the directory containing the applet's class file. For example, CODEBASE="usr" indicates that the applet is in a directory called usr that is a subdirectory of the Web page's directory.

If the applet makes use of class files that are not part of the standard Java API, these class files must be located in the same directory as the applet's class file.

The HEIGHT and WEIGHT attributes should be familiar to anyone who has used them to place an image on a Web page—they work the same with <APPLET> as they do with <IMG>. The ALIGN attribute used with images also can be used with <APPLET>. The ALIGN attribute determines how the applet is positioned in relation to the other parts of the Web page and can have the values TOP, MIDDLE, or BOTTOM.

Using Parameters

Parameters can be sent to an applet by using the <PARAM> tag and its two attributes: NAME and VALUE. Here's a line from the preceding example:

```
<PARAM NAME="blink" VALUE="100">
```

The value of the NAME attribute assigns a name to an applet parameter, and VALUE gives the parameter a value. The preceding statement sends a parameter named blink with a value of 100.

> **NOTE**
>
> The name of a parameter is not case sensitive, so the capitalization of the value assigned to NAME does not matter.

Parameters are sent to an applet when it is loaded; you can send as many parameters as you want. All parameters are sent to applets as strings and must be converted to other data types if they are needed as integers or other types.

For a parameter to be used by a Java applet, the applet must retrieve the parameter. This requires the getParameter() method, which is available to all applets because it is part of the Applet class.

For example, use the following line in a Java applet to store the `blink` parameter in a variable called `blinkValue`:

```
String blinkValue = getParameter("blink");
```

If you want to retrieve the value and convert it to an integer, use the following code:

```
int blinkValue = -1;
try { blinkValue = Integer.parseInt(getParameter("blink")); }
catch (NumberFormatException e) { }
```

This example uses the `parseInt()` method of the `java.lang.Integer` class to convert a `String` into an `int`. The `try` and `catch` block is used to trap errors if the `String` cannot be converted into a number.

Putting the Applet on the Web

When you have created an applet and added it to HTML pages, you easily can make it available on the World Wide Web. Put all `.class` files required by the applet on your Web site, making sure to put the files in the same directory as the `CODEBASE` attribute if it has been used. If not, put the `.class` files in the same directory as the Web page that includes the applet.

That's all it takes. Unlike CGI programming (which requires special access to the computer providing the Web pages), Java applets can be added by anyone who can put pages on a Web site.

An Example: The `ColorCycle` Applet

In the next chapter, you will delve into specific details of applet programming, including user interface design and event handling. For now, it is worthwhile to take a look at a working example of an applet to get a clearer picture of how applets are designed.

The `ColorCycle` applet is a simple applet with one button labeled *Next Color*. When the button is clicked with the mouse, the background color of the applet changes.

The program demonstrates basic applet structure and a simple bit of event handling—how to respond to a mouse click on a button.

Programming the Applet

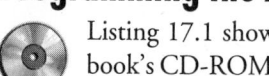 Listing 17.1 shows the full source code of `ColorCycle.java`. It can be found on the book's CD-ROM in the directory `\WIN95NT4\SOURCE\CHAP17` (Windows 95 and Windows NT 4 users) or in the directory `\SOURCE\CHAP17` (Macintosh users), along with the rest of the Java and HTML source code in this chapter. Windows NT 3.51 users must install the source code on their hard drives or select these files from the zipped source code located on the CD-ROM.

Listing 17.1. The source code of `ColorCycle.java`.

```
1: import java.awt.*;
2:
3: public class ColorCycle extends java.applet.Applet {
4:     float hue = (float).5;
5:     float saturation = (float)1;
6:     float brightness = (float)0;
7:     Button b;
8:
9:     public void init() {
10:         b = new Button("Next Color");
11:         add(b);
12:     }
13:
14:     public void start() {
15:         setBackground(Color.black);
16:         repaint();
17:     }
18:
19:     public boolean action(Event evt, Object o) {
20:         if (brightness < 1)
21:             brightness += .25;
22:         else
23:             brightness = 0;
24:         Color c = new Color(Color.HSBtoRGB(hue, saturation, brightness));
25:         setBackground;
26:         repaint();
27:         return true;
28:     }
29: }
```

Don't worry if some aspects of this program are unfamiliar to you at this point. Several aspects of this applet are discussed fully in the next chapter, including the creation of user interface components such as buttons and the `action()` method.

The following things are taking place in the applet:

- **Line 1:** The applet imports several classes by using the wildcard character with `java.awt.*`. The awt stands for Abstract Windowing Toolkit, the set of classes used to handle most visual elements of Java programming—graphics, fonts, a user interface—and also to respond to user input from the keyboard and mouse.

- **Lines 4 through 6:** Three instance variables are created to store the HSB values of the color being displayed. HSB (Hue, Saturation, and Brightness) is a method of describing a color as three numeric values from 0 to 1.

- **Line 7:** A `Button` object is created.

- **Lines 9 through 12:** In the `init()` method of the applet, which is called automatically when the applet is first run, the `Button` object b is instantiated and is assigned the label *Next Color*.

■ **Lines 14 through 17:** In the start() method of the applet, which is called after init() and whenever a Web user returns to the page containing the applet, the background color of the applet is set to black by using the Color constant Color.black. Additionally, a call to the repaint() method tells the applet that the window must be redrawn because something—in this case, the background color— has changed.

■ **Line 19:** The action() method is called whenever a user interface component generates an action event. In this applet, an event occurs when the Next Color button is clicked. There is more on this in the next chapter.

■ **Lines 20 through 23:** The value of brightness is changed so that the background cycles through several colors ranging from black to light blue.

■ **Lines 24 through 26:** A Color object is created to store the value of the background color, which is created based on the values of the variables hue, saturation, and brightness. The background color is changed and another call to repaint() is made.

■ **Line 27:** The boolean value true is returned at the end of the action() method, indicating that the action event generated by clicking the button was taken care of.

17

INTRODUCTION
TO APPLET
PROGRAMMING

Designing the HTML Page

Once the applet has been written and compiled using your development software, you can put it on a Web page using the HTML tags <APPLET>, </APPLET>, and <PARAM> described earlier in this chapter.

 Listing 17.2 shows the full text of an HTML page that loads the ColorCycle.class applet (the source code can also be found on the CD-ROM that accompanies this book). The CODEBASE attribute is not used with the <APPLET> tag, so the ColorCycle.class file must be placed in the same directory as the Web page containing the applet.

Listing 17.2. The source code of ColorCycle.html.

```
1: <html>
2: <body>
3: <applet code=ColorCycle.java height=250 width=250>
4: </applet>
5: </body>
6: </html>
```

Although the applet loses something in the translation from color to black and white, Figure 17.3 shows how the ColorCycle applet looks when loaded with Netscape Navigator 2.02 for Windows 95, one of the current Web browsers equipped to handle Java programs.

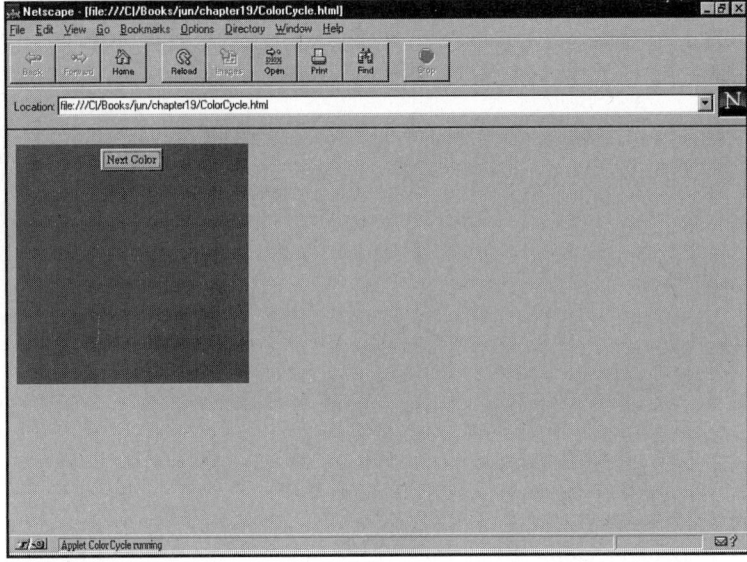

Summary

This chapter provided a framework for the development of applets, but the actual details of creating a user interface and responding to interaction with the mouse and keyboard are coming up next.

As you will find when programming your own applets, the Java API has built-in functionality to handle a lot of the work for you. The user interface provides a lot of components such as buttons, text fields, and choice boxes, and subclassing makes it possible to extend these components without requiring a lot of new code.

Also, other tasks that can be arduous in some languages—such as animation and event handling—are relatively easy using Java.

One of Java's original design goals (back when the language was still known as Oak) was to be simple. When it comes to object-oriented programming, some folks might argue that it can never be simple. However, applet programming is a good area for novice Java programmers to begin because it can be easy to develop useful Web programs without a lot of coding.

Programming Applets

by Rogers Cadenhead

IN THIS CHAPTER

CHAPTER 18

The proliferation of windowing software in the past five years, led by Microsoft Windows and Apple Macintosh systems, has created an expectation among users that software should make use of these features. In Java, windowing and other graphical user interface functions are handled by the Abstract Windowing Toolkit (AWT).

The AWT is one of the most useful packages included with the Java API. The AWT is a set of classes used to build a graphical user interface for Java applications and applets. It enables programmers to easily create the following features for programs:

- Windows and dialog boxes
- Pull-down menus
- Buttons, labels, checkboxes, and other simple user interface components
- Text areas, scroll bars, and other more sophisticated user interface components
- Layout managers to control the placement of user interface components

The AWT also includes classes to handle graphics, fonts, and color in Java programs, and an Event class to enable programs to respond to mouse clicks, mouse movements, and keyboard input.

Today, the Java Developers Kit (JDK) is not the only choice available to programmers. There are numerous ways to develop a graphical user interface for Java programs, such as SunSoft Java WorkShop and Rogue Wave JFactory. Java WorkShop includes a Visual Java tool for the drag-and-drop development of windows, dialog boxes, and other elements that are common to windowing systems. JFactory is an interface builder that can be used with different Java programming environments.

However, there are several reasons to begin learning about interface development by using only the AWT. First, it's still the most commonly used interface designer for Java, so the majority of source code that's publicly available uses AWT classes to control its interface. Second, many of the other windowing design systems use the AWT as the underlying code to handle the interface.

This chapter focuses on how the AWT can be used in the development of applets. However, the same methods apply to the creation of applications. Many of these features and additional aspects of Java interface programming are covered in Chapter 16, "The Windowing (AWT) Package."

Simple Components

When you use the Abstract Windowing Toolkit, you make up the graphical user interface with components. Each element you can manipulate with a windowing program is represented by its own component. There are components for buttons you can press, components for text fields you can type into, and components for scroll bars you can control. There also are components for some things you cannot directly manipulate, such as labels—lines of text used on an interface, such as the words Enter password: next to a text field on a login window.

To use these components in a program, you must put them into some kind of container. A *container* is a blank slate where graphical user interface components can be put. All containers in Java are subclasses of the `Container` class.

There are two basic types of containers:

- **The `Window` class**: Pop-up windows separate from the main program. There are two subclasses of `Window`: `Frame` (windows that have a border and menu bar) and `Dialog` (a special window used in applications to select a file).

- **The `Panel` class**: A container that represents a section of an existing window. The `Applet` class is a container that is a subclass of the `Panel` class. You can place components directly on an applet or use `Panel` objects to subdivide the applet into smaller sections.

A `Panel` container is not visible when it is added to an applet. Its purpose is to provide a way to organize components when they are being laid out in a window.

 Listing 18.1 is the full source code for an applet that has a new `Panel` added to its surface. It does not produce any output other than a blank window. However, it is useful as a template for the components you will learn to add throughout this chapter. This file—and all the other listings in this chapter—are included on the CD-ROM that accompanies this book in the `/SOURCE/CHAP18` subdirectory.

Listing 18.1. The source code of `Sample.java`.

```
1: import java.awt.*;
2:
3: public class Sample extends java.applet.Applet {
4:     Panel p = new Panel();
5:
6:     public void init() {
7:         add(p);
8:     }
9: }
```

The method call that puts the `Panel` object `p` on the applet window is the statement `add(p);`. The `add()` method is used whenever a component of any kind is added to a container.

By replacing the line `Panel p = new Panel()` with the variable declarations of components you will create, and replacing the line `add(p);` with the components to be added to a container, you can use this source code to try each component out.

By default, components are added to a container in left-to-right, top-to-bottom order. If a component does not fit on a line, it is placed at the leftmost edge of the next line. You can control how components are organized by using a layout manager, as you learn later in this chapter. Until then, the examples use the default layout style.

Buttons

The Button component is a rectangular button that can be pushed by clicking it with a mouse. Figure 18.1 shows an example of a simple one-button applet.

FIGURE 18.1.

A Button *component.*

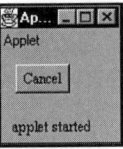

The following code is used to create a Button component and add it to an applet window:

```
Button b = new Button("Cancel");
add(b);
```

The add(b) method does not refer to a specific container object, so it defaults to the applet itself, adding the button to the applet surface. If you wanted to create a new Panel and add a new Button component to that panel, use the following code:

```
Panel p = new Panel();
Button b = new Button("Send");
p.add(b);
```

Text Fields

The TextField component is an input box in which a user can type a single line of text. The number of characters that can be visible in the text field is configurable. Figure 18.2 shows an example of an applet with a text field.

FIGURE 18.2.

A TextField
component.

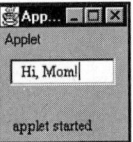

The following code is used to create a TextField component and add it to an applet window:

```
TextField t = new TextField(12);
add(t);
```

The parameter 12 in the constructor TextField(12) sets up the text field so that around 12 characters can be displayed in the field at one time. The user can type more characters than that, but only some of the characters will be displayed.

If a string is specified as a parameter to the constructor, as in the statement TextField t = TextField("your name"); the text field is created with the string as the default text in the input area of the field.

You can specify default text and a width at the same time by using a statement such as the following:

```
TextField country = new TextField("United States", 20);
```

Labels

The Label component is a string of text displayed on the container; it cannot be modified by the user. Figure 18.3 shows an example of an applet with a label next to a text field.

FIGURE 18.3.

A Label *component to the left of a text field.*

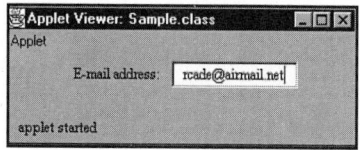

The following code is used to create a Label component and add it to an applet window:

```
Label l = new Label("E-mail address: ");
add(l);
```

The parameter in the constructor Label("E-mail address: ") identifies the text to be displayed.

Checkboxes

The Checkbox component is a toggle box that can be either selected—marked with a checkmark—or unselected. The checkbox usually has a line of text next to it explaining what the box signifies. Figure 18.4 shows an example of an applet with a checkbox.

FIGURE 18.4.

A Checkbox *component.*

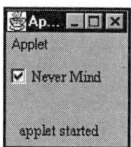

The following code is used to create a Checkbox component and add it to an applet window:

```
Checkbox c = new Checkbox("Never Mind");
add(c);
```

The parameter in the constructor CheckBox("Never Mind") identifies the text to be displayed. If you omit this parameter, a checkbox is displayed without any text next to it.

A checkbox is often used with a group of related checkboxes so that only one of the boxes can be selected at one time. To group checkboxes together, you use the CheckboxGroup class. The setCheckboxGroup() method associates a checkbox with a particular group; the setCurrent() method of CheckboxGroup can be used to make one of the boxes the selected box. The following code shows the use of CheckboxGroup:

```
CheckboxGroup cbg = new CheckboxGroup();
Checkbox c1 = new Checkbox("To-MAY-to");
c1.setCheckboxGroup(cbg);
add(c1);
Checkbox c2 = new Checkbox("To-MAH-to");
c2.setCheckboxGroup(cbg);
add(c2);
Checkbox c3 = new Checkbox("Let's call the whole thing off.");
c3.setCheckboxGroup(cbg);
cbg.setCurrent(c3);
add(c3);
```

Figure 18.5 shows this applet with the third checkbox selected.

FIGURE 18.5

A group of Checkbox
components.

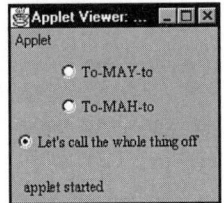

Choice List

The Choice component is a pop-up list of strings from which a single string can be selected. Its function is similar to a group of checkboxes because a choice list provides a group of options and enables one to be selected. Figure 18.6 shows an example of an applet with a choice list.

FIGURE 18.6.

A Choice *component.*

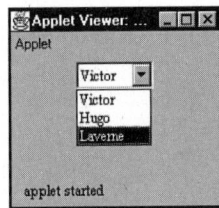

The addItem() method of the Choice class is used to build the choice list. The following code is used to create a choice list, add items to it, and then add the list to an applet window:

```
Choice c = new Choice();
c.addItem("Victor");
c.addItem("Hugo");
c.addItem("Laverne");
add(c);
```

Organizing the Interface

Up to this point, all the components have been added to a container in a manner similar to the way HTML elements are arranged on a Web page. Things are loosely organized from left to right and top to bottom, and the look of the container is highly dependent on the size of its display area.

This approach fits Java's requirement to be multiplatform. Because the language must work on any system that has a Java implementation, the windowing environment must be flexible. The Java applet you program looks dramatically different when shown on a Windows 95 system, a Macintosh system, and a SPARC workstation.

However, Java has a system of organizing user interface components that makes it possible for your applet's interface to work on each of the platforms—and to look close enough in appearance on different platforms to operate reliably. These organization tools are called *layout managers.*

When you added components to a container—the main applet window—in each of the previous examples, you were using the default layout manager: a class called FlowLayout. There are three other layout managers you can use as you organize your interface: BorderLayout, GridLayout, and GridBagLayout.

To start using a layout manager for a container, call the setLayout() method before you add any components. This approach is further described in the following sections.

The FlowLayout Class

The FlowLayout class is the default layout manager for all Panels—including the Applet class—and it is the one that's the simplest to use. Components placed under the rules of FlowLayout are arranged in order from left to right. When a component is too big to be added to the current row, a new line of components is begun below the first line.

Each row of components can be aligned to the left, right, or centered. The only parameter used with the add() method is the name of the object to add.

The following setLayout() statement sets up a container to use the FlowLayout manager:

```
setLayout( new FlowLayout() );
```

Figure 18.7 shows an example of an applet with all components arranged according to the rules of the FlowLayout manager.

The BorderLayout Class

The BorderLayout class is the default layout manager for all Window, Dialog, and Frame classes. In a border layout, components are added to the edges of the container and the center area is allotted all the space that's left over. The add() method takes an additional parameter—a string that can be North, South, East, West, or Center. This parameter specifies the location in the border layout for the component. For example, the following statements create five buttons and add them to a container laid out with the BorderLayout manager:

FIGURE 18.7.

*Components arranged
by the* FlowLayout
manager.

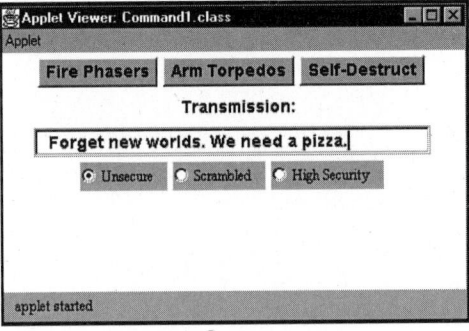

```
Button b1 = new Button("Climb");
Button b2 = new Button("Dive");
Button b3 = new Button("Left");
Button b4 = new Button("Right");
Button b5 = new Button("Fire!");
setLayout( new BorderLayout() );
add("North", b1);
add("South", b2);
add("West", b3);
add("East", b4);
add("Center", b5);
```

The setLayout(new BorderLayout()); statement shows the use of the setLayout() method to select a layout manager for the container. Figure 18.8 shows the resultant applet. Be sure to correctly capitalize the directional parameter to the add() method—unlike other aspects of the language that are not case sensitive, BorderLayout requires the directions to be capitalized consistently as North, South, East, West, and Center.

FIGURE 18.8.

*Components arranged
by the* BorderLayout
manager.

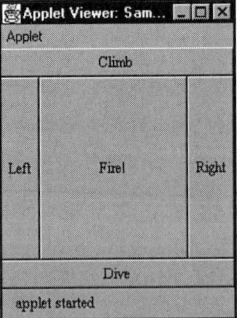

The GridLayout Class

The GridLayout class puts each component into a spot on a grid and makes each component equal in size. The grid is given specific dimensions when created, and each component is added to the grid in order, starting in the upper-left corner. This is similar to the way that components are added according to the rules of FlowLayout, but with GridLayout, components are given equal amounts of space on the container.

Components placed under the rules of GridLayout are arranged in order from left to right. When there are no more grids remaining on a row, the next component to be added is placed in the leftmost grid on the next line, if one is available. The only parameter used with the add() method is the name of the object to add.

The following setLayout() statement sets up a container to use the grid layout manager with four rows and six columns:

```
setLayout( new GridLayout(4, 6));
```

Figure 18.9 shows an example of an applet with all components arranged according to the rules of the GridLayout manager.

FIGURE 18.9.

Components arranged by the GridLayout *manager.*

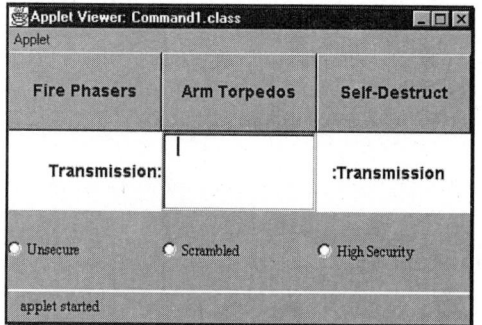

The GridBagLayout Class

The GridBagLayout class is similar to the GridLayout manager except that GridBagLayout provides much more control over how the grid is organized and how components are presented. Cells in the grid are not required to take up the same amount of space, and components can be aligned in different ways in each grid cell.

A special GridBagConstraints object is used to determine how a component will be placed into a cell and how much space that cell will occupy. Unlike the FlowLayout and GridLayout managers, with the GridBagLayout manager, components can be added to the grid in any order.

The first step needed to use a GridBagLayout is to set up the layout and the GridBagConstraints object, as shown here:

```
GridBagLayout gl = new GridBagLayout();
setLayout ( gl );
GridBagConstraints gb = new GridBagConstraints();
```

Before a component can be added to the container, instance variables of the GridBagConstraints object are used to determine the component's location and alignment within its grid cell.

The following `GridBagConstraints` variables can be set:

- `gridx` and `gridy`: These variables specify the cell in the grid where the component should be placed. `gridx` represents the rows, and `gridy` represents the columns. The (1,1) position is in the upper left corner.

- `gridheight` and `gridwidth`: These variables specify the number of cells a component should occupy. `gridheight` determines the number of rows, and `gridwidth` determines the number of columns.

- `fill`: This variable specifies the directions in which a component should expand if it has room to grow inside its cell. This can happen because of larger components in other cells. The constants `GridBagConstraints.HORIZONTAL`, `GridBagConstraints.VERTICAL`, `GridBagConstraints.BOTH`, and `GridBagConstraints.NONE` can be used with this variable. The following is an example of a statement that sets the `fill` variable:

  `gb.fill = GridBagConstraints.BOTH;`

- `anchor`: This variable specifies the way a component should be aligned in its cell. The following `GridBagConstraints` constants can be used: NORTH, NORTHEAST, EAST, SOUTHEAST, SOUTH, SOUTHWEST, WEST, NORTHWEST, CENTER.

Following is an example that places a component using the `GridBagLayout` manager:

```
// declare variables
GridBagLayout gl = new GridBagLayout();
GridBagConstraints gb = new GridBagConstraints();
Label l1 = new Label("Full e-mail address:");
// choose a layout manager
setLayout ( gl );
// set up the constraints
gb.gridx = 1;
gb.gridy = 2;
gb.gridwidth = 2;
gl.setConstraints(l1, gb);
// set up the component
l1.setAlignment(Label.RIGHT);
// add the component
add(l1);
```

In this example, the component is placed in row 1 and column 2 of the grid, and the component takes up two cells in width.

Figure 18.10 shows an example of an applet with all components arranged according to the rules of the `GridBagLayout` manager.

Nested Panels

Although the Abstract Windowing Toolkit offers several different kinds of layout managers, there are many times when one specific manager does not fit the user interface you are trying to create.

FIGURE 18.10.

Components arranged by the GridBagLayout *manager.*

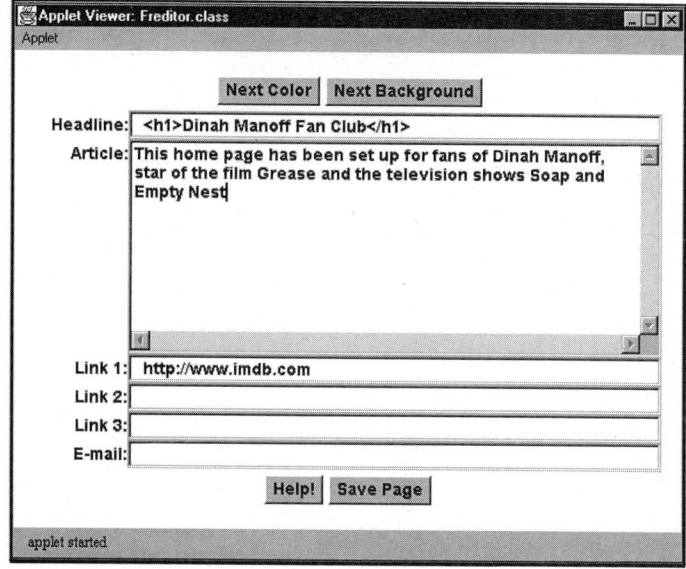

The solution to this problem is to nest one type of container inside another so that the nested container can use one type of layout manager, and the larger container can use another.

You can nest containers as many times as needed: containers can contain other containers, and each can use its own layout manager.

The following code creates a container that uses the BorderLayout manager and then adds a panel of choice boxes to that container. Because no layout manager is specified for the buttons, they default to the FlowLayout manager:

```
setLayout( new BorderLayout() );
Button b1 = new Button("Purchase");
add("North", b1);
Button b2 = new Button("Exit");
add("West", b2);
Button b3 = new Button("Help");
add("East", b3);
Button b4 = new Button("Browse Catalog");
add("South", b4);
Panel p = new Panel();
// add check boxes to panel
Checkbox c1 = new Checkbox("Brazil: $9.95");
p.add(c1);
Checkbox c2 = new Checkbox("Time Bandits: $12.95");
p.add(c2);
Checkbox c3 = new Checkbox("12 Monkeys: $39.95");
p.add(c3);
// add panel to main container
add("Center",p);
```

18

PROGRAMMING
APPLETS

Figure 18.11 shows the applet that uses this code. Using nested panels and different types of layout managers makes it possible to create many different types of user interface windows.

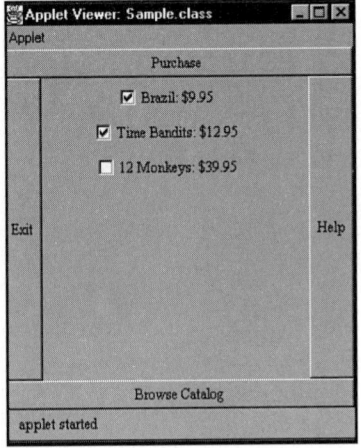

Advanced Components

In addition to the components you have learned to create up to this point, the AWT offers some more sophisticated elements such as text areas, scrolling lists, and scroll bars.

Text Areas

The TextArea component is an extended input box that enables more than one line of text to be entered. The number of lines and the number of characters per line that are visible in the text area are configurable. Figure 18.12 shows an example of an applet with a text area.

FIGURE 18.12.

A TextArea *component.*

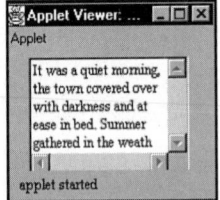

The following code is used to create a TextArea component and add it to an applet window:

```
TextArea t = new TextArea(5,20);
add(t);
```

The parameters 5 and 20 specify the text area's number of lines and the number of characters per line, respectively. If the text extends beyond the borders of the text area, a scroll bar appears to enable the user to scroll to the different sections of the text area.

If a string is specified as a parameter to the constructor, as in the statement `TextArea t = TextArea("It was a dark and stormy night.", 7, 25);` the text area is created with the string as the default text in the input area of the field. To cause parts of this text to start at the beginning of the next line, use a newline character (`\n`) in the text of the parameter. For example, to put the text `stormy night.` at the beginning of a new line, use the following statement:

```
TextArea t = TextArea("It was a dark and\nstormy night.", 7, 25);
```

Scrolling Lists

The `List` component is a scrolling list of strings from which one or more strings can be selected. Figure 18.13 shows an example of an applet with a scrolling list.

FIGURE 18.13.

A `List` component.

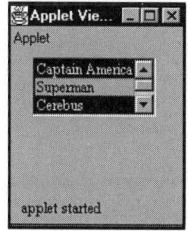

The `addItem()` method of the `List` class is used to build the scrolling list. The following code is used to create a scrolling list, add items to it, and then add the list to an applet window:

```
List l = new List(3,true);
l.addItem("Captain America");
l.addItem("Superman");
l.addItem("Cerebus");
l.addItem("Nexus");
add(l);
```

The `List()` constructor can be used with no parameters or with two parameters; the `List l = new List(3, true);` statement uses two parameters. The first parameter indicates the number of list items to display in the list window; the second parameter determines how many list items can be selected. If the second parameter is `true`, multiple items can be selected. Otherwise, only one choice from the list can be made.

Scroll Bars

The `Scrollbar` component is an up-down or left-right slider that can be used to set a numeric value. The component can be used by clicking the mouse on an arrow or grabbing the box on the slider. Figure 18.14 shows an example of an applet with a scroll bar.

The first parameter of the `Scrollbar` constructor determines whether it is a vertical or horizontal scroll bar. If you want the bar to be vertical, use the constant `Scrollbar.VERTICAL`. Otherwise, use the constant `Scrollbar.HORIZONTAL`. There are four other parameters that follow the alignment parameter. These parameters determine the slider's initial setting, the size of the scrollable area, the minimum value, and the maximum value.

Figure 18.14.

A Scrollbar *component.*

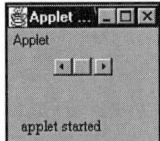

Consider the following statement:

```
Scrollbar sb = new Scrollbar(Scrollbar.HORIZONTAL, 50, 30, 10, 90);
```

This creates a horizontal Scrollbar component with the slider initially set to 50. The visible part of the scrollable area has a value of 30 from one end to the other. The minimum value when the slider is all the way to the left is 10, and the maximum value when the slider is all the way to the right is 90.

The following code is used to add a scroll bar to an applet window:

```
Scrollbar s = new Scrollbar(Scrollbar.HORIZONTAL,50,100,1,100);
add(s);
```

Canvases

The Canvas component is a section of a window used primarily as a place to draw graphics. In that respect, it is more similar to a container than a component—however, a Canvas cannot be used as a place to put components. Figure 18.15 shows an example of a canvas, which appears as a white area on a darker applet background.

Figure 18.15.

A Canvas *component.*

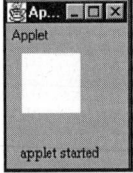

The following code is used to create a Canvas component, resize it to 50-by-50 pixels, set the background of the canvas to the color white, and add the canvas to an applet window:

```
Canvas c = new Canvas();
c.resize(50,50);
c.setBackground(Color.white);
add(c);
```

Event Handling

At this point, you have the tools necessary to build an impressive graphical user interface for a Java applet. You can use text fields to enter characters, click buttons, move scroll bars from side to side, and so on.

However, the interface has no way to respond to any of this user input. In a windowing environment such as the one provided by the Abstract Windowing Toolkit, user input—whether from the mouse, keyboard, or other means—generates an event.

An *event* is a way for a program to communicate that something has taken place. Events generate automatic calls to methods in the same way that a paint() method can be called automatically when an applet window has to be redrawn, or an init() method is called automatically when an applet is first run.

Events can involve a user interface element—such as a button that has been clicked. Events can also be something unrelated to the interface—such as an error condition that causes the program to stop execution.

In Java, the class java.awt.Event handles all events related to the user interface.

For the purpose of controlling the user interface components you can create for use with applets, there are two kinds of events to consider: action events and scroll-list events.

Action Events

An action() event is generated by most user interface components to signify that an event has taken place. This means different things depending on the component:

- For buttons, an event means that the button has been clicked.
- For checkboxes, an event means that the box has been selected or deselected.
- For lists or choice lists, an event means that one of the list items has been selected.
- For text fields, an event means that the Enter key has been pressed to indicate that user input is completed.

The action() method of the Event class takes the following form:

```
public boolean action(Event e, Object o) {
    // method code here
}
```

All user interface components that generate an action event do so by calling the action() method. To determine which component generated the event—and to gather some other information about what occurred—there are two parameters to the action() method: an instance of the Event class and an Object.

The Event class has several instance variables that provide information about the event that has taken place. The one you use most with action() events is the target variable, which indicates which component generated the event.

 The code in Listing 18.2 creates three buttons on an applet window and sets a TextField in response to the button that was pressed. You can also find this code on the CD-ROM that accompanies this book. Windows 95 and Windows NT 4 users will find the code for this chapter in \WIN95NT4\SOURCE\CHAP18. Macintosh users will find code in \SOURCE\CHAP18. Windows NT 3.51 users must install the source code to their hard drives or select the files from the zipped source code on the CD-ROM.

Listing 18.2. The full source code of Buttons.java.

```
 1: import java.awt.*;
 2:
 3: public class Buttons extends java.applet.Applet {
 4:     Button b1 = new Button("Swing Away");
 5:     Button b2 = new Button("Bunt");
 6:     Button b3 = new Button("Renegotiate Contract");
 7:     TextField t = new TextField(50);
 8:
 9:     public void init() {
10:         add(b1);
11:         add(b2);
12:         add(b3);
13:         add(t);
14:     }
15:
16:     public boolean action(Event e, Object o) {
17:         if (e.target instanceof Button) {
18:             String s = (String)o;
19:             if ( s.equals("Swing Away") )
20:                 t.setText("A long fly to center ... caught.");
21:             else if ( s.equals("Bunt") )
22:                 t.setText("You reach on a throwing error!");
23:             else
24:                 t.setText("You're now America's newest multimillionaire!");
25:         }
26:         return true;
27:     }
28: }
```

 To test the applet, create an HTML file with the source code from Listing 18.3 (this code is also found on the CD-ROM that accompanies this book).

Listing 18.3. The HTML source code of Buttons.html.

```
1: <html>
2: <body>
3: <applet code="Buttons.class" height=100 width=475>
```

```
4: </applet>
5: </body>
6: </html>
```

Figure 18.16 shows this applet being run.

FIGURE 18.16.

The Buttons *applet.*

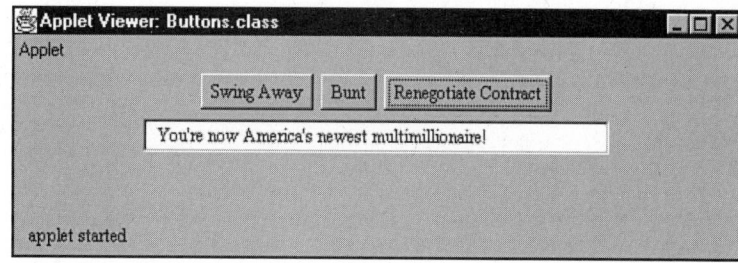

Scroll Bar Events

The action() method is generated by every component described in this chapter except for one: Scrollbar. The Scrollbar component uses the handleEvent() method.

The handleEvent() method of the Event class takes the following form:

```
public boolean handleEvent(Event e) {
    // method code here
}
```

Unlike the action() method, handleEvent() takes only one parameter: an instance of the Event class. Using the target variable of the Event class, you can determine which component generated the event and respond to it.

 The following example sets a value in a text field based on user input to a scroll bar. To try it out, type the code in Listing 18.4 into a text editor and save it as Scroller.java (alternatively, you can copy the code from the CD-ROM that accompanies this book).

Listing 18.4. The full source code of Scroller.java.

```
1: import java.awt.*;
2:
3: public class Scroller extends java.applet.Applet {
4:     Scrollbar s = new Scrollbar(Scrollbar.HORIZONTAL,
5:                        50,100,0,100);
6:     Label l = new Label("Choose Your Own Tax Rate: ");
7:     TextField t = new TextField("50%", 3);
8:
9:     public void init() {
10:         add(s);
11:         add(l);
12:         add(t);
13:     }
```

continues

Listing 18.4. continued

```
14:
15:     public boolean handleEvent(Event e) {
16:         if (e.target instanceof Scrollbar) {
17:             int taxrate = ((Scrollbar)e.target).getValue();
18:             t.setText(taxrate + "%");
19:             return true;
20:         }
21:     return false;
22:     }
23: }
```

Compile the file and create a Web page to put the applet on. Enter the code in Listing 18.5 and save it as Scroller.html (you can also find this code on the CD-ROM that accompanies this book).

Listing 18.5. The HTML source code of Scroller.html.

```
1: <html>
2: <body>
3: <applet code="Scroller.class" height=200 width=200>
4: </applet>
5: </body>
6: </html>
```

When you use a Web browser or the applet viewer JDK utility to view the page, it should resemble Figure 18.17.

Figure 18.17.

The Scroller *applet.*

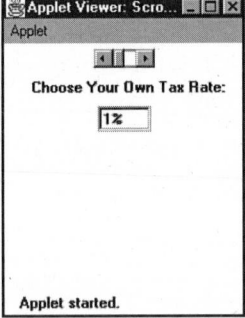

Summary

This introduction to applet programming and the Abstract Windowing Toolkit showed you that a lot of Java's functionality is built into its class libraries. For many applets, creating the user interface represents the bulk of the work because a lot of the code needed to control the interface has already been written.

Each of the user interface components has methods you can use to retrieve or change their values, enable or disable their operation, and perform other tasks. The full reference to these methods is available in the Java API documentation that comes with the Java Developers Kit.

Once you have acquired some experience developing applets with the AWT, you will be in a much better position to take advantage of the other visual programming tools that have been introduced for Java.

18

PROGRAMMING
APPLETS

CHAPTER 19

Java Graphics Fundamentals

by Michael Morrison

IN THIS CHAPTER

Few Java applets would be interesting without at least some degree of graphics. Knowing this, it's important for you to understand the fundamentals of Java graphics so that you can make the most of graphics in your applets. This chapter focuses on some of the basic Java graphics techniques that will be important as you start building your own applets. Although some of the graphics techniques you learn about in this chapter may seem fairly simple, keep in mind that they form the basis for more advanced graphics.

The chapter begins by explaining the Java graphics coordinate system and the class used as the basis for most of the Java graphics operations. The chapter then moves on to text and how it is drawn using the standard Java graphics features. You finish up the chapter by learning how images are used in the context of a Java applet. By the end of the chapter, you will have a solid understanding of graphics and how they are handled in Java applets.

The Graphics Coordinate System

All graphical computing systems use some sort of coordinate system to specify the nature of points in the system. Coordinate systems typically spell out the origin (0,0) of a graphical system, as well as the axes and directions of increasing value for each of the axes. The traditional mathematical coordinate system familiar to most of us is shown in Figure 19.1.

FIGURE 19.1.
The traditional coordinate system.

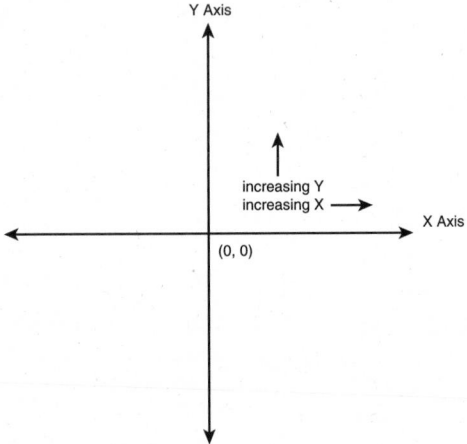

The graphical system in Java uses a coordinate system of its own to specify how and where drawing operations take place. Because all drawing in Java takes place within the confines of an applet window, the Java coordinate system is realized by the applet window. The coordinate system in Java has an origin located in the upper-left corner of the window; positive X values increase to the right and positive Y values increase down. All values in the Java coordinate system are positive integers. Figure 19.2 shows how this coordinate system looks.

FIGURE 19.2.

The Java graphics coordinate system.

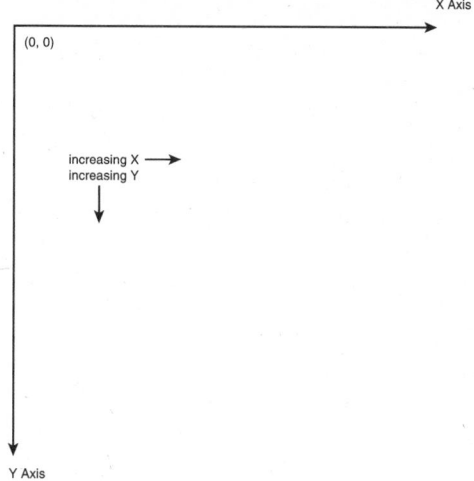

X Axis

(0, 0)

increasing X ⟶
increasing Y

Y Axis

The Basics of Color

A topic that impacts almost every area of Java graphics is color. Therefore, it's important to understand the underlying nature of color and how it is modeled in Java and in computer systems in general. Most computer systems take a similar approach to representing color. The main function of color in a computer system is to accurately reflect the physical nature of color within the confines of a graphical system. This physical nature isn't hard to figure out; anyone who has experienced the joy of Play-Doh can tell you that colors react in different ways when they are combined with each other. Like Play-Doh, a computer color system must be able to mix colors with accurate, predictable results.

Color computer monitors provide possibly the most useful insight into how software systems implement color. A color monitor has three electron guns: red, green, and blue. The output from these three guns converge on each pixel of the screen, exciting phosphors to produce the appropriate color (see Figure 19.3). The combined intensities of the guns determine the resulting pixel color. This convergence of different colors from the monitor guns is very similar to the convergence of different colored Play-Doh.

NOTE

Technically speaking, the result of combining colors on a monitor is different than that of combining similarly colored Play-Doh. Color combinations on a monitor are *additive*, meaning that mixed colors are emitted by the monitor, whereas Play-Doh color combinations are *subtractive*, meaning that mixed colors are absorbed. The additive or subtractive nature of a color combination depends on the physical properties of the particular medium involved.

Figure 19.3.

Electron guns in a color monitor converging to create a unique color.

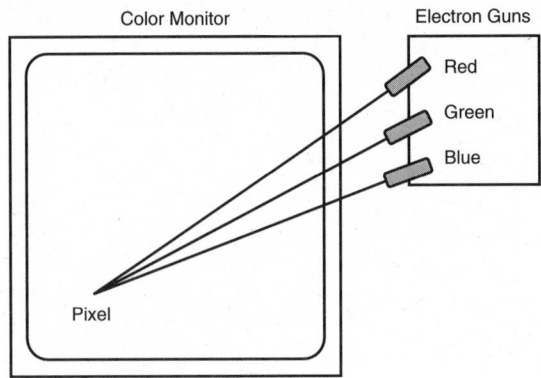

The Java color system is very similar to the physical system used by color monitors; it forms unique colors by using varying intensities of the colors red, green, and blue. Therefore, Java colors are represented by the combinations of the numeric intensities of the primary colors (red, green, and blue). This color system is known as RGB (Red Green Blue) and is standard across most graphical computer systems.

> **NOTE**
>
> Although RGB is the most popular computer color system in use, there are others. Another popular color system is HSB, which stands for Hue Saturation Brightness. In this system, colors are defined by varying degrees of hue, saturation, and brightness. The HSB color system is also supported by Java.

Table 19.1 shows the numeric values for the red, green, and blue components of some basic colors. Notice that the intensities of each color component range from 0 to 255 in value.

Table 19.1. RGB component values for some basic colors.

Color	Red	Green	Blue
White	255	255	255
Black	0	0	0
Light Gray	192	192	192
Dark Gray	128	128	128
Red	255	0	0
Green	0	255	0

Color	Red	Green	Blue
Blue	0	0	255
Yellow	255	255	0
Purple	255	0	255

Java provides a class, Color, for modeling colors. The Color class represents an RGB color and provides methods for extracting and manipulating the primary color components. The Color class also includes constant members representing many popular colors. You typically use the Color class to specify the color when you are using many of Java's graphical functions, which you learn about next.

The Graphics Class

Most of Java's graphics functions are accessible through a single class, Graphics, found in the Java AWT (Abstract Windowing Toolkit) package. The Graphics class models a graphics context. A *graphics context* is an abstract representation of a graphical surface that can be drawn on. A graphics context is basically a way to allow you to draw in a generic manner, without worrying about where the drawing is physically taking place.

Graphics contexts are necessary so that the same graphics routines can be used regardless of whether you are drawing to the screen, to memory, or to a printer. The Graphics class provides you with a graphics context to which you perform all graphics functions. As you learn about the functionality provided by the Graphics class, keep in mind that its output is largely independent of the ultimate destination, thanks to graphics contexts.

Graphical output code in a Java applet is usually implemented in the applet's paint() method. A Graphics object is passed into the paint() method, which is then used to perform graphical output to the applet window (output surface). Because the Graphics object is provided by paint(), you never explicitly create a Graphics object. Actually, you couldn't explicitly create a Graphics object even if you wanted to because it is an abstract class.

Even though graphics operations often take place within the context of an applet window, the output of the Graphics object is really tied to a component. A *component* is a generic graphical window and forms the basis for all other graphical elements in the Java system. Java components are modeled at the highest level by the Component class, which is defined in the AWT package.

An applet window is just a specific type of component. Thinking of graphics in terms of the Component class rather than an applet window shows you that graphics can be output to any object derived from the Component class. As a matter of fact, every Component object contains a corresponding Graphics object that is used to render graphics on its surface.

Java graphics contexts (`Graphics` objects) have a few attributes that determine how different graphical operations are carried out. The most important of these attributes is the color attribute, which determines the color used in graphics operations such as drawing lines. You set this attribute using the `setColor()` method defined in the `Graphics` class. `setColor()` takes a `Color` object as its only parameter. Similar to `setColor()` is `setBackground()`, which is a method in the `Component` class that determines the color of the component's background. `Graphics` objects also have a font attribute that determines the size and appearance of text. This attribute is set using the `setFont()` method, which takes a `Font` object as its only parameter. You learn more about drawing text and using the `Font` object in "Drawing Text," later in this chapter.

Most of the graphics operations provided by the `Graphics` class fall into one of the following categories:

- Drawing graphics primitives
- Drawing text
- Drawing images

Drawing Graphics Primitives

Graphics primitives consist of lines, rectangles, circles, polygons, ovals, and arcs. You can create pretty impressive graphics by mixing these primitives together; the `Graphics` class provides methods for drawing these primitives. There are also methods that act on primitives that form closed regions. *Closed regions* are graphical elements with a clearly distinctive inside and outside. For example, circles and rectangles are closed regions, whereas lines and points are not. You can also use the methods defined in the `Graphics` class to erase the area defined by a primitive or fill it with a particular color.

Lines

Lines are the simplest of the graphics primitives and are therefore the easiest to draw. The `drawLine()` method handles drawing lines, and is defined as follows:

```
void drawLine(int x1, int y1, int x2, int y2)
```

The first two parameters, *x1* and *y1*, specify the starting point for the line; the *x2* and *y2* parameters specify the ending point. To draw a line in an applet, call `drawLine()` in the applet's `paint()` method, as in this example:

```
public void paint(Graphics g) {
  g.drawLine(5, 10, 15, 55);
}
```

The results of this code are shown in Figure 19.4.

FIGURE 19.4.
A line drawn using the drawLine() *method.*

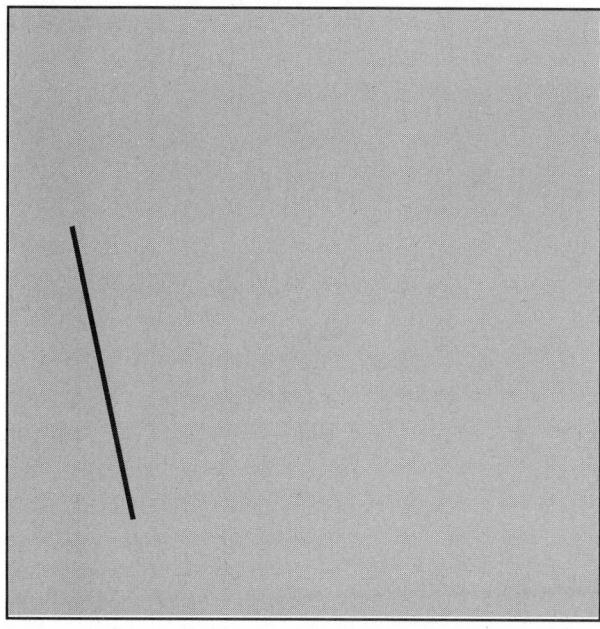

> **NOTE**
>
> Most graphical programming environments provide a means to draw lines (and other graphics primitives) in various widths. Java doesn't currently provide a facility to vary the width of lines, which is a pretty big limitation. Release 1.1 of Java will probably alleviate this problem.

Rectangles

Rectangles are also very easy to draw in Java. The drawRect() method enables you to draw rectangles by specifying the upper-left corner and the width and height of the rectangle. The drawRect() method is defined in Graphics as follows:

```
void drawRect(int x, int y, int width, int height)
```

The *x* and *y* parameters specify the location of the upper-left corner of the rectangle; the *width* and *height* parameters specify their namesakes, in pixels. To draw a rectangle using drawRect(), just call it from the paint() method like this:

```
public void paint(Graphics g) {
  g.drawRect(5, 10, 15, 55);
}
```

The results of this code are shown in Figure 19.5.

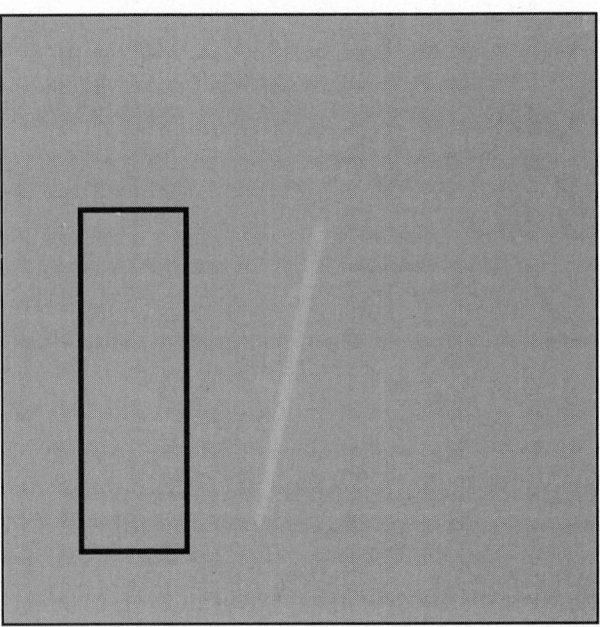

There is also a drawRoundRect() method that allows you to draw rectangles with rounded corners:

```
void drawRoundRect(int x, int y, int width, int height, int arcWidth,
  int arcHeight)
```

The drawRoundRect() method requires two additional parameters than drawRect(): *arcWidth* and *arcHeight*. These parameters specify the width and height of the arc forming the rounded corners of the rectangle. Following is an example of using drawRoundRect() to draw a rectangle with rounded corners:

```
public void paint(Graphics g) {
  g.drawRoundRect(5, 10, 15, 55, 6, 12);
}
```

The results of this code are shown in Figure 19.6.

In addition to these two basic rectangle-drawing methods, there is also a method for drawing 3D rectangles with shadow effects along the edges, draw3DRect(). However, the current limitation of Java only supporting a line width of one pixel makes the 3D effect pretty subtle.

The Graphics class also provides versions of each of these rectangle-drawing methods that fill the interior of a rectangle with the current color in addition to drawing the rectangle itself. These methods are named fillRect(), fillRoundRect(), and fill3DRect(), respectively. The support for drawing both unfilled and filled rectangles is common throughout the Graphics class when dealing with closed regions.

FIGURE 19.6.

*A rounded rectangle
drawn using the*
drawRoundRect()
method.

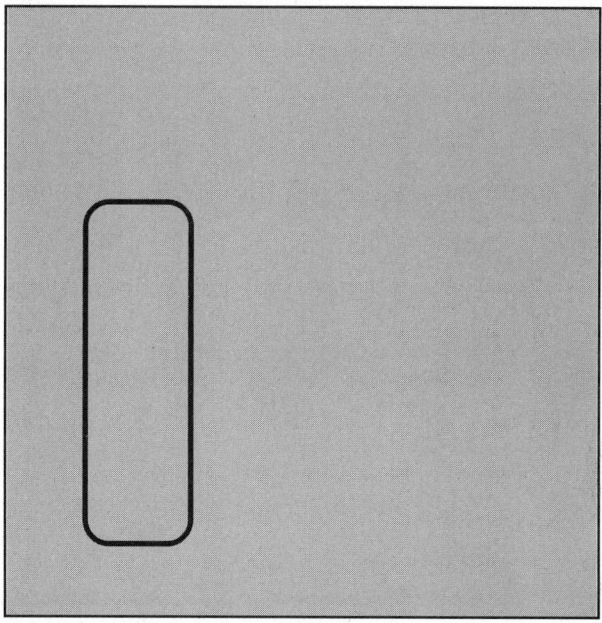

FIGURE 19.6.

*A rounded rectangle
drawn using the*
drawRoundRect()
method.

NOTE

To draw a perfect square using any of the rectangle drawing methods, you simply use an equivalent width and height.

Polygons

Polygons are shapes consisting of a group of interconnected points; each point in a polygon is connected in a series by lines. To draw a polygon, you provide a list of points in the order that they are to be connected to form the polygon shape. Polygons are not closed regions by default; to make a polygon a closed region, you must provide the same point as the starting and ending point for the polygon.

Java provides two approaches to drawing polygons: a method and a class. The most straightforward approach is using the drawPolygon() method, which is defined as follows:

```
void drawPolygon(int xPoints[], int yPoints[], int nPoints)
```

The first two parameters, *xPoints* and *yPoints*, are arrays containing the x and y components of each coordinate in the polygon. For example, *xPoints*[0] and *yPoints*[0] form the starting point for the polygon. The last parameter to drawPolygon(), *nPoints*, is the number of points in the polygon; this value is typically equal to the length of the *xPoints* and *yPoints* arrays.

The following example uses the `drawPolygon()` method to draw a closed polygon:

```
public void paint(Graphics g) {
  int xPts[] = {5, 25, 50, 30, 15, 5};
  int yPts[] = {10, 35, 20, 65, 40, 10};

  g.drawPolygon(xPts, yPts, xPts.length);
}
```

The results of this code are shown in Figure 19.7.

FIGURE 19.7.

A closed polygon drawn using the `drawPolygon()` *method.*

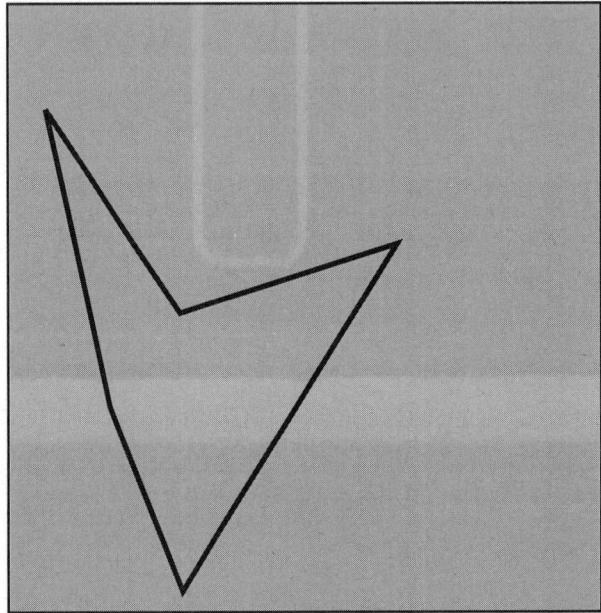

> **NOTE**
>
> The polygon in Figure 19.7 is closed because the same point (5, 10) is defined both at the beginning and end of the polygon coordinate list. Without duplicating this point at the end of the list, the last point would not have been connected back to the first point and the polygon would have remained an open region.

The other approach to drawing polygons involves using the `Polygon` class to construct a `Polygon` object. Once you have a `Polygon` object, you can simply pass it to `drawPolygon()` instead of passing the x and y point arrays. You construct a `Polygon` object using one of the `Polygon` class's constructors, which are defined as follows:

```
Polygon()
Polygon(int xpoints[], int ypoints[], int npoints)
```

The first constructor simply creates a default polygon with an empty coordinate list; the second constructor is initialized with a coordinate list much like the one taken by the `drawPolygon()` method just described. Regardless of how you create a `Polygon` object, you can add points to the polygon by using the `addPoint()` method, which is defined as follows:

```
void addPoint(int x, int y)
```

The following example uses a `Polygon` object to draw a closed, filled polygon:

```
public void paint(Graphics g) {
  int     xPts[] = {5, 25, 50, 30, 15, 5};
  int     yPts[] = {10, 35, 20, 65, 40, 10};
  Polygon poly = new Polygon(xPts, yPts, xPts.length);

  g.fillPolygon(poly);
}
```

The results of this code are shown in Figure 19.8.

FIGURE 19.8.

A closed polygon drawn using a Polygon *object and the* fillPolygon() *method.*

I mentioned in the previous section that many of the methods for drawing graphics primitives in Java support both unfilled and filled versions. Figure 19.8 is an example of using the filled version for polygons, `fillPolygon()`.

You may not see why there is ever a need for using a `Polygon` object, considering the fact that I used basically the same technique for representing the set of points that make up the polygon. The truth is that `Polygon` objects are very useful whenever you know you'll need to draw a particular polygon again. Consider the asteroids floating around in a space game; you could easily model the asteroids as polygons and use a `Polygon` object to represent each. When it comes time to draw the asteroids, all the messy coordinates are already stored within each `Polygon` object, so you only have to pass the object to the `drawPolygon()` or `fillPolygon()` method.

Ovals

Another useful graphics primitive supported by Java is the oval, which is a rounded, closed region. You specify an oval using a coordinate for the top left corner of the oval, along with the width and height of the oval. This is basically the same approach used when drawing rectangles with square corners; the difference of course being that ovals are round regions, not rectangular regions. The primary method for drawing ovals is `drawOval()`, which is defined as follows:

```
void drawOval(int x, int y, int width, int height)
```

The *x* and *y* parameters specify the location of the upper-left corner of the oval; the *width* and *height* parameters specify their namesakes. You draw an oval using `drawOval()` like this:

```
public void paint(Graphics g) {
  g.drawOval(5, 10, 15, 55);
}
```

The results of this code are shown in Figure 19.9.

FIGURE 19.9.

An oval drawn using the `drawOval()` *method.*

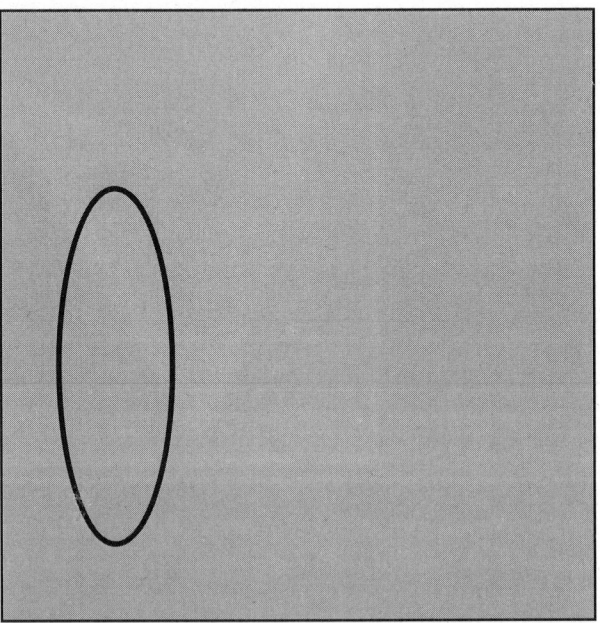

Like the drawing methods you learned about for other graphics primitives, the `Graphics` class also provides a method to draw filled ovals, `fillOval()`.

Arcs

Unlike the graphics primitives you've learned about so far, arcs are a little more complex to handle. An arc is basically a section of an oval; just picture erasing part of an oval and what you have left is an arc. Because an arc is really just part of an oval, you draw an arc in relation to the complete oval it is a part of. In other words, to specify an arc, you must specify a complete oval along with what section of the oval the arc comprises. If you still don't quite follow, maybe taking a look at the Java method for drawing arcs will help clear things up:

```
void drawArc(int x, int y, int width, int height, int startAngle, int arcAngle)
```

As you can see, the first four parameters are the same ones used in the `drawOval()` method. In fact, these parameters define the oval of which the arc is a part. The remaining two parameters define the arc as a section of this oval. To understand how these parameters define an arc, refer to Figure 19.10, which shows an arc as a section of an oval.

FIGURE 19.10.

An arc defined as a section of an oval.

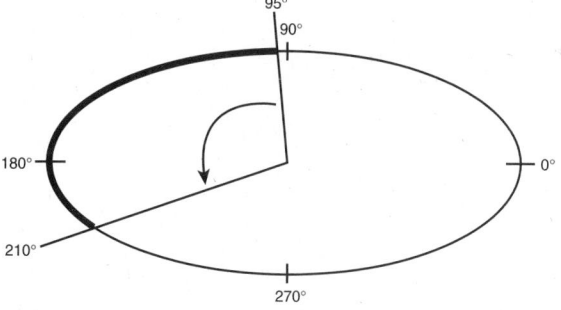

As you can see in Figure 19.10, an arc can be defined within an oval by specifying the starting and ending angles for the arc. Alternatively, you can specify just the starting angle and a number of degrees to sweep in a particular direction. In the case of Java, an arc is defined in the latter manner: with a starting angle and a sweep angle, or arc angle. The sweep direction in Java is counterclockwise, meaning that positive arc angles are counterclockwise and negative arc angles are clockwise. The arc shown in Figure 19.10 has a starting angle of 95 degrees and an arc angle of 115 degrees. The resulting ending angle is the sum of these two angles, which is 210 degrees.

Following is an example of drawing a similar arc using the `drawArc()` method:

```
public void paint(Graphics g) {
  g.drawArc(5, 10, 150, 75, 95, 115);
}
```

The results of this code are shown in Figure 19.11.

FIGURE 19.11.

An arc drawn using the `drawArc()` *method.*

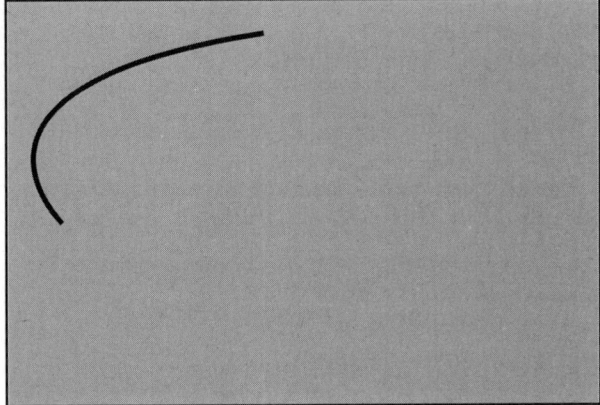

Like most of the graphics primitives in Java, there is a method for drawing filled arcs, `fillArc()`. The `fillArc()` method is very useful because you can use it to draw pie-shaped pieces of a circle or oval. For example, if you are writing an applet that needs to draw a pie graph for a set of data, you can use the `fillArc()` method to draw each piece of the pie.

Drawing Text

Because Java applets are entirely graphical in nature, you must use the `Graphics` object even when you want to draw text. Fortunately, drawing text is very easy and yields very nice results. You will typically create a font for the text and select it as the font to be used by the graphics context before actually drawing any text. As you learned earlier, the `setFont()` method selects a font into the current graphics context. This method is defined as follows:

```
void setFont(Font font)
```

The `Font` object models a textual font and includes the name, point size, and style of the font. The `Font` object supports three different font styles, which are implemented as the following constant members: `BOLD`, `ITALIC`, and `PLAIN`. These styles are really just constant numbers and can be added together to yield a combined effect. The constructor for the `Font` object is defined as follows:

```
Font(String name, int style, int size)
```

As you can see, the constructor takes as parameters the name, style, and point size of the font. If you are wondering exactly how font names work, you simply provide the string name of the font you want to use. The names of the most common fonts supported by Java are TimesRoman, Courier, and Helvetica. To create a bold, italic, Helvetica, 22-point font, you use the following code:

```
Font f = new Font("Helvetica", Font.BOLD + Font.ITALIC, 22);
```

> **CAUTION**
>
> Some systems may support other fonts beyond the three common fonts mentioned here (TimesRoman, Courier, and Helvetica). Even though you are free to use other fonts, keep in mind that these three common fonts are the only ones guaranteed to be supported across all systems. In other words, it's much safer to stick with these fonts.

After you've created a font, you will often want to create a `FontMetric` object to find out the details of the font's size. The `FontMetric` class models very specific placement information about a font, such as the ascent, descent, leading, and total height of the font. Figure 19.12 shows what each of these font metric attributes represent.

FIGURE 19.12.

The different font metric attributes.

You can use the font metrics to precisely control the location of text you are drawing. After you have the metrics under control, you just need to select the original `Font` object into the `Graphics` object using the `setFont()` method, as in the following:

```
g.setFont(f);
```

Now you're ready to draw some text using the font you've created, sized up, and selected. The `drawString()` method, defined in the `Graphics` class, is exactly what you need. `drawString()` is defined as follows:

```
void drawString(String str, int x, int y)
```

The `drawString()` method takes a `String` object as its first parameter, which determines the text to be drawn. The last two parameters specify the location at which the string is drawn; *x* specifies the left edge of the text and *y* specifies the baseline of the text. The baseline of the text is the bottom of the text, not including the descent. Refer to Figure 19.12 if you are having trouble visualizing this.

The `DrawText` sample applet (see Listing 19.1) demonstrates drawing a string centered in the applet window. Figure 19.13 shows the `DrawText` applet in action.

Listing 19.1. The DrawText sample applet.

```java
// DrawText Class
// DrawText.java

// Imports
import java.applet.*;
import java.awt.*;

public class DrawText extends Applet {
  public void paint(Graphics g) {
    Font        font = new Font("Helvetica", Font.BOLD +
      Font.ITALIC, 22);
    FontMetrics fm = g.getFontMetrics(font);
    String      str = new
      String("The highest result of education is tolerance.");

    g.setFont(font);
    g.drawString(str, (size().width - fm.stringWidth(str)) / 2,
      ((size().height - fm.getHeight()) / 2) + fm.getAscent());
  }
}
```

FIGURE 19.13.

The DrawText *sample applet.*

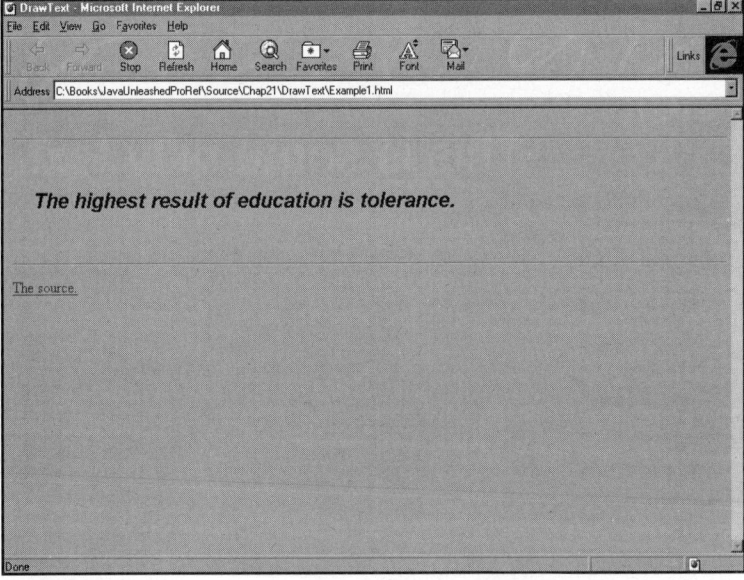

The DrawText applet uses the font-related methods you just learned to draw a string centered in the applet window. You may be wondering about the calls to the size() method when the location to draw the string is being calculated. The size() method is a member of Component and returns a Dimension object specifying the width and height of the applet window.

That sums up the basics of drawing text using the Graphics object. Now it's time to move on to one of the most important aspects of Java graphics: images.

Drawing Images

Images are rectangular graphical objects composed of colored pixels. Each pixel in an image describes the color at that particular location of the image. Pixels can have unique colors that are usually described using the RGB color system. Java provides support for working with 32-bit images, which means that each pixel in an image is described using 32 bits. The red, green, and blue components of a pixel's color are stored in these 32 bits, along with an alpha component. The *alpha component* of a pixel refers to the transparency or opaqueness of the pixel.

Before getting into the details of how to draw an image, you need to first learn how to load images. The getImage() method, defined in the Applet class, is used to load an image from a URL. getImage() comes in two versions, which are defined as follows:

```
Image getImage(URL url)
Image getImage(URL url, String name)
```

These two versions essentially perform the same function; the only difference is that the first version expects a fully qualified URL, including the name of the image, and the second version enables you to specify a separate URL and image name.

You probably noticed that both versions of getImage() return an object of type Image. The Image class represents a graphical image, such as a GIF or JPEG file image, and provides a few methods for determining the width and height of the image. Image also includes a method for retrieving a graphics context for the image, which enables you to draw directly onto an image.

The Graphics class provides a handful of methods for drawing images, which follow:

```
boolean drawImage(Image img, int x, int y, ImageObserver observer)
boolean drawImage(Image img, int x, int y, int width, int height,
  ImageObserver observer)
boolean drawImage(Image img, int x, int y, Color bgcolor, ImageObserver observer)
boolean drawImage(Image img, int x, int y, int width, int height, Color bgcolor,
  ImageObserver observer)
```

All these methods are variations on the same theme: they all draw an image at a certain location as defined by the parameters *x* and *y*. The last parameter in each method is an object of type ImageObserver, which is used internally by drawImage() to get information about the image.

The first version of drawImage() draws the image at the specified *x* and *y* location—*x* and *y* represent the upper-left corner of the image. The second version draws the image inside the rectangle formed by *x*, *y*, *width*, and *height*. If this rectangle is different than the image rectangle, the image is scaled to fit. The third version of drawImage() draws the image with transparent areas filled in with the background color specified in the *bgcolor* parameter. The last version of drawImage() combines the capabilities in the first three, enabling you to draw an image within a given rectangle and with a background color.

The process of drawing an image involves calling the getImage() method to load the image, followed by a call to drawImage(), which actually draws the image on a graphics context. The

DrawImage sample applet (shown in Listing 19.2) shows how easy it is to draw an image (see Figure 19.14). This applet shows how easy it is to immortalize your friends by plastering their image on the Web; it displays a picture of my good friend, Keith Nash, who is clearly having a bad hair day!

Listing 19.2. The DrawImage sample applet.

```
// DrawImage Class
// DrawImage.java

// Imports
import java.applet.*;
import java.awt.*;

public class DrawImage extends Applet {
  public void paint(Graphics g) {
    Image img = getImage(getCodeBase(), "Dude.gif");

    g.drawImage(img, (size().width - img.getWidth(this)) / 2,
      (size().height - img.getHeight(this)) / 2, this);
  }
}
```

FIGURE 19.14.

The DrawImage *sample applet.*

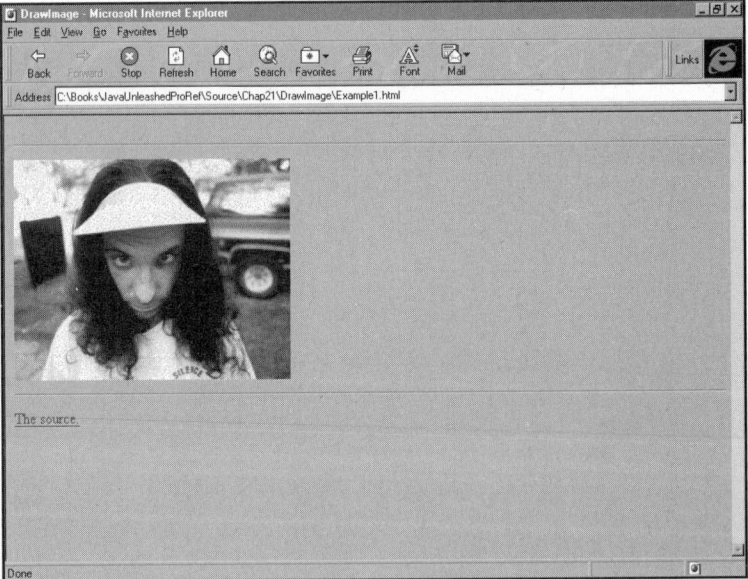

The DrawImage sample applet loads an image in the paint() method using getImage(). The getCodeBase() method is used to specify the applet directory where applet resources are usually located, while the image name itself is simply given as a string. The image is then drawn centered in the applet window using the drawImage() method. It's as simple as that!

Summary

This chapter bombarded you with a lot of information about the graphics support in Java. Most of it was centered around the `Graphics` object, which is fortunately pretty straightforward to use. You began by learning about color and what it means in the context of Java. You moved on to drawing a variety of different graphics primitives. You then learned how text is drawn in Java through the use of fonts and font metrics. Finally, you concluded the chapter by taking a look at images and how they are drawn.

This chapter showed you that Java not only provides a rich set of graphics features, but that is also has a very clean interface through which you can explore the use of graphics in your own applets. If the graphics features you learned about in this chapter seem a little tame, you may be ready to jump into the next chapter, which covers animation programming.

Basic Animation Programming

by Christopher A. Seguin

IN THIS CHAPTER

CHAPTER 20

History, as the cliché claims, repeats itself. Consider this: Between 4,000 and 6,000 years ago, the Sumerians began communicating using pictograms. In 1827, Joseph Niepce produced the first photographs on a metal plate. Eighty-eight years later, the motion picture camera was created and in 1937, the first full-length animation feature was released. Since then, animation has transformed from a novelty to an art form. We regularly see animation in commercials, television, and movies.

The history of the Web is similar. At first, Web pages could contain only text and links to other pages. In the early 1990s, a browser called Mosaic was released that added the ability to incorporate pictures and sound. Mosaic started a flurry of interest in the Internet. But after a while, even the carefully designed Web pages with elaborate background images and colored text began to grow stale. Java, a recent extension to the World Wide Web, allows programs to be added to Web pages.

Animations have been available on the Web since the early versions of Mosaic, where Mosaic would download the MPEG file and launch a separate viewer. With the release of Netscape version 1.1, CGI files could use a push-and-pull method of creating animations. The browser would receive instructions to reread the information or read the next URL address after a set delay. The client could keep the connection open and push new information onto the browser every so often. However, this type of animation was available only on Netscape. And it was slow. One of the popular uses of Java is to create animations. Because the Java animations are on the page, they serve to call attention to the Web page, rather than away from the page the way a separate viewer does. Java is also faster than the Netscape method and works on any browser that supports Java.

This chapter covers the following topics:

- The `Animator` class
- Design of simple animation systems
- Double buffering
- Advanced animation techniques

The design of simple animation systems is explained with animated text and images. This chapter covers double buffering, which is the easiest way to eliminate animation flicker. The advanced animation techniques include in-betweens, backgrounds, z-order, and collision detection.

The Animator Class

Before we dive into the programming of animation applets, let's start with the hands-down easiest way to create an animation: use someone else's applet. Herb Jellinek and Jim Hagen at Sun Microsystems have created an `Animator` class, an applet that creates an animation. This class is provided as a demonstration program with the Java Developers Kit.

To use the `Animator` applet, do the following:

1. After installing Sun's Java Developers Kit, copy the following three files to your classes directory: `Animator.class`, `ParseException.class`, and `ImageNotFoundException.class`. These files can be found in the examples provided with the JDK provided by Sun and are located on the CD-ROM that accompanies this book. They should be in a directory called `java/demo/Animator`.

2. Create the image and sound files for your animations.

3. Put the applet tag on your Web page. Table 20.1 shows the parameters that the `Animator` applet reads from your HTML file.

4. View your animation on your favorite Java-enabled browser.

Table 20.1. Animator applet parameters.

Tag	Description	Default
IMAGESOURCE	The directory that contains the image files	The same directory that contains the HTML file
STARTUP	The image to be displayed while the program loads the other images	None
BACKGROUNDCOLOR	A 24-bit number that specifies the color of the background	A filled, light-gray rectangle that covers the entire applet
BACKGROUND	The image to be displayed in the background	A filled, light-gray rectangle that covers the entire applet
STARTIMAGE	The number of the first image	1
ENDIMAGE	The number of the last image	1
NAMEPATTERN	Specifies the name of the image files	T%N.gif (%N means number, so T%N.gif use images called T1.gif, T2.gif, T3.gif,...")
IMAGES	A list of indexes of the images to be displayed, in the order in which they are to be displayed	None
HREF	The page to visit on a mouse click	None
PAUSE	The number of milliseconds for the pause between frames	3900

20

BASIC ANIMATION PROGRAMMING

continues

Table 20.1. continued

Tag	Description	Default
PAUSES	The number of milliseconds for the pause between each frame	The value of PAUSE
REPEAT	A boolean value: Does the animation cycle through the images? (yes or true/no or false)	true
POSITIONS	The coordinates of where each image will be displayed in the applet	(0,0)
SOUNDSOURCE	The directory that contains the sound files	The value of IMAGESOURCE
SOUNDTRACK	The background music	None
SOUNDS	The sounds to be displayed for each image in the animation	None

Most of the tags are straightforward in their use, but some tags need additional explanation. We'll begin with the images and then describe how to use the tags that accept multiple inputs.

The default name of images used by the Animator class must start with the letter T followed by a number. For example, if you have three GIF files that form the changing part of the animation, you can name them T1.gif, T2.gif, and T3.gif. However, you can change this default by using the NAMEPATTERN parameter. For example, if your images are called myImage1.jpg, myImage2.jpg, and myImage3.jpg, you would use the following parameter:

```
<PARAM NAME=NAMEPATTERN VALUE="myImage%N.jpg">
```

The background image and startup image have no constraints on their names.

There are two ways to specify the order of the images. First, you can specify the first and last image with the STARTIMAGE and ENDIMAGE tags. If the value of the STARTIMAGE tag is greater than the value of the ENDIMAGE tag, the images are displayed starting at STARTIMAGE and decrementing to ENDIMAGE. Second, you can specify the order of the images with the IMAGES tag. This tag takes multiple inputs, so let's consider how to give multiple inputs to the Animator applet.

Several tags take multiple inputs. The Animator class has implemented these tags using a ¦ as a separator between values. For example, the IMAGES tag requires the list of numbers of the images to be displayed. If you want to display the images T1.gif, T3.gif, and T2.gif in that order, you would write this:

```
<PARAM NAME=IMAGES VALUE=1¦3¦2>
```

The SOUNDS tag works the same way except that values can be left blank. A blank value in the SOUNDS tag means that no sound is played for that image. The PAUSES tag also takes multiple inputs, but if an input is left out, it defaults to the standard pause between images. For example, the following statements display the first image for 1000ms (1000 milliseconds), the second image for 250ms, and the third image for 4ms:

```
<PARAM NAME=PAUSE VALUE=250>
<PARAM NAME=PAUSES VALUE=1000¦¦4>
```

The POSITION tag is a set of coordinates. As with the IMAGES and SOUNDS tags, the coordinates are separated by a ¦ character. The x and y values of the coordinate are separated by an @ character. If a coordinate is left blank, the image remains in the same location as the previous image. For example, if you want to draw the first and second images at (30, 25), and the third image at (100, 100), you would write this code:

```
<PARAM NAME=POSITION VALUE=30@25¦¦100@100>
```

The Animator class enables you to create an animation quickly and easily. If, however, you have more than one moving object or you want to draw your objects as the animation runs, you have to write your own animation applet. The next section begins with the design of an animator and gives four examples.

Simple Animation

Let's dive right into programming simple animations in Java. Although these animations may not be perfectly smooth in their presentation, they do explain the basic design of an animation. We will also look at what makes a good animation. Let's begin by creating an abstract animated object interface, and then create several examples of the animation in action.

The `AnimationObject` Interface

When writing a program in an object-oriented language, the first step is to decompose the problem into things that interact. The things, called *objects*, that are similar are grouped into classes. The class holds all the information about an object. Sometimes, classes are very similar, and you can have a class to represent the similarities of the class. Such a class is called a *base class*. If the base class doesn't actually store information, but provides a list of methods that all the members of the class have, the class is called an *abstract class*.

Java is an objected-oriented language, so in creating a design for a program, first find similarities in the components of the program. When designing an animation, begin by looking for similarities. Each image or text message that moves is an object. But if you consider these objects, you find that they are very similar. Each object has to be able to paint itself in the applet window. In addition to painting the object, something about the objects is changing (or it wouldn't be an animation). So the object must know when to change.

Let's create a class with the following two methods:

- `paint()`—directs the object to paint itself
- `clockTick()`—tells the object to change

Java provides two ways to create an abstract class. First, if there is some basic method that is used for any object of the class, you can create an abstract class. The methods that are the same can be filled in. If there is no similarity in the actual methods, you can create an interface. The advantage of using an interface is that a class can inherit from multiple interfaces, but it can inherit only from a single class.

Because a moving text object and an image have nothing in common other than the names of their `paint()` and `clockTick()` methods, I have created the following interface:

```
public interface AnimationObject {
    public void paint (Graphics G, Applet parent);
    public void clockTick ();
}
```

This skeleton enables you to simplify the design of the applet object. For example, the `paint()` routine just erases the screen and sends each animation object a `paint()` method:

```
public void paint (Graphics g) {
    update (g);
    }
public void update (Graphics g) {
    //  Erase the screen
    g.setColor (Color.lightGray);
    g.fillRect (0, 0, nWidth, nHeight);
    g.setColor (Color.black);

    //  Paint each object
    for (int ndx = 0; ndx < AnimatedObjects.length; ndx++)
        AnimatedObjects[ndx].paint (g, this);
    }
```

For now, assume that the `update()` method and the `paint()` method are essentially the same, although a description of the difference is given later in this chapter in the section on double buffering. The `update()` method is straightforward, but it may cause your animation to flicker. Code to fix the flicker is given in the section on double buffering.

The `run()` method is only three steps. First, the applet tells each object that one time unit has passed, and then the applet repaints itself. Finally, the program pauses. Here's what the `run()` method looks like:

```
public void run() {
        int ndx = 0;

        //  Set the priority of the thread
        Thread.currentThread().setPriority(Thread.MIN_PRIORITY);
```

```
//  Do the animation
while (size().width > 0 &&
       size().height > 0 &&
       kicker != null) {

    for (ndx = 0; ndx < AnimatedObjects.length; ndx++)
        AnimatedObjects[ndx].clockTick ();

    repaint();

    try { Thread.sleep(nSpeed); }
        catch (InterruptedException e) {}
    }
}
```

The hard part is initially creating the applet, and that depends on how difficult it is to create each of the animation objects. Let's start with moving text.

Moving Text

NOTE

The code in this section is in Example 20.1 in file exmp20_1.java on the CD-ROM that accompanies this book.

Everyone has seen animated text, such as weather warnings that slide across the bottom of the TV screen during storms. Let's start with an animation object that moves a text message around the applet drawing area and consider why this is effective.

Java provides the drawString (String s, int x, int y) routine in the java.awt.Graphics class that draws a string at a specific location. To animate text, the applet repeatedly draws the string at a different location.

If we want to scroll text across the applet, what do we have to store? First, we need a text message. For this example, assume that the message slides only to the left. (It's easy to extend this code so that the message can also slide right, up, or down.) In addition to the message, we need some internal variables to store the x and y locations of where the message should be printed next.

The next question is, "How do you compute when the message is no longer visible?" We have to know about the length of the message and the width of the applet to determine when the message disappears from view and where it should reappear. We won't be able to determine the length of the message until we have the java.awt.Graphics object, so we'll postpone this computation until the first time we paint() the text message.

Let's begin by creating an object that stores each of these values:

```
class TextScrolling implements AnimationObject {

    //  Internal Variables
    String pcMessage;

    int nXPos;
    int nYPos;
    int nAppletWidth;
    int nMessageWidth;
```

Now we need to initialize these variables in the constructor method. The constructor needs the text message and the applet width. The other values are computed in the paint() method. Here's the constructor:

```
public TextScrolling (String pcMsg, int nWide) {
        pcMessage = pcMsg;

        nAppletWidth = nWide;
        nMessageWidth = -1;

        nXPos = nWide;
        nYPos = -1;
        }
```

Use the drawString() method to draw the text message. The paint() routine is more complex, however, because we have to compute nYPos and nMessageWidth. The constructor assigned both of these variables the value -1 to flag them as unknown values. Now that a Graphics object is available, their values can be computed:

```
public void paint (Graphics g, Applet parent) {
        if (nYPos < 0) {
            //  Determine the y position
            nYPos = (g.getFontMetrics ()).getHeight ();

            //  Determine the size of the message
            char pcChars [];
            pcChars = new char [pcMessage.length()];
            pcMessage.getChars (0, pcMessage.length(),
                            pcChars, 0);
            nMessageWidth = (g.getFontMetrics ()).charsWidth
                            (pcChars, 0, pcMessage.length());
        }

        //  Draw the object here
        g.drawString (pcMessage, nXPos, nYPos);
        }
```

TIP

Drawing in an applet is easy because the applet draws only the graphics that fall inside its boundaries. This process is called *clipping*—limiting the drawing area to a specific rectangle. All graphics output that falls outside the rectangle is not displayed. You can further limit the region where the graphics are drawn using java.awt.Graphics.clipRect().

Now, whenever the clock ticks, the message shifts to the left. You can do this by adjusting the nXPos variable. We reset the nXPos whenever the message is no longer visible:

```
public void clockTick () {
        //  Do nothing until the message width is known
        if (nMessageWidth < 0)
            return;

        //  Move Right
        nXPos -= 10;
        if (nXPos < -nMessageWidth)
            nXPos = nAppletWidth - 10;
        }

//  END of TextScrolling Object
}
```

At this point, I could point out the lack of computation in the paint() and clockTick() meth-ods and say how it is important to avoid extensive computations during an animation. But either you already know that, or you would discover it very quickly with the first complex animation you write.

How can you avoid complex computations? You have two options:

- Perform the computations offline
- Do each computation once and save the results

In this animation object, the value of the variables nMessageWidth and nYPos were computed once in the paint() routine. Before then, the information wasn't available.

Let's consider some more examples. First, we'll write two programs to display a series of images in an applet and to move a single image around an applet. These programs demonstrate the first possibility. For the second possibility, we draw and copy a stick person.

Images

In the past ten years, computer animations of many different objects have been created using the physical equations that model movement. Interactions between rigid bodies are easy to animate, but more advanced techniques have created realistic animations of rubber bands and elastic cubes that deform as they interact. The computations required for these are extensive and are not suitable for the online nature of applets.

The first animation object uses the flip-book principle of animation. For this approach, you generate all the pictures in advance and allow Java to display the images in sequence to create the illusion of motion. This second approach is useful for rigid body motion and interactions, where you take a single image and move it around the applet drawing area.

But first, let's review some information about images.

20

**BASIC ANIMATION
PROGRAMMING**

The MediaTracker Class

Images take a while to load into the computer's memory, and they look very strange if you display them before they are completely ready. Have you ever seen the top of a head bouncing around a Web page? Very unnerving :-) To avoid this gruesome possibility, the creators of Java have provided a MediaTracker class. A MediaTracker object enables you to determine whether an image is correctly loaded.

> **NOTE**
>
> Although the MediaTracker class will eventually be able to determine whether an audio object has loaded correctly, it currently supports only images.

The MediaTracker object provides three types of methods:

- Those that register or check in images
- Those that start loading images
- Those that determine whether the images are successfully loaded

The methods that register images are named AddImage(); there are two versions of this method:

- AddImage (Image *img*, int *groupNumber*) begins tracking an image and includes the image in the specified group
- AddImage (Image *img*, int *groupNumber*, int *width*, int *height*) begins tracking a scaled image

You can organize images with the group number. Doing so enables you to check logical groups of images at once.

The methods that start loading the images are listed here:

- checkAll (true) starts loading all the images and returns immediately
- checkID (int *groupNumber*, true) starts loading all the images in the group specified by *groupNumber* and returns immediately
- waitForAll() starts loading all images and returns when all images are loaded
- waitForID(int *groupNumber*) starts loading all images in the group specified by *groupNumber* and returns when all images in the group are loaded

> **NOTE**
>
> In checkAll() and checkID(), the last input is true. It is not a variable but the boolean constant.

Because the routines that start with check return immediately, you can continue with other processing and occasionally monitor the progress with checkID(groupNumber) and checkAll().

> **TIP**
>
> Be careful not to monitor an image that has already been loaded. You should only track the loading of an image once. If you ask the media tracker to wait for an image that has already been loaded, it might never return.

The final two methods that determine whether the images loaded successfully are shown here:

- isErrorAny() returns true if any errors were encountered loading any image
- isErrorID(int *groupNumber*) returns true if any errors were encountered loading the images in the specified group

Now we are ready to start working with the image object animators. Let's begin with a *changing* image animation. Then we'll discuss a special type of changing image where all the individual frames are *tiled* in one large image and a different frame is shown at each time step. Finally, we'll create a *moving* image animation.

Changing Images

The flip-book method of animation in Java is the most popular on Web sites. Flip books contain pictures but no words. The first picture is slightly different from the second, and the second picture is slightly different from the third. When you thumb through a flip book as shown in Figure 20.1, the pictures appear to move. In this section, we create an applet that takes a series of images and repeatedly displays them in the applet window to create the illusion of motion.

> **NOTE**
>
> The code in this section is in Example 20.2 in file exmp20_2.java on the CD-ROM that accompanies this book.

This program has to store two values: the images to be displayed and the MediaTracker to determine whether the images are ready. Internally, we will also keep track of the number of the image to be displayed next:

```
class ChangingImage extends AnimationObject {

    //  Internal Variables
    Image ImageList [];
    int nCurrent;
    MediaTracker ImageTracker;
```

FIGURE 20.1.
*Thumbing through a
flip book creates the
illusion of motion.*

The constructor initializes the variables with the constructor's inputs and starts the animation sequence with the first image:

```
public ChangingImage (Image il[], MediaTracker md,
            Applet parent) {
     ImageList = il;
     nCurrent = 0;
     ImageTracker = md;
     }
```

As mentioned earlier, it is important to check that the image is available before it is drawn:

```
public void paint (Graphics g, Applet Parent) {
     //  Draw the object here
     if (ImageTracker.checkID(1)) {
         g.drawImage (ImageList [nCurrent], 100, 100, Parent);
         }
     else
         System.out.println
            ("Not Ready Yet " + (nCurrent+1));
     }
```

Remember that this object is only one part of a possibly large animation; you may have to sacrifice the first few pictures to keep all the parts of the animation together. Therefore, the object doesn't check the ImageTracker to see whether the images are ready in the clockTick method:

```
public void clockTick () {
     nCurrent++;
     if (nCurrent >= ImageList.length)
         nCurrent = 0;
     }

//  END of ChangingImage Object
}
```

With this approach, most of the work is done ahead of time, either as you draw all the images or by a computer program that generates and saves the images. In Java, this method is how you animate objects with elastic properties or realistic lighting because of the amount of computation involved.

Tiling Image Frames

>
>
> **NOTE**
>
> The code in this section is in Example 20.3 in file `exmp20_3.java` on the CD-ROM that accompanies this book.

One problem with loading multiple images is that you have to make a separate connection for each image file you want to download. This operation takes extra time because of the overhead involved in making a connection back to the server. One way to get around this delay is to place all the images side by side in a single image file. Figure 20.2 shows an example of laying the images side by side.

FIGURE 20.2.

Frames are stored side by side in a single image.

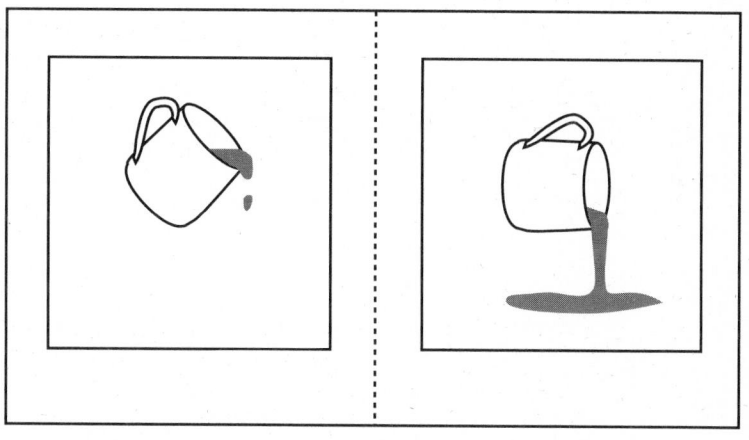

Frame 1   Frame 2

With this arrangement, you have to read only one large image from the server—hence, you make only one connection. But how do you draw the image since you don't want to write all the images onto the screen at the same time? The solution is to use `java.awt.Graphics.clipRect()`. First, block out the area we want to draw in. This should have the x and y coordinates of where you want the image to be, and the size of the frame. Let's call the location of the image `nX` and `nY`; call the width and height of the frame `nFrameWidth` and `nFrameHeight`:

```
public void paint (Graphics g, Applet Parent) {
    //  Draw the object here
    g.clipRect (nXPos, nYPos, nFrameWidth, nFrameHeight);
    g.drawImage (Picture, nXImagePos, nYPos, Parent);
    }
```

The tricky part was recognizing this use of the clipRect() method. The only thing left is to explain the nXImagePos variable. All we have to do is shift what part of the image is in the visible part. The shifting is done in the variable nXImagePos. Let's say that we have nImageWidth that stores the width of the entire image (with all the frames); when we do a clock tick, we just decrease the nXImagePos until it becomes less than the nImageWidth parameter, at which point we reset it to zero:

```
public void clockTick () {
    nXImagePos -= nFrameWidth;
    if (nXImagePos <= nImageWidth)
        nXImagePos = 0;
    }
```

Because that is so easy, why isn't it done all the time? Well, you will run into problems with this approach if you use multiple changing images in your animations. clipRect() computes the intersection of the current clipping rectangle (which initially is the entire area of the applet) and the rectangle that was just given as the input to clipRect. So there is no way to make the clipping region bigger! This AnimationObject must be the only one of its type, and it must be the last object to be painted. If only there was a way to break up the framed image once you've loaded it into the applet....

We don't have the mechanism yet to do this operation, but I promise to show you how before the end of the chapter.

Moving Images

NOTE

The code in this section is in Example 20.4 in file exmp20_4.java on the CD-ROM that accompanies this book.

For rigid bodies, there is an easier way to create a 2D animation: You can take an image of the object and move it around the applet drawing area. An example of a *rigid body* is a rock or a table (they don't deform or change while they move). A cube of gelatin, on the other hand, wiggles as it moves and deforms when it runs into another object.

The MovingImage class is very similar to the ChangingImage class described in the preceding section. The variables are a picture and the x and y locations where it will be drawn. In this object, the nCurrent variable keeps track of the location in the object's path, rather than the image:

```
class MovingImage extends AnimationObject {
    //  Internal Variables
    Image Picture;
    MediaTracker ImageTracker;
    int nCurrent;

    int pnXPath [];
    int pnYPath [];
```

The constructor for MovingImage is nearly identical to the constructor for ChangingImage except that it has two extra variables to save:

```
public MovingImage (Image img, MediaTracker md,
                int pnXs [], int pnYs [],
                Applet parent) {
    Picture = img;
    nCurrent = 0;

    ImageTracker = md;

    pnXPath = pnXs;
    pnYPath = pnYs;
    }
```

Instead of changing images, we simply draw the image at the next location in the path:

```
public void paint (Graphics g, Applet Parent) {
    //  Draw the object here
    if (ImageTracker.checkID(1))
        g.drawImage (Picture,
                    pnXPath[nCurrent], pnYPath[nCurrent],
                    Parent);
}
```

The clockTick() program is nearly identical to the method written for the ChangingImage object.

The Copy Area

NOTE

The code in this section is in Example 20.5 in file exmp20_5.java on the CD-ROM that accompanies this book.

Remember that we are trying to minimize the amount of computation performed during an animation. If we don't have an image we can use, we have to draw the image using graphic primitives. Suppose that we want to slide a stick figure across the applet. Here is a small method that draws a stick person at a specified location:

```
public void drawStickFigure (Graphics g, int nX, int nY) {
        g.drawOval (nX +  10, nY +  20, 20, 40);
        g.drawLine (nX +  20, nY +  60, nX +  20, nY + 100);
        g.drawLine (nX +  10, nY +  70, nX +  30, nY +  70);
```

```
g.drawLine (nX +  10, nY + 150, nX +  20, nY + 100);
g.drawLine (nX +  20, nY + 100, nX +  30, nY + 150);
}
```

The original stick figure is drawn in black on a lightGray background. To continue the animation, we can erase it by redrawing the figure in lightGray over the black figure, and then drawing a new figure in black a little to the right. For such an uncomplicated drawing, this method is effective. For the purpose of this illustration, however, let's animate the stick figure using the copyArea() method:

```
public void paint (Graphics g, Applet Parent) {
        if (bFirstTime) {
            bFirstTime = false;
            drawStickFigure (g, nX, nY);
            }
        else {
            g.copyArea (nX, nY, 35, 155, 5, 0);
            }
        }
```

The first time the paint() method is called, the figure is drawn using the drawStickFigure() routine. After the first time, the paint() routine recopies the stick figure a few pixels to the right. To erase the old copy of the figure, some blank space is copied with the stick figure. The result: the figure slides across the applet.

There are two problems with this animation so far. The first problem is that sometimes part of the stick figure is left behind. When you make a repaint() method call to draw the next frame in the animation, you sometimes get repainted and you sometimes do not. Whether or not the repaint() call is processed depends on how much additional computation is being done at the time. If multiple repaint requests have been made since the drawing thread has last been allowed to execute, it combines all of these repaints into a single call. To solve this problem, you just have to remember where the stick figure was last drawn in the applet window, and copy the figure with extra blank space from there. You can do this easily in the paint() routine:

```
public void paint (Graphics g, Applet Parent) {
    static int nLastX;
    if (bFirstTime) {
        bFirstTime = false;
        drawStickFigure (g, nX, nY);
        nLastX = nX;
        }
    else {
        int nSkipped = nX - nLastX;
        g.copyArea (nX - (nSkipped - 5), nY, 30 + nSkipped, 155, nSkipped, 0);
        nLastX = nX;
        }
    }
```

The second problem is that our previous animations repeatedly cycle across the screen. Once our little figure is out of the viewing area, it is gone for good. If only there was a way to draw an image in Java and save it. Then we could use the animation techniques in the previous section to move the image around the applet drawing area repeatedly.

Fortunately, such a facility is available in Java. In addition to enabling us to create an image offline so that it can be used repeatedly, this facility generates a cleaner flicker-free animation.

Double-Buffered Animation

Double buffering is a common trick to eliminate animation flicker. Instead of drawing directly onto the applet's drawing area where a person can see it, a second drawing area is created in the computer's main memory. The next frame of the animation is drawn on the drawing area in main memory. When the frame is complete, it is copied onto the screen where a person can see it. It sounds complicated, but it is really quite simple.

To double buffer your animation, you have to do the following:

- Create an off-screen image and get the associated graphics object
- Draw on the off-screen graphics object
- Copy the off-screen image onto the applet's graphic object

> **NOTE**
>
> An example that shows the flickering effect and the improvement created by using double buffering is in Example 20.6 in file exmp20_6.java on the CD-ROM that accompanies this book.

The first step requires that you create an image in which you will do all the work. To create the off-screen image, you must know the height and width of the drawing area. Once that is determined, you can get the graphics object from the image with the getGraphics() method:

```
offScreenImage = createImage(width, height);
offScreenGraphic = offScreenImage.getGraphics();
```

The graphics object extracted from the image is now used for all drawing. This part of the program is the same as the paint() program explained in "Simple Animation," earlier in this chapter—except that, instead of using g, you use offScreenGraphic:

```
//  Erase the screen
offScreenGraphic.setColor (Color.lightGray);
offScreenGraphic.fillRect (0, 0, width, height);
offScreenGraphic.setColor (Color.black);

//  Paint each object
for (int ndx = 0; ndx < AnimatedObjects.length; ndx++)
    AnimatedObjects[ndx].paint (offScreenGraphic, this);
```

Finally, you copy the off-screen image into the applet's graphics object:

```
g.drawImage(offScreenImage, 0, 0, this);
```

You have succeeded in improving the clarity of your animation. You may wonder why this change improves the animation. After all, the number of pixels that are drawn has increased! There are three reasons for this improvement:

- Most machines have an efficient way to copy a block of bits onto the screen, and an image is just a block of bits.

- No extra computations interrupt the drawing of the picture. These extra computations come from drawing lines, determining the boundaries of a filled area, and looking up fonts.

- Video memory cannot be cached in the CPU, while an off-screen image can be anywhere in memory.

- All the image appears at once, so even though more work is done between frames, a human perceives that all the work is done instantaneously.

Now we have reduced the flicker by creating an off-screen image. In the first section, the theme was to reduce the computation the applet performed. Using the off-screen image increases the computations but improves the visual effect. Now we will eliminate the extra computations in the program by using the off-screen image.

The update() and paint() Methods

> **NOTE**
>
> To see when the paint() and update() methods are called, the ChangingImage example has been modified to print a message to the output describing which method was called. This method is in Example 20.7 in exmp20_7.java on the CD-ROM that accompanies this book.

Earlier, I said that the paint() and update() methods were essentially the same. In fact, most of the sample code that Sun Microsystems provides does basically what I did in the "Simple Animation" section: the update() method calls the paint() method. So what is the difference?

The paint() method is called when the applet begins execution and when the applet is exposed. An applet is said to be *exposed* when more area or a different area can be viewed by the user. For example, when an applet is partially covered by a window, it must be redrawn after the covering window is removed. The removal of the covering window exposes the applet (changes the screen to enable the user to see more of a viewing area of a window). See Figure 20.3 for an example.

FIGURE 20.3.

Moving another window exposes the applet.

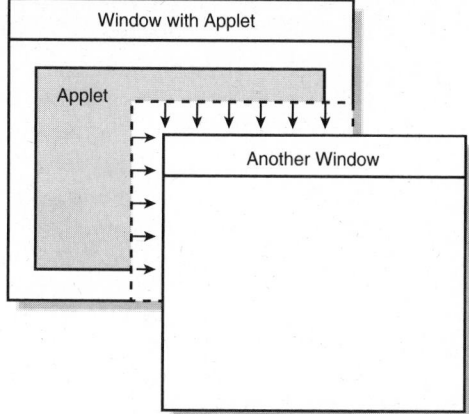

The update() method is called whenever a repaint() method is called. For example, in the run() method of the applet, a repaint() method is called on every iteration through the loop.

So what does that mean? If the paint() method calls the update() method, the applet does extra work by recomputing what the image should be. Yet less than a second ago, update() created a perfectly good picture—and it is still available for paint() to use. It is better if the paint() method copies the image created by update() onto the screen again.

Here is a more efficient pairing of paint() and update():

```
public void paint (Graphics g) {
    if (offScreenImage != null)
        g.drawImage(offScreenImage, 0, 0, this);
}

public void update (Graphics g) {
    if (offScreenImage != null) {
        //  Erase the screen
        offScreenGraphic.setColor (Color.lightGray);
        offScreenGraphic.fillRect (0, 0, nWidth, nHeight);
        offScreenGraphic.setCOlor (Color.black);

        //  Paint each object
        for (int ndx = 0; ndx < AnimatedObjects.length; ndx++)
            AnimatedObjects[ndx].paint (offScreenGraphic,
                                        this);

        g.drawImage(offScreenImage, 0, 0, this);
    }
}
```

TIP

One problem with this approach is that the paint() method is called as the applet begins running. At this time in the execution of the applet, there is no image to display because update() has not yet been called. The effect: The first screen the user sees is a filled white rectangle that covers the entire applet. You can remedy this situation by printing a text message in the off-screen image when it is created.

Because it takes only three lines of code to overload the paint() and the update() methods, we've been doing this from the very beginning. However, you don't have to overload the update() method. You could just put all your drawing commands in the paint() method, and your code would work just fine. The default method for update() erases the screen with the background color and calls the paint() method. And our earlier code has already showed us what happens if you do this—it creates lots of flicker. If you want a cleaner-looking animation, you should always overload the update() method.

Breaking Tiled Images

Earlier in this chapter, I said that the problem with using tiled images to store the frames of an animation is that you can use only one of them. But now that we have the mechanism to create an off-screen image, we can break the tiled image into multiple off-screen images after the image with the frames is loaded.

The easy way to do this is to create a new object similar to the ChangingImage object. Most of the code is identical to the ChangingImage object except that once the MediaTracker reports that the image is completely loaded, the object should break the image into its separate frames. We can do this in the prepare() method. First, we create an array of the images called ImageList. Then we create an off-screen image for each. Now we just act as if we are doing double buffering—we get the graphic and draw each frame using the graphic:

```
private void prepare () {
    ImageList = new Image [nFrameCount];
    Graphic tempGraphic;
    for (int ndx = 0; ndx < nFrameCount; ndx++) {
        ImageList [ndx] = createImage(nFrameWidth, nFrameHeight);
        tempGraphic = pimgFrames [ndx].getGraphics();
        tempGraphic.drawImage (imgAllFrames, -1 * ndx * nFrameWidth, 0, this);
        }
}
```

The double-buffered approach is one of the most widely used algorithms to improve animation. Part of the reason that this algorithm is widely used is that it is so simple. The next section discusses other algorithms that help improve your animation or simplify your life.

Advanced Tricks of the Trade

The following sections present four tactics for better animations. First, you learn about *in-betweens*, which reduce the amount of time you spend creating the animation. Second, *backgrounds* provide an alternative method to erase the screen and spice up the animation. Third, we consider the *order* in which images are drawn in the applet to produce the illusion of depth. Finally, we discuss *collisions*.

In-Betweens

When the first movie-length animation was finished, it required over two million hand-drawn pictures. Because there were only four expert artists, it would have been impossible for these people to create the entire film. Instead, the master artists drew the main, or key, frames (the frames specified by the creator of the animation). Other artists drew the in-between frames (frames created to move objects between their key positions).

This approach is used today to create animations, except that now the computer creates the in-between frames. Generally, a computer needs more key frames than does a human artist because computers don't have common-sense knowledge about how something should move. For example, a falling rock increases speed as it falls (which is obvious), but a computer does not know this obvious fact. You can compensate for the computer's lack of common sense by specifying how the objects move between key positions. Four common trajectories are shown in Figure 20.4.

FIGURE 20.4.

These graphs show four different trajectories for moving objects.

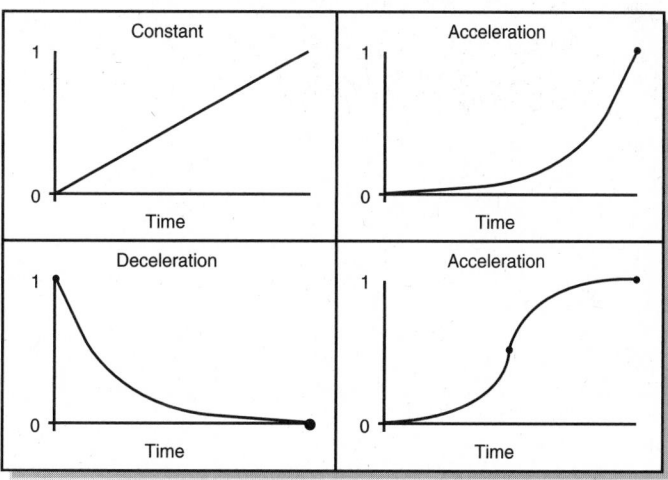

To see how in-betweens work, consider Figure 20.5, which shows a ball moving upwards using the acceleration trajectory from Figure 20.4. At first, the ball object moves slowly, but then the distance between successive positions of the ball increases. The successive positions of the balls are numbered, with 1 being the starting image and 10 being the final image.

FIGURE 20.5.

The motion of an image corresponds to the location on the trajectory graph.

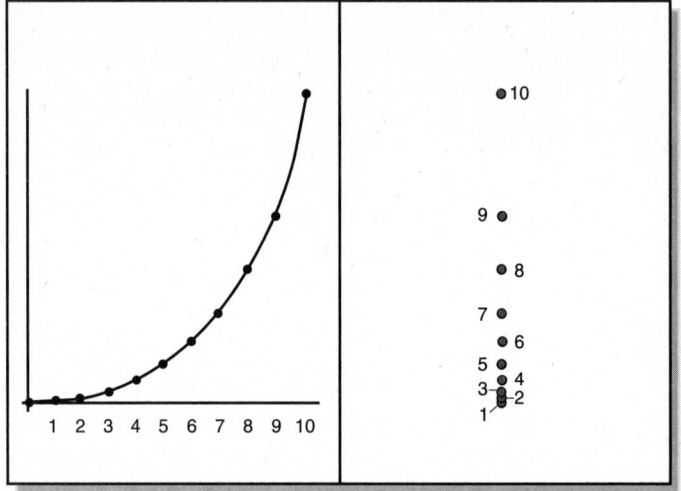

You can create these object paths with the following code:

```
class InBetweenGenerator extends Object {

    public int[] InBetweens (int pnValues[], String sTypes[],
                             int pnWidths [])
        {
        int pnResult [];
        int ndx;
        int nArraySize = 1;

        //  Create the array of the correct size
        for (ndx = 0; ndx < pnWidths.length; ndx++) {
            nArraySize += 1 + pnWidths [ndx];
            }

        pnResult = new int [nArraySize];

        //  Fill in the array
        int nItem = 0;
        for (ndx = 0; ndx < pnWidths.length; ndx++) {
            pnResult [nItem] = pnValues [ndx];
            fillIn (pnResult, nItem + 1,
                    pnWidths[ndx], sTypes [ndx],
                    pnValues[ndx], pnValues[ndx+1]);
            nItem += (pnWidths[ndx] + 1);
            }
```

```
        pnResult [nItem] = pnValues [pnWidths.length];

        return pnResult;
        }
```

First, we call the method `InBetweens()`, which creates an array and fills it in. Each segment of the array can contain a different type of motion. For each type of motion, we will fill in a separate portion of the array using the method `fillIn()`:

```
void fillIn (int pnArray [], int nStart, int nHowMany,
            String sType, int nLow, int nHigh)
    {
    double dIncr = 1.0 / ((double) (nHowMany + 2));
    double dTemp = dIncr;

    for (int ndx = 0; ndx < nHowMany; ndx++) {
        pnArray [ndx + nStart] = (int) (nLow +
            (nHigh - nLow) * interpolate (sType, dTemp));
        dTemp += dIncr;
        }
    }
```

How these values are filled in depends on the type of interpolation occurring between each point. We can compute the actual value with the following method:

```
double interpolate (String sType, double dValue)
    {
    if (sType.equalsIgnoreCase ("c")) {
        return dValue;
        }
    else if (sType.equalsIgnoreCase ("a")) {
        return dValue * dValue;
        }
    else if (sType.equalsIgnoreCase ("d")) {
        return (dValue * (2.0 - dValue));
        }
    else { //  Both
        if (dValue < 0.5) {
            double dTemp = 2.0 * dValue;
            return 0.5 * dTemp * dTemp;
            }
        else {
            double dTemp = 2.0 * dValue - 1.0;
            double dTemp2 = 0.5 * dTemp * (2.0 - dTemp);
            return 0.5 + dTemp2;
            }
        }
    }

//  End of InBetweenGenerator
}
```

In-betweens reduce the amount of information an animation artist must enter to create the desired animation. The next section presents a few hints for using a background image. Basically, a *background image* is a combination image that contains all the unchanging pictures. Using a background can reduce the computations involved in the animation.

NOTE

One thing in-betweens allow you to do is to specify the velocity or acceleration of the object.

Background

Another trick animators use is to draw the background on one sheet of paper and then draw the characters and moving objects on a piece of plastic. Because the background remains the same, it is drawn once. By overlaying the different plastic pictures, you can create the illusion of movement in a world. The same trick can be used with a computer. You first create a background image and save it. Then, instead of erasing the image with the `fillRect()`, you use `drawImage()` to initialize the off-screen image and draw the moving parts on top of the background.

The borders of your moving images should be transparent—just as though the characters were drawn on plastic. The GIF89a graphics image format allows you to designate one of the colors in a GIF image as transparent. When Java recognizes one of the pixels in the image as being the transparent color, it does not draw anything, so the background shows through. You can either create your images with a software program that allows you to specify the transparent color, or you can use a separate program to read the graphics file and set the transparent color. One program that allows you to specify the transparent color is called `giftrans`, available at anonymous ftp sites such as this one:

`http://www-genome.wi.mit.edu/WWW/tools/graphics/giftrans/`

This site contains a DOS executable file and the C source code. Many more sites have this program, and you can find at least 20 more by searching Lycos or Yahoo with the keyword `giftrans`.

NOTE

You can load either JPG or GIF images for animations in Java, but there is no facility to specify transparent regions in images stored in the JPG format.

Z-Order

You will notice in your animations that some objects appear to be in front of others because of the way they are painted. For example, the last object painted appears to be the closest object to the viewer. Such an arrangement is called a *2-$\frac{1}{2}$- dimensional picture*.

We can specify the order in which the objects are drawn by associating a number with each AnimationObject. This number reflects how far forward in the viewer's field of vision the object is. This number is called the *z coordinate*, or the *z-order number*. Because the x axis is generally from left to right on the screen, and the y axis is up and down, the z axis comes out of the screen at you.

The z-order number can be stored in a base class from which the other animated objects are subclassed. Let's call this new object a DepthObject. Although we could store an integer in this class of objects, we might tempt users of the DepthObject to manipulate the number directly. Instead, we'll use good data-hiding techniques and require the implementation of a method that returns the z-order number:

```
public interface DepthObject implements AnimationObject {
    public int queryZOrder ();
}
```

The next step is to create an object to store all the animated objects and keep them in order. This object should be able to add a new animated object at any time, as well as paint each object and inform them all of the passage of time:

```
public class ThreeSpaceAnimation {
    Vector vecAnimations;

    public int addElement (DepthObject doNew) {
        int nStart = 0;
        int nEnd = vecAnimations.size ();
        int nOrder = doNew.queryZOrder ();

        try {
            while (nStart + 1 <= nEnd) {
                int nCurrent = (nStart + nEnd) / 2;
                int nCurrentDepth = ((DepthObject) vecAnimations.elementAt
➡(nCurrent)).queryZOrder ();
                if (nCurrentDepth < nOrder)
                    nStart = nCurrent;
                else if (nCurrentDepth == nOrder) {
                    nStart = nCurrent;
                    nEnd = nCurrent;
                    }
                else
                    nEnd = nCurrent;
                }

            if (((DepthObject) vecAnimations.elementAt (nStart)).queryZOrder () >
➡nOrder) {
                // Insert before
                vecAnimations.insertElementAt (doNew, nStart);
                }
            else if (((DepthObject) vecAnimations.elementAt (nEnd)).queryZOrder ()
➡< nOrder) {
                // Insert after
                vecAnimations.insertElementAt (doNew, nEnd+1);
                }
            else {
```

```
                    //  Insert between
                    vecAnimations.insertElementAt (doNew, nEnd);
                    }
              } catch (ClassCastException cce) {}
          }

    public void clockTick () {
        allAnimationObjects = vecAnimations.elements ();
        while (allAnimationObjects.hasMoreElements ()) {
            try {
                AnimationObject aniObj = (AnimationObject)
➥allAnimationObjects.nextElement ();
                aniObj.clockTick ();
                } catch (ClassCastException cce) {}
            }
        }
    public void paint (Graphics g, Applet parent) {
        allAnimationObjects = vecAnimations.elements ();
        while (allAnimationObjects.hasMoreElements ()) {
            try {
                AnimationObject aniObj = (AnimationObject)
➥allAnimationObjects.nextElement ();
                aniObj.paint (g, parent);
                } catch (ClassCastException cce) {}
            }
        }
```

Before we finish with this class, note that the way DepthObject was created allows the object to change its depth at any time. To make changing the depth more efficient, we will ask the object to send a message to the ThreeSpaceAnimation to inform it of the change. The method to inform the object is called informDepthChange and it takes the object that is changing as input:

```
public void informDepthChange (DepthObject obj) {
    vecAnimations.removeElement (obj);
    addElement (obj);
    }
```

Collision Detection

One final item to cover is how you can tell if two objects have collided. In many animations where the path of each object is predetermined, this question is not important. But sometimes, you may want to create an animated object controlled by the user (in a video game, for example). In such situations, it becomes important to determine when two objects collide.

The easiest way to detect collisions is to simply consider whether the two images overlap. This calculation is easy because we can extract the size of the images from the images themselves. But it is not very accurate, especially if there are transparent pixels along the edge. For an example of this approach, see Figure 20.6.

FIGURE 20.6.

*An example of collision
detection using a
rectangle covering the
entire image.*

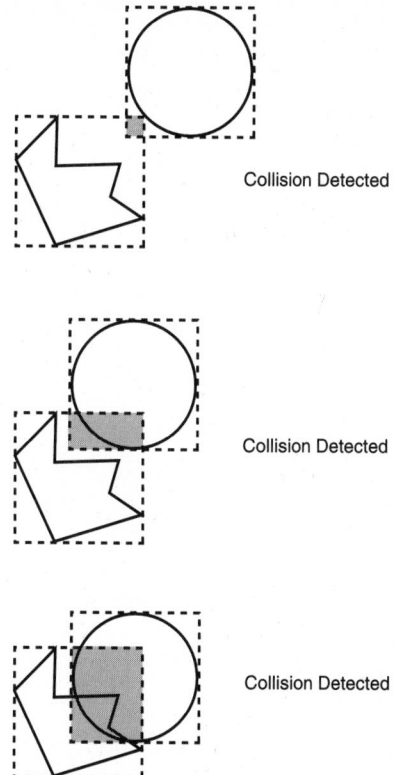

Collision Detected

Collision Detected

Collision Detected

The hard way to detect a collision is to check each pixel in each image and see whether two non-transparent pixels are at the same location. Figure 20.7 shows this option. This is a very costly operation because you have to check each pixel; this approach is really not suited to an interpreted language like Java.

As a compromise, a third method is suggested. You can associate with each image a smaller rectangle that lies inside the image. This smaller rectangle more closely matches where the nontransparent pixels are (see Figure 20.8). There are two reasons that this algorithm is better. First, comparing two rectangles to determine whether they intersect is much quicker than comparing all the colored pixels of each image to determine if they overlap. Second, a large portion of the image near the edge may be transparent. Generally, you don't want to make this transparent region an invisible force field that transforms near misses into collisions.

If you choose the correct rectangle for each image, the rectangle will cover most of the colored pixels and not too many of the transparent pixels. Choosing the best rectangle is the hard part, and I can't help you there, but we can plan to make collision detection a part of the animation design by creating an interface. This interface, called `Collidable`, returns the bounding rectangle. You determine whether an object can collide by casting it to an instance of this interface. If it can be cast, then you check its rectangle with the object that it collides with.

FIGURE 20.7.
*Exact collision detection
is possible if you
compare nontrans-
parent pixels.*

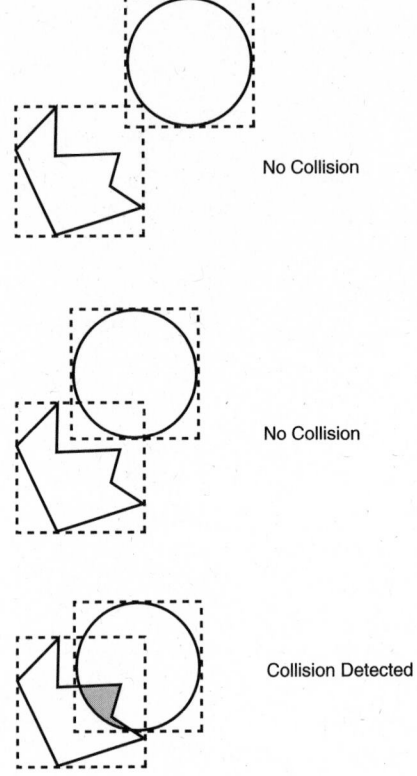

No Collision

No Collision

Collision Detected

```
public interface Collidable {
    public Rectangle queryHitArea ();
    }
```

With this interface, we can check to see whether two animated objects collide with the following code:

```
if ((animatedObject1.queryHitArea ()).intersects (animatedObject2.queryHitArea ())) {
    // The two objects have collided
    }
else {
    //   The two objects missed each other
    }
```

This algorithm makes use of the Rectangle object provided in java.awt.

FIGURE 20.8.

Using a smaller rectangle for detecting collisions is faster and has fewer errors than using the image's entire area.

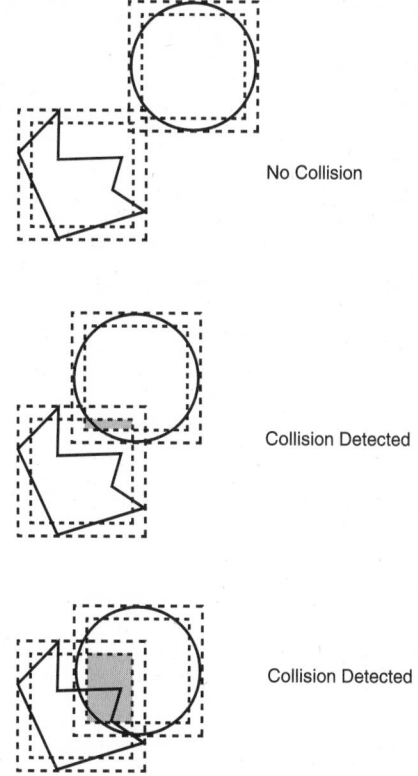

No Collision

Collision Detected

Collision Detected

Example Object Animator

Now let's take some of the ideas discussed in this chapter and make a multiple-object animator. In this section, we'll see some of the highlights of this chapter. First, we want the code to be able to read from the HTML file the number and motion of the animation objects. Second, we'll review how some of the advanced animation techniques are used in this example.

NOTE

  The full source code for this example is provided on the CD-ROM that accompanies this book. The code for this example is in `exmp20_8.java`.

To enable the program to read the motion specifications from the applet tag, we have to do the following:

20

BASIC ANIMATION PROGRAMMING

- Store the images and animation objects in a vector
- Generalize the ChangingImage and MovingImage to a single object
- Add routines to the init() method to load the required information

The first step is to store the images and the animation objects in a vector. The applet then dynamically stores however many objects or images there will be in the animation. For more information about how to use a vector, see Chapter 13, "The Utilities Package."

The effect of an AnimatedImage object is a moving changing picture. It requires an array of images and two arrays for the path the object travels. However, the AnimatedImage object sometimes is used as a ChangingImage object, and it would be easier on the user if numbers could be passed for the path variables. The constructor has been overloaded for this purpose. The other change is the use of a vector to store the images, which allows us to store an arbitrary number of images.

The init() method is standard, but the applet generates the tags it needs as it runs. It does this by concatenating strings with numbers:

```
String at = getParameter ("IL" + 3);
```

This arrangement enables us to load an arbitrary number of animation objects. For the tags and what they mean, consult Table 20.2.

Table 20.2. Tags for exmp20_8.java (located on the CD-ROM).

Tag	Description
IL?	Image letter, what should prefix the image filenames
IC?	The number of images
IO?	Image offset, which image you should start with
KF?	The number of key frames
X?_?	The x coordinates of the key frame
Y?_?	The y coordinates of the key frame
XT?_?	The type of motion between x values
YT?_?	The type of motion between y values
W?_?	The number of points between values

The first ? in the tag refers to the number of the animated object. The second ? in the tag is the number of the frame. For example, X3_7 refers to the x value of the third animated object in the seventh key frame.

Now consider some of the advanced techniques and how they were used in this example. This program provides the functionality to create in-betweens and to use a background image. To keep the animation from flickering, this code also uses the double-buffered approach to painting the image.

The paths of the moving objects are specified in the HTML file, but they are filled in as suggested by the user with the `InBetweenGenerator` object. This object requires three values: the key locations, how many frames to produce between each set of key locations, and the type of motion between each key location. It then generates an array of integers that represent the path that object traverses. To extend the `InBetweenGenerator` object to create another type of motion between end points, rewrite the `interpolation()` method to include your new motion. All the equations in this method take a number between 0 and 1, and return a number between 0 and 1. However, if you want the object to overshoot the source or the destination, you can create equations that produce values outside this range.

Notice that a background image is an image that doesn't move and doesn't change. To create a background for the animation, just make the background image the first animated object.

FOR MORE INFORMATION

Here are some Web sites you can browse for more information about animations. The best collection of Java applets is Gamelan, and it has a page on animations. Its URL is as follows:

`http://www.gamelan.com/Gamelan.animation.html`

The following sites have many links to animations. Viewing some of these sites can give you ideas for your animations:

- `http://www.xm.com/cafe/AnimatePLUS/slideshow.html`
  Description of the slideshow applet

- `http://www.auburn.edu/~harshec/WWW/Cinema.html`
  An example of the slideshow in action

- `http://www-itg.lbl.gov/vbart/`
  BART schedule animation

- `http://www.intrinsa.com/personal/steve/ClickBoard/ClickBoard.html`
  Interactive animation

- `http://www.sealevelsoftware.com/sealevel/javademo.htm`
  Animation of falling raindrops

- `http://www.dimensionx.com/dnx/StreamingAnimation/index.html`
  Smooth-loading animation

- `http://www.geom.umn.edu/~daeron/apps/flag.html`
  United States flag blowing in the wind

More information about animation can be found at this URL:
http://java.sun.com/people/avh/javaworld/animation/

20

BASIC ANIMATION PROGRAMMING

Summary

In this chapter, we created the `AnimationObject` interface that simplifies design. This animation class was then used to create moving text, to create a flip-book-style animation, to animate an image that contains frames, and to create a moving-image animation. Double buffering was used to eliminate flicker, and we discussed the difference between the `paint()` and `update()` methods. The final algorithms discussed were the use of in-betweens, background images, z-order numbers, and collision detection.

What really launched Java into the spotlight for many people was its capability to perform animations on the World Wide Web. With the release of Netscape 2.0, Java is not the only way to create animations on Web pages. Increasingly, there are specialized programs that help you create animations that can be visible on Web pages. One of these is Shockwave for Director, which enables you to create animations in Director; Shockwave also allows the animations to be viewed. VRML is a language that specifies three-dimensional animations by specifying the locations, objects, and a viewing path. However, VRML currently requires special graphics hardware to view. It seems, then, that Java is still the least expensive way to create an animation.

Creating User Interface Components

by David R. Chung

IN THIS CHAPTER

CHAPTER 21

The Java Abstract Window Toolkit (AWT) consists of classes that encapsulate basic GUI controls. Because Java is a multiplatform solution, the AWT provides a lowest common denominator interface. Any interface you develop should appear about the same on any platform. Often, the AWT is called *Another Window Toolkit* or (affectionately) *Awful Window Toolkit*. Chapter 16, "The Windowing (AWT) Package," provides an overview of the AWT.

Now don't be mislead—the AWT provides many useful controls and your applications or applets may not require anything more. Sometimes, however, an application needs something extra. This chapter examines two methods for creating custom user interface components: subclassing and combining controls.

Subclassing Controls

Subclassing is just a fancy object-oriented term for changing the way a class works. The actual method is to create a new class from the old one and add new features along the way. In this chapter, you learn how to extend the TextField class to create a password control. The new class will be a TextField that allows users to enter a password. Instead of displaying the password, the control displays asterisks as the user types.

The passField Class

You create the passField class by subclassing the TextField class. The control allows the user to type passwords. When the user enters a character, you catch the keyDown event. You keep track of the key the user pressed and place an asterisk in the control (to keep the password hidden).

Notice that this control does not actually verify that the password is valid. Instead, the control keeps track of user input and hides the actual characters. Later in the chapter, you see how to combine this control with others to create a useful password control.

Member Data

The passField class has to keep track of the characters entered by the user. To do so, we need a data member of type String:

```
class passField extends java.awt.TextField {

    String pass ;
```

The class constructor has to know how many characters the control can contain. To convey that information, the class constructor takes an integer parameter, chars. Because passField is derived from TextField, the first line in the constructor must be a call to the superclass constructor.

Creating User Interface Components

CHAPTER 21

451

21

CREATING USER
INTERFACE
COMPONENTS

> **NOTE**
>
> To understand how classes are derived from (or extend) other classes, you must be familiar with some object-oriented terminology. In this example, passField is derived from TextField. TextField is referred to as the *superclass*, *parent*, or *base class*, while passField is referred to as the *subclass*, *child*, or *derived class*.

The call to super(int) actually calls TextField(int). The next line in the constructor simply creates the String:

```
public passField( int chars ) {

    super( chars ) ;

    pass = new String() ;

}
```

The reason for subclassing this control is to hide user input. To do this, the control must handle user input in the derived class before the TextField class does. To handle user input, this control overrides the Component class's keyDown() method. This method is called every time a key is pressed.

The overridden keyDown() method must do the following:

- Add an asterisk to the control
- Store the actual key value entered
- Position the cursor at the end of the string

Because this class does not actually display the user-entered values, the call to getText() returns a String full of asterisks. Next, the method adds an asterisk to the String and puts it back in the control. The select() method is used to position the cursor at the end of the line; because the two parameters are the same, nothing is actually selected.

```
public boolean keyDown( Event e, int key ) {

    String text = getText() ;
    setText( text + "*" ) ;
    select( text.length() + 1, text.length() + 1 ) ;
```

The next item of business is to store the keystroke in a String. Because the key parameter is an int, you must cast it to a char and then use the String.valueOf() method to convert it to a String. This new String is then concatenated onto the existing String. Finally, the keyDown() method has to return true because it has fully handled the keystroke.

```
    pass = pass + String.valueOf( (char)key ) ;

    return true ;
}
```

The getString() method is provided to allow Containers that use this control to get the user-entered value:

```
public String getString() {
    return pass ;
}

}
```

To test the passField class, let's embed it in a simple applet, as shown here:

```
import java.awt.*;

public class testPassField extends java.applet.Applet {

    public void init() {
        add( new passField( 40 ) ) ;
    }

}
```

Figure 21.1 shows the testPassField applet.

FIGURE 21.1.

The testPassField *applet.*

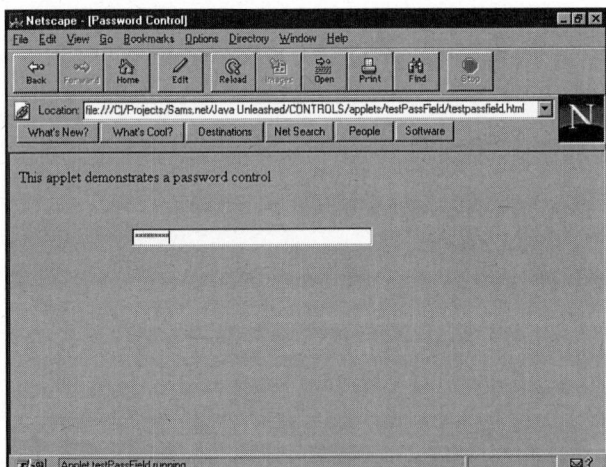

If you run the applet and type some letters, you will see some strange behavior. When you press Backspace, instead of erasing an asterisk as you might expect, the control adds another one! The reason is when the keyDown() method gets a keystroke—any keystroke—it simply adds it to the string and displays another asterisk.

To fix this behavior, you must somehow handle certain keystrokes differently. One possibility is to add the following code to the beginning of the keyDown() method:

```
        if ( arg < 20 ) {
            return false ;
        {
```

Creating User Interface Components

CHAPTER 21

453

21

CREATING USER
INTERFACE
COMPONENTS

This is only a partial solution, but it is a beginning. If the keystroke has an ASCII value less than 20 (that is, if it is a nonprinting character), then keyDown() should return false. If keyDown() or any other event-handling method returns false, the Event is passed on to the superclass method. In this example, this small modification causes the control to accept Backspaces. To really make this method useful, you must also change the value of the String to reflect any deletions.

Combining Controls

If you have ever served on a committee, you know how hard it is for a group of people to work together to reach a common goal. Without leadership, everyone seems to go their own way. Without well-coordinated communication, duplication of effort can occur. Likewise, if you try to put together a Java applet by combining several AWT controls, it may seem like you have a big committee—lots of activity but no leadership and no communication.

However, if you combine your controls into *composite controls*, they will then act like all the rest of the AWT controls. You can use the new composite controls anywhere you use regular AWT controls. To demonstrate composite controls, the following sections explain how to create a scrolling picture window control. This control takes an image and makes it scrollable. All the interaction between the AWT components that make up the control is handled internally. To use the control, all you have to do is create one and add it to your applet's layout.

Using Panels to Combine User Interface Elements

The base class for all composite controls is Panel. The Panel class allows you to embed other AWT components. This class is derived from Container, so it can contain user interface (UI) components. The Panel class also contains functions for *managing* embedded components.

Some functions in the Panel class can retrieve references to the embedded components. These functions allow the class to iteratively call methods in the embedded components. Other functions handle layout issues.

PANELS ARE COMPONENTS, TOO

The primary advantage of using Panel as your composite component base class is that it is a Component itself. Consequently, you can use your composite components like any other AWT components. You can take these new components and combine them to form composite components from other composite components and so on.

The new components can be added to layouts; they can generate existing events or create new ones. They are full-fledged UI components and can be used anywhere that AWT components are used.

continues

continued
The composite controls will be more versatile if you implement them with the appropriate layout manager. Because you want the controls to be self-contained, they should be able to lay themselves out properly no matter what size they are.

A Scrolling Picture Window Example

In this example, you create a scrolling picture window. You derive a class from `Panel` called `ScrollingPictureWindow`. The class contains three member objects: an `ImageCanvas` object (derived from `Canvas`) to hold the picture and two scroll bars.

This composite control provides a self-contained way of displaying a picture. A user simply has to pass an `Image` object to the control and the control does the rest. The control handles scrolling and updating the image. Figure 21.2 shows the scrolling picture window applet.

FIGURE 21.2.

The `testPictureWindow` *applet.*

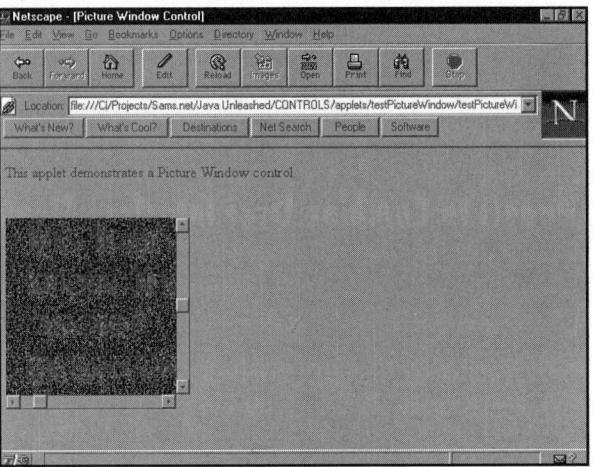

The `testPictureWindow` applet uses a `ScrollingPictureWindow` object. The applet creates the `ScrollingPictureWindow` in *exactly* the same way that you would use an AWT control. The source code for the `testPictureWindow` applet is given in Listing 21.1.

Listing 21.1. The source code for the `testPictureWindow` applet.

```
import java.applet.*;
import java.awt.*;
import ScrollingPictureWindow ;

public class TestPictureWindow extends Applet {
```

Creating User Interface Components

CHAPTER **21**

455

21

CREATING USER
INTERFACE
COMPONENTS

```
    ScrollingPictureWindow pictureWindow ;

public void init() {

    Image img = getImage( getCodeBase(), "picture.gif" ) ;
    pictureWindow = new ScrollingPictureWindow( img ) ;
    setLayout( new BorderLayout() );
    add( "Center", pictureWindow ) ;


    }

};
```

The ImageCanvas Class

The ImageCanvas class is derived from Canvas. Canvas is provided in the AWT as a generic class for painting and drawing. You use this class to display your Image. The class contains one instance variable:

```
Image canvasImg ;
```

The ImageCanvas constructor takes an Image object as a parameter. Because object parameters are passed by reference, this makes a local reference to the Image object in the class:

```
public ImageCanvas( Image img ) {
    canvasImg = img ;
}
```

The only other method provided in the ImageCanvas class is paint(). The paint() method actually draws the image. Before doing any painting, however, the control has to determine whether its parent is enabled. This check allows the entire control to be turned off.

Because the picture scrolls, the class has to know where to draw it. The location of the image depends on the position of the scroll bars. In your scheme, the ScrollingPictureWindow object handles communication between the member objects. You have to query the ScrollingPictureWindow object to determine where to draw the image:

```
    public void paint(Graphics g) {

        if ( getParent().isEnabled() ) {
            g.drawImage( canvasImg,
                -1 * ((ScrollingPictureWindow)getParent()).imgX,
                -1 * ((ScrollingPictureWindow)getParent()).imgY,
                this ) ;
        }

    }
```

To get the information, use the getParent() method. The getParent() method is a member of the Component class. This method returns a reference to the Container object that holds the Component.

When you call `getParent()`, you get a reference to the `ScrollingPictureWindow` object. Because this reference is the `Container` type, you have to cast it to a `ScrollingPictureWindow` reference. Now you can access the public instance variables in the `ScrollingPictureWindow` object.

The `imgX` and `imgY` members contain the x and y coordinates of the point (in terms of the `Image`) that will be displayed in the upper-left corner of the window. If you want the point (10,5) to be displayed in the upper-left corner, pass `-10` and `-5` to `drawImage()`.

Instance Variables

The `ScrollingPictureWindow` class contains several instance variables. These variables include the embedded controls and state variables. The embedded controls are stored as follows:

```
public ImageCanvas imageCanvas ;
Scrollbar    vertBar ;
Scrollbar    horzBar ;
Image        image ;
```

The last instance variable in this list is a reference to an `Image` object, which is passed in by the *owner* of your class object.

The remaining instance variables all contain information about the state of the control. The first two contain the size in pixels of the entire image:

```
int imgWidth ;
int imgHeight ;
```

The next two instance variables contain the current position of the image. These variables also reflect the current position of the scroll bars. Because the scroll bars and the image are tied together, both classes use these variables. The scroll bars set their values, and the `ImageCanvas` uses these values to place the image.

```
int imgX ;
int imgY ;
```

The last variable is used by the scroll bars. This value specifies the amount the scroll bar moves when you request a page up or page down.

```
int page ;
```

Class Construction

The class constructor performs all the initialization for your class. The constructor must do the following:

- Initialize the state variables
- Determine the size of the image
- Instantiate the member controls
- Set up the `GridBagLayout` layout manager
- Set the constraints for each control

Initialize State Variables

Begin construction by setting the local `Image` reference to the `Image` argument:

```
public ScrollingPictureWindow ( Image img ) {

    image = img ;
```

The next step in the construction process is simple. You have to initialize `imgX` and `imgY` to 0. What this really does is set the initial position of the image and scroll bars. These two instance variables contain the x and y offsets at which to display the image:

```
    imgX = 0 ;
    imgY = 0 ;
```

The `ImageCanvas` class needs these variables to determine how to place the image. The `ImageCanvas paint()` method accesses these instance variables directly and uses them in its call to `drawImage()`.

Determine the Image Size

Your composite control has to know how large the image is. Once you have this information, you know it will remain constant. Unfortunately, determining the image size is not as straightforward as you may think.

Your class has been designed to take an `Image` object as a parameter, giving the users of the class a great deal of flexibility in loading the image any way they want. The image you receive may be one of many in an array. It may be in use by other objects in the applet. It may also have been just recently loaded by the calling applet. It is this last case that causes problems.

In your class constructor, it is possible that the reference you receive is to an image that is not yet fully loaded. To get the image size, you make a call to `Image.getHeight()`. If the image is not fully loaded, however, `getHeight()` returns -1. To get the size of the image, you must loop until `getHeight()` returns a value other than -1. Both `while` loops that follow have `null` bodies:

```
while ((imgHeight = image.getHeight(this)) == -1 ) {
    // loop until image loaded
}

while ((imgWidth  = image.getWidth(this)) == -1 ) {
    // loop until image loaded
}
```

Instantiate Member Controls

Next you must create the embedded member objects. The `ImageCanvas` takes the `Image` as a parameter. The scroll bar constructors each take a constant that determines whether the scroll bar is vertical or horizontal:

```
imageCanvas = new ImageCanvas( image ) ;

vertBar = new Scrollbar( Scrollbar.VERTICAL ) ;
horzBar = new Scrollbar( Scrollbar.HORIZONTAL ) ;
```

Set Up `GridBagLayout`

You use a `GridBagLayout` to lay out the embedded control. `GridBagLayout` is the most versatile layout manager in the AWT, and it provides precisely the control you need to arrange the components. `GridBagLayout` is the most powerful layout manager.

First you create a `GridBagLayout` object. Then you call `setLayout()` to make it the current layout manager:

```
GridBagLayout gridbag = new GridBagLayout();

setLayout( gridbag ) ;
```

Set Up Constraints for Each Control

The `GridBagLayout` class uses the `GridBagConstraints` class to specify how the controls are laid out. First, you create a `GridBagConstraints` object. Then you use the `GridBagConstraints` object to determine how to lay out the individual components:

```
GridBagConstraints c = new GridBagConstraints();
```

You add the `ImageCanvas` object to your panel first. Because the `ScrollingPictureWindow` control is supposed to act like the native AWT controls, it must be resizeable. You have to specify that the control can grow in both x and y directions, so you set the `fill` member to `BOTH`:

```
c.fill      = GridBagConstraints.BOTH ;
```

Because you want the image to fill all the available space with no padding, set the `weight` parameters to `1.0`:

```
c.weightx   = 1.0;
c.weighty   = 1.0;
```

Finish laying out the image by calling `setConstraints()` to associate the `ImageCanvas` object with the `GridBagConstraints` object. Then add the image to the layout:

```
gridbag.setConstraints(imageCanvas, c);
add( imageCanvas ) ;
```

Next you lay out the scroll bars. Start with the vertical scroll bar. The vertical scroll bar should shrink or grow vertically when the control is resized, so you set the `fill` member to `VERTICAL`:

```
c.fill      = GridBagConstraints.VERTICAL ;
```

Look at your layout in terms of rows. You see that the first row contains two controls: the `ImageCanvas` and the vertical scroll bar. You indicate that the scroll bar is the last control in the row by setting the `gridwidth` member to `REMAINDER`.

```
c.gridwidth  = GridBagConstraints.REMAINDER ;
```

Complete the vertical scroll bar layout by associating it with the constraint object and then add it to the layout:

Creating User Interface Components

CHAPTER 21

459

21

CREATING USER
INTERFACE
COMPONENTS

```
gridbag.setConstraints(vertBar, c);
add( vertBar ) ;
```

Finally, lay out the horizontal scroll bar. Because this scroll bar should be horizontally resizeable, set its `fill` member to `HORIZONTAL`:

```
c.fill       = GridBagConstraints.HORIZONTAL ;
```

The reason for using a `GridBagLayout` layout manager is to prevent the horizontal scroll bar from filling the entire width of the control. You want to guarantee that the horizontal scroll bar remains the same width as the `ImageCanvas` object. Fortunately, the `GridBagConstraint` class provides a means of tying the width of one object to the width of another.

You use the `gridWidth` member of the `GridBagConstraint` class to specify the width of the scroll bar in terms of grid *cells*. Set this member to 1 so that the horizontal scroll bar takes up the same width as the `ImageCanvas` object (they are both one cell wide). It is the `ImageCanvas` object that sets the cell size.

```
c.gridwidth  = 1 ;
```

The last thing you have to do is add the horizontal scroll bar. First associate it with the constraints object and then add it to the layout:

```
gridbag.setConstraints(horzBar, c);
add( horzBar ) ;
```

Depending on where your control is used, it may be resizeable. You handle resizing by overriding the `Component.reshape()` method. This method is called every time a control is resized. The first thing that your function does is call the superclass's `reshape()` method. The superclass method does the real work of sizing. Because you are using a `GridBagLayout`, the `LayoutManager` resizes the individual components.

```
public synchronized void reshape(int x,
                                 int y,
                                 int width,
                                 int height) {

    super.reshape( x, y, width, height ) ;
```

You let the superclass do the resizing, so now you must update the image and scroll bars. First, determine whether the width of the control is greater than the image width plus the width of the vertical scroll bar. If the control width is greater, disable the horizontal scroll bar:

```
if ( width > imgWidth +
              vertBar.preferredSize().width ) {

    horzBar.disable() ;
```

If the control width is not greater, enable the horizontal scroll bar:

```
} else {

        horzBar.enable() ;
```

Next, determine how to reposition the horizontal scroll bar. Start by getting the size of the entire control and the width of the vertical scroll bar:

```
11111 Rectangle bndRect = bounds() ;
int barWidth = vertBar.preferredSize().width ;
```

> **NOTE**
>
> When working with scroll bars, you have to set several values:
> - The thumb position
> - The maximum and minimum values
> - The size of the viewable page
> - The page increment

Now you can calculate the maximum value for the scroll bar. You always set the minimum of the scroll bar to 0. The maximum value is the image width minus the width of the ImageCanvas. You set the page size and page increment to one-tenth of the maximum size:

```
int max = imgWidth - (bndRect.width - barWidth);
page = max/10 ;
```

Before setting the new values, you must determine how to translate the old position to the new scale. Start by getting the old maximum value. If the old value is 0, you make the position 0:

```
int oldMax = horzBar.getMaximum() ;

        if ( oldMax == 0) {

            imgX = 0 ;
```

If the old maximum is not 0, you calculate the new position. First, express the old position as a fraction of the old maximum. Then multiply the fraction by the new maximum. The resulting value gives you the new position:

```
} else {

imgX = (int)(((float)imgX/(float)oldMax) *
                        (float)max) ;

}
```

The last thing you have to do is set the scroll bar parameters:

```
    horzBar.setValues( imgX, page, 0, max ) ;
    horzBar.setPageIncrement( page ) ;

}
```

Use the same algorithm to set the vertical scroll bar.

Event Handling

The scrolling picture window control is especially concerned about scroll bar events. All other types of events are passed on and handled outside your program.

You start by overriding the Component.handleEvent() method. In this method, you look for events generated by the horizontal scroll bar. If the event is one of the seven scroll bar events, you reset the imgX variable and call repaint(). You return true if you can handle the event.

```
public boolean handleEvent(Event e) {

        if ( e.target == horzBar ) {

            switch( e.id ) {

                case Event.SCROLL_PAGE_UP:
                case Event.SCROLL_LINE_UP:

                case Event.SCROLL_ABSOLUTE:

                case Event.SCROLL_LINE_DOWN:
                case Event.SCROLL_PAGE_DOWN:

                imgX = horzBar.getValue() ;
                imageCanvas.repaint();

                return true ;

            }
```

The code for handling the vertical scroll bar is the same as for the horizontal scroll bar. If you do not handle the event, call the superclass handleEvent() method and return:

```
    return super.handleEvent(e) ;

}
```

Putting It Together

You now have a composite control that can become a drop-in replacement for other AWT controls. It handles its own events and responds to external resizing. The complete ScrollingPictureWindow class appears in Listing 21.2.

Listing 21.2. The ScrollingPictureWindow class.

```
import java.awt.*;

public class ScrollingPictureWindow extends Panel {

    public ImageCanvas imageCanvas ;
    Scrollbar     vertBar ;
    Scrollbar     horzBar ;
    Image         image ;
```

continues

Listing 21.2. continued

```java
    int imgWidth ;
    int imgHeight ;

    int imgX ;
    int imgY ;

    int page ;

    public ScrollingPictureWindow ( Image img ) {

        image = img ;

        imgX = 0 ;
        imgY = 0 ;


        while ((imgHeight = image.getHeight(this)) == -1 ) {
        // loop until image loaded
        }

        while ((imgWidth  = image.getWidth(this)) == -1 ) {
        // loop until image loaded
        }


        imageCanvas = new ImageCanvas( image ) ;

        vertBar = new Scrollbar( Scrollbar.VERTICAL ) ;
        horzBar = new Scrollbar( Scrollbar.HORIZONTAL ) ;

        GridBagLayout gridbag = new GridBagLayout();

        setLayout( gridbag ) ;

        GridBagConstraints c = new GridBagConstraints();

        c.fill      = GridBagConstraints.BOTH ;
        c.weightx   = 1.0;
        c.weighty   = 1.0;
        gridbag.setConstraints(imageCanvas, c);
        add( imageCanvas ) ;

        c.fill      = GridBagConstraints.VERTICAL ;
        c.gridwidth = GridBagConstraints.REMAINDER ;
        gridbag.setConstraints(vertBar, c);
        add( vertBar ) ;

        c.fill      = GridBagConstraints.HORIZONTAL ;
        c.gridwidth = 1 ;
        gridbag.setConstraints(horzBar, c);
        add( horzBar ) ;
    }

public synchronized void reshape(int x,
                                 int y,
                                 int width,
                                 int height) {
```

```
super.reshape( x, y, width, height ) ;

if ( width > imgWidth + vertBar.bounds().width ) {

    horzBar.disable() ;

} else {

    horzBar.enable() ;

    Rectangle bndRect = bounds() ;

    int barWidth = vertBar.preferredSize().width ;

    int max = imgWidth - (bndRect.width - barWidth);
    page = max/10 ;

    int oldMax = horzBar.getMaximum() ;

    if ( oldMax == 0) {

        imgX = 0 ;

    } else {

    imgX = (int)(((float)imgX/(float)oldMax) *
                                (float)max) ;
    }

    horzBar.setValues( imgX, page, 0, max ) ;
    horzBar.setPageIncrement( page ) ;

}

if (height > imgHeight + horzBar.bounds().height) {

    vertBar.disable() ;

} else {

    vertBar.enable() ;

    Rectangle bndRect = bounds() ;

    int barHeight = horzBar.preferredSize().height ;

    int max = imgHeight - (bndRect.height - barHeight) ;

    page = max/10 ;

    int oldMax = vertBar.getMaximum() ;

    if ( oldMax == 0) {

        imgY = 0 ;
```

continues

Listing 21.2. continued

```
                } else {

            imgY = (int)(((float)imgY/(float)oldMax) *
                                        (float)max) ;
            }

            vertBar.setValues( imgY, page, 0, max ) ;
            vertBar.setPageIncrement( page ) ;

        }
    }

    public boolean handleEvent(Event e) {

        if ( e.target == horzBar ) {

            switch( e.id ) {

                case Event.SCROLL_PAGE_UP:
                case Event.SCROLL_LINE_UP:

                case Event.SCROLL_ABSOLUTE:

                case Event.SCROLL_LINE_DOWN:
                case Event.SCROLL_PAGE_DOWN:

                imgX = horzBar.getValue() ;
                imageCanvas.repaint();

                return true ;

            }

        } else if ( e.target == vertBar ) {

            switch( e.id ) {

                case Event.SCROLL_PAGE_UP:
                case Event.SCROLL_LINE_UP:

                case Event.SCROLL_ABSOLUTE:

                case Event.SCROLL_LINE_DOWN:
                case Event.SCROLL_PAGE_DOWN:

                imgY = vertBar.getValue() ;
                imageCanvas.repaint();

                return true ;

            }

    }
```

Creating User Interface Components

CHAPTER 21

465

21

CREATING USER
INTERFACE
COMPONENTS

```
        return super.handleEvent(e) ;

    }


};

class ImageCanvas extends Canvas {

    Image canvasImg ;

    public ImageCanvas( Image img ) {
        canvasImg = img ;
    }

    public void paint(Graphics g) {

        g.drawImage( canvasImg,
            -1 * ((ScrollingPictureWindow)getParent()).imgX,
            -1 * ((ScrollingPictureWindow)getParent()).imgY,
            this ) ;

    }
}
```

A Password-Protected Picture Control

The versatility of composite, or extended, controls becomes apparent when they are combined into a single applet. The applet presented in this section is a password-protected picture control. This control combines a passField control with a ScrollingPictureWindow control. Figures 21.3 and 21.4 show the testPassWindow applet.

FIGURE 21.3.

The testPassWindow *applet before entering the password.*

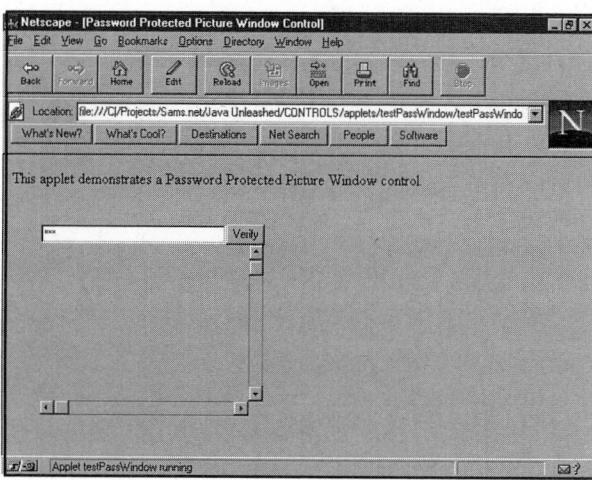

FIGURE 21.4.

The testPassWindow
*applet after entering the
password.*

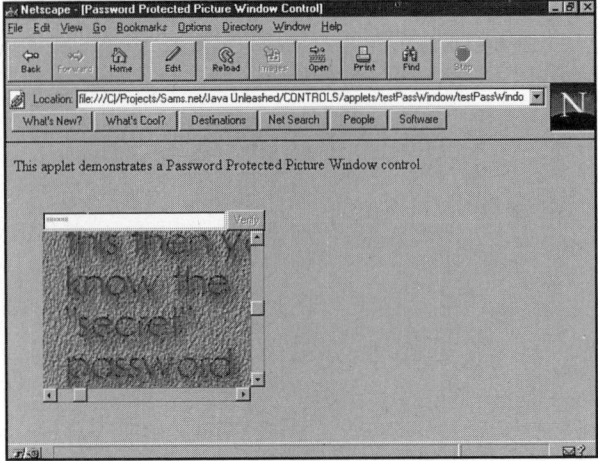

The following applet code combines passField, ScrollingPictureWindow, and Button objects. Because the passField and ScrollingPictureWindow classes are self-contained, they are used here just like the AWT Button control. Because Java applets are reusable components themselves, the applet is like a new control itself. In fact, in Java, you create applets to embed in your Web pages the same way you create controls to embed in your applets.

```
import java.applet.*;
import java.awt.*;

public class testPassWindow extends Applet {

    passField               passwordField ;
    Button                  verifyButton ;
    ScrollingPictureWindow pictureWindow ;
```

The init() method creates the member objects and then places them in the control using a GridBagLayout (see Chapter 16, "The Windowing (AWT) Package," for details on GridBagLayout and the associated GridBagConstraints classes). Notice that the passField and ScrollingPictureWindow controls are used as if they were *native* AWT controls.

```
public void init() {

    GridBagLayout gridbag = new GridBagLayout();
    setLayout( gridbag ) ;

    {
    GridBagConstraints c = new GridBagConstraints();

    passwordField = new passField( 30 ) ;

    c.gridx      = 1 ;
    c.gridy      = 1 ;
```

```
gridbag.setConstraints(passwordField, c);
add( passwordField ) ;
}


{
GridBagConstraints c = new GridBagConstraints();

verifyButton  = new Button( "Verify" ) ;

c.gridx     = 2 ;
c.gridy     = 1 ;

gridbag.setConstraints(verifyButton, c);
add( verifyButton ) ;
}


{
GridBagConstraints c = new GridBagConstraints();

Image img = getImage( getCodeBase(), "picture.gif" ) ;
pictureWindow = new ScrollingPictureWindow( img ) ;

c.fill      = GridBagConstraints.BOTH ;
c.gridx     = 1 ;
c.gridy     = 2 ;
c.gridwidth = 2 ;
c.weighty   = 1 ;

gridbag.setConstraints(pictureWindow, c);
add( pictureWindow ) ;
}

pictureWindow.disable() ;

}
```

To tie all these controls together, it is necessary to handle Button events. In this example, the Applet class does the event handling. This combination of the password control and the picture window control is a good candidate for placement in a Panel so that it would become one big composite control.

```
public boolean action( Event evt, Object arg ) {

    if ( evt.target instanceof Button ) {
        if ( ((String)arg).equals( "Verify" ) ){

            if ( passwordField.getString().equals(
                                           "secret" ) ) {

                pictureWindow.enable() ;
                pictureWindow.imageCanvas.invalidate() ;
                pictureWindow.imageCanvas.repaint() ;

                verifyButton.disable() ;

                passwordField.disable() ;
```

```
                }
           return true ;
           }

      }

      return false ;
   }

};
```

Summary

Sometimes, your applets or applications require user interface functionality beyond what is provided by the AWT. You can use subclassing or composite controls to extend the AWT and create new classes from the basic AWT classes.

When you extend the AWT, you can create self-contained controls that respond to their own events. Your enhanced controls can often be used as drop-in replacements for associated AWT controls.

The `passField` class developed in this chapter is an example of a subclassed control. This class takes the basic functionality of an AWT `TextField` and enhances it. The result is a control that can be plugged in anywhere you might use a `TextField`.

The `ScrollingPictureWindow` class created in this chapter is a good example of a composite control. This class combines the techniques of subclassing and encapsulation. It also is a subclass of `Panel` and serves to encapsulate the `Canvas` control and two scroll bars.

When you design an applet or application in Java, you have at your disposal the basic AWT controls. Now you can create enhanced controls by combining and subclassing them. These new controls will become part of your personal Java toolbox and you can use them in all your future Java programming projects.

Working with Dialog Boxes

by K.C. Hopson

IN THIS CHAPTER

CHAPTER

22

This chapter focuses on the Dialog class, which is the basis for writing dialog boxes in Java. The class is illustrated through several dialog box examples which provide tips about how to use some of the more obscure features of the Abstract Windowing Toolkit (AWT). The FileDialog class is discussed at the end of this chapter.

To get a proper understanding of the Dialog class, however, it is important to review how the Window and Frame classes work. This chapter begins with a quick review of these two classes.

Windows and Frames

The Window class is used in AWT to create popup windows that appear outside the constraints of the normal browser area allocated to an applet. Because the Window class is derived from the Container class, it can contain other components. Unlike applet components tied directly to a browser page, Window classes are not restricted to a prespecified area of the screen. Window objects can be resized as their immediate requirements dictate. AWT can perform this automatically through the Window class's pack() method; this method works with the Window layout (by default, BorderLayout) to arrive at the optimal presentation of the window given its contained components and screen resolution. Typically, pack() is called before a window is displayed. Windows are not made visible until the show() method is called. Windows are removed from the screen and their resources are freed when the dispose() method is invoked.

The Frame class extends the Window class by adding a title bar, a border for resizing, support for menus, and the ability to modify the system cursor to various states such as waiting or moving. For most GUI platforms, the frame's title bar is tied to system control boxes, such as minimize, maximize, or destroy. Consequently, the Frame class has all the elements necessary to make an applet look like a "real" application, complete with menus and system controls.

Figure 22.1 and Listing 22.1 present a simple Frame applet that changes the cursor to a state based on the button selected.

Listing 22.1. Code for the Frame class that changes the cursor state.

```
import java.awt.*;
import java.lang.*;
import java.applet.*;

// This applet simply starts up the frame used to
// show different frame cursors...
public class FrameCursorApplet extends Applet  {
    public void init() {
        // Create the frame with a title...
        new FrameCursor("Frame Cursors");
    }
}

// The frame for letting the user pick different
// cursors to display...
class FrameCursor extends Frame {
```

```
// Create the frame with a title...
public FrameCursor(String title) {
    // Call the superclass constructor...
    super(title);
    // Create a grid layout to place the buttons...
    setLayout(new GridLayout(3,2));
    // Add the buttons for choosing the cursor...
    add(new Button("Default"));
    add(new Button("Wait"));
    add(new Button("Hand"));
    add(new Button("Move"));
    add(new Button("Text"));
    add(new Button("SE Resize"));
    // Pack and display...
    pack();
    resize(300,200); // Make it a reasonable size...
    show();
}

// Handle events...
public boolean handleEvent(Event e) {
    switch(e.id) {
        case e.WINDOW_DESTROY:
            dispose();  // Erase frame
            return true;
        case Event.ACTION_EVENT:
            if (e.target instanceof Button)
                SetCursor((Button)e.target);
            return true;
        default:
            return false;
    }
}

// Set the cursor based on the button chosen...
void SetCursor(Button btn) {
    // Get the label of the button...
    String selection = btn.getLabel();
    //Set the cursor based on that label...
    if (selection.equals("Wait"))
            setCursor(Frame.WAIT_CURSOR);
    else if (selection.equals("Hand"))
            setCursor(Frame.HAND_CURSOR);
    else if (selection.equals("Move"))
            setCursor(Frame.MOVE_CURSOR);
    else if (selection.equals("Text"))
            setCursor(Frame.TEXT_CURSOR);
    else if (selection.equals("SE Resize"))
            setCursor(Frame.SE_RESIZE_CURSOR);
    else // Just use the default...
            setCursor(Frame.DEFAULT_CURSOR);
}
}
```

22

WORKING WITH
DIALOG BOXES

FIGURE 22.1.

A Frame *applet that changes the state of the cursor.*

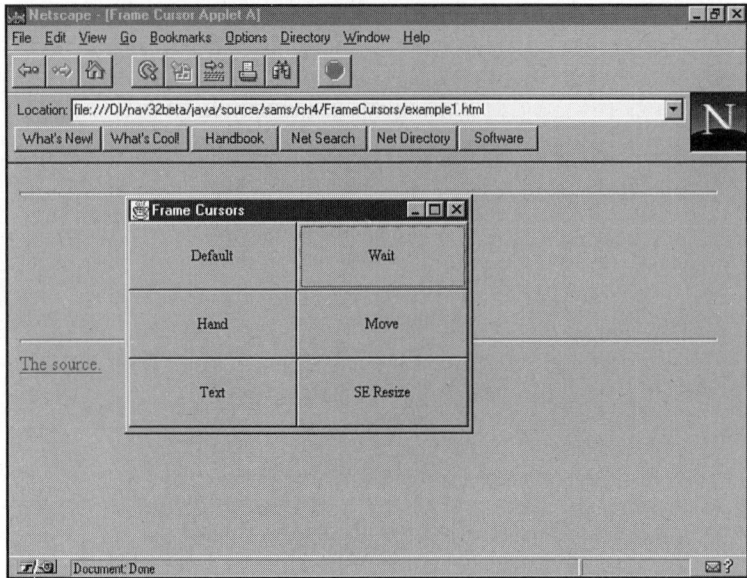

The applet class, FrameCursorApplet, does little more than launch the main frame, FrameCursor. The constructor for this frame begins by calling the frame superconstructor. The sole parameter is the caption displayed on the title bar. The layout for the frame is then set: Although the default is BorderLayout, in this case you want a 3-by-2 grid matrix, hence the use of GridLayout. Next, the buttons are added to the frame, with names representing the cursor state to be selected. After all the components have been added, the pack() method is invoked so that the button placement can be optimized. Because this optimized placement results in a small frame (six buttons sized tightly around the label text doesn't take much space), the resize() method is called to make the frame larger. Finally, the frame is displayed with the show() method.

When a button is selected, the custom method setCursor() is invoked. This method takes the button label and figures out which cursor should be displayed. The Frame class's setCursor() method is used to set the cursor state; its parameter is a static integer defined as part of the Frame class.

The current state of the cursor can be retrieved with the getCursorType() method. The getTitle() and setTitle() frame methods can be used to get and set the title bar caption. Similarly, the getIconImage() and setIconImage() methods can be used to get and set the image display of an iconized frame.

Introduction to the Dialog Class

Like the Frame class, the Dialog class is a subclass of the Window class. Dialog boxes differ from frames in a couple of subtle ways, however. The most important of these differences is that dialog boxes can be *modal*. When a modal dialog box is displayed, input to other windows in the applet is blocked until the dialog box is disposed. This feature highlights the general purpose of dialog boxes, which is to give the user a warning or a decision to be made before the program can continue. Although support for nonmodal, or *modeless*, dialog boxes is supported, most dialog boxes are modal.

There are two constructors for the Dialog class. Both take a Frame object as a parameter; they also take a boolean flag that indicates whether the dialog box should be modal. If the flag is set to true, the dialog box is modal. The constructors differ only in a parameter that specifies whether the dialog box should have a title caption. It is this constructor that is used in the example that follows.

Figure 22.2 shows a variation of the applet introduced in the preceding section, except that a dialog box is used to change the cursor state. Listing 22.2 shows the code for the Dialog class, called ChangeCursorDialog. Note how similar the dialog box here is to the frame in Figure 22.1.

FIGURE 22.2.

Using a dialog box to change the state of the cursor.

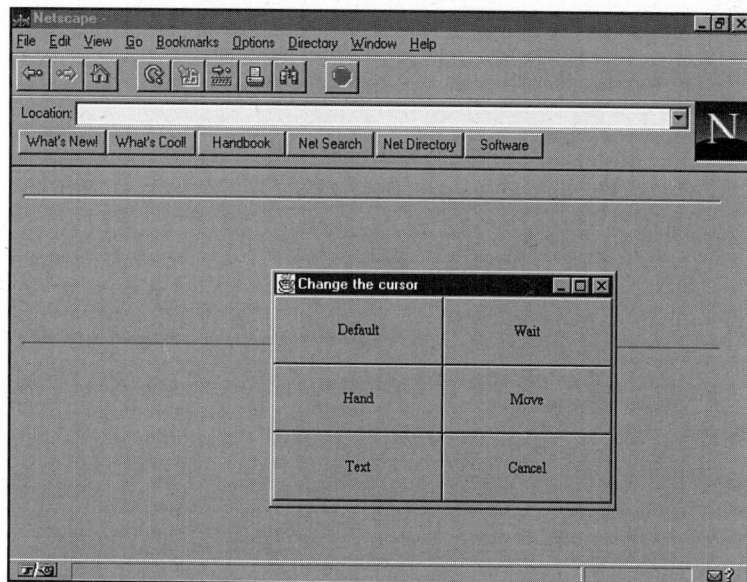

Listing 22.2. Code for the Dialog class that changes the cursor state.

```
import java.awt.*;
import java.lang.*;
import java.applet.*;

// Dialog that presents a grid of buttons
// for choosing the Frame cursor. A Cancel
// button exits the dialog...
class ChangeCursorDialog extends Dialog {
FrameMenuCursor fr;
```

continues

Listing 22.2. continued

```java
// Create the dialog and store the title string...
public ChangeCursorDialog(Frame parent,boolean modal,String title) {

  // Create dialog with title
  super(parent,title,modal);
  fr = (FrameMenuCursor)parent;
  // The layout is Grid layout...
  setLayout(new GridLayout(3,2));

  // Add the button options
  add(new Button("Default"));
  add(new Button("Wait"));
  add(new Button("Hand"));
  add(new Button("Move"));
  add(new Button("Text"));
  add(new Button("Cancel"));

  // Pack and size for display...
  pack();
  resize(300,200);
}
// Look for button selections to
// change the cursor...
public boolean action(Event e,Object arg) {
     // If button was selected then exit dialog..
  if (e.target instanceof Button) {
        // And possibly change the cursor...
        if (arg.equals("Default"))
           fr.setCursor(Frame.DEFAULT_CURSOR);
        if (arg.equals("Wait"))
           fr.setCursor(Frame.WAIT_CURSOR);
        if (arg.equals("Hand"))
           fr.setCursor(Frame.HAND_CURSOR);
        if (arg.equals("Move"))
           fr.setCursor(Frame.MOVE_CURSOR);
        if (arg.equals("Text"))
           fr.setCursor(Frame.TEXT_CURSOR);
        dispose();
     }
     return false;
}
}
```

You can declare the dialog box and instantiate it as follows:

```java
ChangeCursorDialog dlg;
dlg = new ChangeCursorDialog(this,true,"Change the cursor");
```

When it is time to display the dialog box, you can declare this method:

```java
dlg.show(); // Make the dialog visible...
```

The Color Dialog Box Example

In this section, a color dialog box is created to further explain how to use the Dialog class. The example lets you associate a color with the foreground and background states of text. Figure 22.3 shows how the dialog box appears in a browser.

FIGURE 22.3.

The color dialog box.

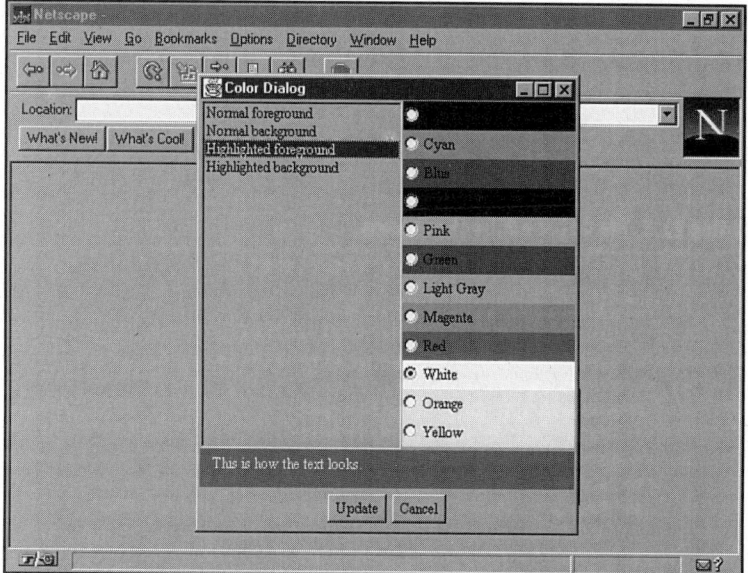

How the Color Dialog Box Is Used

When the dialog box appears, a list control at the top left of the dialog box shows which elements of the text can be modified. These colors are normal foreground, normal background, highlighted foreground, and highlighted background. When you select a list item, the radio button for the corresponding color is highlighted. A text display underneath the list shows what the text would look like with the given colors. The text display shows either the normal state (with both foreground and background colors) or the background state. If you select a new color with the radio buttons, the Canvas object is updated to show what the new foreground and background combination would look like. The text can be updated with the color settings for the current list item when you select the Update button.

The Construction of the Color Dialog Box

Four classes are used to construct the color dialog box. The ChooseColorDialog class is a subclass of Dialog and controls the main display and control of the dialog box. The colorDisplay class is a Canvas class derivative that draws text with colors corresponding to the selected foreground and background display. The ColoredCheckbox class draws a checkbox associated with a certain Color object; the background of the box is drawn according to that color. The

ColoredCheckboxGroup class groups ColoredCheckbox items together so that they can function as part of a radio button group.

The discussion of the color dialog box begins with its underlying components. Listing 22.3 shows the code for the ColoredCheckbox class. Its most interesting feature is that it associates itself with a given Color object. It paints its background according to the Color object and, through the setIfColorMatches() method, turns its checkbox on if the color sent to it matches its internal color. The checkbox in this case is a radio button because the class is associated with a CheckboxGroup object. Checkbox objects have radio buttons only if they are associated with a CheckboxGroup object; only one radio button in a checkbox group can be selected at a time. If no checkbox group is specified for a checkbox object, there are no restrictions on which boxes can be selected.

Listing 22.3. The ColoredCheckbox class.

```
// Class for creating a checkbox associated
// with a given color...
class ColoredCheckbox extends Checkbox {
    Color color;  // The color of this checkbox...
    // Constructor creates checkbox with specified color...
    public ColoredCheckbox(Color color, String label,
            CheckboxGroup grp, boolean set) {
        // Call the default constructor...
        super(label,grp,set);
        this.color = color;
        setBackground(color);
    }
    // Sets itself to true if it matches the color
    public void setIfColorMatches(Color match) {
        if (color == match)
            setState(true);
        else
            setState(false);
    }
    // Return the color matching this box...
    public Color getColor() {
        return color;
    }
}
```

The ColoredCheckboxGroup is used to contain ColoredCheckbox objects. Its constructor creates a preselected number of colored checkboxes to be associated with a Panel object. Here are the first few lines of the ColoredCheckboxGroup class declaration:

```
class ColoredCheckboxGroup extends CheckboxGroup {
    // Array to hold checkboxes...
    ColoredCheckbox c[] = new ColoredCheckbox[12];
    // Constructor. Create the checkboxes with
    // no default color chosen...
    public ColoredCheckboxGroup(Panel p) {
        // Call the default constructor...
        super();
```

```
// Create the checkboxes and store in panel and reference array...
c[0] = new ColoredCheckbox(Color.black,"Black",this,false);
p.add(c[0]);
c[1] = new ColoredCheckbox(Color.cyan,"Cyan",this,false);
p.add(c[1]);
```

Strangely enough, `ColoredCheckboxGroup` is not a `Container` object. Consequently, the checkboxes must be associated with a `Panel` object to meet the needs at hand. Note the use of the `Color` constants in constructing the `ColoredCheckbox` objects. The reference array (variable c) is used in the other method of the class, `setMatchingColor()`, which is used to set the radio button of the `ColoredCheckbox` object that matches a certain color:

```
public void setMatchingColor(Color match) {
    for (int i = 0; i < c.length; ++i)
        c[i].setIfColorMatches(match);
}
```

Because `ColoredCheckbox` objects are self-identifying by color, this technique prevents a long and cumbersome walk through hard-coded color names to see which radio button should be turned on.

The `colorDisplay` class is a `Canvas` derivative that draws text (specified in the `displayText` String variable) with a specified foreground and background color. Listing 22.4 highlights some of the more interesting features of the class.

Listing 22.4. Portions of the `colorDisplay` class.

```
// The layout will call this to get the minimum size
// of the object.  In this case, you want it to be at
// least big enough to fit the display text...
   public Dimension minimumSize() {
      // Get the metrics of the current font...
      FontMetrics fm = getFontMetrics(getFont());
      return new Dimension(fm.stringWidth(displayText),
         2 * fm.getHeight());
   }

   // Paint the colors and text...
   public synchronized void paint(Graphics g) {
      if ((foreground == null) || (background == null))
         return;
      // Set background...
      Dimension dm = size();
      g.setColor(background);
      g.fillRect(0,0,dm.width,dm.height);
      // Draw the string
      g.setColor(foreground);
      // Set dimensions. Move just from left...
      FontMetrics fm = getFontMetrics(getFont());
      int x = fm.charWidth('W');
      // And center in height...
      int y = fm.getHeight();
      g.drawString(displayText,x,y);
   }
```

22

WORKING WITH
DIALOG BOXES

The `paint()` method draws the canvas if a background and foreground color have been selected. The method starts by getting the size of its drawing area through the `size()` method; this method is a standard part of subclasses of `Component`. It then fills in the background color through the `setColor()` and `fillRect()` methods of the `Graphics` class. The `paint()` method then sets the color of the text to be displayed (the foreground). By getting the current `FontMetrics`, the canvas can figure out a good location for the text string; the `getHeight()` method returns the total height of the font. The `drawString()` method then draws the text at the specified location.

The `minimumSize()` method is used with layouts, which are discussed in Chapter 21, "Creating User Interface Components." When AWT constructs the display of a group of components, it works with the layouts to decide what position and size a component should have. Sometimes, you may want a component to exercise some input into what its size will be. You can invoke two methods of the `Component` class to do this. The `preferredSize()` method returns the dimensions of the preferred size of the component. The `minimumSize()` method returns the smallest size in which the component should be made. For the `colorDisplay()` class, the `minimumSize()` method returns that the component should be wide enough to display the text string and twice as high as its current font. The method does this by getting the `FontMetrics` information of the current font and calling the `stringWidth()` and `getHeight()` methods respectively.

Finally, the dialog box is ready to be constructed. Listing 22.5 highlights the declarations and methods used to construct the color dialog box.

Listing 22.5. The construction of the `ChooseColorDialog` class.

```
// Dialog box for choosing display colors...
public class ChooseColorDialog extends Dialog {
    Frame fr;     // What to update...
    ColoredCheckboxGroup colorGrp;  // To hold radio buttons of colors...
    List choiceList;  // List of color choices...
    colorDisplay d; // This is the text display...
    // Defines for listbox values...
    static int NORMAL_FORE = 0;
    static int NORMAL_BACK = 1;
    static int HILITE_FORE = 2;
    static int HILITE_BACK = 3;
    // Construct dialog to allow color to be chosen...
    public ChooseColorDialog(Frame parent,boolean modal) {
        // Create dialog with title
        super(parent,"Color Dialog",modal);
        fr = parent;
        // Create the dialog components...
        createComponents();
        pack();   // Compact...
        // Resize to fit everything...
        resize(preferredSize());
    }
```

```
// The layout will call this to get the preferred size
// of the dialog.  Make it big enough for the listbox text
// the checkboxes, canvas, and buttons...
    public Dimension preferredSize() {
        // Get the metrics of the current font...
        FontMetrics fm = getFontMetrics(getFont());
        int width = 3 * fm.stringWidth("Highlighted foreground");
        int height = 24 * fm.getHeight();
        return new Dimension(width,height);
    }

    // Create the main display panel...
    void createComponents() {
    // Use gridbag constraints...
    GridBagLayout g = new GridBagLayout();
    setLayout(g);
    GridBagConstraints gbc = new GridBagConstraints();
    // Set the constraints for the top objects...
    gbc.fill = GridBagConstraints.BOTH;
    gbc.weightx = 1.0;
    gbc.weighty = 1.0;
    gbc.gridheight = 10;

    // Add the listbox of choices...
    choiceList = new List();
    choiceList.addItem("Normal foreground");
    choiceList.addItem("Normal background");
    choiceList.addItem("Highlighted foreground");
    choiceList.addItem("Highlighted background");
    g.setConstraints(choiceList,gbc);
    add(choiceList);

    // Create the checkbox panel
    Panel checkboxPanel = new Panel();
    checkboxPanel.setLayout(new GridLayout(12,1));
    // Create the checkbox group and add radio buttons...
    colorGrp = new ColoredCheckboxGroup(checkboxPanel);
    colorGrp.setMatchingColor(Color.magenta);

    // Create checkbox panel to right...
    gbc.gridwidth = GridBagConstraints.REMAINDER;
    g.setConstraints(checkboxPanel,gbc);
    add(checkboxPanel);

    // Display the color chosen...
    d = new colorDisplay("This is how the text looks.");

    // Add to grid bag...
    gbc.weighty = 0.0;
    gbc.weightx = 1.0;
    gbc.gridwidth = GridBagConstraints.REMAINDER;
    gbc.gridheight = 1;
    g.setConstraints(d,gbc);
    add(d);

    // Two buttons: "Update" and "Cancel"
    Panel p = new Panel();
```

continues

Listing 22.5. continued

```
    p.add(new Button("Update"));
    p.add(new Button("Cancel"));

    // Add to grid bag...
    gbc.gridwidth = GridBagConstraints.REMAINDER;
    g.setConstraints(p,gbc);
    add(p);
  }
```

The createComponents() method adds the components to the dialog box by using the complex GridBagLayout class. The main thing to be done here is to have most of the space that is taken up by the list control set to half the dialog box size; the color checkboxes take up the other half (refer back to Figure 22.3). The key reason for doing this is to set the GridBagConstraint's weighty and gridheight variables to the appropriate values. By setting the former to 1.0, you tell the layout that the associated components should be given preeminence in terms of the layout's height. When weighty is set to 0.0, the height of the corresponding components is given lower priority.

The preferredSize() method in Listing 22.5 returns the desired dimensions of the dialog box. It should be 3 times as wide as the longest string in the list component, and 24 times as high as the current font. With these settings, everything should fit comfortably in the dialog box.

Using the Dialog Box

Once the dialog box is displayed, its event loop is entered. Listing 22.6 details the dialog box's handleEvent() method. This code has several subtleties worth noting. Most of the work is performed when an action occurs, as indicated by the ACTION_EVENT method. When a button is selected, the argument of the Event object is set to the name of the button. The handleEvent() method looks at this name to decide what to do. If the name is Cancel, the dialog box is removed from the screen with the dispose() method, and control returns to the calling frame. You can use the Update button to set the colors according to what is currently highlighted.

Listing 22.6. The handleEvent() method of the ChooseColorDialog class.

```
// Wait for Cancel or OK buttons to be chosen...
public boolean handleEvent(Event e) {
    switch(e.id) {
        case Event.ACTION_EVENT:
            // Kill the dialog...
            if (e.arg.equals("Cancel")) {
                dispose();  // Remove Dialog...
                return true;
            }  // end if
            // Update colors...
            if (e.arg.equals("Update")) {
                //  INSERT YOUR CODE HERE!
                return true;
```

```
      } // end if
      if (e.target instanceof Checkbox) {
         selectedRadioItem();
         return false;
      }
      return false;
   // User selected a listbox item...
   case Event.LIST_SELECT:
      // Set up caption colors and color choice highlight...
      if (e.target instanceof List) {
         selectedChoiceListItem();
         return false;
      } // end list if
      return false;
   default:
      return false;
   } // end switch
}
```

If the target of the ACTION_EVENT is a checkbox, a radio button is selected and the selectedRadioItems() method is called. This method sets the colorDisplay object's foreground or background colors according to the radio button chosen and the current selection in the list.

If you click a list item, a LIST_SELECT event is issued. In this case, the selectedChoiceListItems() method is invoked. This method sets the colorDisplay object's settings according to the current list selection; this process must take into account both the foreground and background colors. The ColoredCheckboxGroup's setMatchingColor() method is called to set the radio button of the ColoredCheckbox object corresponding to the current list color.

Calling the Dialog Box

The Frame object is responsible for bringing up the color dialog box. It can declare a variable of the colorDialog class as follows:

```
ChooseColorDialog colorDialog;  // Color Dialog...
```

In its constructor, the frame instantiates the color dialog box with the following call:

```
colorDialog = new ChooseColorDialog(this, true);
```

This code fragment states that the frame is the parent of the dialog box and its appearance is modal. Recall that a modal dialog box does not allow input to other windows while it is being displayed.

A dialog box does not automatically appear when it is constructed; to make the dialog box, you must specifically call the show() method. The color dialog box overrides the show() method so that it can do some setup before the dialog box appears:

```
public synchronized void show() {
     super.show(); // Call the default show method...
     // Set the listbox default...
```

```
      choiceList.select(0);
      // Set up caption colors and color choice highlight...
      selectedChoiceListItem();
}
```

The last method called, selectedChoiceListItem(), sets the radio buttons and display canvas to values corresponding to the current list selection.

The Font Dialog Box Example

This discussion of the font dialog box example will not be as lengthy as the preceding overview of the color dialog box. In many ways, the two examples are similar, so a detailed explanation of the font dialog box isn't required.

Figure 22.4 shows the font dialog box. It is based on the ChooseFontDialog class, which displays its components in a two-column style similar to the color dialog box. The current font family, style, and size are shown in a Canvas display object of the fontDisplay class. This class is very similar to the colorDisplay class.

FIGURE 22.4.

The font dialog box.

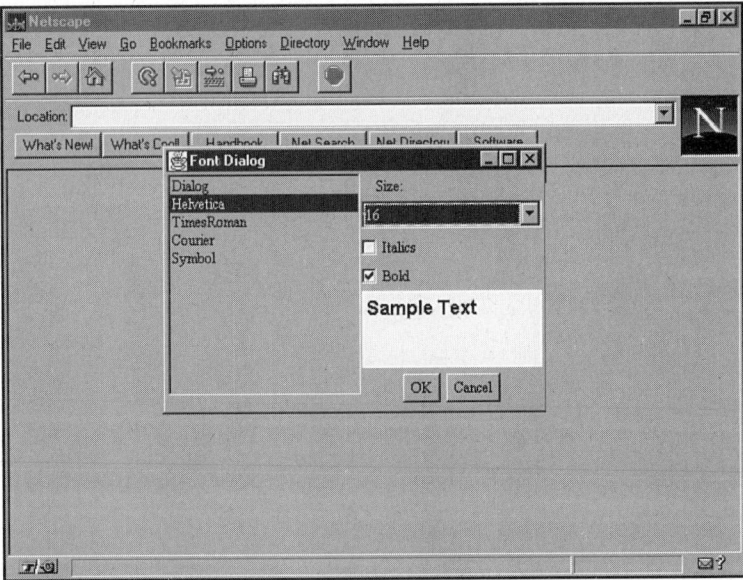

The list component on the left side of the dialog box shows the fonts available on the current platform. It uses the AWT Toolkit class to get this information. Here is the code that creates the control and adds the font families:

```
// Add the listbox of choices...
   // Get the selection from the toolkit...
   choiceList = new List();
```

```
String fontList[] = Toolkit.getDefaultToolkit().getFontList();
for (int i = 0; i < fontList.length; ++i)
   choiceList.addItem(fontList[i]);
```

A choice box is added to the dialog box to enumerate font sizes that can be used. Two checkboxes are used to set the bold and italicized styles. If none of these are set, the font's style is set to plain.

Every time one of these controls is changed, the font display is updated with a new font. This happens in the paintSample() method. Listing 22.7 shows the code for the paintSample() method and also features the full source code of the font dialog box.

Listing 22.7. The full source code of the font dialog box.

```
// Dialog box for choosing display colors...
public class ChooseFontDialog extends Dialog {
   Frame fr;    // What to update...
   List choiceList;   // List of color choices...
   fontDisplay d; // This is the text display...
   Choice choiceSize;  // Size of font...
   Checkbox checkItalics;
   Checkbox checkBold;
   Font currentFont;  // Current font in sample...
   Font defaultFont; // Store font dialog was created with...
   // Construct dialog to allow color to be chosen...
   public ChooseFontDialog(Frame parent,boolean modal) {
      // Create dialog with title
      super(parent,"Font Dialog",modal);
      fr = parent;
      defaultFont = getFont();
      // Create the dialog components...
      createComponents();
   }
   // Get the default font and set up display...
   private void setDefaultFont() {
      // SET YOUR DEFAULT FONT HERE!
      currentFont = getFont();
      // Get default list...
      String s = currentFont.getName();
      int index = findListString(choiceList,s);
      if (index >= 0)
            choiceList.select(index);
      else
            choiceList.select(0);
      // Get default size
      int sizeFont = currentFont.getSize();
      index = findChoiceString(choiceSize,
         String.valueOf(sizeFont));
      if (index >= 0)
            choiceSize.select(index);
      else
            choiceSize.select(0);
      // Set the style displays...
      int styleFont = currentFont.getStyle();
```

continues

22

WORKING WITH
DIALOG BOXES

Listing 22.7. continued

```java
        if ((styleFont & Font.BOLD) != 0)
            checkBold.setState(true);
    else
            checkBold.setState(false);
        if ((styleFont & Font.ITALIC) != 0)
            checkItalics.setState(true);
    else
            checkItalics.setState(false);
    // Set the canvas style...
    d.setFont(currentFont);
}

// Wait for Cancel or OK buttons to be chosen...
public boolean handleEvent(Event e) {
  switch(e.id) {
     case Event.ACTION_EVENT:
        // Kill the dialog...
        if (e.arg.equals("Cancel")) {
         dispose();  // Remove Dialog...
         return true;
        }  // end if
        // Update colors on the text…
        if (e.arg.equals("OK")) {
            //   YOUR UPDATE CODE GOES HERE!
            dispose();
            return true;
        }  // end if
        if (e.target instanceof Choice) {
            paintSample();
            return false;
        }  // end list if
        if (e.target instanceof Checkbox) {
            paintSample();
            return false;
        }  // end list if
        return false;
     // User selected a listbox item...
     case Event.LIST_SELECT:
        // Set up caption colors and color choice highlight...
        if (e.target instanceof List) {
            paintSample();
            return false;
        }  // end list if
        return false;
     default:
        return false;
    } // end switch
}

// The layout will call this to get the preferred size
// of the dialog.  Make it big enough for the components
public Dimension preferredSize() {
    // Get the metrics of the current font...
    FontMetrics fm = getFontMetrics(getFont());
    int width = 3 * fm.stringWidth("Highlighted foreground");
    int height = 14 * fm.getHeight();
    return new Dimension(width,height);
}
```

```
// Create the main display panel...
private void createComponents() {
 // Use gridbag constraints...
 GridBagLayout g = new GridBagLayout();
 setLayout(g);
 GridBagConstraints gbc = new GridBagConstraints();
 // Set the constraints for the top objects...
 gbc.fill = GridBagConstraints.BOTH;
 gbc.weightx = 1.0;
 gbc.weighty = 1.0;
 gbc.gridheight = 10;
 // Add the listbox of choices...
 // Get the selection from the toolkit...
 choiceList = new List();
 String fontList[] = Toolkit.getDefaultToolkit().getFontList();
 for (int i = 0; i < fontList.length; ++i)
    choiceList.addItem(fontList[i]);
    g.setConstraints(choiceList,gbc);
    add(choiceList);
 // Set the default values...
 gbc.weighty = 0.0;
 gbc.weightx = 1.0;
 gbc.gridheight = 1;
 gbc.gridwidth = GridBagConstraints.REMAINDER;
 // Create a label for display...
 Label l = new Label("Size:");
 // Add to grid bag...
 g.setConstraints(l,gbc);
 add(l);
 // Create the choice box...
 choiceSize = new Choice();
 choiceSize.addItem("8");
 choiceSize.addItem("10");
 choiceSize.addItem("12");
 choiceSize.addItem("14");
 choiceSize.addItem("16");
 choiceSize.addItem("20");
 // Add to grid bag...
 g.setConstraints(choiceSize,gbc);
 add(choiceSize);
 // Add Italics...
 checkItalics = new Checkbox("Italics");
 g.setConstraints(checkItalics,gbc);
 add(checkItalics);
 // Add Bold...
 checkBold = new Checkbox("Bold");
 g.setConstraints(checkBold,gbc);
 add(checkBold);
 // Display the color chosen...
 d = new fontDisplay("Sample Text");
 // Add to grid bag...
 g.setConstraints(d,gbc);
 add(d);
 // Two buttons: "OK" and "Cancel"
 Panel p = new Panel();
 p.add(new Button("OK"));
 p.add(new Button("Cancel"));
```

continues

Listing 22.7. continued

```
    // Add to grid bag...
    gbc.gridwidth = GridBagConstraints.REMAINDER;
    g.setConstraints(p,gbc);
    add(p);
}

// Setup defaults upon showing...
public synchronized void show() {
    super.show(); // Call the default constructor...
    // Set the font dialog started off with...
    setFont(defaultFont);
    // Set up defaults...
    setDefaultFont();
    pack();  // Compact...
    // Resize to fit everything...
    resize(preferredSize());
}

// Set the display canvas to show itself with
// the currently selected font
private synchronized void paintSample() {
    // Get the family to display
    String fontName = choiceList.getSelectedItem();
    // Get its point size
    String fontSize = choiceSize.getSelectedItem();
    // Set its style
    int fontStyle = Font.PLAIN;
    if (checkItalics.getState())
        fontStyle += Font.ITALIC;
    if (checkBold.getState())
        fontStyle += Font.BOLD;
    // Create a font with the proper attributes...
    currentFont = new Font(fontName,fontStyle,
        Integer.parseInt(fontSize));
    // Set the new font on the canvas...
    d.setFont(currentFont);
    // Repaint it so the new font is displayed..
    d.repaint();
}

// Return index of string in list...
// -1 means not found
public int findListString(List l,String s) {
    for (int i = 0; i < l.countItems(); ++i) {
        if (s.equals(l.getItem(i)) )
            return i;
    }
    return -1;
}

// Return index of string in choice...
// -1 means not found
public int findChoiceString(Choice c,String s) {
    for (int i = 0; i < c.countItems(); ++i) {
        if (s.equals(c.getItem(i)) )
            return i;
    }
```

```
        return -1;
    }
}

// A small class that illustrates the
// current highlight and background
class fontDisplay extends Canvas {
    String displayText;
    // Construct the display by storing the
    // text to be displayed...
    public fontDisplay(String displayText) {
        super();
        this.displayText = displayText;
    }
    // The layout will call this to get the minimum size
    // of the object.  In this case we want it to be at
    // least big enough to fit the display test...
    public Dimension minimumSize() {
        // Get the metrics of the current font...
        FontMetrics fm = getFontMetrics(getFont());
        return new Dimension(fm.stringWidth(displayText),
            4 * fm.getHeight());
    }

    // Paint the colors and text...
    public synchronized void paint(Graphics g) {
        // Set background...
        Dimension dm = size();
        g.setColor(Color.white);
        g.fillRect(0,0,dm.width,dm.height);
        // Draw the string
        g.setColor(Color.black);
        // Set dimensions. Move just from left...
        FontMetrics fm = getFontMetrics(getFont());
        int x = fm.charWidth('I');
        // And center in height...
        int y = fm.getHeight();
        g.drawString(displayText,x,y);
    }
}
```

The FileDialog Class

The FileDialog class is a subclass of Dialog used to provide a platform-independent approach to letting the user select the files to be loaded or saved. Instances of the FileDialog class usually mirror the underlying GUI conventions. For example, a FontDialog object for loading a file on the Windows 95 environment follows the Windows 95 Open dialog box conventions.

The FileDialog can be constructed to be in a mode to load a file or save a file. These dialog boxes look similar but perform slightly differently. For example, the Save version of the dialog box notifies the user that a file exists if a filename is given for a preexisting file. Here's the code you need to construct dialog boxes for both the load and save cases:

```
FileDialog openFileDialog;  // File Open Dialog...
FileDialog saveFileDialog;  // File Save Dialog...
openFileDialog = new FileDialog(this,"Open File",
            FileDialog.LOAD);
saveFileDialog = new FileDialog(this,"Save File",
            FileDialog.SAVE);
```

The integer flag in the last parameter of the constructors indicates the mode in which the dialog box should function.

When the dialog box is displayed with the show() method, it acts in a modal fashion so that input to the frame is blocked while it is displayed. After a choice has been made, the chosen file and directory can be retrieved with the getFile() and getDirectory() methods. The former returns a null value if the user cancels out of the dialog box.

It is interesting to note that the FileDialog objects constructed here do not appear when the applet is run in Netscape Navigator. For security reasons, Netscape does not allow any file-based methods to be invoked from an applet. In the latest incarnation of Microsoft Internet Explorer, you actually get a security exception if you even attempt to reference the FileDialog class! Consequently, the FileDialog class is really useful only for standalone applications.

Summary

As the examples in this chapter have shown, most of the work in creating a dialog box is setting up the component controls. The techniques for doing this are very similar to creating controls in an applet, with the difference that you may have to call pack() or the preferredSize() method to get the exact appearance you are after.

The other big issue with dialog boxes is related to security. Some browsers, like Netscape Navigator, consider dialog boxes to be a possible security threat. For this reason, a warning or an "untrusted window" message may appear in the browser status bar. In the worst case, the dialog box may not even appear or may be flagged with a security exception! As stated before, this is the case with the FileDialog class in Microsoft's Internet Explorer. For these reasons, dialog boxes must be used with great caution in applets. When all is said and done, dialog boxes may be best suited for standalone Java applications.

V
PART

IN THIS PART

Networking with Java

CHAPTER 23

Introduction to Network Programming

by Mike Fletcher

IN THIS CHAPTER

One of the best features of Java is its networking support. Java has classes that range from low-level TCP/IP connections to ones that provide instant access to resources on the World Wide Web. Even if you have never done any network programming before, Java makes it easy.

The following chapters introduce you to the networking classes and how to use them. A guide to what is covered by each chapter follows:

- **Chapter 23, "Introduction to Network Programming"**
  The chapter you are reading contains an introduction to TCP/IP networking, a list of the concepts you should be familiar with before reading the rest of the networking section, and an overview of the networking facilities provided by Java.

- **Chapter 24, "Developing Content and Protocol Handlers"**
  This chapter discusses what protocol and content handlers are and how they can be applied, and provides an introduction to writing your own handlers.

- **Chapter 25, "Client/Server Fundamentals"**
  This chapter covers the basics of client/server programming and how Java supports the client/server model.

- **Chapter 26, "Java Socket Programming"**
  This chapter shows you how to use Java's low-level TCP/IP socket facilities.

- **Chapter 27, "Multiuser Network Programming"**
  This chapter presents techniques for creating applets that allow multiple users to interact with each other.

Prerequisites

Although networking with Java is fairly simple, there are a few concepts and classes from other packages you should be familiar with before reading this part of the book. If you are interested only in writing an applet that interacts with an HTTP daemon, you probably can concentrate just on the URL class for now. For the other network classes, you need at least a passing familiarity with the World Wide Web, java.io classes, threads, and TCP/IP networking.

World Wide Web Concepts

If you are using Java, you probably already have a familiarity with the Web. You need some knowledge of how Uniform Resource Locators (URLs) work to use the URL and URLConnection classes.

java.io Classes

Once you have a network connection established using one of the low-level classes, you will use java.io.InputStream and java.io.OutputStream objects or appropriate subclasses of these objects to communicate with the other endpoint. Also, many of the java.net classes throw a java.io.IOException when they encounter a problem.

Threads

Although not strictly needed for networking, threads make using the network classes easier. Why tie up your user interface waiting for a response from a server when a separate communication thread can wait? Server applications also can service several clients simultaneously by spawning off a new thread to handle each incoming connection.

TCP/IP Networking

Before using the networking facilities of Java, you should be familiar with the terminology and concepts of the TCP/IP networking model. The next part of this chapter gets you up to speed.

Internet Networking: A Quick Overview

TCP/IP (Transmission Control Protocol/Internet Protocol) is the set of networking protocols used by Internet hosts to communicate with other Internet hosts. If you have ever had any experience with networks or network programming in general, you should be able to skim this section and check back when you find a term you are not familiar with. A list of references is given at the end of this section if you want more detailed information.

TCP/IP and Networking Terms

Like any other technical field, computer networking has its own set of jargon. These definitions should clear up what the terms mean:

- **host.** An individual machine on a network. Each host on a TCP/IP network has at least one unique address (see *IP number*).

- **hostname.** A symbolic name that can be mapped into an IP number. Several methods exist for performing this mapping, such as DNS (Domain Name Service) and Sun's NIS (Network Information Services).

- **IETF.** The Internet Engineering Task Force, a group responsible for maintaining Internet standards and defining new ones.

- **internet.** A network of networks. When capitalized as the *Internet*, the term refers to the globally interconnected network of networks.

- **intranet.** A term used to describe a network using TCP/IP protocols which either is not connected to the Internet or is connected through a firewall.

- **IP number.** A unique address for each host on the Internet (unique in the sense that a given number can be used only by one particular machine, but a particular machine may be known by multiple IP numbers). Currently, this is a 32-bit number that consists of a network part and a host part. The network part identifies the network on which the host resides; the host part is the specific host on that network. Sometimes, the IP number is referred to as the *IP address* of a host.

- **packet.** A single message sent over a network. Sometimes, a packet is referred to as a *datagram*, but the former term usually refers to data at the network layer and the latter term refers to a higher-layer message.

- **protocol.** A set of data formats and messages used to transmit information. Different network entities must speak the same protocol if they are to understand each other.

- **protocol stack.** Networking services can be thought of as different layers that use lower-level services to provide services to higher-level services. The set of layers that provides network functionality is known as a *protocol stack*.

- **RFC.** Request For Comments—documents in which proposed Internet standards are released. Each RFC is issued a sequential number, which is how they are usually referenced. Examples are RFC 791, which specifies the Internet Protocol (the IP of TCP/IP), and RFC 821, which specifies the protocol used for transferring e-mail between Internet hosts (SMTP).

- **router.** A host that knows how to forward packets between different networks. A router can be a specialized piece of network hardware or can be something as simple as a machine with two network interfaces (each on a different physical network).

- **socket.** A communications *endpoint* (that is, one end of a conversation). In the TCP/IP context, a socket usually is identified by a unique pair consisting of the source IP address and port number and the destination IP address and port number.

The Internet Protocols

TCP/IP is a set of communications protocols for communicating between different types of machines and networks (hence the name *internet*). The name TCP/IP comes from two of the protocols: the Transmission Control Protocol and the Internet Protocol. Other protocols in the TCP/IP suite are the User Datagram Protocol (UDP), the Internet Control Message Protocol (ICMP), and the Internet Group Multicast Protocol (IGMP).

These protocols define a standard format for exchanging information between machines (known as *hosts*) regardless of the physical connections between them. TCP/IP implementations exist for almost every type of hardware and operating system imaginable. Software exists to transmit IP datagrams over network hardware ranging from modems to fiber-optic cable.

TCP/IP Network Architecture

There are four layers in the TCP/IP network model. Each of the protocols in the TCP/IP suite provides for communication between entities in one of these layers (see Figure 23.1). These lower-level layers are used by higher-level layers to get data from host to host. The layers are as follows, with examples of which protocols live at each layer:

- Physical (Ethernet, Token Ring, PPP)
- Network (IP)

- Transport (TCP, UDP)
- Application (telnet, HTTP, FTP, Gopher)

FIGURE 23.1.

The TCP/IP protocol stack.

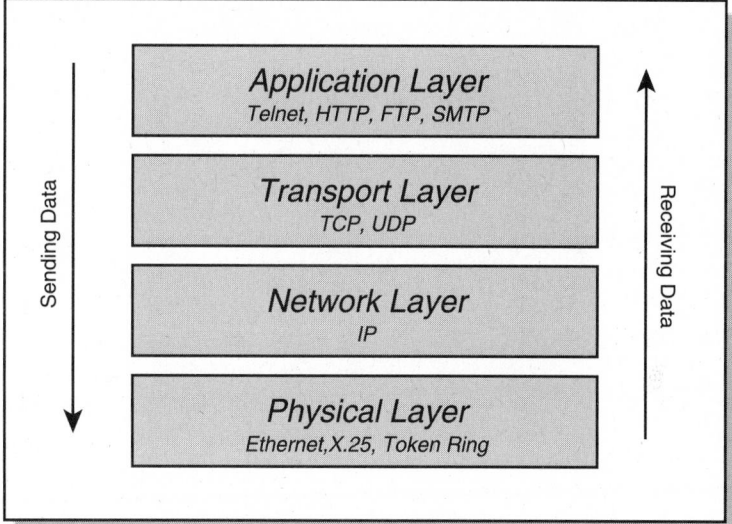

Each layer in the stack takes data from the one above it and adds the information needed to get the data to its destination, using the services of the layer below. One way to think of this layering is like the layers of an onion. Each protocol layer adds a layer to the packet going down the protocol stack (see Figure 23.2). When the packet is received, each layer peels off its addressing to determine where next to send the packet.

FIGURE 23.2.

Addressing information is added and removed at each layer.

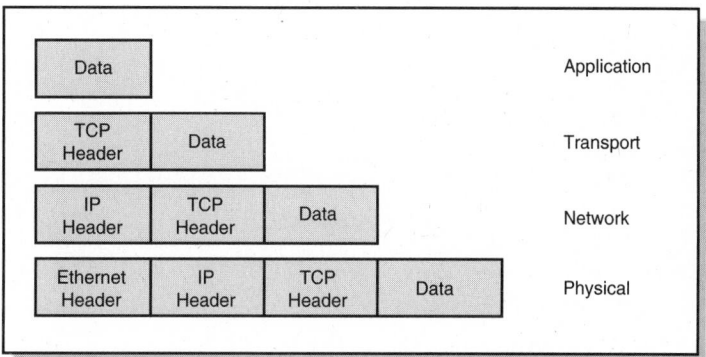

Suppose that your Web browser wants to retrieve something from a Web server running on a host on the same physical network. The browser sends an HTTP request using the TCP layer. The TCP layer asks the IP layer to send the data to the proper host. The IP layer then uses the physical layer to send the data to the appropriate host.

At the receiving end, each layer strips off the addressing information that the sender added and determines what to do with the data. Continuing the example, the physical layer passes the received IP packet to the IP layer. The IP layer determines that the packet is a TCP packet and passes it to the TCP layer. The TCP layer passes the packet to the HTTP daemon process. The HTTP daemon then processes the request and sends the data requested back through the same process to the other host.

When the hosts are not on the same physical network, the IP layer handles routing the packet through the correct series of hosts (known as *routers*) until the packet reaches its destination. One of the nice features of the IP protocol is that individual hosts do not have to know how to reach every host on the Internet. The host simply passes to a default router any packets for networks it does not know how to reach.

For example, a university may have only one machine with a physical connection to the Internet. All the campus routers know to forward all packets destined for the Internet to this host. Similarly, any host on the Internet only has to get packets to this one router to reach any host at the university. The router forwards the packets to the appropriate local routers (see Figure 23.3).

FIGURE 23.3.
An example of IP routing.

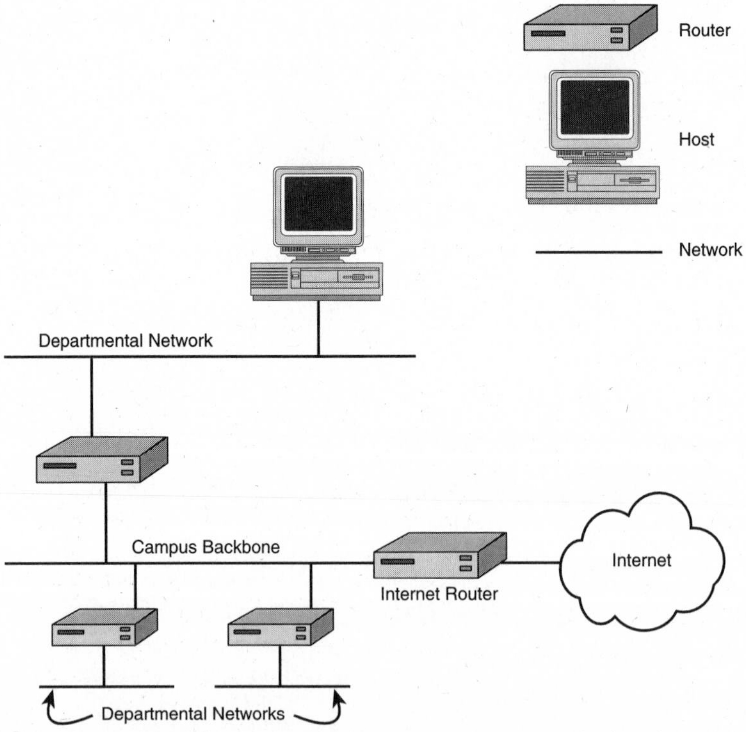

NOTE

A publicly available program for UNIX platforms called `traceroute` is useful if you want to find out what routers are actually responsible for getting a packet from one host to another and how long each hop takes. The source for `traceroute` can be found by consulting an Archie server for an FTP site near you, or from `ftp://ee.lbl.gov`.

The Future: IP Version 6

Back when the TCP/IP protocols were being developed in the early 1970s, 32-bit IP numbers seemed more than capable of addressing all the hosts on an internet. Although there currently is no lack of IP numbers, the explosive growth of the Internet in recent years is rapidly consuming the remaining unassigned addresses. To address this lack of IP numbers, a new version of the IP protocols is being developed by the IETF.

This new version, known as either IPv6 or IPng (IP Next Generation), will provide a much larger address space of 128 bits. This address space will allow for approximately 3.4×10^{38} different IP addresses. Where IP addresses used to be expressed as four decimal numbers (with values 0 to 255) separated by a period (.), as in `192.242.139.42`, IPv6 addresses are expressed as eight groups of four hexadecimal digits separated by colons, like this:

`5A02:1364:DD03:0432:0031:12CA:0001:BEEF`

IPv6 will be backward compatible with current IP implementations to allow older clients to interoperate with newer ones. Provisions are contained in the protocol for tunneling IPv6 traffic over an IPv4 network (and vice versa). Other benefits of the new version are as follows:

- Improved support for *multicasting* (sending packets to several destinations at one time).
- Simplified packet header formats.
- Support for authentication and encryption of packet contents at the network layer.
- Support for designating a connection as a special flow which should be given special treatment (such as real-time audio data that needs quick delivery).

Several new protocols are being added to the TCP/IP suite. The RTP (Real Time Protocol) and RTCP (Real Time Control Protocol) protocols provide support for applications such as video and audio conferencing. Some protocols are being done away with and the functionality they provide is being merged into other existing protocols. IGMP (Internet Group Membership Protocol), which provided support for membership in multicast groups, has been done away with; multicast membership is now handled with ICMP messages.

These enhancements to TCP/IP should allow the Internet to continue the phenomenal growth it has experienced over the past few years.

Where to Find More Information

This chapter was not meant to completely cover the subject of TCP/IP. If your curiosity has been piqued, the following online documents and books may be of interest to you.

RFCs

The first and definitive source of information on the IP protocol family are the Request For Comments documents defining the standards themselves. An index of all of RFC documents is available through the Web at `http://ds.internic.net/ds/rfc-index.html`. This page has pointers to all currently available RFCs (organized in groups of 100) as well as a searchable index.

Table 23.1 gives the numbers of some relevant RFCs and what they cover. Keep in mind that a given RFC may have been made obsolete by a subsequent RFC. The InterNIC site's index will note in the description any documents that were made obsolete by a subsequent RFC.

Table 23.1. RFC documents.

RFC Number	Topic
791	The Internet Protocol (IPv4)
793	The Transmission Control Protocol (TCP)
768	The User Datagram Protocol 2(UDP)
894	Transmission of IP Datagrams over Ethernet Networks
1171	The PPP Protocol
1883	IP Version 6
1602	The Internet Standards Process: How an RFC Becomes a Standard
1880	Current Internet Standards

Books on TCP/IP

A good introduction to TCP/IP is the book *TCP/IP Network Administration* by Craig Hunt (O'Reilly and Associates, ISBN 0-937175-82-X). Although it was written as a guide for system administrators of UNIX machines, the book contains an excellent introduction to all aspects of TCP/IP, such as routing and the Domain Name Service (DNS).

Another book worth checking out is *The Design and Implementation of the 4.3BSD UNIX Operating System* by Samuel J. Leffler, et al. (Addison-Wesley, ISBN 0-201-06196-1). In addition to covering how a UNIX operating system works, it contains a chapter on the TCP/IP implementation.

If you are a beginner, another way to get started get started with TCP/IP is by reading *Teach Yourself TCP/IP in 14 Days* by Timothy Parker (Sams Publishing, ISBN 0-672-30549-6).

IPng and the TCP/IP Protocols by Stephan A. Thomas (John Wiley & Sons, ISBN 0-471-13088-5) offers an overview of version 6 of the Internet protocols.

Network Class Overview

This section gives a short overview of the capabilities and limitations of the different network classes provided in the `java.net` package. If you have never done any network programming, this section should help you decide what type of connection class you need to base your application. The overview will help you pick the Java classes that best fit your networking application. An overview of Java security, as it relates to network programming, is also provided.

Which Class Is Right for Me?

The answer to this question depends on what you are trying to do and what type of application you are writing. Each network protocol has its own advantages and disadvantages. If you are writing a client for someone else's protocol, the decision probably has been made for you. If you are writing your own protocol from scratch, the following should help you decide which transport method (and hence, which Java classes) best fit your application.

The URL Class

The URL class is an example of what can be accomplished using the other, lower-level network objects. The URL class is best suited for applications or applets that need to access content on the World Wide Web. If all you need to use Java for is writing Web browser applets, the URL and URLConnection classes in all likelihood will handle your network communications needs.

The URL class enables you to retrieve a resource from the Web by specifying the Uniform Resource Locator for it. The content of the URL is fetched and turned into a corresponding Java object (such as a String containing the text of an HTML document). If you are fetching arbitrary information, the URLConnection object provides methods that will try to deduce the type of the content either from the filename in the URL or from the content stream itself.

The Socket Class

The Socket class provides a reliable, ordered stream connection (that is, a TCP/IP socket connection). The host and port number of the destination are specified when the Socket is created.

The connection is reliable because the transport layer (the TCP protocol layer) acknowledges the receipt of sent data. If one end of the connection does not get an acknowledgment back within a reasonable period of time, the other end re-sends the unacknowledged data (a technique known as *Positive Acknowledgment with Retransmission,* often abbreviated as PAR). Once you have written data into a Socket, you can assume that the data will get to the other side (unless you receive an IOException, of course).

The term *ordered stream* means that the data arrives at the opposite end in the exact same order it is written. However, because the data is a stream, write boundaries are not preserved. What this means is that if you write 200 characters, the other side may read all 200 at once. It might get the first 10 characters one time and the next 190 the next time data is received from the socket. In any case, the receiver cannot tell where each group of data was written.

The reliable stream connection provided by Socket objects is well suited for interactive applications. Examples of protocols that use TCP as their transport mechanism are telnet and FTP. The HTTP protocol used to transfer data for the Web also uses TCP to communicate between hosts.

The ServerSocket Class

A ServerSocket class represents what Socket-type connections communicate with. Server sockets listen on a given port for connection requests when their accept() method is called. The ServerSocket offers the same connection-oriented, ordered stream protocol (TCP) that the Socket object does. In fact, once a connection has been established, the accept() method returns a Socket object to talk with the remote end.

The DatagramSocket Class

The DatagramSocket class provides an unreliable, connectionless, datagram connection (that is, a UDP/IP socket connection).

Unlike the reliable connection provided by a Socket, there is no guarantee that what you send over a UDP connection actually gets to the receiver. The TCP connection provided by the Socket class takes care of retransmitting any packets that get lost. Packets sent through UDP simply are sent out and forgotten, which means that if you need to know that the receiver got the data, you will have to send back some sort of acknowledgment. This arrangement does not mean that your data will never get to the other end of a UDP connection. If a network error happens (your cat jiggles the Ethernet plug out of the wall, for example), the UDP layer does not try to send it again or even know that the packet did not get to the recipient.

Connectionless means that the socket does not have a fixed receiver. You can use the same DatagramSocket to send packets to different hosts and ports; however, you can use a Socket connection only to connect to a given host and port. Once a Socket is connected to a destination, that destination cannot be changed. The fact that UDP sockets are not bound to a specific destination also means that the same socket can listen for packets as well as originating them. There is no UDP DatagramServerSocket equivalent to the TCP ServerSocket.

Datagram refers to the fact that the information is sent as discrete packets rather than as a continuous ordered stream. The individual packet boundaries are preserved. It may help to think of this process as dropping fixed-size postcards in a mailbox. If you send four packets, the order in which they arrive at the destination is not guaranteed to be the same in which they were sent. The receiver may get them in the same order they were sent, or the packets may arrive in reverse order. In any case, each packet is received whole.

Given the above constraints, why would anyone want to use a `DatagramSocket`? There are several advantages to using UDP:

- **You have to communicate with several different hosts.** Because a `DatagramSocket` is not bound to a particular host, you can use the same object to communicate with different hosts by specifying the `InetAddress` when you create each `DatagramPacket`.

- **You are not worried about reliable delivery.** If the application you are writing does not have to know that the data it sends was received at the other end, using a UDP socket eliminates the overhead of acknowledging each packet as TCP does. Another case is if the protocol you are implementing has its own method of handling reliable delivery and retransmission.

- **The amount of data being sent does not merit the overhead of setting up a connection and the reliable delivery mechanism.** An application that is sending only 100 bytes for each transaction every 10 minutes is an example of this situation.

The NFS (Network File System) protocol version 2, originally developed by Sun with implementations available for most operating systems, is an example application that uses UDP for its transport mechanism. Another example of an application in which a `DatagramSocket` may be appropriate is a multiplayer game. The central server must communicate with all the players involved and does not necessarily have to know that a position update got to the player.

> **NOTE**
>
> An actual game that uses UDP for communication is Netrek, a space combat simulation loosely based on the Star Trek series. Information on Netrek can be found using the Yahoo subject catalog at this URL:
>
> `http://www.yahoo.com/Recreation/Games/Internet_Games/Netrek/`
>
> There is also a Usenet newsgroup:
>
> `news:rec.games.netrek`

Decisions, Decisions

Now that you know what the classes are capable of, you can choose the one that best fits your application. Table 23.2 sums up the type of connection each of the base networking classes creates. The *Direction* column indicates where a connection originates: *Outgoing* indicates that your application is opening a connection out to another host; *Incoming* indicates that some other application is initiating a connection to yours.

Table 23.2. Summary of low-level connection objects.

Class	Connection Type	Direction
Socket	Connected, ordered byte stream (TCP)	Outgoing
ServerSocket	Connected, ordered byte stream (TCP)	Incoming
DatagramSocket	Connectionless datagram (UDP)	Incoming or Outgoing

You should look at the problem you are trying to solve, any constraints you have, and the transport mechanism that best fits your situation. If you are having problems choosing a transport protocol, take a look at some of the RFCs that define Internet standards for applications (such as HTTP or SMTP). One of them might be similar to what you are trying to accomplish. As an alternative, you can be indecisive and provide both TCP and UDP versions of your service, duplicating the processing logic and customizing the network logic. Trying both transport protocols with a pared-down version of your application can give you an indication of which protocol better serves your purposes. Once you've looked at these factors, you should be able to decide which class to use.

Java Security and the Network Classes

One of the purposes of Java is to enable executable content from an arbitrary network source to be retrieved and run securely. To accomplish this goal, the Java runtime enforces certain limitations on what classes obtained through the network may do. You should be aware of these constraints because they affect the design of applets and how the applets must be loaded. You must take into consideration whatever security constraints are imposed by your target environment and your development environment as well when you design your application or applet.

For example, Netscape Navigator 2.0 allows code loaded from local disk more privileges than code loaded over a network connection. A class loaded from an HTTP daemon may create only outgoing connections back to the host from which it was loaded. If the class is loaded from the local host (that is, if it is located somewhere in the class search path on the machine running Navigator), the class can connect to an arbitrary host. Contrast this with the applet viewer provided with Sun's Java Developers Kit. The applet viewer can be configured to act similarly to Navigator or to enforce no restrictions on network connectivity.

If you need full access to all Java's capabilities, there is always the option of writing a standalone application. A standalone application (that is, one not running in the context of a Web browser) has no restrictions on what it is allowed to do. Sun's HotJava Web browser is an example of a standalone application.

> **NOTE**
>
> For a more detailed discussion of Java security and how it is designed into the language and runtime, take a look at Chapter 35, "Java Security."
>
> In addition, Sun has several white paper documents and a collection of frequently asked questions available at `http://www.javasoft.com/sfaq/`.

These checks are implemented by a subclass of `java.lang.SecurityManager`. Depending on the security model, the object will allow or deny certain actions. You can check beforehand whether a capability your applet needs is present by calling the `SecurityManager` yourself. The `java.lang.System` object provides a `getSecurityManager()` method that returns a reference to the `SecurityManager` active for the current context. If your applet needs to open a `ServerSocket`, for example, you can call the `checkListen()` method yourself and print an error message (or pop up a dialog box) alerting the users and referring them to installation instructions.

Summary

This chapter is a roadmap to the next four chapters. It has shown what concepts you need to be familiar with before you dive into network programming in Java. You should be comfortable with how TCP/IP networking operates in general (or at least know where to look for more information). You also should now have an idea of which Java class provides what functionality.

Developing Content and Protocol Handlers

by Mike Fletcher

IN THIS CHAPTER

CHAPTER

24

Java's URL class gives applets and applications easy access to the World Wide Web using the HTTP protocol. This is fine and dandy if you can get the information you need into a format that a Web server or CGI script can access. However, wouldn't it be nice if your code could talk directly to the server application without going through an intermediary CGI script or some sort of proxy? Wouldn't you like your Java-based Web browser to be able to display your wonderful new image format? This is where protocol and content handlers come in.

What Are Protocol and Content Handlers?

Handlers are classes that extend the capabilities of the standard URL class. A *protocol handler* provides a reference to a java.io.InputStream object (and a java.io.OutputStream object, where appropriate) that retrieves the content of a URL. Content handlers take an InputStream for a given MIME type and convert it into a Java object of the appropriate type.

MIME Types

MIME (Multipurpose Internet Mail Extensions) is the Internet standard for specifying the type of content a resource contains. As you may have guessed from the name, it originally was proposed for the context of enclosing nontextual components in Internet e-mail. MIME allows different platforms (PCs, Macintoshes, UNIX workstations, and others) to exchange multimedia content in a common format.

The MIME standard, described in RFC 1521, defines an extra set of headers similar to those on Internet e-mail. The headers describe attributes such as the method of encoding the content and the MIME content type. MIME types are written as *type/subtype*, where *type* is a general category such as text or image and *subtype* is a more specific description of the format such as html or jpeg. For example, when a Web browser contacts an HTTP daemon to retrieve an HTML file, the daemon's response looks something like this:

```
Content-type: text/html

<HEAD><TITLE>Document moved</TITLE></HEAD>
<BODY><H1>Document moved</H1>
```

The Web browser parses the Content-type: header and sees that the data is text/html—an HTML document. If it was a GIF image file, the header would have been Content-type: image/gif.

IANA (Internet Assigned Numbers Authority), the group that maintains the lists of assigned protocol numbers and the like, is responsible for registering new content types. A current copy of the official MIME types is available from ftp://ftp.isi.edu/in-notes/iana/assignments/media-types/. This site also has specifications or pointers to specifications for each type.

Getting Java to Load New Handlers

The exact procedure for loading a protocol or content handler depends on the Java implementation. The following instructions are based on Sun's Java Developers Kit and should work for any implementation derived from Sun's. If you have problems, check the documentation for your particular Java version.

In the JDK implementation, the URL class and helpers look for classes in the sun.net.www package. Protocol handlers should be in a package called sun.net.www.protocol.*ProtocolName*, where *ProtocolName* is the name of the protocol (such as ftp or http). The handler class itself should be named Handler. For example, the full name of the HTTP protocol handler class, provided by Sun with the JDK, is sun.net.www.protocol.http.Handler. To load your new protocol handler, you must construct a directory structure corresponding to the package names and add the directory to your CLASSPATH environment variable. Assume that you have a handler for a protocol—let's call it the foo protocol—and that your Java library directory is .../java/lib/ (...\java\lib\ on Windows machines). You must take the following steps to load the foo protocol:

- Make directories .../java/lib/sun, .../java/lib/sun/net, and so on. The last directory should be named like this:

  .../java/lib/sun/net/www/protocol/foo

- Place your Handler.java file in the last directory (that is, it should be named like this:

  .../java/lib/sun/net/www/protocol/foo/Handler.java)

- Compile the Handler.java file.

 If you place the netClass.zip file containing the network classes (located on the CD-ROM that accompanies this book) in your CLASSPATH, the example handlers should load correctly.

Creating a Protocol Handler

Let's start extending Java with a handler for the finger protocol. The finger protocol is defined in RFC 762. The server listens on TCP port 79. It expects either the user name for which you want information followed by ASCII carriage return and linefeed characters, or (if you want information on all users currently logged in) just the carriage return and linefeed characters. The information is returned as ASCII text in a system-dependent format (although most UNIX variants give similar information). We will use an existing class (fingerClient) to handle contacting the finger server and concentrate on developing the protocol handler.

Design

The first decision we must make is how to structure URLs for our protocol. We'll imitate the HTTP URL and specify that finger URLs should be of the following format:

```
finger://host/user
```

In this syntax, *host* is the host to contact and *user* is an optional user to ask for information about. If the user name is omitted, we will return information about all users.

Because we already have a `fingerClient` class written, we need to write only the subclasses to `URLStreamHandler` and `URLConnection`. Our stream handler will use the client object to format the returned information using HTML. The handler will write the content into a `StringBuffer`, which will be used to create a `StringBufferInputStream`. The `fingerConnection`, a subclass of `URLConnection`, will take this stream and implement the `getInputStream()` and `getContent()` methods.

In our implementation, the protocol handler object does all the work of retrieving the remote content; the connection object simply retrieves the data from the stream provided. Usually, the connection object handler would retrieve the content. The `openConnection()` method would open a connection to the remote location, and the `getInputStream()` would return a stream to read the contents. In our case, the protocol is very simple (compared to something as complex as FTP) and we can handle everything in the protocol handler.

The `fingerConnection` Source

The source for the `fingerConnection` class should go in the same file as the `Handler` class. The constructor copies the `InputStream` passed and calls the `URLConnection` constructor. It also sets the `URLConnection` member to indicate that the connection cannot take input. Listing 24.1 contains the source for this class.

Listing 24.1. The `fingerConnection` class.

```
class fingerConnection extends URLConnection {
  InputStream in;

  fingerConnection( URL u, InputStream in ) {
    super( u );
    this.in = in;
    this.setDoInput( false );
  }

  public void connect( ) {
    return;
  }

  public InputStream getInputStream( ) throws IOException {
    return in;
  }

  public Object getContent( ) throws IOException {
    String retval;
    int nbytes;
    byte buf[] = new byte[ 1024 ];
```

```
   try {
     while( (nbytes = in.read( buf, 0, 1024 )) != -1 ) {
       retval += new String( buf, 0, 0, nbytes );
     }
   } catch( Exception e ) {
     System.err.println(
       "fingerConnection::getContent: Exception\n" + e );

     e.printStackTrace( System.err );
   }

   return retval
  }
}
```

Handler Source

First, let's rough out the skeleton of the Handler.java file. We need the package statement so that our classes are compiled into the package where the runtime handler will look for them. We also import the fingerClient object here. The outline of the class is shown in Listing 24.2.

Listing 24.2. Protocol handler skeleton.

```
package sun.net.www.protocol.finger;

import java.io.*;
import java.net.*;
import sun.net.www.protocol.finger.fingerClient;


// fingerConnection source goes here

public class Handler extends URLStreamHandler {
  // openConnection() Method
}
```

The openConnection() Method

Now we'll develop the method responsible for returning an appropriate URLConnection object to retrieve a given URL. The method starts out by allocating a StringBuffer to hold our return data. We also will parse out the host name and user name from the URL argument. If the host was omitted, we default to localhost. The code for openConnection() is given in Listings 24.3 through 24.6.

Listing 24.3. The openConnection() method: parsing the URL.

```
public synchronized URLConnection openConnection( URL u ) {
  StringBuffer sb = new StringBuffer( );
```

continues

Listing 24.3. continued

```
String host = u.getHost( );
String user = u.getFile( ).substring( 1, u.getFile( ).length() );

if( host.equals( "" ) ) {
  host = "localhost";
}
```

Next, the method writes an HTML header into the buffer (see Listing 24.4). This allows a Java-based Web browser to display the finger information in a nice-looking format.

Listing 24.4. The openConnection() method: writing the HTML header.

```
sb.append( "<HTML><head>\n" );
sb.append( "<title>Fingering " );
sb.append( (user.equals("") ? "everyone" : user) );
sb.append( "@" + host );
sb.append( "</title></head>\n" );

sb.append( "<body>\n" );
sb.append( "<pre>\n" );
```

We'll then use the fingerClient class to get the information into a String and then append it to our buffer. If there is an error while getting the finger information, we will put the error message from the exception into the buffer instead (see Listing 24.5).

Listing 24.5. The openConnection() method: retrieving the finger information.

```
try {
  String info = null;
  info = (new fingerClient( host, user )).getInfo( );

  sb.append( info )
} catch( Exception e ) {
  sb.append( "Error fingering: " + e );
}
```

Finally, we'll close off the open HTML tags and create a fingerConnection object that will be returned to the caller (see Listing 24.6).

Listing 24.6. The openConnection() method: finishing the HTML and returning a fingerConnection object.

```
  sb.append( "\n</pre></body>\n</html>\n" );

  return new fingerConnection( u,
    (new StringBufferInputStream( sb.toString( ) ) ) );
}
```

Using the Handler

Once all the code is compiled and in the right locations, load the urlFetcher applet provided on the CD-ROM that accompanies this book and enter a finger URL. If everything loads right, you should see something like Figure 24.1. If you get an error that says something along the lines of BAD URL "finger://...": unknown protocol, check that you have your CLASSPATH set correctly.

FIGURE 24.1.

The urlFetcher *applet displaying a* finger *URL.*

```
                        Applet Viewer: urlFetcher.class
Applet

          Location:  finger://outland                    Fetch   Clear URL

       <HTML><head>
       <TITLE> Fingering everyone@outland </TITLE></head>
       <BODY>
       <pre>
       Login      Name            TTY Idle    When     Where
       fletch    Mike Fletcher     co   2d Tue 16:21
       fletch    Mike Fletcher     a   11: Mon 00:07
       fletch    Mike Fletcher     p0   2d Thu 10:28   :0.1
       fletch    Mike Fletcher     p3   2d Thu 10:32   :0.1
       fletch    Mike Fletcher     p4   10 Sun 19:01   mothra:S.0
       fletch    Mike Fletcher     p5   2d Tue 17:13   :0.1
       fletch    Mike Fletcher     p6   4d Mon 12:18   :0.0
       fletch    Mike Fletcher     p7   2d Fri 10:08   :0.0
       fletch    Mike Fletcher     p8   2d Tue 15:13   :0.0
       fletch    Mike Fletcher     pa    9 Mon 01:13   mothra:S.1
       fletch    Mike Fletcher     pb   10 Sat 22:11   mothra:S.2
       fletch    Mike Fletcher     pc   2d Fri 14:45   :0.1
       fletch    Mike Fletcher     pd   59 Fri 22:39   mothra:S.3
       fletch    Mike Fletcher     pe 1:02 Fri 22:58   mothra:S.4

          Content Type:   text/html            Content Size:  1195

       Content Retrieved.
```

Creating a Content Handler

The content handler example presented in this section is for the MIME-type text/tab-separated-values. If you have ever used a spreadsheet or database program, this type will be familiar. Many applications can import and export data in an ASCII text file, where each column of data in a row is separated by a tab character (\t). The first line is interpreted as the names of the fields, and the remaining lines are the actual data.

Design

Our first design decision is to figure out what type of Java object or objects to use to map the tab-separated values. Because this is a textual content, some sort of String object would seem to be the best solution. The spreadsheet characteristics of rows and columns of data can be represented by arrays. Putting these two facts together gives us a data type of String[][], or an array of arrays of String objects. The first array is an array of String[] objects, each representing one row of data. Each of these arrays consists of a String for each cell of the data.

We'll also need to have some way of breaking the input stream into separate fields. We will make a subclass of java.io.StreamTokenizer to handle this task. The StreamTokenizer class provides methods for breaking an InputStream into individual tokens. You may want to browse through the entry for StreamTokenizer in the API reference if you are not familiar with it.

Content Handler Skeleton

Content handlers are implemented by subclassing the java.net.ContentHandler class. These subclasses are responsible for implementing a getContent() method. We'll start with the skeleton of the class and then import the networking and I/O packages as well as the java.util.Vector class. We also will define the skeleton for our tabStreamTokenizer class. Listing 24.7 shows the skeleton for this content handler.

Listing 24.7. Content handler skeleton.

```
/*
 * Handler for text/tab-separated-values MIME type.
 */

// This needs to go in this package for JDK-derived
// Java implementations

package sun.net.www.content.text;

import java.net.*;
import java.io.*;

class tabStreamTokenizer extends StreamTokenizer {
  public static final int TT_TAB = ''\t'

  // Constructor
}

import java.util.Vector;

public
  class tab_separated_values extends ContentHandler {

  // getContent method

}
```

The `tabStreamTokenizer` Class

We will first define the class that breaks the input into the separate fields. Most of the functionality we need is provided by the StreamTokenizer class, so we only have to define a constructor that specifies the character classes needed to get the behavior we want. For the purposes of this content handler, there are three types of tokens: TT_TAB tokens, which represent fields; TT_EOL tokens, which signal the end of a line (that is, the end of a row of data); and TT_EOF tokens, which signal the end of the input file. Because this class is relatively simple, it is presented in its entirety in Listing 24.8.

Listing 24.8. The `tabStreamTokenizer` class.

```
class tabStreamTokenizer extends StreamTokenizer {
  public static final int TT_TAB = '\t';

  tabStreamTokenizer( InputStream in ) {
    super( in );

    // Undo parseNumbers() and whitespaceChars(0, ' ')
    ordinaryChars( '0', '9' );
    ordinaryChar( '.' );
    ordinaryChar( '-' );
    ordinaryChars( 0, ' ' );

    // Everything but TT_EOL and TT_TAB is a word
    wordChars( 0, ('\t'-1) );
    wordChars( ('\t'+1), 255 );

    // Make sure TT_TAB and TT_EOL get returned verbatim.
    whitespaceChars( TT_TAB, TT_TAB );
    ordinaryChar( TT_EOL );
  }

}
```

The getContent Method

Subclasses of `ContentHandler` must provide an implementation of `getContent()` that returns a reference to an `Object`. The method takes as its parameter a `URLConnection` object from which the class can obtain an `InputStream` to read the resource's data.

The getContent Skeleton

First, we'll define the overall structure and method variables. We need a flag (which we'll call done) to signal when we've read all the field names from the first line of text. The number of fields (columns) in each row of data will be determined by the number of fields in the first line of text and will be kept in an int variable called numFields. We also will declare another integer, index, for use while inserting the rows of data into a `String[]`.

We need some method of holding an arbitrary number of objects because we cannot tell the number of data rows in advance. To do this, we'll use the `java.util.Vector` object, which we'll call lines, to keep each `String[]`. Finally, we will declare an instance of our tabStreamTokenizer, using the `getInputStream()` method from the `URLConnection` passed as an argument to the constructor. Listing 24.9 shows the skeleton code for the `getContent()` method.

24

CONTENT AND
PROTOCOL
HANDLERS

Listing 24.9. The getContent() skeleton.

```
public Object getContent( URLConnection con )
  throws IOException
{
  boolean done = false;
  int numFields = 0;
  int index = 0;
  Vector lines = new Vector();

  tabStreamTokenizer in =
    new tabStreamTokenizer( con.getInputStream( ) );

  // Read in the first line of data (Listing 31.10 & 31.11)

  // Read in the rest of the file (Listing 31.12)

  // Stuff all data into a String[][] (Listing 31.13)
}
```

Reading the First Line

The first line of the file will tell us the number of fields and the names of the fields in each row for the rest of the file. Because we don't know beforehand how many fields there are, we'll keep each field in a Vector called firstLine. Each TT_WORD token that the tokenizer returns is the name of one field. We know we are done once it returns a TT_EOL token and can set the done flag to true. We will use a switch statement on the ttype member of our tabStreamTokenizer to decide what action to take. This is done in the code in Listing 24.10.

Listing 24.10. Reading the first line of data.

```
Vector firstLine = new Vector( );

while( !done && in.nextToken( ) != in.TT_EOF  ) {
  switch( in.ttype ) {
  case in.TT_WORD:
    firstLine.addElement( new String( in.sval ) );
    numFields++;
    break;

  case in.TT_EOL:
    done = true;
    break;
  }
}
```

Now that we have the first line in memory, we need to build an array of String objects from those stored in the Vector. To accomplish this, we'll first allocate the array to the size just determined. Then we will use the copyInto() method to transfer the strings into the array just allocated. Finally, we'll insert the array into lines (see Listing 24.11).

Listing 24.11. Copying field names into an array.

```
// Copy first line into array
  String curLine[] = new String[ numFields ];
  firstLine.copyInto( curLine );
  lines.addElement( curLine );
```

Read the Rest of the File

Before reading the remaining data, we have to allocate a new array to hold the next row. Then we loop until encountering the end of the file, signified by TT_EOF. Each time we retrieve a TT_WORD, we insert the String into curLine and increment index.

The end of the line lets us know when a row of data is done, at which time we will copy the current line into Vector. Then we will allocate a new String[] to hold the next line and set index back to zero (to insert the next item starting at the first element of the array). The code to implement this is given in Listing 24.12.

Listing 24.12. Reading the rest of the data.

```
curLine = new String[ numFields ];

while( in.nextToken( ) != in.TT_EOF ) {
  switch( in.ttype ) {
  case in.TT_WORD:
    curLine[ index++ ] = new String( in.sval );
    break;

  case in.TT_EOL:
    lines.addElement( curLine );
    curLine = new String[ numFields ];
    index = 0;
    break;
  }
}
```

Stuff All Data into String[][]

At this point in the code, all the data has been read in. All that remains is to copy the data from lines into an array of arrays of String, as shown in Listing 24.13.

Listing 24.13. Returning TSV data as String[][].

```
String retval[][] = new String[ lines.size() ][];
lines.copyInto( retval );

return retval;
```

Using the Content Handler

To show how the content handler works, we'll modify the urlFetcher applet used earlier in this chapter to demonstrate the finger protocol handler. We'll change it to use the getContent() method to retrieve the contents of a resource rather than reading the data from the stream returned by getInputStream(). We'll show the changes to the doFetch() method of the urlFetcher applet necessary to determine what type of Object was returned and display it correctly. The first change is to call the getContent() method and get an Object back rather than getting an InputStream. Listing 24.14 shows this change.

Listing 24.14. Modified urlFetcher.doFetch() code: call getContent() to get an Object.

```
try {
  boolean displayed = false;
  URLConnection con = target.openConnection();
  Object obj = con.getContent( );
```

Next come tests using the instanceof operator. We handle String objects and arrays of String objects by placing the text into the TextArea. Arrays are printed item by item. If the object is a subclass of InputStream, we read the data from the stream and display it. Image content is just noted as being an Image. For any other content type, we simply throw our hands up and remark that we cannot display the content (because the urlFetcher applet is not a full-fledged Web browser). The code to do this is shown in Listing 24.15.

Listing 24.15. Modified urlFetcher.doFetch() code: determine the type of the Object and display it.

```
if( obj instanceof String ) {
  contentArea.setText( (String) obj );
  displayed = true;
}

if( obj instanceof String[] ) {
  String array[] = (String []) obj;
  StringBuffer buf = new StringBuffer( );

  for( int i = 0; i < array.length; i++ )
    buf.append( "item " + i + ": " + array[i] + "\n" );

  contentArea.setText( buf.toString( ) );
  displayed = true;
}

if( obj instanceof String[][] ) {
  String array[][] = (String [][]) obj;
  StringBuffer buf = new StringBuffer( );

  for( int i = 0; i < array.length; i++ ) {
    buf.append( "Row " + i + ":\n\t" );
    for( int j = 0; j < array[i].length; j++ )
      buf.append( "item " + j + ": "
                  + array[i][j] + "\t" );
```

```
      buf.append( "\n" );
    }

    contentArea.setText( buf.toString() );
    displayed = true;
  }

  if( obj instanceof Image ) {
    contentArea.setText( "Image" );
    diplayed = true;
  }

  if( obj instanceof InputStream ) {
    int c;
    StringBuffer buf = new StringBuffer( );

    while( (c = ((InputStream) obj).read( )) != -1 )
      buf.append( (char) c );

    contentArea.setText( buf.toString( ) );
    displayed = true;
  }

  if( !displayed ) {
    contentArea.setText( "Don't know how to display "
      obj.getClass().getName( ) );
  }

  // Same code to display content type and length

} catch( IOException e ) {
  showStatus( "Error fetching \"" + target + "\": " + e );
  return;
}
```

The complete modified applet source is on the CD-ROM that accompanies this book as `urlFetcher_Mod.java` in the `tsvContentHandler` directory. Figure 24.2 shows what the applet will look like when displaying text/tab-separated-values. The file displayed in the figure is included on the CD-ROM as `example.tsv`.

Most HTTP daemons should return the correct content type for files ending in `.tsv`. Many Web browsers have a menu option that shows you information such as the content type about a URL (for example, the View | Document Info option in Netscape Navigator). You can use this feature to see what MIME type the sample data is being returned as. If the data does not show up as text/tab-separated-values, try one of the following things:

■ Ask your Webmaster to look at the MIME configuration file for your HTTP daemon. The Webmaster will either be able to tell you the proper file suffix or modify the daemon to return the proper type.

24

CONTENT AND
PROTOCOL
HANDLERS

■ If you can install CGI scripts on your Web server, you may want to look at a sample script on the CD-ROM that accompanies this book (named tsv.sh); it has the content handler example that returns data in the proper format.

FIGURE 24.2.

The urlFetcher_Mod *applet.*

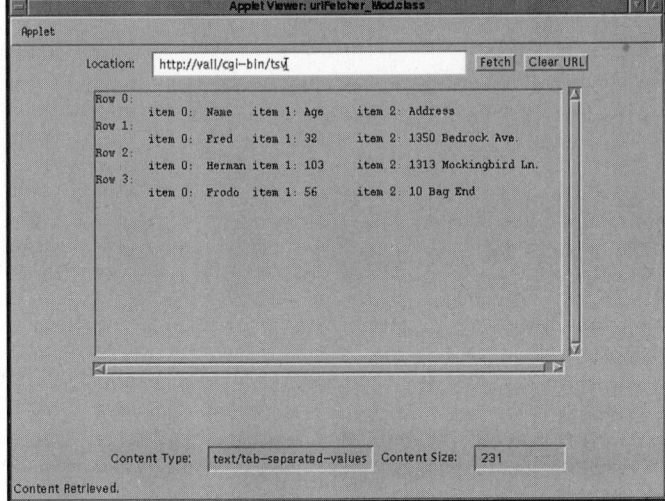

Summary

After reading this chapter, you should have an understanding of how Java can be extended fairly easily to deal with new application protocols and data formats. You now know what classes you have to derive your handlers from (URLConnection and URLStreamHandler for protocol handlers, ContentHandler for content handlers) and how to get Java to load the new handler classes.

CHAPTER 25

Client/Server Fundamentals

by George Reese

IN THIS CHAPTER

A network connects two or more computers together to perform tasks individual computers cannot do on their own. In business, government, education, and research, the network has been a common way of extending the power of the computer. On the simplest level, a network enables multiple users to share the same work. For example, almost anywhere you see a network, you see people working on the same documents and spreadsheets.

On a more complex level, a network enables a single computer to share the hardware resources of other computers. One computer may be a powerful graphics machine and another may be a powerful number cruncher. If you put the two together, you can perform tasks that require both heavy graphics and heavy number crunching in an optimized fashion.

Over the past decade, the client/server architecture has grown to be the most common design for network applications. Client/server is based on the idea that one computer specializing in information presentation displays the data stored and processed on a remote machine.

Today, the Internet provides home computers with the same networking power institutions outside the home have traditionally used. Many of the Internet applications you have come to know are client/server applications: the Web, e-mail, ftp, telnet, and so on. Specifically, your home PC serves as the *client* side of the architecture. It displays information located on *servers* around the world.

This chapter takes a look at the basics of client/server programming and how Java supports the client/server architecture. The first step, of course, is to understand exactly what it is that the client/server architecture tries to accomplish. We then take a look at the basic building blocks of client/server programming: sockets. Finally, we take a look at ways we can extend that architecture to build powerful Internet applications.

Basic Client/Server Architecture

The most basic form of the client/server architecture involves two computers: one computer, the server, is responsible for storing some sort of data and handing it to the other computer, the client, for user interaction. The user can modify that data and save it back to the server. The Web implements this simple form of client/server architecture for multiple client machines. Your computer, the client, uses a Web browser to display HTML documents stored across the Internet on a Web server.

There are four software components to the Web system:

- A browser such as Netscape that displays HTML documents on a client machine.
- A server program running on the server that hands HTML documents to client browsers.
- The HTML documents stored on the server machine.
- The communications protocol that handles the communication of data between the client and server.

The diagram in Figure 25.1 shows how this architecture fits together.

FIGURE 25.1.
The client/server architecture of the Web.

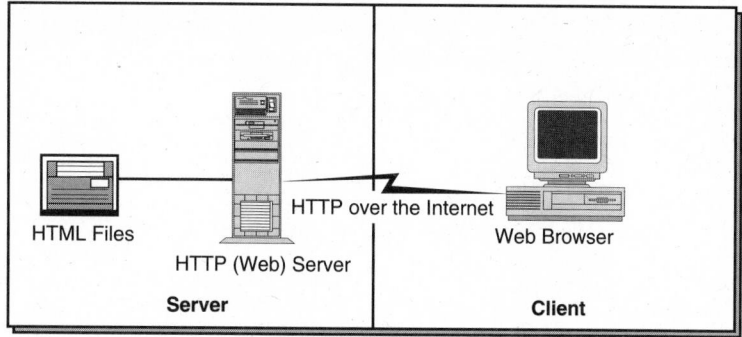

Dividing the Work

The client/server architecture provides us with a logical breakdown of application processing. In an ideal environment, the server side of the application handles all common processing, and the client side handles user-specific processing. With the Web, the server stores the HTML documents that are shown to all the clients. Each client, on the other hand, has different display needs. For example, a user at a dummy terminal is limited to using the character-mode Lynx client. A Windows user, on the other hand, can use a GUI browser to use the power of the graphical interface to display the document using full multimedia. The presentation of the HTML documents presented by the server is thus left up to the client.

Client/Server Communication

Internet applications communicate using Internet Protocol (IP) sockets. IP is a basic networking protocol on top of which other protocols exist to serve varying purposes. The details of how IP works are very boring and, outside of addressing, are fortunately unimportant to anyone who wants to write network applications.

Each computer in an IP network has an *IP address*, which is a 32-bit number usually broken into four 8-bit quads. An IP address looks like this: 206.11.201.18. The first two numbers (the high-order bits) form the network address. The low-order bits specify which computer on that network the address is for. Using this multinetwork addressing scheme, computers on different networks can communicate with each other.

IPV6: THE NEXT GENERATION

The current 32-bit scheme can address 4 billion hosts on 16.7 million networks. Optimistic projections suggest that we will run out of these addresses some time between 2005 and 2011. On November 17, 1994, the Internet Engineering Task Force (IETF) accepted a

continues

continued

recommendation for a new version of IP called IPng (IP: Next Generation) to handle this problem and related issues. This new IP specification, also called IPv6, uses a 128-bit addressing scheme. Under pessimistic projections, IPng provides 1,564 IP addresses for each square meter of the planet Earth. Optimistic projections suggest that it will provide over 3 quintillion addresses for each square meter of the Earth's surface. This new specification is designed to interoperate with the existing IP standards so that each machine on the Internet can simply do a software upgrade when ready.

When I want to send some information from my machine to yours, my application uses your machine's IP address to send that data to your machine. If your machine has the address 199.199.181.120, for example, my machine first checks whether it knows where that specific IP address is. Because my machine is a simple client on the 206.11 network, it is very unlikely that it has any idea where your machine is. But it *does* know of a *default gateway* machine to which it sends data for all unknown computers.

When a gateway receives data addressed for a specific IP, it in turn checks to see whether it knows about the specific computer in question. In this case, my default gateway is likely a router for my local network. It probably knows about the existence of machines only on the local network. It thus forwards my data onto its default gateway, which is responsible for knowing about a lot of networks. Although this router also does not know where the 199.199.181.120 machine is, it does have a specific gateway for the 199.199 network. It therefore forwards the data to that gateway. After traveling through a series of gateways, the data eventually reaches a machine that knows exactly where your machine can be found. Figure 25.2 shows the flow of how a machine handles each set of IP data (also referred to as a *packet*).

On any given machine, you may have a lot of applications communicating with other computers on the network. The packet I sent you now has to be able to tell your machine exactly which application it is destined for. It does this using the final piece to IP addressing: the port number. Just as an apartment number tells the post office which apartment in a building a specific letter should be sent to, a port number tells a computer which application should receive an IP packet.

NOTE

With all this talk about IP numbers, you may be wondering how IP names fit into the picture. IP names are actually aliases placed on top of IP through a system called DNS (Domain Name Service). DNS provides a system for turning names such as byzantium.imaginary.com into numbers like 206.11.201.18 and then reversing the process. It is important to note that IP itself has no knowledge of machines names; such processing is handled at a higher level.

FIGURE 25.2.

How a computer handles an IP packet.

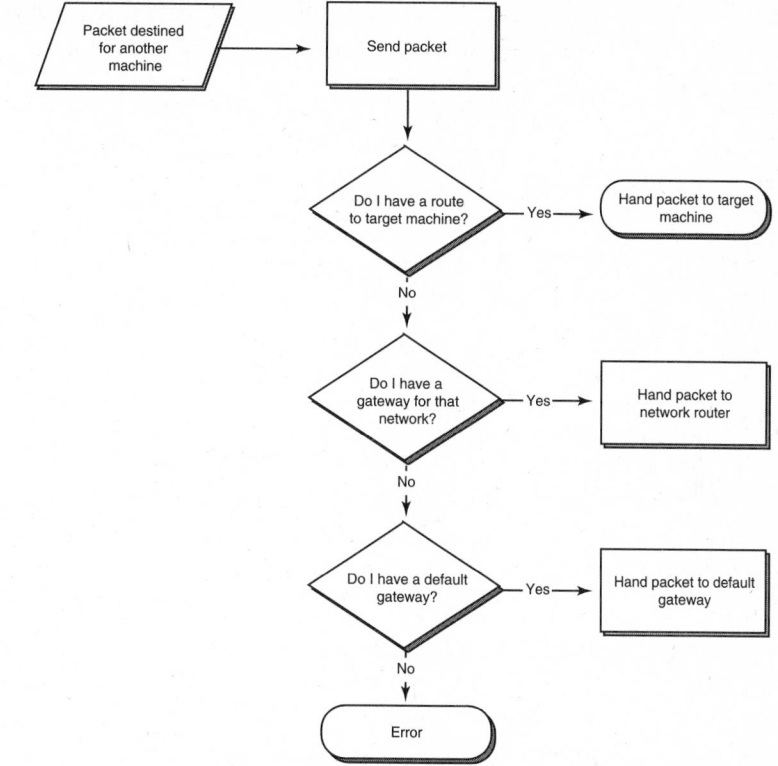

However, all you really need to know about IP specifically is how to address the data you want to send. In fact, the port number just described is not even part of the IP. IP simply describes how to get a packet from point A to point B. Any network application you write will instead be coded against higher level protocols which, in turn, handle IP management. The two most common protocols are these:

- TCP/IP (Transmission Control Protocol/Internet Protocol)
- UDP/IP (User Datagram Protocol/Internet Protocol)

TCP/IP, referred to in older texts as DARPA Internet Protocols, is actually a suite of protocols that provides applications with a reliable data communication layer. When you send a TCP/IP packet, you know either that the packet will reach its destination or that you will be informed of any problems with the transmission of the data. All this is done by encapsulating packet transmission inside a network session. When you want to communicate with another computer using TCP/IP, you create a connection that allows you to send multiple packets. The target application is listening to the network on a target port. Your client application connects to that listen port and negotiates a new private port through which data can be transmitted for as long as the connection is open.

The downside to TCP/IP is the overhead required to manage all that error handling as well as the need to take up ports on both machines to maintain a constant connection. UDP/IP, on the other hand, is a protocol for transmitting packets across the network without the reliability overhead incurred by TCP/IP. If you use UDP/IP, your application sends individual packets (called *datagrams*) to the target computer's listen port and hopes for the best. Sometimes the packets get to their destination, sometimes they do not. For a detailed discussion of socket programming, take a look at Chapter 26, "Java Socket Programming."

Using TCP/IP

Our client/server application starts with the server. Java provides a ServerSocket class that listens to a port and waits for clients to connect. When an application creates a ServerSocket, it passes a port number to the constructor. The application then repeatedly calls the ServerSocket accept() method. That method blocks application processing until a client connects. Once a client does connect, accept() returns a Java Socket object representing the connection to the client machine. The server then creates a new thread for the processing of data related to this connection. The listen thread calls accept() to wait for the next connection. Listing 25.1 shows the basic flow of server processing.

Listing 25.1. Basic server processing using the Java TCP/IP classes.

```java
import java.net.ServerSocket;
import java.net.Socket;

public class Server implements Runnable {
  private Socket client;

  public Server(Socket socket) {
    Thread thread;

    client = socket;
    thread = new Thread(this);
    thread.start();
  }

  static public void main(String args[]) {
    ServerSocket listen_socket;

    try {
      listen_socket = new ServerSocket(10000);
    }
    catch( java.io.IOException e ) {
      System.err.println("Failed to create listen socket.");
      e.printStackTrace();
      System.exit(-1);
      return;
    }
    while( true ) {
      Socket socket;
      try {
```

```
      socket = listen_socket.accept();
      new Server(socket);
    }
    catch( java.io.IOException e ) {
      e.printStackTrace();
    }
  }
}

public void run() {
  // Handle all processing for a specific client here
}
}
```

On both the client and server ends, your application sends and receives data through Socket objects. The run() method in the Server in Listing 25.1 is used to get and receive information from the client. For each instance of the Server class created from the static main() method, the application has a corresponding instance of the Socket class to communicate with a specific client.

As with other forms of I/O, socket I/O is managed with the Java streams. Listing 25.2 shows how we can implement the run() method of a Server class to simply echo information the client sends back to it.

Listing 25.2. The run() method from the Server class.

```
public void run() {
  java.io.DataInputStream input;
  java.io.PrintStream output;
  String data;

  try {
    input = new java.io.DataInputStream(client.getInputStream());
    output = new java.io.PrintStream(client.getOutputStream());
  }
  catch( java.io.IOException e ) {
    e.printStackTrace();
    return;
  }
  while( true ) {
    try {
      data = input.readLine();
      output.println("Received (" + data.length() + "): " + data);
    }
    catch( java.io.IOException e ) {
      break;
    }
  }
}
```

You can test this program using the telnet client to connect to port 10000 on the machine running the Server application. To do this, type **telnet localhost 10000** at your UNIX or DOS command line. When using the telnet application for testing, however, you should keep in mind that telnet is a protocol on top of TCP/IP. It actually sends more characters than you type as part of its protocol. Because the Server application does not know the telnet protocol, it ends up sending back to you what you typed plus all the telnet protocol information.

Of course, it may be more useful to try out the Server application using an application that shows how a client uses Java sockets. Listing 25.3 shows such a client application.

Listing 25.3. A Java client application.

```java
import java.net.Socket;

public class Client {
  static public void main(String args[]) {
    Socket socket;

    try {
      java.io.DataInputStream input;
      java.io.PrintStream output;

      socket = new Socket("localhost", 10000);
      while( true ) {
        try {
          String tmp;
          java.io.DataInputStream user_input =
            new java.io.DataInputStream(System.in);

          input = new java.io.DataInputStream(socket.getInputStream());
          output = new java.io.PrintStream(socket.getOutputStream());
          tmp = user_input.readLine();
          output.println(tmp);
          tmp = input.readLine();
          System.out.println(tmp);
        }
        catch( java.io.IOException e ) {
          e.printStackTrace();
          return;
        }
      }
    }
    catch( java.io.IOException e ) {
      e.printStackTrace();
    }
  }
}
```

Because of the way Java sockets are engineered, client and server operations are nearly identical. The major differences are that the server communicates with multiple clients but the client communicates with only a single server, and that the server has to create a listen port for initial connections.

What we have developed in this chapter so far simply takes raw data from one end and sends it right back. In a real application, we probably want something more like a dialog to occur between the client and server applications—we want to interpret the data. Once you have the basic blocks for communicating between the client and server, you need to build your own customer protocol on top of that communication layer to give that data meaning.

Using UDP/IP

You may wonder at first why you would use an unreliable communications protocol like UDP. After all, if you are sending data, can't you assume that you want it to get to its destination? Not necessarily. Sometimes, an application sends information, and the arrival of individual packets is unimportant. For example, a server repeatedly broadcasting sports scores 24 hours a day does not really care whether a given score arrives at its destination. It does care, however, about the overhead any error correction might introduce. Such an application is a perfect situation for UDP/IP.

Listing 25.4 shows a `DatagramServer` class that performs two main tasks:

1. Listens for incoming datagram packets from clients that request scores to be sent to them.

2. Sends out scores to all clients who have shown interest.

Listing 25.4. A simple datagram server.

```
import java.net.DatagramPacket;
import java.net.DatagramSocket;
import java.net.InetAddress;

public class DatagramServer implements Runnable {
  private java.util.Hashtable listeners = new java.util.Hashtable();

  public DatagramServer() {
    Thread thread = new Thread(this);
    thread.start();
  }

  static public void main(String args[]) {
    DatagramSocket socket;
    DatagramPacket packet;
    DatagramServer server;
    byte[] buffer = new byte[255];

    server = new DatagramServer();
    packet = new DatagramPacket(buffer, buffer.length);
    try {
      socket = new DatagramSocket(10000);
    }
    catch( java.net.SocketException e ) {
      e.printStackTrace();
      return;
```

25

continues

Listing 25.4. continued

```java
        }
      while( true ) {
        String tmp;

        try {
          socket.receive(packet);

          tmp = new String(buffer, 0, 0, packet.getLength());
          if( tmp.equals("close") ) {
            server.removeListener(packet.getAddress());
          }
          else {
            server.addListener(packet.getAddress());
          }
        }
        catch( java.io.IOException e ) {
          e.printStackTrace();
        }
      }
    }

    public void run() {
      while(true) {
        synchronized(listeners) {
          java.util.Enumeration addresses = listeners.keys();

          // Send a score to the current list
          while( addresses.hasMoreElements() ) {
            InetAddress addr = (InetAddress)addresses.nextElement();
            DatagramPacket packet;
            DatagramSocket socket;
            String str = "a score";
            byte[] msg = new byte[str.length()];

            try {
              socket = new DatagramSocket();
            }
            catch( java.net.SocketException e ) {
              e.printStackTrace();
              break;
            }
            str.getBytes(0, msg.length, msg, 0);
            try {
              packet = new DatagramPacket(msg, msg.length, addr, 11000);
              socket.send(packet);
            }
            catch( java.io.IOException e ) {
              e.printStackTrace();
            }
          }
        }
        // unsynchronize the listeners and allow any new additions
        try {
          Thread.sleep(500);
        }
        catch( InterruptedException e ) {
```

```
      }
      // remove old listeners
      synchronized(listeners) {
        java.util.Enumeration addresses = listeners.keys();

        while(addresses.hasMoreElements()) {
          InetAddress addr = (InetAddress)addresses.nextElement();
          int count = ((Integer)listeners.get(addr)).intValue();

          if( count > 1200 ) {
            listeners.remove(addr);
          }
          else {
            listeners.put(addr, new Integer(count + 1));
          }
        }
      }
    }
  }

  public void addListener(InetAddress ip) {
    listeners.put(ip, new Integer(0));
  }

  public void removeListener(InetAddress ip) {
    listeners.remove(ip);
  }
}
```

For simplicity's sake, this example simply sends the string a score out repeatedly. For a real application, you would, of course, want to provide the server with some way of retrieving real scores instead. Listing 25.5 is equally simple. It connects to the server and displays the scores as they come across.

Listing 25.5. A corresponding datagram client for displaying scores from the server.

```
import java.net.DatagramPacket;
import java.net.DatagramSocket;
import java.net.InetAddress;

public class DatagramClient {
  static public void main(String args[]) {
    DatagramSocket socket;
    DatagramPacket packet;
    byte[] buffer = new byte[255];
    int count = 0;

    packet = new DatagramPacket(buffer, buffer.length);
    try {
      socket = new DatagramSocket(11000);
    }
    catch( java.net.SocketException e ) {
      e.printStackTrace();
      return;
```

25

CLIENT/SERVER
FUNDAMENTALS

continues

Listing 25.5. continued

```java
  }
  try {
    DatagramPacket p;
    DatagramSocket s;
    String str = "keep alive";
    byte[] msg = new byte[str.length()];

    count = 0;
    try {
      s = new DatagramSocket();
      str.getBytes(0, msg.length, msg, 0);
      p = new DatagramPacket(msg, msg.length,
                        InetAddress.getByName("localhost"), 10000);
      s.send(packet);
    }
    catch( java.net.SocketException e ) {
      e.printStackTrace();
    }
  }
  catch( java.io.IOException e ) {
    e.printStackTrace();
  }
  while( true ) {
    String tmp;

    count++;
    try {
      socket.receive(packet);

      tmp = new String(buffer, 0, 0, packet.getLength());
      System.out.println(tmp);
    }
    catch( java.io.IOException e ) {
      e.printStackTrace();
    }
    if( count > 5000 ) {
      DatagramPacket p;
      DatagramSocket s;
      String str = "keep alive";
      byte[] msg = new byte[str.length()];

      count = 0;
      try {
        s = new DatagramSocket();
      }
      catch( java.net.SocketException e ) {
        e.printStackTrace();
        break;
      }
      str.getBytes(0, msg.length, msg, 0);
      try {
        p = new DatagramPacket(msg, msg.length,
                          InetAddress.getByName("localhost"), 10000);
        s.send(packet);
      }
    }
```

```
        catch( java.io.IOException e ) {
          e.printStackTrace();
        }
      }
    }
  }
}
```

UDP/IP sockets require a lot more base manipulation than do TCP/IP sockets because you have to make a new connection for every single packet you send. The payoff is enhanced performance for communication, which does not depend on any one socket actually arriving at its destination.

Two-Tier versus Three-Tier Design

Now that you understand how to make computers talk to one another on the Internet with Java, it helps to understand how to design any client/server application you might build. As discussed earlier, the client/server architecture assigns processing responsibility where it logically belongs. A simple system can be broken into two layers: a server where data and common processing occurs and a client where user-specific processing occurs. This kind of architecture is more commonly known as a *two-tier architecture*. For the types of applications we have discussed, a simple two-tier breakdown works well.

Business applications—and, increasingly, Internet applications—are generally much more complex than the applications discussed in this chapter. These kinds of applications can involve relational databases and complex server-side processing. Client machines are becoming increasingly powerful. At the same time, the benefit of client/server development has enabled applications to move processing off the server and onto the client to facilitate the use of cheaper servers. This trend has led to what is known as the problem of the fat client.

A *fat client* in a client/server system is a client that has absorbed an inordinate amount of the system's processing needs. Although a fat client architecture is as capable as any other client/server configuration, it is harder to scale as your application grows over time. Using a common client/server tool such as PowerBuilder, your client application has direct knowledge of exactly how your data is stored and what it looks like in the data store (usually a database). If you ever change where that data is stored or how it is stored, you have to do significant rework of your client application.

The solution to the problem of the fat client is a three-tier client/server architecture that creates another layer of processing across the network. In Figure 25.3, you can see how the three-tier design divides application work into the following three tasks:

- User interface
- Data processing or business rules
- Data storage

FIGURE 25.3.
*The three-tier client/
server architecture.*

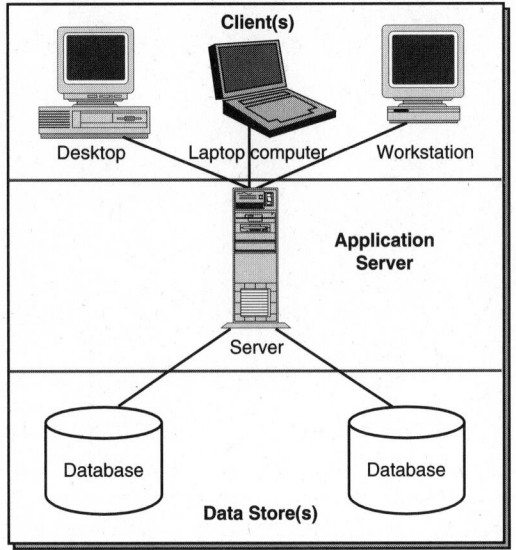

One of the primary advantages of a three-tier architecture is that, as your data storage needs grow, you can change the way data is stored without affecting your clients. The middle layer of the system, commonly referred to as the *application server*, can thus concentrate on centralizing business rule processing. (Business rule processing is the processing of data going to and from clients in a way that is common to all clients.)

Beyond Sockets

This chapter has outlined the nuts and bolts of how communication between machines works in a client/server environment and how you might construct client/server applications to best perform the tasks you need them to perform. Much of the code you have seen in this chapter, unfortunately, really has little to do with the central job your application is doing. It is simply about making two or more computers talk to each other.

New technologies are on the horizon to help deliver you from the tedium of socket programming in a client/server environment. The most exciting of these technologies is distributed objects. A *distributed application* is a single application that has individual objects located on many machines. In an ideal world, these objects communicate with one another through simple method calls. Unfortunately, the ideal world is not here yet.

With the 1.1 release, Java provides a new API designed to allow you to distribute your Java applications. This new API, called Remote Method Invocation (RMI), enables a program on one machine to communicate with a program on another machine using simple Java method calls. Instead of writing a complex socket interface and application-specific communication protocol, your application acts as if all the separate pieces were part of a single program on one machine. You call methods in any object, no matter where they exist, just as you do any other Java method.

A discussion of RMI is beyond the scope of this chapter. Nevertheless, as a seamless method-based communication API, RMI does provide an attractive alternative to writing socket code. Unfortunately, RMI works only when all the pieces of your application are Java pieces. In a hybrid system, sockets provide the best method of enabling communication among networked machines.

Summary

The client/server architecture is a very powerful design used by almost every application you use on the Internet. At its core, it is simply about making an application on one computer talk with an application on another computer. On the Internet, this is always done using the keystone of the Internet: IP.

In most of the applications you build today, you use Java's socket objects to do TCP/IP and UDP/IP communication. Understanding how these protocols work is not only critical to writing client/server applications that use the Java socket code, but it is also key to understanding the problems that can occur using any protocols built on top of them—such as RMI.

Java Socket Programming

by Stephen Ingram

IN THIS CHAPTER

CHAPTER

26

For full Java client/server applet connectivity, an applet server is required. This chapter initiates the development of a Java HTTP server. Before beginning the development of the server, however, you need some background knowledge of socket programming. This chapter begins with a socket overview followed by an exploration of Java's socket classes. The remainder of the chapter focuses on the construction of a Java HTTP Web server.

After reading this chapter, you should be able to do the following:

- Understand the socket abstraction
- Know the different modes of socket operation
- Have a working knowledge of the HTTP protocol
- Be capable of applying the Java socket classes
- Understand applet socket use and limitations
- Comprehend the HTTP Java server

An Introduction to Sockets

The computers on the Internet are connected by the TCP/IP protocol. In the 1980s, the Advanced Research Projects Agency (ARPA) of the U.S. government funded the University of California at Berkeley to provide a UNIX implementation of the TCP/IP protocol suite. What was developed was termed the *socket interface* (although you may hear it called the Berkeley-socket interface or just Berkeley sockets). Today, the socket interface is the most widely used method for accessing a TCP/IP network.

A *socket* is nothing more than a convenient abstraction. It represents a connection point into a TCP/IP network, much like the electrical sockets in your home provide a connection point for your appliances. When two computers want to converse, each uses a socket. One computer is termed the *server*—it opens a socket and listens for connections. The other computer is termed the *client*—it calls the server socket to start the connection. To establish a connection, all that's needed is a server's destination address and port number.

Each computer in a TCP/IP network has a unique address. *Ports* represent individual connections within that address. This is analogous to corporate mail—each person within a company shares the same address, but a letter is routed within the company by the person's name. Each port within a computer shares the same address, but data is routed within each computer by the port number. When a socket is created, it must be associated with a specific port—this process is known as *binding to a port*.

Socket Transmission Modes

Sockets have two major modes of operation: connection-oriented and connectionless modes. *Connection-oriented sockets* operate like a telephone: they must establish a connection and then hang up. Everything that flows between these two events arrives in the same order it was sent.

26

Connectionless sockets operate like the mail: delivery is not guaranteed, and multiple pieces of mail may arrive in a different order than they were sent.

The mode you use is determined by an application's needs. If reliability is important, connection-oriented operation is better. File servers must have all their data arrive correctly and in sequence. If some data is lost, the server's usefulness is invalidated. Some applications—time servers, for example—send discrete chunks of data at regular intervals. If data were to get lost, the server would not want the network to retry because by the time the resent data arrived, it would be too old to have any accuracy. When you need reliability, be aware that it does come with a price. Ensuring data sequence and correctness requires extra processing and memory usage; this extra overhead can slow down the response times of a server.

Connectionless operation uses the User Datagram Protocol (UDP). A *datagram* is a self-contained unit that has all the information needed to attempt its delivery. Think of it as an envelope—it has a destination and return address on the outside and contains the data to be sent on the inside. A socket in this mode does not have to connect to a destination socket; it simply sends the datagram. The UDP protocol promises only to make a best-effort delivery attempt. Connectionless operation is fast and efficient, but not guaranteed.

Connection-oriented operation uses the Transport Control Protocol (TCP). A socket in this mode must connect to the destination before sending data. Once connected, the sockets are accessed using a *streams interface*: open-read-write-close. Everything sent by one socket is received by the other end of the connection in exactly the same order it was sent. Connection-oriented operation is less efficient than connectionless operation, but it's guaranteed.

Sun Microsystems has always been a proponent of internetworking, so it isn't surprising to find rich support for sockets in the Java class hierarchy. In fact, the Java classes have significantly reduced the skill needed to create a sockets program. Each transmission mode is implemented in a separate set of Java classes. This chapter discusses the connection-oriented classes first.

Java Connection-Oriented Classes

The connection-oriented classes within Java have both a client and a server representative. The client half tends to be the simplest to set up, so we cover it first.

Listing 26.1 shows a simple client application. It requests an HTML document from a server and displays the response to the console.

Listing 26.1. A simple socket client.

```
import java.io.*;
import java.net.*;
```

continues

Listing 26.1. continued

```java
/**
 * An application that opens a connection to a Web server and reads
 * a single Web page from the connection.
 */
public class SimpleWebClient {
    public static void main(String args[])
    {
        try
        {
            // Open a client socket connection
            Socket clientSocket1 = new Socket("www.javasoft.com", 80);
            System.out.println("Client1: " + clientSocket1);

            // Get a Web page
            getPage(clientSocket1);
        }
        catch (UnknownHostException uhe)
        {
            System.out.println("UnknownHostException: " + uhe);
        }
        catch (IOException ioe)
        {
            System.err.println("IOException: " + ioe);
        }
    }

    /**
     * Request a Web page using the passed client socket.
     * Display the reply and close the client socket.
     */
    public static void getPage(Socket clientSocket)
    {
        try
        {
            // Acquire the input and output streams
            DataOutputStream outbound = new DataOutputStream(
                clientSocket.getOutputStream() );
            DataInputStream inbound = new DataInputStream(
                clientSocket.getInputStream() );

            // Write the HTTP request to the server
            outbound.writeBytes("GET / HTTP/1.0\r\n\r\n");

            // Read the response
            String responseLine;
            while ((responseLine = inbound.readLine()) != null)
            {
                // Display each line to the console
                System.out.println(responseLine);

                // This code checks for EOF.  There is a bug in the
                // socket close code under Win 95.  readLine() will
                // not return null when the client socket is closed
                // by the server.
                if ( responseLine.indexOf("</HTML>") != -1 )
                    break;
            }
```

```
        // Clean up
        outbound.close();
        inbound.close();
        clientSocket.close();
    }
    catch (IOException ioe)
    {
        System.out.println("IOException: " + ioe);
    }
  }
}
```

NOTE

The examples in this chapter are coded as applications to avoid security restrictions. Run the code from the command line `java ClassName`.

Recall that a client socket issues a connect call to a listening server socket. Client sockets are created and connected by using a constructor from the `Socket` class. The following line creates a client socket and connects it to a host:

```
Socket clientSocket = new Socket("merlin", 80);
```

The first parameter is the name of the host you want to connect to; the second parameter is the port number. A host name specifies only the destination computer. The port number is required to complete the transaction and allow an individual application to receive the call. In this case, port number `80` was specified, the well-known port number for the HTTP protocol. Other well-known port numbers are shown in Table 26.1. Port numbers are not mandated by any governing body, but are assigned by convention—this is why they are said to be "well known."

Table 26.1. Well-known port numbers.

Service	*Port*
echo	7
daytime	13
ftp	21
telnet	23
smtp	25
finger	79
http	80
pop3	110

Because the `Socket` class is connection oriented, it provides a streams interface for reads and writes. Classes from the `java.io` package should be used to access a connected socket:

```
DataOutputStream outbound = new DataOutputStream( clientSocket.getOutputStream() );
DataInputStream inbound = new DataInputStream( clientSocket.getInputStream() );
```

Once the streams are created, normal stream operations can be performed. The following code snippet requests a Web page and echoes the response to the screen:

```
outbound.writeBytes("GET / HTTP/1.0\r\n\r\n);
String responseLine;
while ( (responseLine = inbound.readLine()) != null)
{
    System.out.println(responseLine);
}
```

When the program is done using the socket, the connection must be closed:

```
outbound.close();
inbound.close();
clientSocket.close();
```

Notice that the socket streams are closed first. All socket streams should be closed before the socket is closed. This application is relatively simple, but all client programs follow the same basic script:

1. Create the client socket connection.

2. Acquire read and write streams to the socket.

3. Use the streams according to the server's protocol.

4. Close the streams.

5. Close the socket.

Using a server socket is only slightly more complicated than using a client socket, as explained in the following section.

Server Sockets

 Listing 26.2 is a partial listing of a simple server application. The complete server example can be found on the CD-ROM that accompanies this book in `SimpleWebServer.java`.

Listing 26.2. A simple server application.

```
/**
 * An application that listens for connections and serves a simple
 * HTML document.
 */
class SimpleWebServer {
    public static void main(String args[])
    {
        ServerSocket serverSocket = null;
```

```java
        Socket clientSocket = null;
        int connects = 0;
        try
        {
            // Create the server socket
            serverSocket = new ServerSocket(80, 5);

            while (connects < 5)
            {
                // Wait for a connection
                clientSocket = serverSocket.accept();

                //Service the connection
                ServiceClient(clientSocket);
                connects++;
            }
            serverSocket.close();
        }
        catch (IOException ioe)
        {
            System.out.println("Error in SimpleWebServer: " + ioe);
        }
    }

    public static void ServiceClient(Socket client)
        throws IOException
    {
        DataInputStream inbound = null;
        DataOutputStream outbound = null;
        try
        {
            // Acquire the streams for IO
            inbound = new DataInputStream( client.getInputStream());
            outbound = new DataOutputStream( client.getOutputStream());

            // Format the output (response header and tiny HTML document)
            StringBuffer buffer = PrepareOutput();

            String inputLine;
            while ((inputLine = inbound.readLine()) != null)
            {
                // If end of HTTP request, send the response
                if ( inputLine.equals("") )
                {
                    outbound.writeBytes(buffer.toString());
                    break;
                }
            }
        }
        finally
        {
            // Clean up
            System.out.println("Cleaning up connection: " + client);
            outbound.close();
            inbound.close();
            client.close();
            client.close();
        }
    }
```

Servers do not actively create connections. Instead, they passively listen for a client connect request and then provide their services. Servers are created with a constructor from the ServerSocket class. The following line creates a server socket and binds it to port 80:

```
ServerSocket serverSocket = new ServerSocket(80, 5);
```

The first parameter is the port number on which the server should listen. The second parameter is optional. The API documentation indicates that this second parameter is a listen time, but in traditional sockets programming, the listen function's second parameter is the listen stack depth. As it turns out, this is also true for the second constructor parameter. A server can receive connect requests from many clients at the same time, but each call must be processed one at a time. The *listen stack* is a queue of unanswered connect requests. The preceding code instructs the socket driver to maintain the last five connect requests. If the constructor omits the listen stack depth, a default value of 50 is used.

Once the socket is created and listening for connections, incoming connections are created and placed on the listen stack. The accept() method is called to lift individual connections off the stack:

```
Socket clientSocket = serverSocket.accept();
```

This method returns a connected client socket used to converse with the caller. No conversations are ever conducted over the server socket itself. Instead, the server socket spawns a new socket in the accept() method. The server socket is still open and queuing new connection requests.

As you do with the client socket, the next step is to create an input and output stream:

```
DataInputStream inbound = new DataInputStream( clientSocket.getInputStream() );
DataOutputStream outbound = new DataOutputStream( clientSocket.getOutputStream() );
```

Normal I/O operations can now be performed by using the newly created streams. This server waits for the client to send a blank line before sending its response. When the conversation is finished, the server closes the streams and the client socket. At this point, the server tries to accept more calls. What happens when there are no calls waiting in the queue? The method waits for one to arrive. This behavior is known as *blocking*. The accept() method blocks the server thread from performing any other tasks until a new call arrives. When five connects have been serviced, the server exits by closing its server socket. Any queued calls are canceled.

NOTE

The SimpleServer application produces no output. To exercise it, you can either use a browser or the SimpleClient application from Listing 26.1. Both cases require the current machine's name. You can substitute localhost if you are unsure of your machine name. Browsers should be pointed to http://localhost/.

All servers follow the same basic script:

1. Create the server socket and begin listening.
2. Call the accept() method to get new connections.
3. Create input and output streams for the returned socket.
4. Conduct the conversation based on the agreed protocol.
5. Close the client streams and socket.
6. Go back to step 2 or continue to step 7.
7. Close the server socket.

Figure 26.1 summarizes the steps needed for client/server connection-oriented applications.

FIGURE 26.1.

Client and server connection-oriented applications.

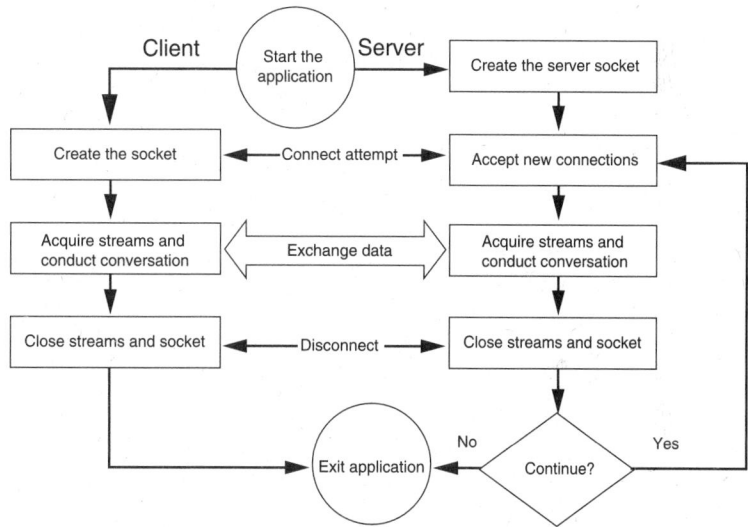

Iterative and Concurrent Servers

The client/server application just presented is known as an *iterative server* because the code accepts a client connection and completely processes it before it accepts another connection. More complex servers are *concurrent servers*: Instead of accepting connections and immediately processing them, a concurrent server spawns a new thread to process each new request, so it seems as though the server is processing many requests simultaneously. All commercial Web servers are concurrent servers.

Java Datagram Classes

Unlike the client and server portions of connection-oriented classes, the datagram versions of the client and server behave in nearly identical manners—the only difference occurs in implementation. For the datagram model, the same class is used for both client and server halves.

The following lines create client and server datagram sockets:

```
DatagramSocket serverSocket = new DatagramSocket( 4545 );
DatagramSocket clientSocket = new DatagramSocket();
```

The server specifies its port using the lone constructor parameter 4545. Because the client calls the server, the client can use any available port. The omitted constructor parameter in the second call instructs the operating system to assign the next available port number. The client could have requested a specific port, but the call would fail if some other socket had already bound itself to that port. It's better not to specify a port unless the intent is to be a server.

Because streams can't be acquired for communication, how do you talk to a DatagramSocket object? The answer lies in the DatagramPacket class.

Receiving Datagrams

The DatagramPacket class is used to receive and send data over DatagramSocket classes. The packet class contains connection information as well as the data. As was explained earlier, datagrams are self-contained transmission units. The DatagramPacket class encapsulates these units. The following lines receive data from a datagram socket:

```
DatagramPacket packet = new DatagramPacket(new byte[512], 512);
clientSocket.receive(packet);
```

The constructor for the packet must know where to place the received data. A 512-byte buffer is created and passed to the constructor as the first parameter. The second constructor parameter is the size of the buffer. Like the accept() method in the ServerSocket class, the receive() method blocks until data is available.

Sending Datagrams

Sending datagrams is really very simple; all that's needed is a complete address. Addresses are created and tracked using the InetAddress class. This class has no public constructors, but it does contain several static methods that can be used to create an instance of the class. The following list shows the public methods that create InetAddress class instances:

Public InetAddress *Creation Methods*

```
InetAddress getByName(String host);

InetAddress[] getAllByName(String host);

InetAddress getLocalHost();
```

Getting the local host is useful for informational purposes, but only the first two methods are actually used to send packets. Both getByName() and getAllByName() require the name of the destination host. The first method merely returns the first match it finds. The second method is needed because a computer can have more than one address. When this occurs, the computer is said to be *multi-homed*. The computer has one name, but multiple ways to reach it.

All the creation methods are marked as static. They must be called as follows:

```
InetAddress addr1 = InetAddress.getByName("localhost");
InetAddress addr2[] = InetAddress.getAllByName("localhost");
InetAddress addr3 = InetAddress.getLocalHost();
```

Any of these calls can throw an UnknownHostException. If a computer is not connected to a Domain Name Server (DNS), or if the host is really not found, an exception is thrown. If a computer does not have an active TCP/IP configuration, then getLocalHost() is likely to fail with this exception as well.

Once an address is determined, datagrams can be sent. The following lines transmit a string to a destination socket:

```
String toSend = "This is the data to send!";
byte[] sendbuf = new byte[ toSend.length() ];
toSend.getBytes( 0, toSend.length(), sendbuf, 0 );
DatagramPacket sendPacket = new DatagramPacket( sendbuf, sendbuf.length, addr,
➡port);
clientSocket.send( sendPacket );
```

First, the string must be converted to a byte array. The getBytes() method takes care of the conversion. Then a new DatagramPacket instance must be created. Notice the two extra parameters at the end of the constructor. Because this will be a send packet, the address and port of the destination must also be placed into the packet. An applet may know the address of its server, but how does a server know the address of its client? Remember that a datagram is like an envelope—it has a return address. When any packet is received, the return address can be extracted from the packet by using getAddress() and getPort(). This is how a server would respond to a client packet:

```
DatagramPacket sendPacket = new DatagramPacket( sendbuf, sendbuf.length,
    recvPacket.getAddress(), recvPacket.getPort() );
serverSocket.send( sendPacket );
```

Unlike connection-oriented operation, datagram servers are actually less complicated than the datagram client.

Datagram Servers

The basic script for datagram servers is as follows:

1. Create the datagram socket on a specific port.
2. Call receive() to wait for incoming packets.
3. Respond to received packets according to the agreed protocol.
4. Go back to step 2 or continue to step 5.
5. Close the datagram socket.

Listing 26.3 shows a simple datagram echo server. This server echoes back any packets it receives.

Listing 26.3. A simple datagram echo server.

```java
import java.io.*;
import java.net.*;

public class SimpleDatagramServer
{
    public static void main(String[] args)
    {
        DatagramSocket socket = null;
        DatagramPacket recvPacket, sendPacket;
        try
        {
            socket = new DatagramSocket(4545);
            while (socket != null)
            {
                recvPacket= new DatagramPacket(new byte[512], 512);
                socket.receive(recvPacket);
                sendPacket = new DatagramPacket(
                    recvPacket.getData(), recvPacket.getLength(),
                    recvPacket.getAddress(), recvPacket.getPort() );
                socket.send( sendPacket );
            }
        }
        catch (SocketException se)
        {
            System.out.println("Error in SimpleDatagramServer: " + se);
        }
        catch (IOException ioe)
        {
            System.out.println("Error in SimpleDatagramServer: " + ioe);
        }
    }
}
```

Datagram Clients

The corresponding client uses the same process with one exception: A client must initiate the conversation. The basic recipe for datagram clients is as follows:

1. Create the datagram socket on any available port.
2. Create the address to send to.
3. Send the data according to the server's protocol.
4. Wait for incoming data.
5. Go to step 3 (send more data), step 4 (wait for incoming data), or step 6 (exit).
6. Close the datagram socket.

Figure 26.2 summarizes the steps needed for client/server datagram applications. The symmetry between client and server is evident in this figure; compare Figure 26.2 with Figure 26.1.

FIGURE 26.2.

*Client and server
datagram applications.*

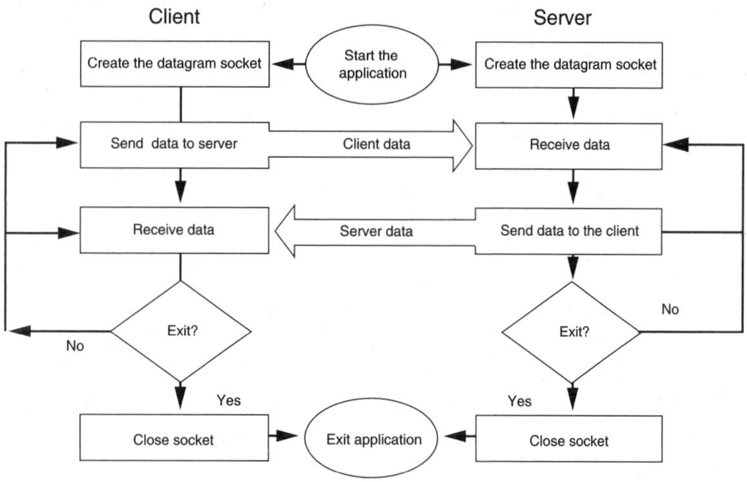

Listing 26.4 shows a simple datagram client. It reads user input strings and sends them to the echo server from Listing 26.3. The echo server sends the data right back, and the client prints the response to the console.

Listing 26.4. A simple datagram client.

```
import java.io.*;
import java.net.*;

public class SimpleDatagramClient
{
    private DatagramSocket socket = null;
    private DatagramPacket recvPacket, sendPacket;
    private int hostPort;

    public static void main(String[] args)
    {
        DatagramSocket socket = null;
        DatagramPacket recvPacket, sendPacket;
        try
        {
            socket = new DatagramSocket();
            InetAddress hostAddress = InetAddress.getByName("localhost");
            DataInputStream userData = new DataInputStream( System.in );
            while (socket != null)
            {
                String userString = userData.readLine();
                if (userString == null || userString.equals(""))
                    return;
                byte sendbuf[] = new byte[ userString.length() ];
```

continues

Listing 26.4. continued

```
                        userString.getBytes(0, userString.length(), sendbuf, 0);
                        sendPacket = new DatagramPacket(
                            sendbuf, sendbuf.length, hostAddress, 4545 );
                        socket.send( sendPacket );
                        recvPacket= new DatagramPacket(new byte[512], 512);
                        socket.receive(recvPacket);
                        System.out.write(recvPacket.getData(), 0,
                            recvPacket.getLength());
                        System.out.print("\n");
                    }
            }
            catch (SocketException se)
            {
                System.out.println("Error in SimpleDatagramClient: " + se);
            }
            catch (IOException ioe)
            {
                System.out.println("Error in SimpleDatagramClient: " + ioe);
            }
        }
}
```

All the examples so far have been Java applications. Running these in an applet presents an extra complication: security.

APPLET SECURITY AND SOCKETS

When writing applications, you don't have to be concerned with security exceptions. This changes when the code under development is executed from an applet. Browsers use very stringent security measures where sockets are concerned. An applet can open a socket only back to the host name from which it was loaded. If any other connection is attempted, a `SecurityException` is thrown.

Datagram sockets don't open connections, so how is security ensured for these sockets? When an inbound packet is received, the host name is checked. If the packet did not originate from the server, a `SecurityException` is immediately thrown. Obviously, sending comes under the same scrutiny. If a datagram socket tries to send to any destination except the server, a `SecurityException` is thrown. These restrictions apply only to the address, not the port number. Any port number on the host may be used.

An HTTP Server Application

Client applets need an HTTP Web server so that they can open sockets. If an applet is loaded into a browser from a hard drive, no socket activity is allowed to take place. This presents a significant hurdle to Java client applet development and testing. A simple solution is to write an HTTP server application. Once written, additional server threads can be added to provide all types of back-end connectivity.

HTTP Primer

Before diving into the project, you need some background information about the HTTP protocol. The Hypertext Transfer Protocol (HTTP) has been in use on the World Wide Web since 1990. All applet-bearing Web pages are sent over the Net with HTTP. Our server will support a subset of HTTP version 1.0 in that only file requests will be handled. As long as browser page requests can be fulfilled, the server will have accomplished its goal.

HTTP uses a stream-oriented (TCP) socket connection. Typically, port 80 is used, but other port numbers can be substituted. All the protocol is sent in plain-text format. An example of a conversation was demonstrated in Listings 26.1 and 26.2. The server listens on port 80 for a client request, which takes this format:

```
GET FILE HTTP/1.0
```

The first word is referred to as the "method" of the request. Table 26.2 lists all the request methods for HTTP/1.0.

Table 26.2. HTTP/1.0 request methods.

Method	Use
GET	Retrieve a file
HEAD	Retrieve only file information
POST	Send data to the server
PUT	Send data to the server
DELETE	Delete a resource
LINK	Link two resources
UNLINK	Unlink two resources

The second parameter of a request is a file path. Each of the following URLs is followed by the request that will be formulated and sent:

```
HTTP://www.qnet.com/
GET / HTTP/1.0

HTTP://www.qnet.com/index.html
GET /index.html HTTP/1.0

HTTP://www.qnet.com/classes/applet.html
GET /classes/applet.html HTTP/1.0
```

The request does not end until a blank line containing only a carriage return (\r) and a line feed (\n) is received. After the method line, a number of optional lines can be sent. Netscape Navigator 2.0 produces the following request:

```
GET / HTTP/1.0
Connection: Keep-Alive
User-Agent: Mozilla/2.0 (Win95; I)
Host: merlin
Accept: image/gif, image/x-xbitmap, image/jpeg, image/pjpeg, */*
```

Responses use a header similar to the request:

```
HTTP/1.0 200 OK
Content-type: text/html
Content-Length: 128
```

Like the request, the response header is not complete until a blank line is sent containing only a carriage return and a line feed. The first line contains a version identification string followed by a status code indicating the results of the request. Table 26.3 lists all the defined status codes. The server sends only two of these: 200 and 404. The text that follows the status code is optional. It may be omitted; if it is present, it might not match the definitions given in the table.

Table 26.3. HTTP response status codes.

Status Code	Optional Text Description
200	OK
201	Created
202	Accepted
204	No Content
300	Multiple Choices
301	Moved Permanently
302	Moved Temporarily
304	Not Modified
400	Bad Request
401	Unauthorized
403	Forbidden
404	Not Found
500	Internal Server Error
501	Not Implemented
502	Bad Gateway
503	Service Unavailable

Immediately after the response header, the requested file is sent. When the file is completely transmitted, the socket connection is closed. Each request-response pair consumes a new socket connection.

That's enough information for you to construct a basic Web server. Full information on the HTTP protocol can be retrieved from this URL:

HTTP://www.w3.org/

A Basic Web Server

The basic Web server follows the construction of the SimpleWebServer from Listing 26.2. Many improvements will be made to method and response handling. The simple server does not parse or store the request header as it arrives. The new Web server will have to parse and store the requests for later processing. To do this, you need a class to contain an HTTP request.

The HTTPrequest Class

Listing 26.5 shows the complete HTTPrequest class. The class must contain all the information that could be conveyed in a request header.

Listing 26.5. The HTTPrequest class.

```
import java.io.*;
import java.util.*;
import java.net.*;
import NameValue;

/**
 * This class maintains all the information from an HTTP request
 */
public class HTTPrequest
{
    public String version;
    public String method;
    public String file;
    public Socket clientSocket;
    public DataInputStream inbound;
    public NameValue headerpairs[];

    /**
     * Create an instance of this class
     */
    public HTTPrequest()
    {
        version = null;
        method = null;
        file = null;
        clientSocket = null;
        inbound = null;
        headerpairs = new NameValue[0];
```

continues

```
    }

    /**
     * Add a name/value pair to the internal array
     */
    public void addNameValue(String name, String value)
    {
        try
        {
            NameValue temp[] = new NameValue[ headerpairs.length + 1 ];
            System.arraycopy(headerpairs, 0, temp, 0, headerpairs.length);
            temp[ headerpairs.length ] = new NameValue(name, value);
            headerpairs = temp;
        }
        catch (NullPointerException npe)
        {
            System.out.println("NullPointerException while adding name-value: " +
➥npe);
        }
    }

    /**
     * Renders the contents of the class in String format
     */
    public String toString()
    {
        String s = method + " " + file + " " + version + "\n";
        for (int x = 0; x < headerpairs.length; x++ )
            s += headerpairs[x] + "\n";
        return s;
    }
}
```

The NameValue class simply stores two strings: name and value. You can find the source code for it in NameValue.java on the CD-ROM that accompanies this book. When you want to add a new pair, a new array is allocated. The new array receives a copy of the old array as well as the new member. The old array is then replaced with the newly created entity.

Two data fields in the class are not directly part of an HTTP request. The clientSocket member allows response routines to get an output stream; the inbound member allows easy closure after a request has been processed. The remaining members are all part of an HTTP request. The toString() method allows class objects to be printed using "plus notation." The following line displays the contents of a request by invoking the toString() method:

```
System.out.println("Request: " + request);
```

Now that the request container is finished, it's time to populate it.

The BasicWebServer Class

The BasicWebServer class is the main class for the server. It can be divided into request and response routines. Because this is a server, the request routines are activated first. After some validation, the response routines are called. Listing 26.6 shows the routines used to parse an HTTP request.

Listing 26.6. HTTP request routines.

```
/**
 * Read an HTTP request into a continuous String.
 * @param client a connected client stream socket
 * @return a populated HTTPrequest instance
 * @exception ProtocolException If not a valid HTTP header
 * @exception IOException
 */
public HTTPrequest GetRequest(Socket client)
    throws IOException, ProtocolException
{
    DataInputStream inbound = null;
    HTTPrequest request = null;
    try
    {
        // Acquire an input stream for the socket
        inbound = new DataInputStream(client.getInputStream());

        // Read the header into a String
        String reqhdr = readHeader(inbound);

        // Parse the string into an HTTPrequest instance
        request = ParseReqHdr(reqhdr);

        // Add the client socket and inbound stream
        request.clientSocket = client;
        request.inbound = inbound;
    }
    catch (ProtocolException pe)
    {
        if ( inbound != null )
            inbound.close();
        throw pe;
    }
    catch (IOException ioe)
    {
        if ( inbound != null )
            inbound.close();
        throw ioe;
    }
    return request;
}

/**
 * Assemble an HTTP request header String
 * from the passed DataInputStream.
 * @param is the input stream to use
```

continues

Listing 26.6. continued

```
 * @return a continuous String representing the header
 * @exception ProtocolException If a pre HTTP/1.0 request
 * @exception IOException
 */
private String readHeader(DataInputStream is)
    throws IOException, ProtocolException
{
    String command;
    String line;

    // Get the first request line
    if ( (command = is.readLine()) == null )
        command = "";
    command += "\n";

    // Check for HTTP/1.0 signature
    if (command.indexOf("HTTP/") != -1)
    {
        // Retreive any additional lines
        while ((line = is.readLine()) != null  &&  !line.equals(""))
            command += line + "\n";
    }
    else
    {
        throw new ProtocolException("Pre HTTP/1.0 request");
    }
    return command;
}

/**
 * Parsed the passed request String and populate an HTTPrequest.
 * @param reqhdr the HTTP request as a continous String
 * @return a populated HTTPrequest instance
 * @exception ProtocolException If name,value pairs have no ':'
 * @exception IOException
 */
private HTTPrequest ParseReqHdr(String reqhdr)
    throws IOException, ProtocolException
{
    HTTPrequest req = new HTTPrequest();

    // Break the request into lines
    StringTokenizer lines = new StringTokenizer(reqhdr, "\r\n");
    String currentLine = lines.nextToken();

    // Process the initial request line
    // into method, file, version Strings
    StringTokenizer members = new StringTokenizer(currentLine, " \t");
    req.method = members.nextToken();
    req.file = members.nextToken();
    if (req.file.equals("/")) req.file = "/index.html";
    req.version = members.nextToken();

    // Process additional lines into name/value pairs
    while ( lines.hasMoreTokens() )
    {
```

```
    String line = lines.nextToken();

    // Search for separating character
    int slice = line.indexOf(':');

    // Error if no separating character
    if ( slice == -1 )
    {
        throw new ProtocolException(
            "Invalid HTTP header: " + line);
    }
    else
    {
        // Separate at the slice character into name, value
        String name = line.substring(0,slice).trim();
        String value = line.substring(slice + 1).trim();
        req.addNameValue(name, value);
    }
  }
}
return req;
}
```

The `readHeader()` method interrogates the inbound socket stream searching for the blank line. If the request is not of HTTP/1.0 format, this method throws an exception. Otherwise, the resulting string is passed to `parseReqHdr()` for processing.

These routines reject any improperly formatted requests, including requests made in the older HTTP/0.9 format. Parsing makes heavy use of the `StringTokenizer` class found in the `java.util` package.

Normally, it is preferable to close the inbound stream as soon as the request has been completely read. If this is done, subsequent output attempts will fail with an `IOException`. This is why the inbound stream is placed into the `HTTPrequest` instance. When the output has been completely sent, both the output and the input streams are closed.

> **CAUTION**
>
> Do not be tempted to close an inbound stream after all input has been read. Closing the input stream causes subsequent output attempts to fail with an `IOException`. Close both streams only after all socket operations are finished.

Currently, the server makes no use of the additional lines in an HTTP request header. The `HTTPrequest` class does save them in an array, however, so they can be used in future enhancements. Wherever possible, the server has been written with future enhancements in mind.

Once you've built the request, you need to form a response. Listing 26.7 presents the response routines used by the server.

Listing 26.7. HTTP response routines.

```
/**
 * Respond to an HTTP request
 * @param request the HTTP request to respond to
 * @exception ProtocolException If unimplemented request method
 */
private void implementMethod(HTTPrequest request)
    throws ProtocolException
{
    try
    {
        if (debug && level < 4)
            System.out.println("DEBUG: Servicing:\n" + request);
        if ( (request.method.equals("GET") ) ||
             (request.method.equals("HEAD")) )
            ServicegetRequest(request);
        else
        {
            throw new ProtocolException("Unimplemented method: " + request.method);
        }
    }
    catch (ProtocolException pe)
    {
        sendNegativeResponse(request);
        throw pe;
    }
}

/**
 * Send a response header for the file and the file itself.
 * Handles GET and HEAD request methods.
 * @param request the HTTP request to respond to
 */
private void ServicegetRequest(HTTPrequest request)
    throws ProtocolException
{
    try
    {
        if (request.file.indexOf("..") != -1)
            throw new ProtocolException("Relative paths not supported");
        String fileToGet = "htdocs" + request.file;
        FileInputStream inFile = new FileInputStream(fileToGet);
        if (debug & level < 4)
        {
            System.out.print("DEBUG: Sending file ");
            System.out.print(fileToGet + " " + inFile.available());
            System.out.println(" Bytes");
        }
        sendFile(request, inFile);
        inFile.close();
    }
    catch (FileNotFoundException fnf)
    {
        sendNegativeResponse(request);
    }
    catch (ProtocolException pe)
    {
```

```
            throw pe;
        }
        catch (IOException ioe)
        {
            System.out.println("IOException: Unknown file length: " + ioe);
            sendNegativeResponse(request);
        }
    }

    /**
     * Send a negative (404 NOT FOUND) response
     * @param request the HTTP request to respond to
     */
    private void sendNegativeResponse(HTTPrequest request)
    {
        DataOutputStream outbound = null;

        try
        {
            // Acquire the output stream
            outbound = new DataOutputStream(
                request.clientSocket.getOutputStream());

            // Write the negative response header
            outbound.writeBytes("HTTP/1.0 ");
            outbound.writeBytes("404 NOT_FOUND\r\n");
            outbound.writeBytes("\r\n");

            // Clean up
            outbound.close();
            request.inbound.close();
        }
        catch (IOException ioe)
        {
            System.out.println("IOException while sending -rsp: " + ioe);
        }
    }

    /**
     * Send the passed file
     * @param request the HTTP request instance
     * @param inFile the opened input file stream to send\
     */
    private void sendFile(HTTPrequest request, FileInputStream inFile)
    {
        DataOutputStream outbound = null;

        try
        {
            // Acquire an output stream
            outbound = new DataOutputStream(
                request.clientSocket.getOutputStream());

            // Send the response header
            outbound.writeBytes("HTTP/1.0 200 OK\r\n");
            outbound.writeBytes("Content-type: text/html\r\n");
            outbound.writeBytes("Content-Length: " + inFile.available() + "\r\n");
```

continues

Listing 26.7. continued

```
            outbound.writeBytes("\r\n");

            // Added to allow browsers to process header properly
            // This is needed because the close is not recognized
             sleep(500);

            // If not a HEAD request, send the file body.
            // HEAD requests solicit only a header response.
            if (!request.method.equals("HEAD"))
            {
                byte dataBody[] = new byte[1024];
                int cnt;
                while ((cnt = inFile.read(dataBody)) != -1)
                    outbound.write(dataBody, 0, cnt);
            }

            // Clean up
            outbound.flush();
            outbound.close();
            request.inbound.close();
        }
        catch (IOException ioe)
        {
            System.out.println("IOException while sending file: " + ioe);
        }
    }
```

Only GET and HEAD requests are honored. The primary goal is to provide an applet server, not a full-featured Web server. File requests are all that are needed for applet loading, although additional handlers can certainly be added for other request methods. The serviceGetRequest() function handles all responses. When the input stream for a file is acquired, the file is opened. At this point, the routine knows whether the file exists and its size. Once a valid file is found, the sendFile() function can be called. The file is read and sent in 1K blocks. This keeps memory usage down while seeking to balance the number of disk accesses attempted. Negative responses are sent only for errors occurring after the request has been built. As a consequence, improperly formatted requests generate no response.

The response routines rely on ProtocolExceptions to signal error conditions. When one of these exceptions reaches the implementMethod() function, a negative response is sent. Notice the catch clause in serviceGetRequest(). The ProtocolException must be caught and thrown again, or the following IOException will catch the event. This happens because ProtocolException is a child class of IOException. If ProtocolException had been placed after the IOException, the compiler would have generated an error:

```
BasicWebServer.java:303: catch not reached.
```

 The remainder of the BasicWebServer application can be found on the CD-ROM that accompanies this book. The remaining code calls the input routine getRequest() and then the output routine implementMethod() for each client connection.

26

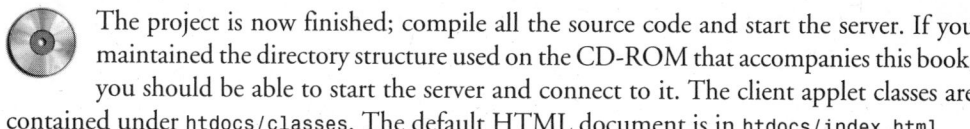 The project is now finished; compile all the source code and start the server. If you maintained the directory structure used on the CD-ROM that accompanies this book, you should be able to start the server and connect to it. The client applet classes are contained under `htdocs/classes`. The default HTML document is in `htdocs/index.html`.

Summary

In this chapter, you learned about the socket abstraction as well as the Java implementation of sockets. Remember that socket use requires at least two applications: a client and a server. The server waits for a client application to call and request attention. Multiple clients can make use of the same server—either at the same time (concurrent server) or one at a time (iterative server). Server behavior was demonstrated with the development of an iterative Java HTTP server. You should now have a working knowledge of HTTP and an appreciation for the limitations imposed by the socket security model. Namely, an applet can only open a socket back to the same server that loaded the applet.

Sockets provide a rich communications medium that allow your Java applications to exploit a wired world.

Multiuser Network Programming

by Michael Afergan

IN THIS CHAPTER

CHAPTER 27

Without doubt, Java is one of the more spectacular products to hit the computer market in recent years. Inasmuch as its initial support came from academia, most initial Java applets have been limited to decorative roles. However, now that Java's popularity has increased, Java has recently been used for more practical purposes. Applets have been used to provide live-time, ticker-like feeds and to create interactive environments for such purposes as retrieving financial information. In essence, by employing the power of Java, users can now do much of what they think they should be able to do on the Internet—but have not been able to do before.

One of the more exciting powers of Java is that it gives programmers the ability to create multiuser environments in which many users can interact and share information. In a simple multiuser environment such as the one in Figure 27.1, several users are connected to each other through a server running on a mutually accessible host. As a result, all actions by one user can instantaneously be displayed on the screens of other users across the world—without any requirement that the users know each other beforehand.

Figure 27.1.
A multiuser environment.

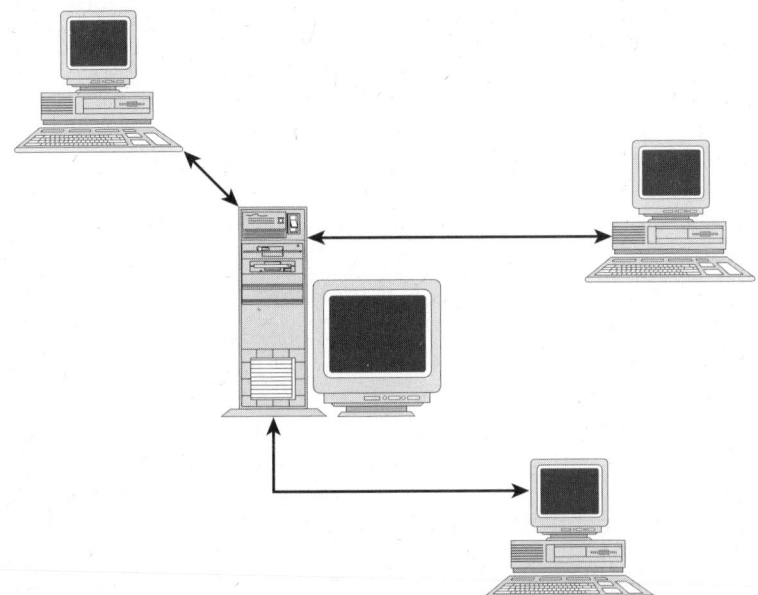

This ability to link computers in live time enables Java programmers to accomplish feats never before possible in a Web page. A business can now set up a system so that people who desire information can talk with a customer service representative directly on the Web page rather than sending e-mail to a service department. Moreover, because of the graphical nature of the Web and Java, the customer service representative can demonstrate information in a visual manner (for example, by pointing out items on a diagram). Additionally, an enterprising company can allow people from around the world to participate in a real-time live auction. In general, by facilitating multiple-user environments that enable such sharing of information, Java has the power to revolutionize the Web.

WHY JAVA?

The concept of servers, sockets, and communication is nothing new, nor is the idea of linking many users together in a live-time environment. In fact, the Web, without Java, can be considered a multiuser environment inasmuch as multiple users can access the same information in the form of a simple HTML page. Furthermore, methods exist by which a user can directly affect what another user sees on a given page (such as the hit counters found at the bottom of many HTML pages).

What, then, does Java offer that is so revolutionary? It offers the capacity to perform actions while the user is viewing the same HTML page. The architecture of the Web enables users to view Web pages from around the world. However, once this page is displayed on your screen, it cannot change. In the example of the hit counters—although more users may access the given page—you are never informed of this fact unless you reload that page. Java, however, brings life into Web pages by means of applets, enabling the pages to perform actions such as communicating with a server. Java enables programmers to create applets as potent and effective as the applications on your own computer. It is this capacity that enables us to create multiuser environments.

This chapter discusses the elements required to create a multiuser environment in Java. Although no entirely new topics in Java are presented, this chapter shows you how to bring several powerful aspects of Java together and highlights some of the more interesting applications of Java. Through explanation of the processes as well as sample code, this chapter enables you, the Java programmer, to code and establish your own multiuser environment. This chapter deals with subjects including the handling of the connections to the server, the graphical interface, and various animation and threading techniques necessary to make your applet Webworthy. Although each of these topics is explained with code, keep in mind that the essence of a multiuser environment is *what* you do, not *how* you do it. Furthermore, the code for each multiuser application depends heavily on the environment itself, and therefore is significantly different in each. Consequently, although the code offered here can supply you with a suitable framework, it may be advisable to envision your own multiuser application. As each topic is presented, imagine how you would deal with each of the issues involved. Remember that in programming—and Java in particular—the limits of the language are the limits of your imagination. Be creative and have fun!

SOCKETS AND NETSCAPE

With any new technology come new concerns and problems. Java is definitely not an exception to this rule. The chief concern of many has been the fact that Java applets can connect to servers from around the world and transmit information from the host that its

continues

continued

owner might not want to make public. Although there are several solutions to this problem, Netscape has chosen to place stringent restrictions on Java socket connections for now.

Currently, Java sockets can connect only to servers running on the host that served the applet. For example, an applet residing in `http://www.xyz.com/page.html` can connect back only to a server running on `www.xyz.com`. Therefore, when developing a multiuser environment as discussed in this chapter, make sure that the server to which the applet connects is running on the same host as the HTML page in which the applet resides. (See Chapter 35, "Java Security," for more details about applet security.)

Our Mission—Should We Choose to Accept It

In this chapter, we develop a multiuser environment for a museum that is opening an exhibition of Haphazard Art. The museum believes that the most beautiful art is created by human-controlled whims and has hired you to create an environment through which users from around the world can "weave" a quilt. The user should be able to access the Web page, select a color and a blank tile, and "paint" the tile. Not only should this tile change colors on the screen of the user, but it also should instantaneously become painted on the screens of all the users around the world who are working on that quilt. (The museum will then save these designs and display them at its upcoming exhibit.)

Although this is a rather simplistic example of the power of multiuser environments, it is an excellent model for the explanation of the concepts involved.

The Requirements of the Server

Although it is not of our direct concern, the server in this environment plays an extremely large role. Because the server can be written in virtually any language, we won't spend much time dealing with it here. However, it is necessary that we discuss the essentials for the server in a multiuser environment.

As you can see from Figure 27.1, the server acts as the intermediate agent between the various users. Thus, the server must be able to do the following:

- Accept multiple connections from clients on a given port
- Receive information from the clients
- Send information to the clients

As the application becomes more involved, it is necessary to add additional functionality to the server. Even in the simple example of the museum quilt, the server must keep track of the color of all the tiles. Furthermore, if a new client begins work on an in-progress quilt, it's necessary for the server to inform the client of the current status of the quilt.

Nevertheless, these subjects are extremely context-dependent and deal more with computer science than with Java. Therefore, we now move on to more exciting matters, such as the socket communication required to provide the interaction.

Integrating a Communication Class in Your Applet

For an effective implementation, it's necessary to create a class that handles all the interaction with the server. This class manages such responsibilities as connecting and disconnecting from the server as well as the actual sending and receiving of data. By encapsulating this functionality in a separate class, we can deal with our problem in a more effective and logical manner.

A more important reason for encapsulating this functionality in a separate class, however, is the fact that, in a multiuser environment, the applet must do two things at the exact same time: listen for user interactions (such as a mouse click) and listen for new information from the server. The best way to do this is to create a separate class to handle the server interaction and make that class a thread. (See Chapter 9, "Threads and Multithreading," for details on creating threads.) This threaded class runs continually for the lifetime of the applet, updating the quilt when required to do so. With this problem out of our hands, we can allow the applet class to respond to user interactions without worrying about the socket connection.

How to Connect to a Server

Assuming that we have a suitable server running, the actual communication is not a very complicated process. In essence, the applet needs only to connect to the server and read and write information to the appropriate streams. Conveniently, Sun has wrapped most of these methods and variables in the `java.net.Socket` class.

Here is the beginning of our `Client` class that handles the actual communication:

```
import java.net.Socket;
import java.io.*;

public class Client extends Thread
{

    private Socket soc;
    public void connect ()
    {
      String      host = "www.museum.com";
      int         port = 2600;

      soc = new Socket(host, port);
    }
}
```

Note that it is necessary for you to know both the name of the host on which the server is running as well as the port on which the server can accept connections.

In theory, the connect() method in the preceding class is sufficient to connect to a server on a known port. However, any experienced programmer knows that what works in theory does not always work in practice. Consequently, it is good practice to place all communication statements in a try-catch block. (Those unfamiliar with the throw and try-catch constructs can refer to Chapter 10, "Exception Handling.") In fact, forgetting to place all statements that deal with the server in a try-catch block will produce a compile-time error with the Java compiler.

Consequently, the preceding method should actually look like this:

```java
import java.net.Socket;
import java.io.*;

public class Client extends Thread
{
    private Socket soc;
    public boolean connect ()
    {
    String          host = "www.museum.com";
    int             port = 2600;

    try {
          soc = new Socket(host, port);
        }
    catch (Exception e)
         return(false);
    return(true);
    }
}
```

Note that the method now returns a boolean variable that corresponds to whether or not it was successful in connecting.

How to Communicate with the Server

Inasmuch as different situations require different constructs, Java supplies several options for the syntax of communication with a server. Although all such approaches can work, some are more useful and flexible than others. Consequently, what follows is a rather generic method of communicating with a server. Keep in mind that there are some nice wrapper methods in the java.io.InputStream subclasses that you may want to use to simplify the processing of the parsing involved with the communication.

Sending Information

Once we have established our connection, the output is then passed through the java.net.Socket.outputStream, which is a java.io.outputStream. Because OutputStream is a protected variable, however, we cannot reference it as simply as you may imagine. To access this stream, we must employ the java.net.Socket.getOutputStream() method. A simple method to send data resembles the following:

```
public boolean SendInfo(int choice) {
   OutputStream out;
   try {
         out = soc.getOutputStream();
         out.write(choice);
         out.flush();
      }
   catch (Exception e)
      return(false);
   return(true);
}
```

Although the preceding code is sufficient to send information across a socket stream, communication is not that simple in a true multiuser environment. Because we will have multiple clients in addition to the server, it is necessary to define a common protocol that all parties can speak. Although this may be as simple as a specific order to a series of integers, it is nevertheless vital to the success of the environment.

PROTOCOLS

Although we will adopt a rather simple protocol for this applet, there are a few issues you should keep in mind when developing more complex protocols:

- Preface each command with a title, such as a letter or short word. For example, B123 could be the command to buy property lot 123, and S123 could be the command to sell lot 123.

- Make all titles of the same format. Doing so makes parsing the input stream much easier. For example, B and S are good titles. B and Sell would cause some headaches.

- Terminate each command with a common character. Doing so signifies the end of information and also gives you a starting point in case some of the information becomes garbled. For the sake of simplicity, the newline character (\n) is usually best.

In the case of our quilt-making applet for the museum, each update packet consists of three things: the x-coordinate of the recently painted tile, the y-coordinate of the recently painted tile, and the color to be applied (which can also be represented by an integer). Additionally, we will use the newline character (\n) as our terminating character. All this can be accomplished with the following method:

```
public boolean SendInfo(int x, int y, int hue) {
   OutputStream out;

   try {
         out = soc.getOutputStream();
         out.write(x);
         out.write(y);
         out.write(hue);
         out.write('\n');
```

```
/*  Now flush the output stream to make sure that everything is sent. */
        out.flush();
    }
catch (Exception e)
    return(false);
return(true);
}
```

Reading Information

Another factor that complicates the reading of information from the socket is that we have absolutely no idea when new information will travel across the stream. When we send data, we are in complete control of the stream and thus can employ a rather simple method as we did earlier. When reading from the socket, however, we do not know when new information will arrive. Thus we need to employ a method that runs constantly in a loop. As discussed previously, the best way to do this is to place our code in the run() method of a threaded class.

A REFRESHER ON THREADS

Before we proceed in our development of this threaded subclass, it is important to review a key concept. As presented in Chapter 9, "Threads and Multithreading," a class that extends the definition of the java.lang.Thread class can continually execute code while other portions of the applet are running. Nevertheless, this is not true of all the methods of the threaded class.

Only the run() method has the power attributed to threads (namely the capacity to run independently of other operations). This method is automatically declared in every thread, but has no functionality unless you override the original declaration in your code. Although other methods can exist within the threaded subclass, remember that only the code contained in the run() method can execute concurrently with the rest of the processes in the application. Furthermore, remember that the run() method of class foo is begun by invoking foo.start() from the master class.

Also note that because we are overriding a method first declared in the java.lang.Runnable interface, we are forced to employ the original declaration: public void run(). Your code won't compile if you choose to use another declaration, such as public boolean run(). (We deal with ways of returning data in the section on sharing information, later in this chapter.)

What results from all this planning is the method shown in Listing 27.1. In reading it, pay attention to how we are able to stop the method from reading from the socket once the user is done; how the method deals with garbled input; and how the method returns information to the main applet. (You will be quizzed later!)

Listing 27.1. Our method to read information from the socket.

```
public void run() {
   int spot = 0;
   int stroke[];
   stroke = new int[10];                          // an array for storing the commands
   DataInputStream in;

   in = new DataInputStream(soc.getInputStream());

   while (running) {
      do {                                         // reads the information
         try {
               stroke[spot] = in.readByte();
            }
         catch (Exception e)
               stroke[spot] = '\n';   // restarts read on error
      } while (  (stroke[spot] != '\n') && (++spot < 9) );
                                       // reads until the newline flag or limit of
      spot = 0;                        // array
                                       // resets the counter
      quilt.sew(stroke[0],stroke[1],stroke[2]);
   }
}
```

Okay. Time is up. Here are the answers.

First of all, remember that we are designing this class to serve within a larger applet. It would be rather difficult for the Client class to decide when the "painting session" is over because it has no idea what is going on inside the applet. Thus, the applet, not the Client class, must have control of when the class will be looking for information. The best way to retain control of the run() method is to create a boolean field (running) inside the Client class itself. This variable can be set to true on connection to the server and can be set to false when the applet decides to close the connection. Thus, once the user has decided to close the connection, the run() method exits the while loop and runs through to its completion.

Second, remember that while we plan on receiving three integers followed by a newline character, in real life, things do not always work as we plan them. Inasmuch as we do not know exactly what the error will be, there is no ideal way of handling garbled information. The run() method in Listing 27.1 uses the newline character as its guide, and continues to read until it reaches one. If, however, there are nine characters before a newline character, it exits the do loop regardless and calls the sew() method. This means that the sew() method in our main applet must be well constructed to handle such errors.

Third, and most important, is the means by which the class returns data to the applet. As discussed earlier, this Client class will be a subclass of our main applet. Consequently, we will be able to call all public methods of the applet class. (In this example, the applet is referenced by the variable quilt.) Although we will discuss this process in more detail later, keep in mind that the last line of code simply passes the appropriate values to a method in the applet that will in turn process them:

```
quilt.sew(stroke[0],stroke[1],stroke[2]);
```

> ## A NOTE FOR ADVANCED READERS
>
> You will notice that in our example, all the information coming across the stream is read in the form of integers. Obviously, in the real world, other data types such as characters—or even mixed data types such as three numbers and a letter—could be passed. Although accommodating these data types would require slight alterations to the preceding code, doing so would not be a dramatic hack.
>
> Although you could deal with such a situation by having separate read() statements for each data type, remember the ASCII relationship between characters and numbers. Because the ASCII value of a number is 48 more than that number (for example, the ASCII value for '1' is 1 + 48), you can choose to read all the data in as integers and then translate certain values to their character equivalents—or vice versa, depending on how you sent the information to the server.
>
> Finally, keep in mind that serverInput is a basic java.lang.Inputstream that can be manipulated in several ways using the powers of the java.lang and java.io classes and methods. (See Chapter 12, "The Language Package," and Chapter 14, "The I/O Package," for more details on java.lang and java.io, respectively.)

How to Disconnect from the Server

So far, we have been able to connect to the server and communicate with it. From the point of view of the user, we have begun the application and have successfully painted our quilt. There is only one essential functionality we haven't included in our Client class thus far: the capacity to disconnect from the server.

Although the capacity to disconnect from the server may appear trivial, it is in fact very essential to a successful multiuser environment. A server can be constructed to accept numerous clients, but because of hardware constraints, there is an inherent limit to the number of clients a server can have connected at the same time. Consequently, if the socket connections remain open even when the clients leave, the server eventually becomes saturated with lingering sockets. In general, it's good practice to close sockets; doing so benefits all aspects of the environment, ranging from the Internet-access software the user is running to the person managing the server.

Without further ado, here is an appropriate disconnect() method for our Client class:

```
public boolean disconnect () {
    running = false;
```

```
try {
      soc.close()
   }
catch (Exception e)
   return(false);
return(true);
}
```

Although the code itself is nothing extraordinary, note the use of the boolean variable running (also used in the run() method). Remember that the function of the running variable is to serve as a flag that allows the client to listen to the socket stream. Inasmuch as we do not want the client to listen to the socket stream after the user has decided to disconnect, we set the variable to false in this method. Also note that the running = false statement comes *before* the soc.close() statement. This arrangement is made because regardless of the success of the disconnect statement, we no longer want to listen to the stream.

The Graphical Interface

Now that we have developed the framework of our Client subclass, let's switch gears to develop the applet class that will act as the heart of our application. Although it is not extremely intricate, the applet must be able to respond to user input and present the user with a friendly and attractive display. Fortunately, as a Web-based programming language, Java is very well suited for this. Each applet you create inherits various methods that enable it to respond to virtually anything the user can do. Furthermore, the java.awt package provides us with some excellent classes for creating good-looking interactive features such as buttons and text areas.

Responding to Input

The most important aspect of a graphical interface is its capacity to monitor the user's responses to the system. As you saw in Chapter 16, "The Windowing (AWT) Package," Java supplies us with an excellent system for doing this in the form of the java.awt.Event class. Additionally, the java.awt.Component class, of which java.applet.Applet is a subclass, provides many methods that we can use to catch and process events. These methods seize control of the applet under appropriate conditions and enable the applet to react to specific user events.

For our museum quilt applet, the user must be able to change the current color, select a tile, and quit the application. If we decide that the user will select the tile through a mouse click and will change colors and quit with the keyboard, we require two interactive methods from the java.awt.Component class: keyDown(*Event*, *int*) and mouseDown(*Event*, *int*, *int*).

In this setup, the keyboard has two purposes: to enable the user to change colors and to enable him or her to quit. If we choose to present the user with a pallet of numbered colors (0 to 9, for example) from which he or she can select, our keyDown() method can be as simple as this:

```
public boolean keyDown(Event evt, int key) {
    if ( (key >= '0') && (key <= '9') ) {        // if a valid key
            current_color = key - 48;            // converts ASCII key to
            return(true);                        // numeric equivalent
    }
    else if ( key = 'Q') {
            leave();                             // a method that will handle
            return(true);                        // cleanup
    }
    return(false);
}
```

In this method, current_color is a field that keeps track of the currently selected color.

If we declare museum to be an instance of the Client socket class (which we have almost completed), the mouseDown() method can be accomplished with the following code:

```
public boolean mouseDown(Event evt, int x, int y) {
    int x_cord, y_cord;

    if ( (x >= xoff) && (x =< xoff + xsize) && (y >= yoff) && (y =< yoff + ysize) {
                                        // checks to see if the click was within the
                                        // grid
        x_cord = (x - xoff)/scale;      // determines the x and y coordinates
        y_cord = (y - yoff)/scale;      // of the click
        museum.sendInfo(x_cord, y_cord, current_color);  // makes use of the
                                                         // sendInfo method to send
                                                         // the data
        return(true);                                    // the click was valid
    }
    return(false);                      // the click was outside the bounds of the
                                        // grid

}
```

Note that in the previous method, it is necessary to have already declared the x and y offsets, the size of each tile (scale), and the size of the grid itself as global fields of the class.

Displaying Information

Chapter 19, "Java Graphics Fundamentals," gave an overview of how to create a background and fill it in with whatever you want. In a dynamic graphical interface, however, various properties will change and thus must be tracked in some manner. Our quilt application may consist of nothing more than a single colored background on which tiles of different colors are drawn. Consequently, the only information we are concerned with is the colors (if any) that have been assigned to the individual tiles.

A simple way of doing this is to create an array of java.awt.Color (hues[ ]) and assign each color to be used a given value (hues[1] = Color.blue, for example). Thus, we can store the design in simple array of integers, such as tiles[ ][ ], with each integer element representing a color. If we do so, our paint() method can be accomplished by the following code:

```
public void paint(Graphics g) {
   for (int i = 0; i < size; i++) {
       for(int j = 0; j < size; j++) {
           g.setColor(hues[ (tiles[i][j]) ]);
           g.fillRect( (i*scale+xoff) , (j*scale+yoff), scale,scale);
       }
   }
}
```

Note that in the preceding example, g.fillRect((i*scale+xoff) , (j*scale+yoff), scale,scale) paints squares with length and width equal to a final field, scale. These squares are located on the grid with respect to the initial x and y offsets.

How to Thread the Client Class

So far, we have been successful in creating the interface that the user will find on our Web page, as well as some of the methods necessary to facilitate the user's interaction with the applet. We have also assembled a Client subclass that will serve as our means of communication. Our next step is to integrate the Client class within the applet class to produce a cohesive application.

Nevertheless, it is important to keep in mind that we are not using this subclass merely as a means of keeping the information separate. The main reason for creating a separate class is that, by making it a thread as well, we can perform two tasks *at the exact same time*.

> **NOTE**
>
> Although it may seem as if we can perform two tasks at the exact same time, this is not entirely true on a standard single-processor computer. What Java does (and other time-sharing applications such as Windows as well) is to allocate "time-slices" to each thread, allowing each thread to run for a brief moment before switching control to another thread. Because this process is automatically done by the Java virtual machine, and because the time for which a given thread is not running is so small, we can think of the two threads as running at the same time.

Although we almost forget about its existence, we must retain some control over the Client class. We do not want it to check for new commands before the socket connection has been opened or after it has been closed. Additionally, we want to be able to control socket events such as opening and closing in a manner that isolates them from the main applet, but also impacts the status of the run() method. Conveniently for us, we developed the Client class in such a manner: We kept the connect() and disconnect() methods separate entities, both of which have control over the run() method (by means of the boolean variable running).

Consequently, within the applet class, the code necessary to control communications is quite simple:

```
public class Project extends Applet {
    public Client museum;

         .
         .
         .

    public void init() {
        museum = new Client();

            .
            .

        museum.connect();
        museum.start();
    }

            .

    public void leave() {
        museum.disconnect();
    }
}
```

First of all, note that this is the first time we have dealt with the applet itself. So far, its only important property is that it is named `Project`.

Also note the use of the constructor `Client()`. Like any other class, the `Client` class requires not only a declaration, but also a `new` statement to actually create and allocate memory for the class. We deal with this constructor again in the next section.

Finally, note that we established the connection by means of the `museum.connect()` statement located in the `init()` method. Most likely (and in the case of the museum applet), you will want to establish the socket stream as soon as the applet starts up. The most logical place for the `museum.connect()` statement is in the `init()` method. Nevertheless, you can place this code anywhere you like in your applet. (You can, for example, have a Connect to Server button somewhere in your applet.)

CAUTION

Although giving the user the ability to initiate connection may be a good idea, be careful that you do not allow the same user to connect to the server more than once without first disconnecting. Neglecting to screen for multiple connections for the same user can lead to all sorts of headaches and improper results.

How to Share Information

We have created the framework of both the Project (applet) and Client classes and have begun the process of intertwining them by creating an instance of the Client class in the Project class. However, there is more to the interaction between the two classes than what we have seen thus far.

Remember that the purpose of the Client subclass is to provide information to the applet. Nevertheless, we are required to employ the run() method of the threaded Client class, which does not allow us to return information through a simple return() statement. Also, in most cases (as well as in the museum application), we must return several pieces of information (the x and y coordinates of the tile being painted as well as its color).

With a little construction, we can easily solve this problem. First, we must enable the Client class to refer to the Project class; this involves a few alterations to the Client class. The changes will allow the Client class to accept the Project applet class in its constructor method and make use of it during its lifetime:

```
public class Client extends Thread
{
    private Project quilt;

    public Client (Project proj) {
        quilt = proj;
    }
...
}
```

> **NOTE**
>
> In this setup, the parent class is required to pass itself as an argument to the constructor method. Therefore, when we add the code to do so to our program, the syntax resembles the following:
>
> ```
> museum = new Client(this);
> ```

What exactly does the preceding code accomplish? First, it establishes a constructor method for the Client class. (Remember that, as in C++, constructor methods must have the same name as the class itself.) Although this constructor may serve other purposes, its most important function is to accept a reference to a Project class as one of its arguments.

Further, the code creates a public variable, quilt, of type Project. By doing so, each method of the Client class can now reference all public methods and variables in the Project class. For example, if we had the following definitions in the Project class, the Client subclass could reference quilt.tiles_remaining and quilt.sew():

```
public int tiles_remaining;

public void sew(int x, int y, int hue) {
...
}
```

The Translating Method

Okay, time for an assessment of where we stand. The museum applet is now able to do the following:

- Connect to the server
- Monitor the user's actions
- Display the current design
- Receive and send information
- Create a client "within" the main applet
- Enable the client to reference the main applet

At this point, whenever the user clicks a square, the "request to paint" is immediately sent to the server by the sendInfo() method. But we have not yet developed a true method of translating a command after it comes back across the server stream.

We have, however, laid the foundation for such a process. By enabling the Client subclass to refer to all public variables and methods of the Project applet class, we have given ourselves access to all the necessary information. In fact, we have many options for updating the data in the applet once it has been parsed from the server stream. Nevertheless, some approaches are much better than others.

The most secure and flexible approach is to create a "translating" method in the applet class, such as the sew() method in the Project class—the sew() method has been mentioned several times in this chapter. This method serves as the bridge between the client and applet classes. Why is this approach the best? Why can't we create some public variables in the Project class that can be changed by the Client class? There are several reasons.

Why Use a Translating Method?

The first reason we use a translating method is that doing so makes life a great deal easier for the programmer. By employing a translating method, we can maintain the encapsulation enjoyed thus far in our application. The sew() method is contained entirely within the Project class and thus has all the necessary resources (such as private variables that would be hidden from the Client subclass). Furthermore, when we actually code the application, we can focus on each class independently. When we code the Client class, we can effectively forget how the sew() method works; when we code the Project class, we can trust that the appropriate information will be sent to it.

The second reason for having the `Client` class rely on a foreign method is flexibility. If we decided to revamp this application and changed the manner in which we store the data, we would have no need to drastically change the `Client` class. In fact, in the worst case, the only changes necessary would be to increase the amount of data being read from the stream and the number of parameters passed to the `sew()` method.

The third reason for employing a translating method is that by linking the two classes with a method rather than direct access, we can prevent the corruption and intermingling of data that can occur when two processes attempt to access the same data at the same time. For example, if we made `tiles[ ][ ]` (the array that contains the design in the applet class) to be `public`, we could change the colors with a statement such as this one:

```
quilt.tiles[(stroke[0])][(stroke[1])] = stroke[2];
```

However, what would happen if, at the exact moment that the `paint()` method was accessing `tiles[1][2]`, the `Client` class was changing its value? What if more data had to be stored (the color, the design, the author's name, and so on)? Would the `paint()` method get the old data, the new data, a mixture, or none? As you can see, this could be a catastrophic problem. However, if we use a separate translating method in our applet class, this problem can easily be solved through use of the synchronized modifier. If our applet grew to the point that this problem presented itself, we could make the `paint()` method synchronized and place any necessary statements in a synchronized block. As a result, these portions of our code would never be able to run at the exact same time, thereby solving our problem.

How to Create a Translating Method

Now that we have seen why the `sew()` method is necessary, let us discuss its actual code. As mentioned earlier, each command in the museum application consists of three integers: the x coordinate, the y coordinate, and the new color. Also remember from the discussion of the `Client` class that the `sew()` method must be able to handle corrupted data. Consequently, the `sew()` method could look something like this:

```
public void sew(int x, int y, int hue) {
   if ( (x>=0) && (x <= size) && ( y >= 0) &&
      (y <= size) && (hue >= 0) && (hue <= _9) ) { // 9 colors
        tiles[x][y] = hue;
        repaint();
   }
}
```

The first statement is self-explanatory, but the second statement deserves some comment (if not a complete explanation). The first statement performs the actual task of changing the color on the tile—even though the user does not see anything unless the `repaint()` method is called. Thus, by setting the array and calling `repaint()`, the `sew()` method updates the quilt in the mind of the computer as well as on the screen itself.

In a moment, we will also harness the `sew()` method to perform another vital function for us.

Now that we have developed the entire functionality of the `Client` subclass, let's tie it together once and for all and put it aside. First look the final product over, as shown in Listing 27.2.

Listing 27.2. The final version of the Client class.

```
import java.net.Socket;
import java.io.*;

public class Client extends Thread
{
    private Socket soc;
    private Boolean running;
    private Project quilt;

    public Client (Project proj) {
      quilt = proj;
    }
    public void connect () {
      String        host;
      int           port = 2600;

      host = "www.museum.com";
      try {
          soc = new  Socket(host, port);
        }
      catch (Exception e)
          return(false);
    }

    public boolean SendInfo(int x, int y, int hue) {
      OutputStream out;

      try {
          out = soc.getOutputStream();
          out.write(x);
          out.write(y);
          out.write(hue);
          out.write('\n');
          out.flush();
        }
      catch (Exception e)
          return(false);
      return(true);
    }

    public void run() {
      int spot;
      int stroke[];
      stroke = new int[10];                    // an array for storing the commands
      spot = 0;
      DataInputStream in;

      in = new DataInputStream(soc.getInputStream());
```

```
    while (running) {
        do {                                // reads the information
            stroke[spot] = in.readByte();
        } while (  (stroke[spot] != '\n') && (++spot < 9) );
                                            // until the newline flag or limit of
                                            // array
    spot = 0;              // resets counter
    quilt.sew(stroke[0],stroke[1],stroke[2]);
    }

    public boolean disconnect () {
      running = false;
      try {
          soc.close()
          }
      catch (Exception e)
            return(false);
      return(true);
    }
}
```

Although none of the methods used in Listing 27.2 are new, there is a very important piece of the class that has been completely installed for the first time—the boolean field running. As a field, it is accessible to all methods within the Client subclass. Nevertheless, by making it private, we have ensured that, if it is changed, its change will be associated with an appropriate change in the status of the socket connection—a connection or disconnection, for example.

Although the Client class may require application-dependent changes, the version shown in Listing 27.2 is sufficient to satisfy most requirements. However, as of yet, we have dealt very little with the applet itself. This is primarily because each multiuser applet is inherently very different. Nevertheless, there are a few topics that should be discussed if you want to develop a quality multiuser applet.

Advanced Topics of Applet Development

What we have developed thus far in the chapter is entirely sufficient to satisfy the demands of the museum. Nevertheless, there are several other topics regarding efficiency, architecture, and appearance that we have not dealt with yet. The next few sections discuss these issues as well as those regarding the development of an effective server on the other end.

Animation and Dynamic Changes to the Screen

Although a programmer may appreciate the intricacies of a multiuser environment, users are attracted to those applications that look nice and help them to do interesting things. Although a multiuser environment is certainly one of the latter variety, we must still keep in mind the first criteria: making the applet look nice and run smoothly.

Although this chapter's purpose is not to deal with such issues as the graphical layout of applets, the communication structures developed in this chapter do have a direct impact on the "smooth-ness" of the changes that will occur on the user's screen. In the case of the museum applet developed earlier in this chapter, every time a user clicks on a tile, his or her request to paint must be sent to the server and then returned to the client. Once this information is finally re-turned to the client, the applet must then repaint each and every tile. Although this process occurs in a matter of seconds, for users who have to wait three seconds to see their changes reflected, as well as users who can actually observe each tile being repainted, this process may be a few seconds too slow.

A SHOT OF JAVA JARGON

As we have learned, the method that actually handles the creation of graphics in a Java applet is paint(). Although various actions such as drawing lines, changing the back-ground color, and displaying messages may be performed in this method, this functionality is nevertheless commonly referred to as the "painting" of the applet.

This slow graphical process can produce a very choppy effect, commonly referred to as "flick-ering," and can nevertheless be easily remedied. Although this requires a few changes to our applet, the main idea behind it is noticing that *we do not have to repaint those items that have not changed.* Even though this may seem a rather elementary observation, when developing an applet, it may seem a great deal easier to simply repaint the entire screen. (In fact, if you take a look at some of the Java applets on the Web, you will notice that many applets exhibit the problem of flickering.)

In the case of our museum applet, you will see that we have to paint only the tile that has been changed. Because we know the coordinates and size of each tile, this should not be much of a problem at all. It would seem as if all we have to do is modify the paint() method to paint only one tile; when the sew() method calls repaint(), only the most recently changed tile must change.

There are two problems with such a simplistic approach. First of all, the paint() method is called not only by explicit calls to repaint(), it is also called whenever the applet "appears" (such as when it first starts up or after the browser has been hidden behind another applica-tion). If we change the paint() method to paint only one tile, we may be left with only one tile on the screen, rather than the full quilt.

Another problem is that we cannot pass information to the paint() method because (as with the run() method for threads) we are overriding an already created method.

Don't worry. These problems can be handled easily. Peruse the additions to our code in List-ing 27.3 and see whether you can determine how the two problems were solved.

Listing 27.3. Revised code to provide smoother animation.

```
public class Project extends Applet {
   private boolean FullPaint;
   private java.awt.Point Changed;

   public void init() {
      ...
     FullPaint = true;
     Changed = new Point();
   }

   public void paint(Graphics g) {
      if (FullPaint) {
         for (int i = 0; i < size; i++)
            for(int j = 0; j < size; j++) {
                g.setColor(hues[ (tiles[i][j]) ]);
                g.fillRect( (i*scale+xoff) , (j*scale+yoff), scale,scale);
            }
      }
      else
         g.fillRect( (Changed.x*scale+xoff) , (Changed.y*scale+yoff), scale,scale);
      FullPaint = true;
   }

   public void sew(int x, int y, int hue) {
      if ( (x>=0) && (x <= size) && ( y >= 0) &&
         (y <= size) && (hue >= 0) && (hue _<= 9) ) { // 9 colors
           tiles[x][y] = hue;
           Changed.x = x;
           Changed.y = y;
           FullPaint = false;
           repaint();
      }
   }
}
```

Okay, let's see how the problems were solved.

Most notably, we added two new variables, one for each problem. The first variable is a boolean named FullPaint. As you can probably guess, its function is to tell the paint() method whether it should repaint all the tiles or just the newest one. Note that the key to this variable is that we want it to be true as much as possible so that we prevent the "one tile quilts" scenario discussed earlier. In this setup, the FullPaint variable is set to false only one line before the call to repaint() and is reset to true at the end of the paint() method.

CAUTION

Remember to reset the FullPaint to true at the end of your paint() statement! If you don't, you'll defeat the purpose of the variable—and ruin the appearance of your applet.

How did we deal with the second problem of being unable to inform the paint() method which tile has changed? Notice the use of the private variable Point Changed. Because the field is accessible by all methods, by setting the x and y values of this variable in the sew() method, we can indirectly pass this information along to the paint() method.

A LOOK INSIDE THE EVOLUTION OF THE LANGUAGE

The code in Listing 27.3 employed Changed, a variable of type Point, which can be found in the java.awt package. This is a useful class, but it has not always been part of Java. When the alpha releases came out, authors (especially those who were making graphical interfaces) were forced to develop their own Point-type classes. Even though this was not much of a problem, Sun chose to respond to this need by including the Point class in the beta and later API libraries.

Ensuring that the Sockets Close Properly

Although we have developed a sufficient disconnect() method, remember that things do not always work as well as they should. In fact, the disconnect() method in the socket class has had some problems in Java—further complicated by the fact that we are running our applet through a browser. As discussed earlier, not closing sockets can become a serious problem in a multiuser environment. It is good practice to develop into your protocol a "close" command. Although it should resemble the other commands in your protocol, the close command need not be anything elaborate. In the museum example, if 123 were the command to paint tile (1,2) in color 3, sending -123 could be the defined close command because it would be an aberration from the rest of the commands—something easily distinguishable.

Are You Still There?

Another related issue is that some users may not tell the applet that they are leaving—so the disconnect() method does not have a chance to execute. For example, the user may go to another HTML page or his or her computer might be struck with a sudden power outage. To handle either case, it is advisable to have some method by which the server can ensure that all its clients are still active.

A simple way of doing this is to develop another command into your protocol, the semantics of which are irrelevant. Regardless of the syntax, the server should send out some kind of "are you there?" command periodically. In terms of the applet itself, you should develop the translating method in such a manner that when such a command is received, it responds with an appropriate answer.

Consequently, if this functionality is built into the applet, the server will know that any client that does not respond within a reasonable amount of time (20 seconds, for example) is no longer active and can be closed.

Requests versus Commands

This chapter has repeatedly referred to the information passed from each client to the server as a *request* that describes what the user would like as opposed to a *command* that defines a particular action to be taken. Furthermore, note that in the system developed in this chapter, although a user may click a square, his or her screen is not updated until the request has been echoed back from the server. These two facts may seem a bit abnormal: It may seem more natural to have the applet update itself and then inform the server of what was done. As you will soon see, these two procedures are very necessary for the exact same reason.

In the example of the museum applet, users can paint only blank (unpainted) tiles. Imagine for a moment what would happen if user A decided to paint tile (1,2) black, and a moment later user B decided to paint tile (1,2) yellow. User A's command is received first and user B's command is received second. (It is impossible for the server to receive two commands at the same time on the same socket. Subsequent commands are normally placed in a queue.) If the applets were designed to paint themselves *before* the commands were echoed, user A and user B would have different images of the same quilt at the same time. Disaster!

Consequently, in a multiuser environment in which the status is really important (or even in a game application), it is essential that you develop your environment in such a manner that the status of whatever is being displayed on the screen (such as the position of the players) is updated *only* by what is returned from the server. That means that the server should be developed so that any invalid requests (such as a request to paint an already painted tile) are simply "sucked up" by the server and are not echoed to any clients. If two users attempt to paint the same tile, only the request of the first user should be honored, and the second request should simply be swallowed up by the server. Even better, you could enable your server to send user-specific error messages that cause some form of error message on the user's screen.

Limiting and Keeping Track of Users

In several situations—such as error messages—the server wants to speak with just one user. Additionally, your situation may require that only five users be in the environment at a given moment. These are real-world problems, but ones that are easily solved.

At the heart of these solutions is the idea of having more than one server for your multiuser environment. Such a configuration may involve one central server that has the power to spawn other servers (on other ports), or a central server that acts as a "gatekeeper," accepting clients only if there are openings (see Figure 27.2).

Either case requires the development of a richer protocol, but also provides you with opportunities for greater power over your environment. For example, you can establish several two-player games managed by a central server. By designing the applet to connect on a given port (1626, for example) and to request entrance to a game, the server on that port can act as a manager by beginning a new game on another port (1627, for example) and informing the applet of the new port number. The applet can then disconnect from port 1626, connect to port 1627, and wait for the central server to send another user to the same port. Once the central server has sent two players to port 1627, it starts a new server on the next available port (1628, for example) and can continue in this manner indefinitely (see Figure 27.3).

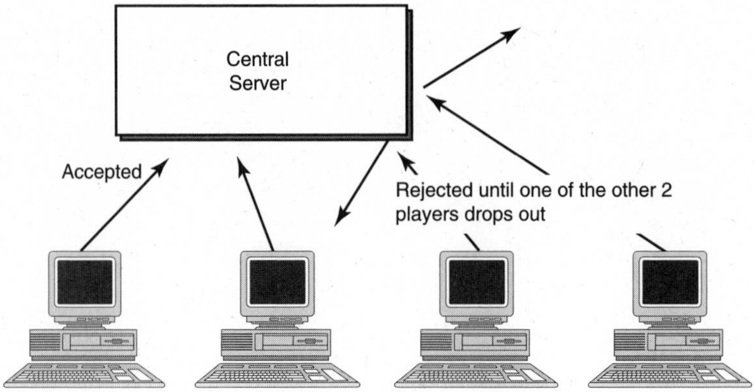

FIGURE 27.2.

An example of a gatekeeper system.

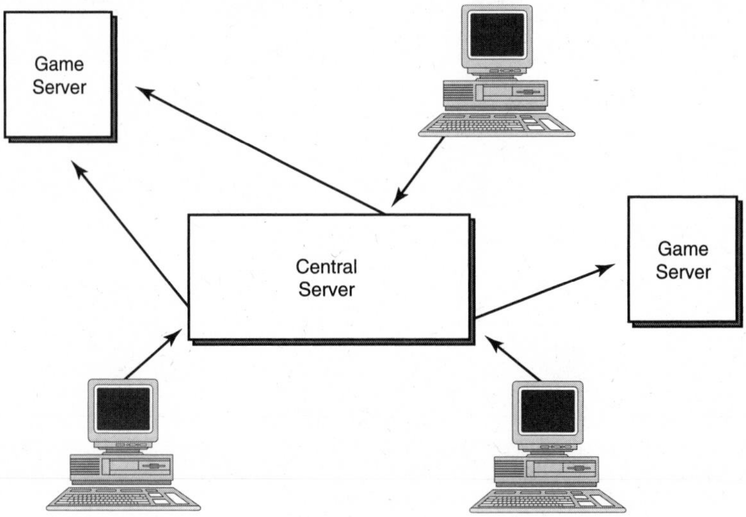

FIGURE 27.3.

An example of a central server/children server system.

In the cases of the central server/children server system and the gatekeeper system, the server can assign each client an identification number at connection time. This arrangement not only allows the server to keep track of who is sending the information, it also enables the server to send user-specific messages (for example, Player One: You can't do that). Both of these tasks can be facilitated by appending a simple identification letter or number to each command in the protocol. (B112 could mean, for example, that player 1 just bought plot 12.)

Summary

Even though this chapter did not deal with many topics, keep in mind that the power of Java is its abstract capability to facilitate a multiuser environment, not its specific lexical constructs. Here are a few issues relating to the Java language that you should keep in mind when developing a multiuser environment:

- Develop a user-friendly graphical interface. By using the `java.awt.Event` class, you can respond to the user's interactions in an effective manner.

- Create a client class that extends the `java.lang.Thread` class. Although you can create as many methods as you want within this class, the best approach is to harness the `run()` method's capacity to run concurrently to develop an effective means of reading data from the stream. Also, remember to use some form of flag that provides you with a way of controlling the lifetime of the `run()` method.

- Develop the framework by which the applet and client classes will be able to communicate. This is best done by making an instance of the client class a field in the applet class. By making the appropriate methods of the client class `public`, your applet class can perform such tasks as connecting, disconnecting, and sending data.

- Create a "translating" method in your applet class. Doing so enables the client class to send the parsed data to the applet class to elicit the proper response.

VI

PART

IN THIS PART

Programming Strategies

Java Debugging

by Tim Park

IN THIS CHAPTER

Bugs are an unfortunate fact of life in software design. Similar to most development environments, Sun has included a debugger with the Java Development Kit (JDK) to help you fix your Java applets and applications. JDB (short for Java DeBugger) isn't a fancy visual debugging environment like the debuggers you may be familiar with from other professional development systems, but it does make the task of finding and exterminating bugs in your Java programs much easier.

Most of this chapter shows you how to use JDB to debug your programs. The last section uses Symantec's Café to show you how to debug your Java programs using Café's very popular visual environment.

Debugging with JDB

In the first part of the chapter, we use a simple Java applet to explain how to use JDB to help you debug your programs. As you can see from the output of the JDB `help` command in Listing 28.1, the range of commands available in JDB is extensive.

Listing 28.1. Output from the JDB `help` command.

```
> help
** command list **
threads [threadgroup]      — list threads
thread <thread id>         — set default thread
suspend [thread id(s)]     — suspend threads (default: all)
resume [thread id(s)]      — resume threads (default: all)
where [thread id] ¦ all    — dump a thread's stack
threadgroups               — list threadgroups
threadgroup <name>         — set current threadgroup

print <id> [id(s)]         — print object or field
dump <id> [id(s)]          — print all object information

locals                     — print all local variables in current stack frame

classes                    — list currently known classes
methods <class id>         — list a class's methods

stop in <class id>.<method> — set a breakpoint in a method
stop at <class id>:<line>   — set a breakpoint at a line
up [n frames]              — move up a thread's stack
down [n frames]            — move down a thread's stack
clear <class id>:<line>    — clear a breakpoint
step                       — execute current line
cont                       — continue execution from breakpoint

catch <class id>           — break for the specified exception
ignore <class id>          — ignore when the specified exception
```

```
list [line number]        — print source code
use [source file path]    — display or change the source path

memory                    — report memory usage
gc                        — free unused objects (gc means garbage collection)

load classname            — load Java class to be debugged
run <class> [args]        — start execution of a loaded Java class
!!                        — repeat last command
help (or ?)               — list commands
exit (or quit)            — exit debugger
>
```

Using JDB to Debug Your Program

From our experience, the easiest way to learn JDB is by using it. Without further ado, then, let's use JDB to debug the simple class that follows. We chose a simple class for the benefit of people skipping ahead to learn how to use the basic features of the debugger. But don't worry if you've read all the previous chapters of this book—we'll still cover all the advanced features of JDB!

AddNumbers is a simple class that implements both the user interface and the algorithm to add two numbers together. Well, at least this is what it's supposed to do. In reality, the class has a simple bug that will be located using JDB (see Listing 28.2).

 On the CD-ROM that accompanies this book, you will find two Java classes: StartApplet, which is the requisite subclass of the Applet class that instantiates the AddNumbers class, and StartApplet.html, which is used by the applet viewer to load the applet. Use the bundled installation program to install the files for this chapter onto your hard drive.

Listing 28.2. The AddNumbers.java file—complete with bug.

```java
import java.awt.*;

public class AddNumbers extends Frame {

  int LeftNumber = 5;
  int RightNumber = 2;

  TextArea taResult;

  public AddNumbers() {

    setTitle("JDB Sample Java Program");
    setLayout(new BorderLayout());

    Panel p = new Panel();
    p.add(new Button("5"));
    p.add(new Button("1"));
```

continues

Listing 28.2. continued

```java
    add("West", p);

    Panel g = new Panel();
    g.add(new Button("2"));
    g.add(new Button("3"));
    add("East", g);

    taResult = new TextArea(2,1);
    taResult.setEditable(false);
    add("South", taResult);

    pack();
    resize(300,200);
    show();

  }

public void ComputeSum () {

  int Total = LeftNumber - RightNumber;

  String ConvLeft  = String.valueOf(LeftNumber);
  String ConvRight = String.valueOf(RightNumber);
  String ConvTotal = String.valueOf(Total);

  taResult.setText(ConvLeft + " + " + ConvRight + " = " +  ConvTotal);

}

public void paint(Graphics g) {

  ComputeSum();

}

public boolean handleEvent (Event evt) {

  switch (evt.id) {

    // Was the termination button pressed?

    case Event.WINDOW_DESTROY: {

      // Yes!  So exit gracefully.

      System.exit(0);
      return true;

    }

    default:

  }
```

```
// Was the "5" button pressed?

if ("5".equals(evt.arg)) {
  LeftNumber = 5;
  ComputeSum();
  return true;
}

// Was the "1" button pressed?

if ("1".equals(evt.arg)) {
  LeftNumber = 1;
  ComputeSum();
  return true;
}

// Was the "2" button pressed?

if ("2".equals(evt.arg)) {
  RightNumber = 2;
  ComputeSum();
  return true;
}

// Was the "3" button pressed?

if ("3".equals(evt.arg)) {
  RightNumber = 3;
  ComputeSum();
  return true;
}

  return false;

 }

}
```

28

JAVA DEBUGGING

Compiling for JDB

Before starting the debugging session, you must first compile the Java applet to include extra information needed only for debugging. This information is needed so that the debugger can display information about your applet or application in a human-comprehensible form instead of a confusing wash of hexadecimal numbers. (Don't laugh—the first debuggers required you to do this translation, so count your lucky stars!)

To compile your program with debugging information enabled, change to the \java\classes\AddNumbers directory and issue the following commands:

```
C:\java\classes\AddNumbers> javac_g -g AddNumbers.java
C:\java\classes\AddNumbers> javac_g -g StartApplet.java
```

The javac_g compiler is functionally identical to the javac compiler used in previous chapters, except that it doesn't perform any optimizations to your applet or application. Optimizations rearrange the statements in your applet or application to make them faster. This rearrangement makes it more difficult to conceptualize program flow when you are debugging, so using javac_g in conjunction with JDB is useful.

The -g command-line option tells the compiler to include line number and object names in the output file. This option allows the debugger to reference objects and line numbers in a program by source code names instead of using the Java interpreter's internal representations.

Setting Up a Debugging Session

The next step in debugging a Java application or applet is to start JDB. There are two ways to do this, depending on whether you are debugging an applet or an application. Because we are debugging an applet in our example, we will use the applet viewer program supplied in the Java Developers Kit to load JDB indirectly. If we were trying to debug an application instead, we would use the following command to start JDB:

```
C:\java\classes\AddNumbers> jdb MyApplication
```

Again, because we are debugging an applet in our example and not an application, do not start JDB in the preceding manner. However, for future reference, after you invoke the debugger, using JDB on a Java application is identical to using it on an applet.

With that important distinction covered, start the applet viewer with the following command:

```
C:\java\classes\AddNumbers> appletviewer -debug StartApplet.html
```

The -debug flag specifies to the applet viewer that it should start up in JDB instead of by directly executing the AddNumbers class.

Once the applet viewer loads, it opens its applet window and displays something similar to the following in the command-line window:

```
C:\java\classes\AddNumbers> appletviewer -debug AddNumbers.html
Initializing jdb...
0x139f2f8:class(sun.applet.Appletviewer)
>_
```

The first thing you should notice about JDB is that it is command-line based. Although this makes the learning curve for JDB a little more steep, it doesn't prevent you from doing anything you may be familiar with in a visual debugging environment.

Before going further, examine the third line of the preceding output. This indicates where the debugger is stopped in its execution of the applet. In this case, it stopped during the execution of Sun's applet.Appletviewer class. This is logical, because applet.Appletviewer is the class that is transparently loaded and executed to load an applet. (See, you're learning things by using JDB already!) The hexadecimal number that prefixes this on the third line is the ID number assigned to the sun.applet.Appletviewer object by the Java interpreter. (Aren't you glad now that you can see the English version because you used the -g option for javac?) The > prompt on the fourth line indicates that there is currently no default thread that we are watching—more on this later.

To understand the bug in `AddNumbers`, we will start the applet running in the debugger as follows:

```
> run
run sun.applet.AppletViewer MA.html
running ...
main[1]
```

The debugger should open the applet's frame and start executing it. Because the debugger and the applet are on different threads of execution, you can interact with the debugger and the applet at the same time. The preceding `main[1]` prompt indicates that the debugger is monitoring the applet thread (the `main` thread); the `[1]` indicates that we currently are positioned at the topmost stack frame on the method call stack (we'll explain what this means later).

Our applet is supposed to take the number of the button pressed on the left and add it to the number of the button pressed on the right. Try this out: press some of the buttons and check the applet's math.

Hmm—unless you learned math differently than we did, there seems to be something wrong with the computation of the applet. (Maybe we found another Pentium processor flaw?)

Basic Debugger Techniques

To find out what is going on, let's examine the `ComputeSum()` method of the `AddNumbers` class. We would like to stop directly in this method without having to move slowly and tediously through the rest of the code.

Setting and Clearing Breakpoints

Fortunately, JDB has a set of commands called *breakpoints* that let you stop directly. We'll use breakpoints to stop program execution in the `ComputeSum()` method; but first, press the 5 and 3 buttons on the applet to make sure that you see the same things as we do when the program is stopped. After pressing 5 and 3, type the following in the debugger window:

```
main[1] stop in AddNumbers.ComputeSum
Breakpoint set in AddNumbers.ComputeSum
main[1]
```

As you probably can guess, the `stop in` command tells JDB to stop when the `ComputeSum()` method in the `AddNumbers` class is entered. This is convenient to do because the computation part of method we are interested in is very close to the start of the method. If the statement was farther down in the method, it would be tedious to manually move down to the statement of interest every time we hit the breakpoint at the beginning of the method. In this case, we would want to use the `stop at` command in JDB.

The stop at command works exactly like the stop in command in JDB, except that you specify the line number you want JDB to stop on instead of the method. For example, look at the handleEvent() method of the AddNumbers class. If you want to stop at the if statement where the program checked for a push of the number 2 button, enter the following:

```
main[1] stop at AddNumbers:90
Breakpoint set in AddNumbers:90
main[1]
```

However, ***don't do this*** because we want to examine the ComputeSum() method and not handleEvent(). We can verify this and see all the breakpoints currently set by using the clear command as follows:

```
AWT-Callback-Win32[1] clear
Current breakpoints set:
      AddNumbers:37
AWT-Callback-Win32[1]
```

As expected, there is only one breakpoint set. Note that it is specified as AddNumbers:37 instead of as AddNumbers:ComputeSum. JDB converts the command stop in AddNumbers.ComputeSum to stop at AddNumbers:37 to make its internal bookkeeping easier.

Of course, the real use of the clear command is to clear breakpoints when they have outgrown their usefulness. *Don't do this now,* but if you need to clear the breakpoint you just set, enter the following:

```
AWT-Callback-Win32[1] clear AddNumbers.ComputeSum
Breakpoint cleared at AddNumbers.ComputeSum
AWT-Callback-Win32[1]
```

Let's get back to debugging our applet. When we left our applet, it was still running and there was no prompt in the JDB window. Why hasn't JDB stopped at ComputeSum()? If you look at the applet code, you notice that the ComputeSum() method is called only when you press a button in the applet. Press the 2 button to provide this ComputeSum() method call:

```
main[1]
Breakpoint hit: AddNumbers.ComputeSum (AddNumbers: 37)
AWT-Callback-Win32[1]
```

As you can see, when you press the 2 button, the debugger stops at the ComputeSum() method as instructed. Note that we are now in a different thread (as shown by the change in prompts from main[1] to AWT-Callback-Win32[1]) because the AWT windowing manager thread calls the handleEvent() method in the AddNumbers class when a button is pressed in the applet.

Although we know we are stopped in the ComputeSum() method, let's get a better sense of our bearings and refresh our memory by looking at where this method is in the source code. Fortunately, the line-number information is stored in the class when you compile with the -g option. You can access this information by using the JDB list command as follows:

```
AWT-Callback-Win32[1] list
33           }
34    35          public void ComputeSum() {
36
```

```
37      =>          int Total = LeftNumber - RightNumber;
38
39                  String ConvLeft  = String.valueOf(LeftNumber);
40                  String ConvRight = String.valueOf(RightNumber);
41                  String ConvTotal = String.valueOf(Total);
AWT-Callback-Win32[1]
```

As expected, this output shows that we are stopped in `ComputeSum()` on the first statement—and as luck would have it, right before the computation statement. The observant reader probably already can tell what is wrong, but just pretend that it's a much more complicated computation and that you can't, okay?

Examining Objects

First, let's check our operands for the computation to make sure that they are correct. JDB provides three commands to display the contents of objects: `locals`, `print`, and `dump`. The `locals` command displays the current values of all of the objects defined in the local scope. The `print` and `dump` commands are very similar and are used to display the contents of any object in any scope, including objects defined in the interface for the class. The main difference is that `dump` displays more information about complex objects (objects with inheritance or multiple data members) than `print` does.

Because `LeftNumber` and `RightNumber` are class members, we'll have to use `print` to display them, as follows:

```
AWT-Callback-Win32[1] print LeftNumber
this.LeftNumber = 5
AWT-Callback-Win32[1] print RightNumber
this.RightNumber = 2
AWT-Callback-Win32[1]
```

The operands seem to be exactly as we entered them in the applet. Let's take a look at the local objects to get a feeling for where we are by using the `locals` command as follows:

```
AWT-Callback-Win32[1] locals
  this = AddNumbers[0,0,300x200,layout=java.awt.BorderLayout,
resizable,title=JDB Sample Java Program]
  Total is not in scope.
  ConvLeft is not in scope.
  ConvRight is not in scope.
  ConvTotal is not in scope.
AWT-Callback-Win32[1]
```

As expected, JDB is telling us that none of the local objects have been instantiated yet, so none of the objects are within the local scope yet. Let's move the execution of the method along one statement so that we can see what the value of the computation is. To do this, use the JDB `step` command as follows:

```
AWT-Callback-Win32[1] step
AWT-Callback-Win32[1]
Breakpoint hit: AddNumbers.ComputeSum (AddNumbers:39)
AWT-Callback-Win32[1]
```

28

JAVA DEBUGGING

JDB moves the execution along one statement and stops. Doing this also triggers another breakpoint, because we are still in AddNumbers.ComputeSum(). Look at the following output to determine how the computation turned out:

```
AWT-Callback-Win32[1] locals
this = AddNumbers[0,0,300x200,layout=java.awt.BorderLayout,
resizable,title=JDB Sample Java Program]
  Total = 3
  ConvLeft is not in scope.
  ConvRight is not in scope.
  ConvTotal is not in scope.
AWT-Callback-Win32[1]
```

We see that Total was instantiated, the addition carried out, and the result put in Total. But wait: 5 + 2 doesn't equal 3! Take a look at the following source code:

```
AWT-Callback-Win32[1] list
35              public void ComputeSum() {
36
37                  int Total = LeftNumber - RightNumber;
38
39      =>          String ConvLeft  = String.valueOf(LeftNumber);
40                  String ConvRight = String.valueOf(RightNumber);
41                  String ConvTotal = String.valueOf(Total);
42
43                  taResult.setText(ConvLeft + " + " + ConvRight + " = " +
AWT-Callback-Win32[1]
```

Oops—a subtraction sign was used instead of an addition sign! So much for finding another bug in the Pentium processor, but congratulations—you've found your first applet bug in JDB.

Additional JDB Functions

We've found our bug, but don't quit out of the applet viewer yet. We'll use it and the AddNumbers class to demonstrate a few more features of JDB that you might find useful in future debugging sessions.

Walking the Method Call Stack with JDB

In the previous section, we used the locals JDB command to look at the objects in the current scope. Using the JDB command up, you can also look at the local objects in previous stack frames (which consist of all the methods that either called ComputeSum() or called a method that called ComputeSum(), and so on). For example, look at the following output to see the state of the handleEvent() method right before it called the ComputeSum() method:

```
AWT-Callback-Win32[1] up
AWT-Callback-Win32[2] locals
this = AddNumbers[0,0,300x200,layout=java.awt.BorderLayout,
resizable,title=JDB Sample Java Program]
```

```
evt = java.awt.Event[id=1001,x=246,y=28,
target=java.awt.Button[5,5,20x24,label=2],arg=2]
AWT-Callback-Win32[2]
```

As you can see, the `handleEvent` stack frame has two objects in its local frame: the pointer to this `AddNumber` instance and the `Event` object passed to `handleEvent()`.

It's possible to use the up command as many times as your method call stack is deep. To undo the up function and return to a higher method call in the stack, use the JDB `down` command as follows:

```
AWT-Callback-Win32[2] down
AWT-Callback-Win32[1] locals
this = AddNumbers[0,0,300x200,layout=java.awt.BorderLayout,
resizable,title=JDB Sample Java Program]
  Total = 3
  ConvLeft is not in scope.
  ConvRight is not in scope.
  ConvTotal is not in scope.
AWT-Callback-Win32[1]
```

As expected, we are now back in the `ComputeSum()` local stack frame.

Using JDB to Get More Information about Classes

JDB also has two functions for getting more information about classes: `methods` and `classes`. `methods` enables you display all the methods in a class. For example, you can examine the `AddNumbers` class with the `methods` command:

```
AWT-Callback-Win32[1] methods
void <init>()
void ComputeSum()
void paint(Graphics)
boolean handleEvent(Event)
AWT-Callback-Win32[1]
```

The `classes` function lists all the classes currently loaded in memory. Here is partial output from the execution of `classes` on `AddNumbers` (the actual output listed more than 80 classes):

```
AWT-Callback-Win32[1] classes
...
...
0x13a5f70:interface(sun.awt.UpdateClient)
0x13a6160:interface(java.awt.peer.MenuPeer)
0x13a67a0:interface(java.awt.peer.ButtonPeer)
0x13a6880:class(java.lang.ClassNotFoundException)
0x13a6ea8:class(sun.tools.debug.Field)
0x13a7098:class(sun.tools.debug.BreakpointSet)
0x13a7428:class(sun.tools.debug.Stackframe)
0x13a7478:class(sun.tools.debug.LocalVariable)
AWT-Callback-Win32[1]
```

28

JAVA DEBUGGING

Monitoring Memory Usage and Controlling `finalize()`

For some large applets or applications, the amount of free memory may become a concern. JDB's `memory` command enables you to monitor the amount of used and free memory during your debugging session, as follows:

```
AWT-Callback-Win32[1] memory
Free: 2554472, total: 3145720
AWT-Callback-Win32[1]
```

JDB also lets you explicitly demand that the `finalize()` method be run on all freed objects through the `gc` (garbage collection) command. This is useful for proving that your applet or application correctly handles deleted objects—which can be difficult to prove normally with small applets and applications because the `finalize()` methods are normally called only when the applet or application has run out of free memory.

Controlling Threads of Execution

As you know from Chapter 9, "Threads and Multithreading," Java applets have multiple threads of execution. Using JDB and the `threads` command, you can view these threads as follows:

```
AWT-Callback-Win32[1] threads
Group sun.applet.AppletViewer.main:
  1. (java.lang.Thread)0x13a3a00          AWT-Win32                   running
  2. (java.lang.Thread)0x13a2a58          AWT-Callback-Win32       running
  3. (sun.awt.ScreenUpdater)0x13a2d98     Screen Updater       running
Group group applet-StartApplet.class:
  4.    (java.lang.Thread)0x13a28f0 class running
AWT-Callback-Win32[1]
```

As you can see from this output, there are four threads of simultaneous applet execution. Two correspond to the AWT window management system (threads 1 and 2), one for updating the screen (thread 3), and one for the actual applet itself (thread 4).

JDB provides two commands for controlling the execution of threads: `suspend` and `resume`. Suspending a thread isn't very worthwhile in our simple example, but in multithreaded applications it can be very worthwhile—you can suspend all but one thread and focus on that thread.

But let's try `suspend` and `resume` on our applet to get a feel for their use. To suspend the AWT-Win32 thread, you should note its ID from the `threads` list and then use this information as the argument to `suspend`, as follows:

```
AWT-Callback-Win32[1] threads
Group sun.applet.AppletViewer.main:
  1. (java.lang.Thread)0x13a3a00              AWT-Win32                   running
  ...
AWT-Callback-Win32[1] suspend 1
AWT-Callback-Win32[1] threads
Group sun.applet.AppletViewer.main:
  1. (java.lang.Thread)0x13a3a00          AWT-Win32                   suspended
  2. (java.lang.Thread)0x13a2a58          AWT-Callback-Win32       running
```

```
   3.  (sun.awt.ScreenUpdater)0x13a2d98 Screen Updater          running
Group group applet-StartApplet.class:
   4.    (java.lang.Thread)0x13a28f0 class                        running
AWT-Callback-Win32[1]
```

As expected, the AWT-Win32 thread is now suspended. Threads are resumed in a completely analogous manner—with the resume command, as follows:

```
AWT-Callback-Win32[1] resume 1
AWT-Callback-Win32[1] threads
Group sun.applet.AppletViewer.main:
   1.  (java.lang.Thread)0x13a3a00        AWT-Win32              running
   2.  (java.lang.Thread)0x13a2a58        AWT-Callback-Win32    running
   3.  (sun.awt.ScreenUpdater)0x13a2d98 Screen Updater          running
Group group applet-StartApplet.class:
   4.    (java.lang.Thread)0x13a28f0 class                        running
AWT-Callback-Win32[1]
```

Using use to Point the Way to Your Java Source Code

To execute the list command, JDB takes the line number and grabs the required lines of Java from the source file. To find that source file, JDB reads your CLASSPATH environmental variable and searches all the paths contained in it. If that path doesn't contain your source file, JDB is unable to display the source for your program.

This wasn't a problem for this example because the search path contained the current directory, but if you set up your applet or application and the source is located in a directory outside the search path, you'll have to use the use command to add to your path. The use command without any arguments displays the current search path as follows:

```
AWT-Callback-Win32[1] use
\java\classes;.;C:\JAVA\BIN\..\classes;
AWT-Callback-Win32[1]
```

Appending a directory to the search path is, unfortunately, slightly tedious. You have to retype the *entire current path* and add the new path. To add the path \myclasses to the preceding path, do the following:

```
AWT-Callback-Win32[1] use \java\classes;.;C:\JAVA\BIN\..\classes;\myclasses
AWT-Callback-Win32[1]
```

Getting More Information about Your Objects with dump

Earlier in this chapter, you saw an example of how to display an object's value using the print command. In this section, we'll look at JDB's dump command, which is a more useful display command for objects containing multiple data members. The AddNumbers class is a good example (note that this in this case refers to the instantiation of AddNumbers for our applet), as follows:

```
AWT-Callback-Win32[1] dump this
this = (AddNumbers)0x13a3000 {
    ComponentPeer peer = (sun.awt.win32.MFramePeer)0x13a31b0
    Container parent = null
```

```
    int x = 0
    int y = 0
    int width = 300
    int height = 200
    Color foreground = (java.awt.Color)0x13a2bb0
    Color background = (java.awt.Color)0x13a2b98
    Font font = (java.awt.Font)0x13a31d0
    boolean visible = true
    boolean enabled = true
    boolean valid = true
    int ncomponents = 3
AWT-Callback-Win32[1] _
```

Contrast this with the output from `print`:

```
AWT-Callback-Win32[1] print this
this = AddNumbers[0,0,300x200,layout=java.awt.BorderLayout,
resizable,title=JDB Sample Java Program]
AWT-Callback-Win32[1]
```

As you can see, the `dump` command displays the data members for the class but `print` displays only the key attributes for the class.

Handling Exceptions with `catch` and `ignore`

JDB has two functions for dealing with exceptions: `catch` and `ignore`. The `catch` function, similar to a breakpoint, enables you to trap exceptions and stop the debugger. This is useful when debugging because it is much easier to diagnose an exception when you know the conditions under which it occurred. To catch an exception, simply type **class** and the name of the exception class. To trap any exception (the `Exception` base class), do the following:

```
AWT-Callback-Win32[1] catch Exception
AWT-Callback-Win32[1]
```

The `ignore` function does exactly the opposite of `catch`. It squelches the specified class of exceptions raised by an applet or application. The use of `ignore` is completely analogous to `catch`, as shown by the following:

```
AWT-Callback-Win32[1] ignore ArrayOutOfBoundsException
AWT-Callback-Win32[1]
```

Continuing Program Execution with `cont`

You may be wondering how to restart execution once you reach a breakpoint and execution has stopped. Why, you use the `cont` command, as shown here:

```
AWT-Callback-Win32[1] cont
```

The program resumes execution and the JDB prompt does not return until a breakpoint or exception is reached.

Leaving JDB Using `exit`

Although it may be obvious to you already, there is one final command that comes in handy at least once in any debugging session. The `exit` command lets you out of the debugger and back into DOS.

Using Symantec Café's Visual Debugger

If you want to be a more efficient Java developer, it is hard to find anything as important as adopting an integrated development environment as your development platform. In our opinion, currently the best such visual environment is Symantec's Café for Java. In addition to excellent debugging support, it also features project management, a visual GUI builder, and object-oriented browsing of your Java classes. Chapter 5, "Third-Party Development Tools," discusses other IDEs.

Loading the `AddNumbers` Project

The first thing we need to do to use Symantec Café's debugger is to load the project file for the `AddNumbers` applet. This project file contains all the information needed to build `AddNumbers.java` and `StartApplet.java`. Use the mouse to pull down the Project menu and select the Open option. The Open Project dialog box appears. In this dialog box, type the path or navigate to the directory containing the same `AddNumbers` applet you used in the first part of this chapter. From this directory, you should be able to see a file named `AddNumbers.prj`. Select this file and click OK to load the project.

Building the `AddNumbers` Project

 The `AddNumbers.prj` project should have come precompiled on the CD-ROM that accompanies this book, but just in case, let's rebuild it in Café. Pull down the Project menu again and select Build. Café pops up a build status window and builds the files one by one.

Running the `AddNumbers` Project

Before we jump into debugging the `AddNumbers` project, let's run it first and make sure that it still adds numbers wrong. To run it, pull down the Project menu and select Execute Program (or press its accelerator key, Ctrl+F5).

Debugging the `AddNumbers` Project

After you play with the `AddNumbers` applet for a while and confirm that it is broken, stop it at the applet's execution. Using the Debug menu, select Start/Restart Debugging. This command should bring up five windows: a source code window displaying StartApplet.java, a Data/Object window, a Call window, a Thread window, and an Output window. A thorough coverage of all these windows would require more than a single chapter. For the purposes of this chapter, we'll explain what all the windows do, but focus on the source code window and the Data/Object window—these are the only windows you'll use for 90 percent of your debugging tasks anyway.

At this point, the debugger is stopped at the first program statement and is waiting for your command. Suppose that from your last test run, you have guessed that the error lies somewhere within the ComputeSum() method in the AddNumbers class. Let's set a breakpoint here using Café and run until we get to this point in the program.

To set a breakpoint, you must first open the AddNumbers.java file. With the AddNumbers file in the editor, move down in the file until you reach the ComputeSum() method. Pull down the Window menu in Café and make sure that the Debug Toolbox option is selected. Next, move the cursor down to line 37, which is the computation of Total. Finally, find the Debug toolbar on your icon bar, which looks like the bar in Figure 28.1.

FIGURE 28.1.
Café's Debug toolbar.

The breakpoint toggle button is the one with the red and green flags on it. Click this button to toggle the breakpoint on for the computation line. A little red diamond should appear next to that line (see Figure 28.2).

With our breakpoint set, we're now ready to let the program execute freely until it reaches the breakpoint. To do this, pull down the Debug menu and select Go Until Breakpoint. This action starts the applet viewer and the AddNumbers applet runs until it reaches the ComputeSum() method as part of the redraw. Execution stops at the line on which we put the breakpoint—as we expect (see Figure 28.3). Notice, however, that Café doesn't execute the line we set as the target of the breakpoint.

Café's Call window (shown in Figure 28.4) shows the stack of method calls that have been made to reach this point in program execution. We know that the ComputeSum() method was reached during the repaint of the window because it was called from the AddNumbers paint() method.

Café's Breakpoint window (shown in Figure 28.5) shows which breakpoint caused the stop in execution. In this example, there is only one breakpoint, so this information isn't very helpful—but for bigger debugging situations, the Breakpoint window is more useful as a central reference for all the breakpoints you have set in your program.

FIGURE 28.2.

Setting a breakpoint in Café.

```
c:\temp2\AddNumbers.java
 File   Edit   Goto   Macro   New!

import java.awt.*;

public class AddNumbers extends Frame {

    int LeftNumber = 5;
    int RightNumber = 2;

    TextArea taResult;

    public AddNumbers() {

        setTitle("JDB Sample Java Program");
        setLayout(new BorderLayout());

        Panel p = new Panel();
        p.add(new Button("5"));
        p.add(new Button("1"));
        add("West", p);

        Panel g = new Panel();
        g.add(new Button("2"));
        g.add(new Button("3"));
        add("East", g);

        taResult = new TextArea(2,1);
        taResult.setEditable(false);
        add("South", taResult);

        pack();
        resize(300,200);
        show();

    }

    public void ComputeSum () {

        int Total = LeftNumber - RightNumber;

        String ConvLeft  = String.valueOf(LeftNumber);
        String ConvRight = String.valueOf(RightNumber);
        String ConvTotal = String.valueOf(Total);

        taResult.setText(ConvLeft + " + " + ConvRight + " = " + ConvTotal)
                                                             Line 37   Col 11
```

28

JAVA DEBUGGING

FIGURE 28.3.

Café stopped at a breakpoint.

```
        taResult = new TextArea(2,1);
        taResult.setEditable(false);
        add("South", taResult);

        pack();
        resize(300,200);
        show();

    }

    public void ComputeSum () {

        int Total = LeftNumber - RightNumber;

        String ConvLeft  = String.valueOf(LeftNumber);
        String ConvRight = String.valueOf(RightNumber);
```

FIGURE 28.4.

Café's Call window.

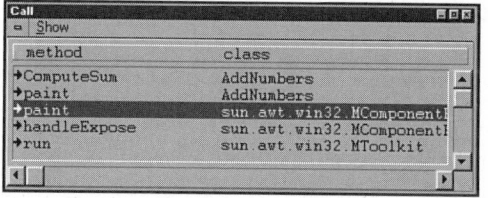

```
Call
 Show
  method              class
→ComputeSum          AddNumbers
→paint               AddNumbers
→paint               sun.awt.win32.MComponent
→handleExpose        sun.awt.win32.MComponent
→run                 sun.awt.win32.MToolkit
```

Figure 28.5.

Café's Breakpoint window.

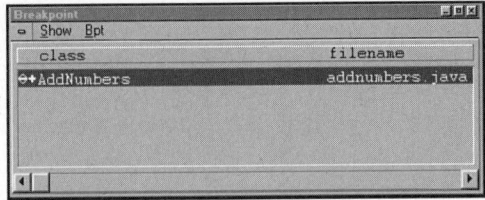

The Thread window shows all the threads in operation for your program. Note that its output is exactly the same, if in a somewhat more readable format, as what we saw when we were using JDB.

But what we're really interested in is the Data/Object window (shown in Figure 28.6). This window contains the current values of all the data members for local objects. In looking at the values of lLeftNumber and lRightNumber, we can tell that the problem isn't caused by the operands to the computation because they are what we expect them to be.

Figure 28.6.

Café's Data/Object window before the Total *computation.*

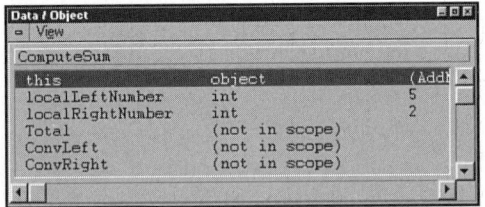

Let's move execution ahead one line so that we can see the result of the execution. To do this, press the F10 key or click the button in the Debug toolbar with the foot "stepping into" a yellow hole. The "stepping into" button differs from the "stepping over" button (the next button on the Debug bar) in that "stepping into" shows the execution of any and all function calls incurred on this line, while "stepping over" shows only the output of the function.

Looking at the Data/Object window, we can now tell that something is wrong with the computation of Total: 5 + 2 certainly doesn't equal 3, as shown in the display of the Data/Object window in Figure 28.7. Hopefully, with this information, the bug is now obvious to you.

To complete the debug cycle, take Café out of debugging mode using the Debug | Stop Debugging menu option. Then change the – operator in the Total computation to a + and rebuild using the Project | Build menu option. Run the program again to show that the program has been fixed.

FIGURE 28.7.

Café's Data Object window after the Total *computation.*

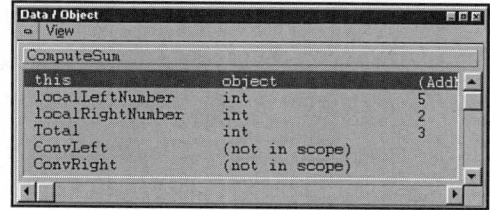

Summary

This chapter helped you learn how to debug by giving you hands-on experience with Sun's Java debugger, JDB, and Symantec's visual environment, Café. Debugging is a learned skill; don't be discouraged if it takes you a long time to debug your first applet or application. As you gain experience doing it, you'll start to recognize the effects of different classes of bugs and be able to solve each bug in a shorter amount of time. Patience is definitely a virtue in software debugging.

Documenting Your Code

by George Reese

IN THIS CHAPTER

CHAPTER 29

If one single thing could define the difference between hackers and serious programmers, it would be documentation. The trademark of a hacker is a quick-and-dirty solution developed without using any commonly understood process or anything other than the code itself to describe what was done. A programmer, on the other hand, develops an application based on documentation derived from a clearly defined development process. As a result, the quality of the applications built by programmers are worlds above the quality of applications built by hackers.

This chapter examines why documentation can make such a huge difference in application quality and how you can effectively document your work to achieve the highest standard. The first task is understanding the role of documentation, especially in complex applications. Sporadic documentation is barely more useful than no documentation at all. The chapter also discusses approaches to object-oriented development, which help produce useful documentation, and the javadoc tool, which provides API documentation.

The Role of Documentation

The complexity of software engineering can equal the complexity of fields like construction and manufacturing. In construction, you create buildings using a process that defines and documents what you are building before you build it. Specifically, an architect puts together a blueprint that others use to define how they will construct the building. Years down the road, if someone decides to expand the building, or simply update it to new fire standards, that old blueprint is brought out and used as the starting point for the changes.

Not all construction projects, however, have the same level of complexity. For example, building a doghouse is not quite the same as building a bridge. You do not really need to document the building of your doghouse; but if you are building a bridge, you better have it blueprinted and tested in computer simulations before constructing it. Why should software development be any different?

Over the life cycle of an application, documentation plays two important roles:

- Prescriptive
- Descriptive

Prescriptive Documentation

Prescriptive documentation outlines how your application *should* be built. How often have you finished a significant portion of an application that you failed to document only to realize that you forgot a piece? Because good documentation follows from a standard engineering process, you are less likely to find that you have missed a key element; and for each element, you will understand it thoroughly before you begin building it. The basic goal of prescriptive documentation is to provide you with a history of the issues you decided were important and how they fit into the application as a whole.

Descriptive Documentation

Descriptive documentation details how an application is actually built. In a well-structured project, your documentation evolves as the project evolves, continuing even after the application has been deployed. If you have ever had to modify someone else's existing code, you know that the tasks of application testing and maintenance are made much easier by well-written documentation. And *much easier* translates into *less time and money.*

The Software Engineering Process

Random documentation does not help you build an application. The documentation you create should tell you, and any potential reader, all the information known about the objects in your system and how they act together. Although scribbling notes into a notebook may be enough to capture this information for yourself, this approach does not help others understand what you are trying to do.

Good documentation comes from a sound software engineering process that challenges you to ask the right questions and record the answers in a standard format. It is often said that "it's the planning, not the plan"; to some degree, that cliché is true. A good software engineering process serves as a sort of preflight checklist that helps you be sure that you do not miss anything crucial before takeoff.

This chapter takes a brief look at object-oriented software engineering and how it relates to the documentation you produce. Many volumes have been written on the subject of object-oriented software engineering, so this short chapter does not attempt to discuss the subject in detail. What I intend to provide is an introduction to the subject that helps you understand its importance and makes you want to learn more.

Object-Oriented Design

Because Java is a purely object-oriented language, the process of designing applications using Java follows well-established object-oriented software engineering methodologies. A *methodology* is simply a step-by-step process for performing a task; at each step along the way, you document what you did. An object-oriented methodology specifically looks at the system as an interplay of objects and thus seeks to understand the objects that make up that system and how they interact with each other.

Any software engineering process can be cleanly divided into six stages:

1. Analysis
2. Design
3. Development

4. Testing

5. Implementation

6. Maintenance

These steps proceed iteratively, meaning that once a subsystem comes out of testing it probably will go back into development (or sometimes even design). This loop will repeat as many times as necessary until all testing requirements are met.

Traditionally, 80 percent of software development is spent in the last stage, maintenance. In other words, the most effort on a system is spent fixing bugs and correcting things done poorly in the first five stages. Because getting something right the first time is always less costly than going back and redoing it, the goal of object-oriented software engineering is to shift time back to the first and second stages so that much less time is spent in the final stage.

Analysis

Before you begin any software development project, you first have to analyze the problem and understand what it is. The task of analysis is to prioritize system components by classifying them as either wants or needs. You must be able to accommodate the proper amount of time for the design and development of your system's needs. If you still have time on your planning chart after the *needs* have been accounted for, you then note which *wants* you will accommodate and which ones you will not. If you plan to implement a want in a future release, you should note that in your documentation so that designers can plan for that future expansion.

> **NOTE**
>
> This chapter offers a very distilled object-oriented software engineering process geared more towards the casual or small-project developer. There are actually several major object-oriented approaches in common use today. This chapter takes the major components of the well-known methodologies and describes their essence. Regardless of what sort of projects you are involved with, I highly recommend that you familiarize yourself with at least two of the major methodologies.
>
> Furthermore, if you are developing software professionally for a large audience, I strongly advise that you follow one of those methodologies for two reasons: First, a well-known methodology provides a common ground of understanding for a diverse set of people— from entry-level developers to senior architects and managers. Second, whenever you tell a potential customer that you follow object-oriented design practices, their first question, oddly enough, will be "Which methodology do you use?"

The documentation of your analysis can be fairly simple. It only has to show which pieces of your system will be considered *in scope*, that is, what will be built in the first release. For everything out of scope, you should note why it is out of scope and whether you plan to address it in a later release.

> **TIP**
>
> If you are building an application for a specific group of people, this is the best time to show them your analysis document and have them sign it. If, at a later date, they come back to you, asking why feature X was not in the system, you can show them their approval of the document.

The following outline captures the essence of what an analysis document should look like:

I.   General Use Cases

II. Context Model

III. Notes

To capture the proper wants and needs, you should sit down with potential users and document general *use cases*, sometimes called *scenarios*. A general use case is a simple statement describing a function of the system. For example, if I were building a program that predicted football games, I might have a use case like this:

The user requests a prediction for two teams.

Your use cases will help you identify high-level components that you can place into a diagram to graphically illustrate which pieces of the application are in scope and which are out of scope. This diagram is called a *context model*. Figure 29.1 shows a sample context model for the football game prediction program.

FIGURE 29.1.

The context model for a football game prediction program.

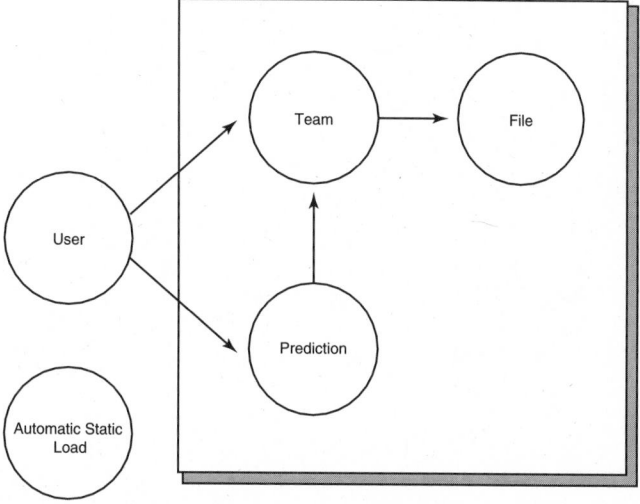

29

DOCUMENTING
YOUR CODE

The content of a context model is simple. You design and build anything inside the box. Anything outside the box is out of scope. If there is a line connecting something inside the box with something outside the box, that means that your system is interfacing with an external system.

The last section of your analysis document should briefly describe any decisions you made about the scope of the application. Specifically, you want to record anything you cut from scope and why you cut it.

Design

By understanding the problem, you can go on to design a solution. During the design process, you break the application into objects and provide descriptions of how they interact to satisfy the general use cases in the analysis document. The end product of your design should be a document that tells you exactly how to build your system without diving into coding details. The outline of a good design document should look something like this:

   I. Object Model

  II. Detailed Use Cases

 III. Object Specifications

To put together the object model, you first have to identify all your objects. Identifying objects is a lot less complex than it sounds. A few people gather around a white board or a piece of paper and name things they think are objects straight off the top of their head. At first, there are no wrong or right answers. Later, as you start applying the objects to use cases, you will see which objects best describe the system and then eliminate from your design those that do not.

The following list of objects comes from a brainstorm session on the design for the football program:

- Team
- Statistic
- Game
- User
- Points-for
- Points-against
- File

Once you feel comfortable with the initial list of objects, the next step is to attempt to identify recurring patterns within those objects. The simplest form is that of inheritance, in which one object is simply an extension of another object. Clearly, the points-for and points-against objects are really extensions of a statistic. But is a statistic really a simple attribute of a team? Or is it a more complex object with independent behaviors? Because converting an object into a simple data type is easier than converting a simple data type into an object during the design process, you should keep anything as an object until you are certain it is not.

Completing the design involves iterating over the process of fitting objects into use cases, fleshing out those use cases, and then identifying opportunities for abstraction until you feel you have a clearly defined architecture for the development of your system. To reach this stage, you need documentation identifying every single object you will build for the system, its attributes, and its behaviors.

The object model is a diagram that illustrates your understanding of the system as a whole. For a small system like the football game prediction program, the diagram can be as simple as the one in Figure 29.2.

FIGURE 29.2.

The object model for the football game predictor.

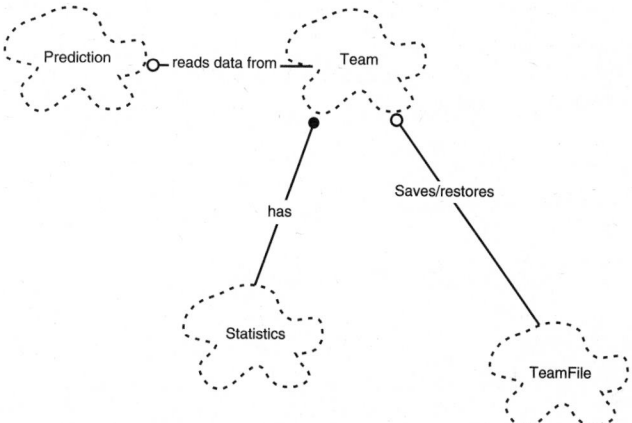

This diagram shows you exactly what you have to code. All that is left to figure out is how to code it. In object-oriented programming, an application consists of objects that are made up of methods and attributes. After putting together the object model, you next must detail each step of the general use cases documented in the analysis documentation. By going into deep detail on the use cases, you can see each thing that a given object does and the data it requires to support that behavior. As you did with the general use cases, you provide simple English sentences that describe what happens. The general use case, "The user requests a prediction for two teams," might be divided into the following detailed scenario:

1. The user executes the program with the two teams as arguments.
2. The prediction object creates a team instance for each of the teams.
3. The prediction object requests relevant statistics from each team.
4. The prediction object calculates an outcome.
5. The prediction object displays the results to the user.

From this detailed use case, you can see that the team object will need methods for retrieving statistics, and the prediction object will need methods to instantiate team objects and predict games.

The final important section of a design document is a list of objects with their attributes and methods, called the *object specification*. Figure 29.3 shows the object specification for the Team object in the football predictor.

FIGURE 29.3.

The object specification for a Team *object.*

Team

Description

The Team class represents a given football team. It is responsible for tracking its statistics and managing information received from recently completed games. In addition, it has a TeamFile object which it uses to save its statistics.

Attributes

Attribute Name	Data Type	Description
name	String	The name of the team.
wins	int	The number of wins to-date.
losses	int	The number of losses to-date.
points_for	int	The number of points scored by the team this season.
points_against	int	The number of points scored by opponents against the team this season.
file	TeamFile	The TeamFile object managing the saving and restoring of team data.

Methods/Events

Method Name	Return Type	Parameters	Description
addGame	void	int points_scored, int points_allows	This method adds a new game to the Team's list of game stats.
getStat	int	String stat	Returns the number of wins, losses, points for, or points against depending on the stat requested.

Into Development and Beyond

The final stages of the software engineering process form the traditional bulk of where work is done. During *development*, you write the code that becomes the system. As you complete each module or subsystem, you *test* it to make sure it works. For the purposes of this chapter, testing is simply making sure that each subsystem does exactly what your design documents say it should do. In a very formal environment, however, the testing process is a very complex subject about which entire books have been written.

Once the application has been thoroughly tested and you know it does everything it is supposed to do, you release the code to the people who will actually use it. Using Java's ability to create zero-install applications, however, the time you spend in the *implementation* stage is greatly reduced. You make the classes available over the Web and let people run the application. The rest of the implementation stage is spent gathering feedback on how the application performs in the real world so that you can prepare and manage the maintenance stage.

After you first release a product, chances are you will want to enhance it and fix any bugs you didn't catch in testing. Perhaps you may even want to reengineer portions of it as your development experience grows. The final phase of software development, *maintenance*, is about doing just that. Of course, the creation of a new release is a full exercise in software development in itself. Maintenance thus brings you full circle back into the analysis stage of software development.

Documenting Code

The documentation created in the analysis and design phases provides the prescriptive documentation you need to build an application. During the iterative process of systems development, however, you will encounter issues that you simply missed in analysis and design. You therefore need a way to communicate to others exactly how your system was built.

Developers commonly write their descriptive documentation from memory after an application is built. They then fail to maintain the documentation along with the application. For someone trying to make a change to an application using poorly maintained documentation, no documentation is almost as good as what they have to work with. Fortunately, Java provides the javadoc utility for documenting your code as you write it.

The javadoc Utility

The javadoc utility is a small Java program that comes with the JDK to help you create object documentation straight from your code. javadoc uses a combination of compiler information and comments made by you to build HTML documentation that describes everything about a Java object. As long as you maintain your comments with your code, your application documentation always reflects the current state of its objects.

If you have visited the JavaSoft API documentation pages at http://java.sun.com:80/products/JDK/CurrentRelease/api/, you have seen the kind of descriptive documentation produced by javadoc. To produce Web pages that properly document your objects, you must include the following in each object source file:

- A description of the object
- A description of all public, protected, or private protected attributes
- A description of all public, protected, or private protected methods

Each description appears in Java code as a comment just before the element it is describing. To mark the comment as a javadoc comment, it must be in the format:

```
/** description */
```

Listing 29.1 shows what the Team class source code looks like.

Listing 29.1. The Team class source file, with javadoc comments.

```java
/**
 * The Team class has statistics and receives updates from users.
 * It represents one football team and maintains the statistics for
 * that team.
 * @version 1.0
 * @author George Reese
 */
public class Team {
  private TeamFile file;
  private int wins, losses, points_for, points_against;

  /**
   * Constructs a new Team object based on a team name.
   * Specifically, it creates a TeamFile object to access
   * the file in which team data is stored.  It then uses
   * the file object to get all of the team's stats
   * from storage.
   * @exception FileException caused by a failure to read storage file
   * @param name the name of the team
   * @see TeamFile#getField
   */
  public Team(String name) {
    file = new TeamFile(name);
    wins = f.getField("wins");
    losses = f.getField("losses");
    points_for = f.getField("points_for");
    points_against = f.getField("points_against");
  }

  /**
   * Adds the statistics for a recently completed game.
   * In this release, we are ignoring ties.
   * @exception FileException thrown by a failed attempt to save the file
   * @param pf the points this team scored in the game
   * @param pa the points scored by the opponent
```

```
 * @see TeamFile#setField
 * @see TeamFile#save
 */
public void addGame(int pf, int pa) {
  if( pf > pa ) wins++;
  else if( pa > pf ) losses++;
  points_for += pf;
  points_against += pa;
  file.setField("wins", wins);
  file.setField("losses", losses);
  file.setField("points_for", points_for);
  file.setField("points_against");
  file.save();
}

/**
 * Allows the Prediction class to get team statistics
 * for this team.
 * @exception NoSuchStatException thrown if a bad stat is requested
 * @param stat the desired stat
 * @return the value for the requested stat
 */
protected int getStat(String stat) {
  if( stat.equals("wins") ) {
    return wins;
  }
  else if( stat.equals("losses") ) {
    return losses;
  }
  else if( stat.equals("points_for") ) {
    return points_for;
  }
  else if( stat.equals("points_against") ) {
    return points_against;
  }
  throw new NoSuchStatException(stat);
}
}
```

29

DOCUMENTING YOUR CODE

Ideally, you should be commenting your code to this degree anyway. Why not have those comments help you get your documentation done?

You may have noticed some fields in the comments beginning with an @ symbol. The javadoc utility enables you to pass certain information using these @ keywords. In the Team class example, I used @version, @author, @exception, @param, @return, and @see to tell javadoc about the class version, class author, method exceptions, method parameters, method return values, and other references.

Table 29.1 lists all the keywords you can use in your `javadoc` comments with their meanings.

Table 29.1. Keywords used by `javadoc`.

Keyword	Description
@author	Used in class comments. Identifies who wrote the class. You can have multiple @author tags for a class.
@exception	Used in method comments. Identifies the full class name for any exceptions thrown by the method. You can have multiple @exception tags for a method.
@param	Used in method comments. Identifies a method parameter. You should specify as many of these as the method has parameters.
@return	Used in method comments. Describes what the method will return.
@see	Used in any comment type. Allows you to reference other classes, attributes, and methods with a hypertext link.
@version	Used in class comments. Identifies the version number for this class.

Among the advantages of this style of documentation is that you can embed HTML tags inside your comments that will appear in your final HTML documentation. You can even go so far as to embed applets inside your applet documentation! More importantly, this kind of documentation enables you to create links to related documentation that is beyond the ability of the @see keyword to handle. The only limitation is that you cannot embed a <HR> or <H1> through <H6> HTML tag inside a comment. Although doing so does not generate an error, it may produce unexpected results in your output documentation.

Once your source files are complete, both in terms of code and commenting, you are ready to build the documentation for the application. To do this, you simply execute the `javadoc` command with the class file as an argument. The `javadoc` command creates five output HTML files with documentation for your class. The generated files are listed here:

- ■ `YourClassName.html` —Detailed documentation for your class.
- ■ `Package-YourPackageName.html`—For each package, one of these files is created listing all the classes in that package.
- ■ `AllNames.html`—A list of attributes and methods for all classes (in this case, just one class) in alphabetical order.
- ■ `packages.html`—A list of all packages in your application.
- ■ `tree.html`—A list of all classes, shown as an inheritance tree.

Of course, you probably want to document more than one class at a time, and you probably do not want that documentation stuck in the same directory as your source code. The javadoc command accepts a host of options so that you can customize your documentation to your needs. Before you worry about those options, however, you should understand what Java does count on. It expects a directory tree that ships with the JDK, containing stock graphics as well as the Java API documentation (javadoc produces documentation that contains appropriate links to Java API documentation).

Managing links to existing documentation is one place in which javadoc gets a little messy. Unfortunately, javadoc likes to pile all your documentation into one huge directory. Additionally, javadoc is not smart enough to determine any class dependencies on its own. If you are generating documentation for classes with dependencies, you must tell javadoc so that it regenerates any old documentation. Finally, the HTML files created by javadoc expect an images subdirectory under the directory in which they are located. You can generally take care of this problem by creating a link to the images directory that came with the JDK.

On the command line, javadoc can take one of two forms:

- javadoc [*options*] *file*
- javadoc [*options*] *package*

You can customize javadoc output with the options listed in Table 29.2.

Table 29.2. Options for use with javadoc.

Option	Comment
-author	If there are @author tags in the comments, list them in the documentation.
-authors	Same as the -author option.
-classpath *path list*	Manually sets the class path for finding source code. Remember that your CLASS PATH environment variable is generally set to where your .class files are located, so you will almost always have to specify this option.
-d *directory*	The directory in which the generated documentation should be placed.
-depend *package list*	A list of dependencies for the package being documented.
-version	As with the @author tag, you must specify that version information should be included in the documentation.
-verbose	Print information about the progress of javadoc as it is generating documentation.

29

DOCUMENTING YOUR CODE

Summary

Although generating documentation may not be the most enjoyable part of software development, it is a necessity. Successful applications built in a timely fashion with small maintenance requirements invariably are well-documented applications flowing from a proven engineering methodology. The analysis and design stages of development provide you with prescriptive documentation that tells you exactly what has to be built before you build it. In the development stage, you can use the `javadoc` utility to create up-to-date descriptive documentation that helps people maintaining and modifying your code down the road—even if you are the one doing the maintenance and modification.

Optimizing Java Code

by Michael Morrison

IN THIS CHAPTER

CHAPTER

30

Even with all its power and wonder, few people can argue the primary drawback to Java as a development platform: execution speed. It's certainly true that the execution speed of Java programs is improving dramatically with the release of just-in-time (JIT) compilers, but there is still much to be desired. Rather than wait around for faster JIT compilers or enhanced Java virtual machines, you can empower yourself by taking control of your Java code and the speed at which it executes.

This chapter looks at Java code optimization and how you can improve the performance of your Java programs. In this chapter, you learn various optimization techniques that can help you become a more efficient Java programmer. To really understand how these optimization techniques help, you have to go under the hood of Java a little. However, I think you'll find that Java code optimization isn't all that difficult. So roll up your sleeves and prepare to get a little dirty.

What Is Code Optimization?

Code optimization is the process of modifying working code to a more optimal state based on a particular goal. The fact that optimization takes place on *working code* is an important point; always perform optimizations on code *after* you get the code working. The type of optimization performed depends on the desired goal; code optimization can be divided into three distinct types, which are based on the needs of the developer:

- Maintainability
- Size
- Speed

Based on this list, you probably realize now that code optimization isn't just about improving performance; speed optimization is simply one type of optimization. Nevertheless, it is usually the most important type of optimization to consider when dealing with Java code.

Maintainability Optimization

Maintainability optimization is performed to help make code more manageable in the future. This type of optimization is usually geared toward the structure and organization of code rather than modifications to the algorithms used in the code. In general, maintainability optimization involves a programmer studying the code at large and making changes to help other programmers understand and modify the code in the future.

Fortunately, the rigid structure of the Java language goes a long way toward keeping things optimized for maintainability. In fact, if you adhere to basic object-oriented design principles, you really don't need to do anything else to keep your code optimized for maintainability.

Size Optimization

Another popular optimization is size optimization, which involves making changes to code that result in a smaller executable class file. The cornerstone of size optimization is code reuse, which comes in the form of inheritance for Java classes. Fortunately, good object-oriented design strategies naturally favor size optimization, so you rarely have to go out of your way to perform this type of optimization. For example, it's simply good design practice to put into a method code that is reused more than once. In this way, most size optimizations naturally take place during the initial code development.

Although it's not typically a huge issue, size optimization can't be completely ignored in Java programming. This is because the size of your compiled Java classes directly impacts the amount of time it takes your program to load and initially execute. If you leverage as much of the standard Java API code as possible and reuse code by deriving from other classes, you're probably doing enough for the cause of reducing class size.

Speed Optimization

Speed optimization is without a doubt the most important type of optimization when it comes to Java programming. Speed optimization includes all the techniques and tricks used to speed up the execution of code. Considering the performance problems inherent in Java, speed optimization takes on an even more important role in Java than it does in other languages such as C and C++. Because the Java compiler has the last word on how code is generated, most speed optimizations are performed with the compiler in mind.

The rest of this chapter focuses on issues of speed optimization and how to get the best performance out of your Java code. At times, you will sacrifice the other types of optimization for the sake of speed. In most cases, this sacrifice is entirely acceptable—even expected—because the organization of the code and size of the executable classes won't matter much if your programs are too slow to be useable.

Optimizing with the JDK Compiler

All optimizations begin and end with the Java compiler. If you don't understand the compiler, you're largely guessing at which optimizations will have a positive effect on your code. So let's take a look at the JDK compiler and see what role it plays in turning out speedy Java bytecodes. Bytecodes comprise the intermediate processor-independent code generated by the Java compiler. Bytecode executables (classes) are interpreted by the Java runtime system.

> **NOTE**
>
> Third-party Java compilers are being released that outclass the JDK compiler in regard to speed optimization. Nevertheless, the JDK compiler is the standard Java compiler and is currently the most reliable.

The JDK compiler (javac) includes a switch for generating optimized Java bytecode executables: -O. In release 1.02 of the JDK, this switch results in only two optimizations taking place: inline methods and exclusion of line numbers. The first of these optimizations is the only one that affects the speed of the executable bytecode; final, static, and private methods are inlined by the compiler, resulting in less method call overhead. *Method inlining* is the process of replacing each call to a method with the actual method code. Inlining can often increase the size of the resulting class file, but it can help improve performance.

The second optimization performed by the JDK compiler results in the exclusion of line number information from the executable class file. This is a size optimization and does nothing in terms of helping speed up the code. However, it does have the side benefit of making the executable class files a little smaller, which improves the download time of Java applets.

The truth is that the JDK compiler does little for you in regard to optimization. This means that you have to plan on doing a lot of optimization by hand. Hopefully, the compiler that ships with Java 1.1 will improve this situation, but you probably can't afford to stand around waiting for miracles.

Costs of Common Operations

Now that you understand what the JDK compiler does (or doesn't do) for you in regard to optimization, it's time to focus on the Java runtime system. By examining the runtime system, you can get an idea of how fast certain types of code run and make smarter decisions about the way you write Java code. What do I mean by *examining the runtime system*? Well, I mean running different types of code and timing each type to see how the speeds match up. This operation gives you a very realistic look at how code differs in terms of execution speed, and consequently gives you a place to start making appropriate code optimizations.

The speed of an operation is often referred to as the *cost* of the operation. Code optimization can almost be likened to accounting, in which you try to keep from blowing a performance budget with your code costs. Jonathan Hardwick performed a very neat analysis on the cost of common Java operations on various systems, the results of which I've included in Tables 30.1 through 30.3. These tables contain approximate times in microseconds for common Java operations. Incidentally, the systems used to perform the cost analysis were a Sun Sparcstation 5 running Solaris, an AMD 486 DX4-120 running Windows 95, and an AMD 486 DX4-120 running Linux 1.2.13.

Table 30.1. The costs of Java variable accesses (speeds measured in microseconds).

Description	Operation	Solaris	486 Win95	486 Linux
Method variable assignment	`i = 1;`	0.4	0.3	0.5
Instance variable assignment	`this.i = 1;`	2.4	0.7	0.9
Array element assignment	`a[0] = 1;`	1.1	1.0	1.3

Table 30.2. The costs of increment with Java data types.

Description	Operation	Solaris	486 Win95	486 Linux
Byte variable increment	`byte b++;`	1.2	1.2	1.3
Short variable increment	`short s++;`	1.4	1.2	1.3
Integer variable increment	`int i++;`	0.3	0.1	0.3
Long variable increment	`long l++;`	1.1	1.1	1.3
Float variable increment	`float f++;`	0.9	1.1	1.2
Double variable increment	`double d++;`	1.0	1.3	1.5

Table 30.3. The costs of miscellaneous Java operations.

Description	Operation	Solaris	486 Win95	486 Linux
Object creation	`new Object();`	10.7	13.8	12.8
Method invocation	`null_func();`	3.1	2.1	2.4
Synchronized method	`sync_func();`	16.3	20.1	15.9
Math function	`Math.abs(x);`	5.6	4.8	5.6
Equivalent math code	`(x < 0) ? -x : x;`	0.6	0.4	0.6

These tables point out lots of interesting information regarding the performance of Java code. From Table 30.1, it's readily apparent that method variables are more efficient to use than instance variables. Furthermore, you can see that array element assignment is slower than method variable assignment because Java performs bounds-checking operations whenever an array element is accessed. Keep in mind that this table isn't meant as an argument to get rid of all your class member data. Rather, think of it as providing insight into making decisions where the design could go either way.

Table 30.2 shows timing data related to the use of the standard Java data types. As you may have expected, the two 32-bit data types (`int` and `float`) showed the best performance because the tests were performed on 32-bit systems. It is interesting to note that the performance differences between using an `int` over a `byte`, `short`, or `long` is much more significant than for using a `float` over a `double`.

Even though the floating-point types show comparable performance to the integer types, don't be misled about using integer math over floating-point math. This timing table reflects only an increment operation, which is much different than more complex operations performed in the context of a practical Java program. Integer math is much more efficient than floating-point math. So use the table as a measure of the relative speeds among integer types, and then try to use integer math throughout your code.

Table 30.3 focuses on a few miscellaneous operations that are worth thinking about. First off, it shows the high cost of creating an object. This should serve as an incentive to eliminate the creation of temporary objects within a loop where the creation occurs over and over. Rather, you can place the temporary object above the loop and reinitialize its members as needed inside the loop.

Table 30.3 also shows the dramatic performance costs of using a normal method versus a synchronized method. Even though synchronization is very important in multithreaded programming, Table 30.3 should be some encouragement to minimize the usage of synchronized methods in situations where you're in a performance squeeze.

Finally, Table 30.3 shows you how using the standard Java math methods can sometimes be a burden. Even something as simple as taking the absolute value of a number imposes much greater performance costs when you call the `Math.abs()` method, as opposed to inlining the equivalent code yourself.

Isolating Sluggish Code

The biggest mistake you can make in regard to optimizing your Java code is trying to optimize *all* the code. Being smart about what code you attack is crucial in not spending years trying to improve the performance of your code. More important, it's a well-established fact that a relatively small portion of code is usually responsible for the bulk of the performance drain. It's your job to isolate this code and then focus your optimization efforts accordingly.

Fortunately, isolating problem code isn't all that difficult if you use the proper tools. The most useful tool in finding bottlenecks in your code is a *profiler*. A profiler's job is to report the amount of time spent in each section of code as a program is executing. The Java runtime interpreter has an undocumented built-in profiler that is easy to use and works pretty well. To use the runtime interpreter profiler, simply specify the -prof option when using the interpreter, like this:

```
java -prof Classname
```

`Classname` is the name of the class you want to profile. Of course, this technique doesn't work too well for applets, because they must be run within the context of the applet viewer tool or a Web browser. Fortunately, you can use the profiler with applets by altering the arguments to the interpreter a little, like this:

```
java -prof sun.applet.AppletViewer Filename
```

In this case, `Filename` is the name of the HTML file containing a link to your applet. When you finish running the applet, the interpreter writes a file named java.prof to the current directory. This file contains profile information for the applet you just ran. The information consists of a list of methods sorted according to how many times each method is called over the course of the program. The methods are listed in order of decreasing method calls, meaning that the first method in the list is called more than any other method.

You can easily use this information as a guide to determine the code on which to focus your optimization efforts. The methods appearing at the top of the java.prof file should receive more of your attention because they are being called much more than methods farther down in the list. Making small performance gains in a method that is called 20,000 times has a much greater impact than speeding up a method that is called only a couple hundred times. The cool thing is that you can try different optimizations and then run the profiler again to see whether the relative times have changed. This is a very practical (if somewhat time-consuming) way to make great strides in speeding up your code.

Optimization Strategies

Now that you've isolated the code that is making your program crawl, it's time to look into exactly what optimizations you can perform to speed things up. You won't always be able to optimize every piece of problem code; the goal is to make big dents in the areas that can be optimized.

Rethink Algorithms

Many C/C++ programmers have traditionally resorted to assembly language when the issue of performance is raised. As a Java programmer, you don't have this option. This is actually a good thing because it forces you to take a closer look at your design approach instead of relying on heavier processor dependence to solve your problems. What the assembly heads don't realize is that much more significant gains can be made by entirely rethinking an algorithm than by porting it to assembly. And trust me, the amount of time spent hand-coding tedious assembly can easily result in a leaner, more efficient algorithm.

This same ideology applies to Java programming. Before you run off writing native methods and expanding loops to get every little ounce of performance (which you learn about in the next sections), take a step back and see whether the algorithm itself has any weaknesses. To put this all into perspective, imagine if programmers had always resorted to optimizing the traditional bubble sort algorithm and had never thought twice about the algorithm itself. The quick sort algorithm, which is orders of magnitude faster than the bubble sort without any optimization, would never have come about.

Use Native Methods

I hate to recommend them, but the truth is that *native methods* (methods written in C or C++ that can be called from Java code) are typically much faster than Java methods. The reason I'm reluctant to promote their use is that they blow the platform-independence benefit of using Java, therefore tying your program to a particular platform. If platform independence isn't high on your list, however, by all means look into rewriting problem methods in C. You learn how to connect Java to C code in Chapter 33, "Integrating Native Code."

Use Inline Methods

Inline methods, whose bodies appear in place of each method call, are a fairly effective means of improving performance. Because the Java compiler already inlines final, static, and private methods when you have the optimization switch turned on, your best bet is to try to make as many methods as possible final, static, or private. If this isn't possible and you still want the benefits of inlined code, you can always inline methods by hand: Just paste the body of the method at each place where it is called. This is one of those cases in which you are sacrificing both maintainability and size for speed. (The things we do for speed!)

Replace Slow Java API Classes and Methods

There may be times when you are using a standard Java API class for a few of its features, but the extra baggage imposed by the generic design of the class is slowing you down. In situations like this, you may be better off writing your own class that performs the exact functionality you need and no more. This streamlined approach can pay off big, even though it comes at the cost of rewriting code that already works.

Another similar situation occurs when you are using a Java API class and you isolate a particular method in it that is dragging down performance. In this situation, instead of rewriting the entire class, just derive from it and override the troublesome method. This is a good middle-of-the-road solution because you leverage code reuse against performance in a reasonable manner.

Use Look-Up Tables

An established trick up the sleeve of every programmer who has wrestled with floating-point performance problems is the look-up table. *Look-up tables* are tables of constant integer values that are used in place of time-consuming calculations. For example, a very popular type of look-up table is one containing values for trigonometric functions, such as sine. The use of trigonometric functions is sometimes unavoidable in certain types of programs. If you haven't noticed, Java's trigonometric functions are all floating-point in nature, which is a bad thing in terms of performance. The solution is to write an integer version of the desired function using a look-up table of values. This relatively simple change is sometimes a necessity considering the performance hit you take by using floating-point math.

Eliminate Unnecessary Evaluations

Moving along into more detailed optimizations, you can often find unnecessary evaluations in your code that serve only to eat up extra processor time. Following is an example of some code that unnecessarily performs an evaluation that acts effectively as a constant:

```
for (int i = 0; i < size(); i++)
  a = (b + c) / i;
```

The addition of b + c, although itself a pretty efficient piece of code, is being calculated each time through the loop. It is better off being calculated before the loop, like this:

```
int tmp = b + c;
for (int i = 0; i < size(); i++)
  a = tmp / i;
```

This simple change can have fairly dramatic effects, depending on how many times the loop is iterated. Speaking of the loop, there's another optimization you might have missed. Notice that size() is a method call, which should bring to mind the costs involved in calling a method (you learned about this performance drag earlier in the chapter). You may not realize it, but size() is called every time through the loop as part of the conditional loop expression. The same technique used to eliminate the unnecessary addition operation can be used to fix this problem. Check out the resulting code:

```
int s = size;
int tmp = b + c;
for (int i = 0; i < s; i++)
  a = tmp / i;
```

Eliminate Common Subexpressions

Sometimes, you may be reusing a costly subexpression without even realizing it. In the heat of programming, it's easy to reuse common subexpressions instead of storing them in a temporary variable, like this:

```
b = Math.abs(a) * c;
d = e / (Math.abs(a) + b);
```

The multiple calls to Math.abs() are costly compared to calling it once and using a temporary variable, like this:

```
int tmp = Meth.abs(a);
b = tmp * c;
d = e / (tmp + b);
```

Expand Loops

One optimization that is popular among C/C++ programmers is loop expansion, or loop unrolling, which is the process of expanding a loop to get rid of the overhead involved in maintaining the loop. You may be wondering exactly what overhead I'm talking about. Well, even a simple counting loop has the overhead of performing a comparison and an increment each time through. This may not seem like much, but when you consider that some code is called thousands of times in a program, it's easy to see how small changes can sometimes yield big results.

Loop expansion basically involves replacing a loop with the brute-force equivalent. To better understand this process, consider the following piece of code:

```
for (int i = 0; i < 1000; i++)
  a[i] = 25;
```

That probably looks like some pretty efficient code and, in fact, it is. But if you want to go the extra distance and perform a loop expansion on it, here's one approach:

```
int i = 0;
for (int j = 0; j < 100; j++) {
  a[i++] = 25;
  a[i++] = 25;
  a[i++] = 25;
  a[i++] = 25;
  a[i++] = 25;
  a[i++] = 25;
  a[i++] = 25;
  a[i++] = 25;
  a[i++] = 25;
  a[i++] = 25;
}
```

In this code, you've reduced the loop overhead by an order of magnitude, but you've introduced some new overhead by having to increment the new index variable inside the loop. Overall, this code does outperform the original code, but don't expect any miracles. Loop expansion can be effective at times, but I don't recommend placing it too high on your list of optimization tricks.

Summary

This chapter covered a somewhat murky area of Java programming: code optimization. You began by learning about the fundamental types of optimization, including the most popular type of Java optimization: speed optimization. You then learned about the optimizations (or lack thereof) provided by the JDK compiler. From there, you got a little dose of realism by looking into the timing costs of common Java operations. You finished the chapter by taking an in-depth look at some practical code optimizations you can apply to your own Java programs.

This chapter rounds out Part VI of this book, "Programming Strategies." Armed with these strategies, you're no doubt ready to press on into Part VII, "Advanced Java." In Part VII, you learn about all kinds of advanced Java programming issues including database connectivity, persistence, and security, among other things.

VII
PART

Advanced Java

Exploring Database Connectivity with JDBC

by George Reese

IN THIS CHAPTER

CHAPTER 31

You have very likely used the file system of your applications' host operating system to save important information related to the work your applications do. For applications such as word processors and graphics applications, storing user data in files works very well. In fact, most traditional PC applications work fine using file-based data storage.

As your applications grow in complexity, however, your data needs can increase in complexity as well. A file system allows an application to save information in a very static manner. If, for example, you want to save information about your compact disc collection, you may choose to store it in a spreadsheet. Your spreadsheet columns would contain information such as artist, title, and release date. You would then save that spreadsheet to a file. But what would you do if you wanted to store a list of songs for each album? How would you find all the songs with the word *rain* in them released since 1979?

A file system does not work well for complex data storage needs such as the one just described. More complex applications, such as those common to the business and research worlds, require the power of a database. A *database* is an application that specializes in providing other applications with access to data in a more complex manner than is allowed by file systems. The only request your application can make of a file system is for it to hand your application a file with a given name. You can ask a database, however, for all the songs with the word *rain* in them released since 1979.

In addition to enabling an application to access data in a more complex way, a database can be used to create a central information store for networked computers. Although the content of such information may not be complex enough to stretch the capabilities of a file system, file systems do not work well on the Internet, where different computers with very diverse operating systems interact.

The original release of Java provided only file system access, with no provisions for database access. In March 1996, JavaSoft began to address the need for database access with the draft release of the Java Database Connectivity (JDBC) specification. This chapter addresses the use of JDBC to give your applications access to databases.

> **NOTE**
>
> This chapter focuses directly on the Java JDBC API. If you are not familiar with databases, take a look at Chapter 43, "Developing Your Own Database Application," which describes in detail the development of a database application.

The JDBC API

To provide a common base API for accessing data, Sun (with support from a number of independent software vendors) developed JDBC. JDBC defines a number of Java interfaces to enable developers to access data independently of the actual database product being used to store the data. In theory, an application written against the basic JDBC API using only SQL-2 can function against any database technology that supports SQL-2.

Database Requirements

Data can be stored in a wide variety of formats using various technologies. Most systems currently use one of three major database management systems:

- Relational databases (RDBMS)
- Object-relational databases (OORDBMS)
- Object-oriented databases (OODBMS)

Relational databases are overwhelmingly the most common. In addition to these systems, there are other things to consider, such as hierarchical databases and file systems. Any low-level API trying to find a least-common denominator among these data storage methods would end up with the null set. JDBC, however, mandates no specific requirements on the underlying DBMS. Rather than dictating what sort of DBMS an application must have to support JDBC, the JDBC specification places all its requirements on the JDBC implementation.

The JDBC specification primarily mandates that a JDBC implementation support at least ANSI SQL-2 Entry Level. Because most common RDBMS and OORDBMS systems support SQL-2, this requirement provides a reasonable baseline from which to build database access. In addition, because SQL-2 is required only at the JDBC implementation level, that implementation can provide its own SQL-2 wrapper around non-SQL data stores. Writing such a wrapper, however, would likely be a huge task.

The JDBC Interfaces

JDBC defines eight interfaces that must be implemented by a driver in order to be JDBC-compliant:

- `java.sql.Driver`
- `java.sql.Connection`
- `java.sql.Statement`
- `java.sql.PreparedStatement`
- `java.sql.CallableStatement`
- `java.sql.ResultSet`
- `java.sql.ResultSetMetaData`
- `java.sql.DatabaseMetaData`

Figure 31.1 shows these interfaces and how they interact in the full JDBC object model.

FIGURE 31.1.

The JDBC object model.

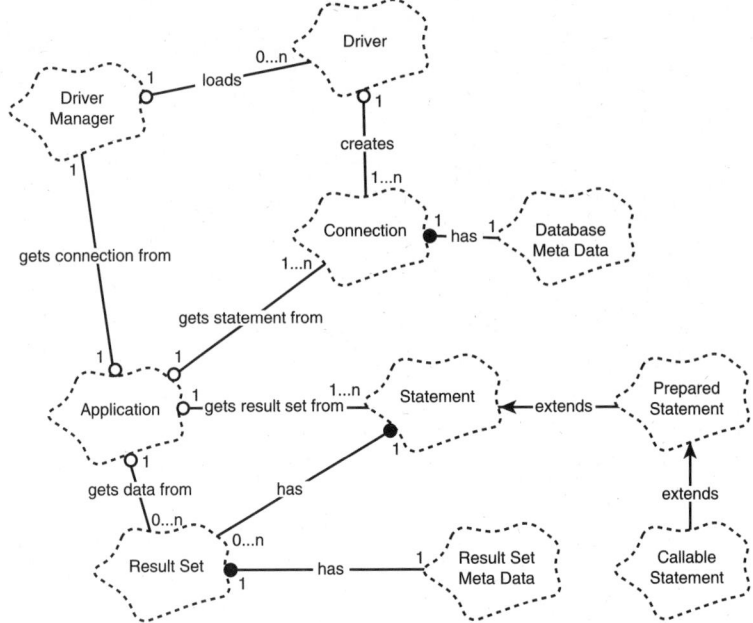

The central object around which the whole concept revolves is the `java.sql.DriverManager` object. It is responsible for keeping track of the various JDBC implementations that may exist for an application. If, for example, a system were aware of Sybase and Oracle JDBC implementations, the `DriverManager` would be responsible for tracking those implementations. Any time an application wants to connect to a database, it asks the `DriverManager` to give it a database connection, using a database URL through the `DriverManager.getConnection()` method. Based on this URL, the `DriverManager` searches for a `Driver` implementation that accepts the URL. It then gets a `Connection` implementation from that `Driver` and returns it to the application.

WHAT IS A DATABSE URL?

To enable an application to specify the database to which it wants to connect, JDBC uses the Internet standard Uniform Resource Locator system. A JDBC URL consists of the following pieces:

`jdbc:<subprotocol>:<subname>`

As with URLs you have seen all over the Internet, the first element is the resource protocol—in this case, a JDBC data source. The *subprotocol* is specific to the JDBC implementation. In many cases, it is the DBMS name and version; for example, syb10 indicates Sybase

System 10. The *subname* element is any information specific to the DBMS that tells it where it needs to connect. For mSQL, the JDBC URL is in this format:

```
jdbc:msql://hostname:port/database
```

JDBC itself does not care what a database URL looks like. The important thing is simply that a desired JDBC implementation can recognize the URL and get the information it needs to connect to a database from that URL.

The `DriverManager` is the only instantiated class provided by JDBC other than exception objects and a few specialized subclasses of `java.util.Date`. Additional calls made by an application are written against the JDBC interfaces that are implemented for specific DBMSs.

The `java.sql.Driver` Interface

A `Driver` is essentially a `Connection` factory. The `DriverManager` uses a `Driver` to determine whether it can handle a given URL. If one of the `Driver`s in its list can handle the URL, that `Driver` should create a `Connection` object and return it to the `DriverManager`. Because an application only indirectly references a `Driver` through the `DriverManager`, applications are rarely concerned with this interface.

The `java.sql.Connection` Interface

A `Connection` is a single database session. As such, it stores state information about the database session it manages and provides the application with `Statement`, `PreparedStatement`, or `CallableStatement` objects for making calls during the session.

The `java.sql.Statement` Interface

A `Statement` is an unbound SQL call to the database. It is generally a simple UPDATE, DELETE, INSERT, or SELECT statement in which no columns must be bound to Java data. A `Statement` provides methods for making such calls and returns to the application the results of any SELECT statement or the number of rows affected by an UPDATE, DELETE, or INSERT statement.

`Statement` has the subclass `PreparedStatement`, which is in turn subclassed by `CallableStatement`. A `PreparedStatement` is a precompiled database call that requires parameters to be bound. An example of a `PreparedStatement` is a stored procedure call that has no OUT or INOUT parameters. For stored procedures with OUT or INOUT parameters, an application should use the `CallableStatement` interface.

The `java.sql.ResultSet` Interface

An application gets data returned by a SELECT query through the implementer of the `java.sql.ResultSet` interface. Specifically, the `ResultSet` object enables an application to retrieve sequential rows of data returned from a previous SELECT call. The ResultSet provides a multitude of methods that enable you to retrieve a given row as any data type to which it makes sense to convert it. For example, if you have a date stored in the database as a datetime, you can retrieve it through the getString() method and use it as a String.

The Meta-Data Interfaces

Meta-data is data about data. Specifically, it is a set of data that gives you information on the database and data retrieved from the database. Java provides two meta-data interfaces: java.sql.ResultSetMetaData and java.sql.DatabaseMetaData. The ResultSetMetaData interface provides a means for getting information about a particular ResultSet. For example, among other things, ResultSetMetaData provides information on the number of columns in the result set, the name of a column, and its type. The DatabaseMetaData interface, on the other hand, gives the application information on the database in general, such as what levels of support it has, its name, version, and other bits.

Simple Database Access Using the JDBC Interfaces

An application for which database independence is paramount should be written to the JDBC specification, using no database-specific calls and making use of no SQL that is not part of the ANSI SQL-2 standard. In such code, no reference should be made to a specific implementation of JDBC. Writing a simple database application using only JDBC calls involves the following steps:

1. Ask the DriverManager for a Connection implementation.
2. Ask the Connection for a Statement or subclass of Statement to execute your SQL.
3. For subclasses of Statement, bind any parameters to be passed to the prepared statement.
4. Execute the statement.
5. For queries, process the result set returned from the query. Do this for each result set (if you have multiple result sets) until there are none left.
6. For other statements, check the return value for the number of rows affected.
7. Close the statement.
8. Process any number of such statements and then close the connection.

The Counter Applet Example

 A simple sample applet that demonstrates bare database connectivity is a common Web counter. A Web counter is an applet that keeps track of how many times a given Web

Exploring Database Connectivity with JDBC

CHAPTER 31

643

31

EXPLORING
DATABASE
CONNECTIVITY

page has been "hit," or accessed. Using the JDBC interfaces, this applet connects to a database, determines how many times the page on which it appears has been hit, updates the page to reflect the new hit, and finally displays the number of hits. To use this example, you need a database engine to run your database and a JDBC driver to access that database engine. If you do not have a database engine, download mSQL and JDBC, which are both free for noncommercial use and are provided on the CD-ROM that accompanies this book. Links to mSQL and the JDBC class may be found through http://www.imaginary.com/Java/. In addition, you need to create a table called t_counter with the fields counter_file (CHAR(100), PRIMARY KEY) and counter_num (INT, NOT NULL). The following mSQL script creates the table:

```
DROP TABLE t_counter\p\g

CREATE TABLE t_counter(
        counter_file    CHAR(100)    PRIMARY KEY,
        counter_num     INT          NOT NULL
)\p\g
```

The applet consists of two classes: Counter and Database. The Counter class is the subclass of the Applet class that provides the user interface to the applet. It contains two instance variables. One, count, is the number this applet is supposed to display—the number of page hits. The other, database, is an instance of the Database class that provides wrappers for the JDBC access needed by the applet.

The Counter class does not define any new methods; rather, it simply overrides the java.applet.Applet.init() and java.applet.Applet.paint() methods. The init() method is used to create a Database instance and find out from it what the page hit count is for display. The paint() method displays the page hit count.

The interesting JDBC-related work is all encapsulated inside the Database class. It has a single instance variable, connection, which is an instance of a JDBC Connection implementation. The connection variable is initialized in the Database class constructor:

```
public Database(String url, String user, String pass)
 throws java.sql.SQLException  {
    connection =
        DriverManager.getConnection(url, user, pass);
}
```

By getting an instantiated Connection object, the applet is ready to do whatever database access it needs to do.

The applet uses the getCount() method to figure out how many page hits this particular access to the Web page represents. That seemingly benign query actually represents several steps:

1. Create a Statement object.
2. Formulate and execute the SELECT query.
3. Process the result.

4. Increment the hit count.

5. Format and execute an UPDATE or INSERT statement.

6. Close the Statement and Connection objects.

Creating the Statement is done through this JDBC call:

```
java.sql.Statement statement = connection.createStatement();
```

For this query, you want the number of hits for this page from the t_counter table:

```
sql = "SELECT counter_num FROM t_counter " +
      "WHERE counter_file = '" + page + "'";
result_set = statement.executeQuery(sql);
```

The result_set variable now holds the results of the query. For queries that return multiple rows, an application loops through the next() method in the result set until no more rows exist. This query, however, should return only one row with one column, unless the page has never been hit. If the page has never been hit, the query does not find any rows, and the count variable should be set to 0:

```
if( !result_set.next() ) count = 0;
```

Otherwise, you must retrieve that row into the count variable as an integer:

```
else count = result_set.getInt(1);
```

After incrementing the count to reflect this new hit, you close out the Statement object and get a new one to prepare for the UPDATE:

```
count++;
statement.close();
statement = connection.createStatement();
```

If this is the first time the page is hit, the applet must insert a new row into the database. Otherwise, it should update the existing row:

```
if( count == 1 ) {
    sql = "INSERT INTO t_counter " +
          "(counter_file, counter_num) " +
          "VALUES ('" + file + "', " + count + ")";
}
else {
    sql = "UPDATE t_counter " +
          "SET counter_num = " + count + " " +
          "WHERE counter_file = '" + file + "'";
}
statement.executeUpdate(sql);
```

The method then cleans up and returns the hit count. Listing 31.1 puts the whole applet together.

Exploring Database Connectivity with JDBC

CHAPTER 31

645

31

EXPLORING
DATABASE
CONNECTIVITY

Listing 31.1. The Counter applet.

```java
import java.sql.Connection;
import java.sql.DriverManager;
import java.sql.ResultSet;
import java.sql.Statement;

public class Counter extends java.applet.Applet {
    Database db;
    String count;

    public void init() {
        String driver = getParameter("driver");
        String url = getParameter("url");
        String user = getParameter("user");
        String pass = getParameter("password");
        String page = getParameter("page");

        try {
            Class.forName(driver);
            db = new Database(url, user, pass);
            count = db.getCount(page);
        }
        catch( java.sql.SQLException e ) {
            e.printStackTrace();
            count = "Database exception";
        }
        catch( Exception e ) {
            e.printStackTrace();
            count = "Unable to load driver";
        }
    }

    public void paint(java.awt.Graphics g) {
        g.setFont(new java.awt.Font(getParameter("font"),
                               java.awt.Font.BOLD, 14));
        g.drawString(count, 5, 15);
    }
}

class Database {
    private Connection connection;

    public Database(String url, String user, String pass)
    throws java.sql.SQLException {
        connection =
            DriverManager.getConnection(url, user, pass);
    }

public String getCount(String page) {
        int count = 0;

        try {
            java.sql.Statement statement =
                connection.createStatement();
            java.sql.ResultSet result_set;
            String sql;
```

continues

Listing 31.1. continued

```
            sql = "SELECT counter_num FROM t_counter " +
                "WHERE counter_file = '" + page + "'";
            result_set = statement.executeQuery(sql);
            if( !result_set.next() ) count = 0;
            else count = result_set.getInt(1);
            count++;
            statement.close();
            statement = connection.createStatement();
            if( count == 1 ) {
                sql = "INSERT INTO t_counter " +
                    "(counter_file, counter_num) " +
                    "VALUES ('" + page + "', " +count+ ")";
            }
            else {
                sql = "UPDATE t_counter " +
                    "SET counter_num = " + count + " " +
                    "WHERE counter_file = '" + page + "'";
            }
            statement.executeUpdate(sql);
            statement.close();
            connection.close();
        }
        catch( java.sql.SQLException e ) {
            e.printStackTrace();
        }
        return ("" + count);
    }
}
```

> **NOTE**
>
> How are drivers registered with the DriverManager? In the preceding example, it was done
> by specifically loading the driver passed into the program through the driver parameter.
> Using the Class.forName() construct, a reference is created to that driver. In its static
> constructor, the driver tells the DriverManager of its existence. A JDBC-compliant driver
> must tell the DriverManager about its existence when it is instantiated. The preferred method
> of listing multiple JDBC drivers for the DriverManager is through the jdbc.drivers property.

Result Sets and the Meta-Data Interfaces

In simple applications such as the Counter applet just described, there is no need to perform
any tricks with the results from a query. The data is simply retrieved sequentially and processed.
More commonly, however, an application will need to process the data in a more complex
fashion. For example, a set of classes may want to deal with data on a more abstract level than

Exploring Database Connectivity with JDBC

CHAPTER 31

647

31

EXPLORING
DATABASE
CONNECTIVITY

the Database class from the Counter example. Such classes may not know exactly what data is being retrieved. They can query the meta-data interfaces to intelligently process the data that they would not otherwise know. Listing 31.2 shows a generic database View class that is populated with database objects based on a result set.

Listing 31.2. A generic database View class.

```java
import java.sql.ResultSet;
import java.sql.ResultSetMetaData;
import java.util.Hashtable;
import java.util.Vector;

public class View {
    private Vector objects;

    public void populate(ResultSet result_set, String cl) {
        ResultSetMetaData meta_data;
        int i, maxi;

        try {
            objects = new Vector();
            meta_data = result_set.getMetaData();
            maxi = meta_data.getColumnCount();
            while( result_set.next() ) {
                Hashtable row = new Hashtable();
                DataObject obj;

                for(i=1; i<=maxi; i++) {
                    String key;
                    Object value;
                    int t;

                    key = meta_data.getColumnLabel(i);
                    t = meta_data.getColumnType(i);
                    value = result_set.getObject(i, t);
                    row.put(key, value);
                }
                obj = (DataObject)Class.forName(cl);
                obj.restore(row);
                objects.addElement(obj);
            }
        }
        catch( java.sql.SQLException e ) {
            e.printStackTrace();
            objects = new Vector();
            return;
        }
    }
}
```

In the View class, reference is made to a DataObject class that implements a restore(java.util.Hashtable) method not listed.

Because this is a generic class to be reused by many applications, it knows nothing about the queries it is executing. Instead, it takes any random result set and assumes that each row corresponds to an instance of the class named by the second parameter of populate().

To get the information it needs for performing the data retrievals, the populate() method first gets the meta-data object for this result set. This method is specifically interested in knowing how many columns are in the result set as well as the names of the columns. To store the columns in a Hashtable object that the DataObject object can use for restoring itself, all data must be in the form of objects. Thus, for each column in the result set, the method finds the row's data type from the meta-data and retrieves the column as an object. The final step is to store that row in the Hashtable.

Stored Procedures

JDBC supports stored procedures and prepared statements through an inheritance hierarchy extended from the Statement class. Stored procedures and prepared statements are precompiled SQL calls sitting on the server. You call a stored procedure like a function, using its name and passing arguments. Prepared statements, on the other hand, you send to the server with placeholders for your input. As you make the actual prepared statement calls, you bind the placeholders to actual Java values. JDBC provides two classes to support this functionality:

- ■ java.sql.PreparedStatement
- ■ java.sql.CallableStatement

The basic difference between these two classes is that PreparedStatement expects only input parameters; CallableStatement allows you to bind input and output parameters. Using stored procedures or prepared statements generally gives your application an added speed advantage, because such statements are stored in a precompiled format in most database engines. In addition, stored procedures allow an application to provide a call-level interface to a database without worrying the Java developer about SQL syntax. Listing 31.3 provides a simple SELECT operation using a stored procedure instead of straight SQL.

Listing 31.3. A simple SELECT operation using stored procedures.

```
import java.sql.*;
import java.util.Properties;

public class ProcSelect {
  public static void main(String args[]) {
    Properties props = new Properties();
    props.put("user",     "po7");
    props.put("password", "po7");
```

```
try {
    Connection c;
    CallableStatement statement;
    ResultSet results;

    c = DriverManager.getConnection("jdbc:weblogic:oracle", props);
    System.out.println("Preparing call...");
    statement = c.prepareCall("BEGIN sp_get_account(?, ?, ?, ?); END;");

    System.out.println("Setting first int...");
    statement.setInt(1, 1);
    statement.registerOutParameter(2, java.sql.Types.INTEGER);
    statement.registerOutParameter(3, java.sql.Types.CHAR);
    statement.registerOutParameter(4, java.sql.Types.INTEGER);
    System.out.println("Executing...");
    statement.execute();
    System.out.println("Getting results...");
    System.out.println("Id: " + statement.getString(2));
    System.out.println("Type: " + statement.getString(3) + "cheese");
    System.out.println("Balance: " + statement.getString(4) + "\n");
}
catch( Exception e ) {
    e.printStackTrace();
}
}
}
```

Other JDBC Functionality

JDBC provides a lot of functionality beyond the commonly used methods already discussed:

- Transaction management
- Cursor support
- Multiple result set processing

Transaction Management

JDBC implementations should default automatically to committing transactions unless the application otherwise requests that transactions require an explicit commit. An application can toggle the automatic commit of the JDBC implementation it is using through the `Connection.setAutoCommit()` method. Here is an example:

```
connection.setAutoCommit(false);
```

Of course, by not setting the `AutoCommit` attribute or by setting it to `true`, the JDBC implementation makes certain that the DBMS commits after each statement you send to the database. When `Connection.setAutoCommit()` is set to `false`, however, the JDBC implementation requires specific commits from the application before a transaction is committed to the database. A series of statements executed as a single transaction looks like this:

```java
public void add_comment(String comment) {
    try {
        Statement s;
        ResultSet r;
        int comment_id;

        connection.setAutoCommit(false);
        s = connection.createStatement();
        r = s.executeQuery("SELECT next_id " +
                           "FROM t_id " +
                           "WHERE id_name = 'comment_id'");
        if( !r.next() ) {
            throw new SQLException("No comment id exists " +
                                   "in t_id table.");
        }
        comment_id = r.getInt(1) + 1;
        s.close();
        s = connection.createStatement();
        s.executeUpdate("UPDATE t_id " +
                        "SET comment_id = " + comment_id + " " +
                        "WHERE next_id = 'comment_id'");
        s.close();
        s = connection.createStatement();
        s.executeUpdate("INSERT INTO t_comment " +
                        "(comment_id, comment_text) " +
                        "VALUES(" + comment_id + ", '" +
                        comment + "')");
        connection.commit();
    }
    catch( SQLException e ) {
        e.printStackTrace();
        try {
            connection.rollback();
        }
        catch( SQLException e2 ) System.exit(-1);
    }
}
```

This approach is used to add a comment to a comment table for some applications. To insert the new comment, the application needs to generate a new `comment_id` and then update the table for generating IDs so that the next one is 1 greater than this ID. Once the application has an ID for this comment, it then inserts the comment into the database and commits the entire transaction. If an error occurs at any time, the entire transaction is rolled back.

JDBC currently has no support for a two-phase commit. Applications written against distributed databases require extra support in the form of third-party APIs to allow your Java applications the ability to do two-phase commits.

Cursor Support

JDBC provides limited cursor support. It enables an application to get a cursor associated with a result set through the `ResultSet.getCursorName()` method. The application can then use the cursor name to perform positioned UPDATE or DELETE statements.

Multiple Result Sets

In some cases, especially with stored procedures, an application can have a statement that returns multiple result sets. JDBC handles this through the method `Statement.getMoreResults()`. Even though there are result sets left to be processed, this method returns true. The application can then get the next `ResultSet` object by calling `Statement.getResultSet()`. Processing multiple result sets simply involves looping through the database as long as `Statement.getMoreResults()` returns true.

Building a JDBC Implementation

Building a JDBC implementation requires a lot more in-depth knowledge of both your DBMS and the JDBC specification than does simply coding the implementation. Most people will never encounter the need to roll their own implementation because database vendors logically want to make them available for their product. Understanding the inner workings of JDBC, however, can help advance your application programming.

JDBC is a low-level interface. It provides direct SQL-level access to the database. Most business applications and class libraries will want to abstract from that SQL-level access to provide such things as object persistence and business-aware database access. A narrow example of such an abstraction is the `Database` class from the `Counter` example used earlier in this chapter.

The ideal object method of accomplishing these goals is to reuse existing JDBC implementations for the DBMS in question and add custom interfaces. If the DBMS is an oddball DBMS, or if you have concerns about the available implementations, writing one from scratch makes sense.

Implementing the Interfaces

The first concern of any JDBC implementation is how it is going to talk to the database. Figure 31.2 shows the architecture of three possible JDBC implementations. Depending on the design goals in question, one of these methods will suit any JDBC implementation:

- A native C library
- A socket interface
- Extending a vendor JDBC implementation

FIGURE 31.2.
Possible JDBC implementation architectures.

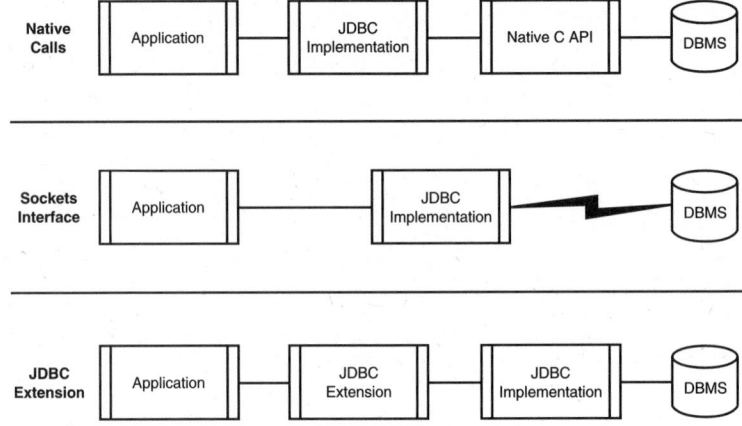

Extending a vendor JDBC implementation, of course, is not really the same as building a JDBC implementation. Because a key to any object-oriented project is reusing code instead of building from scratch, however, it is listed here.

With all three architectures, the application is apparently isolated from the actual communication mechanism. In truth, however, the native C library method places severe restrictions on any application using a JDBC implementation built on top of it. Because it uses native calls, it is naturally not portable across operating systems. In addition, because of virtual machine restrictions on most browsers, native calls are either fully restricted or severely limited.

Using one of these mechanisms for database communication, you must construct the four basic interfaces: java.sql.Driver, java.sql.Connection, java.sql.Statement, and java.sql.ResultSet. These interfaces provide minimum functionality so that testing against simple queries and updates can be done. Once these are functional, the implementation needs the meta-data interfaces as well as the Statement subclasses to be complete and to be JDBC compliant.

Extending JDBC

Nothing requires an application to use the JDBC interface to access a database. In fact, before JDBC, developers were programming with Java classes written specifically to go against several major database engines. JDBC isolates the database access behind a single interface. This isolation can provide developers with the ability to write database access in Java without having to know which database engine their application is actually hitting. With a single prevalent database API, finding people with experience programming against it proves much simpler than finding people to program against a proprietary API. JDBC is, however, a low-level specification that requires developers to write both SQL code and Java code.

Both examples in this chapter demonstrate two different ways in which you can extend JDBC. In the Counter applet, earlier in this chapter, a database class was created as a wrapper around the JDBC implementation. The applet itself was divided into a representational portion, the Counter class, and a functional portion, the Database class. If changes are made to the visual representation, such as making the hit count appear through an odometer graphic, no changes must be made to the functional logic because it is isolated in a separate class. In fact, if the applet were more complex, requiring multiple developers, all the SQL would still be isolated in a class specifically interested in the functional behavior of the application. This reduces the amount of people needed to write SQL code.

The View class example, also presented earlier in this chapter, uses a more abstract way of extending JDBC. The View class assumes that rows in result sets translate into business objects. In an application using this class, View objects are created whose purpose is to make JDBC calls and populate the applications with meaningful objects.

Another manner in which JDBC can be extended is to take advantage of database-specific features. Although it is prudent to question the need to make use of any proprietary features of a given DBMS, it is equally important that you do not ignore the extra power a specific DBMS gives you. It is, after all, very rare that an application actually needs to switch database engines.

Summary

Although the original Java release did not address the issue of database access, the JDBC specification attempts to address this issue by defining a set of interfaces that can give applications access to data independently of the DBMS being used to store that data. Although this back-end independence can be very liberating, it is important to balance it with the advantages of the DBMS being used.

Many books cover only the subjects of database application design and programming. This chapter does not attempt to delve into those matters; instead, it focuses on using Java in database programming. Programmers interested in using Java to write database applications should become familiar with the general subject matter.

In spite of the vastness of the subject matter, this chapter should whet your appetite for database programming and prepare you for Chapter 43, "Developing Your Own Database Application," which goes into the details of building a Java database application. Much of the Java experience you already have translates into many of the issues specific to Java database programming. Your next step should therefore be to get access to a database and start coding.

CHAPTER 32

Persistence

by Eric Williams

IN THIS CHAPTER

Persistence in an object-oriented programming language deals with the ability of objects to exist beyond the lifetime of the program in which they were created. This chapter addresses the topic of persistence from a number of perspectives.

First, it looks at what persistence is and what it means for Java objects to be persistent. An overview of several forms of persistence is presented.

Then the chapter delves into implementing file-based persistence, a strategy in which the programmer does most of the work to store objects persistently in a file. A `Persistent` framework is also introduced to provide developers with a framework in which to implement persistence in their own classes.

Finally, the chapter covers the subject of Persistent Java (PJava), a research project at the University of Glasgow. This project's stated goals include building a prototype persistent storage interface for implementing orthogonal persistence in Java. An overview of persistent stores is presented before the discussion of PJava.

What Is Persistence?

Persistence describes something that exists beyond its expected lifetime. As applied to an object-oriented programming language, persistence describes objects that exist for an extended period of time, often beyond the lifetime of the original program that created the objects.

Object Lifetime

New Java programmers learn that objects have a *lifetime*. An object begins its life when created by the new operator (for example, `new String("hi")`). After it is created, the object exists until destroyed by the Java virtual machine's garbage collector. (An object can be garbage collected only when the Java program no longer holds a reference to the object.) Objects can also be destroyed implicitly, when the Java program ends. This code snippet demonstrates the essential concepts of Java object lifetimes:

```
{
  Date d = new Date();              // Date object starts its life
  System.out.println(d.toString());
}
// Date object is no longer reachable, and may be destroyed
```

In this example, a new `Date` is created within a program block (`{}`) and stored in a variable (`d`) local to that block. After reaching the ending curly brace (`}`), the local variable `d` exists no longer. From that moment, the `Date` object that was created is no longer reachable and may be garbage collected.

Persistence as Extending an Object's Lifetime

Persistence is a way to extend the lifetime of an object beyond the lifetime of the program that created it. To understand why it is useful to have persistent objects, consider an AddressBook class that contains names, addresses, and telephone numbers:

```
public class AddressBook {
  public String[] names = null;
  public String[] addresses = null;
  public String[] phonenums = null;
}
```

A person writes information in an address book so that it is available at a later date, when the information is needed. Most people are unlikely to remember addresses and telephone numbers, so they write that information into a book. If you try to use the AddressBook class to represent a real address book, you will find that it does not support the "save it now, use it later" paradigm. All instances of the AddressBook class are destroyed when the Java program ends.

To be useful, an AddressBook object must exist for an extended period of time. It must be *persistent* (probably for years). Every time the user looks up, adds, or modifies address information, the AddressBook object is needed. Because the program that uses the AddressBook isn't always running, the AddressBook must be preserved during the time the program is not running.

Persistence is usually implemented by preserving the state (attributes) of an object between executions of the program. To preserve its state, the object is converted to a sequence of bytes and stored on a form of long-term media (usually a disk). When the object is needed again, it is restored from the long-term media; the restoration process creates a new Java object that is identical to the original. Although the restored object is not "the same object," its state and behavior are identical. (Object identity in a persistent system is an important issue, and is discussed in greater detail later in this chapter.) The following example outlines an API for a helper class that might be used to provide save and restore capabilities for AddressBook objects:

```
class AddressBookHelper {
  public static void store(AddressBook book, File file) {...}
  public static AddressBook restore(File file) {...}
}
```

To save an AddressBook to a file, you must explicitly write a few lines of code to store the object. The code might look like the following:

```
File output = new new File("address.book");  // persistent media
AddressBookHelper.store(addrBook, output);
```

Restoring an AddressBook from a file would look similar:

```
File input = new File("address.book");  // persistent media
AddressBook addrBook = AddressBookHelper.restore(input);
```

Forms of Persistence in Java

There are several forms of persistence available to Java programmers. The forms discussed in this chapter include file-based persistence, relational databases, and object databases. These forms of persistence differ in several categories, including logical organization of an object's state, the amount of work required of the application programmer to support persistence, concurrent access to the persistent object (from different processes), and support for transactional *commit* and *rollback* semantics.

Files

Files are often used to store information between invocations of a program. Data stored in a file can be simple (a text file) or complex (a circuit diagram). In daily use of a computer, you often interact with objects that are stored in files (word processing documents, spreadsheets, network diagrams, and so on).

Files can be used as the basis for a persistence scheme in Java. Although Java 1.0 does not support a built-in mechanism to store objects in files, Java 1.0 does provide a portable streaming library (`DataInput` and `DataOutput`). This library makes it easier for the programmer to save and restore objects.

A file-based persistence mechanism requires the programmer to put a bit of work into achieving persistence. The programmer must choose an external representation of the object and write the code that saves and restores the objects.

Usually, concurrency control and transactional semantics do not apply to file-based persistence. Storing objects in files is usually appropriate for single-user applications that follow the `File/Open` and `File/Save` model.

> **NOTE**
>
> JavaSoft has recently introduced a new API that simplifies the process of storing objects in files (and streaming objects across the network). Information about the Object Serialization API can be found at `http://chatsubo.javasoft.com/current/`.

RDBMS

Relational database management systems (RDBMS) can also store persistent objects, but the characteristics of a relational database are different from file-based persistence. A relational database is organized into tables, rows, and columns, rather than the unstructured sequence of bytes represented by a file. An effort is under way to standardize the use of relational databases in Java (the JDBC API).

There are two major ways to store objects in a relational database. The first option is to interact with the database on its terms. The JDBC API provides interfaces that directly represent relational database structures. These structures can be used and manipulated as-is. The other option is to write your own Java classes and "map" between the relational data structures and your classes. This type of mapping is a well-understood problem for which many commercial solutions are available (Java implementations will no doubt be available soon).

When using a relational database, unless you are using a tool to perform database-to-class mapping, you must write a large volume of code to interact with the database. Managing objects in the database requires you to write SQL statements (inserts, updates, deletes, and so on), which are forwarded to the database through the JDBC API.

Although using a relational database is more work, there are a few benefits. Relational databases usually support concurrency control and transactional properties. Multiple users can access the database without stepping on each other's changes because the database uses locks to safeguard access. Additionally, almost all relational databases support ACID properties (*atomicity, concurrency, isolation, durability*). These properties protect the integrity of the data by ensuring that blocks of work (referred to as *transactions*) either complete successfully or are rolled back without affecting other users.

> **NOTE**
>
> The JDBC API has been officially standardized. Although few vendors are shipping products that support the API, almost all relational database vendors have publicly committed to providing implementations of the JDBC API.

ODBMS

Object database management systems (ODBMS) support persistence in a different manner than file-based persistence and relational databases. The philosophy behind object databases is to make the programmer's job simpler. Object databases (as the name implies) store objects; the programmer does not have to write SQL statements or methods to package and unpackage objects—the object database interface usually takes care of those details.

Object databases usually support concurrency control and ACID properties, like relational databases do. They provide for concurrency access to the database, and they also provide commit and rollback transactional control. (Object databases are covered in greater depth later in this chapter, in the "The PersistentJava (PJava) Project" section.)

NOTE

As this book went to press, there were no commercial object databases available for Java. Three vendors (Versant, O2, and Object Design) had publicly stated their intent to release Java object database products, but none was available. On the academic front, the PersistentJava project was nearing completion of its first implementation.

Implementing a Simple File-Based Persistent Store

The following sections present an example of how to implement a simple file-based persistent store (that you can use to add *persistability* to your classes). First, you look at how to read and write primitive data using standard classes and interfaces provided by Java. Then you look at how to read and write whole objects, not just primitive data types. Finally, you learn how to apply these new interfaces to make your classes persistent.

IO Helpers—`DataInput` and `DataOutput`

Before discussing how to store whole objects in files, it is important to learn how to store primitive Java data values in files (`int`, `float`, `String`, and so on). The `java.io` package provides two interfaces (`DataInput` and `DataOutput`) that contain a standard API for reading and writing primitive Java types. Table 32.1 provides a summary of the methods in `DataInput` and `DataOutput`.

Table 32.1. The `DataInput` and `DataOutput` APIs.

Data Type	`DataInput`	`DataOutput`
boolean	readBoolean()	writeBoolean()
byte	readByte()	writeByte()
char	readChar()	writeChar()
short	readShort()	writeShort()
int	readInt()	writeInt()
long	readLong()	writeLong()
float	readFloat()	writeFloat()
double	readDouble()	writeDouble()
String	readUTF()	writeUTF()

> **NOTE**
>
> Even though String is not strictly an elemental data type (it is a class), DataInput and DataOutput define an API for reading and writing Strings. The primary reason is that the String data type is a major part of the language—DataInput and DataOutput without String support would be a less-than-functional solution. The String data type is also handled differently; Strings are encoded in a way that compacts the representation, when possible.

The DataInput and DataOutput interfaces are simple to use. The following example demonstrates a few of the DataInput and DataOutput methods:

```
class Person {
  String name = null;
  int age = 0;
  ...
  void write(DataOutput out) {
    out.writeUTF(name);      // write the name string
    out.writeInt(age);       // write the age
  }
  ...
  void read(DataInput in) {
    name = in.readUTF();     // read the name string
    age = in.readInt();      // read the age
  }
}
```

DataInput and DataOutput provide a platform-independent solution for the data representation problem. Data written to a file (or socket) on one platform can be read by Java programs on different platforms because the representation of the data types is standardized. An int or String written to a file on a Windows NT machine can be read from that file on a Solaris machine, Macintosh, and so on. If Java did not provide a standard interface for data formatting, every programmer would solve this problem independently. The result would be a Tower of Babel, which would make communicating between Java programs problematic (especially because Java is targeted for the network computing industry).

Sun has solved the data representation problem before. Years ago, Sun created the eXternal Data Representation (XDR) format and an accompanying C library. XDR was created to provide a standard format for data interchange over networks and to serve as the data format for Remote Procedure Calls (RPC). Today, XDR is still widely used.

Although similar to XDR, the format required by DataInput and DataOutput is not identical to XDR. Java's solution is less complicated and more compact. The DataInput/DataOutput format requires the following:

- Data is represented in binary form (not ASCII), for compactness.
- Data is represented in network byte-order (big-endian).

■ For elemental data types, data is stored in exactly the same number of bytes as guaranteed by the JVM—that is, a byte is stored as one byte; a char, as two bytes; an int, as four bytes, and so on.

■ No padding or byte-alignment is required.

■ Strings are *encoded* using a special format that reduces the number of bytes written (especially if you are using the Latin character set).

Primitive data types can be written to or read from files, sockets, or any type of stream using the DataInput and DataOutput interfaces.

When reading and writing files, there are two implementations of the DataInput and DataOutput interfaces to choose from (in the java.io package). The RandomAccessFile class implements both DataInput and DataOutput. The more frequently used classes are DataInputStream (which implements DataInput) and the DataOutputStream (which implements DataOutput). To write data to a file, you should use a DataOutputStream as a filter over a FileOutputStream. Here's an example:

```
void write(File file, String s, int i, float f) {
  // first open the FileOutputStream
  FileOutputStream fileout = new FileOutputStream(file);

  // then open the DataOutputStream "on top of" the
  // FileOutputStream that's already open
  DataOutputStream dataout = new DataOutputStream(fileout);

  // then write to the DataOutputStream, which will be
  // streamed "into" the FileOutputStream
  dataout.writeUTF(s);
  dataout.writeInt(i);
  dataout.writeFloat(f);
  dataout.close();
}
```

Reading from a file is as simple as the last example. You open a DataInputStream over a FileInputStream and make calls to the DataInput reading methods.

The Persistent Framework

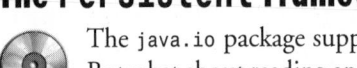 The java.io package supplies the necessary classes to read and write primitive data. But what about reading and writing entire objects? Although DataInput/DataOutput is a powerful concept (the portable data format), these interfaces do not contain methods to read or write entire objects. Objects seem to be "left as an exercise for the reader." I decided to take up the challenge and implement a simple framework for reading and writing objects. The interfaces and classes in this framework are present on the accompanying CD-ROM. Feel free to use the provided framework in your code.

You have already encountered the concepts that go into reading and writing primitive data. DataInput and DataOutput can handle the streaming of primitive types, but they do not handle class types. To stream class types, we need a new concept—the concept of "a class whose instances can stream themselves." This can be generalized in an interface, called Persistent:

```
import PersistentInput;
import PersistentOutput;
import java.io.IOException;

/**
 * Persistent interface. Provides a class with the ability to write
 * itself to a stream, and to read itself from a stream.<p>
 *
 * @see PersistentInput
 * @see PersistentOutput
 * @author  Eric R Williams
 */
public interface Persistent {

  /**
   * Writes self to the specified output stream.<p>
   *
   * @param out the persistent output interface to write self to.
   * @exception IOException if an I/O problem occurs.
   */
  public void write(PersistentOutput out) throws IOException;

  /**
   * Reads self from the specified input stream.<p>
   *
   * @param in the persistent input interface to read self from.
   * @exception IOException if an I/O problem occurs.
   */
  public void read(PersistentInput in) throws IOException;
}
```

> **NOTE**
>
> Note the use of javadoc-style comments in the preceding example. Documenting your code using the javadoc standard format is always a good idea. This format helps you produce online documents describing your code, and it is generally expected by other developers. For the remainder of this chapter, however, the javadoc-style comments have been removed to cut down on the size of the code listings.

The Persistent interface provides a standard way to add persistence (and streamability) to classes. To add persistence to a class, implement the Persistent interface in that class. There are only two methods to implement: one to write the object to an output stream (write(PersistentOutput)) and one to read the object from an input stream (read(PersistentInput)).

If you examine the Persistent interface, you encounter two additional classes: PersistentOutput and PersistentInput. They are actually not classes, but interfaces. These interfaces extend the DataInput and DataOutput interface models to provide support for reading and writing Persistent objects, as follows:

```
import Persistent;
import java.io.DataOutput;
import java.io.IOException;

public interface PersistentOutput extends DataOutput {
   void writePersistent(Persistent obj) throws IOException;
}
```

PersistentOutput defines an API that extends the DataOutput interface and adds a new method (to write Persistent objects). The new method, writePersistent(Persistent), is declared in a style consistent with the other methods declared in the DataOutput interface.

A similar interface is defined to extend DataInput—the PersistentInput interface:

```
import Persistent;
import java.io.DataInput;
import java.io.IOException;

public interface PersistentInput extends DataInput {
   Persistent readPersistent() throws IOException;
}
```

These three interfaces—Persistent, PersistentInput, and PersistentOutput—form a framework that makes it easy to add persistence to your classes. There are two additional classes in the Persistent framework: PersistentInputStream and PersistentOutputStream. These classes are discussed in detail in a later section.

Using the Simple Persistent Store

Now that you have been introduced to the Persistent framework, let's examine how to apply that framework to make objects persistent. This process involves modifying a class you have already written to add the Persistent interface to that class. We will use a simple class created to demonstrate the Persistent framework: the Shape class. The original code for Shape (without persistence) is listed here:

```
import java.io.*;
import java.awt.Point;
public class Shape {
  private Point[] vertices;
  private String  name;

  public Shape(Point[] vertices, String name) {
        this.name = name;
        this.vertices = vertices;
  }
```

```
public Shape(int size, String name) {
    this.name = name;
    vertices = new Point[size];
    for (int i=0; i<size; i++) {
      vertices[i] = new Point(0, 0);
    }
}

public Point getPoint(int pos) {
    return vertices[pos];
}

public String getName() {
    return name;
}
}
```

Shape is a simple class; it has only two attributes: a name and an array of points (the boundaries of the shape). The Shape class depends on java.awt.Point to represent Point objects.

To add persistence to the Shape class, we need to make a few changes to the class source code:

■ Add implements Persistent to the class declaration line

■ Add a no-parameter constructor (the reason for this will be discussed later)

■ Code the write(PersistentOutput) method, which is required by the Persistent interface

■ Code the read(PersistentInput) method, which is also required by the Persistent interface

The first two items on this list are trivial. They involve minor changes to the class. The latter two items are more involved tasks.

Before we start coding the read() and write() methods, we need to choose an external format for the Shape class. The external format is a specification of the order and structure of the object's attributes. One convenient notation used to express this format is similar to C struct declarations. (This notation is used in the Java Virtual Machine Specification to describe the layout for Java .class files.) We can represent the Shape class using the following structure:

```
int vertex_count;
struct {
  int x;
  int y;
} vertices [vertex_count];
String name;
```

This notation specifies that the first element in the format is labeled vertex_count and is an int. The second element is labeled vertices; it is an array of length vertex_count (which was already specified). The array is composed of a compound structure containing two ints, x and y, respectively. The last element is a String, labeled name. In this notation, the labels exist for human consumption only—they are not included in the stored objects. Labels help readers of the format understand what data is being represented.

Once you choose an external format for the Shape class, you can begin to construct the routines to read and write a Shape. Here is an implementation of the write(PersistentOutput) method:

```
public void write(PersistentOutput out) throws IOException {
  out.writeInt(vertices.length);          // write # of points
  for(int i=0; i<vertices.length; i++) {  // write each point
    out.writeInt(vertices[i].x);
    out.writeInt(vertices[i].y);
  }
  out.writeUTF(name);                      // write shape name
}
```

Only two of the DataOutput interface methods are used in this example: writeInt() and writeUTF(). As you can see, this method logically carries out the agreed-on format—array length, followed by the array of points, and then followed by a string. The process of writing an object to a file is not difficult; it is expressed in about five lines of code.

The following is an implementation of the read(PersistentInput) method:

```
public void read(PersistentInput in) throws IOException {
  vertices = new Point[in.readInt()];      // read # of points
  for(int i=0; i<vertices.length; i++) {   // read each point
    vertices[i] = new Point(in.readInt(), in.readInt());
  }
  name = in.readUTF();                      // read shape name
}
```

The read() method implements the agreed-on format. Again, the method is short and simple to understand, using just two methods from the DataInput interface: readInt() and readUTF(). First, it reads the vertices' array size, followed by each vertex (a Point consisting of two ints, x and y), and finally reads a String, the name of the shape.

Now that we have seen the pieces, let's put it all together. The following code listing includes the Shape class (renamed to PShape), plus the additions that have been made (in **bold**) to support persistence:

```
package COM.MCP.Samsnet.jun;

import java.io.*;
import java.awt.Point;
import COM.MCP.Samsnet.jun.Persistent;
public class PShape implements Persistent {
  private Point[] vertices;
  private String  name;

  public PShape() {      // need a no-parameter constructor
    vertices = null
    name = null
  }

  public PShape(Point[] vertices, String name) {
    this.name = name;
    this.vertices = vertices;
  }
```

```java
    public PShape(int size, String name) {
      this.name = name;
      vertices = new Point[size];
      for (int = 0l i<size; i++) {
        vertices[i] = new Point(0, 0);
      }
    }

    public Point getPoint(int pos) {
      return vertices[pos];
    }

    public String getName() {
      return name;
    }

    public void write(PersistentOutput out) throws IOException {
      out.writeInt(vertices.length);           // write # of points
      for(int i=0; i<vertices.length; i++) {   // write each point
        out.writeInt(vertices[i].x);
        out.writeInt(vertices[i].y);
      }
      out.writeUTF(name);                       // write shape name
    }

    public void read(PersistentIntput in) throws IOException {
      vertices = new Point[in.readInt()];       // read # of points
      for(int i=0; i<vertices.length; i++) {    // read each point
        vertices[i] = new Point(in.readInt(), in.readInt());
      }
      name = in.readUTF();                       // read shape name
    }

    public String toString() {
      StringBuffer b = new StringBuffer(name);
      for (int i=0; i<vertices.length; i++) {
        b.append(" (" + vertices[i].x + "," + vertices[i].y + ")");
      }
      return b.toString();
    }

    public boolean equals(Object obj) {
      boolean isequal = false;
      if (obj instanceof PShape) {
        PShape shape = (PShape)obj;
        isequal = (this.name.equals(shape.name))
            && (this.vertices.length == shape.vertices.length);

        int i=0;
        while (isequal && i<vertices.length) {
            if (! this.vertices[i].equals(shape.vertices[i])) {
              isequal = false;
              break;
            }
                    i++;
        }
      }
          return isequal;
    }
}
```

To validate the persistence of the shape class, we need to have a test class that does the following:

- Creates a Shape object
- Writes it to a file using a PersistentOutputStream
- Reads it back from the file using a PersistentInputStream
- Compares the two objects

 The following class, PShapeTest, validates the persistence of PShape. (All these classes are on the accompanying CD-ROM, so feel free to run this test.)

```
package COM.MCP.Samsnet.jun;

import COM.MCP.Samsnet.jun.PShape;
import COM.MCP.Samsnet.jun.PersistentOutputStream;
import COM.MCP.Samsnet.jun.PersistentInputStream;
import java.io.*;
public class PShapeTest {
  public static void main(String[] args) {
    try {
      PShape square = new PShape(4, "SquareOne");
      square.getPoint(0).move(0, 0);
      square.getPoint(1).move(1, 0);
      square.getPoint(2).move(1, 1);
      square.getPoint(3).move(0, 1);

      PersistentOutputStream out =      // create a PersistentOutputStream
          new PersistentOutputStream(   // on top of a FileOutputStream
              new FileOutputStream("pshape.sav"));

      out.writePersistent(square);      // *** write the Shape ***
      out.close();

      PersistentInputStream in =        // create a PersistentInputStream
          new PersistentInputStream(    // on top of a FileInputStream
              new FileInputStream("pshape.sav"));

      PShape shape2 =
          (PShape) in.readPersistent(); // *** read the Shape ***
      in.close();

      if (square.equals(shape2)) {
        System.out.println("everything is ok!");
      }
    } catch (Exception ee) {
      System.err.println(ee.toString());
      ee.printStackTrace();
    }
  } // main
} // class
```

The Implementation of `PersistentInputStream` and `PersistentOutputStream`

The only missing pieces now are the classes that provide implementations for the `PersistentOutput` and `PersistentInput` interfaces. As interfaces, they are API specifications only; implementations are required if you are going to use the interfaces.

Let's start with `PersistentOutput`. The `PersistentOutput` interface is very complicated; it contains all the methods of `DataOutput` (approximately 14 methods), plus `writePersistent()`. That's a lot of methods to implement! Fortunately, reuse by inheritance comes in handy; a class that nearly matches the needs already exists. By subclassing `DataOutputStream`, all the `DataOutput` methods defined in `DataOutputStream` are inherited (and do not have to be reimplemented). You only have to implement a constructor and a `writePersistent()` method. Here's a listing of the `DataOutputStream` class:

```
import java.io.*;
import Persistent;
import PersistentOutput;

public class PersistentOutputStream extends DataOutputStream
    implements PersistentOutput {
public PersistentOutputStream(OutputStream out) {
    super(out);
  }

  public final void writePersistent(Persistent obj) throws IOException {
    if (obj == null) {                      // treat null in a special way
      writeUTF("null");                     // write "null" as the class name
    } else {
      writeUTF(obj.getClass().getName());   // write the object's class name
      obj.write(this);                      // then write the object itself
    }
  }
}
```

The `writePersistent()` method writes the string `"null"` if the specified `Persistent` object is null. Otherwise, the method writes the class name of the object (a `String`), followed by the object writing itself to the stream (using the `write(PersistentOutput)` method of the `Persistent` interface). The `PersistentOutputStream` does not have to understand the format a `Persistent` object uses when it writes itself to the stream. Moving the writing logic to the classes that implement `Persistent` is what the `Persistent` interface is all about.

The `PersistentInputStream` is slightly more complicated, but it still inherits most of its behavior from `DataInputStream`, as shown here:

```
import java.io.*;
import Persistent;
import PersistentInput;

public class PersistentInputStream extends DataInputStream
    implements PersistentInput {
```

```
public PersistentInputStream(InputStream in) {
   super(in);
}

public final Persistent readPersistent() throws IOException {
   Persistent obj = null;
   String classname = readUTF();             // read the class name
   if ("null".equals(classname)) {
      obj = null;                            // if "null", return null
   } else {
      try {
         // retrieve the Class object for the specified class name
         Class clazz = Class.forName(classname);

         // build a new instance of the Class (throws an exception if
         // the class is abstract or does not have a no-param constructor
         obj = (Persistent) clazz.newInstance();

         // let the object read itself from the stream
         obj.read(this);
      } catch (ClassNotFoundException ee) {    // catch all kinds of
         throw new IOException(ee.toString());  // exceptions and rethrow
      } catch (InstantiationException ee) {
         throw new IOException(ee.toString());
      } catch (IllegalAccessException ee) {
         throw new IOException(ee.toString());
      }
   }
   return obj;
}
}
```

The readPersistent() method reads the name of the object's class from the stream. If that name is equal to "null", the null value is returned. Otherwise, the method locates the Java Class object corresponding to the class name and uses the Class to create a new instance of the Persistent object. The new Persistent object then reads itself from the stream in the read(PersistentInput) method.

You may wonder about the exception handling in the readPersistent() method. Why does it have so many catch statements? They were used to keep the readPersistent() method consistent with the methods of DataInput, all of which throw only IOException. If you do not catch the listed exceptions and rethrow them as IOExceptions, the exception class names must be declared in the throws clause of the readPersistent() method—which would be inconsistent with DataInput.

NOTE

The object creation step in the PersistentInputStream class requires the use of the Class method newInstance(), which is Java's generic interface for creating an object, given the Class instance. To allocate a new object of a class using newInstance(), the class must have a public constructor that takes no parameters (this is the constructor method that will be invoked by newInstance()). A public no-parameter constructor was added to the PShape class to support the use of newInstance().

The `PersistentInputStream` and `PersistentOutputStream` implementation of reading and writing `Persistent` objects has several limitations:

- If you attempt to read a persistent object for which the Java class has not yet been loaded, an exception is thrown.

- Object identity is not considered. Two references to a single object are written as two objects on a `PersistentOutputStream`.

- Cyclical data structures cause the `PersistentOutputStream` to enter a recursive loop, eventually exhausting stack space and throwing an exception. (An example of a cyclical structure is one in which two objects contain references to each other.)

The `Persistent` framework classes are simple and straightforward. In short order, you can add "persistence" to your classes; you can store objects in files or send them across a network to another computer. These interfaces and classes are not a general solution to the problem of persistence, but it's a good solution when you have to store or send simple objects. Additionally, the `Persistent` framework is a useful tool to teach some of the concepts of persistence.

The PersistentJava (PJava) Project

In October 1995 (the early days of Java, before the language skyrocketed in popularity), Sun funded a year-long research project at the University of Glasgow to investigate adding *persistence* to the Java programming language. The Glasgow researchers have proposed a design specification for adding "orthogonal" persistence to Java. They have also begun building a persistent storage interface to link Java to a persistent store.

Persistent Store Concepts

Few programmers are familiar with persistent stores or object databases. The following brief sections introduce the basic concepts involved in a persistent store.

> **NOTE**
>
> The phrases *persistent store* and *object database* are often used interchangeably. Because the authors of the PJava design refer to PJava as an "interface to a persistent store," this chapter refers to PJava as a "persistent storage" interface.

Persistent Stores versus Relational Databases

Foremost, a persistent store is a *kind of* database. You are probably familiar with the term *database* (a storage pool for information). Most commercially available databases support long-term data storage on disk, structural organization of the data, methods to retrieve data from the database, methods to update data already stored in the database, row or page locking to prevent concurrent access problems, isolation of uncompleted transactions from other transactions, and so on. Most persistent stores meet these criteria.

By far the most common type of client-server database system is the relational database (for example, Oracle, Informix, Sybase, DB2, and so on). Contrasting a persistent store with a relational database is a useful exercise to understand what a persistent store is and what it is not.

Relational databases are organized in tabular data structures: tables, columns, and rows. Data from different tables can be joined to create new ways of looking at the data. SQL is used to send commands to the database, such as commands to create new rows of data, to update rows, and so on. SQL commands can also be used from other programming languages because they are sent to the database server for processing.

Relational databases, with their tabular data structures, do not mesh well with object-oriented (OO) programming languages. There are three major problems encountered using relational databases from an OO language. First, relational data structures do not provide for class encapsulation. OO programmers are encouraged to model their domain using classes, providing an API to class users, and "hiding" all data within the class. Relational structures expose all data and do not allow encapsulation by an API. Second, OO classes support a rich set of data types that are difficult or impossible to model efficiently in a relational structure. Examples include multidimensional arrays, dictionaries, and object references. Last, it is difficult to represent class inheritance in a relational database. Although it is possible, deep class inheritance trees can result in *n*-way joins on the database server, which have poor performance.

Tools that attempt to solve the object and relational mismatch are available. These tools map relational data structures into OO classes using relatively simple rules (for example, map tables to classes, columns to attributes, and foreign key attributes to object relationships). Although some of these products have been successful, this approach has had problems. These products suffer from performance issues, particularly when complex navigation is performed through the mapped data structures. Additionally, these products limit the type-expressiveness of the language because not all the data types expressible in the object-oriented language are easily expressible in a relational database.

Persistent stores are different from relational databases. Persistent stores do the following:

- Eliminate the use of relational data structures (instead, whole objects are stored directly in the database)
- Enable the programmer to write classes in a normal, object-oriented fashion to represent data that will be made persistent
- Enable the programmer to take advantage of more data types than is possible when using a relational database
- Provide a simpler interface than a relational database interface

Creating and Using Persistent Objects

Different persistent storage interfaces have different methods for creating persistent objects (or making existing objects persistent). Some interfaces require the programmer to specify whether an object is to be persistent at the time an object is created. Other persistent stores implement a concept referred to as *persistent roots*. Persistent root objects are explicitly identified as objects that are persistent; any object that is referred to by the persistent root is also considered persistent. All objects that are reachable in this fashion (from the persistent root) are also considered to be persistent and are saved in the persistent store. This concept is called *persistence through reachability*.

Retrieving objects from a persistent store is significantly different from retrieving data through SQL. When using SQL, the programmer must explicitly request data (using SELECT statements); with persistent stores, programmers seldom make explicit queries for objects. Persistent stores usually provide a mechanism to request only "top-level" objects, either through direct query or through a request for a particular persistent root.

Persistent storage interfaces almost universally employ a process known as *swizzling* (or *object faulting*) to retrieve objects from the database. Objects are retrieved on the fly, as they are needed. After obtaining a reference to a top-level object, programmers normally use that object to access related objects. When attempting to access an object that has not yet been retrieved from the database, the object is *swizzled* in. The attempt to access the object is trapped by the database interface, which then retrieves the object's storage block from the database, restores the object, and then allows the object access to continue.

Finally, persistent stores usually have a mechanism to identify objects uniquely: the object ID. Every object in a persistent store is assigned its own unique object ID, which can be used to differentiate objects of the same class whose values are equal.

PJava Design

The first PersistentJava design, known as PJava0, was published in January 1996. An additional paper (Atkinson, et al. '96) was published in February and describes the design issues of PJava0. (Both of these papers are available from http://www.dcs.gla.ac.uk/~susan/pjava.) The PJava0 design goals, principles, and architecture are outlined in the following sections.

Project Goals

The stated goal of the PersistentJava project is to provide orthogonal persistence in Java. The PJava researchers are creating a persistent storage mechanism that can store objects of any type in the persistent store. This is the operating meaning of *orthogonal*—the independence of the persistence from the data type. Any object, without respect to type, can be made persistent.

Many persistent stores and object databases do not support orthogonal persistence. Orthogonal persistence is extremely hard to implement in most programming languages. It means that programmers can write code without considering that they might be dealing with persistent objects. This forces the persistent storage interface to be extremely flexible in how it deals with data types. Additionally, this makes implementing a programming-language independent database server difficult because a very tight binding is made to one language's type system.

The Glasgow team has set out with a goal of orthogonal persistence; doing so has implications they must handle. Any object, be it of a user-defined or system-defined class, can be persistent. Persistent objects can include `Object`, `Panel`, `SecurityManager`, `Button`, `Class`, `Hashtable`, and so on.

An additional goal of the research project is the building of a prototype application that uses the prototype persistent storage interface. The application is referred to as *Forest*, a distributed software configuration management and build system ([Atkinson, et al. 96] Atkinson, Daynès & Spence. *Draft PJava Design 1.2*. Department of Computer Science, University of Glasgow. January 1996).

Design Principles

The PJava team used several principles to guide their design:

- Data type independence from persistence (orthogonal)
- Persistence through reachability from persistent roots
- No changes to the Java language
- Support for different styles of transactions
- Persistence without modification to existing Java code
- Flexibility, to allow for integration with multiple persistent stores

The PJava team intentionally left out one potential design goal: "No changes to the Java virtual machine." In fact, the team has actively pursued the modification of the JVM; it is a central part of the architecture (and probably the only feasible way to implement orthogonal persistence). Unfortunately, JavaSoft has stated that they will not incorporate the PJava changes into the commercial JVM, effectively relegating PJava to the academic community for the time being.

The foremost point to remember about the design of PersistentJava is that it does not require the programmer to change any existing classes. It does not require the programmer to use a "special" version of the system classes. It does, however, require the programmer to use a customized virtual machine.

Storing and Retrieving Objects

One of the first things you want to know as the user of a persistent store is how to make objects persistent. How do you store objects in the database? PersistentJava incorporates the concept of a persistent root. The *Draft PJava Design 1.2* document states that an early revision of the design included a `PersistentRoot` class—objects of type `PersistentRoot` (or a subclass thereof) have the property of "being a persistent root." However, the design was changed; any object may be registered as a persistent root, thus making the "root" property independent of data type.

Here is an example of how to make an object a persistent root in PJava0:

```
// make obj a persistent root (pstore is a PJavaStore)
pstore.registerPRoot("root-1", obj);
```

To retrieve a persistent root from the database, follow this example:

```
// get the handle for all Open Orders
Orders[] orders = (Orders[]) pstore.getPRoot("OpenOrders");
```

> **NOTE**
>
> The preceding code example is the only PJava code sample included with this book. As this book goes to press, the PJava0 implementation has yet to be completed.

Recall from the earlier discussion of persistent roots (in the section "Persistent Store Concepts") that roots are only the starting point for the identification of persistent objects. By adding a single persistent root to the database, you may be adding thousands of objects to the persistent Java store.

Now you can store root objects in the persistent store and retrieve them. But how do you access other objects? Does a similar "ask the database for the object" interface exist? The answer is both yes and no. When you use a root object to access related objects, you call methods on and retrieve the attributes of those objects. When you attempt to access a related object that has not yet been brought from the database, the modified virtual machine intercepts this action, bringing the object from the database for you. You are not required to do anything special. Use objects as you normally would—the object retrieval mechanism is transparent.

The PJava virtual machine (a modified JVM) performs work that is not visible to the programmer—the VM monitors access to objects. When an attempt is made to access a persistent object that has not yet been accessed, PJava goes into action. Part of the PJava system is called on to retrieve the object. It determines whether the storage block containing the object has already been loaded; if not, it makes a trip to the persistent store. When the object's storage is loaded, PJava converts the byte-oriented storage into a Java object. The PJava VM then allows your code to continue accessing the object. This mechanism of transparent object retrieval is often called *swizzling*, or *object faulting* (a legacy of certain object databases that perform this operation using OS page-faulting mechanisms).

Transactions

The next thing you may want to know about PJava is how to begin and end a transaction. The designers of PJava wanted to allow multiple transaction styles, so they created a transaction root class, TransactionShell. This class has two provided subclasses: NestedTransaction and OLTPTransaction, but the programmer can subclass TransactionShell to create new transactional styles.

Transactions in PJava can either be launched synchronously (that is, in the same thread) or asynchronously (in a different thread) by invoking the start() method of the transaction object. The TransactionShell class executes the user's transaction logic through a Runnable object, whose run() method is invoked as the "main" method of the transaction. To obtain the result of the transaction (whether it succeeds or fails), call the claim() method. If you want to stop an asynchronously running transaction, you can invoke the kill() method on that transaction.

In PJava, you can run one transaction nested within another transaction using the NestedTransaction class. Nested transactions enable you to perform updates in a child transaction without affecting the state of the parent transaction. A child transaction that completes successfully passes all its updates (the modified objects) to its parent transaction. If the child transaction aborts, none of its updates are ever reflected in the parent transaction. You also can spawn parallel, independent NestedTransactions. In this case, each of the sibling transactions is isolated from all others, and can commit or abort independently.

An additional transaction class, OLTPTransaction, also is available. An OLTPTransaction is a traditional transaction style that cannot be executed asynchronously and cannot be nested.

Summary

Persistence involves extending the lifetime of an object beyond the lifetime of the program in which it was created. In this chapter, you have seen several possible ways to implement persistence:

- Saving the representation of an object directly to a file using the DataOutput and DataInput interfaces
- Using the Persistent framework provided with this chapter
- Using some form of database library (for example, JDBC)
- Using a persistent store, like the one being created by researchers at the University of Glasgow

Integrating Native Code

by Tim Park

IN THIS CHAPTER

This chapter explains how to use the native method interface to speed up your Java programs and to interface with legacy C and C++ libraries. *Native methods* are the mechanism in Java that allows you to interface with programs written in C. *Legacy* C and C++ libraries are any libraries that were developed first for the C/C++ platform, but that you now want to interface with in Java. We'll first look at three examples of how to use the native method interface, working through the basics of Java native method programming. After learning the basics, we will then use a simple 3D graphics library to show how you can use the native method interface as a bridge to legacy C++ code.

The first example uses the `Triangle` class to explain the process of developing a native method and the files the Java Developers Kit (JDK) generates to link together Java and C. Then you discover how to access member variables from within a native method for that class. Finally, you see how to pass back a simple type using the return stack.

The second example uses the `SortedList` class to explore passing strings to and from native methods. You also see first-hand how much more complicated a native method can be when you do memory allocation in C rather than as a member variable of Java.

A common application of native methods is to improve the speed with which Java can process arrays of data. The third example explores the mechanisms necessary for accessing arrays from within a native method.

In the second part of this chapter, you will look at `My3D`, a C++ graphics library. The second part of the chapter also helps you work through the steps necessary to build a Java interface library to `My3D`.

A Java Class with Native Methods

Listing 33.1 gives you a first look at a Java class containing native methods. This class encapsulates the base and height of a triangle and contains a native method named `ComputeArea()` that calculates the area of the triangle.

Listing 33.1. `Triangle.java` contains a native method called `ComputeArea()`.

```
public class Triangle {
  public void SetBase(float fInBase) {
    fBase = fInBase;
  }
  public void SetHeight(float fInHeight) {
    fHeight = fInHeight;
  }
  public native float ComputeArea();

  // Load the native routines.
  static {
    System.loadLibrary("Triangle");
```

```
    }
    float fBase;
    float fHeight;
}
```

As you can see, the definition for ComputeArea() is only slightly different from the definition of a normal method. The keyword native is added just after the scope of the method and just before the return type. This tells the javac compiler and the Java interpreter that they should look for the function body in a dynamically linked library (a DLL, in a Microsoft Windows environment, which is named Triangle.DLL) that is loaded using loadLibrary(), a static method in the Java system package. The loadLibrary definition directly following the ComputeArea() definition specifies where this dynamically loaded library can be found.

> **NOTE**
>
> The Triangle class shown in Figure 33.1 and all the files you use in the remainder of this chapter can be found on the CD-ROM that accompanies this book.

Compiling the Java Class

 To build your class, copy the entire \WIN95NT4\SOURCE\CHAP33\TRIANGLE directory from the CD-ROM that accompanies this book into \java\classes\Triangle on your own computer. Macintosh users will find the code in \SOURCE\CHAP33\TRIANGLE; Windows NT 3.51 users must either install the source code to their hard drives or select the files from the zipped source code on the CD-ROM. From \java\classes\Triangle, compile the Triangle class using javac just as you normally would:

```
C:\java\classes\Triangle> javac Triangle.java
```

In a normal Java program, this statement would do it—your class would be ready. In a native application, however, you have to generate or supply three more source files to tie everything together.

Using javah to Generate the Header File

The first file you need to generate for a native application is a header file for the Java Triangle class (see Listing 33.2). This header file gives the native C code routine a layout of how data is arranged within your Java class. It also provides a prototype of how the methods from your object-oriented naming-space class files translate into C's flat naming space.

To generate the stub header file from the Triangle.class file, execute javah in the C:\java\classes\native directory:

```
C:\java\classes\Triangle> javah Triangle.java
```

Listing 33.2. The `Triangle.h` file (generated by `javah`).

```
/* DO NOT EDIT THIS FILE - it is machine generated */
#include <native.h>
/* Header for class Triangle */

#ifndef _Included_Triangle
#define _Included_Triangle

typedef struct ClassTriangle {
    float fBase;
    float fHeight;
} ClassTriangle;
HandleTo(Triangle);

#ifdef __cplusplus
extern "C" {
#endif
__declspec(dllexport) float Triangle_ComputeArea(struct HTriangle *);
#ifdef __cplusplus
}
#endif
#endif
```

The header file defines a new type called `ClassTriangle`. This structure enables access to the internal variables of the `Triangle` class. Each *intrinsic type* (types not defined by the Java class library or the developer) in Java has a corresponding type in Java. Table 33.1 shows this correlation (for Windows 95 and Microsoft development platforms; other combinations may have slight differences).

Table 33.1. Java and C type correspondence.

Java Type	*C Type*
float	float
double	double
int	long
short	int
long	long
boolean	long
byte	char

For developer-defined objects or Java library objects (for example, `String` objects), there can be cases where there are no one-to-one type correspondences with C. This can be a major headache in Java—but we tackle this problem in the second native method interface example.

The second part of the `javah`-generated header file contains the prototypes for the native functions defined in the Java class. For the `Triangle` class, there is only one prototype: the `ComputeArea()` method. The return type is `float` (as expected from the type-translation chart in Table 33.1), but the function contains an unexpected input parameter of type `struct Htriangle *`. This parameter is a handle to the instance of the `Triangle` class that called the native function. This handle lets you access the `Triangle` class variables through the class's `ClassTriangle` structure. You see how to access these variables later in this chapter when you implement the native function in C.

Using `javah -stubs` to Generate a Stub File

Your next task in implementing a native method is to build a stub file from Java's class file representation of the `Triangle` class. This stub file is responsible for finding the parameters and return values on Java's call stack and translating them into parameters for the native C method. The Java interpreter calls this stub, which in turn calls the native method from the DLL you loaded with the `System.loadLibrary()` call a few sections earlier.

To create the stub file, type the following at the command line:

```
C:\java\classes\Triangle> javah -stubs Triangle
```

This statement creates the file `Triangle.c` (see Listing 33.3).

Listing 33.3. The `Triangle.c` file generated by `javah -stubs`.

```
/* DO NOT EDIT THIS FILE - it is machine generated */
#include <StubPreamble.h>

/* Stubs for class Triangle */
/* SYMBOL: "Triangle/ComputeArea()F", Java_Triangle_ComputeArea_stub */
__declspec(dllexport) stack_item *Java_Triangle_ComputeArea_stub(stack_item
*_P_,struct execenv *_EE_) {
    extern float Triangle_ComputeArea(void *);
    _P_[0].f = Triangle_ComputeArea(_P_[0].p);
     return _P_ + 1;
}
```

Developing an Implementation C File

This is a lot of work for one puny native method. Fortunately, you'll use a makefile to automate your work in future sessions. The worst is over—you're ready to build an implementation of the native function.

For the Java interpreter to find the native function, the interpreter has to match the prototype in the `Triangle.h` file type for type.

Here is the prototype from the generated header file:

```
__declspec(dllexport) float Triangle_ComputeArea(struct HTriangle *);
```

In the implementation file, you must match exactly everything from the `float` return type to the right.

As shown in Listing 33.3, the implementation file must also include two header files: `StubPreamble.h` and `Triangle.h`. `Triangle.h` is the file you generated with `javah` in the previous sections. `StubPreamble.h` is a Java library that includes definitions needed to enable you to access your Java data parameters and use certain Java C interpreter calls.

The final building block you need to implement the native `ComputeArea()` function is a way of accessing the class variables from within the native function. You accomplish this using the `unhand` macro provided by the `StubPreamble.h` header file. The `unhand` macro takes a pointer to a handle to a class, such as `struct Htriangle*`, and returns a pointer to a `ClassClass` structure, such as the `ClassTriangle` structure described previously. As you may remember, this structure contains the representation of the variables in the Java class.

> **CAUTION**
>
> Because static variables do not belong to any one instantiation of a Java class, you cannot view or modify them from a native function in C. If you need a static variable that you can modify from your native method, define it in C instead and create accessor methods in the Java class to access it.

To access the value of the `fBase` class variable, use the following syntax:

`unhand(hthis)->fBase`

By doing this for `fHeight` as well, you can compute the area of the triangle and return it to the Java interpreter and your Java program, as shown in Listing 33.4.

Listing 33.4. `TriangleImp.c`.

```
extern "C" {
  #include <StubPreamble.h>
  #include "Triangle.h"

  float Triangle_ComputeArea(struct HTriangle *hthis) {
    return(0.5f * unhand(hthis)->fBase * unhand(hthis)->fHeight);
  }
}
```

Building the Triangle DLL

With the four implementation files for the native-method-containing Java class completed, you now need only to compile two C source files and link them with the Java library to form the Triangle DLL file.

This discussion uses command lines in Visual C++ 4.0 for Windows 95 to develop the native functions. Because Windows 95 is the most prevalent Java platform in use today, you'll learn how to link the library by using Visual C++. The instructions for compiling in UNIX are very similar. Consult the manual supplied with your JDK for instructions.

Before you start your build, you have to add a few environmental variables so that the Visual C++ compiler can find your tools and Java/Netscape can find your native DLL files. Add the following lines to your autoexec.bat file (use the paths for the standard directories):

```
SET LIB=\msdev\lib;\java\lib
SET INCLUDE=\java\include;\java\include\win32;\msdev\include
SET CLASSPATH=\java\classes;.;C:\netscape20\Program\java\classes
```

With these changes made, reexecute your autoexec.bat file by rebooting your computer. Then move back to your Java source directory and compile the implementation of the native Triangle class with the following command line. (Note that cl is the Microsoft Visual C++ command-line compiler. For other development platforms, substitute the equivalent command.)

```
C:\java\classes\Triangle> cl /c W3dTriangleImp.c
```

Likewise, compile the stub file with this command line:

```
C:\java\classes\Triangle> cl /c W3dTriangleImp.c
```

Finally, link these two OBJ files with the Java interpreter library (javai.lib) to form the finished DLL file:

```
cl Triangle.obj TriangleImp.obj -FeTriangle.dll -MD -LD javai.lib
```

Listing 33.5 shows a skeleton makefile used to build Java native applications. It includes all the commands and dependencies necessary to build a Triangle DLL. By replicating the dependency section and changing the names, you can reuse this makefile to build your own native functions.

33

**INTEGRATING
NATIVE CODE**

Listing 33.5. Triangle.mak.

```
OBJS    = Triangle.obj TriangleImp.obj
LIBS    = javai.lib
COMPFLAGS = /c /MLd /Gm /Od /Zi

Triangle.dll: $(OBJS)
    cl $(OBJS) -FeTriangle.dll -MD -LD $(LIBS)

# Build Triangle class

Triangle.class: Triangle.java
    javac Triangle.java

Triangle.h: Triangle.class
    javah Triangle
```

continues

Listing 33.5. continued

```
Triangle.obj: TriangleImp.cpp Triangle.h
    cl $(COMPFLAGS) W3dTriangleImp.c

Triangle.c: Triangle.class
    javah -o Triangle.c -stubs Triangle

Triangle.obj: Triangle.c
    cl $(COMPFLAGS) Triangle.c
```

Let's build a test class to demonstrate the new `Triangle` class in action. Listing 33.6 shows a test application that uses the `Triangle` class. After building it with `javac`, use the `Java` interpreter to run the application.

Listing 33.6. TestTriangle.java.

```
public class TestTriangle {
  public static void main(String argv[]) {
    Triangle theTri;
    theTri = new Triangle();
    theTri.SetBase(2.0f);
    theTri.SetHeight(6.0f);
    System.out.println("The Area of the Triangle is"+theTri.ComputeArea());
  }
}
```

Following is the output of the `TestTriangle` execution:

```
C:\java\classes\Triangle> java TestTriangle
The Area of the Triangle is 6.0
```

Hooray! Your first native method works correctly.

Accepting and Returning Java Classes

Now let's look at a class that has native methods that accept a Java class as one of its parameters.

The class `SortedList`, shown in Listing 33.7, maintains a sorted list of strings. Because sorting is a compute-intensive task, let's write the sorting algorithm as a native method. Native methods are good at compute-intensive tasks because C code runs as compiled instructions for the underlying hardware; Java, on the other hand, runs virtual machine instructions that are very far from the underlying hardware.

Listing 33.7. `SortedList.java`.

```
public class SortedList {
  public native void constructorA();
  public SortedList() {
    constructorA();
  }

  public native void constructorB(int nInitialAllocation);
  public SortedList(int nInitialAllocation) {
    constructorB(nInitialAllocation);
  }

  public native void AddString(String szString);
  public native String GetString(int nIndex);

  public native int HowMany();

  static {
    System.loadLibrary("SortedList");
  }
}
```

The first thing you notice about the native `SortedList` class is that there are two Java constructors that immediately call native C constructor implementations. This is done for two reasons. First, Java doesn't allow constructors to be native, so for classes that require native constructors, you must wrap this call to the native function inside the Java constructor. Secondly, native functions cannot be overloaded within Java because all C function names must be unique and cannot depend on type, and because the process for converting a Java method to a C function name in Java always follows *Package_Class_Method*. For Java classes with overloaded constructors, therefore, you must overload the constructors in Java and then call the corresponding native methods. Not pretty, but the end user of your Java class won't notice the difference.

The next thing you should note about the `SortedList` class is that the class takes and returns a `String` from its `AddString()` and `GetString()` methods, respectively. This arrangement is different than what we did in the first example because here you are dealing with a Java class, `String`, that has no direct counterpart type in C/C++. (Although `(char *)` may seem like a direct counterpart, it isn't because it doesn't encapsulate a string's length.)

The C/C++ implementation of the `SortedList` implementation is shown in Listing 33.8. The compiler directive `extern "C" {` in the first line tells the compiler that the definitions of functions and variables contained within its braces should be defined internally using a C-style definition rather than a C++ style. The difference between these two definitions is that the C++-style definition includes information about the types passed to and returned from the function; the C-style definition contains only the function name. If you leave out the `extern "C" {` directive, all the functions are defined in the C++ style by default. The linker then, looking for a definition to match the C-style definitions of the stub file, will be unable to link the functions together correctly because they will be defined using the C++ style. Also notice that the extern "C" { directive surrounds the Java include files. These include files also have prototypes for Java interpreter functions that must be defined using the C-style definition.

From the length of the implementation file, you should note the complexity of implementing data management for your Java native class in C. Because C isn't object oriented, special wrapper code must be developed for any native Java class that manages its data in C.

TIP

Store your data in Java and use unhand() to access it whenever it yields acceptable performance. Doing so can cut down your development time and simplify your code considerably because it will be unnecessary to write wrapper code to manage the instantiations of your Java class.

You can't follow the preceding tip for the SortedList implementation, because the overhead from converting strings back and forth from Java and C will choke the sorting routine and rob you of much of the C performance advantage. By moving the data management to C, you only have to convert strings in the AddString() and GetString() methods and not in the performance-critical BubbleSort() function.

Now let's focus on the interface for data from and to Java, starting with the AddString() native method.

Implementing AddString()

The AddString() method takes a String and adds it to the list maintained by the given object. The prototype for the native C function looks like this:

```
void SortedList_AddString(struct HSortedList *hthis,
                          struct Hjava_lang_String *AddString);
```

This is pretty much as you expect: the first parameter is the handle to the Java SortedList object and the second is the handle to the Java string being passed. Notice that the structure name follows the *package_package_...._class* nomenclature.

Java strings are not passed by value, as were all the types you considered previously. Instead, a handle to the Java string is passed. If you haven't run into them before, handles can be likened to a license plate on a car—they uniquely identify an object. Handles are used to avoid the overhead in passing large objects to functions and to provide security that doesn't exist if a pointer is given to reference the object. With a pointer, you can do almost anything to the object. With a handle, you are constrained to the API given to you, providing as much security as desired by the API designer.

Because Java strings and C strings are stored differently, you must use the `makeCString()` interpreter API call to convert your string first. `makeCString()` converts the `String` referenced by a handle and allocates enough memory for the converted string, for which it returns a `(char *)` pointer. Here is a use of `makeCString()`, copied from the `AddString()` function:

```
//Add String to the end of the List specified by hList.
lLists[hList][nStringsUsed[hList]++] = makeCString(AddString);
```

You should include `javaString.h` in your `#include` section whenever you use the `makeCString()` function or the `makeJavaString()` function described in the next section. This `include` file defines the prototypes for these two interpreter functions.

Implementing `GetString()`

As you may expect, the `GetString()` native function has a similar conversion need. To return the `String` referenced by the passed index, Java has to convert the C string stored in the C string table back into a handle to a Java `String`. The analogous Java interpreter function call needed to convert C `(char *)` variables into strings is called `makeJavaString(char* theString, int strlength)`. `makeJavaString()` takes a `char *` and a string length as an `int`, instantiates a `String` variable in Java with that value, and returns a handle to that string (`struct Hjava_lang_String *`). The `GetString()` native function uses `makeJavaString` to return the `[nIndex]`th `String` in the `[hList]`th `List` as follows:

```
return (makeJavaString(lLists[hList][nIndex],strlen(lLists[hList][nIndex])));
```

Note that the `GetString()` function returns a handle to a Java string (`struct Hjava_lang_String*`) just as the `AddString()` native function accepted one.

The complete `SortedList` implementation is shown in Listing 33.8. This listing shows how all the parts described in the previous sections fit together.

Listing 33.8. `SortedListImp.cpp`.

```cpp
extern "C" {
  #include <StubPreamble.h>
  #include <javaString.h>
  #include "SortedList.h"
  #include <string.h>

  /* nLists is a long that contains the number of lists that lString
     has been allocated to contain. */
  long nLists;
  long nListsAllocated = 0;
  long nListsUsed = 0;
  long *nStringsAllocated;
  char ***lLists;
  long *nStringsUsed;
```

33

INTEGRATING
NATIVE CODE

continues

Listing 33.8. continued

```c
long SortedList_ResizeNumLists(long nNewAllocation) {
  char*** NewlLists;
  long*   NewnStringsAllocated;
  long*   NewnStringsUsed;

  NewlLists             = new char** [nNewAllocation];
  NewnStringsAllocated  = new long    [nNewAllocation];
  NewnStringsUsed       = new long    [nNewAllocation];

  long i;
  for (i=0; (i < nListsAllocated) && (i < nNewAllocation); i++) {
    NewlLists[i]             = lLists[i];
    NewnStringsAllocated[i]  = nStringsAllocated[i];
    NewnStringsUsed[i]       = nStringsUsed[i];
  }

  for (; (i < nNewAllocation); i++) {
    NewlLists[i]             = NULL;
    NewnStringsAllocated[i] = 0;
    NewnStringsUsed[i]      = 0;
  }

  delete lLists;
  delete nStringsAllocated;
  delete nStringsUsed;

  lLists            = NewlLists;
  nStringsAllocated = NewnStringsAllocated;
  nStringsUsed      = NewnStringsUsed;

  return (nNewAllocation);
}

long SortedList_ResizeNumStrings(long hList, long nNewAllocation) {
  char** NewlStrings = new char* [nNewAllocation];

  long i;
  for (i=0; (i < nListsAllocated) && (i < nNewAllocation); i++) {
    NewlStrings[i] = lLists[hList][i];
  }
  for (; (i < nNewAllocation); i++) {
    NewlStrings[i] = NULL;
  }

  delete lLists[hList];
  lLists[hList] = NewlStrings;
  return (nNewAllocation);
}

void SortedList_constructorA(struct HSortedList *hthis) {
  if (nListsAllocated == 0)
    nListsAllocated = SortedList_ResizeNumLists(1);

  long i;
  int done = FALSE;
```

```
    if (nListsUsed == nListsAllocated)
      nListsAllocated = SortedList_ResizeNumLists(nListsAllocated*2);

    nStringsAllocated[nListsUsed] = 0;
    nStringsUsed[nListsUsed]      = 0;

    unhand(hthis)->hList = nListsUsed++;
}

void SortedList_constructorB(struct HSortedList *hthis,
                             long InitialAllocation) {
    if (nListsAllocated == 0)
      nListsAllocated = SortedList_ResizeNumLists(1);

    long i;
    int done = FALSE;

    if (nListsUsed == nListsAllocated)
      nListsAllocated = SortedList_ResizeNumLists(nListsAllocated*2);

    nStringsUsed[nListsUsed]      = 0;
    nStringsAllocated[nListsUsed] = SortedList_ResizeNumStrings(nListsUsed,
                                                     InitialAllocation);
    unhand(hthis)->hList = nListsUsed++;
}

void BubbleSort(char* lSortStrings[], int nElements) {
    long i,j;
    int changed=TRUE;

    for (j=0; (j < nElements-1) && changed; j++) {
        changed = FALSE;
        for (i=0; i < nElements-1; i++) {
            if (strcmp(lSortStrings[i], lSortStrings[i+1]) > 0) {
                char* temp = lSortStrings[i];
                lSortStrings[i] = lSortStrings[i+1];
                lSortStrings[i+1] = temp;
                changed = TRUE;
            }
        }
    }
}

void SortedList_AddString(struct HSortedList *hthis,
                          struct Hjava_lang_String *AddString) {
    int hList = unhand(hthis)->hList;
    if (nStringsUsed[hList] == nStringsAllocated[hList])
      nStringsAllocated[hList] =
              SortedList_ResizeNumStrings(hList, nStringsAllocated[hList]*2);

    lLists[hList][nStringsUsed[hList]++] = makeCString(AddString);
    BubbleSort(lLists[hList], nStringsUsed[hList]);
}

struct Hjava_lang_String* SortedList_GetString(struct HSortedList *hthis,
          long nIndex) {
    int hList = unhand(hthis)->hList;
```

33

continues

Listing 33.8. continued

```
    if (nIndex > nStringsUsed[hList]) {
      return(NULL);
    }

    return (makeJavaString(lLists[hList][nIndex],strlen(lLists[hList][nIndex])));
  }

  long SortedList_HowMany(struct HSortedList* hthis) {
    return(nStringsUsed[unhand(hthis)->hList]);
  }
}
```

Building and Running a Class That Uses SortedList

A simple applet that uses the native SortedList class is shown in Listing 33.9. SortPresidents was written as an applet just to show that applets also can call native functions. (There is one important caveat: The native code DLL must be already installed on the client machine within a directory contained in your PATH statement before the applet is presented to Netscape or the applet viewer.) SortPresidents takes a list of presidents' names, sorts them based on last name, and prints the results. Notice how SortedList still "feels" like a Java class to the user. You should strive for this feeling in your native Java class design.

Listing 33.9. SortPresidents.java.

```
import java.applet.*;

public class SortPresidents extends Applet {

  public void init() {
    thePresidents = new SortedList();
    thePresidents.AddString("Washington, George");
    thePresidents.AddString("Lincoln, Abraham");
    thePresidents.AddString("Kennedy, John F");
    thePresidents.AddString("Nixon, Richard");
    thePresidents.AddString("Carter, Jimmy");
    thePresidents.AddString("Reagan, Ronald");
    thePresidents.AddString("Bush, George");
    thePresidents.AddString("Clinton, Bill");

    int i;
    int nNames = thePresidents.HowMany();

    System.out.println("There are "+nNames+" entries in our string list.");
    for (i=0; i < nNames; i++)
      System.out.println(thePresidents.GetString(i));
  }
  SortedList thePresidents;
}
```

To build your `SortedList` class, copy the entire `\WIN95NT4\SOURCE\CHAP33\SORTEDLIST` directory on the CD-ROM that accompanies this book into `\java\classes\SortedList` on your machine. Macintosh users will find the code in `\SOURCE\CHAP33\SORTEDLIST`; Windows NT 3.51 users must either install the source code to their hard drives or select the files from the zipped source code on the CD-ROM. From there, you use `nmake` and the `SortedList.mak` makefile to build the `SortedList` class. This makefile looks identical to the one used to build the `Triangle` class in the last section.

Your build of `SortedList` should look something like this:

```
C:\java\classes\SortedList> nmake SortedList.mak

Microsoft (R) Program Maintenance Utility   Version 1.60.5270
Copyright (c) Microsoft Corp 1988-1995. All rights reserved.
        javac SortedList.java
        javah SortedList
        ...
```

We also should compile our sample applet `SortPresidents`, which uses the `SortedList` class:

```
C:\java\classes\SortedList> javac SortPresidents.java
```

 You are now ready to run the applet, as shown in Listing 33.10. The HTML file `RunIt.html` is bundled on the CD-ROM that accompanies this book; it contains a link to this applet.

Listing 33.10. SortedList build.

```
C:\java\classes\SortedList> appletviewer RunIt.html
There are 8 entries in our string list.
Bush, George
Carter, Jimmy
Clinton, Bill
Kennedy, John F
Lincoln, Abraham
Nixon, Richard
Reagan, Ronald
Washington, George
```

Accessing Arrays of Classes

Because of the drastic performance advantage that C has in performing array-based operations, it is very common to pass arrays into a native routine. In this section, you explore how to pass and receive arrays from a native method. To demonstrate passing arrays to and from Java, the `GradeBook` class and its C implementation are shown in Listings 33.11 and 33.12 (in the following section). The `GradeBook` class implements a simple grade-tracking and average-computing system.

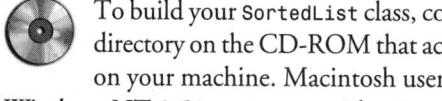

33

The `GradeBook` class supports only one instantiation (unlike the previous `SortedList` class). `GradeBook` is designed this way to simplify the implementation of `GradeBook` and to remove the details present in the `SortedList` class from the last section. A real application that wants to use more than one `GradeBook` class requires a rewrite of the class to support multiple instantiations.

Listing 33.11. GradeBook.java.

```
public class GradeBook {
  public native void constructor(int nStudents, int nTests);
  public GradeBook(int nStudents, int nTests) {
    constructor(nStudents, nTests);
  }

  public native void  NameStudents(String lStudents[]);
  public native int   AddTest(float lScores[]);

  public native float GetTestAvg(int nTestNumber);
  public native float GetStudentAvg(String szStudentName);

  public native int   HowManyTests();
  static { System.loadLibrary("GradeBook"); }
}
```

Looking closer at the Java `GradeBook` class, you should see two new data types that have not previously been passed into a native method. First, the `NameStudents()` method accepts a `String` array that contains the list of students enrolled for the class. Second, the `AddTest()` method accepts an array of `float` for the list of scores achieved by the respective students on a test. In the implementation file, let's use this example to see how you can decode Java arrays into C arrays.

This native class exploits C's array-operation performance advantage over Java to improve the speed of searching for a student's records and computing test and class averages.

Accessing a String Array

The implementation file for the `GradeBook` class is shown in Listing 33.12. The file's general skeleton is very similar to the last two classes you have considered.

Listing 33.12. GradeBookImp.cpp.

```
extern "C" {
  #include <StubPreamble.h>
  #include "GradeBook.h"
  #include <string.h>
  #include <javaString.h>

  long    nStudents;
  char**  lStudents;
  long    nTests;
  float** lTests;
```

```
void GradeBook_constructor(struct HGradeBook *hthis, long nStudentsIN,
                           long nTotalTests) {
  nStudents = nStudentsIN;
  lStudents = new char* [nStudents];
  nTests    = 0;
  lTests    = new float* [nTotalTests];
}

long GradeBook_AddTest(struct HGradeBook    *hthis,
                       struct HArrayOfFloat *lTestScoresIN) {
  float* lJavaTestScores = (float *)(unhand(lTestScoresIN)->body);
  float* lCTestScores = new float[nStudents];

  int i;
  for (i=0; i < nStudents; i++) {
     lCTestScores[i] = lJavaTestScores[i];
  }

  lTests[nTests] = lCTestScores;
  nTests++;
  return (nTests);
}

void GradeBook_NameStudents(struct HGradeBook*    hthis,
                            struct HArrayOfString* JavalStudents) {

  struct Hjava_lang_String* hStudentName;
  int i;
  for (i=0; i < nStudents; i++) {
     hStudentName = (struct Hjava_lang_String *)(unhand(JavalStudents)->body)[i];
     lStudents[i] = makeCString(hStudentName);
  }
}

float GradeBook_GetTestAvg(struct HGradeBook* hthis,
                           long nTestNumber) {
  int i;
  float* lTestScores = lTests[nTestNumber-1];
  float  fScoreAccum = 0;

  for (i=0; i < nStudents; i++) {
     fScoreAccum += lTestScores[i];
  }
  return (fScoreAccum/((float)nStudents));
}

float GradeBook_GetStudentAvg(struct HGradeBook* hthis,
                              struct Hjava_lang_String* hStudentName) {

  char* szSearchStudent = makeCString(hStudentName);

  long cStudentIndex, bDone;
  for (cStudentIndex=0, bDone=FALSE; (cStudentIndex < nStudents) && !bDone;) {
     if (strcmp(szSearchStudent, lStudents[cStudentIndex]) == 0) {
        bDone = TRUE;
```

continues

33

INTEGRATING
NATIVE CODE

Listing 33.12. continued

```
        } else {
          cStudentIndex++;
        }
      }

    if (!bDone)                    // Student not found!
      return (-1.0f);

    for (long cTestNum=0, float fTestScoreAccum=0.0f; cTestNum < nTests;
        cTestNum++) {
      fTestScoreAccum += lTests[cTestNum][cStudentIndex];
    }
    float fTestAvg = fTestScoreAccum/((float)nTests);
    return(fTestAvg);
  }

  long GradeBook_HowManyTests(struct HGradeBook* hthis) {
    return(nTests);
  }
```

The `NameStudents()` method is responsible for associating the names of all the students in the class with the test scores. This arrangement enables the user of this class to pull a student's record using the student's name as a query. Here is the `NameStudents()` prototype:

```
void GradeBook_NameStudents(struct HGradeBook*      hthis,
                            struct HArrayOfString* JavalStudents) {
```

Notice that Java has a special handle type for an array of `String`: `struct HArrayOfString*`. This handle contains only one element, `body`, that you need to consider. The `body` element is common to all `struct HArrayOfObject*` handles in native method programming and is a pointer to a list of handles (or, in the case of intrinsic Java types that have C equivalents, the actual array of values). For `struct HArrayOfString`, `body` points to a list of `String` handles that contain the names of all the students in the class.

Reading in the names of the students in the class is as easy as writing a loop that grabs each student's string handle and converts it to a C (`char *`) using `makeCString()`, as described in the previous section. To grab the individual string handle and convert it, you use the following construct in `NameStudents()`:

```
struct Hjava_lang_String* hStudentName = (struct Hjava_lang_String *)
               (unhand(JavalStudents)->body)[i];
lStudents[i] = makeCString(hStudentName);
```

This method accesses the `body` variable by first unhanding the `JavalStudents` (`struct HArrayOfString*`) variable using `unhand()`. As explained previously, `body` is a pointer to a list of `String` handles; to obtain the ith name handle in the list, you simply suffix an array index `[i]` to the body pointer. By iterating with a loop over the entire class list, you can fill `lStudents`— the C (`char *`) version of the class list—with the names of the students in the class. `lStudents` is then used by the `GetStudentAvg()` native method to search for the student's grade records by name.

Accessing a Float Array

Accessing an array of an intrinsic Java type is easier than accessing an array of Java classes. In the GradeBook class, the AddTest() method accepts a list of float test scores for each student. Its native method implementation prototype looks like this:

```
long GradeBook_AddTest(struct HGradeBook    *hthis,
                       struct HArrayOfFloat *lTestScoresIN);
```

Again, you have a handle to an array of objects, but this time, the handle is to ArrayOfFloat. Accessing ArrayOfFloat is very similar to accessing the String array, but because float is an intrinsic type, you can simply cast the body pointer into a (float *). This pointer can then be used as a normal (float *) to copy the elements of the array from the Java array object into your C array object:

```
float* lJavaTestScores = (float *)(unhand(lTestScoresIN)->body);
float* lCTestScores = new float[nStudents];

int i;
for (i=0; i < nStudents; i++) {
   lCTestScores[i] = lJavaTestScores[i];
}
lTests[nTests] = lCTestScores;
nTests++;
```

A sample Java application, TeachersPet, uses the GradeBook class and is shown in Listing 33.13. This application creates a new GradeBook with five students and three sets of test results. With this database created, the application then finds the overall average for each student and the average for the class as a whole.

Listing 33.13. TeachersPet.java.

```
public class TeachersPet {

  public static void main(String argv[]) {
    int nStudents = 5;
    int nTests = 3;

    GradeBook myClass = new GradeBook(nStudents, nTests);

    String lszStudents[] = new String[nStudents];
    lszStudents[0] = new String("Susan Harris");
    lszStudents[1] = new String("Thomas Thompson");
    lszStudents[2] = new String("Blake Cronin");
    lszStudents[3] = new String("Rotten Johnson");
    lszStudents[4] = new String("Harrison Jackson");

    myClass.NameStudents(lszStudents);

    float lTest1Grades[] = new float[nStudents];
    lTest1Grades[0] = 93;
    lTest1Grades[1] = 86;
    lTest1Grades[2] = 89;
```

continues

33

INTEGRATING
NATIVE CODE

Listing 33.13. continued

```
    lTest1Grades[3] = 65;
    lTest1Grades[4] = 78;
    myClass.AddTest(lTest1Grades);

    float lTest2Grades[] = new float[nStudents];
    lTest2Grades[0] = 100;
    lTest2Grades[1] = 83;
    lTest2Grades[2] = 91;
    lTest2Grades[3] = 55;
    lTest2Grades[4] = 83;
    myClass.AddTest(lTest2Grades);

    float lTest3Grades[] = new float[nStudents];
    lTest3Grades[0] = 89;
    lTest3Grades[1] = 94;
    lTest3Grades[2] = 82;
    lTest3Grades[3] = 59;
    lTest3Grades[4] = 85;
    myClass.AddTest(lTest3Grades);

    for (int cStudent = 0, float fStudentAvg=0.0f; cStudent < nStudents;
        cStudent++) {
      fStudentAvg = myClass.GetStudentAvg(lszStudents[cStudent]);
      System.out.println(lszStudents[cStudent]+"'s average on the 3 tests is
                          "+fStudentAvg);
    }

    for (int cTest = 1, float fClassAvg=0.0f, float fTestAvg = 0.0f;
        cTest < nTests+1; cTest++) {
      fTestAvg   = myClass.GetTestAvg(cTest);
      System.out.println("The class average on Test #"+cTest+" is "+fTestAvg);
      fClassAvg += fTestAvg;
    }

    fClassAvg /= ((float)nTests);
    System.out.println("\nThe class average on the 3 tests is "+fClassAvg);
  }
}
```

Compile the GradeBook class library and the sample application TeachersPet, just as you did with the preceding two examples, and give the application a test run:

```
C:\java\classes\SortedList> java TeachersPet

Susan Harris's average on the 3 tests is 94
Thomas Thompson's average on the 3 tests is 87.6667
Blake Cronin's average on the 3 tests is 87.3333
Rotten Johnson's average on the 3 tests is 59.6667
Harrison Jackson's average on the 3 tests is 82

The class average on Test #1 is 82.2
The class average on Test #2 is 82.4
The class average on Test #3 is 81.8

The class average on the 3 tests is 82.1333
```

Interfacing to Existing C and C++ Libraries

Having explored the basics of the native method interface, let's shift to one of the most common uses of native methods—as an interface to existing C and C++ libraries. First, you learn a methodology for building an interface to existing C libraries using a very simple signal-processing library as an example.

Next, you investigate interfacing to C++ libraries by developing a wrapper system for overcoming Java's C-only native method interface using a very simple 3D library as an example. As you go along, you examine all the problems in interfacing to this library.

Interfacing to Legacy C Libraries

A tremendous number of C libraries exist in the development world today—primarily because of the popularity of the C language. Because of either the time necessary to develop these legacy libraries, or the sheer performance required of them, it may be very difficult to port a C library entirely to Java. Instead, it may be necessary to develop a Java interface to the library.

Interfacing C with Java is difficult for one main reason: Java is entirely object oriented. Unlike C++, Java does not enable you to use procedural functions within the context of an object-oriented program. Every construct must involve an object of some sort.

There are two general methods of working around Java's object requirement. First, you could sit down with the list of functions in the C library and carve it up into functionally related blocks. For each block of the library, you could then develop a class that contains each function as a static Java method within the class. The class is, of course, then titled with some moniker that indicates the relation of all the functions it contains.

Although this is probably the fastest way to convert your library over to Java, it may not be the smartest. Although your current C library users will have no difficulties getting used to the Java interface, your new Java users may have some difficulty because the interface won't be object oriented. As a solution to this dilemma, consider the feasibility of developing an object-oriented interface to your library. In the next section, we look at how this can be done.

Building an Object-Oriented Wrapper Around the C Library

Listing 33.14 shows the `DataSample` object, which implements storage for a set of signal samples and provides methods to calculate the real FFT, the cosine FT, and the sin FT. Notice how it isn't just a static wrapper for the FFT functions, but rather a class library that encapsulates data-sampling functions with a set of FFT functions added.

Listing 33.14. The DataSample class.

```
package mySigProcLib;

class DataSample {
   public void AddSample(float sample) {
         // ...Some signal management logic here...
   }

   public void DeleteSample(int I) {
         // ...Some more signal management logic here...
   }

   public native void realFFT(float FFTresult[]);
   public native void cosFFT(float FFTresult[]);
   public native void sinFFT(float FFTresult[]);

   int nSamples;
   float fSamples[];
}
```

The implementation of the DataSample class is shown in Listing 33.15. There's nothing new in this implementation, but it does show how to structure your C implementation to achieve the feel of an object-oriented library in your Java interface object.

Listing 33.15. The implementation of the DataSample class.

```
#include <native.h>
#include <FFT.h>

void mySigProcLib_DataSample_realFFT(struct mySigProcLib_DataSample* hthis,
                        struct HArrayOfFloat* FFTresult) {
  realFFT(unhand(unhand(hthis)->fSamples)->body,
         unhand(hthis)->nSamples,
         unhand(FFTresult)->body);
}

void mySigProcLib_DataSample_cosFFT(struct mySigProcLib_DataSample* hthis,
                                struct HArrayOfFloat* FFTresult) {
  cosFFT(unhand(unhand(hthis)->fSamples)->body,
        unhand(hthis)->nSamples,
        unhand(FFTresult)->body);
}

void mySigProcLib_DataSample_sinFFT(struct mySigProcLib_DataSample* hthis,
                                struct HArrayOfFloat* FFTresult) {
  realFFT(unhand(unhand(hthis)->fSamples)->body,
         unhand(hthis)->nSamples,
         unhand(FFTresult)->body);
}
```

Developing Java Interface Classes from Legacy C++ Libraries

With the explosion of interest in object-oriented design has come an explosion in the number of available C++ class libraries. This section extends the discussion of interfacing to cover the development of an interface to existing C++ libraries. To make the description of this design process more concrete, we'll take an existing C++ class library and develop a parallel set of Java classes that transparently classes provide the same look and feel as the C++ classes.

The My3D C++ Graphics Class Library

To demonstrate an interface between Java objects and C++ objects, let's use a few components of a very primitive 3D graphics class library, My3D.

Assume that the My3D C++ library is either too performance-sensitive to be converted to Java, or that redevelopment of the Java library would involve so much time that developing a Java interface to the C++ class is a better investment.

The My3D World Object

Listing 33.16 contains the World object, the first C++ object we'll consider in this simple 3D library. The World object is responsible for handling the details of attaching and detaching objects from a 3D scene. The methods AttachNode() and DetachNode(), as you may have guessed, are responsible for taking a Node object and attaching or detaching the Node from the scene graph.

The World class also contains a list of pointers to Node objects in the private section of the definition, which is used to store the scene graph. However, as you'll see when you implement the World class, this information isn't necessary to interface the class with Java—you really have to know only the public methods and variables for the class.

Listing 33.16. World C++ class definition.

```
class World {
  public:
    void AttachNode (Node* theNode);
    Node* DetachNode (Node* RemoveNode);

  private:
    Node** NodeList;
};
```

The My3D Node Object

The next class in the My3D C++ class library is the Node class, shown in Listing 33.17. This class contains the mechanisms necessary to give an object in World a location. This superclass is the base class for all objects that appear in the rendered 3D scenes. The class contains only two accessor methods, SetLocation() and GetLocation(), which are used to set and retrieve the position of the node in space. The data structure PointFW_t is used to encapsulate these points (see Listing 33.18).

Listing 33.17. Node C++ class definition.

```
class Node {
   public:
      void SetLocation (PointFW_t& loc);
      PointFW_t GetLocation();

   private:
      PointFW_t theLocation;
}
```

Listing 33.18. PointFW_t C++ class definition.

```
typedef struct PointFW_t {
  float x;
  float y;
  float z;
  float w;
} PointFW_t;
```

The My3D Light Object

The Light class is a subclass of Node, which makes it attachable within your World scenes (see Listing 33.19) and gives it position. The Light object models a light in the scene by adding a direction and color to the subclass with the associated accessors, Set/GetDirection() and Set/GetColor().

Listing 33.19. Light C++ class definition.

```
class Light : public Node {
  public:
      void SetDirection (PointF_t& dir);
      PointF_t& GetDirection();
      void SetColor (ColorF_t& theColor);
      ColorF_t& GetColor();

  private:
      PointF_t  TheDirection;
      ColorF_t  TheColor;
};
```

The My3D PointF_t and ColorF_t Objects

The Light class also introduces two new data structures, PointF_t and ColorF_t (see Listings 33.20 and 33.21). The PointF_t data structure encapsulates a vector that points in the direction <x,y,z>. The ColorF_t type represents a color with the red, green, and blue components, <r,g,b>.

Listing 33.20. PointF_t C++ struct definition.

```
typedef struct PointF_t {
  float x;
  float y;
  float z;
} PointF_t;
```

Listing 33.21. ColorF_t C++ struct definition.

```
typedef struct ColorF_t {
  float r;
  float g;
  float b;
} ColorF_t;
```

The My3D Geometry Object

The final class in the My3D graphics library (if only real 3D graphics class libraries could be so simple!) is the Geometry class. This class is also a subclass of Node, which enables the class library user to specify a geometric object in the graphics scene. The constructor for the Geometry class takes all the information necessary to specify the object in space: the number of polygons and vertices, the points in space for all the vertices and the vertex normals, and the ordering of which points go with which polygon.

Two methods control rotations and scaling around its central location specified with SetLocation() from the Node class: RotateObject() and ScaleObject(). The Geometry class is shown in Listing 33.22.

Listing 33.22. Geometry C++ class definition.

```
class Geometry : public Node {
   public:
      Geometry(long INnPolygons, long INnVertices,
              PointF_t* INpVertices, PointF_t* INpNormals,
              long* INVerOrder);

      void RotateObject(double theta, PointF_t* RotationAxis);
      void ScaleObject(PointF_t* ScaleFactors);
```

continues

Listing 33.22. continued

```
  private:
    long nPolygons;
    long nVertices;
    PointF_t* pVertices;
    PointF_t* pNormals;
    PointF_t* pFacets;
    PointF_t* pTexture;
    ColorFA_t* pColors;
    long* VerOrder;
}
```

The InterfaceObject Base Class

Now you can move on to the real task of building Java objects that interface with the C++ classes you have just developed. Before doing this, however, you first need a class that encapsulates all the interface information you need about your C++ class, the InterfaceObject class (see Listing 33.23).

Listing 33.23. Java InterfaceObject definition.

```
package My3D;

public class InterfaceObject {

  public int KindOf() {
    return (ObjKindOf);
  }

  // Returns true if the object type passed to IsOf matches this
  // object's type.

  public boolean IsOf(int k) {
    if (k == ObjKindOf) {
      return(true);
    } else {
      return(false);
    }
  }

  public int hCPPObj;
  public int ObjKindOf;

  static {
    System.load("my3d.dll");
  }
}
```

The InterfaceObject class is the base for all your object classes. It contains two methods to help with object identification (you'll see where this is useful in a few sections): KindOf() and IsOf(). KindOf() is used to access the object type. This object type is a constant that uniquely identifies the object's type. The IsOf() method tests the object type passed to it, to see whether it is the same as this object's type, by using the internal constant as a check.

The InterfaceObject class also encapsulates two variables: hCPPObj and ObjKindOf. ObjKindOf contains the ordinal type of the object. hCPPObj contains a handle to the parallel C++ instantiation of this object. You'll see how both these variables are set in the next section.

The My3D World Java Object Definition

Let's start interfacing your library to Java with the World class; the implementation of the Java class is shown in Listing 33.24.

Listing 33.24. World Java class definition.

```
package My3D;

public class World extends InterfaceObject {
  public native void constructor();
  public World() {
    constructor();
  }

  public native void finalize();
  public native void AttachNode (Node theNode);
  public native Node DetachNode (Node afterNode);
}
```

Your first impression of this class should be that it looks very similar to the C++ one. This is good! However, you have to learn a few more things about native implementations before this illusion can become a reality for your Java class library users.

The My3D World Constructor Interface

Let's start at the beginning, with the Java World class constructor. As you saw in Listing 33.24, the World Java implementation class calls a native constructor in its constructor. You want your native constructor to accomplish the following tasks:

1. Instantiate the parallel C++ object—in this case, a C++ World object.

2. Store the pointer to this instantiated class and store an integer reference to the array position of this pointer in the Java interface object (which is referred to as the *handle* in the rest of this section).

3. Initialize the reference counter for this pointer to 1, to indicate that only one Java object is using it.

4. Remember what kind of object it is by saving the class type as a constant in the Java object.

The native constructor implementation for the World class is shown in Listing 33.25.

33

INTEGRATING
NATIVE CODE

Listing 33.25. World interface constructor.

```c
long    My3D_World_AllocLength = 0;
#define INITIAL_My3D_World_ALLOC 2

World** My3D_World_ObjPtr = NULL;
long*   My3D_World_ObjRef = NULL;

void My3D_World_constructor(struct HMy3D_World *jthis) {
  if (My3D_World_AllocLength == 0) {
    My3D_World_AllocLength =
        My3D_World_Resize(INITIAL_My3D_World_ALLOC);
  }

  // Search for an empty position (empty position == NULL).
  long pos;
  for ( pos=0;
      (pos != My3D_World_AllocLength) &&
      (My3D_World_ObjPtr[pos] != NULL);
       pos++ )
    ;

  if (pos == My3D_World_AllocLength) {
    // All allocated positions are full.
    // So use exponential allocation to create some more.
    My3D_World_AllocLength =
        My3D_World_Resize(My3D_World_AllocLength*2);
  }

  My3D_World_ObjPtr[pos] = new World();

  // Stub for handling out of memory condition.
  assert (My3D_World_ObjPtr[pos] != NULL);

  // Increment Reference counter.
  My3D_World_IncRefCntr(pos);

  // Store handle (== position in array) for this
  // object.
  unhand(jthis)->hCPPObj = pos;
}
```

The My3D_World_Resize() Function

In every instantiable class considered in this chapter, your interface functions maintain a list of pointers to all the C++ objects you have instantiated indirectly by instantiating its Java interface class. In the preceding constructor, the first statement checks to see whether this list should be initialized:

```c
if (My3D_World_AllocLength == 0) {
    My3D_World_AllocLength =
        My3D_World_Resize(INITIAL_My3D_World_ALLOC);
}
```

My3D_World_Resize() is a helper function responsible for increasing and decreasing the amount of allocation for the pointer list to World objects. There is a similar function for each of the interface files considered in this chapter. The code for the My3D_World_Resize() function is shown in Listing 33.26.

Listing 33.26. My3D_World_Resize() function definition.

```
long My3D_World_Resize(long newsize) {

    World** NewObjPtr = new World* [newsize];
    long*   NewRefPtr = new long[newsize];

    long i;
    for (i=0; i != My3D_World_AllocLength; i++) {
        NewObjPtr[i] = My3D_World_ObjPtr[i];
        NewRefPtr[i] = My3D_World_ObjRef[i];
    }

    for (; i != newsize; i++) {
        NewObjPtr[i] = NULL;
        NewRefPtr[i] = 0;
    }

    delete My3D_World_ObjPtr;
    delete My3D_World_ObjRef;

    My3D_World_ObjPtr = NewObjPtr;
    My3D_World_ObjRef = NewRefPtr;

    return (newsize);
}
```

Unused pointers in the C++ object array are set to NULL in the My3D_World_Resize() function. After checking in the interface constructor code to see whether the pointer list has been initialized, the constructor next tries to find an empty slot in the pointer list:

```
long pos;
for ( pos=0;
      (pos != My3D_World_AllocLength) &&
      (My3D_World_ObjPtr[pos] != NULL);
       pos++ )
    ;
```

The loop quits before it reaches My3D_World_AllocLength if it does find an empty slot. If it doesn't, the constructor allocates new pointer space:

```
if (pos == My3D_World_AllocLength) {
   // All allocated positions are full.
   // So use exponential allocation to create some more.
   My3D_World_AllocLength =
       My3D_World_Resize(My3D_World_AllocLength*2);
}
```

Notice that the constructor allocates pointer space exponentially—every time the constructor is forced to resize the pointer list, it does so to twice the size of the last pointer list size. This helps reduce the number of times that memory allocation is needed for large object databases, without wasting memory for small object databases. Because memory allocation is such an expensive event, you should implement this or an equivalent scheme in your interface code unless the size of the pointer array is known beforehand or the number of objects typically needed is very small (for example, fewer than eight).

With an empty spot on the list found for the instantiated pointer, the constructor allocates a `World` object and stores it in the list:

```
My3D_World_ObjPtr[pos] = new World();
```

The `World` object's constructor doesn't take any arguments, and for that reason, none are passed into the `World` constructor. If your constructor does take arguments, this is where you should change your routines to pass them in. If your class contains multiple constructors, you have to create multiple constructor interfaces in your implementation file to handle each variant—ugly, but because C does not have any functionality such as overloading in C++, it is the only way to accomplish this.

Directly following this allocation is an `assert()` function call that checks to make sure that the memory allocation occurred safely. If it didn't, the library will fail with the assertion. For your library, you should replace this assertion statement so that your program can handle any problems in a graceful manner.

The Reference Counter Functions

As you'll see in later sections, the underlying C++ library can sometimes return pointers to objects during calls to C++ methods. To mimic this operation in your Java library, you will want to add functionality to translate this pointer to one of the Java objects. Because multiple Java interface objects can refer to a single C++ pointer, you must maintain a reference counter to keep track of how many objects have a copy:

```
My3D_World_IncRefCntr(pos);
```

This reference counter is implemented as an array of integers called `My3D_World_ObjRef`. The reference count for an object is stored in the same position in the array as its pointer is in `My3D_World_ObjPtr` (or equivalently, at the `hCPPObj` position stored in the Java interface object). The implementation of the `IncRefCntr()` and `DecRefCntr()` functions is shown in Listing 33.27.

Listing 33.27. IncRefCntr function definition.

```
void My3D_World_IncRefCntr(long ThehCPPObj) {
    My3D_World_ObjRef[ThehCPPObj]++;
}
```

The `DecRefCntr()` function, used when a Java interface object using a pointer moves out of scope, decrements the reference counter. It then checks to see whether any other Java objects are still using this pointer, indicated by the reference count being greater than 0. If not, `DecRefCntr()` deletes the underlying object. The implementation of `DecRefCntr()` is shown in Listing 33.28.

Listing 33.28. DecRefCntr() function definition.

```
void My3D_World_DecRefCntr(long ThehCPPObj) {

    My3D_World_ObjRef[ThehCPPObj]—;
    if (My3D_World_ObjRef[ThehCPPObj] == 0)
      My3D_World_ObjPtr[ThehCPPObj]->Destroy();
    }

}
```

The final statement in the `World` constructor assigns the position in the pointer list to the Java interface object's `hCPPObj` variable so that when a C++ object pointer is needed, it is available by lookup in the pointer table. This completes all the tasks you set out to do in your `World` constructor.

Passing a Call from Java to C++

Now let's focus on how you implement the methods within the Java `World` interface. This task really boils down to translating a call to one of these Java methods to an equivalent call with the same data (but possibly in a different C++ format) to the C++ version of the class.

Listing 33.29 shows the implementation for the `AttachNode()` method:

Listing 33.29. AttachNode() implementation.

```
  void My3D_World_AttachNode (struct HMy3D_World *hthis, struct HMy3D_Node *hNode)
{
    My3D_World_ResolvePtr(hthis)->AttachNode(My3D_Node_ResolvePtr(hNode));
  }
```

The `AttachNode()` function prototype should look very familiar to you from earlier in this chapter. This function is passed the Java `World` object handle as the first parameter and a handle to the `Node` to be attached as the second parameter. You haven't explored the interface constructor of the `Node` object yet, but you really don't need to—it is completely analogous to the one you saw for the `World` object. Literally, only the names have been changed.

The body of the `AttachNode()` native method contains only one statement: The call to `My3D_World_ResolvePtr()` looks up the `World` C++ pointer referenced by this and calls this `World` object's `AttachNode()` method with the `Node` object referenced by the `hNode` and resolved by using `My3D_Node_ResolvePtr()`.

Using My3D_*xxxx*_ResolvePtr()

The My3D_World_ResolvePtr() and My3D_Node_ResolvePtr() functions referenced earlier are used to find the C++ pointers to the Node and World objects. These functions take a handle to an InterfaceObject and return the C++ pointer to the Java interface object. They do this translation using the hCPPObj handle for the World class. The implementation is shown in Listing 33.30.

Listing 33.30. ResolvePtr() function definition.

```
World* My3D_World_ResolvePtr(struct HMy3D_World *jthis) {
    return( My3D_World_ObjPtr[unhand(jthis)->hCPPObj] );
}
```

ResolvePtr() is a very simple function. It retrieves the object handle stored in hCPPObj and returns the World object pointer referenced by it. You'll see a more complicated example of this function when you consider the implementation of this function for an abstract class such as the Node class.

The DetachNode() method is the final explicit method needed for the World object. Its implementation is shown in Listing 33.31.

Listing 33.31. DetachNode() function definition.

```
struct HMy3D_Node* My3D_World_DetachNode(struct HMy3D_World *hthis,
                                struct HMy3D_Node *hNode) {

    Node* CPPNode = My3D_World_ResolvePtr(hthis)->DetachNode
                    (Node_ResolvePtr(hNode));

    ClassClass *ccNode = NULL;
    ccNode = FindClass(NULL, "My3D/Node\0", TRUE);
    assert(ccNode != NULL);

    struct HMy3D_Node *hNode =
        (struct HMy3D_Node*)execute_java_constructor(NULL,"My3D/Node\0",
        ccNode,"()");
    assert(hNode != NULL);

    My3D_Node_PtrEmul(CPPNode, hNode);
    return(hNode);
}
```

There are a lot of new things in the implementation of the My3D_World_DetachNode() function. First, it returns a class that isn't one of the standard set of objects available in Java. This is the main reason that the function is so complicated. Earlier in this chapter, you learned how to return a java.lang.String class. However, the String class has a Java interpreter call, makeJavaString(), that enables you to instantiate a String for the return. Because Node is a developer-defined class and is not from the Java class library, there is no equivalent call for Node in the Java interpreter API. Instead, you have to learn how to use the interpreter calls to instantiate and return arbitrary Java objects.

The first two lines of the function are pretty straightforward. The function resolves the pointer for the World object and the passed Node object and calls the DetachNode() method. The DetachNode() method returns a pointer to the Node detached, which it stores in CPPNode.

Now you want to find the handle of the Java object that corresponds to the returned C++ pointer of the detached Node and create a Node handle that encapsulates this handle to return.

Before you instantiate a Java Node class, you must fill out a ClassClass structure (as discussed earlier in this section). You did this in My3D_World_DetachNode() using the following statement:

```
ccNode = FindClass(NULL, "My3D/Node\0", TRUE);
```

This statement tells the Java interpreter to look up the class information for the My3D.Node Java class. The first parameter, for which you passed NULL, enables you to specify an interpreter to service this request through an ExecEnv* (the type ExecEnv is defined in interpreter.h, but an understanding of its contents is not necessary for this discussion). Passing NULL indicates that you want to use the default interpreter to look up this information. Unless you are writing native programs that use multiple interpreters (you know if you are—it's a painful experience), you can ignore this parameter and pass NULL.

The third parameter tells the interpreter whether to resolve the name passed into FindClass. You should always pass TRUE for this parameter. Sun hasn't documented exactly what this function does if you don't, so as of this writing, there is no definitive reason.

Next, you want to instantiate a Java Node that you can use to return the C++ Node returned from the DetachNode() method. To do this, you use the Java interpreter function execute_java_constructor():

```
hNode = (struct HMy3D_Node*)
        execute_java_constructor(NULL,"My3D/Node\0",
                              ccNode, "()");
```

The execute_java_constructor() function takes an ExecEnv* as the first parameter and the name of the class as the second, just as the FindClass() function call did. For the third parameter, you should pass the ClassClass structure returned by FindClass() in the last step.

The final parameter specifies the signature of the Node constructor you want to call. This signature indicates the types you want to pass and receive from the invoked Java method. The signature passed in the preceding code ("()") is the simplest—a constructor that accepts no parameters and returns nothing. All constructors do not have a return type, but if you have a constructor in the Node class that accepts an int as a parameter for the constructor, its constructor would have been "(I)". The return type is specified after the closing parenthesis for methods that return values. For this hypothetical constructor that accepts an integer, you pass the integer parameter for the constructor as the fifth parameter. This parameter list is unbounded, like the parameter list for `printf()` in the C language, so to pass in additional parameters, you merely keep adding them to the list. For example, the following statement passes a 4 to a hypothetical `Node` constructor that accepts an integer:

```
hNode = (struct HSolidCoffee_PointFW_t*)
                execute_java_constructor(NULL,"My3D/Node\0",
                        ccNode,"(I)", 4);
```

Now that you have a Java `Node` instantiated, you want to do the following:

1. Find the Java `Node` handle that corresponds to the C++ `Node` pointer returned by `DetachNode()` and set `hNode`'s `hCPPObj` to it.

2. Increment the reference counters to the C++ pointer and decrement the reference counter for the current `hNode` pointer.

3. Copy the handle into the `hNode` object so that it points at the correct object.

All this is done by the function `PtrEmul()`, as used in the `My3D_World_DetachNode()` function:

```
My3D_Node_PtrEmul(CPPNode, hNode);
```

The `My3D_Node_PtrEmul()` implementation is shown in Listing 33.32. It emulates a pointer reference system for your interface code.

Listing 33.32. Node `PtrEmul()` function definition.

```
void My3D_Node_PtrEmul(Node* pNode, struct HMy3D_Node* hNode) {
  long hRetNode = My3D_Node_FindHandle(pNode);
  My3D_Node_IncRefCntr(hRetNode);
  My3D_Node_DecRefCntr(unhand(hNode)->hCPPObj);
  unhand(hNode)->hCPPObj = hRetNode;
}
```

The `My3D_Node_PtrEmul()` function is relatively straightforward (you learn the internals later in this chapter). For now, all you need to know is that `My3D_Node_FindHandle()` returns the handle to the `Node` object (or any of its subclasses) to which the C++ pointer refers.

After finding the corresponding handle for the `Node` C++ object, the function increments its reference count because another Java `Node` object will now be using this pointer. The function then decrements the reference count for the target's current `Node` C++ object because it is no longer referenced by this Java `Node`. Finally, the function copies the handle into the target, completing the copy.

With that done, you now have a handle to a Java `Node` object that refers to the `Node` returned by `DetachNode()`. To complete the interface function, you merely return this handle to the caller, which is done with the last statement of the function.

The World Class's FindHandle() Function

To complete the discussion of the Java World interface object, let's look at its My3D_World_FindHandle() implementation. The My3D_World_FindHandle() function is responsible for taking a pointer to a World object and translating it back into a handle that can be used to reference the World object's My3D_World_ObjPtr array. The implementation for this is shown in Listing 33.33.

Listing 33.33. World FindHandle() implementation.

```
long My3D_World_FindHandle(World *FindWorld) {
  for (long pos=0; (pos != My3D_World_AllocLength) &&
                   (My3D_World_ObjPtr[pos] != FindWorld); pos++);

  // Stub for appropriate handling of pointer not
  // found errors.
  assert (pos != My3D_World_AllocLength);

  return (pos);
}
```

Because in the 3D graphics library, you expect that there is only a small number of pointer lookups using the FindHandle() function, this lookup function is written using a simple linear search function. If a large number of lookups is anticipated, this function should be rewritten with a hashing search method to reduce its performance impact.

The World Class's Finalize() Method

The final interface function for the World class is the interface for the My3d_World_finalize() method. If you are not familiar with this method, it is called when the Java garbage collector has to dispose of an object because it has moved out of scope. This method enables the object to clean up after itself and perform any last-minute maintenance tasks before the allocation for its data is freed. For your Java interface objects, you use this function to decrement the reference counter for the indicated object to keep your reference count coherent. The implementation of My3D_World_finalize() is shown in Listing 33.34.

Listing 33.34. World finalize() implementation definition.

```
void My3D_World_finalize(struct HMy3D_World *jthis) {
  My3D_World_DecRefCntr(unhand(jthis)->hCPPObj);
}
```

33

INTEGRATING
NATIVE CODE

The Node Java Interface Object

The next interface implementation is the interface to the Node object. Listing 33.35 shows the Java object definition. It doesn't look much different from its C++ counterpart (which is helpful for any converts you may have from your C++ product).

Listing 33.35. Node Java class definition.

```
public class Node extends InterfaceObject{
  public native void SetLocation (PointFW_t loc);
  public native PointFW_t GetLocation();
  public native finalize();
}
```

You have to define the Java version of the C++ PointFW_t structure so that you can present the implementation of the SetLocation() and GetLocation() methods. The Java version is very similar to the C++ version, and its implementation is shown in Listing 33.36.

Listing 33.36. PointFW_t Java class definition.

```
class PointFW_t {
  float x;
  float y;
  float z;
  float w;
};
```

The native implementation of the SetLocation() method is shown in Listing 33.37.

Listing 33.37. SetLocation() implementation.

```
void My3D_Node_SetLocation (struct HMy3D_Node      *hthis,
                            struct HMy3D_PointFW_t *hLocation) {
  PointFW_t CPPLocation;
  CPPLocation.x = unhand(hLocation)->x;
  CPPLocation.y = unhand(hLocation)->y;
  CPPLocation.z = unhand(hLocation)->z;
  CPPLocation.z = unhand(hLocation)->z;

  My3D_Node_ResolvePtr(hthis)->SetLocation(CPPLocation);
}
```

This implementation is very similar to the AttachNode() interface function from earlier in this chapter, but because the PointFW_t class is a simple C++ object, you create a C++ PointFW_t structure with each invocation of SetLocation() to pass the location into the C++ method instead of maintaining a list of PointFW_t pointers.

NOTE

You explicitly copy the members of the structure instead of de-referencing the pointer because of the chance of a mismatch between Java's representation of the `PointFW_t` class and C++'s representation. Specifically, the order of the elements of C++'s representation may be the reverse of the Java implementation, yielding `SetLocation (<w,z,y,x>)` when C++'s implementation is `SetLocation (<x,y,z,w>)`. Although the correlation is one-to-one with Visual C++ 4.0 and JDK 1.0, it isn't set in stone. The safe programming practice is to assume no correlation and copy the elements one by one. In any case, compared to the overhead of calling the native method, the performance impact of these four copies is negligible.

The native implementation of the `GetLocation()` method is shown in Listing 33.38.

Listing 33.38. `GetLocation()` implementation.

```
struct HMy3D_PointFW_t* My3D_Node_GetLocation() {
    PointFW_t CPPLocation = My3D_Node_ResolvePtr(hthis)->GetLocation();

    ClassClass *ccNode = FindClass(NULL, "My3D/PointFW_t\0", TRUE);
    assert(ccNode != NULL);

    struct HMy3D_PointFW_t *hLocation = (struct HSolidCoffee_PointFW_t*)
            execute_java_constructor(NULL, "My3D/PointFW_t\0", ccNode, "()");
    assert(hLocation != NULL);

    unhand(hLocation)->x = CPPLocation.x;
    unhand(hLocation)->y = CPPLocation.y;
    unhand(hLocation)->z = CPPLocation.z;
    unhand(hLocation)->w = CPPLocation.w;
    return(hLocation);
}
```

The implementation of `GetLocation()` is very similar to the `DetachNode()` implementation. The only difference is the deletion of the `PtrEmul()` call and its replacement with a straight element-by-element copy of the returned `PointFW_t` location.

Before you leave the `Node` object, notice that the `Node` Java object doesn't have a constructor. This is important because it means that no C++ `Node` objects can be instantiated. This was intended in the C++ design, because only the `Light` and `Geometry` objects were designed to be instantiated. You'll see how this works into the design when you consider the implementation of the `My3D_World_PtrEmul()` function later in this chapter. Before you do that, let's lay the groundwork by discussing the two subclasses of `Node`: `Light` and `Geometry`.

The Light Java Interface Object

Listing 33.39 shows the Java implementation for the interface class to the `Light` object. Because `Light` is a subclass of `Node` in the C++ definition, it is also a subclass in the Java version. Whenever possible, you should strive to keep your object hierarchies the same between your Java and C++ versions to prevent difficulties in interfacing the two libraries and to preserve the same hierarchy with which your C++ users are familiar.

Because it can be instantiated, `Light` does have a constructor. The implementation of this constructor follows nearly exactly the same format as the `World` constructor.

The `SetDirection()` and `GetDirection()` methods also introduce a new class, `PointF_t`. The definition of this class is very similar to the `PointFW_t` class and is shown in Listing 33.40.

Listing 33.39. Light Java class definition.

```
public class Light extends Node {
  private native void constructor();
  public Light() {
    constructor();
  }

  public native void finalize();
  public void SetDirection(PointF_t dir);
  public void PointF_t GetDirection();
}
```

Listing 33.40. PointF_t Java class definition.

```
class PointF_t {
  float x;
  float y;
  float z;
};
```

The native implementation of the `SetDirection` and `GetDirection` interfaces for the `Light` class are shown in Listing 33.41.

Listing 33.41. SetDirection and GetDirection implementation.

```
void My3D_Light_SetDirection (struct HMy3D_Light      *hthis,
                              struct HMy3D_PointF_t *hDirection) {
    PointF_t CPPDirection;
    CPPDirection.x = unhand(hDirection)->x;
    CPPDirection.y = unhand(hDirection)->y;
    CPPDirection.z = unhand(hDirection)->z;
    CPPDirection.z = unhand(hDirection)->z;

    My3D_Light_ResolvePtr(hthis)->SetDirection(CPPDirection);
}
```

```
struct HMy3D_PointF_t* My3D_Light_GetDirection() {

  PointF_t CPPDirection = My3D_Light_ResolvePtr(hthis)->GetDirection();

  ClassClass *ccLight = FindClass(NULL, "My3D/PointF_t\0", TRUE);
  assert(ccLight != NULL);

  struct HMy3D_PointF_t *hDirection = (struct HSolidCoffee_PointF_t*)
                    execute_java_constructor(NULL, "My3D/PointF_t\0",
                          ccLight,"()");
  assert(hDirection != NULL);
  unhand(hDirection)->x = CPPDirection.x;
  unhand(hDirection)->y = CPPDirection.y;
  unhand(hDirection)->z = CPPDirection.z;
  unhand(hDirection)->w = CPPDirection.w;
  return(hDirection);
}
```

As you can see, the implementation of the SetDirection and GetDirection classes is very similar to the implementation of the SetLocation() and GetLocation() methods in the Node class.

The Geometry Java Interface Object

The final interface class you need to know is the Geometry class. The Java interface class for the Geometry object is shown in Listing 33.42 and consists of the constructor and finalize methods for the Geometry class. The rest of the functionality for the Geometry class is provided by the Node class that it extends. Don't worry if you don't understand how the Geometry object specifies a polygon—it really isn't important to the discussion that follows. Instead, focus on how the interface between the Java and the C++ class works.

Listing 33.42. Geometry Java class definition.

```
public class Geometry extends Node {
  private native void constructor(int nPolygons, int nVertices,
                  PointF_t pVertices[], PointF_t pNormals[],
                  PointF_t pFacets[], PointF_t pTexture[],
                  ColorFA_t pColors[], int VerOrder[]);

  public Geometry(int nPolygons, int nVertices, PointF_t pVertices[],
                  PointF_t pNormals[], PointF_t pFacets[],
                  PointF_t pTexture[], ColorFA_t pColors[],
                  int VerOrder[]) {
    constructor();
  }
  public native void finalize();
}
```

The `Geometry` class introduces one final class to your expanding library: the `ColorFA_t` class, which is responsible for specifying the colors of all the vertices in the object. Listing 33.43 shows the implementation of the `ColorFA_t` class.

Listing 33.43. ColorFA_t Java struct definition.

```
class ColorFA_t {
  float r;
  float g;
  float b;
  float a;
};
```

The implementation for the `Geometry` class constructor is shown in Listing 33.44. This constructor demonstrates how to handle arrays of passed objects in your interface code, which is a common source of confusion for native method users.

Listing 33.44. Geometry constructor implementation.

```
long     My3D_Geometry_AllocLength = 0;
#define  INITIAL_My3D_Geometry_ALLOC 2

Geometry**  My3D_Geometry_ObjPtr = NULL;
long*    My3D_Geometry_ObjRef = NULL;

void My3D_Geometry_constructorb(
      struct HMy3D_Geometry *jthis,
      short cNP, short cNV, HArrayOfObject* pAP,
      HArrayOfObject* pAN, HArrayOfObject* pFN,
      HArrayOfObject* pAT, HArrayOfObject* pAC,

  if (My3D_Geometry_AllocLength == 0) {
    My3D_Geometry_AllocLength =
        My3D_Geometry_Resize(INITIAL_My3D_Geometry_ALLOC);
  }

  long pos;
  for ( pos=0;
      (pos != My3D_Geometry_AllocLength) &&
      (My3D_Geometry_ObjPtr[pos] != NULL);
       pos++ )
    ;

  if (pos == My3D_Geometry_AllocLength) {
    My3D_Geometry_AllocLength =
        My3D_Geometry_Resize(My3D_Geometry_AllocLength*2);
  }

  int PassNP = cNP;
  int PassNV = cNV;
```

```
// Copy the Vertex points from the Java Array into a C++ array
int len = obj_length(pAP);
PointF_t* PassAP = new PointF_t[len];
struct HMy3D_PointF_t* hAP;

for (i=0; i != len; i++) {
    hAP = (struct HMy3D_PointF_t *) (unhand(pAP)->body)[i];
    PointF_t* PtrAP = (PointF_t *) unhand(hAP);
    PassAP[i] = *PtrAP;
}

// Copy the Normals from the Java Array into a C++ array
len = obj_length(pAN);
PointF_t* PassAN = new PointF_t[len];
struct HMy3D_PointF_t* hAN;

for (i=0; i != len; i++) {
    hAN     = (struct HMy3D_PointF_t *) (unhand(pAN)->body)[i];
    PointF_t* PtrAN = (PointF_t *) unhand(hAN);
    PassAN[i] = *PtrAN;
}

// Copy the Facet Normals from the Java Array into a C++ array.
len = obj_length(pFN);
PointF_t* PassFN = new PointF_t[len];
struct HMy3D_PointF_t* hFN;

for (i=0; i != len; i++) {
    hFN = (struct HMy3D_PointF_t *) (unhand(pFN)->body)[i];
    PointF_t* PtrFN = (PointF_t *) unhand(hFN);
    PassFN[i] = *PtrFN;
}

// Copy the Texture points from the Java Array into a C++ array.
len = obj_length(pAT);
PointF_t* PassAT = new PointF_t[len];
struct HMy3D_PointF_t* hAT;

for (i=0; i != len; i++) {
    hAT = (struct HMy3D_PointF_t *) (unhand(pAT)->body)[i];
    PointF_t* PtrAT = (PointF_t *) unhand(hAT);
    PassAT[i] = *PtrAT;
}

// Copy the Color points from the Java Array into a C++ array.
len = obj_length(pAC);
ColorFA_t* PassAC = new ColorFA_t[len];
struct HMy3D_ColorFA_t* hAC;

for (i=0; i != len; i++) {
    hAC = (struct HMy3D_ColorFA_t *) (unhand(pAC)->body)[i];
    ColorFA_t* PtrAC = (ColorFA_t *) unhand(hAC);
    PassAC[i] = *PtrAC;
}
```

33

INTEGRATING
NATIVE CODE

continues

Listing 33.44. continued

```
// Make a pointer to the vertex orders.
len = obj_length(pAV);
Fixed16_t* PassAV = (Fixed16_t *)(unhand(pAV)->body);

My3D_Geometry_ObjPtr[pos] = new Geometry(PassNP, PassNV,
                PassAP, PassAN, PassFN, PassAT, PassAC, PassAV);

assert (My3D_Geometry_ObjPtr[pos] != NULL);
My3D_Geometry_IncRefCntr(pos);
unhand(jthis)->hCPPObj = pos;

// Delete all the temporary variables.
delete PassAP;
delete PassAN;
delete PassFN;
delete PassAT;
delete PassAC;

}
```

Take, for example, the pAP array, which contains handle HArrayOfObject. When unhand() is applied to the handle HArrayOfObject, unhand() returns an array of handles to PointF_t objects for each of the points in its body element. By iterating down this array of handles, you can translate these Java PointF_t objects into C++ PointF_t objects.

Listing 33.45 shows the implementation of the My3D_Node_ResolvePtr() function.

Listing 33.45. Node C++ ResolvePtr() implementation.

```
Node* My3D_Node_ResolvePtr(struct HMy3D_Node *hNode) {

    switch (unhand(jthis)->ObjKindOf) {

        case LIGHT:
            return ( ((Node*) My3D_Light_ResolvePtr(hNode));
            break;

        case GEOMETRY:
            return ( ((Node*) My3D_Geometry_ResolvePtr(hNode));
            break;

        default:
            assert(0);
            return (NULL);
            break;
    };
}
```

Obviously, this is much different from the implementations of My3D_xxxx_ResolvePtr() for other interface classes—none of the other classes you have considered have subclasses.

Because you want your Java subclasses of Node to be able to stand in for methods requiring a Node (just as when Node was used in your C++ library), special mechanisms must be built in your superclass interface implementation to handle this requirement.

For example, when you attach a Light object to World using the method AttachNode(Node), you use the properties of Light as a subclass of Node to enable it to stand in as a Node to be attached. Remember the implementation of the My3D_World_AttachNode() for the World interface; you used the following statement to call AttachNode():

```
My3D_World_ResolvePtr(hthis)->AttachNode(My3D_Node_ResolvePtr(hNode));
```

Because there are two subclasses to Node—Light and Geometry—the hNode handle passed to My3D_Node_ResolvePtr() could be either a Light or a Geometry object. This is the reason for the switch statement in the My3D_*xxxx*_ResolvePtr() function implementation—you have to know to which object this handle refers. With the object determined, you can then call the My3D_*xxxx*_ResolvePtr() function for the appropriate object to retrieve the pointer.

With this in mind, case statements were added for both the Light and Geometry objects in the ResolvePtr function. The LIGHT and GEOMETRY constants can be anything, but they must be different. This Java interface defines them in a global header file (see Listing 33.46), which also contains all the public interface functions for each of the objects for linking.

Listing 33.46. Global header file.

```
#define WORLD       1
#define GEOMETRY    2
#define LIGHT       3

Node* My3D_Node_ResolvePtr(struct HMy3D_Node *hNode);
Node* My3D_Node_FindHandle (Node* CPPNode);
void  My3D_Node_DecRefCntr(struct HMy3D_Node *hNode);
void  My3D_Node_IncRefCntr(struct HMy3D_Node *hNode);
```

Unfortunately, to do the inverse and find a Java Node handle given a Node*, you must modify the C++ subclass to tell you what class it represents. To do this in your graphics library, add to the C++ class a method int KindOf() that returns the object type as defined in the global header file in Listing 33.46. With this information, the class can chain the request of My3D_*xxxx*_FindHandle() down to the correct class interface code, as shown in Listing 33.47.

Listing 33.47. Node C++ FindHandle() implementation.

```
struct HMy3D_Node* My3D_Node_FindHandle (Node* CPPNode) {

  switch (CPPNode->KindOf()) {
      case LIGHT:
        return (My3D_Light_FindHandle(CPPNode));
        break;
```

Listing 33.47. continued

```
    case GEOMETRY:
      return (My3D_Geometry_FindHandle(CPPNode));
      break;

    default:
      assert(0);
      return (NULL);
      break;
  };
}
```

In the same manner, the `My3D_Node_IncRefCntr()` and `My3D_Node_DecRefCntr()` interface functions also need this mechanism. Their implementation is shown in Listing 33.48.

Listing 33.48. Node C++ DecRefCntr() implementation.

```
void My3D_Node_IncRefCntr (struct HMy3D_Node* hNode) {

  long hNode;
  switch (unhand(hNode)->ObjKindOf) {
    case LIGHT:
      My3D_Light_IncRefCntr(hNode);
      break;

    case GEOMETRY:
      My3D_Geometry_IncRefCntr(hNode);
      break;

    default:
      assert(0);
      break;
  };
}

void My3D_Node_DecRefCntr (struct HMy3D_Node* hNode) {

  long hNode;
  switch (unhand(hNode)->ObjKindOf) {
    case LIGHT:
      My3D_Light_DecRefCntr(hNode);
      break;

    case GEOMETRY:
      My3D_Geometry_DecRefCntr(hNode);
      break;

    default:
      assert(0);
      break;
  };
}
```

The final component you should integrate into your interface is automatic handling of Java objects that move out of scope. When a Java object moves out of scope, the method `finalize()` is called. The behavior you want in your interface code is to adjust the reference counters appropriately. You accomplish this simply by linking the call to `My3D_xxxx_finalize()` with a call to `My3D_xxxx_DecRefCntr()`, as shown in Listing 33.49 for the `World` class. All Java classes that link to C++ classes that can be instantiated should include interface code for `finalize()` methods like this (that is, in the classes you have seen in this chapter, the `Node` class should be the only class that doesn't include code like this).

Listing 33.49. IncRefCntr() implementation.

```
void My3D_World_finalize(struct HMy3D_World* hthis) {
  My3D_World_DecRefCntr(unhand(hthis)->hCPPObj);
}
```

A Sample Program

That covers most of what you need to know to build a Java interface to a C++ library! A sample program using the `My3D` interface library is shown in Listing 33.50. Because this simple 3D library doesn't have enough functionality to render the scene, you can't run the program; but note how the semantics of the Java version of the `My3D` application are the same as the semantics of a normal Java program, meeting the design goals at the beginning of the chapter.

Listing 33.50. Sample3DProg implementation.

```
import My3D;

class Sample3DProg {

  void main(String argv[]) {
    World theWorld = new World();
    PointF_t LightDir = new PointF_t();
    LightDir.x = 0.0f;
    LightDir.y = 0.0f;
    LightDir.z = 1.0f;

    PointF_t LightLoc = new PointFW_t();
    LightDir.x = 0.0f;
    LightDir.y = 0.0f;
    LightDir.z = 10.0f;
    LightDir.w = 1.0f;

    Light theLight = new Light();
    theLight.SetLocation(LightLoc);
    theLight.SetDirection(LightDir);
  }
}
```

Summary

This chapter covered a lot of ground! Take some time to let it soak in before you continue. The first section of the chapter explained the basics of the Java native method interface and how Java passes data to your C/C++ program and how C/C++ programs should pass data back to Java.

The second half of the chapter dealt with the issues of building a set of Java interface libraries to legacy C and C++ libraries. Because of limitations on the scope of this chapter, we didn't get a chance to go into how to handle all the limitations of Java's lack of some object-orientation features (such as multiple inheritance issues and templates). If you're interested in how to handle these types of problems, take a look at Chapter 31 in *Tricks of the Java Programming Gurus*, published by Sams.net.

Java Under the Hood: Inside the Virtual Machine

by Stephen Ingram

IN THIS CHAPTER

CHAPTER

34

This chapter takes an in-depth look at the internals of the Java virtual machine (VM). Although an understanding of Java's internals is not required to be an effective Java programmer, comprehension of this chapter provides the basis for making the transition to expert-level Java coding. In any event, the VM internals shed light on the mindset of Java's original designers. Exploration at this level is a fascinating journey because of the elegance behind the Java architecture.

Looking at a virtual machine from the outside in is probably the best way to understand its workings. Incremental learning results when you move from the known to the unknown, so this chapter starts with the item you are most familiar with: the class file.

The Class File

The class file is similar to standard language object modules. When a C language file is compiled, the output is an object module. Multiple object modules are linked together to form an executable program. In Java, the class file replaces the object module and the Java virtual machine replaces the executable program.

You'll find all the information needed to execute a class contained within the class file; you'll also find extra information that aids debugging and source file tracking. Remember that Java has no "header" include files, so the class file format also has to fully convey class layout and members. Parsing a class file yields a wealth of class information, not just its runtime architecture.

Layout

The overall layout of the class file uses an outer structure and a series of substructures that contain an ever-increasing amount of detail. The outer layer is described by the following `ClassFile` structure:

```
ClassFile
{
    u4 magic;
    u2 minor_version;
    u2 major_version;
    u2 constant_pool_count;
    cp_info constant_pool[constant_pool_count - 1];
    u2 access_flags;
    u2 this_class;
    u2 super_class;
    u2 interfaces_count;
    u2 interfaces[interfaces_count];
    u2 fields_count;
    field_info fields[fields_count];
    u2 methods_count;
    method_info methods[methods_count];
    u2 attributes_count;
    attribute_info attributes[attribute_count];
}
```

In addition to the generic class information (`this_class`, `super_class`, `version`, and so on), there are three major substructures: `cp_info`, `field_info`, and `method_info`. The `attribute_info` structure is considered a minor substructure because attributes recur throughout the class file at various levels. Fields and methods contain their own set of attributes and some individual attributes also contain their own private attribute arrays.

The symbols u2 and u4 represent unsigned 2-byte and unsigned 4-byte quantities.

The Class Viewer

Simply regurgitating class file structures does not provide the best basis for actual learning. To better convey the overall class file structure, I wrote an interactive Java application that presents a class file in a tree format. Figure 34.1 shows the tool in action. With this tool, you can view any class and save it in ASCII format. Navigation is performed with the keyboard: The arrow keys provide movement and the spacebar expands and contracts the nodes.

 The Viewer.class tool and source code are provided on the CD-ROM that accompanies this book. Because it's an application, run the tool from the command line with this statement: `java Viewer`

FIGURE 34.1.

The class Viewer *application in action.*

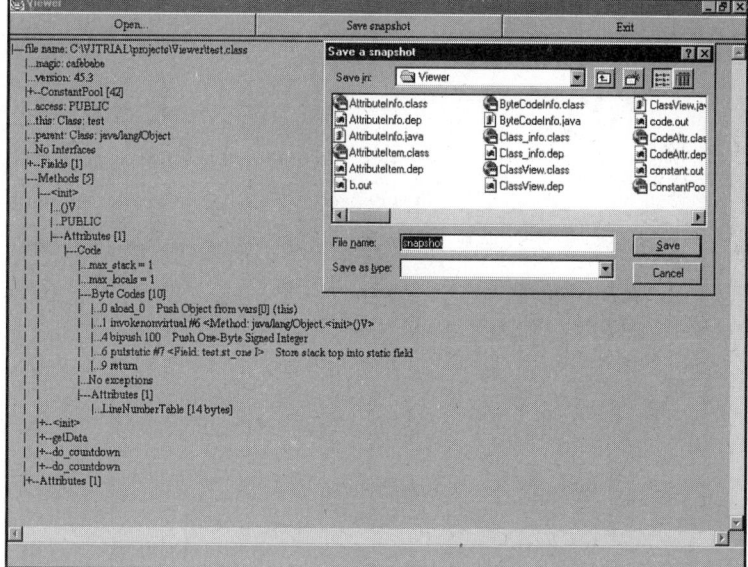

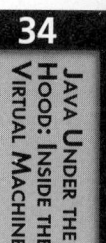

34

JAVA UNDER THE
HOOD: INSIDE THE
VIRTUAL MACHINE

Now that you have a tool, you need a simple class to explore. Here's one, just waiting for you:

```java
public class test
{
    public static int st_one;

    public test()
    {
        st_one = 100;
    }

    public test(int v)
    {
        st_one = v;
    }

    public native boolean getData(int data[] );

    public int do_countdown()
    {
        int x = st_one;

        System.out.println("Performing countdown:");
        while ( x-- != 0 )
            System.out.println(x);
        return st_one;
    }

    public int do_countdown(int x)
    {
        int save = x;

        System.out.println("Performing countdown:");
        while ( x-- != 0 )
            System.out.println(x);
        return save;
    }
}
```

This class doesn't actually do very much, but it does provide a basis for class file exploration. Once compiled, the outer layer of the resulting class file is as follows:

```
----file name: test.class
    |....magic: cafebabe
    |....version: 45.3
    |+---ConstantPool [42]
    |....access: PUBLIC
    |....this: Class: test
    |....parent: Class: java/lang/Object
    |....No Interfaces
    |+---Fields [1]
    |+---Methods [5]
    |+---Attributes [1]
```

The magic number of a class is 0xcafebabe. If a class file does not contain this number, the Java virtual machine will refuse to load the class. This number must appear in a class file or the file is assumed to be invalid. The current major version is 45; the current minor version is 3. Future Java compilers will increment these numbers when the underlying class file format changes. Version numbers allow future Java machines to recognize and disallow execution of older class files.

Access Flags

Access flags are used throughout the class file to convey the access characteristics of various items. The flag itself is a collection of 11 individual bits. Table 34.1 lays out the masks.

Table 34.1. Access flag bit values.

Flag Value	Indication
ACC_PUBLIC = 0x0001	Global visibility
ACC_PRIVATE = 0x0002	Local class visibility
ACC_PROTECTED = 0x0004	Subclass visibility
ACC_STATIC = 0x0008	One occurrence in system (not per class)
ACC_FINAL = 0x0010	No changes allowed
ACC_SYNCHRONIZED = 0x0020	Access with a monitor
ACC_VOLATILE = 0x0040	No local caching
ACC_TRANSIENT = 0x0080	Not a persistent value
ACC_NATIVE = 0x0100	Native method implementation
ACC_INTERFACE = 0x0200	Class is an interface
ACC_ABSTRACT = 0x0400	Class or method is abstract

Access flags are present for a class and its fields and methods. Only a subset of values appears in any given item. Some bits apply only to fields (for example, VOLATILE and TRANSIENT); others apply only to methods (for example, SYNCHRONIZED and NATIVE).

Attributes

Attributes, like access flags, appear throughout a class file. They have the following form:

```
GenericAttribute_info
{
    u2 attribute_name;
    u4 attribute_length;
    u1 info[attribute_length];
}
```

A generic structure exists to enable loaders to skip over attributes they don't understand. The actual attribute has a unique structure that can be read if the loader understands the format. As an example, the following structure specifies the format of a source file attribute:

```
SourceFile_attribute
{
    u2 attribute_name;
    u4 attribute_length;
    u2 sourcefile_index;
}
```

The name of an attribute is an index into the constant pool. You learn about the constant pool in the next section. If a loader does not understand the source file attribute structure, it can skip the data by reading the number of bytes specified in the *length* parameter. For the source file attribute, the length is 2.

Constant Pool

The *constant pool* forms the basis for all numbers and strings within a class file. Nowhere else do you find strings or numbers. Any time you need to reference a string or number, you substitute an index into the constant pool. Consequently, the constant pool is the dominant feature of a class. The pool is even used directly within the virtual machine itself.

There are 12 different types of constants:

- `CONSTANT_Utf8 = 1`
- `CONSTANT_Unicode = 2`
- `CONSTANT_Integer = 3`
- `CONSTANT_Float = 4`
- `CONSTANT_Long = 5`
- `CONSTANT_Double = 6`
- `CONSTANT_Class = 7`
- `CONSTANT_String = 8`
- `CONSTANT_Fieldref = 9`
- `CONSTANT_Methodref = 10`
- `CONSTANT_InterfaceMethodref = 11`
- `CONSTANT_NameAndType = 12`

Each constant structure leads off with a tag identifying the structure type. Following the type is data specific to each individual structure. The layout of each constant structure is shown in Listing 34.1.

Listing 34.1. The layout of all 12 constant structures.

```
CONSTANT_Utf8_info
{
    u1 tag;
    u2 length;
    u1 bytes[length];
}

CONSTANT_Unicode_info
{
    u1 tag;
    u2 length;
    u2 words[length];
}

CONSTANT_Integer_info
{
    u1 tag;
    u4 bytes;
}

CONSTANT_Float_info
{
    u1 tag;
    u4 bytes;
}

CONSTANT_Long_info
{
    u1 tag;
    u4 high_bytes;
    u4 low_bytes;
}

CONSTANT_Double_info
{
    u1 tag;
    u4 high_bytes;
    u4 low_bytes;
}

CONSTANT_Class_info
{
    u1 tag;
    u2 name_index;
}

CONSTANT_String_info
{
    u1 tag;
    u2 string_index;
}
```

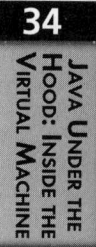

continues

Listing 34.1. continued

```
CONSTANT_Fieldref_info
{
    u1 tag;
    u2 class_index;
    u2 name_and_type_index;
}

CONSTANT_Methodref_info
{
    u1 tag;
    u2 class_index;
    u2 name_and_type_index;
}

CONSTANT_InterfaceMethodref_info
{
    u1 tag;
    u2 class_index;
    u2 name_and_type_index;
}

CONSTANT_NameAndType_info
{
    u1 tag;
    u2 name_index;
    u2 signature_index;
}
```

The CONSTANT_Utf8 structure contains standard ASCII text strings. These are not null-terminated because they use an explicit *length* parameter. Notice that most of the constants reference other constants for information. Methods, for example, specify a class and type by providing indexes to other constant pool members. Constant pool cross-references eliminate repetition of data.

The constant pool for the sample test class appears as follows:

```
¦---file name: test.class
    ¦...magic: cafebabe
    ¦...version: 45.3
    ¦---ConstantPool [42]
    ¦      ¦...String #28 -> Performing countdown:
    ¦      ¦...Class: java/lang/System
    ¦      ¦...Class: java/lang/Object
    ¦      ¦...Class: java/io/PrintStream
    ¦      ¦...Class: test
    ¦      ¦...Method: java/lang/Object.<init>()V
    ¦      ¦...Field: test.st_one I
    ¦      ¦...Field: java/lang/System.out Ljava/io/PrintStream;
    ¦      ¦...Method: java/io/PrintStream.println(I)V
    ¦      ¦...Method: java/io/PrintStream.println(Ljava/lang/String;)V
    ¦      ¦...NameAndType: st_one I
    ¦      ¦...NameAndType: println (I)V
    ¦      ¦...NameAndType: out Ljava/io/PrintStream;
    ¦      ¦...NameAndType: println (Ljava/lang/String;)V
```

```
    |   |...NameAndType: <init> ()V
    |   |...Utf8 [7] println
    |   |...Utf8 [4] (I)V
    |   |...Utf8 [3] ()I
    |   |...Utf8 [13] ConstantValue
    |   |...Utf8 [4] (I)I
    |   |...Utf8 [19] java/io/PrintStream
    |   |...Utf8 [10] Exceptions
    |   |...Utf8 [15] LineNumberTable
    |   |...Utf8 [1] I
    |   |...Utf8 [10] SourceFile
    |   |...Utf8 [14] LocalVariables
    |   |...Utf8 [4] Code
    |   |...Utf8 [21] Performing countdown:
    |   |...Utf8 [3] out
    |   |...Utf8 [21] (Ljava/lang/String;)V
    |   |...Utf8 [16] java/lang/Object
    |   |...Utf8 [6] <init>
    |   |...Utf8 [21] Ljava/io/PrintStream;
    |   |...Utf8 [16] java/lang/System
    |   |...Utf8 [12] do_countdown
    |   |...Utf8 [5] ([I)Z
    |   |...Utf8 [6] st_one
    |   |...Utf8 [7] getData
    |   |...Utf8 [9] test.java
    |   |...Utf8 [3] ()V
    |   |...Utf8 [4] test
    |...access: PUBLIC
    |...this: Class: test
    |...parent: Class: java/lang/Object
    |...No Interfaces
    |+--Fields [1]
    |+--Methods [5]
    |+--Attributes [1]
```

NOTE

The Viewer tool substitutes pool indexes with actual pool data whenever possible.

Fields

Field structures contain the individual data members of a class. Any class item that is not a method is placed into the fields section of the class file. The `field` structure looks like this:

```
field_info
{
    u2 access_flags;
    u2 name_index;
    u2 signature_index;
    u2 attribute_count;
    attribute_info attributes[attribute_count];
}
```

The sample test class contains one field:

```
¦---file name: test.class
     ¦...magic: cafebabe
     ¦...version: 45.3
     ¦+--ConstantPool [42]
     ¦...access: PUBLIC
     ¦...this: Class: test
     ¦...parent: Class: java/lang/Object
     ¦...No Interfaces
     ¦---Fields [1]
     ¦     ¦---st_one
     ¦           ¦...I
     ¦           ¦...PUBLIC STATIC
     ¦           ¦...No attributes
     ¦+--Methods [5]
     ¦+--Attributes [1]
```

Methods

The method section of the class file contains all the executable content of a class. In addition to the method name and signature, the structure contains a set of attributes. One of these attributes has the actual bytecodes that the virtual machine will execute. The method structure is shown here:

```
method_info
{
    u2 access_flags;
    u2 name_index;
    u2 signature_index;
    u2 attributes_count;
    attribute_info attributes[attribute_count];
}
```

The sample test class contains the following method section:

```
¦---file name: test.class
     ¦...magic: cafebabe
     ¦...version: 45.3
     ¦+--ConstantPool [42]
     ¦...access: PUBLIC
     ¦...this: Class: test
     ¦...parent: Class: java/lang/Object
     ¦...No Interfaces
     ¦+--Fields [1]
     ¦---Methods [5]
     ¦     ¦---<init>
     ¦     ¦     ¦...()V
     ¦     ¦     ¦...PUBLIC
     ¦     ¦     ¦---Attributes [1]
     ¦     ¦           ¦---Code
     ¦     ¦                 ¦...max_stack = 1
     ¦     ¦                 ¦...max_locals = 1
     ¦     ¦                 ¦+--Byte Codes [10]
```

```
│   │                   │...No exceptions
│   │                   │+--Attributes [1]
│   │---<init>
│   │       │...(I)V
│   │       │...PUBLIC
│   │       │---Attributes [1]
│   │            │---Code
│   │                   │...max_stack = 1
│   │                   │...max_locals = 2
│   │                   │+--Byte Codes [9]
│   │                   │...No exceptions
│   │                   │+--Attributes [1]
│   │---getData
│   │       │...([I)Z
│   │       │...PUBLIC NATIVE
│   │       │...No attributes
│   │---do_countdown
│   │       │...()I
│   │       │...PUBLIC
│   │       │---Attributes [1]
│   │            │---Code
│   │                   │...max_stack = 2
│   │                   │...max_locals = 2
│   │                   │+--Byte Codes [33]
│   │                   │...No exceptions
│   │                   │+--Attributes [1]
│   │---do_countdown
│   │       │...(I)I
│   │       │...PUBLIC
│   │       │---Attributes [1]
│   │            │---Code
│   │                   │...max_stack = 2
│   │                   │...max_locals = 3
│   │                   │+--Byte Codes [29]
│   │                   │...No exceptions
│   │                   │+--Attributes [1]
│+--Attributes [1]
```

Each method has a name and signature. Signatures are used by Java to determine calling arguments and return types. The format of a signature is as follows:

`"(args*)return_type"`

Arguments can be any combination of the characters listed in Table 34.2. Class name arguments are written as follows:

`Lclass_name;`

The semicolon (;) signals the end of the class name, just as the right parenthesis signals the end of an argument list. Arrays are followed by the array type:

```
[B for an array of bytes
[Ljava/langString; for an array of objects (in this case, Strings)
```

Table 34.2. Method signature symbols.

Type	*Signature Character*
byte	B
char	C
class	L
end of class	;
float	F
double	D
function	(
end of function	)
int	I
long	J
short	S
void	V
boolean	Z

All the methods except getData() have a code attribute. This method is marked as NATIVE, so the Java virtual machine expects the code to be in a native library. Each non-native method contains a code attribute that has the following format:

```
Code_attribute
{
    u2 attribute_name;
    u4 attribute_length;
    u2 max_stack;
    u2 max_locals;
    u4 code_length;
    u1 code[code_length];
    u2 exception_table_length;
    ExceptionItem exceptions[exception_table_length];
    u2 attributes_count;
    attribute_info attributes[attribute_count];
}
```

Code attributes contain a private list of other attributes. Typically, these are debugging lists, such as line-number information.

Exception Handling

The pc register points to the next bytecode to execute. Whenever an exception is thrown, the method's exception table is searched for a handler. Each exception table entry has this format:

```
ExceptionItem
{
    u2 start_pc;
    u2 end_pc;
    u2 handler_pc;
    u2 catch_type;
}
```

If the pc register is within the proper range and the thrown exception is the proper type, the entry's handler code block is executed. If no handler is found, the exception propagates up to the calling method. The procedure repeats itself until either a valid handler is found or the program exits.

Now that you've hit the code attribute, it's time to jump into the virtual machine.

The Virtual Machine

The Java virtual machine interprets Java bytecodes that are contained in code attributes. The virtual machine is stack based. Most computer architectures perform their operations on a mixture of memory locations and registers. The Java virtual machine performs its operations exclusively on a stack. This was done primarily to support portability. No assumptions could be made about the size or number of registers in a given CPU. Intel microprocessors are especially limited in their register composition.

Registers

The virtual machine does contain some registers, but these are used for tracking the current state of the machine:

- The pc register points to the next bytecode to execute
- The vars register points to the local variables for a method
- The optop register points to the operand stack
- The frame register points to the execution environment

All these registers are 32 bits wide and point into separate storage blocks. The blocks, however, can be allocated all at once because the code attribute specifies the size of the operand stack, the number of local variables, and the length of the bytecodes.

Operand Stack

Most Java bytecodes work on the operand stack. For example, to add two integers together, each integer is pushed onto the operand stack. The addition operator removes the top two integers, adds them, and places the result in their place back on the stack:

..., 4, 5 -> ..., 9

> **NOTE**
>
> Operand stack notation is used throughout the remainder of this chapter. The stack reads from left to right, with the stack top on the extreme right. Ellipses indicate indeterminate data buried on the stack. The arrow indicates an operation; the data to the right of the arrow represents the stack after the operation is performed.

Each stack location is 32 bits wide. Longs and doubles are 64 bits wide, so they take up two stack locations.

Local Variables

Each code attribute specifies the size of the local variables. A local variable is 32 bits wide, so long and double primitives take up two variable slots. Unlike C, all method arguments appear as local variables. The operand stack is reserved exclusively for operations.

Before detailing the bytecodes, I think a more holistic view of the virtual machine's operations would be instructive.

The Virtual Machine in Action

Consider the following method from the sample test class:

```
public int do_countdown(int x)
    {
        int save = x;

        System.out.println("Performing countdown:");
        while ( x-- != 0 )
            System.out.println(x);
        return save;
    }
```

The class file specifies that this method has a maximum operand stack of two and a local variable block of three. Figure 34.2 shows the initial state of these two blocks.

Notice how the method's input argument is placed into the local variable block. Java contains an extensive set of bytecodes dedicated to moving data between the local variable block and the operand stack. All data must be moved to the stack before it can be used. This is an important distinction between Java machine code and register-based machine architectures. Register machines reference memory directly from the contents of a register. Java must first move the contents of a variable to its operand stack before it can reference the location.

FIGURE 34.2.

The initial state of the operand stack and local variable blocks.

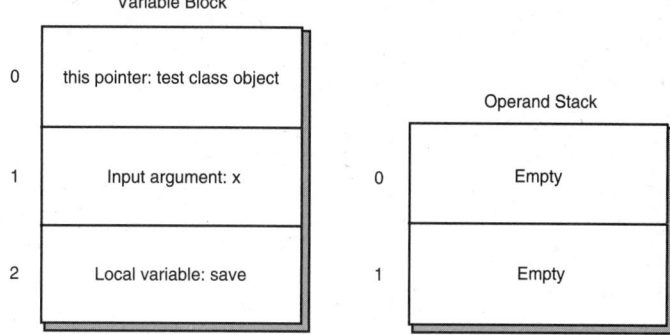

The do_countdown(int x) method contains 29 bytecodes. These two instructions store the input argument x into the local variable save:

```
0 iload_1    Move argument x onto the operand stack
1 istore_2   Store top of stack (x) into variable save
```

The next three bytecodes first load a target object (System.out) and a String onto the operand stack. At this point, println(String) is invoked. Notice that before the invocation, both elements of the operand stack are occupied. After the invocation, the operand stack is completely empty because invokevirtual removes all the stack elements it uses:

```
2 getstatic #8 <Field: java/lang/System.out Ljava/io/PrintStream;>
5 ldc1 #1 <String #28 -> Performing countdown:>
7 invokevirtual #10 <Method: java/io/PrintStream.println(Ljava/lang/String;)V>
```

This instruction transfers control to the test portion of the method's while loop. Most modern compilers code a loop with the loop test at the bottom:

```
10 goto 20
```

The loop body calls println(int):

```
13 getstatic #8 <Field: java/lang/System.out Ljava/io/PrintStream;>
16 iload_1    Move argument x onto the operand stack
17 invokevirtual #9 <Method: java/io/PrintStream.println(I)V>
```

Okay, this next bit is a little tricky. First, the current value of x is placed onto the stack. Next, 1 is subtracted from variable x. Finally, the value on the stack is checked for zero. Notice that the value on the stack is x before it was decremented. If the stack value is not zero, the body of the loop will be executed:

```
20 iload_1    Move argument x onto the operand stack
21 iinc 1 -1  Decrement argument x by one
24 ifne 13    Branch if stack top (x before decrement) not zero
```

The final two bytecodes move the value of variable save onto the stack and then return this value to the calling method:

```
27 iload_2    Move variable save onto the operand stack
28 ireturn    Move integer on stack onto calling method's operand stack
```

The Verifier

When a class is loaded, it is passed through a bytecode verifier before it is executed. The verifier checks the internal consistency of the class and the validity of the code. Java uses a late binding scheme that puts the code at risk. In traditional languages, the object linker binds all the method calls and variable accesses to specific addresses. In Java, the virtual machine doesn't perform this service until the last possible moment. As a result, it is possible for a called class to have changed since the original class was compiled. Method names or their arguments may have been altered, or the access levels may have been changed. One of the verifier's jobs is to make sure that all external object references are correct and allowed.

No assumptions can be made about the origin of bytecodes. A hostile compiler could be used to create executable bytecodes that conform to the class file format, but specify illegal codes.

The verifier uses a conservative four-pass verification algorithm to check bytecodes.

Pass 1

The first pass through the verifier reads in the class file and ensures that it is valid. The magic number must be present and all the class data must be present with no truncation or extra data after the end of the class. Any recognized attributes must have the correct length and the constant pool must not have any unrecognized entries.

Pass 2

The second pass through the verifier involves validating class features other than the bytecodes. All methods and fields must have a valid name and signature, and every class must have a super class. Signatures are not actually checked, but they must appear valid. The next pass is more specific.

Pass 3

The third pass is the most complex because the bytecodes are validated. The bytecodes are analyzed to make sure that they have the correct type and number of arguments. In addition, a data-flow analysis is performed to determine each path through the method. Each path must arrive at a given point with the same stack size and types. Each path must call methods with the proper arguments, and fields must be modified with values of the appropriate type. Class accesses are not checked in this pass. Only the return type of external functions is verified.

Forcing all paths to arrive with the same stack and registers can lead the verifier to fail some otherwise legitimate bytecodes. This is a small price to pay for this high level of security.

Pass 4

The fourth pass loads externally referenced classes and checks that the method name and signatures match. This pass also validates that the current class has access rights to the external class. After complete validation, each instruction is replaced with a _quick alternative. These _quick bytecodes indicate that the class has been verified and need not be checked again.

Bytecodes

The bytecodes can be divided into 11 major categories:

- Pushing constants onto the stack
- Moving local variable contents to and from the stack
- Managing arrays
- Generic stack instructions (dup, swap, pop, and nop)
- Arithmetic and logical instructions
- Conversion instructions
- Control transfer and function return
- Manipulating object fields
- Method invocation
- Miscellaneous operations
- Monitors

Each bytecode has a unique tag and is followed by a fixed number of additional arguments. Notice that there is no way to work directly with class fields or local variables. They must be moved to the operand stack before any operations can be performed on the contents.

Generally, there are multiple formats for each individual operation. The addition operation provides a good example. There are actually four forms of addition: iadd, ladd, fadd, and dadd. Each type assumes the top two stack items are of the correct format: integers, longs, floats, or doubles.

Pushing Constants onto the Stack

Java uses the following instructions for moving object data and local variables to the operand stack.

Push One-Byte Signed Integer:

```
bipush=16 byte1       Stack: ... -> ..., byte1
```

Push Two-Byte Signed Integer:

```
sipush=17 byte1 byte2     Stack: ... -> ..., word1
```

Push Item from the Constant Pool (8-bit index):

```
ldc1=18 indexbyte1     Stack: ... -> ..., item
```

Push Item from the Constant Pool (16-bit index):

```
ldc2=19 indexbyte1 indexbyte2    Stack: ... -> ..., item
```

Push Long or Double from Constant Pool (16-bit index):

```
ldc2w=20 indexbyte1 indexbyte2    Stack: ... -> ..., word1, word2
```

Push Null Object:

```
aconst_null=1    Stack: ... -> ..., null
```

Push Integer Constant -1:

```
iconst_m1=2    Stack: ... -> ..., -1
```

Push Integer Constants:

```
iconst_0=3    Stack: ... -> ..., 0
iconst_1=4    Stack: ... -> ..., 1
iconst_2=5    Stack: ... -> ..., 2
iconst_3=6    Stack: ... -> ..., 3
iconst_4=7    Stack: ... -> ..., 4
iconst_5=8    Stack: ... -> ..., 5
```

Push Long Constants:

```
lconst_0=9    Stack: ... -> ..., 0, 0
lconst_1=10   Stack: ... -> ..., 0, 1
```

Push Float Constants:

```
fconst_0=11    Stack: ... -> ..., 0
fconst_1=12    Stack: ... -> ..., 1
fconst_2=13    Stack: ... -> ..., 2
```

Push Double Constants:

```
dconst_0=14    Stack: ... -> ..., 0, 0
dconst_1=15    Stack: ... -> ..., 0, 1
```

Accessing Local Variables

The most commonly referenced local variables are at the first four offsets from the vars register. Because of this, Java provides single-byte instructions to access these variables for both reading and writing. A two-byte instruction is needed to reference variables greater than four deep. The variable at location zero is the class pointer itself (the this pointer).

Load Integer from Local Variable:

```
iload=21 vindex   Stack: ... -> ..., contents of varaible at vars[vindex]
iload_o=26        Stack: ... -> ..., contents of variable at vars[0]
iload_1=27        Stack: ... -> ..., contents of variable at vars[1]
iload_2=28        Stack: ... -> ..., contents of variable at vars[2]
iload_3=29        Stack: ... -> ..., contents of variable at vars[3]
```

Load Long Integer from Local Variable:

```
lload=22 vindex   Stack: .. -> ..., word1, word2  from vars[vindex] & vars[vindex+1]
lload_0=30        Stack: .. -> ..., word1, word2  from vars[0] & vars[1]
lload_1=31        Stack: .. -> ..., word1, word2  from vars[1] & vars[2]
lload_2=32        Stack: .. -> ..., word1, word2  from vars[2] & vars[3]
lload_3=33        Stack: .. -> ..., word1, word2  from vars[3] & vars[4]
```

Load Float from Local Variable:

```
fload=23 vindex   Stack: ... -> ..., contents from vars[vindex]
fload_0=34        Stack: ... -> ..., contents from vars[0]
fload_1=35        Stack: ... -> ..., contents from vars[1]
fload_2=36        Stack: ... -> ..., contents from vars[2]
fload_3=37        Stack: ... -> ..., contents from vars[3]
```

Load Double from Local Variable:

```
dload=24 vindex   Stack: ... -> ..., word1, word2  from vars[vindex] &
vars[vindex+1]
dload_0=38        Stack: ... -> ..., word1, word2  from vars[0] & vars[1]
dload_1=39        Stack: ... -> ..., word1, word2  from vars[1] & vars[2]
dload_2=40        Stack: ... -> ..., word1, word2  from vars[2] & vars[3]
dload_3=41        Stack: ... -> ..., word1, word2  from vars[3] & vars[4]
```

Load Object from Local Variable:

```
aload=25 vindex   Stack: ... -> ..., object  from vars[vindex]
aload_0=42        Stack: ... -> ..., object  from vars[0]
aload_1=43        Stack: ... -> ..., object  from vars[1]
aload_2=44        Stack: ... -> ..., object  from vars[2]
aload_3=45        Stack: ... -> ..., object  from vars[3]
```

Store Integer into Local Variable:

```
istore=54 vindex  Stack: ..., INT -> ...  into vars[vindex]
istore_0=59       Stack: ..., INT -> ...  into vars[0]
istore_1=60       Stack: ..., INT -> ...  into vars[1]
istore_2=61       Stack: ..., INT -> ...  into vars[2]
istore_3=62       Stack: ..., INT -> ...  into vars[3]
```

Store Long Integer into Local Variable:

```
lstore=55 vindex Stack: ..., word1, word2 -> ...   into vars[vindex] &
vars[vindex+1]
lstore_0=63        Stack: ..., word1, word2 -> ...  into vars[0] & vars[1]
lstore_1=64        Stack: ..., word1, word2 -> ...  into vars[1] & vars[2]
lstore_2=65        Stack: ..., word1, word2 -> ...  into vars[2] & vars[3]
lstore_3=66        Stack: ..., word1, word2 -> ...  into vars[3] & vars[4]
```

Store Float into Local Variable:

```
fstore=56 vindex Stack: ..., FLOAT -> ...   into vars[vindex]
fstore_0=67        Stack: ..., FLOAT -> ...  into vars[0]
fstore_1=68        Stack: ..., FLOAT -> ...  into vars[1]
fstore_2=69        Stack: ..., FLOAT -> ...  into vars[2]
fstore_3=70        Stack: ..., FLOAT -> ...  into vars[3]
```

Store Double into Local Variable:

```
dstore=57 vindex Stack: ..., word1, word2 -> ...   into vars[vindex] &
vars[vindex+1]
dstore_0=71        Stack: ..., word1, word2 -> ...  into vars[0] & vars[1]
dstore_1=72        Stack: ..., word1, word2 -> ...  into vars[1] & vars[2]
dstore_2=73        Stack: ..., word1, word2 -> ...  into vars[2] & vars[3]
dstore_3=74        Stack: ..., word1, word2 -> ...  into vars[3] & vars[4]
```

Store Object into Local Variable:

```
astore=58 vindex Stack: ..., OBJ -> ...   into vars[vindex]
astore_0=75        Stack: ..., OBJ -> ...  into vars[0]
astore_1=76        Stack: ..., OBJ -> ...  into vars[1]
astore_2=77        Stack: ..., OBJ -> ...  into vars[2]
astore_3=78        Stack: ..., OBJ -> ...  into vars[3]
```

Increment Local Variable (incrementing applies only to integers):

```
iinc=132 vindex constant   Stack: ... -> ...   vars[vindex] += constant
```

Managing Arrays

Arrays are treated as objects, but they don't use a method table pointer. Because of this unique-ness, arrays have special bytecodes to create and access them.

Allocate a New Array:

```
newarray=188 type Stack: ..., size -> ..., OBJ
```

Allocate a New Array of Objects:

```
anewarray=189 classindex1 classindex2 Stack: ..., size -> ..., OBJ
```

Allocate a New Multidimensional Array:

```
multianewarray=197 indexbyte1 indexbyte1 indexbyte2  Stack: ..., size1, size2,
etc. -> ..., OBJ
```

Get the Array Length:

```
arraylength=190 Stack: ..., OBJ -> ..., length
```

Load Primitives from the Array:

```
iaload=46 Stack: ..., OBJ, index -> ..., INT
laload=47 Stack: ..., OBJ, index -> ..., LONG1, LONG2
faload=48 Stack: ..., OBJ, index -> ..., FLOAT
daload=49 Stack: ..., OBJ, index -> ..., DOUBLE1, DOUBLE2
aaload=50 Stack: ..., OBJ, index -> ..., OBJ
baload=51 Stack: ..., OBJ, index -> ..., BYTE
caload=52 Stack: ..., OBJ, index -> ..., CHAR
saload=53 Stack: ..., OBJ, index -> ..., SHORT
```

Store Primitives into the Array:

```
iastore=79 Stack: ..., OBJ, index, INT -> ...
lastore=80 Stack: ..., OBJ, index, LONG1, LONG2 -> ...
fastore=81 Stack: ..., OBJ, index, FLOAT -> ...
dastore=82 Stack: ..., OBJ, index, DOUBLE1, DOUBLE2 -> ...
aastore=83 Stack: ..., OBJ, index, OBJ -> ...
bastore=84 Stack: ..., OBJ, index, BYTE -> ...
castore=85 Stack: ..., OBJ, index, CHAR -> ...
sastore=86 Stack: ..., OBJ, index, SHORT -> ...
```

Generic Stack Instructions

Following are the basic operations that alter the stack.

Do Nothing:

```
nop=0   Stack: ... -> ...
```

Pop Stack Values:

```
pop=87  Stack: ..., VAL -> ...
pop2=88  Stack: ..., VAL1, VAL2 -> ...
```

Duplicate Stack Values and Possibly Insert Below Stack Top:

```
dup=89      Stack: ..., V -> ..., V, V
dup2=92     Stack: ..., V1, V2 -> ..., V1, V2, V1, V2
dup_x1=90   Stack: ..., V1, V2 -> ..., V2, V1, V2
dup2_x1=93  Stack: ..., V1, V2, V3 -> ..., V2, V3, V1, V2, V3
dup_x2=91   Stack: ..., V1, V2, V3 -> ..., V3, V1, V2, V3
dup2_x2=94  Stack: ..., V1, V2, V3, V4 -> ..., V3, V4, V1, V2, V3, V4
```

Swap Two Stack Items:

```
swap=95     Stack: ..., V1, V2 -> ..., V2, V1
```

Arithmetic and Logical Instructions

All the arithmetic operations operate on four possible types: integer, long, float, or double.
Logical instructions operate only on integer and long types.

Addition:

```
iadd=96  Stack: ..., INT1, INT2 -> ..., INT1+INT2
ladd=97  Stack: ..., L1_1, L1_2, L2_1, L2_2 -> ..., L1+L2 (high), L1+L2 (low)
fadd=98  Stack: ..., FLOAT1, FLOAT2 -> ..., FLOAT1+FLOAT2
dadd=99  Stack: ..., D1_1, D1_2, D2_1, D2_2 -> ..., D1+D2 (high), D1+D2 (low)
```

Subtraction:

```
isub=100 Stack: ..., INT1, INT2 -> ..., INT1-INT2
lsub=101 Stack: ..., L1_1, L1_2, L2_1, L2_2 -> ..., L1-L2 (high), L1-L2 (low)
fsub=102 Stack: ..., FLOAT1, FLOAT2 -> ..., FLOAT1-FLOAT2
dsub=103 Stack: ..., D1_1, D1_2, D2_1, D2_2 -> ..., D1-D2 (high), D1-D2 (low)
```

Multiplication:

```
imul=104 Stack: ..., INT1, INT2 -> ..., INT1*INT2
lmul=105 Stack: ..., L1_1, L1_2, L2_1, L2_2 -> ..., L1*L2 (high), L1*L2 (low)
fmul=106 Stack: ..., FLOAT1, FLOAT2 -> ..., FLOAT1*FLOAT2
dmul=107 Stack: ..., D1_1, D1_2, D2_1, D2_2 -> ..., D1*D2 (high), D1*D2 (low)
```

Division:

```
idiv=108 Stack: ..., INT1, INT2 -> ..., INT1/INT2
ldiv=109 Stack: ..., L1_1, L1_2, L2_1, L2_2 -> ..., L1/L2 (high), L1/L2 (low)
fdiv=110 Stack: ..., FLOAT1, FLOAT2 -> ..., FLOAT1/FLOAT2
ddiv=111 Stack: ..., D1_1, D1_2, D2_1, D2_2 -> ..., D1/D2 (high), D1/D2 (low)
```

Remainder:

```
irem=112 Stack: ..., INT1, INT2 -> ..., INT1%INT2
lrem=113 Stack: ..., L1_1, L1_2, L2_1, L2_2 -> ..., L1%L2 (high), L1%L2 (low)
frem=114 Stack: ..., FLOAT1, FLOAT2 -> ..., FLOAT1%FLOAT2
drem=115 Stack: ..., D1_1, D1_2, D2_1, D2_2 -> ..., D1%D2 (high), D1%D2 (low)
```

Negation:

```
ineg=116 Stack: ..., INT -> ..., -INT
lneg=117 Stack: ..., LONG1, LONG2 -> ..., -LONG1, -LONG2
fneg=118 Stack: ..., FLOAT -> ..., -FLOAT
dneg=119 Stack: ..., DOUBLE1, DOUBLE2 -> ..., -DOUBLE1, -DOUBLE2
```

Integer Logical Instructions:

>>> *denotes an unsigned right shift*

```
ishl=120  Stack: ..., INT1, INT2 -> INT1<<(INT2 & 0x1f)
ishr=122  Stack: ..., INT1, INT2 -> INT1>>(INT2 & 0x1f)
iushr=124 Stack: ..., INT1, INT2 -> INT1>>>(INT2 & 0x1f)
```

Long Integer Logical Instructions:

>>> *denotes an unsigned right shift*

```
lshl=121  Stack: ..., L1, L2, INT -> L1<<(INT & 0x3f), L2<<(INT & 0x3f)
lshr=123  Stack: ..., L1, L2, INT -> INT1>>(INT & 0x3f), L2>>(INT & 0x03)
lushr=125 Stack: ..., L1, L2, INT -> INT1>>>(INT & 0x3f), L2>>>(INT & 0x3f)
```

Integer Boolean Operations:

```
iand=126  Stack: ..., INT1, INT2 -> ..., INT1&INT2
ior=128   Stack: ..., INT1, INT2 -> ..., INT1|INT2
ixor=130  Stack: ..., INT1, INT2 -> ..., INT1^INT2
```

Long Integer Boolean Operations:

```
land=127  Stack: ..., L1_1, L1_2, L2_1, L2_2 -> ..., L1_1&L2_1, L1_2&L2_2
lor=129   Stack: ..., L1_1, L1_2, L2_1, L2_2 -> ..., L1_1|L2_1, L1_2|L2_2
lxor=131  Stack: ..., L1_1, L1_2, L2_1, L2_2 -> ..., L1_1^L2_1. L1_2^L2_2
```

Conversion Instructions

Because most of the previous bytecodes expect the stack to contain a homogenous set of operands, Java uses conversion functions. In code, you can add a float and an integer, but Java will first convert the integer to a float type before performing the addition.

Integer Conversions:

```
i2l=133      Stack: .., INT -> ..., LONG1, LONG2
i2f=134      Stack: .., INT -> ..., FLOAT
i2d=135      Stack: .., INT -> ..., DOUBLE1, DOUBLE2
int2byte=145 Stack: .., INT -> ..., BYTE
int2char=146 Stack: .., INT -> ..., CHAR
int2short=147 Stack: .., INT -> ..., SHORT
```

Long Integer Conversions:

```
l2i=136      Stack: .., LONG1, LONG2 -> ..., INT
l2f=137      Stack: .., LONG1, LONG2 -> ..., FLOAT
l2d=138      Stack: .., LONG1, LONG2 -> ..., DOUBLE1, DOUBLE2
```

Float Conversions:

```
f2i=139      Stack: .., FLOAT -> ..., INT
f2l=140      Stack: .., FLOAT -> ..., LONG1, LONG2
f2d=141      Stack: .., FLOAT -> ..., DOUBLE1, DOUBLE2
```

Double Conversions:

```
d2i=142      Stack: .., DOUBLE1, DOUBLE2 -> ..., INT
d2l=143      Stack: .., DOUBLE1, DOUBLE2 -> ..., LONG1, LONG2
d2f=144      Stack: .., DOUBLE1, DOUBLE2 -> ..., FLOAT
```

Control Transfer and Function Return

All branch indexes are signed 16-bit offsets from the current pc register.

Comparisons with Zero:

```
ifeq=153 branch1 branch2    Stack: ..., INT -> ...
ifne=154 branch1 branch2    Stack: ..., INT -> ...
iflt=155 branch1 branch2    Stack: ..., INT -> ...
ifge=156 branch1 branch2    Stack: ..., INT -> ...
ifgt=157 branch1 branch2    Stack: ..., INT -> ...
ifle=158 branch1 branch2    Stack: ..., INT -> ...
```

Comparisons with Null:

```
ifnull=198 branch1 branch2    Stack: ..., OBJ -> ...
ifnonnull=199 branch1 branch2 Stack: ..., OBJ -> ...
```

Compare Two Integers:

```
if_icmpeq=159 branch1 branch2  Stack: ..., INT1, INT2 -> ...
if_icmpne=160 branch1 branch2  Stack: ..., INT1, INT2 -> ...
if_icmplt=161 branch1 branch2  Stack: ..., INT1, INT2 -> ...
if_icmpge=162 branch1 branch2  Stack: ..., INT1, INT2 -> ...
if_icmpgt=163 branch1 branch2  Stack: ..., INT1, INT2 -> ...
if_icmple=164 branch1 branch2  Stack: ..., INT1, INT2 -> ...
```

Compare Two Long Integers:

```
lcmp=148  Stack: ..., L1_1, L1_2, L2_1, L2_2 -> ..., INT (One of [-1, 0, 1])
```

Compare Two Floats:

```
l->-1 on NaN, g->1 on NaN.
fcmpl=149  Stack: ..., FLOAT1, FLOAT2 -> ..., INT (One of [-1, 0, 1])
fcmpg=150  Stack: ..., FLOAT1, FLOAT2 -> ..., INT (One of [-1, 0, 1])
```

Compare Two Doubles:

```
l->-1 on NaN, g->1 on NaN.
dcmpl=151  Stack: ..., D1_1, D1_2, D2_1, D2_2 -> ..., INT (One of [-1, 0, 1])
dcmpg=152  Stack: ..., D1_1, D1_2, D2_1, D2_2 -> ..., INT (One of [-1, 0, 1])
```

Compare Two Objects:

```
if_acmpeq=165 branch1 branch2  Stack: ..., OBJ1, OBJ2 -> ...
if_acmpne=166 branch1 branch2  Stack: ..., OBJ1, OBJ2 -> ...
```

Unconditional Branching (16-bit and 32-bit branching):

```
goto=167 branch1 branch2                     Stack: ... -> ...
goto_w=200 branch1 branch2 branch3 branch4   Stack: ... -> ...
```

Jump Subroutine (16-bit and 32-bit jumps):

```
jsr=168 branch1 branch2                      Stack: ... -> ..., returnAddress
jsr_w=201 branch1 branch2 branch3 branch4    Stack: ... -> ..., returnAddress
```

Return from Subroutine:

The return address is retrieved from a local variable, not the stack.

```
ret=169 vindex    Stack: ... -> ...    (returnAddress <- vars[vindex])
ret_w=209 vindex1 vindex2    Stack: ... -> ...    (returnAddress <- vars[vindex])
```

Return Primitives:

The current stack frame is destroyed. The top primitive is pushed onto the caller's operand stack.

```
ireturn=172  Stack: ..., INT -> [destroyed]
lreturn=173  Stack: ..., LONG1, LONG2 -> [destroyed]
freturn=174  Stack: ..., FLOAT -> [destroyed]
```

```
dreturn=175  Stack: ..., DOUBLE1, DOUBLE2 -> [destroyed]
areturn=176  Stack: ..., OBJ -> [destroyed]
return=177   Stack: ... -> [destroyed]
```

Calling the Breakpoint Handler:

```
breakpoint=202  Stack: ..., -> ...
```

Manipulating Object Fields

A 16-bit index into the constant pool is used to retrieve the class and field name. These names are used to determine the field offset and width. The object reference on the stack is used as the source or target. Values are 32 or 64 bits, depending on the field information in the constant pool.

```
Getstatic=178  index1 index2  Stack: ..., -> ..., VAL
Putstatic=179  index1 index2  Stack: ..., VAL -> ...
Getfield=180   index1 index2  Stack: ..., OBJ -> ..., VAL
Putfield=181   index1 index2  Stack: ..., OBJ, VAL -> ...
```

Method Invocation

There are four types of method invocation:

- ■ `invokevirtual=182`—This a the normal method dispatch in Java. Use the index bytes to create a 16-bit index into the constant table of the current class. Extract the method name and signature. Search the method table of the stack object to determine the method address. Use the method signature to remove the method arguments from the operand stack and transfer them to the new method's local variables.

- ■ `invokenonvirtual=183`—Used when a method is called with the super keyword. Use the index bytes to create a 16-bit index into the constant pool of the current class. Extract the method name and signature. Search the named class's method table to determine the method address. Extract the object and arguments and place them in the new method's local variables.

- ■ `invokestatic=184`—Used to call static methods. Create a 16-bit index into the current class's constant pool. Extract the method and search the named class's method table for the address. Transfer the arguments as before. There is no object to pass.

- ■ `invokeinterface=185`—Invoke an interface function. Again, a 16-bit index is created to find the method name and signature. This time, however, the number of arguments is determined from the bytecodes, not the signature.

```
virtual index1 index2              Stack: ..., OBJ, [arg1, [arg2, ...]] -> ...
nonvirtual index1 index2           Stack: ..., OBJ, [arg1, [arg2, ...]] -> ...
static index1 index2               Stack: ..., [arg1, [arg2, ...]] -> ...
interface index1 index2 nargs resv Stack: ..., OBJ, [arg1, [arg2, ...]] -> ...
```

Miscellaneous Operations

The following instructions don't fall under any other heading; they deal with generic object operations, such as creation and casting.

Throw Exception:

```
athrow=191  Stack: ..., OBJ -> [undefined]
```

Create a New Object:

```
new=187 index1 index2  Stack: ... -> ..., OBJ
```

Check a Cast Operation:

```
checkcast=192 index1 index2  Stack: ..., OBJ -> ..., OBJ
```

Instanceof:

```
instanceof=193 index1 index2  Stack: ..., OBJ -> ... INT (1 or 0)
```

Monitors

Monitor instructions are used for synchronization.

Enter a Monitored Region of Code:

```
monitorenter=194  Stack: ..., OBJ -> ...
```

Exit a Monitored Region of Code:

```
monitorexit=195  Stack: ..., OBJ -> ...
```

Summary

This chapter revealed the internal structure of the Java virtual machine through use of the Viewer tool. You learned to interpret signatures and read Java machine code. The elegance of the Java class file was also presented.

Keep this information in mind when you are working with Java. An appreciation for the internal structure will help you become an expert Java programmer. I hope this introduction has heightened your curiosity; feel free to use the Viewer program to explore some of your own Java classes.

Java Security

by Glenn Vanderburg

IN THIS CHAPTER

CHAPTER 35

Java's popularity and high profile are the product of several different characteristics, but none is more important than Java's claim to be a "secure" language. Java isn't *the* first language to have built-in security features, but it is *one* of the first; the others have been research projects or special-purpose languages. Certainly none can come close to Java's general-purpose, mainstream appeal.

This chapter presents a brief survey of Java security. First, you'll learn why security is important, and what kinds of threats Java protects against. You'll also learn the details of how Java security works, and how applications make use of the security features to implement their own security policies. Finally, the chapter discusses the quality of Java's security facilities: how strong they are, what weaknesses remain, and how Java security compares with other systems.

Why Is Security Important?

Since the introduction of Java nearly a year ago, it's been amusing to watch the varying reactions to Java's security claims. Java's creators recognize that security is important, and believe that they have devised a good solution. There are many who agree with them, but there are also many who don't, and the dissenters range all over the spectrum. Some decry the whole idea of indiscriminately bringing untrusted, possibly rogue programs onto your machine from the Internet, claiming that no language security model can be solid enough to hold up against clever crackers. Others wonder what all the fuss is about, and ask whether security is needed at all—wouldn't it be better if applets could actually read and write your files and do useful work for you? Many developers take a middle view; they understand the need for security in general, but they're frustrated when their own Java programs aren't allowed to do benign, helpful things.

All these groups have some good points, but they miss other important points about Java security, or Internet security in general.

Is Java Security a Mirage?

If your computer and the data stored in it are important to you, it's easy to understand why you may not want to run Java applets at all. Java's creators claim that it's secure, but what if they're wrong? You would be opening the door for some malevolent programmer to enter your computer and steal, destroy, or alter important data.

But the same is true of software that you manually load from the Internet and install on your machine. Even if you never do that, you also risk your data when you purchase a shrink-wrapped program from a store and install it from disks or CD. Those programs could destroy or alter your data immediately, or steal it the next time you are connected to the Internet. Although this may sound unlikely to you, it has happened. Several companies have accidentally shipped viruses to their customers along with products. Early beta versions of the Microsoft Network software performed some data collection that many users considered to be an invasion of privacy.

Java may actually improve the overall security of our computers because it guards against accidents almost as much as it guards against deliberate damage. Most of us have had the experience of installing a buggy new program that caused problems on our computers so severe that we had to reinstall the operating system. In many cases, such experiences result in the loss of important data. Although Java may not completely eliminate such problems, Java applets won't be able to inflict such damage, even accidentally.

In fact, the only perfectly secure computer is one that is unplugged. To do useful things, you have to take some risks, and the essence of security is to have acceptable levels of risk and inconvenience. This is true of all security, not just computer security. That's not to say that good security has to be a lot of trouble, but perfect security is always more trouble than it's worth.

Is Java Security Really Necessary?

On the other extreme, if what's on your computer isn't vitally important to you, or if you're simply not convinced anyone would want to steal or destroy it, you may see Java's security restrictions as a nuisance. It would be great if applets, fetched on demand from Web pages (and free of charge) could actually be *useful* applications that you could use to accomplish your work.

That certainly would be great, even if the applets weren't free. Unfortunately, there are a couple things about this scenario that should make you uneasy. Traditional software requires your conscious intervention before it can do anything on your computer: you have to acquire and install it first, and then actually run it. An applet, on the other hand, can be invoked without forethought when you browse to a Web page that contains it. Furthermore, you may never know the applet is there—it may not take up any visible space on the Web page. So an applet can run on your system without any initiative on your part, and it may not leave a trace behind. With an applet, you have no choice, and the applet has no accountability.

You may wonder why anyone would want to attack your system. The unfortunate fact is that many crackers choose their targets randomly. They aren't searching for any particular data, or seeking to harm any particular individual. Instead, they are vandals, or they just want to practice their skills or find some random computer they can use to hide their tracks while they attack their true target. They search for vulnerable systems and zero in on them. Historically, most cracking incidents have focused on UNIX systems, but with the increasing prevalence of Windows and Macintosh systems on the Internet, things are bound to change.

Programs automatically fetched to your system and run locally really are different from those you install deliberately, and their security needs are different. Think of workers who come to your home: it's fine to let selected people in when you're there and expecting them, but you wouldn't leave all your doors open all the time just in case someone came by to do some work on your house.

35
JAVA SECURITY

Why Is Java Security So Strict?

Many users and applet developers understand the need for security, but wish it weren't so strict and inflexible. They say that users should be able to disable or weaken Java's security if they want to. To a large degree, they're right, and you can expect Java applications to have more flexibility in the future.

Java security isn't all or nothing. The application can grant or deny access to applets based on a wide variety of criteria: the name of the applet, where it came from, the type of resource it's trying to access, even the particular resource. An application can choose to let applets read some files, but not others, for example.

If that's the case, then why is Java security in early applications (such as Netscape Navigator and Microsoft Internet Explorer) so inflexibly strict? There are two reasons.

The first is that such configurable, flexible security is difficult to get right. It is usually easy to build a high, impenetrable wall with no holes at all, but a wall with selective holes is much harder to develop. Flexible, selective schemes involve a lot of extra complexity, and with complexity comes the potential for mistakes. In addition, there are subtle, difficult questions surrounding flexible security schemes. For example, employees may have very different ideas about acceptable security than their employer does—how much control should be given to the users and how much to the site security administrator? Faced with numerous tough questions like that, the people behind Java decided to be careful at first. They are starting with an extremely conservative security model, which will become less rigid as time goes on. This is probably a good strategy because a big security scare early in Java's lifetime would have really dampened enthusiasm for the language.

The other problem is that there isn't yet a good criterion for deciding which applets should be trusted and which should not. The best solution is probably to trust applets based on who wrote them, but that's difficult to verify. JavaSoft has developed a model based on digital signatures, but they've been delayed in releasing it because of U.S. government export restrictions. Currently, the government regulations only permit them to export a particularly weak form of signature system, and they expect to be able to use something strong enough to provide real security. Hopefully, these issues will be resolved and a system for signing Java classes will be available by early 1997.

Later in this chapter, you'll read more about the details of the security model and how the application security manager can make fine-grained decisions about access to system resources.

What Are the Dangers?

To really understand the Java security model—why it's important, how it works, and how to work with it—you should have a good idea about the kinds of security attacks that are possible and which system resources can be used to mount such attacks. Java takes care to protect these resources from untrusted code. If you are using a Java application that allows you to configure applet security, or if you are writing a Java application that loads classes from the Net, it helps to understand just what doors you might be opening when you give an applet access to a particular resource.

The Kinds of Attacks

There are several different kinds of security attacks that can be mounted on a computer system. Some of them are surprising to people who are new to computer security issues, but they are very real and can be devastating under the right circumstances. Table 35.1 lists some common types of attacks.

Table 35.1. Some common types of attacks against computers.

Type of Attack	*Description*
Theft of information	Nearly every computer contains some information that the owner or primary user of the machine would like to keep private.
Destruction of information	In addition to data that is private, *most* of the data on typical computers has some value, and losing it would be costly.
Theft of resources	Computers contain more than just data. They have valuable, finite resources that cost money: disk space and a CPU are the best examples. A Java applet on a Web page could quietly begin doing some extensive computation in the background, periodically sending intermediate results back to a central server, thus stealing some of your CPU cycles to perform part of someone else's large project. This would slow down your machine, wasting another valuable resource: your time.
Denial of service	Similar to theft of resources, denial-of-service attacks involve using as much as possible of a finite resource, not because the attacker really needs the resource, but simply to prevent someone *else* from being able to use it. Some computers (like mail servers) are extremely important to the day-to-day operations of businesses, and attackers can cause a lot of damage simply by keeping those machines so busy with worthless tasks that they can't do their real jobs.

continues

35

JAVA SECURITY

Table 35.1. continued

Type of Attack	Description
Masquerade	By pretending to be from another source, a malicious program can persuade a user to reveal valuable information voluntarily.
Deception	If a malicious program were successful in interposing itself between the application and some important data source, the attacker could alter data—or substitute completely different data—before giving it to the application or the user. The user would take the data and act on it, assuming it to be valid.

In addition to these common attacks, Java applets can try another kind of attack. Because applets are fetched to your machine and run locally, they can try to assume your identity and do things while pretending to be you. For example, machines behind corporate firewalls often trust each other more than they trust machines on the wider Internet, so once an applet has started running on your machine behind the firewall, it may try to access other machines, exploiting that trust. (That's the reason current Java applications only let applets make network connections to the machine from which they were fetched.) Another example is mail forging: once on your machine, an applet may attempt to send threatening or offensive mail which appears to be from you. Of course, Internet mail can be forged from other machines besides your own, but doing it from your own machine makes it a little more convincing.

How Does Java Security Work?

Now that you understand why security features are important and what kinds of threats exist, it's time to learn how Java's security features work and how they protect against those threats.

The Java security model is composed of three layers, each dependent on those beneath it. The following sections cover each of the layers, describing how the security systems works.

The Three Layers of Security

The first line of defense against untrusted programs in a Java application is a part of the basic design of the language: Java is a *safe* language. When programming language theorists use the word *safety*, they aren't talking about protection against malicious programs. Rather, they mean protection against *incorrect* programs. Java achieves this in several ways:

■ Array references are checked at runtime to ensure that they are within the bounds of the array. This check prevents incorrect programs from running off the end of an array into storage that doesn't belong to the program or that contains values of the wrong type.

- Casts are carefully controlled so that they can't be used to violate the language's rules, and implicit type conversions are kept to a minimum.

- Memory management is automatic. This arrangement prevents "memory leaks" (when unused storage is never reclaimed) and "dangling pointers" (when valid storage is freed prematurely).

- The language does not allow programmers to manipulate pointers directly (although they are used extensively behind the scenes). This feature prevents many invalid uses of pointers, some of which could be used to circumvent the preceding restrictions.

All these qualities make Java a "safe" language. Put another way, they ensure that code written in Java actually does what it appears to do, or fails. The surprising things that can happen in C (such as continuing to read data past the end of an array as though it were valid) cannot happen. In a safe language, the behavior of a particular program with a particular input should be entirely predictable—no surprises.

The second layer of Java security involves careful verification of Java class files—including the virtual machine bytecodes that represent the compiled versions of methods—as they are loaded into the virtual machine. This verification ensures that a garbled class file won't cause an error within the Java interpreter itself, but it also ensures that the basic language safety is not violated. The rules about proper language behavior that were written into the language specification are good, but it's also important to make sure that those rules aren't broken. Checking everything in the compiler isn't good enough, because it's possible for someone to write a completely new compiler that omits those checks. For that reason, the Java library carefully checks and verifies the bytecodes of every class that is loaded into the virtual machine to make sure that those bytecodes obey the rules. Some of the rules, such as bounds checking on references to array elements, are actually implemented in the virtual machine, so no real checks are necessary. Other rules, however, must be checked carefully. One particularly important rule that is verified rigorously is that objects must be true to their type—an object that is created as a particular type must never be able to masquerade as an object of some incompatible type. Otherwise, there would be a serious loophole through which explicit security checks could be bypassed.

This verification process doesn't mean that Java code can't be compiled to native machine code. As long as the validation is performed on the bytecodes first, a native compiled version of a class is still secure. "Just-in-time" (JIT) compilers run within the Java virtual machine, compiling bytecodes to native code as classes are loaded, just after the bytecode verification stage. This compilation step doesn't usually take much time, and the resulting code runs much faster.

The third and final layer of the Java security model is the implementation of the Java class library. Classes in the library provide Java applications with their only means of access to

35

JAVA SECURITY

sensitive system resources, such as files and network connections. Those classes are written so that they always perform security checks before granting access.

This third layer is the portion of the security system that an application can control—not by changing the library implementation, but by supplying the objects that actually make the decisions about whether to grant each request for access. Those objects—the security manager and the class loaders—are the core of an application's security *policy*, and you'll read more about them (including how to implement them) a little later in this chapter.

Protected System Resources

The first two layers of the Java security model are primarily concerned with protecting the security model itself. It's the third layer, the library implementation, in which explicit measures are taken to protect against the kinds of attacks listed in Table 35.1. To help thwart those attacks, Java checks each and every attempt to access particular system resources that could be used in an attack. Those resources fall into six categories, as listed in Table 35.2.

Table 35.2. Resources checked by Java security.

Resource	Description
Local file access	The capability to read or write files and directories. These capabilities can be used to steal or destroy information, as well as to deny service by destroying important system files or writing a huge file that fills the remaining space on your disk. Applets can also use local file access to deceive you by writing an official-looking file somewhere that you will find later and believe to be trustworthy.
System access	The capability to execute programs on the local machine, plus access to system properties. These capabilities can be used for theft or destruction of information or denial of service in much the same way that direct file access can: by executing commands that manipulate your files. Additionally, system properties may contain information that you view as private or that can help an attacker break into your system using other means.
Network access	The capability to create network connections, both actively (by connecting to some machine) and passively (by listening and accepting incoming connections). Applets that actively create connections may be trying to

Resource	Description
	usurp the user's identity, exploiting the trust that other machines place in him or her. Applets that try to listen for incoming connections may be taking over the job of a system service (such as a Web server).
Thread manipulation	The capability to start, stop, suspend, resume, or destroy threads and thread groups, as well as other sorts of thread manipulation such as adjusting priorities, setting names, and changing the daemon status. Without restrictions on such capabilities, applets can destroy work by shutting down or disabling other components of the applications within which they run, or do so to other applets. Rogue applets can also mount denial of service attacks by raising their own priority while lowering the priorities of other threads (including the system threads that may be able to control the errant applets).
Factory object creation	The capability to create factory objects that find and load extension classes from the network or other sources. An untrustworthy factory object can garble user data, transparently substitute incoming data from a completely different source, or even steal outgoing data— without the user of the application realizing what's happening. See "Further Reading," later in this chapter, for pointers to more information about factory objects.
Window creation	The capability to create new top-level windows. New top-level windows may appear to be under the control of a local, trusted application rather than an applet, and they can prompt unwary users for important information such as passwords. The Java security system permits applications to forbid applets from creating new windows, and it also permits tagging applet-owned windows with a special warning for users.

The third layer of the security model isn't just concerned with protecting system resources; it also provides protection for some Java runtime resources, to protect the integrity of the security model itself. You'll learn more about that kind of protection in "Protection for Security Facilities," later in this chapter.

35

JAVA SECURITY

Example: Reading a File

Let's look at an example to see how the security model works in practice. This example concentrates on what happens in the third layer, for two reasons: The lower two layers sometimes deal with some rather esoteric issues of type theory, and they are not within the programmer's control. The top layer, on the other hand, is relatively straightforward and can be controlled by Java application programmers.

Suppose that the Snark applet has been loaded onto your system and wants to read one of your files—say, diary.doc. To open the file for reading, Snark must use one of the core Java classes—in particular, FileInputStream or RandomAccessFile in the java.io package. Because those core classes are a part of the security model, before they allow reading from that particular file, they ask the system security manager whether it's okay. Those two classes make the request in their constructors; FileInputStream uses code like this:

```
// Gain access to the system security manager.
SecurityManager security = System.getSecurityManager();
if (security != null) {
    // See if reading is allowed.  If not, the security manager will
    // throw a SecurityException.  The variable "name" is a String
    // containing the file name.
    security.checkRead(name);
}
// If there is no security manager, anything goes!
```

The security manager is found using one of the static methods in the System class. If there is no security manager, everything is allowed; if there is a security manager, it is queried to see whether this access is permitted. If everything is fine, the SecurityManager.checkRead() method returns; otherwise, it throws a SecurityException. Because this code appears in a constructor, and because the exception isn't caught, the constructor never completes, and the FileInputStream object can't be created.

How does the security manager decide whether the request should be allowed or not? The SecurityManager class, an abstract class from which all application security managers are derived, contains several native methods that can be used to inspect the current state of the Java virtual machine. In particular, the execution stack—the methods in the process of executing when the security manager is queried—can be examined in detail. The security manager can thus tell which classes are involved in the current request, and it can decide whether all those classes can be trusted with the resource being requested.

In the Snark example, the security manager examines the execution stack and sees several classes, including Snark. That means something to us, but it probably doesn't mean a lot to the security manager. In particular, the security manager has probably never heard of a class called Snark, and presumably it doesn't even know that Snark is an applet. Yet that's the really important piece of information: if one of the classes currently on the execution stack is part of an applet or some other untrusted, dynamically loaded program, then granting the request could be dangerous.

At this point, the security manager gets some help. For each class on the execution stack, it can determine which class loader is responsible for that class. *Class loaders* are special objects that load Java bytecode files into the virtual machine. One of their responsibilities is to keep track of where each class came from and other information that can be relevant to the application security policy. When the security manager consults Snark's class loader, the security manager learns (among other things) that Snark was loaded from the network. At last, the security manager knows enough to decide that Snark's request should be rejected.

An Applet's View of Java Security

Before we plunge ahead into the deeper details of how security managers and class loaders work, let's step to the other side of the security model for a moment and see what it looks like to untrusted classes. We've seen what happens backstage—but what does it look like if you don't have a backstage pass?

Applets and other untrusted (or partially trusted) classes, such as "servlets" in Java-based Web servers, or protocol handlers and content type handlers in HotJava, run within the confines of the application security policy. (In fact, depending on the security policy itself, it's possible that *all* classes except for the security manager and class loaders run under some security restrictions.) Such "unprivileged" classes are the kind that most Java programmers will be writing, so it's important to understand what the Java security facilities look like from the point of view of ordinary code.

Security violations are signaled when the security manager throws a SecurityException. It is certainly possible to catch that SecurityException and ignore it, or try a different strategy, so an attempt to access a secured resource doesn't have to mean the end of your applet. By trying different things and catching the exception, applets can build a picture of what they are and are not allowed to do. It's even possible to call the security manager's access checking methods directly, so that you can find out whether a certain resource is accessible before actually attempting to access it.

> **NOTE**
>
> Such probing may seem sneaky, but there are plenty of legitimate uses for it. If you are writing a word processing applet, for example, it is a good idea to make the applet probe first to determine whether it is allowed to write a file to the local disk, before allowing the user to spend three hours typing an important document. As a user, wouldn't you much rather know from the beginning that saves are not allowed?

How to Build a Security Policy

This section delves a little deeper into the implementation of security managers and class loaders—deep enough to help you implement such classes yourself, should you need to. If you are building Java applets or other dynamic extensions, class libraries, or even standalone Java applications that don't need dynamic network extensibility, you may want to skip this section and proceed to "How Good Is Java Security?" later in this chapter. But if you are building a Java-based application that needs to host applets or other untrusted classes, this section is important for you because those are the kinds of applications that need a security policy.

Unfortunately, the JDK doesn't come with a working security policy mechanism that's ready for an application to use. The SecurityManager class that comes with the JDK is an abstract class, so no instances can be created. It wouldn't be useful anyway, because every access-checking method throws a SecurityException immediately, in every case—whether any untrusted classes are active or not! Clearly, no program could accomplish anything useful with that security manager on watch.

Therefore, if your application plans to host untrusted classes, you need a new SecurityManager and one or more ClassLoader implementations. You'll probably have to build them yourself, because nobody is yet offering reusable security policy implementations that Java programmers can use "out of the box." I expect such third-party security support to be available at some point, but until that happens, the next sections explain how to do it yourself.

Building a Class Loader

Unlike most other portions of an application, class loaders must work both sides of the security fence. They must take care to consult the security manager before allowing certain operations, and they must cooperate with the security manager to help it learn about classes and make decisions about access requests. They must also avoid breaking any of the assumptions about classes on which the security manager relies.

When defining a class, the class loader must identify the package in which the class belongs and call SecurityManager.checkPackageDefinition() before actually loading the class into that package. Membership in a package gives a class special access to other classes in the package and can provide a way to circumvent security restrictions.

When the class loader defines a class, it must also *resolve* the class. Resolving a class involves locating and loading (if necessary) other classes that the new class requires. This is done by calling a native method called ClassLoader.resolveClass(Class). If other classes are needed during the resolution process, the Java runtime calls the loadClass(String, boolean) method in the same `ClassLoader` that loaded the class currently being resolved. (If the `boolean` parameter is `true`, the newly loaded class must be resolved also.)

The class loader must be careful not to load a class from an untrusted source that will mirror a trusted class. The `CLASSPATH` list should be searched first for system classes. This is especially important during the resolution process.

Additionally, the class loader should check with the security manager about whether the class being resolved is even allowed to use the classes in the requested package. The security manager may want to prevent untrusted code from using entire packages.

Listing 35.1 gives an example of the steps you can take to load a class securely.

Listing 35.1. Loading a class securely.

```
protected Class loadClass(String cname, boolean resolve) {

    // Check to see if I've already loaded this one from my source.
    Class class = (Class) myclasses.get(cname);

    if (class == null) {
        // If not, then I have to do security checks.

        // Is the requestor allowed to use classes in this package?
        SecurityManager security = System.getSecurityManager();
        if (security != null) {
            int pos = cname.lastIndexOf('.');
            if (pos >= 0) {
                security.checkPackageAccess(cname.substring(0, pos));
            }
        }

        try {
            // If there's a system class by this name, use it.
            return findSystemClass(cname);
        }
        catch (Throwable e) {
            // otherwise, go find it and load it.
            class = fetchClass(cname);
        }
    }

    if (class == null) throw new ClassNotFoundException();

    if (resolve) resolveClass(class);

    return class;
}
```

In the preceding listing, the real work of actually retrieving a class and defining it is done in the `fetchClass()` method. The primary security responsibility of that method is to call `SecurityManager.checkPackageDefinition(package)` before actually defining the class, as described previously.

The way this resolution process works (with the `ClassLoader` that loaded the class being responsible for resolving class dependencies) is one reason why applications typically define one class loader for each different source of classes. When a class from one source has a dependency on some class named `MyApplet`, for example, it would probably be a mistake to resolve the dependency using a class with the same name from another source.

The other side of the class loader's responsibility for security is to maintain information about classes and provide that information to the security manager. The type of information that is important to the security manager depends on the application. Currently, most Java applications base security decisions on the network host from which a class was loaded, but other information may soon be used instead. With digital signature facilities available, it will be feasible to allow certain classes special privileges based on the organization or authority that has signed those classes.

Building a Security Manager

Implementing a security manager can involve a lot of work, but if you have a coherent security policy, the process isn't particularly complicated. Most of the work involved stems from the fact that `SecurityManager` has a lot of methods you must override with new, more intelligent implementations that make reasonable access decisions instead of automatically disallowing everything.

Once the security manager has decided to allow an operation, all it has to do is return. Alternatively, if the security manager decides to prohibit an operation, it just has to throw a `SecurityException`. Communicating the decision is easy—the hard part is deciding.

The section, "Example: Reading A File," earlier in this chapter, contains a simple example of the workings of the Java security system. That example omitted a few details for the sake of simplicity, but now you need to know the whole story. The security manager can examine the execution stack to find out which classes have initiated an operation. If an object's method is being executed at the time the security manager is called, the class of that object is requesting the current operation (either directly or indirectly). The important thing about the objects on the stack, from the security manager's point of view, is not the objects themselves but their classes and those classes' origins. In Java, each object contains a pointer to its `Class` object, and each class can return its class loader through the `getClassLoader()` method. The implementation of `SecurityManager` uses those facts, along with native methods that can find the objects on the stack itself, to find out the classes and class loaders that have objects on the execution stack. Figure 35.1 shows the Java execution stack while the security manager is executing.

FIGURE 35.1.

The security manager and the Java execution stack.

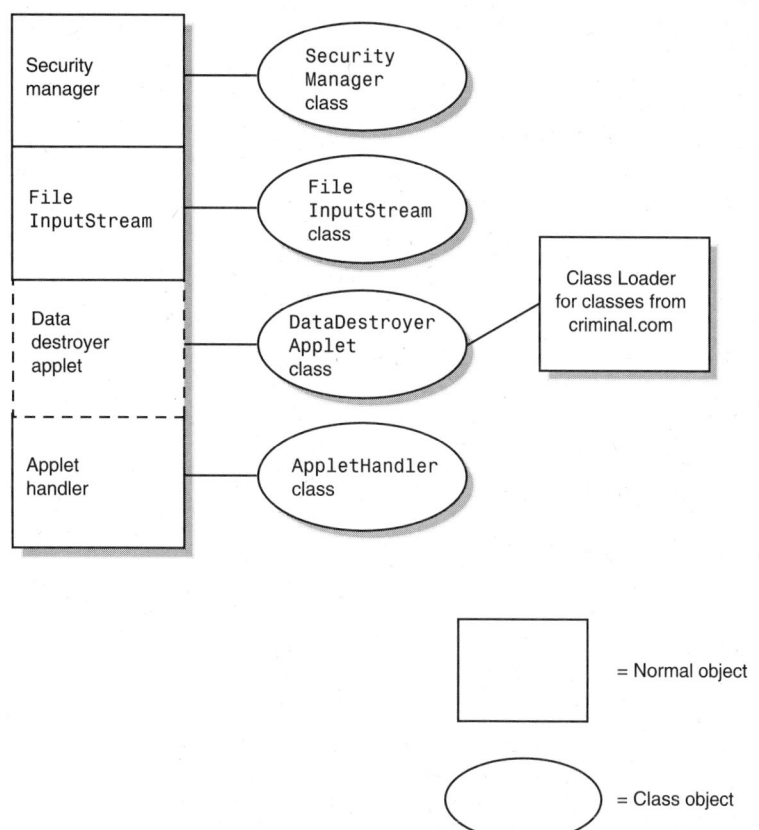

NOTE

Because the security manager really doesn't care about the objects themselves—just the classes and class loaders—the documentation for the SecurityManager class blurs the distinction a bit. It refers to "the classes on the execution stack" and "the class loaders on the execution stack." This chapter uses the same phrases. Strictly speaking, the classes in question aren't actually on the stack, but they have instances that are. Likewise, the class loaders aren't really on the stack, but they are responsible for classes that are. It's just a lot easier to talk about "a ClassLoader on the stack" than "an object on the stack that is an instance of a class that was loaded by a ClassLoader."

The JDK applet viewer application and Netscape Navigator 2.0 have simple security models: if a class is not a system class (that is, if it wasn't loaded from CLASSPATH), it isn't trusted and isn't allowed to do very much. If your security model is that simple, your security manager will be simple, too. Calling `SecurityManager.inClassLoader()` tells you whether the operation is being requested by untrusted code. It returns `true` if there is any class loader at all on the stack. System classes loaded from `CLASSPATH` don't have a class loader, so if there's a class loader on the stack anywhere, there's an untrusted class in control.

If an operation is to be prohibited in general, but allowed if it comes from a particular trusted class, you can investigate further. `SecurityManager.classLoaderDepth()` tells you how deep on the stack the first class loader is. When `classLoaderDepth()` is used with `SecurityManager.classDepth(String)`, it's possible to determine whether a particular trusted class is really in control.

Imagine a distributed calendar management system that makes use of applets. Such a system might include a trusted class, `Invite`, which records an invitation of some sort in your local calendar file. Applets can use the `Invite` class to issue invitations. You wouldn't want an untrusted applet to write directly to your calendar file, but `Invite` can be trusted to write only invitations and not to do any damage or reveal any private information. In such an application, the security manager's `checkWrite()` method might contain code like this:

```
if (classDepth("Invite") < classLoaderDepth()) {
    // The Invite class is in control, so we can allow the request.
    return;
}
else {
    throw new SecurityException("attempted to write file" + filename);
}
```

The `inClass(String)` method can also be helpful in this situation, if you're confident that the class you're interested in doesn't call any untrusted classes along the way. Be careful, however, because `inClass()` simply tells you that the specified class is on the stack somewhere. It says nothing about how deep the class is or what classes lie above it on the stack.

Currently, Java applications typically don't support multiple levels of trust—a class is either trusted or it's not. In the future, when digital signature technology is available for Java classes, it will be possible to verify the source of Java classes and loosen the security restrictions appropriately. If you are designing an application with such a capability, you may need more information about the class loader responsible for the object requesting an operation. The `currentClassLoader()` method returns the `ClassLoader` object highest on the stack. You can query that object for application-specific information about the source of the class.

Finally, if all those other methods aren't enough to implement your security policy, `SecurityManager` provides the `getClassContext()` method. It returns an array of `Class` objects, in the order that they appear on the stack, from top to bottom. You can use any `Class` methods on these objects to learn various things: `getName()`, `getSuperclass()`, and `getClassLoader()`, among others.

Building your application's security manager takes work, and it can be complicated, but it doesn't have to be a nightmare. Just be sure to design a coherent security policy *first*.

Installing and Using Your Security Policy

We've talked about implementing class loaders and security managers, but there's one crucial question left: how are those new implementations installed so that they are called when classes need to be loaded from the network and when security decisions need to be made?

To answer that question, let's start with the security manager. One particular `SecurityManager` instance serves as the security manager for an application. That instance is installed by using `System.setSecurityManager()`. Here's how to install a security manager in your application:

```
System.setSecurityManager(new mySecurityManager());
```

Likewise, the security manager can be accessed by using `System.getSecurityManager()`. Any Java method can query the security manager, but it's crucial that the methods that provide access to sensitive system resources query the security manager before they permit the access. Such checks are very simple, and all the Java library classes that consult the security manager use nearly identical code to do it. For example, here's the `File.delete()` method:

```
/**
 * Deletes the specified file. Returns true
 * if the file could be deleted.
 */
public boolean delete() {
    SecurityManager security = System.getSecurityManager();
    if (security != null) {
        security.checkDelete(path);
    }
    return delete0();
}
```

`delete0()` is the method that really does the work of deleting the file. (It's declared `private` so that other classes can't call it directly.) Before calling it, the `delete()` method checks with the security manager to see whether the operation is permitted. If everything is fine, the security manager's `checkDelete()` method simply returns, and the `delete0()` method is called. If the operation is not allowed, `checkDelete()` throws a `SecurityException`. Because `delete()` makes no attempt to catch the exception, it propagates up to the caller, and `delete0()` is never called.

In the `delete()` method, if there is no security manager defined, access is always granted. The same is true for all the methods that perform security checks. If no security manager is defined, everything is allowed. Thus, it's important that any application that is going to be loading untrusted classes create a security manager *before* the first untrusted class is loaded into the virtual machine.

What about the class loaders? How are they called to load classes from the network?

Classes are loaded either explicitly by the application or automatically by objects called *factory objects*. Some applications may have optional functionality that is loaded on demand. In that case, it may make sense for the application to have built-in knowledge of the classes required for those optional features. In other situations, the classes are supplied by third parties and should be loaded in response to some of the data that is being handled by the application. In such cases, it makes sense to have factory objects that will search for a class that can handle the situation and load it. The core Java library can use factory objects to load protocol handlers and content type handlers in conjunction with the URL class. See "Further Reading," later in this chapter, for pointers to more information on factory objects.

In either case, a class loader is called explicitly by application code, whether a factory object or some other part of the application, so no "installation" of ClassLoader objects is usually necessary.

Protection for Security Facilities

Earlier in this chapter, you learned about the system resources that are protected by the Java security facilities. The security system must also take care to protect certain parts of the security model itself, so that applets cannot subvert the security system and slip in through the back door.

The first line of special protection for the security system is the mechanism for installing the security manager. Obviously, if an applet could install its own security manager, it could do anything it pleased. Therefore, installation of the security manager must be protected. But there's a "chicken and egg" problem here: when the security manager is first installed, there's no security manager to rule on whether it should be allowed!

The resolution of this problem is simple. If no security manager is installed, any class can install one. Once a security manager is active, however, it is *always* a security violation to attempt to replace it. This implies that applications must take care to establish their security policies before any untrusted code is brought into the virtual machine. Another implication is that during any individual execution, an application can have only one security manager. Thus, if it's desirable to adjust the security policy of an application while it is running, those adjustments must be catered to in the security manager itself—they can't be accomplished by changing the security manager.

The other defenses for the security system are more conventional in that they involve library routines that consult the security manager for access decisions. The protected aspects of the security system fall into two categories:

- **Interpreter manipulation.** The capability to stop the execution of the Java virtual machine or load new libraries of native methods into the virtual machine.

- **Class loading.** The capability to create new ClassLoader objects. Additionally, class loaders consult the security manager when loading classes to see whether a new class can be created within a particular package and whether the new class is allowed to access certain packages. For example, untrusted classes are not permitted to be in any of the core Java library packages.

How Good Is Java Security?

There remains one big topic to cover in this chapter: just how good is Java security? Does it really do all that it claims to do, and is it really the best thing out there, or does it have some serious weaknesses? Should we really be trusting our systems to Java applets?

Of course, the precise answer depends on who you ask. Network security is a complex topic, and we don't yet fully understand every detail of it. Nevertheless, some rough consensus is beginning to emerge about the strength of Java's security facilities. In the following sections, I attempt to answer the questions objectively, based on my own analysis as well as on the opinions of others, including some experts in the security community.

What the Java Security Model Does Not Address

Java security doesn't try to solve every security problem. There are some potential attacks that Java doesn't currently attempt to prevent (although work is in progress to extend the security facilities into these areas as well). These attacks involve the abuse of resources that aren't necessarily sensitive, such as CPU cycles, memory, and windows.

The current Java security model takes a "yes or no" approach to security: a class is either allowed access to a resource or it is not. There is no provision for allowing an untrusted class to use only a certain amount of some resource. Java does not enforce resource quotas. It doesn't even keep track of resource usage so that the application can enforce quotas.

Applets can exploit this fact to mount attacks of varying severity: denial-of-service attacks that render your machine unusable by allocating all your memory or some other finite resource; annoyances that make noises or pop up big, bouncing windows on your screen, flash, and then disappear before you can destroy them; or resource theft attacks, where an applet stealthily lurks in the background, using your machine to perform part of some large calculation while you wonder why your computer seems a little slower than usual today.

Java's designers didn't simply forget about these issues. They decided not to deal with them at the time because they are extremely difficult to handle correctly. Especially when it comes to CPU time, it's difficult (and often impossible) to determine whether a class is doing useful work or simply wasting the resource. Researchers are currently investigating ways to prevent (or limit) these kinds of attacks, and future versions of Java will attempt to deal with them as well as possible.

Java Security Bugs

In addition to those attacks that were intentionally excluded from the scope of the Java security facilities, there have been a few accidental flaws. Several have been found by Drew Dean,

35

JAVA SECURITY

Ed Felten, and Dan Wallach, a team of researchers at Princeton University. Others were found by David Hopwood, an Oxford researcher who is now working for Netscape, helping to strengthen Java security in Netscape products.

All these security holes permitted very serious attacks that could result in loss or theft of valuable data. It's comforting, though, that each of the holes was the result of a simple bug in the code that implemented part of the security architecture, rather than any fundamental flaw in the architecture itself. In each case, the bugs were fixed within a few days of discovery. In fact, the process in which researchers carefully examine Java for security weaknesses is one of the important reasons why Sun made the Java source code available for study. Java security is now much stronger because several security bugs have been found and eliminated.

That holes have been found in Java security is a reminder that we should be cautious, but there's no reason for panic. In truth, all network-oriented applications are candidates for serious security holes, and such problems are actually quite common in network applications. It's common for security considerations to be almost an afterthought. Java actually seems to be stronger than that of many other programs because certain aspects of its security architecture have been central to Java's design from the beginning, and because all the Java hype has prompted some intense scrutiny.

Is the Architecture Sound?

What are the chances that someone will discover a really fundamental security flaw in Java—a serious flaw in the security architecture itself?

It's impossible to say for sure, of course, but we do know enough about security to be able to analyze the Java security model and make some guesses. It turns out that the Java security architecture is not perfect, and there are some things to watch out for. Dean, Felten, and Wallach, the Princeton researchers mentioned earlier, have expressed some concern about the complexity of Java's security architecture, but most who have studied the matter seem to believe that the outlook is good.

The biggest weakness in the Java security model is its complexity. Complexity begets mistakes. The problem is exacerbated by the fact that application authors currently must implement their own security manager and class loaders. Hopefully, a few flexible, configurable security policy implementations will be made available for reuse, so that they can be carefully tested and debugged once, and used many times. Such a development would greatly reduce the potential for new security holes.

Another weakness is that the security responsibility is split between the security manager and the class loaders. It would be better if the job were localized in one class.

Although we may wish things were simpler, as a whole, the Java security architecture appears to be strong enough, and we can expect it to grow stronger with time.

Java versus ActiveX

Microsoft has its own proposal for dynamically loaded code on the Internet: ActiveX. ActiveX is essentially a way to leverage the existing body of OLE controls that already exists for the Windows environment. Questions have been raised about the security implications of the proposal, however. ActiveX certainly has considerable value in some situations, but there are good reasons to be worried about potential security problems.

ActiveX controls can be written in Java, and you can bet that Java-based controls will begin appearing in the near future. However, most of the large existing body of controls have been written in C or C++, and have been compiled into native Intel machine code. The ActiveX answer to securing these controls is based on a digital signature technology called Authenticode. Developers and software vendors sign their controls, and the ActiveX system verifies that signature against a registry of signature authorities, thereby verifying the origin of the control. Users can configure ActiveX to allow only controls from certain vendors to run on their system; for example, if you trust Microsoft and Corel, but nobody else, you can configure ActiveX to automatically fetch and run controls from those two companies, but refuse all others.

That sounds okay, right? After all, its sounds a lot like the code-signing system for Java classes which will be used to help loosen the rigidly conservative Java security policy.

Actually, however, the two systems aren't very similar. To understand why, you have to look at what a signature on a piece of software really means. A signature really only means "I signed this and it hasn't been changed since I did." The person or authority who applies the signature might actually mean more than that, but the Authenticode proposal doesn't require any guarantees. Even if guarantees were present, it's unlikely that they would be very strong, based on the weak (or nonexistent) warranties that are found on most software today.

So a signature is not a guarantee of safety. If that's the case, what makes the Java code-signing technology better than Authenticode? The difference is that ActiveX security is all-or-nothing; Java security can be extremely fine-grained and flexible. If you (or the ActiveX system) choose to allow a native-code ActiveX control to run on your system, that control has complete access to your system. It can read any file you can read, delete or change any file you can, make any network connection it chooses—even format your hard disk. Java, on the other hand, can grant access to classes selectively, even choosing which files a particular class is allowed to read. A word processing applet, invoked specifically to edit one particular document, can be allowed to write to that document and no other.

Authenticode is not really a security architecture; it's a trust management architecture. Furthermore, it's a very limited trust management architecture because it doesn't have any understanding of partial trust.

Some people are saying that ActiveX will probably be widely used on corporate intranets, with Java ruling the roost on the Internet at large. That's probably a good prediction—certainly

ActiveX will be very useful on intranets because the security issues aren't quite as important there. However, even that thought makes me uneasy, because of a prediction of my own. I believe that, over the next five to ten years, the walls between corporate intranets and the Internet will become more porous, often coming down altogether. Companies that rely heavily on intranet applications built with ActiveX will be at a disadvantage when that time comes.

FURTHER READING

Several Web pages, and at least one other book, provide more in-depth treatment of Java security topics. JavaSoft maintains an FAQ page on applet security issues (`http://java.sun.com/sfaq/`); the Princeton researchers who have found several serious Java security bugs maintain a similar page with an outsider's perspective (`http://www.cs.princeton.edu/sip/java-faq.html`).

For more information about the second layer of the security model (validation and verification of Java class files and bytecodes as they are loaded into the interpreter), read *The Java Virtual Machine Specification*, by Tim Lindholm and Frank Yellin. The book is a technical description of the architecture of the virtual machine and contains a precise description of the steps taken by the class verifier.

To see examples of applets that exploit some of the weaknesses in the current Java security facilities, take a look at Mark LaDue's Hostile Applets page (`http://www.math.gatech.edu/~mladue/HostileApplets.html`). (Don't worry, you can go at least that far without fear; Mark keeps the hostile applets off the main page.)

For more information about programming with the Java security system, read *Tricks of the Java Programming Gurus* (published by Sams.net). It provides deeper coverage of several topics that readers of this chapter might find interesting, including:

- What information end users need to know about security
- Design considerations for security policies
- More details about the security facilities and security policy implementation
- Building factory objects and other ways of loading classes from the network (with sample code)
- Using a scripting language to provide security policy configurability
- Giving both users and site administrators some say in security configuration
- Integrating native method libraries (even dynamically loaded libraries) into the security model (with sample code)
- A thorough discussion of hostile applets and the current weaknesses in the security model (with sample code)

Summary

Java's security model is possibly the least understood aspect of the Java system. Because it's unusual for a language environment to have security facilities, some people have been bothered by the danger; at the same time, because the security restrictions prevent some useful things as well as harmful things, some people have wondered whether security is really necessary.

Java security is important because it makes exciting new things possible with very little risk. Early security holes caused by implementation bugs are being closed, and technology is being fielded that permits the strict security policy to be carefully and selectively relaxed. Resources that can be used to destroy or steal data are protected, and researchers are examining ways to prevent applets from using other resources to cause annoyance or inconvenience.

Application developers can design their own security policies and supply parts of the third layer of the Java security model to implement those policies in their applications.

The Java security architecture is sound. Early weaknesses and bugs are not a surprise, and the process that has exposed those flaws has also helped remove them.

PART

IN THIS PART

- Building VRML 2.0 Behaviors in Java 775

- Integrating Java and JavaScript 809

- Integrating Java and ActiveX 823

- Using Java with VBScript 833

Integrating Java with Other Technologies

Building VRML 2.0 Behaviors in Java

by Justin Couch

IN THIS CHAPTER

So far in this book, you have seen Java being used to create whole standalone applications or applets to put in Web pages. But Java has other uses as well.

If you have been closely reading the computing press, you may have noticed sections creeping in about another Web technology called VRML—the Virtual Reality Modeling Language. VRML is designed to produce the 3D equivalent of HTML: a three-dimensional scene defined in a machine-neutral format that can be viewed by anyone with the appropriate viewer.

Until recently, VRML has not really lived up to its name. The first version of the standard produced only static scenes and was a derivative of Silicon Graphic's Open Inventor file format. A user could wander around in a 3D scene, but had no way to interact with the scene apart from clicking on the 3D-equivalent of hypertext links. This was a deliberate decision on the part of the designers. In December 1995, the VRML mailing list decided to drop planned revisions to version 1.0 and head straight to the fully interactive version 2.0.

One of the prime requirements for VRML 2.0 was the ability to support programmable behaviors. Of the seven proposals, the Moving Worlds submission by Sony and SGI came out as the favorite among the 2000 members of the VRML mailing list. Contained in what has now become the draft proposal for VRML 2.0 was a Java API for creating behaviors.

To effectively combine VRML and Java, you need a good understanding of how both languages work. This chapter introduces the Java implementation of the VRML API and shows you how to get the most from a dynamic virtual world.

Making the World Behave

Within the virtual reality environment, any dynamic change in the scenery is regarded as a *behavior.* A behavior can be something as simple as an object changing color when it is touched or as complex as autonomous agents that look and act like humans (such as Neal Stephenson's Librarian from *Snow Crash*).

To understand how to integrate behaviors, you have to understand how VRML works. Although this section doesn't provide a lengthy discussion of VRML, it does cover a few basic concepts. To start, VRML is a separate language from the Java used in the scripts. S"pL provides a class to interact only with a preexisting scene, which means that you cannot use VRML as a 3D toolkit. A standalone application can use the VRML class libraries to create a collection of VRML nodes, but without a preexisting browser open, there is no way of making these nodes visible on-screen. In the future, you will be able to write a browser using Java3D that is responsible for the visualization of the VRML file structure, but there is no method to do so currently.

Building VRML 2.0 Behaviors in Java

CHAPTER 36

777

36

BUILDING
VRML 2.0
BEHAVIORS

The second concept to understand is that within VRML there is no such thing as a monolithic application. Java started the ball rolling by introducing individual classes that could be loaded on the fly and VRML takes it one step further. Each object has its own script attached to it. Creating a highly complex world means writing lots of short scripts.

Scripting under VRML has a defined set of functionality for which any language can be used. When the final 2.0 specification was released, there were appendixes for Java and JavaScript. Much of the lightweight work can be performed with JavaScript. Although this is the preferred method for short calculations, when more complex work must be done, the world creator uses Java-based scripting. Typically, such heavyweight operations combine the VRML API with the thread and networking classes. However, at the time of this writing, VRML browsers understood either JavaScript or Java, but not both (the browsers don't take advantage of the built-in Java and JavaScript interpreters provided by Netscape Navigator and MS Internet Explorer).

> **NOTE**
>
> It is expected that Netscape's version of Live3D that supports VRML 2.0 will handle both JavaScript and Java because the browser already does.

To keep down the amount of programming, the VRML specification writers added a number of nodes to take care of commonly required functionality. These nodes can divided into two groups: interpolators and sensors. *Interpolators* are available for color, scalar values, points (morphing), vectors, position, and orientation. *Sensors* cover a more varied range: geometric shapes (cylinder, disk, plane, and sphere), proximity, time, and touch. These all can be directly inserted into a scene and connected to the various primitives to create effects without having to write a line of code. Simple effects, such as an automatically opening door, can be created by adding a sensor, interpolator, and primitives to the scene.

Getting Started: Where Are those Class Files?

To start compiling the example code in this chapter, you must obtain the VRML packages. These come with the individual browser you are using. The examples in this chapter were compiled and tested using Sony's Community Place. Normally, Community Place puts the class files in a directory under itself; typically, the directory is as follows:

```
C:\Program Files\Sony\Community Place Browser\lib\java
```

If you add this directory to your CLASSPATH statement, you should be able to compile.

CAUTION

Although Netscape's Live3D browser also includes VRML class files, they are not VRML 2.0 files. The version of Live3D that ships with Navigator 3.0 does not support VRML 2.0. If you have the Netscape directory already in your CLASSPATH statement, you must remove it to compile the examples in this chapter. Also watch out for any other VRML classes in your directory—particularly because each browser comes with its own library. Multiple VRML classes caused me several days of frustration as I tried to sort out where all the conflicts were.

Overview of VRML

The VRML world description uses a traditional scene-graph approach reminiscent of PEX/PHIGS and other 3D toolkits. This description applies not only to the file structure but also to the inner workings. Each node within the scene has a parent and many nodes can have children. For a complete structural description of VRML, I recommend that you purchase a good book on VRML, especially if you intend to undertake serious behavioral programming. (Naturally, I recommend *Laura Lemay's Web Workshop: 3D Graphics and VRML 2*, authored by yours truly.)

How Does VRML Work?

When I say that VRML uses a *scene graph structure*, I talk about the way information is constructed in the file. The text in the file consists of a number of different things.

Each object within the scene is represented by what is called a *node*. The node can be a geometrical object (such as a sphere), a color or texture, or even something to modify the children of this node by scaling or rotating it. In the text file, you can pick out the nodes because their names all begin with capital letters.

After you have declared the node you want to use, you give it some properties. These properties are termed *fields* in VRML parlance. A field controls one little property of that node. A sphere has only one property—its radius. If you want to give the sphere a color, you must use another node to describe the color properties. You also need another node that joins these two pieces of information together (a color does not need to belong to a shape, nor does a shape have to have a color). You see some examples of this use of nodes later in this chapter.

The arrangement of these parent/child relationships is governed very heavily by the specification. For example, you cannot give a sound node a cone node for the child.

Fields are probably the most important thing you must understand in this chapter. Any behavior that you will be creating depends on the script modifying these field values. When you read

Building VRML 2.0 Behaviors in Java

CHAPTER 36

779

36

BUILDING
VRML 2.0
BEHAVIORS

the VRML specification, you can see that each node is defined to have a collection of fields; each field has a default value. If you do not declare a value for that field in the VRML file, the field uses the default value.

To make sure that the browser knows when one node finishes and the next starts, VRML uses curly braces { } to delimit the node. This arrangement is the same as bracketing a block of code in Java.

Giving a Node a Name

As you discover shortly, if you want to create behaviors, you must make a series of explicit connections between various fields and nodes. A scene can well consist of a couple hundred boxes, so how do you know which box you are trying to connect to? Very simple: VRML provides a method of giving explicit names to nodes.

To name a node, you simply use the VRML keyword DEF, specify a word for its name, and then provide the node type itself. To create a sphere called mysphere, for example, you use the following code:

```
DEF mysphere Sphere {}
```

Whenever you refer to mysphere, you now refer to this node. You can refer to mysphere wherever you like in the file after it has been declared. You can name a node whatever you like—including using the names of other node types (although this is definitely *not* recommended). You can name another node with the same name in the file. In this case, the last node declared is the winner—all references relate to it.

Understanding Field Types

Surprisingly—for a language that was first created before Java became popular—the VRML nodes can be represented in a semi-object-oriented manner that meshes well with Java. Each node has a number of fields that can be accessible to other nodes only if explicitly declared so. The nodes can also be declared read-only or write-only or have defined methods to access their values. In VRML syntax, the four types of access are described as follows:

Access	*Description*
field	Hidden from general access.
eventIn	Sends a value to a node—a write-only field.
eventOut	Sends a value from a node—a read-only field.
exposedField	Publicly accessible for both read and write.

Apart from seeing these in the definitions of the nodes defined by VRML, you will deal with them in the writing of the behavior scripts. Most scripts are written to process a value being passed to it in the form of an eventIn, which then passes the result back through the eventOut. Any internal values are kept in field values. Script nodes are not permitted to have an exposedField because of the updating and implementation ramifications within the event system.

Although a node may consist of a number of input and output fields, it does not insist that they all be connected. Usually the opposite is true—only a few of the available connections are made. By connecting only the required fields, you can create a more general-purpose script and share it with a number of nodes.

VRML requires explicit connection of nodes using the ROUTE keyword as follows:

```
ROUTE fromNode.fieldname1 TO toNode.fieldname2
```

You can connect a route from any field to any other field. The only restriction is that the two fields must be of the same type. No casting of types is permitted. *FromNode* and *toNode* are the names of nodes you have declared previously with the DEF keyword.

This route mechanism can be very powerful when combined with scripting. The specification allows both fan in and fan out of ROUTEs. *Fan in* occurs when many nodes have ROUTEs to a single eventIn field of a node. *Fan out* is the opposite: one eventOut is connected to many other eventIns. This arrangement enables sensors and interpolators to feed the one script with information, thus saving coding effort. Currently, the only problem is that there is no way to find out which node generated an event for an eventIn. Fan out is also handy when one script controls a number of different objects at once (for example, a light switch that turns on multiple lights simultaneously).

If two or more events cause a fan-in clash on a particular eventIn, the results are undefined. The programmer should be careful to avoid such situations. A typical situation in which this occurs is when two animation scripts set the position of an object.

VRML Data Types

All VRML data types follow the standard programming norms. There are integer, floating point, string, and boolean standard types as well as specific types for dealing with 3D graphics such as points, vectors, image, and color. To deal with the extra requirements of the VRML scene-graph structure, behavior nodes and time types have been added. The node data type contains an instance pointer to a particular node in the scene graph. Individual fields within a node are not accessible directly. Individual field references in behaviors programming is rarely needed because communication is based on an event-driven model. When field references are needed within the API, a node instance and field string description pair are used.

Building VRML 2.0 Behaviors in Java
CHAPTER 36

781

36

BUILDING
VRML 2.0
BEHAVIORS

Apart from the `boolean` and `time` types, these values can be either single or multivalued. The distinction is made in the field name: use the `SF` prefix for single-valued fields and `MF` for multivalued fields. A `SFInt32` field contains a single integer; a `MFInt32` field contains an array of integers. For example, the script node definition in the next section contains an `MFString` and a `SFBool`. The `MFString` is used to contain a collection of URLs, each kept in its own separate substring, but the `SFBool` contains a single `boolean` flag that controls a condition.

CAUTION

One small thing to watch for is the use of booleans. In VRML, they are declared in uppercase letters but in Java, they are declared in lowercase letters.

The VRML Script Node

The `Script` node provides the means to integrate a custom behavior into VRML. Behaviors can be programmed in any language supported by the browser and for which an implementation of the API can be found. In the draft versions of the VRML 2.0 specification, sample APIs were provided for Java and JavaScript. The `Script` node is defined as follows:

```
Script {
    field       MFString    behavior        []
    field       SFBool      mustEvaluate    FALSE
    field       SFBool      directOutputs   FALSE

    # any number of the following
    eventIn         eventTypeName   eventName
    eventOut        eventTypeName   eventName
    field           fieldTypeName   fieldName       initialValue
}
```

Unlike a standard HTML, VRML enables multiple target files to be specified in order of preference. The behavior field contains any number of strings specifying URLs or URNs to the desired behavior script. For Java scripts, this is the URL of the `.class` file but is not limited to just one script type.

Apart from specifying what the behavior script is, VRML also lets you control how the script node performs within the scene graph. The `mustEvaluate` field tells the browser about how often the script should be run. If the field is set to `TRUE`, the browser must send events to the script as soon as they are generated, forcing an execution of the script. If the field is set to `FALSE`, in the interests of optimization, the browser may elect to queue events until the outputs of the script are needed by the browser. A `TRUE` setting is most likely to cause browser performance to degrade because of the constant context-swapping needed rather than batching to keep it to a minimum. Unless you are performing something that the browser is not aware of (such as using the networking or database functionality), you should set the mustEvaluate field to FALSE.

The directOutputs field controls whether the script has direct access for sending events to other nodes. Java methods require the node reference of other nodes when setting field values. If, for example, a script is passed an instance of a group node, and the directOutputs field is set to TRUE, the script can send an event directly to that node. To add a new default box to this group, the script would contain the following code:

```
SFNode    group_node = (SFNode)getField("group_node");
group_node.postEventIn("add_children", (Field)CreateVRMLfromString("Box{}"));
```

If directOutputs is set to TRUE, the script node must have an eventOut field with the corresponding event type specified (an MFNode, in this case), and a ROUTE connecting the script with the target node.

There are advantages to both approaches. When the scene graph is static in nature, the second approach (using known events and ROUTEs) is much simpler. However, for a scene in which objects are being generated on the fly, static routing and events do not work and the first approach is required.

VRML Data Types in Java

The whole of the API is built around two Java abstract classes defined in the VRML packages: vrml, vrml.node, and vrml.field. The API also has a class specifically for the browser, which is in the vrml package.

> **NOTE**
>
> An *interface* is a class that has been declared but that has no body (the local platform provides the implementation). A *package* is a collection of classes grouped together for convenience.

The Field class is empty so that individual classes can be created to mimic the VRML field types. There are two types of Field classes: read-only and unlimited access. The read-only version starts with Const<*fieldtype*>; the unlimited-access version has the same name as the field type. The types returned by these classes are standard Java types, with a few exceptions. MF types return an array of that type, so the call to the getValue() method of an MFString would return an array of type String. The basic outline of a Field type class is demonstrated by the MFString class:

```
public class MFString extends MField
{
    public MFString(String s[]);

    public void getValue(String s[]);

    public void setValue(String s[]);
    public void setValue(int size, String s[]);
    public void setValue(ConstMFString s);

    public String get1Value(int index);

    public void set1Value(int index, String s);
    public void set1Value(int index, ConstSFString s);
    public void set1Value(int index, SFString s);

    public void addValue(String s);
    public void addValue(ConstSFString s);
    public void addValue(SFString s);

    public void insertValue(int index, String s);
    public void insertValue(int index, ConstSFString s);
    public void insertValue(int index, SFString s);
}
```

The method names are pretty straightforward. You can set values using both the standard VRML type as well as the read-only field value—an arrangement that comes in handy when you're setting values based on the arguments presented.

For the nonconstant fields, each class has at least setValue() and getValue() methods that return the Java equivalent of the VRML field type. For example, a SFRotation class returns an array of floats mapping to the x, y, z and orientation, but the MFRotation class returns a two-dimensional array of floats. The multivalued field types also have a set1value() method that enables the caller to set an individual element.

> **CAUTION**
>
> SFString and MFString field types need special attention. Java defines character strings as Unicode characters but VRML defines characters as UTF-8. Unicode and UTF-8 are different encodings of the ISO 10646 standard for international text. Ninety-nine percent of the time, this difference should not present any problems, but it pays to be aware of it.

Integrating Java Scripts with VRML

So far, we have been looking almost entirely at VRML. But this is a Java book, right? So I had better get back to the Java. In previous sections of this chapter, you met the VRML Script node. The Script node allows you to say to the browser, "Hey, browser! Here is my script that I want to execute." Now we have to define what the browser is supposed to execute.

The Script Class Definition

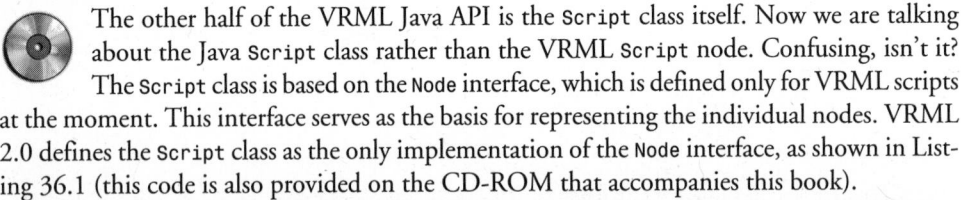

The other half of the VRML Java API is the Script class itself. Now we are talking about the Java Script class rather than the VRML Script node. Confusing, isn't it? The Script class is based on the Node interface, which is defined only for VRML scripts at the moment. This interface serves as the basis for representing the individual nodes. VRML 2.0 defines the Script class as the only implementation of the Node interface, as shown in Listing 36.1 (this code is also provided on the CD-ROM that accompanies this book).

> **NOTE**
>
> It is expected that later versions of VRML should have individual classes for each node type, just as there are individual classes for each field type.

Listing 36.1. The Script abstract class definition.

```
public abstract class Script extends BaseNode {
    // This method is called before any event is generated
    public void initialize();
    // Get a Field by name.
    //    Throws an InvalidFieldException if fieldName isn't a valid
    //    event in name for a node of this type.
    protected final Field getField(String fieldName);
    // Get an EventOut by name.
    //    Throws an InvalidEventOutException if eventOutName isn't a valid
    //    event out name for a node of this type.
    protected final Field getEventOut(String fieldName);
    // processEvents() is called automatically when the script receives
    //    some set of events. It should not be called directly except by its
subclass.
    //    count indicates the number of events delivered.
    public void processEvents(int count, Event events[]);
    // processEvent() is called automatically when the script receives
    // an event.
    public void processEvent(Event event);
    // eventsProcessed() is called after every invocation of processEvents().
    public void eventsProcessed()
    // shutdown() is called when this Script node is deleted.
    public void shutdown();
}
```

Every script is a subclass of the Script class. However, you can't just go out and write your own script right now. You need some more introduction to how it works.

The getField() method returns the value of the field nominated by the given string. This is how the Java script gets the values from the VRML Script node fields. The getField() method is used for all fields and exposedFields. To the Java script, eventOut looks like any other field. There is no need to write an eventOut function—the value is set by calling the appropriate field type's setValue() method.

Dealing with Event Input

Earlier in this chapter, the VRML event system was introduced. Somehow, you need to get the event from the scene graph into the Java script.

> **NOTE**
>
> In early draft versions of the VRML specification, you were simply able to declare a public method that had the same name as the eventIn declared in the VRML Script node. Problems occurred because you could not write a VRML browser in Java alone. So the approach was changed to the event-handling style you are familiar with from the AWT classes.

First, VRML defines its own Event class as follows:

```
class Event {
    public String getName();
    public ConstField getValue();
    public double getTimeStamp();
    public Object clone();
}
```

> **CAUTION**
>
> The VRML Event class is not the same as the AWT Event class. Although it is not possible to put both into a script file (the browser would ignore the AWT calls), things could get very confusing. However, the AWT and VRML event handling systems do share a common philosophy.

Now you need a method that is passed an event when it happens. VRML gives you a choice of two: The processEvents() method is used when there's more that one event generated at a particular timestamp, and the processEvent() method is called when there's only one event to be taken care of at that time.

 The processEvents() method takes an array of event objects that you then analyze and pass to the various methods. This is no different from the way the AWT event-handling system works. A typical segment of code is shown in Listing 36.2 (this code can also be found on the CD-ROM that accompanies this book).

Listing 36.2. An example Java class for a script.

```
import vrml.*;
import vrml.field.*;
import vrml.node.*;

class replace_script extends Script {
    // now we get all the class variables
    private SFBool pointerOver;

    //initialisation
    public void initialize() {
        pointerOver = (SFBool)getField("pointerOver");
    }

    // now the eventIn declarations - only do the isClicked event for now
    private void isOver(ConstSFBool value) {
        if(value.getValue() == false)
            pointerOver.setValue(false);
        else
            pointerOver.setValue(true);
    }

    // now the event handling function
    public void processEvents(int count, Event events[]) {
        int     i;
        for(i=0; i < count; i++)
        {
            if (events[i].getName().equals("isOver"))
                isOver(events[i].getValue());
            // collection of other else if statements here
        }
    }
}
```

The second event-handler method is `processEvent()`; because it deals with just a single event, the argument is only a single `Event` object. Therefore, the only difference between this method and the `processEvents()` method is that you don't need the `for` loop. The big `if...else` ladder of string comparisons remains, however.

When should you use the different event-handling functions? Take the following piece of VRML code as an example (this example comes straight from the VRML specification):

```
Transform {
    children [
        DEF TS TouchSensor {},
        Shape {
            appearance Appearance {
                material Material { emissiveColor 0 0 1 }
            }
            geometry Cone {} }
    ]
```

Building VRML 2.0 Behaviors in Java

CHAPTER 36

787

36

BUILDING
VRML 2.0
BEHAVIORS

```
}
DEF SC Script {
    url     "Example.class"
    eventIn SFBool isActive
    eventIn SFTime touchTime
}
ROUTE TS.isActive  TO SC.isActive
ROUTE TS.touchTime TO SC.touchTime
```

Whenever TouchSensor is touched, it generates two simultaneous events, so the script receives the two events. In this case, you need the processEvents() method to deal with a number of simultaneous events. If you were interested only in the isActive event, you could use the processEvent() method.

If you're not sure whether the script will receive more than one simultaneous event, you can declare both methods. To save duplicating large amounts of code, you can put all the code to call the internal methods in the processEvent() method and just put a for loop that calls processEvent() with each individual event object in processEvents(). If this confuses you, have a look at the following code fragment:

```
void public processEvent(Event e) {
    if(e.getName().equals("someEvent"))
        // call internal method
  else if ......
}

void public processEvents(int count, Event events[]) {
    int    i;
    for (i=0; i < count; i++)
        processEvent(events[i]);
}
```

Notice that a bit more work must be done to get an initial Java class file running. One advantage is that you declare only the fields you need to use. In Listing 36.2 you just wanted to use the pointerOver field from the VRML definition, so you left the rest out. The Java code is compiled independently of VRML source code, allowing you to take a staged approach to developing the code, adding variables and event handlers only when they're needed.

Setting Up the Class to Run

In the preceding code fragment, you may have noticed that an extra method was declared. This initialize() method is where you do all the initialization of values used by the script. VRML has some interesting problems: The time at which the class is first initialized may be different than the time at which values in the scene graph are ready.

If you used the constructor function to initialize the field values, you cannot guarantee that the values will be valid. The initialize() method is called when the scene graph contains valid data: that is, after the whole VRML scene has been loaded but before any events are created.

One of the first things that must be done during initialization is to match the fields declared in the VRML script node definition to the Java variables. The Script class contains two methods: one to get the fields and another to get eventOuts. These methods are passed a string to return the information in a form suitable for Java. Look back at the initialize() method from Listing 36.2:

```
public void initialize() {
    pointerOver = (SFBool)getField("pointerOver");
}
```

The getEventOut() method call would look the same. To Java, sending an event to another node looks the same as simply assigning a value to that variable. The Java internals and the browser take care of the rest.

The First Behavior: A Color-Changing Box

The first behavior can now be defined by putting all that you have learned so far together: A box that, when touched, toggles color between red and blue. This sample behavior requires five components: a box primitive, a touch sensor, a material node, the script node, and the Java script. In this example, the static connections between the script and the other nodes are used because the scene stays the same and we change just a property.

The basic input scene consists of a box placed at the origin with a color and touch sensor around it:

```
Transform {
    children [
        Shape {
            geometry Box {size 1 1 1}
            appearance Appearance {
                DEF box_material Material {
                    diffuseColor    1.0 0. 0. #start red.
                }
            }
        } # end of shape definition
        # Now define a TouchSensor node. This node takes in the
        # geometry of the parent transform. Default behavior OK.
        DEF box_sensor TouchSensor {}
    ]
}
```

Now you have to define a script to act as the color changer. You have to take input from the touch sensor and output the new color to the Material node. You also have to internally keep track of the color. You can do this by reading the value from the Material node, but for demonstration purposes, an internal flag is included in the script. No fancy processing or event sending to other nodes is necessary, so both the mustEvaluate and directOutputs fields can be left at the default setting of `null`. Our completed VRML `Script` definition looks like this:

```
DEF color_script Script {
    behavior    "color_changer.class"

    # now define our needed fields
    field       SFBool       isRed         TRUE
    eventIn     SFBool       clicked
    eventOut    SFColor      color_out
}
```

Now you have to connect the preceding two pieces of code (the script and the box) together using ROUTEs:

```
ROUTE box_sensor.isOver TO color_script.clicked
ROUTE color_script.color_out TO box_material.diffuseColor
```

 Finally, you add the script to make everything work. Listing 36.3 shows the complete source code for the color-changing box. This code can also be found on the CD-ROM that accompanies this book.

Listing 36.3. Java source for the color-changing box.

```
import vrml.*;
import vrml.field.*;
import vrml.node.*;

class color_changer extends Script {

    // declare the field
    private SFBool    isRed;

    // declare the eventOut
    private SFColor   color_out;

    //initialization
    public void initialize() {
        isRed = (SFBool)getField("isRed");
        color_out = (SFColor)getEventOut("color_out");
    }

    // declare eventIns
    private void clicked(ConstSFBool isClicked) {
        float red[] = {1.0, 0, 0};
        float blue[] = {0, 0, 1.0};

        // called when the user clicks or touches the box or
        // stops touching/click so first check the status of the
        // isClicked field. We will only respond to a button up.
        if(isClicked.getValue() == false) {
```

continues

Listing 36.3. continued

```
            // now check whether the box is red or green
            if(isRed.getValue() == true) {
                isRed.setValue(false);
                color_out.setValue(red);
            }
            else {
                isRed.setValue(true);
                color_out.setValue(blue);
            }
        }
    }

    // finally the event processing call
    public void processEvent(Event e) {
        clicked((ConstSFBool)e.getValue());
    }
}
```

That's it. You now have a box that changes color when you click it. Creating more complex behaviors is just a variation on this scheme using more Java code and fields. User input usually comes from sensors or interpolators, which are usually directly wired to a series of other event-generating and event-receiving structures.

More complex input from external systems is also possible. Scripts are not restricted to input methods based on eventIns. One example is a stock market tracker that runs as a separate thread. The tracker could constantly receive updates from the network, process them, and then send the results through a public method to the script, which would put the appropriate results into the 3D world.

The Browser Class

Behaviors using the method presented in the color-changing box example in the preceding section work for many simple systems. Effective virtual reality systems, however, require more than just being able to change the color and shape of objects that already exist in the virtual world. Consider a virtual taxi: A user must step inside and instruct the cab where to go. The cab moves off, leaving the user in the same place. The user does not "exist" as part of the scene graph—the user is known to the browser but not to the VRML scene-rendering engine. Clearly, a greater level of control is needed.

Changing the Current Scene

The VRML 2.0 specification defines a series of actions that must be provided if the programmer is to set and retrieve information about the world. Within the Java implementation of the API, this functionality is provided as the Browser class. This class provides all the functions a programmer needs that are not specific to any particular part of the scene graph.

To define system-specific behaviors, the first functions you must define are these:

```
public String getName();
public String getVersion();
```

These strings are defined by the browser writer and identify the browser in some unspecified way. If this information is not available, empty strings are returned.

If you are programming expensive calculations, you may want to know how they affect the rendering speed (frame rate) of the system. The getCurrentFrameRate() method returns the value in frames per second. If this information is not available, the return value is 100.0.

```
public float getCurrentFrameRate();
public float getCurrentSpeed();
```

The difference between navigation speed and current speed is in the definition. VRML 2.0 defines NavigationInfo as a node that contains default information about how to act if given no other external cues. The *navigation speed* is the default speed in units per second. There is no specification about what this speed represents, only hints. A reasonable assumption is the movement speed in WALK and FLY navigation modes and in panning and dollying in EXAMINE mode. The *current speed* is the actual speed at which the user is travelling at that point in time. The current speed is the speed the user has set with the browser controls.

> **NOTE**
>
> For a complete description of the different navigation types (WALK, FLY, and so on), see the VRML specification for the NavigationInfo node.

Having two different descriptions of speed may seem wasteful, but it comes in quite handy when moving between different worlds. The first world may be a land of giants, where traveling at 100 units per second is considered slow, but in the next world, which models a molecule only 0.001 units across, this speed would be ridiculous. The navigation speed value can be used to scale speeds to something that is reasonable for the particular world.

Modifying the Scene

There is only so much you can do with what is already available in a scene. Complex worlds use a mix of static and dynamically generated scenery to achieve their impressive special effects.

The first thing you may want to do is find out where you are from the URL:

```
public String getWorldURL();
```

GetWorldURL() returns the URL of the root of the scene graph rather than the URL of the currently occupied part of the scene. VRML enables a complex world to be created using a series of small files included into the world—a process called *inlining* in VRML parlance.

The following four methods allow you to modify the scene in some way. To completely replace the scene graph with a new file, call the loadURL() method. As with all URL references within VRML, an array of strings is passed. The array of strings is a list of URLs and URNs to be loaded in order of preference. If the load of the first URL fails, the method attempts to load the second, and so on until the method is successful or the end of the list is reached. If the load fails, the method should notify the user in some browser-specific manner.

As this book goes to press, the exact specification of URNs is still being debated. URNs are legal within fields that contain strings for URLs; the VRML specification states that if the browser is not capable of supporting the URNs, they are to be silently ignored. The specification also states that it is up to the browser whether the loadURL() call blocks or starts a separate thread when loading a new URL. This URL may be another VRML world or any other valid URL such as an HTML page.

So far, the methods described enable the programmer to change individual components of the world. The other requirement is to completely replace the world with some internally generated one. Doing so enables you to use VRML to generate new VRML worlds on the fly. This still assumes that you already are part of a VRML world—you cannot use this approach in an application to generate a 3D graphics front-end.

If you have generated an array of nodes within your script (see the createVRML calls in the next section), ReplaceWorld()is what you have to call. This is a non-returning call that unloads the old scene and replaces it with the given collection of nodes:

```
public static void loadURL(String[] url);
public void replaceWorld(Node[] nodes);
public static Node[] createVrmlFromString(String vrmlSyntax);
   throws InvalidVRMLSyntaxException;
public static void createVrmlFromURL(String[] url,
                                     Node    node,
                                     String  event);
   throws InvalidVRMLSyntaxException;
```

In addition to replacing the whole scene, you may want to add bits at a time. You can do so in one of two ways. If you are very familiar with VRML syntax, you can create strings on the fly and pass them to the createVrmlFromString() method. The node that is returned can then be added into the scene as required.

Building VRML 2.0 Behaviors in Java
CHAPTER 36

793

36
BUILDING
VRML 2.0
BEHAVIORS

Perhaps the most useful of the above methods is the createVrmlFromURL() method. You may notice from the definition that in addition to a list of URLs, createVrmlFromURL() also takes a node instance and a string that refers to an eventIn field name. This call is a nonblocking call that starts a separate thread to retrieve the given file from the URL, converts it to the internal representation, and then sends the newly created list of nodes to the specified node's eventIn field. The eventIn type is required to be an MFNode. The Node reference can be any sort of node, not just a part of the script node. This arrangement enables the script writer to add these new nodes directly to the scene graph without having to write extra functionality in the script.

With both the create methods, the returned nodes do not become visible until they have been added to some preexisting node that already exists within the scene. To add them to the scene, you can either pass them to a grouping node (for example, Transform or Group) or call the replaceWorld() method that we looked at a little earlier. Although it is possible to create an entire scene on the fly within a standalone applet, there is no way to make it visible because this applet does not have a previous node instance to which you can add the dynamically generated scene.

Once you have created a set of new nodes, you want to be able to link them together to get the same behaviors system as the original world. The Browser class defines these methods for dynamically adding and deleting ROUTEs between nodes:

```
public void addRoute(Node fromNode, String fromEventOut,
                     Node toNode,   String toEventIn)
    throws InvalidRouteException;
public void delRoute(Node fromNode, String fromEventOut,
                     Node toNode,   String toEventIn)
    throws InvalidRouteException;
```

For each of these methods, you must know the node instance for both ends of the ROUTE. In VRML, you cannot obtain an instance pointer to an individual field in a node. It is also assumed that if you know you will be adding a route, you also know what fields you are dealing with, so a string is used to describe the field name corresponding to an eventIn or eventOut. Exceptions are thrown if either of the nodes or fields do not exist or an attempt to delete a nonexistent ROUTE is made.

You now have all the tools required to generate a world on the fly, respond to user input, and modify the scene. The only thing that remains is to add the finesse to create responsive worlds that don't get bogged down in Java code.

Creating Efficient Behaviors

In all animation programming, the ultimate goal is to keep the frame rate as high as possible. In a multithreaded application like a VRML browser, the less time spent in behaviors code, the more time that can be spent rendering. Virtual reality behavior programming in VRML is still very much in its infancy. This section outlines a few common-sense approaches to keep up reasonable levels of performance, not only for the renderer, but also for the programmer.

The first technique is to use Java only where necessary. This many sound a little strange from a book about Java programming, but consider the resources required to have not only a 3D-rendering engine but a Java VM loaded to run even a simple behavior; also consider that the majority of viewers will be people using low-end PCs. Because most VRML browsers specify that a minimum of 16MB of RAM is required (with a recommendation of 32MB), also loading the Java VM into memory would require lots of swapping to keep the behaviors going. The inevitable result is bad performance. For this reason, the interpolator nodes and JavaScript were created: built-in nodes for common, basic calculations and a small, light language to provide basic calculation capabilities. Limit your use of Java to the times when you require the capabilities of a full programming language, such as multithreading and network interfaces.

When you do have to use Java, keep the amount of calculation in the script to a minimum. If you are producing behaviors that require either extensive network communication or data processing, these behaviors should be kept out of the script node and sent off in separate threads. The script should start the thread as either part of its constructor or in response to some event; it should then return as soon as possible.

In VR systems, frame rate is king. Don't aim to have a 100-percent-correct behavior if doing so leads to twice the frame rate. Will a 90-percent-correct behavior do? It is quite amazing how users don't notice an incorrect behavior, but as soon as they notice the picture update slowing down, they start to complain. Every extra line of code in the script delays the return of the CPU back to the renderer. In military simulations, the goal is to achieve 60fps; even for Pentium-class machines, the goal should be to maintain at least 10fps. Much of this comes down not only to how detailed the world is, but also to how complex the behaviors are. As always, the tradeoff between accuracy and frame rate depends on the individual programmer and the application requirements. Users usually accept that a door does not open smoothly as long as they can move around without watching individual frames redraw.

Be careful with the event-processing loop. Your behaviors code will be distributed on many different types of machines and browsers. Each browser writer knows best how to optimize the event-handling mechanism to mesh with its internal architecture. With windowing systems, dealing with the event loop is a *must* if you are to respond to user input, but in VR, you no longer have control over the whole system. The `processEvents()` method applies only to an individual script; you cannot use it as a common method across all scripts. Although you may think you are optimizing the event handling, you are only doing so for a single script. In a reasonably sized world, you may have another few hundred scripts running, so the optimization of an individual script generally isn't worth the effort.

Building VRML 2.0 Behaviors in Java
CHAPTER 36

795

36

BUILDING
VRML 2.0
BEHAVIORS

Changing the Scene

Add to the scene graph only what is necessary. If it is possible to modify existing primitives, do so instead of adding new ones. Every primitive added to a scene requires the renderer to convert it to its internal representation and then reoptimize the scene graph to take account of the new objects. When it modifies existing primitives, the browser is not required to re-sort the scene graph structure, saving computation time. For example, a cloudy sky is better simulated using a multiframed texture map image format (such as MJPEG or PNG) on the background node than using lots of primitives that are constantly modified or dynamically added.

If your scene requires objects to be added and removed on the fly, and many of these objects are the same, don't simply delete the objects from the scene graph. It is better to remove them from a node but keep an instance pointer to them so that they can be reinserted at a later time. At the expense of a little extra memory, this approach saves time. If you don't take the time now, you may have to access the objects later from a network or construct them from the ground up from a string representation.

Another trick is to create objects but not add them to the scene graph. VRML lets you create objects but not add them to the scene graph. Any object not added isn't drawn. Node types such as sensors, interpolators, and scripts have no need to be added. Doing so causes extra events to be generated, resulting in a slower system. Normal Java garbage collection rules apply for when these nodes are no longer referenced. VRML, however, adds one little extra: Adding a ROUTE to any object is the same as keeping a reference to the object. If a script creates a node, adds one or more ROUTEs, and then exits, the node stays allocated and functions as though it were a normal part of the scene graph.

There are dangers in this approach. Once you have lost the node instance pointer, there is no way to delete it. You need this pointer if you are to delete the ROUTE. Deleting ROUTEs to the object is the only way to remove these floating nodes. Therefore, you should always keep the node instance pointers for all floating nodes you create so that you can delete the ROUTEs to them when they're no longer needed. You must be particularly careful when you delete a section of the scene graph that has the only routed eventIn field to a floating node that also contains an eventOut to a undeleted section of the scene graph. This arrangement creates the VRML equivalent of memory leaks. The only way to remove this node is to replace the whole scene or to remove the part of the scene that the eventOut references.

Circular Event Loops

The ROUTE syntax makes it very easy to construct circular event loops. Circular loops can be quite handy. The VRML specifications state that if the browser finds event loops, it processes each event only once per timestamp. Events generated as a result of a change are given the same timestamp as the original change. This happens because events are considered to happen instantaneously. When event loops are encountered in this situation, the browser enforces a breakage of the loop. The sample script from the VRML specification using JavaScript shows this:

```
DEF S Script {
    eventIn  SFInt32    a
    eventIn  SFInt32    b
    eventOut SFInt32    c
    field    SFInt32    save_a    0
    field    SFInt32    save_b    0
    url      "data:x-lang/x-vrmlscript, TEXT;
        function a(val) { save_a = val; c = save_a+save_b;}
        function b(val) { save_b = val; c = save_a+save_b;}
}
ROUTE S.c to S.b
```

S computes c=a+b with the ROUTE, completing a loop from the output c back to the input b. After the initial event with a=1, S leaves the eventOut c with a value of 1. This causes a cascade effect, in which b is set to 1. Normally, this should generate an eventOut on c with the value of 2, but the browser has already seen that the eventOut c has been traversed for this timestamp and therefore enforces a break in the loop. This leaves the values save_a=1, save_b=1, and the eventOut c=1.

Dynamic Worlds: Creating VRML on the Fly

Earlier in this chapter, you learned that it was not possible to create a world from a completely standalone application. Although it would be nice to have this facility, it would be the same as being able to create a whole HTML page in the same manner. To create an HTML page applet, you must first start it from an <APPLET> tag. A Java-enabled page may consist of no more than an opening <HTML> tag followed by an <APPLET> tag pair and a closing </HTML> tag. VRML is no different. You can enclose a whole 3D application based on VRML in a similar manner.

Although this approach is not quite as efficient as creating a 3D application using a native 3D toolkit such as Java3D, VRML can be considered an abstraction that enables programmable behaviors in a simplified manner—much like using a GUI builder to create an application rather than writing it all by hand.

The next section develops a framework for creating worlds on the fly. Such a framework can have quite a few different applications—from developing cyberspace protocol-based seamless worlds, to acting as a VR-based scene editor, to generating VRML or other 3D format output files. The explanations of the development process in the next sections assume that you are familiar with at least VRML 1.0 syntax.

There are three ways to create a world on the fly. These are given by the three methods in the Browser class described earlier in the chapter: createVrmlFromURL(), createVrmlFromString(), and `loadURL()`. The example we develop in the following sections is very simple but demonstrates each of these calls. The VRML scene consists of three objects: the sphere, the cone, and the cube of the VRML logo. Touching each of the objects causes a different action to happen (which is explained as we go along).

The VRML Source File

Just as in HTML, you must start with a skeleton file in which you include the Java application. In VRML, however, you have to do a little more than just include an applet and a few PARAM tags.

The first thing you need in the VRML file is at least one node to which you can add things. Remember that there is no method of adding a primitive to the root of the scene graph, so a pseudo root to which objects are added is required. For simplicity, a `Group` node is used. There is nothing that has to be specified, so we can leave the fields alone. The `Group` node has two `eventIn` fields that are used later: `add_children` and `remove_children`. The definition is shown here:

```
DEF root_node Group {}
```

A few objects have to be put into the scene that are representative of the three methods of adding an object to the world. Taking the three primitives that form the VRML logo, the box will represent creating objects from a downloaded file, the sphere will create and add an object from an internal text description, and the cone takes the user to another VRML world by using the call to `loadURL()`. These primitives are surrounded in a `Transform` node to make sure that they are located in different parts of the world (all objects are located at the origin by default). The box definition follows:

```
Transform {
    translation    2 0 0
    children [
        DEF box_sensor TouchSensor{}
        Box { size    1 1 1}
        # script node will go here
    ]
}
```

Notice that DEF is used only for the `TouchSensor` itself and not the whole object. The `TouchSensor` is the object from which events are taken. If there was no sensor, the box would exist as itself. Any mouse click (or touch, if you are using a data glove) on the box does nothing. The other two nodes are similar in definition.

For demonstration purposes, separate scripts have been put with each of the objects. It makes no difference if you have lots of small scripts or one large one. For a VR scene creator, it is probably better to have one large script to keep track of the scene graph for the output file representation, but a virtual factory can have many small scripts, perhaps with some "centralized" script acting as the system controller.

Defining the Script Nodes

Once the basic file is defined, you must add behaviors. The VRML file stands on its own at this point. You can click objects, but nothing happens. Because each object has its own behavior, the requirement for each script is different. Each script requires one eventIn, which is the notification from its TouchSensor.

Because the example presented does not have any real-time constraints, the mustEvaluate field is left with the default setting of FALSE. For the cone, no outputs are sent directly to nodes, so the directOutputs field is left at FALSE. For the sphere, outputs are sent directly to the Group node, so it is set to TRUE. The box must be set to TRUE as well, for reasons explained in the next section.

Besides the eventIn, the box's script also requires an eventOut to send the new object to the Group node acting as the scene root. Good behavior is desirable if the user clicks on the box more than once, so an extra internal variable is added, keeping the position of the last object that was added. Each new object added is translated two units along the z axis from the previous one. A field is also needed to store the URL of the sample file that will be loaded. The box script definition follows:

```
DEF box_script Script {
    url             "boxscript.class"
    directOutputs   TRUE
    eventIn     SFBool    isClicked
    eventIn     MFNode    newNodes
    eventOut    MFNode    childlist
    field       SFInt32   zposition    0
    field       SFNode    thisScript   USE box_script
    field       MFNode    newUrl    []
}
```

Notice that there is an extra eventIn. Processing must be done on the node returned from the createVrmlFromURL() method, so you must provide an eventIn for the argument. If you do not need to process the returned nodes, you can use the root_node.add_children eventIn instead as the target eventIn for the create call.

The other interesting point to note is that the script declaration includes a field that is a reference to itself. A Java class can always refer to itself using this when it needs an event.

To explain the use of direct outputs, the sphere uses the postEventIn method to send the new child directly to root_node. To do this, a copy of the name that was defined for the Group is taken, which, when resolved in Java, essentially becomes an instance pointer to the node. Using direct writing to nodes means that you no longer require the eventOut from the box's script but you keep the other fields:

```
DEF sphere_script Script {
    url             "sphere_script.class"
    directOutputs   TRUE
```

Building VRML 2.0 Behaviors in Java

CHAPTER 36

799

36

BUILDING
VRML 2.0
BEHAVIORS

```
    eventIn    SFBool    isClicked
    field      SFNode    root       USE root_node
    field      SFInt32   zposition   0
}
```

The script for the cone is very simplistic. When you click the cone, all it does is fetch a named URL and set it as the new scene graph. In this case, the URL being used belongs to the independent virtual community called Terra Vista, of which I am a member. At the time of this writing, Terra Vista is a complete VRML 1.0c distributed community that is starting to move towards version 2.0. By the time you read this, it should give you many examples of how to use both simple and complex behaviors.

```
DEF cone_script Script {
    url        "cone_script.class"
    eventIn    SFBool    isClicked
    field      MFString   target_url ["http://www.alaska.net/~pfennig/flux/
flux.wrl"]
}
```

 Now that the scripts are defined, you must wire them together. A number of ROUTEs are added between the sensors and scripts, as shown in the complete code in Listing 36.4. This code can also be found on the CD-ROM that accompanies this book.

Listing 36.4. The main world VRML description.

```
#VRML V2.0 utf8
#
# Demonstration dynamically created world
# Created by Justin Couch 1996

# first the pseudo root
DEF root_node Group {}

# The box
Transform {
    translation    2 0 0
    children [
        DEF box_sensor TouchSensor{},
        Shape {
            appearance Appearance {
                material Material { emissiveColor 1 0 0 }
            }
            geometry Box { size    1 1 1}
        },
        DEF box_script Script {
            url            "boxscript.class"
            directOutputs      TRUE
            eventIn    SFBool    isClicked
            eventIn    MFNode    newNodes
            eventOut   MFNode    childlist
            field      SFInt32   zPosition    0
            field      SFNode    thisScript   USE box_script
            field      MFString  newUrl ["sample_world.wrl"]
        }
    ]
```

continues

Listing 36.4. continued

```
}
ROUTE box_sensor.isActive TO box_script.isClicked
ROUTE box_script.childlist TO root_node.addChildren

# The sphere
Transform {
    # no translation needed as it is at the origin already
    children [
        DEF sphere_sensor TouchSensor {},
        Shape {
            appearance Appearance {
                material Material { emissiveColor 0 1 0 }
            }
            geometry Sphere { radius    0.5 }
        },
        DEF sphere_script Script {
            url            "sphere_script.class"
            directOutputs    TRUE
            eventIn    SFBool    isClicked
            field      SFNode    root        USE root_node
            field      SFInt32   zPosition   0
        }
    ]
}

ROUTE sphere_sensor.isActive TO sphere_script.isClicked

# The cone
Transform {
    translation    -2 0 0
    children [
        DEF cone_sensor TouchSensor {},
        Shape {
            appearance Appearance {
                material Material { emissiveColor 0 0 1}
            }
            geometry Cone {
                bottomRadius    0.5
                height          1
            }
        },
        DEF cone_script Script {
            url      "cone_script.class"
            eventIn    SFBool    isClicked
            field      MFString   targetUrl ["http://www.alaska.net/~pfennig/
➥flux/flux.wrl"]
        }
    ]
}

ROUTE cone_sensor.isActive TO cone_script.isClicked
```

The box sensor adds objects to the scene graph from an external file. This external file (defined in Listing 36.5 and found on the CD-ROM that accompanies this book) contains a `Transform` node with a single box as a child. Because the API does not permit users to create node types, and because you have to place the newly created box at a point other than the origin, you have to use a `Transform` node. Although you could just load in a box from the external scene and then create a `Transform` node with the `createVrmlFromString()` method, doing so requires more code and slows down execution speed. Remember that behavior writing is about getting things done as quickly as possible, so the more you move to external static file descriptions, the better.

Listing 36.5. The external VRML world file.

```
#VRML V2.0 utf8
#
# Demonstration sample world to be loaded
# Created by Justin Couch May 1996

Transform {
    children [
        Shape {
            appearance Appearance {
                material Material { emissiveColor 0.4 0.41 0.1 }
            }
            geometry Box { size     1 1 1}
        }
    ]
}
```

The Java Behaviors

Probably the most time-consuming task for someone writing a VRML scene with behaviors is deciding how to organize the various parts in relation to the scene graph structure. In a simple file like this, there are two ways to arrange the scripts. Imagine what could happen in a moderately complex file of two or three thousand objects.

 All the scripts in this example are simple. Listing 36.6 is the source for the script that belongs to the box (and the source can be found on the CD-ROM that accompanies this book). When the node is received back in `newNodes` eventIn, the node must be translated to the new position. Ideally, you should be able to do this directly by setting the `translation` field but you cannot. The only way to do this is to post an event to the node, naming that field as the destination—the reason for setting `directOutputs` to `TRUE`. After this is done, you can then call the `add_children` eventIn. Because each of the scripts is short, the `processEvents()` method is not used.

Listing 36.6. Java source for the box script.

```java
import vrml.*;
import vrml.node.*;
import vrml.field.*;

class box_script extends Script {
    private SFInt32  zPosition;
    private SFNode   thisScript;
    private MFString newUrl;

    // declare the eventOut field
    private MFNode   childList;

    // initialization
    public void initialize() {
        zPosition = (SFInt32)getField("zPosition");
        thisScript = (SFNode)getField("thisScript");
        newUrl     = (MFString)getField("newUrl");
        childList  = (MFNode)getEventOut("childList");
}

    // now declare the eventIn methods
    private void isClicked(ConstSFBool clicked) {
        // check to see if picking up or letting go
        if(clicked.getValue() == FALSE)
            Browser.createVrmlFromURL(newUrl.getValue(),
                                      thisScript, "newNodes");
    }

    private void newNodes(ConstMFNode nodelist, SFTime ts) {
        Node[]  nodes = (Node[])nodelist.getValue();
        float[3] translation;

        // Set up the translation
        zPosition.setValue(zPosition.getValue() + 2);
        translation[0] = zPosition.getValue();
        translation[1] = 0;
        translation[2] = 0;

        // There should only be one node with a transform at the
        // top. No error checking.
        nodes[0].postEventIn("translation", (Field)translation);

        // now send the processed node list to the eventOut
        childList.setValue(nodes);
    }

    //event handling
    public void processEvents(int count, Event events[]) {
        int i;

        for(i = 0; i < count; i++) {
            if(e.getName().equals("isClicked"))
                isClicked((ConstSFBool)e.getValue());
```

```
        else if(e.getName().equals("newNodes"))
            newNodes((ConstMFNode)e.getValue());
    }
  }
}
```

The sphere class in Listing 36.7 is similar to the previous code, except that you have to construct the text string equivalent of the sample_world.wrl file. This is a straightforward string buffer problem. All you have to do is make sure that the Transform node has the correct value for the translation field. You can find this code on the CD-ROM that accompanies this book.

Listing 36.7. Java source for the sphere script.

```
import vrml.*;
import vrml.field.*;
import vrml.node.*;

class sphere_script extends Script {
    private SFInt32  zPosition;
    private SFNode   root;

    //initialization
    public void initialize() {
        zPosition = (SFInt32)getField("zPosition");
        root      = (SFNode)getField("root");
    }

    // now declare the eventIn methods
    public void processEvent(Event e) {
        StringBuffer vrml_string = new StringBuffer();
        MFNode        nodes;
        ConstSFBool  clicked = (ConstSFBool)e.getValue();

        // set the new position
        zPosition.setValue(zPosition.getValue() + 2);

        // check to see if picking up or letting go
        if(clicked.getValue() == FALSE) {
            vrml_string.append("Transform {");
            vrml_string.append("translation ");
            vrml_string.append(zPosition.getValue());
            vrml_string.append(" 0 0 ");
            vrml_string.append("children [ ");
            vrml_string.append("sphere { radius 0.5} ] }");

            nodes.setValue(Browser.createVrmlFromString(vrml_string));

            root.postEventIn("addChildren", (Field)nodes);
        }
    }
}
```

The cone_script class in Listing 36.8 (and found on the CD-ROM that accompanies this book) is the easiest of the lot. As soon as it receives confirmation of a touch, it starts to load the world with the provided URL.

There is only one interesting part: When retrieving the value of the boolean passed to it, we use two getValue() methods. The first returns the ConstField from the event and the second returns the **boolean** value that was actually passed with the event. To make sure that everything is understandable, I used an intermediate variable to keep from confusing the two methods.

Listing 36.8. Java source for the cone script.

```
import vrml.*;
import vrml.field.*;
import vrml.node.*;

class cone_script extends Script {
    SFBool   isClicked;
    MFString targetUrl;

    // initialization
    public void initialize() {
        isClicked = (SFBool)getField("isClicked");
        targetUrl = (MFString)getField("targetUrl");
    }

    // The eventIn method
    public void processEvent(Event e) {
        ConstSFBool val = (ConstSFBool)e.getValue();

        if(val.getValue() == FALSE)
            Browser.loadURL(targetUrl.getValue());
    }
}
```

By compiling the preceding Java code and placing these and the two VRML source files in your Web directory, you can serve this basic dynamic world to the rest of the world and everyone will get the same behavior as you—regardless of the system they're running.

Creating Reusable Behaviors

It would be problematic if you had to rewrite the code in the preceding example every time you wanted to use it in another file. You could always just reuse the Java bytecodes, but this means that you would need identical copies of the script declaration every time you wanted to use it. Reusing the bytecodes is not a particularly nice practice from the software-engineering point of view, either. Eventually, you will be caught in the cut-and-paste error of having extra pieces of ROUTEs floating around (and extra fields) that could accidentally be connected to nodes in the new scene, resulting in bugs that are difficult to trace.

Building VRML 2.0 Behaviors in Java

CHAPTER 36

805

36

BUILDING
VRML 2.0
BEHAVIORS

VRML 2.0 provides a mechanism similar to the C/C++ #include directive and typedef statements all rolled into one: the PROTO and EXTERNPROTO statement pair. The PROTO statement acts like a typedef: you use PROTO with a node and its definition and then you can use that name as though it were an ordinary node within the context of that file.

If you want to access that prototyped node outside of that file, you can use the EXTERNPROTO statement to include it in the new file and then use it as though it were an ordinary node.

Although this approach is useful for creating libraries of static parts, where it really comes into its own is in creating canned behaviors. A programmer can create a completely self-contained behavior and in the best object-oriented traditions, provide only the interfaces to the behaviors he or she wants. The syntax of the PROTO and EXTERNPROTO statements follow:

```
PROTO prototypename [ # any collection of
    eventIn         eventTypeName eventName
    eventOut        eventTypeName eventName
    exposedField    fieldTypeName fieldName initialValue
    field           fieldTypeName fieldName initialValue
] {
    # scene graph structure. Any combination of
    # nodes, prototypes, and ROUTEs
}

EXTERNPROTO prototypename [ # any collection of
    eventIn         eventTypeName eventName
    eventOut        eventTypeName eventName
    exposedField    fieldTypeName fieldName
    field           fieldTypeName fieldName
]
"URL" or [ "URN1" "URL2"]
```

You can add a behavior to a VRML file just by using the *prototypename* in the file. For example, if you have a behavior that simulates a taxi, you may want to have many taxis in a number of different worlds that represent different countries. The cabs are identical except for their color. Note again the ability to specify multiple URLs for the behavior. If the browser cannot retrieve the first URL, it tries another until it gets a cab.

A taxi can have many behaviors (such as speed and direction) that users of a cab do not really care about when they want to use it. (Well, if they were going in the wrong direction once they got in, they might care!) To incorporate a virtual taxi into your world, all you really care about is a few things, such as being able to signal a cab, getting in, telling it where to go, paying the fare, and then getting out when it has reached its destination. From the world authors' point of view, how the taxi finds its virtual destination is unimportant. A declaration of the taxi prototype file might look like the following:

```
#VRML V2.0 utf8
#
# Taxi prototype file taxi.wrl
PROTO taxicab [
```

```
    exposedField SFBool     isAvailable   TRUE
    eventIn      SFBool     inCab
    eventIn      SFString   destination
      eventIn      SFFloat   payFare
    eventOut     SFFloat    fareCost
    eventOut     SFInt32    speed
    eventOut     SFVec3f    direction
    field        SFColor    color        1. 0 0
    # rest of externally available variables
] {
    DEF root_group Transform {
          # Taxi geometry description here
    }
    DEF taxi_script Script {
        url    ["taxi.class"]
        # rest of event and field declarations
    }
    # ROUTE statements to connect it altogether
}
```

To include the taxi in your world, the file would look something like this:

```
#VRML V2.0 utf8
#
# myworld.wrl
EXTERNPROTO taxi [
    exposedField SFBool     isAvailable
    eventIn      SFBool     inCab
    eventIn      SFString   destination
    eventIn      SFFloat    payFare
    eventOut     SFFloat    fareCost
    eventOut     SFInt32    speed
    eventOut     SFVec3f    direction
    field        SFColor    color
    # rest of externally available variables
]
[ " http://myworld.com/taxi.wrl", "http://yourworld.com/taxi.wrl"]

# some scene graph
#....
Transform {
    children [
        # other VRML nodes. Then we use the taxi
        DEF my_taxi taxi {
            color  0 1. 0
        }
    ]
}
```

Here is a case in which you are likely to use the postEventIn() method to call a cab. Somewhere in the scene graph, you would have a control that your avatar queries a nearby cab for its
isAvailable field. (An *avatar* is the virtual body used to represent you in the virtual world.) If
it is TRUE, the avatar sends the event to flag the cab. Apart from the required mechanics to signal the cab with the various instructions, the world creator does not care how the cab is implemented. By using the EXTERNPROTO call, the world creator and its users can always be sure that

Building VRML 2.0 Behaviors in Java

CHAPTER 36

807

36

BUILDING
VRML 2.0
BEHAVIORS

they are getting the latest version of the taxi implementation and that there will be uniform behavior regardless of which world they are in.

The Future: VRML, Java, and AI

The information presented in this chapter relied on static predefined behaviors available either within the original VRML file or from somewhere on the Internet.

The ultimate step in creating VR worlds is autonomous agents that have some degree of artificial intelligence. Back in the early days of programming, self-modifying code was common, but it faded away as more resources and higher-level programming languages removed the need. A true VR world brings this kind of coding back.

The Librarian from Stephenson's cyberpunk novel *Snow Crash* is just one example of how an independent agent can act in a VR world. Stephenson's model is very simple—a glorified version of today's 2D HTML-based search engine that, when requested, would search the U.S. Library of Congress for information on the desired and related topics (the Librarian also has speech recognition and synthesis capabilities). The next generation of intelligent agents will include learning behavior as well.

The VRML API enables you to take the next step—a virtual assistant that can modify its own behavior to suit your preferences. This is not just a case of loading in some canned behaviors. With the combination of JavaScript and Java behaviors, a programmer can create customized behaviors on the fly by concatenating the behavior strings and script nodes, calling the `createVrmlFromString()` method, and adding it to the scene graph in the appropriate place. This sort of work takes a lot of CPU time just to react to other users in the environment, so it is probably not feasible with current Pentium-class machines; the next generation of processors will probably make it so.

Controlling the VRML World from Applets

What you have learned so far in this chapter is fairly restricted. These scripts cannot interact with anything outside the VRML browser. If you have a multiframed document, there is no way an applet can communicate with the internal scripts. During the drafting of the VRML 2.0 specification, there were some moves to get an external interface as well. Although this was dropped from the final specification, design of the external interface is starting to happen.

At the time of this writing, there was no firm decision on which of the proposals was favored, but a decision should be reached by the time you read this. If you want to know more about this, check out the latest version of the VRML specification, which can be found at this site:

```
http://vag.vrml.org/
```

Summary

With the tools presented in this chapter, you should be able to create whatever you require of the real cyberspace. There is only so much you can do with a 2D screen in terms of new information-presentation techniques. The third dimension provided by VRML enables you to create experiences that are far beyond that of the Web page. 3D representation of data and VR behavior programming is still very much in its infancy. The limits are set only by your imagination—and CPU horsepower, of course!

Sony's Community Place (`http://www.spiw.com/vs`) and DimensionX's Liquid Reality (`http://www.dimensionx.com/products/lr`) were the only products available at the time of this writing and did not contain a complete implementation of the final spec. So take everything with a grain of salt and test everything properly. I'm bound to have got something wrong!

If you are serious about creating behaviors, learning VRML thoroughly is a must. There are many little problems that catch the unwary, particularly in the peculiarities of the VRML syntax when you are ordering objects within the scene graph. An object placed at the wrong level severely restricts its actions. A book on VRML is a must for this work—my introductory book, *Laura Lemay's Web Workshop: 3D Graphics and VRML 2* fits nicely with this chapter.

Whether it is creating reusable behavior libraries, an intelligent postman that brings the mail to you wherever you are, or simply a functional Java machine for your virtual office, the excitement of behavior programming awaits you.

Integrating Java and JavaScript

by Rick Darnell

IN THIS CHAPTER

CHAPTER 37

You've learned a lot so far about how to make Java a part of your Web pages. Standing alone, Java is a significant development because of its ability to stretch the behavior of your Web pages far beyond what was ever imagined for the World Wide Web.

Java can become even more powerful when harnessed with JavaScript. As you know from other chapters, although Java is powerful enough to add animation, sound, and other features to an applet, it's very cumbersome to directly interact with an HTML page. JavaScript isn't big or powerful enough to match Java's programming power, but it is uniquely suited to work directly with the elements that comprise an HTML document.

By combining the best features of both Java and JavaScript, your applet can interact with your Web page, offering a new level of interactivity.

Setting the Stage

For Java and JavaScript to interact on your Web pages, they both must be active and enabled in the user's browser.

To make sure that both features are active in Netscape Navigator when the user views Java applets, include these simple directions:

1. Choose Options, Network Preferences from the menu bar. The Preferences dialog box appears.

2. Select the Languages tab from the Preferences dialog box (see Figure 37.1).

3. Both Java and JavaScript are enabled by default. If this has changed, make sure that both checkboxes are selected.

FIGURE 37.1.

The Languages tab in the Network Preferences dialog box controls whether or not Java applets and JavaScript commands are processed for HTML documents.

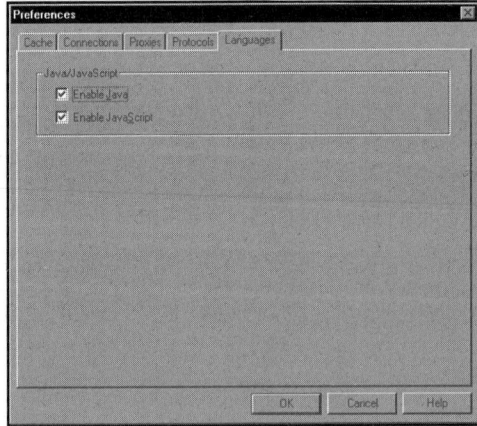

The steps to include to make sure that both languages are active in Microsoft Internet Explorer are similar to the steps for Navigator:

1. Choose View, Options from the menu bar. The Options dialog box appears.

2. Select the Security tab from the Options dialog box (see Figure 37.2).

3. Make sure that the Enable Java Programs checkbox is selected. The scripting languages available in Internet Explorer, JavaScript, and VBScript are automatically enabled; there is no way to disable them.

FIGURE 37.2.

Internet Explorer controls which language features are enabled from the Security tab in the Options dialog box.

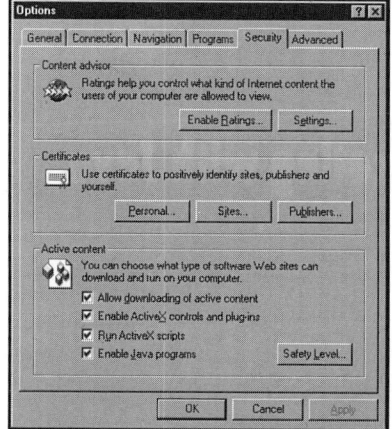

NOTE

Netscape Navigator also includes a Java Console for displaying applet-generated messages (see Figure 37.3). In addition to system messages such as errors and exceptions, the Java Console is where any messages generated by the applet using the `java.lang.System` package (including `System.out.println`) are displayed. To display the console, select Options, Show Java Console from the Netscape Navigator menu bar.

Microsoft Internet Explorer can show the results of system messages also, but not in real time as Navigator's Java Console can do. All messages are saved in `javalog.txt` in `C:\Windows\Java`. To make sure that this feature is active, select View, Options from the menu bar, select the Advanced tab in the Options dialog box, and make sure that the Java Logging checkbox is selected.

continues

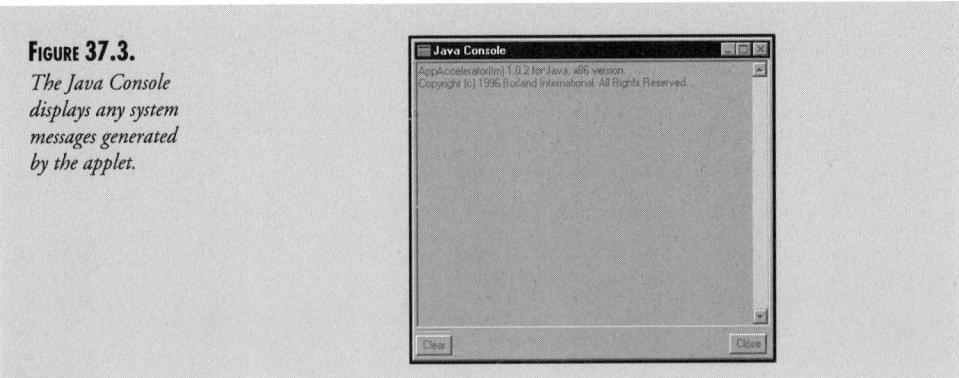

FIGURE 37.3.
The Java Console displays any system messages generated by the applet.

Communicating with Java

The first and most commonly used feature of communication is to modify applet behavior from JavaScript. This is really quite easy to do with the right information, and it allows your applet to respond to events on the HTML page, including interacting with forms.

Java object syntax is very similar to other JavaScript object syntax, so if you're already familiar with this scripting language, adding Java control is an easy step.

Calling Java Methods

With Navigator 3.0, Netscape is providing a brand-new, never-before-seen object called `Packages`; the `Packages` object allows JavaScript to invoke native Java methods directly. This object is used in much the same way as the `Document` or `Window` objects are in regular JavaScript.

> **NOTE**
>
> As you'll recall from earlier discussions, groups of related classes are combined in a construct called a *package*. Classes from a package can be used by outside classes by using the `import` command.
>
> Just to confuse things, that's not the case with the JavaScript version of `Packages`. In JavaScript, `Packages` is the parent object used to invoke native Java methods, such as `Packages.System.out.println("Say Howdy")`.

CAUTION

Invoking native Java methods from JavaScript is possible only within Netscape Navigator 3.0 or later. Microsoft Internet Explorer doesn't include support for the JavaScript-to-Java packages in its 3.0 release, but may include its own version of this capability in later versions.

The source of the problem is that JavaScript is implemented individually for each browser; what Netscape includes for JavaScript isn't the same as what Microsoft includes. In the fast-paced world of browsers, however, you can expect Microsoft to catch up quickly.

Internet Explorer still includes support for all the now-standard features of JavaScript, including control and manipulation of windows, documents, and forms.

Here is the syntax to call a Java package directly:

```
[Packages.]packageName.className.methodName
```

The object name is optional for the three default packages—`java`, `sun`, and `netscape`. These three can be referenced by their package name alone, as shown here:

```
java.className.methodName
sun.className.methodName
netscape.className.methodName
```

Together with the package name, the object and class names can result in some unwieldy and error-prone typing. This is why you can also create new variables using the `Package` product. The following code assigns a Java package to the variable `System` and then uses the `System` variable to call a method in the package:

```
var System = Package.java.lang.System;
System.out.println("Hello from Java in JavaScript.");
```

Controlling Java Applets

Controlling an applet with a script is a fairly easy matter, but it does require some knowledge of the applet you're working with. Any public variable, method, or property within the applet is accessible through JavaScript.

TIP

If you're changing the values of variables within an applet, the safest way to do so is to create a new method within the applet for the purpose. This method can accept the value from JavaScript, perform any error checking, and then pass the new value along to the rest of the applet. This arrangement helps prevent unexpected behavior or applet crashes.

You have to know which methods, properties, and variables in the applet are public. Only the public items in an applet are accessible to JavaScript.

> **TIP**
>
> Two public methods are common to all applets and you can always use them—start() and stop(). These methods provide a handy way to control when the applet is active and running.

There are five basic activities common to all applets, as opposed to one basic activity for applications. An applet has more activities to correspond to the major events in its life cycle on the user's browser. None of the activities have any definitions. You must override the methods with a subclass within your applet. Here are the five activities common to all applets:

- **Initialization.** Occurs after the applet is first loaded. This activity can include creating objects, setting state variables, and loading images.
- **Starting.** After being initialized or stopped, an applet is started. The difference between being initialized and starting is that the former only happens once; the latter can occur many times.
- **Painting.** The paint() method is how the applet actually gets information to the screen, from simple lines and text to images and colored backgrounds. Painting can occur a lot of times in the course of an applet's life.
- **Stopping.** Stopping suspends applet execution and stops the applet from using system resources. This activity can be an important addition to your code because an applet continues to run even after a user leaves the page.
- **Destroying.** This activity is the extreme form of stop. Destroying an applet begins a clean-up process in which running threads are terminated and objects are released.

With this information in hand, getting started begins with the applet tag. It helps to give a name to your applet to make JavaScript references to it easier to read. The following snippit of code shows the basic constructor for an HTML applet tag that sets the stage for JavaScript control of a Java applet. The tag is identical to the tags you used in previous chapters to add applets, except that a new attribute is included for a name:

```
<APPLET CODE="UnderConstruction" NAME="AppletConstruction" WIDTH=60 HEIGHT=60>
</APPLET>
```

Assigning a name to your applet isn't absolutely necessary because JavaScript creates an array of applets when the page is loaded. However, doing so makes for a much more readable page.

> **CAUTION**
>
> Like the JavaScript `Packages` object, the JavaScript `applets` array is currently available only in Netscape Navigator 3.0 or later. This doesn't leave Microsoft Internet Explorer completely out in the cold–JavaScript can still reference an applet in Explorer using the applet's name.

To use a method of the applet from JavaScript, use the following syntax:

```
document.appletName.methodOrProperty
```

> **TIP**
>
> Netscape Navigator 3.0 uses an `applets` array to reference all the applets on a page. The `applets` array is used according to the following syntax:
>
> ```
> document.applets[index].methodOrProperty
> document.applets[appletName].methodOrProperty
> ```
>
> These two methods also identify the applet you want to control, but the method using the applet's name without the `applets` array is the easiest to read and requires the least amount of typing.
>
> Like other arrays, one of the properties of `applets` is `length`, which returns how many applets are in the document.
>
> This array of applets is not currently available in the Microsoft Internet Explorer 3.0 implementation of JavaScript.

One of the easy methods of controlling applet behavior is starting and stopping its execution. You start and stop an applet using the `start()` and `stop()` methods that are common to every applet. Use a form and two buttons to add the functions to your Web page (see Figure 37.4). The following code snippet is a basic example of the HTML code needed to add the buttons, with the name of the applet substituted for *appletName*.

```
<FORM>
<INPUT TYPE="button" VALUE="Start" onClick="document.appletName.start()">
<INPUT TYPE="button" VALUE="Stop" onClick="document.appletName.stop()">
</FORM>
```

You can also call other methods, depending on their visibility to the world outside the applet. JavaScript can call any method or variable with a `public` declaration.

FIGURE 37.4.

One of the simplest methods of controlling an applet is to use buttons that start and stop it.

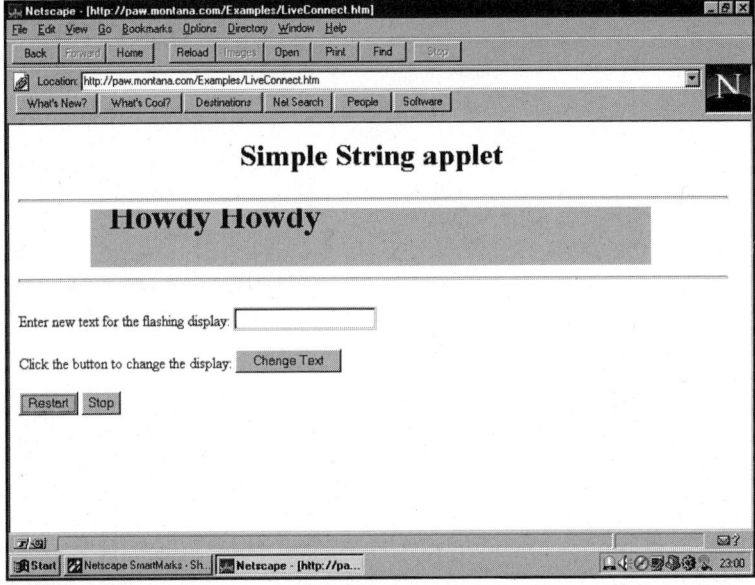

TIP

Any variable or method within the applet that doesn't include a specific declaration of scope is `protected` by default. If you don't see the `public` declaration, it's not.

The syntax to call applet methods from JavaScript is simple and can be integrated with browser events, such as the button code snippet just shown. The basic syntax for calling an applet method from Java is shown here:

```
document.appletName.methodName(arg1,...,argx)
```

To call the `stop()` method from the `underConstructionApplet` applet within an HTML page, the syntax is as follows (assuming that the applet is the first one listed on the page):

```
document.underConstructionApplet.stop();
```

Here's how you do it with Navigator (again, assuming that the applet is the first one listed on the page):

```
document.applets[0].stop();
```

Integrating the `start()` and `stop()` methods for this applet with the applet tag and button code snippet used earlier results in the following code:

```
<APPLET CODE="UnderConstruction" NAME="underConstructionApplet" WIDTH=60
➥HEIGHT=60></APPLET>
```

```
<FORM>
<INPUT TYPE="button" VALUE="Start"
➥onClick="document.underConstructionApplet.start()">
<INPUT TYPE="button"  VALUE="Stop"
➥onClick="document.underConstructionApplet.stop()">
</FORM>
```

Communicating with JavaScript

With the addition of a new set of classes provided with Netscape Navigator 3.0, Java can take a direct look at your HTML page through JavaScript objects. To implement this functionality, you must import the `netscape.javascript.JSObject` class when the applet is created.

> **TIP**
>
> In most applets, the `java` package is all you need. The `netscape` package includes methods and properties for Java to reach out to JavaScript and HTML (as covered later in this chapter). The last package, `sun`, includes platform-specific and system utility classes.

> **TIP**
>
> The `netscape.javascript.JSObject` class is included with the other class files in the Netscape folder in the `java_30` file. In Windows, the complete location is `\Program Files\Netscape\Navigator\Program\java\classes`. To enable the Java compiler to find the packages, you'll have to create a new set of folders under `\Java\Lib` called `\netscape\javascript` and then copy `java_30` to the new location.
>
> The `netscape.javascript.JSObject` class extends the standard Java `Object` class, so the newly created `JSObject` objects are treated as other Java objects.

To include the `JSObject` class as part of your applet, use the `import` command as you normally do to include any other class package:

```
import netscape.javascript.JSObject;
```

Another important addition is necessary in the applet tag—`MAYSCRIPT`. This security feature gives specific permission for the applet to access JavaScript objects. Here's how to include the tag:

```
<APPLET CODE="colorPreview.class" WIDTH=50 HEIGHT=50 NAME="Preview" MAYSCRIPT>
```

Without the `MAYSCRIPT` parameter, any attempt to access JavaScript from the applet results in an exception. If you want to exclude an applet from accessing the page, simply leave out the `MAYSCRIPT` parameter.

Java and JavaScript Values

The JSObject class gives Java the ability to look at and change objects defined through JavaScript. This requires certain assumptions, especially when passing or receiving values from Java. To ensure compatibility, every JavaScript value is assigned some form from java.lang.Object:

- **Objects.** Any object sent or received from Java remains in its original object wrapper.

- **Java numbers.** Because JavaScript doesn't support the variety of numerical types Java does (byte, char, short, int, long, float, and double), numerical types lose their specific type and become a basic JavaScript number.

- **JavaScript numbers.** There's no way to tell what kind of number Java may be receiving from JavaScript, so all JavaScript numbers are converted to Java float types.

- **Booleans and strings.** These types are passed essentially unchanged. Java booleans become JavaScript booleans and vice versa. The same is true for strings.

Looking at the JavaScript Window

To get a handle on JavaScript objects—including form items and frames—you must first create an object to hold the current Navigator window. The getWindow() method provides the means.

First, you have to create a new variable of type JSObject:

```
JSObject jsWin;
```

Then, using the JSObject class, assign the window to the variable:

```
jsWin = JSObject.getWindow(this);
```

> **TIP**
>
> This type of work is typically accomplished within the applet's init() method.

After you have a handle on the window, you can start to break it apart into its various components with getMember(). This method returns a specific object from the next level of precedence. For example, to get a handle on a form on a Web page with a form called response, you can use the following set of statements:

```
jsWin = JSObject.getWindow(this);
JSObject jsDoc = (JSObject) jsWin.getMember("document");
JSObject responseForm = (JSObject) jsDoc.getMember("response");
```

In JavaScript, this form is referred to as `window.document.response`. Note that each JavaScript object is assigned to its own variable in Java and is not a property of a parent object. The form in Java is contained in `responseForm`, not in `jsWin.jsDoc.responseForm`.

NOTE

All parts of an HTML document exist in JavaScript in set relationships to each other. This arrangement is called *instance hierarchy* because it works with specific items on the page, rather than general classes of items.

At the top of the pyramid is the `window` object. It is the parent of all other objects. Its children include `document`, `location`, and `history`, which share a precedence level. The `document` object's children include objects specific to the page, such as forms, links, anchors, and applets.

The Java `netscape` package recognizes and uses this hierarchy through its `getWindow()` and `getMethod()` methods. The first gets the `window` object (the highest object); the latter returns individual members of the next level.

So far, you've retrieved only broad objects, such as windows and forms. Getting a specific value from JavaScript follows the same principles, although now you need a Java variable of the proper type to hold the results instead of an instance of `JSObject`.

TIP

Don't forget about passing numbers between JavaScript and Java. All JavaScript numbers are converted to a float. You can cast it to another Java type if needed once the value is in the applet.

Using the form described earlier in this section, suppose that there is a text field (`name`), a number (`idNum`), and a checkbox (`member`). You can retrieve each of these values from JavaScript using the following commands:

```
jsWin = JSObject.getWindow(this);
JSObject jsDoc = (JSObject) jsWin.getMember("document");
JSObject responseForm = (JSObject) jsDoc.getMember("response");
JSObject nameField = (JSObject) responseForm.getMember("name");
JSOBject idNumField = (JSObject) responseForm.getMember("idNum");
JSOBject memberField = (JSObject) responseForm.getMember("memberField");
String nameValue = (String) nameField.getMember("value");
Float idNumValue = (Float) idNumField.getMember("value");
Boolean memberValue = (Boolean) memberField.getMember("checked");
```

This chunk of code becomes a bit unwieldy, especially when you need several values from Java-Script. If you need to access more than several elements on a page, it can help to create a new method to handle the process.

The `getElement()` method defined in the next code snippet accepts the name of a form and element on an HTML page as arguments and returns a `JSObject` that contains it:

```
protected JSObject getElement(String formName, String elementName) {
    JSObject jsDoc = (JSObject) JSObject.getWindow().getMember("document");
    JSObject jsForm = (JSObject) jsDoc.getMember(formName);
    JSObject jsElement = (JSObject) jsElement.getMember(elementName);
    return jsElement;
}
```

This simple method creates the intervening `JSObject` objects needed to get to the form element, making the retrieval as easy as knowing the form and element name. If the form or form element is not included on the page, the method throws an exception and halts the applet.

To change a JavaScript value, use the `JSObject` `setMember()` method in Java. The syntax is `setMember(`*name*`, `*value*`)`, with the *name* of the JavaScript object and its new *value*. The following snippet uses the `getElement()` method just defined to get the `name` element from the `response` form, and then uses the `JSObject` method `setMember()` to set its value to `Your Name Here`. This is equivalent to the `this.`*name* `= `*newValue* statement in JavaScript.

```
JSObject nameField = getElement("response","name");
nameField.setMember("name","Your Name Here");
```

The `getWindow()` and `getMember()` methods just described are the basic methods used when interfacing with JavaScript. Together, they make receiving values from an HTML page with JavaScript a straightforward task—even if the process is a little cumbersome in the number of statements required.

Getting Values Using Indexes

If your applet is designed to work with a variety of HTML pages that may contain different names for forms and elements, you can use the JavaScript arrays with the `JSObject` slot methods. If the desired form is always the first to appear on the document and the element is the third, then the form name is `forms[0]` and the element is `elements[2]`.

After retrieving the document object using `getWindow()` and `getMember()`, use `getSlot(`*index*`)` to return a value within it. For example, in an HTML document containing three forms, the second is retrieved into Java using the following commands:

```
JSOBject jsWin = JSObject.getWindow(this);
JSObject jsDoc = (JSObject) jsWin.getMember("document");
JSObject jsForms = (JSObject) jsDoc.getMember("forms");
JSObject jsForm1 = (JSObject) jsForms.getSlot(1);
```

Using setSlot(), the same process is used to load a value into an array. The syntax is shown here:

```
JSObject.setSlot(index,value);
```

In this syntax, the index is an integer and the value is a String, boolean, or float.

> **TIP**
>
> The one rule that must stand firm is the placement of the form and the elements within it. When the applet is used with more than one document, the forms and elements must be in the same relative place every time to avoid exceptions and unpredictable results.

Using JavaScript Methods in Java

The netscape class package provides two methods to call JavaScript methods from within an applet: call() and eval(). The syntax differs slightly for the two methods, but the outcome is the same.

> **TIP**
>
> You need a handle for the JavaScript window before you can use the call() and eval() methods.

There are two ways to invoke these methods. The first uses a specific window instance; the second uses getWindow() to create a JavaScript window just for the expression:

```
jsWin.callOrEval(arguments)
JSOBject.getWindow().callOrEval(arguments)
```

The call() method separates the method from its arguments. This is useful for passing Java values to the JavaScript method. The syntax is call("method", args), where method is the name of the method you want to call and the arguments you want to pass are contained in an array.

The eval() method, on the other hand, uses a string that appears identical to the way a method is called within JavaScript. The syntax is eval("expression"), where expression is a complete method name and its arguments, such as document.writeln("Your name here.'"). Here's what it looks like when you include the string with the eval() expression:

```
eval("document.writeln(\"Your name here.\");")
```

> **TIP**
>
> To pass quotation marks as quotation marks to JavaScript within a Java string, use the backslash character before each occurrence.

Summary

Now you have a whole set of tools to get from JavaScript to Java and back again. The marriage of these two Web technologies can open up a whole new world of how to interact with your users. By using simple statements and definitions—already a part of both languages—you can make a previously static Web page communicate with an applet embedded in it; in return, the Web page can react to the output of the applet.

JavaScript-to-Java communication is a simple extension of JavaScript's functionality. As long as your applets have names, any applet's `public` method is accessible to your HTML page. And using the new Netscape package `netscape.javascript` makes the process a two-way street, allowing your Java applet to invoke JavaScript functions and look at the structure of your Web page as represented by the JavaScript document object.

This combination is one more set of capabilities in your toolbox that you can use to meet your users' needs.

Integrating Java and ActiveX

by Michael Morrison

IN THIS CHAPTER

With the full force of Microsoft behind it, it's no surprise that ActiveX has received tons of press attention lately. As an Internet developer, you probably have some degree of confusion about how ActiveX fits into the Internet landscape. More specifically, you may be worried about what impact ActiveX will have on Java. This chapter takes a close look at Java and ActiveX and where each fits in the world of Internet development. This chapter also dicusses an ActiveX technology that enables the integration of Java and ActiveX.

The goal of this chapter is to give you some perspective on the relationship between Java and ActiveX. In doing so, you learn the details surrounding what each technology offers and why they don't necessarily have to be viewed as direct competitors. You also learn about a specific technology that aims to allow Java and ActiveX to happily coexist.

Technological Goals

In a general sense, Java and ActiveX both try to achieve the same goal: to bring interactivity to the Web. Because this is a very general goal, you probably realize that many different approaches can be taken to reach it. Java and ActiveX definitely take different routes to delivering interactivity to the Web, and for good reason—they're widely divergent technologies that come from two unique companies. Let's take a look at each technology and see what it accomplishes in its quest to liven up the Web.

The Java Vision

First and foremost, Java is a programming language. It certainly is other things as well, but the underlying strength of the Java technology is the structure and design of the Java language itself. The architects at Sun wanted to take many of the powerful features in C++ and build a tighter, easier-to-use, and more secure object-oriented language. They succeeded in a big way: Java is indeed a very clean, easy-to-use language with lots of advanced security features. The time spent designing the Java language is paying off well for Sun because the language's structure is the primary cause of the C++ programmer migration to Java.

However, the Java language without its standard class libraries and Internet support would be nothing more than competition for C++. In fact, the Java language, as cool as it is, would probably fail in a head-to-head match with C++ strictly from a language perspective. This is because C++ is firmly established in the professional development community, and programmers need a very compelling reason to learn an entirely new language. Sun realized this, and was smart enough to present Java as much more than just another programming language.

The basic Java technology consists of the Java language, the Java class libraries, the Java runtime system, and the JavaScript scripting language. It's the combination of all these parts that makes the Java technology so exciting. Java is the first large-scale effort at creating a truly cross-platform programming language with lots of functionality from the start. Couple the slick language and cross-platform aspects of Java with its capability to seamlessly integrate Java programs into the Web environment and you can easily see its appeal.

This integration of the Web into the Java technology is no accident; Sun simply saw the potential to capitalize on a technology they had been developing for a while by fitting it to the rapidly growing needs of the Internet. This pretty much sums up the primary aim of Java: To provide a means to safely integrate cross-platform interactive applications into the Web environment using an object-oriented language. Keep in mind, however, that new innovations such as JavaOS and Java microprocessors are rapidly altering and expanding Sun's vision of the Java technology.

The ActiveX Vision

Microsoft has different ideas for the Internet than Sun. Unlike Sun, Microsoft initially didn't realize the immediate potential of the Internet, or at least didn't see how fast it was all happening. In fact, it wasn't until the excitement surrounding Java had begun to peak that Microsoft finally decided they had to rethink things in regard to the Internet and the Web.

The connection was finally made somewhere in Redmond that the Internet would significantly affect personal computing. They couldn't just sit idly by and see what happened; they could either take action to capitalize on the Internet or get burnt by not accepting it as a major shift in the way we all use computers. When Microsoft finally came to terms with the fact that the Internet was rapidly changing the face of computing—even personal computing—the company quickly regrouped and decided to figure out a way to get a piece of the Internet action. Keep in mind that Microsoft has never been content with just *a* piece of the action; they want the *largest* piece of the action!

Unlike Sun, Microsoft already had a wide range of successful commercial software technologies; they just had to figure out which one of them would scale best to the Internet. It turned out that one of their most successful technologies was ideally suited for the Internet: OLE (Object Linking and Embedding). They saw OLE as a powerful, stable technology with lots of potential for the Internet, and they were right; ActiveX is basically OLE revamped for the Internet.

Unlike Java, however, ActiveX isn't meant to be just a way to add interactivity to the Web. Sure, that's part of it, but Microsoft isn't the type of company to just hand out technologies for the good of humanity. OLE is a technology deeply ingrained in most of Microsoft's commercial products, as well as many other commercial Windows applications. By simply migrating OLE to the Internet (through ActiveX), Microsoft effectively assumes a huge market share of Internet products overnight. Suddenly, every piece of code written based on OLE can now be considered ActiveX-enabled with little extra work. Microsoft's new goal of migrating desktop software to the Internet suddenly looks quite attainable.

38

INTEGRATING JAVA AND ACTIVEX

Although Microsoft is certainly looking to bring interactive applications to the Web with ActiveX, they are also looking to make sure that many of those interactive applications are Microsoft applications. This situation also ensures that Windows remains a strong presence on the Internet because OLE is essentially a Windows-derived technology. Although strategically ideal, the selection of OLE as the technological underpinnings for ActiveX has much more to do with the fact that OLE is a slick technology already tweaked for distributed computing; it's just the icing on the cake that OLE is already firmly established in the PC software community.

Microsoft isn't the only company to benefit from the positioning of ActiveX. Every PC software developer that uses OLE in its applications will benefit from ActiveX just as easily as Microsoft. Because the PC development community is by far the largest in the industry, end users also benefit greatly because many software companies will be building ActiveX applications from existing OLE code that is already stable.

In the discussion of ActiveX thus far, little has been said about programming languages. Unlike Java, ActiveX has nothing to do with a specific programming language; you can write ActiveX code in any language you choose that supports Microsoft's COM specification. Just in case you don't realize it, this is a big deal! Although Java is a very cool language, many programmers don't like being forced to learn a new language just to exploit the capabilities of the Internet. On the other hand, writing ActiveX controls in C++ is a little messier than writing Java applets in Java.

Under the Hood

Okay, so you have an idea about what each technology is trying to accomplish—but what does each actually deliver? It turns out that Java and ActiveX are surprisingly different in their implementations, especially considering how similar their ultimate goals are.

Under Java's Hood

The Java technology can be divided into four major components:

- The Java language
- The Java class libraries
- The Java runtime system
- The JavaScript scripting language

The Java language provides the programmatic underpinnings that make the whole Java system possible. It is the Java language that shines the brightest when comparing Java to ActiveX. The Java class libraries, which go hand in hand with the language, provide a wide array of features guaranteed to work on any platform. This is a huge advantage Java has over almost every other programming language in existence. Never before has a tight, powerful language been delivered that offers a rich set of standard classes in a cross-platform manner.

The Java runtime system is the component of Java that gets the least press attention, but ultimately makes many of Java's features a reality. The Java runtime system includes a virtual machine, which stands between Java bytecode programs and the specific processor inside a computer system. It is the responsibility of the virtual machine to translate platform-independent bytecodes to platform-specific native machine code. In doing so, the virtual machine provides the mechanism that makes Java platform-independent. Unfortunately, the virtual machine is also responsible for the performance problems associated with Java. These problems will go away, however, as just-in-time Java compilers evolve to become more efficient.

The JavaScript scripting language is the Java component that allows you to embed scripted Java programs directly into HTML code. The primary purpose of JavaScript is to allow Web developers who aren't necessarily programmers to add interactivity to their Web pages in a straightforward manner.

Under ActiveX's Hood

The ActiveX technology can be broken down into the following major components:

- ActiveX controls
- ActiveX scripting (VBScript)
- ActiveX documents
- ActiveX server scripting (ISAPI)

ActiveX controls are self-contained executable software components that can be embedded within a Web page or a standalone application. Acting as an extension to OLE controls, ActiveX controls can be employed to perform a wide range of functions, both with or without specific support for the Internet. ActiveX controls are essentially Microsoft's answer to Java applets, although ActiveX controls are significantly more open-ended than Java applets.

> **NOTE**
>
> Although ActiveX controls are similar to Java applets, ActiveX controls are true software components. Java Beans components, when they become available in the very near future, will be the closer Java equivalent to ActiveX controls.

Whereas ActiveX controls are Microsoft's answer to Java applets, VBScript is Microsoft's answer to JavaScript. Built on the highly successful Visual Basic programming language, VBScript provides much of the same functionality as JavaScript, but in an environment already familiar to many PC developers.

ActiveX documents are similar to ActiveX controls, except that they are focused on the representation and manipulation of a particular data format, such as a Word document or an Excel spreadsheet. There is no logical equivalent in Java to ActiveX documents; ActiveX documents are a piece of the ActiveX technology that is completely foreign to Java.

The final component of ActiveX is the ISAPI scripting language and server support. ISAPI provides a more powerful answer to CGI scripting, which has long been used to provide pseudo-interactivity for Web pages. ISAPI even goes a step further by providing a means to build filters into Web servers. Java servlets will eventually provide a similar functionality as ISAPI scripting.

Practical Implications

By now, you not only understand what Java and ActiveX are trying to accomplish, but you have a good idea of how each is going about delivering on its promises. I've mentioned some of the differences between each technology while describing the relevant aspects of them, but it's time to dig in and take a look at what these differences really mean.

Although ActiveX as a technology delivers a little more than Java does as far as the individual components, the primary interest for most developers is how ActiveX and Java stack up from the standpoint of adding interactivity to Web pages. This question forces you to analyze the differences between ActiveX controls and Java applets because those are currently the primary aspects of each technology that deliver Web page interactivity.

Probably the most significant divisive issue between ActiveX and Java is security. No one argues the fact that security is an enormous issue when it comes to the Internet. Both Sun and Microsoft saw the importance of security and took appropriate actions in designing their respective technologies. However, they each took a different approach, resulting in drastically different usage issues. You already learned about some of these security issues in Chapter 35, "Java Security," but I'm going to go over them again briefly here because they are so critical in the discussion of Java and ActiveX.

Let's first consider Sun's approach to security: Java's security consists primarily of verifying the bytecodes as a program is being interpreted on the client end. It also does not allow applets access to a client user's hard drive. The first solution of verifying bytecodes, although imposing somewhat of a performance hit, is reasonable. However, the limitation of not being able to access the hard drive is pretty harsh. No doubt, Sun took the safest route—it's very unlikely that anyone can corrupt a user's hard drive using Java, considering that you can't access it. Because of this limitation, it's also equally unlikely that developers will be able to write Java applets that perform any significant function beyond working with data on a server.

Now consider Microsoft's security approach with ActiveX: ActiveX employs a digital signature attached to each control; the signature specifies the original author of the control. The signature is designed so that any tampering with an executable after its release invalidates the signature. What this means is that you have the ability to know who the original author of a control is, and therefore limit your use of controls to only those written by established software vendors. If someone hacks into a control developed by an established vendor, the signature protects you. Granted, this approach pushes some responsibility back onto the user, but it's a practical reality that freedom never comes without a certain degree of added responsibility.

When it comes to security, I think Microsoft has capitalized on what a lot of people are starting to perceive as a major flaw in Java. For the record, Microsoft implemented the signature approach in ActiveX after the release of Java, meaning that they had the advantage of seeing how Sun tackled the security issue and were then able to improve on it. There is nothing wrong with this, it's just an example of how every technology, no matter how powerful and popular, is always susceptible to another one coming along and taking things a step further.

Before you think that Microsoft has won the security issue, let me add that Sun is in the process of adding an extensive digital signature model to Java. Digital signatures will more than likely lift the tight security restrictions on Java applets and put the security issue for both technologies on common ground.

A Peaceful Coexistence

Even though I've presented Java and ActiveX as competing technologies in a lot of ways, please understand that I don't see Java and ActiveX as an either/or proposition. The software development community is far too diverse to say that one technology surpasses another in every possible way. In addition, consider that both of these technologies are in a constant state of flux, with new announcements and releases popping up weekly. In my opinion, it's foolish to think that a single software technology will take the Internet by storm and eliminate all others. Java will naturally find its way to where it is best suited, as will ActiveX. Likewise, smart software developers will keep up with both technologies and learn to apply each in cases where the benefits of one outweighs the other.

And in case you're getting nervous about having to learn two completely new types of programming, here's some reassuring news: Microsoft has released a technology that allows developers to integrate Java applets with ActiveX controls. What does that mean? Well, because ActiveX is language independent, you can write ActiveX controls in Java. Furthermore, it means you can access ActiveX controls from Java applets and vice versa. To me, this is a very exciting prospect: the ability to mix two extremely powerful yet seemingly divergent technologies as you see fit.

The technology I'm talking about is an ActiveX control that acts as a Java virtual machine. What is a Java virtual machine? A *Java virtual machine* is basically a Java interpreter, which means it is ultimately responsible for how Java programs are executed. By implementing a Java virtual machine in an ActiveX control, Microsoft has effectively integrated Java into the ActiveX environment. This integration goes well beyond just being able to execute Java applets like they are ActiveX controls; it provides a means for ActiveX controls and Java applets to interact with each other.

Microsoft's willingness to embrace Java as a means of developing ActiveX objects should give you a clue about the uniqueness of each technology. It could well end up that Java emerges as the dominant programming language for the Internet, while ActiveX emerges as the distributed interactive application standard. I know this seems like a confusing situation, but it does capitalize on the strengths of both Java and ActiveX. On the other hand, the Java Beans component technology could emerge as a serious contender on the component front and give ActiveX some competition.

The main point is that ActiveX and Java are both strong in different ways, which puts them on a collision course of sorts. The software development community is pretty objective; if programmers can have the best of both worlds by integrating ActiveX and Java, then why not do it? No doubt both Sun and Microsoft will have a lot to say about this prospect in the near future. The ActiveX Java virtual machine is a major step in the right direction.

Integrating Java and ActiveX

As you just learned, the ActiveX Java virtual machine (VM) control allows Java programs to run within the context of an ActiveX control. What does this really mean from the perspective of a developer wanting to mix Java and ActiveX? It means you can treat a Java class just like an ActiveX control and interact with it from other ActiveX controls. In other words, the Java VM control gives a Java class the component capabilities of an ActiveX control.

You now understand that Java classes and ActiveX controls can interact with each other through the Java VM control, but you're probably still curious about the specifics. One of the most important issues surrounding Java's integration with ActiveX is the underlying Component Object Model (COM) protocol used by ActiveX. COM is a component software protocol that is the basis for ActiveX. The importance it has in regard to Java is that Java's integration with ActiveX really has more to do with COM than with the specifics of ActiveX. So, when I refer to Java integrating with ActiveX, understand that the COM protocol is really what is making things happen under the hood.

This brings us to the different scenarios under which Java and ActiveX can coexist. Keep in mind that some of these scenarios require not only the Java VM control at runtime but also support for Java/ActiveX integration at development time. In other words, you may have to use a development tool that supports Java/ActiveX integration, such as Microsoft Visual J++. Following is a list of the different situations possible when integrating Java and ActiveX using the Java VM control:

- Using an ActiveX control as a Java class
- Using a Java class as an ActiveX control
- Manipulating a Java applet through ActiveX scripting

Using an ActiveX Control as a Java Class

It is possible to use an ActiveX control just as you would a Java class in Java source code. To do this, you must create a Java class that wraps the ActiveX control and then import the class just as you would any other Java class defined in another package. The end result is that an ActiveX control appears just like a Java class at the source code level. Because we are talking about Java source code here, the Java compiler has to play a role in making this arrangement work. So, this approach requires support for Java/ActiveX integration in the Java compiler. The Visual J++ Java compiler includes this exact support.

Visual J++ includes a tool that automatically generates Java wrapper classes for ActiveX controls. You can then import these wrapper classes into your Java code and use them just like any other Java class. Of course, behind the scenes, the ActiveX control is actually doing all the work, but from a strictly programming perspective, the Java wrapper class is all you have to be concerned with.

Using a Java Class as an ActiveX Control

Just as you can use an ActiveX control as a Java class, you can also use a Java class as an ActiveX control. Because ActiveX controls are manipulated through interfaces, you have to design Java classes a little differently so that they fit into the ActiveX framework. You must first define an interface or set of interfaces for the class, using the Object Description Language (ODL) that is part of COM. You then implement these interfaces in a Java class. Finally, you assign the Java class a global class identifier and register it as an ActiveX control using a registration tool such as JavaReg, which ships with Visual J++.

I know this procedure is a little messier than simply compiling a Java class, but consider what you are gaining by taking these extra steps. You are using one set of source code and just one executable to act as both a Java object and an ActiveX control, with relatively little work. Users can then take advantage of all the benefits of component software by using your Java class as an ActiveX control.

Manipulating a Java Applet through ActiveX Scripting

Another less obvious scenario involving Java and ActiveX is your ability to manipulate Java applets through ActiveX scripting code. The ActiveX scripting protocol, which supports both VBScript and JavaScript, allows you access to all public methods and member variables defined in a Java applet. The ActiveX protocol is specifically designed to expose the public methods and member variables for Applet-derived classes, so any other classes you want scripting access to must be manipulated indirectly through public methods in the applet. You learn the specifics of using VBScript to control Java applets in Chapter 39, "Using Java with VBScript."

Summary

This chapter took an objective look at Java and ActiveX and where they fit in the quest to make the Web interactive. You learned not only about the philosophy and reasoning behind each technology, but also why the technologies don't necessarily have to be considered competition for each other. You finished up the chapter by learning about Microsoft's plans to integrate Java and ActiveX. This combination of two powerful technologies, although a little confusing at first, is crucial for Web developers because it lessens the need to pick one technology over the other. Possibly the biggest benefit is the peace of mind in knowing that you can continue working with Java without fear that Microsoft and ActiveX will sabotage your efforts.

This chapter touched on the ability to use VBScript to control Java applets. The next chapter gives the details about how VBScript works and what benefits it offers.

CHAPTER 39

Using Java with VBScript

by John J. Kottler

IN THIS CHAPTER

The World Wide Web is one of the fastest growing forms of communication today. Not only in the sheer volume of users and computers attached to the Internet, but also in the quality of material found at the countless Web sites. Just over a year ago, typical commercial Web sites featured graphics and text with very little else. Today, however, it is common to find sites that incorporate numerous technologies such as enhanced multimedia, client-side scripting, and Java or ActiveX applications.

But just as creating a useful Web site requires more than pretty pictures, interactive Web sites require much more attention to the coordination of events that a user experiences. Throughout this book, you have learned how to assemble the newest technologies available using traditional HTML as well as script languages like JavaScript and VBScript. In this chapter, you learn how to harness the power of Java applets and share data between those applets and the Web browser using the VBScript language. This chapter does not attempt to teach you the Java language or VBScript; instead, it demonstrates how to integrate the two technologies.

Wake Up and Smell the Java

No other development language has recently caught the attention of the media and computer industry like Sun Microsystems' Java (`www.javasoft.com`). Java grew from an initiative within Sun to create a development environment for small electronic devices such as pagers and cellular phones. Because of this initial requirement, Java appealed to Web site developers who wanted to create usable applications on their pages. For Internet development, it is necessary that applications do not use a large amount of space because the size of the application directly relates to the amount of time required to download it from the Internet. The Java language is based on the C++ computer programming language, with which many developers are already acquainted. These two reasons alone have greatly contributed to the popularity of Java.

Additionally, this robust development language allows developers to create truly unique Windows-style applications that run effortlessly within the confines of an Internet Web browser. Java has become the development language of choice for many Web developers because it offers various advantages for use with the Internet:

- Java is an object-oriented development environment, which allows developers to create modules for applications that can be shared and reused by other applications.
- Java produces highly secure executable programs that cannot be altered or misused.
- Java is a development environment in which a program can be written once, but executed on any type of machine.

In a world as diverse as the Internet, each of these features is indispensable. But as appealing as Java is by itself for use on the Internet, it is a development language that is not intended for the faint of heart. The ease of HTML is replaced with a C++ programming language syntax that is foreign to many users. Therefore, it is common to find many sites reusing common Java applets that can be tweaked appropriately for the site, instead of creating entirely new ones. But how is this "tweaking" accomplished and how can these Java applets communicate with more familiar HTML Web pages?

The VBScript Glue

Java applets alone on a Web page cannot communicate directly with each other or with other elements on the Web page. When creating truly interactive Web pages, this communication is essential. Imagine an orchestra in which all members played their own instruments however they wanted. The result would be far from pleasant! However, if everyone followed a musical "script" that coordinated their efforts and communicated to them when to do what, the result would be a beautiful arrangement.

The same holds true for Web page development. Although not quite as dramatic as independent musicians in an orchestra, multiple Java applets executing aimlessly on a page add little value to the overall use of the page. But when the applets are directed appropriately using predefined commands like those found in a scripting language embedded within the Web browser, the result is significantly more valuable. In a sense, scripting languages such as VBScript and JavaScript are the glue that hold Web pages and objects on those pages together.

In this chapter, you will learn how the VBScript scripting language ties Java applets and Web page material together. With VBScript, you can modify and interrogate the nature of Java applets, which allows you to create pages that extend beyond the traditional capabilities of HTML. You will also learn how it is possible to implement a mechanism for which a Java applet can notify VBScript when a particular event occurs.

> **NOTE**
>
> To establish this communication between Java applets and VBScript, it is essential that you understand the basic concepts of object-oriented technology. You may want to review Chapter 2, "Object-Oriented Programming and Java," to brush up on your object-oriented skills.

The Infamous Marquee

In this section, you learn how to use VBScript to control and be controlled by a Java applet. The examples that follow use a `Marquee` applet. Developers who are familiar with the extended HTML tags that Microsoft's Internet Explorer provides will recall the `<MARQUEE>` tag. This tag allows the Web page designer to specify text that scrolls across the Web page. This same effect can be accomplished using the `Marquee` Java applet, which can then be used on any Java-enabled Web browser. Figure 39.1 shows a sample of this applet in use with a blue textual message that scrolls from right to left on top of a white background. Portions of the Java source code for this applet are given in Listing 39.1. A complete copy of the source code for this application is available on the CD-ROM that accompanies this book.

FIGURE 39.1.

The Marquee *Java applet scrolls text horizontally within a defined region of the Web page.*

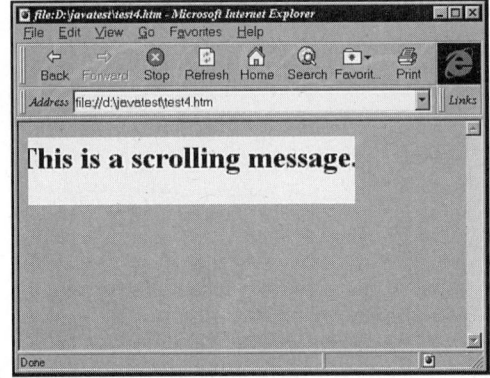

Listing 39.1. The Java source code for the Marquee **applet features public variables (properties) and methods for VBScript.**

```java
import java.awt.*;

public class Marquee extends java.applet.Applet implements Runnable {
//  These are PUBLIC variables, meaning that they can act as
//  properties which can be modified by JavaScript/VBScript
    public  String  MessageText;
    public  int     MouseClick=0;

//  If a user clicks within the Java applet, this event will
//  be triggered.
    public boolean mouseDown(Event evnt, int x, int y){
        MouseClick=1;
        return true;
    }

//  When the mouse button is released after being clicked,
//  this event will be triggered.
    public boolean mouseUp(Event evnt, int x, int y){
        MouseClick=0;
        return true;
    }

//  This method will be used by JavaScript/VBScript to update
//  text that appears within the Java applet.
    public void setText(String s) {
        MessageText=s;
    }
```

```
        }

//  NOTE:
//  The full source for the init, paint, update and thread control
//  routines can be found on the CD-ROM that accompanies this book.


    }

}
```

Marquee's Properties

The Marquee applet in Listing 39.1 allows the user to specify numerous settings using <PARAM> tags for the applet when embedding the applet on a Web page. However, these tags only specify settings when the applet is first started. You cannot dynamically change settings in the Marquee applet using the <PARAM> tag.

Therefore, the Marquee applet also contains two additional properties declared in the Java application as public variables. The public statement allows other applications or scripting languages such as VBScript to "see" these variables as properties to the Java object. In Listing 39.1, notice that MouseClick and MessageText are two properties that can be interrogated and set by VBScript.

With these two properties available to VBScript, it is possible for a VBScript application to examine what the current message is and change it while the applet is running. The MouseClick property can be set or read as well; however, it is dedicated in this case for handling events as discussed later in this chapter.

Marquee's Method

Because all the functions in the Marquee Java applet are public functions, they are all technically available for another application such as a Web browser to invoke. However, an additional method specifically for the Marquee applet has been provided to set the scrolling text. The setText() method instructs the Java applet to change the content of the message being scrolled. Notice that the setText() method expects a string as a parameter to the method. This string is the text you pass from VBScript to the Java applet and is the text that should be displayed in the marquee.

Marquee's Event

At the top of Listing 39.1, notice that two events are trapped in the Marquee applet: mouseDown and mouseUp. When a user presses the mouse button down over the Marquee applet, the mouseDown event is triggered in the Java applet. Likewise, when a user releases the mouse button, the mouseUp event is triggered. These events are typical for creating interactive Java applets. In the case of the Marquee applet, we are going to use these events to capture when a user clicks on the applet. If a user clicks on the applet, we want to notify a VBScript application on a Web page to take appropriate action. Later in this chapter, you learn how to simulate event trapping in VBScript.

Embedding Marquee on a Page

Now that you have a Java applet that you want to use on a Web page, you must place it on the page. Both Netscape Navigator 2.x and 3.x as well as the Microsoft Internet Explorer 3.x support Java applets and their respective tags: <APPLET> and <PARAM>. You can use these two tags to instruct the browser to insert the Java Marquee applet and set its properties accordingly. Listing 39.2 shows the Marquee applet embedded within a simple HTML page.

Listing 39.2. The <APPLET> and <PARAM> tags are used to embed the Marquee Java applet on a Web page.

```
<HTML>
<TITLE>
Sample Java Applet
</TITLE>

<BODY>
<APPLET NAME=Marquee CODE="Marquee.class" WIDTH=350 HEIGHT=70>
<PARAM NAME=BGCOLOR VALUE ="FFFFFF">
<PARAM NAME=TEXTCOLOR VALUE="FF0000">
<PARAM NAME=SPEED VALUE="5">
<PARAM NAME=TEXT VALUE="Enter your text here.">
</APPLET>
</BODY>
</HTML>
```

NOTE

Each Java applet on a Web page must be uniquely identified by a name (which is specified by the "Name" property of the <APPLET> tag) to be used properly within scripts. Names for applets allow scripts to determine which applets should be affected. The names assigned to applets must consist of standard alphanumeric characters and cannot contain spaces.

Controlling Java with VBScript

So you have a Web page with a Java applet that displays scrolling text. Now what? In some cases, this may be just enough. At times, a Web page developer may want to scroll important messages or advertisements using a marquee and little else. However, there may be times when the marquee's message should change dynamically. For example, a marquee that displays Good Morning to a user should display Good Evening at night. You can develop a VBScript routine that first determines the time of day and then sets the marquee's message appropriately.

Invoking Java Methods

Let's make the Marquee applet interactive to the user. People love seeing their name in lights, so we will create a Web page that accepts text input from an HTML input control and sets the marquee's text to what the user enters. Listing 39.3 shows a simple Web page with the Marquee applet, an entry field, and a button that updates the marquee when clicked. Figure 39.2 gives you an idea of what this page looks like.

Listing 39.3. The Marquee applet can be updated using VBScript.

```
<HTML>
<BODY>
<APPLET  NAME=Marquee CODE="Marquee.class" WIDTH=350 HEIGHT=70>
<PARAM   NAME=BGCOLOR VALUE="FFFFFF">
<PARAM   NAME=TEXTCOLOR VALUE="FF0000">
<PARAM   NAME=SPEED VALUE="5">
<PARAM   NAME=TEXT VALUE="Enter your text here.">
</APPLET>

<FORM>
<INPUT   NAME="InputText"
         TYPE=TEXT
         SIZE=35
        VALUE="Enter your text here."
>
<INPUT   TYPE=BUTTON
         WIDTH=200
         VALUE="Change Text"
      onClick="document.Marquee.setText(form.InputText.value)"
>
</FORM>
</BODY>
```

Figure 39.2.

An entry field can be used to type a message to be displayed in the Marquee *applet.*

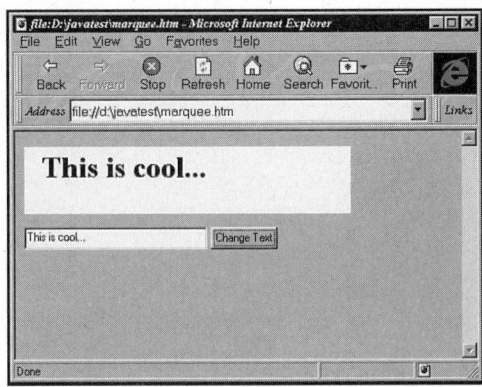

If you are familiar with VBScript or JavaScript, you will quickly realize that calling methods of Java applets is similar to calling VBScript/JavaScript or ActiveX functions. In Listing 39.3, the entry field named InputText holds whatever text the user enters. When a user clicks the Change Text button, a single line of VBScript code is invoked. This single line simply calls the setText() method of the Marquee applet, passing the string from the input field as a parameter for the method.

In general, applet methods can be addressed in VBScript using the following notation:

```
result = document.Applet Name.Applet Method(Method Parameter)
```

In this syntax, Applet Name is the name you used in the <APPLET> tag that uniquely identifies the Java applet on the Web page. Likewise, Applet Method is the name of the method an applet supports that you want to invoke. In addition, some methods may return a value that can be stored in a variable in VBScript, can be tested, or can be used in conjunction with other VBScript functions. According to the source code in Listing 39.1 for the Marquee applet, the void statement for the setText() method indicates that no value is to be returned. If an applet performed some mathematical computation, that method could return the result to VBScript.

It is common to invoke a method in a Java applet with some form of data passed to the method. For example, if you were going to use a modem to dial a phone number, you would pass the phone number to the dialing function in the modem. Just as a Java applet does not necessarily return a result value, a method can be designed that does not require input parameters.

Reading and Writing Properties

Just as you can use methods provided by a Java applet in VBScript, you can also alter the properties of an object or determine the properties' current values. To the current Marquee example, let's add a second button for a crude guessing game. When a user types a phrase and clicks the Change Text button, the Java applet changes the text in the marquee. When a user then clicks the new Guess Secret Message button, the VBScript code checks the text in the Java applet to see whether it is the secret message. The Guess Secret Message button then posts a message indicating whether or not you guessed the message correctly. Listing 39.4 presents the new HTML file for this simple game page; Figure 39.3 shows the screen after guessing the correct phrase.

Listing 39.4. The `MessageText` property of the `Marquee` applet can be read by VBScript and tested to create interactive Web pages.

```
<HTML>
<BODY>

<APPLET NAME=Marquee CODE="Marquee.class" WIDTH=350 HEIGHT=70>
<PARAM NAME=BGCOLOR VALUE="FFFFFF">
<PARAM NAME=TEXTCOLOR value="FF0000">
<PARAM NAME=SPEED value="5">
<PARAM NAME=TEXT VALUE="Enter your text here.">
</applet>

<FORM>
<INPUT   NAME="InputText"
         TYPE=text
         SIZE=35
         VALUE="Enter your text here."
>
<INPUT   TYPE=button
         WIDTH=200
         VALUE="Change Text"
      onClick="document.Marquee.setText(form.InputText.value)"
>
<P>
<INPUT   TYPE=button
         VALUE="Guess Secret Message"
      LANGUAGE="VBScript"
       onclick="if document.Marquee.MessageText='VBScript & Java' then
                    alert('You guessed the secret message!')
                else
                    alert('Nope sorry, try again.')
                end if"
>
</FORM>
</BODY>
```

Just like Java methods, properties for applets can be addressed using the following syntax:

To read a property's value:

```
result = document.Applet Name.Applet Property
```

To set a property:

```
document.Applet Name.Applet Property = Value
```

In this syntax, `Applet Name` indicates the name of the Java applet that was used in the `<APPLET>` tag for the Web page; `Applet Property` is the name of the variable you want to view or change in the Java application. Properties can be stored in variables in VBScript, used in conditional testing, or combined with other VBScript applications. You can also set properties by assigning values to them. In a sense, properties can be treated as variables in your VBScript applications.

Figure 39.3.

A simple guessing game can be made because VBScript can read the MessageText *property in the* Marquee *applet.*

In the computer modem example, the auto-answer capability can be turned on or off. A program can examine the auto-answer property and determine whether it is enabled or disabled. If it is disabled, this property can be changed to a desired setting.

> **NOTE**
>
> The names of methods, properties, and respective parameters for various Java applets vary widely. You must consult either the documentation included with the applet or its source code to determine which capabilities are available for the applet.
>
> If you are creating your own Java applets, note that functions and variables declared in a Java applet's source code that are to be treated as methods or properties for VBScript must be `public`. If functions or variables are not public, other applications or languages cannot "see" or use them as methods.

Properties versus Methods

As we examined the Marquee Java applet along with its properties and methods, you may have asked yourself this common question: "When should I use properties and when should I use methods?" In the Marquee example, the results of the setText() method could have just as easily been implemented by adjusting the MessageText property. If you are creating original Java applets, the decision is up to you when to create methods or properties for use by VBScript. You can base this decision on what makes logical sense. When using commercial or prewritten Java applets or applets without source code, however, you may not have a choice. Each developer will undoubtedly create Java methods and properties to be used by VBScript as logically as possible, although the logic may escape you at times.

In general, *properties* are the characteristics of an object and should be used to change the description of an object. Assume that we have a Java applet that plays video content. Some properties for that object are the filename of the video file to play, the current playback position in the video stream, and the option to display or hide VCR-style control buttons.

Methods, on the other hand, are typically used to instruct an object to actually perform an *action*. Properties typically set static values that in themselves do nothing; methods do the actual work. However, some methods perform differently based on current properties for an object. Using the video player example again, assume that there are methods for playing or stopping content. We can assume that the playback method plays from the current playback position in the video stream. If the stop and playback methods were invoked immediately after each other, playback would continue from wherever it had stopped last. If, on the other hand, a VBScript program stopped playback, changed the playback position property, and then issued a request to play the stream, the playback method would play from the new position indicated by the position property.

Triggering VBScript with Java Events

So far, you have learned how to control Java applets by invoking methods or changing an applet's properties. The third key component to object-oriented technology has not been addressed: events. In the beginning of this chapter, you saw that the Marquee applet traps an event when a user presses the mouse button down and traps another when the button is released. The Marquee applet was designed so that when a user clicks on the marquee, a specific action can be taken by the VBScript application for a Web page. For this example, the VBScript application will simply post a message indicating that a user has clicked the marquee.

VBScript (and JavaScript, for that matter) allows developers to control Java applets through methods and properties, but makes no provision for handling events trapped by a Java applet. Other technologies such as ActiveX provide a mechanism by which, if a particular event occurs in the ActiveX control, corresponding VBScript code can be executed in place of the typical ActiveX code.

NOTE

VBScript allows the trapping of events within a VBScript application. Events for ActiveX objects, for example, can be defined and trapped in VBScript by including a subroutine for each event. This subroutine's name must be identified using the ActiveX object name (determined in the `<OBJECT>` tag for the ActiveX control), followed by an underscore (_), and the name of the event to handle in VBScript.

For example, the `ActiveMovie` ActiveX control, which is used to display video content and Microsoft NetShow media, contains an `Error` event. As its name implies, this event is triggered whenever an error is encountered. If a VBScript subroutine is created for this event, all error handling can be customized by VBScript rather than using the default actions provided by `ActiveMovie`. The following code shows how to implement this error handling for `ActiveMovie` using VBScript:

```
sub MyActiveMovieControl_Error()
    ' Code to perform when errors occur…
end sub
```

When proper subroutines are established in VBScript for events, actions triggered in an ActiveX control can notify the VBScript application automatically and the results can be handled by custom VBScript code.

More information about Microsoft ActiveX and NetShow can be found at the Microsoft Web site:

`www.microsoft.com/netshow`

Because there is no inherent way to handle Java events in VBScript, we must simulate the process of notifying VBScript when particular events take place in the applet. To do this, we must use the properties of the object that VBScript can access and use a VBScript function that polls these properties on a regular interval. If properties are polled on a consistent basis, we can determine when they change their state in VBScript. If we set aside properties specifically tied to events triggered in the Java applet, the VBScript application can poll for those event properties to change, indicating that an event occurred.

The Timer Event

Because we want to check a Java applet's property on a timed interval, the first step in executing this scenario is to use an ActiveX timer control in VBScript. A timer control can be found at Microsoft's Web site at this URL:

`http://activex.microsoft.com/controls/iexplorer/ietimer.ocx`

Listing 39.5 displays the tags necessary to embed an ActiveX timer control into an HTML file.

Listing 39.5. The timer control is an ActiveX control that can be used easily with VBScript.

```
<OBJECT
          ID="TimerControl"
     CLASSID="clsid:59CCB4A0-727D-11CF-AC36-00AA00A47DD2"
     CODEBASE="http://activex.microsoft.com/controls/
               iexplorer/ietimer.ocx#Version=4,70,0,1161"
        TYPE="application/x-oleobject"
       ALIGN=middle
>
<PARAM NAME="Interval" VALUE="100">
<PARAM NAME="Enabled" VALUE="True">
</OBJECT>
```

This control expects numerous parameters, but the two of importance are `Interval` and `Enabled`. The `Enabled` parameter is equivalent to a switch that turns the timer control on or off. When set to `true`, the timer is turned on.

When the timer is enabled, a `Timer` event is sent to the VBScript for the Web page on a regular interval. This interval is determined by the `Interval` parameter in the `<OBJECT>` tag for the timer control. Time is measured in milliseconds; a value of 1000 is equivalent to a one-second interval. In the example code shown in Listing 39.5, the interval is set to 100 milliseconds, which is rather quick. The interval is made short because we do not want a user to experience a long delay between clicking the Java applet to trigger an event and seeing the results posted by VBScript. The shorter this delay is, the quicker the response.

> **NOTE**
>
> The `Interval` property of the `Timer` ActiveX control can be adjusted to trigger the `Timer` event after any given amount of time. Longer delays are suitable for other types of applications that may use timers (such as a clock that updates every second or minute). But a shorter duration is required to emulate the *immediate* triggering of VBScript code by a Java applet.

When the parameters are set appropriately for the timer control, the timer triggers an event in VBScript every given number of milliseconds. In this example, the VBScript event `TimerControl_Timer` is executed every 100 milliseconds. The code in the `TimerControl_Timer` function can then read a Java applet's property and determine when it has changed. Listing 39.6 shows a sample of appropriate VBScript code for detecting changes in the `Marquee` applet's `MouseClick` property.

39

USING JAVA WITH
VBSCRIPT

Listing 39.6. Once a timer control is enabled on a Web page, VBScript can check Java properties on a regular basis to determine when they change.

```
<SCRIPT LANGUAGE="VBScript">
sub TimerControl_Timer()
    if document.Marquee.MouseClick=1 then
        document.Marquee.MouseClick=0
        alert("You clicked on the Java applet!")
    end if
End Sub
</SCRIPT>
```

In this case, the mouseDown event in the Marquee applet's source code assigns the public variable MouseClick the value of 1. Likewise, the mouseUp event resets this property to 0. Because these properties are available for interrogation in VBScript and are tied closely to the events in the applet, they can be used to notify VBScript when the event has occurred.

TIP

As shown in Listing 39.6, it is recommended that you reset the properties for an event where appropriate. Although the Java applet should reset the property automatically, there may be occasions when it will not. Resetting the properties when you are finished using them is good practice to avoid these events from triggering more than the number of times expected.

For example, in Listing 39.6, if the mouseClick property was not reset, a new alert box would appear every 100 milliseconds!

NOTE

Although we have discussed how to implement a timer in VBScript using only ActiveX controls, you can also implement this same technique using JavaScript. Instead of using a timer control, JavaScript uses the setTimeOut() function available in the language. This function instructs JavaScript to execute a particular function on a regular interval. By placing the setTimeOut() function within the function to be called regularly, a looping condition can occur, in which the function is called continuously on a given interval. The only exception to note in this implementation is the use of the <BODY> tag, which uses the onLoad event to initiate the entire timer process. The following code shows how to implement a timer in JavaScript:

```
<BODY onLoad="tf=setTimeOut('TimerFunc()',100)">
...
</BODY>

<SCRIPT LANGUAGE="JavaScript">
function TimerFunc(){
```

```
        tf=window.setTimeout("TimerFunc()",100);

    if (document.Marquee.MouseClick==1){
        document.Marquee.MouseClick=0;
        alert("You clicked on the Java applet!");
    }
    }
</SCRIPT>
```

On the Java Side

As you can see, it is possible to trigger VBScript functions when an event occurs in a Java applet on a Web page. However, for this to work correctly, there must be appropriate properties available for VBScript to use.

In the Marquee applet, a special MouseClick property was designed explicitly for this purpose. When a user clicks the mouse button over the Java applet, the applet's mouseDown event is triggered, setting the MouseClick property to 1. The VBScript code for the Web page can then interrogate the MouseClick property to "see" when it changes from 0 to 1 and act accordingly. Likewise, the mouseUp event for the Marquee applet resets the MouseClick property to 0 so that a user can click the applet and trigger the VBScript again in the future.

The MouseClick property was specifically designed for use with VBScript to indicate when the mouse button is down or up. When designing your own Java applets or modifying applets for which you have the source code, it is easy to add dedicated properties for events to be captured by VBScript. When reusing Java applets that you cannot modify, it becomes increasingly difficult to implement similar event trapping techniques in VBScript—mainly because you cannot add your own custom properties to interrogate with VBScript.

If you use Java applets for which you do not have the source, you may still be able to trap events with VBScript. To do so, however, you must think of other properties that the applet does support that may indicate when particular events occurred. Consider the fictitious video player applet discussed earlier. Assume that we do not have the source code for this applet and want to create a routine in VBScript that performs a specific action when the playback stops. If the applet supports a CurrentPosition property, we can still implement a "stop" event in VBScript. If this CurrentPosition property updates continuously to indicate the position in the video file at which playback is located, it is possible to simply watch this property with a VBScript timer subroutine to determine when the position does not move anymore. This is essentially the same as indicating that the playback of the video stream has stopped.

39

USING JAVA WITH
VBSCRIPT

Summary

In this chapter, you learned how to interface Java applets with VBScript. You saw how to change properties of Java applets and invoke methods that applets support. You also learned how to simulate event trapping in VBScript and JavaScript. With this knowledge, you can implement more complex Web pages that effectively communicate with Java applets to create unique applications. In Chapter 40, "Developing Intranet Applications with Java," you learn how to leverage Java technology to increase the functionality of an internal organization's intranet.

IX

PART

IN THIS PART

Applied Java

CHAPTER 40

Developing Intranet Applications with Java

by Jerry Ablan

IN THIS CHAPTER

Now that you know all about Java, you probably want to put it to good use. Writing applets that animate text and graphics on your personal Web pages gets stale after a while. Most likely, you want to build something to show your boss at work. So why not develop some intranet applications?

Intranets are the hot new internal webs springing up all over the corporate landscape. Some intranets are broad and diverse while others are skimpy. In addition to providing timely company information such as corporate news and the current price of the company stock, these webs can bring the employees closer. Just like the water cooler of the past, the intranet is the new corporate hangout.

But many companies don't even have intranets. Some companies still don't have e-mail. If your company does not yet have an intranet, perhaps developing an application in Java can help get the project started. You never know....

This chapter covers some basic topics regarding intranet applications and Java. In particular, it covers the following areas:

- The anatomy of an intranet application
- Putting together an application framework for intranet applications
- Using the framework to build intranet applications

This chapter discusses an intranet application framework developed in the book *Developing Intranet Applications with Java* (published by Sams.net). The book takes you step-by-step through the design and implementation of an intranet application framework, and then through eight sample intranet applications.

> **NOTE**
>
> The framework software developed in *Developing Intranet Applications with Java* is called the *Java Intranet Framework*, or JIF. Applications created with JIF are called *jiflets*. For your convenience, the JIF source code is provided on the CD-ROM that comes with this book.

The Anatomy of an Intranet Application

Intranet applications are like a corporate application suite, which includes word processors, project planners, spreadsheets, and many other useful and productive applications. Intranet applications encompass all departments and touch many types of data. But unlike the business productivity application suites available today, your intranet applications should all share a common foundation.

Creating a suite of applications from scratch is tedious and boring. Cutting and pasting code is easy, but that goes against all object-oriented programming practices. What is needed is a basic structure from which you can build your applications. This foundation should be flexible, stable, and extensible. Once developed, it will become your intranet application framework.

The next sections introduce you to four standards that all your applications can share. These standards provide a flexible, stable, and extensible foundation for developing intranet applications. Together, these four standards produce a prototype, or a model application, you can use as a base when developing other intranet applications.

A Quick Overview of Intranet Applications

On an intranet, the applications that are built share much of the same functionality. Sure, they all do different things, but they do a lot of the same things. These commonalties should become the foundation for your intranet application framework. They are the base and are truly your application standards.

Your primary design goal should be to provide a set of standard application features. These features create a familiar atmosphere for all your intranet applications. Familiarity provides users with a sense of comfort because they don't have to learn an entirely new program. Apple Computer capitalized on this idea years ago when it introduced the Macintosh computer. If you learned how to use the Mac, then you knew how to run almost every Macintosh application ever written. It was the consistency and adherence to set standards that made this possible. Microsoft Windows has since capitalized on the same concept. The design presented in this chapter is not quite a Macintosh but it does provides something similar: consistency.

The following four standard features are what we suggest you should provide in your intranet application design:

- Standard configuration file processing
- Standard logging to screen or disk
- Standard database connectivity
- Standard look and feel

The following sections examine each feature individually, show an example, and then point you in the right direction to find more information regarding each particular standard.

Configuration File Processing

Using configuration parameters in programming can be a real hassle unless a stable foundation is in place. Generally, you end up coding a new configuration scheme with each application. What you can create is a class that provides a solid method of getting configuration parameters. This method encompasses configuration files on disk and overridden parameters passed in by way of the command line of the application.

The configuration file in Listing 40.1 is an example of the kind of configuration files the applications have.

Listing 40.1. A sample configuration file.

```
# Configuration file for Employee Maintenance
WindowTitle=Employee Maintenance
server=tcp-loopback.world
user=munster
password=
```

At the start of the application, you can read the configuration file into memory. The parameters can then be merged with any configuration parameters passed in by way of the command line. The applications then need a consistent method of retrieving these parameters from the configuration parameter storage area. A good idea is to model the retrieval method after the method used in regular Java applets.

> **NOTE**
>
> In the `jif.util` package, found on the CD-ROM that accompanies this book, is the Java class that implements the design goal of a consistent way to get configuration parameters. It is called `ConfigProperties`.

Logging to Disk or Screen

For tracking problems during the development cycle and for error logging after your application has been deployed, a log file is just the ticket. A common log file is even better for all your applications and users. A common log file is easily searched and filtered for errors. This standard logging mechanism is the first standard feature you should consider developing.

To facilitate such a log file, you must create it on disk. You should append to the log file each time; it should never be overwritten. If you overwrite the file, then information from a previous session would be lost. You know how annoying that can be!

But what if the disk log fails to open, or if it can't be written to? You need a backup log. The failed log entries could go to the screen.

This screen logging facility produces the same log information to a window, using the `System.out` facility. When an application fails to create a disk log, all log output can then go to the screen. You can also automatically use this screen log if no disk log is specified or if there is an error creating one.

Common Log Entries

The entries in the log file should follow a standard—a standard that is easy to view and search. This log-file format should be used across all your intranet applications—and possibly your non-intranet applications as well. This log-file format should be simple enough so that other programs may even use it.

In the future, you may find that you will use a third-party network management tool that can monitor your intranet applications and their log files. These tools can be a lifesaver in a pinch, so why not think about their needs as well?

Therefore, the following log-file format is a good idea of what to go with as the design. It includes all the information needed in an easy-to-use format:

```
application¦user¦date¦level¦entry
```

In this format, the following fields are used:

Field	Description
application	The name of the application
user	The user who is running the application
date	The date of the log entry
level	A single character that indicates the severity of the entry

The severity levels are up to you to define. As a suggestion however, we offer the following:

Suggested Rating	Meaning	Comment
D	Debug	This level is useful for displaying information to the log file during the development stage. When you deploy the application, these messages can easily be filtered from the output.
I	Informational	This level is for information that is not important. Startup and shutdown messages are considered informational.
W	Warning	This level is for semi-important information. When things don't go exactly as planned, but your program can continue, this is a good place for a warning.

continues

40

DEVELOPING INTRANET APPLICATIONS

Suggested Rating	Meaning	Comment
E	Error	This level is for important information. When your program encounters any kind of error, this is the level to use.
F	Fatal	This level is for very important information. When your program can no longer run because of some event, this is the level to use.

Listing 40.2 shows some sample log entries.

Listing 40.2. Sample log entries.

```
Employee¦960909¦I¦Application [Employee] started at Sun Sep 09 22:27:33  1996
Employee¦960909¦I¦Server = mars.mcs.net
Employee¦960909¦I¦Title = Employee Maintenance
Employee¦960909¦I¦User = munster
Employee¦960909¦I¦Password = spot
Employee¦960909¦I¦Application [Employee] ended at Sun Sep 09 22:28:38  1996
```

At startup, all your intranet applications should write several things to the log:

- A startup message showing the application and time/date of startup
- Optionally, the contents of the configuration file
- Optionally, any arguments passed in on the command line

At shutdown, your application can write a corresponding entry to its startup message. Refer back to Listing 40.2 for examples of shutdown entries.

NOTE

In the `jif.log` package, found on the CD-ROM that accompanies this book, are the Java classes that implement the design goal of consistent, or common, log file formatting. They are called `DiskLog` and `ScreenLog`.

Database Connectivity

Connecting to databases with Java is a key point in your intranet application design stage. Various methods are currently available. Some are HTTP server extensions that return data in HTML format. Others are nonportable system-dependent solutions. A more Java-like option is JDBC.

It appears today that JDBC is the strongest supported database standard for Java. For this reason alone, JDBC has been chosen as the database connectivity package for the intranet application in this chapter. Using JDBC allows us to choose from almost any database and provides the flexibility to change databases once coding is complete.

To simplify database connectivity just a bit, we can create a class that encapsulates the more monotonous aspects of connecting and disconnecting from a database server. This new class provides a connection strategy that is simple to use and easily extensible. This class also encapsulates much of the rudimentary JDBC initialization and cleanup. All we have to do is extend this class for each database we need to connect with.

Listing 40.3 shows how easy your JDBC database connection class should be to use.

Listing 40.3. How we want to use our database connector class.

```
//  Make the connection...
if ( myConnector.connect( "username", "password", "dbservername" ) )
{
    //  Connection successful…
}
else
{
    //  Connection failed…
}
```

As you can see, the `connect()` method is called with the connection parameters necessary to make the connection. The exception handling is handled for you in the class, returning nothing but a simple `true` or `false`. This return value indicates the connection state as well.

NOTE

On the CD-ROM that accompanies this book, in the `jif.sql` package, are the Java classes that implement the design goal of consistent database connectivity. The `DBConnector` class is the abstract base for many of the database classes. Also provided in the `jif.sql` package on the CD-ROM are classes that connect to Oracle, Sybase, Microsoft SQL Server, ODBC, and mSQL.

40

DEVELOPING INTRANET APPLICATIONS

Look and Feel

The final standard your intranet applications should follow is that they should have a consistent look and feel. This is achieved through the use of standard font and a consistent component layout.

Figure 40.1 shows the standard look and feel of the model intranet application. This application is the ever-present and highly overrated Hello World example.

FIGURE 40.1.
The standard intranet application look and feel.

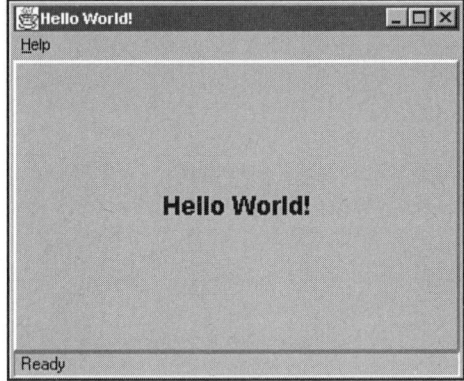

Referring to Figure 40.1, you see the following standard application attributes:

- **A standard Java font.** We choose Dialog, size 12. In Windows 95, the standard font is 8-point MS Sans Serif.
- **A status bar.** The status bar is along the bottom and is used to display messages to the user.

You may notice that there is a menu option shown in Figure 40.1. However, no menu standard is included as part of the standard look and feel for intranet applications. Because the menu varies from application to application, it is not fair to impose a rigid menu structure on applications that may not even need a menu. Therefore, menus are not part of the application design.

NOTE

 On the CD-ROM that accompanies this book, in the jif.awt package, are the Java classes that implement the design goal of a consistent look and feel. The StatusBar class in particular provides a single-line text output area for your applications. There are many other user interface classes in the jif.awt package as well. These can all be used to enhance and beautify your intranet applications.

Creating an Intranet Application Framework

Now you have an idea of the types of building blocks you can use in your intranet applications. We've covered four standard features that can create a sense of consistency for you and your users. Now we can take these features and mold them into an *application framework.*

An application framework is, in its simplest form, an application that does nothing. However, a better definition is this: An application framework provides developers with the necessary foundation from which they can build solid applications.

> **NOTE**
>
> Those of you familiar with Borland C++ or Visual C++ are aware of the benefits of a foundation framework. Using the tools provided by Borland C++ or Visual C++, you can generate a complete application shell in minutes. You, the programmer, are left with the job of providing content for the application. The tedious parts like printing and window management are already done for you. Application frameworks are one of the better advances in developer technology in years.

We'll name our framework the *Java Intranet Framework* because it provides a framework for creating intranet applications with Java. Not to mention the cool acronym: JIF!

How to Package the Application Framework

The best way to package the application framework is in groups of functionality. As you recall, we have four functionality groups: utilities, logging, database, and user interface. These fit perfectly into four functionality packages.

Naming our packages is quite simple: We use `jif` as our base package name and then add on the specifics. For example, the utilities package is called `util`, similar to the `java.util` package. Table 40.1 shows the package names we have chosen, along with the class functionality contained within each.

Table 40.1. The Java Intranet Framework packages.

Package Name	Description
jif.awt	Standard user interface classes and `java.awt` extensions
jif.log	Standard logging classes
jif.sql	Standard database connectivity classes and `java.sql` extensions
jif.util	Standard utility classes and `java.util` extensions

40

DEVELOPING
INTRANET
APPLICATIONS

The `jif.sql` package name does not really contain SQL functionality. However, the name is chosen to be consistent with the JDBC class hierarchy that lives in the `java.sql` package.

TIP

Placing Java classes into packages is simple. In each file, add a line of code that defines the package to which the class belongs. These statements are package statements as discussed in Chapter 8, "Classes, Packages, and Interfaces."

In addition to adding the package statements to your source code, you must also move all the classes into a directory hierarchy that represents the package hierarchy.

Constructing the Foundation

Now that we're headed toward building a framework, we need to use our classes to construct our foundation so that we can build intranet applications. What we really need is something to model our framework on.

An excellent implementation of application direction and structure is Java's own `Applet` class. This class is a self-contained mini-application that runs in a special applet viewer program or from an HTML World Wide Web page.

Making the Framework Easy to Use

To make our jiflets easy to work with, we've modeled them after Java's own `Applet` class. The jiflet is a Java application that provides the standard features of our intranet application in an easy-to-use wrapper. These features include all four outlined earlier, plus many of the features in a standard Java applet.

One such feature is an `init()` method that is called automatically by the framework. The `init()` method is a centralized location in which you can place all your initialization code.

Another feature our jiflet should contain is a standard way to get configuration parameters. We can retrieve parameters from the configuration file with a method like the `java.Applet.getParameter()` method.

In fact, the following methods are available both in applets and jiflets:

- ```
public void init()
```
- ```
public boolean isActive()
```
- ```
public void destroy()
```
- ```
public String getParameter( String name )
```
- ```
public void resize(Dimension d)
```
- ```
public void resize(int width, int height)
```
- ```
public void showStatus(String msg)
```

The only features really missing from jiflets that appear in applets are the multimedia methods. These multimedia methods provide a clean way for applets to load images and sound files off of a network. Because jiflets represent intranet applications, these features are not usually necessary.

With the design goals laid out, let's look into the implementation of the classes.

# The Jiflet Class

The `Jiflet` class is the intranet application version of Java's own `Applet` class. It provides you with a framework to develop intranet applications quickly and easily. It brings together all the usefulness of the other JIF packages into a single, easy-to-use component.

Let's take a look at the `Jiflet` class in detail. We start with the instance variables, move to the constructors, and then on to each of the methods. After finishing this chapter, you should have a good understanding of the `Jiflet` class: how to use it and how to use it to develop intranet applications with Java.

## Instance Variables

The `Jiflet` class contains the following instance variables:

```
protected boolean        activeFlag = false;
protected DiskLog        appLogFile;
protected String         appName;
protected boolean        appVerbosity = false;
protected ConfigProperties  configProperties;
protected ScreenLog      defaultLog;
private DBConnector      myConnector = null;
protected StatusBar      myStatusBar = null;
private int              oldCursor = -1;
```

Let's look at each one and how it is used.
```

activeFlag

```
protected boolean               activeFlag = false;
```

The `activeFlag` variable is used to denote the activeness of a jiflet. Its state can be queried with the `Jiflet.isActive()` method. The `activeFlag` variable is set to `true` right before the `run()` method is called and set to `false` after the `destroy()` method is called.

appLogFile

```
protected DiskLog               appLogFile;
```

The `appLogFile` variable is the log file object for the jiflet. During construction, this object is created like so:

```
appLogFile = new DiskLog( logPath, DiskLog.createLogFileName(), appName );
```

In this syntax, `logPath` is a configurable location in which all log files are placed. The `DiskLog.createLogFileName()` method creates a standard log filename. Finally, `appName` is used on the standard log entry to identify the application that generates it.

appName

```
protected String                appName;
```

The `appName` string holds the name of the application that is running. This string is usually passed in at construction.

appVerbosity

```
protected boolean               appVerbosity = false;
```

If you choose, your jiflet can be configured to report more information about certain things. This *verbosity* level is turned on or off with the `appVerbosity` boolean instance variable. It defaults to `false` and can be set with the `Jiflet.setVerboseMode()` method.

configProperties

```
protected ConfigProperties      configProperties;
```

The `configProperties` object holds the combined program arguments and the configuration parameters read from the application's configuration file. Access to this variable is through the `Jiflet.getParameter()` methods.

defaultLog

```
protected ScreenLog         defaultLog;
```

The `defaultLog` variable is a default log in case the real application log cannot be created. This log writes its entries to the standard out of the operating system.

myConnector

```
private DBConnector         myConnector = null;
```

The `myConnector` variable holds the `DBConnector` object associated with this jiflet. This variable can be set and retrieved with the `Jiflet.setConnector()` and `Jiflet.getConnector()` methods.

myStatusBar

```
protected StatusBar         myStatusBar = null;
```

The `myStatusBar` variable holds the instance of the `StatusBar` object created for the jiflet. The status can be set and cleared with the `Jiflet.showStatus()` and `Jiflet.clearStatus()` methods.

oldCursor

```
private int                 oldCursor = -1;
```

The `oldCursor` private variable is used to store the value of the cursor while a "wait" cursor is displayed. This variable is used by the `Jiflet.startWait()` and `Jiflet.endWait()` methods.

Constructors

There are four ways to construct a jiflet. These are defined by four separate constructors. Each of these four constructors is useful for different purposes. For the most part, most of your jiflets use the fourth incarnation. Let's take a look at each constructor.

Three of the constructors call the fourth constructor. This master constructor is where all the jiflet initialization takes place. Listing 40.4 shows the complete source code for this constructor.

Listing 40.4. The jiflet's master constructor.

```
/**
 * Creates a Jiflet with a title, a name, arguments, and optionally
 * verbose.
 *
 * @param title The window title
 * @param name The name of the application
 * @param args The arguments passed in to the program
```

continues

Listing 40.4. continued

```java
 * @param verbosity On/Off setting indicating verbosity of log entries
 * @see #setVerboseMode
 */
public
Jiflet( String title, String name, String args[], boolean verbosity )
{
    //    Call the superclass...
    super( title );

    //    Copy title to name...
    if ( name.equals( "" ) )
        name = title;

    //    Set the color...
    setBackground( Color.lightGray );

    //    Center and show our window!
    center();

    //    Add a status bar...
    enableStatusBar();

    //    Save my application name...
    appName = name;

    //    Create a default log...
    defaultLog = new ScreenLog( appName );

    //    Parse any passed in arguments...
    //    Parse the configuration file if available...
    configProperties = new ConfigProperties( args, appName + ".cfg" );

    //    Reset the title...
    setTitle( getParameter( "Title", title ) );

    //    Construct a log file name...
    String logPath = getParameter( "LogPath", "" );

    //    Open the log file...
    try
    {
        if ( logPath.equals( "" ) )
        {
            appLogFile = new DiskLog( appName );
        }
        else
        {
            appLogFile = new DiskLog( logPath,
                DiskLog.createLogFileName(),
                appName );
        }
    }
```

```
catch ( IOException e )
{
    //     Write errors to the screen...
    errorLog( "Error opening log file for [" +
        appName + "] (" + e.toString() + ")" );

    appLogFile = null;
}

//     Turn on verbose mode...
setVerboseMode( verbosity );

//     Denote construction...
log( "Application [" + appName + "] started at " +
    ( new Date() ).toString() );

//     Call my init!
init();

//     We are now active!
activeFlag = true;

//     Call my run...
run();
}
```

Because the `Jiflet` class descends from Java's `Frame` class, we need to call the superclass's constructor with a title. This is what we do first. Then we do the following:

- The background color is set to light gray.
- The jiflet is centered on the screen.
- The status bar is created and enabled.
- The default log is opened.
- The configuration file is read into memory and combined with the program arguments.
- The `LogPath` configuration option is retrieved from the configuration.
- The actual disk log file is created.
- Verbose mode is turned on or off depending on the value passed in.
- A message is written to the log, stating that the jiflet has started.
- The user's implemented `init()` method is called.
- The `run()` method is called. By default, the `show()` method of the `Frame` is called to display the jiflet on the screen.

Listing 40.5 shows the other three constructors available for creating `Jiflet` objects.

Listing 40.5. Three more constructors for creating `Jiflet` objects.

```
public
Jiflet()
{
    this( "Generic Jiflet", "Jiflet", null, false );
}

public
Jiflet( String title )
{
    this( title, "", null, false );
}

public
Jiflet( String title, String name, String args[] )
{
    this( title, name, args, false );
}
```

As you see, all three of these constructors call the main constructor, setting some values to `null` or blanks.

Methods

Many methods are available in the `Jiflet` class. The following sections document their arguments and what purpose they serve.

setVerboseMode()

```
public void
setVerboseMode( boolean whichWay )
```

The `setVerboseMode()` method turns on or off verbose mode. If verbose mode is turned on, all log entries created with the `Jiflet.verboseLog()` method are actually passed to the log object. If verbose mode is turned off, all log entries created this way are ignored.

> **TIP**
>
> The `setVerboseMode()` method, in conjunction with `Jiflet.verboseLog()`, offers an excellent debugging tool. Simply enable verbose mode when you need more detail; in your code, provide that detail with the `Jiflet.verboseLog()` method.

verboseLog()

```
//**************************************************************************
//* verboseLog                                                            *
//**************************************************************************

    public void
    verboseLog( char logLevel, String logEntry )

    public void
    verboseLog( String logEntry )
```

The verboseLog() method creates a log entry that is written to the log file only if the verbose mode flag is set to true.

The second constructor defaults to a log level of I (for informational).

errorLog()

```
//**************************************************************************
//* errorLog                                                              *
//**************************************************************************

    public void
    errorLog( String logEntry )
```

The errorLog() method allows you to create error log entries without specifying an error logging level each time. It is simply a convenience method.

log()

```
//**************************************************************************
//* log                                                                   *
//**************************************************************************

    public void
    log( char logLevel, String logEntry )

    public void
    log( String logEntry )
```

The log() method creates a log entry that is written to the log file. If there is an error or the log file is not open, the output goes to the screen.

The second constructor defaults to a log level of I (for informational).

handleEvent()

```
//**************************************************************************
//* handleEvent                                                           *
//**************************************************************************

    public boolean
    handleEvent( Event anEvent )
```

The handleEvent() method overrides the default Frame.handleEvent() method. It listens for destruction events so that the jiflet can close itself down cleanly.

action()

```
//****************************************************************************
//* action                                                                   *
//****************************************************************************

    public boolean
    action( Event event, Object arg )
```

The action() method receives ACTION_EVENT events from the event system. It listens for menu events and passes them to Jiflet.handleMenuEvent().

handleMenuEvent()

```
//****************************************************************************
//* handleMenuEvent                                                          *
//****************************************************************************

    protected boolean
    handleMenuEvent( Event event, Object arg )
```

The handleMenuEvent() method is a place holder for menu events. This method does nothing in the Jiflet class. It must be overridden by derived classes to include any functionality.

shutDown()

```
//****************************************************************************
//* shutDown                                                                 *
//****************************************************************************

    public boolean
    shutDown( int level )
```

The shutDown() method is the central point of exit for the jiflet. With the exception of a program crash, the jiflet always exits through this method. The method is responsible for writing a log entry for the application ending, and it calls the Jiflet.destroy() method. The level argument is passed to the operating system as a return value for the calling program.

suicide()

```
//****************************************************************************
//* suicide                                                                  *
//****************************************************************************

    public void
    suicide( Exception e, String logLine, int level )

    public void
    suicide( String logLine )

    public void
    suicide( String logLine, int level )

    public void
    suicide( Exception e )
```

```
    public void
    suicide( Exception e, String logLine )
```

The suicide() method allows a jiflet to gracefully kill itself. Depending on the circumstances, you may or may not want a log entry written, and you may or may not have an exception that caused your program's death.

center()

```
//***********************************************************************
//* center                                                             *
//***********************************************************************

    public void
    center()
```

The center() method centers the jiflet window on the screen.

enableStatusBar()

```
//***********************************************************************
//* enableStatusBar                                                    *
//***********************************************************************

    public void
    enableStatusBar( String text )

    public void
    enableStatusBar()
```

The enableStatusBar() method creates a status bar with or without text and adds it to the jiflet's layout.

clearStatus()

```
//***********************************************************************
//* clearStatus                                                        *
//***********************************************************************

    public void
    clearStatus()
```

The clearStatus() method clears the text in the status bar.

showStatus()

```
//***********************************************************************
//* showStatus                                                         *
//***********************************************************************

    public void
    showStatus( String text )
```

The showStatus() method sets the text in the status bar.

40

DEVELOPING
INTRANET
APPLICATIONS

setConnector()

```
//*********************************************************************
//* setConnector                                                     *
//*********************************************************************

    protected void
    setConnector( DBConnector aConnector )
```

The setConnector() method sets the DBConnector object associated with this jiflet.

getConnector()

```
//*********************************************************************
//* getConnector                                                     *
//*********************************************************************

    public DBConnector
    getConnector()
```

The getConnector() method returns the previously associated DBConnector object to the caller.

startWait()

```
//*********************************************************************
//* startWait                                                        *
//*********************************************************************

    public void
    startWait()
```

The startWait() method is a luxury method. It changes the cursor to the system default "wait" cursor. Usually an hourglass, this cursor indicates that a lengthy process is occurring.

endWait()

```
//*********************************************************************
//* endWait                                                          *
//*********************************************************************

    public void
    endWait()
```

The endWait() method returns the cursor to its previous state if called after a Jiflet.startWait() call. Otherwise, this method does nothing.

getParameter()

```
//***********************************************************************
//* getParameter                                                        *
//***********************************************************************

    public String
    getParameter( String key )

    public String
    getParameter( String key, String defaultValue )
```

The `getParameter()` method is identical to Java's `Applet.getParameter()` method. It returns the value associated with the *key* passed. You can also pass in a default value in case the key is not found. These parameters are looked for in the `configProperties` instance variable.

canClose()

```
//***********************************************************************
//* canClose                                                            *
//***********************************************************************

    public boolean
    canClose()
```

The `canClose()` method is called before the jiflet is allowed to close. It provides you with a place to catch an unwanted departure. The default implementation returns `true`. Override this method to add your own functionality. An example of its use is to catch users before they exit to see whether they have saved their work.

Within your overridden copy, you can ask users whether they want to save their work. If they say no, return `true`, closing the jiflet. If they say yes, save their work and then return `true`, closing the jiflet. You can also offer them a cancel option, which returns `false`.

isActive()

```
//***********************************************************************
//* isActive                                                            *
//***********************************************************************

    public boolean
    isActive()
```

The `isActive()` method returns `true` if the jiflet is currently active; otherwise it returns `false`. The `isActive()` method is similar to the `Applet.isActive()` method. A jiflet is considered active right before its `run()` method is called.

Wrapping Up Jiflets

Now that we have this new `Jiflet` class, we need to place it somewhere. Again we borrow from the example set by Sun and place it in a package called `jif.jiflet`. This package contains the `Jiflet` class.

Programming with Jiflets

Now that we've created a class that implements the design goals, let's take it for a test drive. Remember that because we've modeled our jiflet on Java's `Applet` class, creating a jiflet should be quite simple.

The Smallest Jiflet

The smallest possible jiflet simply prints a string on the screen and does nothing else. Listing 40.6 shows the source code for our smallest jiflet.

Listing 40.6. The smallest jiflet.

```
//*******************************************************************
//* Imports                                                         *
//*******************************************************************

import                    jif.jiflet.Jiflet;
import                    java.awt.Label;

//*******************************************************************
//* SmallJiflet                                                     *
//*******************************************************************

public class
SmallJiflet
extends Jiflet
{

//*******************************************************************
//* main                                                            *
//*******************************************************************

    public static void
    main( String[] args )
    {
        new SmallJiflet();
    }

//*******************************************************************
//* init                                                            *
//*******************************************************************

    public void
    init()
    {
```

```
        add( "Center", new Label( "I'm a small jiflet" ) );
        pack();
    }

//**************************************************************************
//* run                                                                    *
//**************************************************************************

    public void
    run()
    {
        show();
    }

}
```

The `main()` method is called by the Java interpreter to run your program. It is required to create the class that is your program. It is in the `main()` method that we create an instance of `SmallJiflet`.

The `pack()` method readjusts the size of the jiflet to accommodate all the user interface objects contained within it. The `pack()` method is necessary because, unlike an applet, we have no predefined width or height.

The output of our small jiflet is shown in Figure 40.2.

FIGURE 40.2.

The output of
`SmallJiflet`.

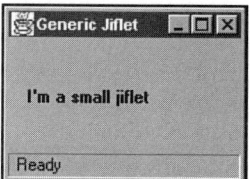

Extending Jiflets for Real-World Use

Now that you have a basic understanding of the Java Intranet Framework (JIF), the rest of this chapter extends the Jiflet concept into a form that can be easily used for building database-aware intranet applications.

A jiflet, as you know, is the smallest application that can be built with JIF. However, it does absolutely nothing but look pretty. After building several applications using the JIF, it becomes apparent that they all share much of the same code. Each application goes through the following life cycle:

1. Construct the jiflet.
2. Construct the user interface.
3. Handle events until the program ends.

Pretty boring, but such is life when you are only binary information. The pattern that becomes evident to you is that each application has a monotonous bunch of initialization code and a user interface that must be copied from application to application. But this base initialization is not in the Jiflet class. Jiflets have to remain pure.

The result is three new abstract classes: SimpleDBJiflet, SimpleDBUI, and DBRecord.

The philosophy is that a SimpleDBJiflet has a user interface defined by a SimpleDBUI. The two work together to present a pleasant atmosphere for the user. Together, they allow the user to manipulate a single set of database data. This database information is represented by the DBRecord class.

By extending these three abstract classes (and filling in the blanks as it were), you can create powerful database applications in a matter of hours!

The DBRecord Class

The DBRecord class is the smallest of the three new classes. This class represents a single set of database data. The data represented by this class is defined in its subclasses, therefore DBRecord is an abstract class. The source code for this class is shown in Listing 40.7.

Listing 40.7. The DBRecord class.

```
//****************************************************************************
//* Package                                                                  *
//****************************************************************************

package                        jif.sql;

//****************************************************************************
//* Imports                                                                  *
//****************************************************************************

//    JIF imports
import                         jif.sql.*;
import                         jif.awt.*;

//    Java imports
import                         java.sql.*;

//****************************************************************************
//* DBRecord                                                                 *
//****************************************************************************

public abstract class
DBRecord
{
```

```
//****************************************************************************
//* Members                                                                  *
//****************************************************************************
    //    An indicator for data changes...
    protected boolean          dataChange = false;
    protected boolean          isNewRecord = false;

//****************************************************************************
//* Constructor                                                              *
//****************************************************************************
    public
    DBRecord()
    {
        clear();
    }

    public
    DBRecord( ResultSet rs )
    {
        parseResultSet( rs );
    }

//****************************************************************************
//* parseResultSet                                                           *
//****************************************************************************
    /**
     * Parses a "SELECT * ..." result set into itself
     */
    public boolean
    parseResultSet( ResultSet rs )
    {
        isNewRecord = false;
        return( isNewRecord );
    }

//****************************************************************************
//* update                                                                   *
//****************************************************************************
    /**
     * Requests update SQL from the JifPanel and sends it to the database
     * via the DBConnector object passed in.
     */
    public abstract boolean
    update( DBConnector theConnector, JifPanel ap );

//****************************************************************************
//* deleteRow                                                                *
//****************************************************************************
    /**
     * Constructs delete SQL for the current row
     */
    public abstract boolean
    deleteRow( DBConnector theConnector );
```

continues

40

DEVELOPING
INTRANET
APPLICATIONS

Listing 40.7. continued

```
//**************************************************************************
//* setDataChange                                                         *
//**************************************************************************

    /**
     * Sets a flag indicating that data has changed...
     */
    public boolean
    setDataChange( boolean onOff )
    {
        dataChange = onOff;
        return( dataChange );
    }

//**************************************************************************
//* clear                                                                 *
//**************************************************************************

    /**
     * Clears all the variables...
     */
    public void
    clear()
    {
        isNewRecord = true;
        setDataChange( false );
    }

//**************************************************************************
//* canSave                                                               *
//**************************************************************************

    /**
     * Checks to see if all required fields are filled in
     */
    public boolean
    canSave()
    {
        //     Everything is filled in!
        return( true );
    }

//**************************************************************************
//* didDataChange                                                         *
//**************************************************************************

    public boolean
    didDataChange()
    {
        return( dataChange );
    }
```

```
//*************************************************************************
//* setNewStatus                                                         *
//*************************************************************************

    public void
    setNewStatus( boolean how )
    {
        isNewRecord = how;
    }

//*************************************************************************
//* getNewStatus                                                         *
//*************************************************************************

    public boolean
    getNewStatus()
    {
        return( isNewRecord );
    }

}
```

The DBRecord class can be constructed with or without data. The data required to construct this class is a JDBC ResultSet object. This object is passed to the parseResultSet() method. In your derived class, you must override this method to read in the data from the ResultSet into instance variables.

To complete the class, you must provide two additional methods in your derived class: update() and deleteRow(). update() is called when someone wants you to save the information that your class contains. deleteRow() is called when someone wants you to delete the information your class contains.

The class provides a clear() method, which you override to clear out your instance variables. The clear() method is called, for example, when the user presses the New or Clear button.

The DBRecord class has two indicators: dataChange and isNewRecord. The boolean value dataChange indicates that the data has changed in the record; the boolean value isNewRecord indicates whether the record exists in the database.

The dataChange value must be manually set and reset. This is done to some degree by the SimpleDBJiflet class. For example, when a record is saved to the database, the dataChange value is set to false. This setting is made by way of the setDataChange() method.

Access methods are provided for you to get at these indicators. getNewStatus() and setNewStatus() allow access to the isNewRecord indicator. setDataChange() and didDataChange() provide access to the dataChange indicator.

Finally, the class provides a method called canSave(). This method returns a boolean value indicating whether the record is eligible for saving to the database. Eligibility depends completely on the table the record represents. The canSave() method allows you to validate the data that the user has entered and give it the thumbs up or down.

NOTE

The DBRecord class is part of the jif.sql package, included on the CD-ROM that accompanies this book.

A complete example is in order. Listing 40.8 is a complete DBRecord derivation for a table that represents Conference Rooms.

Listing 40.8. A DBRecord subclass.

```
//****************************************************************************
//* Package                                                                  *
//****************************************************************************

package                         jif.common;

//****************************************************************************
//* Imports                                                                  *
//****************************************************************************

//    JIF imports
import                          jif.sql.*;
import                          jif.awt.*;

//    Java imports
import                          java.sql.*;

//****************************************************************************
//* ConfRoomRecord                                                           *
//****************************************************************************

/**
 * A class that encapsulates a row in the conference room table...
 */
public class
ConfRoomRecord
extends DBRecord
{

//****************************************************************************
//* Constants                                                                *
//****************************************************************************

    public final static String    TABLE_NAME = "conf_room";

//****************************************************************************
//* Members                                                                  *
//****************************************************************************

    //    A variable for each table column...
    public int                  room_nbr = -1;
    public int                  floor_nbr = -1;
    public String               desc_text = "";
```

```
//****************************************************************************
//* Constructor                                                            *
//****************************************************************************

    public
    ConfRoomRecord()
    {
        clear();
    }

    public
    ConfRoomRecord( ResultSet rs )
    {
        parseResultSet( rs );
    }

//****************************************************************************
//* parseResultSet                                                         *
//****************************************************************************

    public boolean
    parseResultSet( ResultSet rs )
    {
        clear();

        try
        {
            //    Suck out the data...
            room_nbr = rs.getInt( "room_nbr" );
            floor_nbr = rs.getInt( "floor_nbr" );
            desc_text = rs.getString( "desc_text" );
            return( super.parseResultSet( rs ) );
        }
        catch ( SQLException e )
        {
            //    Signal an error...
            clear();
            return( false );
        }
    }

//****************************************************************************
//* update                                                                 *
//****************************************************************************

    /**
     * Requests update SQL from the JifPanel and sends it to the database
     * via the DBConnector object passed in.
     */
    public boolean
    update( DBConnector theConnector, JifPanel ap )
    {
        boolean         success = true;

        try
```

continues

40

DEVELOPING
INTRANET
APPLICATIONS

Listing 40.8. continued

```java
        {
            //    No update if nothing to do...
            if ( dataChange )
            {
                String     sql;

                //    Generate some SQL!
                if ( getNewStatus() )
                    sql = ap.generateInsertSQL( TABLE_NAME );
                else
                    sql = ap.generateUpdateSQL( TABLE_NAME );

                if ( !sql.equals( "" ) )
                    theConnector.getStatement().executeUpdate( sql );
            }
        }
        catch ( SQLException e )
        {
            theConnector.errorLog( e.toString() );
            success = false;
        }

        return( success );
    }

//****************************************************************************
//* deleteRow                                                                *
//****************************************************************************

    /**
     * Removes this record from the database...
     */
    public boolean
    deleteRow( DBConnector theConnector )
    {
        boolean          success = true;

        //    Nothing to do...
        if ( getNewStatus() )
            return( false );

        String sql = "delete from " + TABLE_NAME + " where room_nbr " +
            "= " + Integer.toString( room_nbr ) + " and floor_nbr " +
            "= " + Integer.toString( floor_nbr );

        try
        {
            theConnector.getStatement().executeUpdate( sql );
        }
        catch ( SQLException e )
        {
            theConnector.errorLog( e.toString() );
            success = false;
        }
        return( success );
    }
```

```
//****************************************************************************
//* clear                                                                    *
//****************************************************************************

    /**
    * Clears all the variables...
    */
    public void
    clear()
    {
        super.clear();

        room_nbr = -1;
        floor_nbr = -1;
        desc_text = "";
    }

}
```

The SimpleDBUI Class

The `SimpleDBUI` class encapsulates the nonvisual side of the user interface that is necessary for proper application functionality. The class extends the `JifPanel` class by providing some default buttons and methods for moving data to and from the user interface components. The source code for this class is shown in Listing 40.9.

Listing 40.9. The SimpleDBUI class.

```
//****************************************************************************
//* Package                                                                  *
//****************************************************************************

package                         jif.awt;

//****************************************************************************
//* imports                                                                  *
//****************************************************************************

import                          java.awt.*;
import                          jif.sql.*;
import                          jif.jiflet.*;
import                          jif.common.*;

//****************************************************************************
//* SimpleDBUI                                                               *
//****************************************************************************

public abstract class
SimpleDBUI
extends JifPanel
{
```

continues

Listing 40.9. continued

```
//*****************************************************************************
//* Members                                                                   *
//*****************************************************************************

    SimpleDBJiflet              myJiflet;

    //    Some standard buttons...
    public Button               saveButton = new Button( "Save" );
    public Button               clearButton = new Button( "Clear" );
    public Button               newButton = new Button( "New" );
    public Button               deleteButton = new Button( "Delete" );
    public Button               chooseButton = new Button( "Choose" );
    public Button               closeButton = new Button( "Close" );

//*****************************************************************************
//* Constructor                                                               *
//*****************************************************************************

    public
    SimpleDBUI( SimpleDBJiflet jiflet )
    {
        setJiflet( jiflet );
        setFont( new Font( "Dialog", Font.PLAIN, 12 ) );
    }

//*****************************************************************************
//* getJiflet                                                                 *
//*****************************************************************************

    public SimpleDBJiflet
    getJiflet()
    {
        return( myJiflet );
    }

//*****************************************************************************
//* setJiflet                                                                 *
//*****************************************************************************

    public void
    setJiflet( SimpleDBJiflet jiflet )
    {
        myJiflet = jiflet;
    }

//*****************************************************************************
//* moveToScreen                                                              *
//*****************************************************************************

    /**
     * Moves data from a DBRecord object to the fields on the screen
     * for editing.
     */
    public abstract void
    moveToScreen();
```

```
//*****************************************************************************
//* clearScreen                                                              *
//*****************************************************************************

    /**
    * Clears the screen fields
    */
    public abstract void
    clearScreen();

//*****************************************************************************
//* moveFromScreen                                                           *
//*****************************************************************************

    /**
    * Moves data from the fields on the screen to a DBRecord object.
    */
    public abstract void
    moveFromScreen();

//*****************************************************************************
//* action                                                                   *
//*****************************************************************************

    public boolean
    action( Event event, Object arg )
    {
        //    Smart JIF components generate ACTION_EVENTs when changed...
        if ( event.target instanceof SQLFactoru )
        {
            //    Notify dad...
            sendJifMessage( event, DATA_CHANGE );
            return( true );
        }

        //    User pressed Save...
        if ( event.target == saveButton )
        {
            //    Notify dad...
            sendJifMessage( event, SAVE );
            return( true );
        }

        //    User pressed New...
        if ( event.target == newButton )
        {
            //    Notify dad...
            sendJifMessage( event, NEW );
            return( true );
        }

        //    User pressed Choose
        if ( event.target == chooseButton )
        {
```

continues

40

DEVELOPING
INTRANET
APPLICATIONS

Listing 40.9. continued

```
            //    Notify dad...
            sendJifMessage( event, CHOOSE );
            return( true );
        }

        //    User pressed Close
        if ( event.target == closeButton )
        {
            //    Notify dad...
            sendJifMessage( event, CLOSE );
            return( true );
        }

        //    User pressed Delete
        if ( event.target == deleteButton )
        {
            //    Notify dad...
            sendJifMessage( event, DELETE );
            return( true );
        }

        //    User pressed Clear
        if ( event.target == clearButton )
        {
            //    Notify dad...
            sendJifMessage( event, CLEAR );
            return( true );
        }

        //    Not handled...
        return( false );
    }

}
```

Being abstract, the `SimpleDBUI` class is not very complex. The first thing you notice about the class is that we create a slew of buttons:

```
public Button          saveButton = new Button( "Save" );
public Button          clearButton = new Button( "Clear" );
public Button          newButton = new Button( "New" );
public Button          deleteButton = new Button( "Delete" );
public Button          chooseButton = new Button( "Choose" );
public Button          closeButton = new Button( "Close" );
```

These are the standard buttons that the `SimpleDBUI` knows about. They are defined as `public` so that you can access them outside the user interface. Unless they are placed on a panel or shown in some manner on the screen, they are really never used; therefore they do not generate messages.

When these buttons are shown on the screen and subsequently clicked by the user, an `ACTION_EVENT` event is generated. This event is translated into a `JifMessage` by the `action()` event handler method. The message is then sent on to the parent, presumably a `SimpleDBJiflet`, and processed there.

The `SimpleDBUI` class is expected to move data in and out of a `DBRecord` class. It does this using three methods: `moveToScreen()`, `moveFromScreen()`, and `clearScreen()`. This class has access to the current `DBRecord` by way of the jiflet. By calling the `SimpleDBJiflet`'s `getDBRecord()` method, a reference to the current `DBRecord` is provided.

The `moveToScreen()` method moves data from the `DBRecord` to the screen components. The `moveFromScreen()` method moves data from the screen components to the `DBRecord`. And `clearScreen()` clears out the screen components. This last method does not touch the `DBRecord` really, but a `clearScreen()` followed by a `moveFromScreen()` clears out the `DBRecord`.

NOTE

The `SimpleDBUI` class is part of the `jif.awt` package, included on the CD-ROM that accompanies this book.

A simple `SimpleDBUI` derivation is shown in Listing 40.10. This is from the Online In/Out Board application. This application is provided for you on the CD-ROM that accompanies this book.

Listing 40.10. A `SimpleDBUI` subclass.

```
//*************************************************************************
//* imports                                                              *
//*************************************************************************

import                       java.awt.*;

import                       jif.awt.*;
import                       jif.sql.*;
import                       jif.jiflet.*;
import                       jif.common.*;

//*************************************************************************
//* InOutBoardUI                                                         *
//*************************************************************************

public class
InOutBoardUI
extends SimpleDBUI
{
```

continues

Listing 40.10. continued

```
//***************************************************************************
//* Members                                                                 *
//***************************************************************************

    List                    empList;

//***************************************************************************
//* Constructor                                                             *
//***************************************************************************

    public
    InOutBoardUI( SimpleDBJiflet jiflet )
    {
        super( jiflet );
        setLayout( new BorderLayout() );

        empList = new List();
        empList.setFont( new Font( "Helvetica", Font.BOLD, 14 ) );
        add( "Center", empList );
        empList.enable();

        JifPanel p = new JifPanel();
        p.setLayout( new FlowLayout( FlowLayout.CENTER, 5, 5 ) );
        saveButton.setLabel( "Toggle" );
        saveButton.disable();
        p.add( saveButton );
        add( "South", p );

        //    Set the focus to the first field...
        setFocus( empList );
    }

//***************************************************************************
//* moveToScreen                                                            *
//***************************************************************************

    /**
     * Moves data from an InOutBoardRecord object to the fields on the screen
     * for editing.
     */
    public void
    moveToScreen()
    {
        if ( getJiflet().getDBRecord() == null )
            return;

        //    Cast one off...
        EmployeeRecord er = ( EmployeeRecord )getJiflet().getDBRecord();

        String s = er.first_name + " " + er.last_name + " is ";

        if ( er.in_out_ind.equalsIgnoreCase( "Y" ) )
            s += "in";
        else
            s += "out";
```

```
            empList.addItem( s );
        }

//*************************************************************************
//* clearScreen                                                         *
//*************************************************************************

    /**
     * Clears the record out...
     */
    public void
    clearScreen()
    {
        empList.clear();
    }

//*************************************************************************
//* moveFromScreen                                                      *
//*************************************************************************

    /**
     * Moves data from the fields on the screen to an EmployeeRecord object.
     */
    public void
    moveFromScreen()
    {
        //    Does nothing…
        return;
    }

}
```

The SimpleDBJiflet Class

The SimpleDBJiflet class pulls together the DBRecord and SimpleDBUI classes into a cool little hunk of code. This class encapsulates much of the necessary menu and database initialization that must be done for each application.

The SimpleDBJiflet class extends the Jiflet class and adds the following functionality:

- A File menu with standard database connectivity
- A Help menu with a working About dialog box
- A standard method of communicating with the user interface
- Record saving and deleting
- Data modification notification

Although they are not functional on their own, these features keep you from doing the legwork of cutting and pasting from app to app. The beauty of object-oriented programming and Java is that you can stuff all this functionality into an abstract base class and fill in the blanks. That is all that has been done here.

NOTE

The SimpleDBJiflet class is part of the jif.jiflet package, included on the CD-ROM that accompanies this book.

The File and Help Menus

The SimpleDBJiflet class creates two menus: a File menu and a Help menu. The File menu contains two items: Connect and Exit.

The first option, Connect, connects and disconnects the application to and from the database. This functionality is provided completely as long as the jiflet has a valid DBConnector set for itself.

After a database connection is established, the Connect menu option changes to Disconnect automatically. When the Disconnect option is selected, it disconnects the application from the database and the option changes back to Connect.

CAUTION

The JDK version 1.0.2 for 32-bit Microsoft Windows systems has a bug that prevents a menu item from changing the text after it is displayed. This should be fixed in the JDK version 1.1 release.

The second menu option, Exit, disconnects any connected DBConnector and closes the application. The Exit option can include writing information to a log file or to the screen. It depends on the configuration of the jiflet.

The Help menu has a single menu item that brings up an About dialog box. If you are not familiar with these critters, they are simply brag boxes for the authors of programs. Some of these dialog boxes actually show useful information, but most just show the program name and a fancy icon along with some copyright information.

Should your jiflet be any different? You're just as proud of your creation as other authors are! Well, set a copyright message with the method setCopyright(), and an About dialog box displays automagically! Figure 40.3 shows the About dialog box for the employee maintenance program. Nothing too fancy, just the text and a little icon.

Figure 40.3.
The employee maintenance About dialog box.

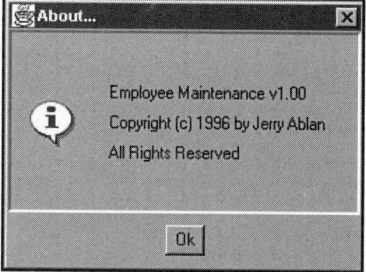

> **TIP**
>
> A nice extension to the `Jiflet` class allows custom icons to be associated with the application. Then in their About dialog boxes, the custom icon displays instead of the stock information icon.

The only code required to get that nice About box in the derived `Employee` program is the following:

```
setCopyright( "Employee Maintenance v1.00\n" +
    "Copyright (c) 1996 by Jerry Ablan\n" +
    "All Rights Reserved" );
```

Not a lot of code for such a nice feature! By the way, the About menu item is disabled until you call the `setCopyright()` method.

Standard Communications: `JifMessage`

In object-oriented programming, objects communicate with each other by way of messages. But at what point should objects know about the inside workings of other objects? Some purists argue, *never*! Some argue, *sometimes*. It is usually, however, a matter of convenience.

While designing many of the applications for this book, I felt that the user interface should be able to manage itself, because it doesn't know about the application driving it. However, I felt that the application needed to know a little about the user interface. Otherwise, you really can't provide any nice bells and whistles. One such feature is to enable and disable the Save button when a data item is modified. This is an excellent visual clue to the user that a change has been made, intentionally or not.

To feel politically correct—OOP-wise—and to not let my user interface design creep into my application design, I created the `JifMessage` interface. Listing 40.11 is the source code for the `JifMessage` interface.

Listing 40.11. The JifMessage interface.

```java
//*******************************************************************************
//* Package                                                                    *
//*******************************************************************************

package                    jif.jiflet;

//*******************************************************************************
//* Imports                                                                    *
//*******************************************************************************

import                     java.awt.Event;

//*******************************************************************************
//* JifMessage                                                                 *
//*******************************************************************************

public interface
JifMessage
{

//*******************************************************************************
//* Members                                                                    *
//*******************************************************************************

    public static final int     NEW = 0;
    public static final int     CLEAR = 1;
    public static final int     SAVE = 2;
    public static final int     DELETE = 3;
    public static final int     CUT = 4;
    public static final int     COPY = 5;
    public static final int     PASTE = 6;
    public static final int     HELP_WINDOW = 7;
    public static final int     HELP_CONTEXT = 8;
    public static final int     HELP_ABOUT = 9;
    public static final int     HELP_HELP = 10;
    public static final int     DATA_CHANGE = 11;
    public static final int     CHOOSE = 12;
    public static final int     CLOSE = 13;

//*******************************************************************************
//* sendJifMessage                                                             *
//*******************************************************************************

    public void
    sendJifMessage( Event event, int msg );

}
```

Again, the JifMessage interface is nothing fancy—simply a list of constants and a consistent method of sending them, which is up to the implementor of this interface. As you can see, many standard actions are represented by the constants in this class: New, Save, Delete, Close, and so on.

After creating this interface, we have to implement it somewhere. I felt that the `JifPanel` class is an excellent spot. Because most user interfaces are created with `JifPanel`s, placing the interface there provides a consistent and standard method of communication with its parent. Listing 40.12 is the code added to the `JifPanel` class to implement this interface.

Listing 40.12. Sending a `JifMessage`.

```
//*******************************************************************************
//* sendJifMessage                                                             *
//*******************************************************************************

    public void
    sendJifMessage( Event event, int msg )
    {
        event.target = this;
        event.arg = new Integer( msg );
        getParent().postEvent( event );
    }
```

Nothing too tricky here, either. The `sendJifMessage()` method takes as arguments an event and the message to send. It changes the target of the event to itself (the `JifPanel` instance) and sets the argument of the event to the message. It then sends the message along to the parent.

Here's a quick example of how it is used. In the `SimpleDBUI` class, there is a built-in Save button. When the user clicks this button, the class automatically sends a `JifMessage.SAVE` event to its parent. The parent needs only to listen for these `JifMessage` events to know what the child wants it to do.

The code for sending from the child looks exactly like this:

```
//    User pressed Save...
if ( event.target == saveButton )
{
    //    Notify dad...
    sendJifMessage( event, JifMessage.SAVE );
    return( true );
}
```

The code for receiving in the parent looks like this:

```
public boolean
action( Event event, Object arg )
{
    switch ( ( ( Integer )arg ).intValue() )
    {
        case JifMessage.DELETE:
            delDlg = new ResponseDialog( this,
                "Delete Confirmation",
                "Are you sure you want to delete this record?",
                "Yes,No" );

            delDlg.show();
```

```
            break;
        }
}
```

Now that there is a standard way of communicating, we can add some standard features like saving and deleting.

Record Saving and Deleting

A nice feature for a program to have is a standard method of saving and deleting. Now that we know when the user wants us to save or delete (by way of a `JifMessage`), we need some standard methods for doing this.

Enter the `saveRecord()` and `deleteRecord()` methods. These two methods provide a way to save and delete the information stored in the `DBRecord` of the jiflet. When the `SimpleDBUI` sends the `SAVE` or `DELETE` `JifMessage` to the jiflet, one of these methods is called.

The methods are declared as shown in Listing 40.13.

Listing 40.13. Declaring the `saveRecord()` and `deleteRecord()` methods.

```
//**************************************************************************
//* saveRecord                                                             *
//**************************************************************************
    public boolean
    saveRecord()
    {
        //    If we are not connected, do nothing...
        if ( !getConnector().connected() )
        {
            MessageBox mb = new MessageBox( this, "Hold on there!",
                "You must connect with the database\n" +
                "before you can save any data.\n\n" +
                "Connect first, then try this again!",
                MessageBox.EXCLAMATION );

            mb.show();
            return( false );
        }

        //    Move the data back to the DBRecord...
        getUIPanel().moveFromScreen();

        //    Check to see if all fields are filled in...
        if ( getDBRecord().canSave() )
        {
            //    Save it...
            if ( getDBRecord().update( getConnector(), getUIPanel() ) )
            {
                //    Indicate that it was saved...
                getDBRecord().setDataChange( false );
                setStatus( "Record saved..." );
```

```
                }
                else
                    setStatus( "Record not saved..." );

                return( true );
            }
            else
            {
                MessageBox mb = new MessageBox( this, "Cannot Save!",
                    "All required fields must be entered!",
                    MessageBox.EXCLAMATION );

                mb.show();
            }

            return( false );
        }


//******************************************************************************
//* deleteRecord                                                              *
//******************************************************************************

    public boolean
    deleteRecord()
    {
        //    If we are not connected, do nothing...
        if ( !getConnector().connected() )
        {
            MessageBox mb = new MessageBox( this, "Hold on there!",
                "You must connect with the database\n" +
                "before you can delete any data.\n\n" +
                "Connect first, then try this again!",
                MessageBox.EXCLAMATION );

            mb.show();
            return( false );
        }

        //    Move the data back to the DBRecord...
        getUIPanel().moveFromScreen();

        //    Kill it!
        if ( getDBRecord().deleteRow( getConnector() ) )
        {
            //    Indicate that it was saved...
            getDBRecord().clear();
            getUIPanel().moveToScreen();
            setStatus( "Record deleted..." );
            return( true );
        }
        else
            setStatus( "Record not deleted..." );

        return( false );
    }
```

Having these methods in the base class allows you to override them in your derived classes, thus enhancing the functionality. One functionality is to modify two tables instead of one. Or perhaps your jiflet does not save any data but you use the Save button and mechanism for some other sort of notification. It is up to you. Be creative!

Data Change Notification

The last function that the `SimpleDBJiflet` class provides is data change notification.

When the `SimpleDBUI` class contains one of the JIF `Component` extensions (such as `JifTextField`), it is notified when the user changes the data. This notification is passed along to the `SimpleDBJiflet` class. The `SimpleDBJiflet` class then manages the enabling and disabling of the Save, New, and Delete buttons.

The status of the record depends on the state of the `DBRecord` at the time. If the record is new, it can't be deleted but it can be saved or cleared (New). If the record has not been changed and is not new, it can be saved, deleted, or cleared. This is not a very complex set of rules, but it is a hassle to code for each application. You'll find it refreshing when your Save button lights up after you type your first character.

Summary

This chapter thoroughly covered an intranet application framework. You had an intimate encounter with the `Jiflet` class, which is part of the Java Intranet Framework. This base, or framework, is provided for you on the CD-ROM that accompanies this book. You can use it to create your own intranet applications with Java.

Java Game Programming

by Tim Macinta

IN THIS CHAPTER

CHAPTER 41

Creating games with Java is a lot like creating games with other languages. You have to deal with the design of movable objects (often referred to as *sprites*), the design of a graphics engine to keep track of the movable objects, and double buffering to make movement look smooth. There is a good chance that future versions of Java will provide built-in support for sprites and double buffering, but for now, we have to add the support ourselves. This chapter covers methods for creating these standard building blocks of games using Java.

Thankfully, Java takes care of a lot of the dirty work you would have to do if you were writing a game in another language. For example, Java provides built-in support for transparent pixels, making it easier to write a graphics engine that can draw nonrectangular objects. Java also has built-in support for allowing several different programs to run at once—perfect for creating a world with a lot of creatures, each with its own special methods for acting. However, the added bonuses of Java can turn into handicaps if they are not used properly. This chapter deals with how to use the advantages of Java to write games and how to avoid the pitfalls that accompany the power.

Graphics: Creating a Graphics Engine

A *graphics engine* is essential to a well-designed game in Java. A graphics engine is an object that is given the duty of painting the screen. The graphics engine keeps track of all objects on the screen at one time, the order in which to draw the objects, and the background to be drawn. By far, the most important function of the graphics engine is the maintenance of movable object blocks.

Movable Object Blocks in Java

So what's the big fuss about movable object blocks (MOBs)? Well, they make your life infinitely easier if you're interested in creating a game that combines graphics and user interaction, as most games do. The basic concept of a movable object is that the object contains both a picture that will be drawn on the screen and information that tells you where the picture is to be drawn on the screen. To make the object move, you simply tell the movable object (more precisely, the graphics engine that contains the movable object) which way to move and you're done—redrawing is automatically taken care of.

The bare-bones method for making a movable object block in Java is shown in Listing 41.1. As you can see, the movable object consists merely of an image and a set of coordinates. You may be thinking, "Movable objects are supposed to take care of all the redrawing that needs to be done when they are moved. How is that possible with just the code from Listing 41.1?" Redrawing is the graphics engine's job. Don't worry about it for now; it's covered a little later.

NOTE

If you don't feel like typing all the code from Listings 41.1 through 41.4, you can find finished versions of all the code in the CHAP41 directory on the CD-ROM that accompanies this book. The files that correspond to Listings 41.1 through 41.4 are called MOB.java, GraphicsEngine.java, Game.java, and example.html. You can see the final version of the GraphicsEngine test by viewing the page entitled example.html with a Java-enabled browser.

Listing 41.1. Use this code to create a bare-bones movable object block (MOB). Save this code in a file called MOB.java.

```
import java.awt.*;

public class MOB {
    public int x = 0;
    public int y = 0;
    public Image picture;

        public MOB(Image pic) {
            picture=pic;
        }
}
```

As you can see in Listing 41.1, the constructor for our movable object block (MOB) takes an Image and stores it away to be drawn when needed. After we've instantiated an MOB (that is, after we've called the constructor), we have a movable object that we can move around the screen just by changing its x and y values. The engine will take care of redrawing the movable object in the new position, so what else is there to worry about?

One thing to consider is the nature of the picture that is going to be drawn every time the movable object is drawn. Consider the place in which the image probably will originate. In all likelihood, the picture will either come from a GIF or JPEG file, which has one very important consequence—it will be rectangular. So what? Think about what your video game will look like if all your movable objects are rectangles. Your characters would be drawn, but so would their backgrounds. Chances are, you'll want to have a background for the entire game; it would be unacceptable if the unfilled space on character images covered up your background just because the images were rectangular and the characters were of another shape.

When programming games in other languages, this problem is often resolved by examining each pixel in a character's image before drawing it to see whether it's part of the background. If the pixel is not part of the background, it's drawn as normal. If the pixel is part of the background, it's skipped and the rest of the pixels are tested. Pixels that aren't drawn usually are referred to as *transparent pixels*. If this seems like a laborious process to you, it is. Fortunately, Java has built-in support for transparent colors in images, which simplifies your task immensely. You don't have to check each pixel for transparency before it's drawn because Java can do that automatically! Java even has built-in support for different levels of transparency. For example, you can create pixels that are 20-percent transparent to give your images a ghostlike appearance. For now, though, we'll deal only with fully transparent pixels.

> **NOTE**
>
> Whether or not you know it, you are probably already familiar with transparent GIFs. If you have ever stumbled across a Web page with an image that wasn't perfectly rectangular, you were probably looking at a transparent GIF.

Java's capability to draw transparent pixels makes the task of painting movable objects on the screen much easier. But how do you tell Java what pixels are transparent and what pixels aren't? You could load the image and run it through a filter that changes the ColorModel, but that would be doing it the hard way. Fortunately, Java supports transparent GIF files. Whenever a transparent GIF file is loaded, all the transparency is preserved by Java. That means your job just got a lot easier.

> **NOTE**
>
> A new Adobe PhotoShop plug-in allows you to save your images as transparent (and interlaced) GIFs. You can download it from http://www.adobe.com.

Now the problem becomes how to make transparent GIFs. This part is easier than you think. Simply use your favorite graphics package to create a GIF file (or a picture in some other format that you can eventually convert to a GIF file). Select a color that doesn't appear anywhere in the picture and fill all areas that you want to be transparent with the selected color. Make a note of the RGB value of the color you use to fill in the transparent places. Now you can use a program to convert your GIF file into a transparent GIF file. I use Giftool, available at http://www.homepages.com/tools/index.html, to make transparent GIF files. You simply pass to Giftool the RGB value of the color you selected for transparency, and Giftool makes that color transparent inside the GIF file. Giftool is also useful for making your GIF files interlaced. *Interlaced GIF files* are the pictures that initially appear with block-like edges and keep getting more defined as they continue to load.

Construction of a Graphics Engine

Now you have movable objects that know where they're supposed to be and don't eat up the background as they go there. The next step is to design something that will keep track of your movable objects and draw them in the proper places when necessary. This is the job of our GraphicsEngine class. Listing 41.2 shows the bare bones of a graphics engine. This is the minimum you need to handle multiple movable objects. Even this engine leaves out several things that nearly all games need, but we'll get to those things later. For now, let's concentrate on how this bare-bones system works to give you a solid grasp of the basic concepts.

Listing 41.2. A bare-bones graphics engine that tracks your movable objects. The code should be saved in a file called GraphicsEngine.java.

```java
import java.awt.*;
import java.awt.image.*;

public class GraphicsEngine {
  Chain mobs = null;

  public GraphicsEngine() {}

  public void AddMOB (MOB new_mob) {
    mobs = new Chain(new_mob, mobs);
  }

  public void paint(Graphics g, ImageObserver imob) {
    Chain temp_mobs = mobs;
    MOB mob;
    while (temp_mobs != null) {
      mob = temp_mobs.mob;
      g.drawImage(mob.picture, mob.x, mob.y, imob);
      temp_mobs = temp_mobs.rest;
    }
  }
}

class Chain {
  public MOB mob;
  public Chain rest;

  public Chain(MOB mob, Chain rest) {
    this.mob = mob;
    this.rest = rest;
  }

}
```

Introducing Linked Lists

Before we detail how the `GraphicsEngine` class works, let's touch on the `Chain` class. The `Chain` class looks rather simple—and it can be—but don't let that fool you. Entire languages such as LISP and Scheme have been built around data structures that have the same function as the `Chain` class. The `Chain` class is simply a data structure that holds two objects. Here, we're calling those two objects `item` and `rest` because we are going to use `Chain` to create a linked list. The power of the `Chain` structure—and those structures like it—is that it can be used as a building block to create a multitude of more complicated structures. These structures include circular buffers, binary trees, weighted di-graphs, and linked lists, to name a few. Using the `Chain` class to create a linked list is suitable for our purposes.

Our goal is to keep a list of the moveable objects that have to be drawn. A linked list suits our purposes well because a linked list is a structure that is used to store a list of objects. It is referred to as a "linked" list because each point in the list contains an object and a link to a list with the remaining objects.

> **NOTE**
>
> The concept of a linked list—the `Chain` class in this case—may be a little hard to grasp at first because it is defined recursively. If you don't understand it right away, don't worry. Try to understand how the `Chain` class is used in the code first and study Figure 41.1; the technical explanation should make more sense.

To understand what a linked list is, think of a train as an example of a linked list: Consider the train to be the first car followed by the rest of the train. The "rest of the train" can be described as the second car followed by the remaining cars. This description can continue until you reach the last car, which can described as the caboose followed by nothing. A `Chain` class is analogous to a train. A `Chain` can be described as a movable object followed by the rest of the `Chain`, just as a train can be described as a car followed by the rest of the train. And just as the rest of the train can be considered a train by itself, the rest of the `Chain` can be considered a `Chain` by itself, and that's why the rest is of type `Chain`.

From the looks of the constructor for `Chain`, it appears that you need an existing `Chain` to make another `Chain`. This makes sense when you already have a `Chain` and want to add to it, but how do you start a new `Chain`? To do this, create a `Chain` that is an item linked to nothing. How do you link an item to nothing? Use the Java symbol for nothing—`null`—to represent the `rest` `Chain`. If you look at the code in Listing 41.2, that's exactly what we did. Our instance variable `mobs` is of type `Chain`, and it is used to hold a linked list of movable objects. Look at the method `AddMOB()` in Listing 41.2. Whenever we want to add another movable object to the list of movable objects we're controlling, we simply make a new list of movable objects that has the new movable object as the first item and the old `Chain` as the rest of the list. Notice that the initial value of `mobs` is `null`, which is used to represent nothing.

NOTE

You may wonder why we even bothered making a method called AddMOB() when it only ended up being one line long. The point in making short methods like AddMOB() is that if GraphicsEngine were subclassed in the future, it would be a lot easier to add functionality if all you have to do is override one method as opposed to changing every line of code that calls AddMOB(). For example, if you wanted to sort all your moveable objects by size, you could just override AddMOB() so that it stores all the objects in a sorted order to begin with.

Painting Images from a List

Now that we have a method for keeping a list of all the objects that have to be painted, let's review how to use the list. The first thing you should be concerned about is how to add new objects to the list of objects that have to be painted. You add a new object to the list by using the AddMOB() method shown in Listing 41.2. As you can see from the listing, all the AddMOB() method does is to replace the old list of objects stored in mobs with a new list that contains the new object and a link to the old list of objects.

How do we use the list of movable objects once AddMOB() has been called for all the movable objects we want to handle? Take a look at the paint() method. The first thing to do is copy the pointer to mobs into a temporary Chain called temp_mobs. Note that the *pointer* is copied, not the actual contents. If the contents were copied instead of the pointer, this approach would take much longer and would be much more difficult to implement. "But I thought Java doesn't have pointers," you may be thinking at this point. That's not exactly true; Java doesn't have pointer arithmetic, but pointers are still used to pass arguments, although the programmer never has direct access to these pointers.

temp_mobs now contains a pointer to the list of all the movable objects to be drawn. The task at hand is to go through the list and draw each movable object. The variable mob is used to keep track of each movable object as we get to it. The variable temp_mobs represents the list of movable objects we have left to draw (that's why we started it off pointing to the whole list). We'll know all our movable objects have been drawn when temp_mobs is null, because that will be just like saying the list of movable objects left to draw is empty. That's why the main part of the code is encapsulated in a while loop that terminates when temp_mobs is null.

Look at the code inside the while loop of the paint() method. The first thing that is done is to assign mob to the movable object at the beginning of the temp_mobs Chain so that there is an actual movable object to deal with. Now it's time to draw the movable object. The g.drawImage() command draws the movable object in the proper place. The variable mob.picture is the picture stored earlier when the movable object was created. The variables mob.x and mob.y are the screen coordinates at which the movable object should be drawn; notice that paint() looks at these two variables every time the movable object is drawn, so changing one of these coordinates while the program is running has the same effect as moving it on the screen. The final argument passed to g.drawImage(), imob, is an ImageObserver that is responsible for redrawing an image when it changes or moves. Don't worry about where to get an ImageObserver from; chances are, you'll be using the GraphicsEngine class to draw inside a Component (or a subclass of Component such as Applet), and a Component implements the ImageObserver interface so that you can just pass the Component to GraphicsEngine whenever you want to repaint.

The final line inside the while loop shortens the list of movable objects that have to be drawn. It points temp_mobs away from the Chain that it just drew a movable object off the top of and points it to the Chain that contains the remainder of the MOBs. As we continue to cut down the list of MOBs by pointing to the remainder, temp_mobs eventually winds up as null, which ends the while loop with all our movable objects drawn. Figure 41.1 provides a graphical explanation of this process.

FIGURE 41.1.

A graphical representation of a Chain.

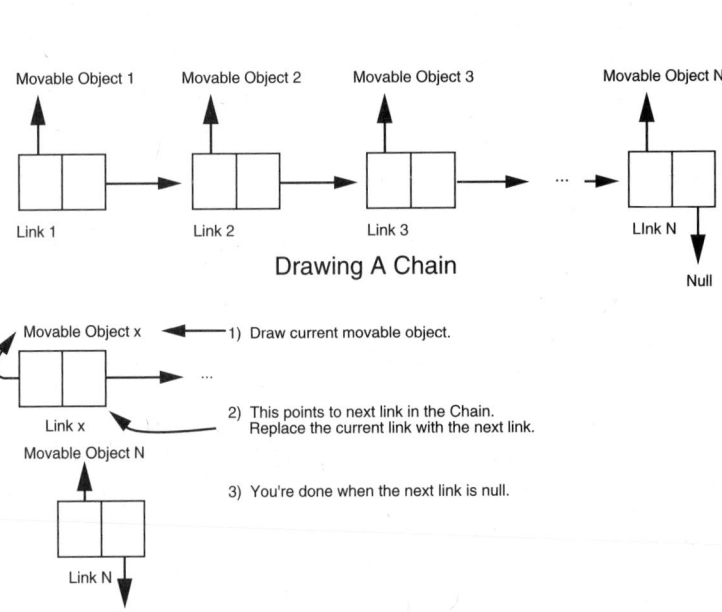

Installing the Graphics Engine

The graphics engine in Listing 41.2 certainly had some important things left out, but it does work. Let's go over how to install the GraphicsEngine inside a Component first, and then go back and improve on the design of the graphics engine and the MOB.

Listing 41.3 shows an example of how to install the GraphicsEngine inside a Component. It just so happens that the Component we're installing it in is an Applet (remember that an Applet is a subclass of Component) so we can view the results with a Web browser. Keep in mind that the same method called to use the GraphicsEngine inside an Applet can also be used to install the GraphicsEngine inside other Components.

> **NOTE**
>
> Remember that you can find all the code presented in the listings in this chapter on the CD-ROM that accompanies this book.

Before trying to understand the code in Listing 41.3, it would be a good idea to type and compile Listings 41.1 through 41.3 so that you can get an idea of what the code does. Save each listing with the filename specified in each listing's header and compile the code by using the javac command on each of those files.

In addition to compiling the code in Listings 41.1 through 41.3, you must also create the HTML file as shown in Listing 41.4. (Use a Java-enabled browser or the JDK applet viewer to view this file once you have compiled everything.) As the final step, you have to place a small image file to be used as the movable object in the same directory as the code and either rename it to one.gif or change the line inside the init() method in Listing 41.3 that specifies the name of the picture being loaded.

Listing 41.3. This sample applet illustrates the GraphicsEngine class. The code should be saved in a file named Game.java.

```java
import java.awt.*;
import java.applet.Applet;
import java.net.URL;

public class Game extends Applet {
  GraphicsEngine engine;
  MOB picture1;

  public void init() {
    try {
      engine = new GraphicsEngine();
      Image image1 = getImage(new URL(getDocumentBase(), "one.gif"));
      picture1 = new MOB(image1);
      engine.AddMOB(picture1);
    }
    catch (java.net.MalformedURLException e) {
      System.out.println("Error while loading pictures...");
      e.printStackTrace();
    }
  }
```

continues

Listing 41.3. continued

```java
public void update(Graphics g) {
  paint(g);
}

public void paint(Graphics g) {
  engine.paint(g, this);
}


public boolean mouseMove (Event evt, int mx, int my) {
  picture1.x = mx;
  picture1.y = my;
  repaint();
  return true;
}

}
```

Listing 41.4. This code must be put into an HTML file in order to view the applet.

```html
<html>
<head>
<title>GraphicsEngine Example</title>
</head>

<body>
<h1>GraphicsEngine Example</h1>

<applet code="Game.class" width=200 height=200>
</applet>
</body>
</html>
```

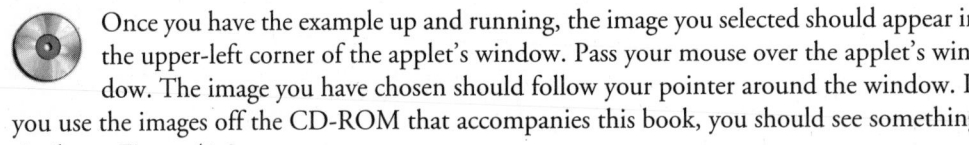 Once you have the example up and running, the image you selected should appear in the upper-left corner of the applet's window. Pass your mouse over the applet's window. The image you have chosen should follow your pointer around the window. If you use the images off the CD-ROM that accompanies this book, you should see something similar to Figure 41.2.

Let's go over how the code that links the GraphicsEngine into the applet called Game works. Our instance variables are engine, which controls all the movable objects we can deliver, and picture1, a movable object that draws the chosen image .

FIGURE 41.2.

This is what the example of the bare-bones GraphicsEngine *should look like.*

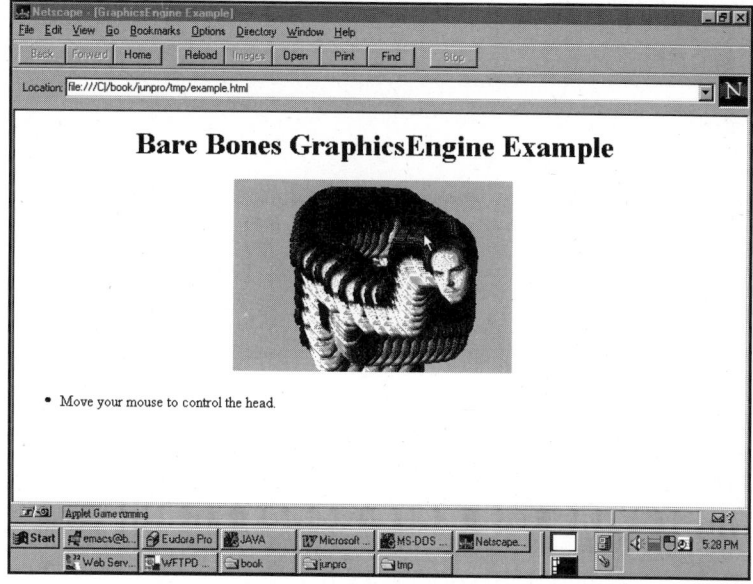

Take a look at the fairly straightforward init() method. You initialize engine by setting it equal to a new GraphicsEngine. Next, the image you chose is loaded with a call to getImage(). This line creates the need for the try and catch statements that surround the rest of the code to catch any invalid URLs. After the image is loaded, it is used to create a new MOB, and picture1 is initialized to this new MOB. The work is completed by adding the movable object to engine so that engine will draw it in the future. The remaining lines (the lines inside the catch statement) are there to provide information about any errors that occur.

The update() method is used to avoid flickering. By default, applets use the update() method to clear the window they live in before they repaint themselves with a call to their paint() method. This can be a useful feature if you're changing the display only once in a while, but with graphics-intensive programs, this can create a lot of flicker because the screen refreshes itself frequently. Because the screen refreshes itself so frequently, once in a while, it catches the applet at a point at which it has just cleared its window and hasn't yet had a chance to redraw itself. This situation is what causes flicker.

The flicker was eliminated here simply by leaving out the code that clears the window and going straight to the paint() method. If you already ran this example applet, you have probably already noticed that although not clearing the screen solves the problem of flickering, it creates another problem: the movable object is leaving streaks! (If you haven't run the applet yet, you can see the streaks in Figure 41.2.) Don't worry; the streaks will be eliminated a little later when we introduce double buffering into our graphics engine.

As you can see, the Game.paint() method consists of one line: a call to the paint() method in engine. It might seem like a waste of time going from update() to paint() to engine.paint() just to draw one image. Once you have a dozen or more movable objects on the screen at once, however, you'll appreciate the simplicity of being able to add the object in the init() method and then forget about it the rest of the time, letting the engine.paint() method take care of everything.

Finally, we have the mouseMove() method. This is what provides the tracking motion so that the movable object follows your pointer around the window. There are, of course, other options for user input that are discussed later in this chapter. The tracking is accomplished simply by setting the coordinates of the movable object to the position of the mouse. The call to repaint() just tells the painting thread that something has changed; the painting thread calls paint() when it gets around to it, so you don't have to worry about redrawing any more. To finish up, true is returned to inform the caller that the mouseMove() event was taken care of.

Improving the Bare-Bones Engine

Now that the framework has been laid for a functional graphics engine, it's time to make improvements. Let's start with movable objects. What should be considered when thinking about the uses movable objects have in games? Sooner or later, chances are that you'll want to write a game with a lot of movable objects. It would be much easier to come up with some useful properties that you want all your movable objects to have now so that you don't have to deal with each movable object individually later.

One area that merits improvement is the order in which movable objects are painted. What if you had a ball (represented by a movable object) that was bouncing along the screen, and you wanted it to travel in front of a person (also represented by a movable object)? How could you make sure that the ball was drawn *after* the person every time, to make it look like the ball was is in front of the person? You could make sure that the ball is the first movable object added to the engine, ensuring that it's always the last movable object painted. However, that approach can get hairy if you have 10 or 20 movable objects that all have to be in a specific order. Also, what if you wanted the same ball to bounce back across the screen later on, but this time *behind* the person? The method of adding movable objects in the order you want them drawn obviously wouldn't work, because you would be switching the drawing order in the middle of the program.

What is needed is some sort of prioritization scheme. The improved version of the graphics engine implements a scheme in which each movable object has an integer that represents its priority. The movable objects with the highest priority number are drawn last and thus appear in front.

Listing 41.5 shows the changes that have to be made to the MOB class to implement prioritization. Listing 41.6 shows the changes that have to be made to the GraphicsEngine class, and Listing 41.7 shows the changes that have to be made to the Game applet. Several other additional features have also been added in these listings, and we'll touch on those later.

> **NOTE**
>
> Our prioritization scheme does not impose any restrictions on the priority of each object. There is no need to give objects sequential priorities (that is, you can give objects priorities like 1, 5, and 20 instead of using priorities 1, 2, and 3). You can also assign the same priority to more than one object if you don't care which object is drawn on top (that is, you can leave all your objects with the default priority of zero).

The heart of the prioritization scheme lies in the new version of GraphicsEngine.paint(). The basic idea is that before any movable objects are drawn, the complete list of movable objects is sorted by priority. The highest priority objects are put at the end of the list so that they are drawn last and appear in front; the lowest priority objects are put at the beginning of the list so that they are drawn first and appear in back. A bubble sort algorithm is used to sort the objects. Bubble sort algorithms are usually slower than other algorithms, but they tend to be easier to implement. In this case, the extra time taken by the bubble sort algorithm is relatively negligible because the majority of time within the graphics engine is eaten up displaying the images.

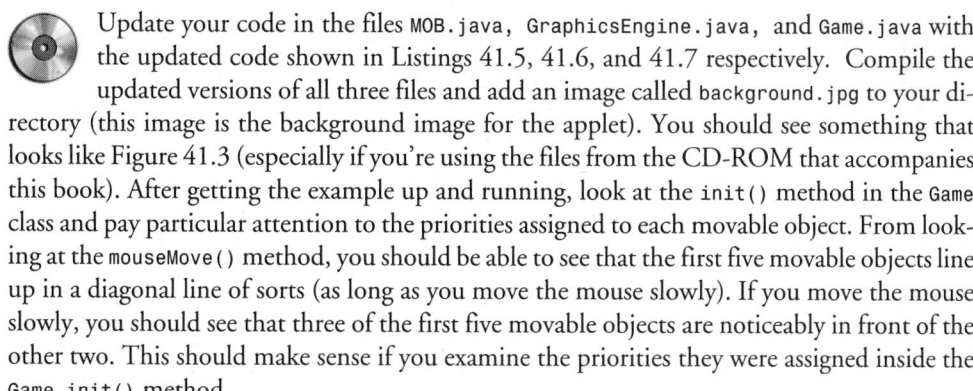 Update your code in the files MOB.java, GraphicsEngine.java, and Game.java with the updated code shown in Listings 41.5, 41.6, and 41.7 respectively. Compile the updated versions of all three files and add an image called background.jpg to your directory (this image is the background image for the applet). You should see something that looks like Figure 41.3 (especially if you're using the files from the CD-ROM that accompanies this book). After getting the example up and running, look at the init() method in the Game class and pay particular attention to the priorities assigned to each movable object. From looking at the mouseMove() method, you should be able to see that the first five movable objects line up in a diagonal line of sorts (as long as you move the mouse slowly). If you move the mouse slowly, you should see that three of the first five movable objects are noticeably in front of the other two. This should make sense if you examine the priorities they were assigned inside the Game.init() method.

Also notice that the bouncing object is always in front of the objects you control with your mouse. This is because it was assigned a higher priority than all the other objects. Now press the S key. The first object that your mouse controls should now be displayed in front of the bouncing object. Take a look at the Game.keyDown() method to see why this occurs. You will see that pressing the S key toggles the priority of picture1 between a priority that is lower than the bouncing object and a priority that is higher than the bouncing object.

FIGURE 41.3.

What the final version of the GraphicsEngine *example should look like.*

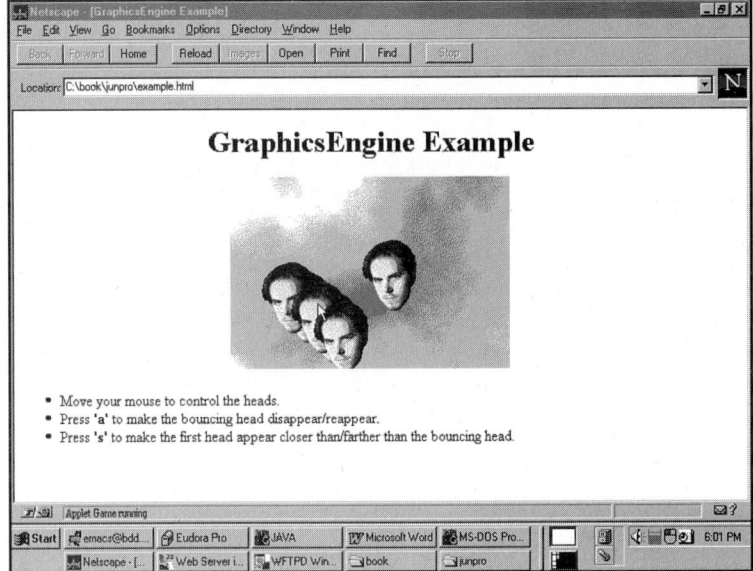

Listing 41.5. The enhanced version of the MOB **class. Save this code in a file named** MOB.java.

```
import java.awt.*;

public class MOB {
  public int x = 0;
  public int y = 0;
  public Image picture;
  public int priority = 0;
  public boolean visible = true;

  public MOB(Image pic) {
    picture=pic;
  }
}
```

Listing 41.6. The enhanced version of the GraphicsEngine **class. Save the code in a file called** GraphicsEngine.java.

```
import java.awt.*;
import java.awt.image.*;

public class GraphicsEngine {
  Chain mobs = null;
  public Image background;
  public Image buffer;
  Graphics pad;
```

41

```
public GraphicsEngine(Component c) {
  buffer = c.createImage(c.size().width, c.size().height);
  pad = buffer.getGraphics();
}

public void AddMOB (MOB new_mob) {
  mobs = new Chain(new_mob, mobs);
}

public void paint(Graphics g, ImageObserver imob) {

  /* Draw background on top of buffer for double buffering. */

  if (background != null) {
    pad.drawImage(background, 0, 0, imob);
  }

  /* Sort MOBs by priority */

  Chain temp_mobs = new Chain(mobs.mob, null);
  Chain ordered = temp_mobs;
  Chain unordered = mobs.rest;
  MOB mob;
  while (unordered != null) {
    mob = unordered.mob;
    unordered = unordered.rest;
    ordered = temp_mobs;
    while (ordered != null) {
   if (mob.priority < ordered.mob.priority) {
     ordered.rest = new Chain(ordered.mob, ordered.rest);
     ordered.mob = mob;
     ordered = null;
   }
   else if (ordered.rest == null) {
     ordered.rest = new Chain(mob, null);
     ordered = null;
   }
   else {
     ordered = ordered.rest;
   }
    }
  }

  /* Draw sorted MOBs */

  while (temp_mobs != null) {
    mob = temp_mobs.mob;
    if (mob.visible) {
   pad.drawImage(mob.picture, mob.x, mob.y, imob);
    }
    temp_mobs = temp_mobs.rest;
  }
```

continues

Listing 41.6. continued

```java
    /* Draw completed buffer to g */

    g.drawImage(buffer, 0, 0, imob);

  }
}

class Chain {
  public MOB mob;
  public Chain rest;

  public Chain(MOB mob, Chain rest) {
    this.mob = mob;
    this.rest = rest;
  }

}
```

Listing 41.7. An extended example showing the properties of the GraphicsEngine class. Save this code in a file called Game.java.

```java
import java.awt.*;
import java.applet.Applet;
import java.net.URL;

public class Game extends Applet implements Runnable {
  Thread kicker;
  GraphicsEngine engine;
  MOB picture1, picture2, picture3, picture4, picture5, picture6;

  public void init() {
    try {
      engine = new GraphicsEngine(this);
      engine.background = getImage(new URL(getDocumentBase(), "background.jpg"));
      Image image1 = getImage(new URL(getDocumentBase(), "one.gif"));
      picture1 = new MOB(image1);
      picture2 = new MOB(image1);
      picture3 = new MOB(image1);
      picture4 = new MOB(image1);
      picture5 = new MOB(image1);
      picture6 = new MOB(image1);
      picture1.priority = 5;
      picture2.priority = 1;
      picture3.priority = 4;
      picture4.priority = 2;
      picture5.priority = 3;
      picture6.priority = 6;
      engine.AddMOB(picture1);
      engine.AddMOB(picture2);
      engine.AddMOB(picture3);
      engine.AddMOB(picture4);
      engine.AddMOB(picture5);
      engine.AddMOB(picture6);
    }
```

```
      catch (java.net.MalformedURLException e) {
        System.out.println("Error while loading pictures...");
        e.printStackTrace();
      }
    }

    public void start() {
      if (kicker == null) {
        kicker = new Thread(this);
      }
      kicker.start();
    }

    public void run() {
      requestFocus();
      while (true) {
        picture6.x = (picture6.x+3)%size().width;
        int tmp_y = (picture6.x % 40 - 20)/3;
        picture6.y = size().height/2 - tmp_y*tmp_y;
        repaint();
        try {
       kicker.sleep(50);
        }
        catch (InterruptedException e) {
        }
      }
    }
    public void stop() {
      if (kicker != null && kicker.isAlive()) {
        kicker.stop();
      }
    }

    public void update(Graphics g) {
      paint(g);
    }

    public void paint(Graphics g) {
      engine.paint(g, this);
    }

    public boolean mouseMove (Event evt, int mx, int my) {
      picture5.x = picture4.x-10;
      picture5.y = picture4.y-10;
      picture4.x = picture3.x-10;
      picture4.y = picture3.y-10;
      picture3.x = picture2.x-10;
      picture3.y = picture2.y-10;
      picture2.x = picture1.x-10;
      picture2.y = picture1.y-10;
      picture1.x = mx;
      picture1.y = my;
      return true;
    }
```

continues

Listing 41.7. continued

```
public boolean keyDown (Event evt, int key) {
  switch (key) {
  case 'a':
    picture6.visible = !picture6.visible;
    break;
  case 's':
    if (picture1.priority==5) {
   picture1.priority=7;
     }
    else {
   picture1.priority=5;
    }
    break;
  }
  return true;
}



}
```

Double Buffering

Two big features also implemented in the improved code are double buffering and the addition of a background image. This is accomplished entirely in GraphicsEngine (as shown in Listing 41.6). Notice the changes in the constructor for GraphicsEngine. The graphics engine now creates an image so that it can do off-screen processing before it's ready to display the final image. The off-screen image is named buffer, and the Graphics context that draws into that image is named pad.

Now take a look at the changes to the paint() method in GraphicsEngine. Notice that, until the end, all the drawing is done into the Graphics context pad instead of the Graphics context g. The background is drawn into pad at the beginning of the paint() method and then the movable objects are drawn into pad after they have been sorted. Once everything is drawn into pad, the image buffer contains exactly what we want the screen to look like; so we draw buffer to g, which causes it to be displayed on the screen.

Invisibility and Other Possible Extensions

Another feature that was added to the extended version of the movable objects was the capability to make your movable objects disappear when they aren't wanted. This was accomplished by giving MOB a flag called visible. Take a look at the end of GraphicsEngine.paint() method in Listing 41.6 to see how this works. This feature would come in handy if you had an object that you wanted to show only part of the time. For example, you could make a bullet as a movable object. Before the bullet is fired, it is in a gun and should not be visible, so you set `visible` to `false` and the bullet isn't shown. Once the gun is fired, the bullet can be seen, so you set `visible` to `true` and the bullet is shown. Run the `Game` applet and press the A key a few times. As you can see from the `keyDown()` method, pressing the A key toggles the `visible` flag of the bouncing object between `true` and `false`.

By no means do the features shown in Listings 41.5, 41.6, and 41.7 exhaust the possibilities of what can be done with the structure of movable objects. Several additional features can easily be added, such as a centering feature for movable objects so that they are placed on the screen based on their center rather than their edge, an animation feature so that a movable object could step through several images instead of just displaying one, the addition of velocity and acceleration parameters, or even a collision-detection method that would allow you to tell when two movable objects have hit each other. Feel free to extend the code as needed to accommodate your needs.

Using the Graphics Engine to Develop Games

We haven't actually written a game yet, but we have laid the foundation for writing games. You now have objects you can move around the screen simply by changing their coordinates. These tools have been the building blocks for games since the beginning of graphics-based computer games. Use your imagination and experiment. If you need more help extending the concepts described here concerning the creation of games with movable objects and their associated graphics engines, pick up a book devoted strictly to game programming. *Tricks of the Game-Programming Gurus* (Sams Publishing) and *Teach Yourself Internet Game Programming with Java* (Sams Publishing) are good examples.

 At the end of this chapter, you will find the source code for and a short discussion of a very simple skiing game that was written using the `GraphicsEngine` built in the first part of this chapter. The skiing game and the source code are also available on the CD-ROM that accompanies this book. Studying the code for the skiing game and making small experimental changes to the code should help you understand how to use the building blocks developed in this chapter to create full-blown games.

Sounds

We've spent all this time learning how to do the graphics for a game in Java, but what about sounds? Sound in Java is very sparse. The Java development team worked hard on the first release of Java, but they unfortunately didn't have time to incorporate a lot of sound support.

> **NOTE**
>
> Although it's possible to develop much better sound control using the undocumented `sun.audio.*` classes, doing so is generally a bad idea for several reasons. First of all, the `sun.audio.*` classes are not part of the core Java API, so there is no guarantee that they will always be there on every implementation of the virtual machine. Second, JavaSoft is currently working on adding better audio support to the Java core classes, so you won't have to worry about the lack of functionality in the future.

Check out `java.applet.AudioClip` in Java release 1.0 to discover the full extent of sound use. There are only three methods: `loop()`, `play()`, and `stop()`. This simple interface makes life somewhat easier. Use `Applet.getAudioClip()` to load an `AudioClip` in the AU format and you have two choices: Use the `play()` method to play it at specific times, or use the `loop()` method to play it continuously. The applications for each are obvious. Use the `play()` method for something that's going to happen once in a while, such as the firing of a gun; use the `loop()` method for something that should be heard all the time, such as background music or the hum of a car engine.

Java-Specific Game Design Issues

When thinking about the design of your game, there are some Java-specific design issues you must consider. One of Java's most appealing characteristics is that it can be downloaded through the Web and run inside a browser. This networking aspect brings several new considerations into play. Java is also meant to be a cross-platform language, which has important ramifications in the design of the user interface and for games that rely heavily on timing.

Picking a User Interface

When picking a user interface, there are several things you should keep in mind. Above all, remember that your applet should be able to work on all platforms because Java is a cross-platform language. If you choose to use the mouse as your input device, keep in mind that regardless of how many buttons your mouse has, a Java mouse has only one button. Although Java can read from any button on a mouse, it considers all buttons to be the same button. The Java development team made the design choice to have only one button so that Macintosh users wouldn't get the short end of the stick.

If you use the keyboard as your input device, it is even more critical for you to remember that although the underlying platforms might be vastly different, Java is platform independent. This becomes a problem because the different machines that Java can run on may interpret keystrokes differently when more than one key is held down at once. For example, you may think it worthwhile to throw a supermove() method in your game that knocks an opponent off the screen, activated by holding down four secret keys at the same time. However, doing this might destroy the platform independence of your program because some platforms may not be able to handle four keystrokes at once. The best approach is to design a user interface that doesn't call into question whether it is truly cross-platform. Try to get by with only one key at a time, and stay away from control and function keys in general because they can be interpreted as browser commands by different browsers in which your applet runs.

Limiting Factors

As with any programming language, Java has its advantages and its disadvantages. It's good to know both so that you can exploit the advantages and steer clear of the disadvantages. Several performance issues arise when you are dealing with game design in Java—some of which are a product of the inherent design of Java and some of which are a product of the environment in which Java programs normally run.

Downloading

One of the main features of Java is that it can be downloaded and run across the Net. Because automatically downloading the Java program you want to run is so central to the Java software model, the limitations imposed by using the Net to get your Java bear some investigation. First, keep in mind that most people with a network connection aren't on the fastest lines in the world. Although you may be ready to develop the coolest animation ever for a Java game, remember that nobody will want to see it if it takes forever to download. It is a good idea to avoid extra frills when they are going to be costly in terms of downloading time.

One trick you can use to get around a lengthy download time is to download everything you can in the background. For example, you can send level one of your game for downloading, start the game, and while the user plays level one, levels two and up are sent for downloading in a background thread. This task is simplified considerably with the java.awt.MediaTracker. To use the MediaTracker class, simply add all your images to a MediaTracker with the addImage() method and then call checkAll() with true as an argument.

> **NOTE**
>
> According to the JavaSoft Web page at http://java.sun.com, Java 1.1 will include the ability to store all your images, classes, and other files in a JAR file. A JAR file is a new type of Java ARchive file, created (among other reasons) to speed up network transfers by reducing the number of connections. For the time being, some browsers, such as Netscape 3.0, allow you to store all your classes in one ZIP file.

Opening a network connection can take a significant amount of time. If you have 30 or 40 pictures to send for downloading, the time this takes can quickly add up. One trick that can help decrease the number of network connections you have to open is to combine several smaller pictures into one big picture. You can use a paint program or an image-editing program to create a large image that is made up of your smaller images placed side by side. You then send for downloading only the large image. This approach decreases the number of network connections you need to open and can also decrease the total number of bytes contained in the image data. Depending on the type of compression used, if the smaller images that make up your larger image are similar, you will probably achieve better compression by combining them into one picture. Once the larger picture has been loaded from across the network, the smaller pictures can be extracted using the `java.awt.image.CropImageFilter` class to crop the image for each of the original smaller images.

Execution Speed

Another thing you should keep in mind with applets is timing. Java is remarkably fast for an interpreted language, but graphics handling usually leaves something to be desired when it comes to rendering speed. Your applet probably will be rendered inside a browser, which slows it down even more. If you are developing your applets on a state-of-the-art workstation, keep in mind that a large number of people will be running Java inside a Web browser on much slower PCs. When your applets are graphics intensive, it's always a good idea to test them on slower machines to make sure that the performance is acceptable. If you find that an unacceptable drop in performance occurs when you switch to a slower platform, try shrinking the `Component` that your graphics engine draws into. You may also want to try shrinking the images used inside your movable objects because the difference in rendering time is most likely the cause of the drop in performance.

Another thing to watch out for is poor threading. A top-of-the-line workstation may allow you to push your threads to the limit, but on a slow PC, computation time is often far too precious. Improperly handled threading can lead to some bewildering results. In the `run()` method in Listing 41.7, notice that we tell the applet's thread to sleep for 50 milliseconds. Try taking this line out and seeing what happens. If you're using the applet viewer or a browser, it will probably lock up or at least appear to respond very slowly to mouse clicks and keystrokes. This happens because the applet's thread, `kicker`, eats up all the computation time and there's not much time left over for the painting thread or the user input thread. Threads can be extremely useful, but you have to make sure that they are put to sleep once in a while to give other threads a chance to run.

Fortunately, there is hope on the horizon concerning the relatively slow execution speed of Java. Just-in-time compilers, which greatly enhance the performance of Java, are starting to appear. Just-in-time compilers compile Java bytecode into native machine code on the fly so that Java programs can be run almost as fast as compiled languages such as C and C++.

A Simple Example: The Skiing Game

The code in Listing 41.8 shows a simple example of a game that has been built using the `GraphicsEngine` developed in the first part of this chapter. The game is also provided in the file `Ski.java` on the CD-ROM that accompanies this book, so you don't have to bother typing it in.

Listing 41.8. A very simple game that shows how to use the `GraphicsEngine` to create games. Save this code in a file called `Ski.java`.

```java
import java.awt.*;
import java.applet.Applet;
import java.net.URL;

public class Ski extends Applet implements Runnable {
  Thread kicker;
  GraphicsEngine engine;
  MOB tree1, tree2, tree3, player;
  int screen_height = 1, screen_width = 1, tree_height = 1, tree_width = 1;
  int player_width = 1, player_height = 1;
  int step_amount = 10;

  public void init() {
    try {
      engine = new GraphicsEngine(this);
      Image snow = getImage(new URL(getDocumentBase(), "snow.jpg"));
      engine.background = snow;
      Image tree = getImage(new URL(getDocumentBase(), "tree.gif"));
      MediaTracker tracker = new MediaTracker(this);
      tracker.addImage(tree, 0);
      tracker.addImage(snow, 0);
      tree1 = new MOB(tree);
      tree2 = new MOB(tree);
      tree3 = new MOB(tree);
      Image person = getImage(new URL(getDocumentBase(), "player.gif"));
      tracker.addImage(person, 0);
      tracker.waitForID(0);
      tree_height = tree.getHeight(this);
      tree_width = tree.getWidth(this);
      player_width =  person.getWidth(this);
      player_height =  person.getHeight(this);
      player = new MOB(person);

      screen_height = size().height;
      screen_width = size().width;

      player.y = screen_height/2;
      player.x = screen_width/2;
```

continues

Listing 41.8. continued

```java
    tree1.x = randomX();
    tree1.y = 0;

    tree2.x = randomX();
    tree2.y = screen_height/3;

    tree3.x = randomX();
    tree3.y = (screen_height*2)/3;

    player.priority = player.y-(tree_height-player_height);
    tree1.priority = tree1.y;
    tree2.priority = tree2.y;
    tree3.priority = tree3.y;

    engine.AddMOB(player);
    engine.AddMOB(tree1);
    engine.AddMOB(tree2);
    engine.AddMOB(tree3);
  }
  catch (Exception e) {
    System.out.println("Error while loading pictures...");
    e.printStackTrace();
  }

}

public void start() {
  if (kicker == null) {
    kicker = new Thread(this);
  }
  kicker.start();
}

public void run() {


  while (true) {
    increment(tree1);
    increment(tree2);
    increment(tree3);
    if (hit(tree1) || hit(tree2) || hit(tree3)) {
      step_amount = 0;
    }
    else step_amount++;
    repaint();
    try {
      kicker.sleep(100);
    }
    catch (InterruptedException e) {
    }
  }

}
```

```java
  public void increment(MOB m) {
    m.y -= step_amount;
    if (m.y < -tree_height) {
      m.y = m.y+screen_height+2*tree_height;
      m.x = randomX();
    }
    m.priority = m.y;
  }

  public boolean hit(MOB m) {
    return
(m.y < player.priority+tree_height/2 &&
m.y >= player.priority &&
m.x > player.x-tree_width &&
m.x < player.x+player_width);
  }

  public int randomX() {
    return (int) (Math.random()*screen_width);
  }

  public void stop() {
    if (kicker != null && kicker.isAlive()) {
      kicker.stop();
      kicker = null;
    }
  }


  public void update(Graphics g) {
    paint(g);
  }

  public void paint(Graphics g) {
    engine.paint(g, this);
  }


  public boolean mouseMove (Event evt, int mx, int my) {
    player.x = mx - player_width/2;
    return true;
  }


}
```

Playing the Game

To play the game, simply use a Java-enabled browser or the JDK applet viewer to view the file called ski.html. You should see something like Figure 41.4. Once the game is properly running, you see a skier and three trees on the screen.

FIGURE 41.4.

A simple skiing game applet that uses the GraphicsEngine.

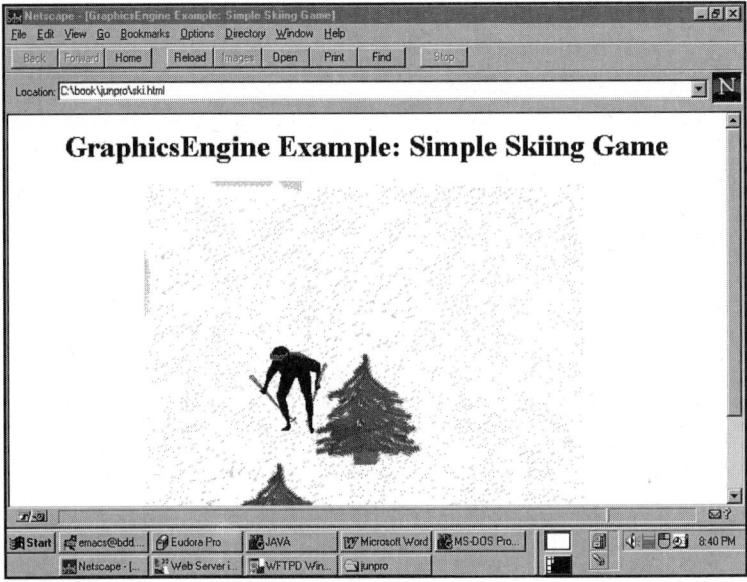

Use the mouse to control the skier. Moving your mouse left and right without holding the mouse button down causes the skier to move left and right. You cannot move the player up and down.

The object of the game is to avoid hitting the trees. Notice that as long as you avoid hitting the trees, you continue to accelerate. Hence, the longer you avoid hitting the trees, the faster you go. Hitting a tree brings the skier to a halt, and you have to start accelerating from a standstill again.

Understanding the Code

The skiing game basically grew out of the GraphicsEngine example developed earlier in this chapter. Support for things that weren't needed (like a bouncing head) was removed, and support for new things (like moving trees) was added. Tweaking code like this is an excellent way to learn a language and to learn new programming methods. Don't be afraid to tweak the code yourself—experimenting with existing code is a great way to build up some experience before attempting to write something from scratch.

Initializing Everything

As its name implies, the init() method is in charge of initializing the applet. It is called once and only once at the beginning of the applet's life cycle. In the case of the skiing game, the init() method takes care of creating the graphics engine to handle all the objects (loading the images for the background, the trees, and the skier; creating new MOBs from these images; adding these MOBs to the graphics engine; and gathering information about the size of the images).

The start() method is also part of the initialization process, but unlike the init() method, it may be called more than once. The idea behind the start() method is that it is called every time the Web page it's in is viewed; the start() method can be called several times if the user goes back to the same Web page several times in the same session.

In this case, the start() method is used just to start a thread. The thread is used to move the trees. The thread is stopped when the user leaves the Web page because the stop() method (which is called every time the Web page is left) contains code that stops the thread.

Creating Movement

The movement of the trees is accomplished inside the run() method. Inside the run() method, the increment() method is called for each of the trees, causing them to move up the screen. Whenever a tree has gone so far up the screen that it is no longer visible, it is placed at the bottom of the screen at a random position, creating the illusion that there are an infinite number of trees when in fact there are only three.

The run() method also checks to see whether or not the skier has hit a tree. If the skier has hit a tree, the variable step_amount is set to zero. If the skier has not hit a tree, the variable step_amount is increased by 1. The variable step_amount is used to decide how far to move the tree up the screen each time. If the skier has hit a tree, the trees don't move at all that particular time (because the skier has stopped). If the skier hasn't hit a tree, the trees move up by step_amount number of pixels. step_amount is increased by 1 each time the skier passes (that is, does not hit) a tree. Because step_amount increases, this makes the trees move up the screen faster, creating the illusion that the skier is accelerating.

Finally, the movement of the skier is controlled completely by the mouse. Because the mouseMove() method is called every time the mouse is moved, all we have to do is override the mouseMove() method so that whenever the mouse moves, we move the player.

Summary

In this chapter, we developed a basic graphics engine with Java that can be used for game creation. This graphics engine incorporated movable objects with prioritization and visibility settings, double buffering, and a background image. We also went over a very simple example of a game that was built using the tools presented in the chapter. However, the focus was on the construction of the tools rather than the construction of the sample game because the tools can be expanded to produce a multitude of games.

This chapter also touched on issues you should keep in mind when developing games with Java. It is important to remember that Java is a cross-platform language and therefore runs on different platforms. When you develop your games, you should be aware that people will want to run them on machines that may not have the same capabilities as your machine.

Advanced Image Processing

*by Stephen Ingram
and K.C. Hopson*

IN THIS CHAPTER

CHAPTER 42

This chapter teaches you the more advanced concepts involved in Java images. It leads off by introducing Java's fundamental image model. It then explores image filters and explains two advanced filters, including a special-effects filter. The chapter ends by using a custom filter to present Mandelbrot sets (a visually striking image from chaos theory).

To really appreciate the power behind Java images, you must understand the consumer/ producer model in detail. Powerful graphics applications use the advantages of this model to perform their visual wizardry. In particular, you can write effective image filters only if you understand the underlying model.

The Image Model

True to Java's object-oriented design, images are not presented by a single class. Rather, a richer and more specialized class system is used. The designers of Java wanted an extensible image system that would allow image manipulation as well as support for a wide variety of image formats. The best way to meet these requirements was to devolve image presentation into its requisite parts. An *image producer* understands a particular image format, but is unaware of the details behind image display. Instead, the producer renders its contents through an *image consumer* interface. By separating production from consumption, Java allows multiple image filters to be inserted between the base image and its eventual display.

Image Producers

The `ImageProducer` interface has the following methods:

- `public void addConsumer(ImageConsumer ic);`
- `public boolean isConsumer(ImageConsumer ic);`
- `public void removeConsumer(ImageConsumer ic);`
- `public void startProduction(ImageConsumer ic);`
- `public void requestTopDownLeftRightResend(ImageConsumer ic);`

Notice that all the methods require an `ImageConsumer` object. There are no back doors; an `ImageProducer` can output only through an associated `ImageConsumer`. A given producer can have multiple objects as client consumers, although this is not usually the case. Typically, as soon as a consumer registers itself with a producer using `addConsumer()`, the image data is immediately delivered through the consumer's interface.

The first three producers' methods involve attachment of consumers. The remaining two producers provide applications with methods for causing a producer to start painting. Usually, it is the AWT that is the caller, not the actual user applets.

Image Consumers

The ImageProducer interface is clean and straightforward, but the ImageConsumer is quite a bit more complex. It has the following methods:

- ◼ `public void setDimensions(int width, int height);`

- ◼ `public void setProperties(Hashtable props);`

- ◼ `public void setColorModel(ColorModel model);`

- ◼ `public void setHints(int hintflags);`

- ◼ `public void setPixels(int x, int y, int w, int h, ColorModel model, byte pixels[], int off, int scansize);`

- ◼ `public void setPixels(int x, int y, int w, int h, ColorModel model, int pixels[], int off, int scansize);`

- ◼ `public void imageComplete(int status);`

Figure 42.1 shows the normal progression of calls to the ImageConsumer interface. Several methods are optional: setProperties(), setHints(), and setColorModel(). The core methods are first setDimensions(), followed by one or more calls to setPixels(). Finally, when there are no more setPixels() calls, imageComplete() is invoked.

FIGURE 42.1.

Normal flow of calls to an ImageConsumer *interface.*

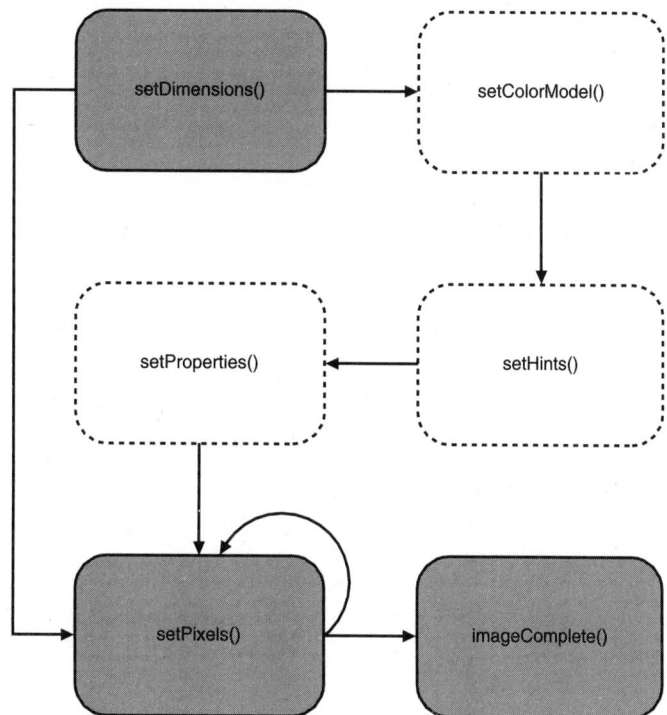

Each image has fixed rectangular dimensions, which are passed in setDimensions(). The consumer has to save this data for future reference. The setProperties() method has no discernible use right now, and most consumers don't do anything with it. The *hintflags* parameter, however, is a different story. *Hints* are supposed to give clues about the format of the producer's data. Table 42.1 lists the values for *hintflags*.

Table 42.1. The values for the *hintflags* parameter for setHints().

Flag Name	Meaning
RANDOMPIXELORDER=1	No assumptions should be made about the delivery of pixels.
TOPDOWNLEFTRIGHT=2	Pixel delivery will paint in top to bottom, left to right.
COMPLETESCANLINES=4	Pixels will be delivered in multiples of complete rows.
SINGLEPASS=8	Pixels will be delivered in a single pass. No pixel will appear in more than one setPixel() call.
SINGLEFRAME=16	The image consists of a single static frame.

When all the pixel information has been transmitted, the producer calls imageComplete(*status*). The *status* parameter has one of three values: IMAGEERROR=1, SINGLEFRAMEDONE=2, or STATICFRAMEDONE=3.

SINGLEFRAMEDONE indicates that additional frames will follow; for example, a video camera would use this technique. Special-effect filters could also use SINGLEFRAMEDONE. STATICFRAMEDONE is used to indicate that no more pixels will be transmitted for the image. The consumer should remove itself from the producer after receiving STATICFRAMEDONE.

Two setPixels() calls provide the image data. Keep in mind that the image size was set in advance by setDimensions(). The array within setPixels() calls does not necessarily contain all the pixels within an image. In fact, the arrays usually contain only a rectangular subset of the total image. Figure 42.2 shows a rectangle of setPixels() within an entire image.

The row size of the array is the scansize. The width and height (*w* and *h*) parameters indicate the usable pixels within the array, and the offset (*off*) contains the starting index. It is up to the consumer to map the passed array onto the entire image. The subimage's location within the total image is contained in the x and y parameters.

The ColorModel contains all needed color information for the image. The call to setColorModel() is purely informational because each setPixels() call passes a specific ColorModel parameter. No assumptions should be made about the ColorModel from setColorModel() calls.

FIGURE 42.2.

The relationship of setPixels() *calls to an entire image.*

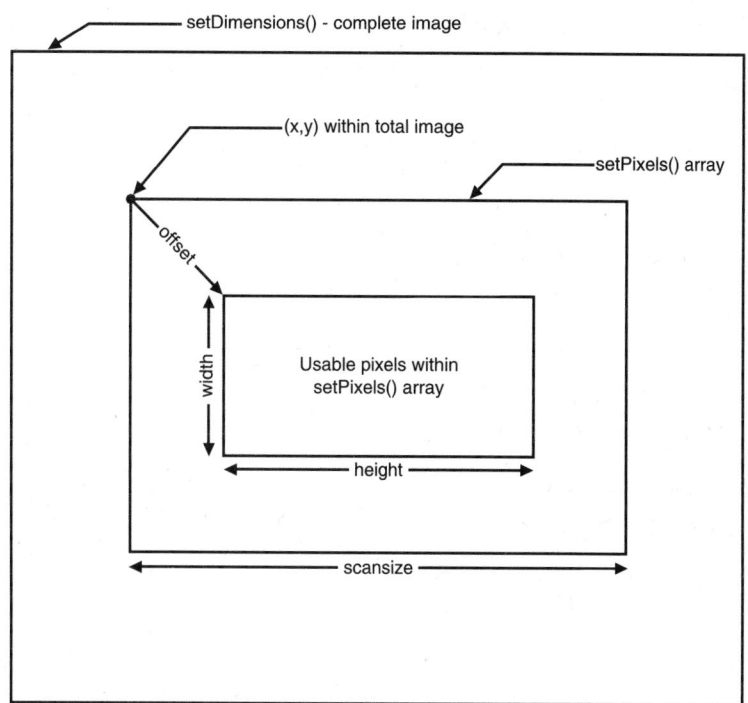

setDimensions() - complete image

(x,y) within total image

setPixels() array

offset

width

Usable pixels within setPixels() array

height

scansize

Filtering an Image

Image filters sit between an ImageProducer and an ImageConsumer and must implement both these interfaces. Java supplies two separate classes for using filters: FilteredImageSource and ImageFilter.

The FilteredImageSource Class

The FilteredImageSource class implements the ImageProducer interface, which allows the class to masquerade as a real producer. When a consumer attaches to the FilteredImageSource, it's stored in an instance of the current filter. The filter class object is then given to the actual ImageProducer. When the image is rendered through the filter's interface, the data is altered before being forwarded to the actual ImageConsumer. Figure 42.3 shows the filtering operation.

The following is the constructor for FilteredImageSource:

```
FilteredImageSource(ImageProducer orig, ImageFilter imgf);
```

42

ADVANCED IMAGE PROCESSING

Producer and filter are stored until a consumer attaches itself to the `FilterImageSource`. The following lines show how an application sets up a filter chain:

```
// Create the filter
ImageFilter filter = new SomeFilter();
// Use the filter to get a producer
ImageProducer p = new FilteredImageSource(myImage.getSource(), filter);
// Use the producer to create the image
Image img = createImage(p);
```

FIGURE 42.3.

Image filtering classes.

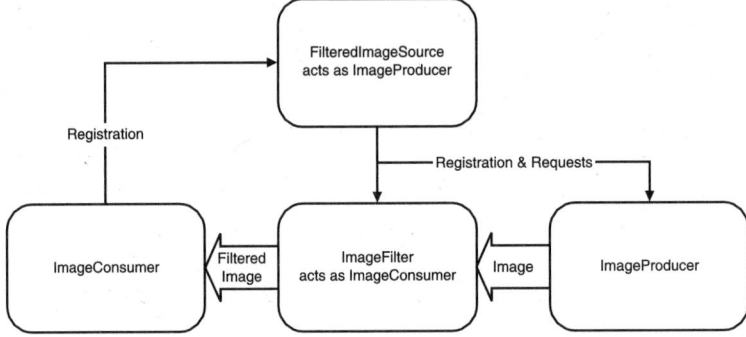

Writing a Filter

Filters always extend the `ImageFilter` class, which implements all the methods for an `ImageConsumer`. In fact, the `ImageFilter` class is itself a pass-through filter. It passes the data without alteration but otherwise acts as a normal image filter. The `FilteredImageSource` class works only with `ImageFilter` and its subclasses. Using `ImageFilter` as a base frees you from having to implement a method you have no use for, such as `setProperties()`. `ImageFilter` also implements one additional method:

```
public void resendTopDownLeftRight(ImageProducer ip);
```

When a `FilteredImageSource` gets a request to resend through its `ImageProducer` interface, it calls the `ImageFilter` instead of the actual producer. `ImageFilter`'s default resend function calls the producer and requests a repaint. There are times when the filter does not want to have the image regenerated, so it can override this call and simply do nothing. One example of this type of filter is described in "Dynamic Image Filter: `FXFilter`," later in this chapter. A special-effects filter can simply remove or obscure certain parts of an underlying image. To perform the effect, the filter must merely know the image dimensions, not the specific pixels it will be overwriting. `setPixel()` calls are safely ignored, but the producer must be prevented from re-painting. If your filter does not implement `setPixels()` calls, a subsequent resend request will destroy the filter's changes by writing directly to the consumer.

> **NOTE**
>
> If `setPixels()` is not overridden in your filter, you will probably want to override `resendTopDownLeftRight()` to prevent the image from being regenerated after your filter has altered the image.

Static Image Filter: Rotation

Rotation is a common image manipulation. Unfortunately, there is no standard Java filter for performing this operation. This apparent oversight provides us with an excellent opportunity to develop your first filter.

Static filters perform their manipulations and then issue a STATICFRAMEDONE. Because all the alterations are applied at one time, the filter is said to be *static*. If a filter applies its changes in stages, it is considered to be a *dynamic* filter.

Pixel Rotation

To perform image rotation, you must use some math. You can perform the rotation of points with the following formulas:

```
new_x = x * cos(angle) - y * sin(angle)
new_y = y * cos(angle) + x * sin(angle)
```

Rotation is around the z-axis. Positive angles cause counterclockwise rotation; negative angles cause clockwise rotation. These formulas are defined for Cartesian coordinates. The Java screen is actually inverted, so the positive y-axis runs down the screen, not up. To compensate for this, invert the sign of the sine coefficients:

```
new_x = x * cos(angle) + y * sin(angle)
new_y = y * cos(angle) - x * sin(angle)
```

Additionally, the sine and cosine functions compute the angle in radians. The following formula converts degrees to radians:

```
radians = degrees * PI/180;
```

This works because there are 2*PI radians in a circle. That's all the math you'll need; now you can set up the `ImageConsumer` routines.

Handling `setDimensions()`

The `setDimensions()` call tells you the total size of the image. Record the size and allocate an array to hold all the pixels. Because this filter will rotate the image, the size may change. In an extreme case, the size could grow much larger than the original image because images are rect-angular. If you rotate a rectangle 45 degrees, a new rectangle must be computed that contains all the pixels from the rotated image (see Figure 42.4).

FIGURE 42.4.
The new bounding rectangle after rotation.

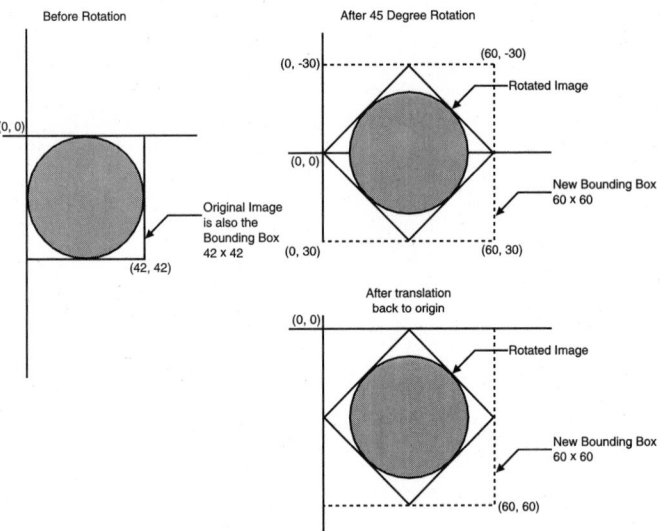

To calculate the new bounding rectangle, each vertex of the original image must be rotated. After rotation, the new coordinate is checked for minimum and maximum x and y values. After all four points are rotated, you'll know what the new bounding rectangle is. Record this infor-mation as rotation space, and inform the consumer of the size after rotation.

Handling setPixels()

The setPixels() calls are very straightforward. Simply translate the pixel color into an RGB value and store it in the original image array allocated in setDimensions().

Handling imageComplete()

The imageComplete() method performs all the work. After the image is final, populate a new rotation space array and return it to the consumer through the consumer's setPixels() rou-tine. Finally, invoke the consumer's imageComplete() method. Listing 42.1 shows the entire filter.

Listing 42.1. The SpinFilter class.

```java
import java.awt.*;
import java.awt.image.*;

public class SpinFilter extends ImageFilter
{
    private double angle;
    private double cos, sin;
    private Rectangle rotatedSpace;
    private Rectangle originalSpace;
    private ColorModel defaultRGBModel;
    private int inPixels[], outPixels[];

    SpinFilter(double angle)
    {
        this.angle = angle * (Math.PI / 180);
        cos = Math.cos(this.angle);
        sin = Math.sin(this.angle);
        defaultRGBModel = ColorModel.getRGBdefault();
    }

    private void transform(int x, int y, double out[])
    {
        out[0] = (x * cos) + (y * sin);
        out[1] = (y * cos) - (x * sin);
    }

    private void transformBack(int x, int y, double out[])
    {
        out[0] = (x * cos) - (y * sin);
        out[1] = (y * cos) + (x * sin);
    }

    public void transformSpace(Rectangle rect)
    {
        double out[] = new double[2];

        double minx = Double.MAX_VALUE;
        double miny = Double.MAX_VALUE;
        double maxx = Double.MIN_VALUE;
        double maxy = Double.MIN_VALUE;
        int w = rect.width;
        int h = rect.height;
        int x = rect.x;
        int y = rect.y;

        for ( int i = 0; i < 4; i++ )
        {
            switch (i)
            {
            case 0: transform(x + 0, y + 0, out); break;
            case 1: transform(x + w, y + 0, out); break;
            case 2: transform(x + 0, y + h, out); break;
            case 3: transform(x + w, y + h, out); break;
            }
```

continues

Listing 42.1. continued

```java
                minx = Math.min(minx, out[0]);
                miny = Math.min(miny, out[1]);
                maxx = Math.max(maxx, out[0]);
                maxy = Math.max(maxy, out[1]);
        }
        rect.x = (int) Math.floor(minx);
        rect.y = (int) Math.floor(miny);
        rect.width = (int) Math.ceil(maxx) - rect.x;
        rect.height = (int) Math.ceil(maxy) - rect.y;
    }

    /**
     * Tell the consumer the new dimensions based on our
     * rotation of coordinate space.
     * @see ImageConsumer#setDimensions
     */
    public void setDimensions(int width, int height)
    {
        originalSpace = new Rectangle(0, 0, width, height);
        rotatedSpace = new Rectangle(0, 0, width, height);
        transformSpace(rotatedSpace);
        inPixels = new int[originalSpace.width * originalSpace.height];
        consumer.setDimensions(rotatedSpace.width, rotatedSpace.height);
    }

    /**
     * Tell the consumer that we use the defaultRGBModel color model
     * NOTE: This overrides whatever color model is used underneath us.
     * @param model contains the color model of the image or filter
     *              beneath us (preceding us)
     * @see ImageConsumer#setColorModel
     */
    public void setColorModel(ColorModel model)
    {
        consumer.setColorModel(defaultRGBModel);
    }

    /**
     * Set the pixels in our image array from the passed
     * array of bytes.  Xlate the pixels into our default
     * color model (RGB).
     * @see ImageConsumer#setPixels
     */
    public void setPixels(int x, int y, int w, int h,
                    ColorModel model, byte pixels[],
                    int off, int scansize)
    {
        int index = y * originalSpace.width + x;
        int srcindex = off;
        int srcinc = scansize - w;
        int indexinc = originalSpace.width - w;
        for ( int dy = 0; dy < h; dy++ )
        {
            for ( int dx = 0; dx < w; dx++ )
            {
                inPixels[index++] = model.getRGB(pixels[srcindex++] & 0xff);
            }
```

```
            srcindex += srcinc;
            index += indexinc;
        }
    }

    /**
     * Set the pixels in our image array from the passed
     * array of integers.  Xlate the pixels into our default
     * color model (RGB).
     * @see ImageConsumer#setPixels
     */
    public void setPixels(int x, int y, int w, int h,
                  ColorModel model, int pixels[],
                  int off, int scansize)
    {
        int index = y * originalSpace.width + x;
        int srcindex = off;
        int srcinc = scansize - w;
        int indexinc = originalSpace.width - w;
        for ( int dy = 0; dy < h; dy++ )
        {
            for ( int dx = 0; dx < w; dx++ )
            {
                inPixels[index++] = model.getRGB(pixels[srcindex++]);
            }
            srcindex += srcinc;
            index += indexinc;
        }
    }

    /**
     * Notification that the image is complete and there will
     * be no further setPixel calls.
     * @see ImageConsumer#imageComplete
     */
    public void imageComplete(int status)
    {
        if (status == IMAGEERROR || status == IMAGEABORTED)
        {
            consumer.imageComplete(status);
            return;
        }
        double point[] = new double[2];
        int srcwidth = originalSpace.width;
        int srcheight = originalSpace.height;
        int outwidth = rotatedSpace.width;
        int outheight = rotatedSpace.height;
        int outx, outy, srcx, srcy;

        outPixels = new int[outwidth * outheight];
        outx = rotatedSpace.x;
        outy = rotatedSpace.y;
        double end[] = new double[2];
        int index = 0;
        for ( int y = 0; y < outheight; y++ )
        {
            for ( int x = 0; x < outwidth; x++)
            {
```

continues

Listing 42.1. continued

```
                // find the originalSpace point
                transformBack(outx + x, outy + y, point);
                srcx = (int)Math.round(point[0]);
                srcy = (int)Math.round(point[1]);

                // if this point is within the original image
                // retreive its pixel value and store in output
                // else write a zero into the space. (0 alpha = transparent)
                if ( srcx < 0 || srcx >= srcwidth ||
                     srcy < 0 || srcy >= srcheight )
                {
                    outPixels[index++] = 0;
                }
                else
                {
                    outPixels[index++] = inPixels[(srcy * srcwidth) + srcx];
                }
            }
        }
        // write the entire new image to the consumer
        consumer.setPixels(0, 0, outwidth, outheight, defaultRGBModel,
                           outPixels, 0, outwidth);

        // tell consumer we are done
        consumer.imageComplete(status);
    }
}
```

The rotation is complex. First, as Figure 42.4 shows (earlier in this chapter), the rotated object is not completely within the screen's boundary. All the rotated pixels must be translated back in relation to the origin. You can do this easily by assuming that the coordinates of rotated space are really 0,0—the trick is how the array is populated. An iteration is made along each row in rotated space. For each pixel in the row, the rotation is inverted. This yields the position of this pixel within the original space. If the pixel lies within the original image, grab its color and store it in rotated space; if it isn't, store a transparent color.

Dynamic Image Filter: FXFilter

The SpinFilter just described is static; the FXFilter described in this section is dynamic. A *static* filter alters an image and sends STATICIMAGEDONE when the alteration is done; a *dynamic* filter makes the effect take place over multiple frames, much like an animation. The FXFilter has four effects: wipe left, wipe right, wipe from center out, and dissolve. Each effect operates by erasing the image in stages. The filter calls imageComplete() many times, but instead of passing STATICIMAGEDONE, it specifies SINGLEFRAMEDONE.

Because each effect is simply a matter of writing a block of a particular color, there is no need to refer to the pixels in the original image. Because you don't need to use the setPixels() method, the filter functions very quickly.

Each of the wipes operates by moving a column of erased pixels over the length of the image. The width of the column is calculated to yield the number of configured iterations. The dissolve works by erasing a rectangular block at random places throughout the image. Of all the effects, dissolve is the slowest to execute because it has to calculate each random location.

In setHints(), the consumer is told that the filter will send random pixels. This causes the consumer to call resendTopDownLeftRight() when the image is complete. The filter must intercept the call to avoid having the just-erased image repainted by the producer in pristine form.

The filter has two constructors. If you don't specify a color, the image dissolves into transparency, allowing you to phase one image into a second image. You can also specify an optional color, which causes the image to gradually change into the passed color. You can dissolve an image into the background by passing the background color in the filter constructor. The number of iterations and paints is completely configurable. There is no hard-and-fast formula for performing these effects, so feel free to alter the values to get the result you want. Listing 42.2 contains the source for the FXFilter filter.

Listing 42.2. The special-effects filter.

```java
import java.awt.*;
import java.awt.image.*;
import java.util.*;

public class FXFilter extends ImageFilter
{
    private int outwidth, outheight;
    private ColorModel defaultRGBModel;
    private int dissolveColor;
    private int iterations = 50;
    private int paintsPer = 2;
    private static final int SCALER = 25;
    private static final int MINIMUM_BLOCK = 7;
    private int dissolve_w, dissolve_h;
    private boolean sizeSet = false;
    private Thread runThread;

    public static final int DISSOLVE = 0;
    public static final int WIPE_LR =  1;
    public static final int WIPE_RL =  2;
    public static final int WIPE_C =   3;
    private int type = DISSOLVE;

    /**
     * Dissolve to transparent constructor
     */
    FXFilter()
    {
        defaultRGBModel = ColorModel.getRGBdefault();
        dissolveColor = 0;
    }
```

Listing 42.2. continued

```java
/**
 * Dissolve to the passed color constructor
 * @param dcolor contains the color to dissolve to
 */
FXFilter(Color dcolor)
{
    this();
    dissolveColor = dcolor.getRGB();
}

/**
 * Set the type of effect to perform.
 */
public void setType(int t)
{
    switch (t)
    {
    case DISSOLVE: type = t; break;
    case WIPE_LR:  type = t; break;
    case WIPE_RL:  type = t; break;
    case WIPE_C:   type = t; break;
    }
}

/**
 * Set the size of the dissolve blocks (pixels removed).
 */
public void setDissolveSize(int w, int h)
{
    if ( w < MINIMUM_BLOCK ) w = MINIMUM_BLOCK;
    if ( h < MINIMUM_BLOCK ) w = MINIMUM_BLOCK;
    dissolve_w = w;
    dissolve_h = h;
    sizeSet = true;
}

/**
 * Set the dissolve paramters. (Optional, will default to 200 & 2)
 * @param num contains the number of times to loop.
 * @param paintsPerNum contains the number of blocks to remove per paint
 */
public void setIterations(int num, int paintsPerNum)
{
    iterations = num;
    paintsPer = paintsPerNum;
}

/**
 * @see ImageConsumer#setDimensions
 */
public void setDimensions(int width, int height)
{
    outwidth = width;
    outheight = height;
    consumer.setDimensions(width, height);
}
```

```java
/**
 * Don't tell consumer we send complete frames.
 * Tell them we send random blocks.
 * @see ImageConsumer#setHints
 */
public void setHints(int hints)
{
    consumer.setHints(ImageConsumer.RANDOMPIXELORDER);
}


/**
 * Override this method to keep the producer
 * from refreshing our dissolved image
 */
public void resendTopDownLeftRight(ImageProducer ip)
{
}


/**
 * Notification that the image is complete and there will
 * be no further setPixel calls.
 * @see ImageConsumer#imageComplete
 */
public void imageComplete(int status)
{
    if (status == IMAGEERROR || status == IMAGEABORTED)
    {
        consumer.imageComplete(status);
        return;
    }
    if ( status == SINGLEFRAMEDONE )
    {
        runThread = new RunFilter(this);
        runThread.start();
    }
    else
        filter();
}

public void filter()
{
    switch ( type )
    {
    case DISSOLVE: dissolve();   break;
    case WIPE_LR:  wipeLR();     break;
    case WIPE_RL:  wipeRL();     break;
    case WIPE_C:   wipeC();      break;
    default:       dissolve();   break;
    }
    consumer.imageComplete(STATICIMAGEDONE);
}

/**
 * Wipe the image from left to right
 */
public void wipeLR()
{
```

continues

Listing 42.2. continued

```java
        int xw = outwidth / iterations;
        if ( xw <= 0 ) xw = 1;
        int total = xw * outheight;
        int dissolvePixels[] = new int[total];
        for ( int x = 0; x < total; x++ )
            dissolvePixels[x] = dissolveColor;

        for ( int t = 0; t < (outwidth - xw); t += xw )
        {
            consumer.setPixels(t, 0, xw, outheight,
                                defaultRGBModel, dissolvePixels,
                                0, xw);
            // tell consumer we are done with this frame
            consumer.imageComplete(ImageConsumer.SINGLEFRAMEDONE);
        }
    }

    /**
     * Wipe the image from right to left
     */
    public void wipeRL()
    {
        int xw = outwidth / iterations;
        if ( xw <= 0 ) xw = 1;
        int total = xw * outheight;
        int dissolvePixels[] = new int[total];
        for ( int x = 0; x < total; x++ )
            dissolvePixels[x] = dissolveColor;

        for ( int t = outwidth - xw - 1; t >= 0; t -= xw )
        {
            consumer.setPixels(t, 0, xw, outheight,
                                defaultRGBModel, dissolvePixels,
                                0, xw);
            // tell consumer we are done with this frame
            consumer.imageComplete(ImageConsumer.SINGLEFRAMEDONE);
        }
    }

    /**
     * Wipe the image from the center out
     */
    public void wipeC()
    {
        int times = outwidth / 2;
        int xw = times / iterations;
        if ( xw <= 0 ) xw = 1;
        int total = xw * outheight;
        int dissolvePixels[] = new int[total];
        for ( int x = 0; x < total; x++ )
            dissolvePixels[x] = dissolveColor;

        int x1 = outwidth /2;
        int x2 = outwidth /2;
        while ( x2 < (outwidth - xw) )
        {
```

```java
        consumer.setPixels(x1, 0, xw, outheight,
                            defaultRGBModel, dissolvePixels,
                            0, xw);
        consumer.setPixels(x2, 0, xw, outheight,
                            defaultRGBModel, dissolvePixels,
                            0, xw);

        // tell consumer we are done with this frame
        consumer.imageComplete(ImageConsumer.SINGLEFRAMEDONE);
        x1 -= xw;
        x2 += xw;
    }
}

/**
 * Dissolve the image
 */
public void dissolve()
{
    // Is the image too small to dissolve?
    if ( outwidth < MINIMUM_BLOCK && outheight < MINIMUM_BLOCK )
    {
        return;
    }
    consumer.imageComplete(ImageConsumer.SINGLEFRAMEDONE);

    if ( !sizeSet )
    {
        // Calculate the dissolve block size
        dissolve_w = (outwidth * SCALER) / (iterations * paintsPer);
        dissolve_h = (outheight * SCALER) / (iterations * paintsPer);

        // Minimum block size
        if ( dissolve_w < MINIMUM_BLOCK ) dissolve_w = MINIMUM_BLOCK;
        if ( dissolve_h < MINIMUM_BLOCK ) dissolve_h = MINIMUM_BLOCK;
    }

    // Initialize the dissolve pixel array
    int total = dissolve_w * dissolve_h;
    int[] dissolvePixels = new int[total];
    for ( int i = 0; i < total; i++ )
        dissolvePixels[i] = dissolveColor;

    int pos;
    double apos;
    for ( int t = 0; t < iterations; t++ )
    {
        for ( int px = 0; px < paintsPer; px++ )
        {
            // remove some pixels
            apos = Math.random() * outwidth;
            int xpos = (int)Math.floor(apos);
            apos = Math.random() * outheight;
            int ypos = (int)Math.floor(apos);
            if ( xpos - dissolve_w >= outwidth )
                xpos = outwidth - dissolve_w - 1;
            if ( ypos - dissolve_h >= outheight )
                ypos = outheight - dissolve_h - 1;
```

continues

Listing 42.2. continued

```
                consumer.setPixels(xpos, ypos, dissolve_w, dissolve_h,
                                   defaultRGBModel, dissolvePixels,
                                   0, dissolve_w);
            }
            // tell consumer we are done with this frame
            consumer.imageComplete(ImageConsumer.SINGLEFRAMEDONE);
        }
    }
}

class RunFilter extends Thread
{
    FXFilter fx = null;

    RunFilter(FXFilter f)
    {
        fx = f;
    }

    public void run()
    {
        fx.filter();
    }
}
```

You need RunFilter for image producers created from a memory image source. GIF and JPEG images both spawn a thread for their producers. Because the filter must loop within the imageComplete() method, you need a separate thread for the production. Memory images do not spawn a separate thread for their producers, so the filter has to spawn its own.

The only way to differentiate the producers is to key on their status. GIF and JPEG image producers send STATICIMAGEDONE, and memory images send SINGLEFRAMEDONE.

NOTE

If you spawn an additional thread for GIF and JPEG images, you won't be able to display the image at all. Producers that are already a separate thread must be operated within their existing threads.

The variables SCALER and MINIMUM_BLOCK apply only to dissolves. Because a dissolve paints into random locations, there are many overlapping squares. If the blocks are sized to exactly cover the image over the configured number of iterations, the image won't come close to dissolving. The SCALER parameter specifies what multiple of an image the blocks should be constructed to cover. Increasing the value yields larger dissolve blocks and guarantees a complete dissolve. A value that's too large will erase the image too quickly and ruin the effect, but a value that's too small will not dissolve enough of the image. A middle value completely dissolves the image, but a dissolve is most effective when most of the image is erased in the beginning stages of the effect.

The Mandelbrot Set Project

A new project, one that views the Mandelbrot set, gives you examples of some of the more advanced concepts you have been introduced to. The Mandelbrot set is the most spectacular example of fractals, which represent one of the hot scientific topics of recent years. With the applets in this chapter, you can view or generate an original Mandelbrot image and zoom in and out of it to produce new portions of the set.

 Because the Mandelbrot set can take a while to generate (it requires millions of calculations), you have a chance to combine threads and image filters so that you can view the set as it's being generated. You may also want to save the Mandelbrot images. The `BmpClass` file, found on the CD-ROM that accompanies this book, converts a BMP-formatted file into a Java image.

Using the Applets

There are two applets in the Mandelbrot example. The first applet, `MandelApp`, generates the full Mandelbrot set. Depending on your computer, this can take a little while; for example, on a 486DX2-50 PC, it takes a couple minutes. When the image is complete (as indicated by a message on the browser's status bar), you can save the image to a BMP formatted file by clicking anywhere on the applet's display area. The file will be called `mandel.bmp`. Remember to run this applet from a program, such as the applet viewer, that lets applets write to disk.

 The other applet, `MandelAppZoom`, is more fully featured. It begins by loading the Mandelbrot bitmap specified by an HTML applet parameter tag. The default `mandel1` corresponds to a BMP file and a data file that specifies x-y parameter values included on this book's CD-ROM.

Once the image is displayed, you can pick regions to zoom in on by clicking on a point in the image and dragging the mouse to the endpoint of the region you want to display. Type z or **z** on the keyboard, and the applet creates the image representing the new region of the Mandelbrot set. The key to this applet is patience; the calculations can take a little while to set up and run. The applet tries to help your patience by updating the status bar to indicate what is going on. Furthermore, the image filter displays each column of the set as the calculations advance.

If you select a region that doesn't appear to have anything interesting to show when you zoom on it, you can stop the calculation by typing a or **A** on the keyboard. The applet takes a moment to wrap up, but then you can proceed. When you have problems finding an interesting region to look at, try increasing the size of the highlighted area. This action yields a bigger area that is generated, giving you a better feel for what should be inspected. You get the best results by working with medium-sized highlighted regions, rather than large or small ones.

The zoom applet maintains a cache of processed images so that you can move back and forth among the processed images. Table 42.2 lists the text codes for using the zoom applet. If you want to use the file-saving capabilities of this program, you must run it from something that does not prevent file saving, such as the applet viewer program. You can also run the program in a browser like Netscape; however, the applet will be able to do everything except save the images as files.

Table 42.2. Codes for controlling the Mandelbrot applet.

Characters	Action
A or a	Abort current Mandelbrot calculation
B or b	Go to previous image
F or f	Go to next image
C or c	Remove all but full image from memory
N or n	Go to next image
P or p	Go to previous image
S or s	Save the current image to a BMP file prefixed by `tempMandel`
Z or z	Zoom in on currently highlighted region

How It Works

Because the Mandelbrot set can take quite a while to generate, it was designed by combining a calculation thread with an image filter so that you can see the results as they are generated. However, understanding how the classes interrelate is a little tricky. Figure 42.5 shows the workflow involved in producing a Mandelbrot image. Understanding this flow is the key to understanding this project.

FIGURE 42.5.

The workflow involved in producing a Mandelbrot image.

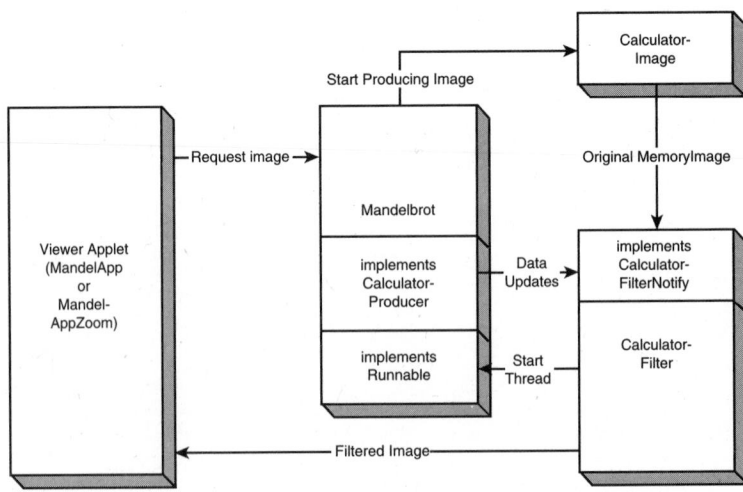

The process begins when an applet displaying Mandelbrot sets constructs a `Mandelbrot` object. The `Mandelbrot` object, in turn, creates an instance of the `CalculatorImage` class. The Mandelbrot set passes itself as a part of the `CalculatorImage` constructor. It is referenced as a `CalculatorProducer` object, an interface that the `Mandelbrot` class implements. This interface implementation is used to communicate with the image filter.

In the next step, the applet requests a `Mandelbrot` image. This is initiated by calling the `getImage()` method of the `Mandelbrot` object, which in turn leads to a call to a like-named method of the `CalculatorImage` object. At this point, the `CalculatorImage` object first creates a color palette by using an instance of the `ImageColorModel` class and then creates a `MemoryImageSource` object. This object, which implements `ImageProducer`, produces an image initialized to all zeros (black); it's combined with an instance of the `CalculatorFilter` class to produce a `FilteredImageSource`.

When the `MemoryImageSource` object produces its empty image, it is passed to the `CalculatorFilter`, which takes the opportunity to produce the calculated image. It does this by kicking off the thread of the image to be calculated. The `CalculatorFilter` doesn't know that it is the Mandelbrot set that's calculated; it just knows that some calculation must occur in the `CalculatorProducer` object in which it has a reference.

Once the `Mandelbrot` thread is started, it begins the long calculations to produce a Mandelbrot set. Whenever it finishes a section of the set, it notifies the filter with new data through the `CalculatorFilterNotify` interface. The filter, in turn, lets the viewing applet know that it has new data to display by updating the corresponding `ImageConsumer`, which causes the applet's `imageUpdate()` method to be called. This call causes a repaint, and the new image data is displayed. This process repeats until the full image is created.

As you have probably observed, this is a complicated process. The `Calculator` classes here are meant to provide a generic approach toward manipulating images that need long calculations. You can replace the `Mandelbrot` class with some other calculation thread that implements `CalculatorProducer`, and everything should work. A good exercise is to replace `Mandelbrot` with another fractal calculation or some other scientific imaging calculation. (I found that replacing `Mandelbrot` with a `Julia` fractal class calculation was very easy.)

 Some of the classes in this project are now presented with their full source code to explain the advanced image processing. The other classes can be found on the CD-ROM that accompanies this book.

The Mandelbrot Class

The `Mandelbrot` class, shown in Listing 42.3, calculates the Mandelbrot set. It implements the `Runnable` interface (so it can run as a thread) and also implements the `CalculatorProducer` interface (so it can update an image filter of progress made in its calculations).

Listing 42.3. The Mandelbrot class.

```java
import java.awt.image.*;
import java.awt.Image;
import java.lang.*;

// Class for producing a Mandelbrot set image...
public class Mandelbrot implements Runnable, CalculatorProducer {
    int width;  // The dimensions of the image...
    int height;
    CalculateFilterNotify filter; // Keeps track of image production...
    int pix[]; // Pixels used to construct image...
    CalculatorImage img;
    // General Mandelbrot parameters...
    int numColors = 256;
    int maxIterations = 512;
    int maxSize = 4;
    double RealMax,ImagineMax,RealMin,ImagineMin;  // Define sizes to build...
    private Boolean stopCalc = new Boolean(false);  // Stop calculations...

    // Create standard Mandelbrot set
    public Mandelbrot(int width,int height) {
        this.width = width;
        this.height = height;
        RealMax = 1.20;   // Default starting sizes...
        RealMin = -2.0;
        ImagineMax = 1.20;
        ImagineMin = -1.20;
    }

    // Create zoom of Mandelbrot set
    public Mandelbrot(int width,int height,double RealMax,double RealMin,
     double ImagineMax,double ImagineMin) {
        this.width = width;
        this.height = height;
        this.RealMax = RealMax;   // Default starting sizes...
        this.RealMin = RealMin;
        this.ImagineMax = ImagineMax;
        this.ImagineMin = ImagineMin;
    }

    // Start producing the Mandelbrot set...
    public Image getImage() {
        img = new CalculatorImage(width,height,this);
        return img.getImage();
    }

    // Start thread to produce data...
    public void start(int pix[],CalculateFilterNotify filter) {
        this.pix = pix;
        this.filter = filter;
        new Thread(this).start();
    }

    // See if user wants to stop before completion...
    public void stop() {
```

```
      synchronized (stopCalc) {
         stopCalc = Boolean.TRUE;
      }
      System.out.println("GOT STOP!");
   }

   // Create data here...
   public void run() {
      // Establish Mandelbrot parameters...
      double Q[] = new double[height];
      // Pixdata is for image filter updates...
      int pixdata[] = new int[height];
      double P,diffP,diffQ, x, y, x2, y2;
      int color, row, column,index;

      System.out.println("RealMax = " + RealMax + " RealMin = " + RealMin +
            " ImagineMax = " + ImagineMax + " ImagineMin = " + ImagineMin);
      // Setup calculation parameters...
      diffP = (RealMax - RealMin)/(width);
      diffQ = (ImagineMax - ImagineMin)/(height);
      Q[0] = ImagineMax;
      color = 0;

      // Setup delta parameters...
      for (row = 1; row < height; row++)
         Q[row] = Q[row-1] - diffQ;
      P = RealMin;

      // Start calculating!
      for (column = 0; column < width; column++) {
         for (row = 0; row < height; row++) {
            x = y = x2 = y2 = 0.0;
            color = 1;
            while ((color < maxIterations) &&
               ((x2 + y2) < maxSize)) {
                  x2 = x * x;
                  y2 = y * y;
                  y = (2*x*y) + Q[row];
                  x = x2 - y2 + P;
                  ++color;
            }
            // plot...
            index = (row * width) + column;
            pix[index] = (int)(color % numColors);
            pixdata[row] = pix[index];
         } // end row
         // Update column after each iteration...
         filter.dataUpdateColumn(column,pixdata);
         P += diffP;
         // See if we were told to stop...
         synchronized (stopCalc) {
            if (stopCalc == Boolean.TRUE) {
               column = width;
               System.out.println("RUN: Got stop calc!");
            }
         }  // end sync
```

continues

Listing 42.3. continued

```
    } // end col

    // Tell filter that we're done producing data...
    System.out.println("FILTER: Data Complete!");
    filter.setComplete();
  }

  // Save the Mandelbrot set as a BMP file...
  public void saveBMP(String filename) {
    img.saveBMP(filename,pix);
  }
}
```

There are two constructors for the `Mandelbrot` class. The default constructor produces the full Mandelbrot set and takes the dimensions of the image to calculate. The `Real` and `Imagine` variables in the constructors and the `run()` method are used to map the x-y axis to the real and imaginary portions of c in the following formula:

$$z_{n+1} = z_n^2 + c$$

The other constructor is used to zoom in on a user-defined mapping.

A few other variables are worth noting. The variable `maxIterations` represents when to stop calculating a number. If this number (set to 512 in the code) is reached, the starting value of c takes a long time to head toward infinity. The variable `maxSize` is a simpler indicator of how quickly the current value grows. How the current calculation is related to these variables is mapped to a specific color; the higher the number, the slower the growth. If you have a fast computer, you can adjust these variables to get a richer or duller expression of the Mandelbrot set.

Once the thread is started (by the `CalculatorFilter` object through the `start()` method), the `run()` method calculates the Mandelbrot values and stores a color corresponding to the growth rate of the current complex number into a pixel array. When a column is complete, it uses the `CalculateFilterNotify` interface to let the related filter know that new data has been produced. It also checks to see whether you want to abort the calculation. Note how it synchronizes the `stopCalc` boolean object in the `run()` and `stop()` methods.

The calculation can take a while to complete (it takes a couple of minutes on a 486-based PC). Nevertheless, this performance is quite a testament to Java! With other interpreted, portable languages, you may be tempted to use the reset button because the calculations would take so long. With Java, you get fast visual feedback on how the set unfolds.

A good exercise is to save any partially developed Mandelbrot set; you can use the `saveBMP()` method here. You also need some kind of data file to indicate where the calculation was stopped.

The `CalculateFilterNotify` Interface

The `CalculateFilterNotify` interface defines the methods needed to update an image filter that works with a calculation thread. As shown in Listing 42.4, the "data" methods are used for conveying a new batch of data to the filter. The `setComplete()` method indicates that the calculations are complete.

Listing 42.4. The `CalculateFilterNotify` interface.

```
/* Interface for defining methods for updating a
   Calulator Filter... */
public interface CalculateFilterNotify {
    public void dataUpdate();   // Update everything...
    public void dataUpdateRow(int row); // Update one row...
    public void dataUpdateColumn(int col,int pixdata[]);  // Update one column...
    public void setComplete();
}
```

The `CalculatorProducer` Interface

The `CalculatorProducer` interface, shown in Listing 42.5, defines the method called when a calculation filter is ready to kick off a thread that produces the data used to generate an image. The `CalculateFilterNotify` object passed to the `start()` method is called by the producer whenever new data is yielded.

Listing 42.5. The `CalculatorProducer` interface.

```
// Interface for a large calculation to produce image...
interface CalculatorProducer {
    public void start(int pix[],CalculateFilterNotify cf);
}
```

The `CalculatorFilter` Class

The `CalculatorFilter` class in Listing 42.6 is a subclass of `ImageFilter`. Its purpose is to receive image data produced by some long calculation (like the Mandelbrot set) and update any consumer of the new data's image. The `CalculatorProducer`, indicated by the variable `cp`, is what produces the data.

Listing 42.6. The `CalculatorFilter` class.

```
import java.awt.image.*;
import java.awt.Image;
import java.awt.Toolkit;
import java.lang.*;
```

continues

Listing 42.6. continued

```java
public class CalculatorFilter extends ImageFilter
 implements CalculateFilterNotify {
   private ColorModel defaultRGBModel;
   private int width, height;
   private int pix[];
   private boolean complete = false;
   private CalculatorProducer cp;
   private boolean cpStart = false;

   public CalculatorFilter(ColorModel cm,CalculatorProducer cp) {
      defaultRGBModel = cm;
      this.cp = cp;
   }

   public void setDimensions(int width, int height) {
      this.width = width;
      this.height = height;
      pix = new int[width * height];
      consumer.setDimensions(width,height);
   }

   public void setColorModel(ColorModel model) {
      consumer.setColorModel(defaultRGBModel);
   }

   public void setHints(int hints) {
      consumer.setHints(ImageConsumer.RANDOMPIXELORDER);
   }

   public void resendTopDownLeftRight(ImageProducer p) {
    }


   public void setPixels(int x, int y, int w, int h,
      ColorModel model, int pixels[],int off,int scansize) {
   }

   public void imageComplete(int status) {
     if (!cpStart) {
        cpStart = true;
        dataUpdate();  // Show empty pixels...
        cp.start(pix,this);
     } // end if
     if (complete)
        consumer.imageComplete(ImageConsumer.STATICIMAGEDONE);
   }

   // Called externally to notify that more data has been created
   // Notify consumer so they can repaint...
   public void dataUpdate() {
     consumer.setPixels(0,0,width,height,
               defaultRGBModel,pix,0,width);
     consumer.imageComplete(ImageConsumer.SINGLEFRAMEDONE);
   }
```

```
// External call to update a specific pixel row...
public void dataUpdateRow(int row) {
    // The key thing here is the second to last parameter (offset)
    // which states where to start getting data from the pix array...
    consumer.setPixels(0,row,width,1,
            defaultRGBModel,pix,(width * row),width);
    consumer.imageComplete(ImageConsumer.SINGLEFRAMEDONE);
}

// External call to update a specific pixel column...
public void dataUpdateColumn(int col,int pixdata[]) {
    // The key thing here is the second to last parameter (offset)
    // which states where to start getting data from the pix array...
    consumer.setPixels(col,0,1,height,
            defaultRGBModel,pixdata,0,1);
    consumer.imageComplete(ImageConsumer.SINGLEFRAMEDONE);
}

// Called from external calculating program when data has
// finished being calculated...
public void setComplete() {
    complete = true;
    consumer.setPixels(0,0,width,height,
        defaultRGBModel,pix,0,width);
    consumer.imageComplete(ImageConsumer.STATICIMAGEDONE);
}
}
```

Because the `ImageFilter` class was explained earlier in this chapter, issues related to this class are not repeated here. However, a couple of things should be pointed out. When the image is first requested, the filter gets the dimensions the consumer wants by calling the `setDimensions()` method. At this point, the `CalculatorFilter` will allocate a large array holding the color values for each pixel.

When the original `ImageProducer` is finished creating the original image, the filter's `imageComplete()` method is called, but the filter must override this method. In this case, the `CalculatorFilter` starts the `CalculatorProducer` thread, passing it the pixel array to put in its updates. Whenever the `CalculatorProducer` has new data, it calls one of the four methods specified by the `CalculateFilterNotify` interface: `dataUpdate()`, `dataUpdateRow()`, `dataUpdateColumn()`, or `setComplete()`. The `dataUpdateColumn()` method is called by the Mandelbrot calculation because it operates on a column basis. In each of these cases, the filter updates the appropriate consumer pixels by using the `setPixels()` method, then calls the consumer's `imageComplete()` method to indicate the nature of the change. For the three "data" methods, the updates are only partial, so a `SINGLEFRAMEDONE` flag is sent. The `setComplete()` method, on the other hand, indicates that everything is complete, so it sets a `STATICIMAGEDONE` flag.

The CalculatorImage Class

The CalculatorImage class, shown in Listing 42.7, is the glue between the CalculatorProducer class that produces the image data and the CalculatorFilter that manages it.

Listing 42.7. The CalculatorImage class.

```java
// This class takes a CalculatorProducer and sets up the
// environment for creating a calculated image.  Ties the
// producer to the CalculatorFilter so that incremental updates
// can be made...
public class CalculatorImage {
    int width;  // The dimensions of the image...
    int height;
    CalculatorProducer cp;  // What produces the image data...
    IndexColorModel palette;  // The colors of the image...
    // Create Palette only once per session...
    static IndexColorModel prvPalette = null;
    int numColors = 256;  // Number of colors in palette...

    // User defines how big of an image they want...
    public CalculatorImage(int width,int height,CalculatorProducer cp) {
        this.width = width;
        this.height = height;
        this.cp = cp;
    }

    // Start producing the Calculator image...
    public synchronized Image getImage() {
        // Hook into the filter...
        createPalette();
        ImageProducer p = new FilteredImageSource(
          new MemoryImageSource(width,height,palette,
              (new int[width * height]),0,width),
              new CalculatorFilter(palette,cp));
        // Return the image...
        return Toolkit.getDefaultToolkit().createImage(p);
    }

    // Create a 256 color palette...
    // Use Default color model...
    void createPalette() {
      // Create palette only once per session...
      if (prvPalette != null) {
          palette = prvPalette;
          return;
      }
      // Create a palette out of random RGB combinations...
      byte blues[], reds[], greens[];
      reds = new byte[numColors];
      blues = new byte[numColors];
      greens = new byte[numColors];
      // First and last entries are black and white...
      blues[0] = reds[0] = greens[0] = (byte)0;
      blues[255] = reds[255] = greens[255] = (byte)255;
```

```
        // Fill in other entries...
        for ( int x = 1;  x < 254; x++ ){
         reds[x] = (byte)(255 * Math.random());
         blues[x] = (byte)(255 * Math.random());
         greens[x] = (byte)(255 * Math.random());
        }
        // Create Index Color Model...
        palette = new IndexColorModel(8,256,reds,greens,blues);
        prvPalette = palette;
    }

    // Save the image set as a BMP file...
    public void saveBMP(String filename,int pix[]) {
        try {
            BmpImage.saveBitmap(filename,palette,
                pix,width,height);
        }
        catch (IOException ioe) {
            System.out.println("Error saving file!");
        }
    }
}
```

When an image is requested with the getImage() method, the CalculatorImage creates a color palette through an instance of the ImageColorModel class and then creates a MemoryImageSource object. This ImageProducer object produces an image initialized to all zeros (black). It is combined with an instance of the CalculatorFilter class to produce a FilteredImageSource. When the createImage() method of the AWT class is called, production of the calculated image begins.

The color palette is a randomly generated series of pixel values. Depending on your luck, these colors can be attractive or uninspiring. The createPalette() method is a good place to create a custom set of colors for this applet—if you want to have some control over its appearance. You should replace the random colors with hard-coded RGB values; you may also want to download a URL file that specifies a special color map.

Summary

This chapter covered advanced image concepts and demonstrated how to write and use image filters, rotation concepts, and special effects. Finally, a Mandelbrot applet was developed to illustrate the principles explained in this chapter.

Images give Java tremendous flexibility. Once you master image concepts, the endless possibilities of the Java graphic system are yours to explore.

Developing Your Own Database Application

by George Reese

IN THIS CHAPTER

CHAPTER

43

Chapter 31, "Exploring Database Connectivity with JDBC," covered Java's JDBC API, which provides Java applications with access to relational databases. A database application, however, is much more complex than simply making JDBC calls. You must first have a properly set up database engine that can handle your application's needs. To understand how a database engine interacts with your application, you must understand the issues surrounding database access, especially as they relate to Java. You also want to display that information to the user. Finally, you have to write the actual application code.

This chapter looks at the different kinds of databases and how they meet the needs of various applications. During this examination, we will glance at object databases but focus on relational databases. To fully understand the issues behind database application development in Java, we will build a guest book database applet that allows people to visit your Web page, sign in, and make comments.

Different Database Systems

A *database* is a storage mechanism that facilitates the retrieval of data. Of course, there is more than one way to do this. The most well-known types of databases include hierarchical, relational, and object databases. Of these three systems, relational databases are overwhelmingly the system of choice.

Hierarchical Databases

If you have done any programming with the Windows registry, you have experience with a hierarchical database. Hierarchical databases, which were the prevalent database system before relational databases took hold, store data in a tree. You access its data by naming the data's location in the hierarchy. Unfortunately, a hierarchical system does not provide any way for data in one branch of the database to relate to data in another branch. Except for very specialized uses (such as the Windows registry), you do not see hierarchical databases very often any more—Java currently has no support for them.

Relational Databases

Relational databases enable you to access data based on its relation to other data. Instead of storing relational data as a tree, a relational database stores data in tables similar to a spreadsheet layout. Each table contains a set of related data. For example, in the guest book applet we are about to build, you have a comments table. As with a spreadsheet, you have columns that include e-mail address, visitor's name, date, and comment. You can also create a people table in which you store detailed information about people you know. For anyone who enters a comment in your comments table, you can cross-reference that information with the people table to get more detailed information about the person making the comments. With a spreadsheet, this arrangement means that you have two separate spreadsheets containing the data but no way to relate the data in the spreadsheets. A relational database, however, contains relationships that allow you to relate data in the `comments` table with data in the `people` table.

Relational databases also provide a special query language, SQL, that allows you to retrieve data based on its relationships. JDBC requires a basic level of SQL support from a relational database. If you have no experience with SQL, I recommend that you pick up a book on it, because a discussion of SQL is beyond the scope of this chapter. SQL is, however, a very simple language to learn. If you understand enough Java to be this far into a Java programming book, you should have only minimal difficulty reading the SQL in this chapter even without any SQL background.

Object Databases

Object databases are a relatively new class of database management systems that are growing in popularity. As an object-oriented programming language, Java supports the idea that the data of an object is inseparable from its behavior. In fact, object-oriented design dictates that an object's data should even be hidden from external systems.

Because a relational database is about storing pure data, it violates the object-oriented concept of encapsulation. In contrast, an object database does not store object data separate from the object itself. When you want to access object data, you access it through that object's data access methods just like you do inside a Java application. In fact, access to object databases in the future may even be as simple as calling specific Java methods. Unfortunately, Java access to object databases at this time is immature to nonexistent.

Structuring Your Relational Database

Before you can get started with any application, you must set up your database. You have to organize your data requirements into related tables of data. Figure 43.1 shows what is called a *logical data model* for the guest book application. It breaks down data into "entities" and shows how they are related to each other.

FIGURE 43.1.

The logical data model for the guest book applet.

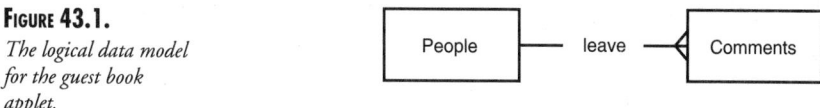

The most important thing to learn from this logical data model is what entities are in the database and in what ways we can relate them. The data model for our application is actually quite simple. A data model for a complex system, however, can span an entire wall.

The logical data model does not really say much about what data we want to store in the database. Once our logical data model is complete, we must define the data we want to store.

In general, each row of each table requires a unique identifier. As a rule of thumb, this unique identifier, referred to as the *primary key*, is never used as a display value and should not have any meaning outside of uniquely identifying a specific row.

With primary keys defined for your database entities, you can begin defining the columns that make up each table. Some of these columns, like the e-mail address column for the `comments` table, have extended information contained in other tables. In the `comments` table, we will use the e-mail address for that person to relate it to the `people` table. Normally, we would use a primary key to create this relationship. Because users entering comments have no knowledge of the `people` table, however, we cannot rely on their ability to determine primary keys for relating `comment` data to `people` data. This relationship is called a *join*. Figure 43.2 shows the detailed table information in a diagram called the *physical data model*.

FIGURE 43.2.

The physical data model for the guest book applet.

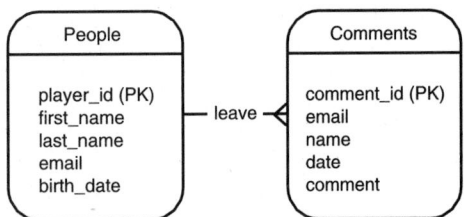

You may run into some situations in which many rows from one database entity are related to many rows of another database entity. Because databases do not allow you to store more than one value in a single field, you have to create a third table to capture this many-to-many relationship. The third table contains two columns representing the primary keys from the other two tables. The intersection of two primary keys defines a unique row and creates the relationship between the two entities.

An example of such a situation is a table relating football players to football teams. A football team has many players; over time, a player can belong to many teams. Figure 43.3 shows the physical data model that relates football players to football teams.

FIGURE 43.3.

The intersection table defining a many-to-many relationship for football players to football teams.

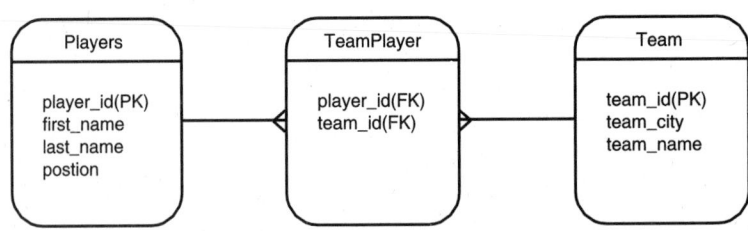

With the entities fully defined in the form of a physical data model, we can now create the database tables using SQL. There are even some data-modeling computer applications that create tables for you based on the data model you draw. I used an mSQL database for the examples in this chapter. Listing 43.1 provides the table creation scripts for mSQL.

> **NOTE**
>
> mSQL is a small relational database engine provided for free to nonprofit users and at a low cost for commercial users. You can find more information about it at `http://www.imaginary.com/Java`.

Listing 43.1. The mSQL creation scripts for setting up the guest book applet support tables.

```
DROP TABLE comments\p\g
CREATE TABLE comments (
    comment_id  INT        PRIMARY KEY,
    email       CHAR(40)   NOT NULL,
    name        CHAR(40)   NOT NULL,
    date        CHAR(30)   NOT NULL,
    comment     CHAR(255)  NOT NULL
)\p\g

DROP TABLE people\p\g
CREATE TABLE people (
    people_id   INT        PRIMARY KEY,
    email       CHAR(40)   NOT NULL,
    first_name  CHAR(30)   NOT NULL,
    last_name   CHAR(30)   NOT NULL,
    birth_date  CHAR(30)
)\p\g

DROP TABLE sys_gen\p\g
CREATE TABLE sys_gen (
    id          CHAR(30)   PRIMARY KEY,
    next_id     INT          NOT NULL
)\p\g
```

Java Database Issues

The biggest challenge of writing an object-oriented application against a relational database is mapping the objects in your object model to entities shown in the data model. On the surface, it looks like a fairly simple task because most of the objects in the object model have entities by the same name in the data model.

Objects in an object-oriented system, however, do not relate in the same way that data relates in a relational database. Because our applet does not have a complex object model, mapping objects to relational entities is not a problem. It is, however, a huge problem for complex Java applications.

Security Issues

Java does put some restrictions on applets for security reasons that can appear to be particularly limiting to the database developer. The following are two particular applet restrictions that affect database programmers:

- Limited access to native calls
- Limited network access

The native call limitation affects programmers who need to use some sort of C library or operating-system-level library to design an applet. This is especially troublesome to applet writers who want to take advantage of a database-specific feature not supported outside of native calls. The mSQL JDBC driver does not use native libraries for database access, so this problem does not affect you if you are using mSQL. Some other drivers for the more common commercial database engines do make use of native library calls. You should refer to your JDBC driver documentation to see whether it is limited in this way.

To veteran client/server developers, however, the most troubling idea is probably that your Web server must be on the same machine to which your applet is connecting for database access. Specifically, most Java virtual machines restrict applets from connecting to any machine except the host that served the applet. The applet therefore cannot connect directly to any local or third-machine databases. As limiting as this particular restriction seems, a three-tier architecture provides a liberating solution.

The Power of Three Tiers

While the two-tier approach does try to centralize business processing on the server, the limitations of just two tiers tend to push a lot of processing onto the client machines. This architecture poses several problems:

- Client-side resource requirements balloon with the extra processing needs. It is not uncommon to find business applications requiring Pentiums with 32M of RAM.
- User interface and business processing tend to get rolled together, especially with the rapid application development tools on the market. With the user interface so closely tied to business processing, changes to one end up having a direct impact on the other, making maintenance a headache.
- With all this redundant processing occurring on many client machines rather than in a central location, new applications are forced to reinvent the wheel when dealing with the same business processing.

With the guaranteed execution environment of the Java virtual machine and an easy-to-use Internet socket interface, Java is actually well suited to the implementation of three-tier systems. A *three-tier application* is one in which a third application layer exists between the client and server layers of the traditional two-tier client/server system. This middle layer has a wide variety of uses depending on the application in question.

The three-tier architecture uses the middle layer to separate business processing from the visual representation of data. This layer, called the *application server*, is responsible for knowing how to find and manipulate business data. The client evolves into a much leaner application responsible only for retrieving information from the application server and displaying it on the screen.

In addition to removing a huge processing burden from client machines, the application server can be used to consolidate enterprise-wide business rules. Where business rules have to be rewritten for each two-tier application thrust on the desktop, application servers process business rules in a single place for use by multiple applications. When the business rules change, a change to the application server takes care of that change for all the applications being run by the business.

Of specific interest to Java developers is the three-tier system's ability to hide any knowledge of the database server from the client. Because Internet clients view the applet or application as interfacing with a single application server, you can use that application server to determine such things as where the data really exists. Additionally, this back-end independence enables applications to scale much easier across CPUs. Figure 43.4 shows a three-tier architecture.

FIGURE 43.4.
A three-tier Java applet or application.

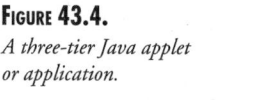

Desktop System running client application   Web Server running HTTP daemon and application server   DBMS Server

It would be overkill to build the guest book applet as a three-tier system. If your application has a complex object model or a need to scale across multiple machines over time, however, a three-tier application is definitely the solution.

Communication among the Tiers

With any three-tier architecture, one of the greatest programming challenges is getting the three layers to communicate with one another. JDBC or some similar set of database access classes should handle the application-server-to-database-server communication in a manner transparent to the application developer. Communication between the client and application server is still undefined.

The two best methods for providing such communication in Java are Java sockets or distributed objects. Compared to sockets from other languages, Java sockets are quite simple to use. Sockets, however, force the developer to make esoteric decisions as to exactly what it is that is being communicated between client and application server, because method calls and object passing are better handled by the distributed objects solution. A socket solution generally best fits an application in which the scope of communication is limited and well defined. A bug-tracking system would be best implemented in this manner.

Distributed objects provide the more elegant solution. From the developer's point of view, the application server objects appear to be part of the same application as the client—they just reside on a central server and are available to other applications simultaneously. The developer handles communication simply through method calls.

Viewing the Data

The magic of any database application is the presentation of relational data in a form that is easy for the user to digest. The first part of the guest book applet provides a display of data in the comments table to potential users. Listing 43.2 shows GuestBookView.java, an applet that handles the viewing functionality of the guest book.

Listing 43.2. The GuestBookView applet that allows users to view comments made by visitors to your Web pages.

```
/**
 * GuestBookView.java
 * A look at all the comments listed in the guest book
 * through the GuestBook applet.
 */

import java.awt.*;
import java.applet.*;

public class GuestBookView extends Applet {
  private GridBagLayout applet_layout;
  private GridBagConstraints applet_constraints;
  private Button retrieve, next, previous;
  private Panel main_panel, comment_panel, status_panel;
  private TextArea comment;
  private TextField email, name;
  private Label status;
  int current_comment = 1;
  int total_comments = 0;

  /**
   * Initialize the appearance of the applet.
   * For the sake of speed, do not download comments until they
   * explicitly perform a retrieval.
   */
  public void init() {
    super.init();
    setLayout(applet_layout = new GridBagLayout());
    applet_constraints = createDefaultConstraints();
    addNotify();
    setBackground(Color.white);
```

```
main_panel = new Panel();
{ // Set up the main panel
  GridBagConstraints constraints;
  GridBagLayout layout;
  Label tmp;

  main_panel.setLayout(layout = new GridBagLayout());
  constraints = createDefaultConstraints();
  constraints.insets = new Insets(2, 10, 2, 10);
  layout.setConstraints(tmp = new Label("Email"), constraints);
  main_panel.add(tmp);
  constraints.gridx = 1;
  layout.setConstraints(email = new TextField(30), constraints);
  main_panel.add(email);
  constraints.gridx = 2;
  layout.setConstraints(retrieve = new Button("Retrieve"), constraints);
  main_panel.add(retrieve);
  constraints.gridx = 0;
  constraints.gridy = 1;
  layout.setConstraints(tmp = new Label("Name"), constraints);
  main_panel.add(tmp);
  constraints.gridx = 1;
  layout.setConstraints(name = new TextField(30), constraints);
  main_panel.add(name);
}
applet_constraints.gridy = 1;
applet_constraints.insets = new Insets(4, 2, 4, 2);
applet_layout.setConstraints(main_panel, applet_constraints);
add(main_panel);
{ // Set up the comments panel
  comment_panel = new Panel();
  comment_panel.setLayout(new CardLayout());
  comment_panel.add("1", getPanel(0, "", "", "", ""));
}
applet_constraints.gridy = 2;
applet_layout.setConstraints(comment_panel, applet_constraints);
add(comment_panel);
{ // Set up the status panel
  GridBagLayout layout;
  GridBagConstraints constraints;

  status_panel = new Panel();
  status_panel.setLayout(layout = new GridBagLayout());
  constraints = createDefaultConstraints();
  // Extra spaces in label for proper spacing in layout
  status = new Label("Ready.                              " +
                     "                                    ");
  previous = new Button("<<");
  next = new Button(">>");
  previous.enable(false);
  next.enable(false);
  constraints.anchor = GridBagConstraints.SOUTHWEST;
  constraints.insets = new Insets(4, 2, 4, 2);
  layout.setConstraints(previous, constraints);
  status_panel.add(previous);
  constraints.gridx = 1;
  layout.setConstraints(next, constraints);
```

continues

Listing 43.2. continued

```java
      status_panel.add(next);
      constraints.gridx = 2;
      layout.setConstraints(status, constraints);
      status_panel.add(status);
    }
    applet_constraints.gridy = 3;
    applet_constraints.anchor = GridBagConstraints.SOUTHWEST;
    applet_layout.setConstraints(status_panel, applet_constraints);
    add(status_panel);
    applet_constraints.anchor = GridBagConstraints.SOUTH;
    try {
      Class.forName("imaginary.sql.iMsqlDriver");
    }
    catch( Exception e ) {
      status.setText("An error occurred finding database drivers.");
    }
  }

  /**
   * Handle the clicking on any of the buttons.
   * For retrieve, go to the database.
   * For previous, go to the previous comment.
   * For next, go to the next comment.
   * For previous or next, make sure to enable and disable as appropriate.
   */
  public boolean action(Event event, Object arg) {
    if( event.target instanceof Button ) {
      if( (Button)event.target == retrieve ) {
        retrieve();
        return true;
      }
      if( (Button)event.target == next ) {
        if( current_comment == total_comments ) {
          return super.action(event, arg);
        }
        ((CardLayout)comment_panel.getLayout()).next(comment_panel);
        current_comment++;
        if( current_comment == total_comments ) {
          next.enable(false);
        }
        if( current_comment > 1 ) {
          previous.enable(true);
        }
        resetStatus();
        return true;
      }
      if( (Button)event.target == previous ) {
        if( current_comment < 2 ) {
          return super.action(event, arg);
        }
        ((CardLayout)comment_panel.getLayout()).previous(comment_panel);
        current_comment--;
        if( current_comment < 2 ) {
          previous.enable(false);
        }
```

```
        if( current_comment < total_comments ) {
          next.enable(true);
        }
        resetStatus();
        return true;
      }
    }
    return super.action(event, arg);
  }

  /**
   * Retrieve data from the database based on any selection
   * criteria.  A user can specify either email address or
   * name.
   */
  private synchronized void retrieve() {
    remove(comment_panel);
    comment_panel = new Panel();
    comment_panel.setLayout(new CardLayout());
    current_comment = 1;
    total_comments = 0;
    try {
      String url = "jdbc:msql://athens.imaginary.com:4333/db_web";
      java.sql.Connection connection;
      java.sql.Statement statement;
      java.sql.ResultSet result;
      String sql;
      int i = 0;

      status.setText("Retrieving from the database, " +
                     "this may take a minute...");
      connection = java.sql.DriverManager.getConnection(url, "borg", "");
      statement = connection.createStatement();
      sql = "SELECT comment_id, email, name, comment, date " +
            "FROM comments " + getWhere();
      result = statement.executeQuery(sql);
      // For each row, add to card layout a panel representing the row
      while(result.next()) {
        Panel tmp;

        i++;
        tmp = getPanel(result.getInt(1),
                       result.getString(2),
                       result.getString(3),
                       result.getString(4),
                       result.getString(5));
        comment_panel.add("" + i, tmp);
      }
      // redo the applet layout
      remove(status_panel);
      applet_constraints.gridy = 2;
      applet_layout.setConstraints(comment_panel, applet_constraints);
      add(comment_panel);
      applet_constraints.gridy = 3;
      applet_constraints.anchor = GridBagConstraints.SOUTHWEST;
      applet_layout.setConstraints(status_panel, applet_constraints);
      add(status_panel);
```

continues

Listing 43.2. continued

```java
        applet_constraints.anchor = GridBagConstraints.SOUTH;
        total_comments = i;
        resetStatus();
      }
    catch( java.sql.SQLException e ) {
      remove(status);
      comment_panel = getPanel(0, "", "", "", "");
      applet_constraints.gridy = 2;
      applet_layout.setConstraints(comment_panel, applet_constraints);
      add(comment_panel);
      applet_constraints.gridy = 3;
      applet_constraints.anchor = GridBagConstraints.SOUTHWEST;
      applet_layout.setConstraints(status_panel, applet_constraints);
      add(status_panel);
      applet_constraints.anchor = GridBagConstraints.SOUTH;
      status.setText("A database error occurred: " + e.getMessage());
      total_comments = 0;
      current_comment = 1;
      next.enable(false);
      previous.enable(false);
    }
    validate();
  }

/**
 * Provides a WHERE clause with an ORDER BY as an extra bonus
 * Needs to make sure user-entered fields do not have database
 * sensitive characters.
 */
private String getWhere() {
  String e = email.getText().replace('\'', '"');
  String n = name.getText().replace('\'', '"');
  String where = "WHERE ";

  if( e.length() < 1 && n.length() < 1 ) return "ORDER BY comment_id";
  if( e.length() > 0 ) {
    where += "email = '" + e + "'";
    if( n.length() > 0 ) {
      where += " AND ";
    }
  }
  if( n.length() > 0 ) {
    where += "name = '" + n + "'";
  }
  return where + " ORDER BY comment_id";
}

/**
 * Creates a panel for database data.
 */
private Panel getPanel(int id, String mail, String nom, String text,
String day) {
  Panel panel =  new Panel();
  GridBagConstraints constraints;
  GridBagLayout layout;
```

```
      TextArea cmt = new TextArea(5, 50);
      TextField eml = new TextField(30);
      TextField nme = new TextField(30);

      panel.setLayout(layout = new GridBagLayout());
      constraints = createDefaultConstraints();
      constraints.gridx = 2;
      constraints.anchor = GridBagConstraints.NORTHWEST;
      constraints.insets = new Insets(2, 2, 2, 2);
      cmt.setText(text);
      eml.setText(mail);
      nme.setText(nom);
      cmt.setEditable(false);
      eml.setEditable(false);
      nme.setEditable(false);
      layout.setConstraints(eml, constraints);
      panel.add(eml);
      constraints.gridy = 1;
      layout.setConstraints(nme, constraints);
      panel.add(nme);
      constraints.gridy = 3;
      constraints.anchor = GridBagConstraints.CENTER;
      layout.setConstraints(cmt, constraints);
      panel.add(cmt);
      return panel;
   }

   /**
    * A way to avoid redoing the creation of constraints
    * being used everywhere in this applet.  This creates
    * a GridBagConstraints object and sets some defaults.
    */
   private GridBagConstraints createDefaultConstraints() {
      GridBagConstraints constraints = new GridBagConstraints();

      constraints.gridx = 0;
      constraints.gridy = 0;
      constraints.gridheight = 1;
      constraints.gridwidth = 1;
      constraints.weightx = 0.0;
      constraints.weighty = 0.0;
      constraints.fill = GridBagConstraints.NONE;
      constraints.anchor = GridBagConstraints.SOUTH;
      return constraints;
   }

   private void resetStatus() {
      // Extra spaces in setText() below for layout reasons
      if( total_comments == 0 ) {
         status.setText("No comments found.                    " +
                        "                    ");
         next.enable(false);
      }
      else if( total_comments == 1 ) {
         status.setText("1 of 1 comment.                    " +
                        "                    ");
         next.enable(false);
      }
```

Listing 43.2. continued

```
    else {
      status.setText(current_comment + " of " + total_comments +
                     " comments.                    " +
                     "                           ");
      if( current_comment < total_comments ) {
        next.enable(true);
      }
      else {
        next.enable(false);
      }
    }
    if( current_comment < 2 ) {
      previous.enable(false);
    }
    else {
      previous.enable(true);
    }
  }
}
```

This example shows the greatest current disadvantage of Java as well as several strengths it has over CGI. Java's weakness lies in the AWT—specifically, the amount of code required to display relational data in a GUI. The applet itself is divided into three display panels:

- A **main panel** that allows a user to specify filter criteria and initiate a search.

- A **comment panel** that displays one comment at a time from the list of comments retrieved from the database.

- A **status panel** that shows status information to the user. In addition, navigation buttons are placed here to flip through the comments being displayed on the comment panel.

The init() method sets up the default display for these three panels. Because the comment panel is actually made up of multiple panels designed to display rows from the database, I have separated the painting of that panel into a distinct method. The layout of all these panels (except the comment panel) depends heavily on the GridBagLayout layout manager. If you are not familiar with that layout manager, take some time to explore it now (refer to Chapter 16, "The Windowing (AWT) Package"). The complex layouts required for the dynamic display of database data often require the use of this difficult layout manager.

The comment panel uses the CardLayout layout manager to flip through comments. The CardLayout enables a panel to display a single component at a time and navigate back and forth among them. Each card of the comment panel's layout is thus a panel displaying one comment from the database.

The retrieval and display of database information occurs in the retrieve() method. When a user clicks the Retrieve button, the action() method triggers the retrieve() method which formulates a SQL statement using the getWhere() method. getWhere() puts together a WHERE clause for a SQL statement based on any data the user has entered into the text fields in the main panel. The retrieve() method then appends the WHERE clause onto the SELECT statement. For each row the applet finds in the database, it creates a panel and adds it to the CardLayout of the comment panel. During the entire process, status information is displayed to the user.

Data Entry

Among the more interesting things you can do in Java that you cannot do using any other means of displaying database information on the Web is the ability to validate data at the client level. Each time a user goes forward or backward through the list of comments, the applet can enable or disable buttons based on whether there are previous or additional comments to view. This ability is more important at data-entry time, where CGI requires users to wait until they have filled out an entire form and submit it before doing any validation. Listing 43.3 shows how we can prevent the user from submitting information until it has been validated.

Listing 43.3. The sibling GuestBook.java applet which handles the data-entry portion of the guest book applet.

```
/**
 * GuestBook.java
 * This applet allows people to enter comments
 * from their web browser and save them to my mSQL
 * database.
 */
import java.awt.*;
import java.applet.*;

public class GuestBook extends Applet {
  private TextField email, name;
  private Label label1, label2, label3, status;
  private TextArea comments;
  private Button save_button;
  private boolean error_disable;

  /**
   * Sets up the applet's look.
   */
  public void init() {
    super.init();
    setLayout(null);
    addNotify();
    resize(351,230);
    setBackground(new Color(16777215));
    email = new java.awt.TextField();
    email.reshape(67,4,157,22);
    add(email);
    label1 = new java.awt.Label("Email ");
    label1.reshape(11,7,45,15);
```

continues

Listing 43.3. continued

```
      add(label1);
      label2 = new java.awt.Label("Name");
      label2.reshape(11,40,48,15);
      add(label2);
      comments = new java.awt.TextArea();
      comments.reshape(11,87,325,109);
      add(comments);
      name = new java.awt.TextField();
      name.reshape(67,37,157,23);
      add(name);
      label3 = new java.awt.Label("Comments");
      label3.reshape(11,68,70,15);
      add(label3);
      save_button = new java.awt.Button("Save");
      save_button.reshape(252,4,87,26);
      add(save_button);
      status = new java.awt.Label("");
      status.reshape(12,202,322,19);
      add(status);
      checkButton();
      error_disable = false;
      try {
        Class.forName("imaginary.sql.iMsqlDriver");
      }
      catch( Exception e ) {
        status.setText("A Java error occurred.");
        error_disable = true;
      }
    }

    /**
     * Checks to make sure enough information exists to
     * allow saving to the database.  This is something
     * you cannot do in CGI-land.
     */
    private boolean validate_value(String str, boolean flag) {
      if( str.length() < 1 ) return false;
      if( flag ) {
        int i = str.indexOf("@");

        if( i == -1 ) return false;
        else return ((i != 0) && (i != str.length()-1));
      }
      return true;
    }

    /**
     * Performs the actual database save.
     */
    private void save() {
      status.setText("Saving to the database, this will take a minute...");
      try {
        String url = "jdbc:msql://athens.imaginary.com:4333/Testdb";
        java.sql.Connection connection;
        java.sql.Statement statement;
```

```
      java.sql.ResultSet result;
      int id = -1;

      connection = java.sql.DriverManager.getConnection(url, "borg", "");
      statement = connection.createStatement();
      result = statement.executeQuery("SELECT next_id FROM sys_gen " +
                                "WHERE id = 'comment_id'");
      if( !result.next() ) {
        throw new java.sql.SQLException("Failed to generate id.");
      }
      id = result.getInt(1) + 1;
      result.close();
      statement.close();
      statement = connection.createStatement();
      statement.executeUpdate("UPDATE sys_gen SET next_id = " + id +
                        " WHERE id = 'comment_id'");
      statement.close();
      statement = connection.createStatement();
      statement.executeUpdate("INSERT into comments " +
                        "comment_id, email, name, comment, date) " +
                        "VALUES (" + id +", '" + getEmail() + "', '" +
                        getName() + "', '" + getComments() + "', '" +
                        (new java.util.Date()).toString() + "')");
      statement.close();
      connection.close();
      email.setText("");
      name.setText("");
      comments.setText("");
      checkButton();
      status.setText("Saved comment id " + id + ".");
    }
  catch( java.sql.SQLException e ) {
      status.setText("A database error occurred: " + e.getMessage());
      error_disable = true;
      checkButton();
    }
  }
}

/**
 * Looks for key presses and other fun events.
 */
public boolean handleEvent(Event event) {
  if( event.target == comments ||
      event.target == name || event.target == email ) {
    if( event.id == Event.KEY_PRESS ) {
      if( event.key == '\t' ) {
        if( event.target == email ) {
          name.requestFocus();
        }
        else if( event.target == name ) {
          comments.requestFocus();
        }
        else {
          email.requestFocus();
        }
        return true;
      }
```

continues

Listing 43.3. continued

```java
        else {
          checkButton();
          return super.handleEvent(event);
        }
      }
    if( event.id == Event.ACTION_EVENT ) {
      if( !save_button.isEnabled() ) {
        return super.handleEvent(event);
      }
      save();
      return true;
    }
  }
  if (event.target == save_button && event.id == Event.ACTION_EVENT) {
    save();
  }
  return super.handleEvent(event);
}

/**
 * Enable or disable the save button as appropriate.
 */
void checkButton() {
  if( error_disable ) {
    save_button.enable(false);
    return;
  }
  save_button.enable(validate_value(comments.getText(), false) &&
                     validate_value(email.getText(), true) &&
                     validate_value(name.getText(), false));
}

public String getEmail() {
  String str = email.getText();

  return str.replace('\'', '"');
}

public String getName() {
  String str = name.getText();

  return str.replace('\'', '"');
}

public String getComments() {
  String str = comments.getText();

  return str.replace('\'', '"');
}
}
```

The Save button that triggers the database save remains disabled until the user has entered the following data:

- An e-mail address in the form of *user@host*. The application does not validate that the user or host is actually real.
- A name of one character or more.
- A comment of one character or more.

When these criteria are met, the Save button becomes enabled and the user can choose to save the data to the database.

One final thing your data-entry processing should be concerned about is making sure that the user does not enter characters that will wreak havoc on your SQL statement. If, for example, a user puts an apostrophe into the comment, that creates a SQL statement with a misplaced single quote. In the guest book applet, I simply converted all instances of ' to ". A more proper way to handle the situation is to escape all instances of ' so that the database engine ignores it. Figure 43.5 shows the final look of the applet.

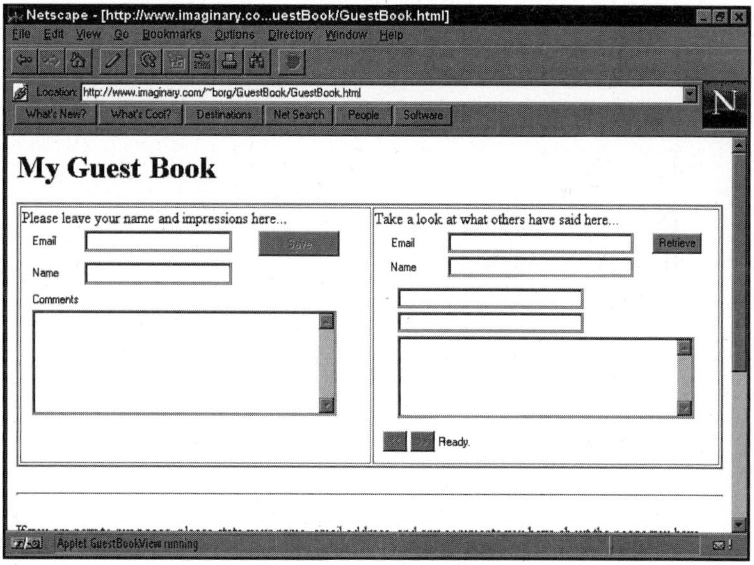

FIGURE 43.5.

A screen shot of the completed guest book applet.

Summary

Database programming is a very complex task that requires several spheres of knowledge:

- Understanding relational databases and your choice of DBMS.
- Understanding how objects can map to relational entities.

- Understanding the Java programming language.
- Understanding how JDBC allows Java applications to access relational databases.

The focus of this chapter was understanding the mapping of relational entities into a graphical user interface. Unlike CGI, Java allows applications to process information dynamically on the browser. The trick to Java is creating a meaningful display of the information you retrieve from the database. In the guest book application developed in this chapter, we used a CardLayout layout manager and some navigational buttons to show visitor comments in a concise way that CGI is unable to handle. As an application grows more complex, however, you will want to map your relational data into business objects. Not only is it impossible for CGI to handle object-to-relational mapping, any attempt to do so produces an application that is impossible to maintain.

X

PART

Emerging Java Technologies

Just-In-Time Compilers

by Michael Morrison

IN THIS CHAPTER

CHAPTER 44

Java programs have been criticized from early on because of their relatively slow execution speeds. Admittedly, compared to natively compiled programs written in languages like C/C++ or Pascal, Java programs are pretty sluggish. However, this complaint has to be weighed heavily against the inherently cross-platform nature of Java, which simply isn't possible with native programs such as those generated by C/C++ and Pascal compilers. In an attempt to alleviate the inherent performance problems associated with processor-independent Java executables, various companies are offering just-in-time (JIT) Java compilers, which compile Java bytecode executables into native programs just before execution.

This chapter explores JIT compilers and how they impact the overall landscape of Java. You learn all about the Java virtual machine and how JIT compilers fit into its organization. Furthermore, you learn about specific types of Java programs that benefit the most from JIT compilation. By the end of this chapter, you'll have a better understanding of this exciting new technology and how it can improve the performance of your own Java programs.

Understanding the Java VM

To fully understand what a just-in-time (JIT) compiler is and how it fits into the Java runtime system, you must have a solid understanding of the Java virtual machine (VM). The Java VM is a software abstraction for a generic hardware platform and is the primary component of the Java system responsible for portability. The purpose of the VM is to allow Java programs to compile to a uniform executable format, as defined by the VM, which can be run on any platform. Java programs execute within the VM itself, and the VM is responsible for managing all the details of actually carrying out platform-specific functions.

When you compile a Java program, it is compiled to be executed under the VM. Contrast this to C/C++ programs, which are compiled to be run on a real (nonvirtual) hardware platform, such as a Pentium processor running Windows 95. The VM itself has characteristics very much like a physical microprocessor, but it is entirely a software construct. You can think of the VM as an intermediary between Java programs and the underlying hardware platform under which all programs must eventually execute.

Even with the VM, at some point, all Java programs must be resolved to a particular underlying hardware platform. In Java, this resolution occurs within each particular VM implementation. The way this works is that Java programs make calls to the VM, which in turn routes them to appropriate native calls on the underlying platform. Knowing this, it's fairly obvious that the VM itself is highly platform dependent. In other words, each different hardware platform or operating system must have a unique VM implementation that routes the generic VM calls to appropriate underlying native services.

Because a VM must be developed for each different platform, it is imperative that it be as lean as possible. Another benefit of having a compact VM is the ability to execute Java programs on systems with fewer resources than desktop computer systems. For example, JavaSoft has plans to use Java in consumer electronics devices such as televisions and cellular phones. A compact, efficient VM is an essential requirement in making Java programs run in highly constrained environments such as these.

Just as all microprocessors have instruction sets that define the operations they can perform, so does the Java VM. VM instructions compile into a format known as *bytecodes*, which is the executable format for Java programs that can be run under the VM. You can think of bytecodes as the machine language for the VM. It makes sense, then, that the JDK compiler generates bytecode executables from Java source files. These bytecode executables are always stored as .class files. Figure 44.1 shows the role of the VM in the context of the Java environment.

FIGURE 44.1.

*The role of the VM in
the Java environment.*

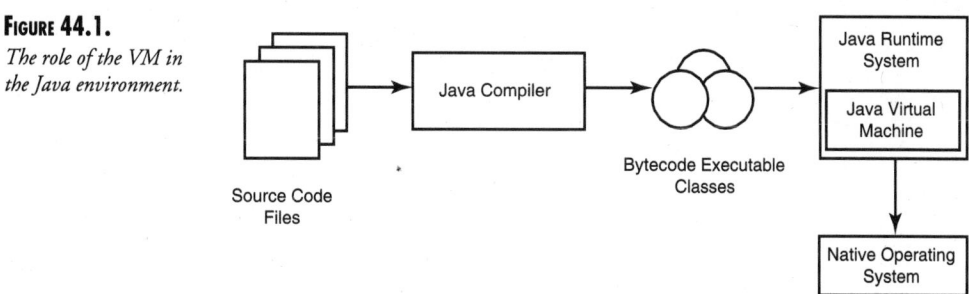

In Figure 44.1, notice how the VM is nestled within the Java runtime system. It is through the VM that executable bytecode Java classes are executed and ultimately routed to appropriate native system calls. A Java program executing within the VM is executed a bytecode at a time. With each bytecode instruction, one or more underlying native system calls may be made by the VM to achieve the desired result. In this way, the VM is completely responsible for handling the routing of generic Java bytecodes to platform-specific code that actually carries out a particular function. The VM has an enormous responsibility and is really the backbone of the entire Java runtime environment. For more gory details about the inner workings of the VM, refer to Chapter 34, "Java Under the Hood: Inside the Virtual Machine."

JIT Compilers and the VM

JIT compilers alter the role of the VM a little by directly compiling Java bytecode into native platform code, thereby relieving the VM of its need to manually call underlying native system services. The purpose of JIT compilers, however, isn't to allow the VM to relax. By compiling bytecodes into native code, execution speed can be greatly improved because the native code can be executed directly on the underlying platform. This stands in sharp contrast to the VM's approach of interpreting bytecodes and manually making calls to the underlying platform. Figure 44.2 shows how a JIT compiler alters the role of the VM in the Java environment.

FIGURE 44.2.

The role of the VM and JIT compiler in the Java environment.

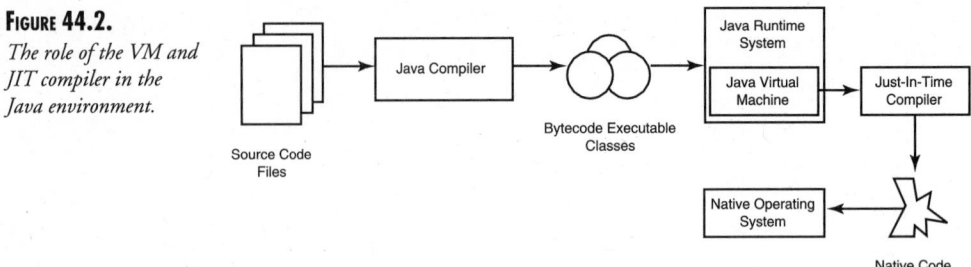

Notice that instead of the VM calling the underlying native operating system, it calls the JIT compiler. The JIT compiler in turn generates native code that can be passed on to the native operating system for execution. The primary benefit of this arrangement is that the JIT compiler is completely transparent to everything except the VM. The really neat thing is that a JIT compiler can be integrated into a system without any other part of the Java runtime system being affected. Furthermore, users don't have to fool with any configuration options; their only clue that a JIT compiler is even installed may simply be the improved execution speed of Java programs.

The integration of JIT compilers at the VM level makes JIT compilers a legitimate example of component software; you can simply plug in a JIT compiler and reap the benefits with no other work or side effects.

Inside a JIT Compiler

Even though JIT compiler integration with the Java runtime system may be transparent to everything outside the VM, you're probably thinking that there are some tricky things going on inside the VM. In fact, the approach used to connect JIT compilers to the VM internally is surprisingly straightforward. In this section, I describe the inner workings of Borland's AppAccelerator JIT compiler, which is the JIT compiler used in Netscape Navigator 3.0. Although other JIT compilers, such as Microsoft's JIT compiler in Internet Explorer, may differ in some ways, they ultimately must tackle the same problems. By understanding Borland's approach with AppAccelerator, you gain insight into the implementation of JIT compilers in general.

The best place to start describing the inner workings of the AppAccelerator JIT compiler is to quickly look at how Java programs are executed *without* a JIT compiler. A Java class that has been loaded into memory by the VM contains a V-table (virtual table), which is a list of the addresses for all the methods in the class. The VM uses the V-table whenever it has to make a call to a particular method. Each address in the V-table points to the executable bytecode for the particular method. Figure 44.3 shows what the physical V-table layout for a Java class looks like.

> **NOTE**
>
> The term *V-table* is borrowed from C++, where it stands for virtual table. In C++, V-tables are attached to classes that have *virtual methods*, which are methods that can be over-ridden in derived classes. In Java, all methods are virtual, so all classes have V-tables.

FIGURE 44.3.

The physical V-table layout for a Java class.

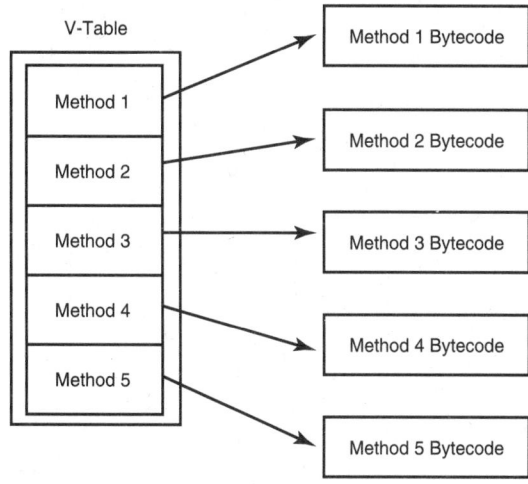

When a JIT compiler is first loaded, the VM pulls a little trick with the V-table to make sure that methods are compiled into native code rather than executed. What happens is that each bytecode address in the V-table is replaced with the address of the JIT compiler itself. Figure 44.4 shows how the bytecode addresses are replaced with the JIT compiler address in the V-table.

FIGURE 44.4.

The physical V-table layout for a Java class with a JIT compiler present.

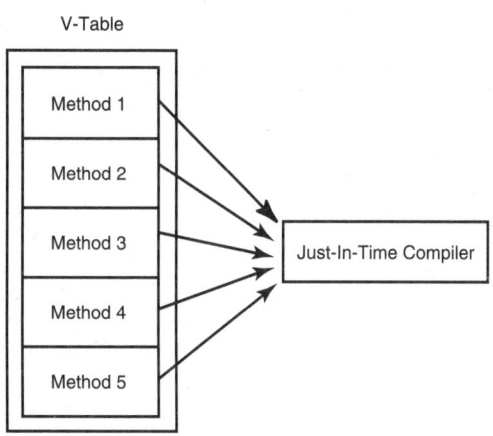

44

JUST-IN-TIME COMPILERS

When the VM calls a method through the address in the V-table, the JIT compiler is executed instead. The JIT compiler steps in and compiles the Java bytecode into native code and then patches the native code address back to the V-table. From now on, each call to the method results in a call to the native version. Figure 44.5 shows the V-table with the last method JIT compiled.

FIGURE 44.5.

The physical V-table layout for a Java class with one JIT-compiled method.

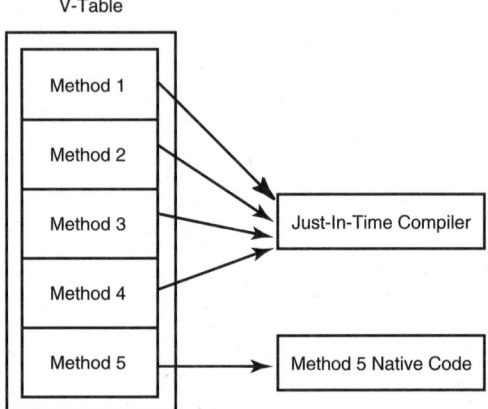

One interesting aspect of this approach to JIT compilation is that it is performed on a method-by-method basis. In other words, the compilation is performed on individual methods, as opposed to entire classes. This is very different from what most of us think of in terms of traditional compilation. Just remember that JIT compilation is anything but traditional!

Another added benefit of the method-by-method approach to compilation is that methods are compiled only when they are called. The first time a method is called, it is compiled; subsequent calls result in the native code being executed. This approach results in only the methods that are actually used being compiled, which can yield huge performance benefits. Consider the case of a class in which only four out of ten methods are being called. The JIT compiler compiles only the four methods called, resulting in a 60-percent savings in compile time (assuming that the compile time for each of the methods is roughly the same).

Just in case you're worried about the original bytecode once a method has been JIT compiled, don't worry, it's not lost. To be honest, I didn't completely tell the truth about how the V-table stores method address information. What really happens is that each method has two V-table entries, one for the bytecode and one for the native code. The native code address is the one that is actually set to the JIT compiler's address. This V-table arrangement is shown in Figure 44.6.

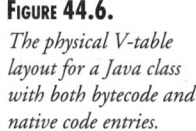

FIGURE 44.6.

The physical V-table layout for a Java class with both bytecode and native code entries.

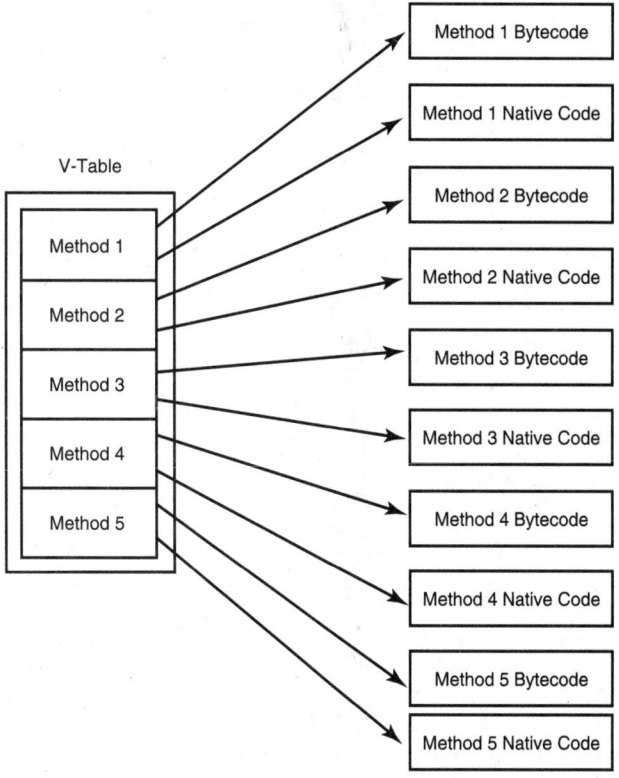

The purpose of having both bytecode and native code entries in the V-table is to allow you to switch between which one is executed. In this way, you can simultaneously execute some methods as bytecode and some using JIT-compiled native code. It isn't immediately apparent what benefits this arrangement will have, but the option of conditionally using the JIT compiler at the method level is something that may come in handy.

Okay, so the JIT compiler is integrated with the VM primarily through the V-table for each class loaded into memory. That's fine, but how is the JIT compiler installed and recognized by the VM in the first place? When the VM is first loaded, it looks for the JIT compiler and loads it if it is found. After loading, the JIT compiler installs itself by hooking into the VM and modifying the class-loading mechanism to reference the compiler. From this point on, the VM doesn't know or care about the compiler. When a class is loaded, the compiler is notified through its hook to the VM and the V-table trickery is carried out.

44

JUST-IN-TIME COMPILERS

Security and JIT Compilers

You may have some concerns about how JIT compilers impact the security of Java programs—because they seem to have a lot of say over what gets executed and how. You'll be glad to know that JIT compilers alter the security landscape of Java very little. The reason is that JIT compilation is performed as the last stage of execution, after the bytecode has been fully checked by the runtime system. This is very important because native code can't be checked for security breaches like Java bytecode can be. So it is imperative that JIT compilation occur on bytecode that has already been security checked by the runtime system.

It is equally important that native code (code that has been JIT compiled) is executed directly from memory and isn't cached on a local file system to be executed later. Again, doing so would violate the whole idea of checking every Java program immediately before execution. Actually, this approach wouldn't qualify as JIT compilation anyway, because the code wouldn't really be compiled just in time.

In terms of security, the cleanest and safest approach to JIT compilation is to compile bytecode directly to memory and throw it away when it is no longer needed. Because native code is disposable in this scenario, it is important that it can be quickly recompiled from the original bytecode. This is where the approach of compiling only methods as they are called really shines.

JIT Compiler Performance

None of the details surrounding JIT compilers would really matter if they didn't perform their job and speed up the execution speed of Java programs. The whole point of JIT compilation is to realize a performance gain by compiling VM bytecode to native code at runtime. Knowing this, let's take a look at just how much of a performance improvement JIT compilers provide.

In assessing JIT compiler performance, it's important to understand exactly where performance gains are made. One common misconception surrounding JIT compilation is the amount of code affected. For example, if a particular JIT compiler improves the execution speed of bytecode by an order of ten (on average), then it seems only logical that a Java program executing under this JIT compiler would run ten times faster. However, this isn't the case. The reason is that many programs, especially applets, rely heavily on the Java AWT, which on the Windows platform is written entirely in native C. Because the AWT is already written in native code, programs that rely heavily on the AWT don't reap the same performance gains as programs that depend on pure Java bytecode. A heavily graphical program that makes great use of the AWT may see performance gains by an order of only two or three.

On the other hand, a heavily processing-intensive Java program that uses lots of floating-point math may see performance gains closer to an order of fifteen. This happens because native Pentium code on a Windows machine is very efficient with floating-point math. Of course, other platforms may differ in this regard. Nevertheless, this will probably remain a common theme across all platforms: nongraphical programs are less affected by JIT compilation than computationally intensive programs.

Now that I've tempered your enthusiasm a little for how greatly JIT compilation impacts performance, let's look at some hard numbers that show the differences between interpreted and JIT-compiled code across different JIT compiler implementations. Figure 44.7 shows a graph of Netscape Navigator 3.0's performance benchmarks for various JIT-compiled Java operations as measured using Pendragon Software's CaffeineMark 2.01 benchmark suite.

FIGURE 44.7.

Performance benchmarks for various JIT-compiled Java operations in Netscape Navigator 3.0.

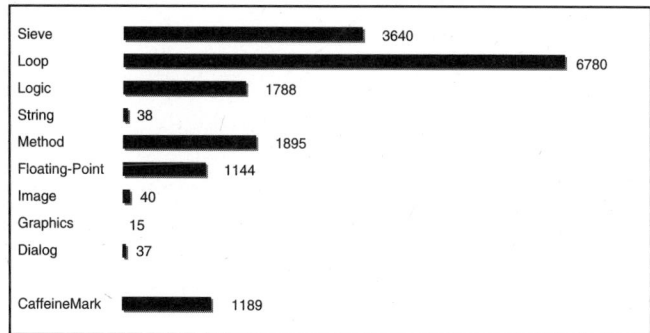

In looking at Figure 44.7, you may be wondering exactly what the numbers mean. The numbers show the relative performance of Netscape Nagivator as compared to the Symantec Café applet viewer running in debug mode. The Café applet viewer produces scores of exactly 100 on all benchmark tests, so scores above 100 represent a higher browser execution speed than the Café applet viewer. Likewise, scores lower than 100 represent slower browser execution. You can see that, in some areas, Navigator blows away the Café applet viewer with scores in the thousands. In other areas, however, the JIT-compiled Navigator code slips a little and is actually slower than the interpreted code. Most of these areas are related to graphics operations, which highlights the fact that Café has more efficient graphics support than Navigator.

Figure 44.8 shows the results of running the same benchmark tests on the JIT compiler in Microsoft Internet Explorer 3.0.

It's interesting to note that Internet Explorer outperformed Navigator on all tests except one. This is expected because Microsoft claims to have the fastest Java implementation around. Even so, this is still the first round of support for JIT compilers, so expect to see plenty of competition in the future between the JIT compiler implementations in different browsers. Marketing hype aside, you can see from these figures that JIT compilation improves performance significantly in many areas regardless of your browser of choice. Navigator and Internet Explorer both show an overall performance improvement that is over eleven times faster than Café's interpreted approach. Just remember that this improvement depends largely on the type of applet you are running and whether it is processing or graphics intensive.

FIGURE 44.8.

Performance benchmarks for various JIT-compiled Java operations in Microsoft Internet Explorer 3.0.

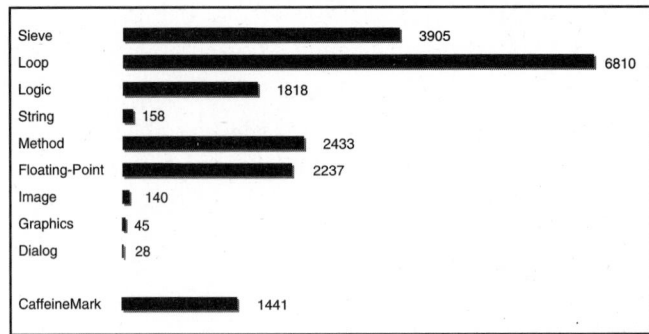

Sieve	3905
Loop	6810
Logic	1818
String	158
Method	2433
Floating-Point	2237
Image	140
Graphics	45
Dialog	28
CaffeineMark	1441

Summary

In this chapter, you learned about just-in-time (JIT) compilers and how they impact the Java runtime system. You began the chapter by peering into the runtime system to see exactly where JIT compilers fit in. In doing so, you learned a great deal about the Java virtual machine (VM), which is largely responsible for the integration of JIT compilers into the runtime system. Once you gained an understanding of how JIT compilers relate to the VM, you moved on to learning about the details of a particular JIT compiler implementation. This look into the inner workings of a real JIT compiler helped give you insight into what exactly a JIT compiler does.

Even though the technical details of JIT compilers are important to understand, little of it would be meaningful if JIT compilers didn't deliver on their promise to improve Java execution speed. For this reason, you spent the last part of the chapter learning about the specific areas where JIT compilers improve Java performance. Furthermore, you saw benchmark tests comparing JIT compiler performance in the two most popular Web browsers available. Through these benchmark tests, you were able to get an idea of how dramatically JIT compilation can improve performance.

Remote Objects and the Java IDL System

by Mike Fletcher

IN THIS CHAPTER

One of Java's most useful new features is its ability to invoke methods on objects running on a remote virtual machine. This Remote Method Invocation (RMI) facility, along with the CORBA (Common Object Broker Request Architecture) IDL (Interface Definition Language) compiler libraries, make Java a very attractive platform for client/server applications.

This chapter covers both the Java native remote method system and the CORBA interface. An overview of the two systems is given first, followed by examples using both.

Using Objects in a Networked Environment

From the start, Java has had network capabilities in the form of the classes in the `java.net` package. The functionality provided by these classes is very low level (raw network streams, or packets). The introduction of the Remote Method Invocation classes and the CORBA interface has raised the level of abstraction. These two packages provide a means of accessing data and methods in the form of objects over a network.

The development and widespread deployment of networks has changed how computers are used. The trend in network computing in the past few years has been towards *client/server* systems. In client/server systems, a local application (the client) provides the interface to a remote database or application (the server). The Web itself is an example of a client/server system, with Web browsers being the client and Web sites the servers.

Client/server systems rely on network services to communicate information between themselves, but for the most part that is all they send: information. Distributed object systems combine client/server systems with another trend in computing: object-oriented programming. Rather than sending just information, distributed object systems transmit both data and code to manipulate that data. Another benefit of distributed objects is the ability of an object on one host to invoke a method on an object located on a remote host across the network.

Imagine that you were writing a tic-tac-toe game to be played over the network. In a conventional client/server approach, you would need to worry about things such as creating network connections between players and developing a protocol for sending moves back and forth. This is not to say that the game could not be developed, simply that there is a lot more work to be done to do so.

With a distributed object system, many of these lower level details are hidden from the programmer. For example, the server object would have a method which registers a player's move. A player's client would simply obtain a reference to the server object and call the appropriate method on this object (just as if the server object resided on the same machine).

A system for distributed objects has to take many things into consideration: How are remote objects referenced? What representation is used for transmitting an object or parameters for a method call (a process known as *marshaling* in distributed object circles)? What character set is used for strings? Are integers represented as little-endian (the low order byte of a word comes first, as with Motorola processors) or big-endian (the high order byte of a word comes first, as with Intel processors)? What happens if there is a network problem during a method call?

Sun is no stranger to solving such problems. Their Remote Procedure Call (RPC) and External Data Representation (XDR) protocols have been in wide use on UNIX platforms for many years. The Network File System (NFS) used to share file systems between machines, and the Network Information System (NIS, formerly known as YP) used to provide a distributed database of configuration information (such as user accounts or hostnames to IP address databases) are both implemented using RPC.

Why Two Different Solutions?

You may be asking yourself why Sun is providing two different solutions to solve the same problem. Each of the remote object systems has its own particular advantages.

The RMI system provides Java-native access to remote objects. Because it is written specifically for Java in Java, the RMI system allows transparent access to remote objects. Once a reference is obtained for a remote object, it is treated just like any other Java object. The code accessing the remote object may not even be aware that the object does not reside on the same host. The downside to this approach is that the RMI system may only be used to interface to servers written in Java.

The IDL interface provides access to clients and servers using the industry standard CORBA protocol specifications. An application that uses the IDL compiler can connect to any object server that complies with the CORBA standards and uses a compatible transport mechanism. Unlike the RMI system, CORBA is intended to be a language-neutral system. Objects must be specified using the OMG Interface Definition Language, and access must be through library routines that translate the calls into the appropriate CORBA messages.

Remote Method Invocation System

The RMI system uses Java interfaces and a special "stub" compiler to provide transparent access to remote objects. An interface is defined specifying the methods provided by the remote object. Next, a server class is defined to implement the interface. The stub compiler is invoked to generate classes that act as the glue between the local representation of an object and the remote object residing on the server.

The RMI system also provides a naming service that allows servers to bind object references to URLs such as `rmi://foohost.com/ObjectName`. A client passes a URL to the `Naming` class's `lookup()` method, which returns a reference to an object implementing the appropriate interface.

Interface Definition Language and CORBA

CORBA is a part of the Object Management Group's (OMG) Object Management Architecture. The OMG is an industry consortium formed in 1989 to help provide standards for object-oriented technology. The architecture consists of four standards:

- **Common Object Broker Request Architecture (CORBA).** This standard specifies the interactions between a client object and an Object Request Broker (ORB). The ORB receives an invocation request, determines which object can handle the request, and passes the request and parameters to the servicing object.

- **Common Object Services Specification (COSS).** COSS provides a standard interface for operations such as creating and relocating objects.

- **Common Facilities.** This standard specifies common application functionalities such as printing, e-mail, and document management.

- **Applications Objects.** These standard objects provide for common business functions.

> **NOTE**
>
> For a more complete introduction to CORBA and related standards, check out the OMG's home page at `http://www.omg.org/`. Another useful URL is `http://www.omg.org/ed.htm` which has pointer to a list of books on distributed objects (and CORBA in particular).

The Java IDL system provides a mapping from the CORBA object model into Java classes. The IDL compiler provides stub classes. These stubs call an ORB core that handles details such as determining the transport mechanism to use (such as Sun's NEO or the OMG's Internet Inter-ORB Protocol (IIOP)) and marshaling parameters.

Using the `java.rmi` Package

Let's take a look at the Java-native remote method system. The following sections provide a more detailed explanation of how the RMI system works and what you need to do to use it. An example service is developed that provides `java.io.InputStream` and `java.io.OutputStream` compatible access to a file located on a remote machine.

An Overview of `java.rmi`

The RMI system consists of several different classes and interfaces. The following sections give brief explanations of what the important ones do and how they are used.

The `java.rmi.Remote` Interface

The RMI system is based on remote interfaces through which a client accesses the methods of a remote object. This interface must be declared to extend `java.rmi.Remote`, and each method of the interface must indicate that it throws a `java.rmi.RemoteException` in addition to any other exceptions.

The `java.rmi.server.RemoteServer` Class

The `RemoteServer` provides a superclass for servers that provide remote access to objects. The second step in developing an RMI server is to create a server class that implements your remote interface. This server class should extend one of the subclasses of `RemoteServer` (`UnicastRemoteServer` is the only subclass provided with the RMI system at this time), and must contain the actual code for the methods declared in the remote interface.

After the server class has been created, the RMI stub compiler (`rmic`) is given the interface for the class and the server that provides the implementation used to create several "glue" classes. These glue classes work behind the scenes to handle all the nasty details such as contacting the remote virtual machine, passing arguments, and retrieving a return value (if any).

The `java.rmi.Naming` Class

The `Naming` class provides a means for server classes to make remote objects visible to clients. All the `Naming` class's methods are static and do not require an instance to use. A server that wants to make an object available calls the `bind()` or `rebind()` method with the name of the object (passed as a `String`) and a reference to an object implementing an interface extending `Remote`. Clients can call the `lookup()` method with a `String` representation of the URL for the object they want to access. RMI URLs are of the form `rmi://host[:port]/name`, where *host* is the hostname the object's server resides on (with an optional port number) and *name* is the name of the object.

Exceptions

The RMI package provides several exceptions used to indicate errors during remote method calls. The most common exception is the generic `RemoteException` used to indicate that some sort of problem occurred during a call. All methods of an interface extending the `Remote` interface must note that they can throw this exception. Several other more specific exceptions such as `StubNotFoundException` (thrown when the RMI system cannot find the glue classes generated by `rmic`) and the `RemoteRuntimeException` (thrown when a `RuntimeException` occurs on the server during a method call) are subclasses of `RemoteException`.

The `Naming` class has two exceptions, `NotBoundException` and `AlreadyBound`, which it throws to indicate that a given name hasn't been bound to an object or has already been bound. All the naming methods can also throw a `java.net.UnknownHostException` if the host specified in the URL is invalid; they can also throw a `java.net.MalformedURLException` if the given URL is not syntactically correct.

RMI Example Architecture

To demonstrate the `java.rmi` package, we will create a (very simple) file server. This server accepts requests from a remote caller and returns a `RemoteObject` that is used by wrapper classes to provide `java.io.InputStream` and `java.io.OutputStream` objects that read or write from the remote file.

The RemoteInputHandle Interface

First off, we define the interface by which our input wrapper class interacts with the remote file (see Listing 45.1). The RemoteInputHandle class provides methods that correspond to those required by the java.io.InputStream abstract class. The interface simply defines the methods required for an InputStream object. Each method can throw a RemoteException as noted in the throws clause.

Listing 45.1. The RemoteInputHandle interface.

```
import java.rmi.*;
import java.io.IOException;

public interface RemoteInputHandle
    extends Remote
{
  public int available( )
    throws IOException, RemoteException;

  public void close( )
    throws IOException, RemoteException;

  public void mark( int readlimit )
    throws RemoteException;

  public boolean markSupported( )
    throws RemoteException;

  public int read( )
    throws IOException, RemoteException;

  public int read( byte b[] )
    throws IOException, RemoteException;

  public int read( byte b[], int off, int len )
    throws IOException, RemoteException;

  public void reset( )
    throws IOException, RemoteException;

  public long skip( long n )
    throws IOException, RemoteException;
}
```

The RemoteInputHandleImpl Class

Next up is the RemoteInputHandleImpl class, which provides the implementation for the RemoteInputHandle interface just defined (see Listing 45.2). The RemoteFileServerImpl class creates a new input handle implementation when a RemoteInputHandle is requested. The constructor for the implementation class takes one argument: the InputStream for which we are providing remote access. This makes the handle more useful because we can provide remote access to any local object that extends `InputStream`. This stream is saved in an instance variable (`inStream`) after the `UnicastRemoteServer` superclass's constructor is called. The superclass constructor is called because it has to set things up to listen for requests from remote clients.

Listing 45.2. The `RemoteInputHandleImpl` class.

```
import java.rmi.*;
import java.rmi.server.UnicastRemoteServer;
import java.rmi.server.StubSecurityManager;

public class RemoteInputHandleImpl
    extends UnicastRemoteServer
    implements RemoteInputHandle
{
  private InputStream inStream;

  public RemoteInputHandleImpl( InputStream in )
    throws RemoteException
  {
    super( );

    inStream = in;
  }
```

Next comes the actual code implementing the methods of the `RemoteInputHandle` interface (see Listing 45.3). Each method simply calls the corresponding method on `inStream` and returns the return value from that call (as appropriate). The RMI system takes care of returning the result—as well as any exceptions that occur—to the calling object on the remote machine.

Listing 45.3. The methods of the `RemoteInputHandleImpl` class.

```
  public int available( )
    throws IOException, RemoteException
  {
    return inStream.available();
  }

  public void close( )
    throws IOException, RemoteException
  {
    inStream.close( );
  }

  public synchronized void mark( int readlimit )
    throws RemoteException
  {
    inStream.mark( readlimit );
  }

  public boolean markSupported( )
    throws RemoteException
  {
```

45

REMOTE OBJECTS
AND THE JAVA
IDL SYSTEM

continues

Listing 45.3. continued

```
      return inStream.markSupported( );
   }

   public int read( )
      throws IOException, RemoteException
   {
      return inStream.read( );
   }

   public int read( byte b[] )
      throws IOException, RemoteException
   {
      return inStream.read( b );
   }

   public int read( byte b[], int off, int len )
      throws IOException, RemoteException
   {
      return inStream.read( b, off, len );
   }

   public synchronized void reset( )
      throws IOException, RemoteException
   {
      inStream.reset( );
   }

   public long skip( long n )
      throws IOException, RemoteException
   {
      return inStream.skip( n );
   }

}
```

The RemoteInputStream Class

The RemoteInputStream class extends the abstract InputStream class and uses the RemoteInputHandle interface. The constructor first contacts a RemoteFileServer to obtain a RemoteInputHandle reference for the path given and then stores this handle in an instance variable. The InputStream methods are mapped into the corresponding calls on the RemoteInputHandle (that is, the RemoteInputStream read() method calls the read() method on the RemoteInputHandle reference obtained by the constructor).

> **NOTE**
>
> You may wonder why we are using a wrapper class when all it does is turn around and call the same method on the interface. The reason is that we want to provide a class that can be used any place an InputStream or OutputStream can be used.

For example, you can create a `PrintStream` using a `RemoteOutputStream` for a log file for an application. Anything you print to this `PrintStream` is written to the log file on the remote machine. Without the wrapper class, you would have to individually extend each class to use the `RemoteInputHandle` or `RemoteOutputHandle` as needed.

We'll start out with the necessary imports and the class definition (see Listing 45.4). We need access to the `java.io` classes because the `RemoteInputStream` extends `InputStream`. We also need access to the RMI `Naming` class so that we can use the `lookup()` method to get a `RemoteInputHandle` from the server. There are two constructors for the class. One takes a pathname as the argument and contacts the file server residing on the same host, and the other takes a remote hostname to contact as well.

Listing 45.4. The `RemoteInputStream` class.

```
import java.io.*;
import java.rmi.RemoteException;
import java.rmi.Naming;
import java.rmi.NotBoundException;

public class RemoteInputStream
    extends InputStream
{
  private RemoteInputHandle in;

  public RemoteInputStream( String path )
    throws IOException, RemoteException, NotBoundException
  {
    String url = "rmi://localhost/RFSI";

    RemoteFileServer rfs = (RemoteFileServer) Naming.lookup( url );

    in = rfs.getInStream( path );
  }

  public RemoteInputStream( String path, String host )
    throws IOException, RemoteException, NotBoundException
  {
    String url = "rmi://" + host + "/RFSI";

    RemoteFileServer rfs = (RemoteFileServer) Naming.lookup( url );

    in = rfs.getInStream( path );
  }
```

Each of the `InputStream` methods is defined next (see Listing 45.5). The code for each method tries to call the corresponding method on the handle object. If a `RemoteException` occurs, an `IOException` is thrown with the message from the `RemoteException` as its message.

Listing 45.5. The InputStream methods of the RemoteInputStream class.

```
public int availabe( )
  throws IOException
{
  try {
    return in.available( );
  } catch( RemoteException e ) {
    throw new IOException( "Remote error: " + e );
  }
}

public void close( )
  throws IOException
{
  try {
    in.close( );
  } catch( RemoteException e ) {
    throw new IOException( "Remote error: " + e );
  }
}

public synchronized void mark( int readlimit )
{
  try {
    in.mark( readlimit );
  } catch( Exception e ) {
    System.err.println(
        "RemoteInputStream::mark: Remote error: " + e );
  }
}

public boolean markSupported( ) {
  try {
    return in.markSupported( );
  } catch( RemoteException e ) {
    return false;            // Assume mark not supported
  }
}

public int read( )
  throws IOException
{
  try {
    return in.read( );
  } catch( RemoteException e ) {
    throw new IOException( "Remote error: " + e );
  }
}

public int read( byte b[] )
  throws IOException
{
  try {
    return in.read( b );
  } catch( RemoteException e ) {
    throw new IOException( "Remote error: " + e );
```

```
    }
  }

  public int read( byte b[], int off, int len )
    throws IOException
  {
    try {
      return in.read( b, off, len );
    } catch( RemoteException e ) {
      throw new IOException( "Remote error: " + e );
    }
  }

  public synchronized void reset( )
    throws IOException
  {
    try {
      in.reset( );
    } catch( RemoteException e ) {
      throw new IOException( "Remote error: " + e );
    }
  }

  public long skip( long n )
    throws IOException
  {
    try {
      return in.skip( n );
    } catch( RemoteException e ) {
      throw new IOException( "Remote error: " + e );
    }
  }
}
```

The Output Side

The remote interface, implementation, and the wrapper class for the output stream version are, for the most part, identical to those for input so they are not given here. The methods in the interface correspond to those for java.io.OutputStream instead of InputStream, and the RemoteOutputStream object extends OutputStream. The complete code for all the output classes is contained on the CD-ROM that accompanies this book.

The RemoteFileServer Interface and RemoteFileServerImpl Class

The RemoteFileServer interface provides two methods that the remote input and output stream classes use to obtain handles (see Listing 45.6).

Listing 45.6. The `RemoteFileServer` interface.

```
public interface RemoteFileServer
    extends java.rmi.Remote
{

public RemoteOutputHandle getOutStream( String path )
    throws java.rmi.RemoteException;

  public RemoteInputHandle getInStream( String path )
    throws java.rmi.RemoteException;
}
```

The server itself is very simple. It consists of a constructor that calls the `UnicastRemoteServer` superclass, a method that does some sanity checking on the pathnames requested, implementations of the interface methods, and a `main()` method that allows the server to be started (see Listing 45.7). We start off as usual with the import statements, class declaration, and the constructor. Note that there is a static class variable `PATH_SEPARATOR`, which should be changed to whatever character separates directory components on your operating system.

Listing 45.7. The `RemoteFileServerImpl` class.

```
import java.io.*;
import java.rmi.*;
import java.rmi.server.UnicastRemoteServer;
import java.rmi.server.StubSecurityManager;

public class RemoteFileServerImpl
    extends UnicastRemoteServer
    implements RemoteFileServer
{
  // Path component separator.  Change as appropriate for your OS.
  public static char PATH_SEPARATOR = '/';

  public RemoteFileServerImpl( )
    throws RemoteException
  {
    super( );      // Call superclass' constructor

    // No class specific initialisation needed.
  }
```

The `checkPathName()` method shown in Listing 45.8 does some rudimentary checking to ensure that the pathname does not point outside the current directory or one of its subdirectories. The code that checks for an absolute path (that is, a path that starts at the root directory or with a specific drive) should be edited as appropriate for your platform.

Listing 45.8. The `RemoteFileServerImpl.checkPathName()` method.

```
public boolean checkPathName( String path )
{

  // No absolute pathnames (i.e. ones beginning with a slash or drive)
  // UNIX Version
  if( path.charAt( 0 ) == PATH_SEPARATOR ) {
    return false;
  }
   // Wintel Version
  /*
     if( path.charAt( 1 ) == ':' && path.charAt( 2 ) == PATH_SEPARATOR ) {
        return false;
     }
  */

// No references to parent directory with ".."
    for( int i = 0; i < path.length() - 1; i++ ) {
      if( path.charAt( i ) == '.'
          && path.charAt( i + 1 ) == '.' ) {
        return false;
      }
    }

    return true;      // Path's OK
}
```

Next comes the code implementing the methods of our remote interface (see Listing 45.9). Each calls `checkPathName()` on the path and then tries to open either a `FileInputStream` or `FileOutputStream` as appropriate. Any exception that occurs while obtaining a stream is rethrown as a `RemoteException` (although there is no reason the interface cannot throw the appropriate exceptions). Once the stream has been opened, a `RemoteInputHandleImpl` or `RemoteOutputHandleImpl` object is created as appropriate with the just-opened stream. The handle is then returned to the caller.

Listing 45.9. The methods of the `RemoteFileServerImpl` class.

```
public RemoteInputHandle getInStream( String path )
  throws java.rmi.RemoteException
{
  FileInputStream file = null; // Used to hold file for input

  // Log that we're opening a stream
  System.err.println( "RFSI::getInStream( \"" + path + "\" )" );

  // Check that the pathname is legal or gripe
  if( !checkPathName( path ) ) {
    RemoteException e =
      new RemoteException( "Invalid pathname '" + path + "'." );
    throw e;
  }
```

45

continues

Listing 45.9. continued

```java
    // Try and open a FileInputStream for the path
    try {
      file = new FileInputStream( path );
    } catch( FileNotFoundException e ) {
      // File doesn't exist, so throw remote exception with that message
      RemoteException r =
        new RemoteException( "File does not exist: "
                             + e.getMessage() );
      throw r;
    } catch( IOException e ) {
      // Problem opening file, so throw exception saying that
      RemoteException r =
        new RemoteException( "Error opening file: "
                             + e.getMessage() );
      throw r;
    }

    // Return value is a RemoteInputHandle for an RIH implementation
    // object created with the file we just opened as it's input stream.
    RemoteInputHandle retval =
      new RemoteInputHandleImpl( file );

    return retval;       // Return handle to caller
  }

  public RemoteOutputHandle getOutStream( String path )
    throws java.rmi.RemoteException
  {
    FileOutputStream file = null; // Used to hold file for output

    // Log that we're opening a stream
    System.err.println( "RFSI::getOutStream( \"" + path + "\" )" );

    // Check that the pathname is legal or gripe
    if( !checkPathName( path ) ) {
      RemoteException e =
        new RemoteException( "Invalid pathname '" + path + "'." );
      throw e;
    }

    // Try and open FileOutputStream for the path
    try {
      file = new FileOutputStream( path );
    } catch( IOException e ) {
      // Problem opening file for output, so throw exception saying so
      RemoteException r =
        new RemoteException( "Error opening file: "
                             + e.getMessage() );
      throw r;
    }

    // Return value is a RemoteOutputHandle for an ROH implementation
    // object created with the file just opened as it's output stream
    RemoteOutputHandle retval = new RemoteOutputHandleImpl( file );

    return retval;       // Return the handle
  }
```

Finally, we come to the `main()` method, which can be used to start a standalone server from the command line (see Listing 45.10). The first thing this method does is to create a `StubSecurityManager`—a `SecurityManager` context appropriate for a standalone remote object server. Next, `main()` creates a `RemoteFileServerImpl` object and binds it to the name `RFSI`. If an exception occurs during object creation or binding, the name of the exception is noted and the server exits.

Listing 45.10. The `RemoteFileServerImpl.main()` method.

```
public static void main( String args[] )
{
  // Create and install stub security manager
  System.setSecurityManager( new StubSecurityManager( ) );

  try {
    System.err.println( "RFSI::main: creating RFSI." );

    // Create a new server implementation object
    RemoteFileServerImpl i = new RemoteFileServerImpl( );

    // Bind our server object to a name so clients may contact us.
    /* The URL will be "rmi://host/RFSI", with host replaced with */
    // the name of the host we're running on.
    String name = "RFSI";
    System.err.println( "RFSI::main: binding to name: " + name );
    Naming.rebind( name, i );

  } catch( Exception e ) {
    // Problem creating server.  Log exception and die.
    System.err.println( "Exception creating server: "
                        + e + "\n" );
    e.printStackTrace( System.err );

    System.exit( 1 );
  }
}
```

The `rfsClient` Class

To demonstrate how to use our remote files, we now develop a very simple client that opens a remote output file and writes a message to it (see Listing 45.11). An input stream is obtained, and the stream's contents are read back. The output filename is defined as `outputfile` and the input filename defaults to `inputfile` (however, if an argument is given on the command line, that name is used instead). The host contacted is defined as the local host, but you can change the URL used to point to a remote machine if you have access to more than one host.

45

REMOTE OBJECTS AND THE JAVA IDL SYSTEM

Listing 45.11. The rfsClient class.

```java
import java.io.*;
import java.rmi.*;

public class rfsClient
{
  public static void main( String args[] ) {
    System.setSecurityManager(
      new java.rmi.server.StubSecurityManager() );

    // Contact remote file server running on same machine
    String url = "rmi://localhost/";

    // Default name of file to read
    String infile = "inputfile";

    // Try and open an output stream to a file called "outputfile"
    try {
      OutputStream out = new RemoteOutputStream( "outputfile");
      PrintStream ps = new PrintStream( out );

      ps.println( "Testing println on remote file." );
      ps.println( new java.util.Date() );

      ps = null;
      out = null;
    } catch( Exception e ) {
      System.err.println( "Error on getOutStream: " + e );
      e.printStackTrace();
      System.exit( 1 );
    }

    // If we were given a command line argument, use that as the
    // input file name
    if( args.length != 0 ) {
      infile = args[ 0 ];
    }

    // Try and open an output stream on a file
    try {
      InputStream in = new RemoteInputStream( infile );
      DataInputStream ds = new DataInputStream( in );

      // Read each line of the file and print it out
      try {
        String line = ds.readLine( );
        while( line != null ) {
          System.err.println( "Read: " + line );
          line = ds.readLine( );
        } catch( EOFException e ) {
          System.err.println( "EOF" );
        }
    } catch( Exception e ) {
      System.err.println( "Error on getInStream: " + e );
      e.printStackTrace( );
      System.exit( 1 );
```

```
    }

    System.exit( 0 );    // Exit gracefully
  }
}
```

Using the IDL Compiler

The following sections cover the CORBA-based IDL compiler and support classes. First, we'll explain exactly what the IDL compiler does and how it maps objects from their IDL definitions to Java equivalents. A simple example using the IDL system is also given.

The IDL to Java Compiler

The IDL compiler takes an object definition in the CORBA IDL format and generates a Java version. Table 45.1 shows several of these mappings.

Table 45.1. Example IDL to Java mappings.

IDL Feature	*Java Mapping*
module	package
boolean	boolean
char	char
octet	byte
string	java.lang.String
short	short
long	int
long long	long
float	float
enum	A Java class with a static final int member for each enum member
struct	A Java class; all methods and instance variables are public
interface	A Java interface; the compiler also generates a stub that implements the interface if you choose
exception	A Java class that extends the omg.corba.UserException class

As Table 45.1 shows, most of the mappings are straightforward. Some IDL constructs do not have a direct Java equivalent. One example of this is a union (a structure that can hold one of several different types of components); in this case, a class with a discriminator (which indicates what type of information the union currently holds) and access methods for each possible content type.

Another difference between Java and the IDL model is in the way parameters are passed to method calls. Java passes all parameters by value; the IDL model defines three ways parameters may be passed: in (which is a pass by value, just as Java does); out (which is a pass by reference—meaning that the parameter is passed so that it can be modified); and inout (which is a cross between a pass by value and a pass by reference—the value remains the same until the method returns).

IDL Support Classes

With the java.rmi system, the remote objects are themselves servers. The CORBA model depends on a separate request broker to receive requests and actually call methods. The IDL system provides a class to represent the ORB. The generic ORB object provides a very important method: resolve(). This method takes a URL and a remote object reference created from a stub class of the appropriate type and binds the reference to the server. The format for IDL URLs is idl:*orb package*://*hostname[:port]*/*object*, where *orb package* is the Java package that provides access to a given type of ORB (sunw.door is the simple ORB that comes with the IDL package, sunw.neo is Sun's NEO ORB, and so on); *hostname* and the optional *port* are used to determine where to contact the ORB; and *object* is the name of the object requested from the ORB.

The CORBA runtime also defines mappings from the standard CORBA exceptions to Java exceptions. All IDL-defined exceptions are subclasses of one of two classes: sunw.corba.SystemException for all exceptions raised by the CORBA system itself, and sunw.corba.UserException, which is used as the superclass for all user-defined exceptions in IDL objects.

IDL System Example

To demonstrate the use of the IDL compiler and the CORBA interface, we will develop a simple example. Our object will represent a conference room. The goal is to allow clients to query the state of the room (whether it is available or in use).

> **NOTE**
>
> This example was created using the Alpha 2 release of the IDL compiler and CORBA classes. Although Sun is very good about freezing APIs before public releases, some changes may have been made. When in doubt, use the documentation that came with the IDL system as the definitive source.

Room IDL Definition

The first step in creating our example is to write the IDL definition for the object. The interface defines an enumerated type, roomStatus, which notes whether the room is in use or available. A room has (for our purposes) two attributes: a name and a status. The interface also provides a method to set the status of the room.

The IDL to Java compile (idlgen) takes this definition and creates several interfaces and classes. These classes are placed in a package called unleashed. The classes implementing the roomStatus enumeration are placed in the unleashed.Room package as shown in Listing 45.12.

Listing 45.12. The IDL for a room (room.idl).

```
module unleashed {
  interface Room {
    // Status of a room
    enum roomStatus { available, inUse };

    // Room name
    readonly attribute string Name;

    // Current room status
    readonly attribute roomStatus Status;

    // Method to set the status of the Room
    void setStatus( in roomStatus newStatus );
  };
};
```

The RoomImpl Class

The first class that must be defined is the implementation object for the room object (see Listing 45.13). This is analogous to creating a subclass of RemoteServer when using the RMI classes. Unlike the RMI system, the server is a separate ORB object.

The implementation must implement the unleashed.RoomServant interface (which was generated by idlgen). The RoomImpl class has two instance variables to hold the name of the room and its status. The constructor takes two arguments, which are copied into these instance variables. Normally, each attribute of an interface has a get() and set() method defined for it (get*Attribute*() and set*Attribute*()). Because both of the attributes on the room interface are read-only, only the getName() and getStatus() methods were defined by the compiler. Our implementation simply returns the contents of the instance variables. The setStatus() method likewise performs a bounds check (using the enumeration class created by the compiler) to set the status member.

Listing 45.13. The unleashed.RoomImpl class.

```
package unleashed;

public class RoomImpl implements unleashed.RoomServant
{
  private String name;
  private int status;

  public RoomImpl( String n, int s )
    throws sunw.corba.EnumerationRangeException
  {
    name = n;
    status = unleashed.Room.roomStatus.narrow( s );
  }

  public String getName( ) {
    return name;
  }

  public int getStatus( ) {
    return status;
  }

  public void setStatus( int newStatus ) {
    status = unleashed.Room.roomStatus.narrow( newStatus );
  }
}
```

The RoomServer Class

Now that we have the implementation for the room object, we have to create a server class (see Listing 45.14). The server uses the simple sunw.door ORB that comes with the IDL system. It first calls sunw.door.Orb.initialize() to start the ORB listening for requests from clients. An implementation object is created and passed to the RoomSkeleton.createRef() method. This method, created by the IDL compiler, returns a RoomRef suitable for passing to the ORB's publish() method. This accomplishes the same thing as using the java.rmi.Naming.bind() method—that is, binding the object reference to a name accessible by a URL.

Listing 45.14. The RoomServer class.

```
package unleashed;

public class RoomServer
{
  static String pathName = "room.server";

  public static void main( String arg[] ) {
    sunw.door.Orb.initialize( );

    try {
      RoomRef r =
        RoomSkeleton.createRef(
          new RoomImpl( "Room 203", unleashed.Room.roomStatus.available ) );
```

```
        sunw.door.Orb.publish( pathName, r );
    } catch( sunw.door.naming.Failure e ) {
        System.err.println( "Couldn't bind object in naming context: " + e );
        System.exit( 1 );
    }

    System.err.println( "Room server setup and bound on port "
                        + sunw.door.Orb.getDefaultPort() );
    }
}
```

The Client Applet

The last step is to create a client to access the remote object. `RoomClient` is an applet that connects to a room object and provides a means of querying the current status and changing the
status. An instance variable of `unleashed.RoomRef` type is used to hold the currently active
remote object reference. The `init()` method creates the user interface. A `TextField` is created
to allow the user to enter the hostname to connect to. Fields are also created to show the name
and status of the room once a server has been contacted. Finally, three buttons are created: one
to cause the applet to connect to the room object, one to request that the room be reserved
(marked as "in use"), and one to request that the room be released (marked as "available").

The `connect()` method uses the hostname entered by the user to construct a URL for the room
server residing on that machine. The URL assumes that the server is running on the default
`sunw.door` ORB port. The `connect()` method next creates a reference to a `RoomStub` and uses
the `sunw.corba.Orb.resolve()` method to resolve the URL to an object reference. If an exception occurs, the error message is displayed in the applet's status area and printed to `System.err`.

The `updateStatus()` method uses the room reference obtained by `connect()` to determine the
name and status of the room. The information is printed to the corresponding field of the interface. Any exceptions are noted in the status line and logged to `System.err`. Both `reserve()`
and `release()` call the `setStatus()` method on the `RoomRef` object. The only difference between the two methods is the constant from the `unleashed.Room.roomStatus` class they use.

Finally, the `action()` method is called whenever the user presses one of the buttons. This method
determines which button was pressed and calls the corresponding method. Listing 45.15 shows
the complete `RoomClient` class; Figure 45.1 shows the `RoomClient` applet in use.

Listing 45.15. The RoomClient class.

```
import java.net.URL;
import java.awt.*;
import java.applet.Applet;
```

continues

Listing 45.15. continued

```java
public class RoomClient extends Applet
{
  unleashed.RoomRef r;
  String serverUrl;

  TextField nameField;
  TextField statusField;
  TextField hostField;
  Button connectButton;
  Button reserveButton;
  Button releaseButton;

  public void init( ) {
    Panel p;

    setLayout( new BorderLayout() );

    p = new Panel();
    p.setLayout( new FlowLayout() );
    p.add( new Label( "Host: " ) );
    p.add( hostField = new TextField( 30 ) );
    add( "North", p );

    Panel stats = new Panel();
    stats.setLayout( new GridLayout( 2, 1 ) );

    p = new Panel( );
    p.setLayout( new GridLayout( 1, 2 ) );
    p.add( new Label( "Room Name: " ) );
    p.add( nameField = new TextField( 30 ) );
    stats.add( p );

    p = new Panel( );
    p.setLayout( new GridLayout( 1, 2 ) );
    p.add( new Label( "Room status: " ) );
    p.add( statusField = new TextField( 10 ) );
    stats.add( p );

    add( "Center", stats );

    p = new Panel( );
    p.setLayout( new GridLayout( 1, 3 ) );
    p.add( connectButton = new Button( "Connect" ) );
    p.add( reserveButton = new Button( "Reserve" ) );
    p.add( releaseButton = new Button( "Release" ) );

    add( "South", p );

    // Name and status fields not editable
    nameField.setEditable( false );
    statusField.setEditable( false );

    updateStatus();
  }
```

```
public void connect( ) {
  String host = hostField.getText();

  if( host == null || host.length() == 0 ) {
    showStatus( "Enter a hostname first." );
    return;
  }

  serverUrl =
    "idl:sunw.door://"
      + host + ":" + sunw.door.Orb.getDefaultPort()
        + "/room.server";
  showStatus( "Connecting to room server on " + host );

  try {
    r = unleashed.RoomStub.createRef();
    sunw.corba.Orb.resolve( serverUrl, r );
  } catch( Exception e ) {
    System.err.println( "Couldn't resolve: " + e );
    showStatus( "Couldn't resolve room server: " + e );
    return;
  }
  updateStatus( );
}

public void updateStatus( ) {

  if( r == null ) {
    nameField.setText( "" );
    statusField.setText( "" );
    showStatus( "Not Connected" );
    return;
  }

  // Get room name and stick it in text field
  try {
    String name = r.getName();
    nameField.setText( name );
  } catch( sunw.corba.SystemException e ) {
    System.err.println( "Error getting room name: " + e );
    showStatus( "Error getting room name: " + e );
  }

  try {
    switch( r.getStatus( ) ) {
    case unleashed.Room.roomStatus.available:
      statusField.setText( "available" );
      break;
    case unleashed.Room.roomStatus.inUse:
      statusField.setText( "in use" );
      break;
    }
  } catch( sunw.corba.SystemException e ) {
    System.err.println( "Error getting room status: " + e );
    showStatus( "Error getting room status: " + e );
  }

}
```

45

**REMOTE OBJECTS
AND THE JAVA
IDL SYSTEM**

continues

Listing 45.15. continued

```java
public void reserve( ) {
  if( r == null ) {
    showStatus( "You must connect to a server first." );
    return;
  }

  try {
    r.setStatus( unleashed.Room.roomStatus.inUse );
  } catch( sunw.corba.SystemException e ) {
    System.err.println( "Error setting room status: " + e );
    showStatus( "Error reserving room: " + e );
  }

  updateStatus( );
}

public void release( ) {
  if( r == null ) {
    showStatus( "You must connect to a server first." );
    return;
  }

  try {
    r.setStatus( unleashed.Room.roomStatus.available );
  } catch( sunw.corba.SystemException e ) {
    System.err.println( "Error setting room status: " + e );
    showStatus( "Error reserving room: " + e );
  }

  updateStatus( );
}

public boolean action( Event e, Object o )
{
  if( "Connect".equals( o ) ) {
    connect();
    return true;
  }

  if( "Reserve".equals( o ) ) {
    reserve( );
    return true;
  }

  if( "Release".equals( o ) ) {
    release( );
    return true;
  }

  return false;
}
}
```

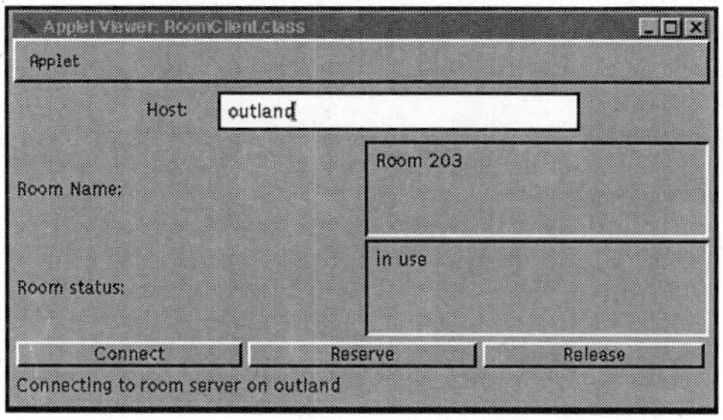

FIGURE 45.1.

The RoomClient *applet in action.*

Summary

You should now have an idea how both of the distributed object systems for Java work. Both systems have their own advantages and disadvantages. Hopefully, you now know enough to choose the one that best fits your application.

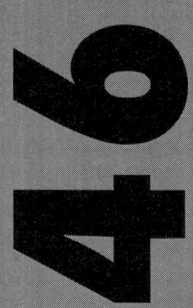

The Standard Extension APIs

by Michael Morrison

IN THIS CHAPTER

Up to this point, everything you've learned about Java has been entirely based on what is known as the *core Java API*, or the Java Base API, version 1.02. This core API currently comprises the entirety of the Java programming environment. JavaSoft recently announced a broad set of extensions to extend this core API in a variety of ways. Some of these extensions will eventually become part of Java 1.1, which is the next major release of Java. Until the official release of Java 1.1, these new extensions will be released individually as standard extensions to the current Java environment. In addition, some of the new extensions will remain as extensions even after the release of Java 1.1 simply because they address development areas that aren't central to the core Java API.

This chapter takes a look at all the new API extensions and what they have to offer you as a Java developer. Most of the API extensions are very new and haven't even reached the specification stage. For this reason, this chapter is meant to give you an idea of where Java is headed with the standard extension APIs. In other words, you may want to check JavaSoft's Web site (www.javasoft.com) to get the latest scoop on the status of these APIs because they are still in the development stage.

Java API Overview

Java release 1.02, which is the latest Java release as of this writing, is now being referred to by JavaSoft as the *core Java API*. The core Java API defines the minimal set of functionality a Java implementation must support to be considered Java compliant. For example, when someone undertakes the job of supporting Java on a particular platform, that person must fully implement the core Java API. This guaranteed support for the core API is what allows Java developers the luxury of being able to write Java programs once and have them run on any Java-compliant platform.

In the near future, JavaSoft plans to expand on the core API by introducing new APIs that address more applied development needs. The new APIs cover a wide range of areas and will ultimately save developers a great deal of time by establishing a consistent approach to certain development issues, reducing the need for custom coding. Some of these new APIs will merge with the new core API (Java 1.1); others will remain extensions. Regardless of their ultimate relationship to the core API, the new extension APIs are referred to as the *standard extension APIs* because they extend the current core API as we know it.

The standard extension APIs are divided into a set of individual APIs that target different development needs. Following are the major components of the standard extension APIs:

- Enterprise API
- Commerce API
- Management API
- Server API
- Media API

- Security API
- Java Beans API
- Embedded API

The rest of this chapter explains each of these APIs and how each impacts the Java software platform.

The Enterprise API

Enterprise computing has become increasingly important in recent years as more and more companies realize the importance of integrating their operations electronically. The unique possibilities afforded by the increased usage of the Internet have only served to magnify the popularity of enterprise computing. JavaSoft took note of Java's lack of support for enterprise systems and announced plans for an Enterprise API.

The Java Enterprise API is designed to allow Java programs a formal mechanism for connecting to enterprise information systems. This is a much needed feature in Java because so many corporate computer systems rely heavily on enterprise information sources. In answering this need, the Enterprise API tackles the problem on three fronts. These fronts come in the form of three API subsets:

- Java Database Connectivity (JDBC)
- Interface Definition Language (IDL)
- Remote Method Invocation (RMI)

JavaSoft has recognized the importance of these three API subsets and plans to directly incorporate them into the core Java API at some point in the future.

Java Database Connectivity (JDBC)

The first of the subset APIs of the Enterprise API is Java Database Connectivity (JDBC). JDBC defines a structured interface to Structured Query Language (SQL) databases. *SQL databases* are databases built on the SQL standard, which is a widely accepted standard that defines a strict protocol for accessing and manipulating data. By supporting SQL, JDBC allows developers to interact with and support a wide range of databases. This means that the specifics of the underlying database platform are pretty much irrelevant when it comes to JDBC, which is very good news to Java developers.

The JDBC API provides Java developers with a consistent approach to accessing SQL databases that is comparable to existing database development techniques. Interacting with a SQL database using JDBC isn't all that much different than interacting with a SQL database using traditional database tools. This should give Java programmers who already have some database experience confidence that they can hit the ground running with JDBC. The JDBC API has already been widely endorsed by industry leaders, including some development tool vendors who have announced future support for JDBC in their development products.

The JDBC API includes classes for common SQL database constructs such as database connections, SQL statements, and result sets. A *result set* is a group of data retrieved from a database after a user request. JDBC programs will be able to use the familiar SQL programming model of issuing SQL statements and processing the resulting data. The JDBC API depends largely on a driver manager that supports multiple drivers connecting to different databases. JDBC database drivers can either be written entirely in Java or they can be implemented using native methods to bridge Java applications to existing database access libraries.

You can get the latest scoop on JDBC from JavaSoft's JDBC Web site, located at `http://splash.javasoft.com/jdbc/`.

Interface Definition Language (IDL)

The Interface Definition Language (IDL) subset of the Enterprise API is aimed at providing a way to connect Java client programs to network servers running on other platforms. IDL is an industry standard protocol for client/server communications across different platforms. The primary usage of the IDL API is to transparently connect Java client programs to legacy systems. A *legacy system* is an outdated system that has yet to be reimplemented using current technologies. Like it or not, there are still plenty of legacy systems in use that house a great deal of important information.

The Java IDL API includes the following components:

- A client framework that allows Java IDL clients to be designed as either applets or standalone applications
- A server framework that allows Java applications to act as network servers for IDL clients
- A development tool that automatically generates stub code for specific remote interfaces

You can get the latest information on IDL from JavaSoft's IDL Web site, located at `http://splash.javasoft.com/JavaIDL-alpha2.0/pages/`.

Remote Method Invocation (RMI)

The Remote Method Invocation (RMI) component of the Enterprise API defines an interface for invoking object methods in a distributed environment. The RMI API serves a crucial purpose in the Enterprise API by providing full support for remote object communications. The RMI API makes it straightforward for Java developers to add remote computing support to their classes. For the latest information on RMI, check out JavaSoft's RMI Web site, located at `http://chatsubo.javasoft.com/current/rmi/`.

The Commerce API

As the role of the Internet continues to evolve from being an information source to being a retail marketplace, the need for a secure commercial transaction protocol is also growing. Both Internet vendors and shoppers alike are eagerly awaiting the inevitable migration of shopping to the Web. Beyond shopping, there are also other important areas of financial transactions (such as investment trading) that would benefit greatly from a secure standard. JavaSoft has provided an answer to the secure purchasing problem with the Commerce API, a Java API extension that provides the overhead for Java programs to support secure purchasing and financial management.

The Java Commerce API aims to provide developers with an elegant solution to the problem of commercial transactions on the Web. The goal is to make purchasing goods a seamless yet secure part of the Web experience. To this end, the Commerce API is being pushed by JavaSoft as an open, extensible environment for financial management on the Web. The long-term plan for the Commerce API is for integration into the Java software platform partially with the core API and partially as a standard extension. It isn't clear yet which components will make it into the core API and which will remain separate.

The Commerce API consists of the following primary components:

■ **Infrastructure.** The infrastructure of the Commerce API is basically the architectural framework that defines the interactions between the other components of the API. This infrastructure is also what gives the API its extensibility to support future commerce extensions.

■ **Information database.** The database component serves as a repository for user information such as payment methods and the user's shipping address. The database component contains encryption features so that user information can be kept completely private. Alternatively, commerce service providers have the option of sharing user information with one another.

■ **Payment cassettes.** The Commerce API makes use of *cassettes*, which are software modules that implement specific financial protocols. A payment cassette defines the protocol for making electronic payments. Examples of payment cassettes include credit cards, debit cards, and eventually digital cash. A user could have multiple payment cassettes that represent different payment instruments, much like we carry different payment instruments in our wallets or purses. In fact, one of the classes in the Commerce API specifically models an electronic wallet.

■ **Service cassettes.** This is the second kind of software module used by the Commerce API to implement specific financial protocols. Service cassettes serve to model any type of value-added financial service such as financial analysis or tax preparation modules. For example, you could feasibly purchase a service cassette to help you balance your electronic checkbook or assess the value of your stock portfolio.

■ **Administrative interfaces.** This component of the Commerce API includes dialog boxes and other graphical interfaces used to retrieve information from the user and to configure commerce options.

For more information on the Commerce API, check out JavaSoft's Commerce API Web site, located at `http://www.javasoft.com/products/commerce/`.

The Management API

The Management API is designed to answer the needs of integrated network management systems. It includes a wide range of interfaces, classes, and applets to facilitate the development of integrated management solutions. The primary goal of the Management API is to provide a unified approach to handling the complexities involved in developing and maintaining resources and services on a heterogeneous network. Using the Management API, Java developers will be able to rapidly develop network management applications supporting a wide range of systems on large and often complex networks. JavaSoft plans to keep the Management API as a separate extension from the core API.

The Management API includes the following core components:

■ **Admin View Module (AVM).** The AVM is an extension of the Java Abstract Windowing Toolkit (AWT) that is enhanced to provide specific support for creating integrated management applications. The classes implemented in the AVM serve as a basis for developing sophisticated graphical user interfaces. For example, the AVM includes support for graphical tables, charts, graphs, and meters.

■ **Base object interfaces.** The base object interfaces define the core object types used for distributed resources and services in a management system. Using the base object interfaces, developers can define abstractions for a variety of attributes associated with a managed enterprise environment.

■ **Managed container interfaces.** The managed container interfaces define a means for grouping together managed objects for better organization. This organization facilitates a more group-oriented approach to keeping up with managed resources, which can be a great benefit in complex systems.

■ **Managed notification interfaces.** The managed notification interfaces define a core foundation of managed event notification services. Developers are free to create more advanced application-specific notification services by extending these services.

■ **Managed data interfaces.** The managed data interfaces provide a means of linking managed object attributes to relational databases using JDBC. In doing so, the managed data interfaces establish a transparent link between management resources and external databases.

■ **Managed protocol interfaces.** The managed protocol interfaces use the Java Security APIs and Java RMI to add secure distributed object support to the core functionality provided by the base object interfaces.

■ **SNMP interfaces.** The Simple Network Management Protocol (SNMP) interfaces extend the managed protocol interfaces to provide support for SNMP agents. SNMP is a relatively simple protocol originally developed to solve communication problems between different types of networks and gather network statistics. Because SNMP is the most popular management protocol in use, its support through the SNMP interfaces is an important part of the Management API.

■ **Applet integration interfaces.** The applet integration interfaces component of the Management API specifies how Java applets can be integrated with the Management API to provide management solutions. Applet developers use the applet integration interfaces to build management support into their applets.

For more information on the Management API, refer to JavaSoft's Management API Web site, located at `http://java.sun.com/products/JavaManagement/`.

The Server API

After the success of Java and its immediate use for developing client-side applets, JavaSoft decided to take steps to make Java a more viable alternative for server-side applications. The Server API is JavaSoft's answer to the need for more complete server-oriented support in Java. The Server API provides a wide range of server functionality including support for administration, accessibility control, and dynamic resource handling. Also included in the Server API is the Servlet API, which provides a framework for extending servers with servlets. A *servlet* is a Java object that extends the functionality of an information server, such as an HTTP server. You can think of servlets as the server equivalents of client-side Java applets.

The Servlet API provides the overhead necessary for creating servlets and interfacing them with information servers. The Servlet API is equipped to handle the entire servlet/server relationship, with an emphasis on keeping things stable and simple. All that is required to run servlets is a server that supports the Servlet API.

JavaSoft has grouped the Server and Servlet APIs under their new Internet server framework known as *Jeeves*. To get more information about the APIs, visit JavaSoft's Jeeves Web site, located at `http://java.sun.com/products/jeeves/`.

The Media API

Possibly the weakest area of the core Java API as we know it is its support for media. Currently, the Java API supports only static GIF and JPEG images and wave sounds in the AU sound format. Clearly, this limited media support won't cut it in the long run. Sure, developers can hack their own media implementations to some extent, but they can already do that in a variety of other languages and platforms. Java was supposed to make things easier, right?

JavaSoft realized this weakness and is remedying things with the Media API, which is slated to include support for a dizzying array of media types that will no doubt put Java on the map as a serious multimedia platform. The Media API includes classes that model media types such as full-motion video, audio, 2D and 3D graphics, telephony, and more. Furthermore, the structure of the API is such that many of these media types will rely on the same underlying facilities. For example, all time-based media (such as video and audio) will use the same underlying timing mechanism, meaning that synchronization won't be a problem.

The Media API is designed to be very open and extensible—which is important considering that the world of multimedia is always changing. JavaSoft plans to integrate the Media API into the Java platform both as core API additions and as standard extension APIs.

The following API subsets comprise the Media API:

- **Media Framework API.** The Media Framework API handles the low-level timing functionality required by many of the other media APIs. This API includes support for timing and synchronization, both of which are critical to media types that must function together in harmony. *Synchronization* refers to how different time-based media elements agree with each other in time. For example, it is important for the sound track of a movie to remain synchronized with the picture.

  Also included in the Media Framework API is support for streaming, compression, and live data sources. *Streaming* is the process of interacting with data while it is still being transferred. For example, a streaming audio player begins playing audio as soon as a certain minimal amount of data has been transferred.

- **2D Graphics API.** The 2D Graphics API extends the functionality of the AWT classes to provide wider support for 2D graphics primitives and a variety of different graphical output devices, such as printers. Another important addition to the 2D Graphics API is the definition of a uniform graphical model that brings many graphics functions into one structure.

- **Animation API.** The Animation API uses the 2D Graphics API as a basis for its implementation of animated 2D graphics objects, or *sprites*. The Animation API also relies on the Media Framework API for maintaining timing and synchronization.

- **3D Graphics API.** The 3D Graphics API provides the overhead necessary to generate high-performance 3D graphics. This API implements 3D graphics by supporting a model of 3D graphical objects that can be rendered at high speeds. The 3D Graphics API also includes support for VRML, which is a very popular 3D modeling language. To pull off all this functionality, the 3D Graphics API relies heavily on the functions provided by many of the other media APIs.

- **Video API.** The Video API brings full-motion video to Java. The API provides the framework for managing and processing video in either a streaming or stored scenario.

- **Audio API.** Similar to the Video API in some ways, the Audio API also provides support for both streaming and stored media. However, the media supported by the Audio API consists of either sampled or synthesized audio. The Audio API even contains classes for implementing 3D spatial audio.

- **MIDI API.** The MIDI (Musical Instrument Digital Interface) API brings timed musical events to Java by way of the popular MIDI standard. MIDI defines a protocol for communicating and storing time-based events, such as those generated by a musical instrument. MIDI is an efficient way to represent both musical pieces as well as more general timing resources. Expect to hear the Web much differently once this API catches on!

- **Share API.** The Share API is probably the most interesting of the media APIs, simply because it's the least obvious. It defines a means by which live, multiparty communication can take place over a network. The Share API provides support for both synchronization and session management. I wouldn't be surprised to see multiplayer games and "chat" applets take on a new feel once this API is out.

- **Telephony API.** The Telephony API provides Java with the ability to interact with telephones. Most of the important telephone functions are supported in this API, including teleconferencing and caller ID, among others.

The Security API

The eagerly awaited Security API will hopefully remedy one of the biggest limitations of Java applets: the inability to read or write files locally. With full support for cryptography, digital signatures, and authentication, Java developers should be able to leverage security issues to some extent and move away from the seemingly overprotective solution currently in place. *Cryptography* encompasses the algorithms and techniques used to render data unrecognizable in the hands of unauthorized parties, thereby enforcing information privacy. A *digital signature* is an electronic identification technique that serves much the same purpose as a handwritten signature. *Authentication* is the process of verifying an action based on a security check.

The cryptographic functions built into the Security API are isolated from the programmatic interface used by applets that want to make security decisions. This layering allows the cryptographic functions to be replaced by third-party alternatives without impacting anything at the applet level, thereby giving Java developers more options when it comes to their security needs. The Security API will eventually be incorporated directly into the core Java API.

The Java Beans API

For some time now, the software development community has been pushing the idea of reusable components. In case you've missed the hype, a *component* is a reusable piece of software that can be easily assembled with other components to create applications with much greater development efficiency. This notion of reusing carefully packaged software was borrowed to some extent from the assembly-line approach that became so popular in America during the industrial revolution—well before the modern computer era. The idea as applied to software is to build small, reusable components once and then reuse them as much as possible, thereby streamlining the entire development process.

JavaSoft's Java Beans technology is a platform-independent component technology based entirely on the Java platform. The Java Beans technology promises to take the component software assembly paradigm to a new level. As of this writing, the Java Beans specification is close to completion with a preliminary API release expected soon after. Java Beans is being implemented as an architecture and platform-dependent API for creating and using dynamic Java software components. Java Beans picks up where other component technologies have left off, using the portable Java platform as the basis for providing a complete component software solution that is readily applicable to the online world.

The Goal of Java Beans

Following the rapid success of the Java runtime system and programming language, JavaSoft realized the importance of developing a complete component technology solution. Their answer is the Java Beans technology, whose design goals can be summarized by the following list of requirements:

- Compact and easy to create and use
- Fully portable
- Builds on the inherent strengths of Java
- Leverages robust distributed computing mechanisms
- Supports flexible design-time component editors

The first requirement of Java Beans (to be compact) is based on the fact that Java Beans components will often be used in distributed environments where entire components may be transferred across a low bandwidth Internet connection. Clearly, components must be as compact as possible to facilitate a reasonable transfer time. The second part of this goal relates to the ease in which the components are built and used. It's not such a stretch to imagine components that are easy to use, but creating a component architecture that makes it easy to build components is a different issue altogether. Existing attempts at component software have often been plagued by complex programming APIs that make it difficult for developers to create components without chronic headaches. So Java Beans components must be not only easy to use, but also easy to develop. For you and me, this is a critical requirement because it means fewer ulcers and more time to embellish components with frilly features.

Java Beans components are largely based on the class structure already in use with traditional Java applet programming, which is an enormous benefit to those of us heavily investing our time and energy in learning Java. JavaSoft has promised that Java applets designed around the AWT package will easily scale to new Java Beans components. This also has the positive side effect of making Java Beans components very compact because Java applets are already very efficient in terms of size.

The second major goal of Java Beans is to be fully portable. JavaSoft is in the process of finalizing a Java Beans API that defines the specific component framework for Java Beans components. The Java Beans API, coupled with the platform-independent Java system it is based on, will comprise the platform-independent component solution alluded to earlier. As a result, developers do not have to worry about including platform-specific libraries with their Java applets. The end result will be reusable components that unify the world of computing under one happy, peaceful umbrella. Okay, maybe that's asking a little too much—I'll settle for just being able to develop a component and have it run unmodified on any Java-supported system.

The existing Java architecture already offers a wide range of benefits easily applied to components. One of the more important, but rarely mentioned, features of Java is its built-in class discovery mechanism, which allows objects to interact with each other dynamically. This results in a system in which objects can be integrated with each other independently of their respective origins or development history. The class discovery mechanism is not just a neat feature of Java, it is a necessary requirement in any component architecture. It is fortunate for Java Beans that this functionality is already provided by Java at no additional cost. Other component architectures have had to implement messy registration mechanisms to achieve the same result.

Another example of Java Beans inheriting existing Java functionality is *persistence*, the ability for an object to store and retrieve its internal state. Persistence is handled automatically in Java Beans by simply using the serialization mechanism already present in Java. Alternatively, developers can create customized persistence solutions whenever necessary.

Although not a core element of the Java Beans architecture, support for distributed computing is a major issue with Java Beans. Because distributed computing requires relatively complex solutions attributed to the complex nature of distributed systems, Java Beans leverages the usage of external distributed approaches based on need. In other words, Java Beans allows developers to use distributed computing mechanisms whenever necessary but it doesn't overburden itself with core support for distributed computing. This may seem like the Java Beans architects are being lazy, but in fact, it is this very design approach that allows Java Beans components to be very compact because distributed computing solutions inevitably require much more overhead.

Java Beans component developers have the option of selecting the distributed computing approach that best fits their needs. JavaSoft provides a distributed computing solution in their Remote Method Invocation (RMI) technology, which is part of the Enterprise API, but Java Beans developers are in no way handcuffed to this solution. Other options include CORBA (Common Object Request Broker Architecture) and Microsoft's DCOM (Distributed Component Object Model), among others. The point is that distributed computing has been cleanly abstracted from Java Beans to keep things tight while still allowing developers who require distributed support a wide range of options.

The final design goal of Java Beans deals with design-time issues and how developers build applications using Java Beans components. The Java Beans architecture includes support for specifying design-time properties and editing mechanisms to better facilitate visual editing of Java Beans components. The result is that developers will be able to use visual tools to assemble and modify Java Beans components in a seamless fashion, much like existing PC visual tools work with components such as VBX or OCX controls. In this way, component developers specify the way in which the components are to be used and manipulated in a development environment. This feature alone will officially usher in the usage of professional visual editors and significantly boost the productivity of applications developers.

How Java Beans Relates to Java

Many developers not completely familiar with the idea of software components will likely be confused by Java Beans's relationship to Java. Hasn't Java been touted as an object-oriented technology capable of serving up reusable objects? Yes and no. Yes, Java provides a means of building reusable objects, but there are few rules or standards governing how objects interact with each other. Java Beans builds on the existing design of Java by specifying a rich set of mechanisms for interaction between objects, along with common actions that most objects must support, such as persistence and event handling.

Although the current Java component model is not bad, it is relatively limited in regard to delivering true reusability and interoperability. At the object level, there is really no straightforward mechanism for creating reusable Java objects that can interact with other objects dynamically in a consistent fashion. The closest thing you can do in Java is to create applets and attempt to allow them to communicate with each other on a Web page, which isn't a very straightforward task. Java Beans provides the framework by which this communication can take place with ease. Even more important is the fact that Java Beans components can be easily tweaked using a standard set of well-defined properties. Basically, Java Beans merges the power of full-blown Java applets with the compactness and reusability of Java AWT components such as buttons.

Java Beans components aren't limited to visual objects such as buttons, however. You can just as easily develop nonvisual Java Beans components that perform some background function in concert with other components. In this way, Java Beans merges the power of visual Java applets with nonvisual Java applications under a consistent component framework.

NOTE

Just in case you're wondering what a *nonvisual component* is, it's any component that doesn't have visible output. When thinking of components in terms of AWT objects like buttons and menus, this may seem a little strange. However, keep in mind that a component is simply a tightly packaged program and has no specific requirement of being visual. A good example of a nonvisual component is a timer component that fires timing events at specified intervals. Timer components are very popular in other component development environments such as Microsoft Visual Basic.

By using visual tools, you can use a variety of Java Beans components without necessarily writing any code. This ability to use a variety of components together regardless of their origin is an enhancement to the current Java model. You can certainly use other prebuilt objects in Java, but you must have an intimate knowledge of the object's interface. Additionally, you must integrate the object into your code programmatically. Java Beans components expose their own interfaces visually, providing a means to edit their properties without programming. Furthermore, when you use a visual editor, you can simply "drop" a Java Beans component directly into an application without writing any code. This is an entirely new level of flexibility and reuse not previously possible in Java alone.

The Nuts and Bolts of Java Beans

Okay, I've rambled enough about Java Beans from the standpoint of what it does and why it's cool. Let's focus now on some specifics regarding how all this is possible. Keep in mind that Java Beans is ultimately a programming interface, meaning that all its features are implemented as extensions to the standard Java class library. The Java Beans API itself is merely a suite of smaller APIs devoted to specific functions, or services. Following is a list of the main component services in the Java Beans API that are necessary to facilitate all the features you've been learning about:

■ **GUI-merging APIs.** The GUI-merging APIs provide a means for a component to merge its GUI elements with a container document, which is usually just the Web page containing the component. A *container document* is a document (typically one in HTML) containing Java Beans components that serves as a parent for all the components it contains. Most container documents have menus and toolbars that display any special features provided by the component. The GUI-merging APIs allow the component to add features to the container document's menu and toolbar. These APIs also define the mechanism facilitating space negotiations between components and their containers. In other words, the GUI-merging APIs also define the layout properties for components.

■ **Persistence APIs.** The persistence APIs specify the mechanism by which components can be stored and retrieved within the context of a containing document. By default, components inherit the automatic serialization mechanism provided by Java. Developers are also free to design more elaborate persistence solutions based on the specific needs of their components.

■ **Event-handling APIs.** The event-handling APIs specify an event-driven architecture that defines how components interact with each other. The Java AWT already includes a powerful event-handling model, which serves as the basis for the event-handling component APIs. These APIs are critical in allowing components the freedom to interact with each other in a consistent fashion.

■ **Introspection APIs.** The introspection APIs define the techniques by which components make their internal structure readily available at design time. These APIs consist of the functionality necessary to allow development tools to query a component for its internal state—including the interfaces, methods, and member variables that comprise the component. The APIs are divided into two distinct sections based on the level at which they are being used. For example, the low-level introspection APIs allow development tools direct access to component internals, which is a function you wouldn't necessarily want in the hands of component users. The high-level APIs use the low-level APIs to determine which parts of a component are exported for user modification. Although development tools will undoubtedly make use of both APIs, these tools will use only the high-level APIs when providing component information to the user.

■ **Application-builder support APIs.** The application-builder support APIs provide the overhead necessary for editing and manipulating components at design time. These APIs are used largely by visual development tools to provide a means to visually lay out and edit components while constructing an application. The section of a component providing visual editing capabilities is specifically designed to be physically separate from the component itself. This arrangement is so that standalone runtime components can be as compact as possible. In a purely runtime environment, components are transferred with only the necessary runtime component. Developers who want to use the design-time component facilities can easily acquire the design-time portion of the component.

By understanding these services and how they work, you'll have much more insight into exactly the type of technology Java Beans is. Each of these services is implemented in the form of smaller APIs contained within the larger Java Beans API. For the latest information on the Java Beans API, refer to JavaSoft's Java Beans Web site, located at `http://splash.javasoft.com/beans/`.

The Embedded API

The last of the standard extension APIs is the Embedded API, which defines a minimal set of Java functionality specifically targeted for embedded systems applications, such as consumer electronics devices. An *embedded system* is a scaled-down computer system programmed to perform a particular function within an electronic device. The Embedded API is the only API that doesn't really add anything to the Java core API. In fact, the Embedded API will more than likely be a subset of the core API because only a partial amount of the core functionality is needed in embedded applications. For example, because most embedded systems have no graphical output to speak of, the entire AWT is really unnecessary. Likewise, a network connection is unlikely in an embedded system, so there is no need to include the Java networking package.

More than likely, the Embedded API will consist of the following packages from the core API: language, utilities, and I/O. Beyond those, it's possible that Embedded API extensions could be developed to support specialized networking and output requirements. Because the Embedded API is itself a subset of the core API, it will more than likely be treated as an extension API.

Summary

In this chapter, you learned about the standard extension APIs that are planned to expand Java in a variety of directions. These APIs will no doubt boost the appeal of Java to new levels because developers will have much more reusable code to leverage when building custom applications and applets. Although this will ultimately mean more learning on the part of developers, it will also result in less time spent writing code that is best suited to a standard extension. Knowing this, many developers will be forced to rethink their current plans based on the availability of the standard extension APIs because there's no need to reinvent the wheel if it's already in the works.

As you learned in this chapter, some of the standard extension APIs will be merged into the core Java API. Much of this merging will no doubt occur in the next major release of Java (Java 1.1). Even though Java 1.1 isn't available at the time of this writing, you can begin using the standard extension APIs as they become available. Stay tuned to JavaSoft's Web site (www.javasoft.com) for the latest news on the standard extension APIs and Java 1.1.

If these new extensions to Java have gotten you excited about the future of Java, you may be eager to read on. Chapter 47, "The Scoop on JavaOS, Java Microprocessors, and JAR Files," takes a look at some interesting new technologies related to Java that you may not have heard about yet—including a Java operating system, Java microprocessors, and a new Java file format.

CHAPTER 47

The Scoop on JavaOS, Java Microprocessors, and JAR Files

by Michael Morrison

IN THIS CHAPTER

This chapter picks up where the previous chapter left off by peering into the crystal ball and taking a look at some of the emerging new Java technologies. More specifically, this chapter discusses JavaOS, Java microprocessors, and the new JAR file format. *JavaOS* is a new compact operating system based on and fully supporting the Java platform. *Java microprocessors* are full-blown microprocessors geared toward supporting the Java virtual machine. *JAR files* are compact archive files designed to package complete Java applets for more efficient storage and transfer.

The Java technologies you learn about in this chapter are still in their early stages as of this writing, which means that I can give you only a preliminary look at what they have to offer. Nevertheless, you should be able to take from this chapter a better understanding of where Java is headed and what it might mean to your own development efforts.

JavaOS

Even though Java has been touted largely as a neat new programming language, it is, in fact, much more than that. Java is also a very powerful and compact runtime system that in many ways mimics the facilities provided by a full-blown operating system. Knowing this, it wasn't a complete surprise to some that JavaSoft decided to build a complete operating system around the Java technology. This new operating system is called JavaOS and is described by JavaSoft as "a highly compact operating system designed to run Java applications directly on microprocessors in anything from net computers to pagers."

The status of the JavaOS project is still largely under wraps as of this writing, but there is enough information out to at least give you an idea of where JavaSoft is headed with it. First and foremost, JavaOS is no doubt planned to ride the wave created by Java and its insanely rapid success. However, don't let that statement mislead you into thinking that JavaOS is any less legitimate than the technology on which it is built. The idea of building a complete operating system on top of the existing Java technology makes perfect sense. If JavaSoft puts as much thought into JavaOS as it did into Java, JavaOS will no doubt be a very interesting and useful operating system—to say the least.

The applications of a compact, efficient operating system that can natively run Java programs are far and wide. In fact, JavaSoft has already made mention of a variety of devices to which the JavaOS technology could be easily applied. These devices include everything from networked computers to cellular telephones; basically any device that could benefit from a compact operating system and support for a powerful programming language like Java.

Overhead

JavaOS has been described by JavaSoft as just enough of an operating system to run the Java virtual machine. With this minimal design goal, it only stands to reason that JavaSoft is largely targeting consumer electronic devices with the JavaOS technology. As part of this approach,

JavaOS is specifically designed to be fully ROMable, meaning that it will work well in the embedded systems common to electronic devices. A *ROMable software technology* is one that can be implemented in Read-Only Memory (ROM). ROM is commonly used in electronic devices to store executable system code because there is typically no other storage means beyond Random Access Memory (RAM), which is temporary.

JavaSoft has made mention of JavaOS being able to run with as little as 512K of ROM and 256K of RAM in an embedded environment. Likewise, an entire JavaOS system running on a networked computer requires only 3M of ROM and 4M of RAM. These last figures include space for JavaOS, the HotJava Web browser, and a cache for downloading Web content and applets. JavaOS's minimal requirements set the stage for some unique products such as compact personal digital assistants (PDAs) with complete Internet support.

Industry Support

Because of the success of Java, JavaOS is able to enjoy industry support before its availability in even a preliminary form. An impressive group of technology companies have already announced plans to license JavaOS. Likewise, an equally important group of software tools companies have announced plans to provide development tools for JavaOS. These two areas of support provide the one-two punch necessary for JavaOS to be a success.

JavaSoft is already working with the software tools companies to define a set of APIs for developing applications for JavaOS. Major players on the Java development scene have already announced intentions to enhance their development environments to support JavaOS embedded systems development. This is a pretty major step in the embedded programming world, where many development tools are still fairly primitive compared to the visual tools used by computer applications developers.

> **NOTE**
>
> On a similar front, both the Solaris and Windows platforms are slated to include full support for Java at the operating system level. However, this support will be aimed more at supporting the Java runtime system than serving as an implementation of JavaOS.

Java Microprocessors

As if Sun isn't branching out enough with JavaOS, they recently surprised the microprocessor world by announcing the development of a line of microprocessors optimized for Java. Microprocessors aren't new to Sun, whose Sun Microelectronics division is responsible for the popular SPARC line of microprocessors. However, the idea of Sun Microelectronics developing microprocessors specifically to support Java no doubt caught a lot of people off guard, including other microprocessor companies!

> **NOTE**
>
> Just so you don't get confused, both JavaSoft and Sun Microelectronics are divisions of Sun Microsystems. Whenever I refer to Sun, I'm referring to the company as a whole.

Java microprocessors are quite obviously yet another move on Sun's part to capitalize on the success of Java. However, like JavaOS, Sun legitimately has an interesting and potentially lucrative angle in developing Java microprocessors. Also like JavaOS, the primary target application for Java microprocessors is embedded systems. Speed is a very critical factor in embedded systems, primarily because of the limited horsepower available in such small systems. Java microprocessors have the potential to significantly increase performance because they are being designed around the highly efficient Java technology. Contrast this with other embedded microprocessors that typically have a more generic design.

Sun is pushing Java microprocessors based on a new microprocessor product paradigm: simple, secure, and small. Add to this Sun's promise of delivering Java microprocessors at a fraction of the cost of traditional microprocessors. Sun is clearly appealing to the consumer electronics market, where a compact, low-cost microprocessor would probably rock a lot of boats. Sun has also announced the development of a full range of component-level and board-level products to support the microprocessors.

Although the prospect of a Java microprocessor may seem strange at first, it's not hard to see Sun's motivation. By 1999, the average American home is expected to contain between 50 and 100 microcontrollers. Worldwide, there are also expected to be more than 145 million cellular phone users, with each phone containing at least one microcontroller. And each microcontroller contains at least one microprocessor. Are you starting to get the picture?

> **NOTE**
>
> A *microcontroller* is a miniature computer system, usually implemented on a single circuit board, scaled down to support a limited function such as those required by consumer electronic devices.

The Java processor family is slated to consist of three lines of microprocessors:

- picoJAVA
- microJAVA
- UltraJAVA

The next few sections describe these different processor lines and the application for which each is targeted.

picoJAVA

The specification for a minimal Java microprocessor is called picoJAVA and serves as the basic design on which all the microprocessors are based. picoJAVA isn't a physical processor that Sun intends to manufacture and sell; rather, it is the core specification on which all Java microprocessors will be designed and built. The picoJAVA specification will be made readily available for licensing to other chip manufacturers who want to develop their own Java micro-processors. The picoJAVA specification is geared toward a microprocessor with the best price/performance ratio that fully supports the Java virtual machine.

microJAVA

The first physical microprocessor in the works at Sun is microJAVA, which builds application-specific I/O, memory, communications and control functions onto the picoJAVA core. microJAVA processors are expected to cost anywhere from $25 to $100, which makes them good candidates for a wide range of electronic devices such as telecommunications equipment and other nonnetwork applications such as printers and video games.

UltraJAVA

Sun's high-end Java microprocessor offering is called UltraJAVA. It is designed to encompass the very fastest Java processors available. The UltraJAVA processor line includes support for advanced graphics by virtue of Sun's Visual Instruction Set (VIS), which defines high-performance hardware graphics extensions. Not surprisingly, the UltraJAVA line of processors is primarily targeting high-end 3D graphics and multimedia applications. With a projected cost starting at $100, the UltraJAVA processor line may still be a bargain.

JAR Files

Another interesting Java technology in the works at Sun is the JAR file format, which is an archive file format aimed at grouping all the files that comprise an applet and its resources. By combining all an applet's resources into one compact file, both local storage and transfer over-head time are reduced. This is a technology that will have huge implications as Java applets gain acceptance and become more widespread because the task of managing a bunch of files over an Internet connection is something that would be nice to avoid.

The JAR file format is being designed to meet the following criteria:

- Compact
- Platform independent

■ Support for Unicode

■ Extensible

By being compact, JAR files can better meet their goal of minimizing the storage space and transfer times associated with Java applets and their resources. Part of the compactness of JAR files is attributable to their support for compression, which can greatly reduce the size of applet resources. Platform independence is a crucial requirement because Java applets are expected to run on a wide range of systems. Unicode support is important so that there is consistency regarding textual information stored in JAR file headers. Finally, the JAR file format must be extensible so that new features such as code signing can be easily incorporated. For more information on the JAR file format, check out JavaSoft's JAR File Format Specification Web site at `http://www.javasoft.com/security/codesign/jar-format.html`.

> **NOTE**
>
> The JAR file format is slated to be included in the upcoming 1.1 release of Java. Java 1.1 will not only include built-in support for JAR files, but also an API for working with and managing JAR files.

Summary

In this chapter, you broke away from the programming aspects of Java and learned about some new technologies that are based on the Java framework. Although these technologies may not directly impact your Java development efforts in the immediate future, they will no doubt play a significant role in Java reaching maturity as a technology with widespread application.

You began the chapter by learning about JavaOS, which is a new operating system based entirely on the Java virtual machine. You followed this up with a look at the new Java microprocessors, which aim to be the first physical Java implementation on silicon. You finished up the chapter by learning about the JAR file format, which provides a means to combine an applet and all its resources into one compact file.

Hopefully, this chapter has sparked your interest in some of the applications of Java beyond the traditional programming areas. If you're still hungry for more applied Java, Chapter 48, "Serving the Net with Jeeves," delves into a new Java Internet server technology called Jeeves.

Serving the Net with Jeeves

by Mike Fletcher

IN THIS CHAPTER

This chapter discusses Jeeves, Sun's Java-based Web server. The chapter starts with an introduction to Web servers for those not familiar with them and continues with a discussion of how Jeeves differs from other servers. An overview of some of Jeeves's features follows, including a sample "servlet" (a Java class that runs in the server to dynamically create content) and an introduction to the servlet API.

How the Other Half Lives: Web Servers

Web servers are the complement to Web browsers. When you type a URL or click a link, your browser contacts the HTTP server residing on the host from which you want to retrieve content. Using the HTTP protocol, the browser indicates what resource it wants to obtain, and the server sends back the requested data (or an error if the request fails).

You may hear an HTTP server sometimes referred to as an HTTP *daemon*. No, it doesn't mean you need to have your PC exorcised. This usage comes from UNIX terminology for a process that provides system services. (In mythology, a daemon is a *helpful* spirit.) A typical UNIX system has several daemon processes that provide services such as FTP, Telnet, and e-mail. Daemons can start running at system boot time, or they can be started by a process called inetd. The inetd daemon determines what service is requested by the port on which the request comes in. For performance reasons, an HTTP daemon is usually started at boot time rather than from inetd to avoid the overhead of starting up a new process every time a Web page is requested.

Originally, Web servers were limited to returning HTML content from files located on the server's file systems. The only interaction between a client and a server originally was a simple search facility. A page would be marked as ISINDEX, which indicated to the client that an argument could be appended to the URL for the page.

To provide interaction between a client browsing the Web and a server returning content, *forms* were added to the HTML standard. With the added capabilities provided by forms, the Web started moving towards its much more interactive form. Web servers also changed to support the new interaction. The Client Gateway Interface (CGI) is a standard interface that allows an HTTP server to interact with an external application. The CGI specification defines things such as how an external application is given command-line options and what environment variables contain information.

What Makes Jeeves Different from Other HTTP Servers?

Although it provides a needed functionality in today's interactive Web, CGI has some problems. One of the worst is that of security. When users access a URL provided by a CGI program, they are running a program on your Web server. If a CGI program is not carefully written, it could allow a malicious user to gain access to your server or destroy data. This problem can be avoided, but it is something to be aware of.

Another problem with CGI programs is that a separate external program must be started up each time someone requests a URL provided by a CGI program. This extra overhead may not be noticed on an average Web server, but it can make a difference. Several alternatives to CGI exist to address this problem, such as the FastCGI specification from Open Market (which uses persistent external processes to handle requests) or Netscape's server API (which is a C interface that allows code that handles requests to be dynamically linked into their Web servers).

Jeeves addresses both these concerns. In addition to providing the usual CGI interface, Jeeves supports "servlets." A *servlet* is a Java object that is run by Jeeves to handle a request from a client. Servlets can be loaded from the local machine on which the Web server is running, or they can be loaded over the network. Untrusted code loaded over the network is treated similarly to classes loaded by a Web browser and is limited in what it can access.

Jeeves also takes advantage of Java's threading capabilities. In addition to using multiple threads to dispatch incoming requests, servlets can be run in their own thread. This reduces the overhead necessary to dispatch requests for dynamic documents, especially on multiprocessor machines.

HTTP Server Administration Made Easy

Most HTTP servers, especially the freely available UNIX versions, must be set up by modifying a set of configuration files with an editor. Unless you are intimately familiar with your server, it is easy to make mistakes. Jeeves's configuration is handled by means of an interactive applet accessed through your browser (see Figure 48.1). Although the information is stored in files that can be edited, Jeeves's fill-in-the-blank configuration is much easier than searching through manual pages for the exact syntax to turn off this or that feature.

To access the server configuration screens from the configuration applet, you must authenticate yourself to the server with a user name and password. The list box on the left of the screen shows the different sections of settings you can configure. To the right are the various fields, buttons, and whatnot that let you do the actual configuring of the server. Table 48.1 explains what the different sections control.

FIGURE 48.1.

The Jeeves configuration applet.

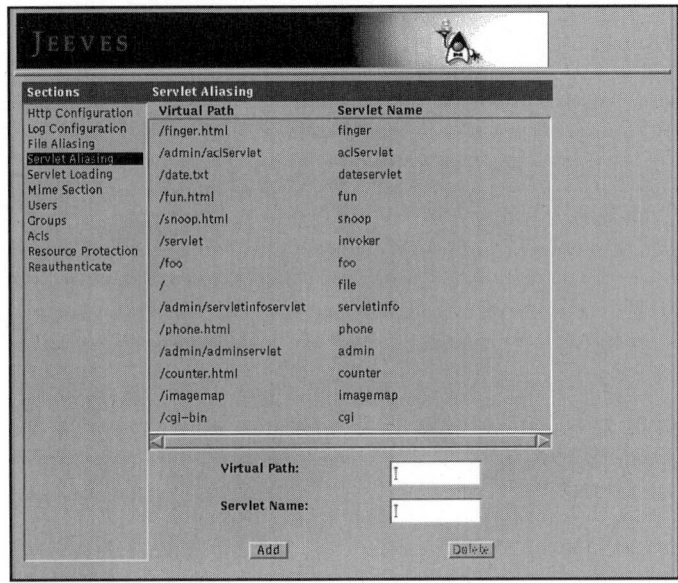

Table 48.1. Jeeves configuration groups.

Section	Explanation
HTTP Configuration	Sets HTTP protocol parameters.
Log Configuration	Defines names used for log files that track server accesses and errors.
File Aliasing	Controls the mapping of URLs to files and directories.
Servlet Aliasing	Controls the mapping of URLs to servlets.
Servlet Loading	Defines where the code for servlets is loaded from and any parameters passed to the servlet.
MIME Section	Sets up mappings from file extensions to the MIME type returned.
Users, Groups, and ACLs	These three sections control the creation, deletion, and modification of access control-related settings.
Resource Protection	This section allows you to grant privileges using the information entered in the preceding sections. More information on this is provided in "Access Control," later in this chapter.
Reauthenticate	This entry lets you enter (authenticate) yourself to the server with your username and password. It allows you to log in as a different user, or to reconnect to the server if you have restarted the server while leaving your browser to run the admin applet.

HTTP Configuration

The HTTP Configuration section of the Jeeves configuration applet allows control of the settings related to the HTTP protocol. The port on which the server listens is set with this section. You can define the maximum number of connections the server will accept. Related to this are the minimum and maximum numbers of threads required to start handling requests.

Jeeves provides support for the HTTP "keep alive" directive. This extension to the HTTP protocol allows a client to ask that a connection be kept open and used to retrieve multiple URLs. The HTTP Configuration section has fields for setting the maximum number of requests for each keep-alive session and a timeout value (to prevent a client from monopolizing a connection).

Log Configuration

The Log Configuration section of the Jeeves configuration applet lets you define the names of the log files to which Jeeves will write information. The level of information written to each log can be specified as a number from zero to 3 (zero turns the log off, 3 provides the most detail).

In addition to the access log (which tracks the resources being accessed by clients) and the error log (which notes errors such as when nonexistent files are requested), Jeeves provides an event log for servlets. Servlets can use the `log()` method of the `java.servlet.Servlet` class to write a `String` to the event log.

File Aliasing

Although the primary purpose of an HTTP server is to return files in response to client requests, you don't want to give out access to your complete file system to just anyone. The File Aliasing section of the Jeeves configuration applet allows you to map URLs to particular directories or files. This facility also lets you give an easy-to-remember URL to a particular resource. For example, if you have a page with a feature that changes monthly, you can set the URL `http://myhost.com/features/current` to point to the current month's page.

Servlet Aliasing and Servlet Loading

The Servlet Aliasing and Servlet Loading sections of the Jeeves configuration applet provide control over a server's Java servlets. Servlet Aliasing is the servlet equivalent of the File Aliasing section (just described). It allows the mappings between URLs and servlet names. The Servlet Loading section sets mappings from servlet names to the Java class for the servlet. The location from which the servlet code is loaded (local disk or from the network) and any parameters to be passed to the servlet can be defined here as well.

MIME Section

The MIME section of the Jeeves configuration applet controls the mappings between file extensions and MIME content types. This lets a browser know what type of resource it is retrieving so that it can handle it properly. For example, if you have several MS Word documents, you can use this configuration to tell Jeeves to return a content type of `application/msword` for all files that have the file extension `.doc`. Assuming that the client's browser is properly configured, it would automatically launch the application to view the file.

Users, Groups, ACLs, and Resource Protection

The Users, Groups, ACLs, and Resource Protection sections of the Jeeves configuration applet allow you to control who can access resources on your server. Refer to the following section, "Access Control," for a detailed description of how Jeeves provides resource controls.

Access Control

Jeeves provides a very flexible system for controlling access to Web pages and servlets. Privileges can be granted to users (referred to as *principals* in this context), groups of users, or network hosts.

Each user has a account name (which must be unique) and a password. The Users section of the configuration applet allows you to create and delete user accounts as well as modify a user's password. Likewise, the Groups section allows the creation and deletion of groups of users. Individual user accounts can be assigned or removed from groups.

Access Control Lists (ACLs) are the basis for resource controls with Jeeves. An ACL can be made up of any combination of users, groups, and network hosts. Membership in an ACL can be either positive (the entity is in the list) or negative (the entity is not in the list). In addition to which entities are in the ACL, the ACL defines which HTTP request (that is, `GET` or `POST`) can be sent. Once you have created an ACL, the Resource Protection section of the configuration applet allows you to assign lists to a particular URL. Figure 48.2 shows what the ACL Configuration screen looks like.

The practical upshot of this arrangement is that Jeeves gives you very flexible control over deciding who can get what from your server. For example, you can create an ACL that contains the hostnames for each department's machines. Engineering documents can be specified as available to the developer ACL and the quality assurance ACL. This information is available only to those two departments—the marketing department's machines are not allowed to retrieve it. If the marketing people want to track who is accessing a particular resource, individual user accounts (or a group) can be placed in an ACL and that ACL can be assigned to the URL in question.

48
SERVING THE NET
WITH JEEVES

FIGURE 48.2.
The Access Control List Configuration section.

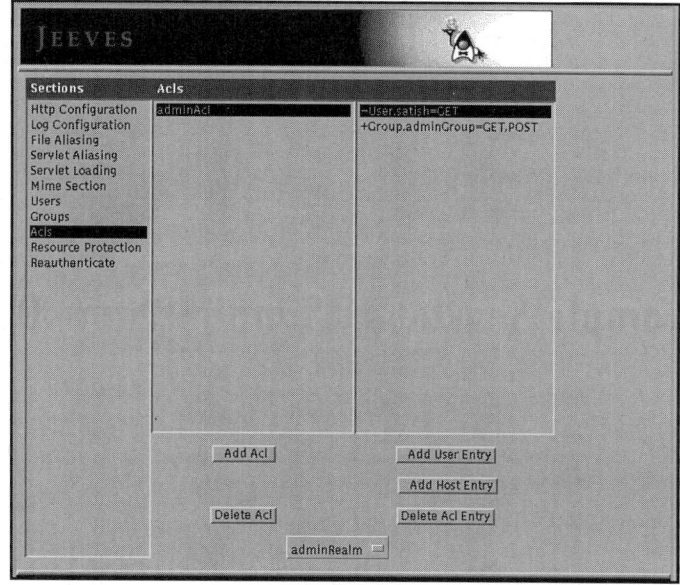

Servlet API

The API for servlets is similar to that for applets. Servlets must extend the java.servlet.Servlet class. Like the java.applet.Applet class, the Servlet class provides methods to retrieve parameters (getInitParameter()). The getServletContext() method obtains a ServletContext object, which provides references to other servlets; the method also provides a way to find out what server the servlet is running on.

If a servlet needs special initialization, an init() method can be provided. This method is called when the servlet class is loaded. A servlet can contain a getServletInfo() method to return information about what the servlet does and who its author is. Jeeves displays this information in the configuration applet.

The most important method for a servlet is the service() method. This method is invoked by the server whenever a request is received. Each time a client requests a URL corresponding to a servlet, Jeeves calls the service() method with two parameters: an object implementing the ServletRequest interface and an object implementing the ServletResponse interface.

The ServletRequest interface provides information similar to that passed to a CGI program in other servers. The interface defines methods to retrieve information such as the URL for the request, the remote host and port the request was received from, and any user authentication information.

The ServletResponse interface contains methods that allow a servlet to communicate the results of a request back to the client that asked for it. A getOutputStream() method provides an OutputStream object that writes to the client. Several methods are provided to set HTTP information such as the response code, the MIME content-type of the reply, and the status message returned.

In addition to the servlet API, Jeeves provides several other APIs such as classes that assist in creating HTML (the sun.server.html package).

Example Servlet: A Simple Phone Database

We finish off this chapter with an example servlet. This servlet reads in a text file containing names, titles, and phone numbers for people and stores this information into a java.util.Hashtable. When a client requests the URL corresponding to the servlet, the servlet returns a form with a text field. The user can enter a name in the field and click the Submit button. The servlet searches its hash table and returns the corresponding phone number if it exists.

First off are the import statements and class definition. Listing 48.1 also defines the Hashtable phoneList and initializes it to null.

Listing 48.1. The phoneSearch servlet.

```
import java.io.*;
import java.util.*;
import java.servlet.*;

public
class phoneSearch extends Servlet {
   // Hashtable to hold phone list information.  Loaded by init()
   Hashtable phoneList = null;
```

Next we define the init() method. As with an applet, this method is called automatically after the class is loaded. The init() code takes care of opening the phone database file and then calls the readDatabase() method to load the information into the hash table. It uses the Servlet.log() method to provide status updates that are written into the server's event log (see Listing 48.2).

Listing 48.2. The phoneSearch.init() method.

```
   // Initialize servlet.  Reads in phone database from file.
   public void init( ) throws Exception
   {
      FileInputStream infile = null; // For reading data file
      String phoneFile = null;       // Filename of database

      // Log when we start up.
      log( "phoneSearch Servlet Started." );
```

```
  // If a filename is given in our parameters use it
  if( (phoneFile = getInitParameter( "file" )) == null ) {
    phoneFile = "phone.txt";    // otherwise default to phone.txt
  }

  // Log what phone database file we're using
  log( "Using phone database file '" + phoneFile + "'." );

  // Try and open the phone database file
  try {
    infile = new FileInputStream( phoneFile );
  } catch( FileNotFoundException e ) {
    log( "Database file '" + phoneFile + "' does not exist." );
    log( "Error was: " + e.getMessage() );
    throw e;    // Rethrow exception
  } catch( IOException e ) {
    log( "I/O Error opening database file '" + phoneFile + "'." );
    log( "Error was: " + e.getMessage() );
    throw e;      // Rethrow exception
  }

  // Read the database into our hashtable
  readDatabase( new DataInputStream( infile ) );

  // Log that we're ready for business.
  log( "Read database.  phoneSearch ready." );

}
```

The `readDatabase()` method takes a `DataInputStream` from which it reads the phone informa-tion (see Listing 48.3). (Lines starting with a # character are ignored.) Each line should have three fields: the person's name, title, and phone number. The format of each line is the three fields separated by pipe (¦) characters. If the line does not contain a ¦ character, we note the line number to the event log and go on to the next line of the file. Correctly formatted lines are split into two parts: the name field, and the title and phone fields. The title and phone string is inserted into the hash table with the name (converted to all lowercase letters) as the key.

Listing 48.3. The `phoneSearch.readDatabase()` method.

```
public void readDatabase( DataInputStream in )
  throws Exception
{
  int pos, oldpos, lineNumber;
  String name, info;

  // Get an empty hashtable
  phoneList = new Hashtable( );

  lineNumber = 0;    // Initilaize line numbers
```

continues

Listing 48.3. continued

```
try {
  try {
    // Read in first line
    String line = in.readLine( );

    // While there are lines to read . . .
    while( line != null ) {
      lineNumber++;    // Increment line count

      // Allow comment lines starting with an octothorpe
      if( line.charAt( 0 ) == '#' ) {
        line = in.readLine( ); // Read next line && loop
        continue;
      }

      // If the line doesn't have a ¦ character log it and go on
      if( (pos = line.indexOf( '¦' )) < 0 ) {
        log( "Malformed phone database line at line " + lineNumber );
        line = in.readLine( ); // Read next line && loop
        continue;
      }

      // Copy name from line
      name = line.substring( 0, pos ).toLowerCase();
      // Leave title and # with ¦ separator as one item
      info = line.substring( pos + 1, line.length() );

      // Place info into hashtable with name as key
      phoneList.put( name, info );

      line = in.readLine( ); // Read next line
    }
  } catch( EOFException e ) {
    ;
  }
} catch( Exception e ) {
  log( "Error while reading database: " + e.getMessage( ) );
  throw e;
}

log( "phoneSearch read " + lineNumber + " lines." );
log( "phoneSearch hashtable has " + phoneList.size() + " items." );

return;    // Done reading database
}
```

The service() method is the heart of any servlet. Whenever Jeeves receives a request for a URL that maps to a servlet, it calls that servlet's service() method. Two parameters are passed with this call: one representing the request (a ServletRequest) and one the servlet's reply (a ServletResponse). The servlet can use information from the ServletRequest to determine how it was called and who called it. The ServletResponse allows the servlet to generate the HTTP headers for its reply, as well as providing an OutputStream on which to write the reply. Listing 48.4 shows the service() method for the phoneSearch data base.

Listing 48.4. The `phoneSearch.service()` method.

```
public void service( ServletRequest req, ServletResponse res )
  throws IOException
{
  PrintStream out = new PrintStream( res.getOutputStream() );

  // Set our content type, that the output shouldn't be cached
  res.setContentType( "text/html" );
  res.setHeader( "Pragma", "no-cache" );
  res.writeHeaders( );     // write out HTTP headers

  // Write out HTML for our search form
  out.println( "<html>" );
  out.println( "<head><title>Phone List Example Servlet</title></head>" );
  out.println( "<body bgcolor=\"#ffffff\">" );

  // Start of form
  out.println( "<form method=\"GET\">" );
  out.println( "<h1>Phone List Servlet</h1><hr>" );

  // Print some instructions for our user
  out.println( "Enter the name of the person you want to search for." );
  out.println( "Names are recorded as all lowercase.  Search terms" );
  out.println( "are converted to all lowercase." );

  // Create a text field for search term
  out.print( "<p><input TYPE=\"text\" NAME=\"search\" VALUE=\"" );

  // See if we were given a query parameter (i.e. someone's called
  // us already).
  String search = req.getQueryParameter( "search" );

  // If we have search will be non-null and we will use that
  // as the default value in our input box
  if( search != null )
    out.print( search );
  out.println( "\">" );     // Finish tag for search INPUT

  // Create a submit button
  out.println( "<input TYPE=\"submit\" NAME=\".submit\"><p><hr>" );

  // If we were given a search parameter and its length is non-zero
  if( search != null && search.length() != 0 ) {
    // Make the search item all lowercase
    search = search.toLowerCase();

    // See if search term is a key in hashtable
    String info = (String) phoneList.get( search );
    if( info != null ) {
      // Find separator in info
      int pos;
      pos = info.indexOf( '¦' );
```

continues

48

SERVING THE NET
WITH JEEVES

Listing 48.4. continued

```
        // Format the data in a spiffy table
        out.println( "<table width=\"75%\" border=\"2\">" );
        out.println( "<tr><th>Name</th><th>Title</th><th>Phone</th></tr>" );

        // Print out a row with the data from the query and hashtable
        out.println( "<tr><td>" + search + "</td>" );
        out.println( "<td>" + info.substring( 0, pos ) + "</td>" );
        out.println( "<td>" + info.substring( pos + 1, info.length() ) + "</td>" );

        out.println( "</table>" ); // Mark the end of our table
      } else {
        // Search term wasn't in hashtable, so let them know that
        out.println( "No one by the name '" + search + "' was found." );
      }
    }

    // Close out form, body, and html tags
    out.println( "<p></form>" );
    out.println( "</body></html>" );

    return;    // We're done
  }
```

Last are the getServletInfo() and destroy() methods (see Listing 48.5). The getServletInfo()
method should return a String with information such as what the servlet does, who the author
is, or version information. The destroy() method for this servlet just logs the fact that it was
called to the event log. If you have a servlet that has, for example, connections to a database or
information that has to be written out to disk, the destroy() method can handle those tasks.

Listing 48.5. The phoneSearch.getServletInfo() and phoneServlet.destroy() methods.

```
// Provide a little information about what servlet does
public String getServletInfo( )
{
  return "Simple Phone Database";
}

public void destroy( )
{
  // Log when we're destroyed
  log( "phoneSearch Servlet destroy() called." );
}
}
```

Using the phoneSearch Servlet

 The simplest way to use the servlet is to compile the code (phoneSearch.java, located
on the CD-ROM that accompanies this book) and place the class file into the servlet
directory under the main Jeeves directory. The phone database file should be placed

in the Jeeves root directory and be named `phone.txt`. If you name the file differently or place it in another directory (in the `servlet` directory, for example), you must specify the location with the `file` parameter in the Servlet Loading section of the configuration applet. Figure 48.3 shows the `phoneSearch` servlet in action.

FIGURE 48.3.

The phoneSearch *servlet in action.*

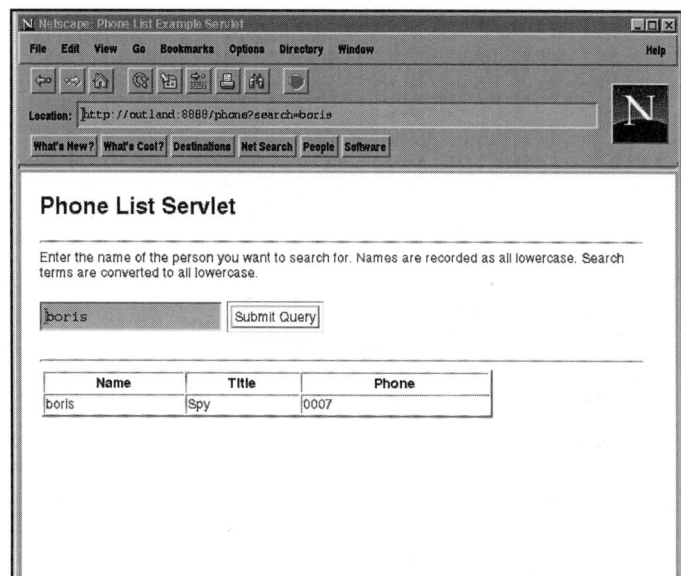

Summary

After reading this chapter, you should have an understanding of Jeeves's capabilities and what sets it apart from other HTTP servers. You should have an idea of how to configure Jeeves to map URLs to different files or servlets, as well as how to write your own servlets to provide dynamic content.

XI
Part

IN THIS PART

Appendixes

Java Language Summary

by Laura Lemay and Michael Morrison

IN THIS APPENDIX

This appendix contains a summary, or quick reference, for the Java language, as described in this book.

Language keywords and symbols are shown in a monospace font. Arguments and other parts to be substituted are in *italic monospace*.

Optional parts are indicated by brackets (except in the array syntax section). If there are several options that are mutually exclusive, they are shown separated by pipes (¦) like this:

```
[ public ¦ private ¦ protected ] type varname
```

Reserved Words

The following words are reserved for use by the Java language itself (some of them are reserved but not currently used). You cannot use these terms to refer to classes, methods, or variable names:

abstract	do	import	public	try
boolean	double	instanceof	return	void
break	else	int	short	volatile
byte	extends	interface	static	while
case	final	long	super	
catch	finally	native	switch	
char	float	new	synchronized	
class	for	null	this	
const	goto	package	throw	
continue	if	private	throws	
default	implements	protected	transient	

Comments

```
/* this is the format of a multiline comment */

// this is a single-line comment

/** Javadoc comment */
```

Literals

`number`	Type `int`
`number[l ¦ L]`	Type `long`
`0xhex`	Hex integer
`0Xhex`	Hex integer
`0octal`	Octal integer
`[ number ].number`	Type `double`
`number[ f ¦ f]`	Type `float`
`number[ d ¦ D]`	Type `double`
`[ + ¦ - ] number`	Signed
`numberenumber`	Exponent
`numberEnumber`	Exponent
`'character'`	Single character
`"characters"`	String
`""`	Empty string
`\b`	Backspace
`\t`	Tab
`\n`	Line feed
`\f`	Form feed
`\r`	Carriage return
`\"`	Double quote
`\'`	Single quote
`\\`	Backslash
`\uNNNN`	Unicode escape (NNNN is hex)
`true`	Boolean
`false`	Boolean

Variable Declaration

[byte ¦ short ¦ int ¦ long] *varname*	Integer (pick one type)
[float ¦ double] *varname*	Float (pick one type)
char *varname*	Character
boolean *varname*	Boolean
classname *varname*	Class type
type *varname, varname, varname*	Multiple variables

The following options are available only for class and instance variables. Any of these options can be used with a variable declaration:

[static] *variableDeclaration*	Class variable
[final] *variableDeclaration*	Constants
[public ¦ private ¦ protected] *variableDeclaration*	Access control

Variable Assignment

variable = value	Assignment
variable++	Postfix Increment
++*variable*	Prefix Increment
variable----	Postfix Decrement
--*variable*	Prefix Decrement
variable += value	Add and assign
variable -- = value	Subtract and assign
*variable *= value*	Multiply and assign
variable /= value	Divide and assign
variable %= value	Modulus and assign
variable &= value	AND and assign
variable ¦ = value	OR and assign
variable ^= value	XOR and assign
variable <<= value	Left-shift and assign
variable >>= value	Right-shift and assign
variable <<<= value	Zero-fill, right-shift, and assign

Operators

`arg + arg`	Addition
`arg - arg`	Subtraction
`arg * arg`	Multiplication
`arg / arg`	Division
`arg % arg`	Modulus
`arg < arg`	Less than
`arg > arg`	Greater than
`arg <= arg`	Less than or equal to
`arg >= arg`	Greater than or equal to
`arg == arg`	Equal
`arg != arg`	Not equal
`arg && arg`	Logical AND
`arg ¦¦ arg`	Logical OR
`! arg`	Logical NOT
`arg & arg`	AND
`arg ¦ arg`	OR
`arg ^ arg`	XOR
`arg << arg`	Left-shift
`arg >> arg`	Right-shift
`arg >>> arg`	Zero-fill right-shift
`~ arg`	Complement
`(type)thing`	Casting
`arg instanceof class`	Instance of
`test ? trueOp : falseOp`	Tenary (if) operator

Objects

`new class();`	Create new instance
`new class(arg,arg,arg...)`	New instance with parameters
`object.variable`	Instance variable
`object.classvar`	Class variable
`Class.classvar`	Class variable

`object.method()`	Instance method (no args)
`object.method(arg,arg,arg...)`	Instance method
`object.classmethod()`	Class method (no args)
`object.classmethod(arg,arg,arg...)`	Class method
`Class.classmethod()`	Class method (no args)
`Class.classmethod(arg,arg,arg...)`	Class method

Arrays

> **NOTE**
>
> The brackets in this section are parts of the array creation or access statements. They do not denote optional parts as they do in other parts of this appendix.

`type varname[]`	Array variable
`type[] varname`	Array variable
`new type[numElements]`	New array object
`array[index]`	Element access
`array.length`	Length of array

Loops and Conditionals

`if ( test) block`	Conditional
`if ( test ) block` `else block`	Conditional with `else`

```
switch (test) {
    case value : statements
    case value : statements
    ...
    default : statement
}
```

switch (only with `int` or `char` types)

```
for (initializer; test; change ) block     for loop


while ( test ) block                        while loop


do block                                    do loop
while (test)


break [ label ]                             Break from loop or switch
continue [ label ]                          Continue loop


label:                                      Labeled loops
```

Class Definitions

```
class classname block                       Simple class definition
```

Any of the following optional modifiers can be added to the class definition:

```
[ final ] class classname block             No subclasses
[ abstract ] class classname block          Cannot be instantiated
[ public ] class classname block            Accessible outside
                                            package
class classname [ extends Superclass ] block     Define superclass
class classname [ implements interfaces ] block  Implement one or more
                                            interfaces
```

Method and Constructor Definitions

The basic method looks like this, where `returnType` is a type name, a class name, or `void`:

```
returnType methodName() block               Basic method
returnType methodName(parameter, parameter, ...) block  Method with
                                            parameters
```

Method parameters look like this:

```
type parameterName
```

Method variations can include any of the following optional keywords:

`[ abstract ]` *returnType methodName() block*	Abstract method
`[ static ]` *returnType methodName() block*	Class method
`[ native ]` *returnType methodName() block*	Native method
`[ final ]` *returnType methodName() block*	Final method
`[ synchronized ]` *returnType methodName() block*	Thread lock before executing
`[ public ¦ private ¦ protected ]` *returnType methodName()*	Access control

Constructors look like this:

classname() block	Basic constructor
classname(parameter, parameter, parameter...) block	Constructor with parameters
`[ public ¦ private ¦ protected]` *classname() block*	Access control

In the method/constructor body, you can use these references and methods:

`this`	Refers to current object
`super`	Refers to superclass
`super.`*methodName*`()`	Calls a superclass's method
`this(...)`	Calls class's constructor
`super(...)`	Calls superclass's constructor
`return [` *value* `]`	Returns a value

Importing

`import` *package.className*	Imports specific class name
`import` *package.**	Imports all classes in package
`package` *packagename*	Classes in this file belong to this package
`interface` *interfaceName* `[ extends` *anotherInterface* `] block`	
`[ public ]` `interface` *interfaceName block*	
`[ abstract ]` `interface` *interfaceName block*	

Guarding

`synchronized ( object ) block`	Waits for lock on object
`try block`	Guarded statements
`catch ( exception ) block`	Executed if exception is thrown
`[ finally block ]`	Always executed
`try block`	Same as previous example (can
`[ catch ( exception ) block ]`	use optional `catch` or `finally`
`finally block`	but not both)

Class Hierarchy Diagrams

by Charles L. Perkins and
Michael Morrison

IN THIS APPENDIX

- About These Diagrams   1060

About These Diagrams

The diagrams in this appendix are class hierarchy diagrams for the package Java and for all the subpackages recursively below it in the Java 1.02 binary release.

Each page contains the class hierarchy for one package (or a subtree of a particularly large package) with all its interfaces included. Each class in this tree is shown attached to its superclasses, even if they are on another page. A detailed key is located on the first page of this appendix.

I supplemented the API documentation by looking through all the source files to find all the (missing) package classes and their relationships.

I've heard there are various programs that automatically lay out hierarchies for you, but I did these the old-fashioned way. (In other words, I *earned* it, as J.H. used to say). One nice side effect is that these diagrams should be more readable than a computer would produce, though you will have to live with my aesthetic choices. I chose, for example, to attach lines through the center of each class node, something that I think looks and feels better overall but which, on occasion, can be a little confusing. Follow lines through the center of the classes (not at the corners, nor along any line not passing through the center) to connect the dots mentally.

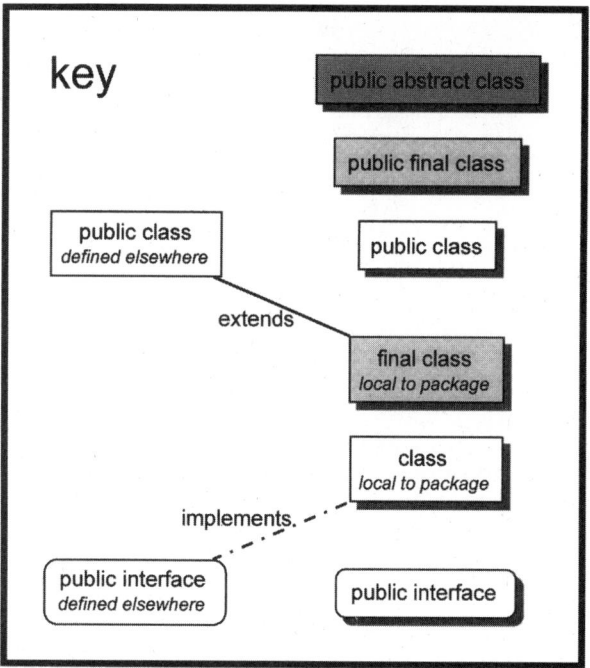

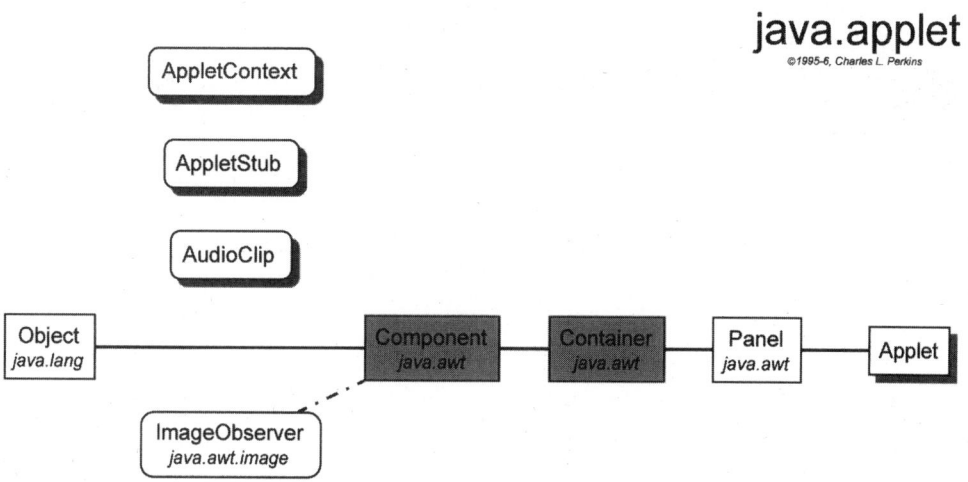

B

CLASS HIERARCHY
DIAGRAMS

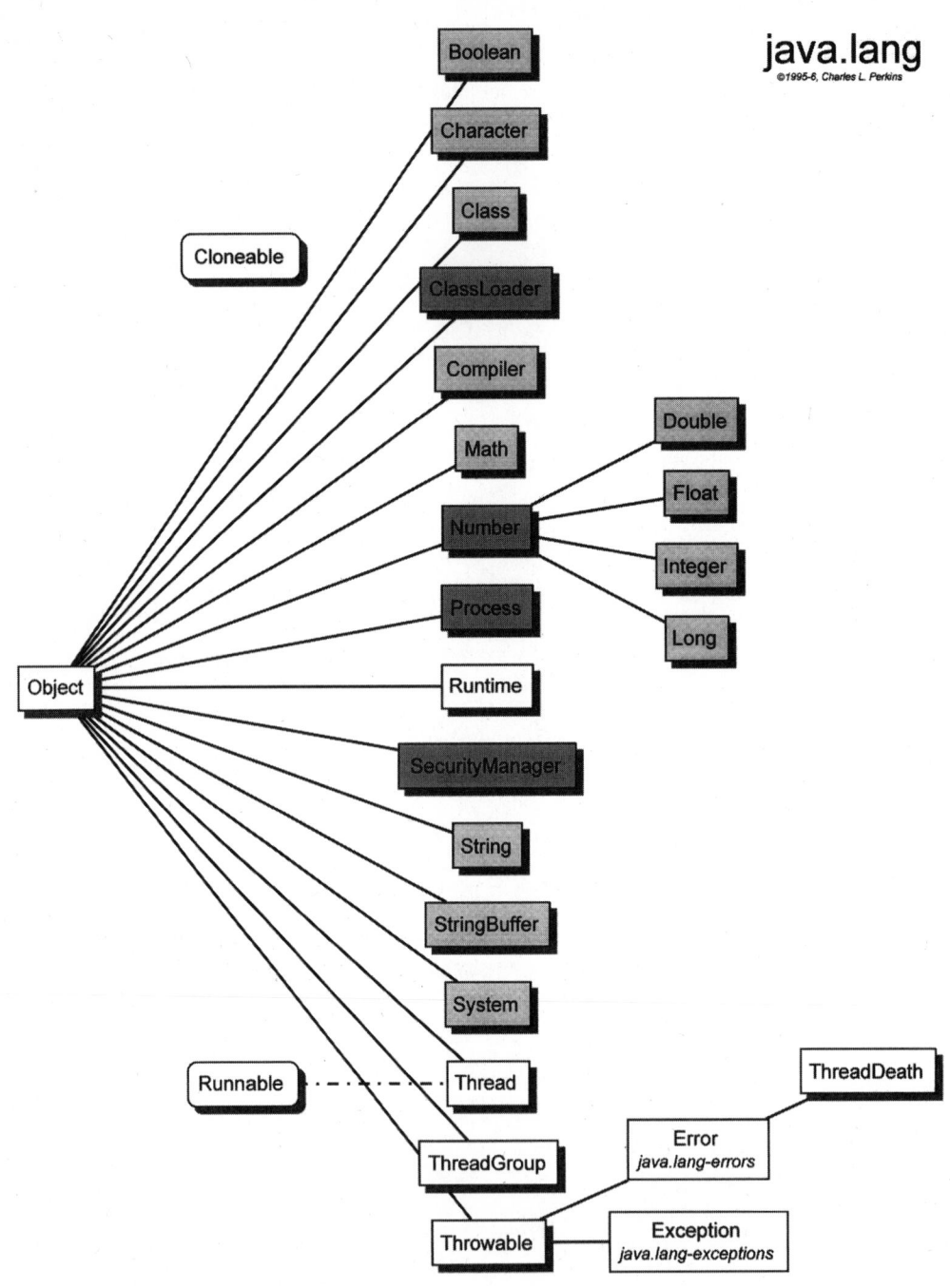

java.lang

©1995-6, Charles L. Perkins

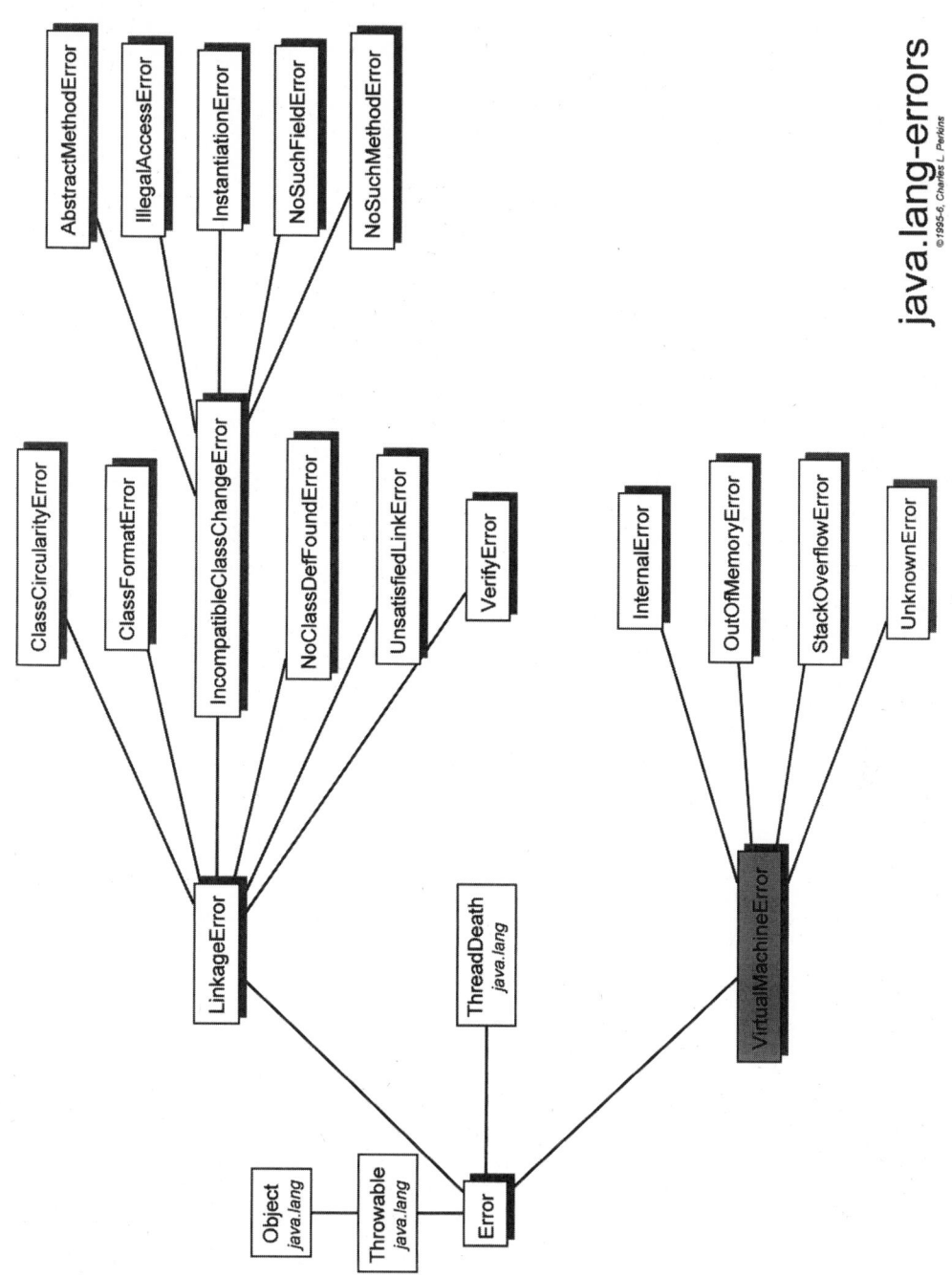

java.lang-errors

©1995-6, Charles L. Perkins

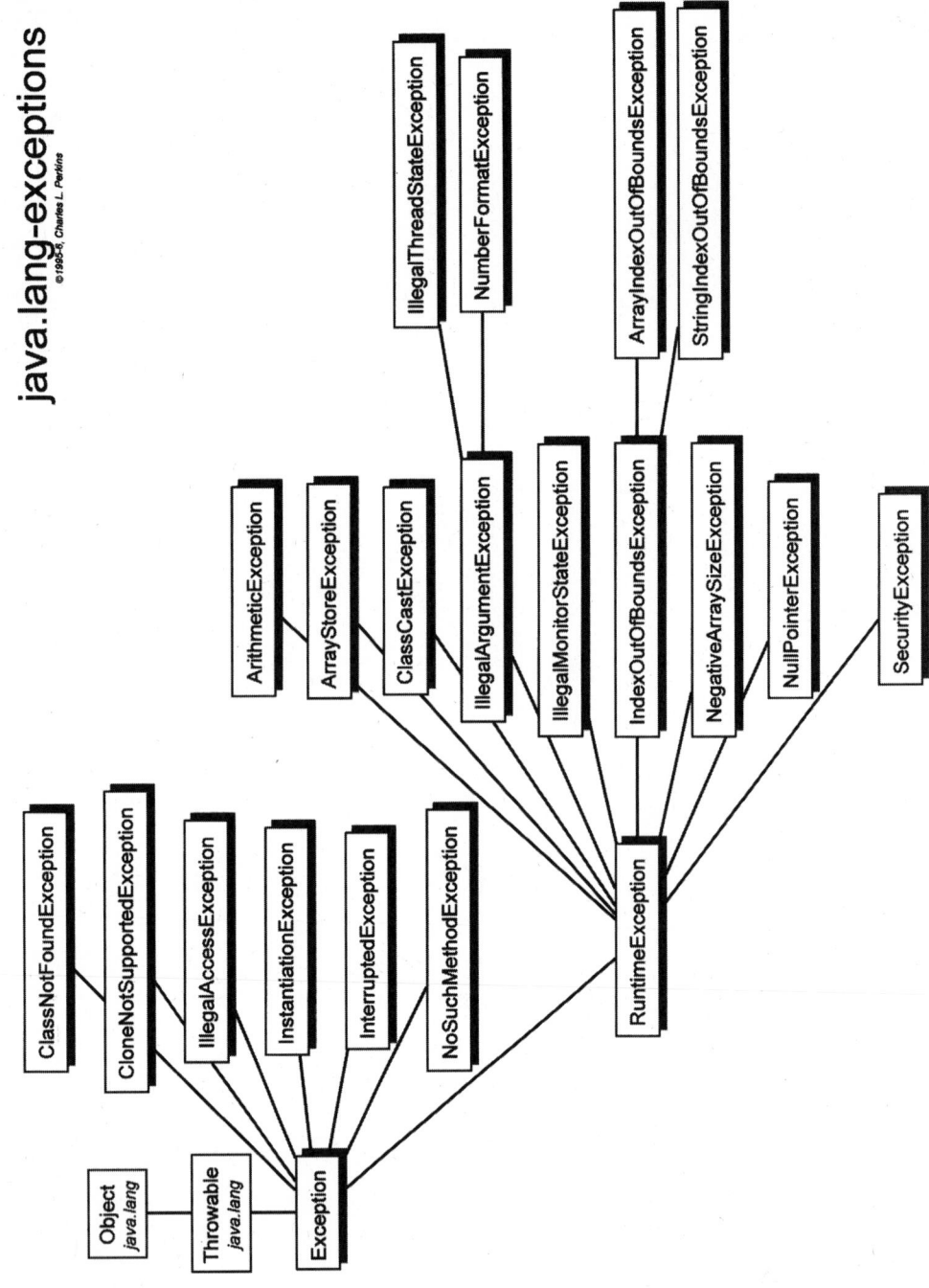

java.lang-exceptions
©1995-6, Charles L. Perkins

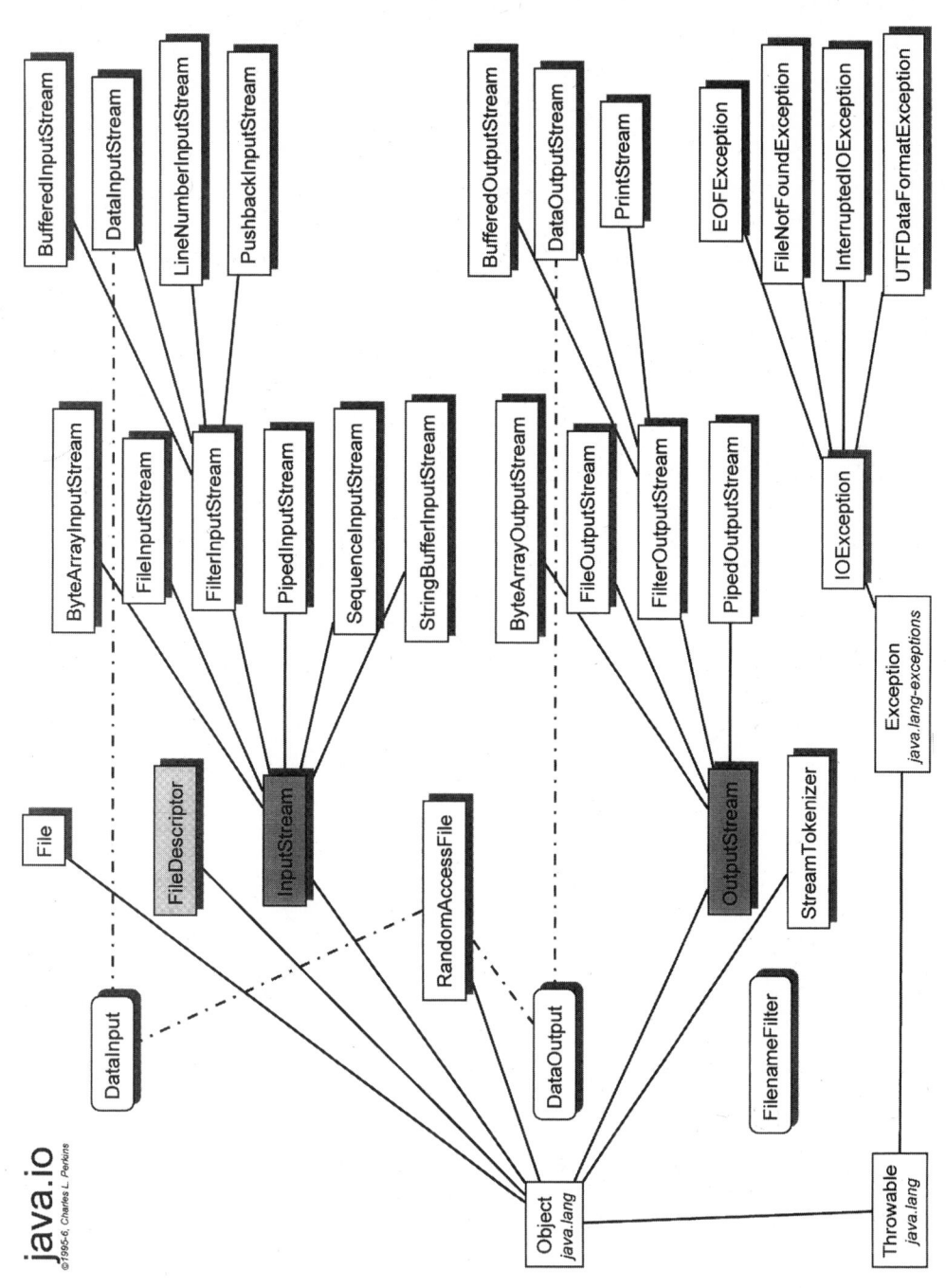

java.io

©1995-6, Charles L. Perkins

B

CLASS HIERARCHY DIAGRAMS

ContentHandlerFactory

SocketImplFactory

URLStreamHandlerFactory

ContentHandler ——— UnknownContentHandler
local to package

DatagramPacket

DatagramSocket

InetAddress

ServerSocket

Socket

SocketImpl ——— PlainSocketImpl
local to package

URL

URLConnection

URLEncoder

URLStreamHandler

Object
java.lang

InputStream
java.io

OutputStream
java.io

FileInputStream
java.io

SocketInputStream
local to package

SocketOutputStream
local to package

FileOutputStream
java.io

Throwable
java.lang

Exception
java.lang-exceptions

IOException
java.io

MalformedURLException

ProtocolException

SocketException

UnknownHostException

UnknownServiceException

java.net
©1995-6, Charles L. Perkins

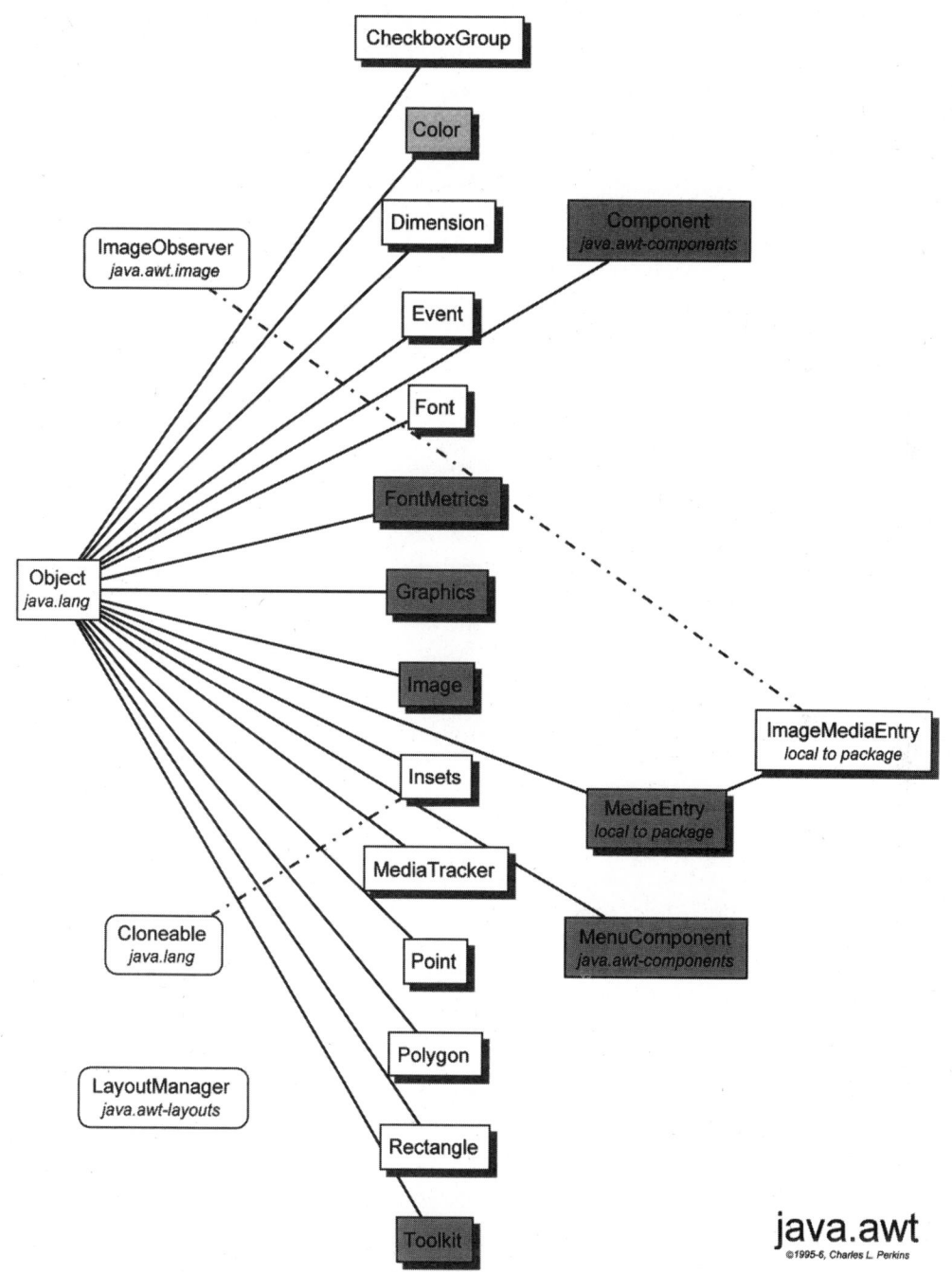

CheckboxGroup

Color

ImageObserver
java.awt.image

Dimension

Component
java.awt-components

Event

Font

FontMetrics

Object
java.lang

Graphics

Image

ImageMediaEntry
local to package

Insets

MediaEntry
local to package

MediaTracker

Cloneable
java.lang

MenuComponent
java.awt-components

Point

LayoutManager
java.awt-layouts

Polygon

Rectangle

Toolkit

java.awt
©1995-6, Charles L. Perkins

B

CLASS HIERARCHY
DIAGRAMS

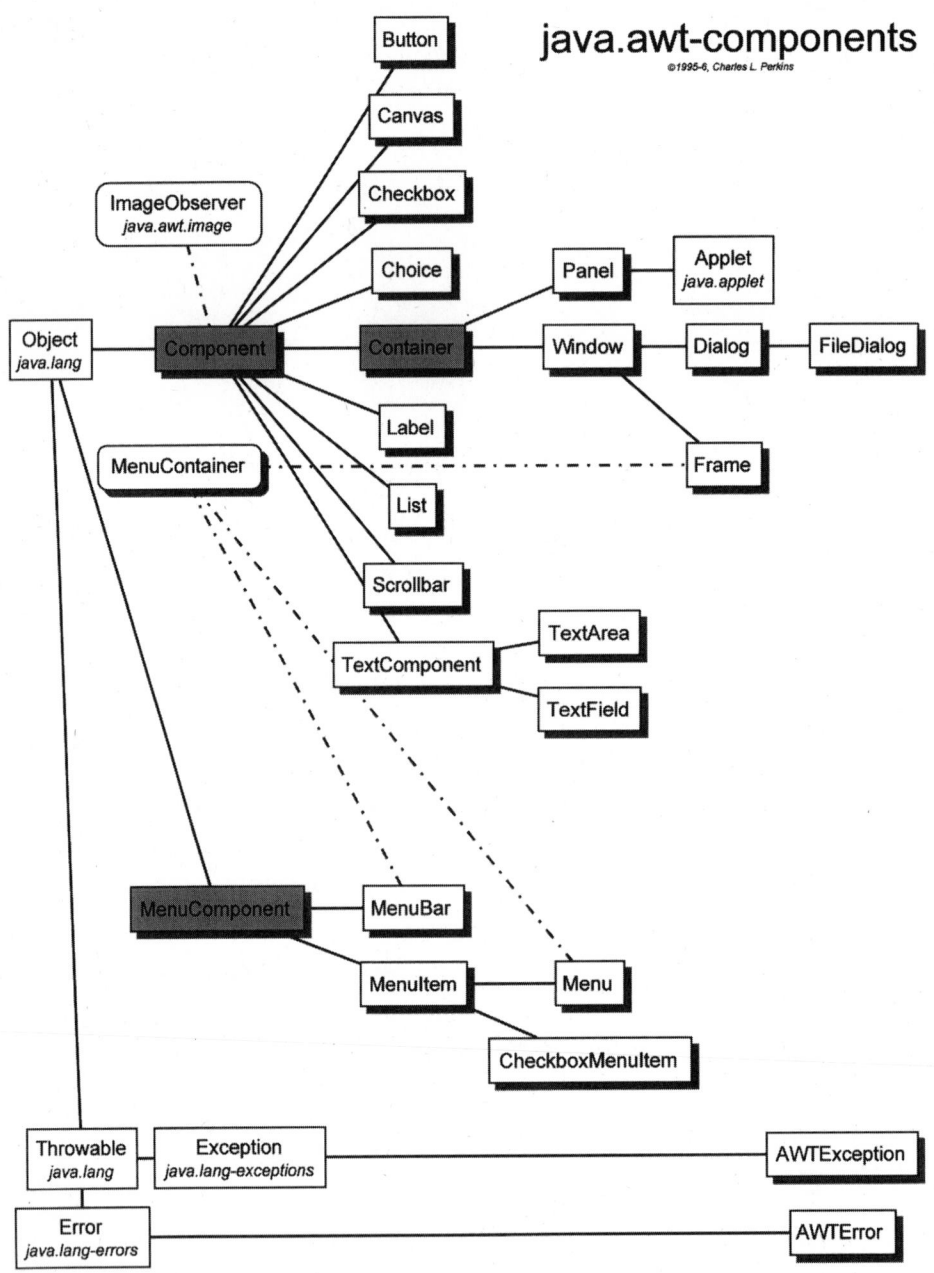

java.awt-components

©1995-6, Charles L. Perkins

java.awt-layouts
©1995-6, Charles L. Perkins

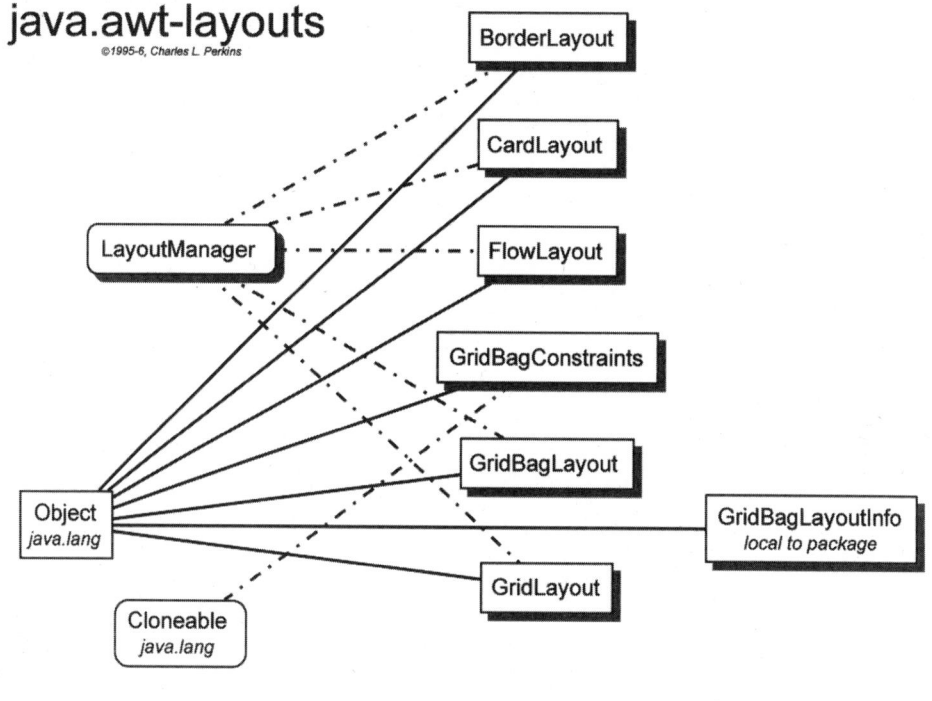

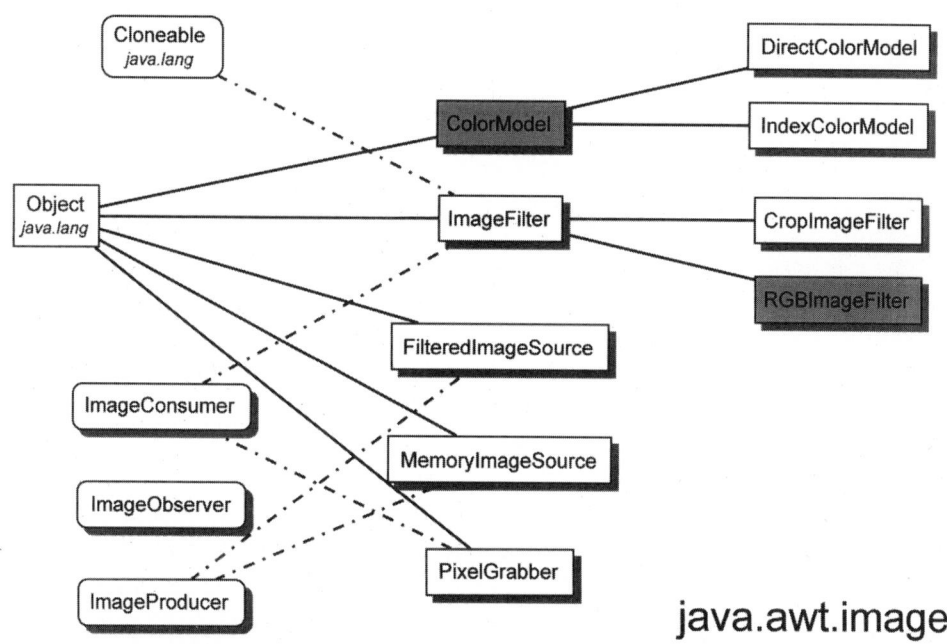

java.awt.image

java.awt.peer

©1995-6, Charles L. Perkins

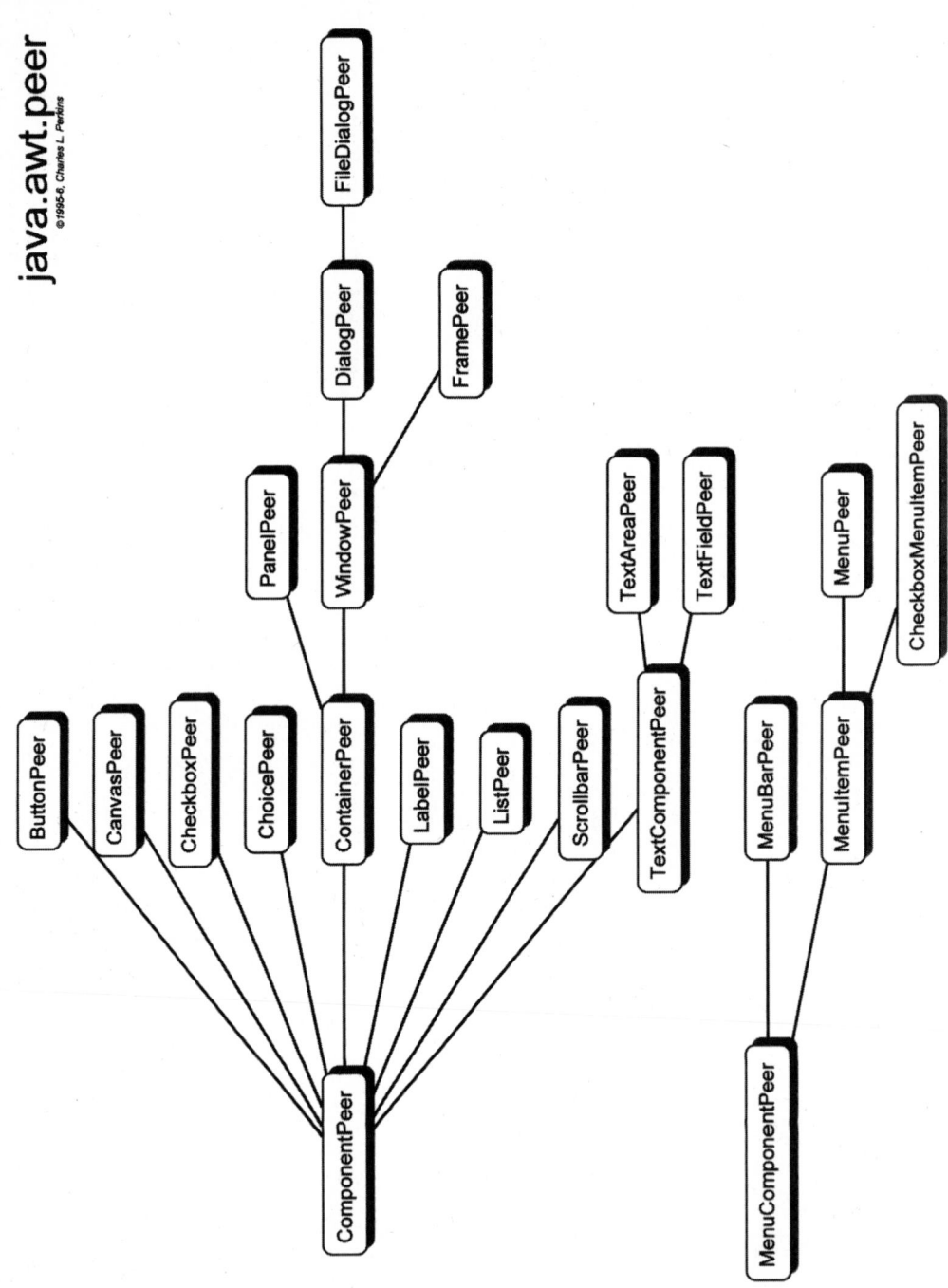

java.util
©1995-6, Charles L. Perkins

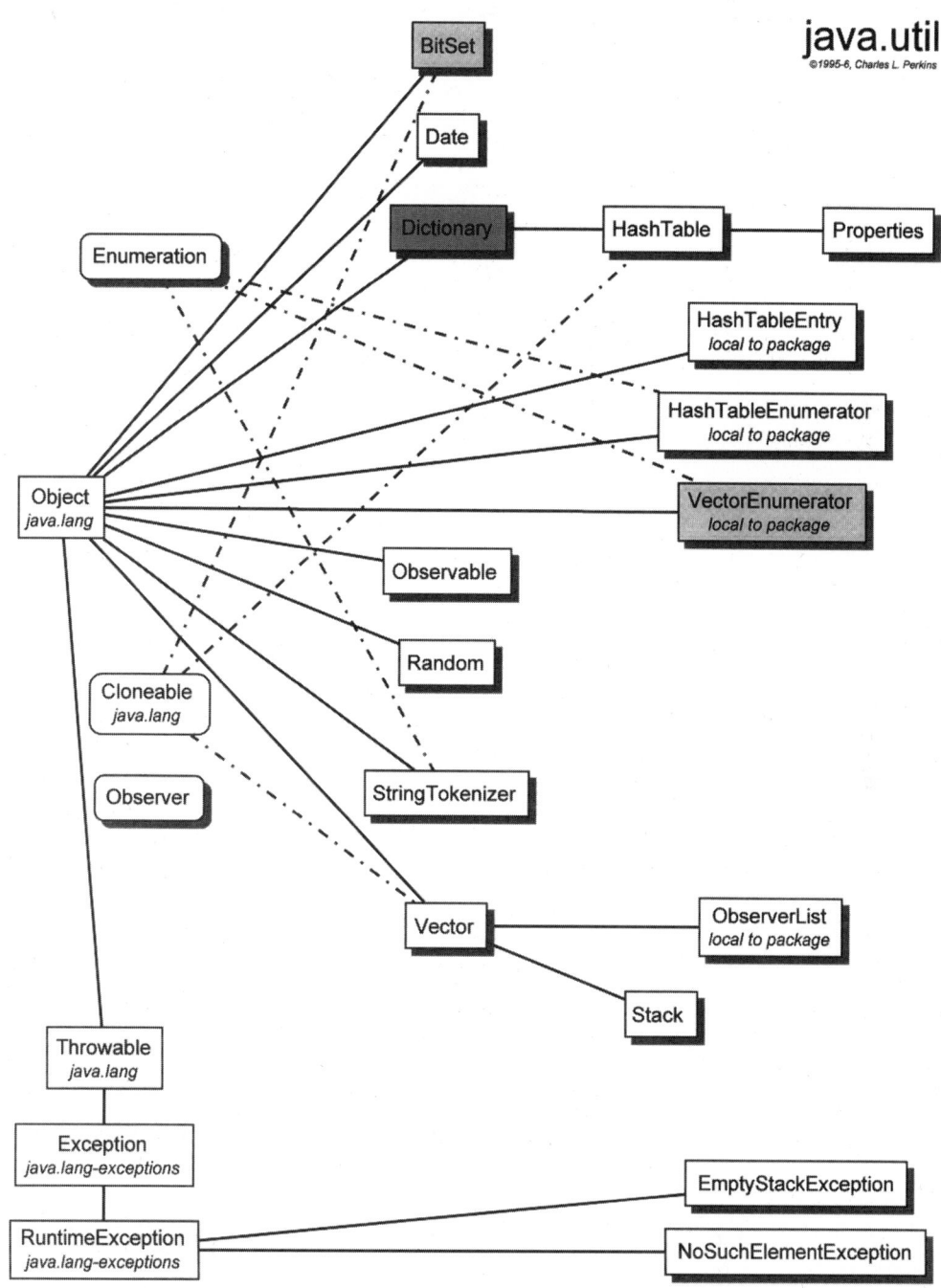

The Java Class Library

by Laura Lemay

IN THIS APPENDIX

APPENDIX C

This appendix provides a general overview of the classes available in the standard Java packages (that is, the classes that are guaranteed to be available in any Java implementation). This appendix is intended for general reference; for more specific information about each variable (its inheritance, variables, and methods), as well as the various exceptions for each package, see the API documentation from Sun at `http://java.sun.com`.

java.lang

The `java.lang` package contains the classes and interfaces that are the core of the Java language.

Interfaces

`Cloneable`	Interface indicating that an object may be copied or cloned
`Runnable`	Methods for classes that want to run as threads

Classes

`Boolean`	Object wrapper for `boolean` values
`Byte`	Object wrapper for byte values (Java 1.1)
`Character`	Object wrapper for `char` values
`Class`	Runtime representations of classes
`ClassLoader`	Abstract behavior for handling loading of classes
`Compiler`	System class that gives access to the Java compiler
`Double`	Object wrapper for `double` values
`Float`	Object wrapper for `float` values
`Integer`	Object wrapper for `int` values
`Long`	Object wrapper for `long` values
`Math`	Utility class for math operations
`Number`	Abstract superclass of all number classes (`Integer`, `Float`, and so on)
`Object`	Generic `Object` class, at top of inheritance hierarchy
`Process`	Abstract behavior for processes such as those spawned using methods in the `System` class
`Runtime`	Access to the Java runtime
`SecurityManager`	Abstract behavior for implementing security policies
`Short`	Object wrapper for `short` values (Java 1.1)
`String`	Character strings

StringBuffer	Mutable strings
System	Access to Java's system-level behavior, provided in a platform-independent way.
Thread	Methods for managing threads and classes that run in threads
ThreadDeath	Class of object thrown when a thread is asynchronously terminated
ThreadGroup	A group of threads
Throwable	Generic exception class; all objects thrown must be Throwable
Void	Object wrapper for void types (Java 1.1)

java.util

The java.util package contains various utility classes and interfaces, including random numbers, system properties, and other useful classes.

Interfaces

Enumeration	Methods for enumerating sets of values
Observer	Methods for enabling classes to observe Observable objects

Classes

BitSet	A set of bits
Date	The current system date as well as methods for generating and parsing dates
Dictionary	An abstract class that maps between keys and values (superclass of HashTable)
Hashtable	A hash table
Observable	An abstract class for observable objects
Properties	A hash table that contains behavior for setting and retrieving persistent properties of the system or a class
Random	Utilities for generating random numbers
Stack	A stack (a last-in-first-out queue)
StringTokenizer	Utilities for splitting strings into individual "tokens"
Vector	A growable array of Objects

java.io

The java.io package provides input and output classes and interfaces for streams and files.

Interfaces

DataInput	Methods for reading machine-independent typed input streams
DataOutput	Methods for writing machine-independent typed output streams
FilenameFilter	Methods for filtering filenames

Classes

BufferedInputStream	A buffered input stream
BufferedOutputStream	A buffered output stream
ByteArrayInputStream	An input stream from a byte array
ByteArrayOutputStream	An output stream to a byte array
DataInputStream	Enables you to read primitive Java types (ints, chars, booleans, and so on) from a stream in a machine-independent way
DataOutputStream	Enables you to write primitive Java data types (ints, chars, booleans, and so on) to a stream in a machine-independent way
File	Represents a file on the host's file system
FileDescriptor	Holds onto the UNIX-like file descriptor of a file or socket
FileInputStream	An input stream from a file, constructed using a filename or descriptor
FileOutputStream	An output stream to a file, constructed using a filename or descriptor
FilterInputStream	Abstract class that provides a filter for input streams (and for adding stream functionality such as buffering)
FilterOutputStream	Abstract class that provides a filter for output streams (and for adding stream functionality such as buffering)
InputStream	An abstract class representing an input stream of bytes; the parent of all input streams in this package
LineNumberInputStream	An input stream that keeps track of line numbers
OutputStream	An abstract class representing an output stream of bytes; the parent of all output streams in this package

PipedInputStream	A piped input stream, which should be connected to a `PipedOutputStream` to be useful
PipedOutputStream	A piped output stream, which should be connected to a `PipedInputStream` to be useful (together they provide safe communication between threads)
PrintStream	An output stream for printing (used by `System.out.println(...)`)
PushbackInputStream	An input stream with a one-byte push-back buffer
RandomAccessFile	Provides random access to a file, constructed from filenames, descriptors, or objects
SequenceInputStream	Converts a sequence of input streams into a single input stream
StreamTokenizer	Converts an input stream into a series of individual tokens
StringBufferInputStream	An input stream from a `String` object

java.net

The java.net package contains classes and interfaces for performing network operations, such as sockets and URLs.

Interfaces

ContentHandlerFactory	Methods for creating `ContentHandler` objects
SocketImplFactory	Methods for creating socket implementations (instance of the `SocketImpl` class)
URLStreamHandlerFactory	Methods for creating `URLStreamHandler` objects

Classes

ContentHandler	Abstract behavior for reading data from a URL connection and constructing the appropriate local object, based on MIME types
DatagramPacket	A datagram packet (UDP)
DatagramSocket	A datagram socket
InetAddress	An object representation of an Internet host (host name, IP address)
MulticastSocket	A server-side socket with support for transmitting data to multiple client sockets (Java 1.1)

`ServerSocket`	A server-side socket
`Socket`	A socket
`SocketImpl`	An abstract class for specific socket implementations
`URL`	An object representation of a URL
`URLConnection`	Abstract behavior for a socket that can handle various Web-based protocols (`http`, `ftp`, and so on)
`URLEncoder`	Turns strings into `x-www-form-urlencoded` format
`URLStreamHandler`	Abstract class for managing streams to object referenced by URLs

java.awt

The `java.awt` package contains the classes and interfaces that make up the Abstract Windowing Toolkit.

Interfaces

`LayoutManager`	Methods for laying out containers
`MenuContainer`	Methods for menu-related containers

Classes

`BorderLayout`	A layout manager for arranging items in border formation
`Button`	A UI pushbutton
`Canvas`	A canvas for drawing and performing other graphics operations
`CardLayout`	A layout manager for HyperCard-like metaphors
`Checkbox`	A checkbox
`CheckboxGroup`	A group of exclusive checkboxes (radio buttons)
`CheckboxMenuItem`	A toggle menu item
`Choice`	A popup menu of choices
`Color`	An abstract representation of a color
`Component`	The abstract generic class for all UI components
`Container`	Abstract behavior for a component that can hold other components or containers
`Dialog`	A window for brief interactions with users
`Dimension`	An object representing width and height

Event	An object representing events caused by the system or based on user input
FileDialog	A dialog box for getting filenames from the local file system
FlowLayout	A layout manager that lays out objects from left to right in rows
Font	An abstract representation of a font
FontMetrics	Abstract class for holding information about a specific font's character shapes and height and width information
Frame	A top-level window with a title
Graphics	Abstract behavior for representing a graphics context and for drawing and painting shapes and objects
GridBagConstraints	Constraints for components laid out using GridBagLayout
GridBagLayout	A layout manager that aligns components horizontally and vertically based on their values from GridBagConstraints
GridLayout	A layout manager with rows and columns; elements are added to each cell in the grid
Image	An abstract representation of a bitmap image
Insets	Distances from the outer border of the window; used to lay out components
Label	A text label for UI components
List	A scrolling list
MediaTracker	A way to keep track of the status of media objects being loaded over the Net
Menu	A menu that can contain menu items and is a container on a menu bar
MenuBar	A menu bar (container for menus)
MenuComponent	The abstract superclass of all menu elements
MenuItem	An individual menu item
Panel	A container that is displayed
Point	An object representing a point (x and y coordinates)
Polygon	An object representing a set of points
Rectangle	An object representing a rectangle (x and y coordinates for the top corner, plus width and height)
Scrollbar	A UI scroll bar object
TextArea	A multiline, scrollable, editable text field
TextComponent	The superclass of all editable text components

`TextField`	A fixed-size editable text field
`Toolkit`	Abstract behavior for binding the abstract AWT classes to a platform-specific toolkit implementation
`Window`	A top-level window and the superclass of the `Frame` and `Dialog` classes

java.awt.image

The `java.awt.image` package is a subpackage of the AWT that provides interfaces and classes for managing bitmap images.

Interfaces

`ImageConsumer`	Methods for receiving image created by an `ImageProducer`
`ImageObserver`	Methods for tracking the loading and construction of an image
`ImageProducer`	Methods for producing image data received by an `ImageConsumer`

Classes

`ColorModel`	An abstract class for managing color information for images
`CropImageFilter`	A filter for cropping images to a particular size
`DirectColorModel`	A specific color model for managing and translating pixel color values
`FilteredImageSource`	An `ImageProducer` that takes an image and an `ImageFilter` object and produces an image for an `ImageConsumer`
`ImageFilter`	A filter that takes image data from an `ImageProducer`, modifies it in some way, and hands it off to an `ImageConsumer`
`IndexColorModel`	A specific color model for managing and translating color values in a fixed-color map
`MemoryImageSource`	An image producer that gets its image from memory; used after constructing an image by hand
`PixelGrabber`	An `ImageConsumer` that retrieves a subset of the pixels in an image
`RGBImageFilter`	Abstract behavior for a filter that modifies the RGB values of pixels in RGB images

java.awt.peer

The `java.awt.peer` package is a subpackage of the AWT that provides the (hidden) platform-specific AWT classes (for example, Motif, Macintosh, Windows 95) with platform-independent interfaces to implement. Thus, callers using these interfaces need not know which platform's window system these hidden AWT classes are currently implementing.

Each class in the AWT that inherits from either `Component` or `MenuComponent` has a corresponding peer class. Each of those classes is the name of the `Component` with `-Peer` added (for example, `ButtonPeer`, `DialogPeer`, and `WindowPeer`). Because each one provides similar behavior, they are not enumerated here.

java.applet

The `java.applet` package provides applet-specific behavior.

Interfaces

`AppletContext`	Methods for referring to the applet's context
`AppletStub`	Methods for implementing applet viewers
`AudioClip`	Methods for playing audio files

Classes

`Applet`	The base applet class

Differences Between Java and C/C++

by Michael Morrison

IN THIS APPENDIX

APPENDIX D

It is no secret that the Java language is highly derived from the C and C++ languages. Because C++ is currently considered one of the languages of choice for professional software developers, it's important to understand what aspects of C++ Java inherits. Of possibly even more importance is what aspects of C++ Java *doesn't* support. Because Java is an entirely new language, it was possible for the language architects to pick and choose which features from C++ to implement in Java and how.

The focus of this appendix is to point out the differences between Java and C++. If you are a C++ programmer, you will be able to appreciate the differences between Java and C++. Even if you don't have any C++ experience, you can gain some insight into the Java language by understanding what C++ discrepancies it clears up in its implementation. Because C++ backwardly supports C, many of the differences pointed out in this appendix refer to C++, but inherently apply to C as well.

The Preprocessor

All C/C++ compilers implement a stage of compilation known as the *preprocessor.* The C++ preprocessor basically performs an intelligent search-and-replace on identifiers that have been declared using the #define directive. Although most advocates of C++ discourage use of the preprocessor (which was inherited from C), it is still widely used by most C++ programmers. Most processor definitions in C++ are stored in header files, which complement the actual source code files.

The problem with the preprocessor approach is that it provides an easy way for programmers to inadvertently add unnecessary complexity to a program. What happens is that many programmers using the #define directive end up inventing their own sublanguage within the confines of a particular project. This results in other programmers having to go through the header files and sort out all the #define information to understand a program, which makes code maintenance and reuse almost impossible. An additional problem with the preprocessor approach is that it is weak when it comes to type checking and validation.

Java does not have a preprocessor. It provides similar functionality to that provided by the C++ preprocessor, but with far more control: Java uses constant data members in place of the #define directive. The result is that Java source code is much more consistent and easier to read than C++ source code. Additionally, Java programs don't use header files; the Java compiler builds class definitions directly from the source code files, which contain both class definitions and method implementations.

Pointers

Most developers agree that the misuse of pointers causes the majority of bugs in C/C++ programming. Put simply, when you have pointers, you have the ability to trash memory. C++

programmers regularly use (and misuse) complex pointer arithmetic to create and maintain dynamic data structures. In return, C++ programmers spend a lot of time hunting down complex bugs caused by their complex pointer arithmetic.

The Java language does not support pointers. Java provides similar functionality by making heavy use of references. Java passes all arrays and objects by reference. This approach prevents common errors caused by pointer mismanagement. The reference approach also makes programming easier in a lot of ways simply because the correct usage of pointers is easily misunderstood by all but the most seasoned programmers.

You may be thinking that the lack of pointers in Java will keep you from being able to implement many data structures, such as dynamic arrays. The reality is that any pointer task can be carried out just as easily—and more reliably—with objects and arrays of objects. You then benefit from the security provided by the Java runtime system; it performs boundary checking on all array indexing operations.

Structures and Unions

There are three types of complex data types in C++: classes, structures, and unions. Java implements only one of these data types: classes. Java forces programmers to use classes when the functionality of structures and unions is desired. Although this sounds like more work for the programmer, it actually ends up being more consistent because classes can imitate structures and unions with ease. The Java designers really wanted to keep the language simple, so it made sense to eliminate aspects of the language that overlapped.

By forcing programmers to think in terms of classes instead of structures and unions, Java enforces a complete object-oriented approach to problem solving. This not only encourages code reuse, it also simplifies code maintenance in the long run.

Functions

In C, code is organized into *functions*, which are global subroutines accessible to a program. C++ added *classes* and in doing so provided class *methods*, which are functions connected to classes. C++ class methods are very similar to Java class methods. However, because C++ still supports C, there is nothing to discourage C++ programmers from using functions. This results in a mixture of function and method use that makes for confusing programs.

Java has no functions. Being a purer object-oriented language than C++, Java forces programmers to bundle all routines into class methods. There is no limitation imposed by forcing programmers to use methods instead of functions. As a matter of fact, implementing routines as methods encourages programmers to organize code better. Keep in mind that, strictly speaking, there is nothing wrong with the procedural approach of using functions, it just doesn't mix well with the object-oriented paradigm that defines the core of Java. However, the Java approach does tend to promote code reuse, which is a distinct advantage over the procedural approach.

Multiple Inheritance

Multiple inheritance is a feature of C++ that allows you to derive a class from multiple parent classes. Although multiple inheritance is indeed powerful, it is complicated to use correctly and causes lots of problems otherwise. It is also very complicated to implement from the compiler perspective.

Java takes the high road and provides no direct support for multiple inheritance. You can implement functionality similar to multiple inheritance by using interfaces in Java. Java interfaces provide object method descriptions, but contain no implementations.

Strings

C and C++ have no built-in support for text strings. The standard technique adopted by C and C++ programmers is to use null-terminated arrays of characters to represent strings.

In Java, strings are implemented as first-class objects (String and StringBuffer), meaning that they are at the core of the Java language. Java's implementation of strings as objects provides several advantages:

- The manner in which you create strings and access the elements of strings is consistent across all strings on all systems.
- Because the Java string classes are defined as part of the Java language, and not part of some extraneous extension, Java strings function predictably every time.
- The Java string classes perform extensive runtime checking, which helps eliminate troublesome runtime errors.

The goto Statement

The dreaded goto statement is pretty much a relic these days—even in C and C++—even though it is technically a legal part of the languages. The goto statement has historically been cited as the cause for messy, impossible-to-understand, and sometimes even impossible-to-predict code known as "spaghetti code." The primary use of the goto statement has merely been as a convenience to substitute for the programmer's not thinking through an alternative, more structured branching technique.

For all these reasons and more, Java does not provide a goto statement. The Java language speci-fies goto as a keyword, but its use is not supported. I suppose the Java designers wanted to eliminate the possibility of even using goto as an identifier! Not including goto in the Java lan-guage simplifies the language and helps eliminate the option of writing messy code.

Operator Overloading

Operator overloading, which is considered a prominent feature in C++, is not supported in Java. *Operator overloading* is a technique of defining different types of functionality for a fun-damental operator, such as the addition operator (+), based on the types of objects being added. Although roughly the same functionality can be implemented by classes in Java, the convenience of operator overloading is still missing. However, in defense of Java, operator over-loading can sometimes get very tricky. No doubt the Java developers decided not to support operator overloading to keep the Java language as simple as possible.

Automatic Coercions

Automatic coercion refers to the implicit casting of data types that sometimes occurs in C and C++. For example, in C++, you can assign a float value to an int variable, which can result in a loss of information. Java does not support C++-style automatic coercions. In Java, if a co-ercion will result in a loss of data, you must always explicitly cast the data element to the new type.

Variable Arguments

C and C++ let you declare functions, such as printf, that take a variable number of arguments. Although this is a convenient feature, it is impossible for the compiler to thoroughly type-check the arguments, which means problems can arise at runtime without your knowing about them. Again, Java takes the high road and doesn't support variable arguments at all.

Command-Line Arguments

The command-line arguments passed from the system into a Java program differ in a couple of ways from the command-line arguments passed into a C++ program. First, the number of parameters passed differs between the two languages. In C and C++, the system passes two arguments to a program: argc and argv. argc specifies the number of arguments stored in argv. argv is a pointer to an array of characters containing the actual arguments. In Java, the system passes a single value to a program: args. args is an array of Strings that contains the command-line arguments.

In C and C++, the command-line arguments passed into a program include the name used to invoke the program. This name always appears as the first argument and is rarely used. In Java, you already know the name of the program because it is the same name as the class, so there is no need to pass this information as a command-line argument. Therefore, the Java runtime system passes only the arguments following the name that invoked the program.

Java Resources

by John December

IN THIS APPENDIX

APPENDIX

E

This appendix lists online information sources about the Java programming language, the Java-enabled browsers, and related technologies.

> **NOTE**
>
> Much of the information in this appendix changes often. For updates on the Java information sources listed in this appendix, visit this URL:
>
> `http://www.december.com/works/java/info.html`

JavaSoft's Java Site

JavaSoft, the developer of Java, offers the best online, one-stop, comprehensive source of technical documentation and information about Java on its Web site at `http://www.javasoft.com/`. This site contains the latest press releases as well as development kits and Java API extensions that you can download.

Java Information Collection Sites

These are high-level Java information collection sites outside of Sun Microsystems:

- **Gamelan:** An excellent collection of Java demos and information; includes a large collection of Java applets; well-organized and frequently updated.

  `http://www.gamelan.com/`

- **JavaScript information:** Contains links to information about JavaScript; includes technical information links plus links to sample applications.

  `http://www.c2.org/~andreww/javascript/`

- **WWW Virtual Library entry for Java:** This site includes links to events, reference information, resources, and selected applications/examples.

  `http://www.acm.org/~ops/java.html`

- **JARS:** Java Applet Rating Service; the hope here is to rate the best applets (top 1 percent, 5 percent, and so on). Includes categories of applets.

  `http://www.jars.com/`

- **Java Developer:** "A public service FAQ devoted to Java Programming," includes resources, a job clearinghouse, and a large section on "How Do I...."

  `http://www.digitalfocus.com/digitalfocus/faq/`

■ **JavaWorld:** An online journal devoted to all aspects of Java, ranging from programming to business-related issues. It is updated monthly and usually contains very timely and interesting articles.

`Http://www.javaworld.com/`

Java Discussion Forums

These are forums where you can take part in or monitor discussions about Java:

■ `comp.lang.java:` Usenet newsgroup for discussing the Java programming language.

`news:comp.lang.java`

■ **Digital Espresso:** The Web formerly known as "J*** Notes"; a weekly summary of the traffic in Java newsgroups and mailing lists.

`http://www.io.org/~mentor/DigitalEspresso.html`

Notable Individual Java Webs

These individual Webs focus on some specific aspect of Java development, information, or products:

■ **Commercial Java Products:** A description of a variety of commercial products related to Java, from *Internet World*.

`http://www.iworld.com/InternetShopper/1Java_products.html`

■ **Java Class Hierarchy Diagrams:** Diagrams that show the class hierarchies for Java packages; very useful for quickly getting an idea of Java class relationships; developed by Charles L. Perkins.

`http://rendezvous.com/java/hierarchy/index.html`

> **NOTE**
>
> These diagrams are also shown in Appendix B.

■ **Programming Active Objects in Java, by Doug Lea:** A discussion of object-oriented design issues and features as they relate to Java.

`http://g.oswego.edu/dl/pats/aopintro.html`

■ **Java Online Bibliography:** A listing of key online articles and press releases about Java and related technology.

`http://www.december.com/works/java/bib.html`

Java Index Sites

These are indexes of Java information:

- **Yahoo Index Entry for Java:**

  `http://www.yahoo.com/Computers_and_Internet/Programming_Languages/Java/`

- **Yahoo Index Entry for HotJava Web Browser:**

  `http://www.yahoo.com/Computers_and_Internet/Internet/World_Wide_Web/Browsers/`
  `➡ HotJava/`

Object-Oriented Information

Because Java is an object-oriented language, these sites can help you connect to more information about object-oriented terminology, design, and programming:

- **Object-Oriented Information Sources Index:** A searchable index to a variety of object-oriented information sources, including research groups, archives, companies, books, and bibliographies.

  `http://cuiwww.unige.ch/OSG/OOinfo/`

- **Object-Oriented Design Online Reference Guide:** A guide to online information sources about object-oriented design. This guide was created by Howie Michalski, Lead Database Engineer, Infrastructure, CompuServe, Inc.

  `http://www.clark.net/pub/howie/OO/oo_home.html`

What's on the CD-ROM?

IN THIS APPENDIX

APPENDIX F

On the *Java Unleashed*, 2nd Edition, CD-ROM that accompanies this book, you will find all the sample files presented in this book along with a wealth of other applications and utilities.

> **NOTE**
>
> Please refer to the readme.wri file on the CD-ROM (Windows) or the Guide to the CD-ROM (Macintosh) for the latest listing of software.

Windows Software

Here's a list of the **Java** products you can find on the CD-ROM:

- Microsoft Visual J++ 1.0 Publishers Edition for Windows 95 and Windows NT 4
- Sun's Java Developers Kit for Windows 95/NT, version 1.0.2
- Sample Java applets
- Sample JavaScripts
- Trial version of Jamba for Windows 95/NT
- JPad IDE
- JPad Pro Java IDE demo
- Kawa IDE
- Studio J++ demo
- Javelin IDE demo
- JDesigner Pro database wizard for Java

Here's a list of the **HTML tools** you can find on the CD-ROM:

- Microsoft Internet Assistants for Access, Excel, PowerPoint, Schedule+, and Word
- W3e HTML Editor
- CSE 3310 HTML Validator
- Hot Dog 32-bit HTML editor demo
- HoTMeTaL HTML editor demo
- HTMLed HTML editor
- HTML Assistant for Windows
- WebEdit Pro HTML editor demo
- Web Weaver HTML editor
- ImageGen

Here are the **graphics, video, and sound applications** you can find on the CD-ROM:

- Goldwave sound editor, player, and recorder
- MapThis image map utility
- Paint Shop Pro 3.12 graphics editor and graphic file format converter for Windows
- SnagIt screen capture utility
- ThumbsPlus image viewer and browser

Here's a list of the **utilities** you can find on the CD-ROM:

- Microsoft Viewers for Excel, PowerPoint, and Word
- Adobe Acrobat viewer
- Microsoft PowerPoint Animation Player and Publisher
- WinZip for Windows NT/95
- WinZip Self-Extractor (a utility program that creates native Windows self-extracting ZIP files)

In addition to all the software products, you can also find electronic versions of the following **books** on the CD-ROM:

- *Tricks of the Java Programming Gurus*
- *Developing Professional Java Applets*

Macintosh Software

Here's a list of the **Java** products you can find on the CD-ROM:

- Sun's Java Developers Kit for Macintosh v1.0.2
- Sample applets
- Sample JavaScripts

Here's a list of the **HTML and graphics applications** you can find on the CD-ROM:

- BBEdit Light
- BBEdit 4.0 demo
- HTML Web Weaver
- HTML Markup
- Web Painter

Here's a list of the **utilities** you can find on the CD-ROM:

■ Adobe Acrobat reader

In addition to all the software products, you can also find electronic versions of the following **books** on the CD-ROM:

■ *Tricks of the Java Programming Gurus*
■ *Developing Professional Java Applets*

About Shareware

Shareware is not free. Please read all the documentation associated with a third-party product (usually contained in a file named `readme.txt` or `license.txt`) and follow all guidelines.

GLOSSARY

anchor. A part of a hypertext document that is either the source or destination of a hypertext link. A link can extend from an anchor to another document, or from another document to an anchor. When anchors are the starting points of these links, they are typically highlighted or otherwise identified in the hypertext browser as *hotspots*.

API (Java) Application Programming Interface. The set of Java packages and classes—included in the Java Developers Kit (JDK)—that programmers use to create applets.

ASCII. American Standard Code for Information Interchange. A 7-bit character code that can represent 128 characters, some of which are control characters used for communications control and are not printable.

applet. A Java program that can be included in an HTML page with the APPLET element and observed in a Java-enabled browser.

application (Java). A computer program—written in Java—that executes independently of a Java-enabled browser through the Java interpreter included in the Java Developers Kit.

attribute. A property of an HTML element, specified in the start tag of the element. The attribute list of the APPLET element is used to identify the location of the applet source code (with the Codebase attribute) and the name of the Java class (with the Code attribute).

block (Java). The code between matching curly braces { and }.

boolean. A data type that has a value of true or false.

browser. A software program for observing the Web. A synonym for a Web client.

bytecode. The machine-readable code that is created as the result of compiling a Java language source file. This is the code distributed across the network to run an applet. Bytecodes are architecture neutral; the Java-capable browser ported to a particular platform interprets them.

cast (verb). To change an expression from one data type to another.

child class. A subclass of a class (its parent class). It inherits public (and protected) data and methods from the parent class.

class. A template for creating objects. A class defines data and methods and is a unit of organization in a Java program. It can pass on its public data and methods to its subclasses.

compiler. A software program that translates human-readable source code into machine-readable code.

constructor. A method named after its class. A constructor method is invoked when an object of that class is made.

content handler. A program loaded into the user's HotJava browser that interprets files of a type defined by the Java programmer. The Java programmer provides the necessary code for the user's HotJava browser to display and interpret this special format.

CPU. Central Processing Unit.

CERN (Centre European pour la Recherche Nucleaire). The European laboratory for particle physics, where the World Wide Web originated in 1989. (See `http://www.cern.ch/`.)

CGI (Common Gateway Interface). A standard for programs to interface with Web servers.

client. A software program that requests information or services from another software application (server) and displays this information in a form required by its hardware platform.

DTD (Document Type Definition). A specification for a markup language such as HTML.

domain name. The alphanumeric name for a computer host; this name is mapped to the computer's numeric Internet Protocol (IP) address.

element. A unit of structure in an HTML document. Many elements have start and stop tags, some have just a single tag, and some can contain other elements.

FTP (File Transfer Protocol). A means to exchange files across a network.

garbage collection. The process by which memory allocated for objects in a program is reclaimed. Java automatically performs this process.

Gopher. A protocol for disseminating information on the Internet using a system of menus.

hotspot. An area on a hypertext document that a user can click to retrieve another resource or document.

HTML (HyperText Markup Language). The mechanism used to create Web pages. Web browsers display these pages according to a browser-defined rendering scheme.

HTTP (HyperText Transfer Protocol). The native protocol of the Web, used to transfer hypertext documents.

home page. An entry page for access to a local web; a page that a person or company defines as a principal page, often containing links to other pages containing personal or professional information.

HotJava. A Web browser designed to execute applets written in the Java programming language.

hypermedia. Hypertext that includes multimedia: text, graphics, images, sound, and video.

hypertext. Text that is not constrained to a single sequence for observation; Web-based hypertext is not constrained to a single server to create meaning.

imagemap. A graphic inline image on an HTML page that potentially connects each pixel or region of an image to a Web resource. The user retrieves the resource by clicking the image.

instance. An object.

interface. A set of methods that Java classes can implement.

Internet. The cooperatively run, globally distributed collection of computer networks that exchange information using the TCP/IP protocol suite.

Java. An object-oriented programming language for creating distributed, executable applications.

Java-enabled browser. A World Wide Web browser that can display Java applets.

link. A connection between one hypertext document and another.

method. A function that can perform operations on data.

MIME (Multipurpose Internet Mail Extensions). A specification for multimedia document formats.

Matrix. The set of all networks that can exchange electronic mail either directly or through gateways. This includes the Internet, BITNET, FidoNet, UUCP, and commercial services such as America Online, CompuServe, Delphi, and Prodigy. This term was coined by John S. Quarterman in his book, *The Matrix* (Digital Press, 1990).

Mosaic. A graphical Web browser originally developed by the National Center for Supercomputing Applications (NCSA). It now includes a number of commercially licensed products.

NCSA (National Center for Supercomputing Applications). Developers and distributors of NCSA Mosaic at the University of Illinois at Champaign-Urbana.

native methods. Class methods declared in a Java class but implemented in C.

navigating. The act of observing the content of the Web for some purpose.

Net. An informal term for the Internet or a subset (or a superset) of the Matrix in context. For example, a computerized conference via e-mail may take place on a BITNET host that has an Internet gateway, thus making the conference available to anyone on either of these networks. In this case, the developer might say, "Our conference will be available on the Net." One might even consider discussion forums on commercial online services to be "on the Net," although these are not accessible from the Internet.

object. A variable defined as being a particular class type. An object has the data and methods as specified in the class definition.

overload (verb). To use the same name for several items in the same scope; Java methods can be overloaded.

packet. A set of data handled as a unit in data transmission.

package (Java). A set of classes with a common high-level function declared with the `package` keyword.

page. A single file of HyperText Markup Language.

parameter (HTML). A name and value pair identified by the Name and Value attributes of the PARAM element used inside an APPLET element.

parameter list (Java). The set of values passed to a method. The definition of the method describes how these values are manipulated.

parent class. The originating class of a given subclass.

protocol handler. A program that is loaded into the user's HotJava browser and that interprets a protocol. These protocols include standard ones such as HTTP or programmer-defined protocols.

robot. A term for software programs that automatically explore the Web for a variety of purposes. Robots that collect resources for later database queries by users are sometimes called *spiders*.

scope. The program segment in which a reference to a variable is valid.

SGML (Standard Generalized Markup Language). A standard for defining markup languages; HTML is an instance of SGML. (See http://www.sgmlopen.org/.)

server. A software application that provides information or services based on requests from client programs.

site. The file section of a computer on which Web documents (or other documents served in another protocol) reside—for example, a Web site, a Gopher site, or an FTP site.

Solaris. Sun Microsystem's software platform for networked applications. Solaris includes an operating system, SunOS.

Sparc (Scalable Processor ARChitecture). A microprocessor architecture based on very efficient handling of a small set of instructions. (See http://www.sparc.com/.)

spider. A software program that traverses the Web to collect information about resources for later queries by users seeking to find resources. Major species of active spiders include Lycos and WebCrawler.

surfing. The act of navigating the Web, typically using techniques for rapidly traversing content to find subjectively valuable resources.

tag. The code used to make up part of an HTML element. For example, the TITLE element has a start tag, <TITLE> and an end tag, </TITLE>.

Unicode. A character set that supports many world languages.

URL (Uniform Resource Locator). The scheme for addressing on the Web. A URL identifies a resource on the Web.

Usenet. A system for disseminating asynchronous text discussion among cooperating computer hosts. The Usenet discussion space is divided into newsgroups, each on a particular topic or subtopic.

TCP/IP (Transmission Control Protocol/Internet Protocol). The set of protocols used for network communication on the Internet.

VRML (Virtual Reality Modeling Language). A specification for three-dimensional rendering used in conjunction with Web browsers.

web. A set of hypertext pages that is considered a single work. Typically, a single web is created by one author or cooperating authors and is deployed on a single server with links to other servers—a subset of the Web.

Web (World Wide Web). A hypertext information and communication system popularly used on the Internet computer network with data communications operating according to a client/server model. Web clients (browsers) can access multiprotocol and hypermedia information using an addressing scheme.

Web server. Software that provides the services to Web clients.

WWW. The World Wide Web.

X (X Window System). A windowing system supporting graphical user interfaces to applications.

See also:

Sun's Java Glossary

```
http://www.javasoft.com/javacontest/java-P1/project_files/faq/glossary.html
```

I

INDEX

Symbols

A

Teach Yourself Java in 21 Days, Professional Reference Edition

Laura Lemay and Michael Morrison

Introducing the first, best, and most detailed guide to developing applications with the hot new Java language from Sun Microsystems. Includes coverage of browsing Java applications with Netscape and other popular Web browsers.

CD-ROM includes the Java Developers Kit.

Price: $59.99 USA/$84.95 CDN   Casual—Accomplished—Expert
ISBN: 1-57521-183-1   1,296 pp.

Teach Yourself JavaScript in a Week, Second Edition

Arman Danesh

Teach Yourself JavaScript in a Week, Second Edition, is a new edition of the best-selling JavaScript tutorial. It has been revised and updated for the latest version of JavaScript from Netscape and includes detailed coverage of new features such as how to work with Java applets with LiveConnect, writing JavaScript for Microsoft's Internet Explorer, and more!

Price: $39.99 USA/$56.95 CDN   Beginning—Intermediate
ISBN: 1-57521-195-5   600 pp.

Java Developer's Reference

Mike Cohn, et al.

This is the information and resource packed development package for professional developers. It explains the components of the Java Developers Kit (JDK) and the Java programming language. Everything needed to program in Java is included within this comprehensive reference, making it the tool developers will turn to over and over again for timely, accurate information on Java and the JDK.

Price: $59.99 USA/$84.95 CDN   Accomplished—Expert
ISBN: 1-57521-129-7   1,296 pp.

JavaScript Developer's Guide

Wes Tatters

The *JavaScript Developer's Guide* is the professional reference for enhancing commercial-grade Web sites with JavaScript. Packed with real-world JavaScript examples, the book shows the developer how to use JavaScript to glue together Java applets, multimedia programs, plug-ins, and more on a Web site.

Price: $49.99 USA/$70.95 CDN   Accomplished—Expert
ISBN: 1-57521-084-3   600 pp.

Teach Yourself SunSoft Java WorkShop in 21 Days

Rogers Cadenhead, Laura Lemay, and Charles E. Perkins

Written in Java itself, the Java WorkShop included with this book is a cross-platform tool that provides a rich set of tools for the beginner or professional Java programmer. The workshop enhances the book to provide the most comprehensive way to learn SunSoft Java WorkShop.

Price: $39.99 USA/$56.95 CDN   Casual—Accomplished
ISBN: 1-57521-159-9   656 pp.

Web Programming with Java

Harris and Jones

This book gets readers on the road to developing robust, real-world Java applications. Various cutting-edge applications are presented, allowing the reader to quickly learn all aspects of programming Java for the Internet.

Price: $39.99 USA/$56.95 CDN   Accomplished—Expert
ISBN: 1-57521-113-0   500 pp.

Web Programming with Visual Basic

Craig Eddy and Brad Haasch

This reference quickly and efficiently shows the experienced developer how to develop Web applications using the 32-bit power of Visual Basic 4. It includes an introduction and overview of Web programming and then quickly delves into the specifics, teaching readers how to incorporate animation, sound, and more into their Web applications.

Price: $39.99 USA/$56.95 CDN   Accomplished—Expert
ISBN: 1-57521-106-8   400 pp.

HTML 3.2 and CGI Unleashed, Professional Reference Edition

John December

Readers will learn the logistics of how to create compelling, information-rich Web pages that grab attention and keep readers returning for more. This comprehensive professional instruction and reference guide for the World Wide Web covers all aspects of the development processes, implementation, tools, and programming.

Price: $59.99 USA/$84.95 CDN   Accomplished—Expert
ISBN: 1-57521-177-7   1,376 pp.

Add to Your Sams.net Library Today
with the Best Books for Internet Technologies

ISBN	Quantity	Description of Item	Unit Cost	Total Cost
1-57521-183-1		Teach Yourself Java in 21 Days Professional Reference Edition (Book/CD-ROM)	$59.99	
1-57521-195-5		Teach Yourself JavaScript in a Week, Second Edition (Book/CD-ROM)	$39.99	
1-57521-129-7		Java Developer's Reference (Book/CD-ROM)	$59.99	
1-57521-084-3		JavaScript Developer's Guide (Book/CD-ROM)	$49.99	
1-57521-159-9		Teach Yourself SunSoft Java WorkShop in 21 Days (Book/CD-ROM)	$39.99	
1-57521-113-0		Web Programming with Java (Book/CD-ROM)	$39.99	
1-57521-106-8		Web Programming with Visual Basic (Book/CD-ROM)	$39.99	
1-57521-177-7		HTML 3.2 & CGI Unleashed, Professional Reference Edition (Book/CD-ROM)	$59.99	
		Shipping and Handling: See information below.		
		TOTAL		

Shipping and Handling: $4.00 for the first book, and $1.75 for each additional book. If you need to have it NOW, we can ship product to you in 24 hours for an additional charge of approximately $18.00, and you will receive your item overnight or in two days. Overseas shipping and handling adds $2.00. Prices subject to change. Call between 9:00 a.m. and 5:00 p.m. EST for availability and pricing information on latest editions.

201 W. 103rd Street, Indianapolis, Indiana 46290

1-800-428-5331 — Orders   1-800-835-3202 — FAX   1-800-858-7674 — Customer Service

Book ISBN 1-57521-197-1

A V I A C O M   S E R V I C E

The Information SuperLibrary™

Bookstore

Search

What's New

Reference

Software

Newsletter

Company Overviews

Yellow Pages

Internet Starter Kit

HTML Workshop

Win a Free T-Shirt!

Macmillan Computer Publishing

Site Map

Talk to Us

CHECK OUT THE BOOKS IN THIS LIBRARY.

You'll find thousands of shareware files and over 1600 computer books designed for both technowizards and technophobes. You can browse through 700 sample chapters, get the latest news on the Net, and find just about anything using our massive search directories.

All Macmillan Computer Publishing books are available at your local bookstore.

We're open 24-hours a day, 365 days a year.

You don't need a card.

We don't charge fines.

And you can be as LOUD as you want.

The Information SuperLibrary
http://www.mcp.com/mcp/   ftp.mcp.com

Installing the CD-ROM

The CD-ROM that accompanies this book contains all the source code and project files developed by the authors, plus an assortment of evaluation versions of third-party products. To install the disc, follow the steps for your appropriate system.

Windows 95/NT 4 Installation Instructions

1. Insert the CD-ROM into your CD-ROM drive.
2. From the Windows 95 desktop, double-click the My Computer icon.
3. Double-click the icon representing your CD-ROM drive.
4. Double-click the icon titled setup.exe to run the CD-ROM installation program.

Windows NT 3.51 Installation Instructions

1. Insert the CD-ROM into your CD-ROM drive.
2. From File Manager or Program Manager, choose Run from the File menu.
3. Type **<*drive*>\setup** and press Enter, where <*drive*> corresponds to the drive letter of your CD-ROM. For example, if your CD-ROM is drive D, type **D:\setup** and press Enter.
4. Follow the on-screen instructions.

Macintosh Installation Instructions

1. Insert the CD-ROM into your CD-ROM drive.
2. When an icon for the CD appears on your desktop, open the disc by double-clicking that icon.
3. Double-click the icon titled Guide to the CD-ROM and follow the on-screen directions.

CUSTOMER REMEDIES. Microsoft's and its suppliers' entire liability and your exclusive remedy shall be, at Microsoft's option, either (a) return of the price paid, or (b) repair or replacement of the SOFTWARE PRODUCT or hardware that does not meet Microsoft's Limited Warranty and which is returned to Microsoft with a copy of your receipt. This Limited Warranty is void if failure of the SOFTWARE PRODUCT or hardware has resulted from accident, abuse, or misapplication. Any replacement SOFTWARE PRODUCT or hardware will be warranted for the remainder of the original warranty period or thirty (30) days, whichever is longer. **Outside the United States, neither these remedies nor any product support services offered by Microsoft are available without proof of purchase from an authorized international source.**

NO OTHER WARRANTIES. To the maximum extent permitted by applicable law, Microsoft and its suppliers disclaim all other warranties, either express or implied, including, but not limited to, implied warranties of merchantability and fitness for a particular purpose, with regard to the SOFTWARE PRODUCT, and any accompanying hardware. This limited warranty gives you specific legal rights. You may have others, which vary from state/jurisdiction to state/jurisdiction.

NO LIABILITY FOR CONSEQUENTIAL DAMAGES. TO THE MAXIMUM EXTENT PERMITTED BY APPLICABLE LAW, IN NO EVENT SHALL MICROSOFT OR ITS SUPPLIERS BE LIABLE.

FOR ANY SPECIAL, INCIDENTAL, INDIRECT, OR CONSEQUENTIAL DAMAGES WHATSOEVER (INCLUDING, WITHOUT LIMITATION, DAMAGES FOR LOSS OF BUSINESS PROFITS, BUSINESS INTERRUPTION, LOSS OF BUSINESS INFORMATION, OR ANY OTHER PECUNIARY LOSS) ARISING OUT OF THE USE OF OR INABILITY TO USE THE SOFTWARE PRODUCT, EVEN IF MICROSOFT HAS BEEN ADVISED OF THE POSSIBILITY OF SUCH DAMAGES. BECAUSE SOME STATES AND JURISDICTIONS DO NOT ALLOW THE EXCLUSION OR LIMITATION OF LIABILITY FOR CONSEQUENTIAL OR INCIDENTAL DAMAGES, THE ABOVE LIMITATION MAY NOT APPLY TO YOU.

9. **NOTE ON JAVA SUPPORT.** THE SOFTWARE PRODUCT CONTAINS SUPPORT FOR PROGRAMS WRITTEN IN JAVA. JAVA TECHNOLOGY IS NOT FAULT TOLERANT AND IS NOT DESIGNED, MANUFACTURED, OR INTENDED FOR USE OR RESALE AS ONLINE CONTROL EQUIPMENT IN HAZARDOUS ENVIRONMENTS REQUIRING FAIL-SAFE PERFORMANCE, SUCH AS IN THE OPERATION OF NUCLEAR FACILITIES, AIRCRAFT NAVIGATION OR COMMUNICATIONS SYSTEMS, AIR TRAFFIC CONTROL, DIRECT LIFE SUPPORT MACHINES, OR WEAPONS SYSTEMS, IN WHICH THE FAILURE OF JAVA TECHNOLOGY COULD LEAD DIRECTLY TO DEATH, PERSONAL INJURY, OR SEVERE PHYSICAL OR ENVIRONMENTAL DAMAGE.

MISCELLANEOUS

If you acquired this product in the United States, this EULA is governed by the laws of the State of Washington.

If you acquired this product in Canada, this EULA is governed by the laws of the Province of Ontario, Canada. Each of the parties hereto irrevocably attorns to the jurisdiction of the courts of the Province of Ontario and further agrees to commence any litigation which may arise hereunder in the courts located in the Judicial District of York, Province of Ontario.

If this product was acquired outside the United States, then local law may apply.

Should you have any questions concerning this EULA, or if you desire to contact Microsoft for any reason, please contact the Microsoft subsidiary serving your country, or write to Microsoft Sales Information Center/One Microsoft Way/Redmond, WA 98052-6399.

LIMITED WARRANTY. Except with respect to Microsoft Internet Explorer and the REDISTRIBUTABLES, which are provided "as is," without warranty of any kind, Microsoft warrants that (a) the SOFTWARE PRODUCT will perform substantially in accordance with the accompanying written materials for a period of ninety (90) days from the date of receipt, and (b) any hardware accompanying the SOFTWARE PRODUCT will be free from defects in materials and workmanship under normal use and service for a period of one (1) year from the date of receipt. Some states and jurisdictions do not allow limitations on duration of an implied warranty, so the above limitation may not apply to you. To the extent allowed by applicable law, implied warranties on the SOFTWARE PRODUCT and hardware, if any, are limited to ninety (90) days and one year, respectively.

e. **Termination.** Without prejudice to any other rights, Microsoft may terminate this EULA if you fail to comply with the terms and conditions of this EULA. In such event, you must destroy all copies of the SOFTWARE PRODUCT. In addition, your rights under this EULA that pertain to the Microsoft Internet Explorer software shall terminate upon termination of your Microsoft operating system product EULA.

6. **REDISTRIBUTABLE COMPONENTS.**

   a. **Redistributable Files.** In addition to the license granted in Section 1, Microsoft grants you a nonexclusive, royalty-free right to reproduce and distribute the object code version of those portions of the SOFTWARE designated in the SOFTWARE as: (i) the files identified in the REDISTRB.WRI file located in the \MSDev\Redist subdirectory on the "Microsoft Visual J++ version 1.00" CD-ROM (collectively, "REDISTRIBUTABLES"), ***provided*** you comply with Section 6.b.

   b. **Redistribution Requirements.** If you redistribute the REDISTRIBUTABLES, you agree to: (i) distribute the REDISTRIBUTABLES in object code form only in conjunction with and as a part of your software application product which adds significant and primary functionality and which is designed, developed, and tested to operate in the Microsoft Windows and/or Windows NT environments; (ii) not use Microsoft's name, logo, or trademarks to market your software application product; (iii) include a valid copyright notice on your software product; (iv) indemnify, hold harmless, and defend Microsoft from and against any claims or lawsuits, including attorney's fees, that arise or result from the use or distribution of your software application product; and (v) not permit further distribution of the REDISTRIBUTABLES by your end user. Contact Microsoft for the applicable royalties due and other licensing terms for all other uses and/or distribution of the REDISTRIBUTABLES.

7. **U.S. GOVERNMENT RESTRICTED RIGHTS.** The SOFTWARE PRODUCT and documentation are provided with RESTRICTED RIGHTS. Use, duplication, or disclosure by the Government is subject to restrictions as set forth in subparagraph (c)(1)(ii) of the Rights in Technical Data and Computer Software clause at DFARS 252.227-7013 or subparagraphs (c)(1) and (2) of the Commercial Computer Software—Restricted Rights at 48 CFR 52.227-19, as applicable. Manufacturer is Microsoft Corporation/One Microsoft Way/Redmond, WA 98052-6399.

8. **EXPORT RESTRICTIONS.** You agree that you will not export or re-export the SOFTWARE PRODUCT to any country, person, entity or end user subject to U.S.A. export restrictions. Restricted countries currently include, but are not necessarily limited to Cuba, Iran, Iraq, Libya, North Korea, Syria, and the Federal Republic of Yugoslavia (Serbia and Montenegro, U.N. Protected Areas and areas of Republic of Bosnia and Herzegovina under the control of Bosnian Serb forces). You warrant and represent that neither the U.S.A. Bureau of Export Administration nor any other federal agency has suspended, revoked or denied your export privileges.

2. **UPGRADES.** If the SOFTWARE is an upgrade, whether from Microsoft or another supplier, you may use or transfer the SOFTWARE only in conjunction with upgraded product. If the SOFTWARE is an upgrade from a Microsoft product, you may now use that upgraded product only in accordance with this EULA.

3. **SUBSCRIPTION UPDATES.** If you have acquired the SOFTWARE PRODUCT as part of a subscription package, then you must treat as an upgrade any subsequent versions of SOFTWARE PRODUCT received as an update to your subscription package.

4. **COPYRIGHT.** All title and copyrights in and to the SOFTWARE PRODUCT (including but not limited to any images, photographs, animations, video, audio, music, text, and "applets" incorporated into the SOFTWARE PRODUCT), the accompanying printed materials, and any copies of the SOFTWARE PRODUCT are owned by Microsoft or its suppliers. The SOFTWARE PRODUCT is protected by copyright laws and international treaty provisions. Therefore, you must treat the SOFTWARE PRODUCT like any other copyrighted material except that you may either (a) make one copy of the SOFTWARE PRODUCT solely for backup or archival purposes or (b) install the SOFTWARE PRODUCT on a single computer provided you keep the original solely for backup or archival purposes. You may not copy the printed materials accompanying the SOFTWARE PRODUCT.

5. **DESCRIPTION OF OTHER RIGHTS AND LIMITATIONS.**

   a. **Limitations on Reverse Engineering, Decompilation, and Disassembly.** You may not reverse engineer, decompile, or disassemble the SOFTWARE PRODUCT, except and only to the extent that such activity is expressly permitted by applicable law notwithstanding this limitation.

   b. **No Separation of Components.** The SOFTWARE PRODUCT is licensed as a single product and neither the software programs making up the SOFTWARE PRODUCT nor any UPDATE may be separated for use by more than one user at a time.

   c. **Rental.** You may not rent or lease the SOFTWARE PRODUCT.

   d. **Software Transfer.** You may permanently transfer all of your rights under this EULA, provided that you retain no copies, you transfer all of the SOFTWARE PRODUCT (including all component parts, the media and printed materials, any upgrades, this EULA, and, if applicable, the Certificate of Authenticity), and the recipient agrees to the terms of this EULA. If the SOFTWARE PRODUCT is an upgrade, any transfer must include all prior versions of the SOFTWARE PRODUCT. Notwithstanding the foregoing, you may permanently transfer all your rights under this EULA that pertain to the Microsoft Internet Explorer only in conjunction with a permanent transfer of your validly licensed copy of a Microsoft operating system product.

END-USER LICENSE AGREEMENT FOR MICROSOFT SOFTWARE

MICROSOFT VISUAL J++, Publisher's Edition

IMPORTANT—READ CAREFULLY: This Microsoft End-User License Agreement ("EULA") is a legal agreement between you (either an individual or a single entity) and Microsoft Corporation for the Microsoft software product identified above and Microsoft Internet Explorer, which include computer software and associated media and printed materials, and may include "online" or electronic documentation (together, the "SOFTWARE PRODUCT" or "SOFTWARE"). By installing, copying, or otherwise using the SOFTWARE PRODUCT, you agree to be bound by the terms of this EULA. If you do not agree to the terms of this EULA, promptly return the unused SOFTWARE PRODUCT to the place from which you obtained it for a full refund.

SOFTWARE PRODUCT LICENSE

The SOFTWARE PRODUCT is protected by copyright laws and international copyright treaties, as well as other intellectual property laws and treaties. The SOFTWARE PRODUCT is licensed, not sold.

1. **GRANT OF LICENSE.** This EULA grants you the following rights:

    a. You may use one copy of the Microsoft Software Product identified above on a single computer. The SOFTWARE is in "use" on a computer when it is loaded into temporary memory (i.e., RAM) or installed into permanent memory (e.g., hard disk, CD-ROM, or other storage device) of that computer. However, installation on a network server for the sole purpose of internal distribution to one or more other computer(s) shall not constitute "use" for which a separate license is required, provided you have a separate license for each computer to which the SOFTWARE is distributed.

    b. You may use copies of the Microsoft Internet Explorer software only in conjunction with a validly licensed copy of Microsoft operating system products (e.g., Windows® 95 or Windows NT®). You may make copies of the SOFTWARE PRODUCT for use on all computers for which you have licensed Microsoft operating system products.

    c. Solely with respect to electronic documents included with the SOFTWARE, you may make an unlimited number of copies (either in hardcopy or electronic form), provided that such copies shall be used only for internal purposes and are not republished or distributed to any third party.